Annual Report Of The Supervising Inspector General, Steamboat Inspection Service To The Secretary Of Commerce

United States. Steamboat-Inspection Service

ANNUAL REPORT

OF THE

SUPERVISING INSPECTOR-GENERAL

STEAMBOAT-INSPECTION SERVICE

TO THE

SECRETARY OF COMMERCE AND LABOR

FOR THE

FISCAL YEAR ENDED JUNE 30, 1906

WASHINGTON
GOVERNMENT PRINTING OFFICE
1906

DEPARTMENT OF COMMERCE AND LABOR

Document No. 69

STEAMBOAT-INSPECTION SERVICE

2

CONTENTS.

REPORT OF THE SUPERVISING INSPECTOR-GENERAL.

APPENDIX.

ANNUAL REPORT

OF THE

SUPERVISING INSPECTOR-GENERAL,

STEAMBOAT-INSPECTION SERVICE.

DEPARTMENT OF COMMERCE AND LABOR,
STEAMBOAT-INSPECTION SERVICE,
Washington, November 19, 1906.

SIR: I have the honor to submit to you the following report of the Steamboat-Inspection Service for the fiscal year ended June 30, 1906, as required by section 4403, Revised Statutes, and under Department regulations relating thereto.

PERSONNEL.

The personnel of this Service at the close of the fiscal year ended June 30, 1906, consisted of 223 officers, clerks, and messengers, as follows: At Washington, the Supervising Inspector-General, chief clerk, 4 clerks, and 1 messenger; and the Service at large, consisting of 9 supervising inspectors (there being at that time a vacancy in the Fourth district), 44 local inspectors of hulls, 44 local inspectors of boilers, 35 assistant inspectors of hulls, 36 assistant inspectors of boilers, and 48 clerks, including 1 clerk to the supervising inspector at New York.

During the fiscal year ended June 30, 1906, there were added to the official force of this Service 5 assistant inspectors of hulls and 5 assistant inspectors of boilers, 1 clerk, and 1 new board of local inspectors (at St. Michael, Alaska). The local boards at Wheeling, W. Va., and Gallipolis, Ohio, were discontinued by act of Congress approved April 9, 1906, and a new board established at Point Pleasant, W. Va.

The additional force was distributed as follows: Two assistant inspectors of hulls and 2 assistant inspectors of boilers at Seattle, Wash.; 2 assistant inspectors of hulls and 2 assistant inspectors of boilers at Milwaukee, Wis.; 1 assistant inspector of hulls and 1 assistant inspector of boilers at Buffalo, N. Y.

The following changes in the personnel of the Service were caused by appointments, resignations, dismissals, and deaths: Appointments of 4 local inspectors of hulls, 3 local inspectors of boilers, 7 assistant inspectors of hulls, 7 assistant inspectors of boilers, and 5 clerks to local inspectors; resignations of 1 supervising inspector, 2 assistant inspectors of boilers, and 3 clerks; dismissals of 1 local inspector of boilers and 1 clerk; deaths of 1 local inspector of boilers and 1 local inspector of hulls; legislated out of office by act of Congress, 1 local inspector of hulls and 1 local inspector of boilers.

SUMMARY OF OFFICE WORK.

The following is a partial summary of the work in the office of the Supervising Inspector-General during the fiscal year ended June 30, 1906:

Acknowledgments received of documents mailed	789
Reports of excursion permits issued	1,520
Letters prepared for Secretary's signature	363
Indorsements on papers passing thru office	165
Permits to use oil as fuel on steamers	100
Temporary permits to use coil boilers	3
Reports of tests of material at mills, and affidavits of boiler makers received, recorded, and filed	918
Miscellaneous accounts examined and approved	605
Personal-expense accounts examined and approved	1,619
Quarterly statements customs officers and inspectors examined, checked, and recorded	190
Weekly reports of inspectors examined and checked	2,340
Reports of casualties and violations of law recorded and filed	1,326
Annual reports of inspectors, lifeboat and life-raft equipment of vessels of over 100 tons	44
Semimonthly reports of vessels visited by supervising inspectors	235
Statements of public property charged to Service received, examined, and checked	108
Index (card system) correspondence (new numbers) [a]	7,353

EXPENDITURES.

Following is a detailed account of the expenditures for the fiscal year ended June 30, 1906:

Salaries, Supervising Inspector-General, supervising inspectors, local and assistant inspectors, clerks, and messengers, paid from the funds in the Treasury not otherwise appropriated, acts approved June 19, 1886, and April 4, 1888, as amended by acts approved March 3, 1905, and act approved April 9, 1906 (appointments authorized by sections 4402, 4404, and 4414, Revised Statutes)	$371,488.77
Traveling expenses (actual and mileage)	59,110.19
Rents, offices	10,141.62
Stationery, supplies, etc., and transportation of same	2,701.21
Telephone rents, telegrams, and postage	2,031.30
Marshals' and witnesses' fees in investigations	1,219.45
Instruments and repairs to instruments	610.28
Typewriting machines, repairs and supplies	605.71
Notary fees, inspection certificates, and expense accounts	570.75
Furniture and repairs to furniture	445.50
Moving offices, San Francisco, Cal., and Point Pleasant, W. Va	364.75
Ice, fuel, gas, and water rents	280.96
Stenographers in cases of investigation	200.10
Clerk, regular meeting of Board of Supervising Inspectors, 1906	175.00
Official badges (Bureau of Engraving and Printing)	87.42
Janitors to inspectors' offices	82.00
Towels, soap, and laundry	63.75
Official railway guides and marine periodicals, etc	37.75
Care clocks in New York office	19.25
Post-office box rent	7.00
Total traveling and miscellaneous expenses	78,753.99

[a] This does not show the actual number of letters received and sent out, for under one file number there may be any number of letters bearing on the same subject. The estimated number of letters or communications received, recorded, answered, and filed is about 15,000, and the estimated number of letters written about 10,000.

Salaries as above noted	$371,488.77
Total expenditures for year ended June 30, 1906	450,242.76
Total expenditures for year ended June 30, 1905	405,729.85
Increase, 1906	44,512.91
Salaries, 1906	371,488.77
Salaries, 1905	325,190.16
Increase, 1906	46,298.61
Contingent expenses, 1905	80,539.69
Contingent expenses, 1906	78,753.99
Decrease, 1906	1,785.70
Traveling expenses, mileage and actual, 1905	63,172.08
Traveling expenses, mileage and actual, 1906	59,110.19
Decrease, 1906	4,061.89
Rents, 1906	10,141.62
Rents, 1905	8,347.08
Increase, 1906	1,794.54

The increase of expenditures under the item of salaries is due to the increase in the salaries of many of the local inspectors by authority of the act of Congress effective July 1, 1905, and a slight increase in the salaries of some of the assistant inspectors, which latter is a matter of discretion with the Secretary. The decrease in contingent expenses is due mainly to the decreased travel of inspectors from that of the previous year, when they were almost constantly engaged in reinspections and other extra duty.

NUMBER, CLASS, AND TONNAGE OF VESSELS INSPECTED.

There is submitted herewith a tabulated statement showing the number, class, and tonnage of vessels regularly inspected by this Service and which have been granted certificates.

Certificates of inspection issued to vessels propelled by steam, sail, or other motors during the fiscal year ended June 30, 1906.

Supervising district.	Local district.	Foreign steamers.		Domestic steamers.		Motor vessels.		Total.		Sail vessels and barges.		Grand total.	
		Number.	Gross tonnage.	Number.	Gross tonnage.	Number.	Gross tonnage.	Number.	Gross tonnage.	Number.	Gross tonnage.	Number.	Gross tonnage.
First district	San Francisco, Cal. [a]	12	54,069	339	306,342	39	4,568	390	364,979	12	12,604	402	377,583
	Portland, Oreg.			151	30,856	4	193	155	31,049	5	7,024	160	38,073
	Seattle, Wash.	14	72,215	291	148,650	15	745	320	221,610	7	6,621	327	228,231
	Juneau, Alaska [b]			116	21,642	4	389	120	22,031			120	22,031
Second district	**New York, N. Y.**	203	1,545,609	1,306	658,244	25	705	1,534	2,204,558	17	7,360	1,551	2,211,918
	Albany, N. Y. [c]	1	1,811	190	43,669	1	46	192	45,526	3	782	195	46,308
	Boston, Mass.	36	323,494	271	86,569	13	1,359	320	411,422	1	237	321	411,659
	Providence, R. I.			202	81,559	6	141	208	81,700	1	243	209	81,943
	New London, Conn.			106	35,943	13	406	119	36,349			119	36,349
	New Haven, Conn.			110	17,343	21	726	131	18,069			131	18,069
	Philadelphia, Pa.	15	107,522	329	162,473	10	507	354	270,502			354	270,502
	Portland, Me.	4	34,634	140	20,548	5	300	149	55,482			149	55,482
	Bangor, Me.	3	855	97	6,870	6	179	106	7,904			106	7,904
Third district	Norfolk, Va.			267	74,825	4	94	271	74,919			271	74,919
	Baltimore, Md.	17	84,800	304	124,142	20	1,251	341	210,193			341	210,193
	Charleston, S. C.			101	9,138	3	61	104	9,199			104	9,199
	Savannah, Ga.			72	46,847	4	98	76	46,945			76	46,945
	Jacksonville, Fla.			65	7,295	6	215	71	7,510			71	7,510
Fourth district	St Louis, Mo.			126	23,271	14	328	140	23,599	1	438	141	24,037
Fifth district	Dubuque, Iowa.			79	6,887	18	913	97	7,800	5	803	102	8,603
	Duluth, Minn.			202	211,725	6	267	208	211,992	1	192	209	212,184
Sixth district	Louisville, Ky.			51	8,907	6	223	57	9,130			57	9,130
	Evansville, Ind.			69	8,677	4	158	73	8,835			73	8,835
	Nashville, Tenn.			86	11,322			86	11,322			86	11,322
	Memphis, Tenn.			75	9,506	2	48	77	9,554			77	9,554
Seventh district	Cincinnati, Ohio.			62	14,738	1	25	63	14,763			63	14,763
	Gallipolis, Ohio [d]			68	7,436			68	7,436	1	152	69	7,588
	Wheeling, W. Va. [d]			21	2,613			21	2,613			21	2,613
	Point Pleasant, W. Va. [e]			9	839			9	839			9	839
	Pittsburg, Pa.			138	24,340			138	24,340			138	24,340
Eighth district	Detroit, Mich.	2	593	130	149,278			132	149,871			132	149,871
	Chicago, Ill.			201	180,628	6	160	207	180,788	1	438	208	181,226
	Grand Haven, Mich.			182	57,625			182	57,625			182	57,625
	Marquette, Mich.	8	4,040	103	15,929			111	19,969	1	148	112	20,117
	Milwaukee, Wis.			281	200,365	1	84	282	200,449			282	200,449
	Port Huron, Mich.	6	9,648	142	89,362	1	28	149	99,038			149	99,038
Ninth district	Cleveland, Ohio.			243	534,187			243	534,187			243	534,187
	Buffalo, N. Y.	11	14,590	333	386,228			344	400,818			344	400,818
	Oswego, N. Y.	20	5,801	122	31,369	2	218	144	37,388			144	37,388
	Toledo, Ohio.	2	1,124	88	51,681	1	26	91	52,831			91	52,831
	Burlington, Vt.	3	772	40	3,237			43	4,009			43	4,009

Tenth district	New Orleans, La	36	108,397	311	50,487	23	630	370	159,514	5	4,151	375	163,665
	Apalachicola, Fla			72	10,198	7	267	79	10,465			79	10,465
	Galveston, Tex	12	47,129	75	25,832	15	406	102	73,367			102	73,367
	Mobile, Ala	16	19,663	137	11,538	14	362	167	31,563			167	31,563
	Total	421	2,436,766	7,903	4,011,160	320	16,126	8,644	6,464,052	61	41,193	8,705	6,505,245
	Total, 1905											8,705	5,910,824
	Increase in tonnage, 1906												594,421

[a] 26 steamers, 2 sail, and 1 motor vessels, with 10,984 gross tonnage, inspected in Hawaiian waters.
[b] 2 steamers, with 688 gross tonnage, inspected by local inspectors, St. Michael, Alaska.
[c] 10 steamers, with 3.561 gross tonnage, inspected in Porto Rican waters.
[d] Board abolished by law May 1, 1906.
[e] Board established by law May 1, 1906, in place of boards at Gallipolis and Wheeling.

Classification of inspections, tonnage, and officers licensed, according to the several divisions of navigation, for fiscal year ended June 30, 1906.

Division.	Vessels inspected.										Number and character of officers licensed.			
	Foreign steamers.		Domestic steamers.		Motor vessels.		Sail vessels and barges.		Total.					
	Number.	Tonnage.	Number.	Tonnage.	Number.	Tonnage.	Number.	Tonnage.	Number.	Tonnage.	Steam vessels.	Motor vessels.	Sail vessels.	Total.
Pacific coast	26	126,284	897	507,490	62	5,895	24	26,249	1,009	665,918	1,205	95	159	1,459
Atlantic coast	279	2,098,725	3,560	1,375,465	137	6,088	22	8,622	3,998	3,488,900	3,051	438	220	3,709
Western rivers			855	121,053	51	1,962	8	1,585	914	124,600	610	33		643
Northern lakes	52	36,568	1,996	1,909,097	11	516	2	586	2,061	1,946,767	1,286	56	2	1,344
Gulf coast	64	175,189	595	98,055	59	1,665	5	4,151	723	279,060	527	195	9	731
Total	421	2,436,766	7,903	4,011,160	320	16,126	61	41,193	8,705	6,505,245	6,679	817	390	7,886

The foregoing statement of the number of all classes of vessels inspected during the fiscal year ended June 30, 1906, shows exactly the same number inspected as in the previous year, but with an increased tonnage of 594,421.

Of all classes of vessels inspected, the Pacific coast has a decrease from the previous year of 199 in number and 72,592 in tonnage, the Atlantic coast a decrease of 64 in number but an increase of 400,129 in tonnage, the western rivers an increase of 65 in number and 1,831 in tonnage, the northern or Great Lakes an increase of 191 in number and 314,780 in tonnage, and the Gulf coast an increase of 7 in number and a decrease of 49,727 in tonnage. Of foreign vessels there is an increase of 93 in the number inspected and 756,390 in tonnage. Domestic vessels show an increase of 282 in number and 402,459 in tonnage.

There were 446 less sail vessels and barges inspected than in the previous year, with a decrease in tonnage of 569,680, which is due to the operation of the law exempting freight sail vessels from inspection.

There were 320 motor vessels inspected, with a tonnage of 16,126, which is an increase over the previous year of 71 in number and 5,252 in tonnage, a condition that indicates emphatically the growing importance of this class of vessels.

The foregoing statistics show that while there was a decrease of 199 vessels of all classes inspected in the Pacific coast districts that condition was due almost entirely to the exemption of freight sail vessels. The increase in other localities was such as to maintain exactly the number of all classes of vessels inspected in 1906 as were inspected in 1905.

MARINE BOILER PLATES TESTED.

During the year ended June 30, 1906, 6,007 marine boiler plates were tested at mills by assistant inspectors of this Service, under the act of Congress approved January 22, 1894. Of this number, 4,728 were accepted and 1,279 rejected, as follows:

Marine boiler plates inspected at mills by assistant inspectors during the fiscal year ended June 30, 1906.

Inspected by Assistant Inspector—	Plates rejected—										Total.		
	Spoiled at shears after inspection.	Lost in shipping house.	Tensile strength.	Elongation.	Lamination.	Light gage.	Heavy gage.	Reduced area.	Bad surface.	Bending test.	Rejected.	Accepted.	Inspected.
P. N. Knaggs, Milwaukee, Wis	....	....	1	....	....	....	....	....	....	15	16	586	602
E. G. Allen, Coatesville, Pa	22	32	42	22	35	1	2	4	59	19	238	2,718	2,956
D. J. Dougherty, Pittsburg, Pa	....	....	302	11	....	57	66	195	32	361	1,025	1,424	2,449
Total	22	32	345	33	35	58	68	199	91	305	1,279	4,728	6,007
Total, 1905	....	....	....	....	....	....	....	....	....	....	....	....	4,206
Increase, 1906	....	....	....	....	....	....	....	....	....	....	....	....	1,801

In addition to these plates, there were inspected at the mills a large number of steel bars for braces and stay bolts in marine boilers, and also several hundred plates for stock and repairs.

There were many requests from other branches and departments of the Government for tests of material at the mills, which tests were completed and reports rendered to the proper officials.

NEW LIFE-PRESERVERS INSPECTED.

During the fiscal year ended June 30, 1906, inspectors of this Service inspected new life-preservers as follows:

Life-preservers inspected during the fiscal year ended June 30, 1906.

Kind.	Past.	Rejected.	Kind.	Past.	Rejected.
Block cork	149,108	1,645	Cork life jackets	490	
Consolidated cork	2,088	70	Balsa wood	1,854	1
Tule	24,228				
Comprest cork	1,915	147	Total	210,131	1,943
Acme	30,448	80			

The above statistics show that of the whole number of new life-preservers submitted for inspection and test, about 0.9 of 1 per cent were rejected, which conclusively indicates that manufacturers are complying closely with the requirements governing the construction and character of this important life-saving equipment.

OFFICERS LICENSED.

There were 7,886 officers of all grades licensed during the fiscal year ended June 30, 1906. The number licensed for each grade, by local districts, is shown in the table on the succeeding page.

Officers licensed during the fiscal year ended June 30, 1906.

Local district.	Masters.	Masters of steam yachts.	Mates of ocean steamers.	Mates of river steamers.	First-class pilots.	Second-class and special pilots.	Chief engineers.	Assistant engineers.	Special engineers.	Joint pilots and engineers.	Operators of motor vessels.	Engineers of motor vessels other than steam.	Masters of sail vessels of over 700 gross tons.	Mates of sail vessels of over 700 gross tons.	Masters or mates of vessels and barges of over 100 gross tons.	Total of all grades.
San Francisco, Cal	146	...	121	11	25	15	122	196	3	2	....	51	60	16	9	777
Juneau, Alaska	4	...	4	7	....	15	9	11	1	1	5	....	....	....	......	57
Portland, Oreg	17	...	5	20	8	27	21	42	5	1	....	5	5	....	1	157
Seattle, Wash	79	...	97	....	1	41	37	96	11	4	....	34	53	15	......	468
St. Michael, Alaska [a]	....	...	....	....	....	....	....	....	....	....	....	....	....	....	......	....
New York, N. Y	214	2	107	19	221	46	381	243	2	3	52	34	34	17	7	1,382
Albany, N. Y	7	...	....	6	10	16	26	37	6	3	....	1	....	....	......	112
Bangor, Me	5	...	7	....	8	12	10	13	....	....	....	10	3	3	......	71
Boston, Mass	87	...	43	1	26	40	71	108	16	5	....	25	39	31	1	493
New Haven, Conn	8	...	....	2	13	14	13	7	....	....	10	21	3	....	......	91
New London, Conn	8	...	....	3	14	20	13	12	2	2	....	12	1	1	......	88
Philadelphia, Pa	40	...	25	9	20	22	39	80	4	3	35	34	15	4	......	330
Portland, Me	11	...	6	....	15	19	12	15	1	4	12	3	13	4	......	115
Providence, R. I	22	...	2	4	17	26	41	34	3	2	16	18	5	1	......	191
Norfolk, Va	35	...	7	....	21	43	43	30	8	3	33	6	8	4	......	241
Baltimore, Md	65	...	19	4	34	52	42	70	5	4	48	31	4	6	......	384
Charleston, S. C	5	...	....	....	10	14	6	13	2	5	4	9	3	1	......	72
Jacksonville, Fla	3	...	1	1	5	14	5	11	3	....	....	16	3	....	......	62
Savannah, Ga	7	...	2	8	1	10	15	15	....	2	....	8	6	3	......	77
St. Louis, Mo	13	...	....	27	38	....	11	24	7	2	....	5	....	....	......	127
Dubuque, Iowa	6	...	....	7	7	26	8	17	8	8	3	9	....	....	......	99
Duluth, Minn	20	...	....	2	21	23	10	23	3	2	....	1	....	....	......	105
Louisville, Ky	5	...	....	1	5	5	7	4	3	....	....	1	....	....	......	31
Evansville, Ind	6	...	....	5	2	10	3	8	....	....	....	6	....	....	......	40
Memphis, Tenn	7	...	....	5	5	6	9	11	....	....	....	4	....	....	......	47
Nashville, Tenn	8	...	....	8	9	4	7	8	1	....	....	2	....	....	......	47
Cincinnati, Ohio	8	...	....	18	14	....	6	4	2	1	....	1	....	....	......	54
Gallipolis, Ohio [b]	19	...	....	21	16	5	2	9	....	....	....	2	....	....	......	74
Pittsburg, Pa	19	...	....	18	9	5	23	16	2	1	....	....	....	....	......	93
Point Pleasant, W. Va. [c]	1	...	....	1	2	1	1	3	....	....	....	....	....	....	......	9
Wheeling, W. Va. [b]	4	...	....	5	3	1	3	6	....	....	....	....	....	....	......	22
Detroit, Mich	12	...	....	....	13	6	34	54	2	2	....	....	....	....	......	123
Chicago, Ill	29	...	....	2	24	21	21	27	3	14	....	7	....	....	......	148
Grand Haven, Mich	12	...	....	....	9	16	18	24	4	4	....	6	....	....	......	93
Marquette, Mich	7	...	....	....	8	18	3	12	1	1	....	....	....	....	......	50
Milwaukee, Wis	15	...	....	....	18	22	20	43	4	1	5	7	....	....	......	135
Port Huron, Mich	40	...	....	....	64	21	27	50	8	3	....	3	....	....	......	216
Cleveland, Ohio	28	...	....	....	43	5	18	26	....	....	....	....	....	....	......	120
Buffalo, N. Y	19	...	....	....	32	31	25	47	7	4	4	....	....	....	2	171
Burlington, Vt	....	...	....	....	....	4	2	5	1	....	....	....	....	....	......	12
Oswego, N. Y	12	...	....	....	19	29	4	13	2	2	....	3	....	....	......	84
Toledo, Ohio	15	...	....	....	16	15	2	18	....	1	16	4	....	....	......	87
New Orleans, La	48	...	8	12	34	66	31	47	7	1	49	60	....	....	......	363
Apalachicola, Fla	15	...	1	3	17	17	11	16	5	....	....	8	1	1	......	95
Galveston, Tex	6	...	6	....	6	21	8	13	9	3	31	19	....	1	......	123
Mobile, Ala	11	...	6	1	13	33	16	33	....	3	22	6	4	2	......	150
Total	1,148	2	467	231	896	857	1,236	1,594	151	97	345	472	260	110	20	7,886

[a] Created May 1, 1906.
[b] Discontinued Apr. 30, 1906.
[c] Created May 1, 1906, by uniting the offices at Gallipolis, Ohio, and Wheeling, W. Va.

Total number of officers, all grades, licensed during fiscal year ended June 30, 1906	7,886
Total number licensed previous year	7,336
Increase over previous year	550

EXAMINATIONS FOR COLOR BLINDNESS.

During the year ended June 30, 1906, 1,504 applicants were examined for color blindness, of which number 39 were found color-blind and rejected and 1,465 were past. As compared with the fiscal year ended June 30, 1905, these figures show an increase of 38 in number of applicants examined and 56 in number of applicants past.

ACCIDENTS AND LIVES LOST.

The total number of accidents resulting in loss of life during the fiscal year ended June 30, 1906, was 65, with a total life loss of 500. Classified according to causes, the accidents and deaths resulted as shown in the following table:

Accidents resulting in loss of life during the fiscal year ended June 30, 1906.

Cause.	Accidents.	Lives lost.
Fire	4	6
Collision	23	45
Explosions or accidental escape of steam	5	12
Breaking of steam pipes, mud drums, etc	3	3
Accidents to machinery	4	4
Snags, wrecks, and sinking	26	253
Accidental drowning	....	123
Miscellaneous	....	54
Total	[a] 65	[b] 500

[a] Increase of 21 over previous year. [b] Increase of 249 over previous year.

Classified according to supervising inspection districts, the loss of life was as follows:

Lives lost as a result of accidents during the fiscal year ended June 30, 1906, by supervising inspection districts.

District.	Fire.	Collision.	Explosions or accidental escape of steam.	Breaking of steam pipes, mud drums, etc.	Accidents to machinery.	Snags, wrecks, or sinking.	Accidental drowning.	Miscellaneous.	Total.
First	1	4	1	1	1	129	15	7	159
Second	1	17	3	....	1	17	17	13	69
Third	3	6	....	....	....	21	15	8	53
Fourth	....	....	....	....	....	....	5	2	7
Fifth	....	....	....	....	1	36	1	3	41
Sixth	....	....	....	....	1	....	14	3	18
Seventh	....	4	2	....	....	1	23	2	32
Eighth	1	8	....	1	....	38	12	8	68
Ninth	....	4	1	....	....	2	2	2	11
Tenth	....	2	5	1	....	9	19	6	42
Total	6	45	12	3	4	253	123	54	500

The above statement marks an increase of about 100 per cent over the loss of life reported for the previous fiscal year, which increase is due principally to the foundering of the steamship *Peconic* on August 28, 1905, at a point off the northeast coast of Florida not actually determined, by which 20 souls perished; the loss of the steamer *Sevona* on Lake Superior on September 1, 1905, by which 7 lives were lost; the loss of the steamer *Iosco* on Lake Superior on September 3, 1905, when 19 lives were lost; the foundering of the steamer *Kaliyuga* on Lake Huron on October 19, 1905, by which 17 lives were lost; the wreck of the steamer *Ira H. Owen* on Lake Superior on November 28, 1905, when 19 souls perished; the stranding of the steamer *Mataafa* at the entrance to Duluth Harbor, Lake Superior, on November 28, 1905, when 9 persons lost their lives, and the wreck of the steamship *Valencia* on the south side of Vancouver Island, British Columbia, on January 22, 1906, by which 121 lives were lost.

The wreck of the steamship *Valencia*, the most serious of the several casualties of the year, was thoroly investigated by the officials of this Service, and was also made the subject of a special investigation by a commission appointed by the Secretary, in accordance with Executive order of February 7, 1906. All of the other casualties were investigated, so far as it was possible for the officers of this Service to obtain any information from the few who were left in some instances, and the entire absence of definite information in others, where whole crews perished with their ships. But the lessons of these disasters have not been lost, and laws and rules and regulations which were formulated with the object and purpose of lessening the frequency and mitigating the horrors of such disasters are already in successful operation.

Of the total number of 500 lives lost, 123 were from accidental drowning and 54 from suicides and other causes that could not be averted. This leaves 323 lives lost that can in any way be charged to accidents on board ship or to collisions or foundering.

During the year 330,235,959 passengers were carried on steamers required by law to make report of the number of passengers carried, a decrease of 12,024,391 from the previous year. A fair estimate of 250,000,000 more that were carried on steamers not required by law to make report makes it safe to calculate that about 580,000,000 passengers were carried by vessels under the jurisdiction of this Service. Of this number, 500 lives were lost, or an average of 1 life for every 1,160,000 passengers carried, and if we take from the total of 500 lives lost 177 that were attributable to suicides and drowning from miscellaneous causes other than wreck or collision, it leaves 323 lives lost from accident, or 1 life for about every 1,796,000 passengers carried.

RECOMMENDATIONS.

In the last annual report of this office I submitted a short legislative history of the Service, the effect of the operation of the law, the deficiencies of the present laws, and a few suggestions and recommendations for remedial legislation. I have the honor to again invite your attention to some of the recommendations that were at that time presented and to bespeak for them the consideration that their importance deserves.

Without entering into the details of these recommendations, I presume to renew my plea for legislation governing the transportation of fuel oil on passenger steamers, and also for some restrictions in its use, with especial reference to the necessity for fixing a minimum flashing point to be allowed all fuel oil. I also renew my suggestion for the amendment of section 4421, Revised Statutes, on the same lines as heretofore proposed.

My former recommendation for the repeal or the amending of section 4433, Revised Statutes, is renewed with all the force at my command, for the reason that recent developments have proven that this section must be repealed or amended in order that an intelligent and practicable rule for determining allowable pressures may be formulated, and so that manufacturers and owners may have the benefit of the improved design and stronger construction of boilers that is demanded by the present advanced practise.

Sections 4438, 4439, and 4445, Revised Statutes, should be amended in order that they may more fully meet their purpose, and my former recommendations upon these sections are exactly in line with this necessity.

Sections 4463, 4464, and 4465, Revised Statutes, referred to in my previous report, should be amended without delay, and in the interest of the safety of the traveling public I beg to renew my former recommendations upon this subject, and earnestly request that you urge upon Congress the necessity of this legislation.

Recent amendments to section 4471 have made that section applicable to its purpose, and it is all right as it now stands.

I beg to renew my recommendation for legislation providing for the punishment of those who interfere with or obstruct an inspector in the performance of his duty.

MEETING OF THE BOARD OF SUPERVISING INSPECTORS.

The regular meeting of the Board of Supervising Inspectors was held in January and February, 1906, when amendments and additions to the rules and regulations were adopted, which, having received the approval of the Secretary, have since had the force of law. Several different tests of life-saving devices were demonstrated satisfactorily and approved, and there was an important destructive test of the Morison furnace in the presence of the full board.

MEETING OF THE EXECUTIVE COMMITTEE.

The executive committee, authorized by the act of Congress approved March 3, 1905, have held two meetings during the fiscal year for the purpose of testing life-saving devices and modifying and amending the rules and regulations. The first of these meetings was on July 1, 1905, and the last on June 28, 1906, and the work of the committee shows conclusively that its establishment was not only important but wise legislation, and its necessity has been fully proven.

EFFECT OF THE PRESENT LAWS.

It is gratifying to note that the amended laws and rules and regulations are working well, and, with but few exceptions, are meeting practically all demands. The Service has been much improved and is steadily progressing, and while it is by no means what it should be nor what we hope to make it, at the same time I would be remiss in my duty were I to omit the positive statement that under the present conditions of inspection the lives of passengers and crews and the property of those interested in or utilizing marine transportation are more carefully safeguarded than ever before in the history of our merchant marine.

FIREPROOF CONSTRUCTION OF EXCURSION STEAMERS.

In my last report I referred briefly to the experiment of a fireproof excursion steamer, and it gives me pleasure to report that this matter has now past its experimental stage. The construction and operation of a fireproof excursion steamer has proven successful beyond the strongest hopes of those who conceived this type of construction, and I renew my recommendation that Congress enact such legislation as will imperatively demand that fireproof construction be required in all excursion steamers hereafter built or contracted for.

CONCLUSION.

During the year I have made an entire tour of the First and Tenth districts, and have visited parts of the Second, Third, Fourth, Fifth, Seventh, Eighth, and Ninth districts, and am glad to report improved conditions in the Service and general satisfaction among the owners and officers of the vessels under the jurisdiction of this Service. I am pleased to note the growing confidence of the public in the safety of marine transportation, due no doubt to the result of the efforts of this Service to require efficient life-saving and fire-fighting equipment, and to the owners who provide it and the officers who maintain it in fit and serviceable condition. The rigid and thoro inspection of all steam vessels and their equipment is a matter of public knowledge, and has had much to do with the return of the confidence that was impaired by previous disasters.

I desire to express my grateful appreciation of your generous support of the efforts of myself and the Service at large to advance the usefulness of the Service in the interest of public safety, and to say that without your sustaining encouragement it would have been impossible to secure the success that has justified our best endeavor.

There are attached hereto for your information and for the information of Congress the statistical details of the operation of this Service and a full list of the vessels under its jurisdiction.

Respectfully,

Geo. Uhler,
Supervising Inspector-General.

Hon. V. H. Metcalf,
Secretary of Commerce and Labor.

APPENDIX.

GENERAL STATISTICS.

STATEMENT EMBRACING THE VARIOUS MATTERS AND OCCURRENCES RELATING TO VESSELS NAVIGATED UNDER THE ACTS OF CONGRESS THAT HAVE BEEN ACTED UPON BY THE SEVERAL BOARDS OF LOCAL AND SUPERVISING INSPECTORS FOR THE YEAR ENDED DECEMBER 31, 1905.

	First district.					Second district.									
	San Francisco, Cal.	Portland, Oreg.	Seattle, Wash.	Juneau, Alaska.	Total.	New York, N. Y.	Boston, Mass.	Philadelphia, Pa.	New London, Conn.	Albany, N. Y.	Portland, Me.	Providence, R. I.	Bangor, Me.	New Haven, Conn.	Total.
Granted certificates of inspection:															
Domestic steam vessels	310	153	294	191	948	1,281	268	309	107	194	147	179	72	101	2,658
Domestic vessels propelled by gas, fluid, naphtha, or electric motors	41	3	11	6	61	26	9	7	15	1	6	8	4	19	95
Domestic sail vessels, barges, etc.	68	10	39	1	118	41	10	6		2	6	3	2	3	73
Foreign steam vessels	9		11		20	175	22	12		1	4		3		217
Total	428	166	355	198	1,147	1,523	309	334	122	198	163	190	81	123	3,043
Refused certificates of inspection:															
Domestic steam vessels				3	3	14				3	1				18
Domestic vessels propelled by gas, fluid, naphtha, or electric motors											1				1
Total				3	3	14				3	2				19
Gross tonnage of vessels inspected:															
Domestic steam vessels	317,523	30,520	123,072	30,567	501,782	657,605	70,322	132,445	55,952	39,109	31,099	66,785	3,375	12,876	1,069,568
Domestic vessels propelled by gas, fluid, naphtha, or electric motors	4,424	93	563	632	5,712	763	996	294	429	46	319	182	106	570	3.705

STATEMENT EMBRACING THE VARIOUS MATTERS AND OCCURRENCES RELATING TO VESSELS NAVIGATED UNDER THE ACTS OF CONGRESS THAT HAVE BEEN ACTED UPON BY THE SEVERAL BOARDS OF LOCAL AND SUPERVISING INSPECTORS FOR THE YEAR ENDED DECEMBER 31, 1905—Continued.

	First district.					Second district.									
	San Francisco, Cal.	Portland, Oreg.	Seattle, Wash.	Juneau, Alaska.	Total.	New York, N. Y.	Boston, Mass.	Philadelphia, Pa.	New London, Conn.	Albany, N. Y.	Portland, Me.	Providence, R. I.	Bangor, Me.	New Haven, Conn.	Total.
Gross tonnage of vessels inspected—Continued.															
Domestic sail vessels, barges, etc.	92,270	11,030	43,930	1,030	148,260	32,193	15,327	9,659	....	515	7,867	3,096	2,383	3,052	74,092
Foreign steam vessels	37,412	....	42,173	....	79,585	1,225,911	205,135	80,889	....	1,811	30,380	....	855	....	1,544,981
Total	451,629	41,643	209,738	32,329	735,339	1,916,472	291,780	223,287	56,381	41,481	69,665	70,063	6,719	16,498	2,692,346
New vessels added to service	13	11	14	11	49	71	7	18	7	9	6	4	6	5	133
Vessels gone out of service	3	11	3	9	26	5	3	6	3	5	6	....	....	1	29
Gross tonnage of new vessels added to service	6,560	2,139	1,389	1,497	11,585	191,818	6,489	11,244	21,741	889	4,623	484	941	214	238,443
Gross tonnage of vessels gone out of service	4,181	1,637	336	1,077	7,231	2,967	1,172	7,364	471	600	125	....	....	136	12,835
Boilers inspected:															
Steel (riveted plates)	676	135	302	225	1,338	2,313	274	354	111	197	160	184	51	82	3,726
Iron (riveted plates)	47	12	27	5	91	285	46	93	10	52	7	13	3	10	519
Pipe	49	13	102	32	196	264	71	35	58	13	38	62	22	22	585
Total	772	160	431	262	1,625	2,862	391	482	179	262	205	259	76	114	4,830
Boilers found defective:															
Steel (riveted plates)	33	....	18	28	79	112	20	61	7	29	8	18	9	17	281
Iron (riveted plates)	1	....	....	....	1	41	12	23	....	12	....	3	1	6	98
Pipe	....	....	1	....	1	....	1	....	....	....	....	3	....	1	5
Boilers gave way under hydrostatic pressure:															
Steel (riveted plates)	8	....	7	....	15	15	1	1	2	1	2	1	1	....	24
Iron (riveted plates)	....	....	....	....	....	2	1	....	....	....	....	2	....	....	5
Boilers condemned from further use:															
Steel (riveted plates)	1	1	....	5	7	....	2	....	....	....	1	1	....	....	4
Iron (riveted plates)	....	1	....	....	1	....	....	1	....	3	....	1	....	....	5
Pipe	....	....	....	....	....	....	2	....	....	....	....	....	....	1	3
Defects in boilers and attachments:															
Sheets	14	....	1	23	38	151	11	19	4	44	2	11	3	18	263
Heads	2	....	....	3	5	9	1	5	....	3	31	....	....	....	49

Steam and mud drums			2	9	11		1	2	4						7
Flues and tubes	21		2	4	27	2,059	9	8		263	1	12	8	7	2,362
Steam pipes		1			1		1	5					3	1	10
Stay bolts	25	1	8	2	36	352	23	19		212	28	20	1	4	659
Braces	15				15		3	18		6	3	6		3	39
Other parts	14		6	1	21	18	5	82				24			129
Tests of samples of steel and iron plates to be used in marine boilers, other than material tested at the mills by assistant inspectors:															
Samples of steel tested	50	8			58	37	7								44
Samples of iron tested						23									23
Steel failed in tensile strength	7				7	4									4
Steel failed in reduction of area	1				1	1	1								2
Iron failed in reduction of area						2									2
Failed in elongation	1				1		1								1
Tests of samples of line-carrying guns:															
Samples tested						92	6								98
Failed in tensile strength						2									2
Failed in reduction of area						15									15
Vessels wrecked or foundered:															
Steam vessels	2	2	1	1	6	3		1	1						5
Sail vessels	1				1										
Barges, etc						2	1		1						4
Accidents to steam and other vessels:															
By collision between vessels	20	3	11		34	127	12	21	5	1	4	5	2	3	180
By fire	5		4		9	11	3	4	5	2	2	2	1	1	31
By sinking						3	1	4	1						9
By grounding	8		4	2	14	3	4	8	5		2		2	1	25
Damaged by snags, ice, or other cause		2	5		7	1	1	16			1	1		2	22
By explosion or accidental escape of steam	1		1		2			2				1	1		4
To machinery	4	2	8		14		1	4	1		2		1		9
Miscellaneous	1		1		2			2							2
Accidents causing loss of life by explosion or accidental escape of steam	1		1		2			1							1
Lives lost:															
By explosion or accidental escape of steam	1		1		2			1							1
By wreck or founder						14	4		7						25

STATEMENT EMBRACING THE VARIOUS MATTERS AND OCCURRENCES RELATING TO VESSELS NAVIGATED UNDER THE ACTS OF CONGRESS THAT HAVE BEEN ACTED UPON BY THE SEVERAL BOARDS OF LOCAL AND SUPERVISING INSPECTORS FOR THE YEAR ENDED DECEMBER 31, 1905—Continued.

	First district.					Second district.									
	San Francisco, Cal.	Portland, Oreg.	Seattle, Wash.	Juneau, Alaska	Total.	New York, N. Y.	Boston, Mass.	Philadelphia, Pa.	New London, Conn.	Albany, N. Y.	Portland, Me	Providence, R. I.	Bangor, Me.	New Haven, Conn.	Total.
Lives lost—Continued.															
By collision between vessels	4	....	....	....	4	5	2	8	....	4	....	....	2	....	21
By accidental drowning	10	2	3	13	28	9	1	3	1	....	....	....	1	....	15
From miscellaneous causes	5	....	2	....	7	4	....	3	....	....	....	1	....	....	8
Passengers lost:															
By collision between vessels	2	....	....	....	2	1	1	....	....	4	....	....	....	....	6
By accidental drowning	1	....	....	....	1	1	....	....	....	....	....	....	....	....	1
From miscellaneous causes	2	....	....	....	2	3	....	2	....	....	....	....	....	....	5
Lives saved by means of life-saving appliances required by law	232	....	....	....	232	5	....	....	....	10	....	....	....	....	15
Passengers carried by steamers	27,300,876	1,793,910	2,530,723	128,835	31,754,344	a199,322,364	22,457,561	28,823,285	1,091,676	3,721,629	2,436,043	2,277,613	754,844	507,613	261,392,628
Amount of property lost:															
By wreck or founder	$495,000	$16,500	$6,000	$6,000	$523,500	$15,000	....	....	$45,000	....	....	....	....	....	$60,000
By collision between vessels	$29,760	$3.200	$1,550	....	$34,510	$53,000	$2,000	....	$2,265	$500	$170	$5,000	....	$8.175	$71,110
By fire	$86,000	$500	$13,800	....	$100,300	$86,000	$2,500	....	$3,500	$7,500	$550	$5,000	$5,000	$7,000	$116,850
By snags	....	$1.000	....	....	$1,000	$1,000	....	....	....	....	....	$1,000	....	$3,000	$5,000
From miscellaneous causes	$54,600	$2,200	$13,720	$56,125	$126,645	....	....	....	$10,000	....	....	....	$125	....	$10,125
Total	$665,360	$23,400	$35,070	$62,125	$785,955	$155,000	$4,500	....	$60,565	$8,000	$720	$11,000	$5,125	$18,175	$263,085
Violations of the steamboat laws:															
Cases investigated by local boards	32	4	32	10	78	53	4	23	17	1	....	4	....	4	106
Cases dismissed	8	....	5	4	17	21	....	9	10	....	....	1	....	....	41
Licenses suspended	25	3	26	8	62	27	4	21	7	....	....	3	....	4	66
Licenses revoked	....	....	6	2	8	4	....	....	....	2	....	....	....	1	7
Cases reported to district attorneys and to chief officers of customs	....	....	....	13	13	20	4	9	4	....	2	2	....	2	43
Appeals taken from decisions of local boards:															
Number of appeals	4	2	....	2	8	9	....	7	....	2	....	....	2	....	20

Decisions revoked	1				1	1									1
Decisions modified	2	1		1	4	7		7		1			2		17
Decisions sustained	1	1			2	1				1					2
Received original license:															
Masters of steam vessels	9	4	13	2	28	18	5	1		2					26
Masters and pilots of steam vessels	9	6	14	3	32	2	2	3			1				8
Mates of steam vessels	72	21	30	8	131	56	32	38	3	5	2	15		4	155
Mates and pilots of steam vessels			18	3	21	1	1	1						1	4
Pilots of steam and other motor vessels	32	17	19	6	74	143	30	14	16	13	9	19	16	14	274
Joint pilots and engineers of steam vessels	1		2	4	7		3	1		1	2				7
Engineers of steam and other motor vessels	117	42	84	33	276	245	81	75	20	23	21	25	15	25	530
Masters of sail vessels and barges	10		15		25	3	6	2		1	8	2			22
Chief mates of sail vessels and barges	20	1	14		35	8	13	2						2	25
Total	270	91	209	59	629	476	173	137	39	45	43	61	31	46	1,051
Received renewal of license:															
Masters of steam vessels	36	1	18	1	56	54	18	7			3				82
Masters and pilots of steam vessels	96	11	31	3	141	133	30	30	4	4	6	12	5	7	231
Mates of steam vessels	70	9	15	3	97	47	13	4			1				65
Mates and pilots of steam vessels	3		3		6	7	4	3			2		2		18
Pilots of steam and other motor vessels	19	6	26	4	55	111	31	27	11	13	16	14	7	12	242
Joint pilots and engineers of steam vessels			1	1	2	6	1		1	2		2			12
Engineers of steam and other motor vessels	225	19	52	6	302	373	102	64	14	37	17	44	20	11	682
Masters of sail vessels and barges	96	7	36		139	32	40	9	1	1	13	8	3	3	110
Chief mates of sail vessels and barges	16		6		22	16	19	5	1		3	2	4		50
Total	561	53	188	18	820	779	258	149	32	57	61	82	41	33	1,492
Refused license:															
Masters of steam vessels	2		1	1	4	2									2
Mates of steam vessels	2		2	1	5	3		3	2	1		4		1	14
Pilots of steam and other motor vessels	2			1	3	5	3	6	2				2		18

a The decrease in the year 1905 from the year 1904 of nearly 4 millions in number of passengers carried in the local inspection district of New York, N. Y., is accounted for by loss of business of the three ferry companies operating in the vicinity of the new Williamsburg Bridge, which lines carried 14,488,331 less passengers in 1905 than in 1904.

STATEMENT EMBRACING THE VARIOUS MATTERS AND OCCURRENCES RELATING TO VESSELS NAVIGATED UNDER THE ACTS OF CONGRESS THAT HAVE BEEN ACTED UPON BY THE SEVERAL BOARDS OF LOCAL AND SUPERVISING INSPECTORS FOR THE YEAR ENDED DECEMBER 31, 1905—Continued.

	First district.					Second district.									
	San Francisco, Cal.	Portland, Oreg.	Seattle, Wash.	Juneau, Alaska.	Total.	New York, N. Y.	Boston, Mass.	Philadelphia, Pa.	New London, Conn.	Albany, N. Y.	Portland, Me.	Providence, R. I.	Bangor, Me.	New Haven, Conn.	Total.
Refused license—Continued.															
Joint pilots and engineers of steam vessels			1	2	3										
Engineers of steam and other motor vessels	3		8	3	14	20	2	14	2		2			1	41
Masters of sail vessels and barges						2									2
Chief mates of sail vessels and barges	2		1		3	1	3	1	1						6
Total	11		13	8	32	33	8	24	7	1	2	4	2	2	83
Licenses suspended or revoked:															
Masters of steam vessels	8		4	1	13										
Masters and pilots of steam vessels	27	3	14		44	18		6	5			1		1	31
Mates of steam vessels	20		1	1	22										
Pilots of steam and other motor vessels			2	1	3	9	1	7	2	2		1		2	24
Engineers of steam and other motor vessels	12	2	11	7	32	4	3	8				1		2	18
Masters of sail vessels and barges	10				10										
Chief mates of sail vessels and barges	5				5										
Total	82	5	32	10	129	31	4	21	7	2		3		5	73

	Third district.						Fourth district.	Fifth district.			Sixth district.				
	Norfolk, Va.	Baltimore, Md.	Charleston, S. C.	Savannah, Ga.	Jacksonville, Fla.	Total.	St. Louis, Mo.	Dubuque, Iowa.	Duluth, Minn.	Total.	Louisville, Ky.	Evansville, Ind.	Nashville, Tenn.	Memphis, Tenn.	Total.
Granted certificates of inspection:															
Domestic steam vessels	256	290	105	83	63	797	131	80	195	275	61	77	89	71	298
Domestic vessels propelled by gas, fluid, naphtha, or electric motors	3	17	4	4	6	34	10	11	4	15	5	5		2	12
Domestic sail vessels, barges, etc.	18	9	3	4		34	2	3	1	4			1		1
Foreign steam vessels		16				16									
Total	277	332	112	91	69	881	143	94	200	294	66	82	90	73	311
Refused certificates of inspection:															
Domestic steam vessels		5	2		2	9	3	3	1	4	26	12		8	46
Domestic vessels propelled by gas, fluid, naphtha, or electric motors					1	1		1		1	1				1
Domestic sail vessels, barges, etc.							1								
Foreign steam vessels		1				1									
Total		6	2		3	11	4	4	1	5	27	12		8	47
Gross tonnage of vessels inspected:															
Domestic steam vessels	57,373	121,549	9,319	50,875	7,226	246,342	26,184	6,568	203,398	209,966	11,694	10,067	10,636	9,086	41,483
Domestic vessels propelled by gas, fluid, naphtha, or electric motors	102	1,136	87	110	188	1,623	225	533	169	702	188	186		48	422
Domestic sail vessels, barges, etc.	25,858	10,669	3,487	4,371		44,385	917	516	192	708			110		110
Foreign steam vessels		91,414				91,414									
Total	83,333	224,768	12,893	55,356	7,414	383,764	27,326	7,617	203,759	211,376	11,882	10,253	10,746	9,134	42,015
New vessels added to service	8	21	8	3	5	45	4	10	7	17	14	4	5	2	25
Vessels gone out of service	1	4	9	1	5	20	14	15	3	18	1	4	3	6	14
Gross tonnage of new vessels added to service	3,361	10,355	689	618	165	15,188	119	426	6,484	6,910	1,990	106	369	95	2,560
Gross tonnage of vessels gone out of service	409	45	194	1,855	92	2,595	3,180	978	10,384	11,362	66	150	160	1,217	1,593

STATEMENT EMBRACING THE VARIOUS MATTERS AND OCCURRENCES RELATING TO VESSELS NAVIGATED UNDER THE ACTS OF CONGRESS THAT HAVE BEEN ACTED UPON BY THE SEVERAL BOARDS OF LOCAL AND SUPERVISING INSPECTORS FOR THE YEAR ENDED DECEMBER 31, 1905—Continued.

	Third district.						Fourth district.	Fifth district.			Sixth district.				
	Norfolk, Va.	Baltimore, Md.	Charleston, S. C.	Savannah, Ga.	Jacksonville, Fla.	Total.	St. Louis, Mo.	Dubuque, Iowa.	Duluth, Minn.	Total.	Louisville, Ky.	Evansville, Ind.	Nashville, Tenn.	Memphis, Tenn.	Total.
Boilers inspected:															
Steel (riveted plates)	245	478	97	99	59	978	155	102	211	313	207	140	158	125	630
Iron (riveted plates)	45	46	8	7	1	107	8	3	11	14	1		4	4	9
Pipe	21	48	16	10	13	108	1	6	44	50	1	3		3	7
Total	311	572	121	116	73	1,193	164	111	266	377	209	143	162	132	646
Boilers found defective:															
Steel (riveted plates)	44	84	27	12	5	172	5	17	29	46	47	23	25	61	156
Iron (riveted plates)	4	13	3			20	1	1	2	3					
Pipe		2	6			8		1		1				1	1
Boilers gave way under hydrostatic pressure:															
Steel (riveted plates)	5	9	10	5	3	32	1		13	13	1			3	4
Iron (riveted plates)		2	1			3									
Pipe			3			3									
Boilers condemned from further use:															
Steel (riveted plates)		17	6		1	24	1		1	1	3	2		2	7
Iron (riveted plates)		10	1			11	1		1	1				1	1
Defects in boilers and attachments:															
Sheets	41	198	15	12	2	268	3	12	15	27	23	23	13	39	98
Heads		39				39		1		1		3	2	1	6
Steam and mud drums	1	4				5	1	5	3	8	2	11	6	8	27
Flues and tubes	1	2,111	2,468	2	3	4,585		8	6	14	117	80	87	396	680
Steam pipes		3	8		2	13	2	3	1	4		6	1	2	9
Stay bolts	24	91	1	9		125		1	112	113		5			5
Braces	1	26				27		5	7	12		4	2		6
Other parts	9	6				15		12		12					
Tests of samples of steel and iron plates to be used in marine boilers, other than material tested at the mills by assistant inspectors:															
Samples of steel tested		8				8		36		36	260				260
Failed in tensile strength								2		2	7				7
Failed in reduction of area								2		2	2				2
Failed in elongation								1		1	2				2

Vessels wrecked or foundered:															
Steam vessels	1			1		2		1	7	8	3	4			7
Motor vessels											1				1
Accidents to steam and other vessels:															
By collision between vessels	15	16	2	1	3	37	1							1	1
By fire	4	5	2	1	3	15	7	1	3	4	1		1	1	3
By sinking	2	2				4	4	1	2	3	3	4	2	1	10
By grounding	4					4							1		1
Damaged by snags, ice, or other cause	1	1	2			4			1	1				1	1
To machinery									2	2					
Miscellaneous	2	2				4			12	12					
Lives lost:															
By wreck or founder				20		20			18	18					
By collision between vessels	2	2		1	1	6									
By fire					1	1								1	1
By accidental drowning	5	3	2		3	13	3	1	2	3	3	3	6	7	19
From miscellaneous causes		1	1		3	5		1	2	3	1		1		2
Passengers lost:															
By accidental drowning	1				2	3	1							3	3
From miscellaneous causes		1	1		2	4	1				1				1
Lives saved by means of life-saving appliances required by law	20					20	1		17	17					
Passengers carried by steamers	4,652,967	3,691,972	593,613	401,653	449,465	9,789,670	2,931,224	1,018,329	655,677	1,674,006	822,419	308,335	269,373	323,617	1,723,744
Amount of property lost:															
By wreck or founder	$202,200				$300	$202,500		$6,000	$930,000	$936,000	$350		$1,000		$1,350
By collision between vessels	$6,800	$4,045	$1,310		$95	$12.250									
By fire	$1.410	$13,500		$300	$900	$16,110	$134,925	$2,000	$850	$2,850	$1.700		$20,000	$40,000	$61,700
By snags	$150		$375			$525			$1,000	$1,000	$2,975	$26,200	$1,500	$150	$30,825
From miscellaneous causes	$500	$500				$1,000		$200	$232,700	$232,900		$3,000	$600	$3,000	$6,600
Total	$211,060	$18,045	$1,685	$300	$1,295	$232.385	$134.925	$8,200	$1,164,550	1,172,750	$5,025	$29,200	$23,100	$43,150	$100,475
Violations of the steamboat laws:															
Cases investigated by local boards	18	11	7	3	3	42	3				10	6	13	8	37
Cases dismissed	9	6		1		16	1				2			2	4
Licenses suspended	4	6	6	2	3	21	6	1		1	3	6	12	4	25
Licenses revoked	2					2					2		2	3	7
Cases reported to district attorneys and to chief officers of customs	2	5		2		9	5	3	3	6	3	4	8	3	18
Appeals taken from decisions of local boards:															
Number of appeals			1			1	1	1	1	2			2		2
Decisions revoked			1			1		1		1			1		1
Decisions modified							1								
Decisions sustained									1	1			1		1

STATEMENT EMBRACING THE VARIOUS MATTERS AND OCCURRENCES RELATING TO VESSELS NAVIGATED UNDER THE ACTS OF CONGRESS THAT HAVE BEEN ACTED UPON BY THE SEVERAL BOARDS OF LOCAL AND SUPERVISING INSPECTORS FOR THE YEAR ENDED DECEMBER 31, 1905—Continued.

	Third district.						Fourth district.	Fifth district.			Sixth district.				
	Norfolk, Va.	Baltimore, Md.	Charleston, S. C.	Savannah, Ga.	Jacksonville, Fla.	Total.	St. Louis, Mo.	Dubuque, Iowa.	Duluth, Minn.	Total.	Louisville, Ky.	Evansville, Ind.	Nashville, Tenn.	Memphis, Tenn.	Total.
Received original license:															
Masters of steam vessels	4					4	12	1		1	2		2		4
Masters and pilots of steam vessels		36	2		1	39		2	9	11	1	6	4	3	14
Mates of steam vessels	7	10		12	1	30	24	2		2	3	4	3	2	12
Mates and pilots of steam vessels		11				11									
Pilots of steam and other motor vessels	23	45	14	10	8	100	27	15	14	29	6	4	9	7	26
Joint pilots and engineers of steam vessels	1	4	3	6	1	15	1	7	1	8					
Engineers of steam and other motor vessels	29	83	18	22	10	162	23	32	17	49	12	10	14	4	40
Masters of sail vessels and barges		2		1		3									
Chief mates of sail vessels and barges	6	3				9									
Total	70	194	37	51	21	373	87	59	41	100	24	24	32	16	96
Received renewal of license:															
Masters of steam vessels	24	4				28	4				1	2	1	5	9
Masters and pilots of steam vessels	21	31	5	8	2	67	3	6	7	13	3	5	2	5	15
Mates of steam vessels	5	1		2	1	9	13	5	1	6	4	3	2	6	15
Mates and pilots of steam vessels	1	2		2		5									
Pilots of steam and other motor vessels	33	22	14	4	12	85	23	15	11	26	3	11	8	13	35
Joint pilots and engineers of steam vessels	1					1	2		1	1					
Engineers of steam and other motor vessels	55	39	9	14	15	132	26	14	14	28	5	11	9	12	37
Masters of sail vessels and barges	11	5	3	8	1	28									
Chief mates of sail vessels and barges	2	6		2		10									
Total	153	110	31	40	31	365	71	40	34	74	16	32	22	41	111

Refused license:															
Masters of steam vessels	3	1				4		1		1	1	1		1	3
Masters and pilots of steam vessels	3					3			2	2					
Mates of steam vessels	2	1			1	4	1				2	2		1	5
Pilots of steam and other motor vessels		3	3			6	1	3	4	7	2	2	2	1	7
Engineers of steam and other motor vessels	1				2	3	2	3		3				2	2
Total	9	5	3		3	20	4	7	6	13	5	5	2	5	17
Licenses suspended or revoked:															
Masters of steam vessels	2					2	2	1		1		1	1		2
Masters and pilots of steam vessels	2	5	2	2	1	12					1	1	1	2	5
Mates of steam vessels													1		1
Pilots of steam and other motor vessels	1	1				2	3					1	2	2	5
Engineers of steam and other motor vessels			4		2	6	1				4	3	9	3	19
Total	5	6	6	2	3	22	6	1		1	5	6	14	7	32

	Seventh district.					Eighth district.						
	Cincinnati, Ohio.	Gallipolis, Ohio.	Wheeling, W. Va.	Pittsburg, Pa.	Total.	Detroit, Mich.	Chicago, Ill.	Grand Haven, Mich.	Marquette, Mich.	Milwaukee, Wis.	Port Huron, Mich.	Total.
Granted certificates of inspection:												
Domestic steam vessels	61	68	24	130	283	150	170	176	102	252	130	980
Domestic vessels propelled by gas, fluid, naphtha, or electric motors	2				2							
Domestic sail vessels, barges, etc		1		1	2		3			2	2	7
Foreign steam vessels						2			6		5	13
Total	63	69	24	131	287	152	173	176	108	254	137	1,000
Refused certificates of inspection: Domestic steam vessels		2	2		4					1	3	4
Gross tonnage of vessels inspected:												
Domestic steam vessels	14,741	8,144	2,919	22,733	48,537	145,769	175,727	53,775	17,296	219,355	74,439	686,361
Domestic vessels propelled by gas, fluid, naphtha, or electric motors	43				43		71			66	44	181
Domestic sail vessels, barges, etc		152		115	267							
Foreign steam vessels						593			2,910		7,482	10,985
Total	14,784	8,296	2,919	22,848	48,847	146,362	175,798	53,775	20,206	219,421	81,965	697,527

STATEMENT EMBRACING THE VARIOUS MATTERS AND OCCURRENCES RELATING TO VESSELS NAVIGATED UNDER THE ACTS OF CONGRESS THAT HAVE BEEN ACTED UPON BY THE SEVERAL BOARDS OF LOCAL AND SUPERVISING INSPECTORS FOR THE YEAR ENDED DECEMBER 31, 1905—Continued.

	Seventh district.					Eighth district.						
	Cincinnati, Ohio.	Gallipolis, Ohio.	Wheeling, W. Va.	Pittsburg, Pa.	Total.	Detroit, Mich.	Chicago, Ill.	Grand Haven, Mich.	Marquette, Mich.	Milwaukee, Wis.	Port Huron, Mich.	Total.
New vessels added to service	5	2	1	1	9	9	4	5	1	9	11	39
Vessels gone out of service	3	4	3	4	14	1	2	5	4	8	11	31
Gross tonnage of new vessels added to service	117	193	86	151	547	52,236	12,728	1,013	16	606	29,153	95,752
Gross tonnage of vessels gone out of service	346	603	186	314	1,449	27	59	3,605	7,067	5,914	12,296	28,968
Boilers inspected:												
Steel (riveted plates)	172	140	35	382	729	196	222	188	104	338	156	1,204
Iron (riveted plates)	1		3	1	5	10	11	19	11	18	10	79
Pipe	2	3	1	20	26	31	23	19	3	18	9	103
Total	175	143	39	403	760	237	256	226	118	374	175	1,386
Boilers found defective:												
Steel (riveted plates)	71	52	14	196	333		30	13	15	12	7	77
Iron (riveted plates)							2	6	1	2	1	12
Pipe				1	1				1	1		2
Boilers gave way under hydrostatic pressure:												
Steel (riveted plates)						3	10	1	1	9	5	29
Iron (riveted plates)						1					1	2
Boilers condemned from further use:												
Steel (riveted plates)		9	1		10						1	1
Iron (riveted plates)		2			2							
Defects in boilers and attachments:												
Sheets	50	17	1	130	198	2	33	14	26		8	83
Heads	12	1		3	16				2			2
Steam and mud drums	2	6	1	25	34			2			2	4
Flues and tubes	50	3	62	39	154	1	28	6	2	4	8	49
Steam pipes			2	2	4			2	6	4		12
Stay bolts		25	4	1	30	1	168	15	175	9	17	385
Braces							8	2	16	2	8	36
Other parts			66		66			2	12	2		16
Tests of samples of steel and iron plates to be used in marine boilers other than material tested at the mills by assistant inspectors: Samples of steel tested							7					7

Vessels wrecked or foundered: Steam vessels	4	3	1	8	16			3	2	1	4	10
Accidents to steam and other vessels:												
By collision between vessels	1	2		12	15	8	7	2	13	4	10	44
By fire			1	2	3	1	1	2	2	2	5	13
By sinking	2	1	1	5	9	1	1				3	5
By grounding				1	1	4	2		17	4	8	35
Damaged by snags, ice, or other cause	3	1	2	5	11				4			4
By explosion or accidental escape of steam		1			1		2					2
To machinery	3		1		4	3	3	3	2	6		17
Miscellaneous							7	10	3	8	1	29
Accidents causing loss of life by explosion or accidental escape of steam		1			1							
Lives lost:												
By explosion or accidental escape of steam, etc.		9			9							
By wreck or founder									38		17	55
By collision between vessels											2	2
By accidental drowning	2	4	7	16	29	2	2	1	6	2	3	16
From miscellaneous causes				1	1				1			1
Passengers lost:												
By accidental drowning			2	3	5	2						2
From miscellaneous causes							3					3
Lives saved by means of life-saving appliances required by law		1			1			35	46	42	156	279
Passengers carried by steamers	1,136,738	1,283,885	621,809	432,700	3,475,132	6,795,439	1,210,837	889,804	1,129,073	451,010	741,404	11,217,567
Amount of property lost:												
By explosion		$30,000			$30,000		$300					$300
By wreck or founder	$37,800	$2,300	$10,000	$27,100	$77,200			$181,500	$105,000	$75,000	$70,000	$431,500
By collision between vessels		$850		$3,455	$4,305	$20,425	$910	$600	$195,200	$16,205	$362,800	$596,140
By fire			$6,000	$28,000	$34,000	$3,500	$3,500	$12,000	$66,000	$41,500	$95,000	$221,500
By snags				$2,000	$2,000				$4,700			$4.700
From miscellaneous causes						$19,975	$23,317	$49,100	$198,425	$20,045	$71,700	$382,562
Total	$37,800	$33,150	$16,000	$60,555	$147.505	$43,900	$28,027	$243,200	$569,325	$152,750	$599,500	$1,636,702
Violations of the steamboat laws:												
Cases investigated by local boards	3	4	3	5	15	2	4		11		5	22
Cases dismissed	1	1		1	3	1			3		1	5
Licenses suspended	1	1	3	6	11	1	9	3	12	1	2	28
Licenses revoked		1	1		2		2			1	1	4
Cases reported to district attorneys and to chief officers of customs	1	2	2	3	8	1	5	5	4	6	1	22
Appeals taken from decisions of local boards:												
Number of appeals			1	1	2	2	4	3	3	5	7	24
Decisions revoked			1		1		1	1		1	4	7
Decisions modified							1		2	1		4
Decisions sustained				1	1	2	2	2	1	3	3	13

STATEMENT EMBRACING THE VARIOUS MATTERS AND OCCURRENCES RELATING TO VESSELS NAVIGATED UNDER THE ACTS OF CONGRESS THAT HAVE BEEN ACTED UPON BY THE SEVERAL BOARDS OF LOCAL AND SUPERVISING INSPECTORS FOR THE YEAR ENDED DECEMBER 31, 1905—Continued.

	Seventh district.					Eighth district.						
	Cincinnati, Ohio.	Gallipolis, Ohio.	Wheeling, W. Va.	Pittsburg, Pa.	Total.	Detroit, Mich.	Chicago, Ill.	Grand Haven, Mich.	Marquette, Mich.	Milwaukee, Wis.	Port Huron, Mich.	Total.
Received original license:												
Masters of steam vessels	2	2	2	...	6	...	...	...	...	...	...	...
Masters and pilots of steam vessels	...	1	...	...	1	...	3	5	3	1	7	19
Mates of steam vessels	4	6	3	7	20	...	...	...	...	...	...	...
Pilots of steam and other motor vessels	3	9	3	4	19	12	18	12	11	31	20	104
Joint pilots and engineers of steam vessels	1	...			1	2	1	1	...	...	2	6
Engineers of steam and other motor vessels	6	14	4	9	33	19	15	11	8	20	15	88
Total	16	32	12	20	80	33	37	29	22	52	44	217
Received renewal of license:												
Masters of steam vessels	6	3	1	3	13	...	...	...	...	...	...	...
Masters and pilots of steam vessels	1	9	2	14	26	16	21	7	3	20	34	101
Mates of steam vessels	11	9	5	6	31	...	...	...	...	...	...	...
Pilots of steam and other motor vessels	7	10	4	4	25	13	15	5	8	15	30	86
Joint pilots and engineers of steam vessels	...	...	...	2	2	...	1	2	...	1	...	4
Engineers of steam and other motor vessels	5	10	2	27	44	53	13	18	9	32	42	167
Total	30	41	14	56	141	82	50	32	20	68	106	358
Refused license:												
Masters of steam vessels	...	...	1	1	2	...	...	...	...	...	...	...
Masters and pilots of steam vessels	...	...	...	...	...	4	1	...	...	2	3	10
Mates of steam vessels	...	...	...	2	2	...	...	...	...	...	...	...
Pilots of steam and other motor vessels	...	...	...	1	1	9	2	3	1	6	11	32
Joint pilots and engineers of steam vessels	...	...	...	...	...	1	...	...	...	...	...	1
Engineers of steam and other motor vessels	2	1	...	5	8	8	3	9	5	1	13	39
Total	2	1	1	9	13	22	6	12	6	9	27	82

Licenses suspended or revoked:												
Masters and pilots of steam vessels			2	2	4		6	3	8	1	1	19
Pilots of steam and other motor vessels		1	1	1	3	1	3		2			6
Engineers of steam and other motor vessels	1	1	1	3	6		2		2	1	2	7
Total	1	2	4	6	13	1	11	3	12	2	3	32

	Ninth district.						Tenth district.				
	Cleveland, Ohio.	Buffalo, N. Y.	Burlington, Vt.	Oswego, N. Y.	Toledo, Ohio.	Total.	New Orleans, La.	Apalachicola, Fla.	Galveston, Tex.	Mobile, Ala.	Total.
Granted certificates of inspection:											
Domestic steam vessels	215	306	39	118	104	782	313	72	77	137	599
Domestic vessels propelled by gas, fluid, naphtha, or electric motors, etc.				1	1	2	18	6	19	13	56
Domestic sail vessels, barges, etc							6	1	1	2	10
Foreign steam vessels		14	3	18	2	37	43		12	11	66
Total	215	320	42	137	107	821	380	79	109	163	731
Refused certificates of inspection:											
Domestic steam vessels			1	5	1	7	14		1		15
Domestic vessels propelled by gas, fluid, naphtha, or electric motors							4				4
Foreign steam vessels							1				1
Total			1	5	1	7	19		1		20
Gross tonnage of vessels inspected:											
Domestic steam vessels	394,101	316,761	3,385	28,977	89,518	832,742	60,120	8,366	34,549	11,200	114,235
Domestic vessels propelled by gas, fluid, naphtha, or electric motors				17	26	43	500	238	571	348	1,657
Domestic sail vessels, barges, etc							5,959	1,079	728	1,520	9,286
Foreign steam vessels		17,244	1,373	5,001	1,124	24,742	132,657		50,056	14,378	197,091
Total	394,101	334,005	4,758	33,995	90,668	857,527	199,236	9,683	85,904	27,446	322,269
New vessels added to service	11	6	1	1	5	24	22	5	14	12	53
Vessels gone out of service	1	2	2	2	1	8	12	1	4	13	30
Gross tonnage of new vessels added to service	47,459	888	5	9	5,907	54,268	12,241	188	3,796	2,681	18,906
Gross tonnage of vessels gone out of service	517	2,253	586	20	12	3,388	3,534	19	61	1,718	5,332

STATEMENT EMBRACING THE VARIOUS MATTERS AND OCCURRENCES RELATING TO VESSELS NAVIGATED UNDER THE ACTS OF CONGRESS THAT HAVE BEEN ACTED UPON BY THE SEVERAL BOARDS OF LOCAL AND SUPERVISING INSPECTORS FOR THE YEAR ENDED DECEMBER 31, 1905—Continued.

	Ninth district.						Tenth district.				
	Cleveland, Ohio.	Buffalo, N. Y.	Burlington, Vt.	Oswego, N. Y.	Toledo, Ohio.	Total.	New Orleans, La.	Apalachicola, Fla.	Galveston, Tex.	Mobile, Ala.	Total.
Boilers inspected:											
Steel (riveted plates)	340	468	23	99	118	1,048	413	74	107	194	788
Iron (riveted plates)	11	14	2	9	10	46	25	2	3		30
Pipe	25	13	20	52	14	124	5	7	7	8	27
Total	376	495	45	160	142	1,218	443	83	117	202	845
Boilers found defective:											
Steel (riveted plates)	36	56		9	15	116	38	5	1	13	57
Iron (riveted plates)	1				2	3	2				2
Pipe			1	5		6		5		1	6
Boilers gave way under hydrostatic pressure:											
Steel (riveted plates)	10	56			10	76	1			1	2
Pipe				2		2					
Boilers condemned from further use:											
Steel (riveted plates)	2			1		3	2				2
Iron (riveted plates)				1		1					
Pipe								5			5
Defects in boilers and attachments:											
Sheets	6	11				17	9	6		17	32
Heads	7					7				6	6
Steam and mud drums		2	1			3	4			4	8
Flues and tubes	15			5		20	104	4		387	495
Steam pipes	2					2	1			2	3
Stay bolts	33	45		3		81				218	218
Braces	3	3				6	1			168	169
Other parts	13	1				14	3			2	5
Tests of samples of steel and iron plates to be used in marine boilers, other than material tested at the mills by assistant inspectors: Samples of steel tested							62				62
Vessels wrecked or foundered: Steam vessels	1	1				2	5	1			6
Accidents to steam and other vessels:											
By collision between vessels	4	3			2	9	4	1	1	3	9
By fire		1	1	1	4	7	4	1	3	1	9
By sinking		2				2	3	1			4
By grounding		1	1	1	1	4					

Damaged by snags, ice, or other cause		6		2		8					
To machinery		1			2	3	1	1	1		3
Miscellaneous		2				2	2				2
Lives lost:											
By wreck or founder	2	1				3	1				1
By collision between vessels		1		1	2	4	1				1
By accidental drowning	1	1				2	9	2		5	16
From miscellaneous causes		1				1	3				3
Passengers lost:											
By accidental drowning							1			1	2
From miscellaneous causes							2			1	3
Lives saved by means of life-saving appliances required by law	10					10					
Passengers carried by steamers	95,577	887,983	178,341	451,001	1,288,520	2,901,422	3,123,871	124,372	21,011	106,968	3,376,222
Amount of property lost:											
By wreck or founder	$12,000	$45,000				$57,000	$300,000	$500			$300,500
By collision between vessels	$7,000	$1,000			$400	$8,400		$200		$50	$250
By fire		$500	$3,000	$7,000	$6,250	$16,750	$10,800	$400	$10,700	$1,800	$23,700
By snags		$11,000				$11,000	$37,922				$37,922
From miscellaneous causes		$13,750			$10,100	$23,850	$10,200		$6,000		$16,200
Total	$19,000	$71,250	$3,000	$7,000	$16,750	$117,000	$358,922	$1,100	$16,700	$1,850	$378,572
Violations of the steamboat laws:											
Cases investigated by local boards	3	3			1	7	4		2	2	8
Cases dismissed							1			2	3
Licenses suspended	1	3			2	6	15		2		17
Licenses revoked							1				1
Cases reported to district attorneys and to chief officers of customs	1	2	1			4	21	3	5	17	46
Appeals taken from decisions of local boards:											
Number of appeals					2	2	3				3
Decisions modified					1	1					
Decisions sustained					1	1	3				3
Received original license:											
Masters of steam vessels							6				6
Masters and pilots of steam vessels	1	4				5	12			5	17
Mates of steam vessels							15	3	4	1	23
Pilots of steam and other motor vessels	20	24	8	18	16	86	64	22	23	21	130
Joint pilots and engineers of steam vessels		2	1	1		4			2	3	5
Engineers of steam and other motor vessels	20	34	6	13	9	82	95	21	35	18	169
Masters of sail vessels and barges		6				6				1	1
Total	41	70	15	32	25	183	192	46	64	49	351

STATEMENT EMBRACING THE VARIOUS MATTERS AND OCCURRENCES RELATING TO VESSELS NAVIGATED UNDER THE ACTS OF CONGRESS THAT HAVE BEEN ACTED UPON BY THE SEVERAL BOARDS OF LOCAL AND SUPERVISING INSPECTORS FOR THE YEAR ENDED DECEMBER 31, 1905—Continued.

	Ninth district.						Tenth district.				
	Cleveland, Ohio.	Buffalo, N. Y.	Burlington, Vt.	Oswego, N. Y.	Toledo, Ohio.	Total.	New Orleans, La.	Apalachicola, Fla.	Galveston, Tex.	Mobile, Ala.	Total.
Received renewal of license:											
Masters of steam vessels							3	1			4
Masters and pilots of steam vessels	19	15		16	5	55	16	17	7	5	45
Mates of steam vessels							10		2	3	15
Mates and pilots of steam vessels							1			1	2
Pilots of steam and other motor vessels	16	18	2	8	7	51	43	14	7	21	85
Joint pilots and engineers of steam vessels		2				2	2				2
Engineers of steam and other motor vessels	37	32	5	8	8	90	50	23	12	26	111
Masters of sail vessels and barges										4	4
Chief mates of sail vessels and barges								1	3		4
Total	72	67	7	32	20	198	125	56	31	60	272
Refused license:											
Masters of steam vessels							1				1
Masters and pilots of steam vessels				1		1					
Mates of steam vessels							1				1
Pilots of steam and other motor vessels		4		1	4	9	3	1		1	5
Engineers of steam and other motor vessels	8	10		2	4	24	5	1		1	7
Masters of sail vessels and barges		1				1					
Total	8	15		4	8	35	10	2		2	14
Licenses suspended or revoked:											
Masters of steam vessels		1				1	2				2
Masters and pilots of steam vessels							4		1		5
Mates and pilots of steam vessels							2				2
Pilots of steam and other motor vessels		2				2	3				3
Engineers of steam and other motor vessels	1				1	2	5		1		6
Total	1	3			1	5	16		2		18

STATEMENT EMBRACING THE VARIOUS MATTERS AND OCCURRENCES RELATING TO VESSELS NAVIGATED UNDER THE ACTS OF CONGRESS THAT HAVE BEEN ACTED UPON BY THE SEVERAL BOARDS OF LOCAL AND SUPERVISING INSPECTORS FOR THE YEAR ENDED DECEMBER 31, 1905—Continued.

RECAPITULATION.

		Total in 1905.	Total in 1904.	Increase (+) or decrease (−).
VESSELS.				
Vessels granted certificates of inspection:				
Domestic steam vessels	7,751			
Domestic vessels propelled by gas, fluid, naphtha, or electric motors	294			
Domestic sail vessels, barges, etc	244			
Foreign steam vessels	369			
		8,658	9,073	−415
Vessels refused certificates of inspection:				
Domestic steam vessels	113			
Domestic vessels propelled by gas, fluid, naphtha, or electric motors	8			
Domestic sail vessels, barges, etc	1			
Foreign steam vessels	2			
		124	69	+55
Gross tonnage of vessels inspected:				
Domestic steam vessels	3,777,200			
Domestic vessels propelled by gas, fluid, naphtha, or electric motors	14,313			
Domestic sail vessels, barges, etc	278,025			
Foreign steam vessels	1,948,798			
		6,018,336	5,876,234	+142,102
New vessels added to service		398	490	−92
Vessels that went out of service		204	207	−3
Gross tonnage of new vessels added to service		444,278	379,200	+65,078
Gross tonnage of vessels that went out of service		77,933	81,429	−3,496
BOILERS.				
Boilers inspected:				
Steel (riveted plates)	10,909			
Iron (riveted plates)	908			
Pipe	1,227			
		13,044	13,424	−380
Boilers found defective:				
Steel (riveted plates)	3,019			
Iron (riveted plates)	254			
Pipe	187			
		3,460	1,169	+2,291
Boilers gave way under hydrostatic pressure:				
Steel (riveted plates)	196			
Iron (riveted plates)	10			
Pipe	5			
		211	216	−5
Boilers condemned from further use:				
Steel (riveted plates)	59			
Iron (riveted plates)	24			
Pipe	8			
		91	57	+34
Defects in boilers and attachments:				
Sheets	1,140			
Heads	135			
Steam and mud drums	97			
Flues and tubes	10,418			
Steam pipes	59			
Stay bolts	1,968			
Braces	295			
Other parts	275			
		14,387		
Tests of samples of steel and iron plates to be used in marine boilers, other than material tested at the mills by assistant inspectors:				
Samples of steel tested	454			
Samples of iron tested	46			
		500	838	−338
Steel failed in tensile strength	17			
Steel failed in reduction of area	7			
Iron failed in reduction of area	4			
Samples failed in elongation	4			
		32	76	−44

STATEMENT EMBRACING THE VARIOUS MATTERS AND OCCURRENCES RELATING TO VESSELS NAVIGATED UNDER THE ACTS OF CONGRESS THAT HAVE BEEN ACTED UPON BY THE SEVERAL BOARDS OF LOCAL AND SUPERVISING INSPECTORS FOR THE YEAR ENDED DECEMBER 31, 1905—Continued.

RECAPITULATION—Continued.

		Total in 1905.	Total in 1904.	Increase (+) or decrease (—).
LINE-CARRYING GUNS.				
Tests of samples of line-carrying guns:				
Samples tested		98	20	+78
Samples failed in tensile strength	2			
Samples failed in reduction of area	15			
		17	7	+10
CASUALTIES—LOSS OF LIFE.				
Vessels wrecked or foundered:				
Steam vessels	62			
Motor vessels	1			
Sail vessels	1			
Barges, etc	4			
		68	68	....
Accidents to vessels:				
By collision between vessels	423			
By fire	103			
By sinking	53			
By grounding	73			
Damaged by snags, ice, or other cause	52			
By explosion or accidental escape of steam	7			
To machinery	38			
Miscellaneous	51			
		800	....	....
Accidents causing loss of life by explosion or accidental escape of steam		4	31	—27
Lives lost:				
By explosion or accidental escape of steam	12			
By wreck or founder	122			
By collision between vessels	39			
By fire	1			
By accidental drowning	144			
From miscellaneous causes	31			
		349	1,270	—921
Passengers lost:				
By collision between vessels	8			
By accidental drowning	18			
From miscellaneous causes	19			
		45	1,054	—1,009
Lives saved by means of life-saving appliances required by law		575	195	+380
PASSENGERS CARRIED.				
Passengers carried on passenger steamers which are required by law to make report		330,235,959	342,260,350	—12,024,391
LOSS OF PROPERTY.				
Amount of property lost:				
By explosion	$30,300			
By wreck or founder	2,589,550			
By collision between vessels	726,965			
By fire	728,685			
By snags	93,972			
From miscellaneous causes	799,882			
		$4,969,354	$3,201,445	+$1,767,909
VIOLATIONS OF LAW.				
Violations of the steamboat laws:				
Cases investigated by local boards		318	....	....
Cases dismissed		90	....	....
Licenses suspended		243	....	....
Licenses revoked		31	....	....
Cases reported to district attorneys and to chief officers of customs		174	....	....
Appeals taken from decisions of local boards:				
Number of appeals		65	....	....
Decisions revoked		13	....	....
Decisions modified		27	....	....
Decisions sustained		24	....	....

STATEMENT EMBRACING THE VARIOUS MATTERS AND OCCURRENCES RELATING TO VESSELS NAVIGATED UNDER THE ACTS OF CONGRESS THAT HAVE BEEN ACTED UPON BY THE SEVERAL BOARDS OF LOCAL AND SUPERVISING INSPECTORS FOR THE YEAR ENDED DECEMBER 31, 1905—Continued.

RECAPITULATION—Continued.

		Total in 1905.	Total in 1904.	Increase (+) or decrease (−).
OFFICERS.				
Received original license:				
Masters of steam vessels	87			
Masters and pilots of steam vessels	146			
Mates of steam vessels	397			
Mates and pilots of steam vessels	36			
Pilots of steam and other motor vessels	869			
Joint pilots and engineers of steam vessels	54			
Engineers of steam and other motor vessels	1,452			
Masters of sail vessels and barges	57			
Chief mates of sail vessels and barges	69			
		3,167	3,323	−156
Received renewal of license:				
Masters of steam vessels	196			
Masters and pilots of steam vessels	697			
Mates of steam vessels	251			
Mates and pilots of steam vessels	31			
Pilots of steam and other motor vessels	713			
Joint pilots and engineers of steam vessels	28			
Engineers of steam and other motor vessels	1,619			
Masters of sail vessels and barges	281			
Chief mates of sail vessels and barges	86			
		3,902	4,350	−448
Refused license:				
Masters of steam vessels	17			
Masters and pilots of steam vessels	16			
Mates of steam vessels	32			
Pilots of steam and other motor vessels	89			
Joint pilots and engineers of steam vessels	4			
Engineers of steam and other motor vessels	143			
Masters of sail vessels and barges	3			
Chief mates of sail vessels and barges	9			
		313	359	−46
Licenses suspended or revoked:				
Masters of steam vessels	23			
Masters and pilots of steam vessels	120			
Mates of steam vessels	23			
Mates and pilots of steam vessels	2			
Pilots of steam and other motor vessels	51			
Engineers of steam and other motor vessels	97			
Masters of sail vessels and barges	10			
Chief mates of sail vessels and barges	5			
		331	179	+152

DOMESTIC VESSELS INSPECTED DURING THE YEAR ENDED DECEMBER 31, 1905.

FIRST SUPERVISING DISTRICT.

LOCAL DISTRICT OF SAN FRANCISCO, CAL.

Names of vessels and class.	Gross tonnage.	Hull built.	Hull rebuilt.	Boilers built.	Boilers rebuilt.	Where built.	Date of inspection.	Where inspected.	Date of previous inspection.	Local district where previously inspected.
Ocean passenger steamers.										
Alameda	3,158	1883		1900		Philadelphia, Pa	Jan. 19, 1905	San Francisco, Cal	Jan. 7, 1904	San Francisco, Cal.
Aurelia	440	1902		1903		Prosper, Oreg	Feb. 14, 1905	do	Feb. 12, 1904	Do.
Alliance	679	1896		1896		Fairhaven, Cal	Feb. 24, 1905	do	Apr. 15, 1904	Do.
Acme	416	1901		1901		Alameda, Cal	Mar. 31, 1905	Alameda, Cal	Mar. 15, 1904	Do.
Australia	2,755	1875		1889		Glasgow, Scotland	May 10, 1905	San Francisco, Cal	Sept. 18, 1901	Do.
Alcazar	263	1887		1897		San Francisco, Cal	June 21, 1905	do	June 18, 1904	Do.
Acapulco	2,572	1873		1884		Wilmington, Del	Sept. 21, 1905	do	Aug. 31, 1904	Do.
Arctic	392	1901		1901		Bay City, Oreg	July 25, 1905	do	July 26, 1904	Do.
Aberdeen	499	1899		1899		Aberdeen, Wash	Sept. 26, 1905	do	Oct. 3, 1904	Do.
Alameda	3,158	1883		1900		Philadelphia, Pa	Nov. 16, 1905	do	Jan. 19, 1905	Do.
Brooklyn	333	1901		1902		Aberdeen, Wash	May 5, 1905	do	Apr. 30, 1904	Do.
Breakwater	1,065	1880	1900	1901		Chester, Pa	May 31, 1905	do	May 31, 1904	Do.
Brunswick	512	1898	1903	1892		North Bend, Oreg	Sept. 20, 1905	do	Sept. 15, 1904	Do.
Bonita	521	1881		1902		San Francisco, Cal	Oct. 17, 1905	do	Oct. 20, 1904	Do.
Buckman	1,820	1901		1901		Toledo, Ohio	Dec. 8, 1905	do	Nov. 28, 1904	Baltimore, Md.
Centennial [a]	2,075	1859	1878	1878		London, England	Dec. 30, 1904	do	Nov. 5, 1903	San Francisco, Cal.
Curaçao [b]	1,503	1895		1895		Philadelphia, Pa	Dec. 31, 1904	do	Dec. 31, 1903	Do.
City of Panama	1,409	1874		1890		Chester, Pa	Jan. 13, 1905	do	Dec. 24, 1903	Do.
Chehalis	663	1901		1901		Fairhaven, Cal	Feb. 13, 1905	do	Feb. 13, 1904	Do.
Chico	362	1890		1900		Tacoma, Wash	Mar. 28, 1905	do	Feb. 20, 1904	Do.
City of Puebla	2,623	1881		1901		Philadelphia, Pa	Mar. 22, 1905	do	Mar. 29, 1904	Do.
City of Sydney	3,016	1875		1890		Chester, Pa	Apr. 10, 1905	do	Mar. 24, 1904	Do.
Charles Nelson	629	1898		1898		Alameda, Cal	June 3, 1905	do	May 30, 1904	Do.
Costa Rica	1,783	1891		1891		Chester, Pa	June 13, 1905	do	June 15, 1904	Do.
Cabrillo	611	1904		1904		Wilmington, Cal	June 21, 1905	San Pedro, Cal	June 21, 1904	Do.
Columbia	2,721	1879		1895		Chester, Pa	July 19, 1905	San Francisco, Cal	July 20, 1904	Do.
Corona	1,492	1888		1895		Philadelphia, Pa	Aug. 28, 1905	do	Sept. 2, 1904	Do.
City of Para	3,532	1878		1892		Chester, Pa	Sept. 29, 1905	do	Oct. 19, 1904	Do.
Coos Bay	544	1884		1904		Marshfield, Oreg	Oct. 3, 1905	do	Sept. 30, 1904	Do.
China	5,060	1889		1889		Glasgow, Scotland	Nov. 13, 1905	do	Oct. 14, 1904	Do.
Centralia	487	1902		1902		Alameda, Cal	Nov. 23, 1905	do	Nov. 17, 1904	Do.
City of Peking	5,079	1874		1897		Chester, Pa	Nov. 27, 1905	do	Dec. 19, 1904	Do.
Coronado	578	1900		1900		Aberdeen, Wash	Dec. 5, 1905	do	Nov. 30, 1904	Do.
City of Panama	1,409	1874		1890		Chester, Pa	Dec. 9, 1905	do	Jan. 13, 1905	Do.
Cascade	515	1904		1904		Fairhaven, Cal	Dec. 26, 1905	do	Dec. 28, 1904	Do.
Del Norte	450	1891		1894		Tiburon, Cal	May 8, 1905	do	Apr. 27 1904	Do.

Enterprise	2,675	1882	....	1886	....	Newcastle-on-Tyne, England.	Apr. 8, 1905	....do	Mar. 25, 1904	Do.
Eureka	484	1900	....	1900	....	Wilmington, Cal	July 1, 1905	....do	July 1, 1904	Do.
Falcon	117	1886	1898	1898	....	San Francisco, Cal	Jan. 16, 1905	San Pedro, Cal	Jan. 19, 1904	Do.
Francis H. Leggett	1,606	1903	....	1903	....	Newport News, Va	Mar. 29, 1905	Alameda, Cal	Mar. 30, 1904	Do.
F. A. Kilburn	728	1904	....	1904	....	Fairhaven, Cal	May 10, 1905	San Francisco, Cal	Apr. 14, 1904	Do.
G. C. Lindauer	453	1902	....	1902	....	Aberdeen, Wash	Mar. 22, 1905	....do	Feb. 16, 1904	Portland, Oreg.
Humboldt	1,075	1897	....	1897	....	Fairhaven, Cal	Feb. 10, 1905	....do	Feb. 29, 1904	San Francisco, Cal.
Homer	501	1892	....	1892	....	Bandon, Oreg	May 26, 1905	....do	Apr. 8, 1904	Do.
Hermosa	483	1902	....	1888	....	Wilmington, Cal	June 19, 1905	San Pedro, Cal	June 17, 1904	Do.
Helen P. Drew	286	1904	....	1904	....	Hoquiam, Wash	Dec. 28, 1905	San Francisco, Cal	Dec. 28, 1904	Do.
Harold Dollar	926	1904	....	1898	....	Fairhaven, Cal	Oct. 11, 1905	....do	Oct. 6, 1904	Do.
Iaqua	712	1900	1901	1900	....	....do	Sept. 7, 1905	....do	Sept. 6, 1904	Do.
Kvichak	1,063	1900	....	1900	....	Portland, Oreg	Mar. 28, 1905	Oakland, Cal	Apr. 12, 1904	Do.
Korea	11,276	1902	....	1902	....	Newport News, Va	Apr. 20, 1905	San Francisco, Cal	Apr. 6, 1904	Do.
M. F. Plant	1,214	1879	....	1889	....	Philadelphia, Pa	Feb. 1, 1905	....do	Jan. 2, 1904	Baltimore, Md.
Manchuria	13,638	1904	....	1903	....	Camden, N. J	Apr. 8, 1905	....do	Apr. 13, 1904	Philadelphia, Pa.
Morning Star	547	1900	....	1900	....	Essex, Mass	July 18, 1905	Honolulu, Hawaii	May 27, 1904	Boston, Mass.
Mariposa	3,158	1883	....	1901	....	Philadelphia, Pa	Sept. 5, 1905	San Francisco, Cal	Sept. 7, 1904	San Francisco, Cal.
Mongolia	13,638	1903	....	1903	....	Camden, N. J	Nov. 6, 1905	....do	Dec. 17, 1904	Philadelphia, Pa.
Mandalay	438	1900	....	1900	....	North Bend, Oreg	Dec. 8, 1905	Alameda, Cal	Dec. 23, 1904	San Francisco, Cal.
Nushagak	714	1904	....	1904	....	Alameda, Cal	Mar. 28, 1905	Oakland, Cal	Mar. 30, 1904	Do.
Navarro	232	1887	....	1895	....	San Francisco, Cal	Apr. 6, 1905	San Francisco, Cal	Apr. 4, 1904	Do.
Newport	2,735	1880	....	1897	....	Chester, Pa	June 17, 1905	....do	June 1, 1904	Do.
Nome City	939	1900	....	1900	....	Fairhaven, Cal	July 11, 1905	....do	July 9, 1904	Seattle, Wash.
Newburg	450	1898	....	1898	....	San Francisco, Cal	July 31, 1905	....do	July 26, 1904	San Francisco, Cal.
National City	310	1888	....	1888	....	....do	Aug. 10, 1905	....do	Aug. 6, 1904	Do.
Northland	845	1904	....	1904	....	Fairhaven, Cal	Sept. 8, 1905	....do	Sept. 1, 1904	Do.
Norwood	760	1904	....	1904	....	Winslow, Wash	Oct. 4, 1905	....do	Oct. 7, 1904	Do.
Olympic	688	1901	....	1901	....	Hoquiam, Wash	June 21, 1905	....do	June 4, 1904	Do.
Phoenix	256	1902	....	1898	....	Alameda, Cal	Jan. 30, 1905	Alameda, Cal	Jan. 23, 1904	Do.
Prentiss	406	1902	....	1902	....	Oakland, Cal	Mar. 27, 1905	San Francisco, Cal	Apr. 4, 1904	Do.
Peru	3,528	1892	....	1892	....	San Francisco, Cal	May 31, 1905	....do	May 17, 1904	Do.
Pomona	1,264	1888	....	1900	....	....do	Aug. 24, 1905	....do	Aug. 12, 1904	Do.
Pomo	368	1903	....	1902	....	Eureka, Cal	Dec. 16, 1905	....do	Dec. 16, 1904	Do.
Queen	2,727	1882	....	1896	....	Philadelphia, Pa	Nov. 27, 1905	....do	Dec. 2, 1904	Do.
Roanoke	2,354	1882	....	1882	....	Chester, Pa	May 9, 1905	....do	May 6, 1904	Seattle, Wash.
Robert Dollar	798	1900	....	1900	....	Grays Harbor, Wash	May 6, 1905	....do	May 17, 1904	San Francisco, Cal.
Rival	266	1888	....	1888	....	San Francisco, Cal	Mar. 31, 1905	....do	Apr. 29, 1904	Do.
Rainier	800	1900	....	1900	....	Hoquiam, Wash	May 22, 1905	....do	May 18, 1904	Do.
Redondo	679	1902	....	1902	....	Toledo, Ohio	June 30, 1905	....do	May 21, 1904	Do.
Sonoma	6,253	1900	....	1900	....	Philadelphia, Pa	Jan. 25, 1905	....do	Jan. 13, 1904	Do.
Samoa	377	1898	....	1898	....	San Francisco, Cal	Feb. 16, 1905	....do	Feb. 15, 1904	Do.
State of California	2,266	1878	....	1885	....	Philadelphia, Pa	Mar. 6, 1905	....do	Mar. 8, 1904	Do.
Santa Monica	497	1902	....	1901	....	San Francisco, Cal	Jan. 16, 1905	....do	Jan. 28, 1904	Do.
Shasta	722	1904	....	1904	....	Hoquiam, Wash	Mar. 7, 1905	....do	Mar. 1, 1904	Do.
Senator	2,409	1898	....	1898	....	San Francisco, Cal	May 1, 1905	....do	May 6, 1904	Do.
Spokane	2,036	1902	....	1902	....	....do	May 18, 1905	....do	Feb. 29, 1904	Do.
St. Paul	2,440	1898	....	1898	....	....do	May 23, 1905	....do	May 25, 1904	Do.
San Jose	2,080	1882	....	1898	....	Chester, Pa	Sept. 5, 1905	....do	Aug. 19, 1904	Do.

a Certificated Jan. 11, 1905.

b Certificated Jan. 5, 1905.

DOMESTIC VESSELS INSPECTED, YEAR ENDED DECEMBER 31, 1905—FIRST SUPERVISING DISTRICT—SAN FRANCISCO, CAL.—Continued.

Names of vessels and class.	Gross tonnage.	Hull built	Hull rebuilt.	Boilers built.	Boilers rebuilt.	Where built.	Date of inspection.	Where inspected.	Date of previous inspection.	Local district where previously inspected.
Ocean passenger steamers—Continued.										
San Juan	2,076	1882		1896		Chester, Pa	Oct. 6, 1905	San Francisco, Cal	Sept. 24, 1904	San Francisco, Cal.
Siberia	11,284	1902		1902		Newport News, Va	Oct. 25, 1905	do	Sept. 27, 1904	Do.
Sierra	5,989	1900		1900		Philadelphia, Pa	Nov. 15, 1905	do	Nov. 3, 1904	Do.
Sonoma	6,253	1900		1900		do	Dec. 9, 1905	do	Jan. 25, 1905	Do.
Unimak [a]	254	1902		1902		Alameda, Cal	Mar. 28, 1905	Oakland, Cal	Mar. 12, 1904	Do.
Umatilla	3,069	1881		1903		Chester, Pa	June 10, 1905	San Francisco, Cal	June 16, 1904	Do.
Ventura	6,253	1900		1900		Philadelphia, Pa	Feb. 16, 1905	do	Feb. 4, 1904	Do.
Vanguard	358	1904		1904		Alameda, Cal	Nov. 20, 1905	do	Nov. 21, 1904	Do.
Warrior	122	1901		1901		Wilmington, Cal	July 3, 1905	San Pedro, Cal	July 18, 1904	Do.
W. H. Kruger	469	1900		1900		Aberdeen, Wash	Apr. 3, 1905	San Francisco, Cal	Mar. 30, 1904	Do.
Zealandia	2,730	1875		1875		Glasgow, Scotland	May 10, 1905	do	June 20, 1902	Do.
Inland passenger steamers.										
A. C. Freese	205	1874	1904	1891		San Francisco, Cal	June 17, 1905	Stockton, Cal	June 19, 1904	San Francisco, Cal.
Arrow	318	1903		1902		Portland, Oreg	June 1, 1905	San Francisco, Cal	June 1, 1904	Seattle, Wash.
Alvira	469	1889		1889		San Francisco, Cal	July 10, 1905	do	July 11, 1904	San Francisco, Cal.
Alice	10	1885		1885		Eureka, Cal	July 27, 1905	Eureka, Cal	July 25, 1904	Do.
Alert	75	1885		1898		San Francisco, Cal	Mar. 10, 1905	San Francisco, Cal	Mar. 7, 1904	Do.
Aurora	406	1885	1898	1898		do	May 23, 1905	do	May 13, 1904	Do.
Apache	938	1880		1898		Oakland, Cal	May 1, 1905	do	Apr. 27, 1904	Portland, Oreg.
Blanco	37	1893		1889		Marshfield, Oreg	July 8, 1905	do	July 10, 1904	San Francisco, Cal.
Columbia [b]	763	1898		1898		San Francisco, Cal	June 26, 1905	do	June 27, 1904	Do.
Constance	422	1874		1896		do	Jan. 4, 1905	do	July 3, 1903	Do.
Caroline	182	1868	1898	1898		Union City, Cal	July 31, 1905	do	Aug. 9, 1904	Do.
Capt. Weber	612	1882		1905		San Francisco, Cal	Oct. 27, 1905	do	Aug. 22, 1904	Do.
Dauntless	269	1903		1903		do	Oct. 12, 1905	do	Nov. 9, 1904	Do.
Defiance [c]	255	1898		1890		Camden, N. J	Sept. 29, 1905	do	Oct. 31, 1904	Do.
Dover	244	1891		1891		Sacramento, Cal	June 9, 1905	Sacramento, Cal	June 17, 1904	Do.
Emerald	[d] 16	1887		1887		San Francisco, Cal	May 26, 1905	Tahoe, Cal	May 26, 1904	Do.
Fort Bragg	317	1898		1898		Fort Bragg, Cal	June 2, 1905	San Francisco, Cal	June 2, 1904	Do.
Flora	185	1885		1889		Sacramento, Cal	June 9, 1905	Sacramento, Cal	June 9, 1904	Do.
Fruta	429	1889		1898		Oakland, Cal	Sept. 29, 1905	do	Oct. 3, 1904	Do.
Gov. Irwin	[d] 80	1878		1894	1904	San Francisco, Cal	Feb. 24, 1905	San Francisco, Cal	Dec. 11, 1903	Do.
Grace Barton	194	1890		1902		do	Mar. 15, 1905	Vallejo, Cal	Mar. 14, 1904	Do.
General Frisbie	544	1901		1901		New Whatcom, Wash	May 9, 1905	San Francisco, Cal	May 6, 1904	Do.
Gold	334	1880		1889		San Francisco, Cal	June 26, 1905	do	June 27, 1904	Do.
Henrietta	39	1898		1898		do	Mar. 25, 1905	do	Mar. 26, 1904	Do.
Hattie Belle	[d] 6	1891	1902	1895		do	May 27, 1905	Tallac, Cal	May 27, 1904	Do.
Herald	293	1878		1887		Stockton, Cal	May 8, 1905	San Francisco, Cal	May 6, 1904	Do.
H. H. Buhue	97	1869	1892	1887		Eureka, Cal	July 26, 1905	Eureka, Cal	July 25, 1904	Do.

H. J. Corcoran	682	1898		1905		Stockton, Cal.	Aug. 2, 1905	San Francisco, Cal.	Aug. 6, 1904	Do.
H. E. Wright	562	1899		1899		do	Dec. 19, 1905	Stockton, Cal.	Dec. 17, 1904	Do.
Isleton	615	1902		1898		Wood Island, Cal.	July 29, 1905	San Francisco, Cal.	Aug. 2, 1904	Do.
J. D. Peters	880	1889	1899	1899		San Francisco, Cal.	May 16, 1905	Stockton, Cal.	May 9, 1904	Do
Jacinto	235	1889		1899		Sacramento, Cal.	June 9, 1905	Sacramento, Cal.	June 9, 1904	Do.
Leader	400	1884	1898	1898		Stockton, Cal.	Oct. 2, 1905	San Francisco, Cal.	Oct. 7, 1904	Do.
Mary Garratt	810	1878	1891	1898		do	Jan. 13, 1905	Stockton, Cal.	Jan. 2, 1904	Do.
Monticello	226	1892		1899		Ballard, Wash.	Apr. 26, 1905	San Francisco, Cal.	Apr. 25, 1904	Do.
Meteor	d 20	1876		1876		Glenbrook, Nev.	May 26, 1905	Tahoe, Cal.	May 26, 1904	Do.
Mamie	d 6	1883		1883		Donahue, Cal.	May 27, 1905	Tallac, Cal.	May 27, 1904	Do.
Modoc	929	1880		1899		Oakland, Cal.	June 13, 1905	San Francisco, Cal.	June 13, 1904	Do.
Nevada e	d 25	1890		1902		Buffalo, N. Y.	May 26, 1905	Tahoe, Cal.	May 26, 1904	Do.
Napa City	178	1891		1898		Benicia, Cal.	July 16, 1905	Stockton, Cal.	July 17, 1904	Do.
Oriole	68	1905		1905		Sacramento, Cal.	Jan. 16, 1905	Sacramento, Cal.	First inspn.	
Onward	388	1877		1888		San Francisco, Cal.	Apr. 12, 1905	San Francisco, Cal.	Apr. 14, 1904	Do.
Onisbo	632	1900		1898		do	June 11, 1905	Wood Island, Cal.	May 28, 1904	Do.
Peerless	22	1893		1904		Eureka, Cal.	Mar. 1, 1905	Eureka, Cal.	Apr. 26, 1904	Do.
Pride of the River	619	1878	1897	1899		San Francisco, Cal.	May 26, 1905	San Francisco, Cal.	May 24, 1904	Do.
Pioneer	195	1902		1900		Honolulu, Hawaii	July 18, 1905	Honolulu, Hawaii	First inspn.	
Pilot	88	1903		1900		San Francisco, Cal.	Aug. 28, 1905	San Francisco, Cal.	Aug. 24, 1904	Do.
Priscilla	51	1902		1902		Alameda, Cal.	Aug. 29, 1905	do	Aug. 27, 1904	Do.
Redondo	77	1905		1905		Hoquiam, Wash.	Jan. 11, 1905	Alameda, Cal.	First inspn.	
Richmond	135	1900		1900		San Francisco, Cal.	Feb. 23, 1905	Point Richmond, Cal.	Feb. 23, 1904	Do.
Resolute	264	1884	1900	1884		Benicia, Cal.	May 22, 1905	San Francisco, Cal.	May 24, 1904	Do.
Red Bluff	246	1894		1894		Sacramento, Cal.	July 15, 1905	Sacramento Cal.	July 15, 1904	Do.
Relief	204	1884		1899		Philadelphia, Pa.	Sept. 29, 1905	San Francisco, Cal.	Sept. 28, 1904	Do.
St. Vallier	92	1899		1899		Cincinnati, Ohio	Jan. 19, 1905	Yuma, Ariz.	Jan. 17, 1904	Do.
Searchlight	98	1903		1902		Needles, Cal.	do	do	Jan. 21, 1904	Do.
Sea Queen	111	1883		1900		San Francisco, Cal.	Feb. 13, 1905	San Francisco, Cal.	Mar. 11, 1904	Do.
Sea Prince	58	1901		1901		do	Mar. 27, 1905	do	Mar. 25, 1904	Do.
Sea Witch	74	1883		1900		do	Mar. 13, 1905	do	Mar. 11, 1904	Do.
Sea King	181	1883		1903		do	Mar. 29, 1905	do	Mar. 28, 1904	Do.
Sea Lark	69	1905		1905		do	Mar. 31, 1905	do	First inspn.	
Sonoma	305	1874	1897	1897		do	Apr. 1, 1905	do	Apr. 4, 1904	Do.
St. Helena	344	1902		1902		do	Apr. 3, 1905	do	Apr. 1, 1904	Do.
San Joaquin No. 4	365	1885		1895		Sacramento, Cal.	July 15, 1905	Sacramento, Cal.	July 2, 1904	Do.
Sea Rover	199	1902		1902		San Francisco, Cal.	Aug. 10, 1905	San Francisco, Cal.	Aug. 10, 1904	Do.
San Joaquin No. 3	220	1877		1899		do	Oct. 5, 1905	Sacramento, Cal.	Sept. 28, 1904	Do.
Tahoe	d 190	1896		1896		Glenbrook, Nev.	May 26, 1905	Tahoe, Cal.	May 26, 1904	Do.
T. C. Walker	786	1885		1893		Stockton, Cal.	June 19, 1905	Stockton, Cal.	June 19, 1904	Do.
Thoroughfare	1,012	1871		1899		San Francisco, Cal.	Sept. 18, 1905	Oakland, Cal.	Sept. 26, 1904	Do.
Union	67	1899		1899		do	Mar. 18, 1905	San Francisco, Cal.	Mar. 17, 1904	Do.
Victory f	137	1877	1899	1904		do	July 20, 1905	Stockton, Cal.	July 19, 1904	Do.
Water Nymph	27	1881		1881		do	Dec. 28, 1905	San Francisco, Cal.	Dec. 28, 1904	Do.
Zinfandel	329	1889		1889		do	May 25, 1905	do	May 28, 1904	Do.

a Formerly Redwood City, 1903.
b Formerly Mary Ellen Galvin, 1898.
c Formerly L. Luckenbach, 1900.
d Estimated.
e Formerly Tallac, 1903.
f Formerly Mary B. Williams, 1899.

DOMESTIC VESSELS INSPECTED, YEAR ENDED DECEMBER 31, 1905—FIRST SUPERVISING DISTRICT—SAN FRANCISCO, CAL.—Continued.

Names of vessels and class.	Gross tonnage.	Hull built.	Hull rebuilt.	Boilers built.	Boilers rebuilt.	Where built.	Date of inspection.	Where inspected.	Date of previous inspection.	Local district where previously inspected.
Ferry steamers.										
Antelope	155	1888		1903		Eureka, Cal	July 27, 1905	Eureka, Cal	July 25, 1904	San Francisco, Cal.
Bay City	1,283	1878		1905		San Francisco, Cal	June 6, 1905	Oakland, Cal	June 20, 1904	Do.
Berkeley	1,945	1898		1898		do	Sept. 21, 1905	do	Oct. 3, 1904	Do.
Cazadero	1,682	1903		1903		Alameda, Cal	Apr. 21, 1905	Sausalito, Cal	Apr. 12, 1904	Do.
Coronado	308	1886		1893		San Francisco, Cal	Aug. 26, 1905	San Diego, Cal	Aug. 24, 1904	Do.
Encinal	2,014	1887		1888		do	Mar. 31, 1905	Oakland, Cal	Mar. 31, 1904	Do.
El Capitan	982	1868	1896	1896		do	May 25, 1905	do	May 7, 1904	Do.
Ellen	328	1883		1899		Vallejo, Cal	Nov. 18, 1905	Vallejo, Cal	Nov. 27, 1904	Do.
Garden City	1,080	1879	1901	1905		San Francisco, Cal	Nov. 22, 1905	Oakland, Cal	June 9, 1904	Do.
James M. Donahue	730	1878		1902		do	June 9, 1905	Tiburon, Cal	do	Do.
Newark	2,197	1877	1902	1902		do	June 23, 1905	Oakland, Cal	June 23, 1904	Do.
Ocean Wave	724	1891	1900	1904		Portland, Oreg	Mar. 8, 1905	Point Richmond, Cal.	Mar. 7, 1904	Do.
Oakland	1,672	1875	1898	1898		Oakland, Cal	Aug. 4, 1905	Oakland, Cal	Aug. 4, 1904	Do.
Piedmont	1,854	1883		1883		do	Oct. 2, 1905	do	Oct. 8, 1904	Do.
Ramona	575	1903		1903		Alameda, Cal	June 17, 1905	San Diego, Cal	June 18, 1904	Do.
Sausalito	1,766	1894		1894		San Francisco, Cal	July 11, 1905	Sausalito, Cal	July 26, 1904	Do.
San Jose	1,115	1903		1903		Alameda, Cal	July 31, 1905	Emeryville, Cal	Aug. 22, 1904	Do.
San Francisco	1,070	1905		1905		do	Apr. 12, 1905	do	First inspn.	
Solano	3,549	1879	1905	1905		Oakland, Cal	Oct. 9, 1905	Port Costa, Cal	Oct. 13, 1904	Do.
San Pablo	1,584	1901		1900		San Francisco, Cal	Oct. 11, 1905	Point Richmond, Cal.	Oct. 7, 1904	Do.
Transit	1,566	1878	1900	1899		do	Jan. 9, 1905	Oakland, Cal	Jan. 11, 1904	Do.
Tiburon	1,248	1884	1894	1884		do	Apr. 21, 1905	Tiburon, Cal	Apr. 22, 1904	Do.
Tamalpais	1,631	1901		1901		do	Mar. 21, 1905	Sausalito, Cal	Apr. 16, 1904	Do.
Ukiah	2,564	1890		1890	1904	Tiburon, Cal	Oct. 2, 1905	Tiburon, Cal	Oct. 24, 1904	Do.
Vallejo	414	1879		1879		Portland, Oreg	Sept. 2, 1905	Vallejo, Cal	Sept. 19, 1904	Do.
Yerba Buena	1,115	1903		1903		Alameda, Cal	Sept. 1, 1905	Oakland, Cal	Aug. 26, 1904	Do.
Ocean freight steamers.										
Asuncion	2,196	1900		1900		Lorain, Ohio	Dec. 27, 1905	San Francisco, Cal	Dec. 27, 1904	San Francisco, Cal.
Alitak	115	1901		1901		Alameda, Cal	Mar. 29, 1905	Oakland, Cal	Mar. 11, 1904	Do.
Argo	180	1898		1897		Ballard, Wash	Mar. 30, 1905	San Francisco, Cal	Mar. 31, 1904	Do.
Argyll	2,953	1892		1892		West Hartlepool, England.	June 26, 1905	Port Harford, Cal	June 11, 1904	Do.
Alcatraz	255	1887		1898		San Francisco, Cal	Oct. 9, 1905	San Francisco, Cal	Oct. 3, 1904	Do.
American	5,591	1900		1900		Chester, Pa	Oct. 18, 1905	do	Oct. 29, 1904	New York, N. Y.
Aztec	3,508	1894		1894		Newcastle-on-Tyne, England.	Dec. 8, 1905	do	Nov. 16, 1904	San Francisco, Cal
Atlas	1,942	1899		1898		Chester, Pa	Dec. 18, 1905	do	Dec. 1, 1904	New York, N. Y.
Bee	601	1904		1898		Aberdeen, Wash	Mar. 16, 1905	do	Mar. 10, 1904	Seattle, Wash.
Coquille River	415	1896		1896		Prosper, Oreg	Apr. 18, 1905	do	Apr. 16, 1904	San Francisco, Cal.
Celia	173	1884		1905		Benicia, Cal	Apr. 29, 1905	do	May 31, 1904	Do.

Czarina	1,045	1883		1896		Sunderland, England	Dec. 14, 1905	....do	Dec. 19, 1904	Do.
Daisy Mitchell	612	1905		1905		Fairhaven, Cal	Aug. 21, 1905	Alameda, Cal	First inspn.	
Edith	2,369	1882		1882		Sunderland, England	Feb. 24, 1905	San Francisco, Cal	Feb. 15, 1904	Do.
Empire	732	1873	1897	1882		Port Madison, Wash	Jan. 25, 1905	....do	Jan. 9, 1904	Do.
Fulton	380	1898	1904	1898		Fairhaven, Cal	June 29, 1905	....do	June 23, 1904	Do.
Geo. F. Haller	139	1901		1901		Alameda, Cal	Apr. 13, 1905	....do	Apr. 15, 1904	Do.
Grace Dollar	429	1898		1898		San Francisco, Cal	May 26, 1905	....do	May 31, 1904	Do.
Gualala	225	1901		1895		Alameda, Cal	Aug. 21, 1905	....do	Aug. 16, 1904	Do.
Greenwood	195	1886		1897		San Francisco, Cal	Oct. 24, 1905	....do	Oct. 21, 1904	Do.
George Loomis	691	1895		1895		....do	Nov. 6, 1905	....do	Oct. 30, 1904	Do.
Jennie	127	1889	1895	1899		Benicia, Cal	Mar. 25, 1905	Oakland, Cal	Mar. 11, 1904	Do
James S. Higgins	382	1904		1904		Aberdeen, Wash	Apr. 18, 1905	San Francisco, Cal	Apr. 18, 1904	Do.
Lakme	529	1888		1889		Port Madison, Wash	Nov. 11, 1905	....do	July 29, 1904	Do.
Mackinaw	2,578	1890		1890		West Bay City, Mich	Feb. 2, 1905	....do	Jan. 2, 1904	Do.
Marshfield	388	1901		1902		Marshfield, Oreg	June 2, 1905	....do	May 25, 1904	Do.
Montara[a]	2,562	1881		1898		Chester, Pa	July 7, 1905	....do	June 6, 1904	Do.
Melville Dollar[b]	1,380	1875		1895		West Bay City, Mich	Nov. 11, 1905	Port Costa, Cal	Nov. 12, 1904	Do.
Maggie	85	1891		1889		Albion River, Cal	Nov. 4, 1905	San Francisco, Cal	Nov. 4, 1904	Do.
Nevadan	4,408	1902		1902		Camden, N. J	Feb. 23, 1905	....do	Mar. 22, 1904	Do.
Nayo	316	1887		1888		San Francisco, Cal	Mar. 27, 1905	....do	Mar. 8, 1904	Do.
Newsboy	208	1888		1888		....do	May 24, 1905	....do	May 7, 1904	Do.
Nebraskan	4,408	1902		1902		Camden, N. J	June 8, 1905	....do	June 16, 1904	Do.
Newport	331	1875		1891		San Francisco, Cal	Oct. 3, 1905	....do	Sept. 3, 1904	Seattle, Wash.
North Fork	322	1888		1888		Fairhaven, Cal	Oct. 21, 1905	....do	Oct. 12, 1904	San Francisco, Cal.
Nevadan	4,408	1902		1902		Camden, N. J	Dec. 26, 1905	....do	Feb. 23, 1904	Do.
Pasadena	300	1887		1887		San Francisco, Cal	Sept. 8, 1905	....do	Aug. 24, 1904	Do.
Pt. Arena	223	1887	1896	1898		....do	Oct. 26, 1905	....do	Oct. 27, 1904	Do.
Rosecrans[c]	2,976	1883		1883		Glasgow, Scotland	Apr. 26, 1905	Alameda, Cal	May 16, 1904	
Signal	475	1887		1891		North Bend, Oreg	Mar. 2, 1905	San Francisco, Cal	Feb. 17, 1904	Do.
South Coast	301	1887		1898		San Francisco, Cal	Mar. 15, 1905	....do	Mar. 9, 1904	Do.
Santa Cruz	511	1868		1889		....do	Mar. 24, 1905	....do	Mar. 22, 1904	Do.
Sequoia	411	1898		1892		....do	May 18, 1905	....do	May 11, 1904	Do.
San Mateo	2,926	1888		1888		South Shields, England.	Aug. 2, 1905	....do	Aug. 6, 1904	Do.
San Gabriel	484	1903		1903		Alameda, Cal	Aug. 11, 1905	Alameda, Cal	Aug. 10, 1904	Do.
South Bay	438	1901		1902		Tacoma, Wash	Aug. 16, 1905	San Francisco, Cal	Aug. 11, 1904	Do.
San Pedro	456	1899		1899		Aberdeen, Wash	Sept. 19, 1905	....do	Sept. 17, 1904	Do.
Santa Barbara	695	1900		1900		San Francisco, Cal	Oct. 26, 1905	....do	Oct. 24, 1904	Do.
Scotia	181	1888		1888		....do	Nov. 16, 1905	....do	Nov. 10, 1904	Do.
Whittier	1,295	1903		1903		....do	Apr. 18, 1905	....do	Apr. 9, 1904	Do.
Westport	211	1888		1888		....do	Aug. 31, 1905	....do	Aug. 26, 1904	Do.
Wasp	563	1905		1905		Fairhaven, Cal	July 18, 1905	Alameda, Cal	First inspn.	
Inland freight steamers.										
Acme	294	1889		1889		Sacramento, Cal	June 9, 1905	Sacramento, Cal	June 9, 1904	San Francisco, Cal.
Alviso	197	1895		1888		Port Costa, Cal	Apr. 11, 1905	San Francisco, Cal	Apr. 13, 1904	Do.
Cochan	234	1899		1872		Yuma, Ariz	June 19, 1905	Yuma, Ariz	Jan. 17, 1904	Do.
City of Dawson	230	1898		1898		San Francisco, Cal	Feb. 27, 1905	Wood Island, Cal	Feb. 8, 1904	Do.
Champion	477	1896	1905	1888		Stockton, Cal	May 16, 1905	Stockton, Cal	First inspn.	

[a] Formerly Willamette, 1902.

[b] Formerly Simon J. Murphy, 1901.

[c] Formerly United States transport.

DOMESTIC VESSELS INSPECTED, YEAR ENDED DECEMBER 31, 1905—FIRST SUPERVISING DISTRICT—SAN FRANCISCO, CAL.—Continued.

Names of vessels and class.	Gross tonnage.	Hull built.	Hull rebuilt.	Boilers built.	Boilers rebuilt.	Where built.	Date of inspection.	Where inspected.	Date of previous inspection.	Local district where previously inspected.
Inland freight steamers—Con.										
Car Float No. 2	1,374	1905		1905		Oakland, Cal	May 26, 1905	Oakland, Cal	First inspn.	
Dimond [a]	225	1898		1898		San Francisco, Cal	Feb. 23, 1905	do	Feb. 23, 1904	San Francisco, Cal.
Dauntless	612	1892		1892		do	Aug. 14, 1905	do	Aug. 13, 1904	Do.
Dimond [a]	225	1898		1898		do	Dec. 9, 1905	San Francisco, Cal	Feb. 23, 1905	Do.
Ellen	57	1885	1898	1898		Fairhaven, Cal	June 23, 1905	Redwood, Cal	June 10, 1904	Do.
Francis	698	1905		1905		San Francisco, Cal	May 16, 1905	San Francisco, Cal	First inspn.	
Ilwaco	120	1891		1889		Portland, Oreg	July 8, 1905	Oakland, Cal	Dec. 10, 1903	Portland, Oreg.
J. R. McDonald	137	1899		1899		Stockton, Cal	Apr. 27, 1905	Stockton, Cal	Apr. 20, 1904	San Francisco, Cal.
Lagunitas	767	1903		1903		Oakland, Cal	Feb. 20, 1905	Sausalito, Cal	Feb. 29, 1904	Do.
Neponset No. 2	224	1884		1888		San Francisco, Cal	May 5, 1905	Sacramento, Cal	May 6, 1904	Do.
Newtown No. 2	217	1902		1905		Benicia, Cal	July 10, 1905	San Francisco, Cal	First inspn.	
Potrero	531	1900		1900		Alameda, Cal	Mar. 27, 1905	do	Mar. 26, 1904	Do.
Retta	[b] 5	1899		1898		Needles, Cal	Feb. 5, 1905	Needles, Cal	Mar. 12, 1903	Do.
Sea Gull	44	1899		1899		San Francisco, Cal	Mar. 3, 1905	Oakland, Cal	Mar. 27, 1902	Do.
Santa Fe	51	1884		1904		Coronado, Cal	Aug. 26, 1905	San Diego, Cal	Aug. 24, 1904	Do.
San Joaquin No. 2	242	1878		1893		Sacramento, Cal	Oct. 5, 1905	Sacramento, Cal	Sept. 28, 1904	Do.
Sunol	294	1890	1897	1897		San Francisco, Cal	Oct. 14, 1905	San Francisco, Cal	Oct. 17, 1904	Do.
San Jose	192	1898		1898		do	Dec. 16, 1905	Sacramento, Cal	Nov. 27, 1904	Do.
Trilby	80	1896		1900		do	July 21, 1905	San Francisco, Cal	First inspn.	
Valletta	419	1901		1898		Benicia, Cal	Aug. 22, 1905	do	Aug. 23, 1904	Do.
Ocean towing steamers.										
Callis	205	1889		1902		San Francisco, Cal	Aug. 24, 1905	Oakland, Cal	Aug. 25, 1904	San Francisco, Cal.
Liberty	60	1889		1899		Bandon, Oreg	Nov. 20, 1905	San Francisco, Cal	Nov. 29, 1904	Do.
Monarch	195	1875		1892		San Francisco, Cal	Oct. 6, 1905	do	Oct. 19, 1904	Do.
Ranger	144	1887		1901		North Bend, Oreg	Sept. 11, 1905	Alameda, Cal	Sept. 8, 1904	Do.
Inland towing steamers.										
Ada Warren	45	1903		1903		San Francisco, Cal	Apr. 27, 1905	San Francisco, Cal	Mar. 7, 1904	San Francisco, Cal.
Annie	20	1887		1900		Alameda, Cal	May 22, 1905	do	May 28, 1904	Do.
A. H. Payson	158	1902		1902		Oakland, Cal	Sept. 20, 1905	Point Richmond, Cal.	Sept. 19, 1904	Do.
Arabs	155	1904		1904		San Francisco, Cal	Oct. 6, 1905	San Francisco, Cal	Oct. 6, 1904	Do.
Auralie	8	1888		1897		do	Dec. 16, 1905	do	Dec. 15, 1904	Do.
Big River	[b] 10	1900		1900		Big River, Cal	Aug. 6, 1905	Big River, Cal	July 31, 1904	Do.
Catalina	36	1888		1888		Wilmington, Cal	Feb. 13, 1905	San Pedro, Cal	Mar. 14, 1904	Do.
Elizabeth	25	1890		1889		San Francisco, Cal	June 12, 1905	San Francisco, Cal	June 13, 1904	Do.
Fox	20	1901		1901		do	Sept. 29, 1905	do	Sept. 28, 1904	Do.
Gov. Perkins	17	1884		1890		do	May 9, 1905	do	Nov. 9, 1901	Do.
Gov. Markham	[b] 80	1892		1892		do	Nov. 22, 1905	do	Nov. 19, 1904	Do.
Ida W	[b] 32	1889		1889		do	Jan. 20, 1905	do	Sept. 11, 1903	Do.

Millie	12	1883		1900		do	Oct. 14, 1905	do	Sept. 21, 1904	Do.
Milton	23	1890		1890		Prosper, Oreg	Dec. 15, 1905	Oakland, Cal	Dec. 14, 1904	Do.
Rival	26	1869	1898	1898		Stockton, Cal	Sept. 21, 1905	do	Oct. 8, 1904	Do.
Reliance	94	1889		1889		Benicia, Cal	Sept. 22, 1905	San Francisco, Cal	Sept. 22, 1904	Do.
Rescue	172	1875		1896		San Francisco, Cal	May 15, 1905	do	May 15, 1904	Do.
Sea Fox	69	1902		1902		Oakland, Cal	Oct. 23, 1905	do	Oct. 22, 1904	Do.
Transit	28	1894	1904	1891		San Francisco, Cal	Aug. 25, 1905	Alameda, Cal	Aug. 23, 1904	Do.
Walter Hackett	44	1867	1894	1893	1893	Empire City, Oreg	Aug. 11, 1905	Oakland, Cal	Aug. 15, 1904	Do.
Steam pleasure yachts.										
Lucero	59	1895		1903		Seattle, Wash	Aug. 25, 1905	San Francisco, Cal	Aug. 26, 1904	Seattle, Wash.
Nemo	[b] 4	1888		(c)		San Francisco, Cal	Dec. 15, 1905	Teal, Cal	Dec. 15, 1905	San Francisco, Cal.
Miscellaneous steam vessels.										
Alexander (whaling)	294	1856	1879	1888		New York, N. Y	Mar. 6, 1905	San Francisco, Cal	Mar. 24, 1904	San Francisco, Cal.
Belvedere (whaling)	440	1880		1904		Bath, Me	Feb. 21, 1905	do	Feb. 23, 1904	Do.
Christopher Columbus (fishing).	41	1898		1898		San Francisco, Cal	Sept. 16, 1905	do	Aug. 13, 1904	Do.
Eva (hoisting)	36	1898		1894		do	Aug. 9, 1905	do	Aug. 8, 1904	Do.
Farragut (fishing)	47	1890		1890		do	Nov. 4, 1905	do	Nov. 5, 1904	Do.
Iolanda (fishing)	53	1905		1905		do	July 1, 1905	do	First inspn.	
Jeanette (whaling)	290	1893		1890		Benicia, Cal	Mar. 8, 1905	do	Mar. 8, 1904	Do.
Norwhal (whaling)	523	1883		1883		San Francisco, Cal	Mar. 7, 1905	do	Mar. 19, 1902	Do.
Pedro Costa (fishing)	51	1903		1903		do	Aug. 19, 1905	do	Aug. 20, 1904	Do.
Renown (hoisting)	42	1896		1896		do	July 22, 1905	do	July 26, 1904	Do.
Thrasher (whaling)	671	1883		1883		Bath, Me	Mar. 7, 1905	do	Mar. 16, 1904	Do.
U. S. Grant (fishing)	35	1885		1889		San Francisco, Cal	May 6, 1905	do	May 9, 1904	Do.
William Baylies (whaling)	380	1886		1894		Bath, Me	Feb. 27, 1905	do	Feb. 26, 1904	Do.
Vessels propelled by gasoline motors.										
Anvil	363	1905				San Francisco, Cal	June 22, 1905	San Francisco, Cal	First inspn.	
Admiral	27	1888				do	July 3, 1905	do	July 2, 1904	San Francisco, Cal.
Argus	566	1902				Marshfield, Oreg	July 26, 1905	do	First inspn.	
Berwick	100	1887				Benicia, Cal	Apr. 6, 1905	do	Apr. 1, 1904	Do.
Bessie K	98	1893				Alameda, Cal	Jan. 31, 1905	do	Jan. 28, 1904	Do.
Corinthian	94	1892				do	Sept. 23, 1905	do	First inspn.	
Commodore	44	1900				San Francisco, Cal	Mar. 18, 1905	do	Mar. 18, 1904	Do.
Charles Hansen	192	1881				Eureka, Cal	Mar. 21, 1905	do	First inspn.	
Confianza	88	1888				Benicia, Cal	May 6, 1905	do	Apr. 16, 1904	Do.
Chetco	103	1887				do	Dec. 13, 1905	do	Sept. 14, 1904	Seattle, Wash.
Expansion	135	1904				Oakland, Cal	Apr. 14, 1905	do	Mar. 31, 1904	San Francisco, Cal.
Etta B	33	1895				Benicia, Cal	May 13, 1905	Oakland, Cal	May 17, 1904	Do.
Elsie	23	1904				San Francisco, Cal	June 21, 1905	San Francisco, Cal	June 20, 1904	Do.
Four Sisters	38	1895				Benicia, Cal	June 20, 1905	do	June 22, 1904	Do.
Gretta A	53	1903				Freeport, Cal	July 15, 1905	Sacramento, Cal	July 15, 1904	Do.
Geo. R. Bailey	26	1904				Alameda, Cal	Aug. 1, 1905	San Francisco, Cal	May 18, 1904	Do.
Ida A	28	1895				San Francisco, Cal.	July 1, 1905	do	July 1, 1904	Do.

[a] Formerly Queen of the Yukon. [b] Estimated. [c] Unknown.

DOMESTIC VESSELS INSPECTED, YEAR ENDED DECEMBER 31, 1905—FIRST SUPERVISING DISTRICT—SAN FRANCISCO, CAL.—Continued.

Names of vessels and class.	Gross tonnage.	Hull built.	Hull rebuilt.	Boilers built.	Boilers rebuilt.	Where built.	Date of inspection.	Where inspected.	Date of previous inspection.	Local district where previously inspected.
Vessels propelled by gasoline motors—Continued.										
Jessie Madsen	32	1893				San Francisco, Cal	July 7, 1905	Oakland, Cal	July 9, 1904	San Francisco, Cal.
Jennie Griffin	17	1884				Benicia, Cal	Aug. 31, 1905	San Francisco, Cal	Aug. 26, 1904	Do.
Jersey [a]	41	1900				Stockton, Cal	May 5, 1905	Stockton, Cal	Apr. 16, 1904	Do.
J. C. Elliott	29	1898				Terminal Island, Cal	Jan. 17, 1905	San Pedro, Cal	Jan. 22, 1904	Do.
Monterey	126	1887				Benicia, Cal	Mar. 25, 1905	San Francisco, Cal	Apr. 5, 1904	Do.
Mizpah	64	1898				Prosper, Oreg	Apr. 10, 1905	do	Apr. 7, 1904	Do.
Mary C	27	1893				Sausalito, Cal	June 13, 1905	do	June 7, 1904	Do.
Nellie	43	1880				Benicia, Cal	Feb. 13, 1905	San Pedro, Cal	Mar. 15, 1904	Do.
Newark	120	1887				do	May 24, 1905	San Francisco, Cal	May 20, 1904	Do.
Nonpareil	52	1900				San Francisco, Cal	Dec. 6, 1905	do	Dec. 8, 1904	Do.
Oakland	146	1905				Coos Bay, Oreg	Aug. 1, 1905	Oakland, Cal	First inspn.	
Pike County	43	1851				Corte Madera, Cal	Mar. 28, 1905	San Francisco, Cal	Mar. 26, 1904	Do.
President	26	1891				San Francisco, Cal	May 26, 1905	Oakland, Cal	May 3, 1904	Do.
Rio Rey	84	1890				Alameda, Cal	Feb. 6, 1905	San Francisco, Cal	Feb. 4, 1904	Do.
Rita Newman	182	1903				Oakland, Cal	Apr. 6, 1905	do	Apr. 11, 1904	Do.
Santa Rosa Island	140	1902				Wilmington, Cal	Jan. 16, 1905	San Pedro, Cal	Jan. 23, 1904	Do.
Starlight	17	1894				California City, Cal	June 5, 1905	San Francisco, Cal	June 10, 1904	Do.
Sotoyome	534	1904				Albion, Cal	July 14, 1905	do	First inspn.	
Surprise	110	1902				San Francisco, Cal	Aug. 5, 1905	do	July 30, 1904	Do.
San Diego	70	1896				do	Aug. 26, 1905	San Diego, Cal	First inspn.	
Suisun City	152	1902				do	Sept. 7, 1905	San Francisco, Cal	Sept. 14, 1904	Do.
Trilby	80	1896				do	May 8, 1905	do	May 7, 1904	Do.
Topo	229	1903				Alameda, Cal	Sept. 27, 1905	do	Sept. 26, 1904	Do.
W. P. Fuller	49	1898				Benicia, Cal	June 28, 1905	do	June 28, 1904	Do.
Freight sail vessels of over 700 tons.										
A. J. Fuller (ship)	1,848	1881				Bath, Me	Mar. 18, 1905	San Francisco, Cal	July 21, 1903	Seattle, Wash.
Alpena (schooner)	823	1901				Port Blakeley, Wash	June 14, 1905	do	Mar. 1, 1904	Do.
Agenor (ship)	1,487	1870				Boston, Mass	June 24, 1905	do	July 17, 1900	Do.
Charles B. Kenney (bark)	1,128	1881				Bath, Me	Mar. 8, 1905	Oakland, Cal	June 17, 1903	San Francisco, Cal.
Charles E. Moody (ship)	2,003	1882				do	Apr. 7, 1905	San Francisco, Cal	Mar. 14, 1904	Do.
Carrollton (bark)	1,450	1872				do	May 5, 1905	do	May 27, 1903	Seattle, Wash.
C. D. Bryant (bark)	929	1878				Searsport, Me	June 9, 1905	do	Oct. 11, 1902	San Francisco, Cal.
Espada (schooner)	777	1902				Fairhaven, Cal	Apr. 10, 1905	do	Sept. 22, 1903	Seattle, Wash.
Echo (barkentine)	707	1896				North Bend, Oreg	Apr. 19, 1905	do	Jan. 5, 1904	San Francisco, Cal.
Fort George (ship) [b]	1,769	1884				Belfast, Ireland	Dec. 31, 1904	do	Dec. 30, 1902	Do.
Gathever (bark)	1,509	1874				Bath, Me	May 8, 1905	do	Apr. 25, 1904	Do.
Hecla (bark)	1,529	1877				do	Apr. 21, 1905	do	Aug. 6, 1903	Seattle, Wash.
Isaac Reed (bark)	1,541	1875				Waldoboro, Me	May 5, 1905	do	Apr. 6, 1904	San Francisco, Cal.

Jabez Howes (ship)	1,648	1877				Newburyport, Mass.	June 1, 1905	do	Oct. 20, 1903	Seattle, Wash.
Louis (schooner)	831	1888				North Bend, Oreg.	Apr. 11, 1905	do	Oct. 24, 1903	Do.
Martha Davis (bark)	870	1873				East Boston, Mass.	Apr. 14, 1905	do	Mar. 17, 1904	San Francisco, Cal.
Manga Reva (ship)	2,214	1891				Glasgow, Scotland	Apr. 27, 1905	do	First inspn.	
O. Kanogan (schooner)	721	1895				Port Blakeley, Wash.	Feb. 15, 1905	do	Jan. 28, 1904	Seattle, Wash.
Pactolus (bark)	1,673	1891				Bath, Me.	Mar. 18, 1905	do	Feb. 18, 1901	San Francisco, Cal.
Palmyra (bark)	1,359	1876				do	Apr. 21, 1905	do	July 2, 1903	Seattle, Wash.
Reaper (bark)	1,468	1876				do	Mar. 6, 1905	do	Apr. 16, 1903	San Francisco, Cal.
Sea King (bark)	1,491	1877				Bowdoinham, Me	Jan. 5, 1905	do	Aug. 13, 1902	Do.
Star of France (ship)	1,644	1877				Belfast, Ireland	Mar. 16, 1905	do	Mar. 17, 1904	Do.
St. David (ship)	1,595	1877				Bath, Me.	Apr. 13, 1905	do	May 27, 1903	Seattle, Wash.
St. James (bark)	1,578	1883				do	June 17, 1905	do	May 31, 1904	Do.
Thos. P. Emigh (barkentine)	1,040	1901				Tacoma, Wash.	Jan. 30, 1905	do	Apr. 10, 1903	San Francisco, Cal.
Sail vessels, barges, etc., of over 100 tons, carrying passengers for hire.										
Amy Turner (bark)	991	1877				Boston, Mass.	Mar. 30, 1905	San Francisco, Cal.	Feb. 29, 1904	San Francisco, Cal.
Archer (barkentine)	900	1876				Sunderland, England.	Feb. 23, 1905	do	Feb. 5, 1904	Do.
Annie Johnson (bark)	1,049	1872				Harrington, England.	Mar. 23, 1905	do	Mar. 2, 1904	Do.
Bohemia (ship)	1,633	1875				Bath, Me.	Mar. 30, 1905	do	Mar. 31, 1904	Do.
Big Bonanza (ship)	1,472	1875				Newburyport, Mass.	Apr. 12, 1905	do	Apr. 12, 1904	Do.
B. P. Cheney (ship)	1,322	1874				Bath, Me.	Apr. 27, 1905	do	Apr. 15, 1905	Do.
Columbia (ship)	1,471	1871				do	Apr. 7, 1905	do	Apr. 7, 1904	Do.
Coalinga (bark)	1,001	1868				Dundee, Scotland.	Apr. 17, 1905	do	Mar. 29, 1904	Do.
Carondelet (bark)	1,438	1872				Port Gamble, Wash.	Apr. 25, 1905	do	Mar. 14, 1904	Do.
Coronado (barkentine) [c]	1,062	1874				Sunderland, England.	Nov. 21, 1905	do	Oct. 15, 1904	Do.
Euterpe (bark)	1,318	1863				Ramsey, England	Mar. 29, 1905	do	Mar. 30, 1904	Do.
Emily F. Whitney (bark)	1,317	1880				Boston, Mass.	Sept. 30, 1905	do	Nov. 18, 1904	Do.
Electra (bark)	985	1868				do	Apr. 11, 1905	do	Apr. 6, 1904	Do.
Falls of Clyde (ship)	1,809	1878				Port Glasgow, Scotland.	Feb. 14, 1905	do	Dec. 29, 1903	Do.
Glendale (schooner)	296	1888				Fairhaven, Cal.	Mar. 29, 1905	do	Apr. 1, 1904	Do.
George Curtis (bark)	1,837	1884				San Francisco, Cal.	June 24, 1905	do	Mar. 15, 1904	Do.
Himalaya (bark)	1,027	1863				Sunderland, England.	Apr. 21, 1905	do	Mar. 29, 1904	Do.
Helene (schooner)	927	1900				Port Blakeley, Wash.	June 29, 1905	do	June 29, 1904	Do.
Indiana (ship)	1,487	1876				Bath, Me.	Apr. 7, 1905	do	Mar. 30, 1904	Do.
Irmgard (barkentine)	670	1889				Port Blakeley, Wash.	Nov. 2, 1905	do	Sept. 29, 1904	Do.
Kaiaulani (bark)	1,570	1899				Bath, Me.	May 12, 1905	do	May 9, 1904	Do.
Lucile (ship)	1,402	1874				Freeport, Me.	Apr. 13, 1905	do	Apr. 13, 1904	Do.
Levi G. Burgess (bark)	1,616	1877				Thomaston, Me.	Apr. 21, 1905	do	Mar. 30, 1904	Do.
Llewellyn J. Morse (ship)	1,392	1877				Brewer, Me.	Mar. 23, 1905	do	Apr. 5, 1904	Do.
M. P. Grace (ship)	1,928	1875				Bath, Me.	Mar. 29, 1905	do	Apr. 12, 1904	Do.
McLaurin (ship)	1,374	1879				Newburyport, Mass.	Apr. 20, 1905	do	Apr. 14, 1904	Do.
Mohican (bark)	852	1875				Chelsea, Mass.	May 17, 1905	do	May 6, 1904	Do.
Oriental (ship)	1,688	1874				Bath, Me.	Apr. 8, 1905	do	Apr. 13, 1904	Do.
Paramita (bark)	1,582	1879				Freeport, Me.	Apr. 19, 1905	do	Apr. 22, 1904	Do.
Roderick Dhu (bark)	1,534	1873				Sunderland, England.	Jan. 10, 1905	do	Oct. [illegible]8, 1903	Do.
St. Katherine (bark)	1,201	1890				Bath, Me.	Feb. 10, 1905	do	Jan. [illegible]4, 1904	Do.

[a] Formerly Dude, 1902. [b] Certificated Jan. 3, 1905. [c] Formerly J. C. Pfluger, 1901.

DOMESTIC VESSELS INSPECTED, YEAR ENDED DECEMBER 31, 1905—FIRST SUPERVISING DISTRICT—SAN FRANCISCO, CAL.—Continued.

Names of vessels and class.	Gross tonnage.	Hull built.	Hull rebuilt.	Boilers built.	Boilers rebuilt.	Where built.	Date of inspection.	Where inspected.	Date of previous inspection.	Local district where previously inspected.
***Sail vessels, barges, etc., of over 100 tons, carrying passengers for hire*—Continued.**										
Santiago (bark)	979	1895				Belfast, Ireland	Feb. 28, 1905	Oakland, Cal	Feb. 16, 1904	San Francisco, Cal.
Star of Russia (ship)	1,981	1874				do	Mar. 24, 1905	San Francisco, Cal	Mar. 25, 1904	Do.
Sea Witch (bark)	1,288	1872				East Boston, Mass	Apr. 1, 1995	do	Apr. 5, 1904	Do.
Standard (ship)	1,534	1878				Phippsburg, Me	Apr. 6, 1905	do	Apr. 6, 1904	Do.
Star of Italy (ship)	1,613	1877				Belfast, Ireland	Apr. 12, 1905	do	May 3, 1904	Do.
Santa Clara (ship)	1,535	1876				Bath, Me	Apr. 13, 1905	do	Mar. 30, 1904	Do.
Servia (bark)	1,866	1883				do	Apr. 28, 1905	do	Sept. 19, 1903	Seattle, Wash.
Tacoma (ship)	1,738	1881				do	Apr. 13, 1905	do	Apr. 11, 1904	San Francisco, Cal.
Will W. Case (bark)	582	1877				Rockland, Me	Apr. 25, 1905	do	Apr. 6, 1904	Do.
William H. Macy (ship)	2,202	1883				Rockport, Me	May 3, 1905	do	Jan. 28, 1904	Do.
W. H. Marston (schooner)	1,169	1901				San Francisco, Cal	Oct. 15, 1905	do	Aug. 11, 1904	Do.
LOCAL DISTRICT OF PORTLAND, OREG.										
Ocean passenger steamers.										
L. Roscoe	117	1903		1903		Hoquiam, Wash	Sept. 14, 1905	Yaquina, Oreg	Sept. 15, 1904	Portland, Oreg.
Sue H. Elmore	232	1900		1900		Portland, Oreg	Oct. 2, 1905	Astoria, Oreg	Oct. 6, 1904	Do.
W. H. Harrison	91	1890		1903		Waldport, Oreg	Sept. 1, 1905	do	Aug. 8, 1904	Do.
Inland passenger steamers.										
Alert	124	1890	1902	1890	1899	Bandon, Oreg	July 11, 1905	Marshfield, Oreg	July 10, 1904	Portland, Oreg.
Alma	13	1896		1886		Sumner, Oreg	do	do	do	Do.
Altona	329	1899		1890		Portland, Oreg	June 8, 1905	Portland, Oreg	June 7, 1904	Do.
America	99	1899		1889		do	May 6, 1905	do	May 5, 1904	Do.
Annarine	5	1897		1901		Rainier, Oreg	May 25, 1905	Tillamook, Oreg	May 26, 1904	Do.
Annie Comings[a]	452	1887	1903	1887	1898	Portland, Oreg	Apr. 17, 1905	Portland, Oreg	Apr. 21, 1904	Do.
Bailey Gatzert	560	1890		1905		Seattle, Wash	May 31, 1905	do	June 4, 1904	Do.
Canby	48	1904		1904		Keno, Oreg	May 2, 1905	Keno, Oreg	First inspn	Do.
Cascades	451	1882	1903	1882	1903	Portland, Oreg	May 16, 1905	Portland, Oreg	May 17, 1904	Do.
Chas. R. Spencer	598	1901	1904	1900		do	Sept. 27, 1905	do	Oct. 6, 1904	Do.
Chester	130	1897		1893		do	Sept. 7, 1905	do	Sept. 14, 1904	Do.
Columbia	84	1902		1902		Newport, Wash	May 13, 1905	Newport, Wash	May 14, 1904	Do.
Colwell	20	1897		1899		Ilwaco, Wash	Apr. 7, 1905	Astoria, Oreg	Apr. 8, 1904	Do.
Coos River	16	1891		1890		Marshfield, Oreg	July 11, 1905	Marshfield, Oreg	July 10, 1904	Do.
Cruiser	62	1886		1900		Coos Bay, Oreg	do	do	do	Do.

Cygnet	4	1892		1892		Portland, Oreg	July 21, 1905	Portland, Oreg	June 1, 1904	Do.
Dalles City	446	1898		1898	1905	do	July 22, 1905	do	July 29, 1904	Do.
Dispatch	250	1903		1899	1898	Parkersburg, Oreg	July 13, 1905	Bandon, Oreg	July 12, 1904	Do.
Echo	76	1901		1901		Coquille, Oreg	July 12, 1905	Coquille, Oreg	July 11, 1904	Do
Electro	81	1901		1901		Astoria, Oreg	Nov. 23, 1905	Astoria, Oreg	Nov. 25, 1904	Do.
Elk	26	1901		1891		Newport, Wash	Jan. 5, 1905	Newport, Wash	Jan. 5, 1904	Do.
Elkkader	31	1902		1901		Portland, Oreg	June 10, 1905	Portland, Oreg	June 9, 1904	Do.
Elmore	493	1895	1903	1900		do	Nov. 24, 1905	do	Nov. 28, 1904	Do.
Eva	130	1894		1887	1894	do	July 10, 1905	Gardiner, Oreg	July 9, 1904	Do.
Favorite	63	1900		1900		Coquille, Oreg	July 13, 1905	Coquille, Oreg	July 11, 1904	Do.
Flyer	36	1890	1901	1890		Porter, Oreg	July 11, 1905	Marshfield, Oreg	July 10, 1904	Do.
George W. Simons [b]	84	1895	1905	1904		Portland, Oreg	June 10, 1905	Portland, Oreg	June 6, 1904	Do.
Glenola [c]	313	1889	1903	1889	1898	do	Apr. 1, 1905	do	Mar. 30, 1904	Do.
Hassalo	679	1899		1899		do	May 6, 1905	do	June 23, 1904	Do.
Harvest Queen	733	1900		1900		do	Aug. 2, 1905	do	Aug. 2, 1904	Do.
Hazel	24	1899		1899		do	July 9, 1905	Florence, Oreg	July 9, 1904	Do.
Hoo Hoo	20	1895		1895		do	Dec. 4, 1905	Portland, Oreg	Dec. 7, 1904	Do.
Ione	242	1889		1889	1901	do	Dec. 1, 1905	do	Dec. 10, 1904	Do.
Iralda	90	1899		1904		do	June 19, 1905	do	June 18, 1904	Do.
Jessie Harkins [d]	71	1903	1905	1905		do	Apr. 10, 1905	do	Nov. 24, 1903	Do.
John McCraken	122	1903		1903		Seattle, Wash	Apr. 1, 1905	do	Mar. 28, 1904	Do.
Jordan	96	1901		1904		Portland, Oreg	Dec. 11, 1905	Astoria, Oreg	Dec. 12, 1904	Do.
Joseph Kellogg	462	1900		1891		do	Sept. 21, 1905	Portland, Oreg	Sept. 28, 1904	Do.
J. Warren	10	1902		1887		Gravel Ford, Oreg	July 12, 1905	Coquille, Oreg	July 11, 1904	Do.
Juno	22	1876	1904	1888	1893	Coos Bay, Oreg	July 10, 1905	Gardiner, Oreg	July 9, 1904	Do.
Katie Weir	6	1886	1900	1895		Portland, Oreg	July 29, 1905	Cascade Locks, Oreg	Aug. 3, 1904	Do.
Klamath	69	1905		1905		Klamath Falls, Oreg	Aug. 20, 1905	Klamath Falls, Oreg	First inspn	
Leona	179	1901		1900		Portland, Oreg	May 24, 1905	Portland, Oreg	May 24, 1904	Do.
Lewiston	548	1905		1899		Riparia, Wash	June 24, 1905	Riparia, Wash	First inspn	
Liberty	174	1903		1903		Bandon, Oreg	July 12, 1905	Coquille, Oreg	July 12, 1904	Do.
Lurline	481	1878	1905	1899		Portland, Oreg	Feb. 27, 1905	Portland, Oreg	Feb. 29, 1904	Do.
Maja	32	1902		1894		Warrenton, Oreg	July 29, 1905	Cascade Locks, Oreg	Aug. 3, 1904	Do.
Marguerite	44	1898		1892	1898	Florence, Oreg	July 9, 1905	Florence, Oreg	July 8, 1904	Do.
Maria	2	1896		1900	1904	Portland, Oreg	May 25, 1905	Tillamook, Oreg	May 26, 1904	Do.
Mascot	267	1890		1890	1903	do	Feb. 13, 1905	Portland, Oreg	Feb. 16, 1904	Do.
Mayflower	82	1891		1901		Astoria, Oreg	June 27, 1905	Astoria, Oreg	July 2, 1904	Do.
Melville	93	1903		1902		Knappton, Wash	June 9, 1905	do	June 10, 1904	Do.
M. F. Henderson	534	1901		1901		Portland, Oreg	Aug. 31, 1905	Portland, Oreg	Sept. 1, 1904	Do.
Modoc	490	1896	1901	1889		do	Nov. 24, 1905	do	Nov. 28, 1904	Do.
Mountain Gem	469	1904		1904		Lewiston, Idaho	Aug. 25, 1905	Riparia, Wash	Aug. 26, 1904	Do.
Nahcotta	149	1899		1898		Portland, Oreg	July 27, 1905	Astoria, Oreg	July 27, 1904	Do.
North West	324	1889	1902	1899		do	Oct. 14, 1905	Portland, Oreg	Oct. 13, 1904	Do.
N. R. Lang	528	1900		1891	1900	do	Sept. 28, 1905	Oregon City, Oreg	Oct. 3, 1904	Do.
Oregona	370	1904		1904		do	June 21, 1905	Portland, Oreg	June 21, 1904	Do.
Pomona	365	1898		1898		do	June 22, 1905	do	July 1, 1904	Do.
Regulator	508	1899		1901		do	Apr. 2, 1905	do	Apr. 6, 1904	Do.
Republic	88	1892	1900	1883	1900	do	June 19, 1905	do	June 20, 1904	Do.
Resolute	24	1900		1900		do	Mar. 27, 1905	do	Mar. 28, 1904	Do.
R. Miler	83	1891	1905	1891		Astoria, Oreg	Apr. 21, 1905	Astoria, Oreg	Apr. 20, 1904	Do.
Ruth	515	1896		1895		Portland, Oreg	Dec. 12, 1905	Portland, Oreg	Dec. 17, 1904	Do.
Sarah Dixon	369	1892		1891		do	Apr. 3, 1905	do	Apr. 2, 1904	Do.

[a] Formerly Wm M. Hoag, 1903. [b] Formerly Sadie B, 1904. [c] Formerly G. W. Shaver, 1903. [d] Formerly gasoline boat.

DOMESTIC VESSELS INSPECTED, YEAR ENDED DECEMBER 31, 1905—FIRST SUPERVISING DISTRICT—PORTLAND, OREG.—Continued.

Names of vessels and class.	Gross tonnage.	Hull built.	Hull rebuilt.	Boilers built.	Boilers rebuilt.	Where built.	Date of inspection.	Where inspected.	Date of previous inspection.	Local district where previously inspected.
Inland passenger steamers—Continued.										
Sareta	34	1903		1899		Newport, Wash	June 17, 1905	Newport, Wash	June 16, 1904	Portland, Oreg.
Shamrock	116	1905		1904		Astoria, Oreg	Jan. 25, 1905	Astoria, Oreg	First inspn	
Spokane	676	1899		1899		Riparia, Wash	Mar. 3, 1905	Riparia, Wash	Mar. 11, 1904	Do.
Spokane	367	1903		1897		Newport, Wash	May 12, 1905	Newport, Wash	May 14, 1904	Do.
Stranger	85	1903		1881	1900	Vancouver, Wash	May 31, 1905	Portland, Oreg	June 1, 1904	Do.
T. J. Potter	1,017	1901		1900		Portland, Oreg	June 13, 1905	do	June 7, 1904	Do.
Telephone	794	1903		1903		do	Aug. 10, 1905	do	First inspn	
T. M. Richardson	36	1888	1905	1905		Oneatta, Oreg	May 18, 1905	Toledo, Oreg	July 7, 1904	Do.
Umpqua	24	1897	1900	1899		San Francisco, Cal	July 10, 1905	Gardiner, Oreg	July 9, 1904	Do.
Undine	327	1888	1905	1887	1905	Portland, Oreg	May 31, 1905	Portland, Oreg	June 1, 1904	Do.
Vanguard	75	1901		1901		Astoria, Oreg	Apr. 8, 1905	Astoria, Oreg	Apr. 8, 1904	Do.
Venus	15	1901		1901		Bandon, Oreg	July 13, 1905	Coquille, Oreg	July 13, 1904	Do.
Welcome	30	1900		1892		Coquille, Oreg	July 12, 1905	do	July 12, 1904	Do.
Wenona	74	1904		1901		Coos Bay, Oreg	Jan. 2, 1905	Astoria, Oreg	First inspn	
Ferry steamers.										
John F. Caples	192	1904		1904		Portland, Oreg	Aug. 5, 1905	Portland, Oreg	Aug. 11, 1904	Portland, Oreg.
Lionel R. Webster	343	1904		1904		do	Aug. 11, 1905	do	do	Do.
New Western Queen	120	1898		1879	1899	The Dalles, Oreg	May 11, 1905	The Dalles, Oreg	May 12, 1904	Do.
Oregon	39	1899		1897		Arlington, Oreg	June 15, 1905	Arlington, Oreg	June 14, 1904	Do.
Tacoma	1,362	1884	1904	1903		Portland, Oreg	Sept. 29, 1905	Kalama, Wash	Oct. 5, 1904	Do.
Vancouver	211	1893	1904	1899		do	Oct. 26, 1905	Vancouver, Wash	Nov. 7, 1904	Do.
W. S. Mason	322	1894	1903	1894		do	Apr. 12, 1905	Portland, Oreg	Apr. 14, 1904	Do.
Ocean freight steamer.										
Sea Foam	339	1905		1905		Aberdeen, Wash	Apr. 5, 1905	Portland, Oreg	First inspn	
Inland freight steamers.										
Columbia	159	1903		1886		Blalock, Oreg	Oct. 24, 1905	Arlington, Oreg	Oct. 26, 1904	Portland, Oreg.
G. M. Walker	154	1897	1905	1883	1899	Portland, Oreg	Oct. 27, 1905	Portland, Oreg	Oct. 6, 1904	Do.
J. M. Hannaford	746	1899		1897		Potlatch, Idaho	May 28, 1905	Lewiston, Idaho	Aug. 12, 1903	Do.
New Volunteer	105	1901		1901		Newport, Wash	June 17, 1905	Newport, Wash	June 16, 1904	Do.
Norma	488	1891	1900	1890	1902	Huntington, Oreg	Oct. 11, 1905	Riparia, Wash	Oct. 12, 1904	Do.
Ocean towing steamers.										
Columbia	132	1892		1892	1900	North Bend, Oreg	July 11, 1905	Marshfield, Oreg	July 10, 1904	Portland, Oreg.
Hunter	104	1883	1901	1901		Coos Bay, Oreg	July 10, 1905	Gardiner, Oreg	July 9, 1904	Do.

North King	80	1901	....	1901	....	Portland, Oreg	Apr. 14, 1905	Astoria, Oreg	Apr. 9, 1904	Do.
North Star	62	1899	....	1899	....	Seattle, Wash	Apr. 7, 1905	....do	....do	Do.
Robarts	48	1887	....	1898	....	San Francisco, Cal	June 6, 1905	Yaquina, Oreg	June 2, 1904	Do.
Samson	278	1898	....	1904	....	Portland, Oreg	Oct. 9, 1905	Astoria, Oreg	Oct. 10, 1904	Do.
Tatoosh	277	1900	....	1899	....	Seattle, Wash	June 27, 1905	....do	July 2, 1904	Do.
Triumph	55	1889	....	1900	....	Parkersburg, Oreg	July 13, 1905	Bandon, Oreg	July 12, 1904	Do.
Wallula	167	1899	....	1899	....	San Francisco, Cal	Apr. 28, 1905	Astoria, Oreg	Apr. 20, 1904	Do.
Inland towing steamers.										
Agnes	21	1904	....	1904	....	Portland, Oreg	May 10, 1905	Portland, Oreg	May 11, 1904	Portland, Oreg.
Albany	431	1896	....	1903	....	....do	Apr. 17, 1905	....do	Apr. 16, 1904	Do.
Antelope	29	1886	....	1886	....	Marshfield, Oreg	July 13, 1905	Coquille, Oreg	July 13, 1904	Do.
Cash [a]	35	1883	1903	1903	....	Seattle, Wash	June 13, 1905	Portland, Oreg	June 11, 1904	Do.
City of Eugene	347	1899	....	1899	....	Eugene, Oreg	June 3, 1905	Oregon City, Oreg	May 31, 1904	Do.
Clara	6	1900	....	1900	....	Astoria, Oreg	June 9, 1905	Astoria, Oreg	June 10, 1904	Do.
Defender	28	1903	....	1903	....	Dalkena, Wash	May 12, 1905	Newport, Wash	May 14, 1904	Do.
Detroit	5	1905	....	1905	....	Lenora, Wash	Sept. 4, 1905	....do	First inspn.	
Edith	74	1877	1896	1900	....	Portland, Oreg	May 9, 1905	Astoria, Oreg	May 6, 1904	Do.
El Hurd	33	1897	1905	1887	....	Astoria, Oreg	June 9, 1905	....do	July 2, 1904	Do.
Enterprise	333	1902	....	1890	....	Portland, Oreg	Feb. 10, 1905	Portland, Oreg	Feb. 12, 1904	Do.
Errand Boy	27	1902	....	1902	....	Bonners Ferry, Idaho	Nov. 19, 1905	Bonners Ferry, Idaho	Nov. 16, 1904	Do.
Fannie	316	1887	....	1887	1898	Portland, Oreg	Apr. 15, 1905	Portland, Oreg	Apr. 15, 1904	Do.
F. B. Jones	324	1901	....	1902	....	....do	Sept. 7, 1905	....do	Sept. 5, 1904	Do.
Florence	2	1901	....	1888	....	Astoria, Oreg	June 9, 1905	Astoria, Oreg	June 10, 1904	Do.
Flyer	3	1898	....	1892	....	Portland, Oreg	Jan. 2, 1905	....do	Dec. 29, 1903	Do.
Game Cock	772	1898	....	1898	....	....do	Apr. 10, 1905	Portland, Oreg	Apr. 12, 1904	Do.
Geo. R. Vosburg	106	1900	....	1900	....	....do	Apr. 22, 1905	....do	Jan. 30, 1904	Do.
Grey Eagle	218	1895	1904	1891	....	Newberg, Oreg	Mar. 20, 1905	Newberg, Oreg	Mar. 22, 1904	Do.
Hercules	560	1899	....	1898	....	Portland, Oreg	May 8, 1905	Portland, Oreg	May 16, 1904	Do.
Hustler	204	1891	....	1891	1904	....do	Apr. 1, 1905	....do	Mar. 29, 1904	Do.
James B. Stephens	31	1885	1905	1888	....	....do	May 22, 1905	Westport, Oreg	May 10, 1904	Do.
La Crosse	10	1905	....	1895	....	Cascade Locks, Oreg	Dec. 13, 1905	Cascade Locks, Oreg	First inspn.	
Lillian B	18	1903	....	1903	....	Portland, Oreg	Nov. 17, 1905	Portland, Oreg	Nov. 14, 1904	Do.
Lottie	69	1903	....	1903	....	Astoria, Oreg	Oct. 30, 1905	Astoria, Oreg	Nov. 3, 1904	Do.
Maria	202	1887	1903	1891	....	Portland, Oreg	Dec. 23, 1905	Portland, Oreg	Dec. 22, 1904	Do.
M. F. Hazen [b]	7	1898	1904	1904	....	Tacoma, Wash	Apr. 21, 1905	Astoria, Oreg	Apr. 29, 1904	Do.
Mildred	9	1899	1904	1904	....	Yaquina, Oreg	Apr. 27, 1905	Portland, Oreg	Apr. 9, 1904	Do.
Mink	14	1883	1896	1883	1898	Marshfield, Oreg	July 9, 1905	Florence, Oreg	July 8, 1904	Do.
Nellie	180	1899	....	1884	1903	Portland, Oreg	Apr. 6, 1905	Portland, Oreg	Apr. 6, 1904	Do.
Nestor	97	1903	....	1902	....	....do	May 22, 1905	Westport, Oreg	May 21, 1904	Do.
Norman	60	1903	....	1903	....	....do	Jan. 14, 1905	Portland, Oreg	Jan. 15, 1904	Do.
No Wonder	269	1889	....	1891	1899	....do	Oct. 27, 1905	....do	Nov. 5, 1904	Do.
Ocklahoma	676	1897	....	1902	....	....do	Sept. 16, 1905	....do	Sept. 26, 1904	Do.
Ottawa	77	1905	....	1893	....	....do	Aug. 4, 1905	....do	First inspn.	
Pearl	10	1897	....	1897	1905	....do	July 29, 1905	Cascade Locks, Oreg	Aug. 3, 1904	Do.
Petrel	13	1902	....	1902	....	....do	Oct. 23, 1905	Portland, Oreg	Oct. 18, 1904	Do.
Paloma	185	1902	....	1883	1902	....do	June 10, 1905	....do	June 8, 1904	Do.
Reta	26	1899	....	1894	....	Prosper, Oreg	July 12, 1905	Coquille, Oreg	July 11, 1904	Do.
Rowena	8	1885	1904	1886	....	Portland, Oreg	June 13, 1905	Portland, Oreg	June 10, 1904	Do.
Sacajawea	59	1905	....	1904	....	Felida, Wash	Sept. 8, 1905	....do	First inspn.	

[a] Formerly Brick, 1903.

[b] Formerly St. Mary, 1904.

DOMESTIC VESSELS INSPECTED, YEAR ENDED DECEMBER 31, 1905—FIRST SUPERVISING DISTRICT—PORTLAND, OREG.—Continued.

Names of vessels and class.	Gross tonnage.	Hull built.	Hull rebuilt.	Boilers built.	Boilers rebuilt.	Where built.	Date of inspection.	Where inspected.	Date of previous inspection.	Local district where previously inspected.
Inland towing steamers—Con.										
Victor	17	1903		1903		St. Helens, Oreg	Dec. 12, 1905	Portland, Oreg	Dec. 8, 1904	Portland, Oreg.
Volga	71	1894		1889		Portland, Oreg	Nov. 17, 1905	do	July 2, 1904	Do.
Wenona	50	1888	1904	1905		do	Oct. 3, 1905	do	Oct. 4, 1904	Do.
Wilavis	16	1901		1901		Rainier, Oreg.	Apr. 24, 1905	Bonneville, Oreg	Apr. 22, 1904	Do.
Steam pleasure yacht.										
Nerka	5	1894		1894		Portland, Oreg	May 11, 1905	Warrendale, Oreg	May 12, 1904	Portland, Oreg.
Miscellaneous steamers.										
Geo. H. Williams (fireboat)	194	1904		1904		Portland, Oreg	May 16, 1905	Portland, Oreg	May 16, 1904	Portland, Oreg.
Mildred (fishing)	2	1904		1898		do	Apr. 24, 1905	Bonneville, Oreg	Apr. 18, 1904	Do.
Vessels propelled by gasoline motors.										
Della	30	1901				Woods, Oreg	Feb. 21, 1905	Astoria, Oreg	Nov. 3, 1903	Portland, Oreg.
Elsie May	32	1899				Wallula, Wash	Sept. 18, 1905	Wallula, Wash	Sept. 17, 1904	Do.
Gerald C	31	1895				Benicia, Cal	Jan. 25, 1905	Astoria, Oreg	Jan. 16, 1904	Do.
Freight sail vessels of over 700 tons.										
Alex. T. Brown (schooner)	788	1903				Ballard, Wash	Apr. 12, 1905	Portland, Oreg	Apr. 19, 1904	Seattle, Wash.
Alvena (schooner)	772	1901				Eureka, Cal	do	do	Apr. 18, 1904	Do.
Ariel (schooner)	726	1900				Benicia, Cal	Feb. 11, 1905	do	July 10, 1903	Do.
Borealis (schooner)	764	1902				Eureka, Cal	July 1, 1905	do	June 20, 1904	Do.
Mabel Gale (schooner)	762	1893				Port Blakeley, Wash.	Feb. 13, 1905	do	Feb. 2, 1904	Portland, Oreg.
Sail vessels, barges, etc., of over 100 tons, carrying passengers for hire.										
Berlin (ship)	1,634	1882				Bath, Me	Apr. 8, 1905	Astoria, Oreg	Mar. 31, 1903	Portland, Oreg.
C. F. Sargent (bark)	1,704	1874				Yarmouth, Me	Apr. 14, 1905	do	Apr. 4, 1904	Do.
Klickitat (barge)	998	1901				Portland, Oreg	June 20, 1905	Portland, Oreg	June 8, 1904	Do.
Koko Head (bark)	1,084	1901				San Francisco, Cal	Mar. 15, 1905	do	Oct. 17, 1903	Seattle, Wash.
St. Nicholas (ship)	1,798	1869				Bath, Me	Apr. 4, 1905	Astoria, Oreg	Feb. 21, 1902	San Francisco, Cal.

LOCAL DISTRICT OF SEATTLE, WASH.

Ocean passenger steamers.										
Al-ki	1,259	1884		1890		Bath, Me	Apr. 7, 1905	Seattle, Wash	Apr. 13, 1904	Seattle, Wash.
Bertha	926	1899		1899		Alameda, Cal	Mar. 23, 1905	do	Apr. 5, 1904	Do.
Corwin	447	1876	1904	1889		Portland, Oreg	May 2, 1905	do	May 11, 1904	Do.
Cottage City	1,885	1890		1903		Bath, Me	May 22, 1905	do	May 25, 1904	Do.
City of Topeka	1,057	1884		1904		Chester, Pa	May 23, 1905	do	June 14, 1904	Do.
City of Seattle	1,411	1890		1890		Philadelphia, Pa	July 8, 1905	do	July 24, 1904	Do.
Dirigo	843	1898		1898		Hoquiam, Wash	June 14, 1905	do	May 13, 1904	Do.
Dora	293	1880		1892		Benicia, Cal	Jan. 16, 1905	do	Feb. 8, 1904	San Francisco, Cal.
Dora [a]	293	1880		1892		do	Oct. 16, 1905	do	Jan. 16, 1905	Seattle, Wash.
Excelsior	830	1893		1893	1893	Eureka, Cal	June 26, 1905	do	June 28, 1904	Do.
Elihu Thomson	896	1888		1888		Newcastle, England	May 6, 1905	Quartermaster, Wash	Sept. 20, 1903	Do.
Farallon	749	1888		1892		San Francisco, Cal	Dec. 5, 1905	Seattle, Wash	Dec. 14, 1904	Do.
Garonne	3,901	1871		1871		Glasgow, Scotland	Apr. 7, 1905	do	Feb. 19, 1904	Do.
Jeanie	1,071	1883		1899		Bath, Me	Apr. 14, 1905	do	Apr. 17, 1904	Do.
Jefferson	1,615	1904		1904		Tacoma, Wash	May 25, 1905	do	July 5, 1904	Do.
Minnesota	20,718	1904		1902		New London, Conn	Oct. 23, 1905	do	Aug. 18, 1904	New London, Conn.
Olympia	2,837	1883		1883		Glasgow, Scotland	May 9, 1905	do	Apr. 27, 1904	Seattle, Wash.
Ohio	3,488	1873		1905		Philadelphia, Pa	May 10, 1905	do	May 11, 1903	Do.
Oregon	2,335	1878		1903		Chester, Pa	May 20, 1905	do	May 14, 1904	Do.
Portland	1,420	1885		1897		Bath, Me	June 11, 1905	do	July 9, 1904	Do.
Ramona	1,061	1902		1902		Alameda, Cal	July 21, 1905	do	Aug. 3, 1904	Do.
Santa Rosa	2,416	1884		1905		Chester, Pa	Apr. 21, 1905	do	Apr. 20, 1904	San Francisco, Cal.
Santa Ana	1,250	1900		1900		Marshfield, Oreg	May 16, 1905	do	May 13, 1904	Seattle, Wash.
Shawmut	9,606	1902		1902		Sparrow Point, Md	do	do	Mar. 28, 1904	Do.
Santa Clara [b]	1,588	1900		1900		Everett, Wash	July 29, 1905	do	July 19, 1904	Do.
Tremont	9,606	1902		1902		Sparrow Point, Md	May 27, 1905	do	May 2, 1904	Do.
Valencia	1,598	1882		1901		Philadelphia, Pa	Apr. 27, 1905	do	Apr. 30, 1904	Do.
Inland passenger steamers.										
Athlon	157	1901		1900		Portland, Oreg	Feb. 13, 1905	Seattle, Wash	Feb. 12, 1904	Seattle, Wash.
Alice Gertrude	413	1898		1898		Seattle, Wash	Apr. 30, 1905	do	May 22, 1904	Do.
Acme	31	1899		1892		do	June 1, 1905	Lake Washington, Wash.	June 1, 1904	Do.
Albion	149	1899		1905		Coupeville, Wash	July 31, 1905	Seattle, Wash	July 23, 1904	Do.
Advance	93	1899		1899		Poulsbo, Wash	Aug. 19, 1905	do	Aug. 22, 1905	Do.
Black Prince	159	1901		1901		Everett, Wash	Mar. 24, 1905	Everett, Wash	Mar. 25, 1904	Do.
Burton	90	1905		1898	1899	Tacoma, Wash	Apr. 7, 1905	Tacoma, Wash	First inspn.	
Blanche [c]	98	1890	1898	1890		Seattle, Wash	July 3, 1905	Seattle, Wash	July 7, 1904	Do.
Buckeye	87	1890		1902		do	Aug. 2, 1905	Bellingham, Wash	May 27, 1904	Do.
Bellingham [d]	333	1882	1891	1891		Astoria, Oreg	Dec. 21, 1905	Seattle, Wash	Dec. 17, 1904	Do.
Capital City [e]	552	1898		1901		Port Blakeley, Wash	Feb. 3, 1905	do	Feb. 1, 1904	Do.
City of Shelton	190	1895		1895		Shelton, Wash	Apr. 1, 1905	Olympia, Wash	Apr. 6, 1904	Do.
Cyrene	25	1891	1904	1904		Seattle, Wash	Apr. 13, 1905	Lake Washington, Wash.	Apr. 14, 1904	Do.

[a] Second inspection. [b] Formerly John S. Kimball, 1904. [c] Formerly C. C. Calkins, 1903. [d] Formerly Willapa, 1903. [e] Formerly Dalton, 1901.

DOMESTIC VESSELS INSPECTED, YEAR ENDED DECEMBER 31, 1905—FIRST SUPERVISING DISTRICT—SEATTLE, WASH.—Continued.

Names of vessels and class.	Gross tonnage.	Hull built.	Hull rebuilt.	Boilers built.	Boilers rebuilt.	Where built.	Date of inspection.	Where inspected.	Date of previous inspection.	Local district where previously inspected.
Inland passenger steamers—Continued.										
Chelan	244	1902		1903		Wenatchee, Wash	May 29, 1905	Wenatchee, Wash	June 6, 1904	Seattle, Wash.
Cascade	34	1904		1904		Snohomish, Wash	June 27, 1905	Everett, Wash	June 24, 1904	Do.
Columbia	341	1905		1905		Wenatchee, Wash	Oct. 17, 1905	Wenatchee, Wash	First inspn	
City of Everett	212	1900		1900	1901	Everett, Wash	Nov. 29, 1905	Seattle, Wash	Nov. 30, 1904	Do.
Crystal	25	(a)	1904	1904		Alameda, Cal	Dec. 6, 1905	Tacoma, Wash	Dec. 6, 1904	Do.
Crest	99	1900	1901	1903		Tacoma, Wash	Dec. 19, 1905	do	Dec. 19, 1904	Do.
Dorothy	59	1903		1903		Barnaby, Wash	Mar. 9, 1905	Kirkland, Wash	Mar. 7, 1904	Do.
Dode	215	1898		1898		Seattle, Wash	Mar. 19, 1905	Seattle, Wash	Apr. 1, 1904	Do.
Dix	130	1904		1904		Tacoma, Wash	May 16, 1905	do	May 26, 1904	Do.
Defiance	171	1901		1903		do	May 17, 1905	do	May 23, 1904	Do.
Dauntless	125	1899		1899		do	June 12, 1905	Port Townsend, Wash	June 15, 1904	Do.
Dove [b]	85	1889	1904	1898		Portland, Oreg	Aug. 23, 1905	Seattle, Wash	Aug. 27, 1904	Do.
Enterprise	129	1903		1903		Wenatchee, Wash	Mar. 21, 1905	Brewster, Wash	Oct. 11, 1903	Do.
Echo	36	1893		1893		Snohomish, Wash	May 29, 1905	Wenatchee, Wash	June 7, 1904	Do.
Edgar	26	1890		1898		San Francisco, Cal	Oct. 7, 1905	Hoquiam, Wash	Oct. 10, 1904	Do.
Fleetwood	64	1902		1901		Aberdeen, Wash	Feb. 25, 1905	Aberdeen, Wash	Feb. 25, 1904	Do.
Falcon	74	1905		1905		Houghton, Wash	Feb. 24, 1905	Lake Washington, Wash.	First inspn	
Fairhaven	319	1889		1889		Tacoma, Wash	Apr. 30, 1905	Seattle, Wash	May 1, 1905	Do.
Florence K	143	1903		1903		do	July 24, 1905	do	July 25, 1904	Do.
Frankie	4	1891		1891		Olympia, Wash	Aug. 23, 1905	Olympia, Wash	June 17, 1904	Do.
Flyer	427	1891	1892	1899	1903	Portland, Oreg	Sept. 29, 1905	Seattle, Wash	Sept. 30, 1904	Do.
Flora Brown	15	1900		1900		South Bend, Wash	Oct. 11, 1905	South Bend, Wash	Oct. 10, 1904	Do.
Geo. E. Starr	472	1879		1903		Seattle, Wash	Feb. 14, 1905	Seattle, Wash	Feb. 22, 1904	Do.
Garland	166	1890		1890		Port Townsend, Wash	Apr. 28, 1905	do	May 25, 1904	Do.
Gerome	110	1902		1903		Wenatchee, Wash	May 4, 1905	Wenatchee, Wash	Oct. 11, 1903	Do.
Goldfinch	10	1905		1902		Everett, Wash	May 27, 1905	Seattle, Wash	First inspn	
Gazelle	75	1898	1904	1898		Pontiac, Wash	June 15, 1905	Lake Washington, Wash.	June 17, 1904	Do.
Greyhound	197	1890	1901	1890	1898	Portland, Oreg	Aug. 30, 1905	Olympia, Wash	Sept. 2, 1904	Do.
Hattie Hansen	113	1893		1903		Lake Washington, Wash.	May 29, 1905	Everett, Wash	June 7, 1904	Do.
Harbor Queen	161	1900		1900		Aberdeen, Wash	Aug. 28, 1905	Aberdeen, Wash	Aug. 31, 1904	Do.
Harbor Belle	179	1902		1903		do	Nov. 6, 1905	do	Nov. 18, 1904	Do.
Inland Flyer	151	1898		1901	1904	Portland, Oreg	Mar. 2, 1905	Seattle, Wash	Mar. 14, 1904	Do.
Irene	105	1899		1902		Ballard, Wash	May 12, 1905	Olympia, Wash	May 13, 1904	Do.
Islander	162	1904		1903		Newhall, Wash	Sept. 11, 1905	Bellingham, Wash	Sept. 19, 1904	Do.
James Roe	c 5	1896		1896		Marysville, Wash	Aug. 17, 1905	Everett, Wash	Sept. 2, 1904	Do.
Lydia Thompson	202	1893		1900		Port Angeles, Wash	Feb. 23, 1905	Seattle, Wash	Mar. 4, 1904	Do.
L. T. Haas	89	1897		1897		Seattle, Wash	Apr. 26, 1905	Lake Washington, Wash.	May 25, 1904	Do.

Manette	125	1902		1898		do	May 2,1905	Seattle, Wash	Apr. 30,1904	Do.
Marguerite	29	1898		1899		Olympia, Wash	May 26,1905	do	June 10,1904	Do.
Marian	28	1903		1903		Tacoma, Wash	June 9,1905	Tacoma, Wash	June 13,1904	Do.
Mercer	53	1904		1904		Seattle, Wash	June 21,1905	Lake Washington, Wash.	July 2,1904	Do.
Multnomah	312	1885		1885	1903	Portland, Oreg	Aug. 4,1905	Olympia, Wash	Aug. 7,1904	Do.
North Star	144	1902		1902		Wenatchee, Wash	May 4,1905	Wenatchee, Wash	June 6,1904	Do.
Norwood	92	1899		1899		Tacoma, Wash	June 13,1905	Seattle, Wash	June 16,1904	Do.
Port Orchard [d]	345	1887	1902	1898		do	Feb. 26,1905	do	Feb. 28,1904	Do.
Prosper	111	1898		1898		Port Townsend, Wash	June 22,1905	do	June 15,1904	Do.
Peerless	57	1902		1899		Houghton, Wash	July 17,1905	do	Mar. 22,1904	Do.
Perdita	209	1903		1900		Seattle, Wash	Aug. 4,1905	do	Aug. 15,1904	Do.
Progress	16	1900		1900		Aberdeen, Wash	Aug. 28,1905	Aberdeen, Wash	Aug. 31,1904	Do.
Queen	59	1892		1891		Astoria, Oreg	Mar. 14,1905	South Bend, Wash	Mar. 17,1904	Do.
Rosalie	318	1893		1893		San Francisco, Cal	May 8,1905	Seattle, Wash	May 14,1904	Do.
Reliance	153	1900		1898		Portland, Oreg	July 5,1905	do	July 7,1904	Do.
Reliable	102	1902		1902	1905	Astoria, Oreg	Aug. 11,1905	South Bend, Wash	Aug. 16,1904	Do.
Ranger	43	1899		1899		Hoquiam, Wash	Aug. 28,1905	Aberdeen, Wash	Aug. 31,1904	Do.
Sarah M. Renton	164	1889		1900		Port Blakeley, Wash	May 3,1905	Seattle, Wash	May 4,1904	Do.
Sentinel	108	1898	1903	1900		Tacoma, Wash	May 8,1905	do	May 9,1904	Do.
State of Washington	605	1889		1889		do	Aug. 6,1905	do	Aug. 7,1904	Do.
Skagit Queen	327	1898		1891		Seattle, Wash	Nov. 20,1905	do	Nov. 21,1904	Do.
Selkirk	223	1899		1904		Wenatchee, Wash	Dec. 18,1905	Wenatchee, Wash	Dec. 30,1904	Do.
Tyrus	174	1904		1903		Tacoma, Wash	May 2,1905	Tacoma, Wash	May 2,1904	Do.
Telegraph	386	1903		1903		Everett, Wash	July 20,1905	Seattle, Wash	July 22,1904	Do.
T. C. Reed	237	1897		1899		Aberdeen, Wash	Sept. 18,1905	do	Sept. 19,1904	Do.
Tyconda	186	1901		1901		Tacoma, Wash	Oct. 19,1905	do	Oct. 24,1904	Do.
Tarrynot	[c]5	1878		1891		Seattle, Wash	Dec. 16,1905	Olympia, Wash	Dec. 16,1904	Do.
Utopia	423	1893		1895		do	Sept. 13,1905	Seattle, Wash	Sept. 19,1904	Do.
Vashon	132	1905		1905		Dockton, Wash	June 19,1905	do	First inspn	
Wildwood	53	1886		1887		Seattle, Wash	Jan. 21,1905	do	Jan. 19,1904	Do.
Whatcom [e]	716	1901		1901		Everett, Wash	Jan. 22,1905	do	Jan. 27,1904	Do.
W. E. Harrington	33	1901		1901	1905	do	May 19,1905	do	Nov. 20,1903	Do.
W. H. Pringle	575	1901		1888		Pasco, Wash	May 29,1905	Wenatchee, Wash	June 7,1904	Do.
Xanthus	49	1901		1901		Seattle, Wash	Aug. 10,1905	Lake Washington, Wash.	Aug. 16,1904	Do.
Ferry steamers.										
Seattle county	272	1888		1888		Portland, Oreg	Dec. 4,1905	Seattle, Wash	Dec. 27,1904	Seattle, Wash.
King County	412	1900		1900		Lake Washington, Wash.	May 9,1905	Lake Washington, Wash.	May 7,1904	Do.
Ocean freight steamers.										
Eureka	2,122	1899		1899	1904	Lorain, Ohio	May 22,1905	Ballard, Wash	May 23,1904	Seattle, Wash.
Hyades	3,753	1900		1900		Sparrow Point, Md	June 28,1905	Tacoma, Wash	May 26,1904	Do.
Lyra	4,417	1901		1901		do	June 7,1905	do	do	Do.
Leelanaw	1,923	1886		1886		Newcastle, England	Nov 13,1905	Seattle, Wash	Nov. 17,1904	Juneau, Alaska.
Meteor	2,301	1901		1901		Toledo, Ohio	Apr. 6,1905	do	Apr. 8,1904	Seattle, Wash.
Pleiades	3,753	1900		1900		Sparrow Point, Md	May 6,1905	Tacoma, Wash	Apr. 9,1904	Do.
Tampico	2,133	1900		1900		Toledo, Ohio	Nov. 12,1905	Seattle, Wash	Nov. 14,1904	Do.

[a] Unknown.
[b] Formerly Typhoon, 1904.
[c] Estimated.
[d] Formerly Skagit Chief, 1902.
[e] Formerly Majestic, 1903.

Domestic Vessels Inspected, Year ended December 31, 1905—First Supervising District—Seattle, Wash.—Continued.

Names of vessels and class.	Gross tonnage.	Hull built.	Hull rebuilt.	Boilers built.	Boilers rebuilt.	Where built.	Date of inspection.	Where inspected.	Date of previous inspection.	Local district where previously inspected.
Inland freight steamers.										
Arthur B	62	1897		1900		Port Townsend, Wash	Apr. 18, 1905	Seattle, Wash	Apr. 19, 1904	Seattle, Wash.
Clara Brown	190	1886		1889		Tacoma, Wash	Jan. 18, 1905	Bellingham, Wash	Jan. 18, 1904	Do
City of Aberdeen	244	1891		1891		Aberdeen, Wash	May 1, 1905	Seattle, Wash	May 20, 1903	Do.
Dredger No 1	282	1898		1898		Portland, Oreg	Aug. 28, 1905	do	Sept. 1, 1904	Do.
Edison	120	1904		1905		Edison, Wash	Apr. 18, 1905	Bellingham, Wash	Sept. 26, 1904	Do.
Fidalgo	295	1904		1879		La Conner, Wash	May 23, 1905	Seattle, Wash	May 19, 1904	Do.
La Conner	297	1898	1903	1898		Seattle, Wash	Aug. 19, 1905	do	Aug. 19, 1904	Do.
Neptune	136	1897		1895		Ballard, Wash	Feb. 7, 1905	do	Feb. 8, 1904	Do.
Rapid Transit	192	1891		1891		Hadlock, Wash	July 31, 1905	do	July 28, 1904	Do.
Samson	328	1903		1892	1903	West Seattle, Wash	June 2, 1905	do	Apr. 20, 1903	Do.
Swinomish	166	1903		1903		La Conner, Wash	Dec. 8, 1905	do	Dec. 14, 1904	Do.
Transport	147	1899	1902	1898		Olympia, Wash	Apr. 22, 1905	do	May 11, 1904	Do.
T. W. Lake	191	1895		1890		Ballard, Wash	Oct. 2, 1905	Tacoma, Wash	Oct. 4, 1904	Do.
Ocean towing steamers.										
Astoria	152	1884		1902		North Bend, Oreg	May 9, 1905	South Bend, Wash	May 13, 1904	Seattle, Wash.
Bahada	132	1903		1903		Seattle, Wash	Feb. 14, 1905	Seattle, Wash	Feb. 13, 1904	Do.
Dolphin	62	1900		1900		do	May 11, 1905	do	Mar. 29, 1904	Do.
Daring	227	1904		1904		Aberdeen, Wash	June 13, 1905	Aberdeen, Wash	June 13, 1904	Do.
Golden Gate	119	1891	1897	1891		Sausalito, Cal	Mar. 30, 1905	Seattle, Wash	Apr. 3, 1903	Do.
J. E. Boyden	87	1888		1888	1903	Seattle, Wash	Mar. 9, 1905	do	Mar. 7, 1904	Do.
J. M. Colman	79	1887		1891		do	Aug. 14, 1905	do	Aug. 29, 1904	Do.
Katy	93	1882		1896	1902	San Francisco, Cal	Aug. 12, 1905	do	Aug. 17, 1904	Do.
Mary C	93	1903		1903		Decatur, Wash	May 11, 1905	do	May 27, 1904	Do.
Magic	67	1893		1893		Port Blakeley, Wash	Nov. 16, 1905	do	Nov. 18, 1904	Do.
Pioneer	160	1878		1889		Philadelphia, Pa	Oct. 12, 1905	do	Oct. 12, 1904	Do.
Printer	110	1889		1903		Hoquiam, Wash	Nov. 6, 1905	Hoquiam, Wash	Nov. 5, 1904	Do.
Queen City	67	1883		1898		Seattle, Wash	May 20, 1905	Seattle, Wash	May 11, 1904	Do.
Richard Holyoke	181	1877	1898	1886		Seabeck, Wash	June 1, 1905	do	May 27, 1904	Do.
Resolute	91	1887		1887		Yaquina, Oreg	Sept. 9, 1905	do	Sept. 7, 1904	Do.
Sea Lion	185	1884		1884		Camden, N. J	Jan. 21, 1905	do	Jan. 21, 1904	Do.
Tacoma	239	1876		1888		San Francisco, Cal	Feb. 7, 1905	do	Feb. 6, 1904	Do.
Tyee	316	1884		1900		Port Ludlow, Wash	July 31, 1905	do	July 21, 1904	Do.
Traveler	145	1886		1893		Coos Bay, Oreg	Oct. 4, 1905	do	Nov. 17, 1904	Do.
Wyadda	132	1903		1903		Seattle, Wash	Feb. 18, 1905	do	Feb. 17, 1904	Do.
Wallowa	184	1889		1904		Portland, Oreg	Mar. 25, 1905	do	Apr. 1, 1904	Do.
Wanderer	212	1890		1902		Port Blakeley, Wash	Apr. 8, 1905	do	Apr. 23, 1904	Do.

Inland towing steamers.										
Alpha	36	1901	....	1901	1904	Richardson, Wash	May 8, 1905	Bellingham, Wash	June 13, 1904	Seattle, Wash.
Active	57	1899	....	1902	....	Tacoma, Wash	....do	Seattle, Wash	May 7, 1904	Do.
Aldulia	*a* 4	1903	....	1898	....	Burton, Wash	May 25, 1905	Tacoma, Wash	July 25, 1904	Do.
Augusta	78	1888	....	1887	1898	Oneatta, Oreg	June 13, 1905	Bellingham, Wash	June 13, 1904	Do.
Alert	*a* 4	1886	....	1897	....	Cosmopolis, Wash	June 8, 1905	Hoquiam, Wash	June 11, 1904	Do.
Agnes	30	1905	....	1905	....	Hoquiam, Wash	Aug. 5, 1905	....do	First inspn	
Bonita	32	1900	....	1900	....	Eagle Harbor, Wash	Apr. 6, 1905	Bellingham, Wash	Oct. 16, 1902	Juneau, Alaska.
Black Cat	16	1900	....	1900	....	Hamilton, Wash	Sept. 11, 1905	....do	Sept. 19, 1904	Seattle, Wash.
Blue Star	32	1892	....	1901	....	Tacoma, Wash	Sept. 19, 1905	Olympia, Wash	Sept. 21, 1904	Do.
C. C. Cherry	54	1896	....	1891	....	Seattle, Wash	Apr. 6, 1905	Bellingham, Wash	Apr. 13, 1904	Do.
Chinook	21	1889	....	1889	....	Astoria, Oreg	....do	....do	Apr. 1, 1904	Do.
Chehalis	55	1890	....	1905	....	Cosmopolis, Wash	Apr. 14, 1905	....do	May 5, 1904	Do.
Celtic	20	1900	....	1905	....	Beach, Wash	May 8, 1905	....do	July 9, 1904	Do.
C. B. Smith	28	1902	....	1902	....	Everett, Wash	Sept. 1, 1905	Everett, Wash	Sept. 2, 1904	Do.
Delta	46	1888	1894	1902	....	Stanwood, Wash	May 29, 1905	....do	June 20, 1904	Do.
Defender	25	1900	....	1900	....	Tacoma, Wash	Oct. 19, 1905	Seattle, Wash	Oct. 10, 1904	Do.
Enola	26	1905	....	1899	....	Ballard, Wash	June 27, 1905	....do	First inspn	
Elf	44	1902	....	1902	....	Tacoma, Wash	May 25, 1905	Tacoma, Wash	May 31, 1904	Do.
Echo	56	1900	....	1900	....	....do	May 30, 1905	....do	June 4, 1904	Do.
Emogene	18	1900	....	1898	....	Monohan, Wash	June 6, 1905	Bellingham, Wash	Apr. 27, 1903	Juneau, Alaska.
Evergreen	30	1901	....	1890	....	Ballard, Wash	June 12, 1905	Seattle, Wash	June 20, 1904	Seattle, Wash.
Enterprise	31	1884	....	1898	....	Port Townsend, Wash	June 17, 1905	....do	June 15, 1904	Do.
Electric	44	1886	....	1887	1905	Astoria, Oreg	July 21, 1905	Bellingham, Wash	May 19, 1902	Juneau, Alaska.
Elk	25	1890	....	1891	....	Houghton, Wash	Oct. 16, 1905	Everett, Wash	Oct. 15, 1904	Seattle, Wash.
Eagle	26	1900	....	1900	....	Eagle Harbor, Wash	Nov. 1, 1905	Seattle, Wash	Oct. 27, 1904	Do.
Favorite	269	1868	....	1902	....	Utsalady, Wash	Feb. 24, 1905	Port Blakeley, Wash	Feb. 27, 1904	Do.
Fearless	86	1901	....	1900	....	Tacoma, Wash	Apr. 1, 1905	Tacoma, Wash	Apr. 4, 1904	Do.
Favorite	34	1886	....	1884	....	Astoria, Oreg	May 18, 1905	....do	May 20, 1904	Do.
Famous	39	1901	....	1900	....	La Conner, Wash	May 19, 1905	Seattle, Wash	May 23, 1904	Do.
Fairfield	30	1898	....	1898	....	Tacoma, Wash	May 30, 1905	Tacoma, Wash	June 4, 1904	Do.
Falcon	43	1902	....	1902	....	....do	Aug. 25, 1905	....do	Aug. 18, 1904	Do.
Gwylan	43	1902	....	1902	....	....do	Mar. 24, 1905	Everett, Wash	Apr. 1, 1904	Do.
Grace Thurston	52	1899	....	1899	....	Everett, Wash	Oct. 16, 1905	....do	Oct. 18, 1904	Do.
Hero	31	1902	....	1902	....	Ballard, Wash	May 8, 1905	Seattle, Wash	May 6, 1904	Do.
Hoquiam	41	1898	....	1898	....	Hoquiam, Wash	May 14, 1905	Aberdeen, Wash	May 17, 1904	Do.
Harold C	27	1903	....	1903	....	Ballard, Wash	June 2, 1905	Seattle, Wash	May 31, 1904	Do.
Hermosa	15	1901	....	1903	....	Olympia, Wash	June 6, 1905	Bellingham, Wash	June 6, 1904	Do.
Harry S	20	1897	....	1900	....	Seattle, Wash	June 20, 1905	Seattle, Wash	June 17, 1904	Do.
Hoosier Boy	31	1898	....	1902	....	....do	Nov. 2, 1905	Anacortes, Wash	Nov. 10, 1904	Do.
Hornet	15	1890	....	1890	....	Port Madison, Wash	Dec. 16, 1905	Seattle, Wash	Dec. 13, 1904	Do.
Independent	49	1899	....	1899	1905	Everett, Wash	May 29, 1905	....do	Nov. 16, 1903	Juneau, Alaska.
Iola	34	1885	....	1885	....	Big Skookum, Wash	June 13, 1905	Aberdeen, Wash	June 14, 1904	Seattle, Wash.
Irene	81	1902	....	1902	....	Tacoma, Wash	Nov. 4, 1905	Everett, Wash	Nov. 12, 1904	Do.
Juneau	60	1898	....	1898	....	Portland, Oreg	Jan. 21, 1905	Seattle, Wash	Mar. 26, 1902	Do.
John Cudahy	125	1900	....	1900	....	Ballard, Wash	Feb. 17, 1905	Bellingham, Wash	May 22, 1903	Do.
Jannet L	12	1905	....	1905	....	Taylors Mill, Wash	Aug. 2, 1905	Taylors Mill, Wash	First inspn	
Juniata	9	1893	....	1899	....	Tacoma, Wash	Oct. 16, 1905	Bellingham, Wash	Oct. 18, 1904	Do.
Katahdin	44	1900	....	1899	....	Ballard, Wash	Apr. 1, 1905	Blaine, Wash	Apr. 1, 1904	Do.

a Estimated.

DOMESTIC VESSELS INSPECTED, YEAR ENDED DECEMBER 31, 1905—FIRST SUPERVISING DISTRICT—SEATTLE, WASH.—Continued.

Names of vessels and class.	Gross tonnage.	Hull built.	Hull rebuilt.	Boilers built.	Boilers rebuilt.	Where built.	Date of inspection.	Where inspected.	Date of previous inspection.	Local district where previously inspected.
Inland towing steamers—Con.										
Keros [a]	21	1887		1902		Portland, Oreg.	Sept. 19, 1905	Seattle, Wash.	July 13, 1904	Seattle, Wash.
Lurline	41	1902		1902		Monohan, Wash.	Jan. 9, 1905	do	Jan. 14, 1904	Do.
Laura	[b] 5	1892		1899		Seattle, Wash.	Apr. 5, 1905	do	Dec. 22, 1903	Do.
Laurel	41	1903		1903		South Bend, Wash.	May 9, 1905	South Bend, Wash.	May 13, 1904	Do.
Lumberman	34	1899		1899		Seattle, Wash.	May 15, 1905	Seattle, Wash.	May 18, 1904	Do.
Laurel	16	1891		1891		Chican, Alaska	June 19, 1905	do	June 21, 1904	Do.
Lily	123	1883		1876		Seattle, Wash.	Sept. 17, 1905	Stanwood, Wash.	Sept. 17, 1904	Do.
Little Giant	8	1891		1888		Port Blakeley, Wash.	Dec. 11, 1905	Tacoma, Wash.	Aug. 2, 1902	Do.
Mystic	27	1894		1895		do	June 20, 1905	Seattle, Wash.	June 21, 1904	Do.
Mariner	89	1903		1903		Tacoma, Wash.	Sept. 23, 1905	Tacoma, Wash.	Sept. 26, 1904	Do.
N. D. Tobey	12	1901		1901	1903	Hadlock, Wash.	July 3, 1905	Port Townsend, Wash.	July 1, 1904	Do.
Olympic	102	1900		1893		Ballard, Wash.	July 5, 1905	Everett, Wash.	July 5, 1904	Do.
Oscar B.	23	1899		1899		Tacoma, Wash.	July 13, 1905	Seattle, Wash.	June 17, 1904	Do.
Pilot	35	1903		1903		Hoquiam, Wash.	do	Hoquiam, Wash.	July 14, 1904	Do.
Pilgrim	12	1904		1904		Everett, Wash.	Dec. 21, 1905	Seattle, Wash.	Dec. 24, 1904	Do.
Royal	59	1891		1890		Benicia, Cal.	Apr. 1, 1905	Blaine, Wash.	Apr. 1, 1904	Do.
R. P. Elmore	85	1890		1890		Astoria, Oreg.	May 4, 1905	Everett, Wash.	May 19, 1904	Do.
Roche Harbor [c]	87	1888		1895		Tacoma, Wash.	May 20, 1905	Tacoma, Wash.	May 20, 1904	Do.
Reef	9	1894		1896	1905	Ballard, Wash.	June 2, 1905	Burrows Landing, Wash.	June 3, 1904	Do.
Rustler	30	1887		1887		Hoquiam, Wash.	June 8, 1905	Hoquiam, Wash.	June 11, 1904	Do.
Ruth [d]	53	1897	1903	1897		Seattle, Wash.	Nov. 2, 1905	Anacortes, Wash.	Nov. 4, 1904	Do.
Success	13	1868	1904	1892	1904	Utsalady, Wash.	Apr. 10, 1905	Lake Washington, Wash.	Apr. 26, 1904	Do.
Sea Foam	19	1893		1891		Astoria, Oreg.	Apr. 12, 1905	Seattle, Wash.	Apr. 11, 1904	Do.
Skookum	302	1904		1903		Aberdeen, Wash.	Apr. 14, 1905	Aberdeen, Wash.	Apr. 21, 1904	Do.
Stimson	25	1892		1892		Ballard, Wash.	July 28, 1905	Ballard, Wash.	Aug. 1, 1904	Do.
Tillicum	116	1902		1902		do	Jan. 17, 1905	do	Jan. 16, 1904	Do.
Tempest	54	1901		1901		Everett, Wash.	May 13, 1905	Everett, Wash.	May 17, 1904	Do.
Thistle	18	1893		1890		Hoquiam, Wash.	May 14, 1905	Aberdeen, Wash.	May 16, 1904	Do.
The Doctor	28	1890		1890		Olympia, Wash.	Sept. 9, 1905	Seattle, Wash.	Sept. 7, 1904	Do.
Tussler	18	1899		1893		do	Nov. 1, 1905	Port Townsend, Wash.	Oct. 19, 1903	Do.
Violet	12	1887		1898	1902	Seattle, Wash.	June 6, 1905	Seattle, Wash.	June 8, 1904	Do.
Volga	19	1888		1900		Astoria, Oreg.	June 28, 1905	Bellingham, Wash.	July 2, 1904	Do.
Wasp	25	1890		1889		Seattle, Wash.	June 10, 1905	Seattle, Wash.	June 8, 1904	Do.
Wilma	[b] 5	1885	1896	1886		South Bend, Wash.	July 13, 1905	Hoquiam, Wash.	July 14, 1904	Do.
Yellow Jacket	60	1900		1900		Seattle, Wash.	Nov. 25, 1905	Seattle, Wash.	Dec. 1, 1904	Do.
Steam pleasure yachts.										
Amerind	14	1902		1902		Tacoma, Wash.	Nov. 21, 1905	Tacoma, Wash.	Nov. 22, 1904	Seattle, Wash.
Bessie [e]	[b] 5	1900		1903		do	Apr. 18, 1905	Bellingham, Wash.	Mar. 28, 1904	Do.

Captola	7	1904		1898		Stanwood, Wash	July 18, 1905	Seattle, Wash	June 2, 1904	Do.
Eula	b 5	1904		1904		Bellingham, Wash	Dec. 4, 1905	Bellingham, Wash	Dec. 2, 1904	Do.
Judix	b 4	1890		1897	1903	Olympia, Wash	July 14, 1905	Olympia, Wash	June 17, 1904	Do.
Loretta	b 5	1899		1898		Newhall, Wash	Apr. 14, 1905	Bellingham, Wash	June 15, 1903	Do.
Lena	b 4	1892		1900		Chicago, Ill	June 21, 1905	Lake Washington, Wash.	June 22, 1904	Do.
Lolo	b 4	1902		1902		Tacoma, Wash	June 9, 1905	Tacoma, Wash	May 20, 1904	Do.
Mary and Edith	b 4	1892		1897		South Bend, Wash	May 9, 1905	South Bend, Wash	Oct. 11, 1903	Do.
May Bird	12	1901		1893		Sing Sing, N. Y	Aug. 18, 1905	Seattle, Wash	June 9, 1904	Do.
Osprey	32	1903		1903		Seattle, Wash	Aug. 3, 1905	....do	Aug. 1, 1904	Do.
Rover	b 4	1903		1903		....do	Feb. 2, 1905	....do	Feb. 2, 1904	Do.
Starling	14	1898		1898		Tacoma, Wash	June 7, 1905	Tacoma, Wash	June 4, 1904	Do.
Miscellaneous steam vessels.										
Anna B. (fishing)	9	1903		1903		Long Branch, Wash	Apr. 1, 1905	Olympia, Wash	Mar. 28, 1904	Seattle, Wash.
Aleut (fishing)	38	1889		1889		Benicia, Cal	Apr. 18, 1905	Blaine, Wash	Apr. 21, 1904	Do.
Arthur G. (fishing)	8	1900		1901		Lopez, Wash	July 1, 1905	Anacortes, Wash	May 7, 1903	Do.
Carlisle (fishing)	20	1901		1901		Whatcom, Wash	Mar. 27, 1905	Fairhaven, Wash	Mar. 28, 1904	Do.
Callender (fishing)	73	1900		1900		Portland, Oreg	Apr. 14, 1905	Bellingham, Wash	Apr. 22, 1904	Do.
Columbia (fishing)	8	1894		1898		New Whatcom, Wash	May 8, 1905	....do	June 6, 1904	Do.
Crescent (fishing)	16	1893		1903		Tacoma, Wash	June 19, 1905	Seattle, Wash	June 15, 1904	Do.
City of Olympia (fishing)	51	1898		1883		Olympia, Wash	June 20, 1905	Bellingham, Wash	June 23, 1904	Do.
De Haro (fishing)	9	1902		1897		Fairhaven, Wash	Mar. 27, 1905	....do	Mar. 28, 1904	Do.
Dispatch (fishing)	24	1891		1896		Astoria, Oreg	May 23, 1905	Seattle, Wash	May 23, 1904	Do.
Elsa (fishing)	13	1904		1903		Seattle, Wash	Mar. 24, 1905	....do	First inspn.	
Eclipse (fishing)	17	1895		1899		Ballard, Wash	Apr. 18, 1905	Bellingham, Wash	Apr. 3, 1903	Do.
E. L. Dwyer (fishing)	64	1892		1892		Astoria, Oreg	May 8, 1905	....do	May 5, 1904	Do.
Edith (fishing)	192	1882		1898		San Francisco, Cal	Sept. 30, 1905	Tacoma, Wash	Sept. 28, 1904	Do.
Fawn (fishing)	11	1900		1901		Decatur, Wash	May 12, 1905	Anacortes, Wash	May 5, 1904	Do.
George T. (fishing)	42	1899		1899		Seattle, Wash	July 14, 1905	Bellingham, Wash	May 19, 1904	Do.
Hector (fishing)	7	1897		1902		Roche Harbor, Wash	May 8, 1905	....do	May 6, 1904	Do.
Kingfisher (fishing)	263	1902		1902		San Francisco, Cal	June 8, 1905	Vancouver, B. C	Mar. 25, 1904	Do.
McKinley (fishing)	45	1902		1902		Tacoma, Wash	Apr. 19, 1905	Seattle, Wash	Apr. 27, 1904	Juneau, Alaska.
Mia (fishing)	9	1894		1891	1901	Marysville, Wash	Sept. 8, 1905	....do	Sept. 9, 1904	Seattle, Wash.
Nemo (fishing)	9	1904		1904		Seattle, Wash	Apr. 13, 1905	....do	Apr. 13, 1904	Do.
Nellie Pearson (fishing)	35	1901		1902		Everett, Wash	May 15, 1905	Everett, Wash	May 19, 1904	Do.
Pacific (dredge)	460	1903		1903		Tacoma, Wash	Apr. 7, 1905	Tacoma, Wash	Aug. 18, 1903	Do.
Philip F. Kelley (fishing)	137	1901		1901		....do	Apr. 12, 1905	Seattle, Wash	Apr. 25, 1904	Do.
Puritan (fishing)	25	1887	1898	1893		Portland, Oreg	May 8, 1905	Bellingham, Wash	May 27, 1904	Do.
Rover (fishing)	b 4	1890		1905		Olympia, Wash	Feb. 3, 1905	Olympia, Wash	Nov. 3, 1903	Do.
Rover (fishing) f	b 4	1890	1905	1905		....do	Dec. 5, 1905	Seattle, Wash	Feb. 3, 1905	Do.
Ryba (fishing)	32	1902		1902		Alameda, Cal	Apr. 18, 1905	Blaine, Wash	Apr. 21, 1904	Do.
Rescue (fishing)	27	1898		1898		South Bend, Wash	Apr. 21, 1905	Anacortes, Wash	Sept. 25, 1903	Do.
Rustler (fishing)	18	1898		1898		La Conner, Wash	June 13, 1905	....do	June 13, 1904	Do.
San Juan (fishing)	284	1904		1904		Seattle, Wash	Jan. 4, 1905	Seattle, Wash	First inspn.	
Salmo (fishing)	57	1889		1889		San Francisco, Cal	Mar. 27, 1905	Bellingham, Wash	Sept. 24, 1903	Do.
Sockeye (fishing)	14	1896		1896		Blaine, Wash	Apr. 18, 1905	Blaine, Wash	Apr. 21, 1904	Do.
Snoqualmie (fire boat)	109	1891		1890		Seattle, Wash	May 11, 1905	Seattle, Wash	May 11, 1904	Do.

a Formerly San Juan, 1903.
b Estimated.
c Formerly Harry Lynn, 1895.
d Formerly Lady of the Lake, 1903.
e Formerly Emma, 1902.
f Second inspection.

DOMESTIC VESSELS INSPECTED, YEAR ENDED DECEMBER 31, 1905—FIRST SUPERVISING DISTRICT—SEATTLE, WASH.—Continued.

Names of vessels and class.	Gross tonnage.	Hull built.	Hull rebuilt.	Boilers built.	Boilers rebuilt.	Where built.	Date of inspection.	Where inspected.	Date of previous inspection.	Local district where previously inspected.
Miscellaneous steam vessels—Continued.										
Steelhead (fishing)	37	1898		1898		Fairhaven, Wash	June 7, 1905	Bellingham, Wash	June 23, 1904	Seattle, Wash.
Sachem (fishing)	36	1902		1901		do	July 11, 1905	do	July 18, 1904	Do.
San Juan (fishing)	284	1904		1904		Seattle, Wash	Dec. 27, 1905	Seattle, Wash	Jan. 4, 1905	Do.
Union (fishing)	19	1898		1892		do	Sept. 19, 1905	do	July 30, 1900	Do.
Victor (fishing)	40	1893		1893		Tacoma, Wash	June 20, 1905	Bellingham, Wash	June 23, 1904	Do.
Viola (fishing)	a 4	1901		1898		Still Harbor, Wash	Sept. 4, 1905	do	Apr. 19, 1904	Do.
Wigwam (fishing)	40	1895		1895		San Francisco, Cal	Apr. 18, 1905	Blaine, Wash	Apr. 21, 1904	Do.
Zapora (fishing)	289	1905		1904		Tacoma, Wash	May 30, 1905	Tacoma, Wash	First inspn.	
Zebeitka (fishing)	10	1902		1889	1903	Seattle, Wash	June 7, 1905	Bellingham, Wash	June 6, 1904	Do.
Freight sail vessels of over 700 tons.										
Alex Gibson (ship)	2,190	1877				Thomaston, Me	Mar. 22, 1905	Port Gamble, Wash	Apr. 8, 1904	San Francisco, Cal.
Charles F. Crocker (barkentine).	855	1891				Alameda, Cal	Mar. 2, 1905	Everett, Wash	Mar. 16, 1904	Seattle, Wash.
Carrier Dove (schooner)	707	1890				Port Blakeley, Wash	Apr. 6, 1905	Aberdeen, Wash	do	Do.
Coryphene (bark)	811	1878				Millbridge, Me	May 1, 1905	Seattle, Wash	July 16, 1903	San Francisco, Cal.
Coloma (bark)	852	1869				Warren, R. I	June 19, 1905	Everett, Wash	May 27, 1904	Do.
Eclipse (ship)	1,595	1878				Bath, Me	Mar. 20, 1905	Port Blakeley, Wash	Mar. 16, 1904	Do.
Emily Reed (ship)	1,564	1880				Waldoboro, Me	May 18, 1905	Tacoma, Wash	Apr. 27, 1900	Seattle, Wash.
Fresno (bark)	1,244	1874				Bath, Me	Feb. 21, 1905	Port Gamble, Wash	Mar. 22, 1904	San Francisco, Cal.
F. M. Slade (schooner)	737	1900				Aberdeen, Wash	Feb. 25, 1905	Aberdeen, Wash	June 25, 1903	Do.
Great Admiral (ship)	1,575	1869				Boston, Mass	Jan. 13, 1905	Winslow, Wash	Feb. 21, 1903	Seattle, Wash.
Gamble (schooner)	726	1901				Port Blakeley, Wash	Mar. 11, 1905	Port Gamble, Wash	Aug. 13, 1903	Do.
General Fairchild (bark)	1,427	1874				Freeport, Me	Apr. 23, 1905	Port Blakeley, Wash	Feb. 4, 1904	Do.
Harvester (bark)	754	1871				Newburyport, Mass	June 22, 1905	Seattle, Wash	Apr. 12, 1904	Do.
Inca (schooner)	1,014	1896				Port Blakeley, Wash	Feb. 8, 1905	Winslow, Wash	Oct. 14, 1903	Do.
James Drummond (ship)	1,556	1881				Pittsburg, Me	Jan. 27, 1905	Hadlock, Wash	Feb. 8, 1904	Do.
John C. Meyer (barkentine)	932	1903				Tacoma, Wash	June 13, 1905	Aberdeen, Wash	Mar. 4, 1904	Do.
John Palmer (barkentine)	1,188	1900				Eureka, Cal	June 27, 1905	Everett, Wash	July 23, 1904	Do.
King Cyrus (schooner)	717	1890				Port Blakeley, Wash	Feb. 10, 1905	Hoquiam, Wash	Feb. 10, 1904	Do.
Lyman D. Foster (schooner)	777	1892				do	Jan. 10, 1905	Winslow, Wash	Dec. 17, 1903	Do.
Louisiana (bark)	1,436	1873				Bath, Me	Mar. 22, 1905	Port Gamble, Wash	Mar. 8, 1904	San Francisco, Cal.
Mary E. Foster (schooner)	950	1898				Port Blakeley, Wash	Feb. 3, 1905	Port Blakeley, Wash	Nov. 23, 1903	Seattle, Wash.
Mahukona (schooner)	738	1901				Hoquiam, Wash	May 15, 1905	Olympia, Wash	May 24, 1904	Do.
Prussia (bark)	1,212	1868				Bath, Me	May 3, 1905	Port Blakeley, Wash	Oct. 23, 1903	San Francisco, Cal.
Sintram (ship)	1,656	1877				Freeport, Me	Apr. 21, 1905	Bellingham, Wash	Apr. 11, 1904	Do.
Soquel (schooner)	765	1902				San Francisco, Cal	May 15, 1905	Olympia, Wash	May 21, 1904	Seattle, Wash.
Willis A. Holden (schooner)	1,188	1902				Ballard, Wash	Jan. 2, 1905	Mukilteo, Wash	Jan. 13, 1904	Do.
Watson A. West (schooner)	818	1901				Aberdeen, Wash	May 14, 1905	Aberdeen, Wash	May 21, 1904	Do.

Wilbert L. Smith (schooner)	848	1903				Ballard, Wash	June 15, 1905	Ballard, Wash	Mar. 22, 1904	Do.
Wm. Nettingham (schooner)	1,204	1902				do	June 29, 1905	do	Apr. 1, 1904	Do.
Sail vessels, barges, etc., of over 100 tons, carrying passengers for hire.										
America (ship)	2,054	1874				Quincy, Mass	Apr. 22, 1905	Seattle, Wash	Apr. 12, 1904	Seattle, Wash.
Albert (bark)	682	1890				Port Blakeley, Wash	Nov. 14, 1905	Port Ludlow, Wash	Dec. 3, 1904	Do.
Blakeley (schooner)	751	1902				do	Feb. 2, 1905	Port Blakeley, Wash	Feb. 11, 1904	Do.
Diamond Head (bark)	1,012	1866				London, England	May 3, 1905	Ballard, Wash	Sept. 5, 1903	Do.
Guy C. Goss (bark)	1,557	1879				Bath, Me	Apr. 17, 1905	Seattle, Wash	Apr. 13, 1904	Do.
J. D. Peters (bark)	1,085	1875				do	Mar. 31, 1905	do	May 22, 1904	Juneau, Alaska.
Kate Davenport (barge)	1,248	1866				do	Apr. 10, 1905	do	Apr. 20, 1904	Seattle, Wash.
Minnie A. Caine (schooner)	880	1900				Seattle, Wash	July 7, 1905	Tacoma, Wash	June 20, 1904	Portland, Oreg.
Robert Lewers (schooner)	732	1889				Port Blakeley, Wash	Oct. 21, 1905	Winslow, Wash	Oct. 20, 1904	Seattle, Wash.
St. Paul (ship)	1,893	1874				Bath, Me	Apr. 17, 1905	Seattle, Wash	Apr. 9, 1904	Do.
Vessels propelled by gasoline motors.										
Alice	42	1904				Ballard, Wash	Apr. 28, 1905	Seattle, Wash	May 3, 1904	Seattle, Wash.
Argosy	23	1905				Tacoma, Wash	Sept. 4, 1905	Tacoma, Wash	First inspn	
Barbara Hernster	148	1887				Fairhaven, Cal	May 10, 1905	Seattle, Wash	Mar. 30, 1904	Do.
Bismarck	23	1893				Seattle, Wash	July 19, 1905	Atlantic City, Wash	July 19, 1904	Do.
Claude B. Hanthorn	26	1888	1905			do	Mar. 8, 1905	Seattle, Wash	Mar. 19, 1901	Portland, Oreg.
Duxbury	37	1896				Benicia, Cal	May 17, 1905	River Park, Wash	Mar. 28, 1904	Seattle, Wash.
Henry Finch	52	1892				Seattle, Wash	July 24, 1905	Seattle, Wash	May 6, 1904	Do.
Island Transfer	17	1905				do	Sept. 29, 1905	Lake Washington, Wash.	First inspn	
Northland	33	1904				Ballard, Wash	May 18, 1905	Seattle, Wash	Mar. 28, 1904	Do.
North	46	1905				do	June 29, 1905	do	First inspn	
P. J. Abler	116	1900	1905			Seattle, Wash	June 10, 1905	do	do	

LOCAL DISTRICT OF JUNEAU, ALASKA.

Ocean passenger steamers.										
Claudine	846	1890		1891		Glasgow, Scotland	Jan. 31, 1905	Honolulu, Hawaii	Feb. 7, 1904	Juneau, Alaska.
Elk No. 1	61	1898 [a]		1898		Port Townsend, Wash	July 23, 1905	St. Michael, Alaska	July 18, 1904	Do.
Gussie Brown	119	1898		1898		San Francisco, Cal	July 17, 1905	do	Sept. 9, 1903	Do.
Helene	618	1897		1896		do	Jan. 24, 1905	Honolulu, Hawaii	Feb. 4, 1904	Do.
Iwalani	588	1881		1898		do	do	do	Feb. 2, 1904	Do.
Kalulani	384	1899		1899		Alameda, Cal	Jan. 18, 1905	Hilo, Hawaii	Jan. 21, 1904	Do.
Kauai [b]	366	1887	1901	1899		San Francisco, Cal	Feb. 2, 1905	Honolulu, Hawaii	Feb. 9, 1904	Do.
Ke Au Hou	263	1894		1894		Port Blakeley, Wash	Feb. 6, 1905	do	Feb. 8, 1904	Do.
Kinau	975	1883		1891	1902	Philadelphia, Pa	Jan. 30, 1905	do	Feb. 1, 1904	Do.
Likelike	374	1904		1904		San Francisco, Cal	Feb. 6, 1905	do	Feb. 29, 1904	San Francisco, Cal.
Maui	631	1897		1897		do	Feb. 8, 1905	do	Feb. 7, 1904	Juneau, Alaska.

[a] Estimated.

[b] Formerly Cosmopolis, 1890.

DOMESTIC VESSELS INSPECTED, YEAR ENDED DECEMBER 31, 1905—FIRST SUPERVISING DISTRICT—JUNEAU, ALASKA—Continued.

Names of vessels and class.	Gross tonnage.	Hull built.	Hull rebuilt.	Boilers built.	Boilers rebuilt.	Where built.	Date of inspection.	Where inspected.	Date of previous inspection.	Local district where previously inspected.
Ocean passenger steamers—Continued.										
Mauna Loa	850	1896 [a]		1896	1904	Port Blakeley, Wash.	Jan. 25, 1905	Honolulu, Hawaii	Feb. 3, 1904	Juneau, Alaska.
Meteor	68	1900		1900		San Francisco, Cal.	July 20, 1905	St. Michael, Alaska	July 27, 1904	Do.
Mikahala	444	1886		1896		Port Blakeley, Wash.	Jan. 26, 1905	Honolulu, Hawaii	Feb. 4, 1904	Do.
Niihau [a]	341	1897		1897		Fairhaven, Cal.	Feb. 2, 1905	do	Feb. 11, 1904	Do.
Noeau	294	1896		1896		Port Blakeley, Wash.	Feb. 7, 1905	do	Feb. 9, 1904	Do.
W. G. Hall	505	1884		1893		do	Jan. 30, 1905	do	do	Do.
Inland passenger steamers.										
Alaskan	138	1886		1899		Oneatta, Oreg.	Apr. 9, 1905	Ketchikan, Alaska	Apr. 9, 1904	Juneau, Alaska.
Alert	24	1893		1893	1903	Port Blakeley, Wash.	Apr. 12, 1905	do	Apr. 12, 1904	Do.
Antelope	10	1901		1898		Wrangell, Alaska	Apr. 24, 1905	Wrangell, Alaska	Apr. 21, 1904	Do.
Arctic	42	1890		1890	1904	Alameda, Cal.	Apr. 11, 1905	Loring, Alaska	Apr. 8, 1904	Do.
Bar	b 4	1901		1900		Juneau, Alaska	May 2, 1905	Juneau, Alaska	May 2, 1904	Do.
Capella	19	1899		1903		Sitka, Alaska	Apr. 24, 1905	Wrangell, Alaska	Apr. 20, 1904	Do.
Carita	14	1895	1900	1888	1904	Port Angeles, Wash.	Apr. 6, 1905	Ketchikan, Alaska	Apr. 7, 1904	Do.
Catherine M	65	1902		1902		Whatcom, Oreg.	Apr. 25, 1905	Wrangell, Alaska	Apr. 20, 1904	Do.
Challenge	54	1901		1901		Ballard, Wash.	Apr. 18, 1905	Klawack, Alaska	Apr. 24, 1904	Do.
Cordova	18	1904		1888		Klinquam, Alaska	do	do	May 10, 1904	Do.
Delta	293	1905		1905		St. Michael, Alaska	July 11, 1905	St. Michael, Alaska	First inspn.	
D. R. Campbell	718	1898		1898		Seattle, Wash.	July 21, 1905	do	July 28, 1904	Do.
Fearless	167	1899		1899		San Francisco, Cal.	Feb. 8, 1905	Honolulu, Hawaii	Feb. 11, 1904	Do.
Florence	90	1898		1898		do	July 21, 1905	St. Michael, Alaska	July 20, 1904	Do.
Florence	51	1904		1904		Seattle, Wash.	May 1, 1905	Juneau, Alaska	Sept. 24, 1904	Seattle, Wash.
Georgia	255	1902		1902		Tacoma, Wash.	May 8, 1905	do	May 8, 1904	Juneau, Alaska.
Good Enough	b 3	1904			1904	Juneau, Alaska	May 6, 1905	do	First inspn.	
Hannah	1,211	1898		1898		Unalaska, Alaska	July 23, 1905	St. Michael, Alaska	Sept. 13, 1904	Do.
Isabelle	162	1902		1898		St. Michael, Alaska	Aug. 15, 1905	Fairbanks, Alaska	Aug. 8, 1904	Do.
Ida May [c]	278	1898		1898		Stockton, Cal.	July 23, 1905	St. Michael, Alaska	July 28, 1904	Do.
John Cudahy	819	1898		1898		Unalaska, Alaska	Aug. 20, 1905	Tanana, Alaska	Aug. 23, 1904	Do.
John J. Healy	450	1896		1896		St. Michael, Alaska	Aug. 7, 1905	Chena, Alaska	July 19, 1904	Do.
Kayak	115	1901		1901		Alameda, Cal.	Apr. 11, 1905	Loring, Alaska	Apr. 8, 1904	Do.
Klondyke	406	1898		1898		Dutch Harbor, Alaska	July 15, 1905	St. Michael, Alaska	July 25, 1904	Do.
Koyukuk	286	1902		1902		Portland, Oreg.	Sept. 6, 1905	Nulato, Alaska	Aug. 9, 1904	Do.
Lavelle Young	506	1898		1891		do	Aug. 6, 1905	Chena, Alaska	Aug. 25, 1904	Do.
Leah	477	1898		1898		St. Michael, Alaska	July 11, 1905	St. Michael, Alaska	July 24, 1904	Do.
Lone Fisherman	12	1883		1898		Seattle, Wash.	May 6, 1905	Juneau, Alaska	Apr. 30, 1904	Do.
Louise	717	1898		1898		Unalaska, Alaska	Aug. 22, 1905	Tanana, Alaska	Aug. 19, 1904	Do.
Margaret	520	1897		1897		St. Michael, Alaska	Aug. 5, 1905	Fairbanks, Alaska	Aug. 26, 1904	Do.
Marion	43	1901		1901		Tacoma, Wash.	Apr. 8, 1905	Hadley, Alaska	Apr. 7, 1904	Do.
Milwaukee	396	1898		1898		Ballard, Wash.	July 15, 1905	St. Michael, Alaska	Sept. 11, 1904	Do.

Monarch	463	1898		1898		....do	Aug. 26, 1905	Tanana, Alaska	Aug. 11, 1904	Do.
Oil City	718	1898		1898		Seattle, Wash	Sept. 1, 1905	....do	Aug. 29, 1904	Do.
Portus B. Weare	400	1892		1892		St. Michael, Alaska	Aug. 8, 1905	Chena, Alaska	July 25, 1904	Do.
Raguhild	73	1900		1900		Ballard, Wash	Apr. 24, 1905	Wrangell, Alaska	Apr. 21, 1904	Do.
Rock Island	533	1898		1898		Seattle, Wash	July 5, 1905	St. Michael, Alaska	Aug. 26, 1904	Do.
Rustler	80	1893	1903	1898		....do	May 6, 1905	Juneau, Alaska	May 2, 1904	Do.
Sarah	1,211	1898		1898		Unalaska, Alaska	Aug. 23, 1905	Tanana, Alaska	July 27, 1904	Do.
Schwatka	484	1898		1898		Port Blakeley, Wash	July 31, 1905	....do	Aug. 23, 1904	Seattle, Wash.
Seattle No. 3	548	1898		1898		Dutch Harbor, Alaska	Aug. 24, 1905	....do	July 25, 1904	Juneau, Alaska.
Susie	1,211	1898		1898		Unalaska, Alaska	July 22, 1905	St. Michael, Alaska	Aug. 15, 1904	Do.
Tanana	495	1904		1904		St. Michael, Alaska	July 30, 1905	Tanana, Alaska	July 19, 1904	Do.
T. C. Power	819	1898		1897		Unalaska, Alaska	Aug. 28, 1905	....do	July 25, 1904	Do.
Tyonic	59	1901		1901		San Francisco, Cal	May 25, 1905	Seldovia, Alaska	May 25, 1904	Do.
Vesper	[b]7	1880		1903		Wilmington, Del	Apr. 7, 1905	Ketchikan, Alaska	Apr. 7, 1904	Do.
Vigilant	50	1894		1903		Ballard, Wash	Nov. 14, 1905	....do	Nov. 6, 1904	Do.
Will H. Isom	983	1901		1901		....do	July 10, 1905	St. Michael, Alaska	July 26, 1904	Do.
Ocean freight steamers.										
J. A. Cummins	79	1886		1895		San Francisco, Cal	Feb. 4, 1905	Honolulu, Hawaii	Feb. 11, 1904	Juneau, Alaska.
James Makee	301	1879		1896		Port Ludlow, Wash	Feb. 1, 1905	....do	Feb. 2, 1904	Do.
Waialeale	268	1886		1897		Port Blakeley, Wash	....do	....do	Feb. 9, 1904	Do.
Inland freight steamers.										
Chinega	188	1903		1903		San Francisco, Cal	June 18, 1905	Kogiung, Alaska	Mar. 19, 1903	San Francisco, Cal.
Ella	419	1905		1905		Seattle, Wash	Aug. 10, 1905	Fairbanks, Alaska	First inspn	
Florence S	100	1898		1898		St. Michael, Alaska	Aug. 14, 1905	....do	Aug. 10, 1904	Juneau, Alaska.
Independence	148	1898		1898		....do	Aug. 18, 1905	Chena, Alaska	Aug. 26, 1904	Do.
Leota	36	1898		1898		Alameda, Cal	July 14, 1905	St. Michael, Alaska	July 19, 1904	Do.
Lillie	31	1901		1901		Seattle, Wash	Sept. 22, 1905	Nome, Alaska	Sept. 23, 1904	Do.
Lotta Talbot	342	1898		1898		....do	Aug. 11, 1905	Fairbanks, Alaska	Sept. 26, 1904	Do.
Luella	115	1898		1898		Stockton, Cal	Aug. 14, 1905	....do	Aug. 13, 1904	Do.
Minneapolis	235	1898		1898		Tacoma, Wash	Aug. 9, 1905	Chena, Alaska	Sept. 6, 1904	Do.
Robert Kerr	718	1898		1898		Seattle, Wash	Aug. 27, 1905	Tanana, Alaska	July 28, 1904	Do.
White Seal	193	1905		(d)		Fairbanks, Alaska	Aug. 17, 1905	Fairbanks, Alaska	First inspn	
Wilbur Crimmin	124	1898		1901		Coupeville, Wash	Aug. 6, 1905	....do	....do	
Ocean towing steamers.										
Charles Counselman	123	1900		1899	1904	Ballard, Wash	Jan. 19, 1905	Hilo, Hawaii	Jan. 21, 1904	Juneau, Alaska.
Dorothy	8	1900		1900		San Francisco, Cal	Sept. 25, 1905	Nome, Alaska	Sept. 12, 1903	Do.
Gertie Storey	73	1889		1899		....do	June 15, 1905	Ugashik, Alaska	June 28, 1904	Do.
Kaena	35	1878		1897		....do	Feb. 9, 1905	Honolulu, Hawaii	Feb. 4, 1904	Do.
Lehua	176	1879		1886		....do	Feb. 8, 1905	....do	Feb. 9, 1904	Do.
Leslie Baldwin	23	1901		1901		....do	Jan. 21, 1905	Kahului, Alaska	Jan. 21, 1904	Do.
Polar Bear	57	1888		1902		Astoria, Oreg	June 20, 1905	Kogiung, Alaska	June 28, 1904	Do.
Rover	44	1901		1899		Hilo, Hawaii	Feb. 3, 1905	Honolulu, Hawaii	Feb. 3, 1904	Do.
Sawtooth	13	1901		1901		Alameda, Cal	Sept. 23, 1905	Nome, Alaska	Oct. 10, 1904	Do.
Shelikof	173	1900		1900		....do	May 30, 1905	Uyak Bay, Alaska	May 27, 1904	Do.
Thistle	102	1887	1897	1897		Benicia, Cal	June 16, 1905	Naknek, Alaska	Mar. 25, 1903	San Francisco, Cal.

[a] Formerly Hueneme, 1899. [b] Estimated. [c] Formerly Rideout, 1905. [d] Unknown.

DOMESTIC VESSELS INSPECTED, YEAR ENDED DECEMBER 31, 1905—FIRST SUPERVISING DISTRICT—JUNEAU, ALASKA—Continued.

Names of vessels and class.	Gross tonnage.	Hull built.	Hull rebuilt.	Boilers built.	Boilers rebuilt.	Where built.	Date of inspection.	Where inspected.	Date of previous inspection.	Local district where previously inspected.
Inland towing steamers.										
Alarm	31	1902		1902		Astoria, Oreg	June 20, 1905	Nushagak, Alaska	June 29, 1904	Juneau, Alaska.
Alaska	46	1888		1902		San Francisco, Cal	Apr. 24, 1905	Wrangell, Alaska	Apr. 20, 1904	Do.
Alaska	60	1899		1898		Seattle, Wash	July 25, 1905	Andreaofsky, Alaska	July 31, 1904	Do.
Alice	55	1897		1904		Tacoma, Wash	Apr. 29, 1905	Petersburg, Alaska	May 11, 1904	Do.
Angeles	62	1889		1889		Portland, Oreg	May 4, 1905	Killisnoo, Alaska	May 5, 1904	Do.
Anna Barron	82	1902		1902		Astoria, Oreg	May 5, 1905	Funter Bay, Alaska	May 4, 1904	Do.
Annie	12	1901		1904		Chinega, Alaska	May 23, 1905	Valdez, Alaska	May 22, 1904	Do.
Aurora	a 4	1893		1901		San Francisco, Cal	May 29, 1905	Karluk, Alaska	May 28, 1904	Do.
Arctic Bird	38	1898		1898		St. Michael, Alaska	Sept. 28, 1905	Chinic, Alaska	Sept. 23, 1904	Do.
Baby Ruth	a 25	1893		1893		San Francisco, Cal	June 5, 1905	Chignik River, Alaska	June 4, 1904	Do.
Baranoff	20	1889		1888		East Portland, Oreg	Apr. 16, 1905	Wrangell, Alaska	Apr. 21, 1904	Do.
Bear	31	1901		1901		Douglas, Alaska	Mar. 31, 1905	Douglas, Alaska	May 6, 1904	Do.
Belle	10	1900		1898		Seattle, Wash	Sept. 22, 1905	Nome, Alaska	Sept. 20, 1904	Do.
Capt. Worden	12	1900	1902	1900		Nome, Alaska	Oct. 6, 1905	do	July 15, 1904	Do.
Cathie Killeran	a 6	1891		1898		San Francisco, Cal	June 14, 1905	Ugashik, Alaska	June 25, 1904	Do.
Charlotte	10	1902		1893		Howkan, Alaska	Apr. 19, 1905	Klawack, Alaska	Apr. 24, 1904	Do.
Chignik	16	1902		1902		San Francisco, Cal	June 5, 1905	Chignik River, Alaska	June 3, 1904	Do.
Clara	a 4	1895		1900		Seattle, Wash	June 25, 1905	Dutch Harbor, Alaska	July 6, 1904	Do.
Clatawa	13	1902		1902		Dolomi, Alaska	Nov. 26, 1905	Wrangell, Alaska	Nov. 7, 1904	Do.
Collis	a 3	1899		1899		San Francisco, Cal	June 15, 1905	Ugashik, Alaska	June 25, 1904	Do.
Cora	a 4	1887		1900		do	Apr. 19, 1905	Klawack, Alaska	Apr. 23, 1904	Do.
Cornelia Cook	60	1900		1899		Portland, Oreg	Apr. 14, 1905	Juneau, Alaska	Apr. 16, 1904	Do.
Cub	19	1898		1898		San Francisco, Cal	Sept. 12, 1905	St. Michael, Alaska	Sept. 11, 1904	Do.
Eleu	a 70	(b)	1905	1899		(b)	Feb. 20, 1905	Honolulu, Hawaii	First inspn	
Ella Rohlffs	64	1889		1889		San Francisco, Cal	Apr. 16, 1905	Labashoe Bay, Alaska	Apr. 20, 1904	Do.
Etolin	a 4	1901		1900		Wrangell, Alaska	Apr. 29, 1905	Petersburg, Alaska	Apr. 27, 1904	Do.
Fawn	a 4	1886		1886		San Francisco, Cal	May 13, 1905	Haines Mission, Alaska	May 7, 1904	Do.
Florence Hume	a 8	1898		1896		do	June 4, 1905	Chignik Bay, Alaska	June 3, 1904	Do.
Fram	a 22	1899		1899		Naknek, Alaska	June 17, 1905	Naknek, Alaska	June 27, 1904	Do.
Gracie Feltz	24	1893		1901		Seattle, Wash	Apr. 11, 1905	Chomly, Alaska	Apr. 8, 1904	Do.
Griffin	11	1899		1905		Friday Harbor, Wash	May 23, 1905	Ellamar, Alaska	May 25, 1904	Seattle, Wash.
Hattie Gage	80	1889		1898		San Francisco, Cal	Apr. 16, 1905	Labashoe Bay, Alaska	May 9, 1904	Juneau, Alaska.
Herald	37	1888		1901		Aberdeen, Wash	Apr. 10, 1905	Metlakatla, Alaska	Apr. 11, 1904	Do.
Herbert	a 12	1898		1898		San Francisco, Cal	June 18, 1905	Kogiung, Alaska	June 27, 1904	Do.
Herbert Hume	a 12	1898		1898		do	May 30, 1905	Uyak Bay, Alaska	May 29, 1904	Do.
Hilda	18	1901		1901		do	June 20, 1905	Nushagak, Alaska	June 28, 1904	Do.
Hilo	13	1900		1900		Hilo, Hawaii	Jan. 18, 1905	Hilo, Hawaii	Jan. 21, 1904	Do.
Hope	9	1898		1898		Wrangell, Alaska	Apr. 24, 1905	Wrangell, Alaska	Apr. 21, 1904	Do.
Ira	a 5	1901		1905		do	Nov. 25, 1905	do	Nov. 15, 1904	Do.
Islam	11	1900		1900		Alameda, Cal	Sept. 28, 1905	Chinic, Alaska	Sept. 12, 1903	Do.
Jupiter	11	1899		1899		Tacoma, Wash	Apr. 14, 1905	Juneau, Alaska	Apr. 29, 1904	Do.
Kamishak	21	1904		1904		Alameda, Cal	May 29, 1905	Karluk, Alaska	Mar. 30, 1904	San Francisco, Cal.

Kariuk	13	1900		1899		San Francisco, Cal	do	do	May 28, 1904	Juneau, Alaska.
Kenai	12	1890		1898		Alameda, Cal	May 30, 1905	Uyak Bay, Alaska	May 29, 1904	Do.
Klawack	21	1887		1895		San Francisco, Cal	Apr. 19, 1905	Klawack, Alaska	Apr. 23, 1904	Do.
Kodat	24	1889		1893		do	May 5, 1905	Funter Bay, Alaska	May 4, 1904	Do.
Koggiung	11	1901		1901		Alameda, Cal	June 20, 1905	Nushagak, Alaska	June 29, 1904	Do.
Leader	a 25	1901		1901		Naknek, Alaska	June 14, 1905	Ugashik, Alaska	June 25, 1904	Do.
Lillian	34	1897		1897		San Francisco, Cal	June 18, 1905	Kogiung, Alaska	June 27, 1904	Do.
Lincoln	65	1902		1902		Tacoma, Wash	Apr. 29, 1905	Petersburg, Alaska	Apr. 29, 1904	Seattle, Wash.
Lizzie M	a 4	1900		1900		Seattle, Wash	Oct. 3, 1905	Nome, Alaska	Sept. 27, 1904	Juneau, Alaska.
Louise	9	1882		1882		San Francisco, Cal	May 4, 1905	Killisnoo, Alaska	May 5, 1904	Do.
Lurline	a 5	1900		1900		do	Jan. 18, 1905	Hilo, Hawaii	Jan. 21, 1904	Do.
Mabel	9	1904		1899		Shakan, Alaska	Nov. 25, 1905	Wrangell, Alaska	Nov. 7, 1904	Do.
Marie G. Haven	25	1883		1903		Portland, Oreg	Apr. 10, 1905	Metlakatla, Alaska	Nov. 1, 1903	Do.
May	a 20	1903		1903		San Francisco, Cal	June 20, 1905	Nushagak, Alaska	June 29, 1904	Do.
Miami	81	1898		1902		Tillamook, Oreg	do	do	June 16, 1904	Seattle, Wash.
Mohawk	18	1901		1901		San Francisco, Cal	June 14, 1905	Ugashik, Alaska	June 25, 1904	Juneau, Alaska.
Mohea	a 5	1893	1903	1898		do	Jan. 18, 1905	Hilo, Hawaii	Jan. 21, 1904	Do.
Nak Nek	36	1903		1903		do	June 17, 1905	Naknek, Alaska	June 26, 1904	Do.
Novelty	56	1884		1899		Coos Bay, Oreg	Apr. 11, 1905	Loring, Alaska	Apr. 8, 1904	Do.
Nuten	22	1901		1901		Astoria, Oreg	June 20, 1905	Nushagak, Alaska	June 29, 1904	Do.
Occident	10	1901		1901		do	do	do	do	Do.
Oneida	21	1901		1901		San Francisco, Cal	do	do	do	Do.
Petrel	27	1899		1900	1903	New Whatcom, Oreg	May 10, 1905	Juneau, Alaska	May 7, 1904	Do.
Pilot	a 5	1896		1896		Juneau, Alaska	May 2, 1905	Treadwell, Alaska	Apr. 29, 1904	Do.
Queen	24	1900		1900		San Francisco, Cal	June 19, 1905	Chogiung, Alaska	June 29, 1904	Do.
Quinnat	31	1901		1901		do	June 17, 1905	Naknek, Alaska	June 27, 1904	Do.
Ralph L	15	1891		1891		do	do	do	June 26, 1904	Do.
Rattler	a 4	1899		1899		Oakland, Cal	June 20, 1905	Nushagak, Alaska	June 29, 1904	Do.
Rebecca	a 7	1898		1898	1903	(b)	Aug. 1, 1905	Tanana, Alaska	Aug. 4, 1904	Do.
Research	45	1898		1898		Liverpool, England	July 12, 1905	St. Michael Alaska	First inspn	
Sayak	a 90	1900		1898		Kogiung, Alaska	June 18, 1905	Kogiung, Alaska	June 27, 1904	Do.
Scout	a 3	(b)		(b)		(b)	Apr. 29, 1905	Petersburg, Alaska	Apr. 20, 1904	Do.
Seaolin	41	1883		1897		San Francisco, Cal	May 10, 1905	Juneau, Alaska	May 3, 1904	Do.
Spray	10	1904		1903		Howkan, Alaska	Apr. 19, 1905	Klawack, Alaska	Apr. 24, 1904	Do.
Starlight	a 4	(b)		1899		(b)	Apr. 24, 1905	Wrangell, Alaska	Apr. 20, 1904	Do.
Togiak	21	1901		1901		San Francisco, Cal	June 19, 1905	Chogiung, Alaska	June 28, 1904	Do.
Tugidak	22	1903		1903		Alameda, Cal	May 29, 1905	Karluk, Alaska	May 28, 1904	Do.
Tyone	a 14	1903		1899		San Francisco, Cal	June 19, 1905	Chogiung, Alaska	June 28, 1904	Do.
Uganuk	13	1900		1900		do	May 29, 1905	Karluk, Alaska	May 28, 1904	Do.
Ugashik	21	1901		1901		do	June 14, 1905	Ugashik, Alaska	June 24, 1904	Do.
Uyak	22	1901		1901		Alameda, Cal	May 30, 1905	Uyak Bay, Alaska	May 29, 1904	Do.
Viking	a 3	1905			1904	Douglas, Alaska	May 2, 1905	Treadwell, Alaska	First inspn	
Vladimer	a 8	1900		1900		San Francisco, Cal	June 25, 1905	Unalaska, Alaska	July 5, 1904	Do.
Waiakea	a 8	1899		1899		do	Jan. 18, 1905	Hilo, Hawaii	Jan. 21, 1904	Do.
White Wing	67	1898		1899		Seattle, Wash	May 4, 1905	Killisnoo, Alaska	Apr. 27, 1904	Do.
Steam pleasure yachts.										
Josephine	a 2	1896		1896		Chicago, Ill	July 21, 1905	St. Michael, Alaska	Sept. 11, 1904	Juneau, Alaska.
Vixen	a 5	1905		1903	1905	Shakan, Alaska	Nov. 11, 1905	Wrangell, Alaska	First inspn	

a Estimated. b Unknown.

DOMESTIC VESSELS INSPECTED, YEAR ENDED DECEMBER 31, 1905—FIRST SUPERVISING DISTRICT—JUNEAU, ALASKA—Continued.

Names of vessels and class.	Gross tonnage.	Hull built.	Hull rebuilt.	Boilers built.	Boilers rebuilt.	Where built.	Date of inspection.	Where inspected.	Date of previous inspection.	Local district where previously inspected.
Miscellaneous steamers.										
Comet (prospecting)	[a] 4	1899		1902		Shakan, Alaska	Apr. 17, 1905	Shakan, Alaska	Apr. 25, 1904	Juneau, Alaska.
Equator (fishing)	76	1888		1897		Benicia, Cal	June 4, 1905	Chignik Bay, Alaska	June 3, 1904	Do.
Eskimo (fishing)	[a] 8	1898		1890		Alameda, Cal	do	do	do	Do.
Ethel and Marion (fishing)	13	1883		1898		San Francisco, Cal	do	do	do	Do.
Ethel (fishing)	[a] 4	1902		1903		Tacoma, Wash	Apr. 21, 1905	Shakan, Alaska	Jan. 7, 1904	Seattle, Wash.
Gleason (prospecting)	[a] 4	1901		1901		Wrangell, Alaska	Apr. 24, 1905	Wrangell, Alaska	Apr. 21, 1904	Juneau, Alaska.
Katahoon (fishing)	31	1903		1903		Tacoma, Wash	Apr. 14, 1905	Juneau, Alaska	May 2, 1904	Do.
Marietta (missionary)	[a] 3	1900		1901		Metlakatla, Alaska	Apr. 12, 1905	Ketchikan, Alaska	Apr. 11, 1904	Do.
Ruth (fishing)	[a] 4	1896		1899		Tacoma, Wash	Apr. 25, 1905	Wrangell, Alaska	Apr. 20, 1904	Do.
St. Joseph (missionary)	69	1898		1898		St. Michael, Alaska	July 11, 1905	St. Michael, Alaska	July 18, 1904	Do.
Thistle (prospecting)	[a] 4	1896		1896	1903	Puyallup, Wash	May 2, 1905	Juneau, Alaska	Apr. 30, 1904	Do.
Vessels propelled by gasoline motors.										
Eclipse	211	1900				Benicia, Cal	Feb. 1, 1905	Honolulu, Hawaii	Feb. 8, 1904	Juneau, Alaska.
Hettie B	27	1894				San Francisco, Cal	Oct. 6, 1905	Nome, Alaska	Oct. 7, 1904	Do.
Malola	32	1898				do	Feb. 6, 1905	Honolulu, Hawaii	Feb. 12, 1904	Do.
Sea Light	20	1894				Hoquiam, Wash	Apr. 7, 1905	Ketchikan, Alaska	Apr. 11, 1904	Do.
Pacific	[a] 25	1905				Copper Mount, Alaska	Nov. 12, 1905	do	First inspn	
Tana	317	1905				Seattle, Wash	Aug. 12, 1905	Fairbanks, Alaska	do	
Freight sail vessel of over 700 tons.										
Rosamond	1,030	1900				Benicia, Cal	Feb. 16, 1905	Elele, Hawaii	Nov. 6, 1903	San Francisco, Cal.

SECOND SUPERVISING DISTRICT.

LOCAL DISTRICT OF NEW YORK, N. Y.

Names of vessels and class.	Gross tonnage.	Hull built.	Hull rebuilt.	Boilers built.	Boilers rebuilt.	Where built.	Date of inspection.	Where inspected.	Date of previous inspection.	Local district where previously inspected.
Ocean passenger steamers.										
Advance	2,605	1883		1904		Chester, Pa	May 23, 1905	New York, N. Y	May 24, 1904	Philadelphia, Pa.
Alamo	2,942	1883		1898		do	Nov. 9, 1905	do	Nov. 23, 1904	New York, N. Y.
Algonquin	2,832	1890		1890		Philadelphia, Pa	Aug. 28, 1905	do	Aug. 30, 1904	Do.
Alliança	2,985	1886		1896		Chester, Pa	June 17, 1905	do	June 16, 1904	Do.
America	141	1903		1903		Tomkins Cove, N. Y	Aug. 17, 1905	do	Aug. 19, 1904	Do.
Angler	409	1878		1890		Wilmington, Del	Mar. 20, 1905	do	Mar. 21, 1904	Do.

Apache	4,145	1901	1902	1901, 1902	......	Philadelphia, Pa	June 9,1905	....do	June 7,1904	Do.
Arapahoe	4,145	1901	1902	1901, 1902	......	....do	Aug. 1,1905	....do	Aug. 2,1904	Do.
Brooklyn	3,636	1880	......	1896	......	Belfast, Ireland	June 15,1905	Brooklyn, N. Y	First inspn.	
Caracas	2,886	1889	1901	1889	1901	Wilmington, Del	Dec. 6,1905	....do	Dec. 8,1904	Do.
Carib	2,087	1882	......	1882	......	Glasgow, Scotland	July 21,1905	New York, N. Y	July 28,1904	Do.
Chalmette	3,205	1879	......	1879	......	Philadelphia, Pa	Sept. 19,1905	....do	Sept. 26,1904	New Orleans, La.
Chas. R. Norman [b]	99	1899	......	1899	......	Port Richmond, N. Y.	Mar. 16,1905	Bayonne, N. J	Mar. 16,1904	New York, N. Y.
Cherokee	2,556	1886	......	1886	......	Philadelphia, Pa	Mar. 15,1905	New York, N. Y	Mar. 21,1904	Do.
City of Augusta	2,869	1880	......	1897	......	Chester, Pa	Feb. 18,1905	Brooklyn, N. Y	Sept. 21,1903	Savannah, Ga.
City of Birmingham	3,066	1888	......	1888	......	....do	July 12,1905	Hoboken, N. J	May 26,1904	Do.
City of Savannah [c]	5,017	1896	......	1898	......	Newport News, Va	June 24,1905	New York, N. Y	Sept. 18,1903	New York, N. Y.
City of Washington	2,683	1877	......	1889	......	Chester, Pa	Feb. 9,1905	....do	Jan. 14,1904	Do.
Coamo	4,384	1891	......	1891	......	Glasgow, Scotland	Aug. 26,1905	Brooklyn, N. Y	Aug. 22,1904	Do.
Colon [d]	5,667	1899	......	1898	......	Philadelphia, Pa	May 18,1905	....do	May 19,1904	Do.
Colorado	2,764	1879	......	1905	......	Chester, Pa	Nov. 6,1905	New York, N. Y	Aug. 2,1904	Do.
Comal	2,934	1885	......	1885	......	....do	Oct. 3,1905	Hoboken, N. J	Oct. 7,1904	Do.
Comanche	3,856	1895	1901	1895	......	Philadelphia, Pa	Nov. 6,1905	New York, N. Y	Nov. 3,1904	Do.
Commander	99	1893	......	1893	......	Wilmington, Del	Apr. 9,1905	Brooklyn, N. Y	Apr. 20,1904	Do.
Concho	3,724	1891	......	1904	......	Chester, Pa	Aug. 19,1905	New York, N. Y	Aug. 13,1904	Norfolk, Va.
Denver	4,549	1901	......	1901	......	Wilmington, Del	Oct. 14,1905	....do	Oct. 22,1904	New York, N. Y.
Edgemont [e]	1,409	1882	......	1882	......	Bath, Me	July 17,1905	....do	July 22,1904	Do.
Edwin Brandow	124	1905	......	1905	......	Tottenville, N. Y	May 6,1905	....do	First inspn.	
Esperanza	4,702	1901	......	1901	......	Philadelphia, Pa	May 1,1905	Brooklyn, N. Y	May 2,1904	Do.
Finance	2,603	1882	......	1904	......	Chester, Pa	June 29,1905	New York, N. Y	June 20,1904	Philadelphia, Pa.
Finland	12,760	1902	......	1902	......	Philadelphia, Pa	Sept. 27,1905	....do	Sept. 15,1904	New York, N. Y.
George Starr	168	1862	1884	1894	......	Keyport, N. J	Feb. 27,1905	Hoboken, N. J	Jan. 20,1904	Do.
Havana	5,667	1898	......	1898	......	Philadelphia, Pa	Dec. 21,1905	....do	Dec. 24,1904	Do.
Iroquois	3,601	1888	......	1888	......	....do	Nov. 3,1905	New York, N. Y	Nov. 7,1904	Do.
Isabel	421	1894	......	1896	......	Noank, Conn	Apr. 18,1905	Hoboken, N. J	May 16,1904	Do.
Jas. A. Lawrence [f]	86	1891	......	1900	......	Athens, N. Y	Apr. 10,1905	Brooklyn, N. Y	Apr. 11,1904	Do.
James S. Whitney	2,707	1900	......	1900	......	Wilmington, Del	Oct. 21,1905	New York, N. Y	Oct. 27,1904	Do.
Jamestown	2,898	1894	......	1903	......	Chester, Pa	Apr. 7,1905	Hoboken, N. J	Apr. 5,1904	Do.
Jefferson	3,127	1899	......	1898	......	....do	May 4,1905	....do	Apr. 29,1904	Norfolk, Va.
John Scully [g]	413	1899	......	1899	......	Camden, N. J	Dec. 28,1904	Port Richmond, N. Y.	Jan. 7,1904	Do.
John B. Collins	325	1901	......	1901	......	Tottenville, N. Y	May 2,1905	New York, N. Y	May 3,1904	New York, N. Y.
John K. Gilkinson	108	1902	......	1902	......	....do	July 24,1905	Hoboken, N. J	July 25,1904	Do.
Kansas City	3,679	1889	......	1889	......	Chester, Pa	Nov. 17,1905	New York, N. Y	Nov. 15,1904	Savannah, Ga.
Kroonland	12,760	1902	......	1902	......	Philadelphia, Pa	July 20,1905	....do	July 8,1904	New York, N. Y.
Lampasas	2,942	1883	......	1896	......	Chester, Pa	July 7,1905	Brooklyn, N. Y	July 15,1904	Do.
Maracaibo	1,771	1899	......	1899	......	Wilmington, Del	Dec. 1,1905	....do	Nov. 30,1904	Do.
Monroe	4,704	1903	......	1903	......	Newport News, Va	Feb. 16,1905	New York, N. Y	Feb. 24,1904	Do.
Monterey	4,702	1901	......	1900	......	Philadelphia, Pa	May 22,1905	Brooklyn, N. Y	May 25,1904	Do.
Morro Castle	6,004	1900	......	1900	......	....do	Nov. 9,1905	....do	Nov. 11,1904	Do.
Mount Desert	457	1879	......	1890	......	Bath, Me	Aug. 16,1905	Mariners Harbor, N. Y.	Apr. 15,1904	Portland, Me.
Navahoe	1,879	1880	......	1880	......	Hamburg, Germany	Feb. 24,1905	New York, N. Y	Mar. 4,1904	New York, N. Y.
New York	2,589	1875	......	1892	......	Wilmington, Del	Apr. 1,1905	Brooklyn, N. Y	Apr. 6,1904	Do.
New York	10,798	1888	......	1903	......	Clydebank, Scotland	Aug. 8,1905	New York, N. Y	July 28,1904	Do.

[a] Estimated.
[b] Formerly Edward T. Dalzell, 1903.
[c] Formerly La Grande Duchesse, 1901.
[d] Formerly Mexico, 1905.
[e] Formerly State of Maine, 1904.
[f] Formerly C. E. Evarts, 1897.
[g] Certificate issued Jan. 3, 1905.

DOMESTIC VESSELS INSPECTED, YEAR ENDED DECEMBER 31, 1905—SECOND SUPERVISING DISTRICT—NEW YORK, N. Y.—Continued.

Names of vessels and class.	Gross tonnage.	Hull built.	Hull rebuilt.	Boilers built.	Boilers rebuilt.	Where built.	Date of inspection.	Where inspected.	Date of previous inspection.	Local district where previously inspected.
Ocean passenger steamers—Continued.										
Niagara	2,265	1877		1901		Chester, Pa	Feb. 2, 1905	Brooklyn, N. Y	Jan. 7, 1904	New York, N. Y.
Nueces	3,367	1887		1903		do	Aug. 9, 1905	New York, N. Y	Aug. 15, 1904	Do.
Orizaba	3,496	1889		1889		do	Oct. 9, 1905	Brooklyn, N. Y	Sept. 13, 1904	Do.
Philadelphia [a]	10,786	1888		1901		Clydebank, Scotland	Oct. 17, 1905	New York, N. Y	Oct. 4, 1904	Do.
Philadelphia	2,520	1885		1885		Philadelphia, Pa	Apr. 13, 1905	Brooklyn, N. Y	Apr. 14, 1904	Do.
Ponce	3,503	1899		1899		Wilmington, Del	Nov. 3, 1905	do	Nov. 4, 1904	Do.
Richmond	1,437	1873		1873		do	Feb. 28, 1905	do	Mar. 12, 1904	Do.
Rio Grande	2,556	1876		1891		Chester, Pa	Oct. 13, 1905	New York, N. Y	Oct. 14, 1904	Do.
Rudolph Brothers	123	1902		1902		Athens, N. Y	May 2, 1905	Brooklyn, N. Y	May 12, 1904	Do.
Sabine [b]	3,328	1889	1900	1900		Chester, Pa	July 25, 1905	Hoboken, N. J	July 9, 1904	Do.
Sagamore	458	1901		1902		Philadelphia, Pa	May 10, 1905	Long Island City, N. Y	May 19, 1904	Do.
St. Paul	11,629	1895		1895		do	Nov. 22, 1905	New York, N. Y	Nov. 22, 1904	Do.
San Jacinto	6,069	1903		1903		Chester, Pa	Dec. 9, 1905	do	Dec. 6, 1904	Galveston, Tex.
San Marcos	2,839	1881		1901		do	Oct. 17, 1905	do	Oct. 19, 1904	New York, N. Y.
Santiago	2,358	1879		1900		do	Nov. 2, 1905	Brooklyn, N. Y	Nov. 1, 1904	Do.
Saratoga	2,820	1878		1897		do	May 27, 1905	do	May 24, 1904	Do.
Seguranca	4,033	1890		1904		do	May 12, 1905	New York, N. Y	May 12, 1904	Do.
Seminole	2,556	1886		1886		Philadelphia, Pa	Dec. 5, 1905	do	Dec. 5, 1904	Do.
Seneca	2,729	1884		1884		Chester, Pa	Feb. 15, 1905	Brooklyn, N. Y	Jan. 25, 1904	Do.
Taurus	916	1881		1901		Philadelphia, Pa	Apr. 13, 1905	do	May 23, 1904	Do.
Theresa Verdon	49	1892		1892		Jersey City, N. J	May 18, 1905	Long Island City N. Y.	May 18, 1904	Do.
Union	96	1900		1900		Brooklyn, N. Y	Feb. 24, 1905	New York, N. Y	Feb. 24, 1904	Do.
Unity	96	1900		1900		do	Mar. 8, 1905	do	Mar. 7, 1904	Do.
Vigilancia	4,115	1890	1902	1902		Chester, Pa	May 8, 1905	Brooklyn, N. Y	May 10, 1904	Do.
W. F. Cogan	55	1903		1902		Tottenville, N. Y	Jan. 23, 1905	Hoboken, N. J	Jan. 21, 1904	Do.
William Fletcher	159	1864	1902	1894		Keyport, N. J	June 3, 1905	do	Mar. 28, 1904	Do.
Wm. E. Chapman	281	1889	1894	1894		Brooklyn, N. Y	Nov. 22, 1905	Brooklyn, N. Y	Jan. 10, 1905	Do.
Wm. E. Chapman	281	1889	1894	1894		do	Jan. 10, 1905	do	Jan. 8, 1904	Do.
Yucatan	3,525	1890		1890		Chester, Pa	Dec. 7, 1905	do	Nov. 29, 1904	Do.
Zulia	1,713	1901		1901		Philadelphia, Pa	June 28, 1905	do	June 28, 1904	Do.
Inland passenger steamers.										
Active	7	(c)		1898		No record	July 20, 1905	Brooklyn, N. Y	June 23, 1904	New York, N. Y.
Adela	24	1887	1892	1887		Newburyport, Mass	May 13, 1905	do	Mar. 24, 1904	Do.
Adelaide	355	1875		1897		Greenport, N. Y	Nov. 11, 1905	do	May 16, 1904	Boston, Mass.
Alberta M	87	1883	1905	1901		Athens, N. Y	Dec. 18, 1905	West New Brighton, N. Y.	Dec. 5, 1904	New York, N. Y.
Albertina	558	1882		1882		Greenpoint, N. Y	Mar. 29, 1905	Red Bank, N. J	May 10, 1904	Do.
Amanda	89	1878	1895	1897		Espy, Pa	May 27, 1905	Harrison, N. J	May 19, 1904	Do.
Anita	14	1872		1887		New York, N. Y	Aug. 22, 1905	Greenwood Lake, N. Y.	Aug. 30, 1904	Do.

Asbury Park	2,078	1903		1903		Philadelphia, Pa	Apr. 17, 1905	Communipaw, N. J	May 7, 1904	Do.
Atlantic	157	1900		1900		Wilmington, Del	Sept. 6, 1905	Brooklyn, N. Y	Sept. 6, 1904	Do.
Belle	39	1900	1903	1890		Newark, N. J	June 23, 1905	Newark, N. J	June 21, 1904	Do.
Benjamin Franklin [d]	489	1894		1899		Tottenville, N. Y	Dec. 31, 1904	New York, N. Y	Jan. 2, 1904	Do.
C. W. Morse	4,307	1903		1904		Wilmington, Del	Apr. 4, 1905	....do	Mar. 11, 1904	Do.
Carrie T	[e] 8	1892		1903		Greenwood Lake, N. Y	July 21, 1905	Greenwood Lake, N. Y.	July 16, 1904	Do.
Cepheus	882	1881		1903		Chester, Pa	May 6, 1905	Brooklyn, N. Y	May 12, 1904	Do.
Cetus	847	1881		1903		Philadelphia, Pa	May 10, 1905	....do	May 14, 1904	Do.
Charles F. Allen	31	1882		1892		Rondout, N. Y	Jan. 12, 1905	Tompkinsville, N. Y	Jan. 11, 1904	Do.
Chrystenah	571	1866	1893	1893		Nyack, N. Y	Apr. 10, 1905	Nyack, N. Y	Apr. 2, 1904	Do.
Clifton	153	1888		1900		Chester, Pa	Apr. 21, 1905	Brooklyn, N. Y	May 5, 1904	Do.
Commerce	127	1901		1901		Athens, N. Y	Sept. 26, 1905	New York, N. Y	Sept. 26, 1904	Do.
Cornelius Van Cott	41	1881	1893	1897		Brooklyn, N. Y	Oct. 9, 1905	....do	Oct. 10, 1904	Do.
Cygnus	857	1881		1903		Chester, Pa	May 12, 1905	Brooklyn, N. Y	May 11, 1904	Do.
Daisy	30	1897		1905		Peekskill, N. Y	June 28, 1905	Yonkers, N. Y	July 1, 1904	Do.
Despatch	21	1899		1899		Camden, N. J	June 19, 1905	Weehawken, N. J	June 20, 1904	Do.
Dreamland [f]	1,285	1878		1895		Wilmington, Del	Apr. 14, 1905	Brooklyn, N. Y	May 27, 1904	Do.
Elberon	360	1888		1886		Nyack, N. Y	May 18, 1905	Hoboken, N. J	June 11, 1904	Do.
Erastus Corning	308	1857		1901		Brooklyn, N. Y	May 3, 1905	Port Richmond, N. Y	May 14, 1904	Do.
Eugene F. Moran	200	1904		1904		Philadelphia, Pa	Aug. 7, 1905	Brooklyn, N. Y	Aug. 5, 1904	Do.
Favorite	399	1894		1894		Tomkins Cove, N. Y	Apr. 8, 1905	Hoboken, N. J	Apr. 9, 1904	Do.
Fidelity	152	1873		1899		Brooklyn, N. Y	Mar. 21, 1905	New York, N. Y	Mar. 21, 1904	Do.
Fireproofer	173	1903		1903		Baltimore, Md	June 6, 1905	Hoboken, N. J	June 9, 1904	Do.
Franklin Edson	112	1885		1895		Brooklyn, N. Y	May 20, 1905	North Brothers Island, N. Y.	May 28, 1904	Do.
Frolic	44	1905		1905		Croton, N. Y	Aug. 22, 1905	Croton, N. Y	First inspn	
Fulton Market	158	1895		1895		Noank, Conn	Dec. 14, 1905	New York, N. Y	Dec. 10, 1904	Do.
General Putnam	285	1902		1902		Wilmington, Del	June 12, 1905	....do	June 13, 1904	Do.
Geo. K. Kirkham	95	1900		1881		Athens, N. Y	Dec. 12, 1905	Hoboken, N. J	Dec. 14, 1904	Do.
Glen	491	1893		1891		Port Richmond, N. Y	Apr. 14, 1905	West Brighton, N. Y	May 17, 1904	Do.
Glenville	268	1886	1896	1886		Brooklyn, N. Y	Jan. 27, 1905	New York, N. Y	Jan. 27, 1904	Do.
Golden Rod	194	1882		1897		Nyack, N. Y	June 7, 1905	Brooklyn, N. Y	Aug. 18, 1897	Do.
Gov. Flower	103	1893		1893		Perth Amboy, N. J	Mar. 18, 1905	Tompkinsville, N. Y	Mar. 21, 1904	Do.
Guiding Star	105	1899		1900		Noank, Conn	Apr. 8, 1905	Brooklyn, N. Y	Apr. 6, 1904	Do.
Harlem River No. 1	50	1892		1904		New York, N. Y	May 17, 1905	New York, N. Y	May 19, 1904	Do.
Harlem River No. 3	63	1901		1903		....do	June 21, 1905	....do	June 25, 1904	Do.
Herman S. Caswell	114	1878		1890		Noank, Conn	Jan. 5, 1905	Brooklyn, N. Y	Feb. 4, 1904	Do.
Herman S. Caswell	114	1878		1890		....do	Nov. 24, 1905	....do	Jan. 5, 1905	Do.
Huntington	345	1903		1903		....do	June 14, 1905	New York, N. Y	June 15, 1904	Do.
J. G. Emmons	156	1854		1880		Athens, N. Y	July 11, 1905	Hoboken, N. J	July 11, 1904	Do.
J. S. Warden	485	1863	1895	1895		Jersey City, N. J	June 20, 1905	Mariners Harbor, N. Y	May 20, 1904	Do.
James W. Wadsworth [g] [h]	85	1880		1892		Northport, N. Y	July 20, 1904	Tompkinsville, N. Y	July 20, 1903	Do.
James W. Wadsworth	85	1880		1892		....do	July 20, 1905	....do	July 20, 1904	Do.
John Lenox	225	1864		1883		Brooklyn, N. Y	Apr. 5, 1905	Port Richmond, N. Y	May 20, 1904	Do.
John Nichols	119	1899		1899		Athens, N. Y	Sept. 19, 1905	Hoboken, N. J	Sept 19, 1904	Do.
John Wise	275	1895		1902		Essex, Mass	June 30, 1905	Brooklyn, N. Y	Sept. 17, 1902	Do.
John E. Moore	135	1853	1883	1896		Hoboken, N. J	Apr. 20, 1905	Hoboken, N. J	Apr. 19, 1904	Do.
John H. Starin	904	1865	1891	1901		Baltimore, Md	May 20, 1905	Port Richmond, N. Y.	June 10, 1904	Do.
Juliette [i]	28	1883	1903	1904		Oswego, N. Y	May 22, 1905	Nyack, N. Y	May 12, 1904	Albany, N. Y.

[a] Formerly Paris, 1901.
[b] Formerly Leona, 1900.
[c] No record; formerly Government vessel.
[d] Certificate issued Jan. 10, 1905.
[e] Estimated.
[f] Formerly Cape May, 1904.
[g] Certificate issued Feb. 21, 1905.
[h] Formerly Ripple.
[i] Formerly George H. Haselton, 1903.

DOMESTIC VESSELS INSPECTED, YEAR ENDED DECEMBER 31, 1905—SECOND SUPERVISING DISTRICT—NEW YORK, N. Y.—Continued.

Names of vessels and class.	Gross tonnage.	Hull built.	Hull rebuilt.	Boilers built.	Boilers rebuilt.	Where built.	Date of inspection.	Where inspected.	Date of previous inspection.	Local district where previously inspected.
Inland passenger steamers—Continued.										
Lackawanna	340	1900		1900		Camden, N. J.	Nov. 3, 1905	Hoboken, N. J.	Nov. 3, 1904	New York, N. Y.
Lima	31	1890		1890		Perth Amboy, N. J.	July 20, 1905	Brooklyn, N. Y.	July 18, 1904	Do.
Little Silver	428	1893		1893		Tomkins Cove, N. Y.	May 26, 1905	Hoboken, N. J.	May 20, 1904	Do.
Lottie B.	21	1901		1901		Tottenville, N. Y.	Aug. 8, 1905	Perth Amboy, N. J.	Aug. 8, 1904	Do.
Manhanset	154	1879		1901		Mystic Bridge, Conn.	Mar. 22, 1905	West New Brighton, N. Y.	Apr. 11, 1904	New London, Conn.
Mary Patten	508	1893	1900	1905		Brooklyn, N. Y.	Apr. 25, 1905	Hoboken, N. J.	May 18, 1904	New York, N. Y.
Massasoit [a]	453	1901		1901		Tomkins Cove, N. Y.	Nov. 21, 1905	New York, N. Y.	Oct. 27, 1904	Do.
Matteawan	774	1862	1896	1902		Keyport, N. J.	Apr. 11, 1905	Port Richmond, N. Y.	May 26, 1904	Do.
Mecca	7	1897	1900	1897		Harrison, N. J.	July 15, 1905	Brooklyn, N. Y.	June 23, 1904	Do.
Minnahanonck	370	1868		1883		New York, N. Y.	Oct. 13, 1905	New York, N. Y.	June 17, 1904	Do.
Montclair	130	1903		1903		Camden, N. J.	July 13, 1905	Hoboken, N. J.	July 12, 1904	Do.
Montclair [b]	85	1876		1876		Greenwood Lake, N. Y.	Sept. 6, 1904	Greenwood Lake, N. Y.	Sept. 4, 1903	Do.
Nantasket	498	1878		1896		Chelsea, Mass.	Apr. 15, 1905	Mariners Harbor, N. Y.	May 11, 1904	Do.
Nassau	400	1898		1898		Noank, Conn.	June 14, 1905	Long Island City, N. Y.	July 9, 1904	Do.
Neptune	73	1875		1891		Mystic, Conn.	June 26, 1905	Jersey City, N. Y.	July 5, 1904	Do.
Nonpareil	167	1904		1904		Noank, Conn.	Nov. 8, 1905	Brooklyn, N. Y.	Nov. 5, 1904	New London, Conn.
Northport	89	1885		1885		Wilmington, Del.	June 21, 1905	Hoboken, N. J.	June 21, 1904	New York, N. Y.
O'Brien Brothers	108	1901		1901		Tottenville, N. Y.	July 14, 1905	Brooklyn, N. Y.	July 15, 1904	Do.
Pauline	71	1889		1893		Salisbury, Mass.	Aug. 22, 1905	New York, N. Y.	Aug. 27, 1904	Do.
Pegasus	847	1881		1881		Philadelphia, Pa.	May 23, 1905	Brooklyn, N. Y.	May 9, 1904	Do.
Perseus	847	1881		1881		do.	May 22, 1905	do.	May 14, 1904	Do.
Pleasure Bay	378	1890		1890		Nyack, N. Y.	May 23, 1905	Hoboken, N. J.	May 24, 1904	Do.
President	112	1898		1898		Tomkins Cove, N. Y.	Aug. 14, 1905	New York, N. Y.	Aug. 15, 1904	Do.
Richmond [c]	688	1902		1889		Noank, Conn.	Apr. 18, 1905	West Brighton, N. Y.	May 24, 1904	Do.
Robert Palmer [d]	112	1902		1902		do.	Nov. 17, 1904	Brooklyn, N. Y.	Nov. 16, 1903	Do.
Robert Palmer	112	1902		1902		do.	Nov. 18, 1905	do.	Nov. 17, 1904	Do.
Rockland	13	1875		1897		Philadelphia, Pa.	June 28, 1905	College Point, N. Y.	June 5, 1898	Do.
Rose A.	52	1905		1905		Brooklyn, N. Y.	May 15, 1905	Brooklyn, N. Y.	First inspn.	
St. Johns	1,098	1878		1886		Wilmington, Del.	May 4, 1905	Hoboken, N. J.	May 24, 1904	Do.
St. Michaels	283	1894		1905		Baltimore, Md.	Aug. 31, 1905	New York, N. Y.	Sept. 1, 1904	Do.
Samuel E. Bouker	135	1902		1902		Noank, Conn.	June 21, 1905	Brooklyn, N. Y.	June 20, 1904	Do.
Sandy Hook	1,559	1889		1904		Wilmington, Del.	Apr. 29, 1905	Communipaw, N. J.	May 18, 1904	Philadelphia, Pa.
Sarah A. Jenks	350	1885		1898		Linwood, Pa.	Nov. 16, 1905	New York, N. Y.	Nov. 16, 1904	New York, N. Y.
Sea Bird	489	1866	1887	1894		Hunters Point, N. Y.	Apr. 27, 1905	Red Bank, N. J.	Apr. 7, 1904	Do.
Sea Gull [e]	365	1864	1900	1890		Keyport, N. J.	Apr. 17, 1905	West Brighton, N. Y.	June 14, 1904	Do.
Seawanhaka [f]	27	1891		1889		Peekskill, N. Y.	May 25, 1905	Oyster Bay, N. Y.	June 9, 1904	Do.
Senekes	40	1892		1895		Moriches, N. Y.	June 24, 1905	Moriches, N. Y.	June 25, 1904	Do.
Shady Side	444	1873		1886		Bulls Ferry, N. Y.	Mar. 30, 1905	Hoboken, N. J.	Mar. 25, 1904	Do.
Shinnecock	1,205	1896		1896		Wilmington, Del.	June 10, 1905	New York, N. Y.	June 14, 1904	Do.
Sirius	993	1881		1901		Chester, Pa.	May 3, 1905	Brooklyn, N. Y.	May 11, 1904	Do.

Thomas Patten	875	1901		1901		Newburg, N. Y	June 7, 1905	Hoboken, N. J	June 13, 1904	Do.
Thomas C. Millard	356	1905		1905		Tottenville, N. Y	Dec. 23, 1905	New York, N. Y	First inspn	
Thomas M. Mulry	69	1900		1900		Athens, N. Y	Mar. 23, 1905	do	Mar. 24, 1904	Albany, N. Y.
Thomas S. Brennan	977	1884		1899		Brooklyn, N. Y	Mar. 8, 1905	do	Mar. 7, 1904	Do.
Unique	91	1900		1900		Rockland, Me	Feb. 3, 1905	Hoboken, N. J	Jan. 16, 1904	New York, N. Y.
Valley Girl	429	1851		1895		New York, N. Y	Apr. 7, 1905	Port Richmond, N. Y	May 20, 1904	Do.
Vigilant	226	1901		1901		Philadelphia, Pa	Sept. 11, 1905	Hunters Point, N. Y	Sept. 9, 1904	Do.
W. V. Wilson	689	1880	1900	1892		Keyport, N. J	May 2, 1905	Belford, N. J	May 11, 1904	Do.
Wanderer	281	1896		1896		Tomkins Cove, N. Y	Apr. 12, 1905	New York, N. Y	Apr. 12, 1904	Do.
Wildwood	22	1905		1905		Greenport, N. Y	Aug. 14, 1905	Hoboken, N. J	First inspn	
William Storie	439	1882		1882		Brooklyn, N. Y	June 14, 1905	do	June 16, 1904	Do.
Ferry steamers.										
Alaska	730	1872		1890		Brooklyn, N. Y	Apr. 8, 1905	Greenpoint, N. Y	Apr. 8, 1904	New York, N. Y.
Albany	1,059	1883		1883		Newburg, N. Y	Feb. 1, 1905	Weehawken, N. J	Feb. 1, 1904	Do.
America	818	1895		1894		Chester, Pa	Feb. 9, 1905	Brooklyn, N. Y	Feb. 11, 1904	Do.
Annex	529	1895		1895		Tompkins Cove, N. Y	Aug. 6, 1905	Hoboken, N. J	Aug. 6, 1904	Do.
Annex 4 [g]	501	1890		1890		Wilmington, Del	Dec. 24, 1904	do	Dec. 24, 1903	Do.
Annex 5	507	1891		1891		do	Mar. 31, 1905	do	Apr. 15, 1904	Do.
Arlington	1,446	1903		1904		Port Richmond, N. Y	Feb. 14, 1905	Jersey City, N. J	Feb. 11, 1904	Do.
Arthur Kill [h]	147	1861	1905	1905		Athens, N. Y	Apr. 22, 1905	Mariners Harbor, N. Y	Jan. 29, 1904	Do.
Atlantic	930	1885	1904	1885		Brooklyn, N. Y	Mar. 14, 1905	Brooklyn, N. Y	Mar. 26, 1904	Do.
B. M. Shanley	414	1899		1899		Wilmington, Del	May 24, 1905	Port Richmond, N. Y	May 24, 1904	Do.
Baltic	637	1863		1863		Greenpoint, N. Y	Mar. 23, 1905	Brooklyn, N. Y	Mar. 26, 1904	Do.
Baltimore	1,080	1882	1902	1901		Wilmington, Del	Oct. 18, 1905	Hoboken, N. J	Oct. 15, 1904	Do.
Bergen	1,120	1888		1889		Newburgh, N. Y	Apr. 27, 1905	do	Apr. 25, 1904	Do.
Binghamton	1,462	1905		1904		Newport News, Va	Mar. 10, 1905	do	First inspn	
Bremen	1,252	1891		1891		Newburg, N. Y	Mar. 7, 1905	do	Mar. 7, 1904	Do.
Bronx [i]	445	1884		1884		Brooklyn, N. Y	June 13, 1905	College Point, N. Y	June 11, 1904	Do.
Brooklyn	930	1885		1885		do	Mar. 10, 1905	Brooklyn, N. Y	Mar. 25, 1904	Do.
Bound Brook	1,016	1901		1901		Wilmington, Del	Oct. 23, 1905	Communipaw, N. J	Oct. 25, 1904	Do.
Bouwery Bay	432	1890		1890		Greenpoint, N. Y	Oct. 16, 1905	Astoria, N. Y	Oct. 15, 1904	Do.
Buffalo	1,021	1897		1896		Wilmington, Del	Apr. 17, 1905	Weehawken, N. J	Apr. 15, 1904	Do.
Castleton	1,587	1888		1888		Baltimore, Md	June 27, 1905	Clifton, N. Y	July 11, 1904	Do.
Chautauqua	663	1868		1878		Brooklyn, N. Y	May 24, 1905	Mariners Harbor, N. Y	May 13, 1904	Do.
Chicago	1,334	1901		1901		Port Richmond, N. Y	Mar. 8, 1905	Hoboken, N. J	Mar. 8, 1904	Do.
Cincinnati	1,255	1891		1891		Elizabeth, N. J	Oct. 13, 1905	do	Oct. 11, 1904	Do.
Clinton	586	1862	1904	1904		New York, N. Y	Mar. 28, 1905	Brooklyn, N. Y	Mar. 29, 1904	Do.
College Point [j]	724	1868		1890		Hoboken, N. J	Jan. 14, 1905	North Beach, N. Y	Jan. 23, 1904	Do.
Colorado	833	1885		1885		Wilmington, Del	Apr. 6, 1905	New York, N. Y	Apr. 7, 1904	Do.
Columbia	810	1895		1895		Chester, Pa	Mar. 7, 1905	Brooklyn, N. Y	Mar. 7, 1904	Do.
Columbia	586	1867		1903		Brooklyn, N. Y	Apr. 20, 1905	do	Apr. 20, 1904	Do.
Dakota	553	1880		1880		do	Sept. 26, 1905	do	Sept. 27, 1904	Do.
Easton	643	1893		1893		Wilmington, Del	Apr. 8, 1905	Communipaw, N. J	Apr. 11, 1904	Do.
Edgewater	709	1902		1902		do	Mar. 20, 1905	New York, N. Y	Mar. 19, 1904	Do.
Elizabeth	1,197	1904		1904		do	Oct. 2, 1905	Communipaw, N. J	Oct. 7, 1904	Do.

[a] Formerly John F. Carroll, 1902.
[b] Certificate issued June 3, 1905.
[c] Formerly Str. Mohawk; built below decks entirely new, 1902.
[d] Certificate issued Jan. 6, 1905.
[e] Formerly Black Bird, 1900.
[f] Formerly Dunderburg, 1900.
[g] Certificate issued Jan. 27, 1905.
[h] Formerly J. C. Doughty, 1899.
[i] Formerly F. P. James, 1902.
[j] Formerly Weehawken, 1897.

DOMESTIC VESSELS INSPECTED, YEAR ENDED DECEMBER 31, 1905—SECOND SUPERVISING DISTRICT—NEW YORK, N. Y.—Continued.

Names of vessels and class.	Gross tonnage.	Hull built.	Hull rebuilt.	Boilers built.	Boilers rebuilt.	Where built.	Date of inspection.	Where inspected.	Date of previous inspection.	Local district where previously inspected.
Ferry steamers—Continued.										
Ellis Island	800	1904		1904		Wilmington, Del	May 10, 1905	Ellis Island, N. Y	May 9, 1904	New York, N. Y.
Elmira	1,460	1905		1904		Newport News, Va	Feb. 7, 1905	Hoboken, N. J	First inspn.	
Englewood[a]	484	1896		1896		Wilmington, Del	Oct. 26, 1905	Edgewater, N. J	Oct. 28, 1904	Do.
Express	945	1889		1889		do	Sept. 15, 1905	New York, N. Y	Sept. 24, 1904	Do.
Fannie McKane	21	1872	1893	1897		Peekskill, N. Y	May 29, 1905	Canarsie, N. Y	May 19, 1904	Do.
Farragut	647	1871		1871		Brooklyn, N. Y	May 10, 1905	Brooklyn, N. Y	Mar. 24, 1904	Do.
Florida	818	1896		1896		Chester, Pa	Aug. 7, 1905	do	Aug. 9, 1904	Do.
Flushing	521	1877		1901		Wilmington, Del	June 8, 1905	Long Island City, N. Y	June 8, 1904	Do.
Frank and Helen McAvoy	75	1903		1904		Brooklyn, N. Y	June 21, 1905	Canarsie, N. Y	June 2, 1904	Do.
Fred B. Randall	50	1889		1889		Bernhards Bay, N. Y	July 15, 1905	Freeport, N. Y	July 7, 1904	Do.
Fulton	647	1871		1871		Brooklyn, N. Y	Mar. 18, 1905	Brooklyn, N. Y	Mar. 23, 1904	Do.
Garden City	825	1872		1893		Chester, Pa	June 16, 1905	Long Island City, N. Y	May 14, 1904	Do.
Goshen	1,459	1905		1903		Wilmington, Del	Jan. 5, 1905	Hoboken, N. J	First inspn.	
Goshen	1,459	1905		1903		do	Dec. 29, 1905	Jersey City, N. J	Jan. 5, 1905	Do.
Greenpoint	460	1852		1873		Williamsburg, N. Y	Sept. 28, 1905	Astoria, N. Y	Sept. 26, 1904	Do.
Haarlaem	382	1889		1890		Greenpoint, N. Y	Nov. 6, 1905	do	Nov. 2, 1904	Do.
Hackensack	917	1871		1894		Hoboken, N. J	Nov. 14, 1905	College Point, N. Y	do	Do.
Hamburg	1,266	1891		1891		Newburg, N. Y	Dec. 23, 1905	Hoboken, N. J	Dec. 23, 1904	Do.
Hamilton	584	1862		1863		Brooklyn, N. Y	Mar. 30, 1905	Brooklyn, N. Y	Apr. 9, 1904	Do.
Harry B. Hollins	1,019	1901		1900		Newburg, N. Y	Dec. 12, 1905	do	Dec. 19, 1904	Do.
Highlander	135	1876	1902	1902		Greenpoint, N. Y	May 5, 1905	West Point, N. Y	May 6, 1904	Do.
Hoboken	831	1881		1881		Newburg, N. Y	Oct. 18, 1905	Hoboken, N. J	Oct. 19, 1904	Do.
Hornet	14	1899		1889		Brooklyn, N. Y	July 18, 1905	Canarsie, N. Y	July 2, 1904	Do.
Hudson City	1,008	1867		1880		do	Sept. 16, 1905	Whitestone, N. Y	Sept. 14, 1904	Do.
Jamaica	435	1884		1903		Wilmington, Del	Sept. 22, 1905	New York, N. Y	Oct. 15, 1904	Do.
James M. Waterbury	412	1878	1904	1900		do	Nov. 9, 1905	do	Nov. 5, 1904	Do.
Jersey City	982	1862	1902	1901		Brooklyn, N. Y	Apr. 25, 1905	Hoboken, N. J	Apr. 22, 1904	Do.
John Englis	1,022	1901		1900		Newburg, N. Y	Nov. 21, 1905	Brooklyn, N. Y	Nov. 25, 1904	Do.
John G. Carlisle	710	1896		1896		Noank, Conn	June 19, 1905	Ellis Island, N. Y	June 17, 1904	Do.
John G. McCullough	1,309	1891		1890		Philadelphia, Pa	Feb. 10, 1905	Jersey City, N. J	Feb. 3, 1904	Do.
Joseph J. O'Donohue	901	1898		1897		Chester, Pa	do	Brooklyn, N. Y	Feb. 10, 1904	Do.
Kentucky[b]	567	1871		1893		Greenpoint, N. Y	Sept. 20, 1905	do	Sept. 22, 1904	Do.
Kingston	1,064	1883	1905	1905		Newburg, N. Y	Dec. 1, 1905	Weehawken, N. J	Dec. 1, 1904	Do.
Lackawanna	822	1880		1880		do	Nov. 28, 1905	Hoboken, N. J	Nov. 24, 1904	Do.
Lakewood	1,016	1901		1901		Wilmington, Del	July 22, 1905	Communipaw, N. J	July 20, 1904	Do.
Long Beach	519	1880		1880		do	Mar. 30, 1905	Long Island City, N. Y	Mar. 30, 1904	Do.
Maine	850	1888		1888		do	Sept. 28, 1905	New York, N. Y	Sept. 29, 1904	Do.
Manhattan Beach	630	1884		1884		Newburg, N. Y	June 5, 1905	Long Island City, N. Y	June 4, 1904	Do.
Maryland	859	1890		1890		Wilmington, Del	Oct. 3, 1905	New York, N. Y	Oct. 16, 1904	Do.
Mascot	32	1884		1883		Port Jefferson, N. Y	June 30, 1905	Bay Shore, N. Y	July 12, 1904	Do.

Mauch Chunk	642	1893		1903		Wilmington, Del	Apr. 17, 1905	Communipaw, N. J	Apr. 9, 1904	Do.
Mermaid	14	1878		1896		Peekskill, N. Y	Aug. 15, 1905	Wards Island, N. Y	Aug. 15, 1904	Do.
Middletown	641	1864		1892		Brooklyn, N. Y	May 13, 1905	Clifton, N. Y	May 12, 1904	Do.
Mineola	620	1868		1899		do	Mar. 20, 1905	Brooklyn, N. Y	Mar. 25, 1904	Do.
Montauk	1,087	1890		1890		Newburg, N. Y	July 10, 1905	do	Aug. 17, 1904	Do.
Montclair	1,095	1886		1886		do	Mar. 31, 1905	Hoboken, N. J	Mar. 28, 1904	Do.
Moonachie	810	1877		1877		Hoboken, N. J	Dec. 9, 1905	do	Dec. 3, 1904	Do.
Musconetcong	846	1885		1885		Newburg, N. Y	Oct. 14, 1905	do	Oct. 12, 1904	Do.
Netherlands	1,129	1893		1893		do	Sept. 16, 1905	do	Sept. 3, 1904	Do.
Newark	1,308	1902		1902		do	Oct. 27, 1905	do	Oct. 20, 1904	Do.
Newburgh	1,053	1883		1883		do	Aug. 25, 1905	Weehawken, N. J	Aug. 31, 1904	Do.
New Brunswick	1,273	1897		1897		Philadelphia, Pa	Jan. 7, 1905	Hoboken, N. J	Jan. 7, 1904	Do.
New Jersey	1,035	1873	1896	1896		Brooklyn, N. Y	June 30, 1905	do	July 1, 1904	Do.
Newtown	450	1879		1901		Wilmington, Del	Oct. 14, 1905	New York, N. Y	Oct. 14, 1904	Do.
New York	896	1892		1892		do	Apr. 10, 1905	Brooklyn, N. Y	Apr. 6, 1904	Do.
New York	642	1863		1904		Brooklyn, N. Y	June 29, 1905	do	June 28, 1904	Do.
Nevada	666	1870	1901	1891		Greenpoint, N. Y	Apr. 21, 1905	Greenpoint, N. Y	Apr. 20, 1904	Do.
North Beach	833	1901		1892		Shooters Island, N. Y	Apr. 15, 1905	North Beach, N. Y	Apr. 14, 1904	Do.
Oak Island	19	1898		1901		Glenwood, N. Y	June 21, 1905	Babylon, N. Y	June 21, 1904	Do.
Ohio	867	1887		1887		Wilmington, Del	Sept. 27, 1905	Brooklyn, N. Y	Sept. 28, 1904	Do.
Orange	1,096	1886		1886		Newburg, N. Y	Nov. 22, 1905	Hoboken, N. J	Nov. 21, 1904	Do.
Oregon	831	1885		1885		Wilmington, Del	Sept. 29, 1905	Brooklyn, N. Y	Sept. 30, 1904	Do.
Oswego	1,055	1883		1883		Newburg, N. Y	June 3, 1905	Wehawken, N. J	June 8, 1904	Do.
Passaic	755	1869	1890	1890		New York, N. Y	June 15, 1905	Jersey City, N. J	June 14, 1904	Do.
Paterson [c]	1,057	1886		1886		Philadelphia, Pa	Sept. 2, 1905	do	Aug. 15, 1904	Do.
Paunpeck	820	1882		1882		Newburg, N. Y	July 15, 1905	Hoboken, N. J	July 13, 1904	Do.
Philadelphia	1,306	1899		1899		Chester, Pa	Apr. 20, 1905	do	Apr. 11, 1904	Do.
Pierrepont	1,095	1889		1889		Newburg, N. Y	Aug. 16, 1905	Brooklyn, N. Y	Aug. 15, 1904	Do.
Pittsburg	1,273	1896		1905		Philadelphia, Pa	Dec. 21, 1905	Hoboken, N. J	Feb. 5, 1905	Do.
Pittsburg	1,273	1896		1896		do	Feb. 5, 1905	do	Feb. 10, 1904	Do.
Plainfield	1,225	1904		1903		Elizabeth, N. J	May 15, 1905	Communipaw, N. J	Apr. 6, 1904	Do.
Point O'Woods II	45	1905		1904		Bay Shore, N. Y	June 27, 1905	Bay Shore, N. Y	First inspn.	
Port Morris	561	1901		1902		Brooklyn, N. Y	Apr. 14, 1905	College Point, N. Y	Apr. 14, 1904	Do.
Princeton	888	1879		1879		do	Oct. 5, 1905	Hoboken, N. J	Oct. 5, 1904	Do.
Public Service [d]	305	1872	1903	1885		Greenpoint, N. Y	Jan. 20, 1905	Port Richmond, N. Y	Jan. 20, 1904	Do.
Public Service [d]	305	1872	1903	1885		do	Dec. 28, 1905	do	Jan. 20, 1905	Do.
Red Bank	1,016	1902		1902		Wilmington, Del	June 20, 1905	Communipaw, N. J	June 6, 1904	Do.
Refuge	33	1892		1892		do	July 18, 1905	Randalls Island, N. Y	July 20, 1904	Do.
Republic	539	1863		1863		Greenpoint, N. Y	Mar. 25, 1905	Brooklyn, N. Y	Mar. 28, 1904	Do.
Richmond	2,006	1905		1905		Port Richmond, N. Y	June 7, 1905	Port Richmond, N. Y	First inspn.	
Ridgewood [e]	981	1873		1898		Chester, Pa	Sept. 14, 1905	Jersey City, N. J	Sept. 13, 1904	Do.
Robert Garrett	1,592	1888		1888		Baltimore, Md	Apr. 24, 1905	Clifton, N. Y	Mar. 12, 1904	Do.
Rockaway	520	1879		1879		Wilmington, Del	May 17, 1905	Long Island City, N. Y	May 17, 1904	Do.
Rockland	393	1888		1888		Athens, N. Y	Mar. 24, 1905	Nyack, N. Y	Mar. 24, 1904	Do.
Rutherford [f]	864	1861		1891		Brooklyn, N. Y	Sept. 8, 1905	Jersey City, N. J	Sept. 1, 1904	Do.
Sag Harbor	630	1884		1884		Newburg, N. Y	Apr. 3, 1905	Long Island City, N. Y	Apr. 2, 1904	Do.
St. Louis	1,273	1896		1896		Philadelphia, Pa	Jan. 26, 1905	Hoboken N. J	Jan. 26, 1904	Do.
Scandinavia	1,462	1905		1905		Newport News, Va	Apr. 7, 1905	do	First inspn.	
Scranton	1,462	1904		1904		do	Feb. 4, 1905	do	do	

[a] Formerly City of Englewood, 1901.
[b] Formerly Northside, 1900.
[c] Formerly John King, 1898.
[d] Formerly Astoria, 1904.
[e] Formerly Erie, 1902.
[f] Formerly Pavonia, 1902.

DOMESTIC VESSELS INSPECTED, YEAR ENDED DECEMBER 31, 1905—SECOND SUPERVISING DISTRICT—NEW YORK, N. Y.—Continued.

Names of vessels and class.	Gross tonnage.	Hull built.	Hull rebuilt.	Boilers built.	Boilers rebuilt.	Where built.	Date of inspection.	Where inspected.	Date of previous inspection.	Local district where previously inspected.
Ferry steamers—Continued.										
Scranton	1,462	1904		1904		Newport News, Va	Dec. 12, 1905	Hoboken, N. J	Feb. 4, 1905	New York, N. Y.
Sea Gull	13	1898		1898		Brooklyn, N. Y	June 22, 1905	Bay Shore, N. Y	June 21, 1904	Do.
Sea Witch	13	1898		1898		do	do	Freeport, N. Y	June 25, 1904	Do.
Secaucus	974	1873	1892	1892		Hoboken, N. J	May 12, 1905	Hoboken, N. J	Apr. 4, 1904	Do.
Shinnecock [a]	650	1866	1898	1898		Brooklyn, N. Y	June 26, 1905	Brooklyn, N. Y	June 23, 1904	Do.
Shooter Island [b]	76	1902		1896		Shooters Island, N. Y	Dec. 29, 1904	Shooters Island, N. Y	Dec. 31, 1903	Do.
Somerset	538	1862		1884		Brooklyn, N. Y	Mar. 8, 1905	Brooklyn, N. Y	Mar. 23, 1904	Do.
Southampton	673	1869		1890		Wilmington, Del	June 14, 1905	Long Island City, N. Y	July 9, 1904	Do.
South Brooklyn	728	1887		1887		Newburg, N. Y	May 5, 1905	Brooklyn, N. Y	Apr. 30, 1904	Do.
Southfield	758	1882		1882		Clifton, N. Y	May 6, 1905	Clifton, N. Y	May 10, 1904	Do.
South Side	494	1853		1905		Williamsburg, N. Y	Sept. 21, 1905	Brooklyn, N. Y	Sept. 23, 1904	Do.
Steinway	354	1884		1884		Brooklyn, N. Y	Apr. 14, 1905	Astoria, N. Y	Apr. 16, 1904	Do.
Sterlington [c]	985	1868		1892		New York, N. Y	June 1, 1905	Jersey City, N. J	May 31, 1904	Do.
Sunshine	21	1880		1905		Newburg, N. Y	June 9, 1905	Canarsie, N. Y	July 22, 1904	Do.
Susquehanna	921	1865		1889		New York, N. Y	Oct. 5, 1905	Jersey City, N. J	Oct. 3, 1904	Do.
Syracuse	1,344	1903		1903		Newburg, N. Y	Apr. 19, 1905	Weehawken, N. J	Apr. 18, 1904	Do.
Tennessee	547	1883		1883		Greenpoint, N. Y	Sept. 19, 1905	Brooklyn, N. Y	Sept. 20, 1904	Do.
Texas	896	1890		1890		Wilmington, Del	Apr. 8, 1905	New York, N. Y	Apr. 9, 1904	Do.
The Bronx	47	1896		1900		Tottenville, N. Y	Nov. 18, 1905	do	Oct. 7, 1904	Do.
Thos. F. Gilroy	24	1894		1894		do	July 3, 1905	do	June 25, 1904	Do.
Tuxedo	1,483	1904		1904		Wilmington, Del	Feb. 16, 1905	Jersey City, N. J	Feb. 15, 1904	Philadelphia, Pa.
Uncas	127	1872	1878	1872		Mystic, Conn	July 28, 1905	Elizabeth, N. J	July 29, 1904	New York, N. Y.
Union	562	1862		1900		Greenpoint, N. Y	Mar. 21, 1905	Brooklyn, N. Y	Mar. 24, 1904	Do.
Vermont	810	1895		1895		Chester, Pa	Apr. 12, 1905	do	Apr. 8, 1904	Do.
Virginia	818	1896		1896		do	Aug. 8, 1905	New York, N. Y	Aug. 11, 1904	Do.
Warren	480	1859		1872		Brooklyn, N. Y	Dec. 23, 1905	Clifton, N. Y	Nov. 21, 1904	Do.
Washington	1,247	1891		1892		Chester, Pa	Sept. 5, 1905	Hoboken, N. J	July 25, 1904	Do.
West Brooklyn	740	1887		1887		Newburg, N. Y	May 26, 1905	Brooklyn, N. Y	May 9, 1904	Do.
Westfield	609	1862		1891		Brooklyn, N. Y	May 22, 1905	Clifton, N. Y	May 14, 1904	Do.
West Point	1,328	1901		1901		Newburg, N. Y	Feb. 11, 1905	Weehawken, N. J	Feb. 13, 1904	Do.
Whitehall	1,088	1890		1890		do	Oct. 14, 1905	Brooklyn, N. Y	Aug. 19, 1904	Do.
Wilkes-Barre	1,197	1904		1904		Wilmington, Del	Sept. 8, 1905	Communipaw, N. J	Sept. 9, 1904	Philadelphia, Pa.
Wm. H. Wickham	25	1883	1901	1900		Brooklyn, N. Y	Sept. 13, 1905	New York, N. Y	Sept. 12, 1904	New York, N. Y.
Winona	649	1869		1901		New York, N. Y	Mar. 16, 1905	Brooklyn, N. Y	Mar. 28, 1904	Do.
Wyoming	833	1885		1885		Wilmington, Del	Apr. 5, 1905	New York, N. Y	Apr. 6, 1904	Do.
Ocean freight steamers.										
Alaskan	8,671	1902		1902		San Francisco, Cal	Mar. 24, 1905	Brooklyn, N. Y	Apr. 14, 1904	San Francisco, Cal.
Aragon	1,450	1896		1896		Wyandotte, Mich	July 11, 1905	Long Island City, N. Y	July 6, 1904	Charleston, S. C.
Aschenbroedel	248	1897		1902		Elizabethport, N. J	Apr. 20, 1905	New York, N. Y	Apr. 8, 1904	New York, N. Y.
Berwind [d]	2,589	1893		1893		Stockton, England	Apr. 15, 1905	Mariners Harbor, N. Y	First inspn	

Catania	3,269	1881		1881		Glasgow, Scotland	Mar. 4, 1905	Brooklyn, N. Y.	Feb. 8, 1904	Do.
City of Everett	2,595	1894	1904	1893		Everett, Wash	Sept. 21, 1905	Long Island City, N. Y.	Sept. 22, 1904	Do.
Cretan [e]	2,350	1882		1882		Chester, Pa.	Mar. 3, 1905	Brooklyn, N. Y.	Mar. 7, 1904	Do.
David [f]	1,337	1873		1890		Dumbarton, Scotland	Jan. 18, 1905	do	Jan. 21, 1904	Philadelphia, Pa.
Dorothy [g]	2,214	1898		1898		West Hartlepool, England.	June 30, 1905	Hoboken, N. J.	June 17, 1904	Baltimore, Md.
El Cid	4,608	1899		1899		Newport News, Va.	Nov. 9, 1905	New York, N. Y.	Nov. 8, 1904	Galveston, Tex.
El Dia	4,613	1901		1901		do	July 31, 1905	do	July 28, 1904	Do.
El Dorado	3,531	1884		1884		Philadelphia, Pa.	Aug. 25, 1905	do	Aug. 30, 1904	Do.
El Mar	3,531	1889		1902		do	Nov. 17, 1905	do	Nov. 16, 1904	Do.
El Monte	3,531	1886		1886		do	July 27, 1905	do	Aug. 6, 1904	New York, N. Y.
El Paso	3,531	1884		1884		do	Sept. 1, 1905	do	Aug. 29, 1904	Galveston, Tex.
Foxhall	843	1885		1899		Newcastle, England	Nov. 4, 1905	Brooklyn, N. Y.	July 22, 1904	Philadelphia, Pa.
H. M. Whitney	2,706	1890		1890		Philadelphia, Pa.	Mar. 28, 1905	New York, N. Y.	Apr. 2, 1904	New York, N. Y.
Harry Luckenbach [h]	2,798	1881	1899	1904		West Hartlepool, England.	Mar. 18, 1905	Brooklyn, N. Y.	Mar. 15, 1904	Do.
Hawaiian	5,597	1900		1900		Chester, Pa	Dec. 19, 1905	do	Dec. 16, 1904	Do.
Lansing	4,560	1890		1890		Newcastle, England	Jan. 12, 1905	do	Jan. 16, 1904	Do.
Lassell	1,972	1879		1880		Helburn, England	July 8, 1905	do	July 16, 1904	Do.
Lewis Luckenbach [i]	3,905	1903		1903		Camden, N. J.	Dec. 31, 1904	do	Jan. 4, 1904	Philadelphia, Pa.
Ligonier	3,737	1903		1902		do	May 9, 1905	do	May 14, 1904	Do.
J. L. Luckenbach	4,920	1886		1897		Glasgow, Scotland	Jan. 27, 1905	Hoboken, N. J.	May 6, 1902	New York, N. Y.
J. M. Guffey	2,520	1902		1902		Camden, N. J.	May 30, 1905	Brooklyn, N. Y.	May 28, 1904	Do.
Julia Luckenbach	3,100	1882		1896		Rotterdam, Holland	Dec. 14, 1905	New York, N. Y.	Dec. 1, 1904	Philadelphia, Pa.
Maine	7,914	1903		1903		Sparrow Point, Md.	Nov. 9, 1905	do	May 25, 1904	Baltimore, Md.
Matanzas	3,094	1883		1903		Belfast, Ireland	Jan. 18, 1905	Brooklyn, N. Y.	Dec. 21, 1903	New York, N. Y.
Maverick	1,561	1890		1898		Baltimore, Md.	Oct. 24, 1905	Long Island City, N. Y.	Nov. 5, 1904	Do.
Northman	2,210	1901		1901		Chicago, Ill.	Apr. 17, 1905	Brooklyn, N. Y.	Apr. 27, 1904	Philadelphia, Pa.
Northtown	2,208	1901		1901		do	May 2, 1905	do	Mar. 29, 1904	Galveston, Tex.
Oregonian	5,597	1901		1900		Chester, Pa.	July 22, 1905	do	Aug. 11, 1904	San Francisco, Cal.
Orion	1,786	1888		1899		Wilmington, Del.	Mar. 22, 1905	do	Mar. 18, 1904	Boston, Mass.
Peconic	1,855	1881		1897		Liverpool, England	Apr. 22, 1905	do	First inspn.	
Pennsylvania	3,343	1873		1891	1898	Philadelphia, Pa.	Dec. 16, 1905	Jersey City, N. J.	Sept. 14, 1904	Providence, R. I.
Postmaster General	434	1898		1898		Noank, Conn.	Sept. 28, 1905	New York, N. Y.	Oct. 3, 1904	New York, N. Y.
Santurce	1,836	1898		1898		Wilmington, Del.	Dec. 28, 1905	Brooklyn, N. Y.	Dec. 6, 1904	Do.
Seaboard	662	1874		1898		do	Nov. 21, 1905	New York, N. Y.	Nov. 16, 1904	Do.
Winifred	2,551	1898		1898		Bath, Me.	Nov. 20, 1905	Brooklyn, N. Y.	Dec. 14, 1904	Do.
Inland freight steamers.										
A. C. Brown	22	1897		1897		Tottenville, N. Y.	July 31, 1905	Perth Amboy, N. J.	July 30, 1904	New York, N. Y.
Acme	128	1890		1901		Lockport, N. Y.	Sept. 13, 1905	Communipaw, N. J.	Sept. 9, 1904	Buffalo, N. Y.
Alert	170	1874		1874		Wilmington, Del.	Nov. 21, 1905	New York, N. Y.	Nov. 14, 1904	New York, N. Y.
Alsenborn	508	1888		1888		Baltimore, Md.	July 19, 1905	do	July 18, 1904	Do.
Amackassin	266	1902		1903		Tomkins Cove, N. Y.	Mar. 4, 1905	Hastings, N. Y.	Mar. 3, 1904	Do.
Amelia	123	1879		1904		Brooklyn, N. Y.	Sept. 25, 1905	Brooklyn, N. Y.	Sept. 24, 1904	Do.
Annie Laurie	352	1884		1888		Communipaw, N. J.	July 19, 1905	Hoboken, N. J.	July 18, 1904	Do.
Armitage Brearley	237	1863	1895	1895		Philadelphia, Pa.	Apr. 22, 1905	Tarrytown, N. Y.	Apr. 23, 1904	Do.

[a] Formerly Monticello, 1898.
[b] Certificate issued Jan. 14, 1905.
[c] Formerly Delaware, 1902.
[d] Formerly Boston City, 1905.
[e] Formerly Guyandotte, 1905.
[f] Formerly Santuit, 1900.
[g] Formerly Wilster, 1902.
[h] Formerly Michigan, 1901.
[i] Certificate issued Jan. 3, 1905.

DOMESTIC VESSELS INSPECTED, YEAR ENDED DECEMBER 31, 1905—SECOND SUPERVISING DISTRICT—NEW YORK, N. Y.—Continued.

Names of vessels and class.	Gross tonnage.	Hull built.	Hull rebuilt.	Boilers built.	Boilers rebuilt.	Where built.	Date of inspection.	Where inspected.	Date of previous inspection.	Local district where previously inspected.
Inland freight steamers—Con.										
Aug. Demarest	122	1888		1903		Buffalo, N. Y	July 22, 1905	West New Brighton, N. Y.	July 12, 1904	New York, N. Y.
Bessie	108	1892		1889		Athens, N. Y	June 19, 1905	Yonkers, N. Y	June 21, 1904	Do.
Border City	84	1872		1885		Fall River, Mass	Apr. 15, 1905	New York, N. Y	Mar. 21, 1904	Do.
Brinton	103	1889		1889		Philadelphia, Pa	May 1, 1905	Hoboken, N. J	Oct. 5, 1903	Do.
Buffalo	431	1905		1905		Newport News, Va	Dec. 7, 1905	do	First inspn.	
Burlington	348	1869		1887		Philadelphia, Pa	Sept. 14, 1905	Jersey City, N. J	Sept. 13, 1904	Do.
Cenerentola	248	1897		1902		Elizabethport, N. J	Mar. 4, 1905	New York, N. Y	Mar. 4, 1904	Do.
Chas. H. Perkins	118	1894		1903		Lockport, N. Y	Oct. 2, 1905	Jersey City, N. J	Sept. 30, 1904	Do.
Charleston	141	1890		1905		Buffalo, N. Y	Aug. 8, 1905	West New Brighton, N. Y.	June 11, 1904	Do.
Cinderella	166	1896		1896		Elizabeth, N. J	Nov. 21, 1905	New York, N. Y	Apr. 29, 1904	Do.
City of Detroit	118	1875		1892		Buffalo, N. Y	June 19, 1905	Jersey City, N. J	Apr. 4, 1903	Albany, N. Y.
City of Yonkers	140	1884		1884		Athens, N. Y	Sept. 25, 1905	Yonkers, N. Y	Sept. 26, 1904	New York, N. Y.
Clara	73	1877		1898		Tottenville, N. Y	Apr. 27, 1905	Brooklyn, N. Y	Apr. 27, 1904	Do.
Commodore	125	1887		1887		Wilmington, Del	Apr. 11, 1905	Hoboken, N. J	Apr. 11, 1904	Do.
Communipaw	93	1872		1886		Keyport, N. J	Oct. 11, 1905	do	Oct. 22, 1904	Do.
Deland	136	1887		1902		Lockport, N. Y	Oct. 24, 1905	Jersey City, N. J	Oct. 18, 1904	Do.
Dennis Valentine	97	1873		1882		Bordentown, N. J	Mar. 7, 1905	Brooklyn, N. Y	Mar. 6, 1904	Do.
E. Frank Coe	153	1895		1895		Athens, N. Y	Jan. 31, 1905	West Brighton, N. Y.	Jan. 25, 1904	Do.
E. T. Douglass	137	1895		1895		Buffalo, N. Y	Sept. 14, 1905	Jersey City, N. J	Sept. 13, 1904	Do.
Edwin Dayton	95	1881		1892		Mystic, Conn	Sept. 8, 1905	New York, N. Y	Sept. 8, 1904	Do.
Eugene Grasselli	157	1899		1899		Camden, N. J	June 19, 1905	Elizabethport, N. J	June 18, 1904	Do.
Express	178	1852	1901	1878		Belleville, N. J	Apr. 17, 1905	Newark, N. J	Apr. 15, 1904	Do.
Fannie Woodall	167	1878		1882		Wilmington, Del	Aug. 7, 1905	Peekskill, N. Y	Aug. 6, 1904	Do.
Florence	110	1892		1892		do	May 25, 1905	Hoboken, N. J	June 9, 1904	Do.
Gen'l McCallum	1,396	1864		1899		Glasgow, Scotland	Oct. 14, 1905	Weehawken, N. J	Nov. 7, 1904	Do.
Globe	137	1900		1900		Richmond, Me	May 22, 1905	New York, N. Y	May 20, 1904	Do.
Gowanda	130	1880		1903		Ithaca, N. Y	Aug. 16, 1905	do	Aug. 20, 1904	Do.
Greenwich	125	1879		1892		Wilmington, Del	Oct. 16, 1905	Newark, N. J	Oct. 17, 1904	Do.
Greylock	87	1866	1901	1896		Port Richmond, N. Y.	May 20, 1905	Elizabethport, N. J	May 18, 1904	Do.
Guy G. Major	174	1901		1900		Newburg, N. Y	July 7, 1905	Port Richmond, N. Y.	July 7, 1904	Do.
Gypsum	81	1889		1889		Perth Amboy, N. J	June 16, 1905	do	June 16, 1904	Do.
H. C. French	142	1888		1888		Lockport, N. Y	July 28, 1905	Brooklyn, N. Y	July 26, 1904	New London, Conn.
Hackensack	124	1863		1884		Belleville, N. J	Oct. 23, 1905	Port Richmond, N. Y.	Oct. 12, 1904	New York, N. Y.
Harry	77	1881		1898		Tottenville, N. Y	Mar. 10, 1905	Newark, N. J	Mar. 14, 1904	Do.
Hattie Thomas	57	1890		1899		New Haven, Conn	Sept. 26, 1905	West New Brighton, N. Y.	Aug. 17, 1904	Do.
Henriette	97	1889		1900		Boston, Mass	Nov. 20, 1905	Newark, N. J	Nov. 19, 1904	Do.
Howard	179	1882		1895		Kingston, N. Y	Apr. 26, 1905	Elizabeth, N. J	Apr. 25, 1904	Do.
Islander	248	1901		1901		Tomkins Cove, N. Y.	Jan. 18, 1905	New York, N. Y	Jan. 18, 1904	Do.

Islander	91	1890		1902		Adams Wharf, N. J	June 5, 1905	Brooklyn, N. Y	June 17, 1904	New London, Conn.
J. H. Taylor	134	1884		1885		Rochester, N. Y	June 2, 1905	New Brighton, N. Y	May 28, 1904	New York, N. Y.
J. W. Wonson	108	1902		1902		Perth Amboy, N. J	July 1, 1905	Brooklyn, N. Y	July 1, 1904	Do.
Jerome B. King	97	1878	1903	1893		Brooklyn, N. Y	June 27, 1905	Port Richmond, N. Y	June 27, 1904	Do.
John E. Tygert	226	1879	1905	1875		Philadelphia, Pa	Nov. 9, 1905	New York, N. Y	July 11, 1904	Do.
John M. Worth	442	1905		1904		Tottenville, N. Y	Feb. 8, 1905	Tottenville, N. Y	First inspn	
Kirk S. Blanchard	112	1887		1896		Rochester, N. Y	Sept. 15, 1905	Jersey City, N. J	Sept. 14, 1904	Do.
Lillian	174	1902		1902		Athens, N. Y	Dec. 1, 1905	New York, N. Y	Nov. 30, 1904	Do.
Lizzie Henderson	146	1876	1896	1901		Philadelphia, Pa	Aug. 26, 1905	Long Island City, N. Y	Aug. 29, 1904	Do.
Lizzie M. Conklin	86	1886		1889		Tottenville, N. Y	Jan. 12, 1905	New York, N. Y	Jan. 16, 1904	Do.
Lorillard Brick Works No. 1	228	1887		1900		Wilmington, Del	Aug. 31, 1905	Perth Amboy, N. J	Aug. 26, 1904	Do.
M. Moran [a]	137	1885		1897		Lockport, N. Y	Dec. 28, 1904	New York, N. Y	Dec. 23, 1903	Do.
Mabel & Ray	26	1899		1901		Stratford, Conn	Jan. 23, 1905	Brooklyn, N. Y	Jan. 25, 1904	Do.
McKeever Bros. [b]	107	1889		1901		Wilmington, Del	Dec. 11, 1905	do	Dec. 7, 1904	Do.
Maid of Kent	171	1881		1881		do	May 6, 1905	Communipaw, N. J	May 5, 1904	Do.
Manager	325	1903		1903		Noank, Conn	Sept. 22, 1905	Brooklyn, N. Y	Sept. 22, 1904	Do.
Marian	128	1889		1898		Buffalo, N. Y	Nov. 23, 1905	West New Brighton, N. Y.	Nov. 1, 1904	Do.
Marie	121	1894		1895		Washington, N. C	July 10, 1905	New York, N. Y	Dec. 1, 1903	Do.
Middlesex	188	1871		1904		Portland, Conn	Jan. 2, 1905	Hoboken, N. J	Dec. 30, 1903	Do.
Morgan	137	1868	1895	1897		Brooklyn, N. Y	Sept. 20, 1905	Shady Side, N. J	Sept. 19, 1904	Do.
Mohawk	2,783	1896	1905	1900		Chester, Pa	Apr. 28, 1905	Brooklyn, N. Y	Apr. 6, 1904	New London, Conn.
Mount Morris	400	1899		1900		Athens, N. Y	Jan. 27, 1905	New York, N. Y	Jan. 27, 1904	New York, N. Y.
Nanticoke	282	1882		1892		Pocomoke City, Md	Apr. 21, 1905	Newark, N. J	Apr. 21, 1904	Do.
National	78	1897		1897		Newburg, N. Y	Jan. 4, 1905	Brooklyn, N. Y	Jan. 4, 1904	Do.
Nellie	141	1884		1884		Wilmington, Del	Sept. 29, 1905	New York, N. Y	Sept. 29, 1904	Do.
New York	126	1882		1900		Brooklyn, N. Y	Oct. 2, 1905	Hoboken, N. J	Aug. 5, 1903	Do.
New York Central No. 4	457	1900		1900		Port Richmond, N. Y	Aug. 7, 1905	Weehawken, N. J	Aug. 8, 1904	Do.
New York Central No. 5 [c]	380	1879		1897		Philadelphia, Pa	Sept. 25, 1905	do	Sept. 26, 1904	Do.
New York Central No. 14 [d]	404	1890		1890		Elm Park, N. Y	Dec. 26, 1905	do	Dec. 27, 1904	Do.
New York Central No. 15 [e]	176	1896		1890		Brooklyn, N. Y	Feb. 14, 1905	do	Feb. 15, 1904	Do.
New York Central No. 16 [f]	404	1891		1890		Elm Park, N. Y	Feb. 27, 1905	do	Feb. 28, 1904	Do.
Ox	109	1866	1898	1885		Brooklyn, N. Y	May 10, 1905	Brooklyn, N. Y	May 9, 1904	Do.
Paragon	142	1898		1905		Lockport, N. Y	May 9, 1905	do	May 19, 1904	Buffalo, N. Y.
Peekskill	190	1889		1894		Grassy Point, N. Y	Apr. 4, 1905	Peekskill, N. Y	Apr. 4, 1904	New York, N. Y.
Peter Hagen	174	1867		1882		Philadelphia, Pa	Aug. 26, 1905	West New Brighton, N. Y.	Aug. 10, 1904	Do.
Phenix	85	1881		1881		Brooklyn, N. Y	July 29, 1905	do	July 29, 1904	Do.
Pioneer	329	1865		1890		do	Dec. 8, 1905	Newark, N. J	Dec. 19, 1904	Do.
Puritan	126	1892		1892		Buffalo, N. Y	Aug. 21, 1905	Jersey City, N. J	Sept. 15, 1904	Do.
Raleigh	260	1872	1894	1884		Portsmouth, Va	July 8, 1905	Nyack, N. Y	July 11, 1904	Do.
Rancocas	150	1886		1897		Wilmington, Del	May 24, 1905	Port Richmond, N. Y	May 28, 1904	New Haven, Conn.
Renovator	310	1865	1893	1900		New York, N. Y	Jan. 13, 1905	Hoboken, N. J	Nov. 30, 1903	New York, N. Y.
Richmond	68	1863	1904	1891		Chester, Pa	Sept. 15, 1905	Jersey City, N. J	Sept. 6, 1904	Do.
Ridgeway Park	87	1881		1902		Wilmington, Del	May 22, 1905	Hoboken, N. J	May 23, 1904	Do.
Riverside	97	1892		1903		do	July 1, 1905	Brooklyn, N. Y	July 1, 1904	Do.
Rockaway	92	1883		1883		Rockaway, N. Y	Aug. 26, 1905	Jersey City, N. J	Sept. 12, 1904	Do.
Rosalie	500	1886		1886		Port Jefferson, N. Y	Mar. 16, 1905	Brooklyn, N. Y	Mar. 17, 1904	Do.

[a] Certificate issued Mar. 10, 1905.
[b] Formerly Walter W. 1899.
[c] Formerly New York Central Lighterage Co. No. 5, 1899.
[d] Formerly New York Central Lighterage Co. No. 14, 1899.
[e] Formerly New York Central Lighterage Co. No. 15, 1899.
[f] Formerly New York Central Lighterage Co. No. 16, 1899.

DOMESTIC VESSELS INSPECTED, YEAR ENDED DECEMBER 31, 1905—SECOND SUPERVISING DISTRICT—NEW YORK, N. Y.—Continued.

Names of vessels and class.	Gross tonnage.	Hull built.	Hull rebuilt.	Boilers built.	Boilers rebuilt.	Where built.	Date of inspection.	Where inspected.	Date of previous inspection.	Local district where previously inspected.
Inland freight steamers—Con.										
Rosebud [a]	200	1898		1898		Astoria, N. Y	Dec. 12, 1905	Brooklyn, N. Y	Sept. 2, 1898	New York, N. Y.
S. D. Combes	86	1900		1900		East Rockaway, N.Y.	Sept. 20, 1905	West New Brighton, N. Y.	Sept. 19, 1904	Do.
Sagamore	253	1879	1904	1889		Greenpoint, N. Y	May 6, 1905	New York, N. Y	May 1, 1904	Do.
Sargent L. Saville	92	1899		1897		Athens, N. Y	Dec. 11, 1905	Brooklyn, N. Y	Nov. 22, 1904	Do.
Sentinel	110	1862	1902	1902		East Haddam, Conn	Oct. 23, 1905	Port Richmond, N. Y.	Oct. 22, 1904	Do.
Shackamaxon	383	1877		1866		Camden, N. J	Mar. 29, 1905	Hoboken, N. J	Mar. 26, 1904	Do.
Shamokin [b]	120	1898		1898		Tomkins Cove, N. Y	Dec. 12, 1905	Jersey City, N. J	Dec. 16, 1904	Do.
Smith, Davis & Co	131	1886		1887		Lockport, N. Y	May 8, 1905	Brooklyn, N. Y	Dec. 12, 1904	Do.
Terminal	129	1891		1891		Brooklyn, N. Y	June 20, 1905	Hoboken, N. J	June 20, 1904	Do.
Trenton	85	1894		1894		Philadelphia, Pa	May 8, 1905	West New Brighton, N. Y.	May 9, 1904	Do.
Two Brothers	139	1881		1889		Brooklyn, N. Y	Jan. 6, 1905	New York, N. Y	July 19, 1901	Do.
U. F. Washburn	141	1890		1894		Lockport, N. Y	June 22, 1905	Communipaw, N. J	June 20, 1904	Do.
Wachusett	75	1891		1890		Newburg, N. Y	Apr. 22, 1905	Constable Hook, N. J	Apr. 23, 1904	Do.
William Marvel	86	1875		1903		Fall River, Mass	Apr. 27, 1905	West New Brighton, N. Y.	Apr. 12, 1904	Do.
Windsor	102	1890		1890		Tottenville, N. Y	Nov. 15, 1905	Port Richmond, N. Y.	Nov. 15, 1904	Do.
Zenobia	142	1881		1896		Lockport, N. Y	Nov. 27, 1905	Brooklyn, N. Y	Sept. 2, 1904	Albany, N. Y.
Ocean towing steamers.										
Abram P. Skidmore	73	1880		1903		Kingston, N. Y	Nov. 27, 1905	Long Island City, N. Y	Nov. 28, 1904	New York, N. Y.
Agnes [c]	54	1878	1900	1878		Brooklyn, N. Y	Sept. 25, 1905	New York, N. Y	Sept. 25, 1904	Do.
Alison Briggs	93	1901		1885		Athens, N. Y	Nov. 8, 1905	....do	Nov. 5, 1904	Do.
Anna W	204	1901		1901		Philadelphia, Pa	Aug. 24, 1905	....do	Aug. 24, 1904	Mobile, Ala.
Arthur W. Palmer	117	1899		1902		Athens, N. Y	Mar. 20, 1905	Brooklyn, N. Y	Mar. 21, 1904	New York, N. Y.
Ashbourne	115	1895		1895		Philadelphia, Pa	Oct. 14, 1905	Perth Amboy, N. J	Oct. 17, 1904	Do.
Astral	616	1903		1903		....do	Oct. 31, 1905	Long Island City, N. Y	Nov. 23, 1904	Do.
Belvidere	106	1888		1888		South Amboy, N. J	Aug. 5, 1905	Hoboken, N. J	Aug. 5, 1904	Do.
Bouker	125	1902		1901		Tottenville, N. Y	Jan. 21, 1905	New York, N. Y	Jan. 21, 1904	Do.
Bulley [d]	99	1894		1894		Camden, N. J	June 14, 1905	Jersey City, N. J	June 18, 1904	Do.
Charles E. Matthews	164	1902		1902		Philadelphia, Pa	Aug. 29, 1905	New York, N. Y	Aug. 29, 1904	Do.
Cheektowaga	331	1902		1900		Port Richmond, N. Y	Sept. 9, 1905	Perth Amboy, N. J	Sept. 9, 1904	Boston, Mass.
Chief	226	1893		1902		Wilmington, Del	Mar. 31, 1905	Brooklyn, N. Y	Jan. 4, 1904	Mobile, Ala.
Christobal [e]	161	1905		1905		Tottenville, N. Y	Feb. 20, 1905	New York, N. Y	First inspn.	
Coastwise	268	1900		1900		Perth Amboy, N. J	Dec. 1, 1905	Port Richmond, N. Y	Dec. 1, 1904	New York, N. Y.
Col. John F. Gaynor	153	1893		1899		Philadelphia, Pa	Sept. 11, 1905	Brooklyn, N. Y	Sept. 9, 1904	Do.
D. S. Arnott	93	1893		1893		Tottenville, N. Y	Nov. 10, 1905	Jersey City, N. J	Nov. 7, 1904	Do.
Daniel Willard	361	1890		1885		Camden, N. J	Apr. 28, 1905	Port Richmond, N. Y	Mar. 23, 1904	Do.
David B. Dearborn	135	1902		1902		Noank, Conn	Nov. 17, 1905	New York, N. Y	Nov. 14, 1904	Do.
Defiance	154	1903		1903		Baltimore, Md	Apr. 12, 1905	Brooklyn, N. Y	Apr. 8, 1904	Do.

De Witt C. Ivins	121	1900		1900		Philadelphia, Pa	Mar. 28,1905	....do	Mar. 28,1904	Do.
E. S. Atwood	94	1890	1902	1890		Noank, Conn	Oct. 16,1905	....do	Oct. 17,1904	Do.
Edgar F. Luckenbach	272	1891		1897		Camden, N. J	Mar. 17,1905	....do	Mar. 14,1904	Norfolk, Va.
Edna V. Crew	161	1901		1900		Noank, Conn	Mar. 14,1905	New York, N. Y	Mar. 9,1904	New York, N. Y.
Edward M. Timmins	68	1889		1889		Sleightsburg, N. Y	Aug. 31,1905	....do	Aug. 30,1904	Do.
Elmer A. Keeler	236	1904		1904		Port Richmond, N. Y	Nov. 20,1905	Port Richmond, N. Y	Nov. 18,1904	Do.
Emma Kate Ross	127	1882		1904		Camden, N. J	Aug. 9,1905	Clifton, N. Y	Aug. 9,1904	Do.
El Amigo	150	1899		1899		Newport News, Va	June 26,1905	New York, N. Y	June 24,1904	Do.
Eli B. Conine	117	1900		1900		Wilmington, Del	Mar. 11,1905	Port Richmond, N. Y	Mar. 10,1904	Do.
Fred B. Dalzell	82	1901		1901		Athens, N. Y	June 23,1905	Brooklyn, N. Y	June 24,1904	Do.
Fred E. Richards	357	1900		1900		Philadelphia, Pa	Sept. 27,1905	....do	Oct. 3,1904	Portland, Me.
George Hughes	177	1900		1893		Pocomoke City, Md	Dec. 4,1905	Hoboken, N. J	Dec. 23,1904	New York, N. Y.
Gerry	273	1900		1900		Wilmington, Del	Mar. 28,1905	Brooklyn, N. J	Feb. 9,1904	Mobile, Ala.
Gypsum King	562	1899		1899		Port Richmond, N. Y	June 24,1905	Port Richmond, N. Y	June 30,1904	New York, N. Y.
H. A. Baxter	87	1889		1905		Milford, Del	Mar. 21, 1905	Jersey City, N. J	Mar. 2,1904	Philadelphia, Pa.
H. B. Chamberlain	164	1902		1902		Philadelphia, Pa	Oct. 2,1905	New York, N. Y	Oct. 1,1904	New York, N. Y.
Harry G. Runkle	164	1902		1902		....do	Sept 25,1905	....do	Sept. 23,1904	Do.
Henry S. Beard	119	1900		1902		Brooklyn, N. Y	Mar. 27,1905	Brooklyn, N. Y	Mar. 28,1904	Do.
Hercules	155	1880		1896		Camden, N. J	Apr. 12,1905	New York, N. Y	Apr. 11,1904	Do.
Hercules	163	1905		1904		Tomkins Cove, N. Y	Mar. 27,1905	....do	First inspn	
Hokendauqua [f] [g]	137	1880		1897		Newburg, N. Y	Dec. 8,1904	Communipaw, N. J	Dec. 21,1903	Do.
Hokendauqua	137	1880		1897		....do	Dec. 8,1905	Perth Amboy, N. J	Dec. 8,1904	Do.
Honeybrook	373	1902		1902		Philadelphia, Pa	Dec. 14,1905	Hoboken, N. J	Dec. 13,1904	Do.
John A. Bouker	119	1896		1896		Noank, Conn	Sept. 8,1905	....do	Sept. 9,1904	Do.
Johnstown	225	1900		1900		Wilmington, Del	Aug. 12,1905	....do	Aug. 12,1904	Do.
Lancaster	223	1902		1902		Richmond, Va	Aug. 2,1905	....do	Aug. 2,1904	Do.
Lehigh	446	1900		1900		Port Richmond, N. Y	May 4,1905	Jersey City, N. J	May 9,1904	Do.
Luzerne [h]	165	1899		1899		....do	Feb. 28,1905	Hoboken, N. J	Mar. 1,1904	Do.
M. Moran	121	1900		1900		Philadelphia, Pa	Apr. 24,1905	Brooklyn, N. Y	Apr. 23,1904	Do.
Maria Hoffman	78	1890		1895		Brooklyn, N. Y	May 15,1905	New York, N. Y	May 14,1904	Do.
Mutual	66	1890		1890		Athens, N. Y	Oct. 14,1905	....do	Oct. 13,1904	Do.
Nottingham	408	1894		1894		Camden, N. J	Aug. 8,1905	Hoboken, N. J	Aug. 5,1904	Do.
O. L. Halenbeck	198	1898		1898		Philadelphia, Pa	Nov. 27,1905	Brooklyn, N. Y	Nov. 28,1904	Do.
Orange	130	1903		1903		Camden, N. J	Aug. 5,1905	Hoboken, N. J	Aug. 3,1904	Do.
Port Chester	138	1902		1902		Tottenville, N. Y	Jan. 13,1905	Long Island City, N. Y	Dec. 31,1903	Do.
Pencoyd	119	1897		1897		Philadelphia, Pa	Oct. 28,1905	Perth Amboy, N. J	Nov. 2,1904	Do.
Plymouth	373	1892		1905		....do	Aug. 29,1905	Hoboken, N. J	Sept. 2,1904	Do.
R. B. Little	99	1896		1903		Port Richmond, N. Y	June 17,1905	Jersey City, N. J	June 14,1904	Providence, R. I.
R. J. Moran	75	1886		1881		Athens, N. Y	Oct. 11,1905	Brooklyn, N. Y	Oct. 3,1904	New York, N. Y.
Resolute	120	1881		1900		Fly Mountain, N. Y	Dec. 20,1905	Jersey City, N. J	Jan. 2,1905	New Haven, Conn.
Robert Robinson	74	1872	1896	1899		Philadelphia, Pa	Sept. 16,1905	....do	Sept. 15,1904	New York, N. Y.
Robert Rogers	179	1904		1904		Tottenville, N. Y	June 19,1905	New York, N. Y	June 16,1904	Do.
S. O. Co. No. 1 [i]	128	1889		1901		Newburg, N. Y	Feb. 4,1905	Long Island City, N. Y	Feb. 2,1904	Do.
S. O. Co. No. 2	157	1898		1898		Philadelphia, Pa	Oct. 25,1905	....do	Nov. 17,1904	Portland, Me.
S. O. Co. No. 3 [j]	94	1890		1890		Athens, N. Y	Oct. 18,1905	....do	Oct. 29,1904	Do.
S. O. Co. No. 4	145	1899		1899		Camden, N. J	May 22,1905	....do	May 21,1904	Do.
S. O. Co. No. 7 [k]	117	1898		1898		Philadelphia, Pa	July 14,1905	....do	July 14,1904	New York, N. Y.

[a] Formerly Ed. Ward, 1905.
[b] Formerly Ruth, 1899.
[c] Formerly Daylight, 1900.
[d] Formerly (a) Dorothy Annan, 1899; (b) George D. Kuper, 1903.
[e] Formerly William J. Dailey, 1905.
[f] Certificate issued Jan. 18, 1905.
[g] Formerly Robert Lockhart, 1899.
[h] Formerly Fred B. Dalzell, 1899.
[i] Formerly Astral, 1899.
[j] Formerly Acme, 1899.
[k] Formerly De Witt C. Ivins, 1899.

DOMESTIC VESSELS INSPECTED, YEAR ENDED DECEMBER 31, 1905—SECOND SUPERVISING DISTRICT—NEW YORK, N. Y.—Continued.

Names of vessels and class.	Gross tonnage.	Hull built.	Hull rebuilt.	Boilers built.	Boilers rebuilt.	Where built.	Date of inspection.	Where inspected.	Date of previous inspection.	Local district where previously inspected.
Ocean towing steamers—Con.										
S. O. Co. No. 12	158	1903		1903		Camden, N. J.	Feb. 17, 1905	Long Island City, N. Y.	Feb. 15, 1904	New York, N. Y.
S. O. Co. No. 14	164	1902		1902		Philadelphia, Pa.	Dec. 9, 1905	do	Dec. 24, 1904	Do.
S. O. Co. No. 15	164	1903		1902		do	Dec. 6, 1905	do	Dec. 27, 1904	Do.
Scranton	300	1902		1903		Camden, N. J.	June 27, 1905	Hoboken, N. J.	June 27, 1904	Do.
Senator Rice	98	1902		1902		Rondout, N. Y.	Dec. 23, 1905	New York, N. Y.	Dec. 15, 1904	Do.
Shawanese	199	1888		1899		Newburg, N. Y.	Oct. 21, 1905	Elizabeth, N. J.	Oct. 27, 1904	Do.
Standard	374	1901		1901		Port Richmond, N. Y.	June 5, 1905	Long Island City, N. Y.	Apr. 28, 1904	Do.
T. J. Scully	130	1904		1904		do	Sept. 20, 1905	Port Richmond, N. Y.	Sept. 20, 1904	Do.
Transit	113	1884	1892	1884		Philadelphia, Pa	June 26, 1905	Perth Amboy, N. J.	July 11, 1904	Do.
W. E. Gladwish	121	1873		1900		do	Apr. 21, 1905	Port Richmond, N. Y.	Apr. 15, 1904	Do.
Walter Tracy	98	1900		1886		Port Richmond, N. Y.	Aug. 26, 1905	do	Aug. 11, 1904	Do.
Walter A. Luckenbach	434	1899		1898		Philadelphia, Pa	Mar. 3, 1905	Brooklyn, N. Y.	Feb. 29, 1904	Norfolk, Va.
Washington	181	1905		1905		Port Richmond, N. Y	Dec. 15, 1905	Port Richmond, N. Y.	First inspn.	
Wellington	334	1904		1904		do	Aug. 14, 1905	do	Aug. 11, 1904	New York, N. Y.
Wilkesbarre	87	1898		1899		Solomons, Md	Aug. 9, 1905	West New Brighton, N. Y.	Aug. 9, 1904	Do.
William H. Taylor	226	1903		1903		Noank, Conn.	Dec. 7, 1905	Communipaw, N. J.	Dec. 12, 1904	Do.
Wyalusing[a]	149	1881	1899	1899		Newburg, N. Y.	Dec. 28, 1905	Perth Amboy, N. J.	Jan. 5, 1905	Do.
Wyalusing[a]	149	1881	1899	1899		do	Jan. 5, 1905	Communipaw, N. J.	Jan. 2, 1904	Do.
Wyomissing	222	1904		1903		Philadelphia, Pa	Jan. 16, 1905	Perth Amboy, N. J.	Jan. 20, 1904	Philadelphia, Pa.
Inland towing steamers.										
A. A. Sumner	119	1896		1896		Newburg, N. Y.	Dec. 19, 1905	Bayonne, N. J.	Dec. 15, 1904	New York, N. Y.
A. C. Rose	150	1888		1888		Philadelphia, Pa	Mar. 8, 1905	Port Richmond, N. Y.	Mar. 8, 1904	Do.
A. C. Sumner	68	1874		1874		Brooklyn, N. Y	Sept. 11, 1905	Jersey City, N. J	Sept. 9, 1904	Do.
A. J. Hoole	21	1872		1884		Buffalo, N. Y.	Apr. 10, 1905	do	July 8, 1903	Do.
A. W. Smith	64	1904		1892		Athens, N. Y.	July 12, 1905	New York, N. Y.	July 12, 1904	Albany, N. Y.
Addie Richardson	14	1886	1900	1892		Monmouth Beach, N. J.	Oct. 20, 1905	Peekskill, N. Y.	Oct. 18, 1904	New York, N. Y.
Adelaide	61	1864	1884	1879		Bordentown, N. J.	Aug. 22, 1905	New York, N. Y.	Aug. 31, 1904	Do.
Admiral Dewey[b]	152	1900		1900		Port Richmond, N. Y	Dec. 31, 1904	Brooklyn, N. Y	Dec. 31, 1903	Do.
Admiral Dewey	152	1900		1900		do	Dec. 15, 1905	do	Dec. 31, 1904	Do.
Admiral Farragut	41	1865	1893	1893		Philadelphia, Pa	Dec. 30, 1905	Perth Amboy, N. J.	May 18, 1904	New London, Conn.
Adonis	40	1902		1902		Athens, N. Y.	Apr. 19, 1905	New York, N. Y.	Apr. 18, 1904	New York, N. Y.
Alexander Barkley	41	1874	1887	1894		Albany, N. Y.	Apr. 25, 1905	do	Apr. 23, 1904	Do.
Alfred J. Murray	27	1892		1892		Brooklyn, N. Y	Sept. 9, 1905	Brooklyn, N. Y	Sept. 10, 1904	Do.
Alice[c]	37	1880		1880		do	Apr. 1, 1905	do	Mar. 31, 1904	Do.
Alice P. Egbert	27	1882		1881		Baltimore, Md.	Mar. 27, 1905	Jersey City, N. J	Mar. 19, 1904	Do.
Allentown[d]	46	1879		1879		Tottenville, N. Y.	Sept. 16, 1905	Perth Amboy, N. J.	Sept. 16, 1904	Do.

Alvin Brown	17	1884	....	1890	....	Richmond, Va	Apr. 29, 1905	Newark, N. J	May 4, 1904	Do.
American[a]	155	1901	....	1902	....	Wilmington, Del	Feb. 11, 1905	West Brighton, N. Y	Feb. 11, 1904	Do.
Anna J. Kipp	42	1873	....	1881	....	Camden, N. J	July 29, 1905	Jersey City, N. J	July 30, 1904	Do.
Annie L	47	1888	....	1903	....	Tottenville, N. Y	July 19, 1905	Brooklyn, N. Y	July 20, 1904	Do.
Annie R. Wood	25	1875	....	1890	....	Philadelphia, Pa	Sept. 30, 1905	Jersey City, N. J	July 19, 1904	Do.
Anthracite	76	1895	....	1903	....	....do	Oct. 23, 1905	West New Brighton, N. Y.	Dec. 16, 1904	Do.
Archy Crossman	51	1888	....	1888	....	Jersey City, N. J	June 29, 1905	Jersey City, N. J	June 27, 1904	Do.
Archibald Watt	32	1888	....	1888	....	Athens, N. Y	July 25, 1905	....do	July 25, 1904	Do.
Arrow	50	1881	....	1880	....	Brooklyn, N. Y	Apr. 8, 1905	New York, N. Y	Apr. 11, 1904	Do.
Arthur Kill	95	1905	....	1904	....	Tottenville, N. Y	Jan. 4, 1905	Perth Amboy, N. J	First inspn.	
Atlantic	77	1873	....	1901	....	Boston, Mass	Apr. 16, 1905	Brooklyn, N. Y	Apr. 1, 1904	Do.
Atlas	33	1864	....	1897	....	Philadelphia, Pa	Mar. 15, 1905	Long Island City, N. Y	Feb. 9, 1904	Do.
B. S. Cronin	16	1882	....	1898	....	Brooklyn, N. Y	June 3, 1905	Brooklyn, N. Y	June 4, 1904	Do.
Bailey[f]	24	1872	1900	1894	....	Elizabeth, N. J	Aug. 1, 1905	....do	Aug. 1, 1904	Do.
Baltic	63	1872	....	1881	....	Brooklyn, N. Y	Nov. 18, 1905	New York, N. Y	Nov. 18, 1904	Do.
Baltimore	177	1893	....	1893	....	Sparrow Point, Md	July 17, 1905	Port Richmond, N. Y	July 15, 1904	Do.
Battler	138	1881	....	1902	....	Philadelphia, Pa	Sept. 8, 1905	Long Island City, N. Y	Sept. 8, 1904	Do.
Bayonne	122	1882	....	1890	....	Noank, Conn	July 31, 1905	Communipaw, N. J	June 23, 1904	Do.
Belle	29	1897	....	1889	....	New Baltimore, N. Y	June 14, 1905	New York, N. Y	June 13, 1904	Do.
Belle McWilliams	68	1864	1894	1897	....	Brooklyn, N. Y	July 7, 1905	Jersey City, N. J	July 19, 1904	Do.
Ben	45	1875	1901	1901	....	....do	Oct. 28, 1905	Brooklyn, N. Y	Oct. 29, 1904	Do.
Bernice[g]	26	1893	....	1892	....	....do	Mar. 14, 1905	Communipaw, N. J	Mar. 14, 1904	Do.
Blue Stone	20	1868	....	1882	....	Philadelphia, Pa	July 12, 1905	West New Brighton, N. Y.	July 6, 1904	Do.
Blue Stone Company	21	1869	1889	1884	....	Malden, N. Y	June 28, 1905	Hoboken, N. J	June 28, 1904	Do.
Brandon	47	1874	....	1888	....	Baltimore, Md	June 6, 1905	Port Richmond, N. Y	June 1, 1904	Do.
Brilliant	44	1873	1882	1882	....	Philadelphia, Pa	Dec. 18, 1905	Long Island City, N. Y	Dec. 17, 1904	Do.
Brooklyn[h]	32	1881	....	1882	....	New York, N. Y	Mar. 28, 1905	Brooklyn, N. Y	Dec. 16, 1903	Do.
Buffalo	79	1873	....	1889	....	Brooklyn, N. Y	Mar. 24, 1905	Jersey City, N. J	Jan. 28, 1904	Do.
C. C. Clarke	150	1886	....	1890	....	Camden, N. J	Dec. 11, 1905	Weehawken, N. J	Dec. 12, 1904	Do.
C. D. Meneely	26	1893	....	1901	....	New Baltimore, N. Y	July 11, 1905	Hoboken, N. J	July 11, 1904	Do.
C. F. Roe	27	1873	....	1883	....	Athens, N. Y	July 14, 1905	New York, N. Y	July 9, 1904	Do.
C. J. Saxe	30	1860	....	1882	....	Jersey City, N. J	July 6, 1905	Jersey City, N. J	July 2, 1904	Do.
C. M. Depew	176	1901	....	1900	....	Newburg, N. Y	Feb. 20, 1905	Weehawken, N. J	Feb. 23, 1904	Do.
C. N. Kimpland	131	1892	....	1892	....	Camden, N. J	Mar. 16, 1905	Brooklyn, N. Y	Mar. 14, 1904	Do.
C. P. Raymond	111	1893	....	1893	....	Athens, N. Y	Aug. 7, 1905	....do	Aug. 5, 1904	Do.
C. W. Standart	59	1874	....	1894	....	Jersey City, N. J	Aug. 4, 1905	....do	Apr. 27, 1904	Do.
Canisteo[i]	51	1864	1882	1880	....	Philadelphia, Pa	Nov. 21, 1905	Jersey City, N. J	Oct. 2, 1903	Do.
Carrie	27	1869	1886	1895	....	New Brunswick, N. J	Aug. 8, 1905	West New Brighton, N. Y.	Aug. 9, 1904	Do.
Carroll Boys	21	1892	....	1892	....	Brooklyn, N. Y	Oct. 4, 1905	Brooklyn, N. Y	Oct. 4, 1904	Do.
Castle Point[j]	43	1864	....	1891	....	Buffalo, N. Y	Apr. 24, 1905	New York, N. Y	Apr. 23, 1904	Do.
Castor	73	1891	....	1891	....	Perth Amboy, N. J	Sept. 22, 1905	Brooklyn, N. Y	Sept. 26, 1904	Do.

[a] Formerly Gov. H. M. Hoyt, 1899.
[b] Certificate issued Jan. 3, 1905.
[c] Formerly: (a) New York Central Lighterage Co. No. 7, 1899; (b) New York Central No. 7, 1892.
[d] Formerly Sallie P. Linderman, 1899.
[e] Formerly John L. Brainard, 1903.
[f] Formerly Annie Williams, 1901.
[g] Formerly Estelle, 1899.
[h] Formerly George S. Townsend, 1904.
[i] Formerly Don Juan, 1902.
[j] Formerly Thomas Shortland, 1899.

DOMESTIC VESSELS INSPECTED, YEAR ENDED DECEMBER 31, 1905—SECOND SUPERVISING DISTRICT—NEW YORK, N. Y.—Continued.

Names of vessels and class.	Gross tonnage.	Hull built.	Hull rebuilt.	Boilers built.	Boilers rebuilt.	Where built.	Date of inspection.	Where inspected.	Date of previous inspection.	Local district where previously inspected.
Inland towing steamers—Con.										
Catasauqua [a]	78	1879		1879		Newburg, N. Y.	Nov. 14, 1905	Jersey City, N. J.	Nov. 11, 1904	New York, N. Y.
Charles McWilliams	83	1866		1904		Philadelphia, Pa.	May 5, 1905	Long Island City, N.Y.	May 5, 1904	Do.
Charles Runyon	78	1884		1884		Tottenville, N. Y.	May 4, 1905	Brooklyn, N. Y.	Apr. 7, 1904	Do.
Charles B. Sanford	151	1871		1891		Philadelphia, Pa.	May 10, 1905	Port Richmond, N. Y.	May 6, 1904	Do.
Charles E. Soper	42	1881		1881		Jersey City, N. J.	Mar. 14, 1905	Jersey City, N. J.	Mar. 14, 1904	Do.
Charles H. Senff	147	1882		1905		Brooklyn, N. Y.	Oct. 10, 1905	Brooklyn, N. Y.	Apr. 4, 1904	Do.
Chas. J. Davis [b]	40	1900	1904	1900		New Baltimore, N. Y.	July 24, 1905	do.	Apr. 25, 1904	Do.
Chas. P. Kuper [c]	51	1892		1892		Tottenville, N. Y.	Sept. 16, 1905	New York, N. Y.	Sept. 15, 1904	Do.
Charles R. Stone	55	1873	1894	1879		Philadelphia, Pa.	July 17, 1905	do.	July 22, 1904	Do.
Chas. W. Russell	29	1893		1888		New Baltimore, N. Y.	July 8, 1905	do.	July 11, 1904	Do.
Charm	47	1868		1885		Philadelphia, Pa.	July 18, 1905	do.	July 18, 1904	Do.
Chief	62	1870		1886		do.	July 14, 1905	do.	July 14, 1904	Do.
Christiana Baird	33	1879		1890		Camden, N. J.	Sept. 16, 1905	Newark, N. J.	Sept. 14, 1904	Do.
Christine [d]	33	1890		1900		Athens, N. Y.	June 12, 1905	West Brighton, N. Y.	June 13, 1904	Do.
Claremont [e]	25	1885		1891		Brooklyn, N. Y.	Aug. 4, 1905	Greenpoint, N. Y.	Aug. 4, 1904	Do.
Clinton	12	1882		1898		Glenwood, N. Y.	Nov. 25, 1905	Oyster Bay, N. Y.	Nov. 19, 1904	Do.
Coleraine	99	1893		1893		Wilmington, Del.	Aug. 11, 1905	West New Brighton, N. Y.	Aug. 1, 1904	Do.
Columbia	96	1882		1872		Brooklyn, N. Y.	Apr. 21, 1905	Hoboken, N. J.	Apr. 21, 1904	Do.
Columbia	106	1898		1898		Madison, Md.	July 7, 1905	Jersey City, N. J.	July 7, 1904	Norfolk, Va.
Coney Island	31	1894		1891		Gravesend, N. Y.	July 5, 1905	Brooklyn, N. Y.	July 6, 1904	New York, N. Y.
Conqueror	21	1901		1901		Long Island City, N.Y.	June 24, 1905	Long Island City, N.Y.	June 19, 1904	Do.
Cornell [f]	37	1866	1898	1887		Dorchester, N. J.	July 24, 1905	New York, N. Y.	July 18, 1904	Do.
Crescent [g]	68	1872	1900	1890		Philadelphia, Pa.	Oct. 7, 1905	Brooklyn, N. Y.	Oct. 8, 1904	Do.
Cyclops	128	1873		1880		Tottenville, N. Y.	Mar. 11, 1905	Port Richmond, N. Y.	Mar. 11, 1904	Do.
D. F. Skinner	30	1890		1891		New Baltimore, N. Y.	July 15, 1905	Long Island City, N.Y.	Apr. 11, 1904	Do.
Daisy	10	1880		1903		Brooklyn, N. Y.	do.	Brooklyn, N. Y.	July 14, 1904	Do.
Dart	21	1901		1901		Long Island City, N.Y.	Oct. 20, 1905	Greenpoint, N. Y.	Oct. 20, 1904	Do.
Defender	36	1896		1896		do.	July 21, 1905	Long Island City, N.Y.	July 16, 1904	Do.
Defiance	42	1883		1901		Philadelphia, Pa.	Feb. 25, 1905	Brooklyn, N. Y.	Feb. 27, 1904	Do.
Delaware	99	1883		1900		South Amboy, N. J.	Sept. 9, 1905	Hoboken, N. J.	Sept. 9, 1904	Do.
Dictator	96	1899		1899		Tottenville, N. Y.	May 11, 1905	Long Island City, N.Y.	Apr. 25, 1904	Do.
Director	21	1899		1898		Long Island City, N.Y.	Mar. 6, 1905	Greenpoint, N. Y.	Mar. 7, 1904	Do.
Dr. Geo. J. Moser	77	1904		1904		Tottenville, N. Y.	Dec. 21, 1905	New York, N. Y.	Dec. 22, 1904	Do.
Downer	65	1905		1888		do.	Sept. 14, 1905	Tottenville, N. Y.	First inspn.	Do.
Drusilla M. Cox	38	1878		1878		Philadelphia, Pa.	June 1, 1905	Greenpoint, N. Y.	June 1, 1904	Do.
Dubois	223	1901		1901		Tottenville, N. Y.	Sept. 18, 1905	New York, N. Y.	Sept. 17, 1904	Do.
E. Luckenbach	88	1880		1895		Newburg, N. Y.	Feb. 1, 1905	Jersey City, N. J.	Jan. 2, 1904	Do.
E. A. Packer	72	1872		1886		Philadelphia, Pa.	June 23, 1905	Brooklyn, N. Y.	June 22, 1904	Do.
E. M. Millard	91	1880	1903	1890		Athens, N. Y.	Nov. 21, 1905	Hoboken, N. J.	Nov. 25, 1904	Do.
East Chester	39	1890		1890		Tottenville, N. Y.	Dec. 13, 1905	Brooklyn, N. Y.	Dec. 9, 1904	Do.

Eddie H. Garrison	38	1888		1904		Brooklyn, N. Y	June 30, 1905	....do	Oct. 29, 1903	Do.
Ed. F. Murray [h]	54	1881	1903	1901		....do	May 9, 1905	New York, N. Y	May 10, 1904	Do.
Edgar Baxter	60	1869	1888	1898		Chester, Pa	Aug. 5, 1905	Brooklyn, N. Y	Aug. 5, 1904	Do.
Edith	37	1897		1897		Tottenville, N. Y	June 13, 1905	Perth Amboy, N. J	June 9, 1904	Do.
Edith Beard	34	1894		1891		Brooklyn, N. Y	July 3, 1905	Brooklyn, N. Y	July 5, 1904	Do.
Edmund L. Levy	51	1870		1883		New Brunswick, N. J.	Dec. 7, 1905	Hoboken, N. J	Dec. 5, 1904	Do.
Edna [i]	53	1882		1882		Philadelphia, Pa	Feb. 3, 1905	....do	Feb. 3, 1904	Do.
Edna B. King	29	1872	1896	1896		....do	Nov. 23, 1905	Brooklyn, N. Y	Nov. 23, 1904	Do.
Edward Annan	46	1873	1891	1890		....do	May 24, 1905	....do	May 23, 1904	Do.
Edward J. Berwind	193	1902		1902		Port Richmond, N. Y.	Oct. 7, 1905	....do	Oct. 10, 1904	Do.
Edwin Hawley	66	1873	1903	1898		Philadelphia, Pa	Sept. 12, 1905	New York, N. Y	Sept. 12, 1904	Do.
Eli Shriver, jr	26	1890		1890		Buffalo, N. Y	Dec. 4, 1905	Brooklyn, N. Y	Nov. 23, 1904	Do.
Elmira	94	1882		1897		Brooklyn, N. Y	Nov. 8, 1905	Jersey City, N. J	Sept. 23, 1904	Do.
Elsie K. [j]	30	1879	1902	1904		Yantacaw, N. J	Feb. 3, 1905	West Brighton, N. Y.	Feb. 3, 1904	Do.
Emerald [k]	44	1880		1885		Brooklyn, N. Y	June 12, 1905	New York, N. Y	June 11, 1904	Do.
Emma A	76	1899		1894	1904	Peekskill, N. Y	May 10, 1905	Peekskill, N. Y	May 9, 1904	Do.
Emma J. Kennedy	57	1873		1891		Philadelphia, Pa	Apr. 8, 1905	West New Brighton, N. Y.	Apr. 8, 1904	Do.
Engels	34	1899		1899		Athens, N. Y	May 26, 1905	Haverstraw, N. Y	May 25, 1904	Do.
Enterprise [m]	153	1901		1900		Bayonne, N. J	Dec. 30, 1904	New York, N. Y	Dec. 10, 1903	Do.
Erie	29	1883		1902		Brooklyn, N. Y	Mar. 29, 1905	Elizabethport, N. J	Mar. 28, 1904	Do.
Erin [n]	67	1861		1886		Chester, Pa	Dec. 11, 1905	New York, N. Y	Dec. 2, 1904	Do.
Escort	29	1883		1886		Baltimore, Md	Sept. 1, 1905	....do	Aug. 31, 1904	Do.
Essex	64	1864		1894		Newburg, N. Y	Jan. 31, 1905	Communipaw, N. J	Jan. 30, 1904	Do.
Eugene Hughes	111	1895		1895		Philadelphia, Pa	Mar. 13, 1905	Brooklyn, N. Y	Mar. 10, 1904	Do.
Eureka	48	1903		1892		Athens, N. Y	May 17, 1905	New York, N. Y	May 16, 1904	Do.
Evelyn	48	1886		1886		New Baltimore, N. Y.	Aug. 10, 1905	Brooklyn, N. Y	Aug. 8, 1904	Do.
Excelsior	65	1881		1881		Athens, N. Y	July 14, 1905	Hoboken, N. J	July 15, 1904	Do.
Express	38	1871		1885		Philadelphia, Pa	Aug. 21, 1905	Jersey City, N. J	Aug. 22, 1904	Do.
F. Woodruff	43	1862	1904	1881		Wilmington, Del	Apr. 14, 1905	Brooklyn, N. Y	Apr. 13, 1904	Do.
F. M. Stinson	28	1873		1903		Athens, N. Y	May 27, 1905	Jersey City, N. J	Oct. 19, 1903	Do.
Fairmount	24	1892		1903		Cambridge, Md	Aug. 21, 1905	Perth Amboy, N. J	Aug. 22, 1904	Do.
Flemington	220	1903		1903		Philadelphia, Pa	Aug. 14, 1905	Communipaw, N. J	Aug. 18, 1904	Do.
Florence	42	1883		1900		Brooklyn, N. Y	Mar. 6, 1905	Greenpoint, N. Y	Mar. 7, 1904	Do.
Florence	27	1867	1885	1885		Buffalo, N. Y	Mar. 24, 1905	Newark, N. J	Mar. 4, 1904	Do.
Flushing	49	1892		1892		Tottenville, N. Y	Sept. 2, 1905	New York, N. Y	Sept. 2, 1904	Do.
Forward	18	1884		1884		Brooklyn, N. Y	July 5, 1905	Brooklyn, N. Y	July 5, 1904	Do.
Franklin N. Brown	95	1887		1896		Elizabethport, N. J	Nov. 22, 1905	New York, N. Y	Nov. 18, 1904	Do.
Fred E. Scammell	32	1891		1891		Brooklyn, N. Y	....do	Jersey City, N. J	Nov. 22, 1904	Do.
Fred J. Fenner	37	1889		1900		Jersey City, N. J	June 17, 1905	....do	June 17, 1904	Do.
Freehold	220	1903		1903		Philadelphia, Pa	Sept. 5, 1905	Communipaw, N. J	Sept. 2, 1904	Do.
Free Lance	33	1887		1892		New London, Conn	Nov. 3, 1905	Jersey City, N. J	Oct. 28, 1904	Do.
Ganoga	204	1900		1900		Port Richmond, N. Y.	Sept. 22, 1905	Brooklyn, N. Y	June 20, 1904	Do.
Gazelle	13	1875		1897		Philadelphia, Pa	May 29, 1905	....do	June 11, 1902	Do.

[a] Formerly Isabel E. Wilbur, 1899.
[b] Formerly Chas. J. Reno, 1904.
[c] Formerly C. Offerman, 1899.
[d] Formerly Wm. H. Walker, 1904.
[e] Formerly Theresa, 1904.
[f] Formerly Gratitude, 1898.
[g] Formerly Sammie, 1900.
[h] Formerly Pontiac, 1903.
[i] Formerly James D. Nicol, 1898.
[j] Formerly Wesley Stoney, 1902.
[k] Formerly Gracie, 1904.
[l] Estimated.
[m] Certificate issued Jan. 4, 1905.
[n] Formerly (a) New York Central Lighterage Co. No. 1, 1899; (b) New York Central No. 1, 1901.

DOMESTIC VESSELS INSPECTED, YEAR ENDED DECEMBER 31, 1905—SECOND SUPERVISING DISTRICT—NEW YORK, N. Y.—Continued.

Names of vessels and class.	Gross tonnage.	Hull built.	Hull rebuilt.	Boilers built.	Boilers rebuilt.	Where built.	Date of inspection.	Where inspected.	Date of previous inspection.	Local district where previously inspected.
Inland towing steamers—Con.										
Gen'l McClellan	18	1904		1904		New York, N. Y	July 31, 1905	New York, N. Y	July 16, 1904	New York, N. Y.
General Newton	40	1880		1895		Athens, N. Y	Oct. 7, 1905	Port Liberty, N. J	Oct. 3, 1904	Do.
Genesee	204	1900		1900		Port Richmond, N. Y	Dec. 2, 1905	Jersey City, N. J	Nov. 26, 1904	Do.
Geneva [a]	109	1897		1888		Brooklyn, N. Y	Oct. 14, 1905	do	Nov. 17, 1904	Do.
George Hill [b]	93	1889		1889		Philadelphia, Pa	Jan. 5, 1905	Brooklyn, N. Y	Jan. 5, 1904	Do.
George B. Roe	42	1882		1905		Tottenville, N. Y	Oct. 19, 1905	Perth Amboy, N. J	Oct. 19, 1904	Do.
George P. Taylor	64	1903		1904		do	Dec. 5, 1905	New York, N. Y	Nov. 25, 1904	Do.
Geo. S. Shultz	43	1872	1894	1881		Philadelphia, Pa	Dec. 9, 1905	do	Nov. 26, 1904	Do.
George S. Tice	74	1885	1897	1898		Newburg, N. Y	Apr. 24, 1905	Jersey City, N. J	Apr. 23, 1904	Do.
George W. Elder	73	1882		1883		Petersburg, Va	July 17, 1905	New York, N. Y	July 16, 1904	Do.
Gladiator	167	1888		1903		Boston, Mass	Feb. 2, 1905	Long Island City, N. Y	Feb. 4, 1904	Do.
Glen Cove	47	1882		1882		Tottenville, N. Y	Sept. 27, 1905	Jersey City, N. J	Sept. 27, 1904	Do.
Glen Iris	63	1863		1889		Buffalo, N. Y	June 7, 1905	Brooklyn, N. Y	June 8, 1904	Philadelphia, Pa.
Glen Island	63	1875	1901	1883		Brooklyn, N. Y	Aug. 28, 1905	Hoboken, N. J	Sept. 6, 1904	New York, N. Y.
Golden Age [c]	35	1881	1897	1897		Greenpoint, N. Y	Nov. 8, 1905	Brooklyn, N. Y	Nov. 5, 1904	Do.
Golden Ray	20	1864	1893	1891		Buffalo, N. Y	Jan. 16, 1905	Long Island City, N. Y	Jan. 14, 1904	Do.
Golden Rod	35	1891		1891		Noank, Conn	Aug. 7, 1905	Brooklyn, N. Y	Aug. 5, 1904	Do.
Golden Rule	39	1891		1891		do	Feb. 23, 1905	New York, N. Y	Feb. 15, 1904	Do.
Goshen [d]	45	1875	1899	1899		Newburg, N. Y	May 8, 1905	Jersey City, N. J	May 7, 1904	Do.
Gowanus	10	1881	1893	1898		Brooklyn, N. Y	Aug. 24, 1905	Brooklyn, N. Y	Aug. 24, 1904	Do.
Greenville	30	1883		1904		do	Nov. 25, 1905	Jersey City, N. J	Nov. 26, 1904	Do.
Guiding Star	29	1868	1903	1883		Philadelphia, Pa	Nov. 28, 1905	Bayonne, N. J	Oct. 29, 1904	Do.
H. B. Moore, jr	52	1896		1896		Tottenville, N. Y	Sept. 21, 1905	Port Richmond, N. Y	Sept. 21, 1904	Do.
H. B. Rawson	54	1889	1903	1890		do	Aug. 7, 1905	Brooklyn, N. Y	Aug. 4, 1904	Do.
H. H. Newkirk	27	1880	1900	1893		Poughkeepsie, N. Y	Jan. 16, 1905	New York, N. Y	Jan. 16, 1904	Do.
Hamburg-American Line No. 2 [e]	52	1903		1903		Tottenville, N. Y	Nov. 24, 1905	do	Nov. 22, 1904	Do.
Harlem River	28	1889		1889		Brooklyn, N. Y	Oct. 19, 1905	do	Oct. 19, 1904	Do.
Harlem River No. 2	49	1896		1889		New York, N. Y	May 24, 1905	do	May 26, 1904	Do.
Harrisburg	225	1900		1900		Wilmington, Del	July 1, 1905	Hoboken, N. J	July 1, 1904	Do.
Harsimus	112	1882		1883		South Amboy, N. J	July 7, 1905	do	July 7, 1904	Do.
Harvey W. Temple	36	1879		1890		Athens, N. Y	Nov. 18, 1905	Newark, N. J	Nov. 9, 1904	Albany, N. Y.
Hazelton [f]	97	1886		1895		Perth Amboy, N. J	Jan. 17, 1905	Jersey City, N. J	Jan. 19, 1904	New York, N. Y.
Henry Maurer	46	1904		1899		Tottenville, N. Y	Sept. 9, 1905	Maurer, N. J	Sept. 9, 1904	Do.
Henry O'Brien	64	1903		1903		do	July 31, 1905	Brooklyn, N. Y	Aug. 1, 1904	Do.
Henry A. Peck	45	1882		1882		City Island, N. Y	Sept. 12, 1905	Newark, N. J	Sept. 12, 1904	Do.
Henry D. McCord	69	1872	1895	1889		Philadelphia, Pa	Aug. 21, 1905	Brooklyn, N. Y	Aug. 22, 1904	Do.
Henry H. Stanwood	44	1898		1893		Athens, N. Y	June 29, 1905	do	June 29, 1904	Do.
Henry L. Wait	39	1862		1877		New Baltimore, N. Y	Dec. 2, 1905	do	Nov. 14, 1904	Do.
Henry R. Heath	42	1880		1885		Eddyville, N. Y	Dec. 12, 1905	Hoboken, N. J	Dec. 13, 1904	Do.

Henry U. Palmer	137	1891	....	1900	....	Philadelphia, Pa	Sept. 11, 1905	Brooklyn, N. Y	Sept. 12, 1904	Do.
Hewitt Boice	38	1863	1887	1887	....	....do	Oct. 16, 1905	New York, N. Y	Oct. 14, 1904	Do.
Hiawatha	69	1903	....	1903	....	Tottenville, N. Y	Dec. 6, 1905	....do	Dec. 1, 1904	Do.
Horace B. Freeman	67	1889	....	1889	....	New Brighton, N. Y	May 13, 1905	Hoboken, N. J	May 9, 1904	Do.
Hortense	15	1879	1893	1893	....	Brooklyn, N. Y	Aug. 3, 1905	Newark, N. J	Aug. 2, 1904	Do.
Howard	43	1881	....	1881	....	Philadelphia, Pa	Sept. 2, 1905	Hoboken, N. J	Aug. 25, 1904	Do.
Hudson	78	1875	....	1890	....	....do	June 27, 1905	Elizabeth, N. J	July 5, 1904	Do.
Hugh Bond	10	1888	....	1887	....	Brooklyn, N. Y	July 19, 1905	Brooklyn, N. Y	July 19, 1904	Do.
Hugh C. Barrett [g]	46	1874	1905	1896	....	Philadelphia, Pa	Oct. 6, 1905	Jersey City, N. J	Oct. 8, 1904	Do.
Irene	11	1893	....	1902	....	Brooklyn, N. Y	May 20, 1905	Brooklyn, N. Y	May 19, 1904	Do.
Irving G. Keller [h]	43	1890	....	1905	....	....do	Mar. 8, 1905	Hoboken, N. J	Feb. 11, 1904	Do.
Ithaca [i]	105	1891	....	1891	....	....do	Jan. 19, 1905	Communipaw, N. J	Jan. 19, 1904	Do.
J. D. Billard [j]	75	1862	....	1902	....	Mystic, Conn	July 17, 1905	Brooklyn, N. Y	July 15, 1904	Do.
J. Fred Lohman	98	1892	....	1892	....	Athens, N. Y	Sept. 18, 1905	....do	Sept. 16, 1904	Do.
J. H. Petersen [k]	36	1872	1899	1889	....	Camden, N. J	Sept. 21, 1905	New York, N. Y	Sept. 24, 1904	Do.
J. H. Randerson	48	1904	....	1904	....	New Baltimore, N. Y	Aug. 13, 1905	....do	Aug. 15, 1904	Albany, N. Y.
Jacob M. Heath	41	1896	....	1903	....	Tottenville, N. Y	Feb. 27, 1905	Brooklyn, N. Y	Feb. 27, 1904	New York, N. Y
James Kay [l]	34	1872	1898	1898	....	Philadelphia, Pa	June 12, 1905	Hoboken, N. J	June 11, 1904	Do.
James McAllister	85	1904	....	1904	....	Athens, N. Y	Dec. 13, 1905	Greenpoint, N. Y	Dec. 12, 1904	Do.
James McDonough [m]	49	1889	....	1889	....	Brooklyn, N. Y	Dec. 16, 1904	Brooklyn, N. Y	Dec. 16, 1903	Do.
James McDonough	49	1889	....	1889	....	....do	Dec. 18, 1905	....do	Dec. 16, 1904	Do.
James McWilliams [n]	149	1882	....	1905	....	Newburg, N. Y	July 27, 1905	Jersey City, N. J	Sept. 8, 1903	Do.
James Roy	45	1869	....	1893	....	Philadelphia, Pa	Nov. 16, 1905	Brooklyn, N. Y	Nov. 16, 1904	Do.
James Watt	74	1873	....	1883	....	Chester, Pa	Mar. 14, 1905	New York, N. Y	Mar. 14, 1904	Do.
James A. Garfield	41	1881	1893	1901	....	Athens, N. Y	Feb. 9, 1905	Brooklyn, N. Y	Feb. 1, 1904	Do.
James D. Leary	76	1886	1899	1886	....	Port Richmond, N. Y	May 1, 1905	Hoboken, N. Y	May 1, 1904	New London, Conn.
James J. McGuirl [o]	85	1892	....	1892	....	Brooklyn, N. Y	Jan. 26, 1905	Brooklyn, N. Y	Jan. 26, 1904	New York, N. Y.
James Van Alst	19	1891	....	1891	....	....do	June 29, 1905	....do	June 29, 1904	Do.
James W. Husted	43	1875	....	1875	....	Philadelphia, Pa	Apr. 11, 1905	....do	Apr. 18, 1904	Do.
Jamestown	118	1890	....	1904	....	....do	Feb. 23, 1905	Jersey City, N. J	Oct. 31, 1903	Do.
Jessie [p]	31	1862	1903	1904	....	....do	Oct. 25, 1905	Hoboken, N. J	Oct. 25, 1904	Do.
John Douglass	52	1902	....	1886	....	Tottenville, N. Y	May 29, 1905	Brooklyn, N. Y	May 28, 1904	Do.
John Fleming	164	1899	....	1900	....	Jersey City, N. J	Mar. 24, 1905	New York, N. Y	Mar. 23, 1904	Do.
John Fuller	79	1864	1881	1886	....	Philadelphia, Pa	Aug. 2, 1905	....do	Aug. 11, 1904	Do.
John Harlin	79	1891	....	1889	....	Charleston, S. C	Oct. 10, 1905	Brooklyn, N. Y	Oct. 10, 1904	Do.
John Lee	41	1882	....	1882	....	Brooklyn, N. Y	Oct. 14, 1905	Greenpoint, N. Y	Oct. 14, 1904	Philadelphia, Pa.
John Sparks	22	1883	1891	1883	....	Tottenville, N. Y	June 17, 1905	Brooklyn, N. Y	June 18, 1904	New York, N. Y
John D. Dailey [q]	79	1873	1898	1898	....	Chester, Pa	Jan. 27, 1905	New York, N. Y	Jan. 26, 1904	Do.
John E. Berwind	75	1888	....	1898	....	Newburg, N. Y	May 15, 1905	Hoboken, N. J	May 16, 1904	Do.
John J. White	13	1872	....	1903	....	New York, N. Y	Aug. 24, 1905	Glen Cove, N. Y	Aug. 27, 1904	Do.
John V. Cowen	160	1900	....	1900	....	Baltimore, Md	July 31, 1905	Port Richmond, N. Y	June 24, 1904	Do.
John S. Smith	70	1872	1891	1898	....	Philadelphia, Pa	July 26, 1905	Hoboken, N. J	July 25, 1904	Do.

[a] Formerly John Taylor, 1899.
[b] Formerly Frank W. Munn, 1901.
[c] Formerly J. J. Driscoll, 1897.
[d] Formerly Governor Morgan, 1899.
[e] Formerly Frank Steers, 1903.
[f] Formerly Mary H. Packer, 1899.
[g] Formerly William C. Nicol, 1905.
[h] Formerly (a) Henry Hoehn, 1901; (b) Gilbert M. Edgett, 1905.
[i] Formerly Rollin H. Wilbur, 1899.
[j] Formerly U. S. S. Rocket.
[k] Formerly Reba, 1899.
[l] Formerly Kate Miller, 1898.
[m] Certificate issued Jan. 20, 1905.
[n] Formerly (a) Robert A. Packer, 1899; (b) Cheektowaga, 1905.
[o] Formerly Fortuna, 1905.
[p] Formerly William H. Beaman, 1903.
[q] Formerly Henry A. Crawford, 1899.

DOMESTIC VESSELS INSPECTED, YEAR ENDED DECEMBER 31, 1905—SECOND SUPERVISING DISTRICT—NEW YORK, N. Y.—Continued.

Names of vessels and class.	Gross tonnage.	Hull built.	Hull rebuilt.	Boilers built.	Boilers rebuilt.	Where built.	Date of inspection.	Where inspected.	Date of previous inspection.	Local district where previously inspected.
Inland towing steamers—Con.										
John T. Pratt	60	1882		1882		Tottenville, N. Y.	Jan. 17, 1905	Hoboken, N. J.	Jan. 15, 1904	Philadelphia, Pa.
Joseph Peene, sr.	86	1889		1900		do	July 29, 1905	Yonkers, N. Y.	July 30, 1904	New York, N. Y.
Juniata	111	1874		1874		Brooklyn, N. Y.	Aug. 19, 1905	Hoboken, N. J.	Aug. 19, 1904	Do.
Kate Buckley	21	1891		1891		do	Sept. 18, 1905	Brooklyn, N. Y.	Sept. 17, 1904	Do.
Kathryn	84	1896		1901		Tottenville, N. Y.	July 22, 1905	New York, N. Y.	July 22, 1904	Do.
Laurida	36	1898		1880		Athens, N. Y.	Sept. 2, 1905	Greenpoint, N. Y.	Sept. 1, 1904	Albany, N. Y.
Leader	44	1878		1878		Philadelphia, Pa.	July 13, 1905	Hoboken, N. J.	Aug. 8, 1904	New York, N. Y.
Leal	20	1905		1905		Steinway, N. Y.	Oct. 26, 1905	Steinway, N. Y.	First inspn.	
Lewis Pulver	71	1886		1900		Athens, N. Y.	Oct. 12, 1905	Hoboken, N. J.	Oct. 14, 1905	Do.
Libbie [a]	29	1881	1898	1885		Poughkeepsie, N. Y.	June 29, 1905	West New Brighton, N. Y.	May 16, 1904	Do.
Liberty	14	1882		1898		Brooklyn, N. Y.	July 8, 1905	Brooklyn, N. Y.	July 9, 1904	Do.
Lila May Hardy	19	1884		1898		Jersey City, N. J.	May 10, 1905	Ellis Island, N. Y.	May 11, 1904	Do.
Linden	66	1881		1884		South Amboy, N. J.	Mar. 6, 1905	Hoboken, N. J.	July 24, 1903	Philadelphia, Pa.
Lowell M. Palmer	119	1887		1904		Philadelphia, Pa.	July 31, 1905	Brooklyn, N. Y.	Aug. 1, 1904	New York, N. Y.
M. Henderer	44	1900		1900		Albany, N. Y.	July 6, 1905	Long Island City, N. Y.	July 6, 1904	Do.
M. D. Wheeler	31	1871	1891	1891		Philadelphia, Pa.	Jan. 20, 1905	West Brighton, N. Y.	Jan. 9, 1904	Do.
Mabel	50	1893		1893		Athens, N. Y.	July 26, 1905	Haverstraw, N. Y.	July 27, 1904	Do.
Mabel	26	1888		1903		Tottenville, N. Y.	June 13, 1905	Perth Amboy, N. J.	June 13, 1904	Do.
McCaldin Bros	63	1886		1886		Perth Amboy, N. J.	June 8, 1905	Brooklyn, N. Y.	June 7, 1904	Do.
Mahanoy	204	1900		1900		Port Richmond, N. Y.	Aug. 11, 1905	do	Aug. 26, 1904	Do.
Mamie	31	1884		1903		Baltimore, Md.	May 17, 1905	do	Apr. 5, 1904	Do.
Manhattan [b]	155	1900		1900		New York, N. Y.	Feb. 11, 1905	New York, N. Y.	Feb. 13, 1904	Do.
Margaret	40	1901		1899		Tottenville, N. Y.	Sept. 25, 1905	do	Sept. 24, 1904	Do.
Margaret A. Lenox	45	1864	1883	1877		New Brunswick, N. J.	July 21, 1905	Hoboken, N. J.	July 22, 1904	Do.
Margaret J. Sanford	77	1883	1895	1895		Jersey City, N. J.	Mar. 21, 1905	Clifton, N. Y.	Mar. 18, 1904	Do.
Marion	93	1896		1896		Tomkins Cove, N. Y.	Dec. 5, 1905	Jersey City, N. J.	Dec. 7, 1904	Do.
Marion	47	1886		1905		South Amboy, N. J.	Nov. 4, 1905	Hoboken, N. J.	Nov. 30, 1903	Do.
Mary Ann	40	1876	1896	1895		Chester, Pa.	July 31, 1905	Perth Amboy, N. J.	July 23, 1904	Do.
Mary Lewis [c]	35	1863		1891		Wilmington, Del.	Aug. 15, 1905	Hoboken, N. J.	Aug. 13, 1904	Do.
Mascot	21	1899		1899		Long Island City, N. Y.	Aug. 12, 1905	Greenpoint, N. Y.	Aug. 10, 1904	Do.
Mascot	20	1890		1890		Brooklyn, N. Y.	Aug. 26, 1905	Newark, N. J.	Aug. 29, 1904	Do.
Mascotte	20	(d)	1886	1886		No record	Sept. 23, 1905	West New Brighton, N. Y.	Sept. 24, 1904	Do.
Mattie	58	1899		1899		Brooklyn, N. Y.	July 29, 1905	New York, N. Y.	July 28, 1904	Do.
Media	103	1889		1889		Philadelphia, Pa.	Nov. 27, 1905	Hoboken, N. J.	Nov. 28, 1904	Do.
Mercedes	67	1881		1890		Camden, N. J.	Apr. 20, 1905	Jersey City, N. J.	Mar. 31, 1904	Do.
Mercer	150	1888		1888		do	Sept. 2, 1905	Hoboken, N. J.	Sept. 2, 1904	Do.
Michael J. Coffey	62	1892		1886		West Troy, N. Y.	Nov. 14, 1905	West New Brighton, N. Y.	Nov. 12, 1904	Do.
Michael T. Barrett [e]	32	1886	1894	1886		Athens, N. Y.	May 25, 1905	Jersey City, N. J.	May 25, 1904	Do.

Mildred [f]	25	1869	1903	1891	....	Philadelphia, Pa	June 3, 1905	....do	June 2, 1904	Do.
Mischief	20	1884	....	1886	....	Greenpoint, N. Y	Nov. 27, 1905	Brooklyn, N. Y	Nov. 14, 1904	Do.
Montauk	121	1895	....	1901	....	Wilmington, Del	May 17, 1905	Long Island City, N. Y	May 19, 1904	Do.
N. B. Starbuck [g]	72	1865	....	1888	....	New Baltimore, N. Y	Dec. 19, 1904	....do	Dec. 19, 1903	Do.
N. B. Starbuck	72	1865	....	1888	....	....do	Dec. 16, 1905	....do	Dec. 19, 1904	Do.
Nanuet	217	1904	....	1904	....	Port Richmond, N. Y	May 23, 1905	Jersey City, N. J	May 20, 1904	Do.
Narragansett	96	1873	....	1891	....	Brooklyn, N. Y	Sept. 2, 1905	Port Richmond, N. Y	Aug. 4, 1904	Do.
Nellie M. Tyerell	10	1879	....	1889	....	Tottenville, N. Y	May 4, 1905	Perth Amboy, N. J	May 5, 1904	Do.
Nettie L. Tice	45	1881	....	1898	....	Newburg, N. Y	June 19, 1905	Hoboken, N. J	June 18, 1904	Do.
Newport	74	1889	....	1889	....	Wilmington, Del	Oct. 23, 1905	....do	Oct. 24, 1904	Do.
Newsboy	[h] 7	1894	....	1902	....	Buffalo, N. Y	Oct. 7, 1905	Brooklyn, N. Y	June 7, 1904	Do.
New York Dock Company	147	1903	....	1903	....	Noank, Conn	Oct. 16, 1905	....do	Oct. 24, 1904	Do.
New York Central No. 1	110	1901	....	1901	....	Newburg, N. Y	Nov. 20, 1905	Weehawken, N. J	Nov. 21, 1904	Do.
New York Central No. 2 [i]	133	1890	....	1890	....	....do	Dec. 4, 1905	....do	Dec. 5, 1904	Do.
New York Central No. 3 [j]	130	1891	....	1904	....	Newport News, Va	May 1, 1905	....do	May 2, 1904	Do.
New York Central No. 7	113	1903	....	1903	....	Newburg, N. Y	Feb. 14, 1905	....do	Feb. 15, 1904	Do.
New York Central No. 9 [k]	134	1884	1902	1891	....	Philadelphia, Pa	Mar. 13, 1905	....do	Mar. 14, 1904	Do.
New York Central No. 10 [l]	77	1886	....	1895	....	Camden, N. J	May 15, 1905	....do	May 16, 1904	Do.
New York Central No. 11	110	1901	....	1901	....	Newburg, N. Y	Nov. 20, 1905	....do	Nov. 21, 1904	Do.
New York Central No. 12 [m]	103	1887	....	1903	....	Camden, N. J	Nov. 10, 1905	....do	Nov. 7, 1904	Do.
New York Central No. 13 [n]	103	1899	....	1898	....	....do	Nov. 27, 1905	....do	Nov. 28, 1904	Do.
New York Central No. 17 [o]	147	1891	....	1890	....	Newburg, N. Y	Jan. 23, 1905	....do	Jan. 25, 1904	Do.
New York Central No. 18 [p]	103	1891	....	1891	....	....do	Apr. 10, 1905	....do	Apr. 11, 1904	Do.
New York Central No. 19 [q]	85	1891	....	1891	....	Tottenville, N. Y	Mar. 20, 1905	....do	Mar. 21, 1904	Do.
New York Central No. 20 [r]	83	1891	....	1891	....	Elm Park, N. Y	June 5, 1905	....do	June 6, 1904	Do.
New York Central No. 21	101	1899	....	1899	....	Newburg, N. Y	Oct. 30, 1905	....do	Oct. 31, 1904	Do.
New York Central No. 22	101	1899	....	1899	....	....do	Dec. 4, 1905	....do	Dec. 5, 1904	Do.
New York Central No. 23	113	1903	....	1903	....	....do	Feb. 6, 1905	....do	Feb. 8, 1904	Do.
Nyack	117	1891	....	1903	....	Philadelphia, Pa	May 18, 1905	Jersey City, N. J	June 1, 1904	Do.
Olympia	116	1896	....	1896	....	Astoria, N. Y	June 27, 1905	New York, N. Y	June 27, 1904	Do.
Oscar G. Murray	165	1900	....	1900	....	Baltimore, Md	Nov. 18, 1905	Clifton, N. Y	Nov. 19, 1904	Do.
Overbrook	179	1894	....	1894	....	Philadelphia, Pa	Feb. 11, 1905	Hoboken, N. J	Jan. 27, 1904	Do.
Overbrook	179	1894	....	1894	....	....do	Dec. 22, 1905	....do	Feb. 11, 1905	Do.
Owasco [s]	117	1887	....	1887	....	Perth Amboy, N. J	Aug. 15, 1905	Communipaw, N. J	Aug. 17, 1904	Do.
P. I. Nevius	40	1878	....	1885	....	Brooklyn, N. Y	Nov. 16, 1905	West New Brighton, N. Y.	Nov. 14, 1904	Do.
P. R. R. No. 7	223	1904	....	1904	....	Richmond, Va	June 13, 1905	Hoboken, N. J	June 13, 1904	Norfolk, Va.
P. R. R. No. 9	223	1904	....	1904	....	....do	Apr. 22, 1905	....do	Apr. 22, 1904	Do.
P. R. R. No. 32	201	1904	....	1904	....	Sparrow Point, Md	May 29, 1905	....do	May 28, 1904	Baltimore, Md.
Palmyra	110	1891	....	1904	....	Elizabeth, N. J	Nov. 25, 1905	....do	Dec. 8, 1904	New York, N. Y.
Passaic	41	1903	....	1903	....	Newark, N. J	Oct. 27, 1905	Newark, N. J	Oct. 24, 1904	Do.

[a] Formerly Samuel W. Morris, 1898.
[b] Formerly Richard Croker, 1902.
[c] Formerly Government vessel Commodore Morris.
[d] No record.
[e] Formerly Wm. B. Snow, 1901.
[f] Formerly E. L. Austin, 1900.
[g] Certificate issued Feb. 14, 1905.
[h] Estimated.
[i] Formerly Chauncey M. Depew, 1900.
[j] Formerly Dorothy, 1900.
[k] Formerly New York Central Lighterage Co. No. 9, 1899.
[l] Formerly New York Central Lighterage Co. No. 10, 1899.
[m] Formerly New York Central Lighterage Co. No. 12, 1899.
[n] Formerly New York Central Lighterage Co. No. 13, 1899.
[o] Formerly New York Central Lighterage Co. No. 17, 1899.
[p] Formerly New York Central Lighterage Co. No. 18, 1899.
[q] Formerly New York Central Lighterage Co. No. 19, 1899.
[r] Formerly New York Central Lighterage Co. No. 20, 1899.
[s] Formerly Nannie Lamberton, 1904.

DOMESTIC VESSELS INSPECTED, YEAR ENDED DECEMBER 31, 1905—SECOND SUPERVISING DISTRICT—NEW YORK, N. Y.—Continued.

Names of vessels and class.	Gross tonnage.	Hull built.	Hull rebuilt.	Boilers built.	Boilers rebuilt.	Where built.	Date of inspection.	Where inspected.	Date of previous inspection.	Local district where previously inspected.
Inland towing steamers—Con										
Patrick McGuirl [a]	70	1892		1892		Perth Amboy, N. J.	Sept. 22, 1905	New York, N. Y.	Sept. 21, 1904	New York, N. Y.
Pennsylvania	91	1874		1889		Camden, N. J.	Feb. 25, 1905	Hoboken, N. J.	Feb. 26, 1904	Do.
Peter L. Colon [b]	39	1865	1900	1880		Chester, Pa.	Oct. 3, 1905	Port Richmond, N. Y.	Oct. 5, 1904	Do.
Philip Hoffman	28	1882	1904	1882		Rondout, N. Y.	July 17, 1905	West New Brighton, N. Y.	July 16, 1904	Do.
Phoenix	118	1898		1897		Tomkins Cove, N. Y.	Mar. 10, 1905	New York, N. Y.	Mar. 10, 1904	Do.
Pollux [c]	86	1893		1893		Philadelphia, Pa.	Oct. 21, 1905	Hoboken, N. J.	Oct. 21, 1904	Do.
Post Boy	11	1894		1893		Buffalo, N. Y.	Aug. 5, 1905	Brooklyn, N. Y.	May 9, 1904	Do.
Protector	35	1894		1898		Long Island City, N. Y.	July 28, 1905	do	July 28, 1904	Do.
Queen Mab	19	1880	1898	1898		Tottenville, N. Y.	May 5, 1905	do	May 6, 1904	Do.
Quickstep	68	1864		1887		New Brunswick, N. J.	Oct. 14, 1905	New York, N. Y.	Oct. 15, 1904	Do.
R. J. Barrett	109	1893		1893		Athens, N. Y.	Oct. 3, 1905	Hoboken, N. J.	Sept. 30, 1904	Do.
R. S. Carter	37	1861	1885	1881		Buffalo, N. Y.	Dec. 4, 1905	Brooklyn, N. Y.	Nov. 28, 1904	Do.
R. W. Burke	49	1873		1873		Philadelphia, Pa.	Feb. 7, 1905	New York, N. Y.	Feb. 4, 1904	Do.
Radnor	122	1896		1896		South Amboy, N. J.	May 10, 1905	Hoboken, N. J.	May 10, 1904	Do.
Ramapo	69	1882		1895		Brooklyn, N. Y.	Apr. 11, 1905	Jersey City, N. J.	Apr. 11, 1904	Do.
Rambler	15	1883		1883		Baltimore, Md.	Nov. 16, 1905	Newark, N. J.	Nov. 17, 1904	Do.
Rambler	34	1891		1891		Tottenville, N. Y.	Nov. 17, 1905	Long Island City, N. Y.	Oct. 31, 1904	Do.
Raymond [d]	17	1879		1886		Camden, N. J.	Mar. 31, 1905	Jersey City, N. J.	Apr. 13, 1904	Do.
Red Ash	117	1888		1888		Brooklyn, N. Y.	Nov. 16, 1905	Communipaw, N. J.	Nov. 17, 1904	Do.
Regina	24	1900		1899		Athens, N. Y.	May 20, 1905	Long Island City, N. Y.	May 21, 1904	Do.
Reliance	62	1903		1903		Long Island City, N. Y.	Nov. 15, 1905	Astoria, N. Y.	Nov. 14, 1904	Do.
Reliance	96	1881		1890		Wilmington, Del.	Nov. 8, 1905	West Brighton, N. Y.	Nov. 17, 1904	Charleston, S. C.
Richmond [e]	99	1891		1896		Buffalo, N. Y.	Jan. 21, 1905	New York, N. Y.	Jan. 11, 1904	New York, N. Y.
Robert Burnett	55	1881		1881		Newburg, N. Y.	July 11, 1905	West Brighton, N. Y.	June 2, 1904	Do.
Robert Robinson	36	1898		1888		New Baltimore, N. Y.	Apr. 15, 1905	Perth Amboy, N. J.	Apr. 13, 1904	Do.
Robert White	35	1896		1898		Athens, N. Y.	July 15, 1905	Brooklyn, N. Y.	July 13, 1904	Do.
Robert E. Petty	60	1893		1893		Tottenville, N. Y.	Dec. 5, 1905	do	Dec. 5, 1904	Do.
Robert M. Duy [f]	26	1870	1897	1898		Philadelphia, Pa.	May 13, 1905	do	May 14, 1904	Do.
Rochester	118	1890		1905		do	Nov. 20, 1905	Jersey City, N. J.	Nov. 23, 1904	Do.
Roselle	220	1903		1903		do	Apr. 10, 1905	Communipaw, N. J.	Apr. 9, 1904	Do.
Rover	22	1899		1899		Long Island City, N. Y.	Mar. 25, 1905	Long Island City, N. Y.	Mar. 25, 1904	Do.
Royal	22	1900		1900		do	Sept. 14, 1905	do	Sept. 14, 1904	Do.
S. L'Hommedieu	100	1898		1898		Noank, Conn.	Oct. 13, 1905	Brooklyn, N. Y.	Oct. 17, 1904	Do.
S. F. Sprague	11	1885		1885		Freeport, N. Y.	Aug. 19, 1905	Jersey City, N. J.	Aug. 19, 1904	Do.
S. R. Callaway	175	1901		1901		Newburg, N. Y.	Jan. 9, 1905	Weekawken, N. J.	Jan. 11, 1904	Do.
S. R. St. John	54	1864		1875		Wilmington, Del.	Oct. 12, 1905	Jersey City, N. J.	Oct. 11, 1904	Do.
S. O. Co. No. 5 [g]	112	1894		1894		Newburg, N. Y.	Sept. 9, 1905	Long Island City, N. Y.	Sept. 12, 1904	Do.
S. O. Co. No. 6 [h]	89	1896		1895		Philadelphia, Pa.	Aug. 12, 1905	do	Aug. 12, 1904	Do.

S. O. Co. No. 8 [e]	71	1892		1892		Tottenville, N. Y.	Dec. 5, 1905	do	Dec. 17, 1904	Do.
S. O. Co. No. 9 [f]	62	1898		1898		Newburg, N. Y.	July 22, 1905	do	July 28, 1904	Do.
S. O. Co. No. 10 [k]	48	1889	1894	1889		Brooklyn, N. Y.	Dec. 12, 1905	do	Dec. 22, 1904	Do.
S. O. Co. No. 11	129	1904		1904		Philadelphia, Pa.	Nov. 25, 1905	do	Nov. 30, 1904	Philadelphia, Pa.
Sadie E. Ellis	40	1879		1902		Tottenville, N. Y.	Dec. 5, 1905	Brooklyn, N. Y.	Dec. 7, 1904	New York, N. Y.
St. Patrick	35	1872		1891		Brooklyn, N. Y.	July 10, 1905	New York, N. Y.	July 9, 1904	Do.
Sarah E. Easton	34	1868	1887	1882		Philadelphia, Pa.	Nov. 22, 1905	West New Brighton, N. Y.	Nov. 29, 1904	Do.
Sarah E. Wetherell	22	1872		1883		Gloucester, Mass.	Nov. 4, 1905	Brooklyn, N. Y.	Nov. 2, 1904	Do.
Sarah J. Weed	61	1874		1900		Brooklyn, N. Y.	Dec. 4, 1905	Greenpoint, N. Y.	Dec. 3, 1904	Do.
Sayre [l]	140	1889		1889		do	Sept. 23, 1905	Jersey City, N. J.	Sept. 22, 1904	Do.
Sea Wall	34	1867		1898		Richmond, Va.	Sept. 15, 1905	New York, N. Y.	Sept. 10, 1904	Do.
Senator D. C. Chase	70	1872	1887	1887		Philadelphia, Pa.	Jan. 11, 1905	Hoboken, N. J.	Jan. 10, 1904	Do.
Seven Brothers	32	1899		1899		Athens, N. Y.	Sept. 23, 1905	Brooklyn, N. Y.	Sept. 24, 1904	Do.
Shamrock [m]	32	1865	1900	1880		Philadelphia, Pa.	July 10, 1905	New York, N. Y.	July 9, 1905	Do.
Shohola	117	1891		1902		do	Feb. 28, 1905	Jersey City, N. J.	Mar. 3, 1904	Do.
Sprite	27	1883		1890		Tottenville, N. Y.	May 9, 1905	Perth Amboy, N. J.	May 9, 1904	Do.
Stamford	55	1899		1897		do	Sept. 28, 1905	Jersey City, N. J.	Sept. 30, 1904	Do.
Stanley H. Miner [n]	31	1896		1892		Athens, N. Y.	Nov. 1, 1905	Brooklyn, N. Y.	Oct. 31, 1904	Do.
Stapleton	38	1902		1902		Tottenville, N. Y.	May 23, 1905	Stapleton, N. Y.	May 21, 1904	Do.
Steers [o]	25	1889		1905		Patchogue, N. Y.	May 9, 1905	Greenville, N. J.	Aug. 18, 1904	Do.
Stella	36	1876		1876		Brooklyn, N. Y.	May 27, 1905	Brooklyn, N. Y.	May 28, 1904	Do.
Sterling	61	1888		1882		Tottenville, N. Y.	Feb. 4, 1905	New York, N. Y.	Feb. 4, 1904	Do.
Success	32	1891		1891		Jersey City, N. J.	July 24, 1905	Jersey City, N. J.	July 23, 1904	Do.
Syosset	176	1899		1899		Philadelphia, Pa.	Aug. 31, 1905	Long Island City, N. Y.	Sept. 1, 1904	Do.
T. W. Wellington	49	1862	1881	1890		do	Nov. 9, 1905	Brooklyn, N. Y.	Sept. 12, 1904	New London, Conn.
Tacoma	82	1889		1899		Brooklyn, N. Y.	Dec. 11, 1905	Jersey City, N. J.	Dec. 12, 1904	New York, N. Y.
Tacoma [p]	82	1889		1899		do	Dec. 12, 1904	do	Dec. 8, 1903	Do.
Theodore Smith	33	1888		1888		Tottenville, N. Y.	Nov. 17, 1905	Communipaw, N. J.	Nov. 16, 1904	Do.
Thomas Flannery	72	1898		1898		do	Nov. 11, 1905	Brooklyn, N. Y.	Nov. 1, 1904	Do.
Thomas Tracy [q]	59	1889		1889		Perth Amboy, N. J.	Mar. 16, 1905	New York, N. Y.	Mar. 16, 1904	Do.
Thomas Walsh	76	1873		1880		New York, N. Y.	Sept. 20, 1905	Brooklyn, N. Y.	Sept. 20, 1904	Do.
Thos. A. Quigley [r]	45	1880		1900		Brooklyn, N. Y.	July 17, 1905	do	July 18, 1904	Do.
Three Brothers	50	1892		1884		Perth Amboy, N. J.	Jan. 7, 1905	New York, N. Y.	Jan. 6, 1904	Do.
Titan	80	1868		1881		Brooklyn, N. Y.	June 6, 1905	Hoboken, N. J.	June 8, 1904	Do.
Tom and Joe [s]	19	1898		1895		Athens, N. Y.	Aug. 28, 1905	Brooklyn, N. Y.	Aug. 26, 1904	Do.
Tom S. Wotkyns	31	1884		1884		do	July 29, 1905	Jersey City, N. J.	July 11, 1904	Do.
Transfer No. 1	136	1878		1885		Philadelphia, Pa.	July 22, 1905	New York, N. Y.	Aug. 18, 1904	Do.
Transfer No. 2	101	1880		1880		do	Aug. 30, 1905	do	Sept. 14, 1904	Do.
Transfer No. 3	130	1886		1895		do	Sept. 6, 1905	do	Sept. 19, 1904	Do.
Transfer No. 4	102	1880		1880		do	Sept. 26, 1905	do	Oct. 1, 1904	Do.
Transfer No. 5	142	1888		1895		Wilmington, Del.	May 1, 1905	do	May 7, 1904	Do.
Transfer No. 6	142	1888		1896		do	Mar. 8, 1905	do	Mar. 29, 1904	Do.
Transfer No. 7	129	1891		1891		Elizabeth, N. J.	May 6, 1905	do	May 7, 1904	Do.

[a] Formerly Andrew J. White, 1905.
[b] Formerly Jacob Sinex, 1900.
[c] Formerly J. L. Luckenbach, 1901.
[d] Formerly Josiah W. Cloud, 1905.
[e] Formerly Pier, 1902.
[f] Formerly O. V. Coffin, 1898.
[g] Formerly Comet, 1899.
[h] Formerly Radiant, 1899.
[i] Formerly Tea Rose, 1899.
[j] Formerly Charles F. Engels, 1899.
[k] Formerly Pearl, 1899.
[l] Formerly Robert H. Sayre, 1904.
[m] Formerly Gen. Geo. G. Meade, 1900.
[n] Formerly T. A. Briggs, 1905.
[o] Formerly E. Bailey & Sons, 1899.
[p] Certificate issued Jan. 21, 1905.
[q] Formerly Jack Dykman, 1899.
[r] Formerly W. H. Bentley, 1900.
[s] Formerly O. V. Sage, 1905.

Domestic Vessels Inspected, Year ended December 31, 1905—Second Supervising District—New York, N. Y.—Continued.

Names of vessels and class.	Gross tonnage.	Hull built.	Hull rebuilt.	Boilers built.	Boilers rebuilt.	Where built.	Date of inspection.	Where inspected.	Date of previous inspection.	Local district where previously inspected.
Inland towing steamers—Con.										
Transfer No. 8	131	1891		1891		Elizabeth, N. J	Apr. 26, 1905	New York, N. Y	May 4, 1904	NewYork, N. Y.
Transfer No. 9	196	1891		1891		do	Mar. 29, 1905	do	Apr. 12, 1904	Do.
Transfer No. 10	217	1889		1893		Wilmington, Del	Aug. 15, 1905	do	Sept. 8, 1904	Do.
Transfer No. 11	248	1898		1898		do	Mar. 15, 1905	do	Apr. 2, 1904	Do.
Transfer No. 12	249	1898		1898		do	Apr. 19, 1905	do	Apr. 30, 1904	Do.
Transfer No. 14	322	1900		1900		Bath, Me	Apr. 5, 1905	do	Apr. 5, 1904	Do.
Transfer No. 15	322	1900		1900		do	Feb. 23, 1905	do	Mar. 23, 1904	Do.
Transfer No. 16	268	1904		1904		Philadelphia, Pa	Mar. 1, 1905	do	Mar. 25, 1904	Philadelphia, Pa.
Transfer No. 17	268	1904		1904		do	Mar. 22, 1905	do	Apr. 7, 1904	New York, N. Y.
Transfer No. 18	268	1904		1904		do	Apr. 12, 1905	do	Apr. 21, 1904	Do.
Transfer No. 19	270	1905		1905		do	Nov. 24, 1905	do	First inspn.	
Transfer No. 20	270	1905		1905		do	Dec. 5, 1905	do	do	
Transport	162	1900		1900		Brooklyn, N. Y	Sept. 18, 1905	Brooklyn, N. Y	Sept. 17, 1904	Do.
Trenton	96	1888		1888		South Amboy, N. J	Aug. 4, 1905	Hoboken, N. J	Aug. 4, 1904	Do.
Triumph	77	1904		1904		Tottenville, N. Y	June 19, 1905	Long Island City, N. Y	First inspn.	
Valiant	57	1884		1883		Perth Amboy, N. J	Mar. 7, 1905	Brooklyn, N. Y	Mar. 7, 1904	Do.
Vaseline	a 9	1884		1890		Brooklyn, N. Y	Aug. 5, 1905	do	Aug. 6, 1904	Do.
Victor	21	1874		1897		New York, N. Y	June 14, 1905	Hoboken, N. J	July 7, 1904	Do.
Vigilant	98	1902		1902		Long Island City, N. Y	Aug. 12, 1905	Greenpoint, N. Y	Aug. 12, 1904	Do.
Virginia Jackson	52	1873		1883		Philadelphia, Pa	July 11, 1905	West New Brighton, N. Y.	July 13, 1904	Do.
Volunteer	64	1888		1903		Bordentown, N. J	Aug. 7, 1905	Brooklyn, N. Y	Aug. 6, 1904	Do.
Volunteer	92	1888		1887		Tottenville, N. Y	July 24, 1905	New York, N. Y	July 25, 1904	Do.
W. A. Forman[b]	39	1901		1901		do	June 30, 1905	Hoboken, N. J	July 8, 1904	Do.
W. A. Sherman[c]	99	1881		1891		Brooklyn, N. Y	May 5, 1905	do	May 2, 1904	Do.
W. F. Kelly[d]	18	1872	1904	1887		do	July 6, 1905	Jersey City, N. J	July 2, 1904	Do.
W. Freeland Dalzell	81	1875	1895	1883		Philadelphia, Pa	Nov. 7, 1905	Brooklyn, N. Y	Nov. 21, 1904	Do.
W. H. Flannery	115	1902		1905		West New Brighton, N. Y.	Oct. 17, 1905	New York, N. Y	Oct. 15, 1904	Do.
Wade[e]	23	1873	1901	1892		Brooklyn, N. Y	Mar. 4, 1905	do	Mar. 16, 1904	Do.
Walter J. Tice	39	1879		1895		Newburg, N. Y	May 8, 1905	Jersey City, N. J	May 7, 1904	Do.
Water Front	46	1902		1902		New Baltimore, Md	Nov. 28, 1905	New York, N. Y	Nov. 26, 1904	Do.
Waverly	217	1904		1904		Port Richmond, N. Y	June 12, 1905	Jersey City, N. J	June 18, 1904	Do.
Welcome	21	1850		1884		East Boston, Mass	June 3, 1905	do	Aug. 20, 1903	Do.
Westchester	20	1896		1896		Long Island City, N. Y	Nov. 6, 1905	Weehawken, N. J	Nov. 7, 1904	Do.
West Farms[f]	19	1893		1904		do	Dec. 31, 1904	Long Island City, N. Y	Sept. 29, 1903	Do.
West Farms	19	1893		1904		do	Dec. 29, 1905	Brooklyn, N. Y	Dec. 31, 1904	Do.
Westwood[g]	43	1864		1884		New York, N. Y	Oct. 10, 1905	Jersey City, N. J	Oct. 17, 1904	Do.
White Ash	117	1888		1888		Brooklyn, N. Y	Dec. 23, 1905	Communipaw, N. J	Nov. 21, 1904	Do.
William Coleman	21	1883		1888		Athens, N. Y	Oct. 24, 1905	Nyack, N. Y	Oct. 17, 1904	Do.
Wm. Orr	31	1888		1888		New Baltimore, N. Y	Aug. 5, 1905	Greenpoint, N. Y	Aug. 4, 1904	Do.

William Schanbel, sr.	45	1884	....	1899	....	Philadelphia, Pa.	May 19, 1905	Perth Amboy, N. J.	May 18, 1904	Do.
William Tracy	62	1903	....	1892	....	Port Richmond, N. Y.	Dec. 18, 1905	New York, N. Y.	Dec. 17, 1904	Do.
Wm. E. Ferguson	71	1876	....	1886	....	Philadelphia, Pa.	Mar. 2, 1905	....do	Mar. 1, 1904	Do.
William F. Reed	30	1885	....	1885	....	Glenwood, N. Y.	Nov. 28, 1905	Jersey City, N. J.	Nov. 23, 1904	Do.
Wm. H. Baldwin	38	1901	....	1901	....	New Baltimore, Md.	Apr. 1, 1905	Brooklyn, N. Y.	Apr. 4, 1904	Do.
William H. Beard	28	1874	....	1904	....	Brooklyn, N. Y.	Sept. 18, 1905	....do	Sept. 21, 1904	Do.
Wm. H. Vanderbilt	78	1871	1890	1890	....	Philadelphia, Pa.	Sept. 11, 1905	Hoboken, N. J.	Sept. 9, 1904	Do.
Wm. J. McCaldin	75	1886	....	1886	....	Athens, N. Y.	Sept. 2, 1905	New York, N. Y.	Aug. 31, 1904	Do.
William M. Wadley [h]	154	1903	....	1903	....	Chester, Pa.	Dec. 22, 1904	....do	Dec. 21, 1903	Philadelphia, Pa.
William M. Wadley	154	1903	....	1903	....	....do	Dec. 20, 1905	....do	Dec. 22, 1904	New York, N. Y.
William N. Beach [i]	49	1873	1902	1881	....	Philadelphia, Pa.	Dec. 21, 1904	Brooklyn, N. Y.	Dec. 21, 1903	Do.
William N. Beach	49	1873	1902	1881	....	....do	Dec. 20, 1905	....do	Dec. 21, 1904	Do.
Wm. S. Anderson	25	1874	....	1881	....	Aquackoneck, N. J.	Mar. 28, 1905	....do	Mar. 24, 1904	Do.
Willie	38	1885	....	1885	....	Brooklyn, N. Y.	Dec. 11, 1905	....do	Dec. 10, 1904	Do.
Willie Welch	46	1903	....	1881	....	South Amboy, N. J.	May 27, 1905	Hoboken, N. J.	May 27, 1904	Do.
Wilmington	225	1900	....	1900	....	Wilmington, Del.	June 17, 1905	....do	June 17, 1904	Do.
Windber [j]	107	1900	1902	1900	....	Noank, Conn.	Nov. 29, 1905	Brooklyn, N. Y.	Dec. 2, 1904	Do.
Winnie	73	1870	....	1886	....	New Brunswick, N. J.	Jan. 9, 1905	Hoboken, N. J.	Jan. 11, 1904	Do.
Wioma	37	1850	1881	1886	....	Norwalk, Conn.	Apr. 22, 1905	Perth Amboy, N. J.	Apr. 23, 1904	Do.
Wisdom [k]	24	1891	....	1892	....	Brooklyn, N. Y.	May 13, 1905	Brooklyn, N. Y.	Apr. 21, 1904	Do.
Wonder	34	1889	....	1889	....	Tottenville, N. Y.	Dec. 11, 1905	Long Island City, N. Y.	Dec. 10, 1904	Do.
Woodbridge [l]	21	1870	....	1893	....	New Brunswick, N. J.	Sept. 26, 1905	Perth Amboy, N. J.	Sept. 16, 1904	Do.
Wrestler	198	1889	....	1903	....	Boston, Mass.	Feb. 28, 1905	Long Island City, N. Y.	Feb. 4, 1904	Do.
Zouave	86	1861	....	1898	....	Albany, N. Y.	July 10, 1905	Jersey City, N. J.	July 9, 1904	Do.
Ocean steam pleasure yachts.										
Admiral	123	1892	1894	1901	....	Providence, R. I.	May 23, 1905	Brooklyn, N. Y.	May 19, 1904	New York, N. Y.
Aileen	178	1899	....	1899	....	Chester, Pa.	June 9, 1905	....do	June 18, 1904	Do.
Alert [m]	99	1899	....	1899	....	Greenport, N. Y.	July 12, 1905	Bergen Point, N. J.	July 12, 1904	Do.
Aloha	306	1899	....	1899	....	Brooklyn, N. Y.	May 4, 1905	Brooklyn, N. Y.	Dec. 22, 1903	Do.
Alvina	526	1901	....	1901	....	Wilmington, Del.	Aug. 23, 1905	....do	June 16, 1904	Do.
Aphrodite	1,147	1899	....	1899	....	Bath, Me.	May 16, 1905	....do	May 1, 1904	Do.
Aquilo	176	1901	....	1901	....	South Boston, Mass.	July 17, 1905	New York, N. Y.	Aug. 16, 1904	Do.
Ardea [n]	58	1886	....	1894	....	Boston, Mass.	May 12, 1905	Nyack, N. Y.	June 2, 1904	Do.
Ariadne	246	1902	....	1902	....	Wilmington, Del.	May 19, 1905	Brooklyn, N. Y.	June 9, 1904	Do.
Arrow	82	1901	....	1901	....	Nyack, N. Y.	May 9, 1905	....do	May 11, 1904	Do.
Atlantic	303	1903	....	1903	....	Shooters Island, N. Y.	Apr. 5, 1905	....do	Sept. 30, 1903	Do.
Calypso	97	1895	....	1895	....	Boston, Mass.	June 20, 1905	....do	July 20, 1904	Do.
Carmina	260	1903	....	1903	....	South Boston, Mass.	June 1, 1905	....do	May 12, 1904	Boston, Mass.
Cayuga	81	1899	....	1899	....	New York, N. Y.	Aug. 21, 1905	....do	Aug. 18, 1904	New York, N. Y.
Celt	217	1902	....	1902	....	Wilmington, Del.	May 3, 1905	....do	May 5, 1904	Do.
Chetolah	91	1891	....	1901	....	Salisbury, Mass.	July 1, 1905	....do	Sept. 4, 1903	Do.

[a] Estimated.
[b] Formerly Agnes H. White, 1905.
[c] Formerly (a) New York Central Lighterage Co. No. 8, 1899; (b) New York Central No. 8, 1904.
[d] Formerly Jessie Russell, 1904.
[e] Formerly (a) Vigilant, 1900; (b) John G. Tait, 1901.
[f] Certificate issued Jan. 16, 1905.
[g] Formerly Champion, 1902.
[h] Certificate issued Jan. 3, 1905.
[i] Certificate issued Jan. 4, 1905.
[j] Formerly D. B. Dearborn, 1902.
[k] Formerly Katie D., 1905.
[l] Formerly Georgianna, 1899.
[m] Formerly Reba, 1904.
[n] Formerly Hanniel, 1904.

Domestic Vessels Inspected, Year ended December 31, 1905—Second Supervising District—New York, N. Y.—Continued.

Names of vessels and class.	Gross tonnage.	Hull built.	Hull rebuilt.	Boilers built.	Boilers rebuilt.	Where built.	Date of inspection.	Where inspected.	Date of previous inspection.	Local district where previously inspected.
Ocean steam pleasure yachts—Continued.										
Chichota [a]	27	1901		1901		Bristol, R. I.	Aug. 28, 1905	Morris Heights, N. Y.	June 11, 1904	New York, N. Y.
Colonia	259	1899		1899		Chester, Pa.	June 13, 1905	Hoboken, N. J.	Aug. 15, 1903	Do.
Columbia	682	1899		1899		Elizabethport, N. J.	June 22, 1905	Brooklyn, N. Y.	Oct. 7, 1903	Do.
Constant	157	1903		1903		Baltimore, Md.	Apr. 21, 1905	do	Mar. 12, 1903	Baltimore, Md.
Corsair	1,136	1899		1899		Newburg, N. Y.	Feb. 13, 1905	Hoboken, N. J.	July 18, 1904	New York, N. Y.
Courier	65	1897		1897		South Boston, Mass.	June 2, 1905	Brooklyn, N. Y.	June 2, 1904	Baltimore, Md.
Crescent [b]	38	1889		1903		East Boston, Mass.	June 3, 1905	do	Feb. 1, 1903	New Orleans, La.
Crescent [c]	116	1889		1897		Bristol, R. I.	May 12, 1905	Morris Heights, N. Y.	May 11, 1904	Albany, N. Y.
Duquesne	82	1895		1902		do	May 23, 1905	Brooklyn, N. Y.	May 26, 1903	New York, N. Y.
Edithia	124	1904	1905	1905		Nyack, N. Y.	May 22, 1905	Morris Heights, N. Y.	First inspn	
Elreba	201	1898		1898		Elizabethport, N. J.	May 10, 1905	Brooklyn, N. Y.	May 12, 1904	Do.
Elsa	94	1888		1897		Brooklyn, N. Y.	June 21, 1905	do	June 18, 1904	Do.
Elsa II	99	1903		1903		Port Jefferson, N. Y.	July 27, 1905	do	July 29, 1904	Do.
Embla	197	1893		1898		Nyack, N. Y.	June 23, 1905	do	June 15, 1904	Do.
Evelyn [d]	40	1892		1903		do	May 24, 1905	Morris Heights, N. Y.	June 23, 1904	Do.
Genesee	212	1900		1900		Elizabeth, N. J.	June 30, 1905	Brooklyn, N. Y.	May 27, 1904	Do.
Halcyon	52	1882	1896	1901		Poughkeepsie, N. Y.	May 22, 1905	Morris Heights, N. Y.	June 29, 1903	Do.
Halcyon	89	1875		1892		Brooklyn, N. Y.	July 27, 1905	Brooklyn, N. Y.	July 6, 1904	Do.
Helenita	304	1902		1902		Morris Heights, N. Y.	May 8, 1905	Morris Heights, N. Y.	June 6, 1904	Do.
Idler	122	1901		1901		South Boston, Mass.	May 11, 1905	Brooklyn, N. Y.	May 20, 1904	Do.
Inga [e]	166	1901		1901		New York, N. Y.	May 4, 1905	do	May 19, 1903	Do.
Inia	63	1903		1903		do	Apr. 26, 1905	Morris Heights, N. Y.	May 31, 1904	Do.
Illini [f]	159	1886	1889	1905		Brooklyn, N. Y.	June 6, 1905	do	Aug. 1, 1903	Do.
Intrepid	330	1903		1904		Newburg, N. Y.	May 3, 1905	Brooklyn, N. Y.	Mar. 29, 1904	Do.
Invincible [g]	340	1893		1893		Philadelphia, Pa.	May 27, 1905	do	June 6, 1904	Do.
Jathniel	140	1889		1896		East Boston, Mass.	July 22, 1905	do	Apr. 21, 1903	Do.
Kanawha	475	1899		1899		New York, N. Y.	May 10, 1905	New York, N. Y.	May 27, 1904	Do.
Kismet	146	1899		1903		Wilmington, Del.	May 24, 1905	Brooklyn, N. Y.	June 22, 1904	Do.
Lagonda	120	1884		1891		Brooklyn, N. Y.	July 3, 1905	do	July 11, 1903	Do.
Linta	78	1905		1905		Morris Heights, N. Y.	June 28, 1905	Morris Heights, N. Y.	First inspn	
Machigonne	95	1904		1904		New York, N. Y.	May 12, 1905	do	June 6, 1904	Do.
Margaret	88	1902		1902		do	May 6, 1905	do	May 23, 1903	Do.
Maspeth	49	1894		1898		Morris Heights, N. Y.	May 24, 1905	do	May 25, 1904	Do.
Mirage	30	1900		1900		Bristol, R. I.	July 6, 1905	Brooklyn, N. Y.	May 26, 1904	Providence, R. I.
Neaira [h]	342	1893		1893		Wilmington, Del.	Apr. 11, 1905	do	June 12, 1903	New York, N. Y.
Niagara	1,443	1898		1898		do	Apr. 12, 1905	Hoboken, N. J.	Apr. 3, 1903	Do.
Norman [i]	135	1895	1900	1900		Chester, Pa.	June 13, 1905	Brooklyn, N. Y.	June 14, 1904	Do.
Nourmahal	768	1884	1898	1902		Wilmington, Del.	July 27, 1905	do	June 30, 1904	Do.
Nylked [j]	63	1886	1902	1899		New York, N. Y.	May 9, 1905	do	June 22, 1904	New London, Conn.
Phantasy [k]	52	1889		1903		do	Oct. 20, 1905	New York, N. Y.	May 23, 1904	New York, N. Y.

Priscilla [l]	65	1893		1899		South Boston, Mass.	June 21, 1905	Brooklyn, N. Y.	July 10, 1903	Do.
Privateer	361	1902		1902		Elizabeth, N. J.	Sept. 22, 1905	New York, N. Y.	Sept. 22, 1904	Do.
Reposo	29	1890		1900		Bristol, R. I.	June 3, 1905	Pelham Manor, N. Y.	June 6, 1904	Do.
Rheclair	539	1902		1901		Port Richmond, N. Y.	May 3, 1905	Brooklyn, N. Y.	May 10, 1904	Do.
Roxana	99	1903		1903		Racine, Wis.	May 29, 1905	Morris Heights, N. Y.	Oct. 22, 1903	Milwaukee, Wis.
Sagamore	322	1888		1888		Bath, Me.	June 16, 1905	Brooklyn, N. Y.	June 4, 1903	New York, N. Y.
Sapphire	120	1888		1897		do.	June 15, 1905	do.	June 3, 1904	Do.
Saranac	42	1896	1898	1898		Morris Heights, N. Y.	June 7, 1905	do.	June 8, 1904	Do.
Scout	30	1900		1900		Bristol, R. I.	May 31, 1905	City Island, N. Y.	May 10, 1904	Providence, R. I.
Seminole [m]	147	1902		1902		Brooklyn, N. Y.	May 23, 1905	Brooklyn, N. Y.	May 19, 1904	New York, N. Y.
Sentinel	74	1883		1893		do.	July 15, 1905	New York, N. Y.	July 14, 1904	Do.
Sultana	390	1890		1901		do.	May 24, 1905	Brooklyn, N. Y.	Dec. 24, 1902	Do.
Taro [n]	87	1890	1895	1897		do.	May 20, 1905	do.	June 3, 1904	Do.
Tech [o]	141	1887		1899		Marcus Hook, Pa.	July 11, 1905	do.	May 21, 1901	Do.
Thetis	407	1892		1899		Buffalo, N. Y.	June 17, 1905	do.	June 22, 1904	Do.
Turbese	157	1902		1890		Greenport, N. Y.	May 11, 1905	do.	May 2, 1904	New London, Conn.
Vedette	93	1878		1892		Newburg, N. Y.	Apr. 18, 1905	Hoboken, N. J.	July 12, 1902	New York, N. Y.
Vergemere [p]	315	1903		1903		Wilmington, Del.	Sept. 27, 1904	City Island, N. Y.	Sept. 30, 1903	Philadelphia, Pa.
Vim	20	1905		1905		Morris Heights, N. Y.	May 22, 1905	Morris Heights, N. Y.	First inspn.	
Viola	93	1895		1895		South Boston, Mass.	Sept. 5, 1905	Brooklyn, N. Y.	Sept. 9, 1904	New York, N. Y.
Virginia	441	1899		1899		Bath, Me.	May 11, 1905	do.	May 11, 1904	Do.
Wadena	246	1891		1902		Cleveland, Ohio	Apr. 25, 1905	do.	May 21, 1902	Do.
Wild Duck	233	1891		1901		Boston, Mass.	July 6, 1905	do.	July 6, 1904	Do.
Inland steam pleasure yachts.										
Adeline	[q]5	1902		1890		Hoboken, N. J.	June 26, 1905	Hoboken, N. J.	June 30, 1904	New York, N. Y.
Adroit [r]	49	1902		1902		New York, N. Y.	July 3, 1905	Morris Heights, N. Y.	July 9, 1904	Do.
Advance	11	1902		1903		do.	June 10, 1905	do.	June 2, 1904	Do.
Alice	[q]5	1900		1900		Newark, N. J.	July 15, 1905	Harrison, N. J.	July 13, 1904	Do.
Alvina II	[q]5	1901		1905		South Boston, Mass.	Aug. 23, 1905	Brooklyn, N. Y.	June 16, 1904	Do.
Ardath	18	1889		1896		Newburg, N. Y.	June 8, 1905	do.	June 7, 1904	Do.
Artemis	36	1897		1903		Brooklyn, N. Y.	June 9, 1905	do.	June 10, 1904	Do.
Augusta	9	1894		1894		Bayonne, N. J.	June 23, 1905	Perth Amboy, N. J.	June 22, 1904	Do.
Belle Hazen	[q]5	1888		1896		Brooklyn, N. Y.	June 24, 1905	Great Neck, N. Y.	June 24, 1904	Do.
Bronx	11	([s])		1898		No record	June 20, 1905	New York, N. Y.	June 20, 1904	Do.
Carley	[q]5	1901		([s])		Brooklyn, N. Y.	Aug. 10, 1905	Brooklyn, N. Y.	First inspn.	
Carola [t]	32	1891		1905		Nyack, N. Y.	July 12, 1905	do.	July 19, 1904	Do.
Charavi	36	1890		1902		Greenport, N. Y.	June 6, 1905	do.	do.	Do.
Charmary [u]	298	1892	1897	1897		Brooklyn, N. Y.	May 2, 1905	do.	May 6, 1904	Do.
Cherokee	82	1903		1903		New York, N. Y.	Apr. 26, 1905	Morris Heights, N. Y.	Apr. 21, 1904	Do.
Cherub	11	1901		1901		Tottenville, N. Y.	May 11, 1905	Perth Amboy, N. J.	Apr. 7, 1904	Do.
Chief	[q]4	1890		1900		Providence, R. I.	July 31, 1905	Bayonne, N. J.	Aug. 1, 1904	Do.
Claymore	32	1893		1902		Nyack, N. Y.	July 6, 1905	Morris Heights, N. Y.	July 2, 1904	New London, Conn.

[a] Formerly Niagara III, 1902.
[b] Formerly Wabeno, 1900.
[c] Formerly Laurita, 1905.
[d] Formerly Linta, 1905.
[e] Formerly Irene, 1902.
[f] Formerly Reva, 1903.
[g] Formerly Intrepid, 1903.
[h] Formerly Au Revoir, 1902.
[i] Formerly Oneonta, 1900.
[j] Formerly Ozhesta, 1902.
[k] Formerly Trophy, 1904.
[l] Formerly Aquilo, 1900.
[m] Formerly Hanoli, 1903.
[n] Formerly (a) Alga, 1898; (b) Tide, 1901.
[o] Formerly Neaira, 1905.
[p] Certificate issued May 27, 1905.
[q] Estimated.
[r] Formerly Vixen, 1904.
[s] No record.
[t] Formerly Geisha, 1904.
[u] Formerly Clermont, 1903.

DOMESTIC VESSELS INSPECTED, YEAR ENDED DECEMBER 31, 1905—SECOND SUPERVISING DISTRICT—NEW YORK, N. Y.—Continued.

Names of vessels and class.	Gross tonnage.	Hull built.	Hull rebuilt.	Boilers built.	Boilers rebuilt.	Where built.	Date of inspection.	Where inspected.	Date of previous inspection.	Local district where previously inspected.
Inland steam pleasure yachts—Continued.										
Columbia	a 5	1886		1900		Bristol, R. I.	Apr. 12, 1905	Brooklyn, N. Y.	Apr. 21, 1904	New York, N. Y.
Diana	12	1892		1891		Mamaroneck, N. Y.	Aug. 12, 1905	Mamaroneck, N. Y.	Aug. 12, 1904	Do.
Francis K.	a 4	(b)		1896		No record	July 20, 1905	East Rutherford, N. J	July 29, 1904	Do.
Grey Fox	66	1902		1902		New York, N. Y.	June 7, 1905	Morris Heights, N. Y.	June 10, 1904	Detroit, Mich.
Hadassah	a 8	1892		1901		Middletown, Conn	June 28, 1905	Perth Amboy, N. J.	June 22, 1904	New York, N. Y.
Happy Days	46	1905		1905		Croton, N. Y.	Nov. 29, 1905	Croton, N. Y.	First inspn.	
Hirondelle	35	1893	1894	1899		Nyack, N. Y.	May 27, 1905	Brooklyn, N. Y.	May 26, 1904	Do.
Hornet	a 5	1883		1902		Greenport, N. Y.	June 15, 1905	Oyster Bay, N. Y.	Aug. 23, 1904	Do.
Impatient	39	1893		1898		Holly Oak, Del.	June 17, 1905	New York, N. Y.	May 18, 1904	Baltimore, Md.
Jule	41	1902		1902		New York, N. Y.	May 24, 1905	Morris Heights, N. Y.	June 1, 1904	New York, N. Y.
Leo	a 5	1890		1893		Peekskill, N. Y.	May 27, 1905	Greenwood Lake, N. Y	Sept. 4, 1903	Do.
Levanter	131	1905		1905		Morris Heights, N. Y.	May 8, 1905	Morris Heights, N. Y.	First inspn.	
Loando	42	1877		1898		Greenpoint, N. Y.	Apr. 25, 1905	Brooklyn, N. Y.	Dec. 4, 1903	Do.
Lucile	41	1885		1899		Bristol, R. I.	June 28, 1905	Morris Heights, N. Y.	May 27, 1904	Do.
Mandalay	32	1883		1890		Brewer, Me.	May 11, 1905	Brooklyn, N. Y.	May 24, 1904	Do.
Mohawk	a 6	1899		1899		Morris Heights, N. Y.	July 25, 1905	New York, N. Y.	May 14, 1904	Do.
Mohican	a 6	1899		1899		do.	July 26, 1905	Ellis Island, N. Y.	July 26, 1904	Do.
Myra	33	1903		1904		Port Jefferson, N. Y.	May 25, 1905	Oyster Bay, N. Y.	May 3, 1904	New Haven, Conn.
Nada	34	1890	1903	1898		Poughkeepsie, N. Y.	Apr. 28, 1905	Brooklyn, N. Y.	May 11, 1904	New York, N. Y.
Nanita[c]	36	1903		1903		New York, N. Y.	May 5, 1905	Morris Heights, N. Y.	Apr. 21, 1904	Do.
Niagara II	a 5	1903		1898		Morris Heights, N. Y.	Apr. 12, 1905	Hoboken, N. J.	Apr. 1, 1903	Do.
Niagara IV	50	1903		1903		New York, N. Y.	May 5, 1905	Morris Heights, N. Y.	May 16, 1904	New Haven, Conn.
Noria	a 5	1894		1894		Boston, Mass.	June 24, 1905	College Point, N. Y.	July 2, 1904	New York, N. Y.
Orienta	88	1901		1901		Elizabeth, N. J.	May 13, 1905	Brooklyn, N. Y.	First inspn.	
Orrmoore	22	1887	1892	1903		Brooklyn, N. Y.	Aug. 30, 1905	Nyack, N. Y.	June 7, 1904	Do.
Papoose	24	1893		1902		Bath, Me.	June 6, 1905	Brooklyn, N. Y.	June 1, 1904	Do.
Pioneer	287	1897		1896		Newburg, N. Y.	June 12, 1905	College Point, N. Y.	do.	Do.
Priscilla	a 4	1898		1897		City Island, N. Y.	July 27, 1905	Hoboken, N. J.	July 16, 1904	Do.
Queens[d]	a 5	1901		1905		New York, N. Y.	May 31, 1905	New York, N. Y.	May 7, 1904	Do.
Rajah	a 5	1889	1903	1887		Boston, Mass.	May 26, 1905	Newark, N. J.	Oct. 9, 1903	Do.
Sappho	56	1879		1894		Brooklyn, N. Y.	May 16, 1905	Brooklyn, N. Y.	May 23, 1904	Do.
Sarah	a 2	1891		1903		do.	Aug. 30, 1905	do.	Aug. 30, 1904	Do.
Scat	20	1902		1902		Nyack, N. Y.	June 10, 1905	Morris Heights, N. Y.	Sept. 25, 1903	Do.
Scud	38	1901		1901		South Boston, Mass.	July 31, 1905	Brooklyn, N. Y.	Aug. 8, 1904	Do.
Seneca	157	1888		1895		Boston, Mass.	May 24, 1905	do.	June 20, 1902	Do.
Sentinel[e]	28	1876		1884		Poughkeepsie, N. Y.	Aug. 10, 1905	New York, N. Y.	Aug. 10, 1904	Do.
State of New York	87	1890		1901		Brooklyn, N. Y.	May 18, 1905	do.	May 20, 1904	Do.
Telka	35	1896		1902		Port Jefferson, N. Y.	May 29, 1905	Brooklyn, N. Y.	July 7, 1902	Boston, Mass.
Theo[f]	10	1899		1904		Shelton, Conn.	Dec. 13, 1904	do.	Dec. 11, 1903	New York, N. Y.
Theo	10	1899		1905		do.	Nov. 28, 1905	Astoria, N. Y.	Dec. 13, 1904	Do.

Theresa	61	1892		1892		Brooklyn, N. Y	Mar. 10, 1905	Brooklyn, N. Y	Mar. 22, 1904	Do.
Trifle	a 3	1891		1899		Nyack, N. Y	Aug. 21, 1905	New York, N. Y	June 28, 1901	Do.
Uno	37	1903	1904	1903		Mariners Harbor, N. Y	July 7, 1905	Bergen Point, N. J	Aug. 3, 1904	Do.
Venture	21	1883	1901	1903		New York, N. Y	July 28, 1905	Nyack, N. Y	Aug. 10, 1904	Do.
Vitesse	67	1905		1905		Morris Heights, N. Y	May 8, 1905	Morris Heights, N. Y	First inspn.	
Vixen	66	1904		1904		New York, N. Y	Apr. 19, 1905	....do	May 20, 1904	Do.
Why Not g	12	1895		1900		Clifton, N. Y	Nov. 5, 1904	Brooklyn, N. Y	Oct. 10, 1902	Do.
Why Not	12	1895		1900		....do	Nov. 27, 1905	....do	Nov. 5, 1904	Do.
Wilhelmina	a 4	1889		1891		Peekskill, N. Y	July 29, 1905	Greenwood Lake, N. Y	June 4, 1904	Do.
Winona	47	1901		1905		New York, N. Y	May 11, 1905	Morris Heights, N. Y	May 10, 1904	Do.
Yacona No. 1	a 2	1902		1902		Bristol, R. I	July 12, 1905	Brooklyn, N. Y	Sept. 8, 1902	Providence, R. I.
Miscellaneous steamers.										
Abram S. Hewitt (fire)	223	1903		1903		Camden, N. J	Oct. 16, 1905	Brooklyn, N. Y	Oct. 15, 1904	New York, N. Y.
Admiral (freight and towing)	107	1880		1885		Brooklyn, N. Y	Nov. 17, 1905	....do	Nov. 11, 1904	Do.
Alfred & Edwin (freight and towing).	102	1872		1879		Philadelphia, Pa	July 29, 1905	Newark, N. J	Aug. 5, 1904	Do.
Argus (oyster)	25	1891		1903		Port Jefferson, N. Y	June 15, 1905	Oyster Bay, N. Y	June 15, 1904	Do.
Aroma Mills (freight and towing).	84	1872		1885		Camden, N. J	Aug. 14, 1905	Brooklyn, N. Y	Aug. 13, 1904	Do.
Bay Port (freight and towing).	1,399	1891		1891		West Superior, Wis	July 14, 1905	....do	June 7, 1904	Buffalo, N. Y.
Bay View (freight and towing).	1,399	1891		1891		....do	Sept. 11, 1905	....do	Aug. 4, 1904	Duluth, Minn.
Brooklyn (freight and towing).	154	1902		1902		Newburgh, N. Y	Feb. 20, 1905	New York, N. Y	Feb. 20, 1904	New York, N. Y
C. L. Haines (freight and towing).	125	1890		1891		Lockport, N. Y	Sept. 21, 1905	West New Brighton, N. Y.	Sept. 26, 1904	New Haven, Conn.
C. L. Marchal (freight and towing).	108	1874	1889	1889		Brooklyn, N. Y	Nov. 8, 1905	Jersey City, N. J	Nov. 9, 1904	New York, N. Y.
Caledonia (water)	21	1882		1904		....do	July 20, 1905	Brooklyn, N. Y	July 16, 1904	Do.
Calvin Tomkins (freight and towing).	187	1888		1889		Perth Amboy, N. J	Mar. 14, 1905	Newark, N. J	Mar. 14, 1904	Do.
Capelton (freight and towing).	99	1880		1880		Philadelphia, Pa	Sept. 14, 1905	New York, N. Y	Aug. 2, 1904	Do.
Captain A. F. Lucas (freight and towing).	4,188	1904		1904		Richmond, Va	Dec. 16, 1905	Brooklyn, N. Y	Dec. 21, 1904	Philadelphia, Pa.
Ceres (elevator)	380	1866	1890	1893		Cutler, Me	Nov. 6, 1905	Hoboken, N. J	Sept. 22, 1904	New York, N. Y.
Champion (wrecking)	342	1899		1899		Tottenville, N. Y	June 15, 1905	Brooklyn, N. Y	June 11, 1904	Do.
Climax (freight and towing)	119	1872	1895	1902		Brooklyn, N. Y	Nov. 4, 1905	....do	Nov. 5, 1904	Do.
Clinton (water)	28	1898		1897		East Rockaway, N. Y.	July 8, 1905	....do	July 8, 1904	Do.
Col. E. L. Drake (freight and towing).	4,205	1903		1903		Philadelphia, Pa	Apr. 20, 1905	....do	Apr. 18, 1904	Philadelphia, Pa.
Croton (water)	54	1881		1902		Athens, N. Y	July 25, 1905	New York, N. Y	July 23, 1904	New York, N. Y.
Daniel Wheeler (freight and towing).	216	1878		1896		Mobile, Ala	Feb. 28, 1905	Brooklyn, N. Y	Feb. 28, 1904	Do.
David A. Boody (fire)	94	1892		1895		Noank, Conn	Oct. 10, 1905	....do	Oct. 20, 1904	Do.
Dayton (freight and towing)	409	1891	1894	1891		Wilmington, Del	Apr. 7, 1905	Jersey City, N. J	Apr. 11, 1904	Do.

a Estimated.
b No record.
c Formerly Levanter, 1905.
d Formerly Dept. of Docks & Ferries No. 5, 1902.
e Formerly Dashaway, 1903.
f Certificate issued Jan. 12, 1905.
g Certificate issued Apr. 29, 1905.

DOMESTIC VESSELS INSPECTED, YEAR ENDED DECEMBER 31, 1905—SECOND SUPERVISING DISTRICT—NEW YORK, N. Y.—Continued.

Names of vessels and class.	Gross tonnage.	Hull built.	Hull rebuilt.	Boilers built.	Boilers rebuilt.	Where built.	Date of inspection.	Where inspected.	Date of previous inspection.	Local district where previously inspected.
***Miscellaneous steamers*—Continued.**										
Despatch (freight and towing).	127	1888	....	1888	....	South Amboy, N. J...	June 15,1905	Hoboken, N. J........	June 15,1904	New York, N. Y.
Dexter K. Cole (oyster)........	31	1893	....	1893	....	South Norwalk, Conn.	July 31,1905	Perth Amboy, N. J...	July 30,1904	Do.
Edward Clark (freight and towing).	242	1876	1890	1876	....	Philadelphia, Pa.....	Aug. 4,1905	New York, N. Y......	Aug. 4,1904	Do.
Elizabeth Washburn (freight and towing).[a]	69	1863	....	1899	....	Haverstraw, N. Y....	Mar. 21,1905	West Brighton, N.Y..	First inspn..	
Ella (freight and towing).....	103	1888	....	1899	....	Wilmington, Del.....	June 7,1905	Newark, N. J........	June 6,1904	Do.
Excelsior (elevator)..........	597	1900	....	1900	....	West Haven, Conn...	Aug. 7,1905	Hoboken, N. J........	Aug. 5,1904	Do.
F. H. Grove (water)..........	26	1886	....	1884	....	Athens, N. Y.........	Jan. 4,1905	New York, N. Y......	Jan. 4,1904	Do.
Falcon (oyster)..............	46	1884	....	1900	....	South Norwalk, Conn.	Oct. 30,1905	Brooklyn, N. Y.......	Nov. 5,1904	Do.
Four Sisters (oyster)[b]........	28	1897	....	1903	....	Glenwood, N. Y......	Dec. 14,1904	Barren Island, N. Y..	Dec. 12,1903	Do.
Four Sisters (oyster)........	28	1897	....	1903	....	....do..............	Dec. 11,1905	Port Richmond, N. Y.	Dec. 14,1904	Do.
Galion (freight and towing)..	237	1891	....	1891	....	Philadelphia, Pa.....	Mar. 13,1905	Jersey City, N. J......	Mar. 14,1904	Do.
General Franz Sigel (freight and towing).	90	1863	....	1900	....	New York, N. Y......	May 26,1905	New York, N. Y......	May 25,1904	Do.
George B. McClellan (fire)....	256	1904	....	1904	....	Camden, N. J.........	Apr. 1,1905	.....do..............	Apr. 1,1904	Philadelphia, Pa.
Gilbert R. Green (freight and towing).	137	1887	....	1897	....	Lockport, N. Y.......	Sept. 16,1905	Jersey City, N. J......	Sept. 16,1904	Buffalo, N. Y.
Hastings (freight and towing).	298	1885	....	1890	....	Wilmington, Del.....	Oct. 2,1905	Hastings, N.Y.......	Nov. 28,1904	New York, N. Y.
Huntington (freight and towing).	221	1888	....	1888	....	Athens, N. Y.........	Apr. 27,1905	.....do..............	Dec. 9,1903	Do.
Hustler (wrecking)...........	192	1891	....	1894	....	.....do..............	Jan. 21,1905	Brooklyn, N.Y.......	Feb. 3,1904	Do.
Hustler (wrecking)...........	192	1891	....	1894	....	.....do..............	Dec. 16,1905	.....do..............	Jan. 21,1905	Do.
I. J. Merritt (wrecking and towing).	354	1884	1894	1899	....	Tottenville, N. Y....	Jan. 20,1905	Stapleton, N. Y......	Jan. 21,1904	Do.
I. J. Merritt (wrecking and towing).	354	1884	1894	1899	....	.....do..............	Dec. 14,1905	.....do..............	Jan. 20,1905	Do.
I. P. Mersereau (oyster)......	31	1881	....	1896	....	.....do..............	Dec. 23,1905	New York, N. Y......	Dec. 22,1904	Do.
Inspector (water)............	67	1893	....	1896	....	Highlands, N. J......	Oct. 24,1905	Clifton, N. Y........	Oct. 24,1904	Do.
International (freight and towing).	101	1879	1902	1879	....	Philadelphia, Pa.....	Sept. 19,1905	Laurel Hill, N. Y.....	Sept. 19,1904	Do.
International (elevator)......	590	1901	....	1901	....	West Haven, Conn...	Nov. 6,1905	Hoboken, N. J........	Nov. 7,1904	Do.
Isis (elevator)...............	591	1898	....	1898	....	Camden, N. J.........	July 28,1905	.....do..............	July 28,1904	Do.
Jas. S. T. Stranahan (freight and towing).	127	1883	....	1881	....	Athens, N. Y.........	Oct. 16,1905	Brooklyn, N. Y......	Oct. 14,1904	Do.
John Campbell (towing and water).	88	1904	....	1904	....	Perth Amboy, N. J..	June 9,1905	.....do..............	June 9,1904	Do.
John H. Hudler (freight and towing).	24	1886	1903	1886	....	Kingston, N. Y......	Aug. 1,1905	Jersey City, N. J.....	Aug. 1,1904	Do.

John V. Craven (freight and towing).	183	1891	....	1891	....	Wilmington, Del	Aug. 26, 1905	West Brighton, N. Y.	Sept. 1, 1904	Do.
Joseph H. Moran (water)....	67	1905	....	1902	....	Tottenville, N. Y.....	Mar. 28, 1905	Brooklyn, N. Y.......	First inspn..	
Jupiter (water)............	54	1882	....	1887	....	Darien, Conn.........	July 27, 1905	.....do...............	July 25, 1904	Boston, Mass.
L. Boyer (freight and towing).	199	1888	....	1888	....	Brooklyn, N. Y.......	Oct. 19, 1905	.....do...............	Oct. 8, 1904	New York, N. Y.
Leader (freight and towing)..	198	1863	1896	1900	....	Kaighns Point, N. J..	Nov. 18, 1905	Newark, N. J..........	Nov. 21, 1904	Do.
Leonard J. Busby (freight and towing).	126	1894	....	1894	....	Tomkins Cove, N. Y..	Oct. 22, 1905	Brooklyn, N. Y.......	Oct. 26, 1904	Do.
Lizzie Wyman (freight and towing).	77	1876	....	1900	....	Damariscotta, Me....	Feb. 27, 1905	.....do...............	Feb. 25, 1904	Do.
Long Island (freight and towing).	163	1885	....	1885	....	Brooklyn, N. Y.......	July 25, 1905	Whitestone, N. Y....	July 15, 1904	Do.
Major Ulrich (water)........	12	1886	....	1886	....	.....do..............	May 2, 1905	Brooklyn, N. Y.......	May 5, 1904	Do.
Manhattan (freight and towing).	159	1884	1899	1905..	....	Rondout, N. Y.......	Dec. 13, 1905	Jersey City, N. J.....	Sept. 28, 1904	Do.
Martha J. Sutter (oyster)....	17	1902	....	1905	....	Bridgeport, Conn....	Nov. 21, 1905	Brooklyn, N. Y.......	Feb. 13, 1904	Do.
Mary J. (freight and towing).	57	1876	1901	1896	....	Buffalo, N. Y.........	Oct. 10, 1905	New York, N. Y.....	Oct. 10, 1904	Do.
Mary E. Gordon (freight and towing).	150	1880	....	1880	....	Rondout, N. Y.......	July 24, 1905	.....do...............	July 25, 1904	Do.
Mastodon (water)............	96	1885	....	1900	....	Greenpoint, N. Y....	Sept. 19, 1905	Brooklyn, N. Y.......	First inspn..	
Mills (dredging).............	2,525	1901	....	1903	....	Sparrow Point, Md..	May 13, 1905	.....do...............	May 14, 1904	Do.
Nellie (water)...............	20	1885	....	1885	....	Brooklyn, N. Y.......	June 10, 1905	.....do...............	June 11, 1904	Do.
Neshanic (freight and towing).[d]	271	1870	....	1886	....	Cornwallis, Nova Scotia.	Feb. 9, 1905	Communipaw, N. J..	Feb. 16, 1904	Do.
Neshanic (freight and towing).[d e]	271	1870	....	1886	....	.....do..............	Sept. 27, 1905	Brooklyn, N. Y.......	Feb. 9, 1905	Do.
New Jersey (pilot)..........	478	1902	....	1902	....	Tottenville, N. Y.....	Sept. 21, 1905	Port Richmond, N. Y.	Sept. 22, 1904	Do.
New York (pilot)............	540	1897	....	1897	....	Wilmington, Del.....	June 20, 1905	.....do...............	June 21, 1904	Do.
New York Central No. 6 (freight and towing).	453	1901	....	1901	....	Port Richmond, N. Y.	Aug. 14, 1905	Weehawken, N. J.....	Aug. 15, 1904	Do.
No. 2 P. D. (police)..........	[c]4	(f)	....	1901	....	Communipaw, N. J..	Mar. 6, 1905	Jersey City, N. J.....	Dec. 18, 1903	Do.
No. 3 P. D. (police)..........	18	1904	....	1904	....	Bayonne, N. J........	Dec. 26, 1905	New York, N. Y......	Dec. 21, 1904	Do.
No. 4 (police)[g]...............	18	1904	....	1904	....	.....do..............	Dec. 30, 1904	Bayonne, N. J........	First inspn..	
No. 5 (police)...............	18	1904	....	1904	....	.....do..............	Jan. 5, 1905	.....do...............	.....do......	
Omi (freight and towing)[h]...	149	1870	1905	1882	....	Newburgh, N. Y......	July 1, 1905	Port Richmond, N. Y.	June 23, 1904	Do.
Orcadia (water).............	31	1880	....	1880	....	Tottenville, N. Y.....	Dec. 12, 1905	Brooklyn, N. Y.......	Dec. 21, 1904	Do.
Pierre C. Van Wyck (freight and towing).	120	1881	....	1889	....	Athens, N. Y..........	June 29, 1905	West New Brighton, N. Y.	June 17, 1904	Do.
Potomac (freight and towing).	155	1895	....	1895	....	Baltimore, Md.......	Mar. 15, 1905	Port Richmond, N. Y.	Mar. 15, 1904	Do.
Reliance (freight and towing).	98	1870	....	1888	....	Philadelphia, Pa.....	Oct. 9, 1905	Jersey City, N. J.....	Oct. 12, 1904	Do.
Renovator (elevator)[i]......	471	1890	....	1898	....	Hoboken, N. J.......	June 22, 1905	Hoboken, N. J........	June 22, 1904	Do.
Roosevelt (survey)..........	614	1905	....	1905	....	Verona, Me...........	July 11, 1905	New York, N. Y......	First inspn..	
Rover (freight and towing)[j].	88	1876	1901	1903	....	Deering, Me..........	Jan. 23, 1905	.....do...............	Jan. 22, 1904	Do.
S. B. Greacen (freight and towing).	148	1900	....	1900	....	Tottenville, N. Y.....	July 10, 1905	Jersey City, N. J.....	July 9, 1904	Do.

[a] Formerly a sailing vessel.
[b] Certificate issued Jan. 4, 1905.
[c] Estimated.
[d] Formerly Etta Moore, 1899.
[e] Practically rebuilt in 1905, and therefore inspected more than sixty days prior to expiration of certificate.
[f] No record.
[g] Certificate issued Jan. 12, 1905.
[h] Formerly Lime Rock, 1905.
[i] Formerly Columbia, 1899.
[j] Formerly Gipsy Girl, 1901.

DOMESTIC VESSELS INSPECTED, YEAR ENDED DECEMBER 31, 1905—SECOND SUPERVISING DISTRICT—NEW YORK, N. Y.—Continued.

Names of vessels and class.	Gross tonnage.	Hull built.	Hull rebuilt.	Boilers built.	Boilers rebuilt.	Where built.	Date of inspection.	Where inspected.	Date of previous inspection.	Local district where previously inspected.
Miscellaneous steamers—Con.										
S. S. Wyckoff (freight and towing).	267	1864		1897		Greenpoint, N. Y	June 6, 1905	Keyport, N. J	June 6, 1904	New York, N. Y.
Safety (freight and towing)	134	1903		1903		Jersey City, N. J	July 31, 1905	West New Brighton, N. Y.	Aug. 1, 1904	Do.
Santos (freight and towing)	216	1902		1902		Shooters Island, N. Y.	Feb. 6, 1905	Brooklyn, N. Y	Feb. 6, 1904	Do.
Scotia (freight and towing)[a]	175	1861	1900	1900		Brooklyn, N. Y	July 15, 1905	do	July 14, 1904	Do.
Seth Low (fire)	82	1885	1904	1899		do	July 6, 1905	do	July 5, 1904	Do.
Silex (freight and towing)	143	1892		1897		Lockport, N. Y	Sept. 29, 1905	New York, N. Y	Sept. 29, 1904	Do.
Suffern (freight and towing)	398	1898		1898		New York, N. Y	Jan. 30, 1905	Jersey City, N. J	Feb. 3, 1904	Do.
T. L. Sturtevant (freight and towing).	120	1881		1893		Philadelphia, Pa	Aug. 4, 1905	Constable Hook, N. J	Aug. 4, 1904	Do.
Themis (elevator)	591	1898		1898		Camden, N. J	Aug. 23, 1905	Hoboken, N. J	Aug. 22, 1904	Do.
The New Yorker (fire)	243	1890		1902		New York, N. Y	Nov. 23, 1905	New York, N. Y	Nov. 10, 1904	Do.
Thomas (dredge)	2,525	1900		{1900 / 1903}		Sparrow Point, Md	Nov. 11, 1905	Jersey City, N. J	Nov. 11, 1904	Do.
Thos. B. Wattson (freight and towing).	134	1868	1881	1881		Chester, Pa	June 7, 1905	Hoboken, N. J	Mar. 29, 1904	Do.
Transit (freight and towing)	138	1879		1879		Greenpoint, N. Y	June 24, 1905	do	June 24, 1904	Do.
Towanda (freight and towing).[b]	172	1861		1884		Glenwood, N. Y	Nov. 24, 1905	Jersey City, N. J	Nov. 17, 1904	Do.
Turtle (freight and towing)	36	1898		1897		Patchogue, N. Y	Sept. 2, 1905	Patchogue, N. Y	Sept. 8, 1904	Do.
Tuscan (fishing)	13	1904		1891		East Rockaway, N. Y.	June 1, 1905	East Rockaway, N. Y.	First inspn	
Valvoline (freight and towing).	87	1897		1887		Athens, N. Y	Oct. 23, 1905	Brooklyn, N. Y	Oct. 22, 1904	Do.
Varina (freight and towing)	117	1893		1892		Penn Grove, N. J	June 13, 1905	do	Apr. 14, 1904	Do.
W. J. Carle (wrecking)	c 4	1889	1902	1901		Communipaw, N. J	Sept. 23, 1905	Shady Side, N. J	Sept. 24, 1904	Do.
Waccamaw (freight and towing).	1,359	1900		1900		Toledo, Ohio	Sept. 11, 1905	Shooters Island, N. Y.	Aug. 29, 1904	Portland, Me.
Waclark (freight and towing).[d]	88	1879		1904		Buffalo, N. Y	Dec. 1, 1905	West New Brighton, N. Y.	Nov. 17, 1904	New York, N. Y.
Western Union (cable)	184	1889		1899		Camden, N. J	Mar. 9, 1905	Jersey City, N. J	Mar. 8, 1904	Do.
William Coley (wrecking)	193	1893		1894		Tottenville, N. Y	June 22, 1905	Stapleton, N. Y	June 22, 1904	Norfolk, Va.
William Dinsdale (water)	44	1889		1889		Brooklyn, N. Y	July 10, 1905	Brooklyn, N. Y	July 9, 1904	New York, N. Y.
William L. Strong (fire)[e]	203	1898		1898		Camden, N. J	Jan. 23, 1905	New York, N. Y	Jan. 23, 1904	Do.
Zophar Mills (fire)	185	1882		1897		Wilmington, Del	July 28, 1905	do	July 29, 1904	Do.
Vessels propelled by gasoline motors.										
A. E. Vreeland	21	1902				Stratford, Conn	Mar. 28, 1905	Port Richmond, N. Y.	Jan. 11, 1904	New York, N. Y.
Admiral	29	1872				New Brunswick, N. J	Mar. 29, 1905	do	First inspn	
Amphion	20	1901				Bridgeport, Conn	May 26, 1905	Canarsie, N. Y	May 24, 1904	Do.

Athene	25	1884				Brooklyn, N. Y	June 21, 1905	do	First inspn	
Captain	22	1871				Bayport, N. Y	Mar. 10, 1905	Tottenville, N. Y	do	
Clochette	17	1872				Bath, Me.	May 19, 1905	Brooklyn, N. Y	do	
Commodore	25	1873				Islip, N. Y	Sept. 12, 1905	Port Richmond, N. Y.	Sept. 13, 1904	Do.
Dora	18	1904				Hoboken, N. J	June 27, 1905	Hoboken, N. J	June 28, 1904	Do.
Duane	16	1890				Tottenville, N. Y	Apr. 27, 1905	Canarsie, N. Y	First inspn	
Fearless	30	1870				Bath, Me	Apr. 29, 1905	New York, N. Y	do	
George T	25	1905				Tottenville, N. Y	Aug. 12, 1905	Tottenville, N. Y	do	
Hercules	20	1896				Providence, R. I	June 16, 1905	Canarsie, N. Y	do	
Joe Pinkett	16	1897				New York, N. Y	June 1, 1905	Brooklyn, N. Y	Apr. 29, 1904	Do
John Lundy	27	1892				Tottenville, N. Y	May 20, 1905	Sheepshead Bay, N. Y	Feb. 26, 1904	Do.
Magic Safety	71	1901				Brooklyn, N. Y	Mar. 22, 1905	Edgewater, N. J	Mar. 26, 1904	Do.
Magnet	69	1903				do	June 29, 1905	do	July 1, 1904	Do.
Mary J	23	1905				New York, N. Y	Apr. 7, 1905	Astoria, N. Y	First inspn	
Point O'Woods	27	1899				Patchogue, N. Y	May 24, 1905	Bay Shore, N. Y	June 7, 1904	Do.
Richmond	18	1905				Tottenville, N. Y	Aug. 12, 1905	Tottenville, N. Y	First inspn	
Rody Green	29	1901				do	Jan. 17, 1905	New York, N. Y	Jan. 16, 1904	Do.
Roulette	83	1884				Boston, Mass	June 16, 1905	Brooklyn, N. Y	June 7, 1904	Do.
Siva	33	1901				Stratford, Conn	Oct. 27, 1905	Oyster Bay, N. Y	Oct. 27, 1904	Do.
Satire	21	1876				Newport, R. I	Aug. 1, 1905	Brooklyn, N. Y	First inspn	
Tip Top	25	1898				New York, N. Y	Mar. 22, 1905	Edgewater, N. J	Aug. 5, 1903	Do.
W. H. Hoy	19	1901				Bridgeport, Conn	June 10, 1905	Glenwood, N. Y	June 10, 1904	Do.
Whileaway	34	1881				Greenport, N. Y	May 13, 1905	Brooklyn, N. Y	First inspn	
Freight sail vessels of over 700 tons.										
Adelaide Barbour (schooner)	1,336	1901				Newburyport, Mass	Feb. 7, 1905	Perth Amboy, N. J	Jan. 19, 1904	New York, N. Y.
Asbury Fountain (schooner) [f]	1,032	1890				Thomaston, Me	Jan. 23, 1905	Communipaw, N. J	Jan. 27, 1904	Savannah, Ga.
Benjamin C. Frith (schooner)	888	1890				do	June 10, 1905	Brooklyn, N. Y	June 8, 1904	Baltimore, Md.
Brina P. Pendleton (schooner)	933	1902				Belfast, Me	Apr. 12, 1905	Warners, N. J	Dec. 9, 1903	New York, N. Y.
Carrie Winslow (bark)	943	1880				Deering, Me	Jan. 24, 1905	Brooklyn, N. Y	July 28, 1903	Portland, Me.
Charles F. Tuttle (schooner)	776	1886				West Haven, Conn	Feb. 4, 1905	do	Jan. 9, 1904	New York, N. Y.
E. B. Sutton (ship)	1,826	1881				Bath, Me	Apr. 7, 1905	do	Nov. 5, 1903	Do.
Edith L. Allen (schooner)	969	1890				Richmond, Me	Feb. 25, 1905	do	Feb. 24, 1904	Do.
Eleanor F. Bartram (schooner).	1,114	1903				East Boothbay, Me	May 20, 1905	Perth Amboy, N. J	Nov. 6, 1903	Portland, Me.
Eleazer W. Clark (schooner)	934	1891				Bath, Me	Apr. 1, 1905	Brooklyn, N. Y	Mar. 17, 1904	New York, N. Y.
Ethel V. Boynton (barkentine).	739	1890				Harrington, Me	Apr. 11, 1905	do	Apr. 19, 1904	Do.
Florence M. Penley (schooner)	1,154	1903				Bath, Me	May 31, 1905	New York, N. Y	Apr. 25, 1904	Galveston, Tex.
Frances C. Tunnell (schooner)	1,476	1901				Millbridge, Me	Mar. 4, 1905	Hoboken, N. J	Mar. 12, 1904	Philadelphia, Pa.
Frederic A. Duggan (schooner).	1,137	1903				Bath, Me	June 2, 1905	Perth Amboy, N. J	May 19, 1904	Portland, Me.
Gracie D. Buchanan (schooner).	1,140	1888				do	Mar. 4, 1905	Jersey City, N. J	Mar. 2, 1904	New York, N. Y.
Henry Lippitt (schooner)	895	1895				Thomaston, Me	Apr. 15, 1905	New York, N. Y	Feb. 16, 1904	Jacksonville, Fla.
Jacob S. Winslow (schooner)	910	1889				Bath, Me	Jan. 17, 1905	Perth Amboy, N. J	Jan. 9, 1904	New York, N. Y.
John Swan (barkentine)	721	1889				Columbia Falls, Me	Jan. 27, 1905	Brooklyn, N. Y	Jan. 13, 1904	Savannah, Ga.
Kenwood (schooner)	929	1901				Boston, Mass	Jan. 6, 1905	do	Dec. 26, 1903	New York, N. Y.

[a] Formerly Havre, 1900.
[b] Formerly Roslyn, 1899.
[c] Estimated.
[d] Formerly Josephine B., 1904.
[e] Formerly Robert A. Van Wyck, 1902.
[f] Formerly Chas. L. Davenport, 1905.

DOMESTIC VESSELS INSPECTED, YEAR ENDED DECEMBER 31, 1905—SECOND SUPERVISING DISTRICT—NEW YORK, N. Y.—Continued.

Names of vessels and class.	Gross tonnage.	Hull built.	Hull rebuilt.	Boilers built.	Boilers rebuilt.	Where built.	Date of inspection.	Where inspected.	Date of previous inspection.	Local district where previously inspected.
***Freight sail vessels of over 700 tons*—Continued.**										
Mannie Swan (barkentine)	776	1892				Camden, Me.	Apr. 3, 1905	Brooklyn, N. Y.	Oct. 20, 1903	New York, N. Y.
Nuuanu (bark)	1,029	1882				Leith, Scotland	Feb. 3, 1905	do.	Dec. 1, 1902	Do.
Republic (schooner)	801	1900				Thomaston, Me.	Mar. 31, 1905	Carteret, N. J.	Feb. 16, 1904	Philadelphia, Pa.
Rose Inness (barkentine)	835	1881				Bath, Me.	May 1, 1905	Hoboken, N. J.	Oct. 29, 1903	Charleston, S. C.
Viking (schooner)	1,017	1888				do.	June 1, 1905	do.	June 22, 1904	New York, N. Y.
Sail vessels, barges, etc., of over 100 tons, carrying passengers for hire.										
Addie (barge)	177	1863	1903			Malden, N. Y.	Sept. 26, 1905	Ellis Island, N. Y.	Sept. 30, 1904	New York, N. Y.
Andrew M. Church (barge)	278	1892				New Baltimore, N. Y.	June 10, 1905	New York, N. Y.	May 27, 1904	Do.
Charles Spear (barge)	326	1864				Coxsackie, N. Y.	do.	Brooklyn, N. Y.	June 17, 1904	Do.
Curry (barge)	205	1882				Communipaw, N. J.	Apr. 1, 1905	Port Richmond, N. Y.	July 15, 1904	Do.
Empire (barge)	375	1900				Noank, Conn.	June 21, 1905	New York, N. Y.	June 23, 1904	Do.
Helen C. Juilliard (barge)	786	1899				Brooklyn, N. Y.	June 22, 1905	do.	June 22, 1904	Do.
Jacob A. Stamler (ship)	1,198	1856				do.	June 30, 1905	Brooklyn, N. Y.	Aug. 18, 1903	Do.
Laura (barge)	176	1857	1899			Athens, N. Y.	June 22, 1905	Ellis Island, N. Y.	June 25, 1904	Do.
Louisa C. (barge)	217	1861				New-Baltimore, N. Y.	June 20, 1905	do.	do.	Do.
P. R. R. 426 (barge)	546	1900				Elizabethport, N. J.	June 12, 1905	Jersey City, N. J.	First inspn.	
Starina (barge)	308	1864	1896			New York, N. Y.	June 3, 1905	Port Richmond, N. Y.	July 8, 1904	Do.
Stephen Warren (barge)	299	1847				do.	Mar. 31, 1905	do.	do.	Do.
Susquehanna (barge)	236	1850				do.	June 12, 1905	Brooklyn, N. Y.	June 17, 1904	Do.
William A. Sumner (barge)	283	1866				East Albany, N. Y.	June 9, 1905	Port Richmond, N. Y.	July 15, 1904	Do.
Wm. C. Moore (barge)	465	1904				Tottenville, N. Y.	May 4, 1905	Ellis Island, N. Y.	May 5, 1904	Do.
40 (car float)	954	1902				Quincy, Mass.	Sept. 13, 1905	New York, N. Y.	Aug. 3, 1904	Do.
44 (car float)	954	1903				do.	Sept. 18, 1905	do.	do.	Do.

LOCAL DISTRICT OF BOSTON, MASS.

Names of vessels and class.	Gross tonnage.	Hull built.	Hull rebuilt.	Boilers built.	Boilers rebuilt.	Where built.	Date of inspection.	Where inspected.	Date of previous inspection.	Local district where previously inspected.
Ocean passenger steamers.										
Admiral Dewey	2,104	1898		1898		Philadelphia, Pa.	Sept. 26, 1905	Boston, Mass.	Oct. 19, 1904	Boston, Mass.
Admiral Farragut	2,104	1898		1898		do.	Oct. 30, 1905	do.	Nov. 22, 1904	Do.
City of Bangor	1,661	1894		1894		Boston, Mass.	Apr. 10, 1905	do.	May 26, 1904	Do.
City of Rockland	1,696	1901		1900		do.	June 19, 1905	do.	June 27, 1904	Do.
Calvin Austin	3,826	1903		1903		Wilmington, Del.	June 3, 1905	do.	June 11, 1904	Do.
Herman Winter	2,625	1887		1886		Philadelphia, Pa.	Mar. 11, 1905	do.	Mar. 21, 1904	Do.

H. F. Dimock	2,625	1884		1884		....do	Sept. 11, 1905	....do	Sept. 15, 1904	New York, N. Y.
Kennebec	1,652	1889		1889		Bath, Me	June 13, 1905	....do	June 8, 1904	Boston, Mass.
Old Dominion	2,222	1872		1872		Wilmington, Del	Apr. 24, 1905	....do	Apr. 28, 1904	New York, N. Y.
Penobscot	1,414	1882		1882		Boston, Mass	June 5, 1905	....do	June 11, 1904	Boston, Mass.
Surprise [a]	821	1874		1891	1905	New York, N. Y	June 14, 1905	....do	July 27, 1903	Do.
St. Croix	1,993	1895		1895		Bath, Me	Dec. 28, 1905	....do	Dec. 31, 1904	Do.
Inland passenger steamers.										
Columbia	19	1892		1892		Middletown, Conn	May 2, 1905	Gloucester, Mass	Apr. 28, 1904	Portland, Me.
Canastota	51	1888		1888		Canastota, N. Y	May 15, 1905	Lynn, Mass	May 17, 1904	Boston, Mass.
Cape Cod	557	1900		1900		Essex, Mass	May 25, 1905	Quincy, Mass	June 14, 1904	Do.
City of Gloucester	560	1883		1883		Brooklyn, N. Y	May 26, 1905	Boston, Mass	June 7, 1904	Do.
Cormorant	99	1893		1903		Boston, Mass	May 13, 1905	....do	May 17, 1904	Do.
Cape Ann	718	1895		1895		Philadelphia, Pa	June 16, 1905	....do	June 23, 1904	Do.
Carlotta	22	1878		1896		Ipswich, Mass	....do	Ipswich, Mass	June 10, 1904	Do.
City of Haverhill	343	1902		1902		Boston, Mass	June 22, 1905	Boston, Mass	June 16, 1904	Do.
Comet	35	1901		1901		Portland, Me	Aug. 19, 1905	....do	Aug. 20, 1904	Do.
Confidence	65	1898		1898		Baltimore, Md	Dec. 7, 1905	....do	Dec. 9, 1904	Do.
E. W. Rice, jr	41	1893		1894		Providence, R. I	May 22, 1905	Lynn, Mass	May 17, 1904	Do.
Genl. Lincoln	398	1878		1897		Chelsea, Mass	Apr. 20, 1905	Hull, Mass	Apr. 15, 1904	Do.
Gov. Andrew	495	1874		1889		Greenpoint, N. Y	May 1, 1905	....do	Apr. 16, 1904	Do.
Gov. Douglass [b]	40	1900		1905		Essex, Mass	June 15, 1905	Beverly, Mass	June 6, 1904	Do.
Gov. Allen	58	1902		1896		Lowell, Mass	July 12, 1905	Lowell, Mass	July 6, 1904	Do.
Gloria	13	1891		1904		Boston, Mass	July 26, 1905	Boston, Mass	July 25, 1904	Do.
Guardian	124	1896		1896		....do	Oct. 5, 1905	....do	Oct. 13, 1904	Do.
Houghs Neck	60	1902		1902		....do	June 15, 1905	....do	June 4, 1904	Do.
Ida M. Chase	38	1901		1901		....do	Dec. 9, 1905	....do	Dec. 12, 1904	Do.
Juno	75	1894		1903		....do	May 18, 1905	....do	May 18, 1904	Do.
John Howard	38	1874		1899		....do	Sept. 20, 1905	....do	Sept. 24, 1904	Do.
King Philip	279	1893		1893		Bath, Me	May 20, 1905	....do	May 3, 1904	Do.
Mayflower	728	1891		1891		Chelsea, Mass	May 23, 1905	Hull, Mass	June 9, 1904	Do.
Myles Standish	700	1895		1898		....do	June 12, 1905	....do	May 5, 1904	Do.
Mercury	150	1890		1903		Boston, Mass	June 2, 1905	Boston, Mass	Mar. 31, 1904	Do.
Merrimac	211	1892		1892		Salisbury, Mass	June 10, 1905	Newburyport, Mass	June 13, 1904	Do.
Monitor	413	1904		1904		Boston, Mass	Sept. 13, 1905	Boston, Mass	Oct. 26, 1904	Do.
Mina and Lizzie	59	1898		1903		South Portland, Me	July 17, 1905	....do	July 22, 1904	Do.
Nantasket	739	1902		1901		Chelsea, Mass	May 18, 1905	Hull, Mass	Apr. 15, 1904	Do.
New Brunswick	935	1860		1888		New York, N. Y	June 29, 1905	Boston, Mass	June 20, 1904	Do.
Nabby C	32	1873		1899		Norfolk, Va	Aug. 16, 1905	Plymouth, Mass	Aug. 15, 1904	Do.
Old Colony	741	1904		1904		Chelsea, Mass	May 31, 1905	Hull, Mass	Apr. 26, 1904	Do.
Providence	4,365	1905		1905		Quincy, Mass	Feb. 20, 1905	Quincy, Mass	First inspn	
Pallas [c]	80	1882		1900	1904	Wilmington, Del	May 12, 1905	Boston, Mass	Feb. 26, 1904	Do.
Philadelphia	189	1882		1891		Athens, N. Y	May 24, 1905	Chelsea, Mass	May 25, 1904	Do.
Powow	48	1904		1904		Kennebunk, Me	June 6, 1905	Newburyport, Mass	June 4, 1904	Do.
Priscilla	67	1901		1901		Essex, Mass	July 6, 1905	Gloucester, Mass	July 14, 1904	Do.
Relief [d]	19	1894		1895		Boston, Mass	July 13, 1905	Boston, Mass	July 11, 1904	Do.
Resolute	25	1888		1888		Kennebunkport, Me	Nov. 21, 1905	....do	Nov. 21, 1904	Do.
Robert S. Bradley	121	1892		1901		Camden, N. J	Dec. 13, 1905	....do	Dec. 15, 1904	Do.
Sylvan Shore	53	1883		1891		Athens, N. Y	May 15, 1905	Lynn, Mass	May 13, 1904	Do.

[a] Name changed to Warren, 1905. [b] Formerly Empress, 1905. [c] Formerly Fred B. Dalzell, 1899. [d] Formerly Pleasure, 1905.

DOMESTIC VESSELS INSPECTED, YEAR ENDED DECEMBER 31, 1905—SECOND SUPERVISING DISTRICT—BOSTON, MASS.—Continued.

Names of vessels and class.	Gross tonnage.	Hull built.	Hull rebuilt.	Boilers built.	Boilers rebuilt.	Where built.	Date of inspection.	Where inspected.	Date of previous inspection.	Local district where previously inspected.
Inland passenger steamers—Continued.										
Susie D	45	1895		1903		Boston, Mass	June 30, 1905	Vineyard Haven, Mass	June 29, 1904	Boston, Mass.
Scylla [a]	67	1881		1881		do	Dec. 4, 1905	Boston, Mass	Dec. 6, 1904	Do.
Vesta	58	1892		1898		Baltimore, Md	May 8, 1905	do	May 7, 1904	Do.
Vigilant	73	1886		1898		Boston, Mass	June 7, 1905	do	June 20, 1904	Do.
Winthrop	91	1893		1893		Essex, Mass	May 22, 1905	Lynn, Mass	May 13, 1904	Do
Ferry steamers.										
Ashburnham	446	1905		1905		Boston, Mass	May 16, 1905	Boston, Mass	First inspn.	
Blonde	15	1888		1900		do	July 26, 1905	Marblehead, Mass	July 27, 1904	Boston, Mass.
Brunette	10	1882		1886		Camden, Me	Sept. 8, 1905	do	Sept. 16, 1904	Do.
City of Lynn	340	1878		1889		Bath, Me	Mar. 27, 1905	Boston, Mass	Mar. 26, 1904	Do.
City of Malden	487	1882		1882		Chelsea, Mass	Mar. 30, 1905	Chelsea, Mass	Mar. 15, 1904	Do.
City of Boston	487	1880		1879		do	Sept. 22, 1905	do	Sept. 23, 1904	Do.
City of Chelsea	504	1874		1895		Wilmington, Del	Dec. 27, 1905	do	Nov. 22, 1904	Do.
Dartmouth	420	1899		1899		Boston, Mass	May 9, 1905	Boston, Mass	May 13, 1904	Do.
D. D. Kelly	550	1879		1879		do	June 16, 1905	do	May 23, 1904	Do.
Genl. Hancock	577	1887		1887		do	July 19, 1905	do	June 24, 1904	Do.
General Sumner	703	1900		1900		do	Sept. 19, 1905	do	Aug. 26, 1904	Do.
Gov. Russell	713	1898		1898		do	Oct. 19, 1905	do	Dec. 8, 1904	Do.
Hugh O'Brien	645	1883		1884		do	May 11, 1905	do	May 2, 1904	Do.
Irene [b]	[c]4	1888		1902		do	June 27, 1905	Edgartown, Mass	June 27, 1904	Do.
Little Giant	26	1878		1902		Gloucester, Mass	Aug. 28, 1905	Gloucester, Mass	Sept. 2, 1904	Do.
Noddle Island	710	1899		1899		Boston, Mass	May 19, 1905	Boston, Mass	May 14, 1904	Do.
Queen	17	1895		1895		do	July 28, 1905	Marblehead, Mass	July 29, 1904	Do.
Revere	550	1875		1876		do	Aug. 23, 1905	Boston, Mass	Aug. 22, 1904	Do.
Swampscott	416	1882		1899		do	Oct. 20, 1905	do	Oct. 29, 1904	Do.
Ocean freight steamers.										
Hector	2,929	1883		1883		Newcastle-on-Tyne, England.	Jan. 5, 1905	Boston, Mass	Dec. 31, 1903	Boston, Mass.
Hector	2,929	1883		1905		do	Nov. 24, 1905	do	Jan. 5, 1905	Do.
Mae	2,103	1899		1899		Toledo, Ohio	Aug. 12, 1905	North Weymouth, Mass.	Aug. 19, 1904	New York, N. Y.
Massasoit [d]	364	1891		1891		Port Huron, Mich	Aug. 21, 1905	Boston, Mass	Aug. 31, 1904	Port Huron, Mich.
Inland freight steamers.										
Abbott Coffin	68	1882		1891		Boston, Mass	June 15, 1905	Gloucester, Mass	June 15, 1904	Boston, Mass.
Ben Harrison	112	1889		1896		Essex, Mass	Aug. 1, 1905	Rockport, Mass	Aug. 1, 1904	Do.

Eagle	65	1887		1903		Gloucester, Mass	Oct. 3, 1905	Gloucester, Mass	Oct. 28, 1904	Do.
Fannie	220	1886		1886		Wilmington, Del	Apr. 11, 1905	Boston, Mass	Apr. 11, 1904	Philadelphia, Pa.
Hetty Agnes	82	1882		1894		Boston, Mass	Apr. 17, 1905	do	Apr. 12, 1904	Boston, Mass.
Jonas H. French	195	1899		1899		Newburyport, Mass	Feb. 16, 1905	do	Feb. 18, 1904	Do.
James Anderson	111	1877		1892		Boston, Mass	Mar. 23, 1905	do	Mar. 23, 1904	Do.
J. E. James	56	1888		1903		do	Nov. 27, 1905	do	Dec. 15, 1904	Do.
Moses Adams	22	1885		1885		Essex, Mass	Jan. 11, 1905	Gloucester, Mass	Jan. 11, 1904	Do.
Merchant	136	1882		1898		Boston, Mass	Mar. 13, 1905	Boston, Mass	Mar. 12, 1904	Do.
N. Hayden	133	1881		1881		do	Nov. 3, 1905	do	Nov. 3, 1904	Do.
Pioneer	15	1888		1895		Edgartown, Mass	June 16, 1905	Woods Hole, Mass	June 22, 1904	Do.
Philip	75	1903		1903		Gloucester, Mass	July 18, 1905	Gloucester, Mass	July 18, 1904	Do.
Sophia	100	1892		1904		Boston, Mass	Sept. 16, 1905	Rockport, Mass	Sept. 15, 1904	Do.
Wm. S. McGowan	124	1880		1880		do	Aug. 24, 1905	Boston, Mass	Aug. 24, 1904	Do.
William H. Moody	259	1898		1897		Essex, Mass	Sept. 23, 1905	Rockport, Mass	Sept. 30, 1904	Do.
Ocean towing steamers.										
Conestoga	617	1904		1904		Sparrows Point, Md	Jan. 30, 1905	Boston, Mass	Jan. 25, 1904	Baltimore, Md.
Cuba	594	1901		1901		Bath, Me	Apr. 28, 1905	do	Apr. 23, 1904	Providence, R. I.
Carlisle	644	1901		1901		Philadelphia, Pa	Oct. 30, 1905	do	Nov. 7, 1904	Philadelphia, Pa.
Dudley Pray	215	1890		1902		Boston, Mass	June 5, 1905	do	June 6, 1904	Boston, Mass.
International	400	1890		1902		Philadelphia, Pa	Jan. 11, 1905	do	Jan. 8, 1904	Do.
International	400	1890		1902		do	Dec. 27, 1905	do	Jan. 11, 1905	Do.
James Woolley	92	1899		1899		Boston, Mass	Sept. 16, 1905	do	Sept. 16, 1904	Do.
John G. Chandler	110	1902		1902		Bath, Me	Aug. 10, 1905	do	Aug. 4, 1904	Do.
Joshua Lovett	169	1888		1897		Boston, Mass	Nov. 10, 1905	do	Sept. 30, 1904	Do.
Lenape	637	1904		1904		Camden, N. J	Nov. 21, 1905	do	Dec. 7, 1904	Philadelphia, Pa.
Paoli	330	1895		1895		Philadelphia, Pa	Oct. 20, 1905	do	Oct. 18, 1904	Providence, R. I.
Sea King	123	1892		1891		do	May 8, 1905	do	May 9, 1904	Philadelphia, Pa.
Storm King	182	1882		1895		do	July 1, 1905	do	June 30, 1904	Boston, Mass.
Teaser	216	1899		1899		Boston, Mass	June 28, 1905	do	June 21, 1904	Do.
Underwriter	327	1863		1902		Philadelphia, Pa	Aug. 17, 1905	do	Oct. 7, 1904	New York, N. Y.
Valley Forge	558	1898		1898		Wilmington, Del	Sept. 29, 1905	do	Oct. 4, 1904	Philadelphia, Pa.
Inland towing steamers.										
Annie	75	1884		1896		Alexandria, Va	Apr. 3, 1905	Boston, Mass	Apr. 1, 1904	Boston, Mass.
Active	28	1880		1881		Boston, Mass	Aug. 4, 1905	do	Aug. 3, 1904	Do.
Ariel	52	1883		1898		Philadelphia, Pa	Aug. 28, 1905	do	Aug. 29, 1904	Do.
Anna Shaw	12	1869		1891		Millville, N. J	Sept. 8, 1905	do	Sept. 9, 1904	Do.
Annie Emmons	28	1892		1886		Athens, N. Y	Oct. 9, 1905	do	Oct. 17, 1904	Do.
A. W. Chesterton	99	1889		1889		Gloucester, Mass	Dec. 1, 1905	do	Dec. 16, 1904	Do.
B. T. Haviland	103	1883		1897		Brooklyn, N. Y	July 24, 1905	do	July 23, 1904	Do.
Bronx	32	1884		1884		do	July 25, 1905	Newburyport, Mass	Aug. 8, 1904	Do.
Betsy Ross	39	1905		1889		Chelsea, Mass	Aug. 8, 1905	Boston, Mass	First inspn	
Blanche	54	1881		1881		Boston, Mass	Nov. 7, 1905	do	Nov. 7, 1904	Do.
Charles H. Hersey	48	1872		1884		Philadelphia, Pa	Mar. 14, 1905	do	Mar. 11, 1904	Do.
Clara E. Uhler	43	1881		1892		do	Apr. 13, 1905	Newburyport, Mass	Apr. 1, 1904	Do.
Cornelia	41	1881		1901		Tottenville, N. Y	May 10, 1905	Boston, Mass	Apr. 23, 1904	Do.
Channing	51	1895		1895		Boston, Mass	June 5, 1905	do	June 4, 1904	Do.

[a] Formerly Ida M. Dalby, 1905.
[b] Formerly Athlete.

[c] Estimated.
[d] Formerly O. O. Carpenter, 1905.

DOMESTIC VESSELS INSPECTED, YEAR ENDED DECEMBER 31, 1905—SECOND SUPERVISING DISTRICT—BOSTON, MASS.—Continued.

Names of vessels and class.	Gross tonnage.	Hull built.	Hull rebuilt.	Boilers built.	Boilers rebuilt.	Where built.	Date of inspection.	Where inspected.	Date of previous inspection.	Local district where previously inspected.
Inland towing steamers—Con.										
Charles F. Dunbar	136	1898		1904		Buffalo, N. Y.	June 14, 1905	Boston, Mass.	June 21, 1904	Oswego, N. Y.
Charlie	10	1903		1885		St. George, Me.	July 24, 1905	do.	July 23, 1904	Boston, Mass.
Charles F. Harris	65	1873	1901	1904		Chester, Pa.	July 31, 1905	Nantucket, Mass.	July 27, 1904	New York, N. Y.
Charles T. Gallagher	90	1904		1904		South Portland, Me.	Aug. 23, 1905	Boston, Mass.	Sept. 3, 1904	Portland, Me.
Charles Mann	79	1903		1903		do.	Sept. 13, 1905	do.	Sept. 12, 1904	Boston, Mass.
Clara Clarita	125	1864		1892		Brooklyn, N. Y.	Nov. 4, 1905	do.	Nov. 1, 1904	Do.
Cocheco	67	1887		1894		Bath, Me.	Nov. 18, 1905	do.	Nov. 19, 1904	Do.
Dione	33	1886		1899		Philadelphia, Pa.	Apr. 29, 1905	do.	Apr. 28, 1904	Do.
D. Roughan	34	1869		1882		Wilmington, Del.	July 10, 1905	do.	July 8, 1904	Do.
Dolphin	47	1896		1899		Brooklyn, N. Y.	Aug. 7, 1905	do.	Aug. 6, 1904	Do.
DeVaux Powel	61	1873		1896		New Baltimore, N. Y.	Dec. 7, 1905	do.	Dec. 10, 1904	Savannah, Ga.
Eveleth	42	1897		1897		Gloucester, Mass.	Feb. 18, 1905	Gloucester, Mass.	Feb. 20, 1904	Boston, Mass.
Elsie	49	1871		1898		Boston, Mass.	Mar. 30, 1905	Boston, Mass.	Mar. 30, 1904	Do.
Eleanor L. Wright	96	1893		1893		Bath, Me.	July 13, 1905	do.	July 12, 1904	Do.
Eddie	17	1885		1882		Baltimore, Md.	Aug. 24, 1905	do.	Aug. 24, 1904	Do.
Emily	36	1871		1889		Boston, Mass.	Dec. 2, 1905	do.	Dec. 3, 1904	Do.
Francis J. Ward	40	1872		1903		do.	Apr. 4, 1905	do.	Apr. 4, 1904	Do.
Francis C. Hersey	79	1903		1903		South Portland, Me.	Nov. 17, 1905	do.	Nov. 16, 1904	Do.
Flyer	45	1864		1902		Brooklyn, N. Y.	Dec. 9, 1905	do.	July 24, 1903	Do.
Florence	36	1883		1883		Boston, Mass.	Dec. 21, 1905	do.	Dec. 21, 1904	Do.
Hazel Dell	44	1888		1888		New Baltimore, N. Y.	July 8, 1905	Newburyport, Mass.	July 8, 1904	Do.
H. T. Minton [a]	24	1872		1889		Pettys Island, N. J.	July 6, 1905	Boston, Mass.	May 20, 1904	Do.
Hamilton A. Mathes	48	1892		1891		Boston, Mass.	Aug. 3, 1905	do.	Aug. 1, 1904	Do.
H. S. Nichols	65	1888		1899		Athens, N. Y.	Sept. 7, 1905	Rockport, Mass.	Sept. 6, 1904	Do.
Henrietta	45	1875		1884		Portland, Me.	Sept. 21, 1905	Boston, Mass.	Oct. 19, 1904	Do.
Henry Preston, sr	38	1882		1900		Greenpoint, N. Y.	Sept. 18, 1905	Beverly, Mass.	Sept. 28, 1904	Do.
H. Chapel	23	1873		1902		Philadelphia, Pa.	Oct. 9, 1905	Boston, Mass.	Nov. 2, 1904	Do.
Irving F. Ross	27	1898		1893		Boston, Mass.	Oct. 21, 1905	do.	Oct. 24, 1904	Do.
Jennie	20	1897		1897		do.	Mar. 23, 1905	do.	Mar. 23, 1904	Do.
Jacob G. Neafie	29	1868		1882		Philadelphia, Pa.	Apr. 7, 1905	do.	Apr. 8, 1904	Do.
Joseph W. Ross	27	1899		1899		Boston, Mass.	July 21, 1905	do.	July 23, 1904	Do.
Joe Call	31	1882		1900		Essex, Mass.	Sept. 18, 1905	Harwichport, Mass.	Sept. 21, 1904	Do.
Kate Jones	122	1879		1901		Camden, N. J.	June 5, 1905	Boston, Mass.	June 3, 1904	Do.
Leader	59	1881		1881		Philadelphia, Pa.	June 20, 1905	do.	June 23, 1904	Do.
Louis Osborn	32	1871		1899		Gloucester, Mass.	June 30, 1905	do.	July 1, 1904	Do.
Minot I. Wilcox	111	1887		1897		Tottenville, N. Y.	Jan. 4, 1905	do.	Dec. 28, 1903	Do.
Metropolitan	71	1892		1899		Boston, Mass.	Apr. 21, 1905	do.	Apr. 18, 1904	Do.
Mattie Sargent	35	1871		1894		Philadelphia, Pa.	June 22, 1905	do.	June 20, 1904	Do.
Marguerite	128	1893		1893		Kennebunk, Me.	June 20, 1905	do.	June 23, 1904	Do.
Maylu	8	1889		1899		Gloucester, Mass.	July 26, 1905	Vineyard Haven, Mass.	June 29, 1904	Do.
Marie	42	1894		1904		Kennebunkport, Me.	Aug. 4, 1905	Boston, Mass.	Aug. 3, 1904	Do.

Minnie and Irvin	17	1879		1884		Greenpoint, N. Y	Nov. 18, 1905	do	May 18, 1904	Do.
Nellie	39	1873		1893		Philadelphia, Pa	June 14, 1905	do	June 14, 1904	Do.
Nonpareil	46	1887		1887		Tottenville, N. Y	Oct. 2, 1905	do	Oct. 10, 1904	Do.
Nellie	46	1902		1902		Essex, Mass	Nov. 10, 1905	Gloucester, Mass	Nov. 14, 1904	Do.
Onward [b]	36	1888		1884		Boston, Mass	Apr. 14, 1905	Boston, Mass	Apr. 18, 1904	Do.
Ocean Queen	15	1890		1901		do	Nov. 24, 1905	do	Nov. 23, 1904	Do.
Peter W. French	48	1887		1887		do	July 10, 1905	do	July 8, 1904	Do.
Peter B. Bradley	81	1877		1886		do	Aug. 24, 1905	do	Aug. 22, 1904	Do.
P. O'Riorden	62	1879		1885		Communipaw, N. J	Aug. 5, 1905	do	Aug. 6, 1904	Do.
Rosebelle	10	1886		1894		Baltimore, Md	June 15, 1905	do	June 14, 1904	Do.
Sadie Ross	49	1894		1903		Boston, Mass	Apr. 11, 1905	do	Apr. 9, 1904	Do.
Startle	46	1889		1889		Gloucester, Mass	Sept. 26, 1905	do	Oct. 14, 1904	Do.
Samuel Little	46	1872		1888		Boston, Mass	Dec. 21, 1905	do	Dec. 21, 1904	Do.
Thomas J. York, jr	45	1881		1895		Philadelphia, Pa	Apr. 6, 1905	do	Apr. 9, 1904	Portland, Me.
Telephone	15	1879		1897		Boston, Mass	July 3, 1905	do	July 2, 1904	Boston, Mass.
Undine	41	1888		1895		Kennebunkport, Me	Aug. 1, 1905	do	Aug. 1, 1904	Do.
Viking	77	1881		1890		Camden, N. J	May 2, 1905	do	May 21, 1904	Do.
Valora	14	1879		1900		Richmond, Me	June 15, 1905	do	June 16, 1904	Do.
Vim	36	1872		1889		Boston, Mass	Sept. 29, 1905	do	Nov. 7, 1904	Do.
Wm. E. Cleary	41	1864		1897		Philadelphia, Pa	Feb. 10, 1905	do	Dec. 28, 1903	Do.
William Sprague	48	1880		1894		Boston, Mass	May 22, 1905	do	May 21, 1904	Do.
Wesley A. Gove	70	1884		1884		do	June 10, 1905	do	June 13, 1904	Do.
Wm. G. Small	28	1901		1893		Phippsburg, Me	Oct. 11, 1905	do	Oct. 15, 1904	Do.
Wm. G. Williams	30	1900		1900		Boston, Mass	Dec. 1, 1905	do	Nov. 30, 1904	Do.
Zetes	44	1900		1899		do	Apr. 12, 1905	do	Apr. 11, 1904	Do.
Ocean steam pleasure yachts.										
Anona	146	1904		1904		Boston, Mass	May 17, 1905	Boston, Mass	May 25, 1904	Boston, Mass.
Cigarette	83	1905		1905		do	Aug. 30, 1905	do	First inspn	
Idalia	201	1899		1898		Chester, Pa	May 25, 1905	do	June 3, 1904	Do.
Juanita	109	1896		1904		Nyack, N. Y	Apr. 21, 1905	do	Apr. 14, 1904	Do.
Lillie G	34	1905		1905		Camden, Me	June 21, 1905	do	First inspn	
Malay	173	1898		1898		Chester, Pa	May 5, 1905	do	Apr. 27, 1904	Do.
Mayflower	41	1888		1888		Boston, Mass	June 26, 1905	Plymouth, Mass	May 29, 1903	Do.
Montclair	71	1898		1898		North Weymouth, Mass.	July 31, 1905	Boston, Mass	June 10, 1904	Do.
Nerita	137	1887		1894		Noank, Conn	Oct. 21, 1905	Quincy, Mass	May 7, 1902	Do.
Pantooset	538	1902		1902		Bath, Me	May 12, 1905	Boston, Mass	Apr. 15, 1904	Do.
Peregrine	246	1896		1895		do	May 29, 1905	do	May 25, 1904	Do.
Rambler [c]	288	1899		1899		Elizabethport, N. J	May 5, 1905	do	May 6, 1904	Do.
Sayonara	130	1896		1905		Chester, Pa	May 23, 1905	do	Apr. 28, 1904	Do.
Wacondah [d]	119	1899		1899		Morris Heights, N. Y	July 19, 1905	do	Aug. 16, 1904	Do.
Inland steam pleasure yachts.										
Alice M	[e] 2	1888		1888		Sheldonville, Mass	Sept. 5, 1905	South Yarmouth, Mass.	Sept. 7, 1904	Boston, Mass.
Bethulia	57	1893		1893		Boston, Mass	June 2, 1905	Boston, Mass	May 18, 1904	New York, N. Y.
Cloella	26	1896		1901		do	May 29, 1905	do	May 25, 1904	Boston, Mass.

[a] Formerly J. C. Cottingham, 1902. [b] Formerly Louisa and Alice, 1902. [c] Formerly Dreamer, 1903. [d] Formerly Aria, 1904. [e] Estimated.

[DOMESTIC VESSELS INSPECTED, YEAR ENDED DECEMBER 31, 1905—SECOND SUPERVISING DISTRICT—BOSTON, MASS.—Continued.

Names of vessels and class.	Gross tonnage.	Hull built.	Hull rebuilt.	Boilers built.	Boilers rebuilt.	Where built.	Date of inspection.	Where inspected.	Date of previous inspection.	Local district where previously inspected.
Inland steam pleasure yachts—Continued.										
Chipeta	44	1893		1896		Jamestown, R. I	May 29, 1905	Boston, Mass	June 7, 1904	Boston, Mass.
Caprice	9	1898		1898		Braintree, Mass	June 21, 1905	Marblehead, Mass	June 21, 1904	Do.
Carmen	a 1	1894		1893		Boston, Mass	July 15, 1905	Boston, Mass	July 13, 1904	Do.
Dolphin	a 4	1879		1885	1901	do	Sept. 15, 1905	do	Oct. 18, 1904	Do.
Ernestine	a 1	1901		1902		St. Joseph, Mich	May 13, 1905	do	May 14, 1904	Do.
Edna	a 5	1898		1898		Cambridgeport, Mass	June 30, 1905	Chelsea, Mass	Jan. 1, 1902	Do.
Etta	a 3	1882		1895		Portsmouth, N. H	Oct. 10, 1905	Boston, Mass	Sept. 24, 1904	Do.
Eleanor	23	1892		1892		Salem, Mass	July 28, 1905	do	July 30, 1904	Do.
Howard	a 1	1896		1892		Sheldonville, Mass	Sept. 5, 1905	South Yarmouth, Mass.	Sept. 7, 1904	Do.
Iris	7	1887		1902		Boston, Mass	May 24, 1905	Boston, Mass	June 3, 1904	Do.
Iolanthe	a 3	1892		1892		do	July 1, 1905	do	June 6, 1904	Do.
Ilybius	12	1894		1904		Braintree, Mass	July 27, 1905	do	July 23, 1904	Do.
John Harvard	7	1900		1900		Boston, Mass	Mar. 28, 1905	do	Mar. 28, 1904	Do.
Jule	26	1904		1903		do	Apr. 14, 1905	do	Apr. 27, 1904	Do.
Johnnie	a 5	1892		1896		Salem, Mass	Sept. 8, 1905	Beverly, Mass	Aug. 1, 1903	Do.
Letitia	a 3	(b)		1897		Unknown	Aug. 2, 1905	Boston, Mass	May 23, 1904	Do.
Leila	9	1903		1901		Boston, Mass	Aug. 16, 1905	Everett, Mass	Aug. 25, 1904	Do.
Lotis	38	1899		1899		do	Sept. 5, 1905	Boston, Mass	Sept. 8, 1904	Do.
Monoloa	75	1904		1904		do	May 6, 1905	do	June 3, 1904	Do.
My Gypsy	26	1893		1901		do	June 5, 1905	do	June 24, 1904	Do.
Mermaid	a 3	1890		1896		Lowell, Mass	June 14, 1905	Lowell, Mass	May 12, 1896	Do.
Mist	12	1904		1904		Bristol, R. I	July 29, 1905	Boston, Mass	May 16, 1904	Providence, R. I.
Miriam	10	1892		1895		Boston, Mass	Aug. 19, 1905	do	Aug. 20, 1904	Boston, Mass.
Nashawena	37	1889		1902		do	June 13, 1905	do	June 13, 1904	Do.
Nordlys	12	1894		1903		Portland, Me	Aug. 12, 1905	Marblehead, Mass	Aug. 5, 1904	Do.
Nautilus	15	1889		1889		Boston, Mass	Sept. 16, 1905	Boston, Mass	June 12, 1904	Providence, R. I.
Percival	a 2	1888		1905		do	June 3, 1905	Lowell, Mass	May 22, 1903	Boston, Mass.
Pilgrim	18	1899		1899		do	Aug. 2, 1905	Boston, Mass	Aug. 4, 1904	Do.
Sagitta	a 4	1887		1887		do	June 16, 1905	Woods Hole, Mass	June 22, 1904	Do.
Sagoyewatha	a 1	1880		1894		Lowell, Mass	June 3, 1905	Lowell, Mass	June 28, 1904	Do.
Sally	9	1897		1897		Braintree, Mass	July 27, 1905	Boston, Mass	July 26, 1902	Do.
Shoe City	a 2	1893		1894		Boston, Mass	Aug. 18, 1905	Barnstable, Mass	Aug. 23, 1904	Do.
Tramp	27	1901		1901		Bristol, R. I	Apr. 6, 1905	Beverly, Mass	June 1, 1904	Do.
Velthra	70	1903		1903		Morris Heights, N. Y	Apr. 12, 1905	Boston, Mass	Apr. 13, 1904	Do.
Veritas	5	1900		1900		do	May 9, 1905	do	May 9, 1904	Do.
Vulcan	19	1891		1899		Detroit, Mich	June 23, 1905	Haverhill, Mass	June 28, 1904	Do.
Wenonah	58	1903		1903		Rockland, Me	May 25, 1905	Boston, Mass	May 28, 1904	Do.
Wild Goose	43	1892		1896		Salem, Mass	June 8, 1905	Marblehead, Mass	June 6, 1904	Do.
Zinganee	30	1902		1902		Bristol R. I	June 12, 1905	Boston, Mass	May 28, 1904	Do.

Miscellaneous steam vessels.										
Angelia B. Nickerson (fishing)	46	1886		1886		Boothbay, Me	Mar. 28, 1905	Boston, Mass	Apr. 11, 1904	Boston, Mass.
Conwell Brothers (fishing)	a 5	1885		1901		Bristol, Me	May 26, 1905	Provincetown, Mass	May 24, 1904	Do.
Charlie (fishing)	a 4	1890		1890		Gloucester, Mass	July 20, 1905	Barnstable, Mass	July 20, 1904	Do.
Engine 44 (fire)	178	1895		1895		Boston, Mass	Mar. 7, 1905	Boston, Mass	Jan. 20, 1904	Do.
Elsie (fishing)	a 4	1889		1904		Gloucester, Mass	June 6, 1905	Provincetown, Mass	June 2, 1904	Do.
Ethel (fishing)	a 4	1889		1903		do	July 14, 1905	Lynn, Mass	July 16, 1904	Do.
Engine 31 (fire)	186	1897		1890		Boston, Mass	Dec. 2, 1905	Boston, Mass	Nov. 30, 1904	Do.
Flora (water)	17	1872		1886		do	Apr. 6, 1905	do	July 20, 1903	Do.
George Leslie (fishing)	5	1890		1899		Gloucester, Mass	June 6, 1095	Provincetown, Mass	June 2, 1904	Do.
Joppaite (fishing)	28	1901		1898		Newburyport, Mass	July 11, 1905	Newburyport, Mass	July 5, 1904	Do.
Lexington (police)	224	1898		1898		Essex, Mass	July 21, 1905	Edgartown, Mass	Aug. 3, 1904	Do.
Laura (fishing)	6	1889		1904		Gloucester, Mass	Sept. 7, 1905	Provincetown, Mass	June 2, 1904	Do.
Persis (fishing)	6	1901		1899		Boston, Mass	Mar. 20, 1905	Truro, Mass	Mar. 18, 1904	Do.
Petrel (fishing)	22	1896		1896		do	July 31, 1905	Nantucket, Mass	July 25, 1904	Do.
Spray (trawler)	283	1905		1905		Quincy, Mass	Dec. 6, 1905	Quincy, Mass	First inspn	
Viola (fishing)	25	1884		1896		New York, N. Y	Apr. 7, 1905	Boston, Mass	July 3, 1900	Do.
Watchman (police)	14	1898		1897		Boston, Mass	Feb. 23, 1905	do	Feb. 23, 1904	Do.
White Bar (fishing)	a 5	1890		1903		Gloucester, Mass	May 26, 1905	Provincetown, Mass	May 24, 1904	Do.
Waquoit (fishing)	17	1887		1904		Boston, Mass	Aug. 30, 1905	Nantucket, Mass	Sept. 26, 1904	Do.
Gasoline motor vessels.										
Constellation (fishing)	137	1902				Essex, Mass	Mar. 16, 1905	Gloucester, Mass	Mar. 20, 1904	Boston, Mass.
Elizabeth Silsbee (fishing)	153	1905				do	Sept. 19, 1905	do	First inspn	
Gleaner (fishing)	44	1903				do	Sept. 5, 1905	Chatham, Mass	Sept. 1, 1904	Do.
Mary E. Harty (fishing)	122	1901				Gloucester, Mass	Mar. 22, 1905	Gloucester, Mass	Apr. 2, 1904	Do.
Shenandoah (fishing)	110	1890				Essex, Mass	Mar. 25, 1905	do	Apr. 11, 1904	Do.
Saladin (fishing)	137	1902				do	do	do	Mar. 26, 1904	Do.
Victor (fishing)	121	1901				do	do	do	Mar. 28, 1904	Do.
Veda M. McKown (fishing)	131	1902				do	do	do	do	Do.
Welcome (towing)	41	1903				Neponset, Mass	June 24, 1905	Boston, Mass	June 25, 1904	Do.
Freight sail vessels of over 700 tons.										
Benj. F. Hunt, jr. (bark)	1,190	1882				Newburyport, Mass	May 24, 1905	Boston, Mass	Dec. 17, 1903	Boston, Mass.
Gardiner G. Deering (schooner)	1,982	1903				Bath, Me	May 10, 1905	do	May 6, 1904	Baltimore, Md.
Harvard (bark)	1,603	1864				Brunswick, Me	June 24, 1905	do	Oct. 1, 1903	Do.
James B. Drake (schooner)	1,153	1904				Bath, Me	Jan. 9, 1905	do	Jan. 18, 1904	Portland, Me.
Joseph B. Thomas (schooner)	1,564	1900				Thomaston, Me	Jan. 10, 1905	Salem, Mass	Dec. 30, 1903	Philadelphia, Pa.
Mabel I. Meyers (barkentine)	750	1891				Searsport, Me	May 22, 1905	Boston, Mass	Nov. 4, 1903	Boston, Mass.
Prescott Palmer (schooner)	2,811	1902				Bath, Me	Jan. 28, 1905	do	Jan. 19, 1904	Baltimore, Md.
Rebecca Palmer (schooner)	2,556	1901				Rockland, Me	Mar. 10, 1905	do	Mar. 3, 1904	Boston, Mass.
Winfield S. Schuster (schooner)	1,481	1904				Rockport, Me	Feb. 11, 1905	do	Feb. 23, 1904	Portland, Me.
Barge of over 100 tons carrying passengers for hire.										
Clifford	237	1876				Bangor, Me	June 28, 1905	Boston, Mass	First inspn	

a Estimated.

b Unknown.

DOMESTIC VESSELS INSPECTED, YEAR ENDED DECEMBER 31, 1905—SECOND SUPERVISING DISTRICT—Continued.

LOCAL DISTRICT OF PHILADELPHIA, PA.

Names of vessels and class.	Gross tonnage.	Hull built.	Hull rebuilt.	Boilers built.	Boilers rebuilt.	Where built.	Date of inspection.	Where inspected.	Date of previous inspection.	Local district where previously inspected.
Ocean passenger steamers.										
Alleghany	2,014	1881		1898		Philadelphia, Pa	Jan. 25, 1905	Philadelphia, Pa	Jan. 29, 1904	Philadelphia, Pa.
Admiral Sampson	2,104	1898		1904		do	Nov. 15, 1905	do	Dec. 1, 1904	Do.
Admiral Schley	2,104	1898		1898		do	Nov. 21, 1905	do	Nov. 10, 1904	Do.
Grecian	2,827	1900		1900		Wilmington, Del	Apr. 4, 1905	do	Apr. 4, 1904	Do.
Huron	3,318	1902		1902		Philadelphia, Pa	Aug. 24, 1905	do	Dec. 6, 1904	New York, N. Y.
Indian	2,110	1890		1890		Wilmington, Del	June 7, 1905	Wilmington, Del	July 22, 1904	Philadelphia, Pa.
Merrimack	2,546	1879	1904	1904		do	Apr. 6, 1905	Philadelphia, Pa	Apr. 13, 1904	Baltimore, Md.
Parthian	2,082	1887	1902	1887		do	July 17, 1905	do	July 10, 1904	Philadelphia, Pa.
Yemassee	1,879	1879	1886	1886		Philadelphia, Pa	Sept. 6, 1905	do	Sept. 7, 1904	Do.
Inland passenger steamers.										
Anthony Groves, jr	605	1893		1893		Philadelphia, Pa	May 11, 1905	South Camden, N. J	June 7, 1904	Baltimore, Md.
Avalon	20	1895		1895		Nyack, N. Y	June 9, 1905	Longport, N. J	June 17, 1904	Philadelphia, Pa.
Aurelia	22	1892	1897	1903		Bordentown, N. J	Dec. 1, 1905	Somers Point, N. J	Dec. 3, 1904	Do.
Annie L. Vansciver	194	1905		1905		Camden, N. J	Dec. 27, 1905	South Camden, N. J	First inspn	
Brandywine	407	1885		1885		Wilmington, Del	Feb. 26, 1905	Wilmington, Del	Feb. 28, 1904	Do.
Bristol[a]	424	1867	1905	1893		do	Apr. 20, 1905	Camden, N. J	May 19, 1904	Do.
Burlington[b]	592	1857	1905	1885		do	Apr. 19, 1905	Wilmington, Del	May 17, 1904	Do.
City of Chester	611	1888		1888	1896	do	Mar. 17, 1905	do	Mar. 16, 1904	Do.
Clio	217	1898		1898		Philadelphia, Pa	Mar. 31, 1905	Philadelphia, Pa	Apr. 1, 1904	Do.
Columbia	663	1876		1876		Wilmington, Del	May 9, 1905	Camden, N. J	May 6, 1904	Do.
Columbia	1,468	1877		1877		Greenpoint, N. Y	May 26, 1905	Gloucester, N. J	June 1, 1904	Do.
Chincoteague	143	1893		1890		Wilmington, Del	Aug. 15, 1905	Wilmington, Del	Aug. 4, 1904	Do.
Elizabeth Monroe Smith	204	1888		1888		do	Apr. 18, 1905	Philadelphia, Pa	May 18, 1904	Do.
Eastside[c]	22	(d)		1882		Unknown	June 20, 1905	do	June 17, 1904	Do.
Emily	25	1871		1895		Philadelphia, Pa	Sept. 13, 1905	Wilmington, Del	Sept. 12, 1904	Do.
Frederica	293	1894		1894		do	Sept. 8, 1905	Philadelphia, Pa	Sept. 16, 1904	Do.
G. F. Brady	238	1897		1897		do	Apr. 15, 1905	do	Apr. 15, 1904	Do.
Henry A. Haber	48	1896		1896		Newburg, N. Y	May 1, 1905	do	May 2, 1904	Do.
Harriet	55	1903		1903		Wilmington, Del	June 3, 1905	Wilmington, Del	June 25, 1904	Do.
John F. Smith	235	1890		1890		do	Apr. 18, 1905	Philadelphia, Pa	May 18, 1904	Do.
John P. Wilson	350	1904		1904		Philadelphia, Pa	Sept. 20, 1905	do	Sept. 28, 1904	Do.
Longport	20	1895		1895		Nyack, N. Y	June 9, 1905	Longport, N. J	June 11, 1904	Do.
Major Reybold	530	1853		1877		Wilmington, Del	Mar. 17, 1905	Salem, N. J	Mar. 15, 1904	Do.
Monmouth	1,440	1888		1905		Philadelphia, Pa	Apr. 29, 1905	Wilmington, Del	Apr. 27, 1904	New York, N. Y.
Mary M. Vinyard	220	1904		1903		Milford, Del	May 13, 1905	Milton, Del	Apr. 2, 1904	Philadelphia, Pa.
Ocean City	33	1900		1900		Greenport, N. Y	June 29, 1905	Longport, N. J	July 22, 1904	Do.
Ocean City	29	1887		1901		Pamrapo, N. J	June 23, 1905	Grassy Sound, N. J	June 24, 1904	Do.
Pleasant Valley	400	1870		1888		Keyport, N. J	May 10, 1905	Gloucester, N. J	May 10, 1904	Do.

P. J. Thistlewood	223	1905		1904		Milford, Del	June 15, 1905	Milford, Del	First inspn.	
Richard Willing	351	1855	1901	1889		Wilmington, Del	Apr. 14, 1905	South Camden, N. J	Mar. 1, 1904	Do.
Riverside	72	1883		1883		Philadelphia, Pa	Sept. 21, 1905	Philadelphia, Pa	Sept. 22, 1904	Do.
Springfield	287	1901		1901		Wilmington, Del	Mar. 16, 1905	Bordentown, N. J	Mar. 22, 1904	Do.
Sylvan Glen	330	1869	1901	1896		Brooklyn, N. Y	Apr. 28, 1905	Gloucester, N. J	May 27, 1904	Do.
Somers Point	20	1895		1895		Nyack, N. Y	June 29, 1905	Longport, N. J	July 11, 1904	Do.
Sylvan Dell	440	1872	1904	1896		Brooklyn, N. Y	Apr. 12, 1905	Gloucester, N. J	June 8, 1904	Do.
Twilight	466	1868		1901		Wilmington, Del	Apr. 14, 1905	North Camden, N. J	Apr. 11, 1904	Do.
Thomas Clyde	625	1878		1878		do	May 16, 1905	do	May 16, 1904	Do.
Taurus	50	1881		1896		do	May 29, 1905	Wilmington, Del	May 31, 1904	Do.
Ulrica	205	1893		1888		do	May 9, 1905	do	May 11, 1904	Do.
Vigilant	79	1894		1894		Philadelphia, Pa	June 21, 1905	Philadelphia, Pa	June 18, 1904	Do.
Virginia	2,027	1905		1905		Wilmington, Del	Oct. 12, 1905	Wilmington, Del	First inspn.	
W. J. Latta	26	1892		1881		Philadelphia, Pa	May 18, 1905	Philadelphia, Pa	May 9, 1904	Do.
West Jersey	29	1901		1901		South Amboy, N. J	July 10, 1905	Maurice River, N. J	July 11, 1904	Do.
Ferry steamers.										
Atlantic	451	1880		1880		Philadelphia, Pa	Apr. 24, 1905	Camden, N. J	Apr. 6, 1904	Philadelphia, Pa.
Arctic	394	1879		1879		Wilmington, Del	Sept. 15, 1905	do	Sept. 15, 1904	Do.
Atlantic City	422	1883		1883		do	Oct. 13, 1905	South Camden, N. J	Oct. 10, 1904	Do.
Baltic	398	1881	1902	1881		do	Sept. 25, 1905	Camden, N. J	Sept. 23, 1904	Do.
Beverly	439	1882		1882		do	Sept. 30, 1905	do	Oct. 6, 1904	Do.
City of Reading	576	1889		1889		do	Mar. 30, 1905	South Camden, N. J	May 3, 1904	Do.
Coopers Point	389	1879		1879		do	June 20, 1905	Camden, N. J	June 6, 1904	Do.
Columbia	388	1877		1877		do	Aug. 21, 1905	do	Aug. 30, 1904	Do.
Cape May	714	1901		1901		do	Oct. 2, 1905	South Camden, N. J	Sept. 30, 1904	Do.
Camden	757	1896		1896		Elizabethport, N. J	Oct. 31, 1905	Camden, N. J	Nov. 9, 1904	Do.
Cranford	1,197	1905		1905		Wilmington, Del	Dec. 28, 1905	Wilmington, Del	First inspn.	
Dauntless	301	1876		1876		Philadelphia, Pa	Mar. 21, 1905	Gloucester, N. J	Mar. 23, 1904	Do.
Delaware	370	1875		1875		Wilmington, Del	May 4, 1905	Camden, N. J	May 4, 1904	Do.
Fearless	656	1893		1893		do	do	Gloucester, N. J	Apr. 21, 1904	Do.
Genl. J. S. Schultz	461	1875		1875		Camden, N. J	Apr. 22, 1905	South Camden, N. J	Apr. 16, 1904	Do.
Ocean City	665	1903		1903		Philadelphia, Pa	May 18, 1905	do	May 31, 1904	Do.
Peerless	298	1872		1872		Wilmington, Del	Mar. 21, 1905	Gloucester, N. J	Mar. 26, 1904	Do.
Philadelphia	703	1896		1896		do	May 2, 1905	South Camden, N. J	May 16, 1904	Do.
Pennsylvania	430	1874		1874		do	July 6, 1905	North Camden, N. J	June 30, 1904	Do.
William E. Doron	171	1893		1893		Philadelphia, Pa	Mar. 8, 1905	Bristol, Pa	Mar. 10, 1904	Do.
Woodbury	858	1905		1905		Wilmington, Del	Oct. 27, 1905	Wilmington, Del	First inspn.	
Wenonah	439	1882		1882		do	Dec. 13, 1905	Camden, N. J	Oct. 17, 1904	Do.
Ocean freight steamers.										
Arizonan	8,671	1903		1903		San Francisco, Cal	Apr. 26, 1905	Philadelphia, Pa	Feb. 25, 1904	New York, N. Y.
Algiers	2,294	1876	1892	1892		Wilmington, Del	July 11, 1905	do	July 11, 1904	New Orleans, La.
Aries	832	(d)		1877		Unknown	Oct. 27, 1905	do	Nov. 12, 1904	Philadelphia, Pa.
Benefactor	843	1870		1880		Chester, Pa	Aug. 22, 1905	do	Aug. 23, 1904	Do.
Chippewaw	2,696	1905		1905		Philadelphia, Pa	May 4, 1905	do	First inspn.	
Californian	5,707	1900		1900		San Francisco, Cal	Aug. 19, 1905	do	Aug. 5, 1904	New York, N. Y.
George W. Clyde	1,848	1872	1876	1876		Philadelphia, Pa	July 24, 1905	do	July 23, 1904	Philadelphia, Pa.

a Formerly Sue, 1904. b Formerly John A. Warner, 1904. c Formerly Relief, 1903. d Unknown.

DOMESTIC VESSELS INSPECTED, YEAR ENDED DECEMBER 31, 1905—SECOND SUPERVISING DISTRICT—PHILADELPHIA, PA.—Continued.

Names of vessels and class.	Gross tonnage.	Hull built.	Hull rebuilt.	Boilers built.	Boilers rebuilt.	Where built.	Date of inspection.	Where inspected.	Date of previous inspection.	Local district where previously inspected.
Ocean freight steamers—Con.										
Goldsboro	681	1882		1882		Philadelphia, Pa	Oct. 5, 1905	Philadelphia, Pa	Oct. 11, 1904	Philadelphia, Pa.
Larimer	3,737	1903		1903		Camden, N. J	June 7, 1905	Gibsons Point, Pa	June 8, 1904	Do.
Mohican	2,255	1904		1904		Philadelphia, Pa	Aug. 25, 1905	Philadelphia, Pa	Aug. 29, 1904	Do.
Northwestern	2,207	1901		1901		Chicago, Ill	Jan. 15, 1905	do	Jan. 16, 1904	New York, N. Y.
Norman	1,203	1862		1891		Philadelphia, Pa	Sept. 8, 1905	do	Sept. 24, 1904	Philadelphia, Pa.
Onondaga	2,696	1905		1905		do	May 31, 1905	do	First inspn.	
Oneida	1,322	1885		1885		Leith, Scotland	June 15, 1905	do	June 14, 1904	New York, N. Y.
Paraguay	2,201	1900		1900		Lorain, Ohio	Dec. 21, 1905	do	Dec. 14, 1904	Do.
Roma	2,939	1889		1889		Sunderland, England	May 23, 1905	Chester, Pa	June 18, 1904	Philadelphia, Pa.
Stillwater	1,019	1883		1883		Glasgow, Scotland	Apr. 8, 1905	Philadelphia, Pa	Mar. 30, 1904	Do.
Shawmut	1,624	1879		1900		Sunderland, England	June 30, 1905	do	July 16, 1904	Do.
Texan	8,633	1902		1902		Camden, N. J	Apr. 13, 1905	do	Nov. 24, 1903	Do.
Toledo	2,277	1902		1902		Toledo, Ohio	Nov. 18, 1905	Marcushook, Pa	Oct. 29, 1904	Do.
Winyah	1,682	1891		1903		Philadelphia, Pa	Jan. 23, 1905	Philadelphia, Pa	Jan. 21, 1904	Do.
Washtenaw	2,896	1887		1887		West Hartlepool, England.	Apr. 4, 1905	Marcushook, Pa	Mar. 29, 1904	Do.
Westover	617	1873	1899	1895		Wilmington, Del	Dec. 1, 1905	Philadelphia, Pa	Nov. 4, 1904	New York, N. Y.
Inland freight steamers.										
Alice Wakeley	135	1888		1895		Ithaca, N. Y	June 9, 1905	North Camden, N. J	May 20, 1904	Philadelphia, Pa.
Admiral	68	1903		1903		Wilmington, Del	July 1, 1905	do	July 23, 1904	Do.
Bessie	185	1881		1881		Boston, Mass	Jan. 17, 1905	North Cramer Hill, N. J.	May 24, 1898	Galveston, Tex.
Black Diamond	91	1887		1887		Wilmington, Del	May 26, 1905	Philadelphia, Pa	May 26, 1904	Philadelphia, Pa.
Chester	419	1902		1902		Chester, Pa	Mar. 6, 1905	do	Mar. 7, 1904	Do.
City of Salem	195	1900		1900		Wilmington, Del	Aug. 7, 1905	Salem, N. J	Aug. 8, 1904	Do.
Delaware	166	1858		1889		do	May 20, 1905	Trenton, N. J	May 21, 1904	Do.
Eaglet	386	1884		1889		Philadelphia, Pa	May 17, 1905	North Cramer Hill, N. J.	May 17, 1904	Do.
Elsie Weatherby	59	1887		1887		Pennsgrove, N. J	June 26, 1905	Camden, N. J	June 28, 1904	Do.
Ethel	266	1902		1902		Wilmington, Del	Aug. 17, 1905	North Cramer Hill, N. J.	Aug. 15, 1904	Do.
F. W. Brune	296	1860	1902	1887		do	Apr. 22, 1905	Trenton, N. J	Apr. 23, 1904	Do.
Florence	181	1899		1873		do	July 1, 1905	North Camden, N. J	July 29, 1904	Do.
George H. Stout	381	1858	1901	1887		New Brunswick, N. J	Apr. 11, 1905	North Cramer Hill, N. J.	Apr. 8, 1904	Do.
Greensborough	163	1892		1893		Baltimore, Md	July 3, 1905	North Camden, N. J	June 23, 1904	Do.
Hugo Keller	129	1890		1896		Ithaca, N. Y	June 16, 1905	Camden, N. J	June 7, 1904	New Haven, Conn.
Martha Stevens	283	1862		1887		Wilmington, Del	May 22, 1905	Trenton, N. J	May 21, 1904	Philadelphia, Pa.
Nellie	143	1890		1886		do	July 28, 1905	North Camden, N. J	July 27, 1904	Do.
Samuel H. Hartman	245	1891		1891		do	Nov. 29, 1905	Philadelphia, Pa	Nov. 25, 1904	Do.

Ruth B. Lute	148	1898		1891		do	June 17, 1905	Lewes, Del	June 10, 1904	Providence, R. I.
Raritan	166	1858		1890		do	May 24, 1905	Trenton, N. J	May 23, 1904	Philadelphia, Pa.
Riverside	452	1895		1895		Chester, Pa	Oct. 2, 1905	Philadelphia, Pa	Oct. 3, 1904	Do.
Tinicum	481	1905		1905		do	Sept. 13, 1905	Chester, Pa	First inspn	
Yuma	447	1889		1882	1889	Brooklyn, N. Y	Apr. 11, 1905	North Cramer Hill, N. J.	Mar. 28, 1904	Do.
Ocean towing steamers.										
Boxer	216	1899		1899		Boston, Mass	May 23, 1905	Philadelphia, Pa	May 19, 1905	Boston, Mass.
Blue Bell	179	1904		1904		Camden, N. J	Oct. 9, 1905	do	Nov. 1, 1904	Philadelphia, Pa.
Catawissa	558	1897		1896		Wilmington, Del	Feb. 1, 1905	do	Jan. 28, 1904	Boston, Mass.
Catherine Moran	213	1904		1904		Philadelphia, Pa	Sept. 18, 1905	do	Sept. 7, 1904	Philadelphia, Pa.
Gettysburg	557	1898		1898		Wilmington, Del	May 16, 1905	do	May 14, 1904	Do.
Ivanhoe	94	1883		1901		Philadelphia, Pa	Mar. 11, 1905	do	Mar. 11, 1904	Do.
John F. Lewis	157	1903		1903		Camden, N. J	Jan. 11, 1905	do	Dec. 29, 1903	Do.
John A. Hughes	157	1902		1902		do	July 22, 1905	do	July 20, 1904	Do.
Juno	84	1878	1899	1889		do	Oct. 10, 1905	South Camden, N. J	Oct. 5, 1904	Do.
L. Y. Schermerhorn	174	1903		1902		do	June 20, 1905	do	Apr. 25, 1904	Do.
Lykens	625	1899		1899		Philadelphia, Pa	July 17, 1905	Philadelphia, Pa	July 14, 1904	Boston, Mass.
North America	289	1876		1895		Camden, N. J	Aug. 15, 1905	do	Aug. 22, 1904	Philadelphia, Pa.
Navigator	414	1858		1898		do	Nov. 20, 1905	South Camden, N. J	Nov. 10, 1904	Do.
Patience	292	1901		1901		do	Nov. 1, 1905	Philadelphia, Pa	Oct. 25, 1904	Do.
Swatara	625	1899		1898		Philadelphia, Pa	Feb. 10, 1905	do	Feb. 9, 1904	Boston, Mass.
Sweepstakes	227	1867		1894		Cleveland, Ohio	May 15, 1905	do	May 13, 1904	Philadelphia, Pa.
Sommers N. Smith	211	1896		1896		Newport News, Va	Sept. 18, 1905	do	Sept. 24, 1904	Do.
S. A. McCaulley	92	1885		1900		Philadelphia, Pa	Oct. 30, 1905	do	Nov. 21, 1904	Do.
Tamaqua	564	1896		1896		do	Mar. 3, 1905	do	Feb. 29, 1904	Do.
Inland towing steamers.										
Altoona	63	1875		1888		Camden, N. J	Apr. 8, 1905	Philadelphia, Pa	Mar. 8, 1904	Philadelphia, Pa.
Amanda Powell	38	1873		1901		do	Apr. 17, 1905	Wilmington, Del	Apr. 25, 1904	Do.
Alert	51	1890		1889		Bordentown, N. J	Apr. 19, 1905	Philadelphia, Pa	Apr. 18, 1904	Do.
Asa W. Hughes	106	1889		1900		Philadelphia, Pa	May 8, 1905	do	May 4, 1904	Do.
Active	60	1887		1887		New Gretna, N. J	June 6, 1905	do	June 3, 1904	Do.
Atkins Hughes	115	1890		1890		Philadelphia, Pa	June 22, 1905	do	June 21, 1904	Do.
American	20	1876	1895	1896		do	July 1, 1905	South Camden, N. J	July 1, 1904	Do.
Atlas	32	1892		1892		Baltimore, Md	June 29, 1905	Philadelphia, Pa	June 28, 1904	Do.
A. M. Bramell	34	1892		1892		Bordentown, N. J	July 15, 1905	do	July 14, 1904	Do.
Arctic	33	1882		1882		Camden, N. J	Aug. 4, 1905	do	Aug. 4, 1904	Do.
Alex. Y. Hanna	44	1890		1890		Philadelphia, Pa	Aug. 29, 1905	North Camden, N. J	Aug. 29, 1904	Do.
Atlantic	50	1862		1884		Baltimore, Md	Sept. 9, 1905	do	Sept. 8, 1904	Do.
Aurelia	6	(a)		1900		Unknown	Sept. 19, 1905	do	Sept. 16, 1904	Do.
Alida	79	1905		1905		Wilmington, Del	Oct. 2, 1905	Wilmington, Del	First inspn	
Atlantic	129	1904		1904		Philadelphia, Pa	Nov. 7, 1905	Philadelphia, Pa	Nov. 30, 1904	Do.
Brilliant	81	1902		1902		do	Feb. 21, 1905	do	Jan. 30, 1904	Do.
Bryn Mawr	74	1903		1903		Camden, N. J	Apr. 26, 1905	North Camden, N. J	Apr. 22, 1904	Do.
Baltic	72	1894		1894		Philadelphia, Pa	Sept. 12, 1905	Philadelphia, Pa	Sept. 17, 1904	Do.
Bristol	48	1893		1893		do	Sept. 16, 1905	do	do	Do.
Brilliant	81	1902		1902		do	Dec. 29, 1905	do	Feb. 21, 1905	Do.

a Unknown.

DOMESTIC VESSELS INSPECTED, YEAR ENDED DECEMBER 31, 1905—SECOND SUPERVISING DISTRICT—PHILADELPHIA, PA.—Continued.

Names of vessels and class.	Gross tonnage.	Hull built.	Hull rebuilt.	Boilers built.	Boilers rebuilt.	Where built.	Date of inspection.	Where inspected.	Date of previous inspection.	Local district where previously inspected.
Inland towing steamers—Con.										
Convoy	78	1873		1873		Philadelphia, Pa	Jan. 10, 1905	Philadelphia, Pa	Jan. 8, 1904	Philadelphia, Pa.
Cheltenham	113	1899		1899		do	June 16, 1905	do	June 20, 1904	Do.
Cecil	59	1904		1890		Solomons, Md	July 24, 1905	Wilmington, Del	July 23, 1904	Baltimore, Md.
Clara	58	1870	1880	1880		New Brunswick, N. J	July 22, 1905	North Cramer Hill, N. J.	July 2, 1904	Philadelphia, Pa.
Curtin	85	1898		1898		Camden, N. J	Oct. 9, 1905	do	Oct. 11, 1904	Do.
Credenda	34	1903		1886		Paulsboro, N. J	Oct. 12, 1905	Wilmington, Del	Sept. 19, 1904	Baltimore, Md.
City Ice Boat No. 1	325	1866		1893		Philadelphia, Pa	Oct. 16, 1905	Holmesburg, Pa	Nov. 17, 1904	Philadelphia, Pa.
City Ice Boat No. 2	458	1868	1904	1903		do	do	do	Nov. 2, 1904	Do.
Charles Killam	24	1891		1891		Bordentown, N. J	Nov. 20, 1905	Philadelphia, Pa	Nov. 25, 1904	Do.
Ellen McAvoy	27	1883		1883		Pettys Island, N. J	July 17, 1905	North Camden, N. J	July 18, 1904	Do.
Esther	27	1895		1896		Camden, N. J	July 19, 1905	Philadelphia, Pa	do	Do.
Evening Star	37	1897		1893		Bordentown, N. J	Aug. 26, 1905	do	Aug. 25, 1904	Do.
El Mora	13	1887		1894		Elizabethport, N. J	Sept. 11, 1905	Wilmington, Del	Aug. 31, 1904	Do.
Eva Belle Cain	20	1871		1893		Philadelphia, Pa	Sept. 13, 1905	Philadelphia, Pa	Sept. 15, 1904	Do.
Esther	7	1902		1897		Chincoteague, Va	July 31, 1905	Exmoor Station, Va	July 30, 1904	Do.
Edna	23	1892		1892		Philadelphia, Pa	Nov. 13, 1905	North Camden, N. J	Nov. 12, 1904	Do.
Frederick Jansen	28	1884		1888		do	Apr. 17, 1905	Wilmington, Del	Apr. 20, 1904	Do.
F. A. Churchman	64	1894		1883		do	Apr. 5, 1905	Philadelphia, Pa	Apr. 4, 1904	Do.
Fred Cramer	19	1899		1885		Milford, Del	Oct. 4, 1905	North Camden, N. J	Oct. 4, 1904	Do.
Frank K. Esherick	69	1890		1890		Philadelphia, Pa	Nov. 16, 1905	Philadelphia, Pa	Nov. 17, 1904	Norfolk, Va.
Gladys [a]	24	1871		1889		do	Mar. 17, 1905	do	Mar. 16, 1904	Philadelphia, Pa.
Granite	29	1904		1885		Milford, Del	Mar. 29, 1905	Wilmington, Del	Mar. 29, 1904	Do.
George W. Smith	34	1883		1882		Brooklyn, N. Y	Oct. 17, 1904	North Camden, N. J	Oct. 15, 1903	Do.
Gwynedd	115	1896		1896		Philadelphia, Pa	Sept. 30, 1905	Philadelphia, Pa	Oct. 3, 1904	Do.
Gard. B. Reynolds	45	1891		1891		do	Dec. 15, 1905	do	Sept. 29, 1904	Do.
Hainesport	67	1904		1904		Madison, Md	Mar. 3, 1905	do	Mar. 24, 1904	Baltimore, Md.
Harry M. Wall	60	1892		1892		Philadelphia, Pa	Mar. 28, 1905	do	Mar. 19, 1904	Philadelphia, Pa.
Harry Schaubel, jr	34	1886		1886		do	Apr. 13, 1905	do	Apr. 13, 1904	Do.
Harford	59	1881		1904		Camden, N. J	June 19, 1905	Camden, N. J	June 17, 1904	Do.
Helen	102	1901		1901		do	do	North Camden, N. J	June 7, 1904	Do.
Harbor	50	1891		1891		Philadelphia, Pa	Sept. 5, 1905	Philadelphia, Pa	Sept. 13, 1904	Do.
Imperator	93	1886		1886		Athens, N. Y	July 24, 1905	do	July 22, 1904	Do.
I. W. Durham	33	1872	1900	1893		Philadelphia, Pa	Sept. 21, 1905	do	Nov. 9, 1903	Do.
Ivanhoe	35	1875		1890		do	Sept. 26, 1905	do	Sept. 26, 1904	Do.
Josephine Lincoln	18	1875	1886	1892		Bordentown, N. J	Mar. 7, 1905	do	Mar. 8, 1904	Do.
Jack Twohy	171	1905		1905		Camden, N. J	Apr. 4, 1905	Camden, N. J	First inspn	
John B. Patton	39	1896		1895		Bordentown, N. J	Apr. 1, 1905	Philadelphia, Pa	Mar. 17, 1904	Do.
John Reese	57	1894		1894		Philadelphia, Pa	May 11, 1905	do	May 12, 1904	Do.
J. McAteer [b]	20	1869		1895		do	May 27, 1905	do	May 28, 1904	Do.
Jas. McCaulley	92	1887		1898		Camden, N. J	June 17, 1905	do	June 23, 1904	Do.
J. S. Lamson	17	1894		1894		Bordentown, N. J	June 27, 1905	do	June 28, 1904	Do.

John I. Brady	72	1897		1893		Philadelphia, Pa	July 17, 1905	do	July 18, 1904	Do.
John E. Mehrer	76	1894		1894		do	Aug. 16, 1905	do	Aug. 15, 1904	Do.
John C. Bradley	45	1881		1896		do	Sept. 19, 1905	do	Oct. 19, 1904	Do.
John J. Hagan	26	1894		1891		do	Oct. 10, 1905	North Cramer Hill, N. J.	Oct. 11, 1904	Do.
Jared Darlington	57	1893		1893		Bordentown, N. J	Oct. 30, 1905	Philadelphia, Pa	Oct. 31, 1904	Do.
Jamesburg	75	1883		1883		South Amboy, N. J	Nov. 13, 1905	Camden, N. J	Nov. 23, 1904	Do.
J. S. W. Holton	62	1892		1892		Philadelphia, Pa	Nov. 21, 1905	Philadelphia, Pa	Dec. 15, 1904	Do.
Kensington	33	1882		1882		Camden, N. J	June 16, 1905	do	June 13, 1904	Do.
Lightning	48	1874		1898		do	May 13, 1905	Camden, N. J	May 9, 1904	Do.
Leader	26	1882		1881		Pettys Island, N. J	June 16, 1905	Philadelphia, Pa	June 15, 1904	Do.
Lillie M. Graham	49	1892		1892		Philadelphia, Pa	June 19, 1905	do	June 6, 1904	Do.
Lookout	35	1862		1875		Camden, N. J	June 28, 1905	do	June 27, 1904	Do.
Laura	28	1879	1895	1894		Philadelphia, Pa	Aug. 10, 1905	do	Aug. 10, 1904	Do.
Lizzie Crawford	52	1882		1896		Camden, N. J	Sept. 5, 1905	do	Sept. 23, 1904	Do.
Laura B	80	1883		1898		Philadelphia, Pa	Sept. 25, 1905	Wilmington, Del	Oct. 4, 1904	Do.
Lorraine	71	1895		1895		do	Nov. 3, 1905	Philadelphia, Pa	Oct. 19, 1904	Do.
M. S. Quay	131	1903		1903		do	Jan. 31, 1905	do	Jan. 29, 1904	Do.
Madeira	51	1892		1892		do	Feb. 24, 1905	do	Feb. 24, 1904	Do.
Maurice	36	1892		1897		do	Mar. 3, 1905	do	Mar. 7, 1904	Do.
Martha	12	1879		1881		Bordentown, N. J	Apr. 3, 1905	Wilmington, Del	Apr. 2, 1904	Do.
Minerva	38	1886		1901		Philadelphia, Pa	Apr. 10, 1905	Philadelphia, Pa	Apr. 11, 1904	Do.
Meteor	95	1881		1881	1889	Wilmington, Del	May 8, 1905	Wilmington, Del	May 9, 1904	Do.
May T. White	38	1880		1886		Philadelphia, Pa	June 17, 1905	South Camden, N. J	June 17, 1904	Do.
M. P. Howlett	53	1868	1898	1898		Baltimore, Md	June 9, 1905	Philadelphia, Pa	June 9, 1904	Do.
Mascot	41	1890		1890		Philadelphia, Pa	June 10, 1905	do	June 11, 1904	Do.
Mary McIlvaine [c]	34	1888		1889		Tottenville, N. Y	June 30, 1905	do	June 30, 1904	Do.
Mary J. Walker	61	1891		1900		Bordentown, N. J	July 20, 1905	do	July 25, 1904	Do.
Majestic	55	1890		1890		do	Aug. 28, 1905	do	Aug. 26, 1904	Do.
Mary R. Corr	25	1882	1905	1905		Pettys Island, N. J	Sept. 19, 1905	North Camden, N. J	Mar. 30, 1904	Do.
Morris	15	1903		1896		Camden, N. J	Oct. 5, 1905	North Cramer Hill, N. J.	May 10, 1904	Do.
Mollie	36	1875		1899		Philadelphia, Pa	Oct. 4, 1905	Philadelphia, Pa	Dec. 3, 1904	Do.
Majestic	113	1900		1900		Baltimore, Md	Oct. 16, 1905	South Camden, N. J	Nov. 5, 1904	Do.
New Castle	110	1902		1902		Camden, N. J	Apr. 20, 1905	Philadelphia, Pa	Apr. 19, 1904	Do.
Nellie E. Rawson	72	1873		1904		Bath, Me	June 2, 1905	Menhaden, N. J	June 11, 1904	Do.
Nellie	41	1894		1894		Philadelphia, Pa	July 24, 1905	Philadelphia, Pa	Aug. 1, 1904	Do.
Newark	59	1883		1888		Newark, N. J	Sept. 9, 1905	North Camden, N. J	Sept. 9, 1904	Do.
Owen Brady	50	1891		1891		Philadelphia, Pa	Mar. 10, 1905	Philadelphia, Pa	Mar. 10, 1904	Do.
Ogontz	113	1899		1899		do	Nov. 21, 1905	do	Nov. 28, 1904	Do.
Pilot Boy	25	1896		1896		do	Apr. 20, 1905	do	Apr. 19, 1904	Do.
Protector	176	1905		1905		do	May 31, 1905	do	First inspn.	
Penllyn	137	1901		1901		do	May 22, 1905	do	May 20, 1904	Do.
Pensauken	15	1894		1886		do	Apr. 29, 1905	Crum Creek, Pa	Apr. 29, 1904	Do.
Peerless	89	1886		1893		Camden, N. J	June 12, 1905	Philadelphia, Pa	June 4, 1904	Baltimore, Md.
Pilot	120	1891		1891		Philadelphia, Pa	July 21, 1905	South Camden, N. J	Aug. 13, 1904	Philadelphia, Pa.
Pioneer [d]	36	1883	1902	1905		Northport, N. Y	July 11, 1905	North Camden, N. J	Aug. 26, 1904	Do.
P. R. R. No. 4	121	1904		1904		Philadelphia, Pa	July 25, 1905	Camden, N. J	July 25, 1904	Do.
Philadelphia	40	1887	1903	1903		Milford, Del	Oct. 26, 1905	Philadelphia, Pa	Dec. 1, 1904	Do.
Rescue	75	1886		1886		Camden, N. J	Apr. 15, 1905	do	Apr. 14, 1904	Do.

[a] Formerly Edith, 1898. [b] Formerly Minnie, 1901. [c] Formerly Loretta K, 1899. [d] Formerly Lizzie E. Woodend, 1902.

DOMESTIC VESSELS INSPECTED, YEAR ENDED DECEMBER 31, 1905—SECOND SUPERVISING DISTRICT—PHILADELPHIA, PA.—Continued.

Names of vessels and class.	Gross tonnage.	Hull built.	Hull rebuilt.	Boilers built.	Boilers rebuilt.	Where built.	Date of inspection.	Where inspected.	Date of previous inspection.	Local district where previously inspected.
Inland towing steamers—Con.										
Rebecca	39	1874		1881		mden, N. J	May 26, 1905	Philadelphia, Pa	May 24, 1904	Philadelphia, Pa.
Robert K. Cassatt [a]	87	1877		1877		Philadelphia, Pa	June 5, 1905	North Cramer Hill, N. J.	June 16, 1904	Do.
Rose Hagan	17	1900		1893		Bordentown, N. J	Oct. 10, 1905	do	Oct. 11, 1904	Do.
Surprise	19	1892		1889		Clifton, N. Y	Aug. 9, 1905	do	Aug. 8, 1904	Do.
Samuel Gedney	48	1873		1895		Camden, N. J	Sept. 23, 1905	South Camden, N. J	Oct. 18, 1904	Do.
Varuna	64	1867	1899	1887	1902	New Brunswick, N. J.	Sept. 25, 1905	Camden, N. J	Oct. 5, 1904	Do.
William Penn [b]	48	1860	1899	1883	1903	Philadelphia, Pa	Mar. 21, 1905	Wilmington, Del	Mar. 18, 1904	Do.
Willie	15	1896		1896		do	Apr. 3, 1905	Philadelphia, Pa	Apr. 11, 1904	Do.
William Cramp	56	1877	1902	1897		do	Apr. 19, 1905	do	May 6, 1904	Do.
William J. Bradley	81	1900		1895		Camden, N. J	Apr. 22, 1905	South Camden, N. J	Apr. 23, 1904	Do.
White and Price	13	1882		1902		Brooklyn, N. Y	Apr. 3, 1905	Philadelphia, Pa	Mar. 31, 1904	Do.
Wanderer	35	1866	1900	1894		Nassau, New Providence.	May 17, 1905	do	May 16, 1904	Do.
William Rowland	129	1905		1905		Chester, Pa	July 12, 1905	Chester, Pa	First inspn.	
William M. Dove	18	1887		1895		Baltimore, Md	Aug. 8, 1905	Philadelphia, Pa	Aug. 5, 1904	Do.
William J. Sewell	61	1893		1893		Philadelphia, Pa	Aug. 21, 1905	do	Aug. 18, 1904	Do.
White Rose	74	1892		1892		New York, N. Y	Aug. 26, 1905	do	Aug. 24, 1904	Do.
Wm. J. Peoples	62	1898		1898		Wilmington, Del	Sept. 9, 1905	do	Sept. 8, 1904	Do.
William McAvoy	31	1893		1893		Bordentown, N. J	Oct. 23, 1905	do	Oct. 24, 1904	Do.
Winfield S. Cahill	54	1892		1902		Baltimore, Md	Oct. 21, 1905	do	Dec. 19, 1904	Do.
Ocean steam pleasure yachts.										
Giralda	184	1896		1896		Port Jefferson, N. Y	May 1, 1905	Essington, Pa	May 6, 1904	Philadelphia, Pa.
Ibis	184	1875	1893	1888		New Brunswick, N. J.	June 3, 1905	North Camden, N. J	May 23, 1902	Do.
Josephine	974	1899		1899		Philadelphia, Pa	Mar. 31, 1905	Philadelphia, Pa	Jan. 9, 1903	Do.
May	652	1891		1891		Troon, Scotland	May 10, 1905	do	May 12, 1904	Do.
Marietta	153	1897		1904		Brooklyn, N. Y	June 12, 1905	do	June 7, 1904	Do.
Sybilla	110	1885	1888	1895		Linwood, Pa	Sept. 29, 1905	Camden, N. J	Nov. 10, 1904	Do.
Inland steam pleasure yachts.										
Alan Gray	[c] 3	1893		1892		Camden, N. J	June 8, 1905	Millsboro, Del	June 2, 1904	Philadelphia, Pa.
Clara and Lillie	8	([d])		1894		Bridesburg, Pa	May 27, 1905	Bridesburg, Pa	May 5, 1904	Do.
Calypso [e]	8	1893		1893	1904	Trenton, N. J	Sept. 14, 1904	Whitehill, N. J	First inspn.	
Cypher	31	1896		1900		South Boston, Mass	July 8, 1905	Greenwich, N. J	July 8, 1904	Do.
Calypso	8	1893		1893	1904	Trenton, N. J	Sept. 16, 1905	Whitehill, N. J	Sept. 14, 1904	Do.
David Rankins [f]	[c] 4	1890		1890		Bordentown, N. J	May 5, 1905	Camden, N. J	Sept. 13, 1903	Do.
Franklin	5	1903		1896		Philadelphia, Pa	Mar. 3, 1905	Delanco, N. J	Mar. 4, 1904	Do
Governor Pennypacker	132	1903		1903		do	Sept. 29, 1905	Philadelphia, Pa	Nov. 28, 1904	Do.
Harriet	52	1891		1902		Saunderstown, R. I	May 16, 1905	Essington, Pa	May 16, 1904	Do.
Hattie Killam	30	1898		1898		Bordentown, N. J	May 10, 1905	Philadelphia, Pa	May 7, 1904	Do.
Israel W. Durham	[c] 2	([d])	1889	1888		Unknown	Aug. 15, 1905	Mount Holly, N. J	Oct. 14, 1903	Do.

Josephine No. 2	c 4	1903		1899		Morris Heights, N. J	Mar. 31, 1905	Philadelphia, Pa	Aug. 29, 1903	Do.
John Exton, jr	8	1904		1904		Trenton, N. J	June 14, 1905	Trenton, N. J	First inspn.	
Muchacho	5	1902		1902		Camden, N. J	July 1, 1905	Chester, Pa	July 2, 1904	Do.
Minnie [g]	22	1885		1885		Linwood, Pa	June 22, 1905	North Cramer Hill, N. J.	June 17, 1904	Do.
May	48	1893		1901		Bordentown, N. J [e]	July 20, 1905	Bordentown, N. J	July 27, 1904	Do.
Narcissa [h]	51	1896		1896		Wilmington, Del	Aug. 4, 1905	Camden, N. J	Aug. 4, 1904	Do.
Orca [i]	37	1901		1901		South Boston, Mass	May 23, 1905	Essington, Pa	June 2, 1904	Do.
Relief	16	1884		1884		Camden, N. J	Aug. 17, 1905	Trenton, N. J	Aug. 18, 1904	Do.
Telfer	c 1	1893		1894		West Creek, N. J	July 20, 1905	Mount Holly, N. J	July 19, 1904	Do.
Visitor	49	1883		1883		Baltimore, Md	Sept. 28, 1905	Philadelphia, Pa	Sept. 28, 1904	Do.
William S. Stokley	83	1875		1895		Philadelphia, Pa	Sept. 22, 1905	do	Sept. 23, 1904	Do.
Miscellaneous steam vessels.										
Alaska (fishing)	229	1881		1893		Boothbay, Me	Apr. 1, 1905	Wilmington, Del	Mar. 25, 1904	Providence, R.I.
Active (fishing)	73	1887		1887		New Gretna, N. J	Apr. 28, 1905	New Gretna, N. J	June 4, 1904	Philadelphia, Pa.
Adroit (fishing)	92	1900		1899		Pocomoke City, Md	May 17, 1905	Beach Haven, N. J	May 19, 1904	Norfolk, Va.
Ardent (fishing)	106	1902		1902		Baltimore, Md	Apr. 21, 1905	do	June 21, 1904	Philadelphia, Pa.
Albert Brown (fishing)	108	1875		1903		Bristol, Me	do	do	May 21, 1904	Norfolk, Va.
Edwin S. Stuart (fire)	150	1893		1898		Brooklyn, N. Y	Mar. 23, 1905	Philadelphia, Pa	Mar. 16, 1904	Philadelphia, Pa.
Fire Fighter (fire)	192	1905		1905		Wilmington, Del	June 1, 1905	Wilmington, Del	First inspn.	
Joseph Wharton (fishing)	245	1904		1904		do	June 17, 1905	Beach Haven, N. J	June 22, 1904	Do.
Jimmie (waterboat)	11	1880		1904		Brooklyn, N. Y	Aug. 18, 1905	Philadelphia, Pa	Aug. 18, 1904	Do.
Mars (wrecking)	278	1890		1889		Camden, N. J	Apr. 11, 1905	do	Apr. 12, 1904	Do.
Nellie B. Dey (fishing)	122	1884		1901		Lennoxville, N. C	Apr. 28, 1905	New Gretna, N. J	May 19, 1904	Norfolk, Va.
Philadelphia (pilot)	359	1898		1898		Philadelphia, Pa	Aug. 18, 1905	Philadelphia, Pa	Aug. 17, 1904	Philadelphia, Pa.
Somerset (wrecking)	179	1854		1879		Cleveland, Ohio	Mar. 24, 1905	Wilmington, Del	Mar. 11, 1904	Providence, R. I.
Samuel H. Ashbridge (police and fire).	268	1900		1900		Philadelphia, Pa	Oct. 20, 1905	Philadelphia, Pa	Oct. 22, 1904	Philadelphia, Pa.
Vessels propelled by gas motors.										
Arrow	41	1874				Rye, N. Y	June 15, 1905	Essington, Pa	First inspn.	
Alaska	24	1868				Marcushook, Pa	Aug. 28, 1905	Wilmington, Del	do	
Anna Bell	28	1888				Paulsboro, N. J	Oct. 26, 1905	Philadelphia, Pa	Oct. 26, 1904	Philadelphia, Pa.
Cambridge	40	1902				Cambridge, Md	June 15, 1905	Wilmington, Del	June 13, 1904	Do.
Commanche	24	1904				Atlantic City, N. J	Sept. 2, 1905	Atlantic City, N. J	Sept. 3, 1904	Do.
Iola	44	1905				Pennsgrove, N. J	Nov. 9, 1905	Hancocks Bridge, N. J.	First inspn.	
Lewis M. Price	93	1904				Cambridge, Md	Sept. 12, 1905	North Camden, N. J	Oct. 4, 1904	Baltimore, Md.
Freight sail vessels of over 700 tons.										
Erskine M. Phelps (ship)	2,998	1898				Bath, Me	May 18, 1905	Philadelphia, Pa	Apr. 19, 1904	Philadelphia, Pa.
Geneva (schooner)	874	1900				Rockland, Me	Jan. 12, 1905	do	Jan. 11, 1904	Portland, Me.
Madeline Cooney (schooner)	790	1892				Waldoboro, Me	Mar. 17, 1905	do	Jan. 14, 1904	Philadelphia, Pa.
Marie Palmer (schooner)	1,904	1900				Bath, Me	June 22, 1905	do	June 15, 1904	Boston, Mass.
Oakley C. Curtis (schooner)	2,374	1901				do	Jan. 17, 1905	do	Jan. 19, 1904	Portland, Me.
Tillie Baker (bark)	719	1876				Harrington, Me	Jan. 14, 1905	do	Jan. 2, 1904	Philadelphia, Pa.

[a] Formerly Elmore A. Kent, 1904.
[b] Formerly Pacific, 1898.
[c] Estimated.
[d] Unknown.
[e] Certificated July, 1905.
[f] Formerly Alicia, 1904.
[g] Formerly U. S. S. Mermaid.
[h] Formerly Millie K. Ridgway, 1900.
[i] Formerly Monaloa, 1904.

DOMESTIC VESSELS INSPECTED, YEAR ENDED DECEMBER 31, 1905—SECOND SUPERVISING DISTRICT—Continued.

LOCAL DISTRICT OF NEW LONDON, CONN.

Names of vessels and class.	Gross tonnage.	Hull built.	Hull rebuilt.	Boilers built.	Boilers rebuilt.	Where built.	Date of inspection.	Where inspected.	Date of previous inspection.	Local district where previously inspected.
Ocean passenger steamer.										
Dakota	20,714	1905		1902		New London, Conn	Mar. 20,1905	Groton, Conn	First inspn	
Inland passenger steamers.										
Connecticut	3,399	1889		1888		Noank, Conn	June 14,1905	Stonington, Conn	June 11,1904	Providence, R. I.
City of Lowell	2,975	1894		1894		Bath, Me	June 1,1905	New London, Conn	June 1,1904	New London, Conn.
Chelsea	564	1892	1902	1904		Wilmington, Del	June 17,1905	Norwich, Conn	June 18,1904	Do.
C. H. Northam	1,436	1873	1878	1896		New York, N. Y	July 11,1905	Stonington, Conn	July 7,1904	New Haven, Conn.
Chester W. Chapin	2,868	1899		1899		Sparrow Point, Md	Oct. 23,1905	New London, Conn	Oct. 31,1904	New London, Conn.
Gypsy	57	1884		1904		Mystic, Conn	May 28,1905	Saunderstown, R. I	May 25,1904	Do.
Greenport	1,413	1866	1896	1891		New York, N. Y	June 7,1905	Greenport, N. Y	June 6,1904	Do.
Hartford	1,488	1899		1899		Baltimore, Md	Sept. 30,1905	Hartford, Conn	Oct. 3,1904	Do.
Kelpie	43	1874	1900	1892		Salisbury, Mass	May 17,1905	Greenport, N. Y	May 12,1904	Do.
Middletown	1,554	1896		1896		Philadelphia, Pa	Mar. 30,1905	Hartford, Conn	Mar. 31,1904	Do.
Madeleine	74	1893		1891		Cape Elizabeth, Me	May 24,1905	New London, Conn	May 26,1904	Do.
Munnatawket	204	1890		1904		New London, Conn	May 10,1905	Fishers Island, N. Y	Apr. 27,1904	Do.
Meteor [a]	423	1883		1900		Philadelphia, Pa	Nov. 16,1904	Sag Harbor, N. Y	Nov. 18,1903	Do.
New Hampshire	2,395	1892		1892		Wilmington, Del	Mar. 31,1905	New London, Conn	Apr. 2,1904	Do.
Orient	471	1896	1902	1896		Chelsea, Mass	June 6,1905	Greenport, N. Y	May 30,1904	Do.
Osprey	57	1882	1902	1886		Mystic Conn	July 10,1905	Riverside, Conn	June 14,1904	Do.
Restless	475	1904		1903		Noank, Conn	June 27,1905	Fishers Island, N. Y	June 23,1904	Do.
Rhode Island	2,888	1882		1890		do	May 11,1905	Stonington, Conn	May 11,1904	Do.
Sylvia	132	1900		1900		Springfield, Mass	Apr. 17,1905	Springfield, Mass	May 23,1904	Do.
Watch Hill	35	1879		1885		Newburg, N. Y	May 18,1905	Westerly, R. I	June 15,1904	New York, N. Y.
Ferry steamers.										
Colonial	38	1905		1902		Noank, Conn	Apr. 28,1905	Noank, Conn	First inspn	
General Spencer [b]	33	1904		1904		Hartford, Conn	Nov. 19,1904	Hartford, Conn	do	
Gov. Winthrop	485	1905		1905		Noank, Conn	Aug. 4,1905	Noank, Conn	do	
General Spencer	33	1904		1904		Hartford, Conn	Nov. 15,1905	Goodspeeds, Conn	Nov. 19,1904	New London, Conn.
J. A. Saunders	192	1902		1902		Saunderstown, R. I	June 19,1905	Saunderstown, R. I	June 25,1904	Do.
Menantic	203	1893		1893		Noank, Conn	May 13,1905	Greenport, N. Y	Apr. 23,1904	Do.
Middlesex	27	1899	1904	1884		East Haddam, Conn	July 15,1905	Hadlyme, Conn	July 23,1904	Do.
Rocky Hill	33	1902		1902		Portland, Conn	Apr. 5,1905	Rocky Hill, Conn	Apr. 7,1904	Do.
West Side	106	1904		1904		Saunderstown, R. I	June 26,1905	Saunderstown, R. I	June 25,1904	Do.
Inland freight steamers.										
Arthur D. Bissell [c]	137	1881	1902	1898		Lockport, N. Y	Dec. 1,1904	Greens Harbor, Conn.	Nov. 21,1903	New Haven, Conn.
Clifford	212	1890	1902	1901		Rocky Hill, Conn	July 14,1905	New London, Conn	July 14,1904	New London, Conn.

Cortis	131	1880		1888		Havana, N. Y	Aug. 23, 1905	Norwich, Conn	Aug. 25, 1904	Do.
E. P. Cook	135	1881	1903	1905		do	Oct. 2, 1905	Greens Harbor Conn.	Sept. 20, 1904	Do.
Holyoake	198	1898		1898		Greenport, N. Y	June 7, 1905	Greenport, N. Y	June 8, 1904	Do.
Mohegan	2,783	1896		1896		Chester, Pa	May 5, 1905	New London, Conn	May 3, 1904	Do.
Notter	130	1885	1899	1892		Buffalo, N. Y	July 10, 1905	Middletown, Conn	July 1, 1904	Do.
Robt. W. Johnson	204	1905		1905		Noank, Conn	Oct. 9, 1905	Noank, Conn	First inspn.	
Seabury	186	1903		1904		Mystic, Conn	Apr. 12, 1905	New London, Conn	do	
Sarah Thorp	201	1887		1905		Hoboken, N. J	Nov. 11, 1905	Sag Harbor, N. Y	Oct. 19, 1904	Do.
Wm. E. Cleary	140	1887		1904		Lockport, N. Y	Nov. 22, 1905	Westerly, R. I	Oct. 31, 1904	New Haven, Conn.
Inland towing steamers.										
Alert	73	1857	1896	1893		Philadelphia, Pa	Jan. 18, 1905	Greens Harbor, Conn.	Jan. 19, 1904	New London, Conn.
Aquidneck	58	1889	1904	1903		Boston, Mass	Feb. 6, 1905	Riverside, Conn	Jan. 30, 1904	Do.
Argo [d]	105	1873	1897	1897		Hartford, Conn	do	do	Feb. 4, 1904	Do
A. M. Smith	37	1871	1902	1891		Philadelphia, Pa	Apr. 27, 1905	Hartford, Conn	Apr. 28, 1904	Do.
Aries	114	1884	1905	1905		do	Dec. 14, 1905	Riverside, Conn	May 18, 1904	Do.
Cassie	31	1887	1899	1886		New London, Conn	Oct. 14, 1905	Greens Harbor, Conn	Oct. 5, 1904	Do.
Dr. S. N. Briggs	22	1869	1904	1897		Philadelphia, Pa	June 17, 1905	Riverside, Conn	June 14, 1904	Do.
Gertrude	122	1883		1898		Brooklyn, N. Y	Aug. 25, 1905	do	Aug. 27, 1904	Do.
Harriet [e]	56	1875	1900	1900		Boston, Mass	June 13, 1905	Greens Harbor, Conn	June 4, 1904	Do.
Harold	186	1889		1904		New London, Conn	Oct. 7, 1905	Riverside, Conn	Oct. 7, 1904	Do.
J. Warren Coulston	52	1872	1901	1889		Philadelphia, Pa	June 10, 1905	Hartford, Conn	June 10, 1904	Do.
J. E. Randerson	46	1903		1903		New Baltimore, N. Y	Nov. 22, 1905	New London, Conn	Nov. 11, 1904	New Haven, Conn.
Lillian	17	1896		1890		Athens, N. Y	Apr. 5, 1905	Hartford, Conn	June 7, 1904	Do.
Luther C. Ward	106	1882		1903		Newburg, N. Y	June 10, 1905	Middletown, Conn	June 10, 1904	New London, Conn.
Miles Standish	55	1905		1904		New London, Conn	Feb. 2, 1905	Riverside, Conn	First inspn.	
Mabel	84	1882		1904		Philadelphia, Pa	Aug. 3, 1905	Hartford, Conn	Aug. 3, 1904	Do.
Nathan Hale	299	1890		1897		New London, Conn	June 27, 1905	Riverside, Conn	June 20, 1904	Do.
Raymond	20	1885	1902	1891		Hartford, Conn	May 27, 1905	Hartford, Conn	May 27, 1904	Do.
R. M. Waterman	174	1896		1896		New London, Conn	Sept. 7, 1905	Riverside, Conn	Sept. 26, 1904	Do.
Shenecossett	15	1889		1889		Noank, Conn	May 26, 1905	Greens Harbor, Conn	Apr. 21, 1904	Do.
Sachem	195	1900		1900		Baltimore, Md	Aug. 28, 1905	Middletown, Conn	Sept. 1, 1904	Do.
T. A. Scott, jr	36	1882	1900	1889	1904	Noank, Conn	July 29, 1905	Greens Harbor, Conn	July 27, 1904	Do.
Westerly	41	1879	1903	1890		Mystic, Conn	Mar. 16, 1905	Westerly, R. I	Mar. 17, 1904	Do.
Ocean steam pleasure yacht.										
Wacouta [f]	803	1894		1894		Bath, Me	Apr. 29, 1905	New London, Conn	Apr. 29, 1904	New London, Conn.
Inland steam pleasure yachts.										
Aunt Polly	176	1900	1902	1900		Brooklyn, N. Y	June 7, 1905	Greenport, N. Y	June 8, 1904	New London, Conn.
Agnes	29	1897		1898		Baltimore, Md	Sept. 15, 1905	New London, Conn	Sept. 17, 1904	Do.
Della	[g] 1	1902		1899		East Hartford, Conn	June 17, 1905	Hartford, Conn	June 22, 1904	Do.
Endion	61	1898		1903		New York, N. Y	May 12, 1905	New London, Conn	May 18, 1904	Do.
Free Lance	132	1895		1895		Elizabethport, N. J	May 1, 1905	Greenport, N. Y	Apr. 23, 1904	Do.
Fedalma	95	1886	1892	1897		New York, N. Y	Nov. 8, 1905	New London, Conn	Aug. 11, 1902	Do.
Gretchen	58	1891	1901	1895		Poughkeepsie, N. Y	Aug. 26, 1905	Greens Harbor, Conn	Sept. 2, 1904	Do.

[a] Certificate issued June 19, 1905.
[b] Certificate issued Apr. 17, 1905.
[c] Certificate issued Feb. 17, 1905.
[d] Formerly M. R. Brazos, 1897.
[e] Formerly William Wooley, 1900.
[f] Formerly Eleanor, 1900.
[g] Estimated.

DOMESTIC VESSELS INSPECTED, YEAR ENDED DECEMBER 31, 1905—SECOND SUPERVISING DISTRICT—NEW LONDON, CONN.—Continued.

Names of vessels and class.	Gross tonnage.	Hull built.	Hull rebuilt.	Boilers built.	Boilers rebuilt.	Where built.	Date of inspection.	Where inspected.	Date of previous inspection.	Local district where previously inspected.
***Inland steam pleasure yachts*—Continued.**										
Hauoli	299	1903		1903		Brooklyn, N. Y	May 19, 1905	Riverside, Conn	June 27, 1904	New London, Conn.
Irene	a 3	1894		1893		Middletown, Conn	Sept. 2, 1905	New London, Conn	Sept. 2, 1904	Do.
Katrina	52	1897		1904		Bristol, R. I	May 27, 1905	Hartford, Conn	May 27, 1904	Do.
Kauyahoora	a 4	1895		1896		Noank, Conn	June 22, 1905	Norwich, Conn	May 17, 1904	Do.
Leda	a 3	1890		1890		Nyack, N. Y	Apr. 17, 1905	Springfield, Mass	May 23, 1904	Do.
Magnet	23	1884		1896		Panope, N. J	May 6, 1905	Greenport, N. Y	May 2, 1904	Do.
Mollie	a 3	1899		1891		Unknown	June 28, 1905	Hartford, Conn	June 10, 1904	Do.
Narwhal b	238	1894		1894		Boston, Mass	May 26, 1905	New London, Conn	May 24, 1904	Do.
Nirvana	80	1893		1898		Poughkeepsie, N. Y	June 12, 1905	do	Apr. 25, 1903	Do.
Nautilus	24	1900		1900		Brooklyn, N. Y	June 23, 1905	Fishers Island, N. Y	June 21, 1904	Do.
Nellie	25	1894		1894		Hartford, Conn	June 28, 1905	Hartford, Conn	June 10, 1904	Do.
Palmer	124	1865	1898	1899		Philadelphia, Pa	May 18, 1905	New London, Conn	Apr. 28, 1903	Do.
Rosalie	372	1903		1902		Noank, Conn	June 12, 1905	Noank, Conn	May 28, 1904	Do.
Racquette	25	1886	1902	1889		Champlain, N. Y	June 17, 1905	Portland, Conn	June 8, 1904	Do.
Stella	a 5	1887		1904		Greenport, N. Y	Apr. 7, 1905	Greenport, N. Y	May 12, 1904	Do.
Sunbeam	11	1903		1903		Bristol, R. I	May 13, 1905	do	May 16, 1904	Providence, R. I.
Suanee	11	1893		1893		Perth Amboy, N. J	June 10, 1905	Middletown, Conn	June 10, 1904	New London, Conn.
Serapis	a 2	1885	1902	1890		New York, N. Y	Aug. 17, 1905	Norwich, Conn	Aug. 17, 1904	Do.
Vergana	128	1897		1897		Newburg, N. Y	May 1, 1905	Greenport, N. Y	May 2, 1904	Do.
Vega	34	1901		1900		Noank, Conn	June 12, 1905	Noank, Conn	June 4, 1904	Do.
Viking	171	1883		1894		Chester, Pa	June 21, 1905	Greenport, N. Y	June 8, 1904	Do.
Watawga	124	1904		1903		Greenport, N. Y	July 19, 1905	do	June 15, 1904	Do.
Miscellaneous steam vessels.										
Annie L. Wilcox (freight and fishing).	129	1878	1894	1904		Mystic, Conn	Apr. 1, 1905	New London, Conn	Apr. 1, 1904	New York, N. Y.
Cambria (oyster)	127	1871	1904	1897		Greenport, N. Y	June 2, 1905	Greenport, N. Y	May 30, 1904	New London, Conn.
Dream (fishing)	22	1893		1898		Bridgeport, Conn	Aug. 2, 1905	Mystic, Conn	Aug. 6, 1904	New Haven, Conn.
E. J. Codd (freight and fishing)	141	1903		1903		Pocomoke City, Md	May 20, 1905	New London, Conn	May 21, 1904	New London, Conn.
Eleanor F. Peck (freight and towing).	357	1884		1883		Brooklyn, N. Y	Apr. 22, 1905	Stonington, Conn	Apr. 21, 1904	Do.
F. H. Beckwith (freight and fishing).	195	1904		1904		Pocomoke City, Md	May 18, 1905	New London, Conn	May 14, 1904	Baltimore, Md.
George Dewey (nondescript)	49	1901		1898		New Suffolk, N. Y	May 1, 1905	Greenport, N. Y	Apr. 23, 1904	New London, Conn.
Henry C. Rowe (oyster)	220	1883		1901		Port Jefferson, N. Y	Apr. 19, 1905	Noank, Conn	Apr. 20, 1904	Do.
J. & G. H. Smith (oyster and towing).	42	1880		1890		East Haven, Conn	Aug. 14, 1905	New London, Conn	Aug. 10, 1904	Do.
Kate C. Stevens (oyster and towing).	104	1887		1900		Stratford, Conn	Apr. 11, 1905	do	Apr. 11, 1904	Do.

Leander Wilcox (freight and fishing).	205	1903	....	1903	....	Noank, Conn.	May 12, 1905	Mystic, Conn.	May 12, 1904	Do.
Starin (fishing)	20	1901	....	1900	....	....do	....do	Noank, Conn.	May 17, 1904	Do.
Walter Royal (nondescript)	9	1900	....	1900	....	Orient, N. Y.	June 7, 1905	Greenport, N. Y.	June 8, 1904	Do.
Motor vessels.										
Arabell (gasoline)	18	1884	1899	....	....	Bath, Me.	May 10, 1905	New London, Conn.	May 12, 1904	New London, Conn.
Ada Bell (gasoline)	17	1876	....	....	....	Noank, Conn.	June 12, 1905	Noank, Conn.	First inspn.	
Charlotte J. Kingsland (gasoline).	27	1868	1902	....	....	Northport, N. Y.	Apr. 3, 1905	....do	Apr. 4, 1904	Do.
Clara E. (gasoline)	29	1903	....	....	....	East Boothbay, Me.	Sept. 8, 1905	New London, Conn.	Sept. 9, 1904	Do.
Edward H. Smeed (gasoline)	26	1894	....	....	....	Noank, Conn.	Apr. 19, 1905	....do	Apr. 14, 1904	Do.
Elinora Hill (gasoline)	19	1885	....	....	....	....do	Apr. 26, 1905	Noank, Conn.	First inspn.	
Elsie (gasoline)	34	1903	....	....	....	East Boothbay, Me.	Nov. 27, 1905	New London, Conn.	Nov. 23, 1904	Do.
Gazelle (gasoline)	34	1896	....	....	....	Noank, Conn.	Apr. 1, 1905	....do	First inspn.	
Laura Reed (gasoline)	24	1895	....	....	....	....do	June 15, 1905	....do	May 28, 1904	Do.
Minnie C. (gasoline)	27	1902	....	....	....	Greenport, N. Y.	June 21, 1905	Greenport, N. Y.	First inspn.	
Mascot (gasoline)	59	1905	....	....	....	....do	Sept. 8, 1905	....do	....do	
Nomad (electric)	21	1901	....	....	....	Noank, Conn.	June 1, 1905	New London, Conn.	May 28, 1904	Do.
Wizard (gas)[d]	52	1880	1904	....	....	Greenport, N. Y.	Jan. 16, 1905	Greenport, N. Y.	Jan. 22, 1904	Do.
W. Talbot Dodge (gasoline)	21	1895	....	....	....	Noank, Conn.	Jan. 19, 1905	New London, Conn.	First inspn.	
W. Talbot Dodge (gasoline)	21	1895	....	....	....	....do	Dec. 15, 1905	....do	Jan. 19, 1905	Do.

LOCAL DISTRICT OF ALBANY, N. Y.

Ocean passenger steamer.										
Porto Rico	1,257	1899	....	1899	....	Toledo, Ohio	Jan. 24, 1905	San Juan, P. R.	Jan. 26, 1904	San Juan, P. R.
Inland passenger steamers.										
Atlantic [e]	95	1897	1903	1897	....	Rondout, N. Y.	Apr. 6, 1905	New Hamburg, N. Y.	Mar. 24, 1904	Albany, N. Y.
Augustus J. Phillips	129	1903	....	1903	....	....do	Apr. 27, 1905	Rondout, N. Y.	May 23, 1904	Do.
Adirondack	3,644	1896	....	1896	....	Brooklyn, N. Y.	May 25, 1905	Albany, N. Y.	May 28, 1904	Do.
Albany	1,415	1880	....	1895	....	Wilmington, N. Y.	May 27, 1905	....do	....do	Do.
Alice May	133	1899	....	1899	....	Albany, N. Y.	Sept. 14, 1905	....do	Sept. 21, 1904	Do.
City of Troy	1,527	1876	1898	1900	....	New York, N. Y.	May 13, 1905	Troy, N. Y.	May 14, 1904	Do.
Central Hudson	1,002	1861	....	1903	....	Jersey City, N. J.	June 17, 1905	Rondout, N. Y.	June 30, 1904	Do.
Cornell	435	1903	....	1903	....	Shooters Island, N. Y.	June 27, 1905	....do	June 27, 1904	Do.
Commodore	145	1905	....	1905	....	Rondout, N. Y.	June 9, 1905	Newburg, N. Y.	First inspn.	
Carrie F	8	1886	....	1886	....	Peekskill, N. Y.	July 25, 1905	....do	July 27, 1904	Do.
City of Hudson	816	1863	1894	1894	....	Mystic, Conn.	Aug. 9, 1905	Stuyvesant, N. Y.	June 30, 1904	Do.
Celina	122	1897	....	1883	....	Monroe, Mich.	Oct. 28, 1905	Albany, N. Y.	June 17, 1904	Do.
Emeline	383	1866	1888	1897	....	No record	Apr. 4, 1905	Newburg, N. Y.	Mar. 28, 1904	Do.
Echo	11	1874	1901	1904	....	City Island, N. Y.	Aug. 15, 1905	Albany, N. Y.	Aug. 15, 1904	Do.
Falcon	119	1880	....	1880	....	Wilmington, Del.	May 1, 1905	Newburg, N. Y.	May 25, 1904	New York, N. Y.

[a] Estimated. [b] Formerly Formosa, 1898. [c] Formerly Nonowantuc, 1904. [d] Formerly sloop-yacht Wizard. [e] Formerly Robert Main, 1904.

DOMESTIC VESSELS INSPECTED, YEAR ENDED DECEMBER 31, 1905—SECOND SUPERVISING DISTRICT—PHILADELPHIA, PA.—Continued.

Names of vessels and class.	Gross tonnage.	Hull built.	Hull rebuilt.	Boilers built.	Boilers rebuilt.	Where built.	Date of inspection.	Where inspected.	Date of previous inspection.	Local district where previously inspected.
Ocean freight steamers—Con.										
Goldsboro	681	1882		1882		Philadelphia, Pa	Oct. 5, 1905	Philadelphia, Pa	Oct. 11, 1904	Philadelphia, Pa.
Larimer	3,737	1903		1903		Camden, N. J	June 7, 1905	Gibsons Point, Pa	June 8, 1904	Do.
Mohican	2,255	1904		1904		Philadelphia, Pa	Aug. 25, 1905	Philadelphia, Pa	Aug. 29, 1904	Do.
Northwestern	2,207	1901		1901		Chicago, Ill	Jan. 15, 1905	do	Jan. 16, 1904	New York, N. Y.
Norman	1,203	1862		1891		Philadelphia, Pa	Sept. 8, 1905	do	Sept. 24, 1904	Philadelphia, Pa.
Onondaga	2,696	1905		1905		do	May 31, 1905	do	First inspn	
Oneida	1,322	1885		1885		Leith, Scotland	June 15, 1905	do	June 14, 1904	New York, N. Y.
Paraguay	2,201	1900		1900		Lorain, Ohio	Dec. 21, 1905	do	Dec. 14, 1904	Do.
Roma	2,939	1889		1889		Sunderland, England	May 23, 1905	Chester, Pa	June 18, 1904	Philadelphia, Pa.
Stillwater	1,019	1883		1883		Glasgow, Scotland	Apr. 8, 1905	Philadelphia, Pa	Mar. 30, 1904	Do.
Shawmut	1,624	1879		1900		Sunderland, England	June 30, 1905	do	July 16, 1904	Do.
Texan	8,633	1902		1902		Camden, N. J	Apr. 13, 1905	do	Nov. 24, 1903	Do.
Toledo	2,277	1902		1902		Toledo, Ohio	Nov. 18, 1905	Marcushook, Pa	Oct. 29, 1904	Do.
Winyah	1,682	1891		1903		Philadelphia, Pa	Jan. 23, 1905	Philadelphia, Pa	Jan. 21, 1904	Do.
Washtenaw	2,896	1887		1887		West Hartlepool, England.	Apr. 4, 1905	Marcushook, Pa	Mar. 29, 1904	Do.
Westover	617	1873	1899	1895		Wilmington, Del	Dec. 1, 1905	Philadelphia, Pa	Nov. 4, 1904	New York, N. Y.
Inland freight steamers.										
Alice Wakeley	135	1888		1895		Ithaca, N. Y	June 9, 1905	North Camden, N. J	May 20, 1904	Philadelphia, Pa.
Admiral	68	1903		1903		Wilmington, Del	July 1, 1905	do	July 23, 1904	Do.
Bessie	185	1881		1881		Boston, Mass	Jan. 17, 1905	North Cramer Hill, N. J.	May 24, 1898	Galveston, Tex.
Black Diamond	91	1887		1887		Wilmington, Del	May 26, 1905	Philadelphia, Pa	May 26, 1904	Philadelphia, Pa.
Chester	419	1902		1902		Chester, Pa	Mar. 6, 1905	do	Mar. 7, 1904	Do.
City of Salem	195	1900		1900		Wilmington, Del	Aug. 7, 1905	Salem, N. J	Aug. 8, 1904	Do.
Delaware	166	1858		1889		do	May 20, 1905	Trenton, N. J	May 21, 1904	Do.
Eaglet	386	1884		1889		Philadelphia, Pa	May 17, 1905	North Cramer Hill, N. J.	May 17, 1904	Do.
Elsie Weatherby	59	1887		1887		Pennsgrove, N. J	June 26, 1905	Camden, N. J	June 28, 1904	Do.
Ethel	266	1902		1902		Wilmington, Del	Aug. 17, 1905	North Cramer Hill, N. J.	Aug. 15, 1904	Do.
F. W. Brune	296	1860	1902	1887		do	Apr. 22, 1905	Trenton, N. J	Apr. 23, 1904	Do.
Florence	181	1899		1873		do	July 1, 1905	North Camden, N. J	July 29, 1904	Do.
George H. Stout	381	1858	1901	1887		New Brunswick, N. J	Apr. 11, 1905	North Cramer Hill, N. J.	Apr. 8, 1904	Do.
Greensborough	163	1892		1893		Baltimore, Md	July 3, 1905	North Camden, N. J	June 23, 1904	Do.
Hugo Keller	129	1890		1896		Ithaca, N. Y	June 16, 1905	Camden, N. J	June 7, 1904	New Haven, Conn.
Martha Stevens	283	1862		1887		Wilmington, Del	May 22, 1905	Trenton, N. J	May 21, 1904	Philadelphia, Pa.
Nellie	143	1890		1886		do	July 28, 1905	North Camden, N. J	July 27, 1904	Do.
Samuel H. Hartman	245	1891		1891		do	Nov. 29, 1905	Philadelphia, Pa	Nov. 25, 1904	Do.

Ruth B. Lute	148	1898		1891		do	June 17, 1905	Lewes, Del	June 10, 1904	Providence, R. I.
Raritan	166	1858		1890		do	May 24, 1905	Trenton, N. J	May 23, 1904	Philadelphia, Pa.
Riverside	452	1895		1895		Chester, Pa	Oct. 2, 1905	Philadelphia, Pa	Oct. 3, 1904	Do.
Tinicum	481	1905		1905		do	Sept. 13, 1905	Chester, Pa	First inspn	
Yuma	447	1889		1882	1889	Brooklyn, N. Y	Apr. 11, 1905	North Cramer Hill, N. J.	Mar. 28, 1904	Do.
Ocean towing steamers.										
Boxer	216	1899		1899		Boston, Mass	May 23, 1905	Philadelphia, Pa	May 19, 1905	Boston, Mass.
Blue Bell	179	1904		1904		Camden, N. J	Oct. 9, 1905	do	Nov. 1, 1904	Philadelphia, Pa.
Catawissa	558	1897		1896		Wilmington, Del	Feb. 1, 1905	do	Jan. 28, 1904	Boston, Mass.
Catherine Moran	213	1904		1904		Philadelphia, Pa	Sept. 18, 1905	do	Sept. 7, 1904	Philadelphia, Pa.
Gettysburg	557	1898		1898		Wilmington, Del	May 16, 1905	do	May 14, 1904	Do.
Ivanhoe	94	1883		1901		Philadelphia, Pa	Mar. 11, 1905	do	Mar. 11, 1904	Do.
John F. Lewis	157	1903		1903		Camden, N. J	Jan. 11, 1905	do	Dec. 29, 1903	Do.
John A. Hughes	157	1902		1902		do	July 22, 1905	do	July 20, 1904	Do.
Juno	84	1878	1899	1889		do	Oct. 10, 1905	South Camden, N. J	Oct. 5, 1904	Do.
L. Y. Schermerhorn	174	1903		1902		do	June 20, 1905	do	Apr. 25, 1904	Do.
Lykens	625	1899		1899		Philadelphia, Pa	July 17, 1905	Philadelphia, Pa	July 14, 1904	Boston, Mass.
North America	289	1876		1895		Camden, N. J	Aug. 15, 1905	do	Aug. 22, 1904	Philadelphia, Pa.
Navigator	414	1898		1898		do	Nov. 20, 1905	South Camden, N. J	Nov. 10, 1904	Do.
Patience	292	1901		1901		do	Nov. 1, 1905	Philadelphia, Pa	Oct. 25, 1904	Do.
Swatara	625	1899		1898		Philadelphia, Pa	Feb. 10, 1905	do	Feb. 9, 1904	Boston, Mass.
Sweepstakes	227	1867		1894		Cleveland, Ohio	May 15, 1905	do	May 13, 1904	Philadelphia, Pa.
Sommers N. Smith	211	1896		1896		Newport News, Va	Sept. 18, 1905	do	Sept. 24, 1904	Do.
S. A. McCaulley	92	1885		1900		Philadelphia, Pa	Oct. 30, 1905	do	Nov. 21, 1904	Do.
Tamaqua	564	1896		1896		do	Mar. 3, 1905	do	Feb. 29, 1904	Do.
Inland towing steamers.										
Altoona	63	1875		1888		Camden, N. J	Apr. 8, 1905	Philadelphia, Pa	Mar. 8, 1904	Philadelphia, Pa.
Amanda Powell	38	1873		1901		do	Apr. 17, 1905	Wilmington, Del	Apr. 25, 1904	Do.
Alert	51	1890		1889		Bordentown, N. J	Apr. 19, 1905	Philadelphia, Pa	Apr. 18, 1904	Do.
Asa W. Hughes	106	1889		1900		Philadelphia, Pa	May 8, 1905	do	May 4, 1904	Do.
Active	60	1887		1887		New Gretna, N. J	June 6, 1905	do	June 3, 1904	Do.
Atkins Hughes	115	1890		1890		Philadelphia, Pa	June 22, 1905	do	June 21, 1904	Do.
American	20	1876	1895	1896		do	July 1, 1905	South Camden, N. J	July 1, 1904	Do.
Atlas	32	1892		1892		Baltimore, Md	June 29, 1905	Philadelphia, Pa	June 28, 1904	Do.
A. M. Bramell	34	1892		1892		Bordentown, N. J	July 15, 1905	do	July 14, 1904	Do.
Arctic	33	1882		1882		Camden, N. J	Aug. 4, 1905	do	Aug. 4, 1904	Do.
Alex. Y. Hanna	44	1890		1890		Philadelphia, Pa	Aug. 29, 1905	North Camden, N. J	Aug. 29, 1904	Do.
Atlantic	50	1862		1884		Baltimore, Md	Sept. 9, 1905	do	Sept. 8, 1904	Do.
Aurelia	6	(a)		1900		Unknown	Sept. 19, 1905	do	Sept. 16, 1904	Do.
Alida	79	1905		1905		Wilmington, Del	Oct. 2, 1905	Wilmington, Del	First inspn	
Atlantic	129	1904		1904		Philadelphia, Pa	Nov. 7, 1905	Philadelphia, Pa	Nov. 30, 1904	Do.
Brilliant	81	1902		1902		do	Feb. 21, 1905	do	Jan. 30, 1904	Do.
Bryn Mawr	74	1903		1903		Camden, N. J	Apr. 26, 1905	North Camden, N. J	Apr. 22, 1904	Do.
Baltic	72	1894		1894		Philadelphia, Pa	Sept. 12, 1905	Philadelphia, Pa	Sept. 17, 1904	Do.
Bristol	48	1893		1893		do	Sept. 16, 1905	do	do	Do.
Brilliant	81	1902		1902		do	Dec. 29, 1905	do	Feb. 21, 1905	Do.

a Unknown.

Domestic Vessels Inspected, Year ended December 31, 1905—Second Supervising District—Philadelphia, Pa.—Continued.

Names of vessels and class.	Gross tonnage.	Hull built.	Hull rebuilt.	Boilers built.	Boilers rebuilt.	Where built.	Date of inspection.	Where inspected.	Date of previous inspection.	Local district where previously inspected.
Inland towing steamers—Con.										
Convoy	78	1873		1873		Philadelphia, Pa	Jan. 10, 1905	Philadelphia, Pa	Jan. 8, 1904	Philadelphia, Pa.
Cheltenham	113	1899		1899		do	June 16, 1905	do	June 20, 1904	Do.
Cecil	59	1904		1890		Solomons, Md	July 24, 1905	Wilmington, Del	July 23, 1904	Baltimore, Md.
Clara	58	1870	1880	1880		New Brunswick, N. J	July 22, 1905	North Cramer Hill, N. J.	July 2, 1904	Philadelphia, Pa.
Curtin	85	1898		1898		Camden, N. J	Oct. 9, 1905	do	Oct. 11, 1904	Do.
Credenda	34	1903		1886		Paulsboro, N. J	Oct. 12, 1905	Wilmington, Del	Sept. 19, 1904	Baltimore, Md.
City Ice Boat No. 1	325	1866		1893		Philadelphia, Pa	Oct. 16, 1905	Holmesburg, Pa	Nov. 17, 1904	Philadelphia, Pa.
City Ice Boat No. 2	458	1868	1904	1903		do	do	do	Nov. 2, 1904	Do.
Charles Killam	24	1891		1891		Bordentown, N. J	Nov. 20, 1905	Philadelphia, Pa	Nov. 25, 1904	Do.
Ellen McAvoy	27	1883		1883		Pettys Island, N. J	July 17, 1905	North Camden, N. J	July 18, 1904	Do.
Esther	27	1895		1896		Camden, N. J	July 19, 1905	Philadelphia, Pa	do	Do.
Evening Star	37	1897		1893		Bordentown, N. J	Aug. 26, 1905	do	Aug. 25, 1904	Do.
El Mora	13	1887		1894		Elizabethport, N. J	Sept. 11, 1905	Wilmington, Del	Aug. 31, 1904	Do.
Eva Belle Cain	20	1871		1893		Philadelphia, Pa	Sept. 13, 1905	Philadelphia, Pa	Sept. 15, 1904	Do.
Esther	7	1902		1897		Chincoteague, Va	July 31, 1905	Exmoor Station, Va	July 30, 1904	Do.
Edna	23	1892		1892		Philadelphia, Pa	Nov. 13, 1905	North Camden, N. J	Nov. 12, 1904	Do.
Frederick Jansen	28	1884		1888		do	Apr. 17, 1905	Wilmington, Del	Apr. 20, 1904	Do.
F. A. Churchman	64	1894		1883		do	Apr. 5, 1905	Philadelphia, Pa	Apr. 4, 1904	Do.
Fred Cramer	19	1899		1885		Milford, Del	Oct. 4, 1905	North Camden, N. J	Oct. 4, 1904	Do.
Frank K. Esherick	69	1890		1890		Philadelphia, Pa	Nov. 16, 1905	Philadelphia, Pa	Nov. 17, 1904	Norfolk, Va.
Gladys [a]	24	1871		1889		do	Mar. 17, 1905	do	Mar. 16, 1904	Philadelphia, Pa.
Granite	29	1904		1885		Milford, Del	Mar. 29, 1905	Wilmington, Del	Mar. 29, 1904	Do.
George W. Smith	34	1883		1882		Brooklyn, N. Y	Oct. 17, 1904	North Camden, N. J	Oct. 15, 1903	Do.
Gwynedd	115	1896		1896		Philadelphia, Pa	Sept. 30, 1905	Philadelphia, Pa	Oct. 3, 1904	Do.
Gard. B. Reynolds	45	1891		1891		do	Dec. 15, 1905	do	Sept. 29, 1904	Do.
Hainesport	67	1904		1904		Madison, Md	Mar. 3, 1905	do	Mar. 24, 1904	Baltimore, Md.
Harry M. Wall	60	1892		1892		Philadelphia, Pa	Mar. 28, 1905	do	Mar. 19, 1904	Philadelphia, Pa.
Harry Schaubel, jr	34	1886		1886		do	Apr. 13, 1905	do	Apr. 13, 1904	Do.
Harford	59	1881		1904		Camden, N. J	June 19, 1905	Camden, N. J	June 17, 1904	Do.
Helen	102	1901		1901		do	do	North Camden, N. J	June 7, 1904	Do.
Harbor	50	1891		1891		Philadelphia, Pa	Sept. 5, 1905	Philadelphia, Pa	Sept. 13, 1904	Do.
Imperator	93	1886		1886		Athens, N. Y	July 24, 1905	do	July 22, 1904	Do.
I. W. Durham	33	1872	1900	1893		Philadelphia, Pa	Sept. 21, 1905	do	Nov. 9, 1903	Do.
Ivanhoe	35	1875		1890		do	Sept. 26, 1905	do	Sept. 26, 1904	Do.
Josephine Lincoln	18	1875	1886	1892		Bordentown, N. J	Mar. 7, 1905	do	Mar. 8, 1904	Do.
Jack Twohy	171	1905		1905		Camden, N. J	Apr. 4, 1905	Camden, N. J	First inspn	
John B. Patton	39	1896		1895		Bordentown, N. J	Apr. 1, 1905	Philadelphia, Pa	Mar. 17, 1904	Do.
John Reese	57	1894		1894		Philadelphia, Pa	May 11, 1905	do	May 12, 1904	Do.
J. McAteer [b]	20	1869		1895		do	May 27, 1905	do	May 28, 1904	Do.
Jas. McCaulley	92	1887		1898		Camden, N. J	June 17, 1905	do	June 23, 1904	Do.
J. S. Lamson	17	1894		1894		Bordentown, N. J	June 27, 1905	do	June 28, 1904	Do.

John I. Brady	72	1897		1893		Philadelphia, Pa	July 17, 1905	do	July 18, 1904	Do.
John E. Mehrer	76	1894		1894		do	Aug. 16, 1905	do	Aug. 15, 1904	Do.
John C. Bradley	45	1881		1896		do	Sept. 19, 1905	do	Oct. 19, 1904	Do.
John J. Hagan	26	1894		1891		do	Oct. 10, 1905	North Cramer Hill, N. J.	Oct. 11, 1904	Do.
Jared Darlington	57	1893		1893		Bordentown, N. J	Oct. 30, 1905	Philadelphia, Pa	Oct. 31, 1904	Do.
Jamesburg	75	1883		1883		South Amboy, N. J	Nov. 13, 1905	Camden, N. J	Nov. 23, 1904	Do.
J. S. W. Holton	62	1892		1892		Philadelphia, Pa	Nov. 21, 1905	Philadelphia, Pa	Dec. 15, 1904	Do.
Kensington	33	1882		1882		Camden, N. J	June 16, 1905	do	June 13, 1904	Do.
Lightning	48	1874		1898		do	May 13, 1905	Camden, N. J	May 9, 1904	Do.
Leader	26	1882		1881		Pettys Island, N. J	June 16, 1905	Philadelphia, Pa	June 15, 1904	Do.
Lillie M. Graham	49	1892		1892		Philadelphia, Pa	June 19, 1905	do	June 6, 1904	Do.
Lookout	35	1862		1875		Camden, N. J	June 28, 1905	do	June 27, 1904	Do.
Laura	28	1879	1895	1894		Philadelphia, Pa	Aug. 10, 1905	do	Aug. 10, 1904	Do.
Lizzie Crawford	52	1882		1896		Camden, N. J	Sept. 5, 1905	do	Sept. 23, 1904	Do.
Laura B	80	1883		1898		Philadelphia, Pa	Sept. 25, 1905	Wilmington, Del	Oct. 4, 1904	Do.
Lorraine	71	1895		1895		do	Nov. 3, 1905	Philadelphia, Pa	Oct. 19, 1904	Do.
M. S. Quay	131	1903		1903		do	Jan. 31, 1905	do	Jan. 29, 1904	Do.
Madeira	51	1892		1892		do	Feb. 24, 1905	do	Feb. 24, 1904	Do.
Maurice	36	1892		1897		do	Mar. 3, 1905	do	Mar. 7, 1904	Do.
Martha	12	1879		1881		Bordentown, N. J	Apr. 3, 1905	Wilmington, Del	Apr. 2, 1904	Do.
Minerva	38	1886		1901		Philadelphia, Pa	Apr. 10, 1905	Philadelphia, Pa	Apr. 11, 1904	Do.
Meteor	95	1881		1881	1889	Wilmington, Del	May 8, 1905	Wilmington, Del	May 9, 1904	Do.
May T. White	38	1880		1886		Philadelphia, Pa	June 17, 1905	South Camden, N. J	June 17, 1904	Do.
M. P. Howlett	53	1868	1898	1898		Baltimore, Md	June 9, 1905	Philadelphia, Pa	June 9, 1904	Do.
Mascot	41	1890		1890		Philadelphia, Pa	June 10, 1905	do	June 11, 1904	Do.
Mary McIlvaine [c]	34	1888		1889		Tottenville, N. Y	June 30, 1905	do	June 30, 1904	Do.
Mary J. Walker	61	1891		1900		Bordentown, N. J	July 20, 1905	do	July 25, 1904	Do.
Majestic	55	1890		1890		do	Aug. 28, 1905	do	Aug. 26, 1904	Do.
Mary R. Corr	25	1882	1905	1905		Pettys Island, N. J	Sept. 19, 1905	North Camden, N. J	Mar. 30, 1904	Do.
Morris	15	1903		1896		Camden, N. J	Oct. 5, 1905	North Cramer Hill, N. J.	May 10, 1904	Do.
Mollie	36	1875		1899		Philadelphia, Pa	Oct. 4, 1905	Philadelphia, Pa	Dec. 3, 1904	Do.
Majestic	113	1900		1900		Baltimore, Md	Oct. 16, 1905	South Camden, N. J	Nov. 5, 1904	Do.
New Castle	110	1902		1902		Camden, N. J	Apr. 20, 1905	Philadelphia, Pa	Apr. 19, 1904	Do.
Nellie E. Rawson	72	1873		1904		Bath, Me	June 2, 1905	Menhaden, N. J	June 11, 1904	Do.
Nellie	41	1894		1894		Philadelphia, Pa	July 24, 1905	Philadelphia, Pa	Aug. 1, 1904	Do.
Newark	59	1883		1888		Newark, N. J	Sept. 9, 1905	North Camden, N. J	Sept. 9, 1904	Do.
Owen Brady	50	1891		1891		Philadelphia, Pa	Mar. 10, 1905	Philadelphia, Pa	Mar. 10, 1904	Do.
Ogontz	113	1899		1899		do	Nov. 21, 1905	do	Nov. 28, 1904	Do.
Pilot Boy	25	1896		1896		do	Apr. 20, 1905	do	Apr. 19, 1904	Do.
Protector	176	1905		1905		do	May 31, 1905	do	First inspn.	
Penllyn	137	1901		1901		do	May 22, 1905	do	May 20, 1904	Do.
Pensauken	15	1894		1886		do	Apr. 29, 1905	Crum Creek, Pa	Apr. 29, 1904	Do.
Peerless	89	1886		1893		Camden, N. J	June 12, 1905	Philadelphia, Pa	June 4, 1904	Baltimore, Md.
Pilot	120	1891		1891		Philadelphia, Pa	July 21, 1905	South Camden, N. J	Aug. 13, 1904	Philadelphia, Pa.
Pioneer [d]	36	1883	1902	1905		Northport, N. Y	July 11, 1905	North Camden, N. J	Aug 26, 1904	Do.
P. R. R. No. 4	121	1904		1904		Philadelphia, Pa	July 25, 1905	Camden, N. J	July 25, 1904	Do.
Philadelphia	40	1887	1903	1903		Milford, Del	Oct. 26, 1905	Philadelphia, Pa	Dec. 1, 1904	Do.
Rescue	75	1886		1886		Camden, N. J	Apr. 15, 1905	do	Apr. 14, 1904	Do.

[a] Formerly Edith, 1898. [b] Formerly Minnie, 1901. [c] Formerly Loretta K, 1899. [d] Formerly Lizzie E. Woodend, 1902.

DOMESTIC VESSELS INSPECTED, YEAR ENDED DECEMBER 31, 1905—SECOND SUPERVISING DISTRICT—PHILADELPHIA, PA.—Continued.

Names of vessels and class.	Gross tonnage.	Hull built.	Hull rebuilt.	Boilers built.	Boilers rebuilt.	Where built.	Date of inspection.	Where inspected.	Date of previous inspection.	Local district where previously inspected.
Inland towing steamers—Con.										
Rebecca	39	1874		1881		mden, N. J	May 26, 1905	Philadelphia, Pa	May 24, 1904	Philadelphia, Pa.
Robert K. Cassatt [a]	87	1877		1877		Philadelphia, Pa	June 5, 1905	North Cramer Hill, N. J.	June 16, 1904	Do.
Rose Hagan	17	1900		1893		Bordentown, N. J	Oct. 10, 1905	do	Oct. 11, 1904	Do.
Surprise	19	1892		1889		Clifton, N. Y	Aug. 9, 1905	do	Aug. 8, 1904	Do.
Samuel Gedney	48	1873		1895		Camden, N. J	Sept. 23, 1905	South Camden, N. J	Oct. 18, 1904	Do.
Varuna	64	1867	1899	1887	1902	New Brunswick, N. J	Sept. 25, 1905	Camden, N. J	Oct. 5, 1904	Do.
William Penn [b]	48	1860	1899	1883	1903	Philadelphia, Pa	Mar. 21, 1905	Wilmington, Del	Mar. 18, 1904	Do.
Willie	15	1896		1896		do	Apr. 3, 1905	Philadelphia, Pa	Apr. 11, 1904	Do.
William Cramp	56	1877	1902	1897		do	Apr. 19, 1905	do	May 6, 1904	Do.
William J. Bradley	81	1900		1895		Camden, N. J	Apr. 22, 1905	South Camden, N. J	Apr. 23, 1904	Do.
White and Price	13	1882		1902		Brooklyn, N. Y	Apr. 3, 1905	Philadelphia, Pa	Mar. 31, 1904	Do.
Wanderer	35	1866	1900	1894		Nassau, New Providence.	May 17, 1905	do	May 16, 1904	Do.
William Rowland	129	1905		1905		Chester, Pa	July 12, 1905	Chester, Pa	First inspn.	
William M. Dove	18	1887		1895		Baltimore, Md	Aug. 8, 1905	Philadelphia, Pa	Aug. 5, 1904	Do.
William J. Sewell	61	1893		1893		Philadelphia, Pa	Aug. 21, 1905	do	Aug. 18, 1904	Do.
White Rose	74	1892		1892		New York, N. Y	Aug. 26, 1905	do	Aug. 24, 1904	Do.
Wm. J. Peoples	62	1898		1898		Wilmington, Del	Sept. 9, 1905	do	Sept. 8, 1904	Do.
William McAvoy	31	1893		1893		Bordentown, N. J	Oct. 23, 1905	do	Oct. 24, 1904	Do.
Winfield S. Cahill	54	1892		1902		Baltimore, Md	Oct. 21, 1905	do	Dec. 19, 1904	Do.
Ocean steam pleasure yachts.										
Giralda	184	1896		1896		Port Jefferson, N. Y	May 1, 1905	Essington, Pa	May 6, 1904	Philadelphia, Pa.
Ibis	184	1875	1893	1888		New Brunswick, N. J	June 3, 1905	North Camden, N. J	May 23, 1902	Do.
Josephine	974	1899		1899		Philadelphia, Pa	Mar. 31, 1905	Philadelphia, Pa	Jan. 9, 1903	Do.
May	652	1891		1891		Troon, Scotland	May 10, 1905	do	May 12, 1904	Do.
Marietta	153	1897		1904		Brooklyn, N. Y	June 12, 1905	do	June 7, 1904	Do.
Sybilla	110	1885	1888	1895		Linwood, Pa	Sept. 29, 1905	Camden, N. J	Nov. 10, 1904	Do.
Inland steam pleasure yachts.										
Alan Gray	c 3	1893		1892		Camden, N. J	June 8, 1905	Millsboro, Del	June 2, 1904	Philadelphia, Pa.
Clara and Lillie	8	(d)		1894		Bridesburg, Pa	May 27, 1905	Bridesburg, Pa	May 5, 1904	Do.
Calypso [e]	8	1893		1893	1904	Trenton, N. J	Sept. 14, 1904	Whitehill, N. J	First inspn.	
Cypher	31	1896		1900		South Boston, Mass	July 8, 1905	Greenwich, N. J	July 8, 1904	Do.
Calypso	8	1893		1893	1904	Trenton, N. J	Sept. 16, 1905	Whitehill, N. J	Sept. 14, 1904	Do.
David Rankins [f]	c 4	1890		1890		Bordentown, N. J	May 5, 1905	Camden, N. J	Sept. 13, 1903	Do.
Franklin	5	1903		1896		Philadelphia, Pa	Mar. 3, 1905	Delanco, N. J	Mar. 4, 1904	Do
Governor Pennypacker	132	1903		1903		do	Sept. 29, 1905	Philadelphia, Pa	Nov. 28, 1904	Do.
Harriet	52	1891		1902		Saunderstown, R. I	May 16, 1905	Essington, Pa	May 16, 1904	Do.
Hattie Killam	30	1898		1898		Bordentown, N. J	May 10, 1905	Philadelphia, Pa	May 7, 1904	Do.
Israel W. Durham	c 2	(d)	1889	1888		Unknown	Aug. 15, 1905	Mount Holly, N. J	Oct. 14, 1903	Do.

Josephine No. 2	c 4	1903		1899		Morris Heights, N. J	Mar. 31, 1905	Philadelphia, Pa	Aug. 29, 1903	Do.
John Exton, jr	8	1904		1904		Trenton, N. J	June 14, 1905	Trenton, N. J	First inspn.	
Muchacho	5	1902		1902		Camden, N. J	July 1, 1905	Chester, Pa	July 2, 1904	Do.
Minnie g	22	1885		1885		Linwood, Pa	June 22, 1905	North Cramer Hill, N. J.	June 17, 1904	Do.
May	48	1893		1901		Bordentown, N. J	July 20, 1905	Bordentown, N. J	July 27, 1904	Do.
Narcissa h	51	1896		1896		Wilmington, Del	Aug. 4, 1905	Camden, N. J	Aug. 4, 1904	Do.
Orca i	37	1901		1901		South Boston, Mass	May 23, 1905	Essington, Pa	June 2, 1904	Do.
Relief	16	1884		1884		Camden, N. J	Aug. 17, 1905	Trenton, N. J	Aug. 18, 1904	Do.
Telfer	c 1	1893		1894		West Creek, N. J	July 20, 1905	Mount Holly, N. J	July 19, 1904	Do.
Visitor	49	1883		1883		Baltimore, Md	Sept. 28, 1905	Philadelphia, Pa	Sept. 28, 1904	Do.
William S. Stokley	83	1875		1895		Philadelphia, Pa	Sept. 22, 1905	do	Sept. 23, 1904	Do.
Miscellaneous steam vessels.										
Alaska (fishing)	229	1881		1893		Boothbay, Me	Apr. 1, 1905	Wilmington, Del	Mar. 25, 1904	Providence, R. I.
Active (fishing)	73	1887		1887		New Gretna, N. J	Apr. 28, 1905	New Gretna, N. J	June 4, 1904	Philadelphia, Pa.
Adroit (fishing)	92	1900		1899		Pocomoke City, Md	May 17, 1905	Beach Haven, N. J	May 19, 1904	Norfolk, Va.
Ardent (fishing)	106	1902		1902		Baltimore, Md	Apr. 21, 1905	do	June 21, 1904	Philadelphia, Pa.
Albert Brown (fishing)	108	1875		1903		Bristol, Me	do	do	May 21, 1904	Norfolk, Va.
Edwin S. Stuart (fire)	150	1893		1898		Brooklyn, N. Y	Mar. 23, 1905	Philadelphia, Pa	Mar. 16, 1904	Philadelphia, Pa.
Fire Fighter (fire)	192	1905		1905		Wilmington, Del	June 1, 1905	Wilmington, Del	First inspn.	
Joseph Wharton (fishing)	245	1904		1904		do	June 17, 1905	Beach Haven, N. J	June 22, 1904	Do.
Jimmie (waterboat)	11	1880		1904		Brooklyn, N. Y	Aug. 18, 1905	Philadelphia, Pa	Aug. 18, 1904	Do.
Mars (wrecking)	278	1890		1889		Camden, N. J	Apr. 11, 1905	do	Apr. 12, 1904	Do.
Nellie B. Dey (fishing)	122	1884		1901		Lennoxville, N. C	Apr. 28, 1905	New Gretna, N. J	May 19, 1904	Norfolk, Va.
Philadelphia (pilot)	359	1898		1898		Philadelphia, Pa	Aug. 18, 1905	Philadelphia, Pa	Aug. 17, 1904	Philadelphia, Pa.
Somerset (wrecking)	179	1854		1879		Cleveland, Ohio	Mar. 24, 1905	Wilmington, Del	Mar. 11, 1904	Providence, R. I.
Samuel H. Ashbridge (police and fire).	268	1900		1900		Philadelphia, Pa	Oct. 20, 1905	Philadelphia, Pa	Oct. 22, 1904	Philadelphia, Pa.
Vessels propelled by gas motors.										
Arrow	41	1874				Rye, N. Y	June 15, 1905	Essington, Pa	First inspn.	
Alaska	24	1868				Marcushook, Pa	Aug. 28, 1905	Wilmington, Del	do	
Anna Bell	28	1888				Paulsboro, N. J	Oct. 26, 1905	Philadelphia, Pa	Oct. 26, 1904	Philadelphia, Pa.
Cambridge	40	1902				Cambridge, Md	June 15, 1905	Wilmington, Del	June 13, 1904	Do.
Commanche	24	1904				Atlantic City, N. J	Sept. 2, 1905	Atlantic City, N. J	Sept. 3, 1904	Do.
Iola	44	1905				Pennsgrove, N. J	Nov. 9, 1905	Hancocks Bridge, N. J.	First inspn.	
Lewis M. Price	93	1904				Cambridge, Md	Sept. 12, 1905	North Camden, N. J	Oct. 4, 1904	Baltimore, Md.
Freight sail vessels of over 700 tons.										
Erskine M. Phelps (ship)	2,998	1898				Bath, Me	May 18, 1905	Philadelphia, Pa	Apr. 19, 1904	Philadelphia, Pa.
Geneva (schooner)	874	1900				Rockland, Me	Jan. 12, 1905	do	Jan. 11, 1904	Portland, Me.
Madeline Cooney (schooner)	790	1892				Waldoboro, Me	Mar. 17, 1905	do	Jan. 14, 1904	Philadelphia, Pa.
Marie Palmer (schooner)	1,904	1900				Bath, Me	June 22, 1905	do	June 15, 1904	Boston, Mass.
Oakley C. Curtis (schooner)	2,374	1901				do	Jan. 17, 1905	do	Jan. 19, 1904	Portland, Me.
Tillie Baker (bark)	719	1876				Harrington, Me	Jan. 14, 1905	do	Jan. 2, 1904	Philadelphia, Pa.

a Formerly Elmore A. Kent, 1904.
b Formerly Pacific, 1898.
c Estimated.
d Unknown.
e Certificated July, 1905.
f Formerly Alicia, 1904.
g Formerly U. S. S. Mermaid.
h Formerly Millie K. Ridgway, 1900.
i Formerly Monaloa, 1904.

DOMESTIC VESSELS INSPECTED, YEAR ENDED DECEMBER 31, 1905—SECOND SUPERVISING DISTRICT—Continued.

LOCAL DISTRICT OF NEW LONDON, CONN.

Names of vessels and class.	Gross tonnage.	Hull built.	Hull rebuilt.	Boilers built.	Boilers rebuilt.	Where built.	Date of inspection.	Where inspected.	Date of previous inspection.	Local district where previously inspected.
Ocean passenger steamer.										
Dakota	20,714	1905		1902		New London, Conn	Mar. 20, 1905	Groton, Conn	First inspn	
Inland passenger steamers.										
Connecticut	3,399	1889		1888		Noank, Conn	June 14, 1905	Stonington, Conn	June 11, 1904	Providence, R. I.
City of Lowell	2,975	1894		1894		Bath, Me	June 1, 1905	New London, Conn	June 1, 1904	New London, Conn.
Chelsea	564	1892	1902	1904		Wilmington, Del	June 17, 1905	Norwich, Conn	June 18, 1904	Do.
C. H. Northam	1,436	1873	1878	1896		New York, N. Y	July 11, 1905	Stonington, Conn	July 7, 1904	New Haven, Conn.
Chester W. Chapin	2,868	1899		1899		Sparrow Point, Md	Oct. 23, 1905	New London, Conn	Oct. 31, 1904	New London, Conn.
Gypsy	57	1884		1904		Mystic, Conn	May 28, 1905	Saunderstown, R. I	May 25, 1904	Do.
Greenport	1,413	1866	1896	1891		New York, N. Y	June 7, 1905	Greenport, N. Y	June 6, 1904	Do.
Hartford	1,488	1899		1899		Baltimore, Md	Sept. 30, 1905	Hartford, Conn	Oct. 3, 1904	Do.
Kelpie	43	1874	1900	1892		Salisbury, Mass	May 17, 1905	Greenport, N. Y	May 12, 1904	Do.
Middletown	1,554	1896		1896		Philadelphia, Pa	Mar. 30, 1905	Hartford, Conn	Mar. 31, 1904	Do.
Madeleine	74	1893		1891		Cape Elizabeth, Me	May 24, 1905	New London, Conn	May 26, 1904	Do.
Munnatawket	204	1890		1904		New London, Conn	May 10, 1905	Fishers Island, N. Y	Apr. 27, 1904	Do.
Meteor [a]	423	1883		1900		Philadelphia, Pa	Nov. 16, 1904	Sag Harbor, N. Y	Nov. 18, 1903	Do.
New Hampshire	2,395	1892		1892		Wilmington, Del	Mar. 31, 1905	New London, Conn	Apr. 2, 1904	Do.
Orient	471	1896	1902	1896		Chelsea, Mass	June 6, 1905	Greenport, N. Y	May 30, 1904	Do.
Osprey	57	1882	1902	1886		Mystic, Conn	July 10, 1905	Riverside, Conn	June 14, 1904	Do.
Restless	475	1904		1903		Noank, Conn	June 27, 1905	Fishers Island, N. Y	June 23, 1904	Do.
Rhode Island	2,888	1882		1890		do	May 11, 1905	Stonington, Conn	May 11, 1904	Do.
Sylvia	132	1900		1900		Springfield, Mass	Apr. 17, 1905	Springfield, Mass	May 23, 1904	Do.
Watch Hill	35	1879		1885		Newburg, N. Y	May 18, 1905	Westerly, R. I	June 15, 1904	New York, N. Y.
Ferry steamers.										
Colonial	38	1905		1902		Noank, Conn	Apr. 28, 1905	Noank, Conn	First inspn	
General Spencer [b]	33	1904		1904		Hartford, Conn	Nov. 19, 1904	Hartford, Conn	do	
Gov. Winthrop	485	1905		1905		Noank, Conn	Aug. 4, 1905	Noank, Conn	do	
General Spencer	33	1904		1904		Hartford, Conn	Nov. 15, 1905	Goodspeeds, Conn	Nov. 19, 1904	New London, Conn.
J. A. Saunders	192	1902		1902		Saunderstown, R. I	June 19, 1905	Saunderstown, R. I	June 25, 1904	Do.
Menantic	203	1893		1893		Noank, Conn	May 13, 1905	Greenport, N. Y	Apr. 23, 1904	Do.
Middlesex	27	1899	1904	1884		East Haddam, Conn	July 15, 1905	Hadlyme, Conn	July 23, 1904	Do.
Rocky Hill	33	1902		1902		Portland, Conn	Apr. 5, 1905	Rocky Hill, Conn	Apr. 7, 1904	Do.
West Side	106	1904		1904		Saunderstown, R. I	June 26, 1905	Saunderstown, R. I	June 25, 1904	Do.
Inland freight steamers.										
Arthur D. Bissell [c]	137	1881	1902	1898		Lockport, N. Y	Dec. 1, 1904	Greens Harbor, Conn	Nov. 21, 1903	New Haven, Conn.
Clifford	212	1890	1902	1901		Rocky Hill, Conn	July 14, 1905	New London, Conn	July 14, 1904	New London, Conn.

Cortis	131	1880		1888		Havana, N. Y	Aug. 23, 1905	Norwich, Conn	Aug. 25, 1904	Do.
E. P. Cook	135	1881	1903	1905		do	Oct. 2, 1905	Greens Harbor, Conn	Sept. 20, 1904	Do.
Holyoake	198	1898		1898		Greenport, N. Y	June 7, 1905	Greenport, N. Y	June 8, 1904	Do.
Mohegan	2,783	1896		1896		Chester, Pa	May 5, 1905	New London, Conn	May 3, 1904	Do.
Notter	130	1885	1899	1892		Buffalo, N. Y	July 10, 1905	Middletown, Conn	July 1, 1904	Do.
Robt. W. Johnson	204	1905		1905		Noank, Conn	Oct. 9, 1905	Noank, Conn	First inspn	
Seabury	186	1903		1904		Mystic, Conn	Apr. 12, 1905	New London, Conn	do	
Sarah Thorp	201	1887		1905		Hoboken, N. J	Nov. 11, 1905	Sag Harbor, N. Y	Oct. 19, 1904	Do.
Wm. E. Cleary	140	1887		1904		Lockport, N. Y	Nov. 22, 1905	Westerly, R. I	Oct. 31, 1904	New Haven, Conn.
Inland towing steamers.										
Alert	73	1857	1896	1893		Philadelphia, Pa	Jan. 18, 1905	Greens Harbor, Conn	Jan. 19, 1904	New London, Conn.
Aquidneck	58	1889	1904	1903		Boston, Mass	Feb. 6, 1905	Riverside, Conn	Jan. 30, 1904	Do.
Argo [d]	105	1873	1897	1897		Hartford, Conn	do	do	Feb. 4, 1904	Do
A. M. Smith	37	1871	1902	1891		Philadelphia, Pa	Apr. 27, 1905	Hartford, Conn	Apr. 28, 1904	Do.
Aries	114	1884	1905	1905		do	Dec. 14, 1905	Riverside, Conn	May 18, 1904	Do.
Cassie	31	1887	1899	1886		New London, Conn	Oct. 14, 1905	Greens Harbor, Conn	Oct. 5, 1904	Do.
Dr. S. N. Briggs	22	1869	1904	1897		Philadelphia, Pa	June 17, 1905	Riverside, Conn	June 14, 1904	Do.
Gertrude	122	1883		1898		Brooklyn, N. Y	Aug. 25, 1905	do	Aug. 27, 1904	Do.
Harriet [e]	56	1875	1900	1900		Boston, Mass	June 13, 1905	Greens Harbor, Conn	June 4, 1904	Do.
Harold	186	1889		1904		New London, Conn	Oct. 7, 1905	Riverside, Conn	Oct. 7, 1904	Do.
J. Warren Coulston	52	1872	1901	1889		Philadelphia, Pa	June 10, 1905	Hartford, Conn	June 10, 1904	Do.
J. E. Randerson	46	1903		1903		New Baltimore, N. Y	Nov. 22, 1905	New London, Conn	Nov. 11, 1904	New Haven, Conn.
Lillian	17	1896		1890		Athens, N. Y	Apr. 5, 1905	Hartford, Conn	June 7, 1904	Do.
Luther C. Ward	106	1882		1903		Newburg, N. Y	June 10, 1905	Middletown, Conn	June 10, 1904	New London, Conn.
Miles Standish	55	1905		1904		New London, Conn	Feb. 2, 1905	Riverside, Conn	First inspn	
Mabel	84	1882		1904		Philadelphia, Pa	Aug. 3, 1905	Hartford, Conn	Aug. 3, 1904	Do.
Nathan Hale	299	1890		1897		New London, Conn	June 27, 1905	Riverside, Conn	June 20, 1904	Do.
Raymond	20	1885	1902	1891		Hartford, Conn	May 27, 1905	Hartford, Conn	May 27, 1904	Do.
R. M. Waterman	174	1896		1896		New London, Conn	Sept. 7, 1905	Riverside, Conn	Sept. 26, 1904	Do.
Shenecossett	15	1889		1889		Noank, Conn	May 26, 1905	Greens Harbor, Conn	Apr. 21, 1904	Do.
Sachem	195	1900		1900		Baltimore, Md	Aug. 28, 1905	Middletown, Conn	Sept. 1, 1904	Do.
T. A. Scott, jr	36	1882	1900	1889	1904	Noank, Conn	July 29, 1905	Greens Harbor, Conn	July 27, 1904	Do.
Westerly	41	1879	1903	1890		Mystic, Conn	Mar. 16, 1905	Westerly, R. I	Mar. 17, 1904	Do.
Ocean steam pleasure yacht.										
Wacouta [f]	803	1894		1894		Bath, Me	Apr. 29, 1905	New London, Conn	Apr. 29, 1904	New London, Conn.
Inland steam pleasure yachts.										
Aunt Polly	176	1900	1902	1900		Brooklyn, N. Y	June 7, 1905	Greenport, N. Y	June 8, 1904	New London, Conn.
Agnes	29	1897		1898		Baltimore, Md	Sept. 15, 1905	New London, Conn	Sept. 17, 1904	Do.
Della	[g]1	1902		1899		East Hartford, Conn	June 17, 1905	Hartford, Conn	June 22, 1904	Do.
Endion	61	1898		1903		New York, N. Y	May 12, 1905	New London, Conn	May 18, 1904	Do.
Free Lance	132	1895		1895		Elizabethport, N. J	May 1, 1905	Greenport, N. Y	Apr. 23, 1904	Do.
Fedalma	95	1886	1892	1897		New York, N. Y	Nov. 8, 1905	New London, Conn	Aug. 11, 1902	Do.
Gretchen	58	1891	1901	1895		Poughkeepsie, N. Y	Aug. 26, 1905	Greens Harbor, Conn	Sept. 2, 1904	Do.

[a] Certificate issued June 19, 1905.
[b] Certificate issued Apr. 17, 1905.
[c] Certificate issued Feb. 17, 1905.
[d] Formerly M. R. Brazos, 1897.
[e] Formerly William Wooley, 1900.
[f] Formerly Eleanor, 1900.
[g] Estimated.

DOMESTIC VESSELS INSPECTED, YEAR ENDED DECEMBER 31, 1905—SECOND SUPERVISING DISTRICT—NEW LONDON, CONN.—Continued.

Names of vessels and class.	Gross tonnage.	Hull built.	Hull rebuilt.	Boilers built.	Boilers rebuilt.	Where built.	Date of inspection.	Where inspected.	Date of previous inspection.	Local district where previously inspected.
Inland steam pleasure yachts—Continued.										
Hauoli	299	1903		1903		Brooklyn, N. Y.	May 19, 1905	Riverside, Conn.	June 27, 1904	New London, Conn.
Irene	a 3	1894		1893		Middletown, Conn.	Sept. 2, 1905	New London, Conn.	Sept. 2, 1904	Do.
Katrina	52	1897		1904		Bristol, R. I.	May 27, 1905	Hartford, Conn.	May 27, 1904	Do.
Kauyahoora	a 4	1895		1896		Noank, Conn.	June 22, 1905	Norwich, Conn.	May 17, 1904	Do.
Leda	a 3	1890		1890		Nyack, N. Y.	Apr. 17, 1905	Springfield, Mass.	May 23, 1904	Do.
Magnet	23	1884		1896		Panope, N. J.	May 6, 1905	Greenport, N. Y.	May 2, 1904	Do.
Mollie	a 3	1899		1891		Unknown	June 28, 1905	Hartford, Conn.	June 10, 1904	Do.
Narwhal[b]	238	1894		1894		Boston, Mass.	May 26, 1905	New London, Conn.	May 24, 1904	Do.
Nirvana	80	1893		1898		Poughkeepsie, N. Y.	June 12, 1905	do	Apr. 25, 1903	Do.
Nautilus	24	1900		1900		Brooklyn, N. Y.	June 23, 1905	Fishers Island, N. Y.	June 21, 1904	Do.
Nellie	25	1894		1894		Hartford, Conn.	June 28, 1905	Hartford, Conn.	June 10, 1904	Do.
Palmer	124	1865	1898	1899		Philadelphia, Pa.	May 18, 1905	New London, Conn.	Apr. 28, 1903	Do.
Rosalie	372	1903		1902		Noank, Conn.	June 12, 1905	Noank, Conn.	May 28, 1904	Do.
Racquette	25	1886	1902	1889		Champlain, N. Y.	June 17, 1905	Portland, Conn.	June 8, 1904	Do.
Stella	a 5	1887		1904		Greenport, N. Y.	Apr. 7, 1905	Greenport, N. Y.	May 12, 1904	Do.
Sunbeam	11	1903		1903		Bristol, R. I.	May 13, 1905	do	May 16, 1904	Providence, R. I.
Suanee	11	1893		1893		Perth Amboy, N. J.	June 10, 1905	Middletown, Conn.	June 10, 1904	New London, Conn.
Serapis	a 2	1885	1902	1890		New York, N. Y.	Aug. 17, 1905	Norwich, Conn.	Aug. 17, 1904	Do.
Vergana	128	1897		1897		Newburg, N. Y.	May 1, 1905	Greenport, N. Y.	May 2, 1904	Do.
Vega	34	1901		1900		Noank, Conn.	June 12, 1905	Noank, Conn.	June 4, 1904	Do.
Viking	171	1883		1894		Chester, Pa.	June 21, 1905	Greenport, N. Y.	June 8, 1904	Do.
Watawga	124	1904		1903		Greenport, N. Y.	July 19, 1905	do	June 15, 1904	Do.
Miscellaneous steam vessels.										
Annie L. Wilcox (freight and fishing).	129	1878	1894	1904		Mystic, Conn.	Apr. 1, 1905	New London, Conn.	Apr. 1, 1904	New York, N. Y.
Cambria (oyster)	127	1871	1904	1897		Greenport, N. Y.	June 2, 1905	Greenport, N. Y.	May 30, 1904	New London, Conn.
Dream (fishing)	22	1893		1898		Bridgeport, Conn.	Aug. 2, 1905	Mystic, Conn.	Aug. 6, 1904	New Haven, Conn.
E. J. Codd (freight and fishing)	141	1903		1903		Pocomoke City, Md.	May 20, 1905	New London, Conn.	May 21, 1904	New London, Conn.
Eleanor F. Peck (freight and towing).	357	1884		1883		Brooklyn, N. Y.	Apr. 22, 1905	Stonington, Conn.	Apr. 21, 1904	Do.
F. H. Beckwith (freight and fishing).	195	1904		1904		Pocomoke City, Md.	May 18, 1905	New London, Conn.	May 14, 1904	Baltimore, Md.
George Dewey (nondescript)	49	1901		1898		New Suffolk, N. Y.	May 1, 1905	Greenport, N. Y.	Apr. 23, 1904	New London, Conn.
Henry C. Rowe (oyster)[c]	220	1883		1901		Port Jefferson, N. Y.	Apr. 19, 1905	Noank, Conn.	Apr. 20, 1904	Do.
J. & G. H. Smith (oyster and towing).	42	1880		1890		East Haven, Conn.	Aug. 14, 1905	New London, Conn.	Aug. 10, 1904	Do.
Kate C. Stevens (oyster and towing).	104	1887		1900		Stratford, Conn.	Apr. 11, 1905	do	Apr. 11, 1904	Do.

Leander Wilcox (freight and fishing).	205	1903	....	1903	....	Noank, Conn	May 12, 1905	Mystic, Conn	May 12, 1904	Do.
Starin (fishing)	20	1901	....	1900	....	do	do	Noank, Conn	May 17, 1904	Do.
Walter Royal (nondescript)	9	1900	....	1900	....	Orient, N. Y	June 7, 1905	Greenport, N. Y	June 8, 1904	Do.
Motor vessels.										
Arabell (gasoline)	18	1884	1899	....	....	Bath, Me	May 10, 1905	New London, Conn	May 12, 1904	New London, Conn.
Ada Bell (gasoline)	17	1876	....	....	....	Noank, Conn	June 12, 1905	Noank, Conn	First inspn	
Charlotte J. Kingsland (gasoline).	27	1868	1902	....	....	Northport, N. Y	Apr. 3, 1905	do	Apr. 4, 1904	Do.
Clara E. (gasoline)	29	1903				East Boothbay, Me	Sept. 8, 1905	New London, Conn	Sept. 9, 1904	Do.
Edward H. Smeed (gasoline)	26	1894	....	....	....	Noank, Conn	Apr. 19, 1905	do	Apr. 14, 1904	Do.
Elinora Hill (gasoline)	19	1885	....	....	....	do	Apr. 26, 1905	Noank, Conn	First inspn	
Elsie (gasoline)	34	1903	....	....	....	East Boothbay, Me	Nov. 27, 1905	New London, Conn	Nov. 23, 1904	Do.
Gazelle (gasoline)	34	1896	....	....	....	Noank, Conn	Apr. 1, 1905	do	First inspn	
Laura Reed (gasoline)	24	1895	....	....	....	do	June 15, 1905	do	May 28, 1904	Do.
Minnie C. (gasoline)	27	1902	....	....	....	Greenport, N. Y	June 21, 1905	Greenport, N. Y	First inspn	
Mascot (gasoline)	59	1905	....	....	....	do	Sept. 8, 1905	do	do	
Nomad (electric)	21	1901	....	....	....	Noank, Conn	June 1, 1905	New London, Conn	May 28, 1904	Do.
Wizard (gas)[d]	52	1880	1904	....	....	Greenport, N. Y	Jan. 16, 1905	Greenport, N. Y	Jan. 22, 1904	Do.
W. Talbot Dodge (gasoline)	21	1895	....	....	....	Noank, Conn	Jan. 19, 1905	New London, Conn	First inspn	
W. Talbot Dodge (gasoline)	21	1895	....	....	....	do	Dec. 15, 1905	do	Jan. 19, 1905	Do.

LOCAL DISTRICT OF ALBANY, N. Y.

Ocean passenger steamer.										
Porto Rico	1,257	1899	....	1899	....	Toledo, Ohio	Jan. 24, 1905	San Juan, P. R	Jan. 26, 1904	San Juan, P. R.
Inland passenger steamers.										
Atlantic[e]	95	1897	1903	1897	....	Rondout, N. Y	Apr. 6, 1905	New Hamburg, N. Y	Mar. 24, 1904	Albany, N. Y.
Augustus J. Phillips	129	1903	....	1903	....	do	Apr. 27, 1905	Rondout, N. Y	May 23, 1904	Do.
Adirondack	3,644	1896	....	1896	....	Brooklyn, N. Y	May 25, 1905	Albany, N. Y	May 28, 1904	Do.
Albany	1,415	1880	....	1895	....	Wilmington, N. Y	May 27, 1905	do	do	Do.
Alice May	133	1899	....	1899	....	Albany, N. Y	Sept. 14, 1905	do	Sept. 21, 1904	Do.
City of Troy	1,527	1876	1898	1900	....	New York, N. Y	May 13, 1905	Troy, N. Y	May 14, 1904	Do.
Central Hudson	1,002	1861	....	1903	....	Jersey City, N. J	June 17, 1905	Rondout, N. Y	June 30, 1904	Do.
Cornell	435	1903	....	1903	....	Shooters Island, N. Y.	June 27, 1905	do	June 27, 1904	Do.
Commodore	145	1905	....	1905	....	Rondout, N. Y	June 9, 1905	Newburg, N. Y	First inspn	
Carrie F	8	1886	....	1886	....	Peekskill, N. Y	July 25, 1905	do	July 27, 1904	Do.
City of Hudson	816	1863	1894	1894	....	Mystic, Conn	Aug. 9, 1905	Stuyvesant, N. Y	June 30, 1904	Do.
Celina	122	1897	....	1883	....	Monroe, Mich	Oct. 28, 1905	Albany, N. Y	June 17, 1904	Do.
Emeline	383	1866	1888	1897	....	No record	Apr. 4, 1905	Newburg, N. Y	Mar. 28, 1904	Do.
Echo	11	1874	1901	1904	....	City Island, N. Y	Aug. 15, 1905	Albany, N. Y	Aug. 15, 1904	Do.
Falcon	119	1880	....	1880	....	Wilmington, Del	May 1, 1905	Newburg, N. Y	May 25, 1904	New York, N. Y.

[a] Estimated. [b] Formerly Formosa, 1898. [c] Formerly Nonowantuc, 1904. [d] Formerly sloop-yacht Wizard. [e] Formerly Robert Main, 1904.

DOMESTIC VESSELS INSPECTED, YEAR ENDED DECEMBER 31, 1905—SECOND SUPERVISING DISTRICT—ALBANY, N. Y.—Continued.

Names of vessels and class.	Gross tonnage.	Hull built.	Hull rebuilt.	Boilers built.	Boilers rebuilt	Where built.	Date of inspection.	Where inspected.	Date of previous inspection.	Local district where previously inspected.
Inland passenger steamers—Continued.										
Glenerie	35	1887		1887		Eddyville, N. Y	Mar. 27, 1905	Rondout, N. Y	Mar. 30, 1904	Albany, N. Y.
Herman Livingston	39	1887	1901	1887		Athens, N. Y	Apr. 20, 1905	Athens, N. Y	Apr. 8, 1904	Do.
Hudson Taylor	39	1879		1888		Philadelphia, Pa	Apr. 23, 1905	Newburg, N. Y	Apr. 25, 1904	Do.
Homer Ramsdell	1,181	1887	1892	1897		Newburg, N. Y	May 23, 1905	do	May 24, 1904	Do.
Ida	765	1881	1894	1894		Wilmington, Del	June 9, 1905	Saugerties, N. Y	Aug. 4, 1904	Do.
Jacob H. Tremper	571	1885	1898	1885		Greenpoint, N. Y	Apr. 5, 1905	Albany, N. Y	Apr. 6, 1904	Do.
John McCausland	33	1885	1899	1885		Rondout, N. Y	May 31, 1905	Rondout, N. Y	June 3, 1904	Do.
James T. Brett	490	1883		1896		Keyport, N. J	July 9, 1905	Albany, N. Y	July 18, 1904	New York, N. Y.
J. E. Gaitley	7	1893		1893		Albany, N. Y	Aug. 8, 1905	do	Aug. 9, 1904	Albany, N. Y.
Kaaterskill	1,361	1882		1882		Athens, N. Y	May 10, 1905	Catskill, N. Y	May 17, 1904	Do.
Lydia	26	1886		1886		New Baltimore, N. Y	July 13, 1905	Albany, N. Y	July 14, 1904	Do.
Mary Powell	983	1861	1897	1904		Jersey City, N. J	May 9, 1905	Rondout, N. Y	Apr. 30, 1904	Do.
Morris Block [a]	73	1893		1898		Norwalk, Fla	May 16, 1905	do	June 13, 1904	Boston, Mass.
Messenger	37	1885	1890	1898		New Haven, Conn	July 5, 1905	Newburg, N. Y	July 5, 1904	Albany, N. Y.
Marlborough	944	1864		1883		Brooklyn, N. Y	Oct. 17, 1905	Rondout, N. Y	Oct. 28, 1904	Do.
Newburgh	1,033	1886		1896		Philadelphia, Pa	Mar. 23, 1905	Newburg, N. Y	Mar. 26, 1904	Do.
Nellie Ralph	[b] 4	1883		1898		Noank, Conn	Apr. 23, 1905	do	Apr. 28, 1904	Do.
New York	1,974	1887		1887		Wilmington, Del	May 28, 1905	Albany, N. Y	June 6, 1904	Do.
Onteora	1,213	1898		1898		Newburg, N. Y	May 11, 1905	Coxsackie, N. Y	May 11, 1904	Do.
Poughkeepsie	810	1862	1898	1898		Brooklyn, N. Y	Apr. 27, 1905	Rondout, N. Y	Apr. 30, 1904	Do.
Queen City	25	1889	1894	1889		Poughkeepsie, N. Y	July 17, 1905	Poughkeepsie, N. Y	July 18, 1904	Do.
Rob	47	1902		1886		Rondout, N. Y	July 21, 1905	Rondout, N. Y	July 20, 1904	Do.
Saratoga	1,438	1877	1899	1900		New York, N. Y	June 2, 1905	Troy, N. Y	June 3, 1904	Do.
Thomas Edmonds	23	1888		1902		Buffalo, N. Y	Oct. 16, 1905	Rondout, N. Y	Oct. 24, 1904	Do.
Ursula	186	1901		1901		Albany, N. Y	Apr. 12, 1905	Albany, N. Y	Apr. 19, 1904	Do.
Ulster	780	1892		1892		Brooklyn, N. Y	June 1, 1905	Saugerties, N. Y	June 2, 1904	Do.
William F. Romer	880	1881		1900		Baltimore, Md	May 19, 1905	Rondout, N. Y	May 20, 1904	Do.
Young America	24	1891		1903		Poughkeepsie, N. Y	May 12, 1905	Athens, N. Y	May 23, 1904	New York, N. Y.
Ferry steamers.										
A. F. Beach	173	1878	1899	1878		Athens, N. Y	June 14, 1905	Catskill, N. Y	June 15, 1904	Albany, N. Y.
Air Line	71	1857		1885		Philadelphia, Pa	Sept. 22, 1905	Saugerties, N. Y	Oct. 4, 1904	Do.
Brinckerhoff	317	1899		1899		Newburg, N. Y	Sept. 18, 1905	Poughkeepsie, N. Y	Sept. 28, 1904	Do.
Chester G. Ham	34	1883	1900	1900		Greenbush, N. Y	Apr. 12, 1905	Albany, N. Y	Apr. 3, 1903	Do.
Charles A. Schultz	25	1886		1886		Newburg, N. Y	Mar. 22, 1905	Rondout, N. Y	Mar. 30, 1904	Do.
Coxsackie	77	1878		1878		New Baltimore, N. Y	July 20, 1905	Coxsackie, N. Y	July 21, 1904	Do.
C. G. Witbeck	19	1885	1897	1891		Albany, N. Y	Aug. 17, 1905	Troy, N. Y	Aug. 15, 1904	Do.
City of Newburgh	418	1879		1895		Newburg, N. Y	Oct. 23, 1905	Newburg, N. Y	Dec. 1, 1904	Do.
Encarnation	44	1890		1899		London, England	Jan. 21, 1905	San Juan, P. R	Jan. 29, 1904	San Juan, P. R.
Fishkill on Hudson	484	1884		1883		Newburg, N. Y	Apr. 11, 1905	Newburg, N. Y	Apr. 28, 1904	Albany, N. Y.

George H. Power	207	1869		1858		Athens, N. Y	Apr. 12, 1905	Athens, N. Y	Apr. 6, 1904	Do.
G. V. S. Quackenbush	248	1878	1901	1878		New Baltimore, N. Y	Apr. 18, 1905	Albany, N. Y	May 13, 1904	Do.
General J. B. Carr	108	1892		1892		Rondout, N. Y	Apr. 27, 1905	....do	May 27, 1904	Do.
Greta	7	1903		1894		Poughkeepsie, N. Y	June 20, 1905	....do	June 21, 1904	Do.
Henry Lobdell	18	1897		1882		West Troy, N. Y	Sept. 26, 1905	Troy, N. Y	Oct. 5, 1904	Do.
Isabella	38	1882		1882		Athens, N. Y	May 23, 1905	Hudson, N. Y	May 5, 1904	Do.
Julia Safford	108	1892		1892		Rondout, N.Y	May 27, 1905	Albany, N. Y	May 27, 1904	Do.
Riverside	51	1870	1880	1887		....do	May 5, 1905	Rondout, N. Y	May 6, 1904	Do.
Thompson S. Craig	43	1890		1890		Athens, N. Y	Mar. 28, 1905	Albany, N. Y	Mar. 31, 1904	Do.
Thomas Rath	59	1875	1896	1875		Lansingburg, N. Y	Mar. 29, 1905	Troy, N. Y	Mar. 29, 1904	Do.
Transport	318	1875		1875		Philadelphia, Pa	Sept. 15, 1905	Rondout, N. Y	Sept. 16, 1904	Do.
Valdes	56	1883				London, England	Jan. 19, 1905	San Juan, P. R	Jan. 23, 1904	San Juan, P. R.
W. H. Frear	261	1899		1899		New Baltimore, N. Y	Apr. 18, 1905	Albany, N. Y	May 13, 1904	Albany, N. Y.
Ocean freight steamer.										
Vasco	298	1893		1892		Newcastle, England	Jan. 24, 1905	San Juan, P. R	Jan. 26, 1904	San Juan, P. R.
Inland freight steamers.										
Adamant	141	1891		1891		Lockport, N. Y	June 13, 1905	Newburg, N. Y	June 9, 1904	Albany, N. Y.
David	87	1885		1893		Mount Pleasant, N. Y	May 24, 1905	Albany, N. Y	May 24, 1904	Do.
Frederick G. Bourne	286	1905		1905		Newburg, N. Y	June 24, 1905	Newburg, N. Y	First inspn.	
Gypsum	141	1899		1893		Lockport, N. Y	Sept. 15, 1905	Rondout, N. Y	Sept. 14, 1904	Do.
Higginson Mfg. Co. No. 4	148	1904		1903		Newburg, N. Y	May 8, 1905	Newburg, N. Y	May 12, 1904	Do.
Higginson Mfg. Co. No. 3	179	1903		1903		....do	June 22, 1905	....do	June 22, 1904	Do.
Livingston	78	1883	1886	1894		Saugerties, N. Y	Aug. 11, 1905	Rondout, N. Y	Aug. 10, 1904	Do.
Mahar & Burns	137	1905		1905		Newburg, N. Y	Nov. 23, 1905	Albany, N. Y	Nov. 11, 1904	Buffalo, N. Y.
Robert Rogers	142	1888		1897		Lockport, N. Y	July 14, 1905	Rondout, N. Y	July 22, 1904	Albany, N. Y.
Saranac	86	1890		1890		Tonawanda, N. Y	Nov. 8, 1905	Newburg, N. Y	Nov. 7, 1904	Do.
William C. Redfield	370	1865		1876		Albany, N. Y	May 17, 1905	Catskill, N. Y	[b]May 17, 1904	Do.
Ocean towing steamers.										
C. W. Morse	509	1899		1899		Bath, Me	Sept. 19, 1905	Rondout, N. Y	Sept. 16, 1904	Albany, N. Y.
Triton	259	1890		1905		Boston, Mass	Apr. 3, 1905	....do	Mar. 31, 1904	New York, N. Y.
Inland towing steamers.										
Aguirre	41	1900		1900		Baltimore, Md	Jan. 27, 1905	Aguirre, P. R	Jan. 28, 1904	Aguirre, P. R.
Annie	30	1868	1901	1884		New Baltimore, N. Y	Apr. 3, 1905	Poughkeepsie, N. Y	Apr. 7, 1904	Albany, N. Y.
Annex	16	1881		1889		Kingston Point, N. Y	May 1, 1905	Newburg, N. Y	May 4, 1904	Do.
A. C. Cheney	186	1877		1891		Newburg N. Y	July 10, 1905	Rondout, N. Y	July 11, 1904	Do.
Alice R	31	1905		1905		New Baltimore, N. Y	June 16, 1905	Albany, N. Y	First inspn.	
B. B. Odell, jr	23	1901		1902		Schenectady, N. Y	Oct. 7, 1905	....do	Oct. 5, 1904	Do.
Clinton	40	1898		1898		Newburgh, N. Y	Mar. 30, 1905	Newburgh, N. Y	Apr. 30, 1904	New York, N. Y.
Coe F. Young	65	1872	1899	1881		Rondout, N. Y	June 5, 1905	Rondout, N. Y	June 6, 1904	Albany, N. Y.
Confidence	53	1892		1903		Bordentown, N. J	Sept. 25, 1905	Newburgh, N. Y	Oct. 7, 1904	Do.
Chas. C. Wing	74	1905		1905		New Baltimore, N. Y	Dec. 9, 1905	Albany, N. Y	First inspn.	
Dr. David Kennedy	16	1880	1902	1877		Rondout, N. Y	Apr. 15, 1905	Rondout, N. Y	Apr. 13, 1904	Do.

[a] Formerly Jeanette, 1905.

[b] Estimated.

DOMESTIC VESSELS INSPECTED, YEAR ENDED DECEMBER 31, 1905—SECOND SUPERVISING DISTRICT—ALBANY, N. Y.—Continued.

Names of vessels and class.	Gross tonnage.	Hull built.	Hull rebuilt.	Boilers built.	Boilers rebuilt.	Where built.	Date of inspection.	Where inspected.	Date of previous inspection.	Local district where previously inspected.
Inland towing steamers—Con.										
Dutchess	21	1891		1889		Newburg, N. Y	June 19, 1905	Wappingers Falls, N. Y.	June 20, 1904	Albany, N. Y.
Ellen M. Ronan	73	1883		1892		Athens, N. Y	Apr. 17, 1905	Rondout, N. Y	Apr. 18, 1904	Do.
Eugenia	15	1865	1889	1891		Buffalo, N. Y	Apr. 24, 1905	Albany, N. Y	Apr. 26, 1904	Do.
E. L. Levy	142	1888		1888		Philadelphia, Pa	May 15, 1905	Rondout, N. Y	May 16, 1904	Do.
F. C. Baker	153	1889		1889		do	do	do	do	Do.
Edwin Terry	90	1883		1883		Camden, N. J	June 15, 1905	do	June 1, 1904	Do.
Empire	41	1889		1895		Athens, N. Y	July 24, 1905	do	July 25, 1904	Do.
Edwin H. Mead	248	1892		1892		Newburg, N. Y	Aug. 7, 1905	do	Aug. 8, 1904	Do.
Evona	15	1875		1882		Camden, N. J	Nov. 11, 1905	Albany, N. Y	Sept. 8, 1900	Do.
Frank	61	1894		1894		Rondout, N. Y	Apr. 17, 1905	Rondout, N. Y	Apr. 18, 1904	Do.
George W. Pratt	41	1882		1882		do	May 1, 1905	do	May 2, 1904	Do.
Gladys	50	1860	1896	1879		Wilmington, Del	May 12, 1905	Albany, N. Y	Aug. 29, 1903	New York, N. Y.
Geo. C. Van Tuyl, jr	21	1900		1894		Albany, N. Y	do	do	May 13, 1904	Albany, N. Y.
Geo. H. Allen, jr	99	1905		1905		New Baltimore, N. Y	do	do	First inspn.	
Geo. D. Cooley	34	1901		1901		Rondout, N. Y	June 6, 1905	do	June 7, 1904	Do.
Geo. W. Aldridge	31	1896		1896		Cohoes, N. Y	June 21, 1905	do	June 23, 1904	Do.
G. C. Adams	80	1878		1881		Jersey City, N. J	July 24, 1905	Rondout, N. Y	July 25, 1904	Do.
Geo. W. Washburne	298	1890		1890		Newburg, N. Y	July 31, 1905	do	Aug. 1, 1904	Do.
George Field	29	1882		1882		Buffalo, N. Y	Aug. 4, 1905	Newburg, N. Y	Aug. 3, 1904	Do.
G. W. Decker	77	1900		1900		Newburg, N. Y	Sept. 18, 1905	Rondout, N. Y	Sept. 19, 1904	Do.
Harrold	19	1891		1902		Jersey City, N. J	Apr. 13, 1905	Newburg, N. Y	Apr. 12, 1904	New York, N. Y.
Hercules	119	1876		1892		Camden, N. J	June 7, 1905	Rondout, N. Y	June 13, 1904	Albany, N. Y.
H. D. Mould	49	1896		1896		Athens, N. Y	July 3, 1905	do	July 6, 1904	Do.
Harry	49	1892		1892		Rondout, N. Y	July 21, 1905	do	July 25, 1904	Do.
Ira M. Hedges	76	1883		1898		Camden, N. J	May 8, 1905	do	May 9, 1904	Do.
Ice King	138	1877	1904	1905		Philadelphia, Pa	June 21, 1905	do	Nov. 30, 1903	Do.
James J. Logan	34	1889		1889		Newburg, N. Y	Mar. 30, 1905	Newburg, N. Y	Mar. 28, 1904	Do.
Jas. A. Morris	26	1894		1894		New Baltimore, N. Y	Apr. 12, 1905	Albany, N. Y	Apr. 5, 1904	Do.
James H. Scott	20	1897		1891		Albany, N. Y	Apr. 24, 1905	do	Apr. 21, 1904	Do.
John H. Cordts	194	1883	1900	1900		Newburg, N. Y	June 12, 1905	Rondout, N. Y	June 13, 1904	Do.
John Duff	22	1901		1901		Athens, N. Y	June 20, 1905	Albany, N. Y	June 22, 1904	Do.
James J. Sweeney	28	1893		1896		Rondout, N. Y	June 27, 1905	Rondout, N. Y	Apr. 5, 1904	Do.
J. H. Williams	90	1904		1904		Newburg, N. Y	July 3, 1905	do	July 2, 1904	Do.
Joel D. Smith	74	1905		1905		New Baltimore, N. Y	June 2, 1905	Albany, N. Y	First inspn.	
J. C. Hartt	222	1883		1883		Philadelphia, Pa	July 10, 1905	Rondout, N. Y	July 11, 1904	Do.
J. Arnold	23	1893		1893		Albany, N. Y	July 18, 1905	Albany, N. Y	July 19, 1904	Do.
John T. Welch	59	1899		1899		Tottenville, N. Y	Aug. 21, 1905	Rondout, N. Y	Aug. 29, 1904	Do.
Julia A. Brainerd	15	1872	1899	1896		Albany, N. Y	Aug. 22, 1905	Albany, N. Y	Aug. 23, 1904	Do.
J. G. Rose	77	1900		1900		Newburg, N. Y	Aug. 23, 1905	Rondout, N. Y	Aug. 22, 1904	Do.
John D. Schoonmaker	56	1888		1881		Rondout, N. Y	Sept. 21, 1905	do	Sept. 23, 1904	Do.
Knickerbocker	123	1873	1904	1904		Philadelphia, Pa	May 26, 1905	do	June [illegible]1, 1904	Do.

Kitty West	25	1888		1893		Baldwinsville, N. Y.	June 8, 1905	Schenectady, N. Y.	May 27, 1904	Do.
M. B. Harlow	57	1891		1897		Alexandria, Va.	Apr. 18, 1905	Albany, N. Y.	Apr. 5, 1904	Do.
Nimrod	11	1887		1902		Brooklyn, N. Y.	Apr. 20, 1905	Waterford, N. Y.	May 23, 1904	New York, N. Y.
Norwich	255	1836	1888	1888		New York, N. Y.	May 22, 1905	Rondout, N. Y.	do	Albany, N. Y.
Osceola	182	1884	1901	1901		Newburg, N. Y.	Apr. 10, 1905	do	Apr. 11, 1904	Do.
Oswego	329	1848	1898	1897		Brooklyn, N. Y.	May 5, 1905	do	May 9, 1904	Do.
Ponce	26	1900		1902		Croton, N. Y.	Jan. 20, 1905	San Juan, P. R.	Jan. 26, 1904	Porto Rico.
Pocahontas	177	1884	1902	1902		Newburg, N. Y.	Apr. 10, 1905	Rondout, N. Y.	Apr. 11, 1904	Albany, N. Y.
P. C. Ronan	29	1895		1887		Albany, N. Y.	May 26, 1905	do	May 29, 1904	Do.
Pittston	94	1852	1885	1885		Brooklyn, N. Y.	Aug. 1, 1904	do	July 31, 1903	Do.
Pittston	94	1852	1885	1885		do	Aug. 3, 1905	do	Aug. 1, 1904	Do.
Primrose	58	1902		1902		Athens, N. Y.	Aug. 7, 1905	do	Aug. 8, 1904	Do.
Paul Le Roux	44	1902		1895		Albany, N. Y.	Aug. 25, 1905	Albany, N. Y.	Aug. 24, 1904	Do.
Pioneer	28	1902		1899		Little Falls, N. Y.	Oct. 28, 1905	do	June 25, 1904	New York, N. Y.
Preston E. Andrews	26	1894		1885		Poughkeepsie, N. Y.	Dec. 20, 1905	do	Oct. 29, 1904	Albany, N. Y.
Roys J. Cram	19	1882		1884		East Saginaw, Mich.	May 17, 1905	do	Sept. 29, 1903	Do.
Robert A. Scott	50	1904		1904		New Baltimore, N. Y.	May 29, 1905	Rondout, N. Y.	May 28, 1904	Do.
R. G. Davis	23	1891		1891		Athens, N. Y.	June 13, 1905	Newburg, N. Y.	June 16, 1904	Do.
R. J. Foster	45	1903		1903		New Baltimore, N. Y.	July 31, 1905	Rondout, N. Y.	Aug. 1, 1904	Do.
R. G. Townsend	83	1882		1882		Camden, N. J.	Sept. 11, 1905	do	Sept. 12, 1904	Do.
Sarah Orbeta	8	1896				San Juan, P. R.	Jan. 21, 1905	San Juan, P. R.	Jan. 21, 1904	Porto Rico.
Silas O. Pierce	129	1867		1897		Athens, N. Y.	May 15, 1905	Rondout, N. Y.	May 2, 1904	Albany, N. Y.
Saranac	56	1886		1886		do	May 29, 1905	do	June 6, 1904	Do.
S. L. Crosby	103	1883		1899		Philadelphia, Pa.	June 5, 1905	do	do	Do.
Terror	69	1854		1887		do	June 1, 1905	do	May 9, 1904	Do.
Thomas Miller, jr.	15	1878		1904		Eddyville, N. Y.	June 6, 1905	Albany, N. Y.	May 2, 1904	Do.
Triton	35	1899		1899		Buffalo, N. Y.	June 20, 1905	do	June 21, 1904	Do.
Thomas Dickson	67	1872		1887		Rondout, N. Y.	July 6, 1905	Rondout, N. Y.	July 11, 1904	Do.
Thomas Chubb	34	1888		1888		Athens, N. Y.	Aug. 1, 1905	Albany, N. Y.	Aug. 2, 1904	Do.
Thomas J. Johnson	73	1905		1905		New Baltimore, N. Y.	July 12, 1905	do	First inspn.	
Union	10	1901		1901		Croton, N. Y.	Jan. 22, 1905	Ponce, P. R.	Jan. 24, 1904	Porto Rico.
Victoria	77	1878		1892		Camden, N. J.	May 24, 1905	Rondout, N. Y.	May 23, 1904	Albany, N. Y.
Wm. S. Earl	33	1859	1903	1883		Philadelphia, Pa.	Apr. 15, 1905	do	Apr. 13, 1904	Do.
W. B. McCulloch[a]	18	1899		1892		Athens, N. Y.	May 12, 1905	Albany, N. Y.	May 13, 1904	Do.
W. E. Street	104	1881		1888		Camden, N. J.	June 12, 1905	Rondout, N. Y.	June 13, 1904	Do.
Wm. E. Cleary	90	1904		1904		Newburg, N. Y.	July 6, 1905	do	July 8, 1904	Do.
Wilson P. Foss	58	1899		1899		Brooklyn, N. Y.	Sept. 11, 1905	do	Sept. 12, 1904	Do.
W. N. Bavier	110	1901		1901		Port Richmond, N. Y.	Sept. 18, 1905	do	Sept. 19, 1904	Do.
Walter B. Pollock	61	1905		1905		New Baltimore, N. Y.	Dec. 2, 1905	Albany, N. Y.	First inspn.	
Yozephie	22	1881		1901		Brooklyn, N. Y.	Aug. 31, 1905	Rondout, N. Y.	Aug. 31, 1904	Do.
Steam pleasure yachts.										
Alice	134	1903	1905	1903		Port Richmond, N. Y.	June 28, 1905	Newburg, N. Y.	June 1, 1904	New York, N. Y.
Chippewa	34	1903		1903		Albany, N. Y.	June 21, 1905	Albany, N. Y.	June 23, 1904	Albany, N. Y.
Cornell	14	1895		1904		Ithaca, N. Y.	June 19, 1905	Poughkeepsie, N. Y.	June 20, 1904	Do.
Daisy	[b]4	1891		1897		New York, N. Y.	July 18, 1905	Albany, N. Y.	July 19, 1904	Do.
Dena	[b]3	1885		1898		Castleton, N. Y.	Aug. 14, 1905	Rondout, N. Y.	Aug. 18, 1904	Do.
Edward C. Brandow	[b]5	1900		1900		Bath on Hudson, N. Y.	Oct. 20, 1905	Albany, N. Y.	Sept. 21, 1904	Do.
Flirt	[b]2	1886		1883		New York, N. Y.	June 30, 1905	Troy, N. Y.	June 23, 1904	Do.

[a] Formerly P. McCabe, jr., 1904.

[b] Estimated.

DOMESTIC VESSELS INSPECTED, YEAR ENDED DECEMBER 31, 1905—SECOND SUPERVISING DISTRICT—ALBANY, N. Y.—Continued.

Names of vessels and class.	Gross tonnage.	Hull built.	Hull rebuilt.	Boilers built.	Boilers rebuilt.	Where built.	Date of inspection.	Where inspected.	Date of previous inspection.	Local district where previously inspected.
Steam pleasure yachts—Con.										
Globe	a 3	1879	1895	1897		Poughkeepsie, N. Y.	July 27, 1905	Troy, N. Y.	July 21, 1904	Albany, N. Y.
Gipsey	9	1879		1889		do	Aug. 31, 1905	Rondout, N. Y.	Aug. 31, 1904	Do
Idea	10	1899		1899		Mayaguez, P. R.	Jan. 26, 1905	Mayaguez, P. R.	Jan. 27, 1903	Mayaguez, P. R.
Juanita	a 4	1893		1895		Schenectady, N. Y.	June 8, 1905	Schenectady, N. Y.	May 27, 1904	Albany, N. Y.
Lotos	a 5	1898		1903		Geneva, N. Y.	July 26, 1905	Cohoes, N. Y.	July 26, 1904	Do.
Louisa A	a 4	1901		1894		Albany, N. Y.	Aug. 25, 1905	Albany, N. Y.	Aug. 9, 1904	Do.
Neptune	17	1897		1896		Waterford, N. Y.	July 26, 1905	Waterford, N. Y.	July 26, 1904	Do.
O. N. B	a 3	1890		1900		Newark, N. J.	July 28, 1905	Rondout, N. Y.	July 20, 1904	Do.
Pigeon	a 4	1892	1901	1894		Peekskill, N. Y.	June 8, 1905	Schenectady, N. Y.	May 29, 1903	Do.
Roamer	a 4	1897		1896		Troy, N. Y.	June 6, 1905	Albany, N. Y.	May 28, 1904	Do.
Triton b	a 4	1891		1891		Albany, N. Y.	May 25, 1905	Troy, N. Y.	June 10, 1895	Burlington, Vt.
Miscellaneous steam vessels.										
Albatross (peddling)	17	1873		1901		Ogdensburg, N. Y.	Apr. 21, 1905	Rondout, N. Y.	Apr. 22, 1904	Albany, N. Y.
Chief (peddling)	a 4	1889		1896		Hampton, Va.	July 28, 1905	do	July 20, 1904	Do.
Edwin Ambrose (peddling)	a 4	1883		1900		Tarrytown, N. Y.	July 25, 1905	Poughkeepsie, N. Y.	July 30, 1904	Do.
Vessel propelled by gasoline motor.										
Ossining	46	1905				Newburg, N. Y.	July 11, 1905	Newburg, N. Y.	First inspn	
Barges over 100 tons carrying passengers for hire.										
Empress c	248	1852				Coxsackie, N. Y.	June 23, 1905	Coeymans, N. Y.	July 16, 1901	Albany, N. Y
J. R. Baldwin	267	1864				New Baltimore, N. Y.	July 6, 1905	Albany, N. Y.	July 22, 1904	Do.

LOCAL DISTRICT OF PORTLAND, ME.

Names of vessels and class.	Gross tonnage.	Hull built.	Hull rebuilt.	Boilers built.	Boilers rebuilt.	Where built.	Date of inspection.	Where inspected.	Date of previous inspection.	Local district where previously inspected.
Ocean passenger steamers.										
Governor Dingley	3,826	1899		1899		Chester, Pa.	Sept. 25, 1905	Portland, Me.	Oct. 4, 1904	Portland, Me.
Horatio Hall	3,167	1898		1898		do	Apr. 3, 1905	do	Mar. 30, 1904	New York, N. Y.
Manhattan	1,892	1891		1891		Bath, Me.	Apr. 29, 1905	do	Apr. 30, 1904	Portland, Me.
North Star	3,159	1901		1901		Chester, Pa.	June 8, 1905	do	June 6, 1904	Do.

Inland passenger steamers.										
Alice Howard	77	1899		1899		Peaks Island, Me	July 3, 1905	Portsmouth, N. H	July 2, 1904	Portland, Me.
Anodyne	13	1895		1892		Bristol, Me	June 30, 1905	Bristol, Me	June 24, 1904	Do.
Aucocisco	167	1897		1897		South Portland, Me	June 23, 1905	Portland, Me	June 3, 1904	Do.
Aziscohos	9	1888		1888		East Boston, Mass	Aug. 19, 1905	Lakeside, N. H	Aug. 20, 1904	Do.
Bay State	2,211	1894		1895		Bath, Me	Mar. 21, 1905	Portland, Me	Mar. 21, 1904	Do.
Bristol	48	1901		1901		Bristol, Me	June 21, 1905	Damariscotta, Me	June 15, 1904	Do.
Catherine	161	1893		1904		Bath, Me	June 9, 1905	Rockland, Me	June 10, 1904	Do.
Corinna	45	1899		1894	1899	Portland, Me	July 14, 1905	Portland, Me	July 15, 1904	Do.
Damarin [d]	55	1873	1894	1894		Bath, Me	June 16, 1905	Bath, Me	June 16, 1904	Do.
Eldorado	96	1893		1892		Buffalo, N. Y	June 29, 1905	do	June 28, 1904	Do.
Emita	99	1880		1894		Athens, N. Y	May 10, 1905	Portland, Me	May 12, 1904	Do.
Engine No. 7 [e]	47	1891		1901		Portland, Me	Apr. 22, 1905	do	Apr. 23, 1904	Do.
Enterprise	183	1882		1895		Wilmington, Del	May 9, 1905	do	June 13, 1904	Do.
Forest Queen	138	1887		1887	1893	Athens, N. Y	May 22, 1905	do	May 23, 1904	Do.
Frank Jones	1,634	1892		1892		Bath, Me	Apr 11, 1905	Rockland, Me	Apr. 11, 1904	Do.
Gardiner	38	1893		1904		do	June 13, 1905	Gardiner, Me	June 14, 1904	Do.
Gov. Bodwell	140	1892		1902		Rockland, Me	July 13, 1905	Rockland, Me	July 6, 1904	Do.
Hattie L.	a 4	1902		1903		Georgetown, Me	June 12, 1905	Bath, Me	June 9, 1904	Do.
Island Belle	153	1891		1891		Buffalo, N. Y	May 15, 1905	do	June 4, 1904	Do.
James T. Furber	22	1892		1893		Kennebunk, Me	July 24, 1905	Portland, Me	July 23, 1904	Do.
J. T. Morse	780	1904		1904		Boston, Mass	Apr. 27, 1905	Rockland, Me	May 10, 1904	Boston, Mass.
Juliette	132	1892		1898		Bath, Me	June 27, 1905	do	June 27, 1904	Portland, Me.
Lizzie M. Snow	17	1889		1880		Brewer, Me	Oct. 2, 1905	Boothbay Harbor, Me	Oct. 5, 1904	Do.
M. and M	98	1886	1899	1899		Thomaston, Me	July 1, 1905	Portland, Me	May 20, 1904	Do.
Maquoit	77	1904		1904		South Portland, Me	May 10, 1905	do	May 10, 1904	Do.
Mascot	36	1894		1895		Brewer, Me	July 5, 1905	Rockland, Me	July 13, 1904	Bangor, Me.
Merryconeag	165	1888		1899		East Deering, Me	June 15, 1905	Portland, Me	June 18, 1904	Portland, Me.
Mineola	295	1901		1901		St. George, Me	June 26, 1905	do	June 6, 1904	Do.
Monhegan	367	1903		1903		Rockland, Me	June 2, 1905	do	July 29, 1904	Do.
Nahanada	91	1888		1901		Bath, Me	May 26, 1905	Bath, Me	May 24, 1904	Do.
Nellie G.	9	1894		1895		Woolwich, Me	Aug. 11, 1905	Boothbay Harbor, Me	Aug. 11, 1904	Do.
New Castle	83	1902		1902		Bristol, Me	June 14, 1905	Damariscotta, Me	June 7, 1904	Do.
Norumbega	304	1902		1902		Bath, Me	Apr. 4, 1905	Rockland, Me	May 6, 1904	Do.
Pemaquid [f]	409	1893		1893		Philadelphia, Pa	May 26, 1905	Bath, Me	May 27, 1904	Do.
Pilgrim	261	1891		1891		Buffalo, N. Y	June 17, 1905	Portland, Me	June 9, 1904	Do.
Portsmouth	121	1904		1904		Kennebunkport. Me	Mar. 24, 1905	Portsmouth, N. H	Mar. 22, 1904	Do.
Princess	18	1903		1903		Portland, Me	July 1, 1905	Portland, Me	July 1, 1904	Do.
Queen City	a 9	1887		1903		Peekskill, N. Y	Aug. 8, 1905	Portsmouth, N. H	Aug. 8, 1904	Do.
Ransom B. Fuller	1,862	1902		1902		Bath, Me	Apr. 18, 1905	Bath, Me	Apr. 16, 1904	Do.
Samoset [g]	294	1897		1897		Philadelphia, Pa	Sept. 7, 1905	Rockland, Me	July 18, 1904	Philadelphia, Pa.
Sappho	275	1886		1895		Bath, Me	May 1, 1905	do	Apr. 15, 1904	Portland, Me.
Sebascodegan	160	1895		1895		South Portland, Me	May 18, 1905	Portland, Me	May 21, 1904	Do.
Sebenoa	89	1880		1897		Bath, Me	May 29, 1905	Rockland, Me	June 3, 1904	Do.
Sieur De Monts [h]	469	1901		1902		Philadelphia, Pa	May 24, 1905	do	June 29, 1904	New York, N. Y.
Stella Pickert	17	1884		1896		Bath, Me	July 8, 1905	do	June 3, 1904	Bangor, Me.
Sylvia [i]	12	1902		1894		Upton, Me	May 20, 1905	Lakeside, N. H	July 16, 1904	Portland, Me.

[a] Estimated.
[b] Formerly Wanderer.
[c] Formerly Merchant
[d] Formerly Samoset, 1894.
[e] Formerly Chebeague, 1895.
[f] Formerly Long Island, 1901.
[g] Formerly Annie L. Vansciver, 1905.
[h] Formerly Quaker City, 1905.
[i] Formerly Eda, 1903.

DOMESTIC VESSELS INSPECTED, YEAR ENDED DECEMBER 31, 1905—SECOND SUPERVISING DISTRICT—PORTLAND, ME.—Continued.

Names of vessels and class.	Gross tonnage.	Hull built.	Hull rebuilt.	Boilers built.	Boilers rebuilt.	Where built.	Date of inspection.	Where inspected.	Date of previous inspection.	Local district where previously inspected.
Inland passenger steamers—Continued.										
Vinal Haven	186	1892		1905		Searsport, Me	May 5, 1905	Portland, Me	July 21, 1904	Portland, Me.
W. G. Butman	43	1896		1901		East Boothbay, Me	June 5, 1905	Rockland, Me	June 1, 1904	Do.
Wiwurna	98	1884		1884		Bath, Me	June 16, 1905	Bath, Me	June 18, 1904	Do.
Ferry steamers.										
Elizabeth City	254	1893		1893		Bath, Me	May 5, 1905	Portland, Me	May 3, 1904	Portland, Me.
General Knox	427	1898		1898		do	Sept. 9, 1905	Bath, Me	Sept. 8, 1904	Do.
Hercules	800	1892		1891		do	Apr. 15, 1905	do	Apr. 16, 1904	Do.
Hockomock	153	1901		1901		do	Apr. 20, 1905	do	Apr. 20, 1904	Do.
Kittery	139	1900		1900		Kennebunkport, Me	July 28, 1905	Portsmouth, N. H	July 27, 1904	Do.
Leo	a 4	1892		1893		do	Aug. 25, 1905	Brunswick, Me	Aug. 26, 1904	Do.
Ocean freight steamers.										
Frances Hyde	739	1905		1905		Bath, Me	Sept. 5, 1905	Bath, Me	First inspn.	
Georgetown	1,358	1900		1900		Buffalo, N. Y	Oct. 27, 1905	Portland, Me	Oct. 25, 1904	Portland, Me.
Inland freight steamers.										
Della Collins	194	1879		1895		East Boston, Mass	Apr. 28, 1905	Gardiner, Me	Apr. 22, 1904	Portland, Me.
Leviathan	109	1899		1890	1899	Richmond, Me	July 17, 1905	Portsmouth, N. H	July 11, 1904	Do.
North Star	29	1887		1900		Alna, Me	Sept. 6, 1905	Wiscasset, Me	Sept. 6, 1904	Do.
Reliance	251	1903		1903		Bath, Me	July 19, 1905	Rockland, Me	July 14, 1904	Do.
Venture	59	1902		1902		South Gardiner, Me	June 19, 1905	Portland, Me	June 14, 1904	Do.
Inland towing steamers.										
Adelia	85	1864	1869	1883		New York, N. Y	June 12, 1905	Bath, Me	June 4, 1904	Portland, Me.
A. F. Kappella	22	1868		1891		Philadelphia, Pa	Apr. 20, 1904	do	Apr. 18, 1904	Do.
Ben Hur	12	1889		1889		Portland, Me	Mar. 23, 1905	Portland, Me	Mar. 24, 1904	Do.
Casco [b]	41	1873		1904		Kaighns Point, N. J	Mar. 27, 1905	do	Mar. 28, 1904	Do.
Charlie Lawrence	48	1874		1887		Philadelphia, Pa	Apr. 22, 1905	Bath, Me	Apr. 14, 1904	Do.
Cumberland [c]	50	1868		1884		do	July 31, 1905	Portland, Me	July 30, 1904	Do.
Diamond	22	1899	1900	1893		Erroll, N. H	May 20, 1905	Lakeside, N. H	May 14, 1904	Do.
Falmouth [d]	37	1884		1903		Brooklyn, N. Y	Sept. 30, 1905	Portland, Me	Sept. 30, 1904	Do.
Farnsworth	34	1877	1905	1896		Allowaystown, N. J	July 21, 1905	Bath, Me	July 18, 1904	Do.
Frederick M. Wilson	26	1872		1890		Philadelphia, Pa	May 29, 1905	Rockland, Me	May 16, 1904	Do.
Harold	19	1895		1898		Brunswick, Me	July 20, 1905	Brunswick, Me	July 19, 1904	Do.
Iva	30	1891		1902		Dover, N. H	Aug. 3, 1905	Kittery, Me	Aug. 3, 1904	Do.
John Chester Morrison [e]	48	1867	1892	1892		South Rondout, N. Y	July 31, 1905	Portland, Me	July 30, 1904	Do.

Joseph Baker	43	1862		1879		Wilmington, Del	May 13, 1905	Saco, Me	May 11, 1904	Do.
Lester L	12	1894		1895		Kennebunkport, Me	June 10, 1905	Portsmouth, N. H	June 8, 1904	Do.
Mary J. Finn	51	1874		1893		Philadelphia, Pa	Aug. 24, 1905	Rockland, Me	Aug. 25, 1904	Boston, Mass.
M. Mitchell Davis	85	1897		1897		Solomans Island, Md	Sept. 29, 1905	Kittery, Me	Oct. 6, 1904	Portland, Me.
Mustado	16	1899		1899		South Bristol, Me	Apr. 26, 1905	Portland, Me	Apr. 25, 1904	Do.
Naos	16	1894		1889		Boston, Mass	July 20, 1905	do	Aug. 10, 1904	Do.
Ocean View	45	1884		1899		Noank, Conn	June 22, 1905	do	June 13, 1904	Do.
Perry	107	1863		1894		Philadelphia, Pa	May 8, 1905	Bath, Me	May 7, 1904	Do.
Piscataqua	99	1891		1891		Boston, Mass	Aug. 14, 1905	Kittery, Me	Aug. 8, 1904	Do.
Portland	94	1902		1902		South Portland, Me	Oct. 23, 1905	Portland, Me	Nov 18, 1904	Do.
Sally	a 4	1898		1904		Randolph, Me	Sept. 4, 1905	Gardiner, Me	Sept. 3, 1904	Do.
Scandinavia	55	1898		1898		Baltimore, Md	Nov. 18, 1905	Portland, Me	Dec. 10, 1904	Do.
Sebago f	28	1883		1902		Portland, Me	Oct. 3, 1905	do	Oct. 5, 1904	Do.
Seguin	96	1884		1890		Bath, Me	Aug. 7, 1905	Bath, Me	Aug. 5, 1904	Do.
Sommers N. Smith	52	1887		1887		Philadelphia, Pa	May 1[illegible], 1905	Rockland, Me	May 9, 1904	Do.
Stella	39	1874		1896		Camden, N. J	Apr. 19, 1905	do	Apr. 4, 1904	Do.
Wawenoc	40	1882		1882		Wiscasset, Me	Mar. 25, 1905	Portland, Me	Jan. 27, 1904	Do.
Willard g	22	1874		1886		Portland, Me	July 18, 1905	do	July 13, 1904	Do.
William H. Clark	69	1883		1883		Boston, Mass	Sept. 1, 1905	Bath, Me	July 19, 1904	Boston, Mass.
William Kemp	49	1873		1899		New Baltimore, N. Y	Oct. 30, 1905	Portsmouth, N. H	Nov. 14, 1904	Do.
Steam pleasure yachts.										
Alice	a 3	1894		1902		Boston, Mass	July 12, 1905	New Castle, N. H	July 9, 1904	Portland, Me.
Alicia	43	1901		1901		East Boston, Mass	June 1, 1905	Boothbay Harbor, Me	June 2, 1904	Do.
Calumet	17	1902		1902		East Boothbay, Me	June 22, 1905	Portland, Me	June 13, 1904	Do.
Cocoo h	a 1	1890		1891		Yarmouth, Me	Mar. 28, 1905	do	Aug. 7, 1891	Do.
Dictator	a 4	1904		1904		Morris Heights, N. Y	June 6, 1905	do	May 14, 1904	New York, N. Y.
Dolly	a 3	1898		1902		Waldoboro, Me	July 7, 1905	Waldoboro, Me	July 5, 1904	Portland, Me.
Dot i	a 2	1894		1894		Portland, Me	Aug. 17, 1905	Portland, Me	Aug. 13, 1904	Do.
Eda j	a 1	1891		1897		do	May 20, 1905	Lakeside, N. H	May 15, 1904	Do.
Effie C. k	a 1	1897		1894		do	July 21, 1905	Portland, Me	July 23, 1904	Do.
Eleanor l	a 3	1900		1891		do	July 20, 1905	do	July 18, 1904	Do.
Gyda	25	1892		1904		Boston, Mass	July 1, 1905	do	June 25, 1904	Do.
Harold	a 2	1887		1902		Gardiner, Me	July 27, 1905	Gardiner, Me	July 14, 1904	Do.
Hester	9	1892		1892		Medford, Mass	Aug. 7, 1905	Portland, Me	Aug. 22, 1903	Boston, Mass.
Isabel	a 1	1903		1891		Waldoboro, Me	Aug. 4, 1905	Waldoboro, Me	Aug. 28, 1903	Portland, Me.
Item	9	1903		1904		Kennebunkport, Me	July 18, 1905	Saco, Me	July 12, 1904	Do.
Jule	19	1899		1899		Weymouth, Mass	July 11, 1905	Boothbay Harbor, Me	July 9, 1904	Boston, Mass.
Juno	28	1880		1902		Bath, Me	June 26, 1905	Bath, Me	June 21, 1904	Portland, Me.
Ladoga	61	1885	1895	1905		Bristol, R. I	May 25, 1905	Rockland, Me	May 18, 1904	Bangor, Me.
Lillian m	8	1897		1899		Wakefield, Mass	Mar. 29, 1905	South Portland, Me	May 4, 1904	Portland, Me.
Maitland	15	1890		1890		Bath, Me	May 30, 1905	Portland, Me	May 18, 1904	Do.
Merlin	a 2	(n)		1894		Unknown	Sept. 30, 1905	West Bath, Me	Oct. 7, 1904	Do.
Owl	a 2	1887		1887		Bath, Me	July 6, 1905	Bath, Me	Oct. 3, 1903	Do.
Philomena	39	1893		1895		Boston, Mass	June 6, 1905	Portland, Me	June 1, 1904	Do.
Seminole	a 3	1891		1896		Cocoa, Fla	Aug. 2, 1905	South Harpswell, Me	Aug. 2, 1904	Do.

a Estimated.
b Formerly Charles A. Warren, 1904.
c Formerly L. A. Belknap, 1903.
d Formerly A. Demerest, 1903.
e Formerly Atlantic, 1892.
f Formerly Fannie G, 1903.
g Formerly Willard Clapp, 1904.
h Formerly Cuckoo, 1905.
i Formerly Kodak, 1899.
j Formerly Marguerite, 1904.
k Formerly Gracie E, 1901.
l Formerly Phyllis, 1903.
m Formerly Cyclops, 1903.
n Unknown.

DOMESTIC VESSELS INSPECTED, YEAR ENDED DECEMBER 31, 1905—SECOND SUPERVISING DISTRICT—PORTLAND, ME.—Continued.

Names of vessels and class.	Gross tonnage.	Hull built.	Hull rebuilt.	Boilers built.	Boilers rebuilt.	Where built.	Date of inspection.	Where inspected.	Date of previous inspection.	Local district where previously inspected.
Steam pleasure yachts—Con.										
Utowana	a 3	1892		1897		Unknown	Aug. 26, 1905	South Freeport, Me	Aug. 25, 1904	Portland, Me.
Velox	a 4	1886		1896		Bath, Me	July 10, 1905	Bath, Me	July 7, 1904	Do.
Volante	10	1894		1903		Portland, Me	Aug. 19, 1905	Lakeside, N. H	Aug. 20, 1904	Do.
Zuella	a 1	1885		1885		Boston, Mass	Aug. 28, 1905	Perkins, Me	Aug. 12, 1904	Do.
Miscellaneous steamers.										
Bonita (towing and fishing)	28	1894		1902		Boston, Mass	Sept. 22, 1905	Boothbay Harbor, Me	Sept. 21, 1904	Portland, Me.
Carita (towing and fishing)	32	1890		1890		do	May 17, 1905	do	May 17, 1904	Do.
Carrie and Mildred (towing and fishing).	22	1896		1904		South Bristol, Me	May 16, 1905	Rockland, Me	Apr. 23, 1904	Do.
Cormorant (towing and fishing).	11	1893	1904	1901		Gloucester, Mass	July 25, 1905	Boothbay Harbor, Me	July 25, 1904	Do.
Elise (fishing)	9	1890	1901	1894		Nyack, N. Y	Sept. 22, 1905	do	May 5, 1904	Do.
Elthier (towing and fishing)	19	1897		1897		Portland, Me	Sept. 25, 1905	Portland, Me	Sept. 26, 1904	Do.
E. N. Brown (fishing)	8	1905		1894		do	June 19, 1905	do	First inspn.	
Fay (pile driver and lighter)	25	1897		1897		Pittston, Me	Apr. 25, 1905	Gardiner, Me	Apr. 22, 1904	Do.
Grace Morgan (fishing)	21	1890		1904		Noank, Conn	Aug. 5, 1905	Rockland, Me	Aug. 6, 1904	Do.
Hermann Reessing (towing and fishing).	26	1882		1903		Milbridge, Me	Aug. 18, 1905	Portland, Me	Aug. 13, 1904	Do.
Hurricane (fishing)	38	1871		1891		Rockland, Me	Oct. 6, 1905	Boothbay Harbor, Me	Oct. 10, 1904	Do.
Isis (fishing)	11	1881	1900	1895		Thomaston, Me	Aug. 16, 1905	do	Aug. 15, 1904	Do.
John L. Lawrence (fishing)	229	1877	1905	1905		New London, Conn	May 27, 1905	Portland, Me	May 6, 1904	Providence, R. I.
Kearsarge (fishing)	16	1894		1896		South Boston, Mass	May 3, 1905	Boothbay Harbor, Me	Apr. 21, 1904	Portland, Me.
Leo (fishing)	9	1890		1904		Portland, Me	May 31, 1905	Bath, Me	May 25, 1904	Do.
Lorna (towing and fishing)	19	1897		1897		do	July 22, 1905	Portland, Me	July 15, 1904	Do.
Lucretia (towing and fishing)	37	1898		1898		Bristol, Me	July 6, 1905	do	June 30, 1904	Do.
Robert and Edwin (towing and fishing).	30	1899		1899		East Boothbay, Me	May 16, 1905	Rockland, Me	May 18, 1904	Do.
Shark (towing and fishing)	13	1893		1901		Gloucester, Mass	June 20, 1905	Boothbay Harbor, Me	June 11, 1904	Do.
Two Brothers (fishing)	a 4	1902		1902		South Portland, Me	May 12, 1905	York Harbor, Me	May 11, 1904	Do.
Vessels propelled by gasoline motors.										
Chester A. Kennedy	19	1905				Portland, Me	Apr. 21, 1905	Portland, Me	First inspn.	
Dorcas	28	1901				Essex, Mass	do	Cape Porpoise, Me	Apr. 19, 1904	Portland, Me.
Effort	22	1854				Boston, Mass	July 15, 1905	Boothbay Harbor, Me	June 4, 1902	Do.
Etta M. Burns	40	1902				East Boothbay, Me	Nov. 9, 1905	Portland, Me	Dec. 14, 1904	Do.
Natalie B. Nickerson	128	1901				do	Mar. 17, 1905	Boothbay Harbor, Me	Mar. 18, 1904	Do.
Olive F. Hutchins	82	1904				do	July 1, 1905	South Portland, Me	July 1, 1904	Do.

Freight sail vessels of over 700 tons.										
Alice May Davenport (schooner).	1,144	1905				Bath, Me.	Jan. 17, 1905	Bath, Me.	First inspn.	
Cora F. Cressy (schooner)	2,499	1902				do	Apr. 14, 1905	Portsmouth, N. H.	Apr. 14, 1904	Norfolk, Va.
Eliza J. Pendleton (schooner)	751	1891				Belfast, Me.	Feb. 2, 1905	Portland, Me.	Nov. 23, 1903	Mobile, Ala.
Governor Powers (schooner)	1,962	1905				Rockland, Me.	Mar. 20, 1905	Rockland, Me.	First inspn.	
Josie R. Burt (schooner)	760	1882				Bath, Me.	June 27, 1905	Bath, Me.	June 25, 1904	New Haven, Conn.
Orleans (schooner)	751	1905				do	Jan. 26, 1905	do	First inspn.	

LOCAL DISTRICT OF PROVIDENCE, R. I.

Inland passenger steamers.										
Allan Joy [b]	1,113	1898	1899	1898		Chester, Pa.	Mar. 28, 1905	Newport, R. I.	May 7, 1904	New Haven, Conn.
Almeda	10	1904		1892		Cumberland, R. I.	May 1, 1905	Pawtucket, R. I.	First inspn.	
Baltimore	161	1881		1889	1901	Athens, N. Y.	June 3, 1905	Providence, R. I.	May 13, 1904	Providence, R. I.
Block Island	757	1882	1899	1901		Noank, Conn.	June 27, 1905	Newport, R. I.	June 27, 1904	New London, Conn.
Boston	3,626	1904		1903		Quincy, Mass.	June 13, 1905	do	July 13, 1904	Boston, Mass.
City of Brockton	2,771	1886		1886		Chelsea, Mass.	Aug. 11, 1905	do	Aug. 29, 1904	Providence, R. I.
City of Fall River	2,533	1883		1902		do	Sept. 18, 1905	do	Sept. 26, 1904	Do.
City of Lawrence	1,678	1868	1897	1888		Wilmington, Del.	June 26, 1905	do	Aug. 11, 1904	New London, Conn.
City of Newport	561	1863		1901		New York, N. Y.	May 18, 1905	Providence, R. I.	May 25, 1904	Providence, R. I.
City of Taunton	2,881	1892		1890	1903	Chelsea, Mass.	Oct. 17, 1905	Newport, R. I.	Nov. 10, 1904	Do.
City of Worcester	2,489	1881		1903		Wilmington, Del.	July 6, 1905	do	Apr. 15, 1904	New London, Conn.
Corsair	70	1888	1902	1897		East Providence, R. I.	June 8, 1905	Providence, R. I.	June 8, 1904	Providence, R. I.
Cygnet	43	1876		1892	1899	Noank, Conn.	May 19, 1905	New Bedford, Mass.	May 19, 1904	Do.
Gay Head	701	1891		1891		Philadelphia, Pa.	Apr. 20, 1905	do	Apr. 14, 1904	Do.
G. W. Danielson	130	1880		1901		Mystic Bridge, Conn.	Feb. 4, 1905	Newport, R. I.	Feb. 5, 1904	Do.
Islander	119	1883	1904	1901		Bath, Me.	June 5, 1905	Providence, R. I.	June 4, 1904	Do.
J. T. Sherman	89	1903		1903		Noank, Conn.	May 19, 1905	New Bedford, Mass.	May 19, 1904	Do.
Larchmont [c]	1,605	1885		1902		Bath, Me.	Mar. 24, 1905	Providence, R. I.	Mar. 28, 1904	Do.
Louise Perry	25	1900		1900		Bourne, Mass.	July 1, 1905	Fairhaven, Mass.	June 3, 1904	Do.
Maine	2,395	1892		1892		Wilmington, Del.	Jan. 24, 1905	Providence, R. I.	Jan. 27, 1904	New London, Conn.
Marthas Vineyard	515	1871		1899		Brooklyn, N. Y.	Mar. 13, 1905	New Bedford, Mass.	Mar. 12, 1904	Providence, R. I.
Mary	360	1882	1900	1891		Marine City, Mich.	July 25, 1905	Providence, R. I.	Mar. 31, 1905	Chicago, Ill.
Mount Hope	880	1888		1900		Chelsea, Mass.	May 29, 1905	do	May 25, 1904	Providence, R. I.
Nantucket	629	1886		1895		Camden, N. J.	June 19, 1905	New Bedford, Mass.	May 28, 1904	Do.
Nashua	2,554	1884		1895		Noank, Conn.	Oct. 5, 1905	Newport, R. I.	Oct. 4, 1904	Do.
New Shoreham	503	1901		1901		East Boston, Mass.	June 2, 1905	Providence, R. I.	May 31, 1904	Do.
Pilgrim	3,483	1882		1904		Chester, Pa.	Nov. 16, 1905	Newport, R. I.	Dec. 6, 1904	Do.
Plymouth	3,770	1890		1905		do	Nov. 7, 1905	do	Dec. 22, 1904	Do.
Pontiac [d]	91	1883	1902	1895		East Providence, R. I.	May 1, 1905	Pawtucket, R. I.	Apr. 28, 1904	Do.
Priscilla	5,292	1894		1894		Chester, Pa.	Mar. 6, 1905	Newport, R. I.	Apr. 4, 1904	Do.
Puritan	4,593	1889		1899		do	Apr. 13, 1905	do	May 21, 1904	Do.
Queen City	115	1881	1889	1900		Brewer, Me.	Apr. 8, 1905	Providence, R. I.	Apr. 9, 1904	Do.
Richard Borden	892	1874	1882	1898	1905	Bulls Ferry, N. J.	May 25, 1905	do	May 26, 1904	Do.

[a] Estimated. [b] Formerly Cape Charles, 1899. [c] Formerly Cumberland, 1902. [d] Formerly Pioneer, 1902.

DOMESTIC VESSELS INSPECTED, YEAR ENDED DECEMBER 31, 1905—SECOND SUPERVISING DISTRICT—PROVIDENCE, R. I.—Continued.

Names of vessels and class.	Gross tonnage.	Hull built.	Hull rebuilt.	Boilers built.	Boilers rebuilt.	Where built.	Date of inspectio	Where inspected.	Date of previous inspection.	Local district where previously inspected.
Inland passenger steamers—Continued.										
S. C. Hart	63	1896		1895		Baltimore, Md	Apr. 6, 1905	New Bedford, Mass	Apr. 7, 1904	Providence, R. I.
Squantum	248	1888		1888		Newburg, N. Y	May 26, 1905	Providence, R. I	Mar. 29, 1904	Do.
Uncatena	652	1902		1902		Wilmington, Del	Sept. 14, 1905	New Bedford, Mass	Sept. 14, 1904	Do.
Warwick [a]	681	1873	1899	1884	1901	Greenport, N. Y	June 20, 1905	Providence, R. I	July 1, 1904	Do.
What Cheer	214	1867	1900	1905		Keyport, N. J	June 30, 1905	do	May 13, 1904	Do.
William G. Payne	1,310	1902		1902		Wilmington, Del	Mar. 31, 1905	Newport, R. I	May 1, 1904	New Haven, Conn.
Ferry steamers.										
Beavertail	284	1896		1896		Wilmington, Del	May 27, 1905	Newport, R. I	May 23, 1904	Providence, R. I.
Bristol	257	1905		1905		do	June 30, 1905	Bristol, R. I	First inspn.	
Conanicut	353	1886		1886		do	Apr. 29, 1905	Newport, R. I	Apr. 22, 1904	Do.
Fairhaven	279	1896		1896		Chelsea, Mass	Jan. 30, 1905	New Bedford, Mass	Feb. 1, 1904	Do.
Fairhaven	279	1896		1896		do	Dec. 5, 1905	Newport, R. I	Jan. 30, 1905	Do.
General	332	1889		1889		Brooklyn, N. Y	Apr. 22, 1905	do	May 18, 1904	Do.
Sagamore	104	1898		1904		Bath, Me	June 1, 1905	Bristol, R. I	June 2, 1904	Do.
William T. Hart	971	1881		1881		Philadelphia, Pa	Sept. 26, 1905	Newport, R. I	Oct. 31, 1904	Albany, N. Y.
Inland freight steamers.										
Conoho	366	1881		1890	1901	Philadelphia, Pa	June 29, 1905	Providence, R. I	Apr. 5, 1904	Baltimore, Md
Pequot [b]	1,360	1864	1884	1901		New York, N. Y	Oct. 7, 1905	Newport, R. I	Oct. 7, 1904	Providence, R. I.
Ocean towing steamers.										
Concord	353	1898		1898		Philadelphia, Pa	Aug. 24, 1905	Fall River, Mass	Sept. 1, 1904	Providence, R. I.
Eureka	353	1898		1898		do	July 31, 1905	do	Aug. 1, 1904	Do.
Nemasket	220	1899	1904	1899	1904	Tottenville, N. Y	Oct. 27, 1905	do	Nov. 7, 1904	Portland, Me.
Prudence	292	1900		1900		Camden, N. J	Dec. 20, 1905	Providence, R. I	Dec. 16, 1904	Philadelphia, Pa.
Tacony	353	1899		1899		Philadelphia, Pa	May 4, 1905	Fall River, Mass	May 2, 1904	Providence, R. I.
Vulcan	62	1882	1891	1896		Athens, N. Y	Aug. 18, 1905	Newport, R. I	Aug. 8, 1904	Philadelphia, Pa.
Waltham	353	1898		1898		Philadelphia, Pa	Oct. 10, 1905	Fall River, Mass	Oct. 13, 1904	Providence. R. I.
Inland towing steamers.										
Archer	74	1889	1905	1892	1903	Fall River, Mass	Apr. 21, 1905	Fall River, Mass	Apr. 5, 1904	Providence, R. I.
Bay Point	23	1886		1904		do	May 20, 1905	Marion, Mass	May 9, 1904	Boston, Mass.
Carrie A. Ramsey	84	1892		1892		Perth Amboy, N. J	June 16, 1905	Providence, R. I	June 14, 1904	Providence, R. I.
Cohannet	69	1900		1900		Bath, Me	Feb. 28, 1905	Fall River, Mass	Feb. 27, 1904	Do.
Cora L. Staples	92	1872	1890	1898		Wilmington, Del	July 25, 1905	do	July 22, 1904	Do.
Eben Hodge	54	1893		1893		Essex, Mass	July 27, 1905	Providence, R. I	Aug. 6, 1904	Do.

Gaspee	113	1893	....	1898	....	Wilmington, Del	Aug. 22, 1905	....do	Aug. 29, 1904	Boston, Mass.
Howell	63	1873	....	1904	....	Philadelphia, Pa	Sept. 28, 1905	....do	Sept. 30, 1904	Providence, R. I.
Jennie	c 4	1891	....	1889	....	Noank, Conn	June 22, 1905	Portsmouth, R. I	June 14, 1897	New London, Conn.
Nat Sutton	66	1887	1902	1902	....	East Providence, R. I.	Oct. 30, 1905	Providence, R. I	Nov. 1, 1904	Providence, R. I.
Nellie	36	1873	....	1886	....	Philadelphia, Pa	Apr. 14, 1905	New Bedford, Mass	Nov. 20, 1903	Do.
Quequechan	76	1903	....	1903	....	Bath, Me	Oct. 21, 1905	Fall River, Mass	Oct. 27, 1904	Do.
Reliance	75	1873	....	1905	....	Greenpoint, N. Y	July 14, 1905	Providence, R. I	Aug. 6, 1904	Do.
Roger Williams	149	1903	....	1903	....	Athens, N. Y	Sept. 19, 1905	....do	Sept. 30, 1904	Do.
Scamp	11	1904	....	1888	....	Newport, R. I	May 12, 1905	Newport, R. I	May 12, 1904	Do.
Solicitor	56	1899	....	1898	....	Baltimore, Md	Jan. 28, 1905	....do	Jan. 28, 1904	Do.
S. Thomas Brown	58	1883	....	1904	....	Wilmington, Del	July 20, 1905	Fall River, Mass	July 18, 1904	Do.
Walter E. Sutton	41	1884	....	1896	....	Camden, N. J	May 22, 1905	Providence, R. I	May 26, 1904	Do.
William H. Gallison	58	1892	....	1886	....	Boston, Mass	Apr. 28, 1905	New Bedford, Mass	Dec. 18, 1904	Boston, Mass.
Ocean steam pleasure yachts										
Abbicarll	58	1898	1899	1898	....	Fall River, Mass	Aug. 24, 1905	Fall River, Mass	Aug. 23, 1904	Providence, R. I.
Aida	27	1882	....	1895	....	Bath, Me	June 23, 1905	East Greenwich, R. I.	June 16, 1904	Do.
Coranto	174	1902	....	1902	....	New York, N. Y	June 22, 1905	Pawtuxet, R. I	Aug. 3, 1904	Do.
Cosette [d]	42	1884	....	1896	....	Bristol, R. I	June 17, 1905	Bristol, R. I	July 3, 1904	Boston, Mass.
Eugenia	113	1904	....	1904	....	....do	Apr. 27, 1905	....do	Apr. 2, 1904	Providence, R. I.
Felicia	213	1898	....	1904	....	Brooklyn, N. Y	June 10, 1905	Bridgeport, R. I	July 28, 1904	Do.
Florence	53	1900	....	1900	....	Bristol, R. I	Mar. 18, 1905	Bristol, R. I	May 5, 1904	Do.
Florence [e]	104	1902	....	1902	....	....do	Apr. 27, 1905	....do	May 26, 1904	Do.
Hiawatha	219	1897	....	1905	....	New York, N. Y	June 12, 1905	Newport, R. I	May 9, 1903	Do.
Little Sovereign	55	1904	....	1904	....	Bristol, R. I	May 16, 1905	Bristol, R. I	May 27, 1904	Do.
Margaret [f]	245	1899	....	1899	....	Chester, Pa	July 12, 1905	Providence, R. I	July 7, 1904	New London, Conn.
Nushka [g]	37	1891	....	1891	1895	Boston, Mass	July 29, 1905	....do	July 30, 1904	New York, N. Y.
Parthenia	141	1903	....	1903	....	Bristol, R. I	Apr. 14, 1905	New Bedford, Mass	May 1, 1903	Providence, R. I.
Polyanthus [h]	45	1895	....	1899	....	....do	June 17, 1905	Bristol, R. I	June 24, 1904	Do.
Roamer	89	1902	....	1902	....	....do	June 5, 1905	....do	June 9, 1904	Do.
Sea Urchin	49	1905	....	1898	....	....do	Nov. 17, 1905	....do	First inspn.	
Thetis	104	1901	....	1901	....	Boston, Mass	Sept. 29, 1905	Pawtuxet, R. I	Oct. 6, 1904	Do.
Wana	88	1903	....	1903	....	Bristol, R. I	June 13, 1905	Bristol, R. I	June 5, 1904	Do.
Inland steam pleasure yachts.										
Adelia	10	1902	....	1902	....	Boston, Mass	Aug. 4, 1905	Pawtuxet, R. I	Aug. 12, 1904	Providence, R. I.
Arab	c 2	1892	....	1892	1905	Fall River, Mass	July 15, 1905	Fall River, Mass	June 6, 1904	Do.
Augusta [i]	38	1887	....	1898	....	Bristol, R. I	Apr. 17, 1905	Bristol, R. I	June 9, 1904	Do.
Azubah [j]	37	1880	....	1904	....	Greenpoint, N. Y	July 22, 1905	Providence, R. I	June 25, 1904	Do.
Canute	11	1892	....	1892	....	Saunderstown, R. I	Oct. 4, 1905	Pawtucket, R. I	Oct. 1, 1904	Do.
Comet	c 1	1888	....	1893	....	East Providence, R. I.	July 22, 1905	East Providence, R. I.	July 21, 1904	Do.
Coryell	13	1899	....	1905	....	Boston, Mass	Apr. 24, 1905	Providence, R. I	June 22, 1904	Boston, Mass.
Despatch	c 4	1897	....	1897	1903	East Providence, R. I.	June 5, 1905	East Providence, R. I.	June 6, 1904	Providence, R. I.
Dolphin	6	1879	....	1887	1903	Bristol, R. I	July 21, 1905	Pawtucket, R. I	July 21, 1904	Do.
Express	34	1903	....	1903	....	....do	Apr. 17, 1905	Bristol, R. I	Aug. 17, 1903	Do.

[a] Formerly Day Star, 1899.
[b] Formerly Thetis, 1884.
[c] Estimated.
[d] Formerly Marina, 1886.
[e] Formerly Quickstep, 1905.
[f] Formerly Eugenia, 1894; Marjorie, 1900.
[g] Formerly Helvetia, 1899.
[h] Formerly Eugenia, 1899.
[i] Formerly Bessie Ross, 1895.
[j] Formerly Forget Me Not, 1900; Elizabeth, 1902.

DOMESTIC VESSELS INSPECTED, YEAR ENDED DECEMBER 31, 1905—SECOND SUPERVISING DISTRICT—PROVIDENCE, R. I.—Continued.

Names of vessels and class.	Gross tonnage.	Hull built.	Hull rebuilt.	Boilers built.	Boilers rebuilt.	Where built.	Date of inspection.	Where inspected.	Date of previous inspection.	Local district where previously inspected.
Inland steam pleasure yachts—Continued.										
Flyaway	a 2	1887		1895		Sheldonville, Mass	Aug. 17, 1905	Tiverton, R. I	Aug. 15, 1904	Providence, R. I.
Genevieve	48	1895		1900		New Bedford, Mass	June 24, 1905	New Bedford, Mass	July 12, 1904	Do.
Gleam	a 2	(b)	1891	1900		Brooklyn, N. Y	Aug. 25, 1905	Pawtucket, R. I	July 25, 1904	Do.
Hope	39	1901		1904		Morris Heights, N. Y.	May 18, 1905	Tiverton, R. I	June 12, 1904	Boston, Mass.
Lora	a 2	1887		1895	1905	East Greenwich, R. I.	July 31, 1905	Drownville, R. I	Aug. 23, 1901	Providence, R. I.
Lucile	19	1884		1905		Bristol, R. I	July 8, 1905	Bristol, R. I	July 7, 1902	Bangor, Me.
Polly	19	1885		1899	1904	do	July 22, 1905	do	July 25, 1904	Providence, R. I.
Squid	a 4	1898		1898	1905	Ogdensburg, N. Y	July 3, 1905	Newport, R. I	Aug. 11, 1904	Do.
Vanish	6	1893		1901	1902	Bristol, R. I	July 3, 1905	do	May 11, 1904	Do.
Ventura c	49	1902		1899		Poughkeepsie, N. Y	June 17, 1905	Pawtuxet, R. I	June 17, 1904	Norfolk, Va.
Venture	8	1904		1896	1900	Pawtuxet, R. I	Sept. 9, 1905	do	Sept. 10, 1904	Providence, R. I.
Wanderer	a 4	1899		1899	1905	Bristol, R. I	June 15, 1905	Newport, R. I	May 16, 1904	New York, N. Y.
Miscellaneous steamers										
Active (oyster)	49	1895	1905	1901		East Providence, R. I.	Oct. 14, 1905	East Greenwich, R. I.	Sept. 8, 1904	Providence, R. I.
Agnes (fishing)	49	1879	1902	1893		Brooklyn, N. Y	Apr. 4, 1905	Providence, R. I	Apr. 9, 1904	Do.
Amagansett (fishing)	118	1879	1898	1890		Kennebunk, Me	Mar. 25, 1905	Portsmouth, R. I	Apr. 29, 1904	Do.
A. M. Hathaway (fishing)	217	1873	1883	1891	1902	Fall River, Mass	do	do	Mar. 25, 1904	Do.
Annie E. Gallup (fishing)	141	1878	1898	1903		do	Mar. 30, 1905	do	May 6, 1904	Do.
Annie M. (oyster)	19	1898		1892		Warwick, R. I	June 23, 1905	Warren, R. I	June 25, 1904	Do.
Arizona (fishing)	201	1882	1903	1898	1905	Mystic, Conn	Mar. 21, 1905	Portsmouth, R. I	Apr. 8, 1904	Do.
A. T. Serrell (fishing)	49	1871		1896	1902	Bordentown, N. J	June 12, 1905	Newport, R. I	June 11, 1904	Do.
Bamgan (fishing)	18	1904		1903		East Providence, R. I	May 22, 1905	East Providence, R. I	May 13, 1904	Do.
Bernice (oyster)	13	1888	1899	1896	1905	do	Sept. 19, 1905	Warren, R. I	Sept. 16, 1904	Do.
B. G. Browning (lighter)	44	1888		1899		Apponaug, R. I	May 2, 1905	Apponaug, R. I	May 3, 1904	Do.
Blue Jay (freight and towing)	18	1900		1900		Fall River, Mass	July 3, 1905	Newport, R. I	June 18, 1904	Do.
Cora P. White (fishing)	106	1877	1904	1895		do	Apr. 3, 1905	Portsmouth, R. I	Apr. 29, 1904	Do.
Enterprise (fishing)	40	1904		1904		do	Apr. 7, 1905	Fall River, Mass	Apr. 21, 1904	Do.
Estelle (fishing)	164	1880	1898	1898		East Deering, Me	May 13, 1905	Portsmouth, R. I	Apr. 15, 1904	Do.
E. T. Deblois (fishing)	81	1877		1900		South Bristol, Me	Apr. 7, 1905	Fall River, Mass	Apr. 30, 1904	Do.
Eugene F. Price (fishing)	126	1874	1905	1890	1903	Bristol, Me	May 6, 1905	Portsmouth, R. I	June 1, 1904	Do.
Falcon (fishing)	154	1879	1902	1895	1902	East Deering, Me	Mar. 25, 1905	do	May 6, 1904	Do.
Fanny Sprague (freight and towing)	56	1872	1898	1890	1902	Boston, Mass	Apr. 3, 1905	do	Apr. 15, 1904	Do.
Fearless (fishing)	121	1877	1904	1903		Fall River, Mass	Apr. 7, 1905	do	May 27, 1904	Do.
F. S. Willard (fishing and towing)	59	1898		1898		South Portland, Me	Apr. 25, 1905	do	Apr. 12, 1904	Do.
George Curtis (fishing)	182	1881	1896	1899		Boothbay, Me	Mar. 21, 1905	do	Apr. 2, 1904	Do.
George F. Morse (fishing)	153	1878	1904	1898		East Deering, Me	May 13, 1905	do	July 11, 1904	Do.
George Hudson (fishing)	143	1880	1904	1894		Kennebunk, Me	Mar. 30, 1905	do	May 27, 1904	Do.

George M. Long (oyster)	98	1895	1905	1895		Noank, Conn	Nov. 28, 1905	Providence, R. I	Nov. 7, 1904	Do.
G. S. Allyn (fishing)	211	1878	1905	1889	1902	Mystic, Conn	June 10, 1905	Portsmouth, R. I	Apr. 2, 1904	Do.
Hattie (fishing)	22	1890		1904		Noank, Conn	Apr. 10, 1905	Newport, R. I	Apr. 21, 1904	Do.
H. E. Hamlin (fishing)	43	1893		1893		Bath, Me	Apr. 18, 1905	Tiverton, R. I	Apr. 14, 1904	Bangor, Me.
Ivernia (oyster)	43	1874		1903		East Haven, Conn	Oct. 23, 1905	Providence, R. I	Oct. 24, 1904	Providence, R. I.
James M. Gifford (fishing)	168	1905		1905		Greenport, N. Y	June 6, 1905	Portsmouth, R. I	First inspn	
James Morgan (oyster)	69	1822	1899	1892		Poughkeepsie, N. Y	Apr. 4, 1905	Providence, R. I	Apr. 6, 1904	Do.
Jennie (oyster)	18	(b)	1887	1899		Unknown	Mar. 24, 1905	do	Oct. 26, 1903	Do.
John W. Dodge (oyster)	59	1887		1895		Pawtuxet, R. I	Aug. 29, 1905	Drownville, R. I	Sept. 3, 1904	Do.
J. W. French (fishing)	129	1875	1898	1899		Damariscotta, Me	Mar. 30, 1905	Portsmouth, R. I	Apr. 15, 1904	Do.
J. W. Stubbs (oyster)	51	1898		1898		Essex, Mass	Apr. 24, 1905	Warren, R. I	Mar. 7, 1904	Do.
Kickemuit (oyster)	59	1888		1888		Noank, Conn	Sept. 30, 1905	Providence, R. I	Oct. 1, 1904	Do.
Kingston (oyster)	65	1902		1902		Kennebunk, Me	Apr. 24, 1905	do	Apr. 21, 1904	Do.
Leonard Brightman (fishing)	133	1874	1890	1890	1903	Bristol, Me	Mar. 21, 1905	Portsmouth, R. I	Apr. 2, 1904	Do.
Mary S. Lewis (oyster)	138	1901		1901		Port Jefferson, N. Y	Jan. 16, 1905	Providence, R. I	Jan. 19, 1904	New Haven, Conn.
Mary S. Lewis (oyster)	138	1901		1901		do	Dec. 28, 1905	do	Jan. 16, 1905	Providence, R. I.
M. Dewing (oyster)	71	1893		1905		Boston, Mass	Aug. 15, 1905	do	Oct. 8, 1904	Do.
Montauk (fishing)	161	1880	1905	1894		Kennebunk, Me	July 7, 1905	Portsmouth, R. I	May 14, 1904	Do.
Nat Strong (fishing)	176	1880	1897	1894		do	May 23, 1905	do	July 16, 1904	Do.
Nellie (oyster)	16	1890		1896		East Providence, R. I	Aug. 29, 1905	Drownville, R. I	Oct. 25, 1904	Do.
Pet (fishing)	21	1897		1890	1905	do	June 13, 1905	New Bedford, Mass	June 8, 1904	Boston, Mass.
Portland (fishing)	118	1879	1898	1890		Kennebunk, Me	Apr. 7, 1905	Portsmouth, R. I	Apr. 29, 1904	Providence, R. I.
Quickstep (fishing)	214	1879	1898	1893	1903	Noank, Conn	Apr. 25, 1905	do	May 27, 1904	Do.
Ranger (fishing)	160	1882		1895		Mystic, Conn	Mar. 30, 1905	do	Apr. 8, 1904	Do.
Richard W. Law (oyster)	113	1888		1888		New Haven, Conn	July 29, 1905	Providence, R. I	Aug. 9, 1904	Do.
Robert Pettis (oyster)	31	1893		1893		do	Sept. 20, 1905	do	Oct. 20, 1904	Do.
Sagamore (freight and towing).	173	1900		1900		Fall River, Mass	May 5, 1905	do	May 4, 1904	Do.
Samuel S. Brown (fishing)	141	1879	1901	1905		Mystic, Conn	May 6, 1905	Portsmouth, R. I	Apr. 2, 1904	Do.
Seaconnet (fishing)	188	1880	1903	1889		Boothbay, Me	Mar. 21, 1905	do	Mar. 25, 1904	Do.
Seven Brothers (fishing)	46	1870	1904	1886	1900	Bristol, R. I	Apr. 15, 1905	do	Apr. 8, 1904	Do.
Sterling (fishing)	127	1879	1898	1895		East Deering, Me	Apr. 3, 1905	do	Apr. 15, 1904	Do.
Success No. 3 (towing and lightering).	91	1904		1904		New Bedford, Mass	July 18, 1905	New Bedford, Mass	July 19, 1904	Do.
Tiger (fishing)	20	1898		1898		Kingston, Mass	Apr. 18, 1905	Fall River, Mass	Apr. 11, 1904	Do.
Vester (fishing)	117	1876	1901	1889	1901	Boothbay, Me	Apr. 3, 1905	Portsmouth, R. I	Apr. 29, 1904	Do.
Vigilant (fishing)	15	1894		1894	1898	Boston, Mass	Apr. 28, 1905	New Bedford, Mass	May 16, 1904	Do.
Walter Adams (fishing)	271	1890		1890		Noank, Conn	Mar. 25, 1905	Portsmouth, R. I	Apr. 2, 1904	Do.
Warwick (oyster)	49	1901		1901		East Providence, R. I	Sept. 12, 1905	Tiverton, R. I	Sept 19, 1904	Do.
William A. Wells (fishing)	68	1873	1903	1899		Bristol, Me	Apr. 3, 1905	Portsmouth, R. I	June 1, 1904	Do.
Winona (fishing)	20	1890		1905		Noank, Conn	Apr. 18, 1905	Fall River, Mass	May 12, 1904	Do.
Xiphias (fishing)	24	1894		1894		do	do	do	Mar. 31, 1904	Do.
Vessels propelled by gasoline motors.										
Arline	23	1900				Lynn, Mass	May 27, 1905	Newport, R. I	Apr. 1, 1904	Providence, R. I.
Caroline[d]	28	1859	1904			Fall River, Mass	June 6, 1904	Bristol, R. I	First inspn	
Caroline	28	1859	1904			do	June 9, 1905	do	June 6, 1904	Do.
Earl and Nettie	24	1893				Bath, Me	Aug. 5, 1905	Newport, R. I	Aug. 5, 1904	Do.
Fosstena	16	1903				Fall River, Mass	Apr. 17, 1905	Dighton, Mass	Nov. 17, 1903	Do.

[a] Estimated. [b] Unknown. [c] Formerly Indienne, 1902. [d] Certificated Apr. 7, 1905.

DOMESTIC VESSELS INSPECTED, YEAR ENDED DECEMBER 31, 1905—SECOND SUPERVISING DISTRICT—PROVIDENCE, R. I.—Continued.

Names of vessels and class.	Gross tonnage.	Hull built.	Hull rebuilt.	Boilers built.	Boilers rebuilt.	Where built.	Date of inspection.	Where inspected.	Date of previous inspection.	Local district where previously inspected.
Vessels propelled by gasoline motors—Continued.										
Gracie Phillips	20	1876				Noank, Conn.	May 8, 1905	Warren, R. I.	June 18, 1904	New London, Conn.
Inez	16	1901				Fall River, Mass.	Apr. 25, 1905	Fall River, Mass.	Mar. 29, 1904	Providence, R. I.
Viking	27	1897				Noank, Conn.	June 9, 1905	Newport, R. I.	June 3, 1904	Do.
Freight sail vessels of over 700 tons.										
Lyman M. Law (schooner)	1,300	1890				West Haven, Conn.	Jan. 20, 1905	Fall River, Mass.	Dec. 28, 1903	Providence, R. I.
Marguerite (schooner)	1,553	1889				Bath, Me.	June 8, 1905	Providence, R. I.	June 4, 1904	Do.
Sail vessel of over 100 tons carrying passengers for hire.										
Cameo	243	1878				Bath, Me.	Oct. 16, 1905	New Bedford, Mass.	Sept. 24, 1904	Providence, R. I.

LOCAL DISTRICT OF BANGOR, ME.

Names of vessels and class.	Gross tonnage.	Hull built.	Hull rebuilt.	Boilers built.	Boilers rebuilt.	Where built.	Date of inspection.	Where inspected.	Date of previous inspection.	Local district where previously inspected.
Inland passenger steamers.										
Bismarck	a 4	1896		1896		Southwest Harbor, Me.	June 8, 1905	Southwest Harbor, Me.	May 31, 1904	Bangor, Me.
Castine	69	1889		1895		Brewer, Me.	June 4, 1905	Bangor, Me.	June 1, 1904	Do.
Cimbria	275	1882	1899	1899	1905	do	May 29, 1905	do	Apr. 18, 1904	Do.
Circe	6	1887		1905		Bath, Me.	July 1, 1905	Seal Harbor, Me.	Aug. 9, 1904	Do.
Creedmoor	19	1884		1884		Brewer, Me.	July 6, 1905	Bar Harbor, Me.	July 6, 1904	Do.
Day Dream	36	1880		1892		Greenpoint, N. Y.	Aug. 9, 1905	Isle-au-Haut, Me.	Aug. 9, 1904	Do.
Eastport	64	1901		1901		Dennysville, Me.	Sept. 19, 1905	Eastport, Me.	Nov. 7, 1904	Do.
Golden Rod	71	1893		1893		Brewer, Me.	June 4, 1905	Bangor, Me.	June 5, 1904	Do.
Henry F. Eaton	240	1901		1901		South Portland, Me.	Apr. 20, 1905	Calais, Me.	June 19, 1904	Do.
Islesford	27	1893		1893		Brewer, Me.	July 1, 1905	Seal Harbor, Me.	July 1, 1904	Do.
Lottie and May	13	1894		1894		East Boothbay, Me.	Aug. 8, 1905	Bucksport, Me.	Aug. 8, 1904	Do.
Lubec	50	1891		1903		Portland, Me.	June 10, 1905	Eastport, Me.	June 13, 1904	Do.
Marjorie	29	1898		1901		Brewer, Me.	Apr. 12, 1905	Bar Harbor, Me.	Apr. 12, 1904	Do.
Minnehaha	18	1879		1900		Portland, Me.	July 18, 1905	Stonington, Me.	July 15, 1904	Do.
Percy V.	37	1883		1891	1903	Bath, Me.	May 31, 1905	Ellsworth, Me.	June 6, 1904	Do.
Rockland	135	1883		1901		Boston, Mass.	June 30, 1905	Bangor, Me.	June 17, 1904	Portland, Me.
Ruth	188	1894		1901		Rockland, Me.	May 17, 1905	Winter Harbor, Me.	May 22, 1904	Bangor, Me.
Silver Star	75	1886	1889	1897		Brewer, Me.	May 28, 1905	Bangor, Me.	May 27, 1904	Do.
Tremont	81	1895		1895		do	May 1, 1905	Castine, Me.	June 7, 1904	Do.

Verona	149	1902		1893	1902	do	May 8, 1905	Bangor, Me	May 20, 1904	Do.
William Conners	15	1891	1905	1904		do	June 2, 1905	do	July 7, 1904	Do.
Ferry steamer.										
Bon Ton No. 2	7	1902		1902		Brewer, Me	Sept. 10, 1905	Brewer, Me	Sept. 18, 1904	Bangor, Me.
Inland freight steamer.										
Sagadahoc	44	1891	1900	1890		Woolwich, Me	June 11, 1905	Bangor, Me	June 4, 1904	Portland, Me.
Inland towing steamers.										
Betsy Ross	33	1903		1903		Boston, Mass	Apr. 13, 1905	Stonington, Me	Apr. 9, 1904	Boston, Mass.
Bismarck	124	1888		1888		Philadelphia, Pa	July 17, 1905	Bangor, Me	July 18, 1904	Bangor, Me.
Delta	31	1863	1905	1895		do	Apr. 24, 1905	do	Oct. 18, 1904	Do.
Ellen	37	1863		1893		do	July 24, 1905	Eastport, Me	July 25, 1904	Do.
Henry Wellman	38	1871	1899	1884		do	Aug. 16, 1905	Calais, Me	Aug. 16, 1904	Do.
Little Round Top	46	1871	1884	1890		Ellsworth, Me	May 5, 1905	Ellsworth, Me	May 3, 1904	Do.
Phillips Eaton	19	1883		1902		Bath, Me	Sept. 16, 1905	West Sullivan, Me	Sept. 23, 1904	Do.
Ralph Ross	93	1870		1890		Philadelphia, Pa	May 4, 1905	Bangor, Me	May 6, 1904	Do.
Samuel B. Jones	33	1872		1895		do	Oct. 24, 1905	Machias, Me	Oct. 26, 1904	Do.
Walter Ross	24	1867		1890		do	Nov. 6, 1905	Bangor, Me	June 29, 1903	Do.
Steam pleasure yachts.										
Aria	192	1903		1903		New York, N. Y	May 19, 1905	Bangor, Me	May 28, 1904	Boston, Mass.
Doris [b]	[a]5	1892		1904		Nyack, N. Y	June 25, 1905	Islesford, Me	Aug. 17, 1903	Bangor, Me.
El Placita	25	1892		1903		Boston, Mass	Aug. 7, 1905	Bar Harbor, Me	Aug. 6, 1904	Do.
Fire Fly	14	1884		1887		do	June 16, 1905	Winter Harbor, Me	June 15, 1904	Do.
Hiawatha	8	1893		1893		Camden, Me	Aug. 15, 1905	Bar Harbor, Me	Aug. 15, 1904	Do.
Hustler	[a]5	1905		1905		Islesboro, Me	July 14, 1905	Bangor, Me	First inspn.	
Iduna	21	1896		1896		South Boston, Mass	June 8, 1905	Islesford, Me	June 23, 1904	Do.
Katrina	20	1890		1894		Bristol, R. I	June 26, 1905	Sorrento, Me	July 12, 1904	New York, N. Y
Kittewan	82	1900		1900		Trenton, N. J	July 12, 1905	Winter Harbor, Me	July 13, 1904	Bangor, Me.
Norma	13	1891		1900		Boston, Mass	do	Bar Harbor, Me	do	Do.
Ouray	[a]4	1890		1903		Sheldonville, Mass	Aug. 7, 1905	do	Aug. 6, 1904	Do.
Princess	44	1890		1902		Boston, Mass	June 13, 1905	Castine, Me	June 7, 1904	Do.
Roque	39	1902		1902		do	July 27, 1905	Jonesport, Me	July 26, 1904	Providence, R. I.
S. V. A. Hunter	[a]3	1891		1904		Southwest Harbor, Me	June 8, 1905	Southwest Harbor, Me	May 31, 1904	Bangor, Me.
Satilla	106	1902		1902		Boston, Mass	May 26, 1905	Camden, Me	May 26, 1904	Philadelphia, Pa.
Solace [c]	[a]4	1892		1905		Southwest Harbor, Me	Aug. 12, 1905	Islesford, Me	Aug. 10, 1904	Bangor, Me.
Whiporee	22	1904		1903		Islesboro, Me	Aug. 14, 1905	Belfast, Me	Aug. 17, 1904	Do.
Wissahickon [d]	74	1900		1900		South Boston, Mass	May 26, 1905	Rockport, Me	June 17, 1904	Do.
Miscellaneous steam vessels.										
Clarence B. Mitchell (towing and fishing).[e]	47	1897		1899		Boston, Mass	June 16, 1905	Prospect Harbor, Me.	June 15, 1904	Bangor, Me.
Creedmoor (towing and fishing).	10	1878	1899	1904		Bristol, R. I	do	do	do	Do.

[a] Estimated. [b] Formerly Madaruja, 1902. [c] Formerly Brunswick, 1900. [d] Formerly Valda, 1902. [e] Formerly Helen, 1900.

DOMESTIC VESSELS INSPECTED, YEAR ENDED DECEMBER 31, 1905—SECOND SUPERVISING DISTRICT—BANGOR, ME.—Continued.

Names of vessels and class.	Gross tonnage.	Hull built.	Hull rebuilt.	Boilers built.	Boilers rebuilt.	Where built.	Date of inspection.	Where inspected.	Date of previous inspection.	Local district where previously inspected.
Miscellaneous steam vessels—Continued.										
Curlew (towing and fishing)	29	1895		1895		Millbridge, Me.	July 27, 1905	Jonesport, Me.	July 27, 1904	Bangor, Me.
Daphne (towing and fishing)	27	1904		1888		Lubec, Me.	Sept. 6, 1905	Eastport, Me.	Sept. 10, 1904	Do.
Doctor (towing and fishing)	16	1889		1889		New York, N. Y.	Aug. 5, 1905	do	Aug. 5, 1904	Do.
Etta (towing and fishing)	33	1883	1901	1896		Boston, Mass.	July 10, 1905	Millbridge, Me.	Sept. 17, 1903	Boston, Mass.
Escort (towing and fishing)	16	1878		1895		Pawtucket, R. I.	May 24, 1905	Calais, Me.	July 6, 1901	Bangor, Me.
Ethel (towing and fishing)	28	1895		1900		Noank, Conn.	Aug. 25, 1905	Eastport, Me.	Aug. 25, 1904	Do.
Frank and Lloyd (towing and fishing)	16	1895		1895		Lubec, Me.	do	do	Aug. 30, 1904	Do.
G. B. Otis (towing and freight)	25	1896	1904	1893		East Providence, R. I.	May 11, 1905	do	May 13, 1904	Do.
Gertrude L. (towing and fishing)	7	1892	1902	1900		Brewer, Me.	July 21, 1905	Bar Harbor, Me.	July 21, 1904	Do.
Haidee (towing and fishing)	17	1884		1898		Freeport, Me.	July 27, 1905	Machias, Me.	July 27, 1904	Do.
Judge Moore (towing and fishing)	27	1885		1899		Tarrytown, N. Y.	June 10, 1905	Eastport, Me.	May 28, 1904	Do.
Luce Brothers (towing and fishing)	88	1877		1893		New London, Conn.	July 8, 1905	do	July 8, 1904	Do.
Mizpah (towing and fishing)	8	1878		1899		Boston, Mass.	June 21, 1905	do	June 21, 1904	Do.
Mona (fishing)	9	1900		1890		East Boothbay, Me.	Oct. 3, 1905	Stonington, Me.	Oct. 6, 1904	Do.
Phantom (towing and fishing)	56	1887	1905	1904		Freeport, Me.	June 10, 1905	Eastport, Me.	Sept. 26, 1904	Do.
Quoddy (towing and fishing)	34	1900		1900		Dennysville, Me.	July 8, 1905	do	July 8, 1904	Do.
R. J. Killick (towing and fishing)	33	1899		1899		Eastport, Me.	Aug. 5, 1905	do	Aug. 5, 1904	Do.
Sawyer (towing and fishing)	34	1895		1901		Millbridge, Me.	June 9, 1905	Milbridge, Me.	June 9, 1904	Do.
Sycamore (fishing)	a 4	1897		1900		Deer Isle, Me.	June 5, 1905	Surry, Me.	June 3, 1904	Do.
Motor vessels.										
E. McNichol (kerosene)	28	1895				Bristol, Me.	May 22, 1905	Jonesport, Me.	First inspn.	
Marion McLoon (gasoline)	30	1905				East Boothbay, Me.	Sept. 21, 1905	Rockland, Me.	do	
Therese White (gasoline)	20	1905				Friendship, Me.	do	do	do	
Verna G. (gasoline)	28	1903				Deer Isle, Me.	June 7, 1905	Brewer, Me.	do	
Freight sail vessels of over 700 gross tons.										
Augusta W. Snow	830	1905				Brewer, Me.	May 15, 1905	Brewer, Me.	First inspn.	
George E. Walcott	1,553	1890				Bath, Me.	June 3, 1905	Bangor, Me.	June 10, 1904	Bangor, Me.

LOCAL DISTRICT OF NEW HAVEN, CONN.

Inland passenger steamers.										
Continental	82	1905		1905		Port Jefferson, N. Y.	June 23, 1905	Stratford, Conn.	First inspn.	
John Sylvester	495	1866	1886	1886		Jersey City, N. J.	June 30, 1905	Bridgeport, Conn.	May 18, 1904	New York, N. Y.
Margaret	a 6	1890		1890		Guilford, Conn.	May 9, 1905	Stony Creek, Conn.	May 7, 1904	New Haven, Conn.
Medea	54	1885		1893		South Norwalk, Conn.	July 1, 1905	South Norwalk, Conn.	June 13, 1904	Do.
Park City	391	1898		1898		Port Jefferson, N. Y.	May 11, 1905	Port Jefferson, N. Y.	May 29, 1904	Do.
Richard Peck	2,906	1892		1892		Wilmington, Del.	July 17, 1905	New Haven, Conn.	July 14, 1904	Do.
Rosedale	938	1877		1890		Norfolk, Va.	May 27, 1905	Bridgeport, Conn.	Mar. 24, 1904	Do.
Victor	188	1854	1871	1883		Athens, N. Y.	May 26, 1905	do	May 29, 1904	Do.
W. I. Stevens	75	1903		1903		Bridgeport, Conn.	June 22, 1905	South Norwalk, Conn.	June 18, 1904	Do.
Ferry steamers.										
Cynthia	21	1900		1892		Saybrook, Conn.	June 15, 1905	New Haven, Conn.	June 16, 1904	New Haven, Conn.
Etta May	99	1888		1897		Port Jefferson, N. Y.	May 26, 1905	South Norwalk, Conn.	May 23, 1904	Do.
Lenoir	133	1887		1887		Baltimore, Md.	May 25, 1905	Bridgeport, Conn.	June 10, 1904	Do.
Pleasure Beach	55	1896		1896		Noank, Conn.	June 5, 1905	do	do	Do.
Ocean freight steamer.										
George Farwell	977	1895		1901		Marine City, Mich.	Sept. 7, 1905	New Haven, Conn.	Sept. 16, 1904	New York, N. Y.
Inland freight steamers.										
Adamant Plaster	24	1894		1894		New Haven, Conn.	June 22, 1905	Fair Haven, Conn.	June 23, 1904	New Haven, Conn.
Bradford	138	1863		1901		Buffalo, N. Y.	Aug. 3, 1905	do	Aug. 4, 1904	Do.
Capt. M. De Puy	136	1887		1887		do	June 24, 1905	Westport, Conn.	July 2, 1904	Do.
Eagle	170	1861	1887	1896		Mystic Bridge, Conn.	Dec. 2, 1905	Norwalk, Conn.	Dec. 2, 1904	Do.
Francis B. Thurber	131	1880		1889		Lockport, N. Y.	Jan. 31, 1905	Westport, Conn.	Jan. 19, 1904	Do.
J. C. Austin	143	1886	1904	1892		do	Nov. 3, 1905	New Haven, Conn.	Nov. 7, 1904	Do.
John B. Dallas	127	1890		1899		do	June 28, 1905	do	July 7, 1904	New London, Conn.
Marion	262	1901		1901		Wilmington, Del.	Dec. 2, 1905	Bridgeport, Conn.	Dec. 14, 1901	Philadelphia, Pa.
New York World	142	1888		1898		Lockport, N. Y.	Sept. 8, 1905	New Haven, Conn.	Sept. 12, 1904	New London, Conn.
Ocean towing steamer.										
Resolute	120	1881	1900	1900		Fly Mountain, N. Y.	Jan. 2, 1905	New Haven, Conn.	Dec. 26, 1903	New Haven, Conn.
Inland towing steamers.										
Ariosa	140	1885		1903		Brooklyn, N. Y.	Jan. 19, 1905	New Haven, Conn.	Jan. 18, 1904	New York, N. Y.
Arthur	33	1894		1894		Athens, N. Y.	June 12, 1905	do	June 13, 1904	New Haven, Conn.
Clara McWilliams [b]	50	1874	1899	1905		Brooklyn, N. Y.	July 10, 1905	do	July 9, 1904	New York, N. Y.
Frederick E. Ives	120	1882	1900	1900		Fly Mountain, N. Y.	Sept. 14, 1905	do	Sept. 13, 1904	New Haven, Conn.
Isis	36	1883	1901	1883		Brooklyn, N. Y.	Apr. 11, 1905	Bridgeport, Conn.	Apr. 11, 1904	Do.
James H. Hogan	32	1886	1895	1902		Jersey City, N. J.	Nov. 6, 1905	New Haven, Conn.	Dec. 27, 1904	Do.

a Estimated.

b Formerly Pretolia, 1901.

Domestic Vessels Inspected, Year ended December 31, 1905—Second Supervising District—New Haven, Conn.—Continued.

Names of vessels and class.	Gross tonnage.	Hull built.	Hull rebuilt.	Boilers built.	Boilers rebuilt.	Where built.	Date of inspection.	Where inspected.	Date of previous inspection.	Local district where previously inspected.
Inland towing steamers—Con.										
John Glen	40	1902	....	1902	....	Athens, N. Y	June 2, 1905	Bridgeport, Conn	May 31, 1904	Albany, N. Y.
John P. Randerson	28	1898	....	1898	....	New Baltimore, N. Y.	July 23, 1905	New Haven, Conn	July 23, 1904	New Haven, Conn.
Rambler	53	1882	1894	1894	....	Tottenville, N. Y	Apr. 15, 1905	do	Apr. 30, 1904	New London, Conn.
Stephen E. Babcock	46	1863	1886	1881	....	East Albany, N. Y	June 15, 1905	Bridgeport, Conn	June 18, 1904	New Haven, Conn.
William	33	1859	1899	1883	....	New Brunswick, N. J.	Sept. 25, 1905	New Haven, Conn	Oct. 13, 1904	Do.
Ocean steam pleasure yachts.										
Akela	72	1899	....	1899	....	New York, N. Y	Aug. 18, 1905	Port Jefferson, N. Y.	Aug. 27, 1904	New Haven, Conn.
Lavrock	67	1899	....	1899	....	Port Jefferson, N. Y.	May 4, 1905	do	May 5, 1904	Do.
Llewellyn	92	1895	....	1905	....	Wilmington, Del	do	do	May 30, 1904	Do.
Neckan	66	1894	....	1901	....	Bristol, R. I	May 11, 1905	do	May 17, 1904	Do.
Oneida [a]	141	1883	....	1894	1904	Chester, Pa	Apr. 18, 1905	Greenwich, Conn	Apr. 25, 1904	Do.
Orion [b]	77	1893	1904	1893	1904	Wyandotte, Mich	June 26, 1905	Port Jefferson, N. Y.	July 5, 1904	Do.
Saghaya	98	1900	....	1900	....	Morris Heights, N. Y.	May 4, 1905	do	May 5, 1904	Do.
Surprise	93	1899	....	1899	....	Wilmington, Del	do	do	do	Do.
Zoraya	129	1901	....	1901	....	Port Jefferson, N. Y.	June 8, 1905	do	Aug. 2, 1904	Do.
Inland steam pleasure yachts.										
Apache	21	1893	....	1902	....	East Boston, Mass	July 15, 1905	Stratford, Conn	July 16, 1904	Oswego, N. Y.
Aurelia	16	1886	....	1886	....	South Boston, Mass	July 1, 1905	Bridgeport, Conn	June 18, 1904	New Haven, Conn.
Dorothy	25	1904	....	1903	....	Clinton, Conn	July 21, 1905	New Haven, Conn	July 23, 1904	Do.
Elihu Yale	c5	1902	....	1902	....	Boston, Mass	Mar. 25, 1905	do	Mar. 25, 1904	Do.
Normandie [d]	13	1889	....	1896	....	Middletown, Conn	June 26, 1905	Northport, N. Y	June 19, 1902	Do.
Sea Bird	53	1892	....	1892	....	Boston, Mass	May 25, 1905	Bridgeport, Conn	May 27, 1904	Do.
Miscellaneous steam vessels.										
Active (oyster)	59	1888	....	1888	....	Port Jefferson, N. Y	Sept. 26, 1905	South Norwalk, Conn.	Oct. 7, 1904	New Haven, Conn.
Addie V. (oyster and towing)	21	1885	....	1893	....	Bayville, N. Y	June 12, 1905	do	June 18, 1904	Do.
Alberta (oyster)	23	1883	....	1892	....	Norwalk, Conn	Oct. 17, 1905	do	Nov. 3, 1904	Do.
Amanda (oyster) [e]	74	1882	1904	1891	....	Port Jefferson, N. Y	June 22, 1905	New Haven, Conn	June 20, 1904	Do.
Bond-Currier (oyster)	94	1886	....	1893	....	Stratford, Conn	Sept. 26, 1905	South Norwalk, Conn.	Oct. 7, 1904	Do.
C. B. Lowndes (oyster)	28	1891	....	1905	....	Bridgeport, Conn	May 1, 1905	Bridgeport, Conn	May 3, 1904	Do.
C. S. Conklin (oyster)	52	1881	....	1891	....	South Norwalk, Conn	Oct. 2, 1905	do	Sept. 6, 1904	Do.
Ceres (oyster and towing)	16	1885	....	1900	....	Norwalk, Conn	Sept. 1, 1905	Port Jefferson, N. Y.	Sept. 2, 1904	Do.
Daisy E. Smith (oyster)	69	1881	....	1895	....	New Haven, Conn	Sept. 12, 1905	New Haven, Conn	Sept. 10, 1904	Do.
Dreadnaught (oyster) [f]	81	1868	1888	1888	....	Bristol, R. I	Sept. 26, 1905	South Norwalk, Conn.	Oct. 7, 1904	Do.
Edith A. (oyster)	31	1891	....	1890	....	South Norwalk, Conn	Feb. 16, 1905	do	Feb. 15, 1904	Do.
Edna Chase (oyster)	113	1900	....	1901	....	Northport, N. Y	July 6, 1905	Northport, N. Y	July 5, 1904	Do.

Emily Mansfield (oyster and towing).	94	1883	1904	1891	....	New Haven, Conn....	Oct. 6, 1905	Fair Haven, Conn....	Oct. 12, 1904	New London, Conn.
Enterprise (oyster)	36	1877	1904	1889	....	South Norwalk, Conn.	Mar. 18, 1905	New Haven, Conn....	Mar. 22, 1904	New Haven, Conn.
F. C. and A. E. Rowland (oyster).	96	1884	....	1896	....	Darien, Conn..........	Sept. 2, 1905	Bridgeport, Conn.....	Sept. 17, 1904	Do.
Florence (oyster)	102	1882	1894	1889	....	Setauket, N. Y.......	Feb. 27, 1905	....do...............	Mar. 7, 1904	Do.
Frank E. Brown (oyster)....	18	1902	....	1902	....	Stratford, Conn......	Apr. 10, 1905	New Haven, Conn....	Apr. 11, 1904	Do.
Frank T. Lane (oyster)......	99	1897	....	1891	....	Tottenville, N. Y....	Nov. 6, 1905	....do...............	Nov. 10, 1904	Do.
H. S. Lockwood (oyster).....	52	1884	....	1898	....	South Norwalk, Conn.	Feb. 23, 1905	South Norwalk, Conn.	Feb. 25, 1904	Do.
Henry J. (oyster)............	42	1882	....	1895	....	Norwalk, Conn.......	June 2, 1905	....do...............	June 4, 1904	Do.
Isaac E. Brown (oyster).....	85	1885	....	1897	....	New Haven, Conn....	May 8, 1905	Fairhaven, Conn......	May 7, 1904	Do.
Ithiel (oyster)	31	1889	....	1899	....	Port Jefferson, N. Y..	Sept. 22, 1905	Sound Beach, Conn....	Oct. 6, 1904	Do.
J. Howard Lowndes (oyster).	72	1886	....	1895	....	South Norwalk, Conn.	Apr. 11, 1905	South Norwalk, Conn.	Apr. 12, 1904	Do.
J. P. Thomas (oyster).......	79	1884	....	1894	....	New Haven, Conn....	June 5, 1905	New Haven, Conn....	June 4, 1904	Do.
Jeremiah Smith (oyster and towing).	172	1885	1904	1901	....	West Haven, Conn....	July 29, 1905	....do...............	July 26, 1904	Do.
Jessie Clayton (oyster).......	56	1885	....	1903	....	Norwalk, Conn......	May 1, 1905	South Norwalk, Conn.	May 3, 1904	Do.
Josephine (oyster)...........	126	1885	....	1897	....	Stratford, Conn......	May 26, 1905	....do...............	May 23, 1904	Do.
Laurel (oyster)..............	51	1884	1904	1904	....	South Norwalk, Conn.	Nov. 4, 1905	....do...............	Nov. 10, 1904	New York, N. Y.
Lizzie H. (oyster)...........	34	1882	....	1893	1900	Tottenville, N. Y....	May 26, 1905	....do...............	May 16, 1904	New Haven, Conn.
Lola M. (oyster).............	45	1891	1902	1902	....	....do...............	Sept. 2, 1905	Northport, N. Y.....	Sept. 3, 1904	Do.
Loretto (oyster).............	27	1886	1902	1902	....	Brooklyn, N. Y......	Aug. 11, 1905	Milford, Conn........	Aug. 13, 1904	Do.
Luzerne Ludington (oyster).	74	1885	....	1896	....	New Haven, Conn....	June 17, 1905	Fair Haven, Conn....	June 17, 1904	Providence, R. I.
Mabel L. Stevens (oyster)....	31	1880	1901	1896	....	South Norwalk, Conn.	Mar. 25, 1905	South Norwalk, Conn.	Mar. 25, 1904	New Haven, Conn.
Martha (oyster)..............	16	1900	....	1899	....	Tottenville, N. Y....	Mar. 17, 1905	....do...............	Mar. 17, 1904	Do.
Mikado (oyster)..............	91	1886	....	1890	....	Stratford, Conn......	Aug. 14, 1905	New Haven, Conn....	Aug. 16, 1904	Do.
Mildred (oyster).............	123	1897	....	1897	....	Tottenville, N. Y....	Feb. 16, 1905	South Norwalk, Conn.	Feb. 15, 1904	Do.
Mystery (oyster).............	97	1886	1902	1899	....	....do...............	Mar. 17, 1905	....do...............	Mar. 17, 1904	Do.
Old Colony (oyster and towing).	207	1901	....	1901	....	Bridgeport, Conn.....	Sept. 1, 1905	New Haven, Conn....	Sept. 13, 1904	Do.
Ostrea (oyster)..............	69	1887	....	1887	....	Port Jefferson, N. Y...	June 12, 1905	South Norwalk, Conn.	June 18, 1904	Do.
Pioneer (oyster) [g]............	44	1869	1889	1901	....	East Haven, Conn....	Apr. 22, 1905	New Haven, Conn....	Apr. 22, 1904	Do.
Precursor (oyster and towing). [h]	57	1885	1904	1896	....	New Haven, Conn....	Sept. 1, 1905	Port Jefferson, N. Y..	Sept. 2, 1904	Do.
Ripple (oyster and towing)..	36	1887	....	1887	....	South Norwalk, Conn.	Jan. 12, 1905	South Norwalk, Conn.	Jan. 11, 1904	Do.
Ruel Rowe (oyster)..........	211	1887	1903	1895	....	Stratford, Conn......	May 8, 1905	Fair Haven, Conn....	May 9, 1904	Do.
Russel T. (oyster)...........	31	1900	....	1900	....	Greenport, N. Y......	May 2, 1905	New Haven, Conn....	May 2, 1904	Do.
Smith Bros. (oyster).........	87	1882	1902	1900	....	New Haven, Conn....	Mar. 14, 1905	....do...............	Mar. 14, 1904	Do.
Spark (oyster)...............	15	1875	1894	1905	....	Brooklyn, N. Y......	Apr. 7, 1905	....do...............	Mar. 19, 1904	Do.
Stratford (oyster and towing). [i]	91	1891	....	1892	....	Bridgeport, Conn.....	Aug. 26, 1905	Bridgeport, Conn.....	Aug. 25, 1904	Do.
Virginia (oyster).............	83	1884	1902	1897	....	New Haven, Conn....	Feb. 7, 1905	....do...............	Feb. 8, 1904	Do.
Waneta (oyster)..............	19	1888	....	1898	....	City Island, N. Y.....	Sept. 26, 1905	South Norwalk, Conn.	Oct. 6, 1904	Do.
Wm. A. Cumming (oyster)...	76	1885	....	1885	....	South Norwalk, Conn.	Apr. 17, 1905	Milford, Conn.........	Apr. 14, 1904	Do.
Wm. H. Lockwood (oyster)..	48	1878	....	1902	....	....do...............	Oct. 16, 1905	Fair Haven, Conn....	Nov. 10, 1904	Do.

[a] Formerly Utowana, 1886.
[b] Formerly Sultana, 1904.
[c] Estimated.
[d] Formerly Alert, 1890.
[e] Formerly The Hoyt Bros. Co., 1890.
[f] Formerly Annie, 1895.
[g] Formerly H. A. Stevens, 1891.
[h] Formerly C. W. Hoyt, 1895.
[i] Formerly William H. Hoyt, 1896.

DOMESTIC VESSELS INSPECTED, YEAR ENDED DECEMBER 31, 1905—SECOND SUPERVISING DISTRICT—NEW HAVEN, CONN.—Continued.

Names of vessels and class.	Gross tonnage.	Hull built.	Hull rebuilt.	Boilers built.	Boilers rebuilt.	Where built.	Date of inspection.	Where inspected.	Date of previous inspection.	Local district where previously inspected.
Vessels propelled by gas motors.										
Ada Velma	18	1883				Northport, N. Y.	Apr. 6, 1905	Northport, N. Y.	Jan. 5, 1904	New Haven, Conn.
Caroline Augusta	27	1874	1892			Gravesend, N. Y.	June 23, 1905	Fair Haven, Conn.	June 18, 1904	Do.
Commander	47	1898				Baltimore, Md.	Mar. 17, 1905	South Norwalk, Conn.	Mar. 17, 1904	Do.
Curiosity	44	1894				Patchogue, N. Y.	Apr. 18, 1905	Southport, Conn.	Apr. 18, 1904	Do.
Curlew	23	1866				Eastport, N. Y.	Aug. 26, 1905	Stamford, Conn.	First inspn.	
Edw. F. Leeds	28	1903				Stratford, Conn.	Oct. 2, 1905	Bridgeport, Conn.	Oct. 10, 1904	Do.
Freddie W. Decker[a]	23	1881				Norwalk, Conn.	Oct. 17, 1905	South Norwalk, Conn.	Oct. 22, 1904	Do.
Hattie M. Bird	17	1883				Patchogue, N. Y.	Aug. 26, 1905	Stamford, Conn.	First inspn.	
Helen Stanley	27	1902				Huntington, N. Y.	July 22, 1905	South Norwalk, Conn.	July 21, 1904	Do.
Herman L. Rogers	26	1889				Stony Brook, N. Y.	Oct. 24, 1905	Cos Cob, Conn.	First inspn.	
Jessie R.	30	1896	1897			Patchogue, N. Y.	Feb. 7, 1905	New Haven, Conn.	Feb. 15, 1904	New London, Conn.
Kansas City	18	1881	1900			Greenport, N. Y.	Nov. 21, 1905	Fair Haven, Conn.	Nov. 22, 1904	New Haven, Conn.
Lena S.	18	1898				Northport, N. Y.	Aug. 26, 1905	South Norwalk, Conn.	Aug. 25, 1904	Do.
Mary E. Suydam	38	1868	1895			do	Aug. 31, 1905	Fair Haven, Conn.	Sept. 2, 1904	New York, N. Y.
Medora Fisher	66	1887	1898			South River, N. J.	Aug. 12, 1905	Stratford, Conn.	First inspn.	
Samuel Chard	22	1901				Greenwich, Conn.	Aug. 26, 1905	Greenwich, Conn.	Aug. 26, 1904	New Haven, Conn.
Stranger	40	1904				Tottenville, N. Y.	Oct. 11, 1905	New Haven, Conn.	Nov. 7, 1904	Do.
Sylvester Decker	26	1903				Bridgeport, Conn.	May 16, 1905	South Norwalk, Conn.	May 16, 1904	Do.
X-Ray	32	1898				do	Nov. 13, 1905	Fair Haven, Conn.	Nov. 25, 1904	Do.
Freight sail vessels of over 700 tons.										
Estelle Phinney (schooner)	922	1891				New London, Conn.	Jan. 11, 1905	New Haven, Conn.	Dec. 22, 1903	Norfolk, Va.
Massasoit (schooner)	1,377	1889				Bath, Me.	June 10, 1905	do	June 2, 1904	New Haven, Conn.
William E. Downes (schooner)	753	1885				do	Jan. 16, 1905	do	Feb. 15, 1904	Savannah, Ga.

THIRD SUPERVISING DISTRICT.

LOCAL DISTRICT OF NORFOLK, VA.

Names of vessels and class.	Gross tonnage.	Hull built.	Hull rebuilt.	Boilers built.	Boilers rebuilt.	Where built.	Date of inspection.	Where inspected.	Date of previous inspection.	Local district where previously inspected.
Ocean passenger steamers.										
Hamilton	3,127	1899		1899		Chester, Pa.	Mar. 18, 1905	Newport News, Va.	Mar. 21, 1904	Norfolk, Va.
Princess Anne	3,078	1897		1897		do	Aug. 24, 1905	do	July 15, 1904	New York, N. Y.
Powhatan	2,898	1894		1905		do	Oct. 28, 1905	do	Aug. 2, 1904	Baltimore, Md.
Richmond	401	1899		1900		Philadelphia, Pa.	Jan. 13, 1905	do	Jan. 11, 1904	Providence, R. I.

Inland passenger steamers.										
Acomack	434	1877	....	1895	....	Brooklyn, N. Y.	Mar. 6, 1905	Norfolk, Va.	Mar. 21, 1904	Norfolk, Va.
Alma	165	1901	....	1901	....	Fairfield, N. C.	May 31, 1905	Elizabeth City, N. C.	May 28, 1904	Do.
Amanda Moore	121	1900	....	1897	....	Scranton, Miss.	June 8, 1905	Norfolk, Va.	June 9, 1904	Apalachicola, Fla.
Albermarle	509	1891	1898	1891	....	Wilmington, Del.	July 21, 1905	....do	Sept. 8, 1904	Norfolk, Va.
Aurora	98	1894	....	1894	....	Washington, N. C.	Sept. 28, 1905	....do	Sept. 27, 1904	Do.
Arm & Hammer	39	1883	1894	1898	....	Brooklyn, N. Y.	Nov. 13, 1905	Edenton, N. C.	Nov. 25, 1904	Do.
Brandon	1,062	1902	....	1901	....	Wilmington, Del.	Jan. 5, 1905	Norfolk, Va.	Jan. 7, 1904	Do.
Berkeley	1,075	1902	....	1902	....	Richmond, Va.	May 8, 1905	Newport News, Va.	May 31, 1904	Do.
Blanche	97	1883	1902	1887	....	Newbern, N. C.	July 6, 1905	Newbern, N. C.	July 6, 1904	Do.
Crescent	33	1896	....	1896	....	Bridgeton, N. J.	June 2, 1905	Norfolk, Va.	May 27, 1904	Do.
C. W. Ridley	10	1894	....	1897	....	Alexandria, Va.	Aug. 25, 1905	....do	Aug. 25, 1904	Do.
Comet	96	1887	1896	1897	....	Baltimore, Md.	Oct. 14, 1905	Berkley, Va.	Oct. 1, 1904	Do.
Delmar	294	1900	....	1900	....	Newburg, N. Y.	Mar. 28, 1905	Norfolk, Va.	Apr. 6, 1904	Do.
Endeavor	315	1896	....	1902	....	Philadelphia, Pa.	May 29, 1905	Newport News, Va.	Mar. 17, 1904	Baltimore, Md.
Frances	80	1893	....	1901	....	Sparrow Point, Md.	Feb. 28, 1905	Norfolk, Va.	Feb. 27, 1904	Do.
Fannie	4	1899	....	1903	....	New York, N. Y.	July 12, 1905	....do	July 7, 1904	Norfolk, Va.
Guide	174	1885	1900	1897	....	Oswego, N. Y.	July 3, 1905	....do	June 27, 1904	Do.
Hustler	29	1875	1893	1904	....	Baltimore, Md.	Mar. 31, 1905	....do	Mar. 16, 1904	Do.
Hampton	580	1901	....	1901	....	Elizabethport, N. J.	Apr. 29, 1905	....do	Mar. 10, 1904	Do.
Hampton Roads	450	1896	....	1904	....	Wilmington, Del.	May 3, 1905	....do	Apr. 29, 1904	Do.
Helen	113	1897	....	1897	....	....do	May 8, 1905	Newport News, Va.	Apr. 25, 1904	Do.
Hatteras	276	1896	....	1882	....	Eddysville, N. Y.	May 11, 1905	Washington, N. C.	May 12, 1904	Do.
Harbinger	54	1869	1900	1897	....	Baltimore, Md.	May 19, 1905	Elizabeth City, N. C.	Mar. 22, 1904	Do.
Haven Belle	106	1885	1896	1885	....	Philadelphia, Pa.	May 31, 1905	Norfolk, Va.	May 9, 1904	Do.
Howard	70	1887	....	1900	....	Newbern, N. C.	July 6, 1905	Newbern, N. C.	July 6, 1904	Do.
Hertford [b]	287	1869	1903	1892	....	Norfolk, Va.	Nov. 1, 1905	Franklin, Va.	Nov. 14, 1904	Do.
Juniper	23	1873	1903	1900	....	....do	Nov. 22, 1905	Berkley, Va.	Nov. 15, 1904	Do.
Katie	89	1892	....	1896	....	Baltimore, Md.	Sept. 5, 1905	Norfolk, Va.	Sept. 1, 1904	Do.
Keystone	168	1875	....	1875	....	Norfolk, Va.	Oct. 21, 1905	Franklin, Va.	Oct. 21, 1904	Do.
Luray	423	1882	....	1901	....	Brooklyn, N. Y.	May 9, 1905	Norfolk, Va.	May 3, 1904	Do.
Lucy	116	1872	....	1884	....	Norfolk, Va.	Oct. 19, 1905	Berkley, Va.	Dec. 8, 1904	Do.
Louisville [c]	87	1883	....	1892	....	Philadelphia, Pa.	Nov. 21, 1905	Norfolk, Va.	Oct. 28, 1904	Do.
Martha E. Dickerman	162	1883	....	1889	....	Norfolk, Va.	May 10, 1905	Edenton, N. C.	May 9, 1904	Do.
Mobjack	610	1899	....	1899	....	Newburg, N. Y.	May 28, 1905	Norfolk, Va.	June 13, 1904	Do.
Mayflower	93	1894	....	1894	....	Philadelphia, Pa.	Aug. 7, 1905	Edenton, N. C.	Aug. 5, 1904	Do.
Memphis [d]	177	1872	1902	1898	....	Chester, Pa.	Aug. 30, 1905	Norfolk, Va.	Aug. 26, 1904	Do.
New York	785	1889	....	1903	....	Wilmington, Del.	Jan. 9, 1905	....do	Jan. 11, 1904	Do.
Nita	40	1898	....	1898	....	Norfolk, Va.	Apr. 21, 1905	....do	Apr. 21, 1904	Do.
Norman L. Wagner	196	1882	....	1896	....	Canajoharie, N. Y.	Apr. 28, 1905	Edenton, N. C.	Apr. 22, 1904	Do.
Nanticoke	458	1875	1899	1899	....	Wilmington, Del.	Oct. 6, 1905	Elizabeth City, N. C.	Sept. 27, 1904	Do.
Neuse	720	1890	....	1905	....	....do	Oct. 31, 1905	Newport News, Va.	Nov. 5, 1904	Do.
Nettie	85	1896	....	1902	....	Berkley, Va.	Nov. 17, 1905	Norfolk, Va.	Nov. 29, 1904	Do.
Old Point Comfort	643	1886	....	1886	1901	Wilmington, Del.	Jan. 19, 1905	....do	Jan. 25, 1904	Do.
Ora	[e] 4	1903	....	1878	....	Winton, N. C.	Feb. 6, 1905	Winton, N. C.	Feb. 2, 1904	Do.
Ocracoke	421	1898	....	1898	....	Tottenville, N. Y.	June 26, 1905	Elizabeth City, N. C.	July 1, 1904	Do.
Old Point Comfort	643	1886	....	1886	1901	Wilmington, Del.	Dec. 9, 1905	Norfolk, Va.	Jan. 19, 1904	Do.
Pennsylvania	1,352	1900	....	1899	....	Chester, Pa.	Jan. 24, 1905	Newport News, Va.	Feb. 13, 1904	Do.
Plymouth	273	1883	1900	1883	....	Norfolk, Va.	Mar. 21, 1905	Edenton, N. C.	Mar. 7, 1904	Do.

[a] Changed from steamer, 1902. [b] Formerly Olive, 1903. [c] Formerly Thomas A. Bain, 1900. [d] Formerly City of Chester, 1900. [e] Estimated.

DOMESTIC VESSELS INSPECTED, YEAR ENDED DECEMBER 31, 1905—THIRD SUPERVISING DISTRICT—NORFOLK, VA.—Continued.

Names of vessels and class.	Gross tonnage.	Hull built.	Hull rebuilt.	Boilers built.	Boilers rebuilt.	Where built.	Date of inspection.	Where inspected.	Date of previous inspection.	Local district where previously inspected.
Island passenger steamers—Continued.										
Piedmont [a]	90	1892		1903		Baltimore, Md.	May 23, 1905	Norfolk, Va.	May 23, 1904	Norfolk, Va.
Pine Beach [b]	291	1881		1895		New York, N. Y.	June 14, 1905	do.	July 8, 1904	Do.
Pinners Point	63	1891		1891		Philadelphia, Pa.	Oct. 2, 1905	Berkley, Va.	Oct. 5, 1904	Do.
Pocahontas	814	1893		1902		Wilmington, Del.	Oct. 22, 1905	Richmond, Va.	Nov. 16, 1904	Philadelphia, Pa.
Philadelphia [c]	87	1883		1883		Philadelphia, Pa.	Nov. 2, 1905	Norfolk, Va.	Nov. 21, 1904	Norfolk, Va.
Pamlico	40	1898		1898		Norfolk, Va.	Nov. 15, 1905	Edenton, N. C.	Dec. 8, 1904	Do.
Pioneer	45	1891		1900		Berkley, Va.	Dec. 4, 1905	Norfolk, Va.	Dec. 3, 1904	Do.
R. L. Myers	128	1885		1879		Washington, N. C.	Oct. 30, 1905	Washington, N. C.	Nov. 9, 1904	Do.
Shiloh	84	1895		1895		Tarboro, N. C.	Dec. 16, 1904	Tarboro, N. C.	Dec. 9, 1903	Do.
Sophie Wood	28	1891		1892		East Lake, N. C.	Jan. 18, 1905	Washington, N. C.	Jan. 18, 1904	Do.
Salisbury [d]	284	1900		1900		Camden, N. J.	May 29, 1905	Newport News, Va.	June 1, 1904	Do.
S. J. Phillips	77	1902		1901		Newbern, N. C.	Nov. 7, 1905	Newbern, N. C.	Nov. 16, 1904	Do.
Shiloh	84	1895		1895		Tarboro, N. C.	Dec. 13, 1905	Tarboro, N. C.	Dec. 16, 1904	Do.
Thomas Newton	47	1881	1903	1896		Norfolk, Va.	May 19, 1905	Elizabeth City, N. C.	June 4, 1904	Do.
Tourist	284	1894		1894		Nyack, N. Y.	June 12, 1905	Norfolk, Va.	June 13, 1904	Do.
Thomas Cunningham, sr	70	1895		1895		Philadelphia, Pa.	Oct. 2, 1905	Richmond, Va.	Oct. 6, 1904	Do.
Teddie	80	1892		1890		Oneida, N. Y.	Oct. 5, 1905	Portsmouth, Va.	Oct. 11, 1904	Do.
Undine	42	1872		1902		Pettys Island, N. J.	May 20, 1905	Norfolk, Va.	May 17, 1904	Do.
Uneeda [e]	16	1888		1898	1903	Haddam, Conn.	Aug. 29, 1905	do.	Aug. 29, 1904	Do.
Virginia	635	1902		1902		Richmond, Va.	Feb. 11, 1905	Newport News, Va.	Feb. 8, 1904	Do.
Volunteer	79	1894		1894		Philadelphia, Pa.	Aug. 1, 1905	Norfolk, Va.	July 29, 1904	Do.
Virginia Dare	187	1888		1888		Wilmington, Del.	Sept. 25, 1905	do.	Sept. 6, 1904	Do.
Wanderer	108	1890	1897	1891	1905	do.	Apr. 19, 1905	Newport News, Va.	Dec. 4, 1904	Do.
Winthrop	39	1901		1901		Winthrop, N. C.	July 6, 1905	Newbern, N. C.	July 6, 1904	Do.
William H. Philips	103	1881		1881		Norfolk, Va.	Aug. 23, 1905	Berkley, Va.	Aug. 29, 1904	Do.
Ferry steamers.										
City of Portsmouth	457	1888		1888		Wilmington, Del.	July 27, 1905	Portsmouth, Va.	July 30, 1904	Norfolk, Va.
Elizabeth	297	1871		1890		Portsmouth, Va.	Jan. 21, 1905	do.	Jan. 22, 1904	Do.
John W. Garrett	1,343	1887		1887		Wilmington, Del.	Nov. 18, 1905	Edenton, N. C.	Nov. 25, 1904	Do.
Norfolk County [g]	819	1891		1891		East Boston, Mass.	Aug. 30, 1905	Portsmouth, Va.	Aug. 26, 1904	Do.
Ocean View [h]	159	1894		1897	1904	Newburg, N. Y.	July 21, 1905	Norfolk, Va.	Aug. 13, 1904	Do.
Superior	570	1862		1872		New York, N. Y.	Feb. 26, 1905	Portsmouth, Va.	Feb. 25, 1904	Do.
Twin City	292	1894		1894		Berkley, Va.	May 12, 1905	do.	May 12, 1904	Do.
Ocean freight steamers.										
Kanawha	2,182	1902		1902		Port Huron, Mich.	May 2, 1905	Newport News, Va.	May 4, 1904	Chicago, Ill.
Kennebec	2,183	1901		1901		do.	do.	do.	May 7, 1904	Do.
Massachusetts	7,913	1902		1901		Camden, N. J.	July 22, 1905	do.	Jan. 30, 1903	Philadelphia, Pa.

Inland freight steamers.										
Aunt Sue	37	1904		1883		Newbern, N. C	Jan. 24, 1905	Newbern, N. C	Jan. 22, 1904	Norfolk, Va.
Adelle	46	1904		1895		do	Nov. 7, 1905	do	Dec. 21, 1904	Do.
Belvidere	29	1896		1896		Hertford, N. C	Aug. 22, 1905	Hertford, N. C	Aug. 18, 1904	Do.
Carolina	79	1893		1884		Vanceboro, N. C	Jan. 24, 1905	Newbern, N. C	Nov. 13, 1903	Do.
Dennis Simmons	199	1891		1904		Wilmington, Del	June 30, 1905	Norfolk, Va	June 28, 1904	Baltimore, Md.
Ellen S	57	1904		1904		Newbern, N. C	Nov. 7, 1905	Newbern, N. C	Dec. 14, 1904	Norfolk, Va.
Goldsboro	99	1901		1900		Washington, N. C	Jan. 24, 1905	do	Jan. 22, 1904	Do.
Ghio	123	1901		1901		do	Apr. 29, 1905	Edenton, N. C	Apr. 22, 1904	Do.
Julian S. Taylor	262	1893		1893		Madison, Md	May 2, 1905	Norfolk, Va	Apr. 23, 1904	Do.
Jefferson	36	1900		1891		Norfolk, Va	May 27, 1905	Berkley, Va	May 27, 1904	Do.
L. H. Cutler	42	1882		1898		Swift Creek, N. C	Mar. 29, 1905	Newbern, N. C	Jan. 22, 1904	Do.
Lydia	9	1880		1898		Elizabeth City, N. C	Aug. 22, 1905	Hertford, N. C	Aug. 18, 1904	Do.
May Bell	92	1892	1901	1902		Grafton, N. C	Nov. 14, 1905	Newbern, N. C	Oct. 24, 1904	Do.
Mattamuskeet	29	1897		1896		Fairfield, N. C	Nov. 28, 1905	do	Nov. 16, 1904	Do.
Newberne	482	1875		1893		Chester, Pa	Mar. 6, 1905	Elizabeth City, N. C	Mar. 5, 1904	Do.
Nina	39	1897		1901		Swansboro, N. C	Oct. 31, 1905	do	Oct. 27, 1904	Do.
Sara Louise	63	1904		1903		Newbern, N. C	Jan. 24, 1905	Newbern, N. C	Jan. 22, 1904	Do.
Transfer	102	1882		1881		Greenpoint, N. Y	Jan. 23, 1905	Norfolk, Va	Jan. 28, 1904	New York, N. Y.
Tarboro	72	1898		1898		Tarboro, N. C	Nov. 13, 1905	Tarboro, N. C	Nov. 22, 1904	Norfolk, Va.
Uncle Sam	80	1900		1881		Newbern, N. C	Feb. 21, 1905	Newbern, N. C	Feb. 19, 1904	Do.
Virginia F. Hawley	115	1871		1905		Havre de Grace, Md	May 22, 1905	Berkley, Va	First inspn	
Windber [i]	2,441	1889	1905	1889		West Hartlepool, England.	June 28, 1905	Newport News, Va	do	
Ocean towing steamers.										
Asher J. Hudson	136	1891		1900		Camden, N. J	Feb. 10, 1905	Norfolk, Va	Feb. 11, 1904	Norfolk, Va.
Boswell [j]	311	1890		1900		do	Oct. 31, 1905	do	Oct. 28, 1904	Do.
Covington	401	1900		1900		Philadelphia, Pa	Nov. 4, 1905	Newport News, Va	Nov. 23, 1904	Do
Edward Luckenbach	401	1899		1899		do	Jan. 10, 1905	Norfolk, Va	Dec. 31, 1903	Do
Murrell [k]	311	1890		1890	1903	Camden, N. J	Oct. 7, 1905	do	Oct. 12, 1904	Do.
Paul Jones	945	1903		1902		New London, Conn	Dec. 18, 1905	Newport News, Va	Dec. 17, 1904	New London, Conn.
Richmond	401	1899		1900		Philadelphia, Pa	Dec. 27, 1905	do	Jan. 13, 1905	Norfolk, Va.
Inland towing steamers.										
Anita	45	1873	1898	1898		Baltimore, Md	Jan. 23, 1905	Norfolk, Va	Jan. 18, 1904	Norfolk, Va.
Allie	7	1888	1902	1888		Newbern, N. C	Apr. 18, 1905	Newbern, N. C	Apr. 8, 1904	Do.
Apollo	105	1895		1895		Baltimore, Md	May 2, 1905	Norfolk, Va	May 3, 1904	Do.
Anna	39	1890	1902	1902		Berkley, Va	May 20, 1905	do	May 16, 1904	Do
Alma	17	1904		1905		Manchester, Va	Aug. 4, 1905	Manchester, Va	First inspn	
Albatross	15	1901		1904		Belhaven, N. C	Sept. 6, 1905	Washington, N. C	Sept. 9, 1904	Do.
Armorica	30	1885		1885		Glenwood, N. Y	Sept. 28, 1905	Norfolk, Va	Sept. 22, 1904	Do.
Albemarle	75	1889		1890		Norfolk, Va	Oct. 28, 1905	Berkley, Va	Nov. 21, 1904	Do.
Alice	72	1902		1902		Baltimore, Md	Oct. 3, 1905	Norfolk, Va	Oct. 1, 1904	Do.
A. B. Covington	56	1893		1903		Washington, N. C	Nov. 15, 1905	do	Nov. 29, 1904	Do.
Bruce	10	1898		1903		do	Apr. 12, 1905	Washington, N. C	Apr. 6, 1904	Do.

[a] Formerly Mary E. Woodall, 1895.
[b] Formerly Belle Horton, 1902.
[c] Formerly W. H. Jackson, 1889.
[d] Formerly Abram Minis, 1903.
[e] Formerly Doc B, 1903.
[f] Estimated.
[g] Formerly U. S. S. East Boston. 1899.
[h] Formerly Vigilant, 1899.
[i] Formerly Daventry, 1905.
[j] Formerly N. & W. 2, 1903.
[k] Formerly N. & W. 1, 1903.

Domestic Vessels Inspected, Year ended December 31, 1905—Third Supervising District—Norfolk, Va.—Continued.

Names of vessels and class.	Gross tonnage.	Hull built.	Hull rebuilt.	Boilers built.	Boilers rebuilt.	Where built.	Date of inspection.	Where inspected.	Date of previous inspection.	Local district where previously inspected.
Inland towing steamers—Con.										
Bel Virginia	29	1873	1895	1896		Berkley, Va	May 11, 1905	Washington, N. C	May 12, 1904	Norfolk, Va.
Bramble	11	1879		1888		Baltimore, Md	July 18, 1905	Norfolk, Va	First inspn	
Boyd	a 3	1903		1881		Chester, Va	Aug. 28, 1905	Richmond, Va	Aug. 5, 1904	Do.
Barney	19	1893		1893		Washington, N. C	Oct. 30, 1905	Washington, N. C	Nov. 9, 1904	Do.
Conqueror	18	1890		1899		Brooklyn, N. Y	Jan. 4, 1905	Norfolk, Va	Dec. 31, 1903	Do.
Carolina	30	1867		1902		Richmond, Va	Jan. 13, 1905	Berkley, Va	Dec. 28, 1904	Do.
Chowan	33	1862	1883	1893		Philadelphia, Pa	Feb. 17, 1905	do	Feb. 15, 1904	Do.
Carrie X	8	1893		1904		Washington, D. C	Mar. 8, 1905	Stonewall, N. C	Mar. 23, 1904	Do.
Clay Foreman	35	1902		1892		Elizabeth City, N. C	Apr. 3, 1905	Elizabeth City, N. C	Apr. 2, 1904	Do.
Col. J. C. Hill	11	1880	1903	1904		Baltimore, Md	do	Norfolk, Va	Apr. 1, 1904	Do.
Croatan	22	1864	1895	1883		Chester, Pa	Sept. 21, 1905	Berkley, Va	Aug. 29, 1904	Do.
Clara A. McIntyre	44	1874	1892	1904		Buffalo, N. Y	Sept. 26, 1905	Elizabeth City, N. C	Sept. 26, 1904	Do.
Crisfield	236	1903		1903		Sparrow Point, Md	Sept. 27, 1905	Newport News, Va	Oct. 10, 1904	Do.
Dorothea	79	1893		1893		do	Mar. 10, 1905	Portsmouth, Va	Feb. 29, 1904	Do.
D. K. Neal	37	1873	1904	1904		Mystic, Conn	Mar. 25, 1905	Elizabeth City, N. C	Mar. 24, 1904	Do.
Dewey	9	1900		1900		Portsmouth, Va	Aug. 18, 1905	Williamsburg, Va	June 2, 1904	Do.
De Boss Lennox	13	1874	1899	1902		Bordentown, N. J	Sept. 19, 1905	Norfolk, Va	Sept. 19, 1904	Do.
Dauntless	11	1890		1904		Berkley, Va	Oct. 10, 1905	do	Oct. 11, 1904	Do.
E. V. McCaulley	136	1887		1900		Camden, N. J	Jan. 26, 1905	do	Dec. 19, 1903	Do.
Emiley B	13	1902		1905		Norfolk, Va	Feb. 21, 1905	do	Feb. 16, 1904	Do.
Eliza Blackwell	27	1905		1905		Portsmouth, Va	Apr. 6, 1905	do	First inspn	
E. W. Marts	27	1892		1903		Baltimore, Md	May 12, 1905	Belhaven, N. C	May 13, 1904	Do.
Emma	27	1885		1885		Portsmouth, Va	May 18, 1905	Franklin, Va	May 16, 1904	Do.
Elena	46	1889		1889		Pettys Island, N. Y	June 28, 1905	Yorkville, Va	June 9, 1904	Do.
E. B. Lane, jr	32	1890		1902		Norfolk, Va	Aug. 22, 1905	Norfolk, Va	Aug. 20, 1904	Do.
Edmund Parkin	34	1898		1898		Newbern, N. C	Sept. 19, 1905	Newbern, N. C	Sept. 19, 1904	Do.
Edward P. Avery	11	1876		1890		Fair Haven, Conn	Dec. 1, 1905	Norfolk, Va	Nov. 28, 1904	Do.
Fannie M. Gilbert	26	1876		1894	1904	Georgetown, D. C	Apr. 20, 1905	do	Apr. 15, 1904	Do.
Florence	20	1896		1903		Washington, N. C	Sept. 5, 1905	Washington, N. C	Sept. 9, 1904	Do.
Grace Titus	42	1863	1902	1898		Philadelphia, Pa	Feb. 17, 1905	Berkley, Va	Feb. 17, 1904	Do.
Glide	30	1881		1891		Bordentown, N. J	Apr. 12, 1905	Washington, N. C	Apr. 6, 1904	Do.
Glendale	21	1898		1899		Turkey Island, Va	May 11, 1905	Norfolk, Va	May 9, 1904	Do.
Grit	31	1888		1888		City Island, N. Y	May 23, 1905	do	May 21, 1904	Do.
General G. Mott	48	1881		1892		Bordentown, N. J	June 5, 1905	do	June 6, 1904	Philadelphia, Pa.
G. F. Derickson	27	1894	1904	1902		Elizabeth City, N. C	June 26, 1905	Elizabeth City, N. C	June 23, 1904	Norfolk, Va.
Germania	73	1892		1892		Sparrow Point, Md	Nov. 15, 1905	Norfolk, Va	Nov. 21, 1904	Do.
Hinton	90	1883		1903		Philadelphia, Pa	Dec. 9, 1905	Newport News, Va	Dec. 2, 1904	Do.
Ida	a 3	1901		1901		Berkley, Va	Oct. 11, 1905	Norfolk, Va	Oct. 2, 1904	Do.
Ida	30	1893		1893		do	Oct. 30, 1905	Franklin, Va	Oct. 31, 1904	Do.
J. W. Branning	31	1894		1889		Portsmouth, Va	Apr. 4, 1905	Edenton, N. C	Apr. 4, 1904	Do.
J. Alvah Clark	43	1873		1896		Philadelphia, Pa	July 26, 1905	Norfolk, Va	July 9, 1904	Do.
Joseph M. Clark	93	1899		1899		Baltimore, Md	Oct. 7, 1905	do	Oct. 6, 1904	Do.

Julian J. Fleetwood	42	1896		1905		Hertford, N. C.	Oct. 11, 1905	Hertford, N. C.	Oct. 11, 1904	Do.
John Taxis	22	1869	1893	1903		Chester, Pa.	Oct. 14, 1905	Norfolk, Va.	Oct. 18, 1904	Do.
Julia	7	1896		1896		Newbern, N. C.	Nov. 14, 1905	Newbern, N. C.	Nov. 16, 1904	Do.
James Smith, jr.[b]	170	1874		1898		Newburg, N. Y.	Nov. 29, 1905	Newport News, Va.	Oct. 19, 1904	Do.
Juliette W. Murray	56	1895		1894		Portsmouth, Va.	Dec. 8, 1905	Norfolk, Va.	Nov. 29, 1904	Do.
Keystone	9	1872		1900		Alexandria, Va.	May 4, 1905	Claremont, Va.	May 5, 1904	Do.
Lucile	19	1899		1898		Berkley, Va.	Mar. 1, 1905	Berkley, Va.	Feb. 24, 1904	Do.
Lillie	53	1883	1890	1901		Canajoharie, N. Y.	Mar. 8, 1905	Newbern, N. C.	Jan. 15, 1902	Do.
Louise	18	1896		1901		Petersburg, Va.	Mar. 13, 1905	Norfolk, Va.	Mar. 9, 1904	Do.
Lumberman	13	1869	1900	1897		Philadelphia, Pa.	Apr. 3, 1905	....do	Apr. 1, 1904	Do.
Lizzie Blades	7	1897		1882		Newbern, N. C.	July 6, 1905	Newbern, N. C.	July 6, 1904	Do.
Lucile Ross	49	1893		1893		Baltimore, Md.	July 21, 1905	Richmond, Va.	July 25, 1904	Do.
Lena Virginia	21	1900		1890		Washington, N. C.	Aug. 9, 1905	Washington, N. C.	Aug. 8, 1904	Do.
Lillie S.	10	1900		1904		New York, N. Y.	Oct. 12, 1905	City Point, Va.	Oct. 13, 1904	Do.
Lillian	18	1905		1899		Elizabeth City, N. C.	Nov. 20, 1905	Winton, N. C.	May 4, 1904	Do.
Lamberts Point[c]	16	1867		1894		Philadelphia, Pa.	Nov. 29, 1905	Elizabeth City, N. C.	Nov. 18, 1904	Do.
Maggie J. Jory	20	1882		1890		Baltimore, Md.	Apr. 8, 1905	Berkley, Va.	Jan. 9, 1904	Do.
Mollie L. Farmer	21	1890		1898		Bethel, N. C.	May 3, 1905	Newbern, N. C.	Apr. 27, 1904	Do.
Maud	9	1894		1894		Richmond, Va.	May 10, 1905	Richmond, Va.	....do	Do.
Mary E. Roberts	91	1873		1884		Chowan, N. C.	May 28, 1905	Berkley, Va.	May 28, 1904	Do.
May Russell	37	1893		1893		Baltimore, Md.	July 8, 1905	Belhaven, N. C.	July 9, 1904	Do.
Mollie	12	1887		1889		Berkley, Va.	July 29, 1905	Norfolk, Va.	July 18, 1904	Do.
Mary Lee	48	1905		1905		Turkey Island, Va.	Aug. 11, 1905	Petersburg, Va.	First inspn.	
Mary Steel	79	1904		1904		Wilmington, Del.	Sept. 15, 1905	Richmond, Va.	Sept. 12, 1904	Do.
Mary & Joseph	25	1885		1899		Berkley, Va.	Sept. 21, 1905	Norfolk, Va.	Sept. 24, 1904	Do.
Malvern Hill	34	1900		1900		Turkey Island, Va.	Nov. 1, 1905	Petersburg, Va.	Nov. 7, 1904	Do.
Marietta	40	1891		1905		Berkley, Va.	Nov. 4, 1905	Berkley, Va.	Oct. 4, 1904	Do.
Mary Belo	9	1904		1882	1904	Newbern, N. C.	Nov. 7, 1905	Newbern, N. C.	Oct. 19, 1904	Do.
Margarette	22	1903		1902		Elizabeth City, N. C.	....do	....do	Nov. 16, 1904	Do.
Mutual	32	1900		1900		Pocomoke City, Md.	Nov. 11, 1905	Norfolk, Va.	Nov. 12, 1904	Do.
Norfolk	211	1895		1903		Wilmington, Del.	Feb. 16, 1905	....do	Feb. 16, 1904	Do.
Norman	30	1901		1896		Elizabeth City, N. C.	Apr. 12, 1905	Washington, N. C.	May 2, 1904	Do.
N. W. A. Cobb	25	1869	1895	1895		Norfolk, Va.	Sept. 16, 1905	Richmond, Va.	Sept. 15, 1904	Do.
Nautilus	46	1899		1899		Washington, N. C.	Dec. 9, 1904	Washington, N. C.	Oct. 15, 1903	Do.
Nautilus	46	1899		1899		....do	Nov. 27, 1905	....do	Dec. 9, 1904	Do.
Pocahontas	94	1888		1902		Camden, N. J.	Feb. 8, 1905	Norfolk, Va.	Jan. 28, 1904	Do.
Powhatan	11	1903		1897		Port Walthall, Va.	Mar. 28, 1905	....do	Jan. 29, 1904	Do.
Petrel	5	1897		1901		Marcushook, Pa.	Oct. 5, 1905	Tunis, N. C.	Oct. 4, 1904	Do.
Portsmouth	214	1886		1903		Wilmington, Del.	Oct. 26, 1905	Norfolk, Va.	Dec. 19, 1904	Do.
Protector	40	1899		1901		Norfolk, Va.	Nov. 4, 1905	....do	Dec. 3, 1904	Do.
Powhatan	56	1898		1897		Pocomoke City, Md.	Nov. 6, 1905	Hampton, Va.	Nov. 11, 1904	Do.
Reliance	75	1881	1888	1888		Camden, N. J.	Jan. 31, 1905	Norfolk, Va.	Jan. 30, 1904	Do.
Rambler	34	1873	1902	1892		Baltimore, Md.	Oct. 18, 1905	....do	Oct. 19, 1904	Do.
Spring Garden	23	1874		1898		Camden, N. J.	Jan. 28, 1905	....do	Jan. 21, 1904	Do.
Sallie	25	1889		1894		Baltimore, Md.	Mar. 22, 1905	....do	Mar. 4, 1904	Do.
Surry	5	1898		1898	1901	Alexandria, Va.	May 4, 1905	Claremont, Va.	May 5, 1904	Do.
Swan	24	1890	1905	1897		Newbern, N. C.	July 6, 1905	Newbern, N. C.	Mar. 7, 1903	Do.
Samuel Eccles, jr.	41	1887		1896		Hertford, N. C.	Oct. 19, 1905	Berkley, Va.	Nov. 21, 1904	Do.
South Baltimore	15	1872	1904	1904		Buffalo, N. Y.	Nov. 25, 1905	Hampton, Va.	Nov. 29, 1904	Do.
Teaser	21	1896		1895		Berkley, Va.	June 30, 1905	Norfolk, Va.	June 29, 1904	Do.
Vanceboro	61	1888	1903	1905		Vanceboro, N. C.	July 7, 1905	Morehead City, N. C.	July 6, 1904	Do.

[a] Estimated. [b] Formerly Manhattan, 1898. [c] Formerly U. S. life-saving launch Sagadahoc.

DOMESTIC VESSELS INSPECTED, YEAR ENDED DECEMBER 31, 1905—THIRD SUPERVISING DISTRICT—NORFOLK, VA.—Continued.

Names of vessels and class.	Gross tonnage.	Hull built.	Hull rebuilt.	Boilers built.	Boilers rebuilt.	Where built.	Date of inspection.	Where inspected.	Date of previous inspection.	Local district where previously inspected.
Inland towing steamers—Con.										
Virginia	59	1860	1896	1897		Philadelphia, Pa	Sept. 21, 1905	Berkley, Va	Sept. 22, 1904	Norfolk, Va.
Viola	9	1886	1896	1896		Delawanna, N. J	Dec. 16, 1904	Washington, N. C	Dec. 17, 1903	Do.
William B. Blades, jr	62	1902		1901		Newbern, N. C	Apr. 18, 1905	Newbern, N. C	Apr. 27, 1904	Do.
Willard	35	1892		1892		Portsmouth, Va	Apr. 20, 1905	Norfolk, Va	Apr. 11, 1904	Do.
W. F. Taylor	38	1867	1903	1897		Richmond, Va	Sept. 5, 1905	Washington, N. C	Sept. 9, 1904	Do.
Wrestler [a]	19	1870		1903		Buffalo, N. Y	Oct. 10, 1905	Norfolk, Va	Oct. 10, 1904	Do.
W. W. Graham	29	1883	1905	1890	1905	Philadelphia, Pa	Nov. 22, 1905	do	July 19, 1904	Do.
Yeopim	15	1881		1899		Drummond Point, N. C.	Apr. 5, 1905	Hertford, N. C	Apr. 11, 1904	Do.
Ocean steam pleasure yacht.										
Marjorie	40	1894		1904		Bristol, R. I	May 13, 1905	Norfolk, Va	May 26, 1904	Baltimore, Md.
Inland steam pleasure yachts.										
Cyrene	10	1882	1895	1902		Astoria, N. Y	Feb. 1, 1905	Norfolk, Va	Feb. 1, 1904	Norfolk, Va.
Daphne	6	1882		1893	1903	Bristol, R. I	Sept. 18, 1905	Belhaven, N. C	Sept. 22, 1904	Do.
Miscellaneous steam vessels.										
Ann Judson (fishing)	13	1901		1901		Winton, N. C	Apr. 10, 1905	Tunis, N. C	Mar. 30, 1904	Norfolk, Va.
Albemarle (fishing)	7	1888		1896		Avoca, N. C	Apr. 13, 1905	Avoca, N. C	Apr. 12, 1904	Do.
Avoca (fishing)	7	1903		1894		do	do	do	do	Do.
Atlantic (fishing)	221	1902		1902		Baltimore, Md	Apr. 27, 1905	Berkley, Va	May 21, 1904	Charleston, S. C.
Accomac (police patrol)	38	1894		1892		Rome, N. Y	July 19, 1905	Norfolk, Va	July 16, 1904	Norfolk, Va.
Alright (fishing) [b]	48	1899	1904	1891		Battery Park, Va	Dec. 2, 1905	do	Dec. 7, 1904	Do.
Bernice (fishing)	18	1901		1902		Norfolk, Va	Dec. 4, 1905	do	Oct. 31, 1904	Do.
Clara Ellen (fishing)	117	1876	1892	1893		Boothbay, Me	Apr. 25, 1905	do	Apr. 13, 1904	Do.
Chesapeake (fishing)	110	1903		1903		Baltimore, Md	May 9, 1905	do	May 20, 1904	Do.
Emily A. Foot (fishing)	108	1875	1901	1899		Boothbay, Me	Apr. 4, 1905	do	Apr. 23, 1904	Baltimore, Md.
Emma K. (fishing)	32	1890		1903		Glen Cove, N. Y	Apr. 11, 1905	Hampton, Va	Apr. 12, 1904	New York, N. Y.
Edgecombe (fishing)	59	1897		1898		Tottenville, N. Y	Dec. 22, 1905	Norfolk, Va	Nov. 6, 1902	Norfolk, Va.
Fish Hawk (fishing)	13	1893		1894		Edenton, N. C	Mar. 20, 1905	Drummond Point, N. C.	Mar. 19, 1904	Do.
Greenfield (fishing)	8	1887		1879		Drummond Point, N. C.	do	do	do	Do.
Golden Rod (fishing)	14	1893		1880		Avoca, N. C	Apr. 13, 1905	Avoca, N. C	Apr. 12, 1904	Do.
James River (police patrol)	8	1900		1901		Pocomoke City, Md	Nov. 15, 1905	Norfolk, Va	Nov. 7, 1904	Do.
Kecoughtan (fishing)	46	1903		1903		do	Feb. 13, 1905	Hampton, Va	Feb. 8, 1904	Do.
Minnie (freight barge)	75	1900		1887		Portsmouth, Va	June 22, 1905	Berkley, Va	Oct. 16, 1902	Do.
P. M. Warren (fishing)	6	1888		1903		Drummond Point, N. C.	Mar. 20, 1905	Drummond Point, N. C.	Mar. 19, 1904	Do.

Perquimans (fishing)	15	1891		1891		Hertford, N. C	Apr. 13, 1905	Avoca, N. C	Apr. 4, 1904	Do.
Relief (pilot)	219	1891		1891		Philadelphia, Pa	Mar. 31, 1905	Berkley, Va	Mar. 21, 1904	Do.
Rescue (wrecking and towing)	537	1899		1899		Tottenville, N. Y	Aug. 11, 1905	Norfolk, Va	Aug. 10, 1904	New York, N. Y.
Rappahannock (police patrol)	30	1895		1900		Middletown, Conn	Dec. 22, 1905	do	Dec. 21, 1904	Norfolk, Va.
Sarah Drummond (fishing)	12	1893		1879		Drummond Point, N. C.	Mar. 20, 1905	Drummond Point, N. C.	Mar. 19, 1904	Do.
Weldon (fishing)	8	1880		1880		Bluff Point, N. C	do	Edenton, N. C	do	Do.
Vessels propelled by gasoline motors.										
Admiral	29	1899				Beaufort, N. C	Jan. 4, 1905	Roanoke Island, N. C.	Jan. 5, 1904	Norfolk, Va.
George S. Cripps	43	1895				St. Michaels, Md	May 8, 1905	Norfolk, Va	May 25, 1904	Baltimore, Md
Louis Feuerstein	30	1901				Pocomoke City, Md	Jan. 20, 1905	do	Dec. 11, 1903	Norfolk, Va.
Freight sail vessels of over 700 tons.										
Addie M. Lawrence (schooner)	2,807	1902				Bath, Me	Jan. 11, 1905	Newport News, Va	Jan. 7, 1904	Norfolk, Va.
Byard Barnes (schooner)	1,005	1891				New London, Conn	Jan. 17, 1905	do	Jan. 4, 1904	New York, N. Y.
Beulah McCabe (schooner)	763	1881				Bath, Me	Mar. 14, 1905	Norfolk, Va	Aug. 8, 1903	Norfolk, Va.
Childe Harold (schooner)	781	1886	1902			do	Mar. 8, 1905	Newport News, Va	Mar. 3, 1904	New York, N. Y.
Eleanor A. Percy (schooner)	3,401	1900				do	Feb. 6, 1905	do	Feb. 11, 1904	Boston, Mass.
Edith G. Folwell (schooner)	1,263	1901				do	Feb. 15, 1905	Lamberts Point, Va	Feb. 16, 1904	New York, N. Y.
Fannie Palmer (schooner)	2,258	1900				Waldoboro, Me	Feb. 20, 1905	Newport News, Va	Feb. 4, 1904	Boston, Mass.
Frontenac (schooner)	1,704	1904				Bath, Me	Mar. 14, 1905	Lamberts Point, Va	Mar. 26, 1904	Portland, Me.
Fannie C. Bowen (schooner)	1,007	1891				Fall River, Mass	Apr. 20, 1905	Norfolk, Va	May 4, 1904	Norfolk, Va.
Helen Thomas (schooner)	1,470	1904				Thomaston, Me	Jan. 27, 1905	Lamberts Point, Va	Jan. 4, 1904	Portland, Me.
Jennie French Potter (schooner).	1,993	1899				Camden, Me	May 20, 1905	Norfolk, Va	May 10, 1904	Norfolk, Va.
Magnus Manson (schooner)	1,751	1904				Bath, Me	Apr. 7, 1905	Newport News, Va	Apr. 2, 1904	Portland, Me.
Martha P. Small (schooner)	2,178	1901				do	May 12, 1905	Lamberts Point, Va	May 9, 1904	Bangor, Me.
Winifred A. Foran (schooner)	858	1881				Weymouth, Mass	June 13, 1905	Newport News, Va	June 10, 1903	New York, N. Y.
Sail vessels, barges, etc., of over 100 tons, carrying passengers for hire.										
Edward H. Cole (schooner)	1,791	1904				Rockland, Me	Mar. 9, 1905	Lamberts Point, Va	Mar. 4, 1904	Bangor, Me.
Louise (barge)[c]	409	1863				Keyport, N. J	June 1, 1905	Newport News, Va	First inspn	
N. Y. P. & N. Railroad (barge No. 11).	293	1891				Berkley, Va	Mar. 4, 1905	Norfolk, Va	do	
N. & C. 8 (barge)	126	1891				do	July 14, 1905	do	July 14, 1904	Norfolk, Va.

[a] Formerly Dr. J. P. Whitbeck, 1899.
[b] Formerly Wright & Willis, 1905.
[c] Formerly John Romer, 1889, then steamer Louise.

DOMESTIC VESSELS INSPECTED, YEAR ENDED DECEMBER 31, 1905—THIRD SUPERVISING DISTRICT—Continued.

LOCAL DISTRICT OF BALTIMORE, MD.

Names of vessels and class.	Gross tonnage.	Hull built.	Hull rebuilt.	Boilers built.	Boilers rebuilt.	Where built.	Date of inspection.	Where inspected.	Date of previous inspection.	Local district where previously inspected.
Ocean passenger steamers.										
Berkshire	2,014	1881		1894		Philadelphia, Pa	Aug. 1, 1905	Baltimore, Md	Aug. 3, 1904	Baltimore, Md.
Dorchester	2,537	1889		1900		Wilmington, Del	Mar. 21, 1905	do	Mar. 31, 1904	Do.
Essex	2,530	1890		1901		Philadelphia, Pa	July 19, 1905	do	July 22, 1904	Do.
Frederick	1,872	1874		1893	1903	Wilmington, Del	Aug. 15, 1905	do	Aug. 23, 1904	Do.
Gloucester	2,541	1893		1903		Sparrow Point, Md	Sept. 12, 1905	do	Sept. 17, 1904	Do.
Howard	2,551	1895		1895		Wilmington, Del	June 7, 1905	do	June 13, 1904	Do.
Itasca [a]	1,416	1871	1897	1897		do	Dec. 19, 1904	do	Dec. 24, 1903	Do.
Itasca	1,416	1871	1897	1897		do	Dec. 18, 1905	do	Dec. 19, 1904	Do.
Juniata	2,551	1897		1897		do	Nov. 24, 1905	do	Sept. 30, 1904	Do.
Kershaw	2,590	1899		1899		do	Feb. 8, 1905	do	Feb. 10, 1904	Do.
Lexington	2,092	1877		1894		Chester, Pa	Sept. 29, 1905	do	Sept. 26, 1904	Do.
Nantucket	2,599	1899		1899		Wilmington, Del	Apr. 19, 1905	do	Apr. 25, 1904	Do.
New Orleans	1,564	1872		1891		do	Apr. 3, 1905	do	Apr. 9, 1904	Do.
Ontario	3,082	1904		1903		Camden, N. J	July 15, 1905	do	July 21, 1904	Philadelphia, Pa.
Watson	1,820	1902		1901		Toledo, Ohio	Mar. 3, 1905	do	Apr. 9, 1904	New York, N. Y.
Inland passenger steamers.										
Annapolis	485	1892	1903	1892		Baltimore, Md	Oct. 3, 1905	Baltimore, Md	Oct. 12, 1904	Baltimore, Md.
Atlanta [b]	2,094	1896		1896		Philadelphia, Pa	Feb. 22, 1905	do	Feb. 29, 1904	Do.
Annie H	7	1891	1899	1890		Poquoson, Va	Aug. 26, 1904	Washington, D. C	July 13, 1903	Do.
Alabama	1,938	1893		1893		Sparrow Point, Md	Apr. 22, 1905	Baltimore, Md	Apr. 26, 1904	Do.
Anne Arundel	795	1904		1904		Baltimore, Md	June 19, 1905	Washington, D. C	June 22, 1904	Do.
Avalon	600	1888		1888		Wilmington, Del	Apr. 21, 1905	Baltimore, Md	May 2, 1904	Do.
Augusta	2,372	1900		1900		Philadelphia, Pa	Nov. 18, 1905	do	Nov. 26, 1904	Do.
Atlantic	33	1894		1894		Baltimore, Md	Sept. 12, 1905	do	Sept. 10, 1904	Do.
Baltimore	1,413	1885		1902		do	June 1, 1905	do	June 7, 1904	Do.
Baltimore	56	1852		1899		do	Nov. 28, 1905	do	Dec. 1, 1904	Do.
Bristol	265	1871		1902		Philadelphia, Pa	Mar. 25, 1905	do	First inspn	
B. S. Ford	417	1877	1887	1885		Wilmington, Del	Apr. 8, 1905	do	May 17, 1904	Do.
Bartholdi	25	1884	1897	1894		Brooklyn, N. Y	Apr. 27, 1905	Washington, D. C	Apr. 27, 1904	Do.
Charlotte	1,746	1889		1889		Philadelphia, Pa	Aug. 21, 1905	Baltimore, Md	Aug. 22, 1904	Do.
Comet	23	1874	1904	1904		Apponong, R. I	Sept. 26, 1905	do	Sept. 16, 1904	Do.
Calvert	889	1902		1902		Philadelphia, Pa	Feb. 7, 1905	do	Feb. 23, 1904	Do.
Charles Macalester	624	1890		1890		Wilmington, Del	Feb. 17, 1905	Washington, D. C	Feb. 12, 1904	Do.
Carrie	45	1879	1903	1901		Espy, Pa	Mar. 20, 1905	Laurel, Del	Feb. 3, 1904	Do.
Chesapeake	316	1884		1891		Baltimore, Md	Apr. 24, 1905	Baltimore, Md	May 5, 1904	Do.
Cambridge	834	1890		1903		do	May 23, 1905	do	May 21, 1904	Do.
Choptank	346	1883		1883		do	June 14, 1905	do	May 5, 1904	Do.
Corsica	368	1882		1882		Wilmington, Del	June 16, 1905	do	June 27, 1904	Do.

Danville	1,297	1882		1885		Baltimore, Md	Aug. 28, 1905	....do	Sept. 3, 1904	Do.
Dixie	11	1897		1895		Pocomoke City, Md	June 17, 1905	Crisfield, Md	June 16, 1904	Do.
Emma K. Reed	83	1904		1904		St. Michaels, Md	July 24, 1905	Baltimore, Md	July 21, 1904	Do.
Ericsson	897	1887		1897		Philadelphia, Pa	Aug. 7, 1905	....do	Aug. 9, 1904	Do.
Emma Giles	549	1887		1904		Baltimore, Md	Mar. 2, 1905	....do	Mar. 31, 1904	Do.
Eastern Shore	791	1883		1904		Wilmington, Del	May 13, 1905	....do	May 13, 1904	Do.
Emma A. Ford	553	1884		1884		....do	May 23, 1905	....do	June 4, 1904	Do.
Edward G. Gummel	59	1905		1905		Solomons, Md	June 3, 1905	....do	First inspn.	
Estelle Randall	211	1898		1898		Baltimore, Md	May 24, 1905	Washington, D. C	May 25, 1904	Do.
Elm City	125	1883		1892		Norfolk, Va	May 20, 1905	West Point, Va	May 20, 1904	Do.
Enoch Pratt	571	1878		1901		Baltimore, Md	June 30, 1905	Baltimore, Md	Apr. 14, 1904	Do.
Elsie	39	1893		1893		....do	....do	....do	June 25, 1904	Do.
Gov. Robt. M. McLane	144	1884	1904	1904		Philadelphia, Pa	Sept. 29, 1905	....do	Oct. 6, 1904	Do.
Gov. P. F. Thomas	144	1884	1903	1894		....do	Oct. 21, 1905	....do	Oct. 12, 1904	Do.
Georgia	1,749	1887		1887		Wilmington, Del	Apr. 4, 1905	....do	Mar. 16, 1904	Do.
Genl. J. A. Dumont [c]	309	1862	1900	1886		Williamsburg, N. Y	Nov. 9, 1904	....do	Nov. 5, 1903	Do.
Gratitude	214	1880		1880		Philadelphia, Pa	Apr. 15, 1905	....do	Apr. 14, 1904	Do.
Granite City	179	1890		1903		Stonington, Conn	June 22, 1905	....do	May 26, 1904	Do.
Greyhound	36	1872		1900		Philadelphia, Pa	Dec. 8, 1905	....do	Dec. 12, 1904	Do.
Hamilton	64	1904		1904		Baltimore, Md	Jan. 3, 1905	....do	Jan. 11, 1904	Do.
Harry Randall	496	1875	1893	1903		Camden, N. J	May 11, 1905	....do	May 27, 1904	Do.
Hygeia	35	1884		1901		Baltimore, Md	June 7, 1905	....do	June 7, 1904	Do.
Helen	550	1871	1905	1898		Wilmington, Del	Aug. 18, 1905	....do	Dec. 29, 1904	Do.
Ivanhoe	14	1889	1900	1902		Baltimore, Md	July 18, 1905	....do	July 4, 1904	Do.
Jesse Tyson	27	1890		1904		....do	Sept. 22, 1905	....do	Sept. 21, 1904	Do.
J. H. Riehl	39	1900		1900		Madison, Md	Feb. 20, 1905	....do	Feb. 20, 1904	Do.
Jane Moseley	800	1873		1880		Brooklyn, N. Y	June 24, 1905	....do	July 6, 1904	Do.
Joppa	607	1885		1885		Wilmington, Del	May 29, 1905	....do	May 31, 1904	Do.
Kitty Knight	236	1860	1902	1902		Greenpoint, N. Y	May 2, 1905	....do	May 11, 1904	Do.
Lannan	25	1891		1900		Baltimore, Md	July 29, 1905	....do	July 30, 1904	Do.
Lord Baltimore	445	1903		1903		Wilmington, Del	Aug. 2, 1905	....do	Aug. 2, 1904	Do.
Louise	1,023	1864	1897	1901		....do	Apr. 26, 1905	....do	May 23, 1904	Do.
Lancaster	919	1892		1892		Sparrow Point, Md	June 3, 1905	....do	June 8, 1904	Do.
Lucerne	34	1886		1895		Baltimore, Md	....do	West Point, Va	June 4, 1904	Do.
Middlesex	1,197	1902		1902		Philadelphia, Pa	Nov. 23, 1905	Baltimore, Md	Nov. 30, 1904	Do.
Major W. Allen	27	1888	1903	1899		Baltimore, Md	Apr. 7, 1905	....do	Apr. 7, 1904	Do.
Maggie	606	1869		1905		Wilmington, Del	May 8, 1905	....do	Apr. 29, 1904	Do.
Mary	75	1896		1905		Baltimore, Md	June 2, 1905	....do	June 2, 1904	Do.
Massapequa	47	1889	1900	1889		Massapequa, N. Y	May 31, 1905	Wagners Point, Md	May 23, 1904	Do.
Minnie Wheeler	261	1881		1891	1904	Baltimore, Md	June 15, 1905	Baltimore, Md	June 7, 1904	Do.
Maryland	871	1902		1902		Wilmington, Del	July 14, 1905	....do	July 19, 1904	Do.
M. W. Hunt	41	1888	1902	1904		Philadelphia, Pa	Aug. 7, 1905	....do	May 11, 1904	Do.
Norfolk	1,248	1891		1900		Wilmington, Del	Mar. 14, 1905	Washington, D. C	Mar. 16, 1904	Do.
Neptune	188	1904		1904		Baltimore, Md	Mar. 28, 1905	Baltimore, Md	Mar. 23, 1904	Do.
Newport News	1,535	1895		1895		Newport News, Va	May 1, 1905	Washington, D. C	May 9, 1904	Do.
Northumberland	993	1900		1900		Philadelphia, Pa	....do	....do	May 4, 1904	Do.
Owen Dillard	16	1905		1896		Tappahannock, Va	Aug. 23, 1905	Urbanna, Va	Aug. 27, 1904	Do.
Penn	445	1903		1903		Wilmington, Del	May 29, 1905	Baltimore, Md	July 25, 1904	Do.
Pocomoke	656	1891		1891		....do	Apr. 25, 1905	....do	May 9, 1904	Do.
Petrel	49	1902		1902		Bullocks Cove, R. I	May 12, 1905	....do	May 11, 1904	Do.

[a] Certificated Mar. 1, 1905. [b] Certificated Apr. 13, 1905. [c] Certificated May 8, 1905.

DOMESTIC VESSELS INSPECTED, YEAR ENDED DECEMBER 31, 1905—THIRD SUPERVISING DISTRICT—BALTIMORE, MD.—Continued.

Names of vessels and class.	Gross tonnage.	Hull built.	Hull rebuilt.	Boilers built.	Boilers rebuilt.	Where built.	Date of inspection.	Where inspected.	Date of previous inspection.	Local district where previously inspected.
Inland passenger steamers—Continued.										
Potomac	763	1894		1894		Philadelphia, Pa	May 9, 1905	Sparrow Point, Md	May 24, 1904	Baltimore, Md.
Queen Caroline	641	1902		1902		Baltimore, Md	May 30, 1905	Baltimore, Md	May 28, 1904	Do.
Rock Creek	199	1895	1904	1904		Essex, Me	Mar. 6, 1905	do	Mar. 10, 1904	Do.
Runaway	24	1874		1874		Brooklyn, N. Y	Apr. 1, 1905	Alexandria, Va	Mar. 23, 1904	Do.
River Queen	578	1864		1884		Keyport, N. J	Apr. 27, 1905	Washington, D. C	Mar. 26, 1904	Do.
Solicitor	19	1898		1898		Baltimore, Md	Feb. 7, 1905	Baltimore, Md	Mar. 13, 1904	Do.
Susquehanna	462	1898		1898		do	Apr. 22, 1905	do	May 4, 1904	Do.
Severn	113	1891	1903	1891		do	June 2, 1905	Annapolis, Md	Mar. 21, 1904	Do.
St. Marys	688	1872	1890	1903		do	May 2, 1905	Baltimore, Md	May 10, 1904	Do.
Tennessee	1,240	1898		1898		Wilmington, Del	July 20, 1905	do	July 25, 1904	Do.
Tred Avon	676	1884		1898		Baltimore, Md	Nov. 18, 1905	do	Aug. 31, 1904	Do.
Tivoli	704	1894		1894		Sparrow Point, Md	Oct. 23, 1905	do	Nov. 3, 1904	Do.
Tangier	680	1875		1886		Wilmington, Del	Mar. 22, 1905	do	Apr. 13, 1904	Do.
T. V. Arrowsmith	527	1860	1895	1892		Keyport, N. J	May 27, 1905	Washington, D. C	May 9, 1904	Do.
Virginia	868	1903		1903		Sparrow Point, Md	Apr. 3, 1905	Salisbury, Md	Apr. 9, 1904	Do.
Venus	55	1893		1905		Baltimore, Md	June 9, 1905	Baltimore, Md	June 9, 1904	Do.
Westmoreland	846	1883		1902		do	Feb. 21, 1905	do	Mar. 10, 1904	Do.
Washington	1,248	1891		1901		Wilmington, Del	Mar. 10, 1905	Washington, D. C	Mar. 17, 1904	Do.
Wakefield	571	1885		1898		do	May 15, 1905	do	May 20, 1904	Do.
Ferry steamers.										
Bronx	1,954	1905		1905		Sparrow Point, Md	July 14, 1905	Sparrow Point, Md	First inspn	
Brooklyn	1,954	1905		1905		do	June 21, 1905	do	do	
City Belle	20	1887	1900	1887		New York, N. Y	May 6, 1905	Port Deposit, Md	May 5, 1904	Baltimore, Md.
Manhattan	1,954	1905		1905		Sparrow Point, Md	May 31, 1905	Sparrow Point, Md	First inspn	
Queens	1,954	1905		1905		do	Aug. 14, 1905	do	do	
Samuel H. Tagart	310	1878	1901	1878		Baltimore, Md	Oct. 19, 1905	Baltimore, Md	Oct. 25, 1904	Do.
S. W. Smith	320	1877	1900	1887		do	Nov. 24, 1905	do	Dec. 8, 1904	Do.
Vivian	8	1899		1899		Snow Hill, Md	Sept. 28, 1905	Oxford, Md	Sept. 30, 1904	Do.
Ocean freight steamers.										
Bluefields [a]	736	1886				Greenock, Scotland	Dec. 19, 1904	Baltimore, Md	Jan. 4, 1904	Baltimore, Md.
Bluefields	736	1886				do	Dec. 11, 1905	do	Dec. 19, 1904	Do.
Chesapeake	1,101	1900		1900		Wilmington, Del	Apr. 21, 1905	do	Apr. 19, 1904	Do.
City of Philadelphia	542	1896		1896		Philadelphia, Pa	Sept. 23, 1905	do	Oct. 6, 1904	Do.
Charles F. Mayer	1,218	1884		1904		Wilmington, Del	Nov. 9, 1905	do	Nov. 17, 1904	Do.
Carolyn	2,241	1889		1889		Whitby, England	Aug. 9, 1905	do	Aug. 15, 1904	Norfolk, Va.
Frostburg	926	1884		1884		Philadelphia, Pa	Sept. 5, 1905	do	Sept. 1, 1904	Baltimore, Md.
George Weems	416	1874		1897		Baltimore, Md	July 22, 1905	do	First inspn	

Hugoma	2,182	1901		1901		Wyandotte, Mich	Sept. 7,1905	Sparrow Point, Md	Oct. 3,1904	Do.
Lewis Luckenbach	3,905	1903		1903		Camden, N. J	Dec. 20,1905	....do	Dec. 31,1904	New York, N. Y.
Manna-Hata	1,103	1900		1900		Wilmington, Del	Apr. 7,1905	Baltimore, Md	May 14,1904	Baltimore, Md.
S. Oteri	1,043	1881		1882	1899	Middlesboro, England	Mar. 30,1905	....do	Mar. 30,1904	Philadelphia, Pa.
Inland freight steamers.										
Belle Miller	255	1896		1896		Elkton, Md	June 16,1905	Baltimore, Md	June 6,1904	Philadelphia, Pa.
Dallas	21	1902		1902		Alexandria, Va	Oct. 23,1905	Washington, D. C	Oct. 15,1904	Baltimore, Md.
Dan'l K. Jackson	71	1902		1898		Washington, D. C	May 10,1905	....do	May 26,1904	Do.
E. James Tull	72	1899		1904		Pocomoke City, Md	July 21,1905	Alexandria, Va	July 22,1904	Do.
Gaston	846	1881		1881		Wilmington, Del	Oct. 3,1905	Baltimore, Md	Oct. 8,1904	Do.
Joshua Leviness	91	1876	1905	1902		City Island, N. Y	Apr. 1,1905	....do	June 4,1904	Do.
Lily and Howard	88	1899		1887		Aquia Creek, Va	Aug. 15,1905	Washington, D. C	Aug. 12,1904	Do.
Mary Tyler	49	1902		1891	1901	Walkerton, Va	Sept. 22,1905	Walkerton, Va	Sept. 24,1904	Do.
Vesper	331	1871		1891		Wilmington, Del	Apr. 4,1905	Baltimore, Md	Apr. 13,1904	Do.
Ocean towing steamers.										
Buccaneer	226	1900		1900		Boston, Mass	May 10,1905	Baltimore, Md	May 12,1904	Baltimore, Md.
Britannia	249	1899		1899		Sparrow Point, Md	Sept. 13,1905	....do	Sept. 7,1904	Do.
Cumberland	377	1898		1898		Baltimore, Md	June 20,1905	....do	June 16,1904	Do.
Columbia	217	1904		1904		Camden, N. J	Sept. 11,1905	....do	Apr. 10,1904	Philadelphia, Pa.
Georges Creek	398	1899		1899		Baltimore, Md	May 9,1905	....do	May 12,1904	Baltimore, Md.
Margaret	203	1904		1904		....do	Aug. 23,1905	....do	Aug. 18,1904	Do.
Monocacy	617	1905		1905		Sparrow Point, Md	Aug. 28,1905	Sparrow Point, Md	First inspn	
Piedmont	391	1899		1899		Baltimore, Md	Mar. 7,1905	Baltimore, Md	Mar. 11,1904	Do.
Savage	410	1899		1899		....do	Nov. 7,1905	....do	Nov. 16,1904	Do.
Sea King	124	1902		1901		....do	May 29,1905	....do	May 26,1904	Do.
Tormentor	226	1900		1900		Boston, Mass	May 24,1905	....do	May 29,1904	Do.
Inland towing steamers.										
Annie	27	1883		1904		Baltimore, Md	Aug. 1,1905	Baltimore, Md	Aug. 6,1904	Baltimore, Md.
Ada	35	1900		1900		....do	Sept. 13,1905	....do	Sept. 13,1904	Do.
Agnes Miller	22	1904		1888		Solomons, Md	Dec. 4,1905	Washington, D. C	Nov. 14,1904	Do.
Alpha	35	1901		1901		....do	July 1,1905	Baltimore, Md	June 17,1904	Do.
Active	118	1905		1905		Baltimore, Md	Sept. 1,1905	....do	First inspn	
Baby	20	1891		1894		Berkley, Va	June 23,1905	Georgetown, D. C	May 20,1904	Do.
Bohemia	117	1899		1898		Philadelphia, Pa	Sept. 30,1905	Baltimore, Md	Sept. 28,1904	Do.
Calvin Whiteley	21	1876	1896	1896		....do	July 22,1905	....do	July 20,1904	Do.
Claribel	23	1875	1904	1886		Belleville, N. Y	Sept. 2,1905	West Point, Va	Aug. 20,1904	Do.
Columbia	19	1871	1899	1899		Philadelphia, Pa	May 19,1905	Baltimore, Md	May 5,1904	Do.
Columbia	84	1896		1895		....do	Feb. 2,1905	....do	Feb. 24,1904	Philadelphia, Pa.
Chesapeake	18	1880	1893	1893		Baltimore, Md	Sept. 1,1905	....do	Dec. 17,1904	Baltimore, Md.
Corona	23	1891		1881		Astoria, N. Y	Mar. 6,1905	....do	Mar. 4,1904	Do.
Capt. Thos. A. P. Champlin	24	1862		1879		Camden, N. J	Mar. 24,1905	....do	Apr. 8,1904	Do.
Chas. J. Baker	19	1880		1904		Baltimore, Md	Apr. 29,1905	....do	Apr. 29,1904	Do.
Clara	24	1902		1894		Bordentown, N. J	Apr. 24,1905	Annapolis, Md	Apr. 25,1904	Do.
Chicago	88	1885		1891		Camden, N. J	Aug 21,1905	Baltimore, Md	Aug. 20,1904	Do.
D. M. Key	16	1877	1903	1878		Glenwood, N. J	June 28,1905	Washington, D. C	June 21,1904	Do.

a Certificated Jan. 5, 1905.

DOMESTIC VESSELS INSPECTED, YEAR ENDED DECEMBER 31, 1905—THIRD SUPERVISING DISTRICT—BALTIMORE, MD.—Continued.

Names of vessels and class.	Gross tonnage.	Hull built.	Hull rebuilt.	Boilers built.	Boilers rebuilt.	Where built.	Date of inspection.	Where inspected.	Date of previous inspection.	Local district where previously inspected.
Inland towing steamers—Con.										
Dauntless	123	1901		1901		Baltimore, Md	Nov. 13, 1905	Baltimore, Md	Nov. 12, 1904	Baltimore, Md.
Dispatch	9	1893		1903		Greenport, N. Y	Nov. 22, 1905	Havre de Grace, Md	Nov. 19, 1904	Do.
Dixie	74	1905		1905		Madison, Md	Oct. 28, 1905	Baltimore, Md	First inspn	
Easby	28	1888		1905		Baltimore, Md	July 17, 1905	do	July 15, 1904	Do.
Eugenia	10	1874	1896	1904		Buffalo, N. Y	July 26, 1905	Alexandria, Va	July 25, 1904	Do.
Emma	52	1862	1891	1898		Baltimore, Md	Sept. 4, 1905	Baltimore, Md	Aug. 30, 1904	Do.
Edith	50	1880	1895	1896		Tottenville, N. Y	Mar. 28, 1905	do	Dec. 4, 1901	Do.
Edith Goddard Winship	36	1887		1897		Baltimore, Md	Apr. 10, 1905	Washington, D. C	Apr. 11, 1904	Do.
E. Clay Timanus	52	1904		1904		do	Oct. 26, 1905	Baltimore, Md	Sept. 28, 1904	Do.
Favorite	40	1898		1898		do	May 17, 1905	do	Apr. 28, 1904	Do.
Geo. C. Fobes	37	1874	1899	1901		Cape Elizabeth, Me	June 12, 1905	do	June 13, 1904	Do.
Game Cock	11	1874	1892	1898		Buffalo, N. Y	Oct. 10, 1905	do	Oct. 13, 1904	Do.
Gen'l I. J. Wistar	60	1886		1899		Philadelphia, Pa	Mar. 3, 1905	Chesapeake City, Md	Mar. 9, 1904	Do.
Geo. F. Randolph	211	1905		1905		Baltimore, Md	Feb. 14, 1905	Baltimore, Md	First inspn	
George W. Pride	17	1874	1897	1893		Wilmington, Del	Mar. 22, 1905	Alexandria, Va	Mar. 23, 1904	Do.
George S. Rieman	21	1879	1899	1892		Baltimore, Md	May 25, 1905	Baltimore, Md	May 25, 1904	Do.
Hanson H. Keys	28	1883	1895	1895		do	Apr. 22, 1905	do	Aug. 8, 1904	Do.
Irene	30	1901		1901		Madison, Md	Aug. 5, 1905	do	Aug. 15, 1904	Do.
Imperial	160	1904		1904		Baltimore, Md	May 23, 1905	do	May 19, 1904	Do.
J. T. Selecman	18	1897		1903		Solomons, Md	Oct. 6, 1905	Washington, D. C	Oct. 7, 1904	Do.
J. W. Thompson	17	1880		1892		Baltimore, Md	Nov. 29, 1905	Baltimore, Md	Dec. 1, 1904	Do.
James O. Carter	26	1896		1903		Solomons, Md	May 5, 1905	Washington, D. C	Apr. 30, 1904	Do.
Keystone	21	1891		1898		St. Leonards, Md	July 24, 1905	Havre de Grace, Md	July 26, 1904	Do.
Little Nora	17	1887		1897		Baltimore, Md	Oct. 24, 1905	Baltimore, Md	Oct. 27, 1904	Do.
Louie	22	1872		1902		do	Dec. 9, 1905	do	Dec. 7, 1904	Do.
Leader [a]	106	1904		1904		do	Dec. 28, 1904	do	First inspn	
Lauretta Spedden	26	1888		1897		do	June 5, 1905	do	June 4, 1904	Do.
Mohawk	10	1872	1899	1893		Buffalo, N. Y	July 21, 1905	do	July 21, 1904	Do.
Morris L. Keen	21	1865	1895	1895		Philadelpdia, Pa	do	do	do	Do.
Major Henry Brewerton	65	1857		1893		Baltimore, Md	Mar. 1, 1905	Alexandria, Va	Mar. 3, 1904	Do.
Martin Dallman	17	1866	1896	1890		Philadelphia, Pa	Apr. 15, 1905	Washington, D. C	Apr. 11, 1904	Do.
Minerva	21	1884		1890		Wilmington, Del	Mar. 21, 1905	Georgetown, D. C	Mar. 21, 1904	Do.
M. W. Adams	73	1903		1901		Solomons, Md	May 8, 1905	Baltimore, Md	May 9, 1904	Do.
Maryland	22	1884		1896		Baltimore, Md	May 16, 1905	do	May 19, 1904	Do.
M. Mitchell Davis	116	1902		1902		Solomons, Md	July 3, 1905	do	June 30, 1904	Norfolk, Va.
Marion Cameron	95	1904		1904		do	Sept. 16, 1905	do	Sept. 24, 1904	Baltimore, Md.
Meta	31	1891		1891		Brooklyn, N. Y	Oct. 4, 1905	do	Oct. 4, 1904	Do.
Oriole	20	1882		1901		Baltimore, Md	June 19, 1905	do	June 14, 1904	Do.
Patapsco	11	1873		1897		do	June 23, 1905	do	June 23, 1904	Do.
Peerless	102	1899		1899		do	Oct. 25, 1905	do	Dec. 8, 1904	Do.
Progress	27	1901		1901		Madison, Md	Apr. 18, 1905	do	Apr. 16, 1904	Do.
Pickwick	81	1898		1904		Norfolk, Va	May 15, 1905	Alexandria, Va	May 13, 1904	Do.

Rosalie	22	1898		1902		Milford, Del	June 6, 1905	do	June 6, 1904	Do.
Rescue	46	1891		1898		Baltimore, Md	June 29, 1905	Baltimore, Md	June 21, 1904	Do.
R. H. Cook	17	1879		1893		Cambridge, Md	July 11, 1905	do	July 9, 1904	Do.
Reuben Foster	16	1878		1904		Baltimore, Md	Aug. 1, 1905	do	June 23, 1904	Do.
Roman	23	1881		1889		Philadelphia, Pa	Sept. 7, 1905	Chesapeake City, Md	Sept. 7, 1904	Do.
Radiant	81	1902		1902		do	Feb. 3, 1905	Baltimore, Md	Feb. 1, 1904	Do.
Roy	46	1897		1891	1900	Portsmouth, Va	Nov. 21, 1905	West Point, Va	Nov. 16, 1904	Norfolk, Va.
Sunbeam	8	1891		1895		Baltimore, Md	June 13, 1905	Washington, D. C	June 10, 1904	Baltimore, Md.
Sidney	22	1881		1901		do	Aug. 2, 1905	Baltimore, Md	Aug. 1, 1904	Do.
Sandow	112	1862	1897	1891		Wilmington, Del	Aug. 31, 1905	do	Aug. 26, 1904	Do.
Startle	54	1883		1898		do	Dec. 1, 1905	Chesapeake City, Md	Dec. 3, 1904	Do.
Sarah	96	1900		1900		Baltimore, Md	Mar. 11, 1905	Baltimore, Md	Mar. 11, 1904	Do.
Sarah C. Hager	13	1879	1902	1880		Brooklyn, N. Y	Mar. 27, 1905	Annapolis, Md	Mar. 26, 1904	Philadelphia, Pa.
Spray	17	1886		1867		Alexandria, Va	Mar. 22, 1905	Alexandria, Va	Apr. 5, 1904	Baltimore, Md.
Southern	54	1905		1905		Baltimore, Md	Aug. 8, 1905	Baltimore, Md	First inspn	
Transfer	101	1872		1886		Wilmington, Del	Oct. 24, 1905	do	Oct. 24, 1904	Do.
Transport	30	1898		1898		Baltimore, Md	May 4, 1905	do	May 18, 1904	Do.
Thomas B. Webster	25	1889		1889		do	May 25, 1905	do	May 14, 1904	Do.
Uncle Sam	26	1901		1905		Madison, Md	Mar. 20, 1905	do	Apr. 8, 1904	Do.
Vigilant	21	1897		1901		Alexandria, Va	Aug. 10, 1905	Washington, D. C	Aug. 10, 1904	Do.
Volunteer	97	1887		1900		Philadelphia, Pa	Jan. 10, 1905	Baltimore, Md	Jan. 9, 1904	Do.
Walter	32	1890		1894		Baltimore, Md	June 12, 1905	do	June 11, 1904	Do.
W. H. Mohler	36	1866	1892	1884		Washington, D. C	Sept. 28, 1905	Washington, D. C	Oct. 3, 1904	Do.
Walter F. Mead	25	1903		1903		New Baltimore, N. Y	May 15, 1905	do	May 6, 1904	Do.
William H. Yerkes, jr	59	1901		1901		Solomons, Md	June 14, 1905	do	June 16, 1904	Do.
Wm. A. Johnson	25	1883		1903		Baltimore, Md	Dec. 1, 1905	Baltimore, Md	Nov. 28, 1904	Do.
Ocean steam pleasure yacht.										
Margaret	179	1904		1904		Mariners Harbor, N. Y.	Dec. 14, 1905	Baltimore, Md	Dec. 16, 1904	New York, N. Y.
Inland steam pleasure yachts.										
Amadis	85	1894		1894		Searsport, Me	May 17, 1905	Baltimore, Md	July 9, 1904	Baltimore, Md.
Augusta	3	1891	1902	1893	1902	Unknown	Aug. 5, 1905	Alexandria, Va	July 20, 1904	Do.
Bye-Bye	5	1905		1905		Washington, D. C	June 10, 1905	Washington, D. C	First inspn	
Chilhowee	95	1898		1898		Baltimore, Md	July 6, 1905	Baltimore, Md	July 22, 1904	Do.
Cygnus	4	1886	1901	1890		Chicago, Ill	May 26, 1905	Washington, D. C	May 25, 1904	Do.
Commodore Bartlett	58	1901		1901		Croton, N. Y	Apr. 13, 1905	Baltimore, Md	Apr. 7, 1904	Do.
Georgetown [b]	4	1892		1903		Nyack, N. Y	May 17, 1905	Georgetown, D. C	Apr. 23, 1904	Do.
Holly	2	1901	1905	1903		Oxford, Md	Apr. 24, 1905	Annapolis, Md	Apr. 10, 1903	Do.
Helen Isabel	7	(c)		1888		Unknown	Aug. 4, 1905	Baltimore, Md	First inspn	
India	4	1888		1892		Camden, N. J	June 10, 1905	Alexandria, Va	June 27, 1903	Do.
Kaleda	79	1898		1898		Boston, Mass	May 3, 1905	Baltimore, Md	Apr. 29, 1904	Do.
Legonia	126	1903		1902		Baltimore, Md	May 24, 1905	do	May 21, 1904	Do.
Little Angus	4	1892	1901	1901		Washington, D. C	June 26, 1905	Washington, D. C	June 27, 1904	Do.
Maraschino	2	1894		1889		do	Aug. 19, 1905	do	May 21, 1904	Do.
Ruby	4	1895		1895		do	June 22, 1905	do	June 21, 1904	Do.
Samuel W. Sutton	4	1893		1893		Alexandria, Va	Aug. 22, 1905	Alexandria, Va	Aug. 20, 1904	Do.
Teaser	2	(c)	1903	1889		Unknown	June 2, 1905	Washington, D. C	Apr. 27, 1904	Do.

[a] Certificated January 16, 1905. [b] Formerly Tyro. [c] Unknown.

DOMESTIC VESSELS INSPECTED, YEAR ENDED DECEMBER 31, 1905—THIRD SUPERVISING DISTRICT—BALTIMORE, MD.—Continued.

Names of vessels and class.	Gross tonnage.	Hull built.	Hull rebuilt.	Boilers built.	Boilers rebuilt.	Where built.	Date of inspection.	Where inspected.	Date of previous inspection.	Local district where previously inspected.
***Inland steam pleasure yachts*—Continued.**										
Thelma	3	1896		1883		Washington, D. C.	July 19, 1905	Washington, D. C.	July 28, 1903	Baltimore, Md
Vim	3	1902		1900		Baltimore, Md	June 1, 1905	Baltimore, Md	June 1, 1904	Do.
Visitor	61	1904		1904		Boston, Mass	May 16, 1905	do	June 14, 1904	Boston, Mass.
Miscellaneous steamers.										
Alden S. Swan (fishing)	136	1902		1902		Pocomoke City, Md	May 4, 1905	Harborton, Va	May 12, 1904	Baltimore, Md.
Adeline (oyster)	15	1875		1899		Cold Spring, N. Y	June 1, 1905	Fredericksburg, Va	June 2, 1904	Do.
Annapolis (ice)	877	1889		1889		Baltimore, Md	Oct. 19, 1905	Baltimore, Md	Oct. 19, 1904	Do.
Cataract (fire)	85	1891	1897	1891		do	Aug. 10, 1905	do	Aug. 12, 1904	Do.
Charles J. Colonna (fishing)	231	1904		1904		Berkley, Va	May 12, 1905	Lilian, Va	June 23, 1904	Philadelphia, Pa.
Chief (oyster)	51	1902		1892		East Providence, R. I.	June 14, 1905	Fredericksburg, Va	June 17, 1904	Providence, R. I.
Chief (oyster)	33	1902	1905	1892		do	Oct. 27, 1905	Whealton, Va	do	Do.
Dorothy F. Wacker (fishing)	221	1897		1897		Pocomoke City, Md	Aug. 15, 1905	Byrdton, Va	Aug. 16, 1904	Baltimore, Md.
Daisy (fishing)	124	1874	1900	1895		Noank, Conn	Apr. 12, 1905	Carters Creek, Va	Apr. 27, 1904	Do.
David K. Phillips (fishing)	116	1877	1898	1882		Damariscotta, Me	May 15, 1905	Harborton, Va	May 16, 1904	Do.
Dorchester (pile driver)	15	1895		1893		Salisbury, Md	May 18, 1905	Cambridge, Md	May 17, 1904	Do.
Elizabeth M. Froehlich (fishing).	129	1892		1905		Baltimore, Md	Apr. 17, 1905	Baltimore, Md	Mar. 30, 1904	Do.
E. Warren Reed (fishing)	156	1899	1905	1905		Pocomoke City, Md	Apr. 27, 1905	do	Apr. 28, 1904	Do.
E. Benson Dennis (fishing)	100	1901		1901		do	May 11, 1905	Crisfield, Md	May 10, 1904	Do.
E. W. Edwards (fishing)	118	1901		1901		Baltimore, Md	Apr. 25, 1905	Fairport, Va	Apr. 26, 1904	Do.
E. J. Tull (fishing)	119	1902	1903	1903		Pocomoke City, Md	do	do	do	Do.
Fairfield (fishing)	131	1900		1901		do	May 13, 1905	Baltimore, Md	May 18, 1904	Do.
F. C. Latrobe (ice)	726	1879		1905		Baltimore, Md	Dec. 8, 1905	do	Oct. 18, 1904	Do.
George P. Squires (fishing)	143	1900		1900		do	July 28, 1905	do	Aug. 1, 1904	Do.
George H. Bradley (fishing)	118	1871		1885		Bath, Me	May 12, 1905	Ocrans, Va	May 13, 1904	Norfolk, Va.
Helen Euphane (fishing)	127	1902		1902		Pocomoke City, Md	May 22, 1905	Baltimore, Md	May 31, 1904	Baltimore, Md.
Hannah A. Lennen (fishing)	136	1901		1901		do	May 4, 1905	Harborton, Va	May 12, 1904	Do.
John Twohy Brusstar (fishing)	107	1894		1903		Baltimore, Md	May 5, 1905	Mila, Va	May 3, 1904	Do.
Lizzie Colburn (fishing)	130	1875		1894		Boothbay, Me	Apr. 12, 1905	Carters Creek, Va	Apr. 8, 1904	Do.
Menhaden (fishing)	93	1905		1897		Pocomoke City, Md	May 11, 1905	Crisfield, Md	First inspn	
Northumberland (fishing)	167	1897		1900		do	Apr. 25, 1905	Reedville, Va	Apr. 28, 1904	Do.
Pocomoke (fishing)	139	1902	1903	1903		do	Apr. 28, 1905	Baltimore, Md	May 3, 1904	Do.
Potomac (fishing)	135	1903		1903		do	do	Reedville, Va	Apr. 26, 1904	Do.
Pile-driver No. 2 (pile driver)	65	1889	1903	1878		Washington, D. C.	June 9, 1905	Washington, D. C.	May 26, 1904	Do.
Pilot (pilot)	189	1880		1901		Wilmington, Del	Oct. 20, 1905	Baltimore, Md	Nov. 2, 1904	Do.
Rappahannock (fishing)	135	1903		1903		Pocomoke City, Md	Apr. 25, 1905	Fairport, Va	Apr. 28, 1904	Do.
R. B. Douglas (fishing)	129	1901		1901		do	May 12, 1905	Baltimore, Md	May 17, 1904	Do.
Samson (pile driver)	16	1904		1905		Cambridge, Md	Aug. 22, 1905	Cambridge, Md	First inspn	
Tangier (fishing)	145	1903		1903		Pocomoke City, Md	Apr. 28, 1905	Baltimore, Md	May. 3, 1904	Do.

Virginia (fishing)	142	1893		1893		Bordentown, N. J	do	Reedville, Va	Apr. 28, 1904	Do.
William S. Brusstar (fishing)	132	1902		1902		Baltimore, Md	Apr. 21, 1905	Baltimore, Md	May 19, 1904	Do.
Wicomico (fishing)	141	1900		1903		Pocomoke City, Md	Apr. 28, 1905	Reedville, Va	Apr. 28, 1904	Do.
Vessels propelled by gasolin motors.										
A. Woodall	92	1903				Cambridge, Md	Sept. 14, 1905	Baltimore, Md	Sept. 20, 1904	Baltimore, Md.
Bertie E. Tull	163	1895				Pocomoke City, Md	Oct. 16, 1905	do	Oct. 14, 1904	Do.
Charles M. Kelley	51	1892				Severn River, Md	Jan. 21, 1905	Annapolis, Md	Jan. 14, 1904	Do.
Chelsea	98	1905				Pocomoke City, Md	Apr. 29, 1905	Baltimore, Md	First inspn	
Erciffe (passenger)	43	1904				Salisbury, Md	June 2, 1905	do	May 27, 1904	Do.
Elizabeth	69	1901				Baltimore, Md	July 18, 1905	do	July 21, 1904	Do.
Gladys	29	1899				Tilghmans Island, Md	May 16, 1905	do	May 7, 1904	Do.
Kitty Woodall	103	1905				Cambridge, Md	Aug. 14, 1905	do	First inspn	
Leland Mills	52	1901				do	July 22, 1905	do	July 18, 1904	Do.
Leader	39	1905				Madison, Md	May 19, 1905	do	First inspn	
Lauretta Curran	23	1901				do	May 24, 1905	do	May 25, 1904	Do.
Louisa	183	1905				Solomons, Md	Sept. 4, 1905	Solomons, Md	First inspn	
Margaret Atkinson	50	1904				Blankford, Md	Sept. 16, 1905	Baltimore, Md	do	
Pioneer	19	1901				Cambridge, Md	July 3, 1905	do	July 5, 1904	Do.
Pioneer	43	1885				Marcushook, Pa	July 8, 1905	do	June 17, 1904	Do.
Sarah E. Vickers	53	1894				Lankford Bay, Md	Aug. 29, 1905	do	First inspn	
Wm. J. Blankfard	26	1900				Cambridge, Md	Dec. 11, 1905	do	Dec. 6, 1904	Do.
Freight sail vessels of over 700 gross tons.										
Acme (ship)	3,288	1901				Bath, Me	Apr. 26, 1905	Baltimore, Md	Dec. 29, 1903	New York, N. Y.
Good News (barkentine)	712	1889				Baltimore, Md	Apr. 13, 1905	do	Apr. 21, 1904	Baltimore, Md.
Iona Tunnell (schooner)	1,315	1899				Millbridge, Me	June 10, 1905	do	June 3, 1904	Norfolk, Va.
Josephine (barkentine)	940	1895				Belfast, Me	Apr. 5, 1905	do	Apr. 18, 1904	Baltimore, Md.
Mount Hope (schooner)	1,105	1887				Camden, Me	June 17, 1905	Curtis Bay, Md	June 16, 1904	Boston, Mass.
Malcolm B. Seavey (schooner)	1,247	1901				Bath, Me	Mar. 20, 1905	do	Mar. 27, 1904	Baltimore, Md.
Mary T. Quimby (schooner)	1,172	1899				Thomaston, Me	Feb. 3, 1905	do	Feb. 3, 1904	Galveston, Tex.
Sail vessels over 100 tons carrying passengers for hire.										
White Wings (barkentine)	678	1898				Baltimore, Md	Jan. 3, 1905	Baltimore, Md	Sept. 1, 1903	Baltimore, Md.
W. H. Dix (schooner)	212	1901				Pocomoke City, Md	Mar. 8, 1905	do	Dec. 3, 1903	Do.

LOCAL DISTRICT OF CHARLESTON, S. C.

Inland passenger steamers.										
Alexander Jones	134	1877		1888		Baltimore, Md	Mar. 8, 1905	Wilmington, N. C	Mar. 9, 1904	Charleston, S. C.
Alice	45	1903		1903		Wilmington, N. C	Dec. 13, 1905	do	Dec. 17, 1904	Do.
A. J. Johnson	57	1899		1896		Clear Run, N. C	Jan. 10, 1905	do	Jan. 9, 1904	Do.

DOMESTIC VESSELS INSPECTED, YEAR ENDED DECEMBER 31, 1905—THIRD SUPERVISING DISTRICT—CHARLESTON, S. C.—Continued.

Names of vessels and class.	Gross tonnage.	Hull built.	Hull rebuilt.	Boilers built.	Boilers rebuilt.	Where built.	Date of inspection.	Where inspected.	Date of previous inspection.	Local district where previously inspected.
Inland passenger steamers—Continued.										
Atlantic City	71	1890		1891		Newark, N. J	Dec. 16, 1905	Charleston, S. C	Dec. 20, 1904	Charleston, S. C.
Ava	a3	1890		1903		Fall River, Mass	Feb. 3, 1905	Wilmington, N. C	Feb. 3, 1904	Do.
Blanche	94	1878		1903		Philadelphia, Pa	July 3, 1905	do	July 2, 1904	Do.
Brigantine	67	1893		1893		do	Oct. 13, 1905	Charleston, S. C	Oct. 15, 1904	Philadelphia, Pa.
C. W. Bailey	32	1897		1900		Charleston, S. C	Aug. 28, 1905	do	Aug. 30, 1904	Charleston, S. C.
Charles M. Whitlock	49	1901		1900		Point Caswell, N. C	Apr. 10, 1905	Wilmington, N. C	Apr. 9, 1904	Do.
City of Fayetteville	194	1902		1901		Jacksonville, Fla	Nov. 21, 1905	do	Dec. 30, 1903	Do.
Compton	247	1889	1904	1889	1904	Wilmington, Del	Mar. 15, 1905	do	Mar. 12, 1904	Norfolk, Va.
Duplin	59	1904		1903		Chinquepin, N. C	Feb. 3, 1905	do	Feb. 26, 1904	Charleston, S. C.
E. T. Williams	97	1898		1898		Madison, Md	Sept. 23, 1905	Georgetown, S. C	Oct. 6, 1904	Do.
Elizabeth	10	1875		1889	1902	Tottenville, N. Y	Mar. 28, 1905	Charleston, S. C	Mar. 23, 1904	Do.
Fearless	18	1871		1889	1901	Brooklyn, N. Y	Sept. 7, 1905	Georgetown, S. C	Sept. 7, 1904	Do.
F. G. Burroughs	283	1898	1901	1883		Conway, S. C	Jan. 12, 1905	do	Jan. 14, 1904	Do.
Frank Sessoms	93	1894	1900	1889		Wilmington, N. C	Nov. 29, 1905	do	Dec. 5, 1904	Do.
Governor Safford	307	1884		1899		Camden, N. J	June 15, 1905	do	June 15, 1904	Do.
Ira	56	1891		1897		Norfolk, Va	Aug. 15, 1905	Wiggins, S. C	Aug. 31, 1904	Norfolk, Va.
Josephine	33	1902		1902		Mount Pleasant, S. C	Mar. 18, 1905	Charleston, S. C	Mar. 11, 1904	Charleston, S. C.
Lillian	17	1889		1893		New York, N. Y	June 12, 1905	Wilmington, N. C	June 10, 1904	Do.
Lorena	9	1904		1897		Santee, S. C	Sept. 7, 1905	Georgetown, S. C	Sept. 7, 1904	Do.
Lotta	141	1881	1900	1894		Athens, N. Y	Apr. 3, 1905	Charleston, S. C	Apr. 6, 1904	Do.
Marion	206	1905		1905		Charleston, S. C	June 7, 1905	do	First inspn	
Marion	62	1879		1889	1901	Baltimore, Md	Apr. 10, 1905	Wilmington, N. C	Apr. 9, 1904	Do.
Mary Draper	46	1869	1897	1903		Jacksonville, Fla	Sept. 20, 1905	Yonges Island, S. C	Oct. 4, 1904	Do.
Mayflower	92	1904		1904		Point Caswell, N. C	Aug. 23, 1905	Wilmington, N. C	Aug. 23, 1904	Do.
Merchant	405	1878		1905		Wilmington, Del	Sept. 19, 1905	Charleston, S. C	Oct. 6, 1904	Do.
Mitchelle C	135	1905		1905		Conway, S. C	Oct. 3, 1905	Conway, S. C	First inspn	
Navassa	36	1869	1899	1888		Philadelphia, Pa	Apr. 10, 1905	Wilmington, N. C	Apr. 9, 1904	Do.
Planter	499	1876		1903		Charleston, S. C	Oct. 26, 1905	Charleston, S. C	Oct. 25, 1904	Do.
Protector	98	1882		1893		Camden, N. J	June 24, 1905	do	June 28, 1904	Do.
Rosa	47	1903		1885		Wilmington, N. C	Sept. 4, 1905	Wilmington, N. C	Sept. 3, 1904	Do.
Ruth	89	1888		1888		Conway, S. C	Feb. 10, 1905	Conway, S. C	Jan. 29, 1904	Do.
Sanders	74	1903		1902		Little River, S. C	Feb. 3, 1905	Wilmington, N. C	Feb. 3, 1904	Do.
Sea Gate	125	1894		1893		Newburg, N. Y	July 21, 1.05	do	July 15, 1904	New York, N. Y.
Southport	34	1898		1898		Peekskill, N. Y	July 3, 1905	do	July 2, 1904	Charleston, S. C.
Talbot	66	1883		1896		Rondout, N. Y	Apr. 30, 1905	Charleston, S. C	May 5, 1904	Do.
Tar Heel	99	1903		1883		Wilmington, N. C	May 22, 1905	Wilmington, N. C	May 21, 1904	Do.
Thistle	13	1895		1903		Charleston, S. C	Sept. 29, 1905	Georgetown, S. C	Oct. 6, 1904	Do.
Waban	163	1899		1898		Philadelphia, Pa	Jan. 16, 1905	Charleston, S. C	Jan. 15, 1904	Do.
Wilmington	161	1882		1901		do	Apr. 24, 1905	Wilmington, N. C	Apr. 22, 1904	Do.
Wm. Elliott	171	1899		1898		Georgetown, S. C	Feb. 8, 1905	Georgetown, S. C	Oct. 6, 1903	Do.
Wm. P. Congdon	68	1889		1889		Camden, N. J	Aug. 11, 1905	do	Aug. 11, 1904	Do.

Ferry steamers.										
Commodore Perry	538	1859		1884		Brooklyn, N. Y.	May 2,1905	Charleston, S. C.	May 4,1904	Charleston, S. C.
Sappho	333	1874	1897	1897		...do	Apr. 13,1905	...do	Apr. 13,1904	Do.
Ocean freight steamer.										
Katahdin	1,380	1895		1895		West Bay City, Mich.	Oct. 24,1905	Georgetown, S. C.	Nov. 10,1904	Charleston, S. C.
Inland freight steamers.										
Bee	16	1905		1889	1905	Strawhorn Landing, N. C.	Dec. 26,1905	Wilmington, N. C.	First inspn.	
Brunswick [b]	67	1896		1896		Wilmington, Del.	Sept. 29,1905	Georgetown, S. C.	Aug. 23,1904	Charleston, S. C.
City of Columbia	189	1905		1905		Columbia, S. C.	July 29,1905	Columbia, S. C.	First inspn.	
E. A. Hawes	49	1895		1885		Point Caswell, N. C.	Feb. 3,1905	Wilmington, N. C.	Feb. 3,1904	Do.
Elk	24	1892	1900	1888		Wilmington, N. C.	Aug. 4,1905	...do	Aug. 3,1904	Do.
Eutaw	547	1882		1894		Charleston, S. C.	Feb. 23,1905	Georgetown, S. C.	Jan. 26,1904	Do.
Franklin Pierce	36	1902		1890		Shallotte, N. C.	Aug. 4,1905	Wilmington, N. C.	Aug. 3,1904	Do.
Nannie B	85	1887		1896		Stella, N. C.	May 6,1905	Charleston, S. C.	Apr. 5,1904	Do.
Romain	62	1905		1904		McClellanville, S. C.	Feb. 6,1905	...do	First inspn.	
Inland towing steamers.										
Almont	a 4	1897		1895	1903	Wilmington, N. C.	Mar. 13,1905	Georgetown, S. C.	Mar. 22,1904	Charleston, S. C.
Big Four	26	1904		1889		Georgetown, S. C.	Jan. 12,1905	...do	Jan. 26,1904	Do.
Black River	6	1902		1887		Wilmington, N. C.	Mar. 30,1905	Wilmington, N. C.	Mar. 24,1904	Do.
Beulah	18	1897		1904		Mount Pleasant, S. C.	June 22,1905	Charleston, S. C.	June 21,1904	Do.
Buck	29	1897		1896		Wilmington, N. C.	Dec. 11,1905	...do	Dec. 13,1904	Do.
Bull River	16	1871	1900	1902		Charleston, S. C.	Nov. 8,1905	...do	Nov. 17,1904	Do.
Cecilia	98	1882		1882		Camden, N. J.	June 24,1905	...do	June 20,1904	Savannah, Ga.
Daniel's Island	18	1888	1904	1905		...do	Nov. 8,1905	...do	Nov. 11,1904	Charleston, S. C.
E. K. Bishop	44	1902		1890		Newbern, N. C.	Mar. 8,1905	Wilmington, N. C.	Mar. 8,1904	Do.
Emma	36	1899		1892		Wilmington, N. C.	Dec. 26,1905	...do	Dec. 17,1904	Do.
Emma A. Twiggs	16	1891		1898		Georgetown, S. C.	Aug. 11,1905	Georgetown, S. C.	Aug. 11,1904	Do.
Fawn	42	1900		1899		Swansboro, N. C.	Apr. 10,1905	Wilmington, N. C.	Apr. 9,1904	Do.
Henry L. Korter	19	1890		1897		Baltimore, Md.	Aug. 17,1905	Charleston, S. C.	June 20,1904	Do.
Henry Lloyd	13	1880		1897		Brooklyn, N. Y.	Jan. 12,1905	Georgetown, S. C.	Jan. 14,1904	Do.
Herbert M	30	1902		1891		Wilmington, N. C.	Sept. 4,1905	Wilmington, N. C.	Sept. 3,1904	Do.
Hope	9	1902		1891		Point Caswell, N. C.	Oct. 14,1905	...do	Oct. 17,1904	Do.
Ida	39	1870		1878		Philadelphia, Pa.	Jan. 28,1905	Charleston, S. C.	Jan. 25,1904	Do.
Imperial	29	1892		1892		New Haven, Conn.	Mar. 30,1905	Wilmington, N. C.	Mar. 8,1904	Do.
Jewel	9	1904		1897		Georgetown, S. C.	Mar. 13,1905	Georgetown, S. C.	Mar. 22,1904	Do.
Jones	29	1900		1900		Charleston, S. C.	Oct. 22,1905	Charleston, S. C.	Oct. 21,1904	Do.
L and L	21	1901		1891		...do	Apr. 3,1905	...do	Apr. 11,1904	Do.
Lark	9	1903		1903		Moncks Corner, S. C.	Oct. 31,1905	...do	Nov. 1,1904	Do.
Lila	a 4	1889		1905		Capers Island, S. C.	May 8,1905	...do	Apr. 16,1903	Do.
Lorena	36	1888		1891		Charleston, S. C.	Apr. 4,1905	...do	Feb. 29,1904	Do.
Lorretta	a 4	(c)		1893		Unknown	Aug. 11,1905	Georgetown, S. C.	Aug. 11,1904	Do.
Madge	a 3	1888		1888		Charleston, W. Va.	Sept. 7,1905	...do	Sept. 7,1904	Do.
Mabel S	48	1896		1890		New London, Conn.	Nov. 3,1905	...do	Nov. 21,1904	Do.
Marion	8	1905		1905		Santee River, S. C.	Dec. 23,1905	...do	First inspn.	
Maryland	16	1881		1895		Baltimore, Md.	Mar. 18,1905	Charleston, S. C.	Mar. 21,1904	Do.

a Estimated. b Formerly Penn-Dell, 1903. c Unknown.

DOMESTIC VESSELS INSPECTED, YEAR ENDED DECEMBER 31, 1905—THIRD SUPERVISING DISTRICT—CHARLESTON, S. C.—Continued.

Names of vessels and class.	Gross tonnage.	Hull built.	Hull rebuilt.	Boilers built.	Boilers rebuilt.	Where built.	Date of inspection.	Where inspected.	Date of previous inspection.	Local district where previously inspected.
Inland towing steamers—Con.										
R. C. Barkley	16	1885		1895		Charleston, S. C	Apr. 17, 1905	Charleston, S. C	Apr. 18, 1904	Charleston, S. C.
R. J. Armstrong	60	1903		1903		Columbia, S. C	Sept. 23, 1905	Georgetown, S. C	May 23, 1904	Do.
Sea Gull	9	1889		1897		Morris Island, S. C	Apr. 7, 1905	Charleston, S. C	Apr. 5, 1904	Do.
Spray	5	1892		1899		Brooklyn, N. Y	Mar. 29, 1905	Jacksonville, N. C	Mar. 25, 1904	Do.
Susie Magwood	19	1886		1893		Charleston, S. C	Jan. 23, 1905	Charleston, S. C	Jan. 19, 1904	Do.
Tom T	41	1898		1888		Newbern, N. C	Mar. 13, 1905	Georgetown, S. C	Mar. 10, 1904	Do.
Willie	a 6	1893		1893	1900	Charleston, S. C	Sept. 7, 1905	do	Sept. 7, 1904	Do.
W. H. Andrews	57	1905		1894		Georgetown, S. C	June 5, 1905	do	First inspn	
Steam pleasure yachts.										
Bertie	7	1892		1893	1901	New York, N. Y	Jan. 12, 1905	Georgetown, S. C	Jan. 14, 1904	Charleston, S. C.
Dove	50	1885	1899	1900		Wilmington, Del	Jan. 16, 1905	Charleston, S. C	Dec. 9, 1903	Do.
E. H. Jackson	85	1891		1891		Charleston, S. C	Oct. 31, 1905	do	Oct. 15, 1904	Do.
Flory	a 4	1896		1892		do	Apr. 20, 1905	do	Apr. 5, 1904	Do.
Husted	16	1895	1905	1901		Peekskill, N. Y	Sept. 7, 1905	Georgetown, S. C	Sept. 7, 1904	Do.
Leila	a 5	1896		1901		do	July 26, 1905	do	July 26, 1904	Do.
Mystic	a 4	1885		1895		Hoboken, N. J	Mar. 1, 1905	Jacksonboro, S. C	Feb. 17, 1904	Do.
Pelican	a 4	1898		1901		St. Joseph, Mich	June 15, 1905	Georgetown, S. C	June 15, 1904	Do.
Petrel	a 4	1901		1901		Croton on Hudson, N. Y.	Sept. 7, 1905	do	Sept. 7, 1904	Do.
Miscellaneous steam vessels.										
Carolina (pile driver)	22	1878		1898		Charleston, S. C	May 10, 1905	Charleston, S. C	Apr. 5, 1904	Charleston, S. C.
Kingfisher (fishing)	93	1872		1890	1901	Bristol, R. I	June 17, 1905	Wilmington, N. C	June 13, 1904	Providence, R. I.
R. C. Cantwell (fishing)	a 2	1902		1902		Wilmington, N. C	Apr. 24, 1905	do	Apr. 22, 1904	Charleston, S. C.
Vessels propelled by gasoline motors.										
Calypso [b]	26	1893				Groton, Conn	June 12, 1905	Wilmington, N. C	First inspn	
Isabel	16	1905				Southport, N. C	Nov. 15, 1905	do	do	
J. C. Allen	20	1901				Shallotte, N. C	Sept. 4, 1905	do	Sept. 3, 1904	Charleston, S. C.
Spray	25	1898				Charleston, S. C	July 19, 1905	Charleston, S. C	July 21, 1904	Do.
Freight sail vessels of over 700 tons.										
Baltimore (bark)	722	1888				Baltimore, Md	Mar. 23, 1905	Charleston, S. C	Feb. 18, 1904	Baltimore, Md.
Clifford N. Carver (schooner)	1,101	1900				Bath, Me	Jan. 28, 1905	do	Jan. 22, 1904	Philadelphia, Pa.
James Pierce (schooner)	1,664	1901				Thomaston, Me	Mar. 24, 1905	Wilmington, N. C	Mar. 24, 1904	Baltimore, Md.

LOCAL DISTRICT OF SAVANNAH, GA.

Ocean passenger steamers.										
Chatham	2,728	1885		1898		Philadelphia, Pa	July 7,1905	Savannah, Ga	July 7,1904	Baltimore, Md.
Chattahoochee	2,627	1882		1900		Chester, Pa	Nov. 13,1905	do	Nov. 23,1904	Savannah, Ga.
City of Atlanta	5,433	1904		1903		do	July 12,1905	do	July 15,1904	Philadelphia, Pa.
City of Columbus	5,433	1904		1904		do	Apr. 25,1905	do	Apr. 26,1904	Do.
City of Macon	5,311	1903		1903		do	May 5,1905	do	May 2,1904	Savannah, Ga.
City of Memphis	5,252	1902		1901		do	Apr. 10,1905	do	Apr. 15,1904	Do.
Nacoochee	2,680	1882		1889		do	Oct. 16,1905	do	Oct. 29,1904	Do.
Tallahassee	2,677	1882		1903		do	May 4,1905	do	May 4,1904	Do.
Inland passenger steamers.										
Annie Laurie	20	1891		1900		Cedar Bayou, La	May 22,1905	Brunswick, Ga	May 28,1904	Savannah, Ga.
Attaquin	112	1898		1898		Boston, Mass	June 15,1905	do	June 15,1904	Boston, Mass.
Cambria	89	1883		1883		Charleston, S. C	Mar. 1,1905	Savannah, Ga	Feb. 27,1904	Savannah, Ga.
City of Bluffton	56	1904		1903		Barrel Landing, S. C.	Mar. 10,1905	do	Mar. 8,1904	Do.
Clayton	275	1890	1900	1900		Matthews Bluff, S. C.	May 11,1905	do	May 10,1904	Do.
Clifton	256	1883	1889	1883	1904	New York, N. Y	June 24,1905	do	June 25,1904	Do.
Cynthia No. 2	108	1882	1900	1890	1904	Philadelphia, Pa	Sept. 8,1905	do	Sept. 16,1904	Do.
Dorothy	74	1891		1896		Westerly, R. I	July 19,1905	Brunswick, Ga	July 16,1904	New York, N. Y.
Edgar F. Coney	153	1904		1904		Camden, N. J	July 24,1905	do	July 19,1904	Philadelphia, Pa.
Egmont	15	1882		1893		Brooklyn, N. Y	Nov. 16,1905	do	Nov. 29,1904	Savannah, Ga.
Emmeline	137	1890		1904		Ashtabula, Ohio	do	do	Nov. 18,1904	Do.
G. T. Melton	347	1900		1894		Piney Bluff, Ga	Feb. 6,1905	Doctortown, Ga	Feb. 1,1904	Do.
Hessie	66	1900		1900		North Amboy, N. J	June 14,1905	Brunswick, Ga	June 15,1904	Do.
Hildegarde	149	1898		1902		Westerly, R. I	July 19,1905	do	July 29,1904	Do.
H. M. C. Smith	98	1891		1891		Camden, N. J	Nov. 14,1905	Savannah, Ga	Oct. 31,1904	Do.
Inca	103	1875	1899	1898		Philadelphia, Pa	Feb. 9,1905	Brunswick, Ga	Feb. 15,1904	Do.
Katie	530	1882		1899		Charleston, S. C	Mar. 25,1905	Savannah, Ga	Mar. 21,1904	Do.
Louise	129	1890		1892		Mount Pleasant, S. C.	Apr. 5,1905	do	Apr. 1,1904	Do.
Louise	355	1901		1896		Jacksonville, Fla	Aug. 5,1905	do	June 30,1904	Do.
Pilot Boy	288	1885		1903		Charleston, S. C	Mar. 30,1905	Beaufort, S. C	Mar. 31,1904	Do.
Passport	94	1874	1904	1904		Northport, N. Y	June 28,1905	Brunswick, Ga	July 25,1904	Do.
Summer Girl	53	1893		1905		Noank, Conn	June 2,1905	Beaufort, S. C	June 3,1904	Do.
Swan	281	1904		1904		Jacksonville, Fla	Dec. 29,1905	Savannah, Ga	Dec. 21,1904	Jacksonville, Fla.
Tupper	60	1902		1902		Brunswick, Ga	June 14,1905	Brunswick, Ga	June 16,1904	Savannah, Ga.
Two States	362	1901		1901		Savannah, Ga	Oct. 16,1905	Savannah, Ga	Oct. 17,1904	Do.
Wilmington	162	1900		1881	1900	Wilmington Island, Ga.	June 1,1905	do	May 25,1904	Do.
Ferry steamer.										
Eclipse	6	1892		1899		Providence, R. I	June 24,1905	Savannah, Ga	June 27,1904	Savannah, Ga.
Ocean freight steamers.										
Mississippi	9,713	1903		1903		Camden, N. J	Oct. 11,1905	Savannah, Ga	Oct. 8,1904	Galveston, Tex.
Viking	234	1894		1894		Wilmington, Del	Mar. 4,1905	do	July 15,1902	New York, N. Y.

[a] Estimated.

[b] Formerly pleasure yacht.

DOMESTIC VESSELS INSPECTED, YEAR ENDED DECEMBER 31, 1905—THIRD SUPERVISING DISTRICT—SAVANNAH, GA.—Continued.

Names of vessels and class.	Gross tonnage.	Hull built.	Hull rebuilt.	Boilers built.	Boilers rebuilt.	Where built.	Date of inspection.	Where inspected.	Date of previous inspection.	Local district where previously inspected.
Inland freight steamers.										
Alice	72	1901		1900		Abbeville, Ga	Dec. 11, 1905	Abbeville, Ga	Dec. 5, 1904	Savannah, Ga.
Augusta	512	1905		1905		Augusta, Ga	Aug. 31, 1905	Augusta, Ga	First inspn	
C. H. Evans	57	1890		1890		Athens, N. Y	June 27, 1905	Brunswick, Ga	June 29, 1904	Do.
Dixie	142	1903		1898		Lumber City, Ga	Oct. 2, 1905	Lumber City, Ga	Sept. 15, 1904	Do.
Emma	84	1902		1887		Augusta, Ga	May 17, 1905	Augusta, Ga	June 14, 1904	Do.
George Garbutt	442	1901		1901		Garbutt Landing, Ga.	Dec. 13, 1905	Brunswick, Ga	Dec. 12, 1904	Do.
Nannine	20	1901		1901		Savannah, Ga	June 5, 1905	Savannah, Ga	June 4, 1904	Do.
Nellie Garbutt	281	1903		1897		Garbutt Landing, Ga.	Oct. 12, 1905	Abbeville, Ga	Oct. 3, 1904	Do.
Ocmulgee	57	1902		1897		Macon, Ga	June 10, 1905	Macon, Ga	Apr. 27, 1904	Do.
R. C. Henry	195	1900		1885		Dublin, Ga	June 23, 1905	Dublin, Ga	June 18, 1904	Do.
Rover	195	1901		1893		do	Oct. 13, 1905	do	Sept. 29, 1904	Do.
Southland	261	1903		1903		do	Jan. 24, 1905	do	Dec. 28, 1903	Do.
Inland towing steamers.										
Angie and Nellie	45	1882		1889		Wilmington, Del	Apr. 7, 1905	Brunswick, Ga	Apr. 6, 1904	Galveston, Tex.
Dandy	115	1888		1899		Camden, N. J	May 15, 1905	Fernandina, Fla	May 11, 1904	Savannah, Ga.
Forest City	86	1872		1886		Philadelphia, Pa	May 31, 1905	Savannah, Ga	May 16, 1904	Do.
Grantham I. Taggart	85	1890	1905	1901		Brooklyn, N. Y	Mar. 23, 1905	do	First inspn	
Harold	34	1877	1897	1897		Fall River, Mass	Apr. 26, 1905	do	Apr. 13, 1904	Do.
Iris	65	1881	1900	1888		Camden, N. J	May 22, 1905	Brunswick, Ga	May 19, 1904	Do.
Jacob Paulsen	97	1890		1890	1903	Philadelphia, Pa	Mar. 14, 1905	Savannah, Ga	Mar. 23, 1904	Do.
J. C. Mallonee	34	1882	1903	1897	1903	Baltimore, Md	Nov. 21, 1905	do	Dec. 7, 1904	Do.
Jennie E	12	1869		1891		New York, N. Y	Sept. 7, 1905	do	Mar. 18, 1904	Do.
Juno	62	1874	1905	1884	1904	Camden, N. J	July 29, 1905	do	Mar. 19, 1904	Do.
Kate Cannon	50	1887		1887		Norfolk, Va	July 15, 1905	do	June 24, 1904	Do.
Maggie	26	1878		1890	1896	Savannah, Ga	Oct. 16, 1905	do	Oct. 12, 1904	Do.
Marion	417	1900		1893		Augusta, Ga	May 17, 1905	Augusta, Ga	May 13, 1904	Do.
Maud	42	1862	1900	1881		Philadelphia, Pa	May 20, 1905	Savannah, Ga	Dec. 10, 1904	Do.
May McWilliams	53	1889		1902		Jersey City, N. J	Apr. 28, 1905	Beaufort, S. C	Apr. 21, 1904	Do.
Osage	5	1901		1900		Bluffton, S. C	Apr. 10, 1905	Savannah, Ga	Mar. 25, 1904	Do.
Regis	91	1891		1891		Camden, N. J	June 30, 1905	do	June 25, 1904	Do.
Sophie	46	1862	1892	1883	1894	Wilmington, Del	Mar. 14, 1905	do	Dec. 11, 1903	Do.
Urbanus Dart	42	1884		1887	1903	Brunswick, Ga	May 22, 1905	Brunswick, Ga	May 18, 1904	Do.
Wade Hampton	113	1877		1897		Charleston, S. C	Nov. 22, 1905	Fernandina, Fla	Nov. 28, 1904	Do.
Steam pleasure yachts.										
Alameda	87	1895		1902		Baltimore, Md	Nov. 20, 1905	Beaufort, S. C	Nov. 15, 1904	Savannah, Ga.
Charlie D	a4	1897		1897		Brunswick, Ga	Feb. 6, 1905	Lumber City, Ga	Feb. 2, 1904	Do.
Eagle	30	1901		1901		Croton, N. Y	Mar. 9, 1905	Savannah, Ga	July 9, 1903	Norfolk, Va.

Elizabeth Gaffney	a 4	1895		1899		St. Marys, Ga	June 28, 1905	Brunswick, Ga	June 28, 1904	Savannah, Ga.
Elsie	a 4	1888		1904		Penrose, N. J	June 26, 1905	Savannah, Ga	June 1, 1904	Do.
Hattie	a 4	1892		1892		New York, N. Y	June 27, 1905	Brunswick, Ga	June 17, 1904	Do.
Hazel	10	1904		1904		Fernandina, Fla	July 25, 1905	Fernandina, Fla	June 29, 1904	Do.
Hornet	24	1891		1894		Nyack, N. Y	Apr. 20, 1905	....do	Apr. 19, 1904	Do.
Jekyl Island	64	1896		1896		Peekskill, N. Y	June 27, 1905	Brunswick, Ga	June 17, 1904	Do.
Jessie	43	1890		1894		Port Jefferson, N. Y	Oct. 10, 1905	Savannah, Ga	Oct. 12, 1904	Do.
Lillie May	a 5	1904		1898		Abbeville, Ga	Oct. 12, 1905	Abbeville, Ga	Oct. 3, 1904	Do.
Nancy	a 4	1888		1899		Newark, N. J	June 29, 1905	Fernandina, Fla	June 6, 1904	Do.
Skibo	45	1901		1901		Elizabethport, N. J	Feb. 2, 1905	....do	Jan. 14, 1904	Do.
Miscellaneous steam vessel.										
John H. Estill (pilot boat)	243	1894		1894		Newport News, Va	Oct. 7, 1905	Savannah, Ga	Oct. 31, 1904	Savannah, Ga.
Vessels propelled by gas motors.										
Imogene	21	1903				Mount Pleasant, S. C	Mar. 15, 1905	Savannah, Ga	Feb. 27, 1904	Savannah, Ga.
John W. Tatum	28	1901				Brunswick, Ga	Dec. 14, 1905	Brunswick, Ga	Dec. 12, 1904	Do.
Num Quam Dormeo	40	1905				....do	June 28, 1905	....do	First inspn	
Pearl	21	1891				Savannah, Ga	Dec. 19, 1905	Savannah, Ga	....do	
Freight sail vessels of over 700 gross tons.										
Chauncey E. Burk (schooner)	916	1891				Camden, N. J	Feb. 14, 1905	Savannah, Ga	Jan. 13, 1904	Philadelphia, Pa.
L. Herbert Taft (schooner)	1,492	1901				Thomaston, Me	Jan. 26, 1905	Fernandina, Fla	Jan. 28, 1904	Galveston, Tex.
Matanzas (schooner)	1,028	1889				Bath, Me	Mar. 1, 1905	Savannah, Ga	July 13, 1904	Savannah, Ga.
R. W. Hopkins (schooner)	935	1896				Thomaston, Me	Jan. 16, 1905	Brunswick, Ga	Jan. 13, 1904	Do.

LOCAL DISTRICT OF JACKSONVILLE, FLA.

Ocean passenger steamers.										
Martinique	996	1897		1897		Bath, Me	Aug. 2, 1905	Miami, Fla	Aug. 3, 1904	Jacksonville, Fla.
Miami	1,741	1897		1897		Philadelphia, Pa	Jan. 9, 1905	....do	Jan. 11, 1904	Do.
Inland passenger steamers.										
Biscayne	301	1888	1904	1888	1904	Abbeville, Ga	Apr. 28, 1905	Miami, Fla	Apr. 27, 1904	Jacksonville, Fla.
Canaveral	46	1891	1903	1904		Jacksonville, Fla	Jan. 11, 1905	Eau Gallie, Fla	Jan. 12, 1904	Do.
City of Jacksonville	459	1882		1903		Wilmington, Del	June 24, 1905	Jacksonville, Fla	June 25, 1904	Do.
Crescent	253	1893	1903	1903		Jacksonville, Fla	Dec. 12, 1905	....do	Dec. 17, 1904	Do.
Fearless	24	1897		1899		Palatka, Fla	June 22, 1905	Palatka, Fla	June 22, 1904	Do.
Frederick de Bary	395	1881	1884	1899		Wilmington, Del	May 12, 1905	Jacksonville, Fla	May 12, 1904	Do.
Gladys	19	1890	1894	1903		Peekskill, N. Y	Feb. 13, 1905	....do	Feb. 9, 1904	Do.
Harry Lee	34	1894		1900		St. Marys, Ga	Aug. 7, 1905	Palatka, Fla	July 29, 1904	Savannah, Ga.

a Estimated.

DOMESTIC VESSELS INSPECTED, YEAR ENDED DECEMBER 31, 1905—THIRD SUPERVISING DISTRICT—BALTIMORE, MD.—Continued.

DOMESTIC VESSELS INSPECTED, YEAR ENDED DECEMBER 31, 1905—THIRD SUPERVISING DISTRICT—JACKSONVILLE, FLA.—Continued.

Names of vessels and class.	Gross tonnage.	Hull built.	Hull rebuilt.	Boilers built.	Boilers rebuilt.	Where built.	Date of inspection.	Where inspected.	Date of previous inspection.	Local district where previously inspected.
Inland passenger steamers—Continued.										
Heck	80	1904		1904		Jacksonville, Fla	Sept. 7, 1905	Jacksonville, Fla	Sept. 3, 1904	Jacksonville, Fla.
Hessie	54	1881		1905		Tottenville, N. Y	Nov. 28, 1905	do	Nov. 30, 1904	Do.
Hiawatha	129	1904		1904		Palatka, Fla	Mar. 20, 1905	Palatka, Fla	Mar. 21, 1904	Do.
Lida	[a] 4	1901		1893		Astatula, Fla	Oct. 24, 1905	Leesburg, Fla	Oct. 27, 1904	Do.
L. McNeil	145	1899		1899		Jacksonville, Fla	Feb. 17, 1905	Jacksonville, Fla	Feb. 19, 1904	Do.
Martha Helen	75	1878	1905	1905		Berkley, Va	May 26, 1905	Miami, Fla	May 27, 1904	Do.
May Garner	101	1893	1901	1893	1901	Jacksonville, Fla	Apr. 7, 1905	Jacksonville, Fla	Apr. 8, 1904	Do.
Okeehumkee	65	1873	1893	1893		Palatka, Fla	Jan. 16, 1905	Palatka, Fla	Jan. 16, 1904	Do.
Three Kids	48	1902		1902		Jacksonville, Fla	Jan. 18, 1905	Eustis, Fla	Jan. 8, 1904	Do.
William Howard	97	1903		1903		Palatka, Fla	Apr. 3, 1905	Silver Springs, Fla	Apr. 1, 1904	Do.
William S. Brusstar	45	1890		1890		Baltimore, Md	Feb. 8, 1905	Miami, Fla	Feb. 8, 1904	Savannah, Ga.
Ferry steamers.										
Duval	348	1904		1904		Jacksonville, Fla	Sept. 14, 1905	Jacksonville, Fla	Sept. 19, 1904	Jacksonville, Fla.
Transport	38	1905		1894		Palatka, Fla	Feb. 10, 1905	Palatka, Fla	First inspn.	
Ocean towing steamers.										
Admiral Dewey	125	1898		1896		Jacksonville, Fla	May 19, 1905	Jacksonville, Fla	May 17, 1904	Jacksonville, Fla.
Biscayne	99	1881	1900	1900		Wilmington, Del	Nov. 9, 1905	do	Nov. 4, 1904	Do.
Dauntless	153	1893		1893		Camden, N. J	Nov. 14, 1905	Miami, Fla	Nov. 7, 1904	Savannah, Ga.
Three Friends	157	1896		1896		Jacksonville, Fla	Mar. 16, 1905	Jacksonville, Fla	Feb. 26, 1904	Jacksonville, Fla.
Inland towing steamers.										
Agnes K	15	1900		1900		New Berlin, Fla	Aug. 9, 1905	Jacksonville, Fla	Aug. 9, 1904	Jacksonville, Fla.
Annie B	9	1900		1901		Jacksonville, Fla	May 8, 1905	do	May 11, 1904	Do.
Annie H	40	1893	1897	1893		Dinsmore, Fla	Nov. 17, 1905	do	Aug. 2, 1904	Do.
Aztec	26	1902		1902		Picolata, Fla	July 24, 1905	Green Cove Springs, Fla.	July 19, 1904	Do.
Bertha Ritter	27	1899		1903		Jacksonville, Fla	Oct. 27, 1905	Jacksonville, Fla	Nov. 19, 1904	Do.
Bessie	16	1898		1897		Picolata, Fla	Jan. 16, 1905	Palatka, Fla	Jan. 16, 1904	Do.
Bon Acord	42	1899		1898		Georgetown, S. C	Aug. 8, 1905	Jacksonville, Fla	Aug. 3, 1904	Do.
Cadillac	29	1904		1902		Jacksonville, Fla	Nov. 16, 1905	do	Nov. 14, 1904	Do.
Eloise	8	1901	1905	1901		do	Sept. 27, 1905	Sanford, Fla	Sept. 20, 1904	Do.
Frank	26	1883		1897		Baltimore, Md	June 17, 1905	Jacksonville, Fla	June 16, 1904	Do.
Homer	68	1894	1904	1904		Newburg, N. Y	Sept. 22, 1905	Palatka, Fla	Oct. 4, 1904	Do.
Hoo Hoo	32	1902		1902		Buffalo Bluff, Fla	Sept. 11, 1905	do	Sept. 10, 1904	Do.
Kathleen	84	1902		1902		Myers, Fla	June 27, 1905	Myers, Fla	Sept. 27, 1903	Apalachicola, Fla.
Klondike	40	1896		1892		Tuckertown, N. J	Sept. 20, 1905	Jacksonville, Fla	Dec. 12, 1903	Do.

Komuk	49	1888	1905	1888	1905	New York, N. Y.	Sept. 21,1905	do	Sept. 27,1904	Do.
Levi H. Pelton	46	1892		1892		Jacksonville, Fla.	Nov. 14,1905	Miami, Fla.	Nov. 19,1904	Jacksonville, Fla.
Mary Howard	38	1900		1900		Palatka, Fla.	Dec. 8,1905	Palatka, Fla.	Dec. 10,1904	Do.
May Haw	9	1894		1894		Crescent City, Fla.	Mar. 31,1905	Crescent City, Fla.	Mar. 28,1904	Do.
Neptune	19	1902		1904		Palatka, Fla.	Oct. 16,1905	Jacksonville, Fla.	Oct. 22,1904	Do.
Nettie J	9	1904		1904		Sanford, Fla.	Sept. 13,1905	Sanford, Fla.	Sept. 2,1904	Do.
Niely V	a 3	1892		1900		Jacksonville, Fla.	Oct. 2,1905	Jacksonville, Fla.	Aug. 9,1904	Do.
Red Wing	19	1893		1897		New Berlin, Fla.	June 12,1905	do	June 11,1904	Do.
Rosa	89	1853	1891	1872		New York, N. Y.	Jan. 12,1905	do	June 29,1903	Do.
Ruby	17	1880	1904	1890		St. Simons, Ga.	Mar. 13,1905	do	Mar. 12,1904	Do.
Ruth E	34	1895		1903		Satsuma, Fla.	Sept. 15,1905	do	Sept. 19,1904	Do.
S. S. Brewster	50	1883		1903		Port Jefferson, N. Y.	Sept. 5,1905	do	Sept. 1,1904	Do.
St. Johns	81	1904		1901		Jacksonville, Fla.	June 30,1905	do	June 29,1904	Do.
Inland steam pleasure yachts.										
Alice W	a 4	1898	1904	1898		Sanford, Fla.	Mar. 23,1905	Welaka, Fla.	Mar. 23,1904	Jacksonville, Fla.
Augusta	28	1893		1893		Boston, Mass.	July 5,1905	Jacksonville, Fla.	June 22,1903	New York, N. Y.
Doozie	47	1901		1904		Racine, Wis.	Dec. 8,1905	Palatka, Fla.	Dec. 1,1904	Jacksonville, Fla.
Edith	16	1892	1904	1897	1904	Bristol, R. I.	Oct. 3,1905	Jacksonville, Fla.	Oct. 10,1904	Do.
Ichthyosaurus	69	1905		1892	1903	Cocoa, Fla.	Jan. 14,1905	Cocoa, Fla.	First inspn.	
Rose	a 2	1901		1900		Waukeegan, Ill.	May 23,1905	Astatula, Fla.	May 20,1904	Do.
Roseville	a 2	1891	1901	1901		Camden, N. J.	Mar. 15,1905	Rockledge, Fla.	Mar. 18,1904	Do.
Vagabondia	98	1902		1902		Jacksonville, Fla.	Oct. 25,1905	Palatka, Fla.	Oct. 25,1904	Do.
Yankee Doodle	a 4	1894	1898	1900		Silver Springs, Fla.	Mar. 23,1905	Welaka, Fla.	Mar. 23,1904	Do.
Vessels propelled by gasoline motors.										
Chase (fishing)	21	1889				Tampa, Fla.	Nov. 7,1905	Miami, Fla.	First inspn.	
Emily B. (freight)	43	1887	1900			Jacksonville, Fla.	Nov. 15,1905	Palm Beach, Fla.	Oct. 7,1904	Jacksonville, Fla.
Lee S. (passenger)	17	1902				do	Mar. 6,1905	Jacksonville, Fla.	First inspn.	
Meta (pilot boat)	43	1872	1905			Pamrapo, N. J.	Sept. 6,1905	do	Aug. 2,1904	Do.
Mount Pleasant (fishing)	20	1902	1904			Elliotts Key, Fla.	May 1,1905	do	First inspn.	
Princess Issena (passenger)	44	1899				Long Island City, N.Y.	Feb. 9,1905	Ormond, Fla.	Feb. 9,1904	Do.

FOURTH SUPERVISING DISTRICT.

LOCAL DISTRICT OF ST. LOUIS, MO.

Inland passenger steamers.										
Bald Eagle	468	1898		1898		Madison, Ind.	May 2,1905	St. Louis, Mo.	May 11,1904	St. Louis, Mo.
Belle of Ottawa	10	1875		1894		Chicago, Ill.	June 21,1905	Beardstown, Ill.	June 23,1904	Do.
Belle of Calhoun	451	1895		1895		St. Louis, Mo.	Aug. 5,1905	St. Louis, Mo.	June 10,1904	Do.
Conquest	209	1899		1899		Sterling Island, Mo.	Mar. 11,1905	do	May 14,1904	Do.

a Estimated.

DOMESTIC VESSELS INSPECTED, YEAR ENDED DECEMBER 31, 1905—FOURTH SUPERVISING DISTRICT—ST. LOUIS, MO.—Continued.

Names of vessels and class.	Gross tonnage.	Hull built.	Hull rebuilt.	Boilers built.	Boilers rebuilt.	Where built.	Date of inspection.	Where inspected.	Date of previous inspection.	Local district where previously inspected.
Inland passenger steamers—Continued.										
Corwin H. Spencer	1,609	1887		1897		Jeffersonville, Ind	Apr. 8, 1905	St. Louis, Mo	Apr. 9, 1904	St. Louis, Mo.
Cantonia	75	1891		1891		Rock Island, Ill	Apr. 24, 1905	Quincy, Ill	do	Do.
City of Providence	1,303	1880		1880		Jeffersonville, Ind	Apr. 26, 1905	St. Louis, Mo	Apr. 22, 1904	Do.
Cape Girardeau	747	1899	1901	1899		Madison, Ind	June 8, 1905	do	Apr. 9, 1904	Do.
City of Memphis	432	1898		1898		Jeffersonville, Ind	June 22, 1905	do	June 24, 1904	Do.
City of Savannah	293	1902		1902		do	July 7, 1905	do	June 29, 1904	Do.
City of Peoria	128	1892		1892		do	July 10, 1905	Havana, Ill	July 25, 1904	Do.
Chester	631	1888		1900		Dubuque, Iowa	Oct. 10, 1905	St. Louis, Mo	Oct. 11, 1904	Do.
Dauntless	26	1898		1898		Hermann, Mo	Apr. 11, 1905	Hermann, Mo	Apr. 11, 1904	Do.
Daily	35	1904		1896		Commerce, Mo	Apr. 21, 1905	Thebes, Ill	Apr. 21, 1904	Do.
Dubuque	748	1895		1899		Dubuque, Iowa	Apr. 22, 1905	St. Louis, Mo	Apr. 23, 1904	Do.
Desplaines	6	1901		1901		St. Joseph, Mich	Apr. 29, 1905	do	Apr. 21, 1904	Do.
D'Artagnan	26	1904		1904		St. Louis, Mo	May 25, 1905	do	Apr. 4, 1904	Do.
Davenport	4	1902		1902		Racine, Wis	Sept. 21, 1905	do	June 17, 1904	Do.
Eleonore	97	1902		1905		Beardstown, Ill	Mar. 27, 1905	Beardstown, Ill	Apr. 18, 1904	Do.
Echo	15	1892		1898		St. Joseph, Mich	Nov. 29, 1905	St. Louis, Mo	June 16, 1904	Do.
Ferd Herold	900	1890		1890		Dubuque, Iowa	June 22, 1905	do	June 24, 1904	Do.
Frank	31	1879		1887	1905	La Crosse, Wis	Dec. 28, 1905	do	June 17, 1904	Dubuque, Iowa.
Gardie Eastman	100	1903		1899		Rock Island, Ill	Mar. 23, 1905	Quincy, Ill	Apr. 6, 1904	Do.
Grey Eagle	555	1892		1905		Jeffersonville, Ind	Aug. 16, 1905	St. Louis, Mo	June 6, 1904	St. Louis, Mo.
Harry Lynds	27	1892		1895		White Cloud, Kans	May 9, 1905	White Cloud, Kans	May 9, 1904	Do.
Henry Wohlt	67	1900		1900		Hermann, Mo	July 24, 1905	Hermann, Mo	Aug. 9, 1904	Do.
India Givens	228	1886		1886		Evansville, Ind	Apr. 15, 1905	St. Louis, Mo	Jan. 14, 1904	Do.
Illinois	168	1901		1888		Quincy, Ill	Sept. 1, 1905	Beardstown, Ill	Aug. 30, 1904	Do.
J. A. Schulte	4	1895		1896		Havana, Ill	Mar. 17, 1905	Havana, Ill	Mar. 18, 1904	Do.
Josie L. K	27	1884		1900		Yankton, S. Dak	May 13, 1905	Yankton, S. Dak	May 13, 1904	Do.
Julius F. Silber	69	1905		1905		Hermann, Mo	July 24, 1905	Hermann, Mo	First inspn	
J. B. Richardson	191	1898		1898		Jeffersonville, Ind	Nov. 15, 1905	St. Louis, Mo	Nov. 18, 1904	Evansville, Ind.
Kennedy	140	1901		1901		Lyons, Iowa	June 1, 1905	do	June 1, 1904	St. Louis, Mo.
Lucius, jr	31	1901		1900		Memphis, Tenn	Feb. 27, 1905	do	Feb. 20, 1904	Do.
Lora	257	1900		1887		Stillwater, Minn	May 3, 1905	do	May 9, 1904	Do.
Little Dick	4	1902		1900		Beardstown, Ill	June 21, 1905	Beardstown, Ill	June 23, 1904	Do.
Mark Twain	224	1873		1889		Madison, Ind	Jan. 7, 1905	St. Louis, Mo	Jan. 7, 1904	Do.
Minnehaha	8	1893		1894		Canton, S. Dak	May 12, 1905	Sioux City, Iowa	May 11, 1904	Do.
Mary C. Lucas	51	1903		1904		St. Louis, Mo	May 29, 1905	St. Louis, Mo	May 28, 1904	Do.
Mary	50	1901		1902		Beardstown, Ill	June 21, 1905	Beardstown, Ill	June 23, 1904	Do.
Nick Sauer	99	1882		1882		Chester, Ill	June 8, 19, 25, 1905.	Chester, Ill., and St. Louis, Mo.	June 7, 1904	Do.
Nadine	27	1892		1889		Lamine, Mo	Nov. 22, 1905	Jefferson City, Mo	May 18, 1904	Do.
Nina	9	1904		1904		Peoria, Ill	Sept. 12, 1905	Havana, Ill	Sept. 13, 1904	Do.

Oom Paul	3	1901	....	1901	....	Alton, Ill	May 18, 1905	Alton, Ill	May 20, 1904	Do.
Peerless	60	1893	....	1893	....	Hermann, Mo	Mar. 1, 1905	Gasconade, Mo	Feb. 13, 1904	Do.
Percy Swain	115	1882	....	1883	....	Reads Landing, Minn	Mar. 23, 1905	Quincy, Ill	Apr. 3, 1904	Do.
Peters Lee	463	1899	....	1899	....	Jeffersonville, Ind	Oct. 7, 1905	St. Louis, Mo	Oct. 10, 1904	Do.
R. C. Gunter	238	1886	....	1883; 1886	....	Chattanooga, Tenn	Apr. 28, 1905	Kansas City, Mo	Apr. 25, 1904	Do.
Silver Crescent	125	1882	....	1882	....	Clinton, Iowa	Mar. 23, 1905	Quincy, Ill	Mar. 23, 1904	Do.
Spread Eagle	691	1893	....	1893	....	Jeffersonville, Ind	Apr. 15, 1905	St. Louis, Mo	Apr. 15, 1904	Do.
Saturn	189	1901	....	1884	....	Rock Island, Ill	May 27, 1905	....do	Apr. 23, 1904	Dubuque, Iowa.
Sidney	617	1880	1903	1880	....	Wheeling, W. Va	June 14, 1905	....do	June 21, 1904	St. Louis, Mo.
Stacker Lee	710	1902	....	1902	....	Jeffersonville, Ind	June 20, 1905	....do	June 28, 1904	Do.
Susie Hazard	98	1881	....	1905	....	St. Louis, Mo	Aug. 2, 1905	....do	Sept. 7, 1904	Do.
Saint Paul	832	1903	....	1883; 1903	....	Dubuque, Iowa	Aug. 31, 1905	....do	Aug. 30, 1904	Do.
Uncle Sam	469	1898	....	1882	1902; 1905	Sterling Island, Ill	May 5-6, 1905	Quincy, Ill	Apr. 7, 1904	Do.
Wm. McClellan [a]	185	1901	....	1892	1901	Jeffersonville, Ind	June 12, 1905	East St. Louis, Ill	June 7, 1904	Do.
W. L. Heckmann	48	1904	....	1904	....	Hermann, Mo	Aug. 30, 1905	Hermann, Mo	Aug. 29, 1904	Do.
Ferry steamers.										
Altonian	92	1880	1898	1881	....	Cincinnati, Ohio	Apr. 1, 1905	Alton, Ill	Apr. 1, 1904	St. Louis, Mo.
Annie Cade	178	1879	....	1879	....	Leavenworth, Kans	Apr. 13, 1905	Kansas City, Mo	Apr. 15, 1904	Do.
Andrew Christy	830	1897	....	1897	....	Jeffersonville, Ind	June 11, 1905	East St. Louis, Ill	June 13, 1904	Do.
Alonzo C. Church	332	1893	....	1893	....	....do	Oct. 7, 1905	....do	Oct. 8, 1904	Do.
City of Warsaw	178	1895	....	1895	....	....do	Mar. 14, 1905	Cape Girardeau, Mo	Mar. 29, 1904	Do.
Carlos S. Greeley	403	1883	....	1884	....	....do	May 3, 1905	Venice, Ill	Sept. 21, 1904	Do.
Dr. Frederick Hill	160	1870	....	1890	....	Metropolis, Ill	Sept. 6, 1905	St. Louis, Mo	Sept. 6, 1904	Do.
Ella May	66	1903	....	1885	....	St. Louis, Mo	Apr. 7, 1905	Quincy, Ill	Apr. 8, 1904	Do.
Florence	170	1889	....	1889	....	Jeffersonville, Ind	May 29, 1905	St. Louis, Mo	May 28, 1904	Do.
George A. Madill	613	1891	1903	1891	....	....do	Oct. 16, 1905	East St. Louis, Ill	Oct. 17, 1904	Do.
Henry Sackman	610	1883	....	1883	....	....do	June 6, 1905	....do	June 11, 1904	Do.
Henry L. Clark	287	1891	....	1891	....	....do	Aug. 3, 1905	....do	Aug. 3, 1904	Do.
Jos. L. Stephens	85	1887	....	1887	....	....do	Apr. 11, 1905	Boonville, Mo	Apr. 11, 1904	Do.
J. T. Davis	124	1880	....	1880	....	Grafton, Ill	May 5, 1905	Quincy, Ill	Apr. 8, 1904	Do.
Lois	35	1896	....	1896	....	Waverly, Mo	Apr. 12, 1905	Lexington, Mo	Apr. 12, 1904	Do.
Mill Boy	41	1893	....	1893	....	Hermann, Mo	Apr. 14, 1905	Osage, Mo	Feb. 4, 1904	Do.
Meeker	42	1897	....	1897	....	Chester, Ill	June 9-10, 1905	Alexandria, Mo	June 8, 1904	Do.
Madison	292	1892	....	1892	....	Jeffersonville, Ind	Sept. 21, 1905	Venice, Ill	June 22, 1904	Do.
Minnie	25	1904	....	1904	....	Osage, Mo	Nov. 24, 1905	Waverly, Mo	Dec. 10, 1904	Do.
New Pike	75	1887	....	1887	....	Madison, Ind	June 16, 1905	Louisiana, Mo	June 18, 1904	Do.
Peoples Ferry	183	1889	....	1889	....	....do	Apr. 7, 1905	Quincy, Ill	Apr. 7, 1904	Do.
Perryville	77	1904	....	1892	....	Jeffersonville, Ind	Dec. 12, 1905	Chester, Ill	Dec. 20, 1904	Do.
Ste. Genevieve	611	1903	....	1903	....	....do	Feb. 21, 1905	Ste. Genevieve, Mo	Feb. 25, 1904	Do.
Saml. B. Wiggins	364	1885	....	1885	....	....do	June 11, 1905	East St. Louis, Ill	June 13, 1904	Do.
W. B. Duncan	575	1881	....	1881	....	....do	Mar. 14, 1905	Thebes, Ill	Mar. 26, 1904	Do.
Inland freight steamers.										
Buck Elk	58	1900	....	1900	....	Hermann, Mo	Apr. 11, 1905	Hermann, Mo	Apr. 11, 1904	St. Louis, Mo.
Columbia	73	1898	....	1900	....	Osage, Mo	Apr. 12, 1905	Miami, Mo	Apr. 12, 1904	Do.

[a] Character changed to towing steamer Dec. 8, 1905.

DOMESTIC VESSELS INSPECTED, YEAR ENDED DECEMBER 31, 1905—FOURTH SUPERVISING DISTRICT—ST. LOUIS, MO.—Continued.

Names of vessels and class.	Gross tonnage.	Hull built.	Hull rebuilt.	Boilers built.	Boilers rebuilt.	Where built.	Date of inspection.	Where inspected.	Date of previous inspection.	Local district where previously inspected.
***Inland freight steamers*—Con**										
J. R. Wells	206	1898		1898		Tuscumbia, Mo	Apr. 4, 1905	Osage, Mo	Apr. 15, 1904	St. Louis, Mo.
Little Joker	4	1903		1895		Venice, Ill	June 16, 1905	Hannibal, Mo	May 4, 1904	Do.
Little Maud	89	1901		1889		Running Water, S. Dak.	June 28, 1905	Running Water, S. Dak.	May 12, 1904	Do.
Messenger Boy	51	1904		1891		Sioux City, Iowa	Aug. 22, 1905	Sioux City, Iowa	Aug. 16, 1904	Do.
Inland towing steamers.										
Adam Given	48	1899		1899		Sioux City, Iowa	May 9, 1905	St. Joseph, Mo	May 9, 1904	St. Louis, Mo.
Blanche	48	1895		1895		Evansville, Ind	Apr. 17, 1905	Alton, Ill	Apr. 17, 1904	Duluth, Minn.
Birmingham	187	1891		1891		Lavenna, Ohio	July 26, 1905	St. Louis, Mo	May 25, 1904	Memphis, Tenn.
Colorado	45	1891		1903		St. Louis, Mo	Mar. 29, 1905	....do	Mar. 28, 1904	St. Louis, Mo.
City of Pekin No. 2	4	1892		1896		Beardstown, Ill	Apr. 18, 1905	Beardstown, Ill	Apr. 18, 1904	Do.
Dolphin No. 3	564	1897		1897		Jeffersonville, Ind	Apr. 24, 1905	St. Louis, Mo	Apr. 29, 1904	Do.
Dorothy	30	1882		1882		Carondelet, Mo	May 9, 1905	St. Joseph, Mo	May 9, 1904	Do.
Ebaugh	50	1902		1900	1902	Pekin, Ill	June 21, 1905	Beardstown, Ill	June 20, 1904	Do.
Eagle	188	1898		1904		Jeffersonville, Ind	Nov. 4, 1905	St. Louis, Mo	Nov. 8, 1904	Do.
Fred Nellis	70	1876	1904	1880		....do	June 13, 1905	Grays Point, Mo	June 8, 1904	Do.
Geo. Gardner	72	1903		1903		Point Pleasant, W. Va	Nov. 20, 1905	St. Louis, Mo	Nov. 29, 1904	Wheeling, W. Va.
Henry C. Haarstick	226	1897		1897		Jeffersonville, Ind	Mar. 20, 1905	East St. Louis, Ill	Mar. 9, 1904	St. Louis, Mo.
Harry Reid	58	1882		1882		Madison, Ind	Mar. 25, 1905	Peruque, Mo	Mar. 22, 1904	Do.
Henry W. Longfellow	46	1881		1898		Lake Minnetonka, Minn.	Sept. 12, 1905	Havana, Ill	Sept. 12, 1904	Do.
Iris	35	1884		1884		Keokuk, Iowa	Mar. 23, 1905	Quincy, Ill	Apr. 7, 1904	Do.
Ida Patton	26	1884		1884		Dubuque, Iowa	July 7, 1905	St. Louis, Mo	May 24, 1904	Do.
Ida Mc	33	1894		1894		Chester, Ill	Oct. 9, 1905	Havana, Ill	June 17, 1904	Do.
James Y. Lockwood	390	1896		1899		McKees Rock, Pa	Apr. 3, 1905	St. Louis, Mo	Apr. 2, 1904	Do.
Junior	33	1899		1890		Kansas City, Mo	May 9, 1905	St. Joseph, Mo	May 9, 1904	Do.
Jessie Bill	60	1882		1882		Wabasha, Minn	June 21, 1905	Beardstown, Ill	July 1, 1904	Dubuque, Iowa.
Louisiana	286	1902		1883		Hastings, Minn	Apr. 5, 1905	St. Louis, Mo	May 28, 1904	Duluth, Minn.
Margaret	100	1896		1900		Paducah, Ky	Mar. 7, 1905	Hannibal, Mo	Feb. 8, 1904	St. Louis, Mo.
Moline	192	1880	1904	1880	1901	Cincinnati, Ohio	Apr. 13, 1905	Kansas City, Mo	Apr. 15, 1904	Do.
New Haven	80	1892	1900	1892		Pomeroy, Ohio	Mar. 25, 1905	St. Louis, Mo	Sept. 9, 1903	Do.
Pinta	8	1890		1890		Louisiana, Mo	June 16, 1905	Louisiana, Mo	June 18, 1904	Do.
R. G. Schmoldt	19	1891	1903	1891	1902	Peoria, Ill	Mar. 27, 1905	Beardstown, Ill	Apr. 18, 1904	Do.
Robt. E. Carr	30	1903		1904		Dubuque, Iowa	Mar. 29, 1905	St. Louis, Mo	June 9, 1904	Do.
Remora	49	1875		1875		Keithburg, Ill	Sept. 5, 1905	Quincy, Ill	June 17, 1904	Do.
Ruth	36	1894		1894		Gasconade, Mo	Nov. 9, 1905	Alton, Ill	Nov. 4, 1904	Do.
Reliance	59	1890		1890		Dubuque, Iowa	Dec. 6, 1905	St. Louis, Mo	Dec. 6, 1904	Do.
T. H. Davis	240	1898		1900		Middleport, Ohio	Feb. 7, 1905	Manning, Mo	Feb. 12, 1904	Evansville, Ind.
Wm. M. Towle	96	1891		1880		Metropolis, Ill	May 13, 1905	Sioux City, Iowa	May 12, 1904	St. Louis, Mo.
Wm. K. Kavanaugh	203	1898		1902		Dubuque, Iowa	Feb. 1, 1905	St. Louis, Mo	Nov. 6, 1903	Do.

Steam pleasure yachts.										
Annie Russell	127	1902	....	1898	....	Dubuque, Iowa	June 5, 1905	St. Louis, Mo	June 1, 1904	St. Louis, Mo.
Bimini	4	1900	....	1900	....	Springfield, Ill	June 21, 1905	Beardstown, Ill	June 23, 1904	Do.
Dolly B	4	1904	....	1904	....	St. Louis, Mo	Oct. 14, 1905	St. Louis, Mo	June 16, 1904	Do.
Esther	16	1904	....	1893	1904	....do	Mar. 2, 1905	East St. Louis, Ill	First inspn.	
Idlewild	4	1879	....	1879	1904	Winona, Minn	July 28, 1905	St. Louis, Mo	July 9, 1904	Do.
Katie S	4	1903	....	1903	....	St. Louis, Mo	July 12, 1905	....do	June 27, 1904	Do.
North Star	10	1905	....	1905	....	....do	July 28, 1905	....do	First inspn.	
Ouatoga	19	1895	....	1895	....	Nyack, N. Y	May 18, 1905	Alton, Ill	May 20, 1904	Do.
Vernon, jr	33	1902	....	1902	....	Manitowoc, Wis	July 10, 1905	Havana, Ill	May 12, 1904	Chicago, Ill.
Vessels propelled by gasoline motors.										
Annie Austin	19	1895	1903	....	....	Vermilion, S. Dak	June 30, 1905	Ponca, Nebr	July 13, 1904	St. Louis, Mo.
Bonhomme	20	1904	....	....	....	Bonhomme, S. Dak	Oct. 20, 1905	Bonhomme, S. Dak	Oct. 20, 1904	Do.
City of Springfield	24	1904	....	....	....	Springfield, S. Dak	June 29, 1905	Springfield, S. Dak	July 15, 1904	Do.
Lloyd	26	1902	....	....	....	Norborne, Mo	Apr. 12, 1905	Miami, Mo	Apr. 26, 1904	Do.
Queen of Decatur	24	1905	....	....	....	Decatur, Nebr	May 11, 1905	Decatur, Nebr	First inspn.	
Romana	20	1892	....	....	....	Osage, Mo	Apr. 14, 1905	Osage, Mo	Apr. 26, 1904	Do.
Susie B	41	1903	....	....	....	Running Water, S. Dak.	May 12, 1905	Running Water, S. Dak.	May 12, 1904	Do.
St. James	19	1902	....	....	....	St. James, Nebr	June 29, 1905	Meckling, S. Dak	July 14, 1904	Do.
Violet	15	1901	....	....	....	Sioux City, Iowa	June 27, 1905	West Blencoe, Iowa	July 12, 1904	Do.
Wellington	17	1903	....	....	....	Wellington, Mo	Aug. 8, 1905	Wellington, Mo	Aug. 9, 1904	Do.
Barges of over 100 tons carrying passengers for hire.										
Kennard	479	1896	....	....	....	McKeesport, Pa	Feb. 7, 1905	Manning, Mo	Feb. 25, 1904	Nashville, Tenn.
Pearl	438	1896	....	....	....	Newport, Ark	July 10, 1905	Havana, Ill	July 25, 1904	St. Louis, Mo.

FIFTH SUPERVISING DISTRICT.

LOCAL DISTRICT OF DUBUQUE, IOWA.

Inland passenger steamers.										
Apollo No. 1	44	1898	....	1892	....	Kilbourn, Wis	July 8, 1905	Kilbourn, Wis	July 7, 1904	Dubuque, Iowa.
Benjamin	25	1904	....	1904	....	Moline, Ill	Nov. 8, 1905	Moline, Ill	First inspn.	
Chaperon	98	1904	....	1904	....	Clinton, Iowa	Apr. 21, 1905	Clinton, Iowa	Apr. 25, 1904	Do.
City of Hudson	61	1899	....	1899	....	Stillwater, Minn	Aug. 3, 1905	La Crosse, Wis	Aug. 4, 1904	Do.
City of Nauvoo	56	1886	....	1886	....	Rock Island, Ill	Apr. 7, 1905	Montrose, Iowa	Apr. 7, 1904	Do.
Columbia	222	1897	....	1900	....	Clinton, Iowa	May 27, 1905	Rock Island, Ill	June 28, 1904	St. Louis, Mo.
Cyclone	138	1891	....	1890	....	Stillwater, Minn	Apr. 17, 1905	Wabasha, Minn	Apr. 12, 1904	Dubuque, Iowa.
Eagle Point	50	1884	1900	1884	....	Dubuque, Iowa	June 6, 1905	Dubuque, Iowa	June 6, 1904	Do.
Eclipse	148	1905	....	1890	....	....do	Apr. 16, 1905	Rock Island, Ill	Apr. 16, 1904	Do.

DOMESTIC VESSELS INSPECTED, YEAR ENDED DECEMBER 31, 1905—FIFTH SUPERVISING DISTRICT—DUBUQUE, IOWA—Continued.

Names of vessels and class.	Gross tonnage.	Hull built.	Hull rebuilt.	Boilers built.	Boilers rebuilt.	Where built.	Date of inspection.	Where inspected.	Date of previous inspection.	Local district where previously inspected.
Inland passenger steamers—Continued.										
Eleanor	48	1903		1887		Kilbourn, Wis	July 6, 1905	Kilbourn, Wis	July 7, 1904	Dubuque, Iowa.
Eloise	89	1889		1889		Harmar, Ohio	May 2, 1905	Burlington, Iowa	May 2, 1904	Do.
E. Rutledge	212	1892		1904		Rock Island, Ill	Mar. 29, 1905	Rock Island, Ill	Mar. 29, 1904	Do.
Fountain City	65	1905		1905		Stillwater, Minn	July 13, 1905	Fountain City, Wis	First inspn.	
Frontenac	146	1896		1888		Wabasha, Minn	Apr. 12, 1905	Winona, Minn	Apr. 12, 1904	Do.
Gallardo	45	1904		1904		La Crosse, Wis	Apr. 13, 1905	La Crosse, Wis	Apr. 11, 1904	Do.
Helen Blair	213	1897		1897		Marietta, Ohio	Apr. 29, 1905	Rock Island, Ill	Apr. 6, 1904	Do.
H. L.	38	1905		1905		Clinton, Iowa	June 17, 1905	Clinton, Iowa	First inspn.	
Ianthe	22	1902		1902		Stillwater, Minn	Sept. 25, 1905	Rock Island, Ill	Oct. 2, 1904	Do.
James P. Pearson [a]	20	1898	1900	1898		Moline, Ill	Sept. 16, 1905	Moline, Ill	Aug. 24, 1904	Do.
Jap	21	1905		1872		La Crosse, Wis	May 12, 1905	La Crosse, Wis	First inspn.	
Jim Leighton	109	1895		1891		Pierre, S. Dak	Apr. 30, 1905	Pierre, S. Dak	Apr. 29, 1904	Do.
Lion	38	1875	1888	1891		Lyons, Iowa	Apr. 11, 1905	Wabasha, Minn	Apr. 12, 1904	Do.
Maine	26	1897		1885		Portage, Wis	July 3, 1905	Dubuque, Iowa	June 28, 1904	Milwaukee, Wis.
Mamie B	8	1900		1895		Lansing, Iowa	May 6, 1905	McGregor, Iowa	May 7, 1904	Dubuque, Iowa.
Maud M	[b] 2	1896		1895		La Crosse, Wis	May 26, 1905	Minneiska, Minn	May 6, 1904	Do.
Mignon	18	1893	1904	1904		Dubuque, Iowa	Mar. 30, 1905	Muscatine, Iowa	Mar. 29, 1904	Do.
Nautilus	10	1899		1899		Burlington, Iowa	June 30, 1905	Burlington, Iowa	July 1, 1904	Do.
O. K. [c]	59	1899		1894		Cincinnati, Ohio	June 7, 1905	Dubuque, Iowa	Feb. 13, 1904	Louisville, Ky.
Ottumwa Belle	81	1895		1895		Canton, Mo	May 3, 1905	Fort Madison, Iowa	May 2, 1904	Dubuque, Iowa.
Potosi	48	1905		1901		Dubuque, Iowa	Sept. 28, 1905	Dubuque, Iowa	First inspn.	
Quincy	806	1896		1896	1905	do	Aug. 16, 1905	Eagle Point, Iowa	May 24, 1904	St. Louis, Mo.
Redfield	10	1895		1894		Racine, Wis	Aug. 18, 1905	do	Aug. 20, 1904	Milwaukee, Wis.
Robert Harris	36	1872	1896	1878		Burlington, Iowa	Apr. 22, 1905	Fountain City, Wis	Apr. 11, 1904	Dubuque, Iowa.
Rob Roy	5	1901		1899		do	May 2, 1905	Burlington, Iowa	May 2, 1904	Do.
Valeria	130	1904		1904		Clinton, Iowa	Aug. 25, 1905	Clinton, Iowa	Aug. 23, 1904	Do.
Verana	16	1905		1900		Minneiska, Minn	Apr. 10, 1905	Lake City, Minn	First inspn.	
Wanderer	84	1898		1898		Clinton, Iowa	Mar. 29, 1905	Clinton, Iowa	Mar. 28, 1904	Do.
Ferry steamers.										
Davenport	195	1904		1904		Rock Island, Ill	Aug. 24, 1905	Rock Island, Ill	Aug. 23, 1904	Dubuque, Iowa.
Nina Dousman	24	1888		1900		Prairie du Chien, Wis	May 9, 1905	Lyons, Iowa	May 9, 1904	Do.
T. J. Robinson [d]	155	1875	1900	1901		Clinton, Iowa	Mar. 20, 1905	Rock Island, Ill	Mar. 21, 1904	Do.
Wabasha	44	1894		1895		Wabasha, Minn	Jan. 5, 1905	Wabasha, Minn	Jan. 5, 1904	Do.
Inland towing steamers.										
A. J. Whitney	72	1880	1905	1892		Rock Island, Ill	Apr. 16, 1905	Davenport, Iowa	May 1, 1904	Dubuque, Iowa.
Arctic	18	1901		1898		Muscatine, Iowa	Mar. 30, 1905	Muscatine, Iowa	Mar. 29, 1904	Do.
Artemus Gates	90	1896		1895		Clinton, Iowa	Sept. 25, 1905	Clinton, Iowa	Oct. 4, 1904	Do.

Beder	14	1891		1895		Moline, Ill	Aug. 24, 1905	Moline, Ill	Aug. 24, 1904	Do.
B. Hershey	170	1877	1890	1891		Rock Island, Ill	Apr. 13, 1905	Lansing, Iowa	Apr. 17, 1904	Do.
Chancy Lamb	194	1892		1884		Dubuque, Iowa	Mar. 29, 1905	Clinton, Iowa	Mar. 28, 1904	Do.
Clipper	12	1899		1885		Buffalo, Iowa	Mar. 22, 1905	Muscatine, Iowa	Mar. 30, 1904	Do.
C. W. Cowles	180	1881		1881		Madison, Ind	Apr. 24, 1905	Dubuque, Iowa	Apr. 23, 1904	Do.
D. Cawley	19	1904		1896		Lyons, Iowa	May 9, 1905	Lyons, Iowa	May 9, 1904	Do.
Edna	14	1899		1884		Rock Island, Ill	Aug. 24, 1905	Rock Island, Ill	Aug. 23, 1904	Do.
E. Douglas	107	1896		1896		Wabasha, Minn	Apr. 11, 1905	West Newton, Minn	Apr. 13, 1904	Do.
Georgie S	54	1884	1898	1896		Savanna, Ill	Apr. 17, 1905	Wabasha, Minn	Apr. 19, 1904	Duluth, Minn.
Gracie Douglas	[b] 4	1904		1884		Diamond Bluff, Wis	May 26, 1905	Red Wing, Minn	Apr. 17, 1904	Dubuque, Iowa.
Great Eastern	2	1898		1889		Stoddard, Wis	May 12, 1905	McGregor, Iowa	Apr. 24, 1903	Do.
Hattie Darling	14	1893		1893		Rock Island, Ill	May 1, 1905	Rock Island, Ill	May 1, 1904	Do.
Hennepin	40	1897		1892		Davenport, Iowa	Apr. 16, 1905	Davenport, Iowa	Apr. 16, 1904	Do.
H. W. B	55	1903		1874		Muscatine, Iowa	June 3, 1905	Burlington, Iowa	June 3, 1904	Do.
Isaac Staples	147	1878	1899	1880		Stillwater, Minn	Apr. 17, 1905	Wabasha, Minn	Apr. 19, 1904	Duluth, Minn.
J. W. Van Sant	228	1890	1900	1890		Le Claire, Iowa	Apr. 4, 1905	Clinton, Iowa	Apr. 4, 1904	Dubuque, Iowa.
Kit Carson	237	1880		1894		Stillwater, Minn	Apr. 25, 1905	North La Crosse, Wis	Apr. 11, 1904	Do.
Lone Star	48	1890		1897		Rock Island, Ill	Aug. 24, 1905	Davenport, Iowa	Aug. 24, 1904	Do.
Lydia Van Sant	93	1898		1904		Le Claire, Iowa	Apr. 6, 1905	Eagle Point, Iowa	Apr. 19, 1904	Do.
Mary K	37	1902		1904		Lyons, Iowa	Mar. 21, 1905	Burlington, Iowa	Mar. 20, 1904	Do.
May Stewart	62	1905		1905		Dubuque, Iowa	May 8, 1905	Dubuque, Iowa	First inspn	
Minnie Schneider	32	1889	1902	1889		Galena, Ill	Apr. 4, 1905	Fulton, Ill	Mar. 28, 1904	Do.
Musser	163	1886		1886		Le Claire, Iowa	Apr. 13, 1905	Lansing, Iowa	Apr. 22, 1904	Do.
Park Bluff	96	1884		1884		Rock Island, Ill	Apr. 3, 1905	Dubuque, Iowa	Apr. 11, 1904	Do.
Phil Scheckel	99	1897		1881		Wabasha, Minn	Apr. 13, 1905	Lansing, Iowa	Apr. 17, 1904	Do.
Prescott	55	1903		1884		Rock Island, Ill	June 24, 1905	Rock Island, Ill	June 23, 1904	Do.
Ravenna	164	1889	1903	1882		South Stillwater, Minn.	Apr. 17, 1905	Wabasha, Minn	Apr. 18, 1904	Duluth, Minn.
R. D. Kendall	82	1896		1896		Rock Island, Ill	Mar. 29, 1905	Rock Island, Ill	Mar. 29, 1904	Dubuque, Iowa.
Scotia	31	1889		1893		La Crosse, Wis	Apr. 25, 1905	North La Crosse, Wis	Apr. 11, 1904	Do.
Turtle	10	1891		1891		Brotherton, Wis	May 6, 1905	Lansing, Iowa	May 7, 1904	Do.
Virginia	79	1905		1884		Wabasha, Minn	Oct. 22, 1905	Wabasha, Minn	First inspn	
Zalus Davis	46	1894		1894		Dubuque, Iowa	Apr. 24, 1905	Dubuque, Iowa	May 21, 1904	Do.
Steam pleasure yachts.										
City of Moline	52	1904		1905		Le Claire, Iowa	May 22, 1905	Moline, Ill	First inspn	
Ms [e]	[b] 2	1895		1895		Fort Madison, Iowa	Aug. 5, 1905	Fort Madison, Iowa	June 2, 1903	Dubuque, Iowa.
Miscellaneous steamers.										
Good Luck (pile driver)	43	1891		1891		Beef Slough, Wis	Apr. 11, 1905	West Newton, Minn	Apr. 13, 1904	Dubuque, Iowa.
Samson (pile driver)	38	1889		1889		do	do	do	do	Do.
Gasoline motor vessels.										
City of Ft. Pierre (inland passenger).	82	1904				Fort Pierre, S. Dak	May 27, 1905	Fort Pierre, S. Dak	June 10, 1904	Dubuque, Iowa.
Frentress (ferry)	58	1903				East Dubuque, Ill	May 25, 1905	Dubuque, Iowa	May 24, 1904	Do.
Iowa (inland passenger)	48	1897				Sioux City, Iowa	Apr. 13, 1905	Chamberlain, S. Dak	Apr. 8, 1904	Do.

[a] Formerly H. A. Barnard, 1903. [b] Estimated. [c] Formerly Burkesville, 1905. [d] Formerly Augusta, 1902. [e] Formerly Katherine H., 1905.

DOMESTIC VESSELS INSPECTED, YEAR ENDED DECEMBER 31, 1905—FIFTH SUPERVISING DISTRICT—DUBUQUE, IOWA—Continued.

Names of vessels and class.	Gross tonnage.	Hull built.	Hull rebuilt.	Boilers built.	Boilers rebuilt.	Where built.	Date of inspection.	Where inspected.	Date of previous inspection.	Local district where previously inspected.
Gasoline motor vessels—Con.										
J. R. (inland passenger)	20	1905				Eagle Point, Iowa	Mar. 31, 1905	Eagle Point, Iowa	First inspn	
J. H. Keene (inland passenger).	97	1903				Chamberlain, S. Dak.	May 25, 1905	Chamberlain, S. Dak.	June 8, 1904	Dubuque, Iowa.
Lillian (ferry)	17	1891				Eagle Point, Iowa	June 29, 1905	Galena, Ill	June 16, 1904	Do.
Little Pearl (ferry)	31	1902				Tower, Nebr	May 3, 1905	Fort Randall, S. Dak.	May 1, 1904	Do.
Oriole (ferry)	31	1903				Wheeler, S. Dak	June 3, 1905	Wheeler, S. Dak	May 3, 1904	Do.
Scotty Philip (inland passenger).	68	1900				Pierre, S. Dak	Apr. 30, 1905	Pierre, S. Dak	Apr. 29, 1904	Do.
Uella May (ferry)	17	1900				Vermilion, S. Dak	Aug. 2, 1905	Platte, S. Dak	Aug. 18, 1904	Do.
Winnie (inland passenger)	64	1903				Chamberlain, S. Dak.	Apr. 15, 1905	Evarts, S. Dak	Apr. 10, 1904	Do.
Barges of over 100 tons carrying passengers for hire.										
Chippewa	213	1900				Wabasha, Minn	May 18, 1905	Winona, Minn	Aug. 1, 1902	Duluth, Minn.
Comfort	153	1902				Prairie du Chien, Wis	June 15, 1905	Kimbels Park, Wis	June 15, 1904	Dubuque, Iowa.
Mae	150	1902				Diamond Bluff, Wis	May 26, 1905	Red Wing, Minn	June 6, 1904	Duluth, Minn.

LOCAL DISTRICT OF DULUTH, MINN.

Names of vessels and class.	Gross tonnage.	Hull built.	Hull rebuilt.	Boilers built.	Boilers rebuilt.	Where built.	Date of inspection.	Where inspected.	Date of previous inspection.	Local district where previously inspected.
Passenger steamers (lake).										
America	681	1898		1898		Wyandotte, Mich	May 23, 1905	Duluth, Minn	May 24, 1904	Duluth, Minn.
Bon Ami	226	1894		1894		Saugatuck, Mich	Apr. 28, 1905	do	May 2, 1904	Do.
C. W. Moore	383	1881		1886		Allegan, Mich	May 21, 1905	do	May 18, 1904	Do.
D. G. Kerr	5,531	1903		1903		Superior, Wis	June 14, 1905	do	June 23, 1904	Buffalo, N. Y.
D. M. Clemson	5,531	1903		1903		do	July 20, 1905	do	July 26, 1905	Duluth, Minn.
Easton	460	1896		1896		Baltimore, Md	May 24, 1905	do	May 24, 1904	Do.
Frank T. Heffelfinger	4,897	1901		1901		Chicago, Ill	Sept. 13, 1905	do	Oct. 10, 1904	Do.
George W. Peavey	4,997	1901		1901		Cleveland, Ohio	July 11, 1905	do	July 20, 1904	Do.
George W. Perkins	6,406	1905		1905		Superior, Wis	July 6, 1905	Superior, Wis	First inspn	
James H. Hoyt	3,934	1902		1902		do	July 13, 1905	Duluth, Minn	Aug. 3, 1904	Cleveland, Ohio.
Lafayette	5,113	1900		1900		Lorain, Ohio	June 7, 1905	Two Harbors, Minn	June 6, 1904	Duluth, Minn.
Mabel Bradshaw	331	1889		1889		Benton Harbor, Mich.	May 13, 1905	Duluth, Minn	May 11, 1904	Do.
Mariposa	2,831	1892		1900		Cleveland, Ohio	July 18, 1905	Two Harbors, Minn	July 16, 1904	Cleveland, Ohio.
Maritana	2,957	1892		1900		Chicago, Ill	May 24, 1905	Duluth, Minn	May 21, 1904	Do.
Mary Mann	11	1891		1884		Osakis, Minn	July 1, 1905	do	Aug. 8, 1903	Duluth, Minn.
Newsboy	199	1889	1903	1889		West Bay City, Mich.	May 31, 1905	do	June 2, 1904	Do.
Sahara	5,785	1904		1904		Lorain, Ohio	June 24, 1905	do	June 22, 1904	Cleveland, Ohio.

Saxona	4,716	1903		1903		Cleveland, Ohio	June 30, 1905	Two Harbors, Minn.	July 2, 1904	Duluth, Minn.
Skater	92	1890		1890		Detroit, Mich	May 29, 1905	Ashland, Wis	May 23, 1904	Do.
S. N. Parent	1,640	1903		1903		Wyandotte, Mich	May 28, 1905	Superior, Wis	May 18, 1904	Oswego, N. Y.
Spokane	2,356	1886		1896		Cleveland, Ohio	May 10, 1905	Duluth, Minn	May 17, 1904	Cleveland, Ohio.
Stella	9	1899		1890		Ashland, Wis	May 29, 1905	Ashland, Wis	May 20, 1904	Duluth, Minn.
Thomas Adams	3,784	1902		1902		Toledo, Ohio	June 19, 1905	Superior, Wis	July 2, 1904	Do.
Victory	4,527	1895	1905	1895		Chicago, Ill	May 8, 1905	Duluth, Minn	May 18, 1904	Milwaukee, Wis.
Wilbert L. Smith	4,319	1903		1903		Lorain, Ohio	July 24, 1905	do	July 19, 1904	Duluth, Minn.
Yosemite	3,879	1901		1901		Wyandotte, Mich	July 28, 1905	Superior, Wis	Aug. 24, 1904	Do.
Passenger steamers (river).										
Columbia	82	1900		1878		Stillwater, Minn	Apr. 10, 1905	Stillwater, Minn	May 23, 1902	Duluth, Minn.
Expansion	78	1900	1903	1903		Bismarck, N. Dak	May 15, 1905	Washburn, N. Dak	May 14, 1904	Do.
Fram	22	1900		1900		East Grand Forks, Minn.	May 12, 1905	East Grand Forks, Minn.	May 8, 1904	Do.
G. A. Mower	29	1886		1885		Arcola, Minn	do	St. Paul, Minn	May 10, 1904	Do.
Grand Forks	99	1895		1882		Grand Forks, N. Dak.	do	East Grand Forks, Minn.	May 8, 1904	
Hiawatha	85	1904		1904		St. Paul, Minn	June 9, 1905	St. Paul, Minn	June 6, 1904	Do.
Itasca	34	1903		1903		Beaudette, Minn	June 20, 1905	Fort Francis, Ont	June 19, 1904	Do.
Moose	40	1893	1904	1895		Harding, Minn	May 9, 1905	International Falls, Minn.	May 10, 1904	Do.
Na Ma Puck	24	1899		1899		Warroad, Minn	June 23, 1905	Beaudette, Minn	June 20, 1904	Do.
Ollie Bell[a]	10	1901		1896		St. Paul, Minn	July 6, 1905	Fort Snelling, Minn	July 6, 1904	Do.
Sea Gull	22	1898		1899		Rainy Lake, Minn	June 21, 1905	Kettle Falls, Minn	June 18, 1904	Do.
Se A Mo	[b] 10	1903		1903		St. Paul, Minn	June 22, 1905	Fort Francis, Ontario	do	Do.
The Purchase[c]	193	1869	1883	1882 1887		Pittsburg, Pa	Apr. 27, 1905	Hastings, Minn	Apr. 18, 1904	Dubuque, Iowa.
Washburn	57	1901		1901		Bismarck, N. Dak	May 16, 1905	Washburn, N. Dak	May 15, 1904	Duluth, Minn.
Winnifred Hayes	7	1897	1905	1897		Harding, Minn	June 21, 1905	Kettle Falls, Minn	June 17, 1904	Do.
Zillah	[b] 40	1884		1890		Dubuque, Iowa	July 14, 1905	Yellowstone Lake	July 21, 1904	Do.
Ferry steamers (lake).										
Belle	37	1885		1892		Benton Harbor, Mich.	Apr. 21, 1905	Duluth, Minn	May 6, 1904	Duluth, Minn.
Estelle	34	1876	1903	1876	1897	Watkins, N. Y	July 20, 1905	do	July 23, 1904	Do.
Hattie Lloyd	34	1883		1890		Duluth, Minn	June 5, 1905	Superior, Wis	May 6, 1904	Do.
Ideal	40	1885		1885		Buffalo, N. Y	May 21, 1905	Duluth, Minn	Apr. 8, 1904	Oswego, N. Y.
Mary Scott	47	1892	1900	1892		Ludington, Mich	May 16, 1905	Ashland, Wis	May 12, 1904	Duluth, Minn.
Swansea	19	1887		1887		Detroit, Mich	July 8, 1905	Duluth, Minn	July 8, 1904	Do.
Ferry steamers (river).										
J. O. Henning[d]	26	1878	1902	1869		Hudson, Wis	Sept. 3, 1904	Hudson, Wis	Sept. 2, 1903	Duluth, Minn.
J. O. Henning	26	1878	1902	1869		do	Sept. 4, 1905	do	Sept. 3, 1904	Do.
Sam Lilly	[b] 12	1899	1902	1901		Buford, N. Dak	May 22, 1905	Mondak, Mont	May 6, 1904	Do.
Two Brothers	29	1894		1894	1905	North Hudson, Wis.	Aug. 22, 1905	Stillwater, Minn	Sept. 17, 1904	Do.

[a] Formerly Bennington, 1901. [b] Estimated. [c] Formerly Mountain Belle, 1904. [d] Certificate issued July 29, 1905.

Domestic Vessels Inspected, Year ended December 31, 1905—Fifth Supervising District—Duluth, Minn.—Continued.

Names of vessels and class.	Gross tonnage.	Hull built.	Hull rebuilt.	Boilers built.	Boilers rebuilt.	Where built.	Date of inspection.	Where inspected.	Date of previous inspection.	Local district where previously inspected.
Freight steamers (lake).										
A. B. Wolvin	2,286	1900		1900		Cleveland, Ohio	May 18, 1905	Two Harbors, Minn.	May 31, 1904	Cleveland, Ohio.
Alex. Nimick	1,968	1890		1890		West Bay City, Mich.	June 23, 1905	Duluth, Minn.	June 20, 1904	Milwaukee, Wis.
Augustus B. Wolvin	6,585	1904		1904		Lorain, Ohio	Apr. 6, 1905	do	May 23, 1904	Cleveland, Ohio.
Charles R. Van Hise	5,117	1900		1900		Superior, Wis.	May 18, 1905	Two Harbors, Minn.	May 24, 1904	Chicago, Ill.
Christopher	4,260	1901		1901		do	Sept. 2, 1905	Duluth, Minn.	Sept. 30, 1904	Duluth, Minn.
Coralia	4,330	1896		1896		Cleveland, Ohio	May 27, 1905	Two Harbors, Minn.	May 23, 1904	Do.
Frank H. Peavey	5,002	1901		1901		Lorain, Ohio	Apr. 7, 1905	Duluth, Minn.	June 23, 1904	Do.
Frank Rockefeller	2,759	1896		1895		Superior, Wis.	May 14, 1905	do	May 16, 1904	Milwaukee, Wis.
Gilchrist	3,871	1901		1901		West Bay City, Mich.	June 3, 1905	Superior, Wis.	June 4, 1904	Buffalo, N. Y.
H. D. Coffinberry	778	1874		1892		East Saginaw, Mich.	May 30, 1905	Duluth, Minn.	May 31, 1904	Cleveland, Ohio.
Homer Warren [a]	448	1863		1880		Cleveland, Ohio	May 15, 1905	do	May 11, 1904	Detroit, Mich.
James J. Hill	6,025	1900		1900		Lorain, Ohio	May 22, 1905	Two Harbors, Minn.	May 26, 1904	Duluth, Minn.
James Watt	4,090	1896		1896		Cleveland, Ohio	May 9, 1905	do	May 7, 1904	Chicago, Ill.
Joliet	1,921	1890		1897		do	May 13, 1905	Duluth, Minn.	May 10, 1904	Cleveland, Ohio.
J. T. Hutchinson	3,734	1901		1901		do	May 2, 1905	do	May 4, 1904	Buffalo, N. Y.
La Salle	1,921	1890		1890		do	May 22, 1905	Two Harbors, Minn.	May 19, 1904	Cleveland, Ohio.
Mahoning	2,189	1892		1892		Wyandotte, Mich	Apr. 12, 1905	Duluth, Minn.	May 4, 1904	Buffalo, N. Y.
Maricopa	4,223	1896		1896		Chicago, Ill	May 18, 1905	Two Harbors, Minn.	May 24, 1904	Chicago, Ill.
Marina	2,431	1891		1890		do	May 13, 1905	Duluth, Minn.	May 9, 1904	Cleveland, Ohio.
Maruba	2,311	1890		1890		Cleveland, Ohio	May 22, 1905	Two Harbors, Minn.	May 19, 1904	Do.
Masaba	2,431	1891		1890		Chicago, Ill	May 24, 1905	Duluth, Minn.	May 24, 1904	Do.
Mataafa [b]	4,840	1899		1899		Lorain, Ohio	May 13, 1905	do	May 8, 1904	Chicago, Ill.
Mecosta	1,776	1888		1888		West Bay City, Mich.	June 12, 1905	Superior, Wis.	June 21, 1904	Milwaukee, Wis.
Northern King	2,476	1888		1888		Cleveland, Ohio	May 17, 1905	Duluth, Minn.	May 10, 1904	Buffalo, N. Y.
Northern Wave	2,476	1889		1888		do	Apr. 8, 1905	do	May 31, 1904	Duluth, Minn.
Oregon	779	1882		1887		West Bay City, Mich.	July 11, 1905	Two Harbors, Minn.	July 11, 1904	Chicago, Ill.
Orinoco	2,226	1898		1898		do	June 12, 1905	Superior, Wis.	June 13, 1904	Milwaukee, Wis.
Panama	2,044	1888		1888		Trenton, Mich	June 15, 1905	Duluth, Minn.	June 18, 1904	Port Huron, Mich.
Robert Wallace	1,640	1903		1903		Buffalo, N. Y.	May 9, 1905	Superior, Wis.	May 21, 1904	Duluth, Minn.
Samuel Mather	1,713	1892		1892		Superior, Wis.	May 15, 1905	Duluth, Minn.	May 13, 1904	Cleveland, Ohio.
S. B. Barker	176	1882	1903	1891		Grand Haven, Mich.	Sept. 12, 1905	Bayfield, Wis.	Sept. 16, 1904	Duluth, Minn.
Schuylkill	2,205	1892		1892		Cleveland, Ohio	Apr. 8, 1905	Duluth, Minn.	May 5, 1904	Chicago, Ill.
Sonoma	4,539	1903		1903		West Bay City, Mich.	May 28, 1905	do	June 3, 1904	Duluth, Minn.
Sir Henry Bessemer	4,321	1896		1896		Cleveland, Ohio	May 26, 1905	Two Harbors, Minn.	May 31, 1904	Chicago, Ill.
Steel King	4,308	1902		1902		Lorain, Ohio	June 8, 1905	Superior, Wis.	June 17, 1904	Milwaukee, Wis.
Superior City	4,795	1898		1898		do	May 14, 1905	Duluth, Minn.	May 13, 1904	Cleveland, Ohio.
Tampa	1,972	1890		1890		West Bay City, Mich.	May 31, 1905	Superior, Wis.	May 28, 1904	Detroit, Mich.
Venezuela	2,125	1897		1897		do	June 21, 1905	Duluth, Minn.	June 20, 1904	Toledo, Ohio.
Veronica	1,093	1886		1886		Milwaukee, Wis.	May 23, 1905	Superior, Wis.	May 24, 1904	Buffalo, N. Y.
William Edenborn	5,910	1900		1900		West Bay City, Mich.	May 25, 1905	Duluth, Minn.	do	Cleveland, Ohio.
William P. Palmer	2,293	1900		1900		Cleveland, Ohio	May 17, 1905	Two Harbors, Minn.	do	Do.

Towing steamers (lake).										
Annie L. Smith	43	1868	1905	1893		Chicago, Ill	Apr. 20, 1905	Duluth, Minn	Apr. 23, 1904	Duluth, Minn.
Ashland [c]	97	1867	1899	1899		Buffalo, N. Y	Oct. 20, 1905	Ashland, Wis	Oct. 24, 1904	Do.
B. B. Inman	89	1895		1895		Port Huron, Mich	July 3, 1905	Duluth, Minn	July 2, 1904	Do.
B. F. Bruce	35	1873	1902	1889		Buffalo, N. Y	May 6, 1905	do	May 11, 1904	Do.
Buffalo	60	1887		1885		do	July 1, 1905	do	June 25, 1904	Do.
Corona	27	1892		1903		Duluth, Minn	Aug. 12, 1905	do	Aug. 9, 1904	Do.
Crosby	35	1889		1889		Benton Harbor, Mich	May 21, 1905	do	May 21, 1904	Do.
D. T. Helm	64	1893		1898		do	Aug. 11, 1905	do	Aug. 9, 1904	Do.
Edna	[d] 10	1895	1905	1895		Superior, Wis	May 31, 1905	do	May 30, 1904	Do.
Edna G	154	1896		1896		Cleveland, Ohio	Apr. 15, 1905	do	May 2, 1904	Do.
E. G. Crosby	84	1892		1892		Grand Haven, Mich	Sept. 22, 1905	Ashland, Wis	Oct. 3, 1904	Do.
E. G. Maxwell	88	1893		1893		do	May 15, 1905	Duluth, Minn	May 14, 1904	Do.
Eliza Williams	37	1872		1888		Buffalo, N. Y	May 5, 1905	Superior, Wis	May 4, 1904	Do.
Excelsior	73	1892		1892		do	June 15, 1905	Duluth, Minn	June 14, 1904	Do.
Fanchon	13	1879	1904	1894		Grand Island, N. Y	Apr. 3, 1905	do	May 30, 1904	Do.
F. H. Stanwood	18	1883	1901	1903		Saugatuck, Mich	June 5, 1905	Superior, Wis	June 1, 1904	Do.
Frank C. Barnes	46	1892		1878		Manistee, Mich	May 26, 1905	Duluth, Minn	Apr. 11, 1904	Grand Haven, Mich.
F. W. Gillett [e]	28	1869	1899	1904		Huron River, Ohio	May 25, 1905	do	May 24, 1904	Duluth, Minn.
Geo. E. Brockway	164	1867		1890		Port Huron, Mich	Apr. 14, 1905	do	Aug. 25, 1904	Marquette, Mich.
George Emerson	35	1884		1884		Buffalo, N. Y	Sept. 16, 1905	Superior, Wis	Sept. 17, 1904	Duluth, Minn.
Gladiator	220	1871	1896	1881		Port Huron, Mich	Apr. 13, 1905	Duluth, Minn	May 3, 1904	Do.
H. B. Abbott	56	1889		1889		Buffalo, N. Y	Aug. 31, 1905	do	June 8, 1904	Do.
Herman Witt	12	1903		1903		Duluth, Minn	July 20, 1905	do	July 23, 1904	Do.
J. D. McFadden	15	1892		1892		do	May 24, 1905	do	Apr. 27, 1904	Do.
John H. Jeffery, jr	12	1892		1892		do	May 8, 1905	do	May 7, 1904	Do.
Keystone	94	1891	1902	1892		Buffalo, N. Y	May 1, 1905	Ashland, Wis	May 12, 1904	Do.
Major Dana	52	1891		1895		Grand Haven, Mich	June 5, 1905	Superior, Wis	May 14, 1904	Do.
Mayflower	22	1883		1889		Detroit, Mich	May 13, 1905	Duluth, Minn	May 5, 1904	Do.
M. D. Carrington	64	1875		1889		Buffalo, N. Y	May 6, 1905	do	do	Do.
Medina	56	1890		1890		do	Sept. 9, 1905	Superior, Wis	Sept. 10, 1904	Port Huron, Mich.
Mentor	29	1868	1890	1893		Cleveland, Ohio	Oct. 10, 1905	Duluth, Minn	July 29, 1904	Superior, Mich.
Minnie Karl	23	1883	1900	1883		Sheboygan, Wis	May 18, 1905	do	May 11, 1904	Duluth, Minn.
Mystic	63	1871		1900		Sandusky, Ohio	do	do	do	Do.
Natt Stickney	77	1880	1905	1888		East Saginaw, Mich	Apr. 29, 1905	Superior, Wis	Apr. 19, 1902	Do.
Nellie M. [f]	[d] 4	1888		1888		Ferrysburg, Mich	Oct. 3, 1905	Duluth, Minn	Oct. 22, 1904	Do.
Nick	9	1901		1901		Duluth, Minn	June 15, 1905	do	June 16, 1904	Do.
Pacific	42	1876		1886		Buffalo, N. Y	Aug. 11, 1905	do	Aug. 20, 1904	Do.
Record	59	1884		1902		Cleveland, Ohio	May 13, 1905	do	May 11, 1904	Do.
Robert Emmett	32	1863	1901	1896		Racine, Wis	Nov. 11, 1905	do	Aug. 17, 1904	Do.
R. W. Currie	36	1882		1882		Algonac, Mich	Sept. 25, 1905	do	Sept. 16, 1904	Do.
Sarah Smith	45	1883	1904	1883		West Bay City, Mich	June 3, 1905	do	May 30, 1904	Do.
Spirit	6	1871		1889		Bay City, Mich	May 10, 1905	do	May 11, 1904	Do.
Superior	70	1896		1896		Benton Harbor, Mich	Sept. 27, 1905	do	Oct. 4, 1904	Do.
Sylph	4	1890		1890		Manitowoc, Wis	July 29, 1905	Superior, Wis	May 19, 1904	Do.
Tempest	14	1884		1898		West Bay City, Mich	Apr. 20, 1905	Duluth, Minn	May 3, 1904	Do.
Tom Dowling	36	1873		1887		Cleveland, Ohio	July 14, 1905	Ashland, Wis	July 13, 1904	Do.

[a] Formerly Atlantic, 1900.
[b] Formerly Pennsylvania, 1900.
[c] Formerly A. C. Van Raalte, 1903.
[d] Estimated.
[e] Formerly Oddfellow.
[f] Formerly Ariel, 1904.

DOMESTIC VESSELS INSPECTED, YEAR ENDED DECEMBER 31, 1905—FIFTH SUPERVISING DISTRICT—DULUTH, MINN.—Continued.

Names of vessels and class.	Gross tonnage.	Hull built.	Hull rebuilt.	Boilers built.	Boilers rebuilt.	Where built.	Date of inspection.	Where inspected.	Date of previous inspection.	Local district where previously inspected.
Towing steamers (lake)—Con.										
Vigilant	372	1896	....	1887	....	Port Huron, Mich	May 5,1905	Duluth, Minn	May 14,1904	Duluth, Minn.
Walter W. Richardson	22	1884	....	1875	....	West Bay City, Mich	July 8,1905	do	July 8,1904	Do.
Zenith	95	1895	....	1895	....	Benton Harbor, Mich	Apr. 24,1905	do	May 5,1904	Do.
Towing steamers (river).										
Alice D	25	1887	1900	1891	....	Stillwater, Minn	May 11,1905	Stillwater, Minn	May 9,1904	Duluth, Minn.
Baby	5	1896	....	1897	....	do	Apr. 10,1105	do	Apr. 8,1904	Do.
Bun Hersey	35	1883	....	1883	....	do	Apr. 26,1905	do	Apr. 25,1904	Do.
Clyde[a]	121	1870	....	1885	....	Dubuque, Iowa	Apr. 18,1905	do	Apr. 18,1904	Do.
Edwin C	8	1898	1905	1903	....	Stillwater, Minn	Apr. 10,1905	do	do	Do.
Ethel[a]	[b] 3	1889	....	1890	....	Superior, Wis	June 16,1905	Knife Lake, Minn	June 9,1904	Do.
Gordon Fawcett	[b] 48	1905	....	1893	....	Kenmare, N. Dak	Sept. 8,1905	Kenmare, N. Dak	First inspn	
Gypsey[c]	55	1891	1900	1891	....	Le Claire, Iowa	May 3,1905	Stillwater, Minn	Apr. 18,1904	Do.
Imelda	[b] 5	1892	1902	1892	1903	Fort Yates, N. Dak	Sept. 27,1905	Washburn, N. Dak	Sept. 12,1904	Do.
Irene M	[b] 10	1900	....	1881	....	Prescott, Wis	June 1,1905	Prescott, Wis	May 17,1904	Do.
Juniata	98	1889	....	1880	....	Winona, Minn	May 3,1905	Stillwater, Minn	Apr. 18,1904	Do.
Knute Nelson	18	1904	....	1904	....	Warroad, Minn	Sept. 19,1905	Beaudette, Minn	Oct. 6,1904	Do.
Lizzie Gardner	82	1871	....	1893	....	Cincinnati, Ohio	Apr. 19,1905	Stillwater, Minn	Apr. 26,1904	Do.
Mars	132	1902	....	1883	....	Lyons, Iowa	Apr. 10,1905	Hastings, Minn	Apr. 8,1904	Do.
Mary B.[d]	90	1890	....	1890	....	Lake City, Minn	Apr. 18,1905	Stillwater, Minn	Apr. 22,1904	Dubuque, Iowa.
Pathfinder	62	1898	....	1882	....	Clinton, Iowa	Apr. 10,1905	Hastings, Minn	Apr. 23,1904	Do.
Rambler	8	1902	....	1899	....	Duluth, Minn	June 16,1905	Birch Lake, Minn	Aug. 9,1904	Duluth, Minn.
St. Croix	8	1898	....	1894	....	Stillwater, Minn	May 11,1905	Stillwater, Minn	May 9,1904	Do.
Sitting Bull	[b] 5	1891	....	1891	....	South Stillwater, Minn.	Aug. 31,1905	do	Aug. 29,1904	Do.
Wanetta	40	1900	....	1874	....	Muscatine, Iowa	Sept. 14,1905	do	Sept. 19,1904	Do.
West Rambo[e]	105	1884	....	1884	....	Le Claire, Iowa	July 8,1904	St. Paul, Minn	July 9,1903	Dubuque, Iowa.
Yukon	[b] 5	1904	....	1892	....	Beaudette, Minn	Sept. 19,1905	Beaudette, Minn	First inspn	
Steam pleasure yachts (lake).										
Captain Tyler	[b] 2	1887	....	1891	1903	Ferrysburg, Mich	Aug. 10,1905	Grand Portage, Minn.	Aug. 11,1904	Duluth, Minn.
Islay	26	1892	....	1894	....	Superior, Wis	July 27,1905	Superior, Wis	July 30,1904	Do.
John A. Bardon[f]	[b] 6	1889	....	1889	....	Waukegan, Ill	Sept. 6,1905	do	Sept. 3,1904	Do.
Lyma Mac[g]	[b] 4	1889	....	1887	....	Spring Wells, Mich	June 23,1905	do	June 25,1904	Do.
Sam S. Fifield	[b] 3	1891	....	1891	....	Ashland, Wis	June 13,1905	Ashland, Wis	June 11,1904	Do.
Sorella	[b] 10	1905	....	1905	....	Superior, Wis	June 23,1905	Superior, Wis	First inspn	
Steam pleasure yachts (river).										
Aloha[h]	[b] 5	1901	....	1901	....	Stillwater, Minn	July 5,1905	St. Paul, Minn	July 5,1904	Duluth, Minn.

Antoinette [i]	[b] 3	1898	1900	1900		St. Paul, Minn	May 19, 1905	do	May 27, 1904	Do.
Beatrice [j]	[b] 4	1904		1889		do	Sept. 24, 1904	do	First inspn	
Beatrice	[b] 4	1904		1889		do	Oct. 16, 1905	do	Sept. 24, 1904	Do.
Earl [k]	[b] 3	1896	1899	1896		Forest Lake, Minn	Sept. 25, 1905	do	Sept. 10, 1904	Do.
Ethel	[b] 3	1905		1901		St. Paul, Minn	June 11, 1905	do	First inspn	
Florence	[b] 4	1901		1900		do	May 19, 1905	do	May 16, 1904	Do.
Julia B	25	1899		1903		Stillwater, Minn	July 27, 1905	Stillwater, Minn	July 30, 1904	Do.
Justine B	[b] 3	1889		1900		Red Wing, Minn	May 12, 1905	Red Wing, Minn	May 17, 1904	Do.
Lotus Lilly	[b] 4	1894		1894		Prescott, Wis	June 1, 1905	Hastings, Minn	May 27, 1904	Do.
Lu Lu	[b] 4	1896		1897		St. Paul, Minn	June 2, 1905	St. Paul, Minn	do	Do.
Midget [l]	[b] 3	1893	1905	1843		do	June 11, 1905	do	do	Do.
Nahma	[b] 8	1905		1905		Avery, Wis	July 4, 1905	do	First inspn	
Owl [m]	[b] 5	1895		1889		Hastings, Minn	June 2, 1905	do	May 27, 1904	Do.
Success	[b] 2	1893		1893		St. Paul, Minn	Oct. 17, 1905	do	Oct. 17, 1904	Do.
Undine	[b] 4	1889		1897		Waukegan, Ill	May 12, 1905	Red Wing, Minn	May 17, 1904	Do.
Miscellaneous steam vessels (lake).										
Arthur (fishing)	25	1890		1892		East Saginaw, Mich	May 16, 1905	Bayfield, Wis	May 12, 1904	Duluth, Minn.
Fashion (fishing)	48	1889		1889		St. Joseph, Mich	Aug. 7, 1905	do	Aug. 5, 1904	Do.
Francis R. Anderson (fishing)	30	1885		1895		Chicago, Ill	May 16, 1905	do	May 12, 1904	Do.
Henry F. Brower (fishing)	30	1882		1882		Grand Haven, Mich	Sept. 22, 1905	Duluth, Minn	do	Do.
Stella B. (fishing)	6	1899		1899		Bayfield, Wis	Nov. 11, 1905	Bayfield, Wis	Nov. 11, 1904	Do.
The Tramp (fishing)	41	1890		1890		Benton Harbor, Mich	Aug. 3, 1905	Duluth, Minn	June 8, 1904	Superior, Mich.
W. G. Harrow (fishing)	84	1893		1905		Port Huron, Mich	May 16, 1905	Bayfield, Wis	May 12, 1904	Buffalo, N. Y.
Miscellaneous steam vessels (river).										
Admiral (pile driver)	42	1897		1897		St. Paul, Minn	Aug. 6, 1905	St. Paul, Minn	Aug. 6, 1904	Duluth, Minn.
Arcola (pile driver)	[b] 30	1899		1898		South Stillwater, Minn.	Aug. 8, 1905	do	Aug. 8, 1904	Do.
Vessels propelled by gas (river).										
Bismarck (passenger) [n]	93	1896				Bismarck, N. Dak	May 15, 1905	Washburn, N. Dak	May 17, 1904	Duluth, Minn.
Cannonball (ferry)	[b] 32	1895	1904			Rock Haven, N. Dak	Apr. 21, 1905	Cannonball, N. Dak	Apr. 22, 1904	Do.
Missouri (ferry)	[b] 20	1902				Winona, N. Dak	Apr. 20, 1905	Winona, N. Dak	Apr. 21, 1904	Do.
Pearl (ferry)	[b] 24	1886				Chamberlain, S. Dak	May 21, 1905	Williston, N. Dak	May 7, 1904	Do.
Barge over 100 gross tons carrying passengers for hire (river).										
Twin Cities	192	1900				Hastings, Minn	Apr. 27, 1905	Hastings, Minn	May 27, 1904	Duluth, Minn.

[a] Formerly Spray, 1903.
[b] Estimated.
[c] Formerly Lumber Boy, 1901.
[d] Formerly Ethel Howard, 1898.
[e] Certificate issued Apr. 27, 1905.
[f] Formerly Jennie V., 1902; Nonpareil, 1905.
[g] Formerly Hiawatha, 1903.
[h] Formerly Rose Queen, 1902.
[i] Formerly Jennie S., 1904.
[j] Certificate issued June 12, 1905.
[k] Formerly Cecil, 1899; Barton, 1902.
[l] Formerly Spray, 1900; Lillian B., 1901.
[m] Formerly Marguerite, 1904.
[n] Formerly John Bloodgood, 1901.

DOMESTIC VESSELS INSPECTED, YEAR ENDED DECEMBER 31, 1905—Continued.

SIXTH SUPERVISING DISTRICT.

LOCAL DISTRICT OF LOUISVILLE, KY.

Names of vessels and class.	Gross tonnage.	Hull built.	Hull rebuilt.	Boilers built.	Boilers rebuilt.	Where built.	Date of inspection.	Where inspected.	Date of previous inspection.	Local district where previously inspected.
Inland passenger steamers.										
Bellevue	89	1890		1900		Levanna, Ohio	July 24, 1905	New Albany, Ind	July 23, 1904	Louisville, Ky.
Bowling Green [a]	123	1904		1904		Jeffersonville, Ind	Sept. 29, 1904	Jeffersonville, Ind	First inspn	
Cando	74	1899		1899		Ashland, Ky	Oct. 20, 1905	Madison, Ind	Oct. 6, 1904	Gallipolis, Ohio.
Chaperon [b]	95	1884	1904	1884		Chambersburg, Ohio	July 10, 1905	Bowling Green, Ky	July 11, 1904	Evansville, Ind.
City of Saltillo	372	1905		1900		Jeffersonville, Ind	June 21, 1905	Jeffersonville, Ind	First inspn	
Falls City	235	1898		1901		Cincinnati, Ohio	Oct. 31, 1905	Louisville, Ky	Nov. 14, 1904	Louisville, Ky.
Gazelle	95	1899		1903		Hawesville, Ky	Aug. 20, 1905	Hawesville, Ky	Aug. 21, 1904	Do.
Helen M. Gould [c]	208	1897		1901		Middleport, Ohio	Dec. 31, 1904	Madison, Ind	Sept. 24, 1903	Gallipolis, Ohio.
Helen M. Gould	208	1897		1901		do	Dec. 17, 1905	Carrollton, Ky	Dec. 31, 1904	Louisville, Ky.
John W. Thomas	208	1897		1890		Jeffersonville, Ind	Mar. 13, 1905	Louisville, Ky	Mar. 8, 1904	Do.
Kentucky [d]	191	1904		1904		do	Oct. 15, 1904	Jeffersonville, Ind	First inspn	
R. Dunbar [e]	252	1895		1895		do	Nov. 21, 1904	New Albany, Ind	Nov. 2, 1903	Evansville, Ind.
Rowena [e]	97	1904		1903		Burnside, Ky	Dec. 29, 1904	Burnside, Ky	First inspn	
Rowena	97	1904		1903		do	Dec. 9, 1905	do	Dec. 29, 1904	Louisville, Ky.
Tacoma [c]	276	1897		1883	1896	Cincinnati, Ohio	Nov. 18, 1904	Madison, Ind	Nov. 18, 1903	Cincinnati, Ohio.
Tarascon	660	1896		1896		Jeffersonville, Ind	Mar. 4, 1905	Louisville, Ky	Feb. 24, 1904	Louisville, Ky.
Tell City	438	1889		1889		do	May 4, 1905	do	May 3, 1904	Do.
Ferry steamers.										
A. Baldwin	199	1905		1905		Jeffersonville, Ind	May 2, 1905	Jeffersonville, Ind	First inspn	
City of Jeffersonville	161	1891		1891		do	Apr. 26, 1905	do	May 5, 1904	Louisville, Ky.
Columbia	260	1892		1892		do	May 18, 1905	do	May 18, 1904	Do.
Hiawatha	256	1882		1882		Dubuque, Iowa	Apr. 8, 1905	Louisville, Ky	Apr. 4, 1904	Do.
L. H. Marrero	163	1905		1905		Jeffersonville, Ind	Nov. 8, 1905	Jeffersonville, Ind	First inspn	
Major	38	1891		1892		Hawesville, Ky	Mar. 19, 1905	Hawesville, Ky	Mar. 18, 1904	Do.
Sunshine	335	1888		1888		Jeffersonville, Ind	May 18, 1905	Jeffersonville, Ind	May 18, 1904	Do.
Three States	175	1905		1905		do	Jan. 5, 1905	do	First inspn	
Trimble	242	1895		1895		Madison, Ind	Apr. 6, 1905	Madison, Ind	Apr. 7, 1904	Do.
W. C. Hite	f356	1897		1897		Jeffersonville, Ind	May 22, 1905	Jeffersonville, Ind	May 21, 1904	Do.
Inland towing steamers.										
Albany	98	1901		1881		Burnside, Ky	Jan. 10, 1905	Burnside, Ky	Jan. 11, 1904	Louisville, Ky.
Allie	53	1903		1895		Bowling Green, Ky	July 27, 1905	Bowling Green, Ky	July 1, 1904	Nashville, Tenn.
Alma	41	1898		1903		Leavenworth, Ind	July 25, 1905	Tell City, Ind	July 25, 1904	Louisville, Ky.
Blue Wing	40	1901		1901		Madison, Ind	Mar. 28, 1905	Madison, Ind	Mar. 26, 1904	Do.

Charley Hook	99	1892		1892		Marietta, Ohio	July 20, 1905	Port Fulton, Ind	July 20, 1904	Pittsburg, Pa.
Crescent	239	1871		1888		Pittsburg, Pa	Jan. 21, 1905	Jeffersonville, Ind	Jan. 18, 1904	Louisville, Ky.
Dove	18	1899		1898		Ghent, Ky	Feb. 28, 1905	Frankfort, Ky	Feb. 10, 1904	Do.
E. T. Slider	92	1900		1900		Jeffersonville, Ind	Dec. 2, 1905	New Albany, Ind	Nov. 29, 1904	Do.
Fawn	46	1896		1900		Evansville, Ind	Oct. 23, 1905	Owensboro, Ky	Nov. 11, 1904	Do.
Gladys	60	1896		1904		Lenoir City, Tenn	Mar. 10, 1905	Frankfort, Ky	Mar. 10, 1904	Do.
H. M. Hoxie	622	1888		1888		Cincinnati, Ohio	Apr. 26, 1905	Jeffersonville, Ind	Apr. 25, 1904	St. Louis, Mo.
Jennie Barbour	93	1905		1905		Jeffersonville, Ind	Oct. 12, 1905	do	First inspn	
John Mackey [g]	124	1892		1892		Marietta, Ohio	Nov. 25, 1904	Valley View, Ky	Nov. 24, 1903	Pittsburg, Pa.
John Mackey	124	1892		1892		do	Nov. 13, 1905	Frankfort, Ky	Nov. 25, 1904	Louisville, Ky.
Joseph B. Williams	801	1876		1902		Pittsburg, Pa	May 2, 1905	West Louisville, Ky	Apr. 29, 1904	New Orleans, La.
Louise	9	1896		1896		Ludlow, Ky	Sept. 11, 1905	Valley View, Ky	Sept. 28, 1904	Louisville, Ky.
Mabel	49	1904		1904		Carrollton, Ky	July 18, 1905	Carrollton, Ky	July 27, 1904	Do.
Major	60	1904		1901		New Orleans, La	Apr. 19, 1905	Louisville, Ky	Apr. 15, 1904	New Orleans, La.
Minnie	63	1895	1898	1894		Madison, Ind	Jan. 4, 1905	Madison, Ind	Oct. 9, 1903	Louisville, Ky.
Nellie Willett	98	1904		1904		Leavenworth, Ind	Mar. 18, 1905	New Albany, Ind	Mar. 19, 1904	Do.
Nugent	97	1904		1904		Jeffersonville, Ind	Oct. 16, 1905	Jeffersonville, Ind	Oct. 15, 1904	Do.
Oakland	628	1872		1902		Pittsburg, Pa	Oct. 21, 1905	do	Oct. 25, 1904	Pittsburg, Pa.
Sabrina	30	1878		1891		Carondelet, Mo	Mar. 22, 1905	Cloverport, Ky	Mar. 23, 1904	Louisville, Ky.
Sam A. Connor	63	1901		1903		Chattanooga, Tenn	Mar. 14, 1905	Louisville, Ky	Jan. 13, 1904	Nashville, Tenn.
Sprague	1,479	1902		1902		Dubuque, Iowa	Oct. 24, 1905	Jeffersonville, Ind	Nov. 9, 1904	Pittsburg, Pa.
Transit	156	1889	1901	1889		Brownsville, Pa	do	do	Nov. 23, 1904	Louisville, Ky.
Vincennes	81	1899		1893		Higginsport, Ohio	May 20, 1905	New Albany, Ind	May 20, 1904	Gallipolis, Ohio.
Vivian	75	1896		1896		Lyons, Iowa	Apr. 23, 1905	Madison, Ind	Apr. 23, 1904	Louisville, Ky.
Wash Gray	105	1896		1895		Jeffersonville, Ind	Mar. 8, 1905	Port Fulton, Ind	Mar. 8, 1904	Do.
Wm. Duffy	78	1897		1905		Higginsport, Ohio	Dec. 7, 1905	Louisville, Ky	Dec. 7, 1904	Do.
Steam pleasure yachts.										
Little Dago	[h]1	1896		1896	1903	Louisville, Ky	July 12, 1905	Hartford, Ky	June 18, 1904	Louisville, Ky.
Paul W. Howard [e]	[h]4	1901		1894		Jeffersonville, Ind	Dec. 27, 1904	Louisville, Ky	Dec. 12, 1903	Do.
Scimitar II	99	1905		1905		do	June 21, 1905	Jeffersonville, Ind	First inspn	
Miscellaneous steam vessel.										
Champion (sawmill)	66	1902		1902		Frankfort, Ky	Apr. 1, 1905	Frankfort, Ky	Nov. 20, 1903	Louisville, Ky.
Vessels propelled by gasoline motors.										
Hanover (passenger)	66	1901				Plow Handle Point, Ind.	Aug. 3, 1905	Madison, Ind	Aug. 5, 1904	Louisville, Ky.
Hanover (passenger)	37	1905				Madison, Ind	Nov. 21, 1905	Louisville, Ky	First inspn	
Leon (ferry)	20	1902				do	July 18, 1905	Carrollton, Ky	July 27, 1904	Do.
White Dove (passenger)	35	1901				do	July 7, 1905	Madison, Ind	July 10, 1904	Do.
White Oak (passenger)	30	1905				Jeffersonville, Ind	Nov. 17, 1905	Jeffersonville, Ind	First inspn	

[a] Certificate filed Jan. 5, 1905.
[b] Formerly J. C. Kerr, 1904.
[c] Certificate filed Jan. 7, 1905.
[d] Certificate filed Jan. 3, 1905.
[e] Certificate filed Jan. 2, 1905.
[f] Tonnage changed 1905 from 641 gross.
[g] Certificate filed Mar. 6, 1905.
[h] Tonnage estimated.

DOMESTIC VESSELS INSPECTED, YEAR ENDED DECEMBER 31, 1905—SIXTH SUPERVISING DISTRICT—Continued.

LOCAL DISTRICT OF EVANSVILLE, IND.

Names of vessels and class.	Gross tonnage.	Hull built.	Hull rebuilt.	Boilers built.	Boilers rebuilt.	Where built.	Date of inspection.	Where inspected.	Date of previous inspection.	Local district where previously inspected.
Inland passenger steamers.										
Alice L. Barr	50	1884	1902	1892		Cincinnati, Ohio	Aug. 26, 1905	Evansville, Ind	Aug. 27, 1904	Evansville, Ind.
Bowling Green	123	1904		1904		Jeffersonville, Ind	Sept. 18, 1905	do	Sept. 28, 1904	Louisville, Ky.
D. A. Nisbet	64	1889	1903	1889		Evansville, Ind	Nov. 4, 1905	do	Nov. 21, 1904	Evansville, Ind.
Francis	93	1903		1903		do	Sept. 5, 1905	do	Sept. 8, 1904	Do.
John S. Hopkins	593	1880	1900	1880	1899	Pittsburg, Pa	Jan. 2, 1905	Elizabethtown, Ill	Dec. 6, 1903	Nashville, Tenn.
Jessie B	78	1891		1891		Dubuque, Iowa	Apr. 27, 1905	Fairview, Ill	Apr. 25, 1904	Dubuque, Iowa.
Jewel	201	1893		1893		Evansville, Ind	May 29, 1905	Evansville, Ind	June 9, 1904	Evansville, Ind.
John S. Hopkins	593	1880	1900	1905		Pittsburg, Pa	Nov. 24, 1905	Mound City, Ill	Jan. 2, 1905	Do.
Joe Fowler	356	1888	1901	1888		Jeffersonville, Ind	do	do	Dec. 10, 1904	Nashville, Tenn.
Kalista	9	1892		1892		Geneva, Ohio	Oct. 12, 1905	Calhoun, Ky	Oct. 12, 1904	Evansville, Ind.
Louisiana	242	1880	1904	1880		Jeffersonville, Ind	May 17, 1905	Cairo, Ill	May 13, 1904	Nashville, Tenn.
Neptune	80	1900		1880		Lyons, Iowa	July 25, 1905	Evansville, Ind	July 23, 1904	Evansville, Ind.
Norway	24	1904		1888		Spottsville, Ky	July 27, 1905	do	July 29, 1904	Do.
Park City [a]	197	1883	1898	1898		Brownsville, Pa	Sept. 13, 1905	do	Sept. 17, 1904	Do.
Royal	47	1904		1900		Golconda, Ill	Feb. 23, 1905	Golconda, Ill	Feb. 13, 1904	Nashville, Tenn.
Red River	97	1899		1899		Jeffersonville, Ind	Dec. 12, 1905	Mound City, Ill	Dec. 6, 1904	New Orleans, La.
Sunbeam	40	1903		1899		Mound City, Ill	Sept. 14, 1905	Evansville, Ind	Aug. 11, 1904	Evansville, Ind.
Ferry steamers.										
Alfred D. Owen	52	1896	1903	1902		Mount Vernon, Ind	Mar. 9, 1905	Mount Vernon, Ind	Feb. 26, 1904	Evansville, Ind.
Clarence Thorn	29	1905		1905		Mount Carmel, Ill	Mar. 20, 1905	Mount Carmel, Ill	First inspn	
Charles Merriam	515	1883	1905	1901		Jeffersonville, Ind	Nov. 9, 1905	Mound City, Ill	June 8, 1904	St. Louis, Mo.
City of McGregor	98	1867	1898	1885		Pittsburg, Pa	May 2, 1905	Cairo, Ill	Apr. 27, 1904	Evansville, Ind.
Georgie	26	1892		1893		Mount Vernon, Ind	May 4, 1905	Shawneetown, Ill	May 4, 1904	Do.
Henderson	93	1900		1893		Evansville, Ind	Aug. 11, 1905	Henderson, Ky	Aug. 8, 1904	Do.
Henry Marquand [b]	395	1873	1904	1902		Jeffersonville, Ind	Aug. 7, 1905	Cairo, Ill	Aug. 3, 1904	Do.
Pacific	457	1878		1898		Metropolis, Ill	Oct. 24, 1905	do	Oct. 27, 1904	St. Louis, Mo.
St. Louis	312	1869	1901	1888	1901	Freedom, Pa	Mar. 16, 1905	Columbus, Ky	Mar. 11, 1904	Evansville, Ind.
Towing steamers.										
Anton Brucken	40	1902		1895		Bruckens Landing, Ky.	Mar. 13, 1905	Evansville, Ind	Mar. 24, 1904	Evansville, Ind.
Ariadne	22	1868		1892		Buffalo, N. Y	Mar. 3, 1905	Cairo, Ill	Mar. 10, 1904	Do.
Annie L	114	1881		1901		Murraysville, W. Va	Oct. 2, 1905	Mount Vernon, Ind	Oct. 7, 1904	Wheeling, W. Va.
Bart E. L. Molo	35	1895		1895		Lyons, Iowa	Feb. 21, 1905	Mound City, Ill	Mar. 3, 1904	Memphis, Tenn.
Belmont	29	1892		1892		Toms Hill, Ind	Mar. 29, 1905	Vincennes, Ind	Mar. 29, 1904	Evansville, Ind.
Bernice	51	1899		1891		Clinton, Iowa	Mar. 25, 1905	New Harmony, Ind	Mar. 18, 1904	Do.
Barrett [c]	913	1889	1903	1896		Madison, Ind	Apr. 20, 1905	Cairo, Ill	Apr. 19, 1904	Do.

Beaver	314	1886	....	1901	....	Cincinnati, Ohio	Nov. 14, 1905	....do	Nov. 15, 1904	Do.
Carrie V	48	1897	....	1897	....	Antiquity, Ohio	Feb. 21, 1905	....do	Feb. 16, 1904	Do.
Charlotte Boeckeler	143	1881	1901	1902	....	New Albany, Ind	Nov. 1, 1905	Evansville, Ind	Nov. 15, 1904	Do.
Condor	177	1900	....	1896	....	Paducah, Ky	Jan. 16, 1905	Joppa, Ill	Jan. 15, 1904	Do.
Duce	8	1891	1904	1893	....	St. Louis, Mo	Nov. 3, 1905	Evansville, Ind	Oct. 24, 1904	St. Louis, Mo.
Eclipse	57	1903	....	1903	....	Higgensport, Ohio	Mar. 7, 1905	Spottsville, Ky	Mar. 5, 1904	Louisville, Ky.
Edgar[d]	39	1891	....	1891	....	Spottsville, Ky	Mar. 24, 1905	Evansville, Ind	Mar. 23, 1904	Evansville, Ind.
Emma	53	1901	....	1901	....	Evansville, Ind	Jan. 28, 1905	Spottsville, Ky	Jan. 29, 1904	Do.
Enos Taylor	64	1893	....	1894	....	Higgensport, Ohio	Mar. 22, 1905	Shawneetown, Ill	Mar. 19, 1904	Gallipolis, Ohio.
Harth	57	1892	....	1892	....	Malden, W. Va	Mar. 30, 1905	De Koven Landing, Ky.	Mar. 25, 1904	Evansville, Ind.
Hermann Paepcke	157	1900	....	1901	....	Higgensport, Ohio	Jan. 20, 1905	Cairo, Ill	Jan. 14, 1904	Do.
Henrietta	153	1879	....	1883	....	Stillwater, Minn	June 8, 1905	Mound City, Ill	May 20, 1904	Nashville, Tenn.
Isabella	78	1880	1903	1881	....	Evansville, Ind	Mar. 6, 1905	Evansville, Ind	Feb. 8, 1904	Evansville, Ind.
Ingleside	36	1890	....	1890	....	....do	Dec. 5, 1905	....do	Nov. 26, 1904	Do.
John S. Summers	66	1901	....	1902	....	Parkersburg, W. Va	Mar. 17, 1905	Joppa, Ill	Mar. 9, 1904	Nashville, Tenn.
J. F. Buckham	93	1896	....	1896	....	Caseyville, Ky	Sept. 8, 1905	Caseyville, Ky	Sept. 13, 1904	Evansville, Ind.
J. B. A.[c]	51	1894	1905	1905	....	Evansville, Ind	Oct. 14, 1905	Evansville, Ind	Nov. 12, 1904	Do.
Key City	98	1891	....	1891	....	Kingston, Tenn	Mar. 10, 1905	Metropolis, Ill	Mar. 7, 1904	Do.
Katherine[f]	146	1889	....	1896	....	Jeffersonville, Ind	May 2, 1905	Cairo, Ill	May 10, 1904	Do.
Kenois	69	1901	....	1905	....	Metropolis, Ill	Aug. 14, 1905	Evansville, Ind	Jan. 22, 1904	Do.
La Fayette	77	1900	....	1897	....	Lafayette, Ind	May 24, 1905	Lafayette, Ind	May 23, 1904	Do.
Little Willie	31	1895	....	1895	....	Troy, Ind	Apr. 12, 1905	Evansville, Ind	Dec. 23, 1903	Louisville, Ky.
Lyda Wheeler	8	1894	....	1894	....	Bellevue, Ohio	Aug. 25, 1905	Livermore, Ky	Aug. 25, 1904	Evansville, Ind.
Little Clyde	99	1894	....	1892	....	Spottsville, Ky	Nov. 25, 1905	Evansville, Ind	Nov. 18, 1904	Do.
Mary Lacy	98	1897	1905	1897	....	Madison, Ind	Apr. 15, 1905	....do	Sept. 21, 1903	Do.
Martha H. Hennen[g]	77	1900	1904	1900	....	Hawesville, Ky	Apr. 25, 1905	....do	May 7, 1904	Do.
Mary M. Michael	234	1881	....	1881	....	New Albany, Ind	Oct. 24, 1905	Cairo, Ill	Sept. 20, 1904	Do.
Maunie	36	1900	....	1901	....	Maunie, Ill	May 10, 1905	Brookport, Ill	May 13, 1904	Do.
Nellie Chadwick	29	1898	1903	1898	....	New Harmony, Ind	Mar. 25, 1905	New Harmony, Ind	Mar. 18, 1904	Do.
New Haven	48	1902	....	1903	....	New Haven, Ill	Mar. 8, 1905	Uniontown, Ky	Mar. 10, 1904	Do.
Nellie Brown	56	1878	....	1899	....	Pittsburg, Pa	Oct. 9, 1905	De Koven, Ky	Nov. 7, 1904	Do.
Old Reliable	64	1900	....	1900	....	Spottsville, Ky	May 23, 1905	Evansville, Ind	May 31, 1904	Do.
Oscar F. Keeler	9	1902	....	1902	....	Mound City, Ill	May 25, 1905	Mound City, Ill	May 26, 1904	Do.
Pacific No. 2	570	1893	....	1893	....	Pittsburg, Pa	Aug. 29, 1905	Cairo, Ill	Aug. 24, 1904	Wheeling, W. Va.
Racket	60	1883	....	1883	....	Manchester, Ohio	Mar. 14, 1905	Calhoun, Ky	Feb. 29, 1904	Evansville, Ind.
Roy H	42	1899	....	1880	....	Meridosia, Ill	July 11, 1905	Grayville, Ill	July 5, 1904	Do.
Ranger	107	1892	....	1892	....	Pittsburg, Pa	Oct. 24, 1905	Cairo, Ill	Oct. 27, 1904	Pittsburg, Pa.
Samuel[h]	48	1882	1901	1890	....	Rock Island, Ill	Nov. 3, 1905	Evansville, Ind	Nov. 26, 1904	Evansville, Ind.
Thomas Parker	57	1894	....	1887	....	St. Louis, Mo	Mar. 7, 1905	Spottsville, Ky	Mar. 9, 1904	Do.
Theseus	58	1886	....	1894	....	Buffalo, N. Y	Oct. 17, 1905	Cairo, Ill	Oct. 17, 1904	Do.
Wabash[i]	141	1881	1903	1881	....	Dubuque, Iowa	Apr. 13, 1905	Henderson, Xy	Apr. 16, 1904	Do.
Wash Honshell	134	1892	....	1893	....	Cincinnati, Ohio	May 9, 1905	Cairo, Ill	Mar. 31, 1904	Pittsburg, Pa.
Steam pleasure yachts.										
Lucille	[j]2	1897	....	1904	....	St. Joseph, Mich	Aug. 11, 1905	Henderson, Ky	Aug. 17, 1904	Evansville, Ind.
Lark No. 2	7	1904	....	1893	....	Terre Haute, Ind	Apr. 21, 1905	Terre Haute, Ind	First inspn	

[a] Formerly Gayosa, 1898.
[b] Formerly H. S. McComb, 1899.
[c] Formerly Louis Houck, 1903.
[d] Formerly Hussar, 1900.
[e] Formerly Herbert Moran, 1900.
[f] Formerly The New Idea, 1896.
[g] Formerly L. H. Buehrman, 1904.
[h] Formerly Duke, 1901.
[i] Formerly F. C. A. Denkman, 1899.
[j] Estimated.

DOMESTIC VESSELS INSPECTED, YEAR ENDED DECEMBER 31, 1905—SIXTH SUPERVISING DISTRICT—EVANSVILLE, IND.—Continued.

Names of vessels and class.	Gross tonnage.	Hull built.	Hull rebuilt.	Boilers built.	Boilers rebuilt.	Where built.	Date of inspection.	Where inspected.	Date of previous inspection.	Local district where previously inspected.
Vessels propelled by gasoline motors.										
Beulah Ray (passenger)	42	1905				Vincennes, Ind	July 19,1905	Vincennes, Ind	First inspn	
City of Terre Haute (passenger).	28	1905				Terre Haute, Ind	Apr. 21,1905	Terre Haute, Ind	do	
Dorcas Bowman (freight and towing).	53	1904				Grayville, Ill	Jan. 18,1905	Grayville, Ind	Jan. 27,1904	Evansville, Ind.
Mary A (ferry)	27	1896	1905			Mount Carmel, Ill	Apr. 17,1905	Mount Carmel, Ill	Apr. 17,1904	Do.
Tecumseh (passenger)	36	1902				Lafayette, Ind	Aug. 5,1905	Terre Haute, Ind	Aug. 2,1904	Do.

LOCAL DISTRICT OF NASHVILLE, TENN.

Names of vessels and class.	Gross tonnage.	Hull built.	Hull rebuilt.	Boilers built.	Boilers rebuilt.	Where built.	Date of inspection.	Where inspected.	Date of previous inspection.	Local district where previously inspected.
Inland passenger steamers.										
Bob Dudley	196	1897		1891		Jeffersonville, Ind	July 15,1905	Nashville, Tenn	July 18,1904	Nashville, Tenn.
Charleston	94	1887		1887		Charleston, W. Va	June 26,1905	Paducah, Ky	June 22,1904	Do.
Catherine P. Le	67	1904		1897		Knoxville, Tenn	Jan. 19,1905	Knoxville, Tenn	First inspn	
C. M. Pate	82	1903		1903		Marietta, Ohio	Nov. 14,1905	Carthage, Tenn	Nov. 28,1904	Wheeling, W. Va.
Clyde	388	1894	1901	1895		Jeffersonville, Ind	Dec. 9,1905	Paducah, Ky	Dec. 5,1904	Nashville, Tenn.
Dick Clyde [a]	76	1881		1883		Rock Island, Ill	Nov. 21,1904	Gainsboro, Tenn	Nov. 18,1903	Evansville, Ind.
Dick Clyde	76	1881	1905	1905		do	Nov. 14,1905	Carthage, Tenn	Nov. 21,1904	Nashville, Tenn.
Dick Fowler	367	1892		1893		Evansville, Ind	Feb. 10,1905	Paducah, Ky	Feb. 3,1904	Do.
Dick Fowler	367	1892		1893		do	Dec. 24,1905	do	Feb. 10,1905	Do.
Dorothy K. James	38	1905		1902		Chattanooga, Tenn	Dec. 26,1905	Chattanooga, Tenn	First inspn	
Gasconade	74	1891		1891		Loutre Island, Mo	Mar. 10,1905	Dayton, Tenn	Mar. 3,1904	Do.
George Cowling	206	1904		1904		Metropolis, Ill	Oct. 29,1905	Metropolis, Ill	Nov. 10,1904	Evansville, Ind.
Guntersville	204	1903		1903		Jeffersonville, Ind	May 9,1905	Guntersville, Ala	May 10,1904	Nashville, Tenn.
H. W. Buttorff	254	1896		1896		do	Nov. 21,1905	Nashville, Tenn	Nov. 28,1904	Evansville, Ind.
Henry Harley	162	1898		1898		do	Aug. 22,1905	Paducah, Ky	Aug. 24,1904	Nashville, Tenn.
Huntsville	172	1903		1893		Guntersville, Ala	Jan. 24,1905	Guntersville, Ala	Jan. 23,1904	Do.
J. S.	292	1901		1901		Jeffersonville, Ind	Apr. 19,1905	Paducah, Ky	Mar. 30,1904	New Orleans, La.
J. T. Reeder	54	1902		1899		Paducah, Ky	Nov. 1,1905	do	Oct. 14,1904	Nashville, Tenn.
Jane Austin	86	1903		1896		Knoxville, Tenn	Aug. 11,1905	Knoxville, Tenn	Aug. 11,1904	Do.
John Ross	138	1905		1891		Decatur, Ala	Nov. 16,1905	Chattanooga, Tenn	First inspn	
Joe Wheeler	192	1898		1886		Chattanooga, Tenn	Jan. 13,1905	Decatur, Ala	Jan. 15,1904	Do.
Joe Wheeler	192	1898		1886		do	Nov. 16,1905	Chattanooga, Tenn	Jan. 13,1905	Do.
Kentucky	191	1904		1904		Jeffersonville, Ind	Oct. 7,1905	Paducah, Ky	Oct. 15,1904	Louisville, Ky.
Lizzie B. Archbold	45	1892		1901		Paducah, Ky	Dec. 2,1905	do	Dec. 17,1904	Nashville, Tenn.
N. B. Forrest	134	1897		1897		Chattanooga, Tenn	Jan. 14,1905	Chattanooga, Tenn	Jan. 13,1904	Do.
N. B. Forrest	134	1897		1897		do	Nov. 16,1905	do	Jan. 14,1905	Do.

R. Dunbar	252	1895		1895		Jeffersonville, Ind	Nov. 20, 1905	Nashville, Tenn	Nov. 21, 1904	Louisville, Ky.
R. P. Hobson	22	1892		1892		Terre Haute, Ind	Apr. 4, 1905	Brownsville, Ky	Oct. 26, 1903	Nashville, Tenn.
Sam Davis	93	1898		1890		Chattanooga, Tenn	July 28, 1905	Decatur, Ala	July 2, 1904	Do.
Shiloh	140	1902		1902		Jeffersonville, Ind	Nov. 18, 1905	Danville, Tenn	Nov. 25, 1904	Do.
Sycamore[b]	98	1889		1888		Evansville, Ind	Aug. 29, 1904	Nashville, Tenn	Aug. 24, 1903	Do.
Tennessee	334	1897		1897		Jeffersonville, Ind	Sept. 16, 1905	Paducah, Ky	Sept. 17, 1904	Do.
W. W.[c]	212	1895		1902		Rock Island, Ill	May 16, 1905	do	Mar. 29, 1904	Dubuque, Iowa.
Warrenn	98	1900		1899		Diamond Bluff, Wis	Nov. 7, 1905	do	Nov. 15, 1904	Louisville, Ky.
Ferry steamers.										
Bettie Owen	344	1891		1880		Paducah, Ky	May 5, 1905	Paducah, Ky	May 13, 1904	Nashville, Tenn.
Blanche K	9	1904		1904		Decatur, Ala	Sept. 18, 1905	Lambs Ferry, Ala	Sept. 20, 1904	Do.
De Koven	399	1894		1894		Jeffersonville, Ind	Oct. 28, 1905	Paducah, Ky	Sept. 22, 1904	Evansville, Ind.
Mattie	4	1900		1889		Decatur, Ala	Apr. 7, 1905	Decatur, Ala	Apr. 6, 1904	Nashville, Tenn.
Inland towing steamers.										
Almande	73	1904		1904		Decatur, Ala	Nov. 27, 1905	Decatur, Ala	Nov. 28, 1904	Nashville, Tenn.
American	171	1904		1904		do	Dec. 19, 1905	do	Dec. 23, 1904	Do.
Brownie	[d]2	1887		1892		Swanton, Vt	July 10, 1905	Paducah, Ky	July 8, 1904	Do.
Buck Lindsay	14	1902		1897		Decatur, Ala	Dec. 20, 1905	Shellmound, Tenn	Dec. 23, 1904	Do.
Catherine P. Le	67	1904		1897		Knoxville, Tenn	Nov. 22, 1905	Knoxville, Tenn	Jan. 19, 1905	Do.
Castalia	90	1892	1903	1901		Sioux City, Iowa	Dec. 2, 1905	Paducah, Ky	Dec. 10, 1904	Do.
Chastang	72	1904		1903		Bridgeport, Ala	Mar. 17, 1905	Bridgeport, Ala	Mar. 16, 1904	Do.
Charles Turner	73	1892		1892		Pittsburg, Pa	Feb. 15, 1905	Paducah, Ky	Feb. 1, 1904	Cincinnati, Ohio.
Clinch	24	1899		1895		Kingston, Tenn	May 2, 1905	Knoxville, Tenn	May 7, 1904	Nashville, Tenn.
Clinton	7	1899		1899		Clinton, Tenn	do	Clinton, Tenn	May 6, 1904	Do.
City of Charleston	92	1900		1888		Charleston, Tenn	Apr. 10, 1905	Paducah, Ky	Apr. 6, 1904	Do.
City of Loudon	23	1902		1876		Kingston, Tenn	Apr. 13, 1905	Loudon, Tenn	Apr. 12, 1904	Do.
City of Idaho	98	1898		1890		Memphis, Tenn	Sept. 22, 1905	Paducah, Ky	Mar. 2, 1904	Memphis, Tenn.
D. W. Hughes	7	1903		1896		Chattanooga, Tenn	Dec. 5, 1905	Chattanooga, Tenn	Dec. 20, 1904	Nashville, Tenn.
Davie Giles	9	1904		1886		do	Mar. 18, 1905	do	Mar. 17, 1904	Do.
Decatur No. 1	48	1900		1900		Decatur, Ala	Aug. 12, 1905	Decatur, Ala	Aug. 18, 1904	Do.
Fritz	200	1894		1897		Cincinnati, Ohio	Mar. 20, 1905	Nashville, Tenn	Mar. 8, 1904	Evansville, Ind.
Fulton	53	1891		1891		Madison, Ind	Jan. 11, 1905	Paducah, Ky	Jan. 12, 1904	Louisville, Ky.
George H. Cowling	88	1896		1896		Metropolis, Ill	Apr. 15, 1905	Nashville, Tenn	Apr. 8, 1904	Evansville, Ind.
Grady	137	1898		1899		Kingston, Tenn	Dec. 16, 1905	Rockwood, Tenn	Dec. 21, 1904	Nashville, Tenn.
Harvester	530	1896		1891		Madison, Ind	Mar. 27, 1905	Paducah, Ky	Mar. 23, 1904	Pittsburg, Pa.
Hosmer	52	1901		1893		Paducah, Ky	Sept. 14, 1905	do	Oct. 14, 1904	Memphis, Tenn.
I. N. Hook	55	1889		1889		Marietta, Ohio	Feb. 9, 1905	do	Feb. 3, 1904	Nashville, Tenn.
Inverness	121	1888		1891		La Crosse, Wis	Apr. 20, 1905	do	Apr. 21, 1904	Do.
J. R. Gunn No. 2	61	1904		1900		Decatur, Ala	Oct. 26, 1905	Decatur, Ala	Sept. 12, 1904	Do.
Jim T. Duffy, jr	97	1897		1897		Jeffersonville, Ind	Mar. 7, 1905	Paducah, Ky	Mar. 4, 1904	Do.
John A. Hart No. 2	6	1903		1903		Chattanooga, Tenn	Apr. 12, 1905	Chattanooga, Tenn	Apr. 11, 1904	Do.
Kuttawa	14	1899		1881		Harris Landing, Ky	July 26, 1905	Paducah, Ky	June 22, 1904	Do.
Lora	44	1895		1891		Chattanooga, Tenn	July 15, 1905	Nashville, Tenn	July 20, 1904	Do.
Lotus	28	1893		1886		Rock Island, Ill	June 7, 1905	Paducah, Ky	May 9, 1904	Evansville, Ind.
Lula E. Warren	90	1896		1893		Johnsonville, Tenn	Mar. 24, 1905	Wilkins Mill, Tenn	Mar. 12, 1904	Nashville, Tenn.
Lyda	80	1903		1895		Jeffersonville, Ind	Sept. 4, 1905	Paducah, Ky	Sept. 16, 1904	Do.

[a] Certificate filed Mar. 15, 1905. [b] Formerly O. E. Stockell, 1896. [c] Formerly City of Winona, 1905. [d] Estimated.

DOMESTIC VESSELS INSPECTED, YEAR ENDED DECEMBER 31, 1905—SIXTH SUPERVISING DISTRICT—NASHVILLE, TENN.—Continued.

Names of vessels and class.	Gross tonnage.	Hull built.	Hull rebuilt.	Boilers built.	Boilers rebuilt.	Where built.	Date of inspection.	Where inspected.	Date of previous inspection.	Local district where previously inspected.
Inland towing steamers—Con.										
Mary N	56	1889		1904		Paducah, Ky	July 5, 1905	Paducah, Ky	July 8, 1904	Nashville, Tenn.
Margaret	328	1894		1896		Evansville, Ind	do	do	do	Do.
Monie Bauer	45	1892		1883		Golconda, Ill	Jan. 21, 1905	do	Jan. 20, 1904	Do.
Monie Bauer	45	1892		1905		do	Dec. 23, 1905	do	Jan. 21, 1905	Do.
Milnor	49	1905		1905		Knoxville, Tenn	Nov. 22, 1905	Knoxville, Tenn	First inspn.	
Oliver King	42	1897		1898		do	Jan. 15, 1905	do	Jan. 14, 1904	Do.
Oliver King	42	1897		1898		do	Nov. 22, 1905	do	Jan. 15, 1905	Do.
Ondine	14	1899		1899		Rock Island, Ill	May 4, 1905	Paducah, Ky	May 5, 1904	Evansville, Ind.
Pavonia	132	1892		1892		Madison, Ind	Sept. 14, 1905	do	Oct. 6, 1904	Nashville, Tenn.
Penguin	60	1877		1879		Burlington, Iowa	July 14, 1905	do	July 7, 1904	Evansville, Ind.
Russel Lord	295	1898		1898		Pittsburg, Pa	Sept. 14, 1905	do	Oct. 6, 1904	Nashville, Tenn.
Sycamore [a]	98	1889		1888		Evansville, Ind	Aug. 22, 1905	do	Aug. 29, 1904	Do.
T. H. Davis	240	1898		1900		Middleport, Ohio	Dec. 22, 1905	Joppa, Ill	Feb. 7, 1905	St. Louis, Mo.
W. T. Gallaher	27	1898		1887		Kingston, Tenn	May 1, 1905	Kingston, Tenn	May 6, 1904	Nashville, Tenn.
Wilford [b]	47	1892		1895		Nashville, Tenn	Feb. 3, 1905	Paducah, Ky	Feb. 3, 1904	Do.
Wilford [b]	47	1892		1895		do	Dec. 23, 1905	do	Feb. 3, 1905	Do.
Miscellaneous steam vessels.										
Clipper (sawmill)	98	1888		1894		Haynes Landing, W. Va.	Sept. 8, 1905	Clifton, Tenn	Sept. 9, 1904	Nashville, Tenn.
Mackie (sand digger)	77	1905		1891		Nashville, Tenn	Apr. 5, 1905	Nashville, Tenn	First inspn.	
T. L. Herbert (sand digger)	80	1900		1900		do	Dec. 7, 1905	do	Dec. 19, 1904	Do.
Barge of over 100 tons carrying passengers for hire.										
Acme	110	1900				Rock Island, Ill	May 16, 1905	Paducah, Ky	June 16, 1904	Dubuque, Iowa.

LOCAL DISTRICT OF MEMPHIS, TENN.

Names of vessels and class.	Gross tonnage.	Hull built.	Hull rebuilt.	Boilers built.	Boilers rebuilt.	Where built.	Date of inspection.	Where inspected.	Date of previous inspection.	Local district where previously inspected.
Inland passenger steamers.										
Alda	73	1891		1891		Boonville, Mo	June 5, 1905	Clarendon, Ark	June 2, 1904	Memphis, Tenn.
A. D. Allen	92	1901		1896		Jeffersonville, Ind	Sept. 25, 1905	Little Rock, Ark	Oct. 7, 1904	Do.
C. E. Taylor	79	1899		1888		Lewisburg, Ark	Mar. 22, 1905	Black Rock, Ark	Mar. 11, 1904	Do.
City St. Joseph	691	1901		1882		St. Joseph, Mo	May 8, 1905	Memphis, Tenn	May 9, 1904	St. Louis, Mo.
Chas. H. Organ	166	1897		1897		Dubuque, Iowa	June 10, 1905	do	June 9, 1904	Memphis, Tenn.
C. H. Hugo	38	1897		1897		New Haven, Mo	Aug. 1, 1905	do	Aug. 4, 1904	Do.
Caruthersville	47	1903		1896		Dyersburg, Tenn	Oct. 6, 1905	Hickman, Ky	Aug. 18, 1904	Do.

Chas. B. Pearce	223	1899		1900		Augusta, Ky	Nov. 16, 1905	Memphis, Tenn	Nov. 22, 1904	New Orleans, La.
Elva	53	1899		1900		Leavenworth, Ind	May 4, 1905	Dardanelle, Ark	May 4, 1904	Memphis, Tenn.
Eva Alma	48	1898		1891		Pomeroy, Ohio	June 20, 1905	Newport, Ark	June 22, 1904	St. Louis, Mo.
G. W. Huff	66	1904		1899		Poplar Bluff, Mo	Feb. 27, 1905	Black Rock, Ark	Feb. 25, 1904	Memphis, Tenn.
Geo. Pope	97	1902		1890		Judsonia, Ark	Apr. 3, 1905	do	Apr. 1, 1904	Do.
Gate City	60	1900		1901		Winona, Minn	June 26, 1905	Caruthersville, Mo	June 7, 1904	Do.
Georgia Lee	595	1898		1898		Jeffersonville, Ind	July 12, 1905	Memphis, Tenn	July 11, 1904	Do.
Henry Sheldon	220	1893	1904	1884		Little Rock, Ark	Feb. 23, 1905	Little Rock, Ark	Feb. 23, 1904	Do.
James Lee	569	1898		1898		Jeffersonville, Ind	Apr. 17, 1905	Memphis, Tenn	Apr. 15, 1904	Do.
Jewel [c]	49	1899		1891		Golconda, Ill	May 25, 1905	Greenville, Miss	May 25, 1904	Do.
J. N. Harbin	142	1895	1905	1895		Pittsburg, Pa	July 11, 1905	Memphis, Tenn	Aug. 3, 1904	Do.
Joy Patton	63	1891		1891		Dubuque, Iowa	Nov. 21, 1905	do	July 1, 1904	Do.
Kate Adams	595	1898		1898		Jeffersonville, Ind	Oct. 2, 1905	do	Oct. 24, 1904	Do.
Luella Brown	102	1890		1890		Wheeling, W. Va	Jan. 30, 1905	Greenville, Miss	Sept. 26, 1903	Do.
L. E. Patton	94	1894		1890		Dubuque, Iowa	Aug. 17, 1905	Memphis, Tenn	Sept. 16, 1904	Do.
Lucille Nowland	472	1898		1898		Pittsburg, Pa	Sept. 26, 1905	do	Oct. 11, 1904	Do.
Maude Kilgore	82	1901		1900 / 1901		Paducah, Ky	Jan. 7, 1905	Helena, Ark	Jan. 14, 1904	Do.
Mildred	29	1904		1891		Augusta, Ark	Feb. 24, 1905	Augusta, Ark	Feb. 22, 1904	Do.
Morning Star	592	1901		1901		Jeffersonville, Ind	May 8, 1905	Memphis, Tenn	May 9, 1904	Louisville, Ky.
Nettie Johnson	72	1904		1905		Memphis, Tenn	Aug. 12, 1905	do	First inspn.	
Rees Lee	463	1899		1899		Jeffersonville, Ind	Sept. 26, 1905	do	Sept. 29, 1904	St. Louis, Mo.
Speed	85	1886		1893		Stillwater, Minn	Mar. 24, 1905	Greenville, Miss	Mar. 25, 1904	Memphis, Tenn.
Sun	84	1898	1902	1898		Hockingport, Ohio	Nov. 6, 1905	Memphis, Tenn	Nov. 14, 1904	Do.
Sadie Lee	247	1901		1901		Jeffersonville, Ind	Nov. 23, 1905	do	Dec. 2, 1904	Do.
Twins	27	1904		1904		Batesville, Ark	June 21, 1905	Wyatts Landing, Ark	Apr. 6, 1904	Do.
W. M. Gladden	27	1903		1890		Little Rock, Ark	Jan. 23, 1905	Lewisburg, Ark	Jan. 21, 1904	Do.
Zerah, jr	132	1901		1905		Helena, Ark	Sept. 30, 1905	Memphis, Tenn	Dec. 6, 1904	Do.
Inland ferry steamers.										
Caroline	69	1901		1894		Van Buren, Ark	Nov. 1, 1905	Van Buren, Ark	Nov. 2, 1904	Memphis, Tenn.
Dewet	16	1902		1903		Morrisons Bluff, Ark	July 8, 1905	Spadra, Ark	July 7, 1904	Do.
Gussie	23	1901		1901		Roseville, Ark	July 7, 1905	Roseville, Ark	do	Do.
General Pierson	485	1877	1899	1898		Metropolis, Ill	Sept. 21, 1905	Memphis, Tenn	Oct. 13, 1904	Do.
John Bertram	390	1880	1902	1880		Jeffersonville, Ind	Apr. 18, 1905	Helena, Ark	Apr. 16, 1904	Do.
Lee White	49	1902		1902		Dardanelle, Ark	June 19, 1905	Lewisburg Ark	June 16, 1904	Do.
Maude F	23	1905		1905		Piney, Ark	May 23, 1905	Piney, Ark	First inspn.	
Webbers Falls	26	1901		1901		Van Buren, Ark	May 5, 1905	Webbers Falls, Ind. T	May 8, 1904	Do.
Inland towing steamers.										
A. R. Hall	60	1896		1897		Dyersburg, Tenn	Feb. 22, 1905	Dyersburg, Tenn	Feb. 2, 1904	Memphis, Tenn
Anna S. Cooper	85	1882		1903		New Orleans, La	May 25, 1905	Greenville, Miss	May 25, 1904	Do.
A. J. Beardsly	96	1896		1901		Bridgeport, Conn	Dec. 7, 1905	Memphis, Tenn	Dec. 20, 1904	New York, N. Y.
Black Hawk	34	1894		1892		Stillwater, Minn	June 22, 1905	do	June 20, 1904	Dubuque, Iowa.
Chicago	48	1895		1894		Lyons, Iowa	Apr. 14, 1905	Greenville, Miss	Apr. 12, 1904	Memphis, Tenn.
Cora Belle	16	1888		1893		North McGregor, Iowa	Aug. 29, 1905	Clarendon, Ark	Sept. 9, 1904	Do.
Climax	58	1893		1893		Burlington, Iowa	Oct. 3, 1905	Arkansas City, Ark	Oct. 5, 1904	Do.
Essie	18	1902		1902		Lutcher, La	Mar. 24, 1905	Greenville, Miss	Mar. 19, 1904	New Orleans, La.

[a] Formerly O. E. Stockell, 1896.   [b] Formerly John T. Carson, 1900.   [c] Formerly City of Golconda, 1902.

DOMESTIC VESSELS INSPECTED, YEAR ENDED DECEMBER 31, 1905—SIXTH SUPERVISING DISTRICT—MEMPHIS, TENN.—Continued.

Names of vessels and class.	Gross tonnage.	Hull built.	Hull rebuilt.	Boilers built.	Boilers rebuilt.	Where built.	Date of inspection.	Where inspected.	Date of previous inspection.	Local district where previously inspected.
Inland towing steamers—Con.										
Fannie Wallace	25	1888		1888		Belpre, Ohio	June 27, 1905	Memphis, Tenn.	June 21, 1904	Nashville, Tenn.
Greyhound	9	1894	1901	1899		Saugatuck, Mich.	Apr. 14, 1905	Greenville, Miss.	Apr. 13, 1904	Memphis, Tenn.
Hazel Rice	137	1895		1895		Marietta, Ohio	Aug. 3, 1905	Helena, Ark.	July 28, 1904	Do.
J. C. Atlee	87	1886		1886		Rock Island, Ill.	May 19, 1905	Memphis, Tenn.	May 16, 1904	Do.
J. M. Linder	73	1899		1899		Paducah, Ky.	Dec. 16, 1905	do	Dec. 22, 1904	Do.
Lake City	17	1904		1893		Lake City, Ark.	July 15, 1905	Marked Tree, Ark.	July 18, 1904	Do.
Minnehaha	46	1896		1896		Paducah, Ky.	Mar. 20, 1905	Memphis, Tenn.	Mar. 15, 1904	Do.
Marie J	76	1896		1896		Helena, Ark.	May 16, 1905	do	May 14, 1904	Do.
Meter	39	1884	1904	1884		Jeffersonville, Ind.	June 15, 1905	do	June 15, 1904	Do.
Mary D	40	1903		1890		Fort Smith, Ark.	Nov. 2, 1905	Muskogee Landing, Ind. T.	Nov. 2, 1904	Do.
Myrtle Corey	9	1898		1898		Fenton, Mo.	Nov. 17, 1905	Little Rock, Ark.	Apr. 5, 1904	Do.
Nettie	94	1897	1902	1890		Little Rock, Ark.	Jan. 18, 1905	Rosedale, Miss.	Jan. 12, 1904	Do.
N. M. Jones	34	1871		1895		Pittsburg, Pa.	Sept. 16, 1905	Memphis, Tenn.	Sept. 16, 1904	Do.
Parker	208	1901		1887		St. Louis, Mo.	Apr. 20, 1905	do	Apr. 21, 1904	St. Louis, Mo.
Roann	39	1899		1901		Lyons, Iowa	May 9, 1905	Arkansas City, Ark.	May 10, 1904	Memphis, Tenn.
Roy	49	1896		1901		Fiske, Mo.	Oct. 28, 1905	Poplar Bluff, Mo.	Oct. 29, 1904	Do.
Satellite	60	1900		1890		Rock Island, Ill.	May 24, 1905	Memphis, Tenn.	May 14, 1904	Do.
Truman	16	1903		1890		Lake Village, Ark.	May 22, 1905	Little Rock, Ark.	May 23, 1904	Do.
Thomas Heidel	10	1887		1902		Paducah, Ky.	July 18, 1905	Greenville, Miss.	July 18, 1904	Do.
Welcome	45	1897		1897		Greenville, Miss.	Mar. 8, 1905	Jacksonport, Ark.	Mar. 8, 1904	Do.
Steam pleasure yacht.										
Ray	a 3	1904		1904		Brownsville, Pa.	Dec. 23, 1905	Memphis, Tenn.	Nov. 26, 1904	Wheeling, W. Va.
Vessels propelled by gasoline motors.										
Charlie V. (freight)	27	1904				Greenville, Miss.	Nov. 22, 1905	Rosedale, Miss.	Nov. 23, 1904	Memphis, Tenn.
Peerless (passenger)	21	1904				Newport, Ark.	Oct. 23, 1905	Clarendon, Ark.	Oct. 24, 1904	Do.

SEVENTH SUPERVISING DISTRICT.

LOCAL DISTRICT OF CINCINNATI, OHIO.

Inland passenger steamers.										
Avalon	361	1898		1898		Clarington, Ohio	July 18, 1905	Cincinnati, Ohio	July 18, 1904	Cincinnati, Ohio.
Ben Hur [b]	284	1887		1887		Point Harmar, Ohio	Nov. 7, 1904	do	Oct. 28, 1904	Wheeling, W. Va.
Bonanza	741	1885		1885		Cincinnati, Ohio	June 26, 1905	do	June 24, 1904	Cincinnati, Ohio.
City of Cincinnati	816	1899		1899		Jeffersonville, Ind	Apr. 6, 1905	do	Apr. 5, 1904	Louisville, Ky.
City of Louisville	1,681	1894		1894		do	May 5, 1905	do	May 7, 1904	Cincinnati, Ohio.
Cricket	65	1900		1900		Parkersburg, W. Va.	Aug. 1, 1905	Newport, Ky	July 29, 1904	Wheeling, W. Va.
Chilo	94	1905		1888		Point Pleasant, W. Va.	Oct. 18, 1905	Cincinnati, Ohio	First inspn	
Courier	296	1885		1892		Freedom, Pa	Aug. 28, 1905	do	Sept. 1, 1904	Cincinnati, Ohio.
Daisy	11	1904		1893		Grant, Ky	Aug. 14, 1905	Mackville, Ky	May 9, 1904	Do.
Greenwood	270	1898		1898		Parkersburg, W. Va.	Oct. 16, 1905	Cincinnati, Ohio	Nov. 3, 1904	Gallipolis, Ohio.
Hattie Brown	58	1884		1884		Belle Vernon, Pa	July 17, 1905	Warsaw, Ky	July 18, 1904	Cincinnati, Ohio.
Henry M. Stanley	293	1890	1899	1890		Murrayville, W. Va	Nov. 28, 1905	Cincinnati, Ohio	Nov. 29, 1904	Do.
Island Queen	1,446	1896		1896		Cincinnati, Ohio	May 6, 1905	do	May 5, 1904	Do.
Indiana	836	1900		1896		Jeffersonville, Ind	July 25, 1905	do	Aug. 15, 1904	Do.
Keystone State	599	1890		1890		Harmar, Ohio	Mar. 9, 1905	do	Feb. 9, 1904	Do.
Lizzie Bay	198	1886		1886		Madison, Ind	June 7, 1905	do	June 7, 1904	Do.
Levi J. Workum	183	1890		1890		Levanna, Ohio	Oct. 23, 1905	do	Nov. 18, 1904	Do.
M. P. Wells	87	1888		1888		Belle Vernon, Pa	July 11, 1905	do	July 11, 1904	Do.
Ohio	8	1904		1891		Cincinnati, Ohio	Apr. 7, 1905	do	First inspn	
Oneida	11	1902		1897		Higginsport, Ohio	Apr. 12, 1905	do	Mar. 31, 1904	Do.
Pauline	11	1896		1900		Petersburg, Ky	Apr. 8, 1905	Aurora, Ind	Apr. 4, 1904	Do.
Pauline	18	1905		1900		do	Sept. 26, 1905	do	First inspn	
Queen City	624	1897		1897		Cincinnati, Ohio	June 24, 1905	Cincinnati, Ohio	June 25, 1904	Do.
Swan	33	1902		1902		Mackville, Ky	Apr. 8, 1905	Aurora, Ind	Apr. 4, 1904	Do.
Silver Star	20	1897		1897		Pittsburg, Pa	Oct. 7, 1905	Cincinnati, Ohio	Nov. 25, 1904	Do.
Tacoma	276	1897		1883		Cincinnati, Ohio	Nov. 20, 1905	do	Nov. 18, 1904	Louisville, Ky.
Virginia	628	1895		1895		do	Apr. 11, 1905	do	Feb. 8, 1904	Cincinnati, Ohio.
Ferry steamers.										
Boone No. 5	38	1900		1900		Constance, Ky	July 24, 1905	Constance, Ky	July 25, 1904	Cincinnati, Ohio.
Eva Evertt	35	1900		1903		Vevay, Ind	July 3, 1905	Ghent, Ky	July 6, 1904	Do.
Laurance	62	1891	1900	1891		Madison, Ind	Aug. 30, 1905	Maysville, Ky	Sept. 14, 1904	Do.
New Richmond	38	1890	1900	1889		Cincinnati, Ohio	July 28, 1905	New Richmond, Ohio	Aug. 8, 1904	Do.
Proctor K. Smiley	66	1895		1895		Ashland, Ky	Mar. 7, 1905	Ripley, Ohio	Mar. 7, 1904	Do.
W. H. Whiteman	31	1892	1900	1882		Newport, Ky	June 20, 1905	Manchester, Ohio	June 23, 1904	Do.
Whisper	33	1881	1902	1881		Ashland, Ky	July 6, 1905	Augusta, Ky	July 7, 1904	Do.
Inland towing steamers.										
Ada V	23	1888		1888		Little Hocking, Ohio	July 8, 1905	Newport, Ky	June 14, 1904	Cincinnati, Ohio.
Alert	48	1905		1902		Delhi, Ohio	Nov. 13, 1905	Higginsport, Ohio	First inspn	

[a] Estimated.

[b] Certificate not filed with chief officer of customs until Jan. 7, 1905.

DOMESTIC VESSELS INSPECTED, YEAR ENDED DECEMBER 31, 1905—SEVENTH SUPERVISING DISTRICT—CINCINNATI, OHIO—Continued.

Names of vessels and class.	Gross tonnage.	Hull built.	Hull rebuilt.	Boilers built.	Boilers rebuilt.	Where built.	Date of inspection.	Where inspected.	Date of previous inspection.	Local district where previously inspected.
Inland towing steamers—Con.										
Convoy	170	1888		1904		Madison, Ind	Mar. 3,1905	Cincinnati, Ohio	Feb. 25,1904	Gallipolis, Ohio.
Crown Hill	120	1882	1895	1897		Middleport, Ohio	Apr. 24,1905	do	Apr. 28,1904	Cincinnati, Ohio.
Clifton	289	1883	1897	1883		Pittsburg, Pa	Sept. 7,1905	do	Sept. 9,1904	Pittsburg, Pa.
Delta	97	1881	1896	1891		do	Apr. 7,1905	do	Apr. 1,1904	Do.
Emma Cooper	79	1878		1902		do	Mar. 14,1905	do	Mar. 11,1904	Cincinnati, Ohio.
Frank Miller	49	1901		1890		Vevay, Ind	Mar. 18,1905	Ludlow, Ky	Feb. 10,1904	Do.
Fallie	302	1894		1894		Pittsburg, Pa	Nov. 1,1905	Cincinnati, Ohio	Nov. 26,1904	Pittsburg, Pa.
Geo. Matheson	124	1878	1893	1893		do	July 7,1905	do	Apr. 16,1904	Cincinnati, Ohio.
Hercules Carrel	217	1871	1888	1883		Cincinnati, Ohio	Nov. 27,1905	do	Dec. 20,1904	Do.
Ironside	282	1869	1900	1900		Pittsburg, Pa	Feb. 6,1905	Moscow, Ohio	Feb. 3,1904	Pittsburg, Pa.
James Moren	602	1895		1895		do	Aug. 25,1905	Coal Haven, Ky	Aug. 25,1904	Wheeling, W. Va.
Joseph Walton	300	1873	1901	1886		do	Nov. 1,1905	Cincinnati, Ohio	Nov. 4,1904	Pittsburg, Pa.
Jack Frost	350	1881		1881		Jeffersonville, Ind	May 18,1905	do	Apr. 2,1904	Cincinnati, Ohio.
J. O. Cole	128	1900		1900		Cincinnati, Ohio	Apr. 10,1905	do	Apr. 5,1904	Do.
Otto Marmet	135	1898		1898		Raymond City W. Va.	Mar. 6,1905	do	Feb. 25,1904	Do.
Reba Reeves	63	1897		1897		Charleston, W. Va	Mar. 25,1905	Fernbank, Ohio	Mar. 28,1904	Gallipolis, Ohio.
Raymond Horner	688	1882		1903		Pittsburg, Pa	May 22,1905	Cincinnati, Ohio	May 20,1904	New Orleans, La.
Val P. Collins	119	1901		1890		Charleston, W. Va	Mar. 17,1905	do	Mar. 18,1904	Cincinnati, Ohio.
Winifrede	97	1903		1904		Marietta, Ohio	May 15,1905	do	May 16,1904	Do.
Wilmot	163	1889		1896		Pittsburg, Pa	Oct. 17,1905	do	Oct. 8,1904	Pittsburg, Pa.
Steam pleasure yachts.										
Dixie [a]	35	1892	1902	1892		Woodville, Wis	June 1,1905	Newport, Ky	June 21,1904	Cincinnati, Ohio.
Eulalie	3	1901		1902		Cincinnati, Ohio	Oct. 11,1905	Cincinnati, Ohio	Oct. 18,1904	Do.
Manoa	4	1903		1893		do	July 18,1905	Newport, Ky	Aug. 3,1904	Do.
S. & W	8	1904		1900		do	June 29,1905	Cincinnati, Ohio	June 28,1904	Do.
Sentinel	[b] 4	1891		1891	1904	Pittsburg, Pa	Oct. 9,1905	do	Nov. 3,1904	Do.
Gasoline motor vessels.										
Hope	18	1905				Cincinnati, Ohio	Apr. 1,1905	Cincinnati, Ohio	First inspn.	
Dan Patch	25	1905				Levanna, Ohio	July 12,1905	Levanna, Ohio	do	

LOCAL DISTRICT OF GALLIPOLIS, OHIO.

Names of vessels and class.	Gross tonnage.	Hull built.	Hull rebuilt.	Boilers built.	Boilers rebuilt.	Where built.	Date of inspection.	Where inspected.	Date of previous inspection.	Local district where previously inspected.
Inland passenger steamers.										
Bessie Smith	127	1899	1905	1897		Smithsonia, Ala	May 4,1905	Parkersburg, W. Va	Mar. 5,1904	Wheeling, W. Va.
Ben Hur	284	1887		1887		Harmar, Ohio	Oct. 9,1905	do	Nov. 7,1904	Cincinnati, Ohio.

Baxter	75	1900		1893		Point Pleasant, W. Va.	Oct. 30, 1905	Charleston, W. Va.	Nov. 9, 1904	Gallipolis, Ohio.
Calvert	110	1899		1890		Charleston, W. Va.	Sept. 26, 1905	Point Pleasant, W. Va.	Oct. 10, 1904	Do.
Chevalier	67	1901		1888		Middleport, Ohio	Oct. 21, 1905	Gallipolis, Ohio	Oct. 28, 1904	Do.
Carrie Brown	92	1903		1902		Point Pleasant, W. Va.	Nov. 11, 1905	do	Nov. 4, 1904	Do.
Daisy	17	1903		1905		Antiquity, Ohio	Mar. 25, 1905	do	Jan. 27, 1904	Do.
Excel	32	1900		1900		Middleport, Ohio	Feb. 13, 1905	Parkersburg, W. Va.	Feb. 1, 1904	Do.
Evergreen	99	1902		1902		Parkersburg, W. Va.	Sept. 1, 1905	Charleston, W. Va.	Sept. 5, 1904	Do.
French	82	1903		1891		do	June 8, 1905	Parkersburg, W. Va.	June 11, 1904	Do.
Frank Tyler	71	1904		1904		do	July 8, 1905	do	July 8, 1904	Do.
Guyandotte	43	1896		1892		Guyandotte, W. Va.	Feb. 15, 1905	Ashland, Ky.	Jan. 26, 1904	Do.
Greyhound	125	1901		1901		Ironton, Ohio	May 26, 1905	Proctorville, Ohio	May 27, 1904	Do.
Gondola	99	1883	1905	1883		Pittsburg, Pa.	Sept. 26, 1905	Point Pleasant, W. Va.	May 11, 1904	Evansville, Ind.
Greenland	294	1903		1898		Marietta, Ohio	Oct. 30, 1905	Charleston, W. Va.	Nov. 3, 1904	Gallipolis, Ohio.
H. K. Bedford	139	1885		1904		Jeffersonville, Ind.	June 2, 1905	Gallipolis, Ohio	July 14, 1904	Wheeling, W. Va.
Kanawha	429	1896		1896		Ironton, Ohio	Sept. 12, 1905	Parkersburg, W. Va.	Sept. 12, 1904	Gallipolis, Ohio.
Klondike	73	1891	1897	1897		Harmar, Ohio	Oct. 28, 1905	Gallipolis, Ohio	Nov. 5, 1904	Do.
Laynesville	38	1904		1890		Laynesville, Ky.	July 11, 1905	South Point, Ohio	July 11, 1904	Do.
Lillian H	41	1905		1895		Gallipolis, Ohio	Nov. 14, 1905	Proctorville, Ohio	First inspn.	
Neva	71	1898		1900		Point Pleasant, W. Va.	Aug. 19, 1905	Gallipolis, Ohio	Aug. 19, 1904	Do.
Sea Gull	27	1902		1901		Pikeville, Ky.	Feb. 14, 1905	Catlettsburg, Ky.	Jan. 25, 1904	Do.
Thealka	45	1899		1891		Paintsville, Ky.	Jan. 26, 1905	Paintsville, Ky.	Jan. 26, 1904	Do.
Valley Belle	118	1898		1898		Parkersburg, W. Va.	Sept. 12, 1905	Parkersburg, W. Va.	Sept. 17, 1904	Do.
Ferry steamers.										
Arion	60	1902		1891		Point Pleasant, W. Va.	Mar. 30, 1905	Proctorville, Ohio	Mar. 31, 1904	Gallipolis, Ohio.
Boone No. 4	24	1891		1887		Constance, Ky.	July 3, 1905	Kanauga, Ohio	July 1, 1904	Do.
Bonne	41	1897		1891		South Point, Ohio	Aug. 5, 1905	Huntington, W. Va.	Aug. 5, 1904	Do.
Champion No. 2	52	1882	1904	1893	1904	Mason City, W. Va.	Jan. 10, 1905	Gallipolis, Ohio	Jan. 14, 1904	Do.
Chesapeake	158	1904		1904		Point Pleasant, W. Va.	Aug. 25, 1905	Portsmouth, Ohio	Aug. 29, 1904	Do.
Champion No. 3	66	1901		1901		Mason City, W. Va.	Oct. 17, 1905	Pomeroy, Ohio	Oct. 28, 1904	Do.
City of Huntington	58	1900		1904		Middleport, Ohio	Oct. 24, 1905	Huntington, W. Va.	Nov. 5, 1904	Do.
Emily	68	1891	1901	1891		Jeffersonville, Ind.	June 27, 1905	Portsmouth, Ohio	June 27, 1904	Do.
Francis	56	1892	1902	1892		Manchester, Ohio	Nov. 27, 1905	Gallipolis, Ohio	Dec. 7, 1904	Do.
Ironton	129	1895	1904	1895		Levanna, Ohio	May 18, 1905	Ironton, Ohio	May 19, 1904	Do.
Little Ben	33	1895		1895		Pomeroy, Ohio	July 15, 1905	Middleport, Ohio	July 15, 1904	Do.
Nina Paden	84	1896	1904	1896		Marietta, Ohio	Sept. 2, 1905	Parkersburg, W. Va.	Sept. 7, 1904	Do.
Winona	63	1893	1904	1902		Cincinnati, Ohio	May 18, 1905	Ashland, Ky.	May 19, 1904	Do.
W. O. Hughart	67	1894		1894		Conway, Mich.	Oct. 17, 1905	Graham Sta., W. Va.	Oct. 28, 1904	Do.
Inland towing steamers.										
Argand	96	1896		1896		Levanna, Ohio	June 19, 1905	Gallipolis, Ohio	July 15, 1904	Evansville, Ind.
Bob Ballard	150	1890		1890		Murraysville, W. Va.	Apr. 18, 1905	Ironton, Ohio	Apr. 18, 1904	Gallipolis, Ohio.
Billy Martin	28	1883	1903	1901		Charleston, W. Va.	Oct. 4, 1905	Dana, W. Va.	Oct. 10, 1904	Do.
Catharine Davis	334	1896		1896		Marietta, Ohio	May 17, 1905	Point Pleasant, W. Va.	May 11, 1904	Do.
Columbia	197	1893	1903	1893		Point Pleasant, W. Va.	June 21, 1905	Gallipolis, Ohio	July 6, 1904	Do.
Douglas Hall	122	1900		1901		Cincinnati, Ohio	Jan. 13, 1905	Oak Forest, W. Va.	Jan. 11, 1904	Cincinnati, Ohio.
D. T. Lane	146	1871	1895	1888		Pittsburg, Pa.	Feb. 17, 1905	Malden, W. Va.	Feb. 19, 1904	Gallipolis, Ohio.
Darling	78	1899		1899		Parkersburg, W. Va.	May 4, 1905	Parkersburg, W. Va.	May 4, 1904	Do.
E. R. Andrews	469	1894		1895		Jeffersonville, Ind.	Sept. 11, 1905	Lock No. 11, W. Va.	Sept. 22, 1904	Do.

a Formerly Eillen. b Estimated.

DOMESTIC VESSELS INSPECTED, YEAR ENDED DECEMBER 31, 1905—SEVENTH SUPERVISING DISTRICT—GALLIPOLIS, OHIO—Continued.

Names of vessels and class.	Gross tonnage.	Hull built.	Hull rebuilt.	Boilers built.	Boilers rebuilt.	Where built.	Date of inspection.	Where inspected.	Date of previous inspection.	Local district where previously inspected.
Inland towing steamers—Con.										
Florence Marmet	263	1900		1889		Point Pleasant, W. Va.	Sept. 11, 1905	Point Pleasant, W. Va.	Sept. 14, 1904	Gallipolis, Ohio.
Genevieve	14	1898		1898		do	Apr. 17, 1905	Gallipolis, Ohio	Apr. 28, 1904	Do.
Gazette	10	1903		1903		Allegheny, Pa	May 23, 1905	Minersville, Ohio	May 23, 1904	Do.
Iron Duke	30	1875	1899	1889		Portsmouth, Ohio	Dec. 11, 1905	Henderson, W. Va	Dec. 17, 1904	Do.
John A. Wood	687	1870	1901	1904		Pittsburg, Pa	Jan. 20, 1905	Millersport, Ohio	Jan. 20, 1904	Pittsburg, Pa.
J. B. Lewis	162	1900		1900		Middleport, Ohio	Aug. 15, 1905	Point Pleasant, W. Va.	Aug. 15, 1904	Gallipolis, Ohio.
J. T. Hatfield	153	1904		1905		Point Pleasant, W. Va.	Dec. 16, 1905	Middleport, Ohio	Dec. 1, 1904	Cincinnati, Ohio.
Katie Mc	41	1902		1903		Proctorville, Ohio	June 17, 1905	Proctorville, Ohio	June 18, 1904	Do.
Leni Leoti	75	1891		1891		Pittsburg, Pa	Oct. 6, 1905	Catlettsburg, Ky	Oct. 7, 1904	Gallipolis, Ohio.
Lucy Marmet	185	1903		1903		Cincinnati, Ohio	Nov. 1, 1905	Point Pleasant, W. Va.	Nov. 25, 1904	Cincinnati, Ohio.
Lucy Coles	41	1902		1902		Point Pleasant, W. Va.	Nov. 15, 1905	Ashland, Ky	Nov. 28, 1904	Gallipolis, Ohio.
Mary Stewart	77	1893		1893		Spottsville, Ky	May 20, 1905	Gallipolis, Ohio	May 20, 1904	Do.
Mountain State	142	1891		1890		Newport, Ky	Sept. 18, 1905	Parkersburg, W. Va	Sept. 27, 1904	Do.
Nellie England	85	1893		1893		Pittsburg, Pa	Oct. 2, 1905	Gallipolis, Ohio	Oct. 29, 1904	Do.
Natchez	12	1903		1897		Catlettsburg, Ky	Oct. 7, 1905	Catlettsburg, Ky	Oct. 7, 1904	Do.
Robert P. Gillham	158	1901		1902		Parkersburg, W. Va	Apr. 5, 1905	Malden, W. Va	Apr. 4, 1904	Do.
Scout	77	1903		1903		Marietta, Ohio	Feb. 17, 1905	Charleston, W. Va	Jan. 28, 1904	Do.
Sea Lion	106	1880	1905	1905		Wheeling, W. Va	Sept. 26, 1905	Point Pleasant, W. Va.	Nov. 28, 1904	Do.
Sam Brown	491	1903		1896		Elizabeth, Pa	Nov. 3, 1905	Gallipolis, Ohio	Nov. 2, 1904	Pittsburg, Pa.
Telephone	73	1894		1894		Knoxville, Tenn	Nov. 14, 1905	Ironton, Ohio	Nov. 26, 1904	Gallipolis, Ohio.
W. B. Calderwood	85	1893		1904		Cincinnati, Ohio	Aug. 1, 1905	Lock No. 11, W. Va	Aug. 1, 1904	Do.
Barge of over 100 tons carrying passengers for hire.										
Little Kanawha	152	1897	1905			Parkersburg, W. Va	Aug. 10, 1905	Parkersburg, W. Va	First insp'n	

LOCAL DISTRICT OF PITTSBURG, PA.

Names of vessels and class.	Gross tonnage.	Hull built.	Hull rebuilt.	Boilers built.	Boilers rebuilt.	Where built.	Date of inspection.	Where inspected.	Date of previous inspection.	Local district where previously inspected.
Inland passenger steamers.										
Admiral Dewey	137	1898		1894		Brownsville, Pa	Dec. 22, 1905	Pittsburg, Pa	Aug. 5, 1904	Pittsburg, Pa.
Audrey	a 5	1904		1904		Pittsburg, Pa	May 17, 1905	Esplen, Pa	May 18, 1904	Do.
Blanch Edna	9	1898		1898		do	May 10, 1905	Point Marion, Pa	May 9, 1904	Do.
Bob Swan	a 4	1903		1903		Allegheny, Pa	Aug. 31, 1905	Allegheny, Pa	Aug. 30, 1904	Do.
Braddock	150	1900		1900		Elizabeth, Pa	Apr. 11, 1905	Pittsburg, Pa	Apr. 11, 1904	Do.
Columbia	332	1902	1903	1902		Brownsville, Pa	Aug. 29, 1905	do	Aug. 29, 1904	Do.
Dolly [b]	a 4	1896		1897		St. Joseph, Mich	May 22, 1905	Esplen, Pa	May 14, 1904	Do.
Fayette [c]	a 4	1899		1895		Point Marion, Pa	May 10, 1905	Point Marion, Pa	May 9, 1904	Do.
Florence Belle	150	1895		1895		Pittsburg, Pa	May 8, 1905	Tarentum, Pa	May 6, 1904	Do.

Francis J. Torrance	667	1900		1900		Marietta, Ohio	May 18, 1905	Pittsburg, Pa	May 13, 1904	Do.
Gazelle	9	1901		1901		Pittsburg, Pa	May 26, 1905	Allegheny, Pa	May 25, 1904	Do.
Hazel L. Watson	10	1901		1901		...do	Apr. 18, 1905	Lock No. 4, Pa	Apr. 18, 1904	Do.
I. C. Woodward	282	1898		1898		Brownsville, Pa	July 31, 1905	Pittsburg, Pa	Aug. 4, 1904	Do.
Isaac M. Mason	114	1893		1893		Pittsburg, Pa	June 15, 1905	...do	June 13, 1904	Do.
J. O. Watson	54	1903		1903		Brownsville, Pa	Apr. 26, 1905	Lock No. 4, Pa	Apr. 26, 1904	Do.
Juniata	150	1900		1900		Elizabeth, Pa	May 17, 1905	Pittsburg, Pa	May 17, 1904	Do.
Liberty	68	1900		1901		Middleport, Ohio	Nov. 15, 1905	...do	Oct. 10, 1904	Gallipolis, Ohio.
Lorena	287	1895		1895		Marietta, Ohio	July 22, 1905	...do	July 26, 1904	Wheeling, W. Va.
Nellie Hudson No. 3	196	1893		1893		Pittsburg, Pa	May 4, 1905	Rosston, Pa	May 4, 1904	Pittsburg, Pa.
Panama	a 4	1901		1901		Allegheny, Pa	Dec. 18, 1905	Allegheny, Pa	Dec. 10, 1904	Do.
Pastime	9	1900		1892		Pittsburg, Pa	Aug. 2, 1905	Pittsburg, Pa	Apr. 4, 1904	Do.
Reliance	8	1904		1904		Allegheny, Pa	June 15, 1905	Allegheny, Pa	May 19, 1904	Do.
Rose Hite	215	1895		1895		Jeffersonville, Ind	Nov. 14, 1905	Pittsburg, Pa	Nov. 29, 1904	Do.
Sanford Hay	10	1901		1905		Pittsburg, Pa	Sept. 7, 1905	Esplen, Pa	Sept. 17, 1903	Do.
Sylvia	a 5	1904		1901		Allegheny, Pa	Mar. 6, 1905	Pittsburg, Pa	Mar. 5, 1904	Do.
Vesta	142	1902		1902		Pittsburg, Pa	Jan. 21, 1905	...do	Jan. 21, 1904	Do.
Wabash	9	1902		1902		Allegheny, Pa	June 5, 1905	...do	June 1, 1904	Do.
Winnifred	10	1892		1892		Pittsburg, Pa	July 11, 1905	Allegheny, Pa	Nov. 27, 1903	Do.
Ferry steamers.										
Short Cut	81	1880		1880		Pittsburg, Pa	June 21, 1905	Allegheny, Pa	June 21, 1904	Pittsburg, Pa.
Steel Queen	177	1901		1901		Jeffersonville, Ind	Oct. 27, 1905	...do	Oct. 28, 1904	Do.
Inland towing steamers.										
Aid d	a 4	1896		1896		Pittsburg, Pa	Apr. 4, 1905	Allegheny, Pa	Mar. 28, 1904	Pittsburg, Pa.
Alice Brown	551	1871	1892	1896		...do	Nov. 3, 1905	Pittsburg, Pa	Nov. 11, 1904	Cincinnati, Ohio.
Andrew Axton	99	1903		1901		Brownsville, Pa	Oct. 26, 1905	...do	Oct. 31, 1904	Pittsburg, Pa.
Bertha	162	1894		1887		Pittsburg, Pa	Oct. 10, 1905	...do	Oct. 7, 1904	Do.
Boaz	623	1882	1902	1902		...do	Feb. 8, 1905	Sewickley, Pa	Feb. 27, 1904	Louisville, Ky.
Burnadina King	50	1896		1889		Parkersburg, W. Va	Sept. 9, 1905	Coraopolis, Pa	Sept. 7, 1904	Gallipolis, Ohio.
Cadet e	122	1902		1892		Elizabeth, Pa	June 28, 1905	Fayette City, Pa	June 27, 1904	Pittsburg, Pa.
Carbon	121	1902		1902		...do	Nov. 8, 1905	Pittsburg, Pa	Nov. 7, 1904	Do.
Charles Brown	544	1872	1900	1900		Pittsburg, Pa	Nov. 24, 1905	...do	Nov. 25, 1904	Wheeling, W. Va.
Charley Jutte	281	1904		1904		Jeffersonville, Ind	Feb. 18, 1905	...do	Feb. 24, 1904	Louisville, Ky.
Charlie Clarke	147	1882	1893	1894		Pittsburg, Pa	Nov. 2, 1905	...do	Nov. 10, 1904	Pittsburg, Pa.
Clara Cavett	166	1877	1901	1891		Point Harmar, Ohio	Mar. 27, 1905	Creighton, Pa	Mar. 25, 1904	Do.
Clipper	185	1895		1895		Pittsburg, Pa	Feb. 7, 1905	Pittsburg, Pa	June 5, 1903	Do.
Clyde e	157	1903		1903		Brownsville, Pa	Sept. 19, 1905	...do	Sept. 23, 1904	Do.
Coal City	361	1864	1896	1896		Pittsburg, Pa	Sept. 2, 1905	...do	Sept. 8, 1904	Wheeling, W. Va.
Cruiser	341	1890		1898		...do	Mar. 14, 1905	...do	Feb. 17, 1904	Evansville, Ind.
Crusader	137	1904		1904		Elizabeth, Pa	Apr. 29, 1905	...do	Apr. 28, 1904	Pittsburg, Pa.
Dewing and Sons	59	1894		1891		Pittsburg, Pa	June 8, 1905	Kittanning, Pa	June 8, 1904	Do.
Diamond	118	1903		1903		Brownsville, Pa	Oct. 23, 1905	Pittsburg, Pa	Oct. 22, 1904	Do.
Ed Roberts	253	1884		1902		Madison, Ind	Sept. 6, 1905	...do	Sept. 22, 1904	Wheeling, W. Va.
Eleanor	106	1901		1884		Brownsville, Pa	Aug. 11, 1905	...do	Aug. 11, 1904	Pittsburg, Pa.
Eliza	250	1896		1886		Jeffersonville, Ind	Dec. 8, 1905	Allegheny, Pa	Nov. 23, 1904	Do.

a Estimated.
b Formerly E. W. Grove, 1904.
c Formerly Wm. Lockard, 1901.
d Formerly Sam'l W. Clarke, 1902.
e Inspected by Wheeling board.

DOMESTIC VESSELS INSPECTED, YEAR ENDED DECEMBER 31, 1905—SEVENTH SUPERVISING DISTRICT—PITTSBURG, PA.—Continued.

Names of vessels and class.	Gross tonnage.	Hull built.	Hull rebuilt.	Boilers built.	Boilers rebuilt.	Where built.	Date of inspection.	Where inspected.	Date of previous inspection.	Local district where previously inspected.
Inland towing steamers—Con.										
Enterprise	297	1903		1903		Elizabeth, Pa.	May 6, 1905	Pittsburg, Pa.	Feb. 6, 1904	Pittsburg, Pa.
F. K. Hulings	84	1900		1900		Pittsburg, Pa.	Oct. 6, 1905	Kittanning, Pa.	Oct. 6, 1904	Do.
Frank Fowler	67	1901		1889		Newport, Ky.	Oct. 31, 1905	Pittsburg, Pa.	Nov. 7, 1904	Do.
Frank Gilmore	243	1883	1889	1889		Pittsburg, Pa.	June 21, 1905	do.	June 23, 1904	Do.
Fred Hartweg	391	1896		1893		do.	Oct. 17, 1905	do.	July 18, 1904	Evansville, Ind.
G. W. Thomas	281	1901		1901		Jeffersonville, Ind.	Oct. 24, 1905	do.	Oct. 24, 1904	Pittsburg, Pa.
Gleaner	714	1896		{1896 1904}		Madison, Ind.	Nov. 27, 1905	do.	Dec. 12, 1904	Wheeling, W. Va.
H. P. Dilworth [a]	123	1900		1890		Ashland, Ky.	Feb. 24, 1905	do.	Feb. 23, 1904	Pittsburg, Pa.
Harmony	96	1888	1905	1888		Pittsburg, Pa.	Apr. 6, 1905	do.	Aug. 11, 1902	Do.
Harry Brown	604	1898		1898		do.	Feb. 17, 1905	do.	Feb. 10, 1904	Evansville, Ind.
Harry No. 2	48	1893		1903		do.	Feb. 28, 1905	Charleroi, Pa.	Feb. 27, 1904	Pittsburg, Pa.
Harry P. Jones [b]	146	1888	1898	1902		do.	Dec. 20, 1905	Pittsburg, Pa.	Dec. 20, 1904	Do.
Helen White	174	1903		1903		Sistersville, W. Va.	Oct. 18, 1905	do.	Oct. 19, 1904	Do.
Henry A. Laughlin	151	1905		1905		Pittsburg, Pa.	Oct. 14, 1905	do.	First inspn.	
Henry Lourey	646	1881		1894		Mound City, Ill.	Nov. 13, 1905	do.	Oct. 10, 1904	St. Louis, Mo.
I. N. Bunton No. 2 [c]	195	1884		1884		Pittsburg, Pa.	Sept. 13, 1905	do.	Sept. 6, 1904	Pittsburg, Pa.
Iron Age	385	1880		1901		do.	Nov. 10, 1905	do.	Nov. 18, 1904	Do.
J. C. Risher	148	1873	1901	1899		do.	Jan. 11, 1905	do.	Jan. 11, 1904	Do.
Jim Brown	153	1881	1898	1893		do.	Oct. 19, 1905	do.	Oct. 26, 1904	Do.
Jim Wood	525	1885	1900	1902		do.	Nov. 20, 1905	do.	Nov. 1, 1904	Do.
John Dippel	28	1873	1903	1903		do.	Jan. 5, 1905	Allegheny, Pa.	Dec. 9, 1903	Do.
John F. Klein	123	1902		1893		Brownsville, Pa.	Dec. 16, 1905	Pittsburg, Pa.	Dec. 15, 1904	Do.
Josh Cook	384	1876	1903	1903		Pittsburg, Pa.	Oct. 7, 1905	do.	Oct. 4, 1904	Do.
Kathryn [d]	67	1890	1898	1890		Elizabeth, W. Va.	Dec. 27, 1904	Allegheny, Pa.	Nov. 12, 1903	Do.
Kathryn	67	1890	1898	1890		do.	Dec. 21, 1905	Creighton, Pa.	Dec. 27, 1904	Do.
Lee H. Brooks	86	1890		1896		Evansville, Ind.	Nov. 6, 1905	Pittsburg, Pa.	Nov. 11, 1904	Do.
Little Fred	126	1881		1885		Pittsburg, Pa.	Aug. 16, 1905	do.	Aug. 18, 1904	Do.
M. Dougherty	43	1893	1903	1903		do.	Mar. 14, 1905	Redman Mills, Pa.	Mar. 14, 1904	Do.
Margaret	128	1901		1901		Allegheny, Pa.	Dec. 9, 1905	Allegheny, Pa.	Dec. 12, 1904	Do.
Mariner	371	1873	1891	1885		Cincinnati, Ohio	Mar. 20, 1905	Pittsburg, Pa.	Mar. 2, 1904	Wheeling, W. Va.
Mermaid	25	1903		1903		Guyandotte, W. Va.	Apr. 7, 1905	Bellevernon, Pa.	Feb. 10, 1904	Gallipolis, Ohio.
P. M. Pfeil	116	1901		1901		Brownsville, Pa.	Oct. 24, 1905	Pittsburg, Pa.	Oct. 24, 1904	Pittsburg, Pa.
R. L. Aubrey	99	1899		1902		Pittsburg, Pa.	Aug. 22, 1905	do.	Aug. 15, 1904	Do.
Return	109	1881	1899	1893		Bakers Landing, W. Va.	Nov. 13, 1905	do.	Nov. 12, 1904	Do.
Rival	244	1904		1892		Marietta, Ohio	Mar. 22, 1905	do.	Mar. 21, 1904	Do.
Robert Jenkins	242	1893	1905	1899	1903	Pittsburg, Pa.	Nov. 4, 1905	do.	Oct. 15, 1904	Do.
Robt. Taylor	128	1901		1893		Higginsport, Ohio	July 12, 1905	Legionville, Pa.	July 11, 1904	Do.
Rover	145	1902		1902		Elizabeth, Pa.	Dec. 23, 1905	Pittsburg, Pa.	Dec. 15, 1904	Do.
S. B. Goucher	84	1903		1903		Marietta, Ohio	Apr. 21, 1905	Allegheny, Pa.	Apr. 20, 1904	Do.
S. P. Gillett	96	1901		1901		Jeffersonville, Ind.	May 15, 1905	Coraopolis, Pa.	May 12, 1904	Do.

Sailor	140	1900		1902		Parkersburg, W. Va.	Oct. 13, 1905	Pittsburg, Pa.	Oct. 20, 1904	Do.
Samuel Clarke	435	1870	1905	1905		Pittsburg, Pa.	Dec. 5, 1905	do.	Sept. 27, 1904	Wheeling, W. Va.
Stella Moren	215	1890		1888		do.	Jan. 25, 1905	do.	Jan. 28, 1904	Pittsburg, Pa.
T. J. Wood	127	1899		1892		Middleport, Ohio	Nov. 4, 1905	do.	Nov. 10, 1904	Do.
The Leader	131	1891		1891		Pittsburg, Pa.	Oct. 16, 1905	Allegheny, Pa.	Oct. 25, 1904	Do.
Tide	124	1900		1902		Elizabeth, Pa.	Feb. 4, 1905	Pittsburg, Pa.	Feb. 5, 1904	Do.
Titan	195	1899		1891		do.	Dec. 14, 1905	do.	Dec. 19, 1904	Do.
Tom Lysle	121	1871	1896	1883		Pittsburg, Pa.	Nov. 8, 1905	do.	Nov. 16, 1904	Do.
Tom Rees No. 2	327	1869	1897	1885		do.	Feb. 13, 1905	do.	Feb. 18, 1904	Cincinnati, Ohio.
Tornado	319	1895		1895		do.	Feb. 9, 1905	do.	Feb. 29, 1904	Pittsburg, Pa.
Twilight	119	1882		1903		do.	Oct. 9, 1905	do.	Oct. 19, 1904	Do.
Two Brothers	71	1884	1895	1901		do.	Aug. 18, 1905	Point Marion, Pa.	Aug. 20, 1904	Do.
Valiant	307	1877	1904	1894		do.	Feb. 8, 1905	Sewickley, Pa.	Feb. 11, 1904	Do.
Volunteer	313	1891	1902	1891		do.	Nov. 9, 1905	Pittsburg, Pa.	Nov. 21, 1904	Do.
Voyager	213	1885	1899	1899		do.	Nov. 2, 1905	do.	Nov. 10, 1904	Do.
Vulcan	193	1899		1899		Brownsville, Pa.	July 20, 1905	do.	June 30, 1904	Do.
W. C. Jutte	113	1901		1901		do.	Mar. 7, 1905	do.	Mar. 10, 1904	Do.
W. H. Flint	221	1901		1901		do.	June 22, 1905	do.	June 11, 1904	Do.
W. W. O'Neil	778	1881	1896	1892		Pittsburg, Pa.	Oct. 12, 1905	do.	Sept. 28, 1904	Cincinnati, Ohio.
Wasp	17	1878		1895		do.	Dec. 15, 1905	do.	Oct. 18, 1904	Pittsburg, Pa.
Steam pleasure yachts.										
National [e]	[f]3	1900		1900		Pittsburg, Pa.	Nov. 6, 1905	Pittsburg, Pa.	Nov. 5, 1904	Pittsburg, Pa.
Oriole	[f]3	1904		1893		do.	Nov. 11, 1905	Esplen, Pa.	Nov. 12, 1904	Do.
Wauneta	10	1901		1905		do.	July 11, 1905	Pittsburg, Pa.	June 30, 1904	Do.
Miscellaneous steam vessels.										
Alice Bell No. 2 (pump)	[f]4	1896		1896		Pittsburg, Pa.	June 28, 1905	Fayette City, Pa.	June 29, 1904	Pittsburg, Pa.
Cascade (dredge)[c]	90	1892		1888		do.	Sept. 13, 1905	Pittsburg, Pa.	Sept. 15, 1904	Do.
Charlotte (dredge)	163	1900		1900		Brownsville, Pa.	Aug. 30, 1905	Sharpsburg, Pa.	Aug. 30, 1904	Do.
Ed Davison (dredge)	92	1888		1888		Pittsburg, Pa.	June 19, 1905	Aspinwall, Pa.	June 22, 1904	Do.
Fay S (dredge)	63	1889		1888		New Martinsville, W. Va.	Sept. 8, 1905	Colona, Pa.	Sept. 9, 1904	Do.
George Brawdy (dredge)[c]	46	1891		1891		Pittsburg, Pa.	Sept. 19, 1905	Freedom, Pa.	Sept. 23, 1904	Do.
Harriet (dredge)	159	1902		1902		Parkersburg, W. Va.	Aug. 1, 1905	Lock No. 2, Ohio River.	Aug. 1, 1904	Do.
Independent (dredge)	176	1900		1880		Brownsville, Pa.	May 3, 1905	Pittsburg, Pa.	May 2, 1904	Do.
J. K. Davison (dredge)	162	1898		1892		Pittsburg, Pa.	July 3, 1905	Sharpsburg, Pa.	July 5, 1904	Do.
National (dredge)	144	1903		1903		Parkersburg, W. Va.	June 26, 1905	Allegheny, Pa.	June 27, 1906	Do.
Pittsburgh (dredge)	148	1891		1901		Pittsburg, Pa.	Oct. 11, 1905	Pittsburg, Pa.	Oct. 10, 1904	Do.
Progress (dredge)[c]	195	1902		1902		Brownsville, Pa.	Sept. 13, 1905	Ross, Pa.	Sept. 12, 1904	Do.
Rebecca (dredge)	159	1901		1882		Parkersburg, W. Va.	Aug. 4, 1905	River View, Pa.	Aug. 3, 1904	Do.
T. J. Garlick (dredge)	179	1902		1902		Brownsville, Pa.	July 15, 1905	Allegheny, Pa.	July 16, 1904	Do.
W. R. Graham (dredge)	137	1898		1898		Pittsburg, Pa.	Apr. 20, 1905	do.	Apr. 25, 1904	Do.
Barge of over 100 tons carrying passengers for hire.										
Beauty	115	1896				Pittsburg, Pa.	Apr. 8, 1905	Pittsburg, Pa.	Aug. 29, 1903	Pittsburg, Pa.

[a] Formerly Yellow Poplar, 1902.
[b] Formerly R. M. Blackburn, 1898.
[c] Inspected by Wheeling board.
[d] Certificate issued Jan. 23, 1905.
[e] Formerly Esplen, 1904.
[f] Estimated.

DOMESTIC VESSELS INSPECTED, YEAR ENDED DECEMBER 31, 1905—SEVENTH SUPERVISING DISTRICT—Continued.

LOCAL DISTRICT OF WHEELING, W. VA.

Names of vessels and class.	Gross tonnage.	Hull built.	Hull rebuilt.	Boilers built.	Boilers rebuilt.	Where built.	Date of inspection.	Where inspected.	Date of previous inspection.	Local district where previously inspected.
Inland passenger steamers.										
Buckeye	74	1896		1896		West Wheeling, Ohio	Aug. 30, 1905	West Wheeling, Ohio	Sept. 1, 1904	Wheeling, W. Va.
Leroy	142	1896		1896		Levanna, Ohio	July 27, 1905	Marietta, Ohio	July 28, 1904	Do.
Outing	8	1903		1903		Geneva, Ohio	July 21, 1905	Zanesville, Ohio	June 24, 1904	Do.
Pioneer City	51	1891		1891		Marietta, Ohio	May 17, 1905	Marietta, Ohio	May 16, 1904	Do.
Ruth No. 2	157	1904		1904		Clarington, Ohio	May 19, 1905	Wheeling, W. Va	May 20, 1904	Do.
Ruth	131	1893		1893		Marietta, Ohio	May 31, 1905	do	June 3, 1904	Do.
Royal [b]	125	1900		1902		Point Pleasant, W. Va	Sept. 22, 1905	do	Sept. 30, 1904	Do.
Sonoma	139	1897		1897		Parkersburg, W. Va.	July 18, 1905	Marietta, Ohio	July 23, 1904	Do.
Valley Gem	156	1897		1898		Marietta, Ohio	Oct. 9, 1905	Zanesville, Ohio	Nov. 7, 1904	Do.
Ferry steamers.										
Charon	97	1889		1889		Brownsville, Pa	Nov. 22, 1905	Bellaire, Ohio	Dec. 5, 1904	Gallipolis, Ohio.
Ella B	23	1897		1899		Delhi, Ohio	Sept. 5, 1905	Toronto, Ohio	Sept. 8, 1904	Wheeling, W. Va.
Nathaniel	52	1887		1897		Steubenville, Ohio	Apr. 11, 1905	Steubenville, Ohio	Apr. 4, 1904	Do.
Orion	66	1884		1896		Bellevernon, Pa	Oct. 31, 1905	Sistersville, W. Va	Nov. 16, 1904	Do.
West End	47	1890		1890		Brownsville, Pa	Apr. 11, 1905	Brilliant, Ohio	Apr. 4, 1904	Do.
Inland towing steamers.										
Exporter	578	1895		1895		Madison, Ind	Sept. 29, 1905	Captina Island, W. Va.	Oct. 6, 1904	Pittsburg, Pa.
Egan [c]	192	1875	1904	1875	1889	Industry, Pa	Nov. 23, 1905	Wheeling, W. Va	Nov. 23, 1904	Evansville, Ind.
Ford City	93	1889		1889		Pittsburg, Pa	May 12, 1905	do	May 11, 1904	Pittsburg, Pa.
M. L. Thornton	26	1903		1891		Guyandotte, W. Va	Sept. 9, 1905	do	Sept. 19, 1904	Gallipolis, Ohio.
Monator	49	1904		1890		Point Pleasant, W. Va.	Nov. 2, 1905	West Wheeling, Ohio	Nov. 10, 1904	Do.
Nellie Bartlett	56	1896		1896		Little Hocking, Ohio	Aug. 3, 1905	Marietta, Ohio	Aug. 2, 1904	Pittsburg, Pa.
Tom Dodsworth	500	1871		1889		Pittsburg, Pa	Oct. 5, 1905	West Marietta, Ohio	Oct. 8, 1904	Wheeling, W. Va.
Varuna	[a] 4	1896		1896		do	Oct. 16, 1905	Steubenville, Ohio	Oct. 27, 1904	Do.
Miscellaneous steamers.										
Catherine (dredge)	86	1904		1887		Clarington, Ohio	Aug. 16, 1905	West Wheeling, Ohio	First inspn.	
Ray (sawmill)	67	1904		1889		Bakers Landing, Ohio	Nov. 10, 1905	Bakers Landing, Ohio	Dec. 5, 1904	Wheeling, W. Va.

EIGHTH SUPERVISING DISTRICT.

LOCAL DISTRICT OF DETROIT, MICH.

Inland passenger steamers.										
Admiral	4,651	1899		1899		Wyandotte, Mich	Apr. 13, 1905	Detroit, Mich	May 3, 1904	Detroit, Mich.
Amasa Stone	6,282	1906		1905		do	Apr. 19, 1905	do	First inspn	
Arundell	339	1878		1893		Buffalo, N. Y	May 31, 1905	do	May 18, 1904	Do.
Bransford	4,657	1902		1902		West Bay City, Mich	Apr. 5, 1905	do	May 5, 1904	Buffalo, N. Y.
C. A. Lorman	41	1893		1904		Detroit, Mich	Apr. 18, 1905	do	Apr. 15, 1904	Detroit, Mich.
City of Alpena	1,735	1893		1893		Wyandotte, Mich	Apr. 8, 1905	do	Apr. 12, 1904	Do.
City of Buffalo	2,940	1896		1895		do	Apr. 11, 1905	do	May 2, 1904	Do.
City of Cleveland	1,923	1886		1886		do	Apr. 1, 1905	do	Apr. 5, 1904	Do.
City of Detroit	1,919	1889		1889		do	Mar. 28, 1905	do	Mar. 31, 1904	Do.
City of Erie	2,498	1898		1897		do	Apr. 11, 1905	do	Apr. 14, 1904	Do.
City of Mackinack	1,749	1893		1893		do	Apr. 27, 1905	do	Apr. 23, 1904	Do.
City of the Straits	1,094	1878		1878		do	May 10, 1905	do	June 8, 1903	Do.
City of Toledo	1,003	1891		1891		Toledo, Ohio	Mar. 31, 1905	do	Apr. 14, 1904	Do.
Columbia	968	1902		1902		Wyandotte, Mich	May 15, 1905	do	June 1, 1904	Do.
Douglas	98	1888		1889		Toledo, Ohio	Apr. 5, 1905	do	Apr. 4, 1904	Do.
Darius Cole	538	1885		1885		Cleveland, Ohio	May 18, 1905	do	May 19, 1904	Do.
Eastern States	3,077	1902		1902		Wyandotte, Mich	Apr. 17, 1905	do	May 4, 1904	Do.
Frank E. Kirby	532	1890		1890		do	Apr. 3, 1905	do	Apr. 6, 1904	Do.
Florence B	28	1891		1901		Detroit, Mich	Apr. 19, 1905	do	May 7, 1904	Do.
F. R. Buell	951	1888		1888	1899	Mount Clemens, Mich	May 29, 1905	do	June 15, 1904	Do.
Greyhound	1,392	1902		1886		Wyandotte, Mich	May 18, 1905	do	May 18, 1904	Do.
Harvey H. Brown	2,673	1894		1894		do	Apr. 13, 1905	do	Apr. 28, 1904	Milwaukee, Wis.
Helen	31	1895		1892	1903	Detroit, Mich	June 7, 1905	do	June 4, 1904	Detroit, Mich.
Hoover & Mason	5,841	1905		1905		Ecorse, Mich	July 18, 1905	Ecorse, Mich	First inspn	
H. G. Dalton	1,614	1903		1903		West Superior, Wis	Aug. 14, 1905	do	Sept. 6, 1904	Duluth, Minn
Idlewild [d]	363	1879		1893		Wyandotte, Mich	May 31, 1905	Detroit, Mich	June 9, 1904	Detroit, Mich.
James R. Elliott	210	1903		1898		Port Huron, Mich	Jan. 27, 1905	do	Feb. 29, 1904	Do.
James E. Davidson	6,206	1905		1905		Ecorse, Mich	May 29, 1905	Ecorse, Mich	First inspn	
J. L. Miner	23	1880		1883		Detroit, Mich	June 29, 1905	Detroit, Mich	July 7, 1904	Do.
James Battle	198	1900		1900		Wyandotte, Mich	Oct. 20, 1905	do	Nov. 2, 1904	Do.
Lyman C. Smith	6,200	1905		1905		do	June 3, 1905	do	First inspn	
Mineral City	57	1895		1898		Mount Clemens, Mich	Apr. 28, 1905	Mount Clemens, Mich	Apr. 30, 1904	Do.
Mascotte	162	1885		1885		Wyandotte, Mich	May 8, 1905	do	May 10, 1904	Do
Owana [e]	747	1899		1898		do	Mar. 31, 1905	Detroit, Mich	May 18, 1904	Do.
Oneida	22	1872		1889		Buffalo, N. Y	May 20, 1905	do	May 21, 1904	Do.
Ogontz	65	1892		1891		Chicago, Ill	July 1, 1905	do	July 2, 1904	Toledo, Ohio.
Peter White	6,184	1905		1905		Ecorse, Mich	Sept. 11, 1905	Ecorse, Mich	First inspn	
Powell Stackhouse	6,171	1905		1905		Wyandotte, Mich	Aug. 9, 1905	Detroit, Mich	do	
State of Ohio [f]	1,221	1880		1880		do	Apr. 11, 1905	do	Apr. 16, 1904	Detroit, Mich.
State of New York [g]	807	1883		1901		do	Apr. 25, 1905	do	Apr. 7, 1904	Do.

[a] Estimated.
[b] Formerly T. N. Barnsdall.
[c] Formerly Jacob Heatherington.
[d] Formerly Grace McMillan, 1882.
[e] Formerly Pennsylvania, 1902.
[f] Formerly City of Mackinack, 1893.
[g] Formerly City of Cleveland, 1885, and City of Alpena, 1893.

DOMESTIC VESSELS INSPECTED, YEAR ENDED DECEMBER 31, 1905—EIGHTH SUPERVISING DISTRICT—DETROIT, MICH.—Continued.

Names of vessels and class.	Gross tonnage.	Hull built.	Hull rebuilt.	Boilers built.	Boilers rebuilt.	Where built.	Date of inspection.	Where inspected.	Date of previous inspection.	Local district where previously inspected.
Inland passenger steamers—Continued.										
Superior	4,544	1905		1905		Ecorse, Mich	Aug. 22, 1905	Ecorse, Mich	First inspn	Detroit, Mich.
Tashmoo	1,344	1900		1900		Wyandotte, Mich	May 18, 1905	Detroit, Mich	May 18, 1904	Do.
Western States	3,077	1902		1902		do	Apr. 18, 1905	do	Apr. 30, 1904	Do.
Wayward	42	1882		1883		Brooklyn, N. Y	June 21, 1905	do	June 14, 1904	Do.
William G. Mather	6,838	1905		1905		Ecorse, Mich	Dec. 5, 1905	Ecorse, Mich	First inspn	
Ferry steamers.										
Ariel	201	1881		1902		Detroit, Mich	Sept. 29, 1905	Detroit, Mich	Oct. 10, 1904	Detroit, Mich.
Detroit	2,089	1904		1904		Ecorse, Mich	Oct. 19, 1905	do	Dec. 15, 1904	Do.
Excelsior	229	1876	1904	1876		Detroit, Mich	Mar. 30, 1905	do	Apr. 19, 1904	Do.
Garland	248	1880		1880		do	Apr. 15, 1905	do	do	Do.
Hattie	66	1882		1882		Fair Haven, Mich	June 9, 1905	do	June 9, 1904	Do.
Michigan Central	1,522	1884		1884		Wyandotte, Mich	Sept. 13, 1905	do	Sept. 16, 1904	Do.
Pleasure	489	1894		1893		West Bay City, Mich	Apr. 20, 1905	do	Apr. 22, 1904	Do.
Promise	473	1892		1892		Detroit, Mich	do	do	Apr. 20, 1904	Do.
Sappho	223	1883		1883		do	do	do	Apr. 19, 1904	Do.
Transport	1,594	1880		1902		Wyandotte, Mich	Sept. 12, 1905	do	Sept. 16, 1904	Do.
Transfer	1,511	1888		1888		Cleveland, Ohio	Sept. 13, 1905	do	Sept. 20, 1904	Do.
Victoria	192	1872	1882	1872		Detroit, Mich	Sept. 19, 1905	do	Sept. 19, 1904	Do.
Inland freight steamers.										
Atlantis	197	1887	1900	1887		Mount Clemens, Mich	Apr. 25, 1905	Detroit, Mich	May 10, 1904	Detroit, Mich.
A. Weston	511	1882		1882		do	May 6, 1905	do	May 13, 1904	Do.
Annie Laura	244	1871	1904	1892		Marine City, Mich	June 10, 1905	River Rouge, Mich	June 9, 1904	Port Huron, Mich.
Byron Whitaker	1,586	1890		1890		Mount Clemens, Mich	Apr. 26, 1905	Detroit, Mich	May 3, 1904	Detroit, Mich.
Bay City [a]	1,252	1890		1890		Duluth, Minn	May 13, 1905	do	May 17, 1904	Chicago, Ill.
Badger State	686	1862		1862		Buffalo, N. Y	Aug. 24, 1905	do	May 14, 1904	Detroit, Mich.
C. H. Starke	317	1881		1890		Milwaukee, Wis	Apr. 6, 1905	do	Apr. 23, 1904	Do.
Clinton	124	1898		1898		Mount Clemens, Mich	Apr. 28, 1905	Mount Clemens, Mich	Apr. 9, 1904	Do.
City of Berlin	2,051	1891		1891		West Bay City, Mich	May 8, 1905	Detroit, Mich	May 28, 1904	Buffalo, N. Y.
Chauncy Hurlburt	1,009	1874		1887		St. Clair, Mich	May 20, 1905	do	May 25, 1904	Cleveland, Ohio.
Charles B. Hill	1,731	1878		1895		Cleveland, Ohio	Sept. 1, 1905	do	Oct. 20, 1904	Buffalo, N. Y.
Desmond	456	1892		1892		Port Huron, Mich	May 30, 1905	do	June 3, 1904	Toledo, Ohio.
Delaware	3,901	1905		1905		Ecorse, Mich	Nov. 13, 1905	Ecorse, Mich	First inspn	
Emerald	297	1871		1884		Marine City, Mich	Apr. 21, 1905	Detroit, Mich	May 6, 1904	Detroit, Mich.
Gettysburg	837	1887		1887		Trenton, Mich	Apr. 4, 1905	do	Apr. 18, 1904	Buffalo, N. Y.
H. S. Pickands	625	1885		1889		Grand Haven, Mich	May 15, 1905	do	May 22, 1904	Detroit, Mich.
H. Houghten	210	1889		1889		West Bay City, Mich	May 24, 1905	do	May 28, 1904	Do.
Huron City	368	1867	1905	1888		Sandusky, Ohio	Sept. 13, 1905	do	Apr. 29, 1902	Port Huron, Mich.

Ionia	1,418	1890		1890		Grand Haven, Mich	May 12, 1905	....do	May 11, 1904	Milwaukee, Wis.
John H. Pauly	197	1880		1886		Oswego, N. Y	Apr. 25, 1905	....do	Apr. 26, 1904	Detroit, Mich.
Linden	894	1895		1895		Port Huron, Mich	Apr. 18, 1905	....do	Apr. 23, 1905	Toledo, Ohio.
Lily	104	1889		1889		Mount Clemens, Mich	Apr. 24, 1905	Mount Clemens, Mich	Apr. 25, 1904	Detroit, Mich.
Miami	228	1888		1888		Miami City, Mich	Apr. 10, 1905	Detroit, Mich	Apr. 20, 1904	Port Huron, Mich.
Mariska	2,325	1890		1890		Cleveland, Ohio	May 18, 1905	....do	May 17, 1904	Chicago, Ill.
Mary	218	1892		1892		Toledo, Ohio	June 6, 1905	....do	June 9, 1904	Detroit, Mich.
Nipigon	626	1883		1890		St. Clair, Mich	Apr. 6, 1905	....do	Apr. 27, 1904	Oswego, N. Y.
Peshtigo	817	1869	1896	1893		Trenton, Mich	May 12, 1905	....do	May 13, 1904	Marquette, Mich.
R. J. Hackett	1,129	1869		1889		Cleveland, Ohio	May 3, 1905	....do	May 19, 1904	Detroit, Mich.
Saginaw	508	1866		1888		Marine City, Mich	Apr. 7, 1905	....do	Apr. 28, 1904	Do.
Samoa	1,095	1880		1889		Detroit, Mich	May 19, 1905	....do	May 19, 1904	Do.
Sonora	3,914	1902		1902		West Superior, Wis	June 8, 1905	River Rouge, Mich	June 15, 1904	Duluth, Minn.
Senator	4,048	1898		1896		Wyandotte, Mich	July 7, 1905	Detroit, Mich	July 18, 1904	Do.
Tempest	369	1876		1876		Grand Haven, Mich	Apr. 4, 1905	....do	Apr. 21, 1904	Detroit, Mich.
Thos. W. Palmer	2,134	1889		1889		Wyandotte, Mich	Apr. 25, 1905	....do	May 12, 1904	Chicago, Ill.
W. R. Stafford	744	1886		1886		West Bay City, Mich	Apr. 19, 1905	....do	May 16, 1904	Buffalo, N. Y.
W. C. Richardson	3,818	1902		1902		Cleveland, Ohio	May 8, 1905	River Rouge, Mich	May 14, 1904	Milwaukee, Wis.
Wyandotte	320	1892		1892		Wyandotte, Mich	May 25, 1905	Ecorse, Mich	May 19, 1904	Detroit, Mich.
Inland towing steamers.										
Adele	9	1889		1889		Mount Clemens, Mich	Aug. 10, 1905	Detroit, Mich	Oct. 23, 1903	Detroit, Mich.
Columbia	114	1900		1900		Ferrysburg, Mich	Apr. 22, 1905	Amherstburg, Ontario	Apr. 21, 1904	Do.
Cadillac	19	1901		1901		Detroit, Mich	Aug. 19, 1905	Detroit, Mich	Aug. 20, 1904	Do.
Dragon	28	1866	1901	1875	1902	Buffalo, N. Y	Nov. 8, 1905	....do	Nov. 8, 1904	Do.
Fannie Tuthill	27	1873		1881		East Saginaw, Mich	June 15, 1905	....do	June 14, 1904	Toledo, Ohio.
F. J. Haynes	27	1895		1892		Port Huron, Mich	June 29, 1905	....do	July 29, 1904	Port Huron, Mich.
Grayling	15	1889		1889		Bay City, Mich	June 15, 1905	....do	June 18, 1904	Detroit, Mich.
John B. Breymann	59	1885	1904	1904		Manitowoc, Wis	Oct. 4, 1905	Amherstburg, Ontario	Oct. 6, 1904	Toledo, Ohio.
Louise	15	1873		1896		Buffalo, N. Y	May 16, 1905	Detroit, Mich	May 14, 1904	Detroit, Mich.
Margretta	18	1892		1892		Ashtabula, Ohio	June 20, 1905	Amherstburg, Ontario	June 15, 1904	Do.
P. B. Luyster	17	1897		1903		Detroit, Mich	Apr. 17, 1905	Detroit, Mich	Apr. 6, 1904	Do.
Pauline Hickler	37	1892		1892		Buffalo, N. Y	Apr. 22, 1905	Amherstburg, Ontario	Apr. 21, 1904	Port Huron, Mich.
Phil Sheridan	35	1889		1903		....do	June 5, 1905	....do	May 5, 1904	Albany, N. Y.
Quickstep	10	1869		1889		....do	Nov. 27, 1905	....do	Apr. 20, 1904	Detroit, Mich.
Saugatuck	88	1875		1880		Chicago, Ill	May 29, 1905	Detroit, Mich	May 31, 1904	Toledo, Ohio.
Shaughraun	45	1883		1894		Buffalo, N. Y	June 5, 1905	Amherstburg, Ontario	June 4, 1904	Buffalo, N. Y.
Samuel J. Christian	55	1864	1904	1874		Kaighns Point, N. J	July 6, 1905	....do	July 6, 1904	Detroit, Mich.
Sidney T. Smith	70	1895		1902		Manitowoc, Wis	July 20, 1905	....do	July 11, 1904	Milwaukee, Wis.
Shaun Rhue	79	1901		1902		Buffalo, N. Y	Sept. 22, 1905	....do	Sept. 21, 1904	Detroit, Mich.
T. W. Snook	168	1873		1879		Mount Clemens, Mich	Aug. 18, 1905	Detroit, Mich	Aug. 18, 1904	Do.
Steam pleasure yachts.										
Adonis	b 6	1904		1904		Detroit, Mich	June 24, 1905	Detroit, Mich	July 1, 1904	Detroit, Mich.
Albatross	74	1893		1897		Wilmington, Del	July 6, 1905	....do	Aug. 25, 1904	Philadelphia, Pa.
Adieu	5	1897		1899		Detroit, Mich	Aug. 24, 1905	....do	June 4, 1904	Detroit, Mich.
Captain Dave	b 6	1901		1896		....do	June 24, 1905	....do	June 11, 1904	Do.
Contaluta	38	1893		1902		....do	June 30, 1905	....do	June 27, 1904	Do.

a Formerly Colgate Hoyt, 1905.

b Estimated.

DOMESTIC VESSELS INSPECTED, YEAR ENDED DECEMBER 31, 1905—EIGHTH SUPERVISING DISTRICT—DETROIT, MICH.—Continued.

Names of vessels and class.	Gross tonnage.	Hull built.	Hull rebuilt.	Boilers built.	Boilers rebuilt.	Where built.	Date of inspection.	Where inspected.	Date of previous inspection.	Local district where previously inspected.
Steam pleasure yachts—Con.										
Dawn	27	1901		1904		Bristol, R. I.	Apr. 21, 1905	Detroit, Mich	Apr. 21, 1904	Detroit, Mich.
Dream	9	1892		1899		Detroit, Mich	July 13, 1905	do	July 18, 1904	Do.
Great Lakes	[a] 7	1894		1894		do	June 26, 1905	do	June 11, 1904	Do.
Ivy	38	1901		1903		do	July 7, 1905	do	July 7, 1904	Do.
Ida M. Allen	[a] 5	1900		1887		do	Sept. 18, 1905	do	June 28, 1904	Do.
J. R. I	[a] 3	1904		1905		do	July 28, 1905	do	Aug. 17, 1904	Do.
Kalolah	42	1896		1896		Bristol, R. I.	June 22, 1905	do	June 23, 1904	Do.
Lena	[a] 6	1891		1890		Detroit, Mich	Apr. 26, 1905	do	Apr. 21, 1904	Do.
Lillie	31	1872		1891		Brooklyn, N. Y	June 30, 1905	do	July 1, 1904	Do.
May D	9	1895		1890		Wyandotte, Mich	July 22, 1905	Wyandotte, Mich	June 30, 1904	Do.
Minnie M	[a] 4	1887		1888		Detroit, Mich	Oct. 7, 1905	Detroit, Mich	Sept. 28, 1903	Do.
Nomad	28	1887	1901	1895		New York, N. Y	Apr. 21, 1905	do	June 9, 1904	Do.
Palos [b]	11	1896		1902		Bristol, R. I	Apr. 7, 1905	do	Apr. 9, 1904	Do.
Pastime	49	1881		1881		South Brooklyn, N. Y	May 18, 1905	do	May 16, 1904	Do.
Pastime (launch)	[a] 1	1891		1891		Detroit, Mich	do	do	do	Do.
Phoenix	15	1902		1904		do	Apr. 7, 1905	do	Apr. 9, 1904	Do.
Rowena	69	1905		1905		do	July 7, 1905	do	First inspn.	
Raymond F	[a] 3	1901		1901		do	Aug. 5, 1905	do	July 2, 1904	Do.
Saxon	[a] 4	1903		1903		do	Aug. 26, 1905	do	May 13, 1904	Do.
Sea Gull	[a] 2	1899	1905	1899		do	Oct. 6, 1905	do	June 30, 1902	Do.
Truant	100	1892		1899		Bristol, R. I	May 23, 1905	do	May 23, 1904	Do.
Vita	69	1888		1888		Trenton, Mich	May 1, 1905	do	Apr. 18, 1904	Do.
Vera B	[a] 6	1903		1899		Detroit, Mich	May 17, 1905	Delray, Mich	Apr. 22, 1904	Do.
Wanda	20	1891		1895	1905	do	July 6, 1905	Detroit, Mich	Aug. 7, 1903	Do.
Miscellaneous steam vessels.										
C. H. Little (sand barge)	324	1903		1888		Detroit, Mich	June 19, 1905	Detroit, Mich	June 20, 1904	Detroit, Mich.
Carrie Martin (fishing)	[a] 8	1885		1887		Vermilion, Ohio	Oct. 26, 1905	do	June 17, 1904	Do.
Fred J. Dunford (lighter)	275	1873	1904	1890		Port Huron, Mich	June 28, 1905	do	June 29, 1904	Cleveland, Ohio.
G. T. Burroughs (sand barge)	130	1881		1887		Chicago, Ill	May 2, 1905	do	Apr. 30, 1904	Do.
No. 1 (pile driver)	55	1887		1889		Detroit, Mich	May 11, 1905	do	May 5, 1904	Detroit, Mich.
No. 4 (pile driver)	58	1883	1899	1893		do	June 14, 1905	do	June 14, 1904	Do.
Reliable (wrecking)	97	1880		1893		do	July 1, 1905	do	June 2, 1904	Do.

LOCAL DISTRICT OF CHICAGO, ILL.

Inland passenger steamers.										
Albert M. Marshall	1,640	1903		1903		Wyandotte, Mich.	July 21, 1905	Chicago, Ill	July 29, 1904	Duluth, Minn.
Argo	1,069	1901		1903		Toledo, Ohio	Apr. 17, 1905	do	Apr. 19, 1904	Chicago, Ill.
Batavia	202	1904		1889		Buffalo, N. Y	July 19, 1905	do	July 20, 1904	Buffalo, N. Y.
Carter H. Harrison	30	1901		1901		Chicago, Ill	Mar. 1, 1905	do	Mar. 3, 1904	Chicago, Ill.
City of Bangor	4,202	1896	1905	1896		West Bay City, Mich.	May 20, 1905	Colehour, Ill	May 11, 1904	Buffalo, N. Y.
City of Benton Harbor	1,286	1904		1904		Toledo, Ohio	May 18, 1905	Chicago, Ill	June 14, 1904	Toledo, Ohio.
City of Chicago	1,164	1890		1890		West Bay City, Mich.	Apr. 14, 1905	do	Apr. 16, 1904	Grand Haven, Mich.
City of Marquette	341	1890		1898		Manitowoc, Wis	June 12, 1905	do	June 13, 1904	Chicago, Ill.
City of Traverse	1,153	1871	1887	1871		Cleveland, Ohio	do	do	June 11, 1904	Do.
Douglass Houghton	5,332	1899		1899		do	July 27, 1905	South Chicago, Ill	July 28, 1904	Do.
E. A. S. Clarke	4,713	1899		1899		do	Aug. 29, 1905	do	Aug. 29, 1904	Cleveland, Ohio.
Eastland	1,961	1903		1903		Port Huron, Mich	May 22, 1905	Colehour, Ill	June 24, 1904	Chicago, Ill.
Elbert H. Gary	6,331	1905		1905		South Chicago, Ill	May 20, 1905	do	First inspn.	
F. & P. M. No. 1	769	1882		1882		Detroit, Mich	Aug. 16, 1905	Chicago, Ill	Aug. 22, 1904	Do.
Frontenac [c]	626	1868	1902	1901		Cleveland, Ohio	May 23, 1905	do	June 6, 1904	Do.
G. Watson French	3,883	1903		1903		West Bay City, Mich.	Apr. 6, 1905	do	May 12, 1904	Buffalo, N. Y.
Geo. C. Howe	1,550	1903		1903		South Chicago, Ill	June 14, 1905	South Chicago, Ill	June 29, 1904	Chicago, Ill.
Georgia [d]	895	1882	1898	1891		Manitowoc, Wis	Apr. 7, 1905	Chicago, Ill	Apr. 7, 1904	Milwaukee, Wis.
Holland [e]	1,148	1881		1881		Wyandotte, Mich	Apr. 24, 1905	do	May 24, 1904	Grand Haven, Mich.
Illinois	287	1898		1898		South Chicago, Ill	Oct. 13, 1905	do	Nov. 1, 1904	Chicago, Ill.
Indiana	1,177	1890		1890		Manitowoc, Wis	Apr. 15, 1905	do	Apr. 14, 1904	Milwaukee, Wis.
Indianapolis	765	1904		1904		Toledo, Ohio	Apr. 10, 1905	Michigan City, Ind	May 20, 1904	Toledo, Ohio.
Iowa	1,157	1896		1896		Manitowoc, Wis	June 11, 1905	Chicago, Ill	June 17, 1904	Chicago, Ill.
J. B. Bradwell	62	1900		1879		do	June 17, 1905	do	June 16, 1904	Do.
James Hay	35	1879	1900	1890		Buffalo, N. Y	June 8, 1905	do	May 30, 1904	Do.
Jesse Spalding	1,043	1899	1905	1899		West Bay City, Mich.	Apr. 13, 1905	do	July 23, 1904	Duluth, Minn.
John B. Cowle	4,731	1902		1902		Port Huron, Mich	June 8, 1905	South Chicago, Ill	June 9, 1904	Buffalo, N. Y.
John W. Gates	5,946	1900		1900		Lorain, Ohio	May 10, 1905	do	May 8, 1904	Chicago, Ill.
Jim Sheriffs	634	1883		1883		Milwaukee, Wis	July 22, 1905	Michigan City, Ind	July 28, 1904	Do.
John P. Hopkins	[a] 5	1894		1899		Chicago, Ill	July 20, 1905	Chicago, Ill	July 20, 1904	Do.
John Sharples	1,614	1903		1903		Superior, Wis	Sept. 7, 1905	do	Sept. 14, 1904	Duluth, Minn.
Kearsarge	3,092	1894		1894		South Chicago, Ill	June 27, 1905	do	June 30, 1904	Chicago, Ill.
L. C. Smith	4,702	1902		1902		West Bay City, Mich.	June 16, 1905	South Chicago, Ill	June 13, 1904	Toledo, Ohio.
L. Edward Hines [f]	982	1893		1902		Marine City, Mich	May 25, 1905	Chicago, Ill	June 8, 1904	Chicago, Ill.
Lena Knobloch	87	1881	1903	1881		Buffalo, N. Y	May 3, 1905	do	May 11, 1904	Do.
M. Talcott	96	1876	1897	1884		Lockport, Ill	June 24, 1905	do	June 26, 1904	Do.
Mary	360	1882	1900	1901		Marine City, Mich	Mar. 31, 1905	Michigan City, Ind	May 7, 1904	Grand Haven, Mich.
Manitou	2,944	1893		1895		South Chicago, Ill	May 24, 1905	Irondale, Ill	May 31, 1904	Chicago, Ill.
Missouri	2,434	1904		1904		do	May 4, 1905	Chicago, Ill	May 9, 1904	Do.
N. J. Nessen [g]	375	1880	1903	1885		Lorain, Ohio	Mar. 27, 1905	do	Apr. 12, 1904	Grand Haven, Mich.
Phenix [h]	1,294	1884	1895	1890		West Bay City, Mich.	Aug. 7, 1905	do	Aug. 17, 1904	Chicago, Ill.
Puritan	1,547	1901		1901		Toledo, Ohio	Apr. 21, 1905	do	May 14, 1904	Do.
Ravenscraig	2,301	1900		1900		Port Huron, Mich	Apr. 29, 1905	South Chicago, Ill	May 5, 1904	Do.

[a] Estimated.
[b] Formerly Item, 1901.
[c] Formerly Lawrence, 1902.
[d] Formerly City of Ludington.
[e] Formerly City of Milwaukee, 1904.
[f] Formerly Santa Maria, 1903.
[g] Formerly H. Luella Worthington, 1903.
[h] Formerly Waldo A. Avery, 1895.

DOMESTIC VESSELS INSPECTED, YEAR ENDED DECEMBER 31, 1905—EIGHTH SUPERVISING DISTRICT—CHICAGO, ILL.—Continued.

Names of vessels and class.	Gross tonnage.	Hull built.	Hull rebuilt.	Boilers built.	Boilers rebuilt.	Where built.	Date of inspection.	Where inspected.	Date of previous inspection.	Local district where previously inspected.
Inland passenger steamers—Continued.										
Relief [a]	34	1878	1904	1903		Chicago, Ill.	July 3, 1905	Chicago, Ill.	July 20, 1904	Chicago, Ill.
Rose Jackson [b]	35	1881	1896	1896		Muskegon, Mich.	Mar. 4, 1905	....do	Mar. 18, 1904	Do.
Samuel F. B. Morse	4,936	1898		1902		West Bay City, Mich.	July 14, 1905	South Chicago, Ill.	July 18, 1904	Cleveland, Ohio.
Swan	94	1888		1888		Sandusky, Ohio	July 24, 1905	Chicago, Ill.	July 25, 1904	Chicago, Ill.
Welcome	93	1877	1904	1892		Chicago, Ill.	May 9, 1905	....do	Apr. 9, 1904	Do.
William E. Corey	6,363	1905		1905		South Chicago, Ill.	Aug. 3, 1905	Colehour, Ill.	First inspn.	
William S. Mack	3,720	1901		1901		Lorain, Ohio	Oct. 5, 1905	Irondale, Ill.	Oct. 10, 1904	Do.
Inland freight steamers.										
A. R. Colborn	251	1882		1892		Saugatuck, Mich.	Apr. 10, 1905	Michigan City, Ind.	Apr. 22, 1904	Chicago, Ill.
Alva	2,419	1893		1893		Cleveland, Ohio	May 29, 1905	South Chicago, Ill.	May 31, 1904	Toledo, Ohio.
Arthur Orr	2,745	1893		1892	1905	South Chicago, Ill.	Apr. 22, 1905	....do	May 16, 1904	Chicago, Ill.
Black Rock	1,997	1897	1903	1897		Port Huron, Mich.	May 2, 1905	Waukegan, Ill.	May 9, 1904	Do.
Briton	2,348	1891		1891		Cleveland, Ohio	May 12, 1905	South Chicago, Ill.	May 23, 1904	Duluth, Minn.
City of London	2,005	1891		1890		West Bay City, Mich.	Apr. 19, 1905	Chicago, Ill.	May 10, 1904	Buffalo, N. Y.
City of Paris	2,062	1891		1891		....do	May 9, 1905	....do	May 11, 1904	Chicago, Ill.
Francis Hinton	397	1889		1889		Manitowoc, Wis.	Apr. 10, 1905	Michigan City, Ind.	Apr. 22, 1904	Do.
George B. Leonard	4,037	1903		1903		South Chicago, Ill.	June 2, 1905	South Chicago, Ill.	June 11, 1904	Buffalo, N. Y.
George Stone	1,841	1893		1892		West Bay City, Mich.	June 20, 1905	....do	June 23, 1904	Milwaukee, Wis.
Imperial	68	1878	1901	1878		Manitowoc, Wis.	Sept. 18, 1905	Chicago, Ill.	Sept. 19, 1904	Chicago, Ill.
Ira H. Owen	1,753	1887		1887		Cleveland, Ohio	May 22, 1905	....do	May 20, 1904	Do.
James H. Prentice	535	1885		1901		Trenton, Mich.	Apr. 12, 1905	....do	May 4, 1904	Do.
John Lambert	1,550	1903		1903		South Chicago, Ill.	June 2, 1905	South Chicago, Ill.	June 18, 1904	Duluth, Minn.
John Plankinton	1,821	1889		1889		West Bay City, Mich.	Apr. 8, 1905	Chicago, Ill.	May 6, 1904	Milwaukee, Wis.
John Schroeder	372	1890		1890		Sheboygan, Mich.	Apr. 20, 1905	Michigan City, Ind.	May 11, 1904	Grand Haven, Mich.
Joseph C. Suit	318	1884	1903	1884		Saugatuck, Mich.	July 24, 1905	South Chicago, Ill.	July 25, 1904	Chicago, Ill.
Kalkaska	679	1884		1901		St. Clair, Mich.	Apr. 12, 1905	Chicago, Ill.	May 4, 1904	Do.
Lehigh	1,704	1880		1897		Wyandotte, Mich.	Apr. 7, 1905	....do	Apr. 21, 1904	Buffalo, N. Y.
Lewiston [c]	1,808	1886		1899		....do	May 3, 1905	....do	May 7, 1904	Do.
Livingstone	2,134	1889		1889		....do	Apr. 22, 1905	South Chicago, Ill.	May 31, 1904	Milwaukee, Wis.
Louis Pahlow	366	1882		1893		Milwaukee, Wis.	Mar. 25, 1905	Chicago, Ill.	May 11, 1904	Chicago, Ill.
Mary H. Boyce	700	1888	1901	1888		Grand Haven, Mich.	Apr. 21, 1905	Colehour, Ill.	Apr. 20, 1904	Milwaukee, Wis.
New Orleans	1,457	1885		1898		Marine City, Mich.	Apr. 25, 1905	Chicago, Ill.	May 18, 1904	Do.
Niko	814	1889		1889		Trenton, Mich.	May 19, 1905	....do	May 17, 1904	Chicago, Ill.
Normandie	567	1894	1905	1894		Green Bay, Wis.	Mar. 27, 1905	....do	Apr. 18, 1904	Milwaukee, Wis.
O. E. Parks	392	1891		1891		Saugatuck, Mich.	May 31, 1905	Michigan City, Ind.	June 23, 1904	Grand Haven, Mich.
P. J. Ralph	964	1889	1901	1889		Marine City, Mich.	Apr. 8, 1905	Chicago, Ill.	Apr. 18, 1904	Chicago, Ill.
Panther	1,634	1890	1900	1889		West Bay City, Mich.	June 13, 1905	South Chicago, Ill.	June 15, 1904	Do.
Parks Foster	1,729	1889		1889		Cleveland, Ohio	Apr. 18, 1905	Chicago, Ill.	May 24, 1904	Do.
Philetus Sawyer	449	1884		1887		Green Bay, Wis.	Apr. 13, 1905	....do	Apr. 14, 1904	Do.

Philip D. Armour	1,990	1889		1889		Detroit, Mich	Apr. 3, 1905	....do	Apr. 16, 1904	Do.
Queen City	3,979	1896		1896		Cleveland, Ohio	May 13, 1905	South Chicago, Ill	May 26, 1904	Duluth, Minn.
R. P. Fitzgerald	1,681	1887		1887		Detroit, Mich	Apr. 8, 1905	Chicago, Ill	Apr. 16, 1904	Chicago, Ill.
Robert W. E. Bunsen	5,181	1900		1900		South Chicago, Ill	June 1, 1905	South Chicago, Ill	June 3, 1904	Duluth, Minn.
Simon J. Murphy	4,869	1900		1900		Wyandotte, Mich	June 6, 1905	....do	June 11, 1904	Milwaukee, Wis.
Sinaloa	4,539	1903		1903		West Bay City, Mich	May 15, 1905	....do	May 11, 1904	Duluth, Minn.
Susquehanna	2,781	1886		1886		Buffalo, N. Y	Apr. 7, 1905	Chicago, Ill	May 7, 1904	Chicago, Ill.
T. S. Christie	517	1885	1902	1883		West Bay City, Mich	Apr. 11, 1905	....do	Apr. 15, 1904	Milwaukee, Wis.
Thomas Cranage	2,219	1893		1893		....do	May 8, 1905	....do	May 11, 1904	Chicago, Ill.
Three Brothers	583	1888	1903	1888		Milwaukee, Wis	Apr. 18, 1905	....do	Apr. 21, 1904	Do.
Trude R. Wiehe	768	1885		1885		West Bay City, Mich	Mar. 25, 1905	....do	May 26, 1904	Duluth, Minn.
W. H. Sawyer	746	1890		1890		....do	June 14, 1905	....do	June 8, 1904	Port Huron, Mich.
Wiley M. Egan	1,877	1887		1887		Cleveland, Ohio	Apr. 12, 1905	....do	Apr. 23, 1904	Chicago, Ill.
William P. Rend	2,323	1888	{ 1902 1905 }	1889		Bay City, Mich	Apr. 13, 1905	....do	Apr. 22, 1904	Milwaukee, Wis.
Zenith City	3,850	1895		1895		South Chicago, Ill	May 16, 1905	South Chicago, Ill	May 26, 1904	Duluth, Minn.
Inland towing steamers.										
A. B. Ward	30	1866	1901	1882		Chicago, Ill	Apr. 26, 1905	Chicago, Ill	Apr. 27, 1904	Chicago, Ill.
Alert	23	1874	1890	1886		....do	May 15, 1905	....do	May 16, 1904	Do.
Andrew H. Green	79	1896		1896		Benton Harbor, Mich	May 8, 1905	....do	May 11, 1904	Do.
Andy	53	1896		1889		....do	May 6, 1905	....do	May 6, 1904	Do.
Arthur D	21	1889	1904	1889		Buffalo, N. Y	Oct. 14, 1905	....do	Oct. 15, 1904	Do.
C. M. Charnley	83	1882		1892		Manitowoc, Wis	Mar. 18, 1905	....do	May 10, 1904	Do.
C. W. Elphicke	43	1889		1892		Saugatuck, Mich	June 13, 1905	South Chicago, Ill	June 11, 1904	Do.
Chicago	40	1881		1887		Milwaukee, Wis	Mar. 24, 1905	Chicago, Ill	May 10, 1904	Do.
Crawford	36	1880		1878		....do	June 6, 1905	....do	May 20, 1904	Marquette, Mich.
Frank R. Crane	16	1878	1902	1902		Chicago, Ill	May 8, 1905	....do	May 16, 1904	Chicago, Ill.
Fred Drews	28	1878	1900	1886		Saugatuck, Mich	May 29, 1905	....do	May 30, 1904	Do.
Geo. D. Nau	74	1896		1896		Green Bay, Wis	Apr. 19, 1905	....do	May 13, 1904	Do.
Harry C. Lydon	67	1898		1898		Benton Harbor, Mich	Mar. 24, 1905	....do	Mar. 25, 1904	Do.
Henry S. Sill	35	1875		1885		Buffalo, N. Y	Aug. 15, 1905	....do	Aug. 6, 1904	Do.
J. C. Ames [d]	537	1881		1896		Manitowoc, Wis	May 12, 1905	South Chicago, Ill	May 16, 1904	Do.
J. C. Evans [e]	79	1876	1898	1898		Milwaukee, Wis	Mar. 7, 1905	Chicago, Ill	Mar. 2, 1904	Do.
J. H. Hackley	45	1874	1887	1889		Buffalo, N. Y	Mar. 11, 1905	....do	Mar. 9, 1904	Do.
James A. Quinn [f]	42	1881	1898	1898		Milwaukee, Wis	Apr. 26, 1905	....do	Mar. 30, 1904	Do.
L. B. Johnson	42	1868	1889	1890		Chicago, Ill	May 11, 1905	....do	May 13, 1904	Do.
Leslie	38	1894		1893		South Haven, Mich	June 30, 1905	South Chicago, Ill	June 30, 1904	Do.
Loraine T	20	1900		1893		Pullman, Ill	May 1, 1905	Kensington, Ill	May 2, 1904	Do.
Louise B	14	1898		1892		....do	....do	....do	....do	Do.
Luther Loomis	29	1889		1894		Chicago, Ill	June 20, 1905	Chicago, Ill	June 20, 1904	Do.
M. G. Hausler	73	1893	1903	1893		Saugatuck, Mich	Mar. 30, 1905	....do	Mar. 30, 1904	Do.
Mentor [g]	22	1882		1896		....do	Oct. 4, 1905	....do	Oct. 3, 1904	Do.
Mollie Spencer	53	1860	1890	1896		Buffalo, N. Y	May 26, 1905	....do	May 6, 1904	Do.
Monarch	90	1889		1888		West Bay City, Mich	Mar. 18, 1905	....do	Apr. 8, 1904	Do.
Mosher	68	1889		1880		Chicago, Ill	Mar. 24, 1905	....do	Mar. 21, 1904	Do.
O. B. Green	56	1881	1902	1897		....do	Mar. 11, 1905	....do	Mar. 9, 1904	Do.
Perfection	70	1892		1892		West Bay City, Mich	Apr. 15, 1905	....do	May 10, 1904	Do.

[a] Formerly Michael Brand, 1893.
[b] Formerly North Muskegon, 1903.
[c] Formerly Susan E. Peck, 1894.
[d] Formerly J. C. Perrett, 1896.
[e] Formerly James McGordon, 1898
[f] Formerly W. H. Wolf, 1898.
[g] Formerly Hattie A. Fox, 1884.

DOMESTIC VESSELS INSPECTED, YEAR ENDED DECEMBER 31, 1905—EIGHTH SUPERVISING DISTRICT—CHICAGO, ILL.—Continued.

Names of vessels and class.	Gross tonnage.	Hull built.	Hull rebuilt.	Boilers built.	Boilers rebuilt.	Where built.	Date of inspection.	Where inspected.	Date of previous inspection.	Local district where previously inspected.
Inland towing steamers—Con.										
Protection	60	1873		1889		Chicago, Ill	Mar. 30, 1905	Chicago, Ill	May 12, 1904	Chicago, Ill.
Rita McDonald	69	1897		1897		West Bay City, Mich	May 9, 1905	do	do	Do.
Ruby	33	1887		1889		Saugatuck, Mich	June 5, 1905	South Chicago, Ill	June 27, 1904	Do.
S. M. Fischer	628	1896		1896		Toledo, Ohio	Apr. 6, 1905	do	Apr. 15, 1904	Do.
Success	26	1863	{ 1886 1902 }	1868		Grand Haven, Mich	June 22, 1905	Chicago, Ill	June 17, 1904	Do.
T. T. Morford	99	1896		1896		Chicago, Ill	Mar. 7, 1905	do	Mar. 7, 1904	Do.
Tacoma	76	1894		1893		Benton Harbor, Mich	Apr. 17, 1905	do	Apr. 20, 1904	Do.
Tom Brown	37	1870	1904	1888	1904	Chicago, Ill	May 25, 1905	do	May 26, 1904	Do.
Wm. Dickinson	78	1893	1904	1893		Benton Harbor, Mich	Mar. 24, 1905	do	Apr. 5, 1904	Do.
Steam pleasure yachts.										
Amanda Cook	a 3	1884		1884		Chicago, Ill	Sept. 18, 1905	Chicago, Ill	June 20, 1904	Chicago, Ill.
Blanche	a 4	1901		1889		do	June 9, 1905	Riverdale, Ill	June 10, 1904	Do.
Bud	a 4	1903		1904		South Chicago, Ill	Aug. 11, 1905	South Chicago, Ill	Aug. 4, 1904	Do.
Cora E	a 4	1888		1900		City Island, New York, N. Y.	Aug. 23, 1905	Chicago, Ill	July 23, 1902	Do.
Delaware	5	1890	1904	1890		Chicago, Ill	June 30, 1905	do	June 30, 1904	Do.
Edward J. Berwind	a 3	1905		1905		do	Feb. 11, 1905	do	First inspn	
Elin	a 3	1886		1901		do	June 9, 1905	Riverdale, Ill	June 10, 1904	Do.
Fire Fly	a 4	1899		1899		Blue Island, Ill	June 14, 1905	Blue Island, Ill	June 15, 1904	Do.
Hattie	a 4	1898		1897		Saugatuck, Mich	Sept. 26, 1905	Colehour, Ill	May 24, 1904	Grand Haven, Mich.
Jeanette	a 1	1899		1900		Chicago, Ill	July 8, 1905	Kensington, Ill	July 22, 1904	Chicago, Ill.
Kenneth	a 2	1902		1900		do	May 19, 1905	Chicago, Ill	June 11, 1904	Do.
Lena	a 4	1890		1890		Manitowoc, Wis	Aug. 23, 1905	do	Aug. 20, 1904	Do.
Marcia	22	1903		1891	1903	South Chicago, Ill	June 29, 1905	do	June 30, 1904	Do.
May Reis	a 4	1899	1905	1901		Kensington, Ill	June 7, 1905	Kensington, Ill	June 7, 1904	Do.
May Queen	26	1904		1904		Chicago, Ill	Aug. 2, 1905	Chicago, Ill	May 21, 1904	Do.
Minnie R	9	1904		1904		Manitowoc, Wis	Sept. 5, 1905	do	Sept. 5, 1904	Do.
River Queen	a 5	1903		1903		Blue Island, Ill	June 9, 1905	Blue Island, Ill	June 10, 1904	Do.
Walworth	18	1882	1895	1896		Chicago, Ill	June 19, 1905	Chicago, Ill	Nov. 5, 1903	Do.
Miscellaneous steamers.										
Atlas (sand lighter)	232	1903		1890		Milwaukee, Wis	Apr. 19, 1905	Chicago, Ill	Apr. 7, 1904	Chicago, Ill.
B. and C. (canal)	99	1876		1893		Lockport, Ill	May 23, 1905	do	May 24, 1904	Do.
Brier (canal) b	87	1882	1902	1903		Chicago, Ill	Mar. 18, 1905	do	Apr. 1, 1904	Do.
Chicago (fire) c	79	1882	1900	1900		West Bay City, Mich	Oct. 6, 1905	do	Oct. 6, 1904	Do.
D. J. Swenie (fire)	143	1886	1902	1902		Chicago, Ill	Nov. 1, 1905	do	Nov. 30, 1904	Do.
E. H. Heath (canal)	99	1876	1898	1887		Lockport, Ill	July 31, 1905	do	July 30, 1904	Do.
Elsie Nell (fishing)	41	1901		1901		Sturgeon Bay, Wis	Nov. 4, 1905	Waukegan, Ill	Nov. 4, 1904	Do.

Excelsior (canal)	92	1882	1895	1891		Lockport, Ill	Aug. 10, 1905	Chicago, Ill	Aug. 11, 1904	Do.
Fearless (canal)	101	1878		1892		do	July 25, 1905	do	Aug. 2, 1904	Do.
Fire Queen (fire)	20	1892		1892		Chicago, Ill	Apr. 4, 1905	do	Apr. 6, 1904	Do.
Harriett M (fishing)	11	1897	1905	1899		South Chicago, Ill	Sept. 20, 1905	South Chicago, Ill	May 4, 1904	Do.
Hoffnung (fishing)	21	1893	1905	1880		Sheboygan, Wis	Sept. 23, 1905	Michgian City, Ind	Sept. 23, 1904	Milwaukee, Wis.
I. & M. C. (canal)	90	1883		1887		Lockport, Ill	July 5, 1905	Chicago, Ill	June 10, 1904	Chicago, Ill.
Montauk (canal)	92	1875		1894		do	May 3, 1905	do	May 4, 1904	Do.
Nashotah (canal)	94	1877	1899	1898		Peoria, Ill	Sept. 15, 1905	do	Sept. 16, 1904	Do.
Niagara (canal)	99	1878	1898	1882		Chicago, Ill	Oct. 6, 1905	do	Sept. 26, 1904	Do.
Victor (canal)	101	1875	1905	1893		Lockport, Ill	May 16, 1905	do	May 5, 1904	Do.
Vessels propelled by gasoline motors.										
Evening Star (passenger)	31	1905				Chicago, Ill	June 10, 1905	Chicago, Ill	First inspn.	
Grace J. (freight)	24	1903				do	Aug. 22, 1905	do	Aug. 30, 1904	Chicago, Ill.
Illinois (passenger)	16	1904				Manitowoc, Wis	May 19, 1905	do	May 18, 1904	Do.

LOCAL DISTRICT OF GRAND HAVEN, MICH.

Inland passenger steamers.										
Ann Arbor No. 1	1,127	1892		1892		Toledo, Ohio	Aug. 15, 1905	Frankfort, Mich	Sept. 13, 1904	Grand Haven, Mich.
Ann Arbor No. 2	1,144	1892		1892		do	Oct. 18, 1905	do	Oct. 18, 1904	Do.
Ann Arbor No. 3	1,677	1898		1903		Cleveland, Ohio	Aug. 2, 1905	do	Aug. 6, 1904	Milwaukee, Wis.
Algomah	486	1881	1898	1898		Detroit, Mich	May 31, 1905	St. Ignace, Mich	June 5, 1904	Grand Haven, Mich.
Apollo	83	1890		1890		Minekanee, Mich	June 20, 1905	Saugatuck, Mich	June 20, 1904	Do.
Beaver	121	1892		1892		Grand Haven, Mich	Apr. 26, 1905	Charlevoix, Mich	Apr. 20, 1904	Do.
City of South Haven	1,719	1903		1903		Toledo, Ohio	June 9, 1905	South Haven, Mich	June 2, 1904	Chicago, Ill.
Charles H. Hackley	1,304	1892		1892		Philadelphia, Pa	Apr. 21, 1905	Muskegon, Mich	May 6, 1904	Grand Haven, Mich.
Chippewa	996	1900		1900		Toledo, Ohio	June 13, 1905	Mackinac Island, Mich	June 7, 1904	Do.
City of Kalamazoo	729	1893		1893		South Haven, Mich	June 10, 1905	South Haven, Mich	May 14, 1904	Chicago, Ill.
Chequamegon	141	1903		1903		Manitowoc, Wis	May 18, 1905	Ludington, Mich	May 20, 1904	Ashland, Wis.
Columbia	139	1892		1892		Grand Haven, Mich	May 11, 1905	Charlevoix, Mich	May 13, 1904	Grand Haven, Mich.
Carrie A. Ryerson	72	1883	1898	1883		do	May 22, 1905	Montague, Mich	May 26, 1904	Do.
Crescent	71	1890		1890		do	June 23, 1905	Charlevoix, Mich	Apr. 29, 1904	Do.
Cayuga	27	1872	1904	1890		Buffalo, N. Y	May 22, 1905	Montague, Mich	May 26, 1904	Do.
Duluth	247	1890		1890		Cleveland, Ohio	May 31, 1905	St. Ignace, Mich	May 27, 1904	Marquette, Mich.
Eagle	182	1873	1896	1894		Detroit, Mich	May 22, 1905	Montague, Mich	June 11, 1903	Grand Haven, Mich.
Elva	85	1889	1904	1889		Chicago, Ill	Apr. 18, 1905	Cheboygan, Mich	May 4, 1904	Do.
Frank Woods	384	1888		1901		Saugatuck, Mich	May 19, 1905	Holland, Mich	May 6, 1904	Do.
F. W. Fletcher	495	1891		1891		Marine City, Mich	Apr. 13, 1905	Manistee, Mich	Apr. 12, 1904	Do.
Fannie M. Rose	33	1893		1898		Grand Haven, Mich	May 24, 1905	Grand Haven, Mich	May 23, 1904	Do.
Grand	219	1905		1905		Grand Rapids, Mich	Oct. 16, 1905	Grand Rapids, Mich	First inspn.	
Glenn	277	1889	1903	1898		South Haven, Mich	July 25, 1905	South Haven, Mich	July 25, 1904	Do.
Glayds	a5	1897		1897		Saugatuck, Mich	May 19, 1905	Holland, Mich	June 10, 1904	Do.
H. W. Williams	691	1897		1897		South Haven, Mich	July 24, 1905	South Haven, Mich	June 2, 1904	Do.

a Estimated. b Formerly Floe, 1903. c Formerly W. H. Alley.

DOMESTIC VESSELS INSPECTED, YEAR ENDED DECEMBER 31, 1905—EIGHTH SUPERVISING DISTRICT—GRAND HAVEN, MICH.—Continued.

Names of vessels and class.	Gross tonnage.	Hull built.	Hull rebuilt.	Boilers built.	Boilers rebuilt.	Where built.	Date of inspection.	Where inspected.	Date of previous inspection.	Local district where previously inspected.
Inland passenger steamers—Continued.										
Hazel	93	1896		1879		Harbor Springs, Mich.	June 29, 1905	Grand Haven, Mich.	June 12, 1904	Grand Haven, Mich.
Hum	32	1876	1904	1891		Brooklyn, N. Y.	July 12, 1905	Charlevoix, Mich.	July 9, 1904	Do.
Harvey Watson	37	1893		1898		Saugatuck, Mich.	May 5, 1905	Holland, Mich.	Apr. 18, 1904	Do.
Illinois	2,427	1899		1899		South Chicago, Ill.	Apr. 6, 1905	Manistee, Mich.	Apr. 11 1904	Chicago, Ill.
Islander	291	1895		1895		Benton Harbor, Mich.	May 9, 1905	Cheboygan, Mich.	May 14, 1904	Grand Haven, Mich.
John D. Dewar	52	1885		1885		Ludington, Mich.	May 2, 1905	Frankfort, Mich.	May 3, 1904	Do.
John A. Aliber	32	1897		1884		Saugatuck, Mich.	Apr. 10, 1905	Saugatuck, Mich.	Apr. 18, 1904	Do.
J. W. Parmelee	30	1883		1883		do	June 1, 1905	Charlevoix, Mich.	June 3, 1904	Do.
Joseph Gordon	22	1881		1891		Bay City, Mich.	July 20, 1905	do	July 19, 1904	Do.
J. S. Crouse	82	1898		1898		Saugatuck, Mich.	Aug. 9, 1905	Holland, Mich.	Aug. 9, 1904	Do.
Kansas	835	1870	1904	1892		Cleveland, Ohio	June 25, 1905	Manistee, Mich.	May 9, 1904	Chicago, Ill.
Lou A. Cummings	62	1883	1903	1883		Grand Haven, Mich.	July 20, 1905	Charlevoix, Mich.	July 21, 1904	Grand Haven, Mich.
Lizzie Walsh	41	1882	1901	1882		do	July 7, 1905	Pentwater, Mich.	July 8, 1904	Do.
Manistique, Marquette and Northern 1.	2,933	1903		1903		Cleveland, Ohio	Apr. 3, 1905	Ludington, Mich.	Apr. 9, 1904	Chicago, Ill.
Mark B. Covell	261	1888		1888		Manitowoc, Wis.	Mar. 30, 1905	Manistee, Mich.	Apr. 11, 1904	Grand Haven, Mich.
May Graham	91	1879	1903	1878		St. Joseph, Mich.	June 6, 1905	St. Joseph, Mich.	May 31, 1904	Do.
Mary	50	1876		1893		Milwaukee, Wis.	July 15, 1905	Ferrysburg, Mich.	July 18, 1904	Do.
Nyack	1,188	1878	1895	1878		Buffalo, N. Y.	Mar. 27, 1905	Grand Haven, Mich.	Apr. 13, 1904	Do.
Naomi	1,181	1881		1899		Wyandotte, Mich.	Jan. 5, 1905	do	Jan. 9, 1904	Do.
Naomi	1,181	1881		1899		do	Nov. 20, 1905	do	Jan. 5, 1905	Do.
Pere Marquette 18	2,909	1902		1902		Cleveland, Ohio	Oct. 12, 1905	Ludington, Mich.	Oct. 19, 1904	Do.
Pere Marquette 17	2,775	1901		1901		do	June 16, 1905	do	July 8, 1904	Do.
Pere Marquette 20	2,626	1903		1903		do	Oct. 19, 1905	do	Nov. 12, 1904	Do.
Pere Marquette	2,443	1896		1896		West Bay City, Mich.	Aug. 4, 1905	do	Aug. 22, 1904	Do.
Pere Marquette 19	2,626	1903		1903		Cleveland, Ohio	Oct. 19, 1905	do	Nov. 12, 1904	Do.
Pentland	827	1894		1894		Grand Haven, Mich.	Apr. 10, 1905	Grand Haven, Mich.	May 16, 1904	Do.
Pere Marquette 2	771	1882		1882		Detroit, Mich.	Mar. 2, 1905	Manistee, Mich.	Mar. 8, 1904	Do.
Petoskey	770	1888		1888		Manitowoc, Wis.	July 25, 1905	South Haven, Mich.	July 25, 1904	Do.
Petrel	a 3	1894		1903		Chicago, Ill.	Aug. 25, 1905	Montague, Mich.	Aug. 13, 1904	Do.
Post Boy	94	1888		1888		West Bay City, Mich.	July 10, 1905	Macatawa Park, Mich.	July 14, 1904	Do.
Rapids	219	1905		1905		Grand Rapids, Mich.	Nov. 9, 1905	Grand Rapids, Mich.	First inspn.	
Soo City	670	1888	1900	1888		West Bay City, Mich.	Apr. 24, 1905	Ferrysburg, Mich.	Apr. 21, 1904	Chicago, Ill.
Saugatuck	228	1887	1901	1887		Saugatuck, Mich.	June 8, 1905	Saugatuck, Mich.	June 9, 1904	Grand Haven, Mich.
Silver Spray	90	1894		1892		Ludington, Mich.	June 1, 1905	Charlevoix, Mich.	June 17, 1904	Do.
Tourist	66	1899		1897		St. Joseph, Mich.	June 29, 1905	St. Joseph, Mich.	June 21, 1904	Do.
Wau Kon	137	1883		1897		Saugatuck, Mich.	May 30, 1905	St. Ignace, Mich.	June 5, 1904	Do.
Willow	18	1903		1903		St. Joseph, Mich.	June 21, 1905	St. Joseph, Mich.	June 21, 1904	Do.
Walter Crysler	26	1882	1892	1882		Buffalo, N. Y.	June 2, 1905	Charlevoix, Mich.	June 3, 1904	Do.
Winnebago	1,091	1903		1903		St. Clair, Mich.	May 26, 1905	Elk Rapids, Mich.	June 17, 1904	Buffalo, N. Y.
Wanena	a 6	1895		1895		Lime Island, Mich.	May 17, 1905	St. Ignace, Mich.	May 20, 1904	Grand Haven, Mich.

Ferry steamers.										
Arthur S	22	1892		1892		Manistee, Mich	July 17, 1905	Holland, Mich	June 10, 1904	Grand Haven, Mich.
Florance	26	1869		1879		Baltimore, Md	June 12, 1905	Lake Harbor, Mich	June 16, 1904	Do.
Ralph M. Cooper	27	1893		1879		Manitowoc, Wis	Aug. 4, 1905	Ludington, Mich	Aug. 4, 1904	Do.
Sainte Marie	1,357	1893		1893		Detroit, Mich	May 10, 1905	St. Ignace, Mich	May 14, 1904	Do.
St. Ignace	1,199	1888		1887		do	Mar. 24, 1905	do	Apr. 2, 1904	Do.
Sport	12	1885	1899	1885		Grand Haven, Mich	June 12, 1905	Lake Harbor, Mich	June 16, 1904	Do.
Summer Girl	a 4	1904		1893		Saugatuck, Mich	June 19, 1905	Saugatuck, Mich	June 20, 1904	Do.
Inland freight steamers.										
Arcadia	230	1888	1904	1888		Milwaukee, Wis	May 3, 1905	Arcadia, Mich	May 12, 1904	Grand Haven, Mich.
Albert Soper	349	1881		1881		Grand Haven, Mich	Mar. 30, 1905	Manistee, Mich	May 10, 1904	Chicago, Ill.
Chas. Reitz	245	1872	1895	1893		Trenton, Mich	Mar. 29, 1905	do	Apr. 11, 1904	Grand Haven, Mich.
Edward Buckley	414	1891		1891		Manitowoc, Wis	Aug. 31, 1905	do	Sept. 1, 1904	Do.
Falcon	865	1881	1901	1897		Marine City, Mich	June 15, 1905	Boyne City, Mich	June 17, 1904	Cleveland, Ohio.
Geo. C. Markham	309	1883	1903	1883		Milwaukee, Wis	Apr. 21, 1905	Muskegon, Mich	Apr. 30, 1904	Grand Haven, Mich.
Helen C.	622	1874	1901	1901		Chatham, Ontario	Apr. 4, 1905	Manistee, Mich	Apr. 11, 1904	Do.
Helen Taylor	43	1894		1867		Grand Haven, Mich	Apr. 11, 1905	Pentwater, Mich	May 9, 1904	Do.
John Otis	301	1864	1895	1883		Chicago, Ill	Apr. 8, 1905	Muskegon, Mich	Apr. 12, 1904	Do.
Liberty	143	1889		1894		Fort Howard, Wis	Aug. 25, 1905	Montague, Mich	Apr. 29, 1904	Do.
Marshall F. Butters	376	1882	1901	1895		Milwaukee, Wis	Apr. 11, 1905	Buttersville, Mich	Apr. 11, 1904	Milwaukee, Wis.
Maggie Marshall	365	1873	1892	1888		Manistee, Mich	July 21, 1905	Manistee, Mich	July 22, 1904	Do.
Mathew Wilson	322	1872	1904	1882		Cleveland, Ohio	Apr. 9, 1905	Muskegon, Mich	Apr. 12, 1904	Do.
Pine Lake	388	1895		1888		Charlevoix, Mich	Apr. 19, 1905	Charlevoix, Mich	Apr. 18, 1904	Do.
Robert C. Wente	335	1888		1888		Gibraltar, Mich	Mar. 29, 1905	Manistee, Mich	Apr. 11, 1904	Do.
Sidney O. Neff	435	1890		1901		Manitowoc, Wis	Apr. 8, 1905	Ferrysburg, Mich	May 16, 1904	Do.
Wotan	886	1898		1898		Marine City, Mich	Mar. 29, 1905	Manistee, Mich	Apr. 6, 1904	Buffalo, N. Y.
Inland towing steamers.										
Allendale	50	1898		1898		Grand Rapids, Mich	Apr. 15, 1905	Ferrysburg, Mich	Apr. 13, 1904	Grand Haven, Mich.
Alice	40	1891		1891		Grand Haven, Mich	Aug. 3, 1905	Harbor Springs, Mich	Aug. 27, 1904	Do.
Anglar	18	1880	1900	1880		Detroit, Mich	Apr. 27, 1905	St. Ignace, Mich	Apr. 22, 1904	Do.
Bonita	58	1903		1903		Ferrysburg, Mich	May 20, 1905	Benton Harbor, Mich	May 31, 1904	Do.
Bob Stephenson	18	1872	1904	1892		Buffalo, N. Y	July 11, 1905	Cheboygan, Mich	July 11, 1904	Do.
Beatrice	a 5	1886		1889		Muskegon, Mich	Aug. 1, 1905	North Muskegon, Mich.	Aug. 2, 1904	Do.
Charles C. Ryan	28	1881	1905	1892		Lockport, N. Y	Sept. 14, 1905	Charlevoix, Mich	July 20, 1904	Do.
C. B. Strohm	25	1889		1889		West Bay City, Mich	Apr. 18, 1905	Cheboygan, Mich	Apr. 2, 1904	Do.
Clayt	10	1887		1887		Indian River, Mich	July 11, 1905	do	July 8, 1904	Marquette, Mich.
Cygnet	12	1878		1897		Buffalo, N. Y	July 12, 1905	do	July 11, 1904	Grand Haven, Mich.
E. D. Holton	24	1874	1903	1899		Milwaukee, Wis	May 2, 1905	Frankfort, Mich	May 2, 1904	Do.
Favorite	409	1864	1896	1880		Fort Howard, Mich	May 30, 1905	Cheboygan, Mich	July 17, 1904	Do.
Frank Perry	496	1905		1905		Ferrysburg, Mich	Sept. 12, 1905	Ferrysburg, Mich	First inspn.	
George Stickney	12	1880		1901		Grand Haven, Mich	July 31, 1905	Grand Haven, Mich	Aug. 3, 1904	Do.
Gunderson Bros. b	46	1892		1893		Sheboygan, Wis	Dec. 1, 1904	do	Nov. 30, 1903	Do.
Hunter Savidge	20	1866	1904	1901		Ferrysburg, Mich	Apr. 22, 1905	Manistee, Mich	May 27, 1904	Do.
Ida M. Stevens	22	1869	1899	1884		Buffalo, N. Y	Sept. 7, 1905	Ludington, Mich	Sept. 9, 1904	Do.

a Estimated.

b Certificated Mar. 2, 1905.

DOMESTIC VESSELS INSPECTED, YEAR ENDED DECEMBER 31, 1905—EIGHTH SUPERVISING DISTRICT—GRAND HAVEN, MICH.—Continued.

Names of vessels and class.	Gross tonnage.	Hull built.	Hull rebuilt.	Boilers built.	Boilers rebuilt.	Where built.	Date of inspection.	Where inspected.	Date of previous inspection.	Local district where previously inspected.
Inland towing steamers—Con.										
J. V. Taylor	40	1881		1881		Buffalo, N. Y	May 17, 1905	Charlevoix, Mich	May 19, 1904	Grand Haven, Mich.
James H. Martin	36	1869	1901	1873		Cleveland, Ohio	July 12, 1905	do	June 3, 1904	Do.
John C. Mann	33	1898		1888		Ashland, Wis	Apr. 12, 1905	Manistee, Mich	Apr. 12, 1904	Do.
Lillie A	11	1891		1891		Bay City, Mich	July 11, 1905	Mackinaw City, Mich	July 11, 1904	Do.
Maggie	30	1891		1871		Leland, Mich	June 30, 1905	Traverse, City, Mich	June 3, 1904	Do.
Maurice W	a 5	1871		1877		Menominee, Mich	June 23, 1905	Cheboygan, Mich	May 10, 1904	Do.
N. McGraft	11	1888		1904		Grand Haven, Mich	June 1, 1905	Petoskey, Mich	June 3, 1904	Do.
Onekama	33	1883		1883		Onekama, Mich	Aug. 2, 1905	Frankfort, Mich	Aug. 5, 1904	Do.
Pup	13	1894		1894		Saugatuck, Mich	Aug. 8, 1905	Saugatuck, Mich	Aug. 11, 1904	Do.
River Queen	82	1866	1900	1889		Marine City, Mich	May 9, 1905	Cheboygan, Mich	May 9, 1904	Marquette, Mich.
R. H. Weidmann	34	1882	1903	1894		Buffalo, N. Y	Sept. 8, 1905	do	Sept. 8, 1904	Grand Haven, Mich.
R. P. Easton	19	1896		1886		Saugatuck, Mich	May 1, 1905	Muskegon, Mich	Apr. 30, 1904	Do.
Ruby	17	1889	1904	1895		Manistee, Mich	Apr. 28, 1905	Manistee, Mich	Apr. 11, 1904	Do.
Sport	45	1873		1899		Wyandotte, Mich	May 12, 1905	Ludington, Mich	May 17, 1904	Do.
Trio	16	1883	1896	1883		Buffalo, N. Y	Apr. 15, 1905	Saugatuck, Mich	Apr. 9, 1904	Milwaukee, Wis.
Steam pleasure yachts.										
Arrow	14	1901		1897		Frankfort, Mich	June 26, 1905	Frankfort, Mich	June 24, 1904	Grand Haven, Mich.
Annie Lowe	a 4	1893		1892		Grand Rapids, Mich	June 8, 1905	Ottawa Beach, Mich	June 10, 1904	Do.
Alfra	a 3	1902		1887		Cheboygan, Mich	May 25, 1905	Cheboygan, Mich	Apr. 22, 1904	Do.
Blanch M	a 3	1902		1904		Grand Rapids, Mich	July 18, 1905	Grand Rapids, Mich	July 11, 1904	Do.
Ella	25	1898		1898		do	Aug. 8, 1905	Holland, Mich	June 10, 1904	Do.
Echo	a 3	1883	1904	1899		New York, N. Y	Aug. 16, 1905	Les Cheneaux Islands, Mich.	Aug. 9, 1904	Do.
Ellen Hall	a 4	1896		1896		Grand Rapids, Mich	Nov. 27, 1905	Spring Lake, Mich	June 23, 1904	Do.
Laura Alice	a 2	1892		1896		Sucker Creek, Mich	Aug. 9, 1905	Muskegon, Mich	Aug. 9, 1904	Do.
Lottie	a 2	1891		1889		Grand Rapids, Mich	July 15, 1905	Grand Haven, Mich	June 23, 1904	Do.
Me Too	a 6	1897		1897		Benton Harbor, Mich	May 16, 1905	Manistee, Mich	May 11, 1904	Do.
Mamie S	a 3	1890	1904	1904		Detroit, Mich	May 5, 1905	Holland, Mich	Aug. 13, 1901	Do.
Marguerite B	a 2	1895		1900		Grand Rapids, Mich	Aug. 10, 1905	Grand Rapids, Mich	June 11, 1904	Do.
Nipsic	a 7	1893		1898		Eagle Harbor, Mich	Aug. 22, 1905	St. Ignace, Mich	Aug. 18, 1905	Do.
Papoose	a 3	1892		1891		Waukegan, Ill	June 21, 1905	South Haven, Mich	June 21, 1904	Do.
Queen Anne	14	1895		1902		Detroit, Mich	June 13, 1905	Cheboygan, Mich	June 6, 1904	Do.
Ramona	a 4	1893		1893		do	Aug. 16, 1905	Les Cheneaux Islands, Mich.	Aug. 19, 1904	Do.
Sea Fox	74	1895	1905	1895		do	June 5, 1905	Ferrysburg, Mich	May 7, 1904	Detroit, Mich.
Sea Bird	21	1900		1900		Ferrysburg, Mich	Oct. 1, 1904	Spring Lake, Mich	Sept. 2, 1903	Grand Haven, Mich.
Sea Bird	21	1900		1900		do	Sept. 30, 1905	do	Oct. 1, 1904	Do.
Sport	a 3	1889		1889		Grand Haven, Mich	July 14, 1905	Point Stuart, Mich	June 23, 1904	Do.
Wanena	a 5	1899		1899		Detroit, Mich	Aug. 7, 1905	Glen Ella, Mich	July 30, 1904	Do.

Miscellaneous steamers.										
Anna (fishing)	25	1892		1904		Grand Haven, Mich	Oct. 9, 1905	Grand Haven, Mich	Oct. 15, 1904	Grand Haven, Mich.
Anspach (fishing)	15	1879	1903	1882		Detroit, Mich	June 26, 1905	Frankfort, Mich	June 24, 1904	Do.
Badger (fishing)	a 4	1899		1903		Milwaukee, Wis	July 19, 1905	St. James, Mich	July 20, 1904	Do.
C. J. Bos (fishing) b	34	1898		1894		Ferrysburg, Mich	Dec. 1, 1904	Grand Haven, Mich	Nov. 13, 1903	Do.
C. J. Bos (fishing)	34	1898		1894		do	Nov. 24, 1905	do	Dec. 1, 1904	Do.
Chas. M. Auger (fishing)	25	1889		1893		Grand Haven, Mich	Mar. 8, 1905	do	Mar. 4, 1904	Do.
C. A. Meister (fishing)	23	1887	1902	1891		do	Mar. 27, 1905	do	Nov. 13, 1904	Do.
Clara A. Elliott (fishing)	21	1882	1901	1884		Saugatuck, Mich	Sept. 13, 1905	St. James, Mich	Sept. 7, 1904	Do.
Cecil W. (fishing)	a 7	1904		1896		Northport, Mich	Dec. 1, 1905	Northport, Mich	Dec. 15, 1904	Do.
Edward K. (fishing)	42	1899		1899		Vermilion, Ohio	Feb. 20, 1905	St. Joseph, Mich	Mar. 3, 1904	Do.
Ella (fishing)	a 3	1896		1896		Amsterdam, Wis	July 19, 1905	St. James, Mich	June 4, 1904	Do.
Frank Edward (fishing)	39	1890		1890		Grand Haven, Mich	Sept. 5, 1905	St. Joseph, Mich	Sept. 12, 1904	Do.
Frank P. Geiken (fishing)	35	1891		1891		do	July 20, 1905	Charlevoix, Mich	July 19, 1904	Do.
Geo. D. Sanford, jr. (fishing)	51	1882		1883		do	May 12, 1905	Ludington, Mich	May 9, 1904	Do.
G. R. Green (fishing)	18	1887		1882		Milwaukee, Wis	May 11, 1905	Charlevoix, Mich	May 13, 1904	Do.
H. J. Dornbos (fishing)	44	1901		1901		Ferrysburg, Mich	July 14, 1905	Grand Haven, Mich	July 14, 1904	Do.
H. M. Van Ells (fishing)	28	1885	1901	1885		Sheboygan, Wis	Sept. 26, 1905	Charlevoix, Mich	Sept. 24, 1904	Milwaukee, Wis.
J. W. Callister (fishing)	35	1890		1902		Grand Haven, Mich	July 29, 1905	Grand Haven, Mich	Aug. 3, 1904	Grand Haven, Mich.
Job (scow)	a 5	1895		1895		Ludington, Mich	Oct. 11, 1905	Ludington, Mich	Aug. 22, 1904	Do.
Lloyd M. (fishing)	31	1882	1900	1904		Buffalo, N. Y	Feb. 20, 1905	St. Joseph, Mich	Mar. 3, 1904	Do.
L. W. Knapp (fishing)	17	1895		1905		Richmond, Ohio	July 20, 1905	Charlevoix, Mich	Sept. 7, 1904	Do.
Little Maeta (fishing)	12	1903		1890		Charlevoix, Mich	Nov. 30, 1905	do	Dec. 2, 1904	Do.
Margret McCann (fishing)	35	1894		1894		Grand Haven, Mich	Apr. 26, 1905	St. James, Mich	Apr. 29, 1904	Do.
Maggie Lutz (fishing)	15	1873		1880		Sheboygan, Wis	May 2, 1905	Frankfort, Mich	May 2, 1904	Do.
Minnie Warren (fishing)	13	1879	1904	1879		Buffalo, N. Y	July 20, 1905	Charlevoix, Mich	July 19, 1904	Do.
Pottawattomie (fishing)	18	1891		1879		Green Bay, Wis	June 20, 1905	Frankfort, Mich	June 24, 1904	Do.
Pioneer (fishing)	13	1904		1888		Cheboygan, Mich	May 30, 1905	Cheboygan, Mich	May 20, 1904	Do.
Sir Arthur (fishing)	28	1892	1903	1901		Benton Harbor, Mich	Feb. 20, 1905	St. Joseph, Mich	Mar. 3, 1904	Do.
Sea Gull (fishing)	a 5	1896	1905	1892		St. Joseph, Mich	Oct. 13, 1905	Charlevoix, Mich	Oct. 4, 1904	Do.
Sea Gull (fishing)	22	1905		1889		Ludington, Mich	Dec. 19, 1905	Ludington, Mich	First inspn	
Tessler (fishing)	57	1905		1905		Ferrysburg, Mich	May 5, 1905	Ferrysburg, Mich	do	
Thomas Kane (fishing)	a 4	1887		1889		Racine, Wis	Sept. 8, 1905	Cheboygan, Mich	Sept. 8, 1904	Do.
Violet (fishing)	18	1890		1884		Benton Harbor, Mich	Apr. 19, 1905	Charlevoix, Mich	Apr. 20, 1904	Do.
Victor (fishing)	13	1897		1884		Toledo, Ohio	Aug. 22, 1905	St. Ignace, Mich	Aug. 18, 1904	Do.

LOCAL DISTRICT OF MARQUETTE, MICH.

Inland passenger steamers.										
Gifford	63	1901		1901		Manitowoc, Wis	May 19, 1905	Manistique, Mich	May 19, 1904	Marquette, Mich.
Gertrude	12	1891		1891		do	June 12, 1905	Hancock, Mich	June 7, 1904	Do.
George Rogers	64	1889		1889		Toledo, Ohio	July 19, 1905	do	Aug. 3, 1904	Do.
International	144	1889		1889		Buffalo, N. Y	Aug. 4, 1905	Sault Ste. Marie, Mich	Aug. 13, 1904	Do.
Lotus	219	1893		1893		Manitowoc, Wis	Aug. 8, 1905	Escanaba, Mich	Aug. 9, 1904	Do.
Plow Boy	114	1887		1871		West Bay City, Mich	June 9, 1905	Houghton, Mich	June 11, 1904	Duluth, Minn.
Search Light	95	1884		1888		South Haven, Mich	May 21, 1905	Escanaba, Mich	May 21, 1904	Grand Haven, Mich.

a Estimated.

b Certificated Jan. 14, 1905.

Domestic Vessels Inspected, Year ended December 31, 1905—Eighth Supervising District—Marquette, Mich.—Continued.

Names of vessels and class.	Gross tonnage.	Hull built.	Hull rebuilt.	Boilers built.	Boilers rebuilt.	Where built.	Date of inspection.	Where inspected.	Date of previous inspection.	Local district where previously inspected.
***Inland passenger steamers*—Continued.**										
Sunbeam	53	1891		1891		Chicago, Ill	Aug. 7, 1905	Nahma, Mich	Aug. 10, 1904	Marquette, Mich.
S. C. Schenck	126	1890		1903		Buffalo, N. Y	Sept. 6, 1905	Sault Ste. Marie, Mich.	Sept. 16, 1904	Do.
Thomas Friant	81	1884		1884		Grand Haven, Mich	July 1, 1905	...do	June 18, 1904	Do.
Valerie	58	1872	1892	1892		Sandusky, Ohio	June 7, 1905	Houghton, Mich	June 7, 1904	Do.
Ferry steamers.										
Annie R. Hennes	47	1884		1897		Buffalo, N. Y	July 20, 1905	Houghton, Mich	July 30, 1904	Marquette, Mich.
E. T. Carrington	52	1876		1882		Bangor, Mich	Sept. 13, 1905	Hancock, Mich	Sept. 15, 1904	Duluth, Minn.
Fortune	199	1875		1890		Detroit, Mich	July 11, 1905	Sault Ste. Mar e, Mich.	July 9, 1904	Marquette, Mich.
Inland freight steamers.										
Argonaut	1,118	1873	1902	1887		Detroit, Mich	May 20, 1905	Escanaba, Mich	May 21, 1904	Marquette, Mich.
Frontenac	2,003	1889		1889	1898	Cleveland, Ohio	June 13, 1905	Marquette, Mich	June 13, 1904	Cleveland, Ohio.
John J. McWilliams	3,400	1895		1894		West Bay City, Mich.	June 8, 1905	Dollar Bay, Mich	June 8, 1904	Milwaukee, Wis.
Kaliyuga	1,941	1887		1897		St. Clair, Mich	June 14, 1905	Marquette, Mich	June 14, 1904	Cleveland, Ohio.
Sultana	3,914	1902		1902		West Superior, Wis	May 5, 1905	...do	May 11, 1904	Duluth, Minn.
Superior	251	1890		1890		Cleveland, Ohio	May 16, 1905	Sault Ste. Marie, Mich.	May 16, 1904	Marquette, Mich.
Inland towing steamers.										
Allenton	24	1878	1894	1894		Buffalo, N. Y	May 3, 1905	Pequaming, Mich	May 4, 1904	Marquette, Mich.
Alice M	a 6	1904		1888		Sault Ste. Marie, Mich.	May 11, 1905	Sault Ste. Marie, Mich.	May 11, 1904	Do.
Alphard	32	1898		1899		Manitowoc, Wis	Sept. 7, 1905	...do	Sept. 14, 1904	Do.
Adventurer	16	1895		1895		Two Harbors, Minn	Sept. 15, 1905	Ontonagon, Mich	Sept. 21, 1904	Do.
C. L. Boynton	103	1894		1894		Port Huron, Mich	May 13, 1905	Sault Ste. Marie, Mich.	May 16, 1904	Do.
Charlie O. Smith	63	1863		1884		Cleveland, Ohio	...do	...do	May 13, 1904	Do.
Cora A. Shelden	54	1883		1905		Saugatuck, Mich	May 31, 1905	Houghton, Mich	June 8, 1903	Do.
Col. Ferry	17	1882		1890		Lake Harbor, Mich	June 16, 1905	Sault Ste. Marie, Mich.	May 12, 1904	Do.
Clara Hickler	15	1882	1898	1882		Buffalo, N. Y	Aug. 2, 1905	Little Rapids, Mich	Aug. 12, 1904	Do.
C. D. Thompson	91	1893		1893		Port Huron, Mich	Sept. 8, 1905	Sault Ste. Marie, Mich.	Sept. 13, 1904	Do.
Daniel L. Hebard	159	1875	1896	1897		Cleveland, Ohio	May 2, 1905	Pequaming, Mich	May 4, 1904	Do.
Duncan Robertson	37	1884		1897		Grand Haven, Mich	May 26, 1905	Marquette, Mich	June 5, 1904	Do.
Effie L.	41	1875	1900	1875		Cleveland, Ohio	Apr. 18, 1905	Sault Ste. Marie, Mich.	Apr. 19, 1904	Milwaukee, Wis.
Edward Gillen	57	1891		1891		Buffalo, N. Y	May 15, 1905	...do	May 18, 1904	Duluth, Minn.
Ethel J. Pryor	18	1890		1892		Houghton, Mich	June 7, 1905	Houghton, Mich	June 6, 1904	Marquette, Mich.
Fred A. Lee	60	1896		1896		Port Huron, Mich	June 15, 1905	Sault Ste. Marie, Mich.	June 14, 1904	Do.
George Cooper	53	1891		1891		Manitowoc, Wis	Apr. 17, 1905	...do	Apr. 19, 1904	Milwaukee, Wis.
G. A. Tomlinson	78	1896		1895		West Bay City, Mich.	May 21, 1905	Escanaba, Mich	May 20, 1904	Marquette, Mich.
Gazelle	36	1878	1904	1886		Buffalo, N. Y	June 17, 1905	Detour, Mich	June 15, 1904	Do.

Hattie Jordan	a 4	1872	1904	1895		....do	May 8, 1905	Escanaba, Mich	May 6, 1904	Do.
H. F. Bues	25	1873		1880		Milwaukee, Wis	May 11, 1905	Sault Ste. Marie, Mich.	May 10, 1904	Do.
Hazel W	a 4	1897		1897		Marquette, Mich	May 17, 1905	....do	May 13, 1904	Do.
H. A. Meldrum	68	1899		1899		Buffalo, N. Y	July 10, 1905	....do	July 9, 1904	Do.
Irene	10	1893	1897	1902		Marinette, Wis	May 27, 1905	Menominee, Mich	May 26, 1904	Do.
Juanita B.[b]	16	1903		1882		Drummond, Mich	Sept. 20, 1904	Cheboygan, Mich	First inspn.	
J. W. Ward	40	1891		1895		Benton Harbor, Mich.	Apr. 15, 1905	Marquette, Mich	May 7, 1904	Do.
J. W. Westcott	18	1880		1898		Buffalo, N. Y	Apr. 26, 1905	Grand Marais, Mich	May 17, 1904	Do.
Jay C. Morse	99	1867		1903		....do	May 3, 1905	Pequaming, Mich	May 3, 1904	Do.
J. Bonner	74	1901		1886 1892		Sturgeon Bay, Wis	May 20, 1905	Nahma, Mich	May 19, 1904	Do.
James W. Croze	22	1882		1863	1882	Houghton, Mich	June 6, 1905	Houghton, Mich	June 6, 1904	Do.
John Torrent	18	1875		1891		Muskegon, Mich	July 15, 1905	Sault Ste. Marie, Mich.	July 9, 1904	Do.
J. J. Evans	14	1881	1895	1885		Tonawanda, N. Y	Oct. 2, 1905	Menominee, Mich	Aug. 16, 1904	Do.
Juanita B	16	1903		1882		Drummond, Mich	Oct. 13, 1905	Detour, Mich	Sept. 20, 1904	Grand Haven, Mich.
Kate	47	1889		1883		Bay Mills, Mich	May 10, 1905	Sault Ste. Marie, Mich.	May 10, 1904	Marquette, Mich.
Lorenzo Dimick	42	1883	1889	1888		Buffalo, N. Y	May 15, 1905	....do	May 12, 1904	Do.
L. Q. Rawson	14	1866		1886		Sandusky, Ohio	July 11, 1905	....do	July 11, 1904	Grand Haven, Mich.
M. F. Merick	133	1873		1896		Detroit, Mich	Apr. 22, 1905	....do	May 5, 1904	Do.
Myrtle	18	1900		1894		Ludington, Mich	May 11, 1905	....do	May 10, 1904	Marquette, Mich.
Marion	63	1898		1900		Buffalo, N. Y	May 15, 1905	Little Rapids, Mich	May 12, 1904	Do.
Maytham	40	1874		1874		....do	June 6, 1905	Houghton, Mich	June 6, 1904	Do.
Mary Bell	38	1870		1898		....do	Nov. 16, 1905	Sault Ste. Marie, Mich	July 8, 1904	Do.
Nellie Cotton	37	1867		1883		....do	May 4, 1905	Houghton, Mich	May 5, 1904	Do.
Portia	a 7	1891		1891		Toledo, Ohio	May 28, 1905	Gladstone, Mich	May 27, 1904	Do
Richard F	a 8	1901		1901		Baraga, Mich	June 24, 1905	Baraga, Mich	July 2, 1904	Do.
Robert E. Burke	73	1899		1898		Manitowoc, Wis	Aug. 3, 1905	Little Rapids, Mich	Aug. 15, 1904	Chicago, Ill.
Sioux	52	1883	1901	1891		Green Bay, Wis	Apr. 19, 1005	Sault Ste. Marie, Mich.	May 9, 1904	Marquette, Mich.
Samson	181	1866		1890		Detroit, Mich	May 12, 1905	....do	May 13, 1904	Do.
Silver Spray	38	1895		1895		West Bay City, Mich	....do	....do	May 11, 1904	Do.
Third Michigan	42	1869	1901	1902		Ferrysburg, Mich	May 16, 1905	....do	May 27, 1904	Grand Haven, Mich.
Thomas Thompson	19	1873		1892		Buffalo, N. Y	Aug. 11, 1905	Menominee, Mich	Aug. 16, 1904	Marquette, Mich.
Thomas Hood	39	1881	1900	1881		....do	Sept. 7, 1905	Little Rapids, Mich	Sept. 14, 1904	Do.
Violet H. Raber	50	1891		1893		Manitowoc, Wis	Apr. 18, 1905	Sault Ste. Marie, Mich.	May 25, 1904	Port Huron, Mich.
Walton B	32	1891		1898		Duluth, Minn	Apr. 19, 1905	....do	May 18, 1904	Duluth, Minn.
Wa Wa	16	1891		1905		Fort Howard, Wis	May 22, 1905	Escanaba, Mich	May 27, 1904	Marquette, Mich.
Wisconsin	56	1885		1885		Green Bay, Wis	June 22, 1905	Marquette, Mich	June 22, 1904	Do.
Steam pleasure yachts.										
C. Brothers	a 8	1902		1903		Port Huron, Mich	Sept. 11, 1905	Emerson, Mich	Aug. 26, 1904	Marquette, Mich.
Elva	8	1893		1896		Detroit, Mich	June 12, 1905	Lake Linden, Mich	June 7, 1904	Do.
Ethel	a 5	1894		1894		Chicago, Ill	June 17, 1905	Detour, Mich	June 16, 1904	Do.
Louise	a 4	1890		1897		Washington Harbor, Mich.	July 20, 1905	Houghton, Mich	July 18, 1904	Do.
Morgan	29	1891		1893		Rome, N. Y	June 8, 1905	....do	June 6, 1904	Do.
Ouananiche	a 5	1904		1892		Sault Ste. Marie, Mich.	May 10, 1905	Sault Ste. Marie, Mich.	May 11, 1904	Do.
Sapho	45	1897		1897		Benton Harbor, Mich.	July 19, 1905	Hancock, Mich	July 20, 1904	Detroit, Mich.

a Estimated.

b Inspection completed and certificate returned in the Superior (Marquette) district, Mar. 29, 1905.

DOMESTIC VESSELS INSPECTED, YEAR ENDED DECEMBER 31, 1905—EIGHTH SUPERVISING DISTRICT—MARQUETTE, MICH.—Continued.

Names of vessels and class.	Gross tonnage.	Hull built.	Hull rebuilt.	Boilers built.	Boilers rebuilt.	Where built.	Date of inspection.	Where inspected.	Date of previous inspection.	Local district where previously inspected.
Miscellaneous steam vessels.										
Alta (fishing)	a 5	(b)		1893		Green Bay, Wis	May 22, 1905	Escanaba, Mich	June 27, 1904	Milwaukee, Wis.
Alice C. (fishing)	81	1901		1901		Manitowoc, Wis	Aug. 5, 1905	Manistique, Mich	Aug. 10, 1904	Marquette, Mich.
Anabel (fishing)	47	1892		1892		do	do	do	do	Do.
Burger (fishing)	47	1903		1903		do	do	do	Aug. 11, 1904	Do.
Ciscoe (fishing)	25	1895		1883		Grand Haven, Mich	Mar. 14, 1905	do	Aug. 11, 1903	Do.
C. W. Endress (fishing)	73	1898		1904		Manitowoc, Wis	Apr. 25, 1905	Grand Marais, Mich	May 12, 1904	Milwaukee, Wis.
Columbia (fishing)	83	1892		1892		Grand Haven, Mich	June 1, 1905	Marquette, Mich	June 1, 1904	Superior, Wis.
E. M. B. A. (fishing)	44	1891		1891		do	Apr. 25, 1905	Grand Marais, Mich	Apr. 26, 1904	Do.
Effie B. (fishing)	43	1896	1901	1896		Ashtabula, Ohio	June 20, 1905	do	July 7, 1904	Cleveland, Ohio.
Ethel J. (fishing)	21	1884	1897	1884		Fairport, Ohio	July 21, 1905	Marquette, Mich	July 20, 1904	Superior, Wis.
Hoffnung Bros. (fishing)	56	1890		1896		Sheboygan, Wis	June 10, 1905	Ontonagon, Mich	July 27, 1904	Do.
Katie Harrison (fishing)	a 5	1903		1903		Green Bay, Wis	May 27, 1905	Menominee, Mich	May 26, 1904	Do.
Little Jerry (fishing)	a 8	1897		1897		Eagle Harbor, Mich	June 9, 1905	Hancock, Mich	June 10, 1904	Do.
Menominee River (fire tug)	73	1879	1898	1882		Green Bay, Wis	May 27, 1905	Menominee, Mich	May 26, 1904	Do.
Minta K. (fishing)	5	1900		1902		Detour, Mich	Sept. 10, 1905	Detour, Mich	Sept. 15, 1904	Do.
Mariposa (fishing)	92	1902		1900		Manitowoc, Wis	Oct. 12, 1905	Grand Marais, Mich	Oct. 19, 1904	Do.
P. W. Arthur (fishing)	21	1875	1903	1898		Milwaukee, Wis	Aug. 9, 1905	Escanaba, Mich	Sept. 5, 1904	Do.
Ruby (fishing)	9	1896		1896		Marinette, Wis	do	do	do	Do.
Theora (fishing)	24	1893		1893		Grand Haven, Mich	Apr. 12, 1905	Marquette, Mich	Apr. 18, 1904	Do.
William Maxwell (fishing)	43	1883	1895	1903		Chicago, Ill	June 7, 1905	Houghton, Mich	June 14, 1904	Buffalo, N. Y.

LOCAL DISTRICT OF MILWAUKEE, WIS.

Names of vessels and class.	Gross tonnage.	Hull built.	Hull rebuilt.	Boilers built.	Boilers rebuilt.	Where built.	Date of inspection.	Where inspected.	Date of previous inspection.	Local district where previously inspected.
Inland passenger steamers.										
Atlanta	1,129	1891		1896		Cleveland, Ohio	Mar. 13, 1905	Manitowoc, Wis	Mar. 30, 1904	Milwaukee, Wis.
Alice Stafford c	843	1882		1887		Benton Harbor, Mich.	May 3, 1905	Milwaukee, Wis	Apr. 9, 1904	Grand Haven, Mich.
Anna C. Minch	4,285	1903		1903		Cleveland, Ohio	Apr. 8, 1905	do	May 12, 1904	Buffalo, N. Y.
Albatross	87	1880	1902	1877		Portage, Wis	June 9, 1905	Omro, Wis	June 4, 1904	Milwaukee, Wis.
Brazil	2,186	1890		1890		Buffalo, N. Y	Mar. 22, 1905	Sheboygan, Wis	May 18, 1904	Do.
Cambria	1,878	1887		1887	1905	Cleveland, Ohio	Apr. 15, 1905	Milwaukee, Wis	May 23, 1904	Duluth, Minn.
City of Racine	1,041	1889		1889		Manitowoc, Wis	May 9, 1905	do	May 9, 1904	Milwaukee, Wis.
Christopher Columbus	1,511	1893		1892		Superior, Wis	June 14, 1905	Manitowoc, Wis	June 9, 1904	Do.
Chicago	746	1874		(b)		Manitowoc, Wis	June 20, 1905	do	June 1, 1904	Do.
Charles S. Neff	992	1901		1901		Port Huron, Mich	May 10, 1905	Milwaukee, Wis	June 18, 1904	Buffalo, N. Y.
Cecelia Hill	93	1896		1896		Fish Creek, Wis	July 17, 1905	Marinette, Wis	Sept. 1, 1903	Milwaukee, Wis.
Charles McVea	331	1888		1888		Saugatuck, Mich	Aug. 26, 1905	Green Bay, Wis	June 9, 1904	Grand Haven, Mich.
Dixie	40	1904		1904		Omro, Wis	Oct. 17, 1905	Omro, Wis	Oct. 20, 1904	Milwaukee, Wis.
E. C. Pope	2,637	1891		1891		Wyandotte, Mich	Apr. 5, 1905	Milwaukee, Wis	June 6, 1904	Do.

Empire State	1,116	1862	1897	1863		Buffalo, N. Y	May 15, 1905	....do	Apr. 25, 1904	Chicago, Ill.
Eugene C. Hart	522	1890		1890		Manitowoc, Wis	June 26, 1905	Green Bay, Wis	June 27, 1904	Milwaukee, Wis.
Evelyn	150	1883	1903	1894		Oshkosh, Wis	July 14, 1905	Oshkosh, Wis	July 15, 1904	Do.
F. B. Squire	4,582	1903		1903		Port Huron, Mich	Apr. 4, 1905	Milwaukee, Wis	Dec. 18, 1903	Port Huron, Mich.
Fawn	24	1896		1898		Appleton, Wis	May 16, 1905	Appleton, Wis	May 17, 1904	Milwaukee, Wis.
Fannie C. Hart	476	1888		1894		Manitowoc, Wis	June 23, 1905	Green Bay, Wis	May 4, 1904	Do.
Fashion	149	1881		1889		Berlin, Wis	Aug. 9, 1905	Oshkosh, Wis	Aug. 9, 1904	Do.
Grand Haven	2,320	1903		1903		Toledo, Ohio	Sept. 11, 1905	Milwaukee, Wis	Sept. 15, 1904	Grand Haven, Mich.
H. B. Hawgood	4,655	1903		1903		Lorain, Ohio	Apr. 25, 1905	....do	May 10, 1904	Buffalo, N. Y.
I. W. Nicholas	2,624	1894		1894		Cleveland, Ohio	July 19, 1905	....do	July 20, 1904	Cleveland, Ohio.
J. S. Keefe	1,640	1903		1903		Buffalo, N. Y	Apr. 12, 1905	....do	May 18, 1904	Duluth, Minn.
John Denessen	39	1883	1901	1883		Fort Howard, Wis	Apr. 11, 1905	Green Bay, Wis	Apr. 18, 1904	Milwaukee, Wis.
John Crerar	1,550	1903		1903		South Chicago, Ill	July 11, 1905	Racine, Wis	July 12, 1904	Chicago, Ill.
Le Fevre	138	1901		1894		Oshkosh, Wis	May 26, 1905	Oshkosh, Wis	May 26, 1904	Milwaukee, Wis.
Lewis Woodruff	4,707	1903		1903		Lorain, Ohio	Aug. 14, 1905	Milwaukee, Wis	Aug. 17, 1904	Buffalo, N. Y.
Mayflower	49	1901		1894		Oshkosh, Wis	June 14, 1905	Oshkosh, Wis	June 14, 1904	Milwaukee, Wis.
Mary C. Elphicke	4,998	1901		1901		South Chicago, Ill	Apr. 8, 1905	Milwaukee, Wis	May 26, 1904	Do.
Maywood	398	1905		1905		Manitowoc, Wis	June 29, 1905	Manitowoc, Wis	First inspn	
Netie Denessen	54	1884	1903	1884		Fort Howard, Wis	Apr. 11, 1905	Green Bay, Wis	Apr. 18, 1904	Do.
Nia	45	1889		1897		Oshkosh, Wis	June 1, 1905	Fond du Lac, Wis	May 24, 1904	Do.
Orion	2,283	1901		1901		Green Bay, Wis	Apr. 19, 1905	Sturgeon Bay, Wis	May 4, 1904	Do.
Ottawa [d]	94	1884		1884		Saugatuck, Mich	May 29, 1905	Manitowoc, Wis	May 27, 1904	Do.
Penobscot	3,506	1895		1895		West Bay City, Mich	Apr. 14, 1905	Milwaukee, Wis	June 4, 1904	Buffalo, N. Y.
Pere Marquette 4	941	1888		1888		Detroit, Mich	June 3, 1905	....do	July 22, 1904	Grand Haven, Mich.
Pere Marquette 3	924	1887	1902	1887		Gibraltar, Mich	June 5, 1905	....do	July 23, 1904	Do.
Pere Marquette 5	1,722	1890	1901	1890		Detroit, Mich	June 7, 1905	....do	Aug. 8, 1902	Do.
Republic	2,991	1890	1903	1890		Cleveland, Ohio	June 17, 1905	....do	June 16, 1904	Cleveland, Ohio.
Roman	2,348	1891		1891		....do	Apr. 15, 1905	....do	May 26, 1904	Duluth, Minn.
Samuel Mitchell	2,277	1892		1892		....do	Apr. 18, 1905	Green Bay, Wis	May 11, 1904	Milwaukee, Wis.
Selwyn Eddy	2,846	1893		1892		Wyandotte, Mich	Apr. 10, 1905	Milwaukee, Wis	May 12, 1904	Buffalo, N. Y.
Sailor Boy	162	1891		1891		West Bay City, Mich	June 2, 1905	Sturgeon Bay, Wis	June 5, 1904	Grand Haven, Mich.
Sheboygan	623	1869	1897	1851		Manitowoc, Wis	May 22, 1905	Manitowoc, Wis	June 1, 1904	Milwaukee, Wis.
Thistle [e]	127	1894	1900	1899		Oshkosh, Wis	July 29, 1905	Oshkosh, Wis	July 29, 1904	Do.
Thomas Maytham	2,329	1892		1892		South Chicago, Ill	Sept. 7, 1905	Milwaukee, Wis	Sept. 24, 1904	Marquette, Mich.
Virginia	1,606	1891		1891		Cleveland, Ohio	June 13, 1905	Manitowoc, Wis	June 1, 1904	Milwaukee, Wis.
Wisconsin	4,858	1904		1904		Superior, Wis	Apr. 22, 1905	Milwaukee, Wis	Apr. 29, 1904	Duluth, Minn.
Wm. F. Fitch	3,629	1902		1902		Wyandotte, Mich	Apr. 5, 1905	....do	May 12, 1904	Milwaukee, Wis.
Inland freight steamers.										
America	2,171	1889		1889		Buffalo, N. Y	June 15, 1905	Milwaukee, Wis	June 14, 1904	Milwaukee, Wis.
Alice M. Gill	264	1887	1903	1887		Grand Haven, Mich	Mar. 31, 1905	Sheboygan, Wis	Apr. 9, 1904	Do.
Adella Shores	734	1894		1894		Gibraltar, Mich	May 9, 1905	Milwaukee, Wis	May 12, 1904	Do.
Aurania	3,218	1895		1899		Chicago, Ill	Apr. 10, 1905	Manitowoc, Wis	Apr. 23, 1904	Buffalo, N. Y.
Appomattox	2,643	1896		1896		West Bay City, Mich	June 28, 1905	Milwaukee, Wis	July 2, 1904	Milwaukee, Wis.
Addie Wade	98	1902		1898		Saugatuck, Mich	June 9, 1905	Sturgeon Bay, Wis	June 9, 1904	Grand Haven, Mich.
Amazonas	2,228	1898		1898		West Bay City, Mich	June 8, 1905	Milwaukee, Wis	June 8, 1904	Detroit, Mich.
B. F. Carter	210	1877	1892	1901		Oshkosh, Wis	May 10, 1905	Oshkosh, Wis	May 10, 1904	Milwaukee, Wis.
Belle	90	1900		1900		St. Joseph, Mich	July 13, 1905	Green Bay, Wis	June 15, 1903	Do.

[a] Estimated.
[b] Unknown.
[c] Now steamer Manistee, 1905.
[d] Formerly A. B. Taylor, 1902.
[e] Formerly J. H. Crawford, 1900.

DOMESTIC VESSELS INSPECTED, YEAR ENDED DECEMBER 31, 1905—EIGHTH SUPERVISING DISTRICT—MILWAUKEE, WIS.—Continued.

Names of vessels and class.	Gross tonnage.	Hull built.	Hull rebuilt.	Boilers built.	Boilers rebuilt.	Where built.	Date of inspection.	Where inspected.	Date of previous inspection.	Local district where previously inspected.
Inland freight steamers—Con.										
Charles Stewart Parnell	1,739	1888		1888		Detroit, Mich	May 1,1905	Milwaukee, Wis	Apr. 28,1904	Buffalo, N. Y.
C. F. Bielman	2,056	1892		1892		West Bay City, Mich.	June 12,1905	do	June 27,1904	Do.
C. W. Elphicke	2,406	1889		1889	1904	Trenton, Mich	May 31,1905	do	June 23,1904	Milwaukee, Wis.
Chas. B. Packard [a]	676	1887	1902	1887		West Bay City, Mich.	Sept. 5,1905	Sturgeon Bay, Wis	Sept. 12,1904	Do.
City of Rossford	355	1899		1899		Toledo, Ohio	Aug. 28,1905	Milwaukee, Wis	Aug. 24,1904	Toledo, Ohio.
City of Genoa	2,446	1892	1900	1891		West Bay City, Mich.	July 10,1905	do	July 19,1904	Chicago, Ill.
Columbia	1,373	1881		1889		Cleveland, Ohio	Nov. 8,1905	Manitowoc, Wis	May 4,1903	Milwaukee, Wis.
David M. Whitney	4,626	1901		1901		Wyandotte, Mich	June 2,1905	Milwaukee, Wis	June 6,1904	Duluth, Minn.
D. C. Whitney	1,090	1882	1903	1882		St. Clair, Mich	June 13,1905	do	June 9,1904	Chicago, Ill.
Ellen	349	1893		1893		Milwaukee, Wis	June 12,1905	do	June 6,1904	Milwaukee, Wis.
Fayette Brown	2,080	1887		1887		Wyandotte, Mich	Apr. 5,1905	do	May 2,1904	Cleveland, Ohio.
Frank H. Hart	4,307	1902		1902		Lorain, Ohio	Apr. 8,1905	do	June 2,1904	Buffalo, N. Y.
Ferdinand Schlesinger	2,607	1891		1891		Milwaukee, Wis	Apr. 6,1905	do	June 6,1904	Milwaukee, Wis.
Fred Pabst	2,430	1890		1890	1905	do	do	do	Apr. 21,1904	Do.
F. A. Meyer [b]	1,264	1888	1904 1905	1888		Detroit, Mich	May 5,1905	do	May 12,1904	Duluth, Minn.
Fleetwood [c]	1,687	1887		1901		West Bay City, Mich.	Apr. 29,1905	do	May 19,1904	Milwaukee, Wis.
F. M. Osborne	4,309	1902		1902		Lorain, Ohio	May 22,1905	do	June 16,1904	Do.
Frank L. Vance	1,952	1887		1887		Cleveland, Ohio	Apr. 27,1905	do	May 13,1904	Do.
George Burnham	332	1880		1884		Green Bay, Wis	Apr. 12,1905	Sturgeon Bay, Wis	Apr. 28,1904	Do.
George Presley	2,164	1889	1900	1889		Cleveland, Ohio	June 19,1905	Milwaukee, Wis	June 18,1904	Buffalo, N. Y.
George N. Orr	2,872	1896		1905		South Chicago, Ill	July 5,1905	Manitowoc, Wis	June 23,1904	Chicago, Ill.
Hilton	166	1867	1904	1889		East Saginaw, Mich	Apr. 11,1905	Milwaukee, Wis	Apr. 13,1904	Milwaukee, Wis.
Hennepin [d]	990	1888	1902	1888		Milwaukee, Wis	May 5,1905	do	May 5,1904	Do.
Harry E. Packer	1,143	1882		1882		Cleveland, Ohio	June 26,1905	Racine, Wis	June 27,1904	Buffalo, N. Y.
Hendrick S. Holden	4,444	1898		1898		do	July 3,1905	Sheboygan, Wis	July 11,1904	Duluth, Minn.
I. Watson Stephenson	639	1895		1895		West Bay City, Mich.	Apr. 27,1905	Marinette, Wis	Apr. 30,1904	Milwaukee, Wis.
I. N. Foster	355	1872	1893	1884		Port Huron, Mich	Apr. 19,1905	Sturgeon Bay, Wis	Apr. 19,1904	Do.
John Oades	1,454	1890		1890	1903	Detroit, Mich	Apr. 4,1905	Milwaukee, Wis	May 3,1904	Do.
J. L. Weeks	4,551	1903		1903		West Bay City, Mich.	Apr. 6,1905	do	Dec. 11,1903	Port Huron, Mich.
J. W. Westcott	522	1883	1898	1884		Marine City, Mich	Apr. 29,1905	do	May 2,1904	Milwaukee, Wis.
John F. Eddy	1,678	1886		1899		Detroit, Mich	May 3,1905	do	May 21,1904	Do.
J. H. Outhwait	1,304	1886	1902	1903		Cleveland, Ohio	May 12,1905	do	June 7,1904	Cleveland, Ohio.
Joseph L. Hurd	557	1869		1884		Detroit, Mich	Apr. 12,1905	Sturgeon Bay, Wis	Apr. 19,1904	Milwaukee, Wis.
J. E. Leimer	139	1901		(e)		Eureka, Wis	May 25,1905	Berlin, Wis	May 24,1904	Do.
J. H. Marston	117	1882		1881		Appleton, Wis	July 13,1905	Green Bay, Wis	July 15,1904	Do.
J. D. Marshall	531	1891		1891		South Haven, Mich	June 6,1905	Milwaukee, Wis	June 8,1904	Do.
John Duncan	1,267	1891		1891		Green Bay, Wis	June 8,1905	do	June 7,1904	Toledo, Ohio.
Lake Shore	3,871	1901		1900		West Bay City, Mich	Apr. 7,1905	do	June 4,1904	Buffalo, N. Y.
Langham	1,810	1888		1888		do	Apr. 11,1905	Green Bay, Wis	Apr. 30,1904	Do.
Lucy Neff [f]	946	1893		1902		do	May 4,1905	Milwaukee, Wis	May 20,1904	Milwaukee, Wis.

Marion	930	1889	....	1889	....	Sheboygan, Wis	Mar. 28, 1905	....do	Mar. 23, 1904	Do.
Minnie E. Kelton	632	1894	1904	1894	....	West Bay City, Mich	Apr. 4, 1905	....do	Apr. 1, 1904	Do.
Merida	3,329	1893	....	1893	1904	....do	Apr. 6, 1905	....do	Apr. 25, 1904	Cleveland, Ohio.
M. C. Neff	276	1888	....	1890	....	Oshkosh, Wis	Apr. 12, 1905	....do	May 4, 1904	Milwaukee, Wis.
Maryland	2,419	1890	....	1890	....	Wyandotte, Mich	Apr. 26, 1905	....do	May 14, 1904	Do.
Majestic	1,985	1889	....	1889	....	West Bay City, Mich	May 19, 1905	....do	May 23, 1904	Do.
Manchester	2,132	1889	....	1889	....	Wyandotte, Mich	May 31, 1905	....do	June 2, 1904	Do.
Nyanza	2,296	1890	1904	1890	....	Bay City, Mich	Apr. 11, 1905	....do	May 3, 1904	Chicago, Ill.
Neosho	1,982	1888	....	1888	....	Cleveland, Ohio	June 22, 1905	....do	June 13, 1904	Do.
Omaha	1,231	1887	....	1887	....	Milwaukee, Wis	May 6, 1905	Sheboygan, Wis	May 19, 1904	Milwaukee, Wis.
Oceanica	1,490	1881	....	1881	....	West Bay City, Mich	July 25, 1905	Milwaukee, Wis	July 25, 1906	Do.
Pueblo	1,349	1891	....	1891	....	Milwaukee, Wis	Apr. 20, 1905	....do	May 19, 1904	Do.
R. A. Seymour, jr	131	1882	....	1874	....	Manitowoc, Wis	May 23, 1905	Port Washington, Wis	May 20, 1904	Do.
Roswell P. Flower	1,593	1887	....	1887	....	Milwaukee, Wis	May 8, 1905	Milwaukee, Wis	May 16, 1904	Do.
R. W. England	3,887	1904	....	1904	....	Ecorse, Mich	June 10, 1905	....do	June 11, 1904	Detroit, Mich.
Rappahannock	2,380	1895	1904	1895	....	West Bay City, Mich	Aug. 28, 1905	....do	Sept. 1, 1904	Do.
Robert Mills	1,790	1888	....	1893	....	Buffalo, N. Y	June 12, 1905	....do	June 16, 1904	Buffalo, N. Y.
Susie Chipman	216	1885	....	1885	1898	Milwaukee, Wis	Mar. 31, 1905	Sheboygan, Wis	Apr. 9, 1904	Milwaukee, Wis.
S. M. Stephenson	546	1880	1901	1883	....	Manitowoc, Wis	May 5, 1905	Depere, Wis	May 14, 1904	Chicago, Ill.
Siberia	1,892	1882	1903	1896	....	West Bay City, Mich	June 19, 1905	Milwaukee, Wis	June 22, 1904	Milwaukee, Wis.
Topeka	1,876	1889	....	1889	....	Milwaukee, Wis	May 4, 1905	....do	May 20, 1904	Do.
Two Myrtles	96	1899	....	1900	....	Manitowoc, Wis	July 24, 1905	Green Bay, Wis	Aug. 1, 1904	Do.
Thomas Davidson	2,226	1888	....	1888	....	Milwaukee, Wis	June 8, 1905	....do	June 9, 1904	Do.
Uganda	2,298	1892	....	1891	....	West Bay City, Mich	Apr. 25, 1905	Sheboygan, Wis	May 4, 1904	Buffalo, N. Y.
Vega	2,143	1893	....	1893	....	Cleveland, Ohio	May 24, 1905	Milwaukee, Wis	June 6, 1904	Do.
Vulcan	1,759	1889	....	1889	....	....do	May 27, 1905	....do	June 8, 1904	Cleveland, Ohio.
William H. Wolf	2,265	1887	....	1887	....	Milwaukee, Wis	Apr. 22, 1905	....do	Apr. 21, 1904	Milwaukee, Wis.
Wawatam	1,879	1891	....	1891	....	Cleveland, Ohio	May 12, 1905	....do	May 16, 1904	Chicago, Ill.
Walter Vail	726	1890	....	1890	....	Bay City, Mich	May 16, 1905	....do	June 7, 1904	Toledo, Ohio.
W. B. Morley	1,747	1892	....	1892	....	Marine City, Mich	June 6, 1905	....do	July 2, 1904	Milwaukee, Wis.
William Chisholm	1,531	1884	....	1896	....	Cleveland, Ohio	June 27, 1905	....do	July 1, 1904	Marquette, Mich.
Yuma	2,194	1893	....	1893	....	....do	Apr. 10, 1905	....do	May 12, 1904	Cleveland, Ohio.
Inland towing steamers.										
Arctic	71	1881	....	1898	....	Milwaukee, Wis	Apr. 3, 1905	Manitowoc, Wis	Mar. 30, 1904	Milwaukee, Wis.
Arleigh H	[h] 5	1905	....	1888	....	Depere, Wis	Aug. 3, 1905	Green Bay, Wis	First inspn.	
Alfred W	55	1905	....	1904	....	Green Bay, Wis	Aug. 22, 1905	....do	....do	
Boscobel	76	1880	....	1875	1895	Portage, Wis	July 14, 1905	Oshkosh, Wis	July 14, 1904	Do.
Calumet	62	1892	....	1892	....	Milwaukee, Wis	Apr. 13, 1905	Milwaukee, Wis	Apr. 8, 1904	Do.
Erna	14	1894	....	1885	....	Benton Harbor, Mich	Apr. 18, 1905	Green Bay, Wis	Apr. 18, 1904	Do.
Ed Watkins	20	1873	....	1892	....	Milwaukee, Wis	Sept. 5, 1905	Sturgeon Bay, Wis	Sept. 12, 1904	Do.
Golden	44	1892	....	1896	....	....do	Apr. 13, 1905	Milwaukee, Wis	Apr. 13, 1904	Do.
George Nelson	45	1886	1891	1874	....	Manitowoc, Wis	June 2, 1905	Sturgeon Bay, Wis	May 2, 1904	Grand Haven, Mich.
Gunderson Bros	46	1892	....	1893	....	Sheboygan, Wis	Dec. 1, 1905	Milwaukee, Wis	Dec. 1, 1904	Do.
H. Ewig	62	1901	....	1901	....	Ferrysburg, Mich	Apr. 7, 1905	Port Washington, Wis	June 3, 1904	Milwaukee, Wis.
H. O. Warren	26	1898	....	1890	....	Oshkosh, Wis	June 14, 1905	Oshkosh, Wis	June 27, 1904	Do.
H. C. Scott [g]	59	1904	....	1875	....	Omro, Wis	Aug. 1, 1905	Omro, Wis	Aug. 2, 1904	Do.

[a] Formerly Elfin Mere, 1902.
[b] Formerly J. Emery Owen, 1905.
[c] Formerly William H. Gratwick, 1901.
[d] Formerly Geo. H. Dyer, 1898.
[e] Unknown.
[f] Formely W. P. Ketchum, 1901.
[g] Formerly D. A. Cady, 1905.
[h] Estimated.

DOMESTIC VESSELS INSPECTED, YEAR ENDED DECEMBER 31, 1905—EIGHTH SUPERVISING DISTRICT—MILWAUKEE, WIS.—Continued.

Names of vessels and class.	Gross tonnage.	Hull built.	Hull rebuilt.	Boilers built.	Boilers rebuilt.	Where built.	Date of inspection.	Where inspected.	Date of previous inspection.	Local district where previously inspected.
Inland towing steamers—Con.										
J. W. Bennett	81	1876		1891		Huron, Ohio	Apr. 18, 1905	Green Bay, Wis	May 12, 1904	Duluth, Minn.
John Leathem	75	1878	1898	1888		Sturgeon Bay, Wis	June 27, 1905	Sturgeon Bay, Wis	June 27, 1904	Milwaukee, Wis.
Josephine	46	1905		1905		Manitowoc, Wis	May 20, 1905	Manitowoc, Wis	First inspn.	
J. J. Hagerman	42	1872	1902	1902		Buffalo, N. Y	June 30, 1905	Milwaukee, Wis	July 1, 1904	Do.
Knight Templar	38	1890		1889		Milwaukee, Wis	May 3, 1905	do	May 3, 1904	Do.
Lorena	34	1882	1892	1882		Saugatuck, Mich	May 25, 1905	Sturgeon Bay, Wis	May 27, 1904	Do.
Leona R.	16	1903		1893		Jackson Harbor, Wis	do	Marinette, Wis	May 25, 1904	Do.
Lillie	a 3	1896	1904	1905		Pullman, Ill	Aug. 3, 1905	Peshtigo Harbor, Wis	Aug. 31, 1904	Do.
M. A. Knapp	60	1893		1893		Benton Harbor, Mich	Apr. 21, 1905	Milwaukee, Wis	Apr. 21, 1904	Do.
Milwaukee	52	1869		1889		Sheboygan, Wis	Apr. 13, 1905	do	Apr. 20, 1904	Do.
M. A. Gagnon	18	1874		1884		Two Rivers, Wis	May 17, 1905	Marinette, Wis	May 16, 1904	Do.
Mae Martel	38	1895		1883		Saugatuck, Mich	May 16, 1905	Green Bay, Wis	May 18, 1904	Do.
M. D. Moore	59	1880		1880		Oshkosh, Wis	July 5, 1905	Oshkosh, Wis	July 5, 1904	Do.
Nellie B	28	1905		1905		do	May 10, 1905	do	First inspn.	
N. Boutin	46	1882		1882		Buffalo, N. Y	May 25, 1905	Green Bay, Wis	Nov. 11, 1903	Duluth, Minn.
O. M. Field	29	1882		1889		Muskegon, Mich	Apr. 27, 1905	Marinette, Wis	Apr. 27, 1904	Marquette, Mich.
S. O. Dixon	29	1892		1887		Manitowoc, Wis	May 2, 1905	Racine, Wis	May 6, 1904	Milwaukee, Wis.
Starke	49	1889		1889		Sheboygan, Wis	June 7, 1905	Milwaukee, Wis	June 7, 1904	Do.
Satisfaction	47	1894		1891		do	June 19, 1905	Sheboygan, Wis	June 18, 1904	Do.
S. W. Hollister [b]	51	1888		1888		Oshkosh, Wis	July 5, 1905	Oshkosh, Wis	July 5, 1904	Do.
S. S. Coe	31	1868	1898	1896		Buffalo, N. Y	Nov. 3, 1905	Milwaukee, Wis	Nov. 4, 1904	Do.
Torrent	203	1869	1902	1902		Cleveland, Ohio	Apr. 18, 1905	Green Bay, Wis	Apr. 21, 1904	Do.
Volunteer	34	1887	1904	1895		Fort Howard, Wis	May 24, 1905	Depere, Wis	May 25, 1904	Do.
W. H. Meyer	94	1899		1899		Benton Harbor, Mich	Apr. 5, 1905	Milwaukee, Wis	Apr. 8, 1904	Do.
Welcome	77	1890		1894		Milwaukee, Wis	May 2, 1905	do	May 2, 1904	Do.
W. H. Simpson	49	1889	1905	1903		Sheboygan, Wis	Sept. 12, 1905	do	Sept. 15, 1904	Do.
Steam pleasure yachts.										
Anna M	92	1895		1895		Oshkosh, Wis	May 26, 1905	Oshkosh, Wis	May 24, 1904	Milwaukee, Wis.
Anna	a 5	1895		1891		Fond du Lac, Wis	May 24, 1905	Fond du Lac, Wis	do	Do.
Bonita	8	1901		1901		Depere, Wis	June 14, 1905	Oshkosh, Wis	June 14, 1904	Do.
Bonita	73	1892		1896		Detroit, Mich	July 17, 1905	Marinette, Wis	July 23, 1904	Do.
Cambria	48	1894		1891	1904	Oshkosh, Wis	May 24, 1905	Neenah, Wis	May 24, 1904	Do.
Coquette	8	1882		1895		do	Aug. 22, 1905	Oshkosh, Wis	Aug. 18, 1904	Do.
Eagle	14	1905		1893		West Depere, Wis	May 5, 1905	Green Bay, Wis	First inspn.	
Ensign	a 3	1900		1900		Milwaukee, Wis	July 21, 1905	Milwaukee, Wis	July 12, 1904	Do.
Elsie	a 4	1893		1896		Appleton, Wis	May 16, 1905	Appleton, Wis	May 17, 1904	Do.
Iyotan	12	1900		1882		Oshkosh, Wis	July 14, 1905	Oshkosh, Wis	July 14, 1904	Do.
Irma	30	1894		1892	1904	do	Sept. 8, 1905	do	Sept. 8, 1904	Do.
Jessie	16	1886		1902		do	July 14, 1905	do	July 14, 1904	Do.
Juneau	a 4	1897		1897		Milwaukee, Wis	July 21, 1905	Milwaukee, Wis	July 8, 1904	Do.

Lockport	19	1898		1898		Oshkosh, Wis	May 26, 1905	Oshkosh, Wis	June 14, 1904	Do.
Mermaid	a 5	1904		1885		Milwaukee, Wis	Aug. 23, 1905	Milwaukee, Wis	Aug. 23, 1904	Do.
Myrtle	a 3	1890		1890		Manitowoc, Wis	June 13, 1905	do	Aug. 11, 1903	Do.
Maggie	9	1885		1885		Oshkosh, Wis	July 14, 1905	Oshkosh, Wis	July 29, 1904	Do.
Okoboji	15	1893		1893		Chicago, Ill	May 24, 1905	Fond du Lac, Wis	May 24, 1904	Do.
Pastime	24	1899		1905		Oshkosh, Wis	Aug. 2, 1905	Berlin, Wis	Aug. 2, 1904	Do.
Pathfinder	159	1896		1899		Racine, Wis	June 15, 1905	Kenosha, Wis	June 23, 1904	Do.
Redfield, jr	30	1904		1895		Oshkosh, Wis	June 14, 1905	Oshkosh, Wis	June 14, 1904	Do.
Sport	a 5	1893		1905		Omro, Wis	July 17, 1905	Portage, Wis	June 28, 1904	Do.
Tia Juana	16	1901		1902		Chicago, Ill	May 24, 1905	Neenah, Wis	May 24, 1904	Do.
Theresa	37	1885		1886		Oshkosh, Wis	Oct. 17, 1905	Oshkosh, Wis	Oct. 19, 1904	Do.
Wisconsin	16	1901		1901		Neenah, Wis	June 21, 1905	Neenah, Wis	June 14, 1904	Do.
Miscellaneous steam vessels.										
Annie D. (fishing)	20	1886		1887		Saugatuck, Mich	May 22, 1905	Sheboygan, Wis	May 16, 1904	Milwaukee, Wis.
Arthur (fishing)	36	1889		1889		Milwaukee, Wis	Sept. 25, 1905	Milwaukee, Wis	Sept. 24, 1904	Buffalo, N. Y.
A. A. Weborg (fishing)	a 5	1901		1896		Green Bay, Wis	July 17, 1905	Gills Rock, Wis	July 20, 1904	Milwaukee, Wis.
Alice A. Leveille (fishing)	a 10	1896		1896		do	Sept. 14, 1905	Green Bay, Wis	Sept. 13, 1904	Do.
A. A. C. Tessler (fishing)	30	1898		1895		Milwaukee, Wis	Sept. 28, 1905	Sheboygan, Wis	Oct. 1, 1904	Do.
Carry Mather (fishing)	21	1880	1903	1887	1894	Muskegon, Mich	July 8, 1905	do	Dec. 7, 1903	Do.
Crystal (fishing)	12	1905		1905		Manitowoc, Wis	Dec. 11, 1905	Milwaukee, Wis	First inspn.	
Dan Costello (fishing)	27	1874	1889	1892		Milwaukee, Wis	Sept. 25, 1905	do	Sept. 10, 1904	Do.
Emily L (fishing)	a 10	1893		1893		Little Suamico, Wis	June 24, 1905	Green Bay, Wis	June 28, 1904	Do.
Emma Bloecker (fishing)	29	1889		1893		Grand Haven, Mich	Sept. 6, 1905	Racine, Wis	Sept. 6, 1904	Do.
Elizabeth G (fishing)	24	1892		1897		Manistee, Mich	Sept. 28, 1905	Sheboygan, Wis	Sept. 29, 1904	Do.
Esther (fishing)	15	1901		1901		Milwaukee, Wis	Oct. 2, 1905	Milwaukee, Wis	Oct. 10, 1904	Do.
Elsa M (fishing)	14	1893		1890		Oshkosh, Wis	Oct. 5, 1905	Baileys Harbor, Wis	Oct. 5, 1904	Do.
Elanor (fishing)	a 5	1904		1904		Marinette, Wis	Nov. 1, 1905	Menekaunee, Wis	Nov. 2, 1904	Do.
Fish Hawk (fishing)	a 3	1892		1891		Little Suamico, Wis	May 17, 1905	Mud Bay, Wis	May 17, 1904	Do.
Fearless (fishing)	28	1893		1893		Manitowoc, Wis	July 20, 1905	Sheboygan, Wis	July 19, 1904	Grand Haven, Mich.
Frederick Koehn (fishing)	39	1886	1894	1894		Milwaukee, Wis	Sept. 28, 1905	do	Oct. 6, 1904	Milwaukee, Wis.
George R. West (fishing)	22	1885		1885		do	June 24, 1905	Milwaukee, Wis	June 24, 1904	Do.
G. M. A. Hermann (fishing)	34	1891		1891		do	Nov. 23, 1905	Kewaunee, Wis	Nov. 26, 1904	Do.
Henry Troy (fishing)	27	1891		1891		Grand Haven, Mich	Mar. 20, 1905	Milwaukee, Wis	Mar. 23, 1904	Do.
Henry Gust (fishing)	37	1893		1893		Milwaukee, Wis	Sept. 2, 1905	do	Sept. 16, 1904	Do.
Hope (fishing)	7	1893		1893		Ashtabula, Ohio	May 23, 1905	Port Washington, Wis	June 3, 1904	Do.
James N. Brooks (fishing)	10	1872	1897	1901		Milwaukee, Wis	Jan. 23, 1905	Algoma, Wis	Jan. 21, 1904	Do.
Jessie Jackson (fishing)	a 4	1894	1905	1894		Marinette, Wis	Aug. 10, 1905	Marinette, Wis	Aug. 10, 1904	Do.
Julia C. Hammel (fishing)	28	1893		1895		Manitowoc, Wis	Oct. 10, 1905	Two Rivers, Wis	Oct. 13, 1904	Do.
John Lain, jr. (fishing)	12	1900		1900		Kewaunee, Wis	Nov. 27, 1905	Milwaukee, Wis	Nov. 29, 1904	Do.
Lindrup (fishing)	42	1891	1899	1887		Manistee, Mich	May 9, 1905	Two Rivers, Wis	May 9, 1904	Do.
Lillie (fishing)	a 5	1900		1900		Marinette, Wis	May 16, 1905	Green Bay, Wis	May 16, 1904	Do.
Luise M. (fishing)	18	1892	1905	1902		Sheboygan, Wis	June 19, 1905	Sheboygan, Wis	June 18, 1904	Do.
Lone Star (pile driver)	a 50	1876		1865		Oshkosh, Wis	July 5, 1905	Oshkosh, Wis	June 28, 1904	Do.
L. P. Hill (fishing)	22	1889		1888		Fish Creek, Wis	Aug. 28, 1905	Marinette, Wis	Sept. 1, 1904	Do.
L. A. Schultz (fishing)	31	1882	1901	1882		Milwaukee, Wis	Nov. 6, 1905	Milwaukee, Wis	Nov. 5, 1904	Do.
Mary L. (fishing)	12	1903		1892		Manitowoc, Wis	Jan. 24, 1905	Kewaunee, Wis	Jan. 22, 1904	Do.
Mary Anderson (fishing)	4	(c)	1905	1905		Green Bay, Wis	July [illegible], 1905	Green Bay, Wis	First inspn.	
Messenger (fishing)	a 8	1895		1895		St. Martins Island, Mich.	Aug. 10, 1905	Detroit Harbor, Wis	Aug. 10, 1904	Do.

a Estimated. b Formerly D. L. Libby, 1901. c Unknown.

DOMESTIC VESSELS INSPECTED, YEAR ENDED DECEMBER 31, 1905—EIGHTH SUPERVISING DISTRICT—MILWAUKEE, WIS.—Continued.

Names of vessels and class.	Gross tonnage.	Hull built.	Hull rebuilt.	Boilers built.	Boilers rebuilt.	Where built.	Date of inspection.	Where inspected.	Date of previous inspection.	Local district where previously inspected.
Miscellaneous steam vessels—Continued.										
Mascot (fishing)	13	1902		1902		Milwaukee, Wis	Sept. 9, 1905	Milwaukee, Wis	Sept. 10, 1904	Milwaukee, Wis.
Major (fishing)	12	1900		1902		Racine, Wis	Oct. 13, 1905	....do	Oct. 20, 1904	Do.
Mary L. (fishing)	12	1903		1892		Manitowoc, Wis	Nov. 23, 1905	Kewaunee, Wis	Jan. 24, 1905	Do.
No. 23, M. F. D. (fire) [a]	133	1897		1897		Sturgeon Bay, Wis	Mar. 8, 1905	Milwaukee, Wis	Mar. 8, 1904	Do.
No. 17, M. F. D. (fire) [b]	136	1893		1893	1904	Sheboygan, Wis	Aug. 22, 1905	....do	Aug. 23, 1904	Do.
No. 15, M. F. D. (fire)	194	1903		1903		Chicago, Ill	Oct. 12, 1905	....do	Oct. 15, 1904	Do.
P. Reckinger (fishing)	42	1892	1904	1892	1904	Sheboygan, Wis	Apr. 7, 1905	Port Washington, Wis	Apr. 9, 1904	Do.
Paul Jones (fishing)	c 5	1900		1888		Milwaukee, Wis	Nov. 27, 1905	Milwaukee, Wis	Nov. 29, 1904	Do.
Sylvia (fishing)	25	1902		1875		Sturgeon Bay, Wis	Apr. 19, 1905	Sturgeon Bay, Wis	May 16, 1904	Do.
Sea Gull (fishing)	c 4	1896		1896		Oostburg, Wis	June 19, 1905	Oostburg, Wis	June 25, 1904	Do.
Smith Bros. (fishing)	c 3	1896		1896		....do	Aug. 19, 1905	Port Washington, Wis	Sept. 29, 1903	Do.
Stokdyk Bros. (fishing)	c 4	1901		1901		Amsterdam, Wis	July 26, 1905	Cedar Grove, Wis	July 26, 1904	Do.
Sidonie (fishing)	13	1897		1892		Manitowoc, Wis	Aug. 1, 1905	Sheboygan, Wis	Aug. 1, 1904	Do.
Southern Cross (fishing)	25	1894		1894		Racine, Wis	Oct. 24, 1905	Baileys Harbor, Wis	Oct. 6, 1904	Do.
Stewart Edward (fishing)	15	1876	1899	1899		Grand Haven, Mich	Nov. 25, 1905	Marinette, Wis	Nov. 25, 1904	Do.
Two Brothers (fishing)	37	1891		1887		Sheboygan, Wis	Sept. 9, 1905	Milwaukee, Wis	Sept. 10, 1904	Do.
Tillie E. (fishing)	c 8	1903		1898		Marinette, Wis	Nov. 2, 1905	Washington Harbor, Wis.	Nov. 2, 1904	Do.
Viking (fishing)	c 6	(d)		1892		Waukegan, Ill	July 5, 1905	Marinette, Wis	July 6, 1904	Do.
Wm. Grosse (fishing)	c 4	1892		1892		Oconto, Wis	June 3, 1905	Green Bay, Wis	May 27, 1904	Do.
Welcome (fishing)	10	1888		1892		Sheboygan, Wis	May 18, 1905	Washington Harbor, Wis.	May 17, 1904	Do.
William Engel (fishing)	47	1901		1901		Manitowoc, Wis	July 14, 1905	Kenosha, Wis	July 13, 1904	Do.
Gasoline motor vessels.										
Ida Caroline	22	1902				Milwaukee, Wis	Apr. 27, 1905	Milwaukee, Wis	Apr. 28, 1904	Milwaukee, Wis.
Maryette	44	1894	1896			Cleveland, Ohio	May 4, 1905	Kewaunee, Wis	First inspn.	

LOCAL DISTRICT OF PORT HURON, MICH.

Names of vessels and class.	Gross tonnage.	Hull built.	Hull rebuilt.	Boilers built.	Boilers rebuilt.	Where built.	Date of inspection.	Where inspected.	Date of previous inspection.	Local district where previously inspected.
Inland passenger steamers.										
City of Holland	439	1893		1893		Saugatuck, Mich	Apr. 13, 1905	St. Clair, Mich	Apr. 18, 1904	Port Huron, Mich.
City of New Baltimore	80	1875		1886		Marine City, Mich	June 22, 1905	Bay City, Mich	June 14, 1904	Do.
Frank J. Hecker	4,978	1905		1905		St. Clair, Mich	Oct. 9, 1905	St. Clair, Mich	First inspn.	
George H. Russel	4,978	1905		1905		....do	July 28, 1905	....do	....do	
Henry C. Frick	6,490	1905		1905		Bay City, Mich	Sept. 15, 1905	Bay City, Mich	....do	
J. C. Ford	609	1889		1889		Grand Haven, Mich	May 19, 1905	Port Huron, Mich	May 28, 1904	Do.
Pilgrim	299	1888		1888		Saugatuck, Mich	June 19, 1905	St. Clair, Mich	June 20, 1904	Do.

Ogemaw	594	1881		1881		St. Clair, Mich	Apr. 11, 1905	Bay City, Mich	May 22, 1904	Detroit, Mich.
Sacopa	6,272	1905		1905		Bay City, Mich	June 26, 1905	do	First inspn.	
Sylvania	6,272	1905		1905		do	May 8, 1905	do	do	
Viking	1,117	1889		1889		Buffalo, N. Y.	Aug. 19, 1905	Alpena, Mich	Aug. 15, 1904	Duluth, Minn.
Ferry steamers.										
Grace Dormer	65	1868	1904	1889		Buffalo, N. Y.	May 17, 1905	Port Huron, Mich	May 18, 1904	Port Huron, Mich.
Harley	23	1881		1891		do	Aug. 9, 1905	do	Aug. 12, 1904	Do.
James Beard	86	1873	1894	1887		Au Sable, Mich	June 12, 1905	do	June 13, 1904	Do.
Nellie H	25	1900		1891		Detroit, Mich.	May 12, 1905	do	May 12, 1904	Do.
Omar D. Conger	196	1882	1901	1901		Port Huron, Mich	Sept. 28, 1904	do	Oct. 27, 1904	Do.
Pere Marquette 14	2,531	1904		1904		Wyandotte, Mich	Dec. 29, 1904	do	Jan. 22, 1904	Detroit, Mich.
Pere Marquette 14	2,531	1904		1904		do	Nov. 3, 1905	do	Dec. 29, 1904	Port Huron, Mich.
Welcome	140	1894		1887		St. Clair, Mich	Sept. 21, 1905	St. Clair, Mich	Sept. 21, 1904	Do.
Inland freight steamers.										
A. D. Hayward	298	1887	1900	1886		Manitowoc, Wis	Apr. 8, 1905	Marine City, Mich	Apr. 29, 1904	Port Huron, Mich.
A. L. Hopkins	639	1880		1888		Marine City, Mich	Apr. 28, 1905	Port Huron, Mich	Apr. 20, 1904	Detroit, Mich.
Alaska	339	1878	1899	1878		Detroit, Mich	May 31, 1905	do	June 7, 1904	Port Huron, Mich.
Benton	304	1867	1900	1886		Buffalo, N. Y.	May 4, 1905	do	May 4, 1904	Do.
Bermuda	1,312	1897		1890		Bay City, Mich	Aug. 10, 1905	Bay City, Mich	Sept. 17, 1904	Toledo, Ohio.
Britannic	1,121	1888		1888		do	Apr. 14, 1905	Port Huron, Mich	May 11, 1904	Port Huron, Mich.
Business	985	1881		1883		Milwaukee, Wis	May 11, 1905	do	May 15, 1904	Do.
C. Hickox	208	1873		1885		Black Creek, Ohio	May 23, 1905	do	May 21, 1904	Do.
Charles A. Street	512	1888		1887		Grand Haven, Mich	Apr. 12, 1905	Marine City, Mich	May 13, 1904	Buffalo, N. Y.
City of Concord	385	1868		1889		Cleveland, Ohio	Oct. 19, 1905	Port Huron, Mich	July 19, 1904	Port Huron, Mich.
Douglas	230	1882		1882		Saugatuck, Mich	Apr. 21, 1905	St. Clair, Mich	Apr. 21, 1904	Do.
E. F. Gould	261	1875		1887		Carrollton, Mich	Apr. 1, 1905	Port Huron, Mich	Apr. 1, 1904	Do.
Eber Ward	1,342	1888		1888		Bay City, Mich	May 10, 1905	do	May 17, 1904	Buffalo, N. Y.
Edward P. Recor	368	1902		1892		Marine City, Mich	May 27, 1905	do	May 28, 1904	Port Huron, Mich.
Emma E. Thompson	276	1875		1889		Saginaw, Mich	July 3, 1905	St. Clair, Mich	July 5, 1904	Chicago, Ill.
Faustin [e]	256	1882	1900	1889		Port Dover, Ontario	Apr. 19, 1905	Michigan Salt Works	Apr. 14, 1904	Port Huron, Mich.
H. E. Runnels	889	1893		1893		Port Huron, Mich	July 13, 1905	Port Huron, Mich	July 20, 1904	Detroit, Mich.
Harlem	2,299	1888	1900	1888		Wyandotte, Mich	May 27, 1905	do	May 28, 1904	Port Huron, Mich.
Harvey J. Kendall	398	1892		1892		Marine City, Mich	Apr. 26, 1905	do	May 18, 1904	Do.
Havana	1,041	1875		1895		Cleveland, Ohio	June 1, 1905	Michigan Salt Works	June 2, 1904	Do.
H. A. Root	198	1886		1886		Saugatuck, Mich	May 22, 1905	Port Huron, Mich	May 30, 1904	Duluth, Minn.
Ida E.	181	1887	1897	1877		Oshkosh, Wis	June 9, 1905	do	June 9, 1904	Port Huron, Mich.
James P. Donaldson	521	1880	1899	1887		Marine City, Mich	Apr. 26, 1905	Michigan Salt Works	Apr. 26, 1904	Do.
Kongo [f]	672	1881	1904	1890		Bay City, Mich	July 8, 1905	Port Huron, Mich	July 13, 1904	Do.
Langell Boys	387	1890		1890		St. Clair, Mich	Apr. 18, 1905	Bay City, Mich	Apr. 26, 1904	Do.
Leland	336	1873		1889		New Jerusalem, Ohio	Aug. 7, 1905	St. Clair, Mich	Aug. 10, 1903	Detroit, Mich.
Lizzie Madden [g]	690	1887		1887	1903	Detroit, Mich	Apr. 11, 1905	Bay City, Mich	Apr. 26, 1904	Port Huron, Mich.
Luna	143	1882		1883		Mount Clemens, Mich	Apr. 4, 1905	Saginaw, Mich	First inspn.	
M. Sicken	212	1884		1884		Marine City, Mich	Apr. 12, 1905	Marine City, Mich	Apr. 14, 1904	Do.
Maggie Duncan	535	1890		1890		Fort Howard, Wis	Apr. 14, 1905	Port Huron, Mich	May 27, 1904	Do.
Maine	332	1862	1899	1885	1903	Cleveland, Ohio	Sept. 7, 1905	Bangor, Mich	Sept. 15, 1904	Do.
Maud	98	1899		1894		Marine City, Mich	May 10, 1905	St. Clair, Mich	May 17, 1904	Do.
Monohansett	572	1872	1905	1882		Gibraltar, Mich	Apr. 20, 1905	Algonac, Mich	May 17, 1904	Cleveland, Ohio.

[a] Formerly Aug. F. Janssen, 1903.
[b] Formerly James Foley, 1903.
[c] Estimated.
[d] Unknown.
[e] Formerly Edward H. Jenks, 1900.
[f] Formerly Saginaw Valley, 1898 and Meriden, 1904.
[g] Formerly Chenango, 1891.

DOMESTIC VESSELS INSPECTED, YEAR ENDED DECEMBER 31, 1905—EIGHTH SUPERVISING DISTRICT—PORT HURON, MICH.—Continued.

Names of vessels and class.	Gross tonnage.	Hull built.	Hull rebuilt.	Boilers built.	Boilers rebuilt.	Where built.	Date of inspection.	Where inspected.	Date of previous inspection.	Local district where previously inspected.
Inland freight steamers—Con.										
Mueller [a]	699	1887		1894		Manitowoc, Wis	May 22, 1905	Port Huron, Mich	June 15, 1904	Chicago, Ill.
Myron [b]	732	1880		1890		Grand Haven, Mich	Apr. 4, 1905	Portsmouth, Mich	Apr. 16, 1904	Port Huron, Mich.
N. Mills	391	1870	1905	1880		Marysville, Mich	Apr. 20, 1905	Marine City, Mich	May 14, 1904	Do.
Oscar T. Flint	823	1889		1898		St. Clair, Mich	Apr. 10, 1905	Algonac, Mich	Apr. 28, 1904	Buffalo, N. Y.
Pawnee	639	1888		1893		Marine City, Mich	Apr. 22, 1905	Port Huron, Mich	Apr. 22, 1904	Do.
Rand	191	1886		1895		Manitowoc, Wis	Apr. 12, 1905	Marine City, Mich	Apr. 12, 1904	Port Huron, Mich.
Robert Holland	423	1872		1886		Marine City, Mich	Apr. 15, 1905	Saginaw, Mich	May 16, 1904	Detroit, Mich.
Russia	1,501	1872		1898		Buffalo, N. Y	Apr. 7, 1905	Port Huron, Mich	Apr. 29, 1904	Buffalo, N. Y.
Sacramento	2,380	1895	1905	1895		Bay City, Mich	July 31, 1905	Bay City, Mich	June 29, 1903	Duluth, Minn.
Sanilac	310	1867	1900	1867	1900	Algonac, Mich	May 6, 1905	Port Huron, Mich	May 17, 1904	Port Huron, Mich.
Shenandoah	2,251	1894		1894		Bay City, Mich	Sept. 16, 1905	do	Sept. 29, 1904	Do.
Simon Langell	845	1886		1904		St. Clair, Mich	Apr. 10, 1905	Algonac, Mich	Apr. 23, 1904	Do.
Stephen C. Hall	447	1880		1894		Grand Haven, Mich	May 21, 1905	Alpena, Mich	May 31, 1904	Do.
Tempest	412	1872		1885		Marine City, Mich	May 3, 1905	Port Huron, Mich	May 18, 1904	Do.
Thomas R. Scott	268	1887		1884		Grand Haven, Mich	Apr. 19, 1905	do	Apr. 23, 1904	Do.
Toltec	767	1889		1890		Marine City, Mich	May 3, 1905	Marine City, Mich	May 5, 1904	Do.
W. P. Thew	206	1884		1899		Lorain, Ohio	Apr. 5, 1905	Port Huron, Mich	Apr. 23, 1904	Do.
Wonder	99	1889	1901	1888		New London, Wis	Nov. 14, 1905	Marine City, Mich	Nov. 14, 1904	Do.
Wyoming	1,952	1887		1887		Buffalo, N. Y	Apr. 21, 1905	Port Huron, Mich	May 7, 1904	Do.
Inland towing steamers.										
A. W. Colton	92	1881		1898		Buffalo, N. Y	May 17, 1905	Port Huron, Mich	May 21, 1904	Port Huron, Mich.
Bob Teed	45	1883		1883		Saugatuck, Mich	May 2, 1905	Harbor Beach, Mich	May 12, 1904	Duluth, Minn.
Cresswell [c]	35	1882	1900	1892		Saginaw, Mich	June 22, 1905	Bay City, Mich	June 14, 1904	Port Huron, Mich.
Fred. B	16	1889		1889		Bay City, Mich	Apr. 24, 1905	Alpena, Mich	Apr. 25, 1904	Do.
Geo. Dewey	[d] 6	1899		1889		Saginaw, Mich	May 24, 1905	Saginaw, Mich	May 16, 1904	Do.
Geo. R. Hand	34	1881	1900	1880		Buffalo, N. Y	Sept. 13, 1905	Port Huron, Mich	Sept. 13, 1904	Do.
Giant	10	1883	1901	1883	1899	do	June 22, 1905	Bay City, Mich	June 18, 1904	Do.
Howard	195	1864	1905	1892		Wilmington, Del	Apr. 18, 1905	do	July 6, 1903	Do.
J. E. Rumbell	92	1883		1887		Portage, Mich	Nov. 11, 1905	Alpena, Mich	Nov. 2, 1904	Superior, Wis.
John Owen	328	1874	1889	1874		Detroit, Mich	May 15, 1905	do	May 31, 1904	Port Huron, Mich.
Manistique	473	1889	1895	1889		Gibraltar, Mich	Aug. 2, 1905	Port Huron, Mich	Aug. 3, 1904	Do.
Myrtie M. Ross	156	1890	1900	1890		South Haven, Mich	May 31, 1905	do	June 3, 1904	Do.
Peter Smith	161	1863		1888		Renfrew, Scotland	May 30, 1905	Bay City, Mich	Oct. 9, 1902	New York, N. Y.
Ralph	42	1874	1898	1877		Saginaw, Mich	May 15, 1905	Alpena, Mich	May 31, 1904	Port Huron, Mich.
Sardinia	35	1903		1881		Bay City, Mich	Oct. 30, 1905	Bay City, Mich	Oct. 29, 1904	Do.
Shiawassee	[d] 4	1898		1889		Port Austin, Mich	May 9, 1905	Saginaw, Mich	First inspn.	
W. B. Castle	124	1862		1889		Cleveland, Ohio	July 19, 1905	Port Huron, Mich	June 29, 1904	Do.
Welcome	58	1890		1890		Buffalo, N. Y	Aug. 28, 1905	do	Sept. 10, 1904	Do.
Willie Brown	19	1871		1889		do	July 20, 1905	Saginaw, Mich	May 27, 1902	Do.
Witch	44	1904		1872		Bay City, Mich	Mar. 22, 1905	Bay City, Mich	Mar. 28, 1904	Do.

Pleasure steamers.										
Capitola	123	1904		1904		Toledo, Ohio	July 20, 1905	Saginaw, Mich	Aug. 30, 1904	Toledo, Ohio.
Catherine	46	1892		1892		Detroit, Mich	June 30, 1905	...do	May 26, 1904	Port Huron, Mich.
Celia S.	d 3	1903		1902		Rogers City, Mich	July 10, 1905	Rogers City, Mich	May 30, 1904	Do.
Cornelia	59	1898		1898		New York, N. Y	May 24, 1905	Saginaw, Mich	May 26, 1904	Do.
Ethan	d 5	1904		1904		Au Sable, Mich	July 26, 1905	Au Sable, Mich	July 5, 1904	Do.
Florence C	d 4	1889		1889		Thunder Bay Isle, Mich.	June 4, 1905	Alpena, Mich	May 31, 1904	Do.
Gas	d 2	1905		1905		Port Huron, Mich	June 24, 1905	Port Huron, Mich	First inspn	
Iona	30	1900		1900		Bristol, R. I	June 8, 1905	St. Clair, Mich	June 10, 1904	Do.
J. I. C.	d 4	1888		1885		Detroit, Mich	June 23, 1905	Port Huron, Mich	June 17, 1904	Do.
Leila	d 5	1891		1891		...do	June 5, 1905	Rogers City, Mich	May 30, 1904	Do.
Mizpah	d 2	1899		1889		Glasgow, Scotland	Nov. 16, 1905	Saginaw, Mich	First inspn	
Plover	d 4	1895		1895		Port Huron, Mich	June 28, 1905	Marysville, Mich	June 28, 1904	Do.
Pryun	56	1900		1900		Detroit, Mich	June 19, 1905	St. Clair, Mich	June 15, 1904	Do.
Red Jacket	d 2	1900		1901		...do	May 9, 1905	Saginaw, Mich	May 16, 1904	Do.
Sea Gull	d 2	1900		1891		Port Huron, Mich	July 4, 1905	Port Huron, Mich	June 29, 1904	Do.
Trilby	d 2	1903		1904		...do	June 3, 1905	...do	First inspn	
Windigo	d 3	1905		1905		Saginaw, Mich	Oct. 13, 1905	Saginaw, Mich	...do	
Winyah	143	1894		1894		Sparrow Point, Md	June 14, 1905	Alpena, Mich	May 31, 1904	Do.
Miscellaneous steam vessels.										
Annie (pile driver)	10	1887		1887		Bay City, Mich	Sept. 11, 1905	Bay City, Mich	Sept. 7, 1904	Port Huron, Mich.
Arthur Jones (fishing)	34	1893		1901		Benton Harbor, Mich.	Sept. 19, 1905	Harbor Beach, Mich.	Sept. 20, 1904	Do.
Clara Belle (fishing)	46	1879		1889		Saginaw, Mich	Aug. 14, 1905	Alpena, Mich	Aug. 13, 1904	Do.
Deer (fishing)	47	1892	1905	1892		Grand Rapids, Mich.	Sept. 14, 1905	Bay City, Mich	Aug. 6, 1904	Do.
Ellen Gertrude (fishing)	14	1896		1876	1903	Harbor Springs, Mich.	June 5, 1905	Rogers City, Mich	May 30, 1904	Do.
Fisherman (fishing)	18	1880		1880		Detroit, Mich	Aug. 14, 1905	Alpena, Mich	Aug. 13, 1904	Do.
Gracie (fishing)	d 4	1899		1890		Harbor Beach, Mich.	June 21, 1905	Au Sable, Mich	First inspn	
Gracie (pile driver)	d 9	1890		1898		Detroit, Mich	July 31, 1905	Bay City, Mich	July 28, 1904	Do.
Hearl (fishing)	d 6	1903		1890		Bay City, Mich	Apr. 3, 1905	Essexville, Mich	Aug. 14, 1903	Do.
Hocage (pile driver)	d 5	1893		1894		Marine City, Mich	June 27, 1905	St. Clair Flats, Mich.	June 4, 1904	Do.
Isabella (fishing)	43	1904		1904		Alexandria Bay, N. Y.	July 15, 1905	Alpena, Mich	July 19, 1905	Oswego, N. Y.
J. E. Betz (fishing)	d 7	1905		1890		Au Sable, Mich	Oct. 16, 1905	Au Sable, Mich	First inspn	
J. M. R. (pile driver)	10	1899		1887		Saginaw, Mich	July 21, 1905	Saginaw, Mich	July 21, 1904	Port Huron, Mich.
Jose Trombly (fishing)	14	1881		1899		Sebewaing, Mich	Apr. 3, 1905	Bangor, Mich	Apr. 20, 1904	Do.
Martha H. (fishing)	d 4	1899		1892		...do	Oct. 5, 1905	Grindstone City, Mich.	Oct. 5, 1904	Do.
Mary E. Pierce (fishing)	21	1871		1893		Buffalo, N. Y	June 13, 1905	Au Sable, Mich	June 14, 1904	Do.
Oom Paul (dredge)	d 9	1890		1882		Saginaw, Mich	May 9, 1905	Carrollton, Mich	May 9, 1904	Do.
Ora Marie (fishing)	d 7	1898		1885		Bayport, Mich	May 25, 1905	Bayport, Mich	May 23, 1904	Do.
Point Abino (dredge)	204	1872	1900	1883		Buffalo, N. Y	June 9, 1905	Port Huron, Mich	June 22, 1904	Do.
R. T. Roy (fishing)	23	1891	1905	1891		Cleveland, Ohio	May 15, 1905	Alpena, Mich	May 19, 1904	Do.
Sea Wing (fishing)	39	1899		1903		Ashtabula, Ohio	Oct. 2, 1905	...do	Oct. 20, 1904	Do.
Vessels propelled by gas motors.										
Apache	16	1903				Bay City, Mich	Apr. 26, 1905	Port Huron, Mich	Apr. 26, 1904	Port Huron, Mich.
George R. Durkee	28	1887				Sebewaing, Mich	Sept. 8, 1905	Sebewaing, Mich	Sept. 12, 1904	Do.

a Formerly Edward S. Tice, 1901. b Formerly Mark Hopkins, 1902. c Formerly Robert Boyd, 1900. d Estimated.

Domestic Vessels Inspected, Year ended December 31, 1905—Continued.

NINTH SUPERVISING DISTRICT.

LOCAL DISTRICT OF CLEVELAND, OHIO.

Names of vessels and class.	Gross tonnage.	Hull built.	Hull rebuilt.	Boilers built.	Boilers rebuilt.	Where built.	Date of inspection.	Where inspected.	Date of previous inspection.	Local district where previously inspected.
Inland passenger steamers.										
A. D. Davidson	1,640	1903		1903		Wyandotte, Mich.	Aug. 5, 1905	Ashtabula, Ohio	Aug. 12, 1904	Milwaukee, Wis.
Angeline	4,644	1899		1899		do	Sept. 9, 1905	Fairport, Ohio	Sept. 10, 1904	Buffalo, N. Y.
Ball Brothers	5,733	1905		1905		Lorain, Ohio	Mar. 29, 1905	Lorain, Ohio	First inspn.	
Castalia	3,125	1890	1905	1889	1904	Cleveland, Ohio	July 8, 1905	Cleveland, Ohio	Mar. 30, 1904	Cleveland, Ohio.
Cornell	5,082	1900		1900		Chicago, Ill.	July 12, 1905	do	July 9, 1904	Chicago, Ill.
Colonel	3,879	1901		1901		Wyandotte, Mich.	July 17, 1905	Fairport, Ohio	July 18, 1904	Marquette, Mich.
Centurion	3,401	1893		1893		West Bay City, Mich.	Sept. 16, 1905	Ashtabula, Ohio	Sept. 17, 1904	Cleveland, Ohio.
Clarence A. Black	4,521	1898		1898		Lorain, Ohio	Sept. 28, 1905	do	Oct. 1, 1904	Do.
Francis L. Robbins	4,222	1905		1905		Cleveland, Ohio	Apr. 10, 1905	Cleveland, Ohio	First inspn.	
Frank H. Goodyear	4,815	1902		1902		Lorain, Ohio	Sept. 5, 1905	Ashtabula, Ohio	Sept. 6, 1904	Duluth, Minn.
George Stephonson	4,563	1896		1896		West Bay City, Mich.	Aug. 8, 1905	do	Aug. 16, 1904	Cleveland, Ohio.
Harvard	5,054	1900		1900		Wyandotte, Mich.	June 7, 1905	Cleveland, Ohio	June 13, 1904	Duluth, Minn.
Hurlbut W. Smith	4,662	1903		1903		Lorain, Ohio	June 15, 1905	Conneaut, Ohio	June 3, 1904	Buffalo, N. Y.
Howard L. Shaw	4,901	1900		1900		Wyandotte, Mich.	Aug. 31, 1905	do	Sept. 9, 1904	Cleveland, Ohio.
Henry Steinbrenner	4,719	1901		1901		Port Huron, Mich.	Oct. 2, 1905	Cleveland, Ohio	Oct. 4, 1904	Toledo, Ohio.
James C. Wallace	6,684	1905		1905		Lorain, Ohio	Apr. 20, 1905	Lorain, Ohio	First inspn.	
Juniata	4,333	1905		1905		Cleveland, Ohio	May 12, 1905	Cleveland, Ohio	do	
John W. Moore	1,961	1890		1890		Toledo, Ohio	July 27, 1905	Lorain, Ohio	July 28, 1904	Marquette, Mich.
James B. Eads	3,746	1894		1894	1904	Cleveland, Ohio	Aug. 14, 1905	Fairport, Ohio	Aug. 22, 1904	Cleveland, Ohio.
John Stanton	6,129	1905		1905		Lorain, Ohio	Oct. 5, 1905	Lorain, Ohio	First inspn.	
Joseph C. Gilchrist	4,725	1903		1903		do	Oct. 9, 1905	Fairport, Ohio	Oct. 28, 1904	Do.
Joseph G. Butler, jr	6,588	1905		1905		do	Nov. 23, 1905	Lorain, Ohio	First inspn.	
Leonard C. Hanna	6,356	1905		1905		Cleveland, Ohio	May 25, 1905	Cleveland, Ohio	do	
Malietoa	5,229	1899		1899		Lorain, Ohio	Aug. 19, 1905	Conneaut, Ohio	Aug. 29, 1904	Do.
Maunaloa	4,951	1899		1899		Chicago, Ill.	Sept. 11, 1905	do	Sept. 12, 1904	Duluth, Minn.
Moses Taylor	4,772	1902		1902		Lorain, Ohio	Sept. 29, 1905	Cleveland, Ohio	Sept. 18, 1904	Milwaukee, Wis.
Marquette and Bessemer No. 2	2,514	1905		1905		Cleveland, Ohio	Oct. 7, 1905	do	First inspn.	
Marquette and Bessemer No. 1	1,732	1903		1903		Buffalo, N. Y.	Dec. 23, 1905	Conneaut, Ohio	Dec. 27, 1904	Cleveland, Ohio.
Philip Minch	5,865	1905		1905		Lorain, Ohio	May 6, 1905	Lorain, Ohio	First inspn.	
Presque Isle	4,578	1898		1898		Cleveland, Ohio	June 21, 1905	Ashtabula, Ohio	June 24, 1904	Do.
Pontiac	2,298	1889		1889		do	June 14, 1905	do	June 13, 1904	Do.
Panay	3,811	1902		1902		Chicago, Ill.	July 10, 1905	Fairport, Ohio	July 13, 1904	Do.
Princeton	5,125	1900		1900		Lorain, Ohio	July 25, 1905	Lorain, Ohio	Aug. 1, 1905	Do.
Perry G. Walker	4,470	1903		1903		Chicago, Ill.	Oct. 10, 1905	Cleveland, Ohio	Oct. 27, 1904	Buffalo, N. Y.
Rensselaer	5,124	1900		1900		Cleveland, Ohio	Aug. 11, 1905	do	Aug. 16, 1904	Chicago, Ill.
R. L. Ireland	4,470	1903		1903		Chicago, Ill.	Aug. 23, 1905	Fairport, Ohio	Sept. 9, 1904	Duluth, Minn.
R. E. Schuck	4,713	1903		1903		Lorain, Ohio	Sept. 19, 1905	Conneaut, Ohio	Oct. 1, 1904	Do.

S. S. Curry	3,931	1893	1905	1893	1905	West Bay City, Mich.	Apr. 29, 1905	Cleveland, Ohio	May 11, 1904	Do.
Stephen M. Clement	5,821	1905		1905		Lorain, Ohio	June 20, 1905	Lorain, Ohio	First inspn.	
Sir William Siemens	4,344	1896		1896		Cleveland, Ohio	July 29, 1905	Cleveland, Ohio	Aug. 1, 1904	'Do.
Tionesta	4,329	1903		1903		Wyandotte, Mich	Apr. 22, 1905	do	Apr. 18, 1904	Detroit, Mich.
William L. Brown	4,998	1901		1901		Chicago, Ill	Apr. 7, 1905	Lorain, Ohio	May 18, 1904	Chicago, Ill.
William A. Paine	5,798	1905		1905		Cleveland, Ohio	Aug. 1, 1905	Cleveland, Ohio	First inspn.	
William A. Rodgers	6,524	1905		1905		Lorain, Ohio	Aug. 3, 1905	Lorain, Ohio	do	
Western Star	4,764	1903		1903		Wyandotte, Mich	Sept. 13, 1905	Fairport, Ohio	Oct. 3, 1904	Buffalo, N. Y.
Yale	3,453	1895		1895		Cleveland, Ohio	July 19, 1905	Cleveland, Ohio	July 23, 1904	Cleveland, Ohio.
Inland freight steamers.										
Alfred Mitchell	1,751	1900		1890		St. Clair, Mich	Apr. 5, 1905	Ashtabula, Ohio	Apr. 26, 1904	Detroit, Mich.
Arizona	765	1868		1893		Cleveland, Ohio	Apr. 6, 1905	Cleveland, Ohio	May 10, 1904	Cleveland, Ohio.
Argo	721	1895		1895		Detroit, Mich	Apr. 13, 1905	do	May 11, 1904	Do.
A. G. Lindsay	1,067	1889		1889		do	May 11, 1900	do	May 14, 1904	Do
Aztec	834	1889		1889		Marine City, Mich	May 17, 1905	do	do	Do.
Albert Y. Gowen	359	1888	1896	1888		Lorain, Ohio	May 27, 1905	do	May 26, 1904	Toledo, Ohio.
Alfred P. Wright	2,207	1888		1902		Cleveland, Ohio	June 23, 1905	do	June 21, 1904	Milwaukee, Wis.
Alvin A. Turner	309	1873		1887		Trenton, Mich	July 18, 1905	do	June 24, 1904	Cleveland, Ohio.
Alvah S. Chisholm	435	1900		1888		Marine City, Mich	do	do	July 22, 1904	Do.
Alexander McDougall	3,686	1898		1898		West Superior, Wis	July 20, 1905	do	July 18, 1904	Do.
Bulgaria	1,888	1887		1897 / 1898		West Bay City, Mich	May 29, 1905	do	May 31, 1904	Milwaukee, Wis.
Corsica	2,364	1888		1887		Cleveland, Ohio	Apr. 13, 1905	do	May 21, 1904	Cleveland, Ohio.
Charles Beatty	986	1902		1902		Toledo, Ohio	Apr. 28, 1905	do	May 11, 1904	Do.
Cuba	1,526	1872		1888		Buffalo, N. Y	do	do	May 3, 1904	Chicago, Ill.
City of Glasgow	2,400	1891		1891		West Bay City, Mich	May 2, 1905	Ashtabula, Ohio	May 7, 1904	Milwaukee, Wis.
Corona	2,408	1888		1888		Cleveland, Ohio	May 16, 1905	do	May 16, 1904	Chicago, Ill.
Crescent City	4,213	1897		1897		Chicago, Ill	do	Conneaut, Ohio	May 13, 1904	Do.
Charles A. Eddy	2,075	1889		1889		Detroit, Mich	May 23, 1905	Cleveland, Ohio	June 17, 1904	Milwaukee, Wis.
Cumberland	1,601	1881		1896		Cleveland, Ohio	June 10, 1905	Ashtabula, Ohio	June 8, 1904	Cleveland, Ohio.
Charles M. Warner	3,812	1903		1903		Chicago, Ill	June 19, 1905	do	June 14, 1904	Buffalo, N. Y.
Colonial	1,713	1882		1896		Cleveland, Ohio	June 21, 1905	do	June 20, 1904	Oswego, N. Y.
City of Naples	2,340	1892	1903	1892	1901	West Bay City, Mich	Aug. 7, 1905	Cleveland, Ohio	Aug. 24, 1904	Buffalo, N. Y.
City of Rome	1,908	1881	1905	1898		Cleveland, Ohio	Sept. 22, 1905	do	July 21, 1904	Milwaukee, Wis.
D. Leuty	646	1882		1882		Lorain, Ohio	May 17, 1905	do	Apr. 27, 1904	Buffalo, N. Y.
Dorothy	505	1891		1891		Bergen, Norway	Sept. 23, 1905	do	Sept. 13, 1904	Baltimore, Md.
Empire City	4,118	1897		1897		Cleveland, Ohio	May 11, 1905	do	May 9, 1904	Cleveland, Ohio.
Essen	334	1892		1892		do	May 20, 1905	do	May 20, 1904	Do.
Francis Widlar	4,682	1904		1904		do	May 25, 1905	do	May 21, 1904	Do.
General	132	1900		1900		West Bay City, Mich	Apr. 13, 1905	do	Mar. 31, 1904	Detroit, Mich.
Griffin	1,879	1891		1891	1900	Cleveland, Ohio	May 17, 1905	do	May 19, 1904	Cleveland, Ohio.
G. J. Grammer	4,471	1902	1905	1902		West Superior, Wis	do	do	May 16, 1904	Do.
German	2,348	1890		1891		Cleveland, Ohio	May 24, 1905	Ashtabula, Ohio	May 21, 1904	Do.
Grecian	2,348	1891		1891		do	May 26, 1905	do	May 24, 1904	Do.
Hiawatha	1,398	1880		1889		Gibraltar, Mich	May 31, 1905	Cleveland, Ohio	June 7, 1904	Buffalo, N. Y.
Harold B. Nye	4,310	1902		1902		Lorain, Ohio	June 19, 1905	Ashtabula, Ohio	June 24, 1904	Cleveland, Ohio.
Henry Cort	2,234	1892		1892	1904	Superior, Wis	July 13, 1905	Cleveland, Ohio	July 14, 1904	Duluth, Minn.
Isabella J. Boyce	368	1889		1889		Manitowoc, Wis	Apr. 3, 1905	do	Mar. 30, 1904	Cleveland, Ohio.
Isaac L. Ellwood	5,904	1900		1900		West Bay City, Mich	May 26, 1905	Ashtabula, Ohio	May 26, 1904	Duluth, Minn.

DOMESTIC VESSELS INSPECTED, YEAR ENDED DECEMBER 31, 1905—NINTH SUPERVISING DISTRICT—CLEVELAND, OHIO—Continued.

Names of vessels and class.	Gross tonnage.	Hull built.	Hull rebuilt.	Boilers built.	Boilers rebuilt.	Where built.	Date of inspection.	Where inspected.	Date of previous inspection.	Local district where previously inspected.
Inland freight steamers—Con.										
Italia	2,305	1889	1900	1889	1903	Marine City, Mich	July 1, 1905	Cleveland, Ohio	July 1, 1904	Duluth, Minn.
James H. Shrigley	459	1881		1892		Milwaukee, Wis	Apr. 24, 1905	do	May 12, 1904	Cleveland, Ohio.
Joseph S. Fay	1,220	1871		1893		Cleveland, Ohio	Apr. 29, 1905	do	May 3, 1903	Marquette, Mich.
John B. Trevor	1,713	1895		1894	1904	Superior, Wis	May 15, 1905	do	May 14, 1904	Cleveland, Ohio.
James B. Neilson	2,234	1892		1892		do	May 29, 1905	Lorain, Ohio	May 28, 1904	Do.
James Galey	4,777	1902		1902		Cleveland, Ohio	June 1, 1905	Conneaut, Ohio	June 8, 1904	Buffalo, N. Y.
John Owen	2,124	1889		1889		Wyandotte, Mich	June 22, 1905	Cleveland, Ohio	June 18, 1904	Milwaukee, Wis.
John Ericsson	3,200	1896		1896		Superior, Wis	July 14, 1905	Ashtabula, Ohio	July 14, 1904	Duluth, Minn.
James B. Colgate	1,713	1892		1892		do	Sept. 12, 1905	Cleveland, Ohio	Sept. 13, 1904	Cleveland, Ohio.
Louisiana	1,929	1887		1892		Marine City, Mich	Apr. 21, 1905	do	May 2, 1904	Do.
Lansing	1,611	1887		1887		Trenton, Mich	June 17, 1905	Fairport, Ohio	June 14, 1904	Buffalo, N. Y.
M. T. Greene	523	1887		1887		Gibraltar, Mich	Apr. 8, 1905	Cleveland, Ohio	Apr. 15, 1904	Chicago, Ill.
Matoa	2,311	1890		1890		Cleveland, Ohio	May 8, 1905	do	May 9, 1904	Cleveland, Ohio.
Manola	2,325	1890		1890		do	May 15, 1905	Lorain, Ohio	May 10, 1904	Do.
Mary A. McGregor	711	1889		1893	1904	Grand Haven, Mich	May 23, 1905	Cleveland, Ohio	May 20, 1904	Do.
Mars	3,748	1901		1901		Wyandotte, Mich	May 31, 1905	Fairport, Ohio	May 31, 1904	Do.
Major	1,864	1889		1889	1903	West Bay City, Mich	June 5, 1905	Ashtabula, Ohio	June 8, 1904	Chicago, Ill.
Monroe C. Smith	4,281	1903		1903		Lorain, Ohio	June 10, 1905	Conneaut, Ohio	do	Milwaukee, Wis.
Massachusetts	1,415	1882		1892		Detroit, Mich	July 19, 1905	Ashtabula, Ohio	July 25, 1904	Cleveland, Ohio.
Neptune	3,717	1901		1901		Lorain, Ohio	June 6, 1905	Cleveland, Ohio	June 2, 1904	Buffalo, N. Y.
Olympia	2,065	1889		1889		Cleveland, Ohio	do	do	June 6, 1904	Do.
Pathfinder	2,424	1892		1892		Superior, Wis	May 15, 1905	do	May 18, 1904	Milwaukee, Wis.
Pioneer	1,123	1892		1892		Detroit, Mich	June 13, 1905	do	June 13, 1904	Cleveland, Ohio.
Rhoda Emily	570	1884		1884		Trenton, Mich	Apr. 10, 1905	do	June 21, 1904	Do.
Robert Fulton	4,219	1896		1896		Wyandotte, Mich	May 4, 1905	Conneaut, Ohio	May 6, 1904	Do.
Randolph S. Warner	3,062	1901		1901		West Superior, Wis	May 9, 1905	Cleveland, Ohio	May 12, 1904	Do.
Robert R. Rhodes	1,576	1887		1898		Cleveland, Ohio	June 2, 1905	do	May 31, 1904	Do.
Rhoda Stewart	447	1873		1880		Algonac, Mich	June 9, 1905	do	June 11, 1904	Port Huron, Mich.
Robert L. Fryer	1,810	1888		1888, 1893		West Bay City, Mich	June 12, 1905	do	June 10, 1904	Milwaukee, Wis.
Rufus P. Ranney	1,627	1881		1896		Cleveland, Ohio	June 19, 1905	Conneaut, Ohio	June 17, 1904	Cleveland, Ohio.
Schoolcraft	745	1884		1895		Gibraltar, Mich	Apr. 10, 1905	Cleveland, Ohio	Apr. 25, 1904	Do.
S. R. Kirby	2,338	1890		1890		Wyandotte, Mich	Apr. 11, 1905	do	May 9, 1904	Milwaukee, Wis.
Saxon	2,348	1890		1891	1905	Cleveland, Ohio	May 19, 1905	Ashtabula, Ohio	May 21, 1904	Duluth, Minn.
Sir William Fairbairn	4,219	1896		1896		Wyandotte, Mich	June 12, 1905	Cleveland, Ohio	June 16, 1904	Do.
Venus	3,719	1901		1901		Lorain, Ohio	May 3, 1905	do	June 2, 1904	Buffalo, N. Y.
Volunteer	2,316	1888		1888		Trenton, Mich	June 22, 1905	do	June 20, 1904	Milwaukee, Wis.
Vermillion	1,827	1887		1887		do	July 29, 1905	do	Aug. 5, 1904	Chicago, Ill.
William Nottingham	4,234	1902		1901		Buffalo, N. Y	May 13, 1905	Ashtabula, Ohio	May 16, 1904	Do.
W. H. Gilbert	2,820	1892		1892		West Bay City, Mich	May 18, 1905	Cleveland, Ohio	May 21, 1904	Duluth, Minn.
William R. Linn	4,328	1898		1898		Chicago, Ill	May 19, 1905	Conneaut, Ohio	May 19, 1904	Do.
William H. Gratwick	4,776	1902		1902		Cleveland, Ohio	June 5, 1905	Ashtabula, Ohio	June 8, 1904	Buffalo, N. Y.

W. W. Brown	3,582	1902		1901		Chicago, Ill	June 16,1905	....do	June 13,1904	Do.
William Edwards	1,272	1879		1891		Abbot Bridge, Ohio	Aug. 10,1905	....do	Aug. 12,1904	Milwaukee, Wis.
Inland towing steamers.										
Annie	78	1889	1905	1889		Lorain, Ohio	May 2,1905	Fairport, Ohio	May 12,1902	Cleveland, Ohio.
Alva B	83	1890		1890		Buffalo, N. Y	June 20,1905	Cleveland, Ohio	June 25,1904	Do.
America	123	1897		1898		....do	Aug. 4,1905	Conneaut, Ohio	Aug. 4,1904	Do.
Anson M. Bangs	178	1897		1897		Wilmington, Del	Aug. 25,1905	Cleveland, Ohio	Aug. 25,1904	Do.
Albany	18	1890		1890		Buffalo, N. Y	Aug. 31,1905	Conneat, Ohio	Sept. 2,1904	Do.
Cris Grover	56	1892		1892		....do	May 27,1905	Cleveland, Ohio	May 27,1904	Do.
Charles Henry	22	1880		1891		Cleveland, Ohio	June 14,1905	....do	June 14,1904	Buffalo, N. Y.
Charles S. Parnell	30	1881		1887		Buffalo, N. Y	Sept. 27,1905	....do	Sept. 28,1904	Do.
Charles Castle	9	1873	1899	1896		....do	Dec. 8,1905	....do	Dec. 2,1904	Cleveland, Ohio.
Dreadnaught	31	1881	1905	1890		Cleveland, Ohio	May 8,1905	....do	May 21,1900	Do.
Dan Connelly	36	1887		1880		....do	June 3,1905	....do	Oct. 31,1900	Toledo, Ohio.
Elmer	31	1882		1882	1902	Mount Clemens, Mich	May 11,1905	....do	May 11,1904	Cleveland, Ohio.
Erastus Day	69	1893		1893		Buffalo, N. Y	June 5,1905	Ashtabula, Ohio	June 6,1904	Do.
Fred King	13	1889		1889		Erie, Pa	Aug. 4,1905	Fairport, Ohio	July 26,1902	Do.
Fabian	71	1894		1894		Buffalo, N. Y	Oct. 11,1905	Ashtabula, Ohio	Oct. 10,1904	Do.
Frank W	93	1891		1891		....do	Nov. 1,1905	Cleveland, Ohio	Nov. 9,1904	Do.
George Pankratz	63	1882		1893		Manitowoc, Wis	June 20,1905	Lorain, Ohio	June 20,1904	Toledo, Ohio.
Henry	30	1876		1892		Buffalo, N. Y	June 14,1905	Cleveland, Ohio	June 14,1904	Cleveland, Ohio.
Harvey D. Goulder	156	1898		1898		....do	Sept. 8,1905	Lorain, Ohio	Sept. 12,1904	Do.
H. L. Chamberlin	56	1889		1889		....do	Oct. 2,1905	Cleveland, Ohio	Oct. 4,1904	Do.
Industry	80	1897		1897		West Bay City, Mich	June 8,1905	Lorain, Ohio	June 7,1904	Toledo, Ohio.
Jas. T. Martin	47	1896		1893		Port Huron, Mich	May 19,1905	Ashtabula, Ohio	May 20,1904	Cleveland, Ohio.
James Byers	54	1888	1904	1888		Buffalo, N. Y	June 14,1905	Conneaut, Ohio	June 20,1904	Do.
Jos. B. Dewey	22	1901		1891		Monroe, Mich	July 31,1905	Cleveland, Ohio	July 2,1904	Do.
Joe Harris	66	1873	1891	1891		Cleveland, Ohio	Aug. 7,1905	....do	Sept. 15,1903	Do.
Kittie Downs	34	1890		1890		Ashtabula, Ohio	June 21,1905	Ashtabula, Ohio	June 27,1904	Do.
Kunkle Brothers	55	1890		1892		....do	Aug. 30,1905	Lorain, Ohio	Sept. 3,1905	Do.
L. P. Smith	73	1894		1891		Cleveland, Ohio	May 27,1905	Cleveland, Ohio	May 26,1904	Do.
Marion	17	1889		1889		East Saginaw, Mich	May 4,1905	Ashtabula, Ohio	May 9,1904	Toledo, Ohio.
Mohawk	13	1889		1905		Tonawanda, N. Y	May 8,1905	Cleveland, Ohio	May 5,1904	Buffalo, N. Y.
Marguerite	27	1894		1891		Cleveland, Ohio	June 12,1905	....do	June 11,1904	Cleveland, Ohio.
Major Symons	43	1900		1900		Buffalo, N. Y	Nov. 6,1905	....do	Nov. 5,1904	Do.
Oscar C. Stedman	68	1896		1896		Cleveland, Ohio	Aug. 2,1905	....do	Aug. 2,1904	Do.
Prodigy	80	1897		1897		West Bay City, Mich	May 10,1905	Lorain, Ohio	May 14,1904	Do.
Pinola	25	1894		1894		Cleveland, Ohio	June 6,1905	Cleveland, Ohio	June 6,1904	Do.
Peerless	76	1893		1893		Sandusky, Ohio	Sept. 6,1905	....do	Sept. 9,1904	Toledo, Ohio.
Selah Chamberlain	33	1884		1884	1904	Lorain, Ohio	June 2,1905	....do	June 2,1904	Cleveland, Ohio.
Sunol	62	1892		1892		Ashtabula, Ohio	Sept. 2,1905	Ashtabula, Ohio	Sept. 4,1904	Do.
T. C. Lutz	136	1896		1896		Chicago, Ill	Apr. 6,1905	Cleveland, Ohio	Apr. 21,1904	Detroit, Mich.
Tom Maytham	39	1880	1896	1880		Buffalo, N. Y	July 18,1905	....do	July 28,1904	Cleveland, Ohio.
Thomas Wilson	71	1888		1888		....do	Aug. 8,1905	Ashtabula, Ohio	Aug. 11,1904	Do.
Wm. Rollar	28	1882		1892		Saugatuck, Mich	Mar. 30,1905	Cleveland, Ohio	Mar. 31,1904	Do.
Wm. Kannedy	86	1893		1893		Buffalo, N. Y	June 3,1905	....do	June 3,1904	Do.
William D	51	1892		1892		Ashtabula, Ohio	June 5,1905	Ashtabula, Ohio	June 6,1904	Do.
W. B. Saunders	103	1905		1905		Cleveland, Ohio	June 9,1905	Cleveland, Ohio	First inspn.	
William L. Scott	54	1890		1890		Buffalo, N. Y	July 29,1905	....do	July 29,1905	Do.
Waldo A. Avery	70	1880		1880		Bay City, Mich	Aug. 15,1905	....do	May 14,1903	Do.

DOMESTIC VESSELS INSPECTED, YEAR ENDED DECEMBER 31, 1905—NINTH SUPERVISING DISTRICT—CLEVELAND, OHIO—Continued.

Names of vessels and class.	Gross tonnage.	Hull built.	Hull rebuilt.	Boilers built.	Boilers rebuilt.	Where built.	Date of inspection.	Where inspected.	Date of previous inspection.	Local district where previously inspected.
Steam pleasure yachts.										
Peerless	227	1886		1886		Philadelphia, Pa	June 7, 1905	Fairport, Ohio	June 1, 1904	Cleveland, Ohio.
Poly Oly	9	1892		1904		Cleveland, Ohio	Aug. 26, 1905	Cleveland, Ohio	Aug. 27, 1904	Do.
Miscellaneous steam vessels.										
Alert (fishing)	42	1896		1896		Buffalo, N. Y	May 5, 1905	Cleveland, Ohio	May 23, 1904	Cleveland, Ohio.
Annie R	32	1900		1900		Ashtabula, Ohio	May 11, 1905	do	May 10, 1904	Do.
Buckeye (fishing)	32	1901		1901		Lorain, Ohio	Mar. 24, 1905	do	Mar. 6, 1904	Do.
Bertha L. Cockell (fishing)	22	1884		1887		Pentwater, Mich	Apr. 17, 1905	do	Apr. 18, 1904	Buffalo, N. Y.
Black Diamond (fueling)	642	1902		1889		Cleveland, Ohio	July 28, 1905	Ashtabula, Ohio	July 29, 1904	Cleveland, Ohio.
C. R. Edson (fishing)	40	1889		1889	1902	do	Mar. 28, 1905	Cleveland, Ohio	Mar. 19, 1904	Do.
Clevelander (fire)	82	1894		1901		do	June 3, 1905	do	June 3, 1904	Do.
Ciscoe (fishing)	15	1891		1891		do	Nov. 4, 1905	Lorain, Ohio	Nov. 4, 1904	Do.
Daisy (fishing)	18	1896		1898		do	do	do	Oct. 15, 1904	Do.
Gull (fishing)	24	1900		1903		Lorain, Ohio	Mar. 18, 1905	do	Mar. 24, 1904	Do.
Geo. B. Raser (fueling)	554	1896		1901		Ashtabula, Ohio	May 22, 1905	Ashtabula, Ohio	May 21, 1904	Do.
Helene (fishing)	24	1883	1903	1883		Fairport, Ohio	July 6, 1905	Lorain, Ohio	June 24, 1904	Marquette, Mich.
Hugh Stocker (fishing)	30	1904		1900		Cleveland, Ohio	July 15, 1905	Cleveland, Ohio	July 15, 1904	Cleveland, Ohio.
Ideal (pile driver)	20	1891		1888		do	Nov. 4, 1905	Lorain, Ohio	Oct. 15, 1904	Do.
J. L. Wyland (fishing)	27	1885		1895		Vermilion, Ohio	Mar. 24, 1905	Cleveland, Ohio	Mar. 24, 1904	Do.
John P. Manning (fishing)	13	1891		1891		Ashtabula, Ohio	Apr. 14, 1905	do	Oct. 10, 1903	Do.
Jesse Enos (fishing)	23	1888		1892		do	June 28, 1905	Fairport, Ohio	June 27, 1904	Do.
James Burns (fishing)	25	1893		1893		Buffalo, N. Y	June 29, 1905	Cleveland, Ohio	June 2, 1904	Do.
Janie E. Smith (fishing)	50	1903		1903		Ashtabula, Ohio	July 17, 1905	Ashtabula, Ohio	July 16, 1904	Do.
John H. Farley (fire)	109	1894		1886		Buffalo, N. Y	Oct. 30, 1905	Cleveland, Ohio	Oct. 31, 1904	Do.
Kewaunee (light-ship)	133	1900		1900		Kewaunee, Mich	Apr. 4, 1905	do	Apr. 13, 1904	Do.
Mentor (lighter)	305	1881	1888	1887	1902	Fort Howard, Wis	Apr. 19, 1905	do	Apr. 12, 1904	Do.
Norma (fishing)	14	1890		1890		Buffalo, N. Y	Apr. 8, 1905	Fairport, Ohio	Apr. 18, 1904	Buffalo, N. Y.
Osceola (fishing)	21	1889		1890		Lakeside, Ohio	Aug. 26, 1905	Cleveland, Ohio	Aug. 5, 1904	Cleveland, Ohio.
Philip G. Schafer (fishing)	29	1903		1903		Buffalo, N. Y	Aug. 18, 1905	Ashtabula, Ohio	Sept. 7, 1904	Buffalo, N. Y.
Rob. E. Goodill (fishing)	17	1890		1904		Erie, Pa	Oct. 21, 1905	Cleveland, Ohio	Oct. 29, 1904	Cleveland, Ohio.
Rowira (fishing)	35	1900		1891		Ferrysburg, Mich	Oct. 26, 1905	do	Oct. 15, 1904	Do.
Susie B (fishing)	19	1892		1890		Lorain, Ohio	Mar. 18, 1905	Lorain, Ohio	Mar. 24, 1904	Do.
Sprudel (fishing)	67	1891		1891		Buffalo, N. Y	June 13, 1905	do	June 11, 1904	Do.
Stephen Chase (fishing)	45	1902		1892		Ashtabula, Ohio	Nov. 13, 1905	Ashtabula, Ohio	Nov. 21, 1904	Buffalo, N. Y.
Thos. Monson (fishing)	25	1888		1888		Lorain, Ohio	Mar. 22, 1905	Cleveland, Ohio	Mar. 16, 1904	Cleveland, Ohio.
Telephone (fishing)	19	1880		1894		do	Nov. 30, 1905	do	Oct. 8, 1904	Do.
Valiant (fishing)	40	1894		1904		Benton Harbor, Mich	Apr. 18, 1905	Lorain, Ohio	Apr. 18, 1904	Buffalo, N. Y.
William H. (fishing)	38	1898		1898		Ashtabula, Ohio	Apr. 12, 1905	Cleveland, Ohio	Apr. 12, 1904	Cleveland, Ohio.
Wm. D. Ames (fishing)	30	1905		1905		Lorain, Ohio	July 6, 1905	Lorain, Ohio	First inspn.	
Will and Harry (fishing)	10	1898		1886		Ashtabula, Ohio	July 26, 1905	Ashtabula, Ohio	July 29, 1904	Do.
William G. Perry (fueling)	481	1901		1904		West Bay City, Mich	Sept. 18, 1905	Cleveland, Ohio	Sept. 20, 1904	Do.

William D (fishing)	8	1899		1888		Erie, Pa	Nov. 17, 1905	do	Nov. 16, 1904	Do.
Youghiogheny (fueling)	177	1889	1903	1893		Ashtabula, Ohio	Aug. 28, 1905	Fairport, Ohio	Aug. 26, 1904	Do.

LOCAL DISTRICT OF BUFFALO, N. Y.

Inland passenger steamers.										
Andrew Carnegie	4,106	1897		1897		Fairport, Ohio	Apr. 11, 1905	Buffalo, N. Y	May 11, 1904	Milwaukee, Wis.
A. E. Stewart	3,943	1902		1902		West Bay City, Mich	July 17, 1905	do	July 18, 1904	Do.
Algona	92	1880	1895	1894		Buffalo, N. Y	Aug. 10, 1905	Charlotte, N. Y	Aug. 15, 1904	Oswego, N. Y.
Alex H. Sloan	25	1887		1899		do	Aug. 16, 1905	Buffalo, N. Y	Aug. 12, 1904	Buffalo, N. Y.
Buffalo	3,951	1899		1899		do	July 1, 1905	do	July 9, 1904	Do.
Corsair	36	1887		1888		do	June 23, 1905	Tonawanda, N. Y	June 17, 1904	Do.
Chicago	3,195	1901		1901		do	Sept. 20, 1905	Buffalo, N. Y	Sept. 29, 1904	Do.
Captain Thomas Wilson	4,719	1900		1900		Port Huron, Mich	Sept. 22, 1905	do	Sept. 23, 1904	Cleveland, Ohio.
Dorothy	90	1901		1901		Buffalo, N. Y	June 3, 1905	do	June 3, 1904	Buffalo, N. Y.
Edwin F. Holmes	4,787	1904		1904		Lorain, Ohio	Apr. 9, 1905	do	Mar. 29, 1904	Cleveland, Ohio.
Etruria	4,653	1902		1902		West Bay City, Mich	Apr. 12, 1905	do	May 10, 1904	Buffalo, N. Y.
Frank W. Gilchrist	4,551	1903		1903		do	Oct. 11, 1905	Erie, Pa	Oct. 20, 1904	Cleveland, Ohio.
Frederick B. Wells	4,897	1901		1901		South Chicago, Ill	Nov. 14, 1905	Buffalo, N. Y	Nov. 10, 1904	Do.
George Dittly	28	1902		1902		Buffalo, N. Y	Aug. 25, 1905	do	Aug. 23, 1904	Buffalo, N. Y.
Geo. E. Lattimer	27	1899		1899		do	Sept. 12, 1905	do	Sept. 14, 1904	Do.
Henry W. Oliver	4,909	1899		1899		Lorain, Ohio	Apr. 10, 1905	do	May 18, 1904	Do.
Henry Koerber, jr	84	1902		1891		Buffalo, N. Y	June 24, 1905	do	June 11, 1904	Do.
Huron	1,945	1898		1898		Lorain, Ohio	Aug. 2, 1905	do	Aug. 29, 1904	Do.
Henry S. Sill	4,720	1903		1903		Superior, Wis	Nov. 3, 1905	do	Nov. 4, 1904	Do.
India	1,239	1871		1871		Buffalo, N. Y	May 3, 1905	do	Apr. 21, 1904	Do.
Japan	1,239	1871		1871		do	May 10, 1905	do	do	Do.
J. M. Jenks	4,644	1902		1902		Lorain, Ohio	June 1, 1905	Erie, Pa	June 9, 1904	Milwaukee, Wis.
John B. Ketchum 2d	908	1892		1892		Toledo, Ohio	July 14, 1905	Niagara Falls, N. Y	July 15, 1904	Buffalo, N. Y.
J. D. Scott	87	1876	1894	1900		Rochester, N. Y	July 22, 1905	Charlotte, N. Y	July 2, 1904	Do.
John M. Nicol	2,126	1889		1889		West Bay City, Mich	July 26, 1905	Buffalo, N. Y	Aug. 18, 1904	Toledo, Ohio.
Kensington	3,762	1903		1903		Port Huron, Mich	Oct. 3, 1905	Erie, Pa	Oct. 4, 1904	Cleveland, Ohio.
Luzon	3,582	1902		1902		Chicago, Ill	Apr. 28, 1905	Buffalo, N. Y	Apr. 28, 1904	Buffalo, N. Y.
Milwaukee	3,327	1902		1902		do	May 19, 1905	do	May 20, 1904	Do.
Moon	97	1905		1895		Buffalo, N. Y	June 9, 1905	do	First inspn.	
Martin Mullen	4,635	1904		1904		Cleveland, Ohio	June 21, 1905	Erie, Pa	June 22, 1904	Cleveland, Ohio.
Maid of the Mist	99	1892		1892		Niagara Falls, N. Y	June 30, 1905	Niagara Falls, N. Y	July 1, 1904	Buffalo, N, Y.
North Land	4,244	1895		1902		Cleveland, Ohio	June 10, 1905	Buffalo, N. Y	June 10, 1904	Do.
North West	4,244	1894		1902		do	June 24, 1905	do	June 11, 1904	Do.
Ossian Bedell	296	1901		1901		Buffalo, N. Y	May 27, 1905	do	May 26, 1904	Do.
P. P. Miller	3,845	1903		1903		Cleveland, Ohio	Oct. 18, 1905	do	Oct. 14, 1904	Chicago, Ill.
Ruth	70	1903		1892		Buffalo, N. Y	June 17, 1905	do	June 3, 1904	Buffalo, N. Y.
Ray	3	1893	1902	1893		Hamlin, N. Y	Aug. 4, 1905	Carlton, N. Y	June 25, 1904	Do.
Silver King	48	1893	1900	1893		Buffalo, N. Y	June 3, 1905	Buffalo, N. Y	June 3, 1904	Do.
Sevona [a]	3,166	1890	1905	1905		West Bay City, Mich	June 27, 1905	do	May 16, 1904	Do.
Silver Dollar [b]	9	1886		1886		Buffalo, N. Y	July 1, 1905	do	May 7, 1903	Do.

[a] Formerly Emily P. Weed, 1897; readmeasured 1905.

[b] Formerly Louis Harbrecht, 1899.

DOMESTIC VESSELS INSPECTED, YEAR ENDED DECEMBER 31, 1905—NINTH SUPERVISING DISTRICT—BUFFALO, N. Y.—Continued.

Names of vessels and class.	Gross tonnage.	Hull built.	Hull rebuilt.	Boilers built.	Boilers rebuilt.	Where built.	Date of inspection.	Where inspected.	Date of previous inspection.	Local district where previously inspected.
Inland passenger steamers— Continued.										
Troy	3,655	1898		1898		Wyandotte, Mich	June 19, 1905	Buffalo, N. Y	June 17, 1904	Buffalo, N. Y.
Titania	73	1875		1898		Buffalo, N. Y	July 14, 1905	Charlotte, N. Y	July 13, 1904	Do.
Umbria	4,803	1904		1904		Cleveland, Ohio	Apr. 9, 1905	Buffalo, N. Y	Apr. 6, 1904	Cleveland, Ohio.
W. S. Grattan	208	1900		1900		Elizabeth, N. J	Sept. 28, 1905	do	Sept. 30, 1904	Buffalo, N. Y.
Ferry steamers.										
C. Persons Sons	49	1899		1899		Buffalo, N. Y	Nov. 15, 1905	Tonawanda, N. Y	Nov. 16, 1904	Buffalo, N. Y.
Niagara	213	1882		1898		do	Oct. 26, 1905	Buffalo, N. Y	Nov. 15, 1904	Do.
The Windsor	193	1894		1893		Summerville, N. Y	May 20, 1905	Charlotte, N. Y	May 11, 1904	Do.
Whitehaven [a]	22	1889	1904	1904		Tonawanda, N. Y	Aug. 10, 1905	Tonawanda, N. Y	Aug. 12, 1904	Do.
Inland freight steamers.										
Alaska	1,288	1871		1886		Buffalo, N. Y	Apr. 9, 1905	Erie, Pa	Apr. 6, 1904	Buffalo, N. Y.
Alcona	990	1878		1896		Gibraltar, Mich	Apr. 12, 1905	Buffalo, N. Y	May 4, 1904	Cleveland, Ohio.
Andaste	1,573	1892		1892		Cleveland, Ohio	May 16, 1905	do	June 18, 1904	Buffalo, N. Y.
Australia	3,845	1897		1902		Chicago, Ill	May 22, 1905	Erie, Pa	May 28, 1904	Milwaukee, Wis.
Ashford	132	1883		1896		Buffalo, N. Y	June 10, 1905	Buffalo, N. Y	May 21, 1904	Albany, N. Y.
Arabia	1,395	1873		1901		do	Sept. 22, 1905	do	June 20, 1904	Chicago, Ill.
Auburn [b]	1,762	1878		1878		Cleveland, Ohio	Oct. 12, 1905	do	May 7, 1904	Do.
Boston	1,829	1880		1898		Wyandotte, Mich	Apr. 14, 1905	do	Apr. 16, 1904	Buffalo, N. Y.
Bethlehem [c]	2,633	1888		1888		Cleveland, Ohio	Apr. 28, 1905	do	May 3, 1904	Do.
Binghamton [d]	1,953	1882		1891		Buffalo, N. Y	May 5, 1905	do	May 5, 1904	Do.
Bay State [e]	1,245	1890		1890	1904	West Superior, Wis	May 23, 1905	Erie, Pa	May 18, 1904	Chicago, Ill.
B. Lyman Smith	4,271	1903		1903		Lorain, Ohio	June 5, 1905	Buffalo, N. Y	June 7, 1904	Milwaukee, Wis.
Codorus	2,165	1892		1892	1904	Buffalo, N. Y	Apr. 6, 1905	do	May 14, 1904	Buffalo, N. Y.
Clarion	1,711	1881		1881		Wyandotte, Mich	Apr. 8, 1905	do	Apr. 21, 1904	Do.
Conemaugh	1,609	1880		1880		Bay City, Mich	Apr. 10, 1905	do	Apr. 14, 1904	Chicago, Ill.
Commodore	2,082	1875		1875		Cleveland, Ohio	Apr. 14, 1905	do	Apr. 16, 1904	Buffalo, N. Y.
Caledonia [f]	2,197	1888		1888		Marine City, Mich	Apr. 15, 1905	do	June 9, 1904	Cleveland, Ohio.
Chili	2,584	1895		1895		Cleveland, Ohio	Apr. 21, 1905	do	May 7, 1904	Buffalo, N. Y.
C. H. Green	694	1881		1894		East Saginaw, Mich	Apr. 28, 1905	Tonawanda, N. Y	May 16, 1904	Do.
Chemung	2,615	1888		1888		Buffalo, N. Y	May 2, 1905	Buffalo, N. Y	May 10, 1904	Chicago, Ill.
Canisteo	595	1886		1886		Mount Clemens, Mich	May 13, 1905	do	May 27, 1904	Milwaukee, Wis.
Cormorant	977	1873		1879		Cleveland, Ohio	May 13, 1905	do	May 13, 1904	Buffalo, N. Y.
C. W. Watson	4,306	1902		1902		Lorain, Ohio	May 15, 1905	do	June 4, 1904	Do.
Charles H. Bradley	804	1890		1890		West Bay City, Mich	May 18, 1905	Tonawanda, N. Y	June 28, 1904	Do.
Cartagena	1,532	1901		1901		do	May 25, 1905	Buffalo, N. Y	June 10, 1904	Milwaukee, Wis.
C. F. Curtis	691	1882	1887	1889		Marine City, Mich	May 29, 1905	Gratwick, N. Y	May 24, 1904	Buffalo, N. Y.
C. H. Dimmers	133	1882		1905		Buffalo, N. Y	June 3, 1905	Buffalo, N. Y	Nov. 21, 1903	Do.

C. C. Hand [g]	2,122	1890		1890		Cleveland, Ohio	[e]June 5,1905	do	June 21,1904	Milwaukee, Wis.
City of Grand Rapids	399	1879		1879		Grand Haven, Mich.	June 12,1905	do	July 15,1903	Buffalo, N. Y.
Clyde	1,306	1881		1901		West Bay City, Mich.	July 14,1905	Gratwick, N. Y	July 14,1904	Milwaukee, Wis.
C. H. Conover	203	1905		1905		Buffalo, N. Y	Aug. 17,1905	Buffalo, N. Y	First inspn.	
Conestoga	1,726	1878		1886		Cleveland, Ohio	Oct. 26,1905	do	July 17,1904	Buffalo, N.Y.
Duluth	4,623	1903		1903		South Chicago, Ill	Apr. 8,1905	do	Dec. 8,1903	Chicago, Ill.
E. M. Peck	1,809	1888		1888		Wyandotte, Mich	Apr. 10,1905	do	May 18,1904	Cleveland, Ohio.
Edward Smith	700	1883		1883		Marine City, Mich	Apr. 17,1905	Tonawanda, N. Y	May 2,1904	Buffalo, N. Y.
E. N. Saunders	4,305	1902		1902		Lorain, Ohio	May 26,1905	Buffalo, N. Y	June 6,1904	Do.
E. A. Shores, jr.	519	1892		1894		Sheboygan, Mich	July 8,1905	do	July 5,1904	Duluth, Minn.
Fred Mercur	1,224	1882		1882		Buffalo, N. Y	June 5,1905	Gratwick, N. Y	June 15,1904	Milwaukee, Wis.
George King	532	1874		1888		Marine City, Mich	Apr. 24,1905	Tonawanda, N. Y	May 14,1904	Port Huron, Mich.
Gogebic	1,680	1887		1887		West Bay City, Mich.	May 7,1905	Buffalo, N. Y	May 11,1904	Do.
G. A. Flagg	3,062	1901		1901		West Superior, Wis.	May 11,1905	do	May 9,1904	Cleveland, Ohio.
George F. Williams	1,888	1893		1889		West Bay City, Mich.	June 16,1905	do	June 20,1904	Milwaukee, Wis.
George Spencer	1,360	1884		1884		Cleveland, Ohio	July 17,1905	Tonawanda, N. Y	July 12,1904	Buffalo, N. Y.
Genesee [h]	134	1887	1902	1903		Buffalo, N. Y	Sept. 12,1905	Buffalo, N. Y	Aug. 22,1904	New London, Conn.
Iosco	2,051	1891		1891		West Bay City, Mich.	Apr. 13,1905	do	May 13,1904	Buffalo, N. Y.
Iron King	1,702	1887		1900		Detroit, Mich	June 8,1905	do	June 24,1904	Milwaukee, Wis.
Iron Age	1,114	1880		1896		do	June 29,1905	Erie, Pa	June 25,1904	Cleveland, Ohio.
John Pridgeon, jr	1,173	1875	1902	1883		do	Apr. 6,1905	Tonawanda, N. Y	Apr. 12,1904	Buffalo, N. Y.
Jesse H. Farwell	1,200	1881		1881		Gibraltar, Mich	Apr. 22,1905	do	May 12,1904	Detroit, Mich.
John C. Pringle [i]	474	1880		1887		Detroit, Mich	Apr. 28,1905	do	May 9,1904	Buffalo, N. Y.
John J. Albright	4,805	1901		1901		Cleveland, Ohio	June 6,1905	Buffalo, N. Y	June 7,1904	Cleveland, Ohio.
Jupiter	3,719	1901		1901		Lorain, Ohio	do	Erie, Pa	June 4,1904	Buffalo, N. Y.
John Harper	1,951	1890		1890		Fairport, Ohio	June 29,1905	do	June 21,1904	Milwaukee, Wis.
L. L. Barth [j]	683	1889		1889		West Bay City, Mich.	Apr. 18,1905	Tonawanda, N. Y	May 14,1904	Chicago, Ill.
Lackawanna	2,015	1888		1888		Cleveland, Ohio	Apr. 17,1905	Buffalo, N. Y	May 20,1904	Buffalo, N. Y.
Mohegan	1,216	1894		1893		Marine City, Mich	Apr. 6,1905	do	Apr. 22,1904	Do.
Mohawk	2,357	1893		1892		Wyandotte, Mich	Apr. 10,1905	do	June 1,1904	Duluth, Minn.
Minneapolis	2,029	1897		1897		South Chicago, Ill	Apr. 30,1905	do	May 6,1904	Buffalo, N. Y.
Mauch Chunk	4,499	1901		1901		Buffalo, N. Y	May 6,1905	do	June 30,1904	Do.
Maurice B. Grover	2,213	1887	1898	1887		Cleveland, Ohio	May 17,1905	do	May 11,1904	Do.
Muncy	3,863	1902		1902		Wyandotte, Mich	Aug. 28,1905	do	Oct. 13,1904	Do.
Mutual	6	1898	1905	1881		Buffalo, N. Y	Nov. 7,1905	do	June 27,1902	Do.
Niagara	1,951	1897		1897		West Bay City, Mich.	Apr. 9,1905	Erie, Pa	May 4,1904	Do.
North Star	2,476	1889		1888		Cleveland, Ohio	Apr. 10,1905	Buffalo, N. Y	Apr. 15,1904	Do.
Northern Light	2,476	1888		1888		do	do	do	do	Do.
Northern Queen	2,476	1889		1888		do	do	do	do	Do.
North Wind	2,476	1888		1888		do	Apr. 11,1905	do	do	Do.
Norwalk	1,007	1891		1891		Mount Clemens, Mich.	May 5,1905	do	May 10,1904	Cleveland, Ohio.
New York Recorder	121	1892		1892		Lockport, N. Y	June 1,1905	do	May 18,1904	Albany, N. Y.
New York	1,921	1879		1879		Buffalo, N. Y	Oct. 4,1905	do	Oct. 3,1904	Buffalo, N. Y.
Onoko	2,164	1882		1892		Cleveland, Ohio	Apr. 12,1905	do	May 12,1904	Milwaukee, Wis.
Owego	2,611	1887		1887		Buffalo, N. Y	May 9,1905	do	May 10,1904	Chicago, Ill.
Oscoda	529	1878		1893		St. Clair, Mich	May 11,1905	do	May 11,1904	Do.

[a] Formerly Ben Harrison, 1904.
[b] Formerly Buffalo, 1899.
[c] Formerly E. P. Wilbur, 1904.
[d] Formerly H. J. Jewett, 1902.
[e] Formerly Joseph L. Colby, 1905.
[f] Formerly William B. Morley.
[g] Formerly R. E. Schuck, 1904.
[h] Formerly Charles Hamilton, 1903.
[i] Formerly Wm. H. Gratwick, 1886.
[j] Formerly Wilhelm, 1903.

DOMESTIC VESSELS INSPECTED, YEAR ENDED DECEMBER 31, 1905—NINTH SUPERVISING DISTRICT—BUFFALO, N. Y.—Continued.

Names of vessels and class.	Gross tonnage.	Hull built.	Hull rebuilt.	Boilers built	Boilers rebuilt.	Where built.	Date of inspection.	Where inspected.	Date of previous inspection.	Local district where previously inspected.
Inland freight steamers—Con.										
Orville A. Crandall	122	1893		1897		Lockport, N. Y.	June 30, 1905	Buffalo, N. Y.	July 5, 1904	New Haven, Conn.
P. H. Birckhead	495	1870*		1889		Marine City, Mich.	Apr. 27, 1905	Tonawanda, N. Y.	May 3, 1904	Buffalo, N. Y.
Pasadena	1,982	1889	1899	1891		Cleveland, Ohio	May 19, 1905	Buffalo, N. Y.	May 18, 1904	Cleveland, Ohio.
Pascal P. Pratt	1,927	1888		1887		do	May 25, 1905	Erie, Pa.	May 23, 1904	Chicago, Ill.
Progress	1,596	1880		1896		Milwaukee, Wis.	June 17, 1905	do	June 14, 1904	Buffalo, N. Y.
Rochester	2,220	1880		1880		Buffalo, N. Y.	Apr. 25, 1905	Buffalo, N. Y.	May 7, 1904	Do.
Rome [a]	1,847	1879		1879		Cleveland, Ohio	do	do	Apr. 16, 1904	Do.
Raleigh	1,205	1871		1887		do	June 1, 1905	Erie, Pa.	June 7, 1904	Do.
Roumania	1,837	1887		1891		Detroit, Mich.	June 20, 1905	Buffalo, N. Y.	June 20, 1904	Detroit, Mich.
Ramapo	3,314	1896	1903	1896		Buffalo, N. Y.	Aug. 18, 1905	do	Aug. 18, 1904	Buffalo, N. Y.
Syracuse	1,917	1884		1884		Wyandotte, Mich.	Apr. 14, 1905	do	May 10, 1904	Chicago, Ill.
Seneca	2,669	1889		1889		Cleveland, Ohio	Apr. 17, 1905	do	Apr. 30, 1904	Do.
St. Paul	2,029	1897		1897		South Chicago, Ill.	do	do	May 6, 1904	Buffalo, N. Y.
Saranac	2,669	1890		1890		Cleveland, Ohio	Apr. 18, 1905	do	May 3, 1904	Do.
Sachem	739	1889		1889		Grand Haven, Mich.	Apr. 22, 1905	do	May 24, 1904	Duluth, Minn.
S. K. Martin [b]	302	1883		1886		Benton Harbor, Mich.	Apr. 27, 1905	Tonawanda, N. Y.	May 3, 1904	Port Huron, Mich.
St. Louis	985	1864		1896		Cleveland, Ohio	May 10, 1905	do	May 5, 1904	Buffalo, N. Y.
S. C. Reynolds	1,895	1890		1890		Buffalo, N. Y.	May 23, 1905	Buffalo, N. Y.	May 24, 1904	Toledo, Ohio.
Saturn	3,717	1901		1901		Lorain, Ohio	June 13, 1905	do	June 18, 1904	Milwaukee, Wis.
Scranton	2,015	1888		1888		Cleveland, Ohio	June 15, 1905	do	July 11, 1904	Duluth, Minn.
Sarah E. Sheldon	693	1872		1872		Black River, Ohio	June 30, 1905	Tonawanda, N. Y.	June 27, 1904	Buffalo, N. Y.
Starrucca	3,398	1897	1903	1896, 1897		Buffalo, N. Y.	Aug. 2, 1905	Buffalo, N. Y.	Aug. 12, 1904	Do.
Tuscarora	2,386	1890		1890		Cleveland, Ohio	Apr. 18, 1905	do	Apr. 30, 1904	Chicago, Ill.
Tioga	2,320	1885	1903	1896, 1897		Buffalo, N. Y.	Apr. 28, 1905	do	May 5, 1904	Buffalo, N. Y.
Tacoma	1,879	1881		1896		Cleveland, Ohio	June 27, 1905	do	July 2, 1904	Milwaukee, Wis.
Utica	3,533	1904		1904		Wyandotte, Mich.	Apr. 8, 1905	do	May 16, 1904	Detroit, Mich.
Uranus	3,748	1901		1901		do	May 24, 1905	do	June 4, 1904	Buffalo, N. Y.
Winnipeg [c]	1,708	1878		1878		Buffalo, N. Y.	Apr. 6, 1905	do	Mar. 30, 1903	Do.
Wissahickon	1,619	1876		1876		do	Apr. 10, 1905	do	Apr. 2, 1903	Chicago, Ill.
W. D. Rees	3,760	1896		1901		Cleveland, Ohio	Apr. 13, 19[illegible]	do	May 11, 1904	Cleveland, Ohio.
Wm. Castle Rhodes	2,176	1900		1900		Lorain, Ohio	Apr. 18, 1905	do	May 10, 1904	Buffalo, N. Y.
Wilkesbarre	4,153	1901		1901		Buffalo, N. Y.	May 12, 1905	do	May 20, 1904	Do.
Walter Scranton	4,803	1901		1901		Cleveland, Ohio	May 31, 1905	do	June 8, 1904	Do.
Wallula	1,924	1882		1882		do	June 19, 1905	do	June 20, 1904	Do.
Yonkers [d]	1,770	1879		1879		do	Apr. 25, 1905	do	Apr. 18, 1904	Do.
Zillah [e]	748	1890		1890		West Bay City, Mich.	Apr. [illegible], 1905	do	Apr. 28, 1904	Do.

Inland towing steamers.										
A. A. Bellinger	14	1888		1889		Buffalo, N. Y.	Apr. 24, 1905	Tonawanda, N. Y.	Apr. 22, 1904	Buffalo, N. Y.
America [f]	42	1894		1890		do	June 8, 1905	Buffalo, N. Y.	June 7, 1904	Do.
Albert Little	18	1888		1893		Tonawanda, N. Y.	June 12, 1905	Tonawanda, N. Y.	May 27, 1904	Do.
Alpha	43	1882	1896	1896		Buffalo, N. Y.	July 31, 1905	Buffalo, N. Y.	Aug. 1, 1904	Do.
Argosy	48	1904	1905	1904		do	Oct. 9, 1905	do	Oct. 8, 1904	Do.
Constitution [g]	46	1900		1900		Green Bay, Wis.	May 16, 1905	Tonawanda, N. Y.	May 20, 1904	Do.
Cascade	72	1895		1894		Buffalo, N. Y.	June 16, 1905	Buffalo, N. Y.	June 17, 1904	Do.
Conneaut	62	1893		1893		do	Oct. 18, 1905	do	Oct. 20, 1904	Do.
Delta	47	1883	1902	1883		Saugatuck, Mich.	June 12, 1905	do	June 11, 1904	Do.
Delaware	19	1903		1903		Buffalo, N. Y.	July 18, 1905	do	July 18, 1904	Do.
Dark [h]	11	1882	1898	1896		do	Aug. 1, 1905	do	July 6, 1904	Do.
Despatch	11	1890		1890		do	Sept. 14, 1905	do	Sept. 19, 1904	Do.
Elk	57	1892		1892		Grand Haven, Mich.	Apr. 29, 1905	do	Apr. 26, 1904	Do.
Erie	43	1897		1885		Detroit, Mich.	May 5, 1905	Tonawanda, N. Y.	Aug. 17, 1903	Do.
E. W. Sutton, jr.	33	1902		1902		Buffalo, N. Y.	Sept. 15, 1905	Buffalo, N. Y.	Sept. 15, 1904	Do.
E. C. Maytham	55	1885	1902	1899		do	Sept. 27, 1905	do	Sept. 25, 1904	Do.
E. E. Frost	10	1885	1897	1883		Oswego, N. Y.	Oct. 18, 1905	do	Sept. 27, 1904	Do.
Frank L. Bapst	42	1895		1901		Buffalo, N. Y.	Apr. 25, 1905	do	Apr. 28, 1904	Do.
Francis A. Bird	14	1893		1893		do	June 10, 1905	Tonawanda, N. Y.	June 10, 1904	Do.
Florence Yates	32	1895	1898	1898		do	Sept. 6, 1905	Charlotte, N. Y.	Sept. 12, 1904	Do.
Grace Danforth	65	1888		1892		do	May 29, 1905	Buffalo, N. Y.	May 31, 1904	Do.
Genevieve	38	1890		1890		do	June 7, 1905	do	May 13, 1904	Do.
Geo. S. Donaldson	13	1883	1901	1902		do	Nov. 8, 1905	do	Oct. 29, 1904	Do.
Hudson	20	1894		1888		do	May 3, 1905	do	May 6, 1904	Do.
Harlem [i]	26	1890		1891		do	May 24, 1905	do	May 17, 1904	Do.
International	61	1884		1893		Cleveland, Ohio.	Apr. 29, 1905	do	Apr. 13, 1904	Do.
J. Kelderhouse	43	1884	1901	1885		Buffalo, N. Y.	May 2, 1905	do	Nov. 2, 1903	Do.
John Perew	20	1900		1892		do	May 24, 1905	do	May 21, 1904	Do.
John Mahar	20	1905		1905		Tonawanda, N. Y.	June 12, 1905	Tonawanda, N. Y.	First inspn.	
J. F. Schoellkopf	28	1904		1904		Niagara Falls, N. Y.	Oct. 16, 1905	Niagara Falls, N. Y.	Oct. 19, 1904	Do.
Myrtle	25	1894		1900		Buffalo, N. Y.	May 24, 1905	Buffalo, N. Y.	May 21, 1904	Do.
Major Kingman	47	1901		1901		do	July 1, 1905	do	July 1, 1904	Do.
Paddy Miles	33	1891		1891		do	May 9, 1905	do	May 2, 1904	Do.
Paul S.	8	1894	1902	1902		Tonawanda, N. Y.	May 16, 1905	Niagara Falls, N. Y.	May 16, 1904	Do.
Puritan	10	1894		1898		Buffalo, N. Y.	May 19, 1905	Buffalo, N. Y.	May 14, 1904	Do.
Petrel	34	1895		1897		Ausable, Mich.	May 24, 1905	Tonawanda, N. Y.	May 24, 1904	Do.
Peter D. Hershey	14	1892		1894		Buffalo, N. Y.	June 4, 1905	Charlotte, N. Y.	June 8, 1904	Oswego, N. Y.
P. B. McNaughton	63	1888		1899		do	June 10, 1905	Buffalo, N. Y.	June 10, 1904	Buffalo, N. Y.
Queen City	21	1875	1898	1886		do	July 6, 1905	do	July 6, 1904	Do.
Robert H. Hebard	65	1889		1889		do	May 29, 1905	do	May 31, 1904	Do.
Rescue	37	1885		1890		Burlington, Vt.	June 6, 1905	Erie, Pa.	May 16, 1904	Burlington, Vt.
Samuel M. Sloan	15	1882		1881		Buffalo, N. Y.	July 5, 1904	Buffalo, N. Y.	June 30, 1904	Buffalo, N. Y.
S. W. Gee	62	1888		1898		do	Nov. 21, 1905	do	Nov. 28, 1904	Do.
Theodore E. Cowles	33	1905		1905		do	May 24, 1905	do	First inspn.	
Townsend Davis	67	1890		1890		do	July 11, 1905	Erie, Pa.	May 10, 1904	Do.
Tam O'Shanter	23	1892		1892		do	July 21, 1905	Buffalo, N. Y.	July 27, 1904	Do.

[a] Formerly Chicago, 1901.
[b] Formerly City of St. Joseph, 1888.
[c] Formerly Juniata, 1905.
[d] Formerly Milwaukee, 1902.
[e] Formerly Edward Smith No. 2, 1900.
[f] Formerly W. J. Connell, 1903.
[g] Formerly Gladys Nau, 1903.
[h] Formerly Ella B., 1902.
[i] Formerly Adam Homer, 1898.

DOMESTIC VESSELS INSPECTED, YEAR ENDED DECEMBER 31, 1905—NINTH SUPERVISING DISTRICT—BUFFALO, N. Y.—Continued.

Names of vessels and class.	Gross tonnage.	Hull built.	Hull rebuilt.	Boilers built.	Boilers rebuilt.	Where built.	Date of inspection.	Where inspected.	Date of previous inspection.	Local district where previously inspected.
Inland towing steamers—Con.										
Tonawanda	31	1893		1891		Tonawanda, N. Y.	Aug. 3, 1905	Tonawanda, N. Y.	Aug. 2, 1904	Buffalo, N. Y.
Trenton	9	1893		1889		Buffalo, N. Y.	Aug. 11, 1905	Buffalo, N. Y.	June 16, 1904	Do.
W. N. Peckham	17	1892		1892		do	May 3, 1905	do	Apr. 30, 1904	Do.
Williams [a]	89	1876	1902	1884		Algonac, Mich.	May 24, 1905	do	May 21, 1904	Do.
William Stevenson	34	1887		1898		Buffalo, N. Y.	May 28, 1905	Erie, Pa.	May 27, 1904	Do.
W. J. Warwick	21	1901		1898		do	Aug. 8, 1905	Buffalo, N. Y.	May 21, 1904	Do.
W. G. Mason	99	1898		1898		Port Huron, Mich.	Aug. 18, 1905	do	Aug. 17, 1904	Do.
William P. Donnelly	54	1903		1903		Buffalo, N. Y.	Nov. 8, 1905	do	Nov. 10, 1904	Cleveland, Ohio.
W. I. Babcock	63	1888		1888		do	Nov. 21, 1905	do	Nov. 21, 1904	Buffalo, N. Y.
Wm. H. Kinch	58	1902		1902		Ferrysburg, Mich.	Dec. 6, 1905	do	Dec. 6, 1904	Do.
Pleasure steamers.										
Anemone	4	1892		1892		Nyack, N. Y.	May 20, 1905	Buffalo, N. Y.	May 12, 1904	Buffalo, N. Y.
Alcina	34	1896		1899		New Haven, Conn.	July 29, 1905	do	July 26, 1904	Do.
Arrow [b]	3	1900		1895		Buffalo, N. Y.	Aug. 14, 1905	do	July 7, 1904	Do.
Burgard [c]	13	1893		1893		do	July 21, 1905	do	July 20, 1904	Do.
Cygnet	4	1888		1891		Geneva, N. Y.	Nov. 22, 1905	Niagara-on-the-Lake, Canada.	Oct. 5, 1904	Do.
Elgrudor	103	1903		1903		City Island, N. Y.	July 31, 1905	Buffalo, N. Y.	Aug. 10, 1904	Do.
Earl G. Danser [d]	8	1893		1893		Buffalo, N. Y.	Sept. 20, 1905	do	July 20, 1904	Do.
Florence T.	7	1903		1902		do	June 24, 1905	do	June 20, 1904	Do.
Guess	4	1903		1905		Geneva, N. Y.	June 22, 1905	Charlotte, N. Y.	First inspn.	
Gypsy	9	1900		1900		Tonawanda, N. Y.	July 3, 1905	Buffalo, N. Y.	July 1, 1904	Do.
John Helder	10	1903		1903		Buffalo, N. Y.	June 24, 1905	do	June 11, 1904	Do.
Louis Miller	9	1887	1900	1901		do	June 23, 1905	Tonawanda, N. Y.	June 17, 1904	Do.
Little Chief	1	1886		1886		Tonawanda, N. Y.	July 25, 1905	Buffalo, N. Y.	First inspn.	
Mystic	74	1867		1886		Mystic, Conn.	June 17, 1905	Erie, Pa.	June 14, 1904	Do.
Orizaba	76	1875		1903		Buffalo, N. Y.	June 15, 1905	Buffalo, N. Y.	June 20, 1904	Do.
Prudence	3	1886		1891		do	June 9, 1905	Tonawanda, N. Y.	Aug. 15, 1902	Do.
Pearl J.	6	1897		1897		Tonawanda, N. Y.	Sept. 9, 1905	do	Aug. 23, 1904	Do.
Walter B.	3	1890		1890		Erie, Pa.	May 27, 1905	do	May 27, 1904	Do.
Miscellaneous steamers.										
Anna F. Onen (fishing)	22	1886	1901	1889		Youngstown, N. Y.	July 6, 1905	Buffalo, N. Y.	July 5, 1904	Buffalo, N. Y.
Arita (fishing)	13	1901		1886		Erie, Pa.	Aug. 7, 1905	Erie, Pa.	do	Do.
Baby (delivery)	3	1879		1889		Buffalo, N. Y.	July 1, 1905	Buffalo, N. Y.	June 29, 1905	Do.
Comet (fishing)	18	1899		1901		do	July 28, 1905	Erie, Pa.	Aug. 3, 1904	Do.
Cornelius W. Desmond (fishing).	32	1899		1902		do	do	do	June 7, 1904	Do.
Charm (fishing)	25	1885	1902	1889		Chicago, Ill.	Sept. 1, 1905	Dunkirk, N. Y.	Sept. 2, 1904	Do.

Columbia (canal)	130	1889	....	1892	....	Lockport, N. Y.	Sept. 16, 1905	Buffalo, N. Y.	Oct. 19, 1904	Do.
C. F. Mischler (fishing)	18	1898	....	1895	....	Ashtabula, Ohio	Oct. 2, 1905	Dunkirk, N. Y.	Oct. 25, 1904	Do.
Duro (pile driver)	18	1905	....	1886	....	Youngstown, N. Y.	Apr. 24, 1905	Youngstown, N. Y.	First inspn.	
Don (fishing)	11	1901	....	1883	....	Erie, Pa.	May 4, 1905	Erie, Pa.	May 4, 1904	Do.
Dan Kunz (sand dredge)	99	1888	....	1888	....	Sandusky, Ohio	May 13, 1905	....do	May 28, 1904	Do.
Doctor (fishing)	20	1901	....	1901	....	Erie, Pa.	June 29, 1905	....do	July 29, 1904	Do.
Du Bois (canal)	136	1883	....	1893	....	Buffalo, N. Y.	July 18, 1905	Buffalo, N. Y.	July 18, 1904	Do.
Elma (fishing)	29	1897	....	1897	....	....do	Apr. 9, 1905	Erie, Pa.	Apr. 18, 1904	Do.
E. C. Oggel (fishing)	25	1874	1901	1898	....	Grand Haven, Mich.	June 29, 1905	....do	July 29, 1904	Do.
Eugene Loesch (fishing)	19	1903	....	1892	1903	Erie, Pa.	....do	....do	July 11, 1904	Do.
Eagle (fishing)	16	1903	....	1892	1903	....do	....do	....do	....do	Do.
Erie (fishing)	21	1902	....	1902	....	....do	Sept. 19, 1905	....do	Oct. 13, 1904	Do.
Frank S., jr. (fishing)	23	1901	....	1901	....	Buffalo, N. Y.	May 13, 1905	Dunkirk, N. Y.	May 12, 1904	Do.
Fisher (delivery) e	9	1896	....	1904	....	....do	July 22, 1905	Buffalo, N. Y.	July 20, 1904	Do.
F. W. Bacon (fishing)	37	1891	....	1893	....	....do	Nov. 6, 1905	Dunkirk, N. Y.	Sept. 24, 1904	Do.
Fred M. Lawrence (canal)	124	1893	....	1894	....	....do	Nov. 22, 1905	Buffalo, N. Y.	Nov. 9, 1904	Do.
Geo. A. Floss (fishing)	24	1903	....	1892	....	....do	July 29, 1905	....do	July 24, 1904	Do.
Grace (fishing)	13	1892	1903	1901	....	....do	Oct. 2, 1905	Dunkirk, N. Y.	Sept. 24, 1904	Do.
George R. Potter (fire)	133	1887	....	1887	....	....do	Nov. 2, 1905	Buffalo, N. Y.	Nov. 21, 1904	Do.
Harry H. Boyd (fishing)	36	1895	....	1903	....	....do	June 29, 1905	Erie, Pa.	July 11, 1904	Do.
Harold J. (fishing)	33	1901	....	1896	....	Erie, Pa.	July 28, 1905	....do	July 29, 1904	Do.
Harry G. Barnhurst (fishing)	36	1885	1900	1885	....	....do	Aug. 5, 1905	....do	Aug. 3, 1904	Do.
H. G. Brooks (fishing)	20	1888	1902	1888	....	Buffalo, N. Y.	Oct. 7, 1905	....do	Oct. 7, 1904	Do.
Ismalia (delivery)	6	1892	....	1892	....	....do	May 9, 1905	Buffalo, N. Y.	May 9, 1904	Do.
John A. Dash (fishing)	13	1886	....	1886	....	Erie, Pa.	May 13, 1905	Erie, Pa.	May 12, 1904	Do.
John M. Hutchinson (fire)	90	1893	....	1896	....	Buffalo, N. Y.	June 29, 1905	Buffalo, N. Y.	June 28, 1904	Do.
John Desmond (fishing)	44	1900	....	1900	....	....do	Aug. 14, 1905	Dunkirk, N. Y.	Aug. 11, 1904	Do.
Jennie A. Desmond (fishing)	14	1887	....	1887	....	....do	Sept. 30, 1905	....do	Oct. 1, 1904	Do.
Jean (fishing)	12	1889	1901	1901	....	....do	Oct. 3, 1905	Erie, Pa.	Oct. 7, 1904	Do.
James W. Morse (canal)	132	1888	....	1894	....	Phoenix, N. Y.	Oct. 25, 1905	Buffalo, N. Y.	Oct. 8, 1904	Do.
Kate White (fishing)	24	1885	1897	1885	....	Erie, Pa.	June 6, 1905	Erie, Pa.	June 14, 1904	Do.
Keystone (fishing)	18	1902	....	1902	....	....do	June 28, 1905	....do	July 11, 1904	Do.
Kate Wilson (fishing)	15	1897	....	1902	....	Buffalo, N. Y.	Oct. 7, 1905	....do	Oct. 13, 1904	Do.
Loretta (delivery)	9	1895	1903	1895	....	....do	May 24, 1905	Tonawanda, N. Y.	June 18, 1904	Do.
Louis Banks (fishing)	23	1897	....	1901	....	....do	July 28, 1905	Buffalo, N. Y.	July 8, 1904	Do.
Lovisa (fishing)	18	1891	....	1891	....	Lorain, Ohio	Sept. 19, 1905	Erie, Pa.	Sept. 19, 1904	Cleveland, Ohio
Lady Wimett (canal)	141	1887	....	1897	....	Lockport, N. Y.	Oct. 30, 1905	Buffalo, N. Y.	Oct. 22, 1904	Buffalo, N. Y.
Lucy (fishing) f	16	1890	....	1890	....	Buffalo, N. Y.	Nov. 1, 1905	Dunkirk, N. Y.	Apr. 25, 1903	Do.
Marcella Roche (delivery)	3	1892	....	1892	....	....do	Apr. 6, 1905	Buffalo, N. Y.	Sept. 2, 1903	Do.
Matt Wagner (fishing)	32	1888	1904	1888	....	....do	Apr. 9, 1905	Dunkirk, N. Y.	Apr. 8, 1904	Do.
Major (sand dredge)	128	1891	1903	1891	....	....do	Apr. 20, 1905	Erie, Pa.	May 10, 1904	Do.
Mansfield (lighter)	382	1892	....	1896	....	Cleveland, Ohio	....do	....do	May 4, 1904	Do.
Myers Boys (fishing)	27	1903	....	1902	....	Buffalo, N. Y.	July 26, 1905	Buffalo, N. Y.	Aug. 11, 1904	Do.
Mark H. Esser (fishing)	34	1900	....	1901	....	Lorain, Ohio	July 28, 1905	Erie, Pa.	July 29, 1904	Do.
Massasauga (canal)	119	1894	....	1904	....	Lockport, N. Y.	Sept. 30, 1905	Buffalo, N. Y.	Oct. 6, 1904	Do.
Owen Rice (pile driver)	16	1903	....	1882	....	Erie, Pa.	Apr. 20, 1905	Erie, Pa.	Apr. 18, 1904	Do.
Peter Coates (fishing)	32	1886	....	1898	....	Grand Haven, Mich.	Apr. 9, 1905	....do	....do	Do.
Planet (fishing)	24	1903	....	1886	....	Buffalo, N. Y.	Aug. 7, 1905	....do	July 29, 1904	Do.
Puritan (fishing)	20	1892	....	1890	....	....do	Nov. 1, 1905	....do	Nov. 10, 1904	Do.

a Formerly Ella M. Smith, 1902.
b Formerly Ella A, 1905.
c Formerly Nettie Baker, 1903.
d Formerly Lillian, 1904.
e Formerly Maud Moon, 1903.
f Formerly Jose.

DOMESTIC VESSELS INSPECTED, YEAR ENDED DECEMBER 31, 1905—NINTH SUPERVISING DISTRICT—BUFFALO, N. Y.—Continued.

Names of vessels and class.	Gross tonnage.	Hull built.	Hull rebuilt.	Boilers built.	Boilers rebuilt.	Where built.	Date of inspection.	Where inspected.	Date of previous inspection.	Local district where previously inspected.
Miscellaneous steamers—Con.										
Queen (canal) [a]	135	1889		1901		Lockport, N. Y.	Aug. 15, 1905	Buffalo, N. Y.	Aug. 22, 1904	Buffalo, N. Y.
Rainbow (fishing)	15	1894		1894		Erie, Pa.	May 4, 1905	Erie, Pa.	May 4, 1904	Do.
Richard K. Fox (canal)	131	1885	1899	1894		Lockport, N. Y.	July 18, 1905	Buffalo, N. Y.	Aug. 3, 1904	Do.
Ryan (canal) [b]	126	1890		1890		Buffalo, N. Y.	Oct. 28, 1905	do	Oct. 20, 1904	Do.
Rocket (fishing)	39	1901		1901		do	Nov. 1, 1905	Erie, Pa.	July 29, 1904	Do.
Silver Spray (fishing)	40	1889	1903	1889		do	June 6, 1905	do	June 14, 1904	Do.
Stranger (canal)	135	1881	1303	1891		do	Sept. 19, 1905	Buffalo, N. Y.	Sept. 6, 1904	Do.
S. L. Clark (canal)	125	1894		1894		Phoenix, N. Y.	Sept. 27, 1905	do	Sept. 14, 1904	Do.
Tim Desmond (fishing)	31	1898		1898		Buffalo, N. Y.	June 29, 1905	Erie, Pa.	July 11, 1904	Do.
Trenton (sand dredge)	517	1905		1898		do	July 13, 1905	Buffalo, N. Y.	First inspn	
The All Blue (delivery)	6	1890		1889		do	July 28, 1905	Tonawanda, N. Y.	July 27, 1904	Do.
Uncle (fishing)	14	1900		1894		Erie, Pa.	do	Erie, Pa.	June 7, 1904	Do.
Viola (fishing)	30	1887	1901	1888		Saugatuck, Mich.	Aug. 14, 1905	Dunkirk, N. Y.	Aug. 11, 1904	Do.
Wm. M. Mills (delivery)	5	1901		1902		Tonawanda, N. Y.	Apr. 14, 1905	Tonawanda, N. Y.	Apr. 12, 1904	Do.
Walter J. (delivery)	9	1896		1895		do	July 3, 1905	Buffalo, N. Y.	Apr. 26, 1904	Do.
W. J. McCarter (fishing)	18	1886	1902	1892		Erie, Pa.	July 28, 1905	Erie, Pa.	July 29, 1904	Do.
Welcome (fishing)	4	1888		1888		do	Sept. 5, 1905	do	Sept. 10, 1904	Do.
William Hengerer (canal)	125	1894		1894		Phoenix, N. Y.	do	Buffalo, N. Y.	Sept. 16, 1904	Do.
W. J. Hingston (fishing)	22	1894		1894		Buffalo, N. Y.	Sept. 19, 1905	Erie, Pa.	July 29, 1904	Do.
William F. Hallstead (fishing)	18	1892	1904	1892		do	Oct. 9, 1905	Dunkirk, N. Y.	Oct. 22, 1904	Do.

LOCAL DISTRICT OF BURLINGTON, VT.

Names of vessels and class.	Gross tonnage.	Hull built.	Hull rebuilt.	Boilers built.	Boilers rebuilt.	Where built.	Date of inspection.	Where inspected.	Date of previous inspection.	Local district where previously inspected.
Inland passenger steamers.										
Alexander	18	1899		1899		Vergennes, Vt.	May 26, 1905	Vergennes, Vt.	May 26, 1904	Burlington, Vt.
Chateaugay	742	1888		1887		Shelburne, Vt.	Apr. 15, 1905	Shelburne, Vt.	Apr. 14, 1904	Do.
Dresden	c 15	1898		1897		Dresden, N. Y.	Apr. 25, 1905	Dresden, N. Y.	Apr. 23, 1904	Do.
Eloise	40	1881		1902		Athens, N. Y.	June 8, 1905	Whitehall, N. Y.	June 9, 1904	Do.
Liberty	18	1900		1900		St. Albans, Vt.	May 31, 1905	St. Albans, Vt.	May 25, 1904	Do.
Maquam	370	1880		1897		Grand Isle, Vt.	June 12, 1905	Shelburne, Vt.	June 14, 1904	Do.
Mariquita	11	1873	1894	1888		Rhinebeck, N. Y.	July 31, 1905	Burlington, Vt.	Aug. 3, 1904	Do.
Ruth M. [d]	c 4	1897		1897		Troy, N. Y.	Aug. 10, 1905	Plattsburg, N. Y.	Aug. 10, 1904	Do.
Saranac	7	1890		1890		Shelburne, Vt.	July 3, 1905	Shelburne, Vt.	July 2, 1901	Do.
Vermont	1,195	1903		1903		do	May 23, 1905	do	May 24, 1904	Do.
Victor	26	1897		1897		Vergennes, Vt.	May 26, 1905	Vergennes, Vt.	May 26, 1904	Do.
Yioco	c 10	1903		1903		Derby, Vt.	Aug. 3, 1905	Newport, Vt.	Aug. 4, 1904	Do.

Ferry steamer.										
G. R. Sherman	92	1890	....	1890	....	Champlain, N. Y.	June 15, 1905	Port Henry, N. Y.	June 16, 1904	Burlington, Vt.
Inland towing steamers.										
Champlain	c5	1899	....	1899	....	Caldwell, N. Y.	Apr. 19, 1905	Whitehall, N. Y.	First inspn.	
Defender	87	1895	....	1895	....	Baltimore, Md.	Apr. 18, 1905	....do	Apr. 18, 1904	Burlington, Vt.
H. G. Tisdale	81	1872	....	1896	....	Philadelphia, Pa.	....do	....do	....do	Do.
J. G. Witherbee	114	1872	....	1891	....	....do	Apr. 19, 1905	....do	....do	Do.
Pastime	c10	1896	....	1892	1903	Swanton, Vt.	June 10, 1905	Burlington, Vt.	June 18, 1904	Do.
Peggy	c3	1882	....	1893	....	Hoboken, N. J.	July 8, 1905	Rouses Point, N. Y.	July 8, 1904	Do.
Robert H. Cook	157	1882	....	1882	....	Buffalo, N. Y.	Apr. 18, 1905	Whitehall, N. Y.	Apr. 18, 1904	Do.
Steam pleasure yachts.										
Amy	c5	1892	....	1897	....	Whitehall, N. Y.	Aug. 14, 1905	Whitehall, N. Y.	Aug. 12, 1904	Burlington, Vt.
Ariel	18	1891	1897	1891	....	Champlain, N. Y.	July 8, 1905	Champlain, N. Y.	July 9, 1903	Do.
Cruiser	c4	1894	....	1895	1901	Boston, Mass.	June 23, 1905	St. Albans, Vt.	May 25, 1904	Do.
[illegible]ida	146	1900	....	1900	....	Morris Heights, N. Y.	June 17, 1905	Shelburne, Vt.	May 12, 1904	Do.
[illegible] L. Bissell	c3	1884	....	1884	....	Valcour, N. Y.	May 20, 1905	Plattsburg, N. Y.	May 18, 1904	Do.
Hilda	c4	1894	....	1901	....	Champlain, N. Y.	Aug. 23, 1905	Champlain, N. Y.	July 16, 1904	Do.
Kestrel	21	1892	....	1892	....	Charlestown, Mass.	June 17, 1905	Burlington, Vt.	June 2, 1904	Do.
Lady Anne [e]	c5	1893	....	1893	....	Bayonne, N. J.	June 28, 1905	Chazy, N. Y.	July 1, 1903	Do.
Marion	c3	1895	....	1896	....	Newport, Vt.	Aug. 3, 1905	Newport, Vt.	Aug. 4, 1904	Do.
Nettie	c4	1894	....	1893	....	Champlain, N. Y.	July 8, 1905	Rouses Point, N. Y.	July 8, 1904	Do.
Neshobe	c8	1896	1903	1895	....	Fort Ann, N. Y.	Aug. 14, 1905	Fort Ticonderoga, N. Y.	Oct. 2, 1903	Do.
Nymph	c9	1888	1898	1888	....	Champlain, N. Y.	July 5, 1905	Vergennes, Vt.	July 19, 1904	Do.
Okadus [f]	49	1897	....	1897	....	Newburg, N. Y.	July 6, 1905	Port Henry, N. Y.	Apr. 16, 1903	New York, N. Y.
Olympia	c5	1899	....	1896	....	St. Albans, Vt.	Aug. 15, 1905	St. Albans, Vt.	Aug. 15, 1904	Burlington, Vt.
Otter [g]	c1	1889	....	1895	....	Boston, Mass.	July 5, 1905	Vergennes, Vt.	Aug. 20, 1902	Do.
Refuge	c4	1901	....	1890	....	Shoreham, Vt.	June 26, 1905	Whitehall, N. Y.	June 9, 1904	Do.
Satellite	27	1887	....	1899	....	Brooklyn, N. Y.	July 8, 1905	Rouses Point, N. Y.	July 8, 1904	Do.
Valcour [h]	61	1895	....	1904	....	Nyack, N. Y.	July 1, 1905	Valcour, N. Y.	June 15, 1904	Do.
Zelina	c3	1885	....	1885	....	Essex, N. Y.	June 29, 1905	Westport, N. Y.	June 3, 1902	Do.

LOCAL DISTRICT OF OSWEGO, N. Y.

Inland passenger steamers.										
Aida	37	1882	....	1896	....	Bristol, R. I.	Oct. 17, 1905	Alexandria Bay, N. Y.	Oct. 12, 1904	New York, N. Y.
Brownie	13	1896	....	1897	1902	Rome, N. Y.	July 10, 1905	Clayton, N. Y.	July 8, 1904	Oswego, N. Y.
Castanet	54	1898	1903	1904	....	Alexandria Bay, N. Y.	May 20, 1905	Alexandria Bay, N. Y.	May 20, 1904	Do.
Columbia	26	1896	....	1890	....	Clayton, N. Y.	June 6, 1905	Clayton, N. Y.	June 1, 1904	Do.
Capt. Dave Wagoner	19	1901	....	1890	....	Alexandria Bay, N. Y.	June 14, 1905	Alexandria Bay, N. Y.	May 20, 1904	Do.

[a] Formerly Lizzie Crandall, 1899.
[b] Formerly Geo. W. Dimmers, 1905.
[c] Estimated.
[d] Formerly Ruth Field McLeod, 1901.
[e] Formerly Irene, 1901.
[f] Formerly Adrea, 1903.
[g] Formerly Camilla, 1905.
[h] Formerly Washita, 1903.

DOMESTIC VESSELS INSPECTED, YEAR ENDED DECEMBER 31, 1905—NINTH SUPERVISING DISTRICT—OSWEGO, N. Y.—Continued.

Names of vessels and class.	Gross tonnage.	Hull built.	Hull rebuilt.	Boilers built.	Boilers rebuilt.	Where built.	Date of inspection.	Where inspected.	Date of previous inspection.	Local district where previously inspected.
Inland passenger steamers—Continued.										
Cornelia	38	1882	1904	1903		Buffalo, N. Y.	June 19, 1905	Oswego, N. Y.	June 6, 1904	Oswego, N. Y.
Captain Visger	29	1895		1896		Alexandria Bay, N. Y.	June 29, 1905	Alexandria Bay, N. Y.	June 9, 1904	Do.
Cortland [a]	54	1895		1895		Buffalo, N. Y.	Oct. 2, 1905	Fair Haven, N. Y.	Oct. 3, 1904	Do.
Day Dream	10	1897		1904		Phoenix, N. Y.	June 2, 1905	Massena, N. Y.	May 11, 1904	Do.
Dewey	13	1899		1899		Dexter, N. Y.	June 26, 1905	Oswego, N. Y.	June 25, 1904	Do.
F. C. Woodworth	89	1901		1893		West Webster, N. Y.	May 29, 1905	Irondequoit Bay, N. Y.	May 27, 1904	Do.
H. P. Bigelow	46	1893		1893		Baldwinsville, N. Y.	June 21, 1905	Alexandria Bay, N. Y.	June 22, 1904	Do.
H. C. Leroy	81	1892	1901	1897		Sodus Point, N. Y.	June 26, 1905	Sodus Point, N. Y.	June 24, 1904	Do.
Islander [b]	118	1880	1902	1900		Clayton, N. Y.	May 6, 1905	Clayton, N. Y.	May 6, 1904	Do.
Indienne	26	1888		1895		Poughkeepsie, N. Y.	May 16, 1905	....do	May 13, 1904	Do.
Island Belle [c]	89	1879	1894	1895		Alexandria Bay, N. Y.	June 1, 1905	Alexandria Bay, N. Y.	July 18, 1904	Do.
Idler	57	1886	1904	1890	1904	Brooklyn, N. Y.	June 21, 1905	....do	June 18, 1904	Do.
I Wonder	16	1897		1895		Alexandria Bay, N. Y.	July 12, 1905	....do	July 15, 1904	Do.
John C. Howard	1,244	1903		1903		St. Clair, Mich.	Aug. 28, 1905	Ogdensburg, N. Y.	July 29, 1904	Do.
Little Mac	25	1886		1895		Buffalo, N. Y.	Aug. 15, 1905	Chaumont, N. Y.	Aug. 15, 1904	Do.
Lookout	28	1894	1903	1883		Hemlock, N. Y.	Aug. 17, 1905	Irondequoit Bay, N. Y.	Aug. 19, 1904	Do.
Mary [d]	174	1893		1893		Monroe, Mich.	June 3, 1905	Ogdensburg, N. Y.	June 1, 1904	Do.
Mabel	27	1901		1903		Clayton, N. Y.	June 22, 1905	Clayton, N. Y.	June 22, 1904	Do.
New Island Wanderer	123	1888		1888		Buffalo, N. Y.	May 4, 1905	Cape Vincent, N. Y.	May 4, 1904	Do.
Niagara	36	1899		1891		Grindstone, N. Y.	May 26, 1905	Clayton, N. Y.	May 21, 1904	Do.
New Westminster	34	1890		1897		Chaumont, N. Y.	July 11, 1905	Alexandria Bay, N. Y.	July 7, 1904	Do.
New York [e]	294	1887	1898	1887		Bath, Me.	July 13, 1905	Kingston, Ontario	June 11, 1904	Do.
Nightingale	56	1890		1896		Clayton, N. Y.	Sept. 4, 1905	Clayton, N. Y.	Aug. 31, 1904	Do.
Outing	15	1892		1896		Ogdensburg, N. Y.	July 26, 1905	Ogdensburg, N. Y.	July 22, 1904	Do.
Riverside	[f] 90	1892	1904	1895		Buffalo, N. Y.	May 19, 1905	Alexandria Bay, N. Y.	May 19, 1904	Do.
Ramona	57	1886		1902		Newburgh, N. Y.	June 9, 1905	Kingston, Ontario	June 10, 1904	Do.
Sirius	22	1885	1900	1895		Clayton, N. Y.	May 13, 1905	Massena, N. Y.	May 12, 1904	Do.
St. Lawrence	312	1884		1884		....do	May 23, 1905	Kingston, Ontario	May 5, 1904	Do.
Sunbeam	51	1888		1888		Buffalo, N. Y.	May 29, 1905	Oswego, N. Y.	May 28, 1904	Do.
Sophia	16	1894	1902	1902		Alexandria Bay, N. Y.	June 21, 1905	Alexandria Bay, N. Y.	June 18, 1904	Do.
Virginia	21	1897		1898		....do	May 18, 1905	....do	May 13, 1904	Do.
Ferry steamers.										
Henry Plumb	92	1874	1893	1874		Buffalo, N. Y.	June 13, 1905	Ogdensburg, N. Y.	June 17, 1904	Oswego, N. Y.
Wm. Armstrong	181	1876	1890	1903		Ogdensburg, N. Y.	Nov. 10, 1905	....do	Dec. 13, 1904	Do.

Inland freight steamers.										
Avon	1,417	1877		1904		Buffalo, N. Y.	Apr. 14, 1905	Ogdensburg, N. Y.	Apr. 14, 1904	Oswego, N. Y.
A. McVittie	2,046	1890		1889		Detroit, Mich.	May 17, 1905	do	May 19, 1904	Chicago, Ill.
F. H. Prince	2,047	1890		1890		do	May 3, 1905	do	May 16, 1904	Oswego, N. Y.
Frank D. Phelps	83	1903		1894		Chaumont, N. Y.	Aug. 26, 1905	Chaumont, N. Y.	Aug. 27, 1904	Do.
Gov. Smith	2,044	1889		1889		Detroit, Mich.	Sept. 13, 1905	Ogdensburg, N. Y.	Sept. 14, 1904	Do.
Grand View	17	1899		1899		Clayton, N. Y.	Sept. 21, 1905	Oswego, N. Y.	July 11, 1904	Do.
Harlow	575	1891		1891		Green Bay, Wis.	Apr. 19, 1905	Ogdensburg, N. Y.	Apr. 30, 1904	Cleveland, Ohio.
Hecla	1,110	1882		1889		Buffalo, N. Y.	Apr. 20, 1905	do	Apr. 22, 1904	Oswego, N. Y.
Hinckley	141	1901		1891		Chaumont, N. Y.	Sept. 4, 1905	Oswego, N. Y.	Aug. 28, 1904	Do.
Henry R. James	2,048	1890		1890		Detroit, Mich.	Sept. 19, 1905	Ogdensburg, N. Y.	June 27, 1904	Do.
John Rugee	1,216	1888		1888		Milwaukee, Wis.	Apr. 13, 1905	do	Apr. 21, 1904	Do.
James R. Langdon	2,044	1889		1889		Detroit, Mich.	Sept. 2, 1905	do	Sept. 6, 1904	Do.
Madagascar	1,697	1894		1894	1904	West Bay City, Mich.	Apr. 19, 1905	do	May 2, 1904	Chicago, Ill.
Monteagle	1,273	1884		1884		Buffalo, N. Y.	Apr. 22, 1905	Oswego, N. Y.	Apr. 19, 1904	Oswego, N.
Nicaragua	1,201	1894		1894		West Bay City, Mich.	July 28, 1905	Ogdensburg, N. Y.	July 28, 1904	Detroit, Mich.
Ringleader	121	1893	1903	1898		Alexandria Bay, N. Y.	June 12, 1905	Oswego, N. Y.	June 13, 1904	Oswego, N. Y.
St. Joseph	304	1867		1889		Buffalo, N. Y.	Apr. 17, 1905	do	Apr. 20, 1904	Do.
Samuel Marshall	755	1888		1888		Grand Haven, Mich.	July 26, 1905	Ogdensburg, N. Y.	Aug. 1, 1904	Detroit, Mich.
Wm. A. Haskell	1,530	1884		1884		Detroit, Mich.	Apr. 13, 1905	do	May 16, 1904	Oswego, N. Y.
Wm. J. Averell	1,603	1884		1884		do	May 3, 1905	do	do	Do.
W. J. Carter	235	1886		1886		Milwaukee, Wis.	May 9, 1905	Oswego, N. Y.	May 6, 1904	Buffalo, N. Y.
Inland towing steamers.										
Charley Ferris	54	1884	1896	1901		Oswego, N. Y.	May 1, 1905	Oswego, N. Y.	May 3, 1904	Oswego, N. Y.
Carrie	6	1896	1903	1889		Grindstone, N. Y.	Oct. 17, 1905	Alexandria Bay, N. Y.	Oct. 15, 1904	Do.
Geo. D. Seymour	76	1875	1901	1901		Buffalo, N. Y.	Apr. 14, 1905	Ogdensburg, N. Y.	Apr. 14, 1904	Do.
John Navagh	19	1883		1883		do	Apr. 28, 1905	Oswego, N. Y.	Apr. 28, 1904	Do.
Lizzie H	15	1888	1896	1888		Alexandria Bay, N. Y.	Sept. 14, 1905	Ogdensburg, N. Y.	Sept. 14, 1904	Do.
Milton	14	1876	1905	1905		Deseronto, Ontario.	June 13, 1905	do	Mar. 27, 1903	Do.
Mary P. Hall	96	1898		1902		Ogdensburg, N. Y.	Aug. 29, 1905	do	Aug. 30, 1904	Do.
Pandora	13	1889		1889		do	May 25, 1905	do	May 12, 1904	Do.
Queen	29	1897		1890		Buffalo, N. Y.	May 18, 1905	Alexandria Bay, N. Y.	May 13, 1904	Do.
Spencer Meade	f 12	1883	1903	1897		do	Aug. 29, 1905	Ogdensburg, N. Y.	Aug. 29, 1904	Do.
Wm. L. Proctor	117	1883		1900		do	Apr. 20, 1905	do	Apr. 22, 1904	Do.
William Avery	9	1869	1904	1897		do	June 5, 1905	Oswego, N. Y.	June 7, 1904	Do.
Steam pleasure yachts.										
Amabel	29	1894		1897		Nyack, N. Y.	June 7, 1905	Alexandria Bay, N. Y.	June 2, 1904	Oswego, N. Y.
Charlietta	17	1895		1903		do	June 15, 1905	Clayton, N. Y.	June 3, 1904	Do.
Crescent	g 4	1890		1895		Brooklyn, N. Y.	July 19, 1905	Alexandria Bay, N. Y.	July 16, 1904	Do.
Calumet	153	1903		1903		Boston, Mass.	July 25, 1905	Clayton, N. Y.	July 21, 1904	Boston, Mass.
Clara	21	1899		1899		Ithaca, N. Y.	Sept. 12, 1905	Ithaca, N. Y.	Oct. 5, 1904	Oswego, N. Y.
Dorothy	g 5	1894		1894		Peekskill, N. Y.	June 16, 1905	Ogdensburg, N. Y.	June 17, 1904	Do.
Esther C.	23	1903		1901		Alexandria Bay, N. Y.	June 7, 1905	Alexandria Bay, N. Y.	June 2, 1904	Do.
Empress	50	1900		1900		Bristol, R. I.	do	do	June 10, 1904	New York, N. Y.

a Formerly Katharine T. Wilbur, 1904.
b Formerly John Thorn, 1888.
c Formerly Island Wanderer, 1894.
d Formerly F. S. Sterling, 1900.
e Formerly Shrewsbury, 1898.
f Readmeasured and tonnage reduced.
g Estimated.

DOMESTIC VESSELS INSPECTED, YEAR ENDED DECEMBER 31, 1905—NINTH SUPERVISING DISTRICT—OSWEGO, N. Y.—Continued.

Names of vessels and class.	Gross tonnage.	Hull built.	Hull rebuilt.	Boilers built.	Boilers rebuilt.	Where built.	Date of inspection.	Where inspected.	Date of previous inspection.	Local district where previously inspected.
Steam pleasure yachts—Con.										
Edna	[a]4	1892		1892		Chaumont, N. Y	July 22, 1905	Chaumont, N. Y	July 9, 1904	Oswego, N. Y.
Ezra Cornell	30	1900		1900		Ithaca, N. Y	Aug. 2, 1905	Cape Vincent, N. Y	July 16, 1903	Do.
Gadabout	9	1892	1896	1900		Phoenix, N. Y	Sept. 5, 1905	Thousand Islands Park, N. Y.	Aug. 13, 1904	Do.
Irene [b]	52	1897		1905		Bristol, R. I	May 19, 1905	Alexandria Bay, N. Y.	June 3, 1904	Do.
Imogene [c]	28	1896		1896		Poughkeepsie, N. Y	June 6, 1905	Clayton, N. Y	June 9, 1904	Do.
Jessie N	19	1883	1900	1899		Alexandria Bay, N. Y.	July 11, 1905	Alexandria Bay, N. Y.	June 3, 1904	Do.
Jean	28	1897		1904		Bristol, R. I	July 17, 1905	Clayton, N. Y	July 18, 1904	Do.
Karma	38	1900		1899		Ogdensburg, N. Y	June 3, 1905	Ogdensburg, N. Y	May 26, 1904	Do.
Louise	49	1893		1893		Bristol, R. I	May 18, 1905	Alexandria Bay, N. Y.	May 19, 1904	Do.
Lotus Seeker	15	1892		1904		do	May 26, 1905	Thousand Islands Park, N. Y.	May 21, 1904	Do.
Lee	4	1902		1895	1903	Clayton, N. Y	July 24, 1905	Clayton, N. Y	June 1, 1904	Do.
Lotus	52	1887		1887		Ogdensburg, N. Y	Sept. 14, 1905	Ogdensburg, N. Y	Sept. 14, 1904	Do.
Minga	22	1903		1903		Morris Heights, N. Y.	May 16, 1905	Clayton, N. Y	May 6, 1904	Do.
Mascot	[d]5	1904		1903		Alexandria Bay, N. Y.	June 6, 1905	Alexandria Bay, N. Y.	June 2, 1904	Do.
Mollie C	17	1899		1899		Boston, Mass	June 8, 1905	Clayton, N. Y	June 9, 1904	Do.
Mamie C	[a]4	1882		1882		Brooklyn, N. Y	June 14, 1905	Alexandria Bay, N. Y.	May 20, 1904	Do.
Mississippi	6	1895		1895		Alexandria Bay, N. Y.	June 28, 1905	do	May 13, 1904	Do.
Marjencha	17	1891	1894	1901		Nyack, N. Y	Aug. 9, 1905	Ogdensburg, N. Y	July 23, 1903	Do.
Navajo	42	1896		1896	1903	do	May 18, 1905	Alexandria Bay, N. Y.	May 20, 1904	Do.
Nereid	36	1882	1903	1901		Bristol, R. I	June 21, 1905	do	June 18, 1904	Do.
Now Then	25	1887		1904		do	July 10, 1905	Clayton, N. Y	July 6, 1904	Do.
Nella [e]	19	1895		1895	1901	Sheldrake, N. Y	July 18, 1905	Alexandria Bay, N. Y.	July 19, 1904	Do.
Nettie	11	1884	1895	1884		Ogdensburg, N. Y	Aug. 9, 1905	Ogdensburg, N. Y	July 8, 1904	Do.
Oswegatchie	32	1902		1902		Chicago, Ill	June 14, 1905	Alexandria Bay, N. Y.	June 22, 1904	Do.
Presto	22	1897		1897		Nyack, N. Y	June 6, 1905	do	May 19, 1904	Do.
Paul	[a]3	1890		1893		Clayton, N. Y	July 11, 1905	do	July 7, 1904	Do.
Professor	[a]4	1893		1893		Ogdensburg, N. Y	Aug. 29, 1905	Ogdensburg, N. Y	July 9, 1896	Do.
Rose [f]	47	1897		1904		New York, N. Y	June 8, 1905	Alexandria Bay, N. Y.	June 2, 1904	Do.
Stroller	26	1901		1901		Bristol, R. I	do	do	May 13, 1904	Do.
Sport	72	1881		1903		Newburgh, N. Y	July 11, 1905	do	July 7, 1904	Do.
Sallie	[a]5	1897		1904		Alexandria Bay, N. Y.	July 18, 1905	do	July 20, 1904	Do.
Surprise	20	1871		1884		Brooklyn, N. Y	July 29, 1905	Sacketts Harbor, N. Y.	July 25, 1904	Do.
Soubrette	[a]4	1891		1888	1899	Ogdensburg, N. Y	Aug. 30, 1905	Alexandria Bay, N. Y.	July 23, 1902	Do.
St. Charles	9	1902		1902		Canastota, N. Y	Sept. 11, 1905	Oswego, N. Y	First inspn.	
Venice [g]	60	1893		1901		Ithaca, N. Y	Aug. 19, 1905	Alexandria Bay, N. Y.	Aug. 20, 1904	Do.
Vesta	70	1893		1896		Brooklyn, N. Y	Aug. 30, 1905	do	Aug. 31, 1904	Cleveland, Ohio.
W. B	50	1889		1893		Poughkeepsie, N. Y	May 18, 1905	do	May 20, 1904	Oswego, N. Y.
Wyanoke	[d]5	1893		1892		Alexandria Bay, N. Y.	June 8, 1905	do	June 9, 1904	Do.

Miscellaneous steam vessel.										
Capt. Hemens (fishing)	34	1902		1891		Buffalo, N. Y.	Apr. 28, 1905	Sacketts Harbor, N.Y.	Aug. 21, 1903	Oswego, N. Y.
Gasoline motor vessel.										
Supply (freight)	17	1904				Alexandria Bay, N.Y.	Sept. 5, 1905	Clayton, N. Y.	Aug. 31, 1904	Oswego, N. Y.

LOCAL DISTRICT OF TOLEDO, OHIO.

Inland passenger steamers.										
Arrow	365	1895		1888		Wyandotte, Mich	Apr. 20, 1905	Sandusky, Ohio	Apr. 23, 1904	Toledo, Ohio.
A. Wehrle, jr	421	1889		1889		Sandusky, Ohio	July 11, 1905	....do	July 19, 1904	Do.
Cherokee	1,304	1889		1889		Marine City, Mich	Aug. 16, 1905	Toledo, Ohio	Aug. 18, 1904	Do.
Falcon	82	1887		1887		Buffalo, N. Y	May 17, 1905	Port Clinton, Ohio	May 23, 1904	Buffalo, N. Y.
Geo. L. Craig	3,762	1903		1903		Toledo, Ohio	Apr. 8, 1905	Toledo, Ohio	Apr. 26, 1904	Do.
Grandon	47	1893		1874		....do	Apr. 20, 1905	Sandusky, Ohio	Apr. 23, 1904	Toledo, Ohio.
Gerald C	36	1893		1894		Wyandotte, Mich	June 29, 1905	Port Clinton, Ohio	July 1, 1904	Do.
Iroquois	1,169	1901		1901		Toledo, Ohio	Apr. 12, 1905	Toledo, Ohio	July 22, 1903	Buffalo, N. Y.
James Fisk, jr	914	1870	1901	1891		Buffalo, N. Y	Apr. 18, 1905	....do	Apr. 19, 1904	Toledo, Ohio.
James P. Walsh	5,630	1905		1905		Toledo, Ohio	June 1, 1905	....do	First inspn.	
J. H. Wade	1,863	1890		1890		Cleveland, Ohio	June 10, 1905	....do	June 16, 1904	Milwaukee, Wis.
James H. Reed	5,598	1903		1903		Wyandotte, Mich	June 14, 1905	....do	....do	Duluth, Minn.
Louise	83	1878	1902	1886		Sandusky, Ohio	Apr. 11, 1905	Sandusky, Ohio	Apr. 11, 1904	Toledo, Ohio.
L. C. Waldo	4,466	1896	1905	1896		West Bay City, Mich	Apr. 18, 1905	Toledo, Ohio	June 15, 1904	Milwaukee, Wis.
Lucile	71	1883	1905	1883		Marine City, Mich	May 26, 1905	Sandusky, Ohio	May 20, 1904	Duluth, Minn.
Lakeside	285	1901		1901		Toledo, Ohio	Aug. 24, 1905	....do	Aug. 24, 1904	Toledo, Ohio.
Lakeside[h]	337	1901	1905	1905		....do	Dec. 16, 1905	Toledo, Ohio	Aug. 24, 1905	Do.
R. B. Hayes	164	1876	1902	1876		Sandusky, Ohio	May 9, 1905	Sandusky, Ohio	May 9, 1904	Do.
Inland freight steamers.										
A. G. Brower	3,582	1902		1901		South Chicago, Ill	May 31, 1905	Toledo, Ohio	June 7, 1904	Milwaukee, Wis.
City of Mt. Clemens	132	1884		1884		Mount Clemens, Mich	Apr. 17, 1905	....do	Apr. 19, 1904	Toledo, Ohio.
Cadillac	1,263	1892		1892		South Chicago, Ill	June 5, 1905	....do	June 13, 1904	Cleveland, Ohio.
Choctaw	1,573	1892		1892		Cleveland, Ohio	June 16, 1905	....do	June 18, 1904	Do.
Charlemagne Tower, jr	1,825	1886		1886		....do	June 17, 1905	....do	June 20, 1904	Milwaukee, Wis.
Case	2,278	1889		1889		....do	June 20, 1905	Huron, Ohio	....do	Do.
David W. Rust	884	1873		1887		East Saginaw, Mich	June 15, 1905	Toledo, Ohio	June 14, 1904	Toledo, Ohio.
E. W. Oglebay	3,666	1896		1896		West Bay City, Mich	May 31, 1905	....do	June 17, 1904	Milwaukee, Wis.
George J. Gould	2,237	1893		1893		Buffalo, N. Y	Apr. 12, 1905	....do	July 17, 1903	Toledo, Ohio.
General Orlando M. Poe	5,619	1900		1902		Cleveland, Ohio	May 9, 1905	Huron, Ohio	May 7, 1904	Chicago, Ill.
Gladstone	2,453	1888	1901	1887		....do	July 27, 1905	Sandusky, Ohio	Aug. 2, 1904	Port Huron, Mich.

a Estimated.
b Formerly Nina, 1903.
c Formerly Willawalla, 1903.
d Estimated. Tonnage reduced.
e Formerly Ezra Cornell 2d, 1900.
f Formerly Raynham, 1901.
g Formerly Clara, 1900.
h Lengthened and tonnage changed, 1905.

DOMESTIC VESSELS INSPECTED, YEAR ENDED DECEMBER 31, 1905—NINTH SUPERVISING DISTRICT—TOLEDO, OHIO—Continued.

Names of vessels and class.	Gross tonnage.	Hull built.	Hull rebuilt.	Boilers built.	Boilers rebuilt.	Where built.	Date of inspection.	Where inspected.	Date of previous inspection.	Local district where previously inspected.
Inland freight steamers—Con.										
Horace S. Wilkinson	3,860	1902		1901		Chicago, Ill	May 31, 1905	Toledo, Ohio	June 8, 1904	Milwaukee, Wis.
Helena	2,083	1888		1888		Sheboygan, Wis	June 6, 1905	do	June 6, 1904	Buffalo, N. Y.
Iroquois [a]	1,957	1892	1904	1892		Marine City, Mich	June 14, 1905	do	June 14, 1904	Detroit, Mich.
J. H. Devereux	1,618	1885		1897		Cleveland, Ohio	do	do	June 15, 1904	Do.
Lagonda	3,647	1896		1896		West Bay City, Mich	May 24, 1905	do	June 6, 1904	Toledo, Ohio.
M. A. Hanna	4,661	1899		1899		Cleveland, Ohio	June 1, 1905	do	June 8, 1904	Cleveland, Ohio.
Merrimac	1,398	1882		1892		Detroit, Mich	June 9, 1905	Sandusky, Ohio	do	Do.
Norma	111	1884	1900	1884		Sandusky, Ohio	May 22, 1905	do	May 21, 1904	Toledo, Ohio.
Neshoto	2,255	1889		1889		Cleveland, Ohio	June 8, 1905	Toledo, Ohio	June 17, 1904	Milwaukee, Wis.
Portage	1,106	1875	1905	1875		Buffalo, N. Y	May 6, 1905	do	June 6, 1903	Duluth, Minn.
William Henry Mack	3,781	1903		1903		Cleveland, Ohio	May 12, 1905	Sandusky, Ohio	May 19, 1904	Buffalo, N. Y.
William E. Reis	4,748	1900		1900		do	May 31, 1905	Toledo, Ohio	June 8, 1904	Cleveland, Ohio.
William H. Gratwick	2,818	1893		1893		West Bay City, Mich	June 6, 1905	do	June 13, 1904	Buffalo, N. Y.
Inland towing steamers.										
American Eagle	110	1880	1902	1880		Sandusky, Ohio	June 22, 1905	do	June 15, 1904	Toledo, Ohio.
Alfred Noble	50	1905		1905		Toledo, Ohio	July 21, 1905	do	First inspn.	
Alpha	86	1881		1881		Chicago, Ill	Nov. 22, 1905	do	Nov. 23, 1904	Do.
Bad Boy	6	1883		1878		Toledo, Ohio	June 30, 1905	do	May 12, 1904	Do.
Charles E. Bolton	20	1882		1882		Lorain, Ohio	May 15, 1905	do	May 9, 1904	Do.
Craig	32	1905		1888		Toledo, Ohio	June 26, 1905	do	First inspn.	
Dan W. Miller	10	1899		1905		do	May 3, 1905	do	May 6, 1904	Do.
Erie	21	1888		1901		Sandusky, Ohio	Aug. 7, 1905	Port Clinton, Ohio	July 28, 1904	Do.
E. E. Rice	38	1888		1888		Saugatuck, Mich	Oct. 5, 1905	Huron, Ohio	Oct. 6, 1904	Cleveland, Ohio.
Frank S. Butler	38	1865		1875		Chicago, Ill	May 1, 1905	Toledo, Ohio	May 7, 1904	Toledo, Ohio.
Fannie L. Baker	43	1888		1891		Detroit, Mich	Nov. 18, 1905	do	Oct. 12, 1904	Do.
G. H. Breymann	60	1903		1893		Toledo, Ohio	May 11, 1905	do	May 11, 1904	Cleveland, Ohio.
Ina	16	1881		1891		Buffalo, N. Y	Apr. 3, 1905	Put in Bay, Ohio	Mar. 29, 1904	Toledo, Ohio.
J. S. Blazier	87	1867	1890	1890		East Saginaw, Mich	July 24, 1905	Toledo, Ohio	July 21, 1904	Cleveland, Ohio.
John E. Monk	36	1887		1887		Sandusky, Ohio	Aug. 11, 1905	Sandusky, Ohio	Aug. 10, 1904	Toledo, Ohio.
L. Birckhead	32	1883	1905	1892		Toledo, Ohio	Oct. 30, 1905	Toledo, Ohio	June 8, 1904	Do.
Miller Bros	13	1900		1904		do	Apr. 26, 1905	do	Apr. 26, 1904	Do.
Pallister	34	1873	1900	1888		do	May 1, 1905	do	Apr. 30, 1904	Do.
Richard B	63	1901		1900		Vermillion, Ohio	Mar. 23, 1905	Port Clinton, Ohio	Mar. 23, 1904	Do.
Roger C. Sullivan	51	1903		1903		Toledo, Ohio	Apr. 15, 1905	Toledo, Ohio	Apr. 15, 1904	Do.
Sheboygan	62	1886	1905	1886		Sheboygan, Wis	May 11, 1905	do	May 7, 1904	Do.
The M. I. Wilcox Co	14	1880	1890	1887		Buffalo, N. Y	May 25, 1905	do	May 27, 1904	Do.
Warnick	24	1880	1899	1881		do	Apr. 1, 1905	do	May 18, 1904	Do.
Wm. McCarthy	80	1897		1897		Benton Harbor, Mich	Apr. 24, 1905	do	Apr. 26, 1904	Do.
Wau Bun [a]	77	1887	1904	1887		Manitowoc, Wis	May 29, 1905	do	June 6, 1904	Milwaukee, Wis.

Steam pleasure yachts.										
Avalon	4	1901	....	1903	....	Toledo, Ohio	May 20, 1905	....do	Sept. 29, 1903	Toledo, Ohio.
Cygnet	8	1886	1901	1900	....	Detroit, Mich	May 24, 1905	....do	May 25, 1904	Do.
Edith	67	1904	....	1904	....	Toledo, Ohio	Aug. 1, 1905	....do	Aug. 4, 1904	Do.
Lotus	2	1891	....	1895	....	Cleveland, Ohio	Oct. 17, 1905	Winous Point, Ohio	Oct. 19, 1904	Do.
Novia	7	1892	....	1900	....	Detroit, Mich	July 18, 1905	Toledo, Ohio	June 30, 1904	Do.
Pluto [b]	4	1883	1901	1887	....	....do	July 12, 1905	....do	July 13, 1903	Do.
Sigma	158	1883	1901	1901	....	Trenton, Mich	....do	....do	June 28, 1904	Do.
Miscellaneous steamers.										
Arctic (pile driver)	23	1891	....	1891	....	Sandusky, Ohio	Mar. 23, 1905	Sandusky, Ohio	Mar. 29, 1904	Toledo, Ohio.
Active (fishing)	18	1894	1897	1894	....	Port Clinton, Ohio	....do	Vermilion, Ohio	Mar. 23, 1904	Do.
A. Foster (sand dredge)	93	1899	....	1904	....	Fremont, Ohio	Sept. 7, 1905	Fremont, Ohio	Sept. 7, 1904	Do.
Bessie (sand dredge)	89	1880	....	1880	....	Fairhaven, Mich	Apr. 20, 1905	Sandusky, Ohio	Apr. 23, 1904	Do.
Commerce (sand dredge)	112	1878	....	1901	....	Milwaukee, Wis	June 19, 1905	Toledo, Ohio	June 17, 1904	Do.
Charles P. Stricker (fishing)	13	1892	....	1892	....	Buffalo, N. Y	July 14, 1905	Vermilion, Ohio	July 19, 1904	Do.
C. H. Lamb (fishing)	22	1891	1899	1891	....	....do	Aug. 4, 1905	Toledo, Ohio	June 28, 1904	Do.
D. Dussault (sand dredge)	55	1886	....	1886	....	Sandusky, Ohio	May 19, 1905	....do	May 23, 1904	Do.
Duchess (fishing)	30	1887	....	1890	....	Geneva, N. Y	May 22, 1905	Sandusky, Ohio	June 4, 1904	Do.
Ella G. (sand dredge)	115	1882	1892	1878	....	Port Clinton, Ohio	Nov. 3, 1905	Toledo, Ohio	Nov. 3, 1904	Do.
Frank & Jim (fishing)	26	1903	....	1884	....	Buffalo, N. Y	Aug. 11, 1905	Sandusky, Ohio	Aug. 11, 1904	Buffalo, N. Y.
Fred Driscoll (fishing)	30	1902	....	1887	....	Lorain, Ohio	Oct. 28, 1905	Vermilion, Ohio	Oct. 29, 1904	Toledo, Ohio.
George E. Fisher (fishing)	25	1883	1895	1883	....	Detroit, Mich	Nov. 13, 1905	Huron, Ohio	Nov. 17, 1904	Do.
John Smith (fishing)	14	1876	{ 1898 1903 }	1878	....	Manistee, Mich	Mar. 23, 1905	....do	Mar. 26, 1904	Buffalo, N. Y.
Jas. P. Devney (fishing)	27	1890	1895	1898	....	Ashtabula, Ohio	Oct. 28, 1905	Vermilion, Ohio	Oct. 29, 1904	Toledo, Ohio.
L. P. Powell (sand dredge)	143	1903	....	1889	....	Marine City, Mich	May 18, 1905	Toledo, Ohio	May 18, 1904	Do.
Laura D. (sand dredge)	135	1891	....	1903	....	Toledo, Ohio	May 25, 1905	....do	May 25, 1904	Do.
Mary and Norman (fishing)	17	1891	1895	1892	....	Ashtabula, Ohio	Mar. 9, 1905	Vermilion, Ohio	Mar. 7, 1904	Do.
Mogul (pile driver)	23	1889	....	1891	....	Huron, Ohio	May [illegible], 1905	Huron, Ohio	May 9, 1904	Do.
Mary H. (sand dredge)	208	1886	1897	1892	....	Nicollet, Wis	June 29, 1905	Sandusky, Ohio	July 2, 1904	Do.
Messenger (fishing)	48	1880	1900	1901	....	Buffalo, N. Y	Nov. 14, 1905	Toledo, Ohio	Nov. 14, 1904	Do.
Oliver H. Perry (fishing)	76	1902	....	1902	....	Ashtabula, Ohio	Sept. 30, 1905	Port Clinton, Ohio	Oct. 4, 1904	Do.
Protection (sand dredge)	161	1888	1904	1903	....	Sault Ste. Marie, Mich	July 11, 1905	Sandusky, Ohio	July 11, 1904	Do.
R. E. Doville (sand dredge)	199	1905	....	1905	....	Toledo, Ohio	Apr. 15, 1905	Toledo, Ohio	First inspn	
Roma (fishing)	15	1900	....	1897	....	Monroe, Mich	Nov. 21, 1905	....do	Dec. 3, 1904	Do.
Syracuse (sand dredge)	85	1897	....	1895	....	Toledo, Ohio	Apr. 8, 1905	....do	Apr. 8, 1904	Do.
Sheldon Bros. (fishing)	13	1900	....	1889	....	Erie, Pa	Nov. 13, 1905	Vermilion, Ohio	Nov. 10, 1904	Buffalo, N. Y.
Silver Spray (fishing)	33	1898	....	1887	....	Sandusky, Ohio	Sept. 26, 1905	Sandusky, Ohio	Sept. 26, 1904	Toledo, Ohio.
Walter D. (sand dredge)	136	1891	....	1891	....	Toledo, Ohio	May 25, 1905	Toledo, Ohio	May 23, 1904	Do.
Wm. F. Plietz (pile driver)	29	1902	....	1888	....	Vermilion, Ohio	Dec. 9, 1905	Vermilion, Ohio	Dec. 9, 1904	Do.
Vessel propelled by gasoline motor.										
Columbus (passenger)	26	1905	....	....	....	Sandusky, Ohio	Aug. 3, 1905	Sandusky, Ohio	First inspn	

[a] Rebuilt and tonnage changed, 1904

[b] Formerly Moxie, 1905.

DOMESTIC VESSELS INSPECTED, YEAR ENDED DECEMBER 31, 1905—Continued.

TENTH SUPERVISING DISTRICT.

LOCAL DISTRICT OF NEW ORLEANS, LA.

Names of vessels and class.	Gross tonnage.	Hull built.	Hull rebuilt.	Boilers built.	Boilers rebuilt.	Where built.	Date of inspection.	Where inspected.	Date of previous inspection.	Local district where previously inspected.
Ocean passenger steamers.										
Alpha	233	1887		1891		Washington, N. C	Apr. 25, 1905	New Orleans, La	Apr. 11, 1904	Mobile, Ala.
Arkadia	2,206	1895		1895		Stockton, England	Nov. 6, 1905	do	Nov. 23, 1904	New Orleans, La.
Comus	4,828	1900		1900		Newport News, Va	Jan. 17, 1905	do	Jan. 19, 1904	Do.
Excelsior	3,542	1882		1882		Wilmington, Del	Sept. 9, 1905	do	Sept. 16, 1904	Do.
Proteus	4,836	1900		1899		Newport News, Va	Mar. 22, 1905	do	Mar. 22, 1904	Do.
San Juan	3,503	1899		1899		Wilmington, Del	Mar. 8, 1905	do	Feb. 18, 1904	Do.
Inland passenger steamers.										
Amy Hewes	85	1903		1903		Franklin, La	Jan. 29, 1905	New Orleans, La	Jan. 27, 1905	New Orleans, La.
Asa	34	1895		1889		Pearlington, Miss	Feb. 7, 1905	Pearlington, Miss	Feb. 9, 1904	Do.
Assistance	100	1888		1888		Camden, N. J	May 4, 1905	Quarantine, La	May 5, 1904	Do.
American	190	1902		1902		New Decatur, Ala	May 13, 1905	New Orleans, La	May 9, 1904	Do.
Adelaide	25	1897		1903		Scranton, Miss	May 19, 1905	do	May 13, 1904	Mobile, Ala.
Alexander M. Stewart	38	1888	1905	1888		Saginaw, Mich	June 15, 1905	Donaldsonville, La	Aug. 29, 1903	New Orleans, La.
Alice	132	1898	1904	1893		Madisonville, La	Sept. 10, 1905	New Orleans, La	Aug. 29, 1904	Do.
Alert	15	1888		1888		New Orleans, La	Oct. 13, 1905	do	Oct. 17, 1904	Do.
Addie T	97	1904		1893		Higginsport, Ohio	Oct. 17, 1905	Vicksburg, Miss	Aug. 30, 1904	Cincinnati, Ohio.
Albert Hanson	92	1896		1896		Franklin, La	Nov. 28, 1905	Franklin, La	Nov. 30, 1904	New Orleans, La.
America	427	1898		1898		Jeffersonville, Ind	Dec. 28, 1905	New Orleans, La	Dec. 30, 1904	Do.
Buras[a]	29	1894		1898		Saugatuck, Mich	Dec. 31, 1904	do	Dec. 30, 1903	Do.
Bob Blanks	265	1904		1904		Jeffersonville, Ind	Jan. 31, 1905	do	Jan. 21, 1904	Louisville, Ky.
Buckingham	25	1901		1900		Belle Isle, La	Feb. 18, 1905	Avery Island, La	Jan. 28, 1904	New Orleans, La.
Betsy Ann	296	1899		1899		Dubuque, Iowa	Apr. 18, 1905	Natchez, Miss	Apr. 14, 1904	Do.
Belle of the Bend	405	1898		1898		Jeffersonville, Ind	do	Vicksburg, Miss	Apr. 16, 1904	Do.
Biloxi	33	1897		1897		Biloxi, Miss	May 17, 1905	Slidell, La	May 30, 1904	Do.
Borealis Rex	89	1888		1888		Stillwater, Miss	May 29, 1905	Morgan City, La	June 7, 1904	Do.
Buras	29	1894		1898		Saugatuck, Mich	Nov. 13, 1905	New Orleans, La	Dec. 31, 1904	Do.
Corsair	95	1884		1883		Camden, N. J	Jan. 18, 1905	do	Jan. 18, 1904	Do.
Charlie Curlin	92	1895		1895		Jeffersonville, Ind	Jan. 26, 1905	Vacherie, La	Jan. 5, 1904	Do.
City of Greenwood	97	1899		1899		do	Feb. 16, 1905	Yazoo City, Miss	Feb. 25, 1904	Do.
Claribel	39	1891		1898		Benton Harbor, Mich	June 22, 1905	New Orleans, La	June 13, 1904	Do.
Carrie B. Schwing	98	1904		1904		Plaquemine, La	July 29, 1905	Plaquemine, La	July 26, 1904	Do.
Cecile	26	1903		1903		Des Allemands, La	Oct. 30, 1905	Des Allemands, La	Sept. 13, 1904	Do.
Columbia	139	1903		1903		Jeffersonville, Ind	Nov. 1, 1905	New Orleans, La	Nov. 2, 1904	Do.
Elk[b]	100	1894		1894		Peoria, Ill	Dec. 13, 1904	Vicksburg, Miss	Dec. 9, 1903	Do.
Electra[c]	372	1897		1897		Jeffersonville, Ind	Dec. 27, 1904	New Orleans, La	Nov. 17, 1903	Do.

El Mozo	103	1890		1890		Algiers, La	Jan. 5, 1905	do	Jan. 5, 1904	Do.
El Vivo	199	1902		1901		New Orleans, La	Feb. 22, 1905	do	Feb. 26, 1904	Do.
E. L. Russell	206	1899		1899		Camden, N. J	Feb. 24, 1905	do	Feb. 17, 1904	Do.
Ellwood	77	1903		1902		Belle Isle, La	Aug. 19, 1905	Burwood, La	Aug. 26, 1904	Do.
Edgar	34	1901		1901		Scranton, Miss	Oct. 27, 1905	Logtown, Miss	Aug. 4, 1904	Do.
Elizabeth Hyde	39	1900		1900		Ferrysburg, Mich	Nov. 11, 1905	Natchez, Miss	Nov. 18, 1904	Do.
Ella Andrews	64	1879		1893		Philadelphia, Pa	Nov. 22, 1905	New Orleans, La	Nov. 23, 1904	Do.
El Mozo	103	1890		1890		Algiers, La	Dec. 27, 1904	do	Jan. 5, 1905	Do.
Fox	35	1878		1903		Philadelphia, Pa	Jan. 4, 1905	do	Dec. 23, 1903	Do.
F. Weyerhauser	216	1893		1895		Rock Island, Ill	Apr. 3, 1905	do	Apr. 2, 1904	Do.
Frank B. Hayne	90	1904		1904		Jeffersonville, Ind	May 5, 1905	Monroe, La	Apr. 31, 1904	Louisville, Ky.
Grover Cleveland	114	1884	1902	1885		New Orleans, La	Mar. 22, 1905	New Orleans, La	Mar. 21, 1904	New Orleans, La.
Grand Isle	47	1899		1903		Ashwood, La	June 23, 1905	do	June 24, 1904	Do.
Gem	97	1898		1898		Jeffersonville, Ind	Sept. 25, 1905	do	Sept. 14, 1904	Do.
Handy [d]	49	1903		1903		do	Dec. 23, 1904	Monroe, La	Dec. 29, 1903	Louisville, Ky.
Hale	53	1901		1901		Harvey, La	Nov. 29, 1905	New Orleans, La	Nov. 9, 1904	New Orleans, La.
Handy	49	1903		1903		Jeffersonville, Ind	Dec. 15, 1905	Monroe, La	Dec. 23, 1904	Do.
Imperial	494	1894		1894		do	Jan. 6, 1905	New Orleans, La	Jan. 7, 1904	Do.
Independent	37	1897		1897		New Orleans, La	Jan. 17, 1905	do	Jan. 18, 1904	Do.
J. W. Swayze [c]	86	1896		1874		Jonesville, La	Dec. 29, 1904	Jonesville, La	Dec. 10, 1903	Do.
Jennie Louise	77	1890		1875		Patterson, La	Apr. 28, 1905	Berwick, La	Apr. 27, 1904	Do.
J. E. Trudeau	242	1889		1889		Jeffersonville, Ind	June 8, 1905	New Orleans, La	June 11, 1904	Do.
Jesse	81	1890	1902	1902		Madisonville, La	Sept. 21, 1905	do	Sept. 22, 1904	Do.
J. P. Schuh	117	1901		1901		Mobile, Ala	Oct. 25, 1905	Plaquemine, La	Aug. 5, 1904	Mobile, Ala.
Little Rufus [f]	278	1903		1903		Stillwater, Minn	Dec. 14, 1904	Natchez, Miss	Nov. 4, 1903	New Orleans, La.
Louisiana	56	1888	1899	1895		New Orleans, La	Apr. 14, 1905	New Orleans, La	Apr. 8, 1904	Do.
Leo	89	1882		1893		Philadelphia, Pa	July 11, 1905	do	July 11, 1904	Do.
Louise	126	1887		1882		New Orleans, La	Sept. 2, 1905	do	Oct. 31, 1904	Do.
Lafourche	398	1888		1888		Jeffersonville, Ind	Oct. 18, 1905	do	Oct. 19, 1904	Do.
Little Rufus	278	1903		1903		Stillwater, Minn	Dec. 11, 1905	Natchez, Miss	Dec. 14, 1904	Do.
Meta	33	1899		1901		Madisonville, La	Mar. 14, 1905	New Orleans, La	Mar. 2, 1904	Do.
Mary B. Curtis	78	1873		1893		Portland, Me	May 23, 1905	do	May 23, 1904	Mobile, Ala.
Mabel Comeaux	397	1891		1891		Jeffersonville, Ind	Oct. 5, 1905	do	Oct. 13, 1904	Do.
Mark A. Morse	17	1901		1901		New Orleans, La	Oct. 15, 1905	Pilot Town, La	Oct. 23, 1904	Do.
Millie W	41	1902		1897		Patterson, La	Nov. 18, 1905	Morgan City, La	Aug. 11, 1904	Do.
Minnie B	30	1882	1903	1903		Chicago, Ill	Dec. 8, 1905	Manchac, La	Dec. 9, 1904	Do.
New Camelia	270	1878	1892	1899		New Orleans, La	Apr. 4, 1905	New Orleans, La	Mar. 26, 1904	Do.
Natchez	584	1891		1891		Jeffersonville, Ind	Oct. 19, 1905	do	Nov. 14, 1904	New Orleans, La.
Polo	41	1904		1904		New Orleans, La	Jan. 20, 1905	Buras, La	Jan. 18, 1904	Do.
Pelican	60	1892	1903	1892		do	Feb. 7, 1905	Pearlington, Miss	Feb. 9, 1904	Do.
Pearlington	30	1891		1900		Pearlington, Miss	do	do	do	Do.
Providence	11	1893		1905		Chicago, Ill	July 31, 1905	New Orleans, La	June 17, 1904	Do.
Peri	71	1893		1905		Berwick, La	Oct. 15, 1905	Berwick, La	Oct. 15, 1904	Do.
R. C. Veit	192	1891		1895		Atkins, N. J	May 16, 1905	New Orleans, La	May 11, 1904	Do.
R. W. Wilmot	569	1898		1898		Cleveland, Ohio	Oct. 16, 1905	do	Oct. 17, 1904	Do.
Robbie	43	1896		1896		Madison, Ind	Oct. 30, 1905	Grand Bayou, La	Sept. 20, 1904	Do.
Roberta	94	1903		1903		Jeffersonville, Ind	Nov. 22, 1905	New Orleans, La	Nov. 23, 1904	Do.
St. Joseph [g]	277	1893		1892		Madison, Ind	Dec. 14, 1904	Natchez, Miss	Dec. 11, 1903	Do.
Sadie Downman	86	1899		1890		Morgan City, La	Jan. 28, 1905	New Iberia, La	Jan. 27, 1904	Do.

[a] Certificated Jan. 10, 1906.
[b] Certificated Feb. 11, 1905.
[c] Certificated Mar. 13, 1905.
[d] Certificated Jan. 4, 1905.
[e] Certificated Jan. 23, 1905.
[f] Certificated Mar. 15, 1905.
[g] Certificated May 3, 1905.

DOMESTIC VESSELS INSPECTED, YEAR ENDED DECEMBER 31, 1905—TENTH SUPERVISING DISTRICT—NEW ORLEANS, LA.—Continued.

Names of vessels and class.	Gross tonnage.	Hull built.	Hull rebuilt.	Boilers built.	Boilers rebuilt.	Where built.	Date of inspection.	Where inspected.	Date of previous inspection.	Local district where previously inspected.
Inland passenger steamers—Continued.										
St. Tammany	75	1904		1904		Slidell, La	Feb. 6, 1905	New Orleans, La	Feb. 2, 1904	New Orleans, La.
Stella	80	1880		1893		Camden, N. J	Mar. 3, 1905	Burwood, La	Feb. 23, 1904	Do.
Sewanee	90	1904		1904		Patterson, La	Mar. 10, 1905	Morgan City, La	Mar. 12, 1904	Do.
Stella	82	1904		1904		Jeffersonville, Ind	Apr. 16, 1905	Yazoo City, Miss	Apr. 11, 1904	Evansville, Ind.
Sarah	92	1885	1903	1903		Logtown, Miss	May 9, 1905	Logtown, Miss	May 6, 1904	New Orleans, La.
Senator Cordill	280	1902		1902		Jeffersonville, Ind	May 13, 1905	Natchez, Miss	May 10, 1904	Do.
St. John	19	1905		1905		Madisonville, La	May 24, 1905	New Orleans, La	First inspn.	
St. James	344	1898		1898		Cincinnati, Ohio	July 24, 1905	do	July 25, 1904	Do.
Samson	159	1881		1889		Camden, N. J	Sept. 6, 1905	do	Sept. 6, 1904	Do.
Saccharine	218	1883		1901		New Orleans, La	Nov. 18, 1905	Morgan City, La	Nov. 29, 1904	Do.
Taurus	228	1885		1897		Philadelphia, Pa	Sept. 18, 1905	New Orleans, La	Sept. 17, 1904	Do.
Underwriter	170	1881		1903		Camden, N. J	Oct. 14, 1905	Pilot Town, La	Oct. 22, 1904	Do.
Verne Swain	155	1904		1904		Stillwater, Minn	June 26, 1905	Natchez, Miss	June 29, 1904	St. Paul, Minn.
Virgie	70	1903		1903		New Orleans, La	Oct. 24, 1905	Donaldsonville, La	Nov. 16, 1904	New Orleans, La.
W. T. Scovell [a]	244	1895		1895		Jeffersonville, Ind	Dec. 27, 1904	New Orleans, La	Dec. 28, 1903	Do.
Wm. Garig	193	1904		1898		do	June 26, 1905	do	June 22, 1904	Louisville, Ky.
W. M. Wood	58	1880		1880		Philadelphia, Pa	Oct. 16, 1905	do	Oct. 21, 1904	New Orleans, La.
Whitewater	61	1875		1893		Camden, N. J	Nov. 8, 1905	do	Nov. 8, 1904	Do.
W. G. Wilmot	150	1892		1892		West Bay City, Mich	Nov. 9, 1905	do	Nov. 12, 1904	Do.
Ferry steamers.										
Ascension	99	1896		1888		Donaldsonville, La	Mar. 1, 1905	New Orleans, La	Aug. 27, 1903	New Orleans, La.
A. M. Halliday	207	1903		1903		Jeffersonville, Ind	May 10, 1905	do	May 9, 1904	Do.
Alice	149	1900		1900		Ramos, La	Aug. 31, 1905	do	Aug. 31, 1904	Do.
Belle of Jefferson	69	1889		1889		Berwick, La	Mar. 25, 1905	do	Mar. 25, 1904	Do.
Brookhill	9	1899		1899		Chicago, Ill	Oct. 18, 1905	Baton Rouge, La	Oct. 25, 1904	Do.
Carrier	1,749	1892		1893		Newberg, N. Y	July 21, 1905	New Orleans, La	July 20, 1904	Do.
El Capitan	88	1903		1903		St. Louis, Mo	Mar. 17, 1905	Natchez, Miss	Mar. 13, 1904	Do.
Emma	90	1882		1882		Algiers, La	May 15, 1905	New Orleans, La	May 15, 1904	Do.
Gouldsboro	469	1875		1900		Carondelet, Mo	June 9, 1905	do	June 10, 1904	Do.
Hettie	119	1898		1897		New Orleans, La	Apr. 6, 1905	do	Apr. 6, 1904	Do.
Hy. Jacobs	77	1903		1903		Berwick, La	July 4, 1905	Morgan City, La	July 14, 1904	Do.
Istrouma	253	1896		1896		Jeffersonville, Ind	Oct. 19, 1905	Baton Rouge, La	Sept. 7, 1904	Do.
Josie	73	1891		1891		do	Aug. 8, 1905	New Orleans, La	Aug. 8, 1904	Do.
Joseph Bisso	110	1903		1903		Patterson, La	Oct. 31, 1905	do	Nov. 2, 1904	Do.
L. S. Thorne	1,217	1899		1898		Dubuque, Iowa	Apr. 15, 1905	do	Apr. 15, 1904	Do.
Ollie	152	1896		1896		Jeffersonville, Ind	July 22, 1905	do	July 19, 1904	Do.
Scioto	84	1889		1889		New Albany, Ind	June 27, 1905	Vicksburg, Miss	June 21, 1904	Do.

Thomas Pickles	237	1892	....	1892	....	Jeffersonville, Ind	Jan. 17, 1905	New Orleans, La	Jan. 16, 1904	Do.
Washington	100	1901	....	1903	....	Osage City, Mo	June 15, 1905	Donaldsonville, La	June 15, 1904	Do.
Ocean freight steamers.										
El Alba	4,614	1901	....	1901	....	Newport News, Va	Jan. 7, 1905	New Orleans, La	Jan. 9, 1904	Galveston, Tex.
Joseph W. Fordney	3,667	1901	....	1901	....	New Castle-on-Tyne, England.	Oct. 17, 1905	.....do	Oct. 21, 1904	Philadelphia, Pa.
Florida	1,596	1887	1903	1887	1895	Glasgow, Scotland	May 18, 1905	.....do	May 27, 1904	Galveston, Tex.
Pathfinder	2,792	1901	....	1901	....	Wilmington, Del	Dec. 28, 1905	.....do	Dec. 27, 1904	Portland, Me.
Inland freight steamers.										
Bagasse	57	1896	....	1878	....	Ramos, La	June 22, 1905	Morgan City, La	June 22, 1904	New Orleans, La.
Corozal	283	1883	....	1883	....	Cincinnati, Ohio	Jan. 5, 1905	New Orleans, La	Jan. 9, 1905	Do.
Capitola	60	1898	....	1898	....	Carrabelle, Fla	Jan. 24, 1905	Columbia, Miss	Jan. 14, 1904	Do.
City of Wheeling	308	1900	....	1889	....	Clarington, Ohio	Feb. 17, 1905	Vicksburg, Miss	Feb. 5, 1904	Do.
Charley B	3	1894	....	1894	....	New Iberia, La	Apr. 20, 1905	Plaquemine, La	Nov. 8, 1904	Do.
Control	103	1904	....	1881	....	Jeffersonville, Ind	June 30, 1905	New Orleans, La	July 3, 1904	Do.
Choctaw	223	1899	....	1886	....	Dardanelle, Ark	Oct. 29, 1905	Greenwood, Miss	Oct. 27, 1904	Do.
Columbia	92	1894	1903	1879	....	Madisonville, La	Nov. 3, 1905	Pearl River, La	Apr. 8, 1903	Do.
Dixie	71	1900	....	1883	....	New Orleans, La	Jan. 16, 1905	New Orleans, La	Nov. 23, 1904	Do.
Dial	98	1891	....	1891	....	Pearlington, Miss	May 9, 1905	.....do	Oct. 23, 1903	Do.
Daisy	33	1880	1890	1897	....	Algiers, La	Aug. 18, 1905	Head of Island, La	Aug. 19, 1904	Do.
El Listo	200	1902	....	1902	....	Newport News, Va	Apr. 26, 1905	New Orleans, La	Apr. 27, 1904	Do.
Elk	21	1901	....	1901	....	Franklin, La	Oct. 15, 1905	Morgan City, La	Aug. 26, 1904	Do.
F. B. Williams	86	1893	....	1900	....	Patterson, La	.....do	Berwick, La	Oct. 14, 1904	Do.
Fearless	70	1901	....	1901	....	Handsboro, Miss	Oct. 17, 1905	Dunbar, La	Oct. 4, 1904	Mobile, Ala.
George L. Bass [b]	53	1885	1899	1885	....	Dubuque, Iowa	Dec. 22, 1904	Boyce, La	Aug. 29, 1903	New Orleans, La.
Gracie Kent	74	1897	....	1897	....	Stillwater, Minn	Apr. 8, 1905	Pearlington, Miss	Apr. 2, 1904	Do.
Grand Caillou	38	1903	....	1901	....	Ashland, La	Oct. 19, 1905	Ashland, La	Oct. 5, 1904	Do.
Henrietta	62	1893	....	1892	....	New Iberia, La	Oct. 3, 1905	Morgan City, La	Oct. 3, 1905	Do.
H. A. Harvey, jr	59	1892	....	1892	....	Harvey, La	Oct. 21, 1905	Berwick, La	Oct. 14, 1904	Do.
H. W. Grady	68	1904	....	1904	....	Franklin, La	Oct. 31, 1905	Patterson, La	Aug. 11, 1904	Do.
Helena	28	1899	....	1892	....	Columbus Junction, Iowa.	Nov. 11, 1905	Natchez, Miss	Oct. 14, 1904	Memphis, Tenn.
Imogen	51	1904	....	[illegible]	....	Birdie, Miss	Feb. 28, 1905	Batesville, Miss	Feb. 6, 1904	New Orleans, La.
Jack Osborne	125	1896	....	1896	....	Cincinnati, Ohio	Mar. 19, 1905	Greenwood, Miss	Mar. 18, 1904	Do.
Lessley [c]	5	1904	....	1886	....	Jonesville, La	Dec. 29, 1904	Jonesville, La	First inspn	
Lillie	61	1893	1905	1881	....	.....do	May 26, 1905	.....do	May 31, 1904	Do.
Laura	38	1895	....	1891	....	Arrow Rock, Mo	Oct. 18, 1905	Houma, La	July 29, 1904	Do.
Mattie	31	1904	....	1881	....	Moseley Bluff, La	Jan. 14, 1905	West Monroe, La	First inspn	
Maggie	50	1894	1903	1881	....	Yazoo City, Miss	Oct. 29, 1905	Greenwood, Miss	Oct. 26, 1904	Do.
New Daniel	49	1901	....	1903	....	Plaquemine, La	Apr. 8, 1905	St. Martinsville, La	Jan. 8, 1905	Do.
Osage	98	1900	....	1894	....	Osage, Mo	Feb. 17, 1905	Vicksburg, Miss	Feb. 14, 1904	Evansville, Ind.
Ozark Queen	210	1896	....	1899	....	Batesville, Miss	Apr. 30, 1905	Donaldsonville, La	Dec. 15, 1903	Memphis, Tenn.
Peruna	65	1901	....	1904	....	Lockport, La	June 8, 1905	Lockport, La	May 26, 1904	New Orleans, La.
Phyllis	30	1902	....	1902	....	New Orleans, La	Oct. 19, 1905	Montegut, La	Sept. 29, 1904	Do.
Ruth	27	1899	....	1896	....	Patterson, La	Dec. 17, 1904	Berwick, La	Dec. 10, 1903	Do.
Ruth	14	1901	....	1901	....	Buras, La	Jan. 12, 1905	New Orleans, La	Dec. 22, 1903	Do.

[a] Certificated Mar. 13, 1905.
[b] Certificated Jan. 16, 1905.
[c] Certificated Jan. 25, 1905.

DOMESTIC VESSELS INSPECTED, YEAR ENDED DECEMBER 31, 1905—TENTH SUPERVISING DISTRICT—NEW ORLEANS, LA.—Continued.

Names of vessels and class.	Gross tonnage.	Hull built.	Hull rebuilt.	Boilers built.	Boilers rebuilt.	Where built.	Date of inspection.	Where inspected.	Date of previous inspection.	Local district where previously inspected.
Inland freight steamers—Con.										
Ratoon	52	1898		1889		Morgan City, La	Jan. 22, 1905	New Iberia, La	Jan. 23, 1904	New Orleans, La.
Reuben G. Bush	6	1894		1894		New Orleans, La	Oct. 19, 1905	Montegut, La	Sept. 28, 1904	Do.
Sugarland	240	1899		1899		Patterson, La	May 29, 1905	Morgan City, La	May 27, 1904	Do.
Troy	64	1903		1899		Jonesville, La	May 26, 1905	Jonesville, La	May 24, 1904	Do.
Wm. Kyle	35	1898		1892		Morgan City, La	Mar. 11, 1905	Franklin, La	Mar. 7, 1904	Do.
Wade	33	1905		1905		Pineville, La	June 11, 1905	Pineville, La	First inspn.	
X. Ray	18	1896		1883		Berwick, La	Jan. 27, 1905	Berwick, La	Jan. 28, 1904	Do.
Zip	17	1904		1903		Bayou des Allemands, La.	Oct. 31, 1905	New Iberia, La	Feb. 12, 1904	Do.
Ocean towing steamer.										
Iris	387	1863		1893		Brooklyn, N. Y	July 21, 1905	New Orleans, La	June 21, 1903	New York, N. Y.
Inland towing steamers.										
Alfred Hennen[a]	31	1897		1897		Hawsville, Ky	Dec. 19, 1904	Baton Rouge, La	Dec. 9, 1903	Evansville, Ind.
Anton Wilbert	52	1901		1900		Plaquemine, La	Jan. 13, 1905	Indian Village, La	Jan. 8, 1905	New Orleans, La.
Archon	48	1903		1903		Evansville, Ind	Apr. 6, 1905	Berwick, La	Apr. 2, 1904	Do.
Anna Tardy	71	1900		1894		do	Apr. 17, 1905	Jefferson, Tex	Nov. 14, 1904	Do.
Ada B	8	1895		1896		Prescott, Wis	Apr. 13, 1905	Lockport, La	Apr. 26, 1904	Do.
Armead	8	1900		1896		Brashear, La	Apr. 29, 1905	Morgan City, La	Apr. 27, 1904	Do.
A. Paddock	18	1896		1901		Harvey, La	July 7, 1905	Des Allemands, La	July 6, 1904	Do.
Belle Prince[b]	68	1870	1893	1897		Freedom, Pa	Dec. 14, 1904	Natchez, Miss	Dec. 10, 1903	Do.
Baton Rouge Belle	39	1871		1886		Pittsburg, Pa	Mar. 16, 1905	New Orleans, La	Mar. 16, 1904	Do.
Bertha C	11	1897		1895		Berwick, La	Apr. 28, 1905	Morgan City, La	Apr. 27, 1904	Do.
Bradwell	44	1898		1889		Manitowoc, Wis	May 23, 1905	New Orleans, La	June 17, 1904	Do.
Bernice	58	1899		1899		Scranton, Miss	July 22, 1905	do	Feb. 19, 1904	Do.
Belle Prince	68	1870	1893	1897		Freedom, Pa	Dec. 19, 1905	Hanson City, La	Dec. 14, 1904	Do.
Cygnet	3	1894		1900		Madisonville, La	Feb. 21, 1905	Springfield, La	Feb. 8, 1904	Do.
Carrie B	28	1896		1896		New Orleans, La	Feb. 22, 1905	Donaldsonville, La	Feb. 26, 1904	Do.
Cypress	8	1896	1903	1899		Thibodaux, La	Mar. 28, 1905	Manchac, La	Mar. 19, 1904	Do.
Cricket	27	1871		1892		Morgan City, La	May 29, 1905	Morgan City, La	May 26, 1904	Do.
Captain	42	1898		1903		Bayou des Allemands, La.	June 8, 1905	Plaquemine, La	June 2, 1904	Do.
Clio	18	1902		1901		Patterson, La	June 23, 1905	Patterson, La	Mar. 8, 1904	Do.
C. J. Reynolds	71	1901		1901		Proctorsville, Ohio	Oct. 10, 1905	Harvey, La	Oct. 8, 1904	Do.
Clyde	19	1902		1891		Pearlington, Miss	Oct. 17, 1905	Logtown, Miss	Nov. 26, 1904	Do.
Dot	6	1901	1904	1902		Berwick, La	May 27, 1905	Morgan City, La	Mar. 26, 1904	Do.
Dewey	5	1898		1881		Starts Landing, La	do	Trinity, La	May 23, 1904	Do.
Dorothy	7	1902		1902		Des Allemands, La	Oct. 30, 1905	Des Allemands, La	Sept. 14, 1904	Do.
Diamond	3	1894		1903		Michigan City, Ind	Nov. 28, 1905	Morgan City, La	Nov. 29, 1904	Do.
Elmer E. Wood	112	1883		1895		Camden, N. J	Jan. 25, 1905	New Orleans, La	Jan. 25, 1904	Do.

Edna	78	1898		1893		Shandy, Tenn	Mar. 20, 1905	[b]Vicksburg, Miss	Mar. 16, 1904	Do.
Export	14	1900		1903		Herman, Mo	Apr. 15, 1905	Jackson, Miss	Mar. 18, 1904	Do.
Expert	32	1901		1899		Madisonville, La	May 7, 1905	Madisonville, La	May 11, 1904	Do.
Edmund	14	1888		1896		Hawsville, Ky	June 8, 1905	New Orleans, La	May 28, 1904	Do.
Endeavor [c]	2	1887	1900	1901		Racine, Wis	June 23, 1905	Morgan City, La	Mar. 5, 1897	Do.
Emma Francis	48	1898		1898		Leavenworth, Ind	July 20, 1905	Logtown, Miss	Apr. 20, 1904	Do.
Ella	3	1896	1899	1898		Bayou Manchac, La	Aug. 18, 1905	Head of Island, La	Aug. 19, 1904	Do.
Eagle	185	1880		1898		Pittsburg, Pa	Nov. 4, 1905	New Orleans, La	Nov. 5, 1904	Do.
Florence	30	1902		1901		Harvey, La	Apr. 7, 1905	....do	Apr. 6, 1904	Do.
Fearless	26	1887		1902		Palatka, Fla	June 20, 1905	Lake Borgne Canal, La	June 15, 1904	Do.
Florence Swayze	4	1891		1883		Knights Landing, La	July 26, 1905	Jonesville, La	July 22, 1904	Do.
Florine	90	1891		1891		New Orleans, La	Aug. 10, 1905	New Orleans, La	Aug. 9, 1904	Do.
F. A. Goebel	61	1886		1886		Freedom, Pa	Nov. 10, 1905	Monroe, La	Nov. 10, 1904	Gallipolis, Ohio.
Frank R. Hill	109	1905		1879		Fulton, Ark	Dec. 16, 1905	Fulton, Ark	First inspn	
G. W. Stockton	4	1882		1889		Madisonville, La	Feb. 4, 1905	New Orleans, La	Jan. 16, 1904	New Orleans, La.
Gile	4	1892		1886		Salmon, La	May 10, 1905	Manchac, La	May 13, 1904	Do.
Guy Hunter	56	1898		1898		Arrow Rock, Mo	Aug. 10, 1905	Strader, La	Aug. 6, 1904	Do.
Gold Dust	8	1905		1899		Natchez, Miss	Nov. 2, 1905	New Orleans, La	First inspn	
George L. Bass	53	1885		1885		Dubuque, Iowa	Dec. 14, 1905	Boyce, La	Dec. 22, 1904	Do.
Hoo-Hoo	82	1895		1903		Patterson, La	Feb. 18, 1905	Avery Island, La	Dec. 1, 1903	Do.
H. C. Warmouth	5	1871	1895	1903		New Orleans, La	Mar. 28, 1905	Pearlington, Miss	Mar. 30, 1904	Do.
Haskell	24	1904		1904		Madisonville, La	Mar. 29, 1905	New Orleans, La	Mar. 27, 1904	Do.
H. C. Brockman	75	1895		1900		Rock Island, Ill	Apr. 4, 1905	Vicksburg, Miss	Apr. 2, 1904	Do.
Hustler	15	1903		1903		Grand Bayou, La	Oct. 31, 1905	Grand Bayou, La	July 27, 1904	Do.
Hornet	6	1900		1894		Greenville, Miss	Nov. 2, 1905	St. Martinsville, La	Aug. 26, 1904	Do.
Harry	37	1878	1898	1901		Franklin, La	Nov. 27, 1905	Houma, La	Nov. 28, 1904	Do.
Ivan	6	1901		1892		Plaquemine, La	Jan. 27, 1905	Melville, La	Jan. 28, 1904	Do.
Independent	164	1901		1901		Port Richmond, N. Y	July 19, 1905	New Orleans, La	July 14, 1904	New York, N. Y.
John F. May	62	1900		1904		Manitowoc, Wis	Jan. 31, 1905	Prophets Island, La	Jan. 20, 1904	New Orleans, La.
Joseph Rogers	13	1894		1894		New Orleans, La	Mar. 13, 1905	New Orleans, La	Mar. 12, 1904	Do.
Jerome	9	1900	1905	1904		Chicago, Ill	Mar. 27, 1905	Baton Rouge, La	July 29, 1903	Chicago, Ill.
Joe	18	1884	1899	1891		Vancluse, Ark	Apr. 26, 1905	New Orleans, La	Feb. 19, 1904	New Orleans, La.
J. B. Finley	679	1889		1899		Elizabeth, Pa	Apr. 27, 1905	....do	Apr. 28, 1904	Do.
John I. Brady	118	1891		1897		Baltimore, Md	May 3, 1905	Belle Isle, La	May 24, 1904	Galveston, Tex.
Jos. Favre Baldwin	50	1902		1899		Madisonville, La	May 30, 1905	Favreport, Miss	May 6, 1904	New Orleans, La.
J. N. Pharr	16	1897		1902		Patterson, La	Nov. 12, 1905	Des Allemands, La	Nov. 14, 1904	Do.
King Bee	8	1895		1901		New Orleans, La	Feb. 24, 1905	Simmsport, La	Feb. 24, 1904	Do.
Kingfisher	28	1901		1895		Fulton, Ark	May 30, 1905	Fulton, Ark	May 27, 1904	Do.
Lola S	8	1904		1904		Simmsport, La	Feb. 24, 1905	Simmsport, La	Feb. 24, 1904	Do.
Lizzie B	5	1891		1890		Natchez, Miss	Apr. 18, 1905	Natchez, Miss	Apr. 14, 1904	Do.
Laurel	67	1903		1903		New Orleans, La	Apr. 27, 1905	Bayou Sara, La	Apr. 29, 1904	Do.
Leona	5	1899		1899		Melville, La	May 20, 1905	Melville, La	May 9, 1905	Do.
Leo	37	1886	1903	1886		Stillwater, Miss	July 17, 1905	West Monroe, La	July 22, 1904	Do.
L. W. Brown	4	1890		1905		New Orleans, La	July 22, 1905	Slidell, La	May 30, 1903	Do.
Lone Star	73	1880		1901		Berwick, La	July 29, 1905	Donaldsonville, La	July 24, 1904	Do.
Laura Sutcliff	42	1904		1884		Franklin, La	Oct. 30, 1905	Franklin, La	Aug. 2, 1904	Do.
Lady Bussey	12	1897		1897		Bayou Ramos, La	Dec. 13, 1905	Melville, La	Dec. 5, 1904	Do.
Magic	19	1902		1896		Madisonville, La	Jan. 22, 1905	Madisonville, La	Dec. 29, 1903	Do.
Modoc	42	1900		1899		Marked Tree, Ark	Feb. 17, 1905	Vicksburg, Miss	Jan. 18, 1904	Memphis, Tenn.
Mamie Coyle	44	1870		1904		Chester, Pa	Feb. 23, 1905	Baton, Rouge, La	Fep. 25, 1904	New Orleans, La.

[a] Certificated Feb. 14, 1905. [b] Certificated Mar. 6, 1905. [c] Formerly pleasure launch Julia.

DOMESTIC VESSELS INSPECTED, YEAR ENDED DECEMBER 31, 1905—TENTH SUPERVISING DISTRICT—NEW ORLEANS, LA.—Continued.

Names of vessels and class.	Gross tonnage.	Hull built.	Hull rebuilt.	Boilers built.	Boilers rebuilt.	Where built.	Date of inspection.	Where inspected.	Date of previous inspection.	Local district where previously inspected.
Inland towing steamers—Con.										
Mamie D	63	1903		1892		Morgan City, La	Mar. 10, 1905	Morgan City, La	Mar. 7, 1904	New Orleans, La.
Maude	20	1905		1899		do	Apr. 22, 1905	do	First inspn	
Maud	10	1902		1901		Berwick, La	Apr. 13, 1905	Plaquemine, La	Apr. 13, 1904	Do.
Mary B	84	1903		1892		New Orleans, La	June 12, 1905	New Orleans, La	May 28, 1904	Do.
Maud Wilmot	57	1878		1892		Pittsburg, Pa	Aug. 22, 1905	do	Aug. 22, 1904	Do.
McDougall	562	1900		1900		Carondelet, Mo	Oct. 9, 1905	do	Oct. 4, 1904	Do.
Naomi	54	1898		1898		Chocolate Bayou, Tex	Apr. 30, 1905	Donaldsonville, La	May 4, 1904	Do.
Native No. 2	42	1899		1899		Scranton, Miss	Sept. 15, 1905	New Orleans, La	Sept. 22, 1904	Do.
Napoleon	43	1888		1880		Paducah, Ky	Oct. 18, 1905	do	Oct. 21, 1904	Do.
Natalbany	21	1903		1903		Springfield, La	Dec. 1, 1905	Springfield, La	Nov. 3, 1904	Do.
Osage	98	1900		1894		Osage, Mo	Feb. 17, 1905	Vicksburg, Miss	Feb. 14, 1904	Evansville, Ind.
Pearl M. [a]	9	1895		1887		Melville, La	Oct. 15, 1904	Berwick, La	Oct. 7, 1903	New Orleans, La.
Picayune	19	1904		1904		New Orleans, La	Jan. 12, 1905	New Orleans, La	First inspn	
Palo Pinto	4	1903		1903		Pearlington, Miss	May 9, 1905	Logtown, Miss	May 6, 1904	Do.
Pearl M	9	1895		1895		Melville, La	Nov. 17, 1905	Berwick, La	Oct. 15, 1904	Do.
Quick Step	66	1893		1893		Dubuque, Iowa	Nov. 24, 1905	Des Allemands, La	Nov. 18, 1904	Memphis, Tenn.
Richmond [b]	21	1888		1888		Saugatuck, Mich	Oct. 15, 1904	Morgan City, La	Oct. 28, 1903	New Orleans, La.
Resolute	207	1882	1895	1882		Pittsburg, Pa	Feb. 1, 1905	New Orleans, La	Feb. 4, 1904	Do.
Rena	8	1890	1896	1897		Lake Borgne Canal, La	Mar. 28, 1905	Manchac, La	Jan. 11, 1904	Do.
Restless	53	1875		1897		Algiers, La	Aug. 8, 1905	New Orleans, La	Aug. 8, 1904	Do.
Richard	5	1904		1898		New Orleans, La	Oct. 12, 1905	do	June 20, 1904	Do.
S. S. Prentiss [c]	61	1878	1899	1899		Pittsburg, Pa	Dec. 14, 1904	Natchez, Miss	Dec. 9, 1903	Do.
Stillwater	7	1902		1882		New Orleans, La	Mar. 27, 1905	Donaldsonville, La	Mar. 28, 1904	Do.
Sibilla	35	1903		1903		Plaquemine, La	May 8, 1905	Indian Village, La	May 8, 1904	Do.
St. Charles	40	1902		1900		Des Allemands, La	May 12, 1905	Avery Island, La	May 10, 1904	Do.
Senator	8	1884	1903	1903		New Orleans, La	Oct. 7, 1905	New Orleans, La	Oct. 6, 1904	Do.
Sparrow	10	1901		1902		Morgan City, La	Oct. 30, 1905	Berwick, La	Oct. 3, 1904	Do.
Sunbeam	4	1893		1902		Biloxi, Miss	do	Franklin, La	Aug. 2, 1904	Do.
Shamrock	23	1893	1903	1893		Morgan City, La	Nov. 18, 1905	Morgan City, La	Nov. 29, 1904	Do.
S. S. Prentiss	61	1878	1899	1899		Pittsburg, Pa	Dec. 11, 1905	Natchez, Miss	Dec. 14, 1904	Do.
Tempest	35	1896		1901		New Orleans, La	Apr. 17, 1905	Vicksburg, Miss	Apr. 18, 1904	Do.
T. L. Morse	34	1904		1887		Berwick, La	Oct. 3, 1905	Morgan City, La	Oct. 15, 1904	Do.
Tilda	30	1881	1888	1888		Memphis, Tenn	Oct. 25, 1905	Plaquemine, La	Oct. 20, 1904	Do.
Vernie Mac	122	1892		1877		Wabasha, Mich	Mar. 20, 1905	Vicksburg, Miss	Mar. 17, 1904	Do.
Vanguard	80	1885		1885		Pittsburg, Pa	do	do	Mar. 31, 1904	Do.
Vincent D	12	1905		1902		Plaquemine, La	Mar. 27, 1905	Morgan City, La	First inspn	
Violet H	18	1895		1884		Hartville, La	Apr. 26, 1905	New Orleans, La	May 24, 1904	Do.
V. L. Watson	55	1900		1900		Harvey, La	Aug. 3, 1905	Bayou Barataria, La	Aug. 3, 1904	Do.
Whiz	9	1893	1901	1903		Morgan City, La	Jan. 14, 1905	Morgan City, La	Jan. 8, 1904	Do.
Wamba	4	1896		1896		Carrollton, Ill	Feb. 27, 1905	Monroe, La	Feb. 24, 1904	Do.
Wm. Drews	55	1902		1902		Morgan City, La	Mar. 10, 1905	Morgan City, La	Mar. 7, 1904	Do.
White Rose	9	1904		1898		Gramercy, La	May 23, 1905	Lutcher, La	Apr. 29, 1904	Do.

Will H. Wood	44	1884	....	1884	....	New Orleans, La.	May 28, 1905	Baton Rouge, La.	May 29, 1904	Do.
Why Not	14	1893	1893	1880	....	Franklin, La.	July 8, 1905	Abbeville, La.	July 30, 1904	Do.
Wolf	13	1905	....	1880	....	Madisonville, La.	Sept. 13, 1905	New Orleans, La.	First inspn.	
W. W. Carre	74	1889	1904	1897	....	do	Sept. 26, 1905	do	Sept. 29, 1904	Do.
Steam pleasure yachts.										
Amateur	3	1903	....	1903	....	New Orleans, La.	May 25, 1905	New Orleans, La.	Mar. 12, 1904	New Orleans, La.
Blanche A	8	1900	....	1900	....	Brashear, La.	Apr. 28, 1905	Morgan City, La.	Apr. 27, 1904	Do.
Carrie H	6	1901	....	1888	....	Des Allemands, La.	Mar. 24, 1905	Des Allemands, La.	Mar. 8, 1904	Do.
Cecil	5	1899	....	1899	....	Morgan City, La.	Nov. 18, 1905	Morgan City, La.	Nov. 29, 1904	Do.
Dew Drop	3	1901	....	1909	....	Franklin, La.	June 7, 1905	Franklin, La.	May 27, 1904	Do.
Felicien	4	1901	....	1901	....	Camden, N. J.	Jan. 20, 1905	Quarantine, La.	Dec. 27, 1903	Do.
Friday	7	1903	....	1903	....	Ramos, La.	Apr. 29, 1905	Morgan City, La.	Apr. 27, 1904	Do.
Grace	3	1891	....	1891	....	New Orleans, La.	July 5, 1905	New Orleans, La.	June 29, 1904	Do.
Idler	3	1888	....	1904	....	Bridgeport, Conn.	June 13, 1905	Dunbar, La.	June 1, 1904	Do.
Mathilde	8	1895	1901	1895	....	New Orleans, La.	Jan. 13, 1905	Indian Village, La.	Jan. 8, 1904	Do.
Marie E	4	1895	....	1895	....	Des Allemands, La.	Mar. 24, 1905	Des Allemands, La.	Dec. 1, 1903	Do.
Marie	37	1896	....	1896	....	Middleton, Conn.	June 27, 1905	New Orleans, La.	June 28, 1904	Do.
Rambler	3	1903	....	1903	....	McComb City, Miss.	Mar. 28, 1905	Manchac, La.	Feb. 18, 1904	Do.
Surprise	3	1905	....	1905	....	Morgan City, La.	July 14, 1905	Morgan City, La.	First inspn.	
Semper Idem	33	1896	....	1896	....	Algiers, La.	Dec. 6, 1905	New Orleans, La.	Dec. 6, 1904	Do.
Thelma	8	1896	....	1903	....	Grand Bayou, La.	Oct. 31, 1905	Grand Bayou, La.	July 28, 1904	Do.
Wachusett	59	1896	....	1902	....	New York, N. Y.	May 13, 1905	New Orleans, La.	May 13, 1904	Do.
Willa	3	1893	....	1901	1905	St. Joseph, Mich.	May 25, 1905	do	Mar. 7, 1904	Do.
Wm. Talbot	6	1903	....	1903	....	Berwick, La.	June 22, 1905	Berwick, La.	June 22, 1904	Do.
Wayzatta	4	1892	1905	1891	....	Wayzatta, Mich.	July 27, 1905	Felsenthal, Ark.	June 12, 1904	Do.
Miscellaneous steam vessel.										
Jennie Wilson (pilot boat)	77	1878	....	1902	....	Camden, N. J.	Nov. 13, 1905	New Orleans, La.	Oct. 23, 1904	New Orleans, La.
Vessels propelled by gasoline motors.										
American Beauty	16	1905	....	....	....	New Orleans, La.	Mar. 2, 1905	New Orleans, La.	First inspn.	
Barataria	16	1904	....	....	....	Morgan City, La.	Sept. 5, 1905	do	Sept. 22, 1904	New Orleans, La.
City of Hartford	29	1893	....	....	....	Jefferson City, La.	Mar. 17, 1905	do	Mar. 18, 1904	Do.
Edith	23	1904	....	....	....	New Orleans, La.	Aug. 31, 1905	do	Aug. 31, 1904	Do.
F. & J.	27	1904	....	....	....	Grand Isle, La.	Dec. 20, 1905	do	Dec. 9, 1904	Do.
Gem	49	1904	....	....	....	Des Allemands, La.	May 6, 1905	do	Apr. 12, 1904	Do.
Grace	23	1904	....	....	....	New Orleans, La.	Aug. 22, 1905	do	Aug. 13, 1904	Do.
Lower Coast	22	1901	....	....	....	do	Jan. 19, 1905	do	Jan. 21, 1904	Do.
Louisville	23	1896	....	....	....	do	June 17, 1905	do	June 1, 1904	Do.
Louisiana	33	1905	....	....	....	Biloxi, Miss.	Nov. 6, 1905	do	First inspn.	
Magnolia	16	1905	....	....	....	New Orleans, La.	Mar. 21, 1905	do	do	
New Venus	18	1904	....	....	....	do	May 18, 1905	do	Apr. 5, 1904	Do.
Neptune	64	1905	....	....	....	do	Nov. 2, 1905	do	First inspn.	
Pansy	16	1905	....	....	....	do	Mar. 20, 1905	do	do	
Robert Bruce	47	1904	....	....	....	do	Mar. 16, 1905	do	Mar. 18, 1904	Do.
Reliance	39	1905	....	....	....	do	Mar. 29, 1905	do	First inspn.	
Success	20	1904	....	....	....	do	Oct. 15, 1905	Pilot town, La.	Oct. 28, 1904	Do.
Tulane	19	1905	....	....	....	do	May 16, 1905	New Orleans, La.	First inspn.	

[a] Certificated Mar. 15, 1905. [b] Certificated Jan. 14, 1905. [c] Certificated Jan. 11, 1905.

DOMESTIC VESSELS INSPECTED, YEAR ENDED DECEMBER 31, 1905—TENTH SUPERVISING DISTRICT—NEW ORLEANS, LA.—Continued.

Names of vessels and class.	Gross tonnage.	Hull built.	Hull rebuilt.	Boilers built.	Boilers rebuilt.	Where built.	Date of inspection.	Where inspected.	Date of previous inspection.	Local district where previously inspected.
Freight sail vessel of over 700 gross tons.										
Cohasset (schooner)	965	1903				New Orleans, La	June 2, 1905	New Orleans, La	May 2, 1904	New York, N. Y.
Barges over 100 gross tons carrying passengers for hire (river).										
Avondale	1,290	1903				Morgan City, La	Jan. 11, 1905	New Orleans, La	Jan. 11, 1904	New Orleans, La.
Endeavor	633	1871				Cincinnati, Ohio	July 11, 1905	do	July 18, 1904	Do.
Chas. Hyde	398	1900				Ferrysburg, Mich	Nov. 11, 1905	Natchez, Miss	Nov. 17, 1904	Do.
El Grande	1,383	1902				Morgan City, La	Dec. 15, 1905	New Orleans, La	Dec. 16, 1904	Do.
Avondale	1,290	1903				do	Dec. 27, 1905	do	Jan. 11, 1904	Do.

LOCAL DISTRICT OF APALACHICOLA, FLA.

Names of vessels and class.	Gross tonnage.	Hull built.	Hull rebuilt.	Boilers built.	Boilers rebuilt.	Where built.	Date of inspection.	Where inspected.	Date of previous inspection.	Local district where previously inspected.
Ocean passenger steamers.										
Gussie	998	1872		1891		Wilmington, Del	June 9, 1905	Tampa, Fla	June 11, 1904	Apalachicola, Fla.
Mascotte	884	1885		1899		Philadelphia, Pa	Jan. 23, 1905	Port Tampa, Fla	Jan. 24, 1904	Do.
Olivette	1,678	1887	1898	1901		do	Dec. 7, 1905	do	Dec. 18, 1904	Do.
Inland passenger steamers.										
Ancient City	44	1884		1901		St. Augustine, Fla	Jan. 22, 1905	Tampa, Fla	Jan. 23, 1904	Apalachicola, Fla.
Annie M	13	1895		1898		Cedar Keys, Fla	Mar. 16, 1905	Apalachicola, Fla	Jan. 2, 1904	Do.
Anah C	a 10	1898		1904		Denaud, Fla	May 7, 1905	Myers, Fla	May 13, 1904	Do.
Anthea	24	1887	1900	1890		Hoboken, N. J	May 8, 1905	do	May 14, 1904	Do.
Annie	a 1	1892	1905	1905		Wewahitchka, Fla	Aug. 30, 1905	Apalachicola, Fla	Apr. 17, 1904	Do.
Albert F. Dewey	134	1895		1895		Newport News, Va	Sept. 14, 1905	Punta Gorda, Fla	Sept. 25, 1904	Do.
Belle of Myers	a 5	1895		1895		Myers, Fla	Nov. 12, 1905	Myers, Fla	Dec. 11, 1904	Do.
Carrie May	a 4	1898		1898	1905	Wewahitchka, Fla	July 10, 1905	Apalachicola, Fla	July 8, 1904	Do.
Crescent City	154	1887	1900	1900	1900	North Point, N. Y	Aug. 21, 1905	do	Sept. 1, 1904	Do.
Era	a 4	1887	1901	1901		Chicago, Ill	July 10, 1905	do	July 18, 1904	Do.
Gertrude	285	1895	1904	1895		Hawesville, Ky	Aug. 24, 1905	Bainbridge, Ga	Aug. 5, 1904	Do.
H. B. Plant	189	1900		1899		Jacksonville, Fla	Jan. 25, 1905	Tampa, Fla	Jan. 24, 1904	Do.
Hattie	a 4	1900		1897		Fort Gadsen, Fla	Aug. 30, 1905	Apalachicola, Fla	Aug. 29, 1904	Do.
Iola	46	1884	1904	1894		Pinellas, Fla	Sept. 3, 1905	Carrabelle, Fla	Sept. 3, 1904	Do.
Jo	a 1	1894		1894		Tarpon Springs, Fla	Jan. 26, 1905	Tarpon Springs, Fla	Jan. 25, 1904	Do.
James H. Clark	45	1900		1890		Buffalo, N. Y	May 11, 1905	Tampa, Fla	May 15, 1904	Do.

J. P. Williams	61	1900		1896		Bainbridge, Ga	June 2, 1905	St. Andrews, Fla	May 20, 1904	Do.
John W. Auchincloss	49	1904		1904		Scranton, Miss	July 3, 1905	Inglis, Fla	July 23, 1904	Do.
John L. Inglis	98	1903		1903		do	Sept. 13, 1905	do	Sept. 23, 1904	Mobile, Ala.
Loretto	13	1904		1903		Apalachicola, Fla	Feb. 20, 1905	Apalachicola, Fla	Feb. 20, 1904	Apalachicola, Fla.
Lottie	65	1882	1902	1899		do	Mar. 27, 1905	do	Mar. 29, 1904	Do.
Little Sam	a 2	1884	1899	1894	1904	do	June 5, 1905	do	June 2, 1904	Do.
Louise	a 4	1891		1905		Jacksonville, Fla	June 10, 1905	Myers, Fla	Dec. 6, 1901	Do.
Lillie	64	1900		1900		Kissimmee, Fla	Sept. 30, 1905	Kissimmee, Fla	Oct. 25, 1904	Do.
Manatee	104	1884		1884	1905	Newburg, N. Y	Jan. 22, 1905	Tampa, Fla	Jan. 24, 1904	Do.
Mistletoe	43	1894		1899		Tampa, Fla	June 8, 1905	do	June 9, 1904	Do.
M. W. Kelly	95	1900		1900		Jeffersonville, Ind	Nov. 9, 1905	Columbus, Ga	Oct. 22, 1904	Do.
Neptune	117	1898		1898		Baltimore, Md	Feb. 14, 1905	Port Tampa, Fla	Feb. 27, 1904	Do.
Naoma No. 3	49	1901		1892		Kissimmee, Fla	June 10, 1905	Kissimmee, Fla	Mar. 22, 1904	Do.
Ocean Gem	a 4	1887	1905	1905		Chicago, Ill	Apr. 25, 1905	Apalachicola, Fla	Aug. 2, 1898	Do.
Phoenix	96	1903		1890		Cleveland, Fla	May 8, 1905	Punta Gorda, Fla	May 14, 1904	Do.
Queen City	150	1891		1883		Columbus, Ga	Mar. 19, 1905	Apalachicola, Fla	Mar. 6, 1904	Do.
Raymond H	55	1905		1900		St. Marks, Fla	Aug. 25, 1905	St. Marks, Fla	First inspn.	
Roseada	53	1893	1903	1899		Kissimmee, Fla	Oct. 25, 1905	Kissimmee, Fla	Oct. 25, 1904	Do.
Suwannee	82	1897		1899		Carlson, Fla	Nov. 12, 1905	Myers, Fla	Dec. 10, 1904	Do.
Tena Ceia	209	1882	1898	1898		Jacksonville, Fla	Jan. 24, 1905	Tampa, Fla	Jan. 24, 1904	Do.
Three States	126	1898	1905	1890		Apalachicola, Fla	July 8, 1905	Apalachicola, Fla	June 4, 1904	Do.
Thetis	61	1898		1898		do	Aug. 8, 1905	Branford, Fla	Aug. 9, 1904	Do.
Thomas A. Edison	33	1901		1901		do	Sept. 14, 1905	Myers, Fla	Sept. 24, 1904	Do.
W. C. Bradley	175	1898		1886		Columbus, Ga	Oct. 30, 1905	Apalachicola, Fla	Oct. 30, 1904	Do.
Ocean freight steamer										
Fanita	432	1868		1900		Wilmington, Del	May 20, 1905	Tampa, Fla	May 25, 1904	Apalachicola, Fla.
Inland freight steamers.										
City of Hawkinsville	175	1896	1901	1901		Hawkinsville, Ga	Feb. 23, 1905	Branford, Fla	Feb. 25, 1904	Apalachicola, Fla.
Forest	59	1902		1897		Pensacola, Fla	Aug. 26, 1905	Albany, Ga	July 12, 1904	Do.
John R. Sharp	50	1903		1895		Bainbridge, Ga	Mar. 8, 1905	Bainbridge, Ga	Mar. 8, 1904	Do.
Juanita	38	1905		1905		Kissimmee, Fla	Aug. 9, 1905	Kissimmee, Fla	First inspn.	
Ochesee	82	1904		1895		Columbus, Ga	Dec. 16, 1905	Apalachicola, Fla	Dec. 24, 1904	Do.
Pollie	a 4	1901		1881		Kissimmee, Fla	Sept. 30, 1905	Kissimmee, Fla	Oct. 25, 1904	Do.
Sego	41	1901		1895		Carrabelle, Fla	Oct. 26, 1905	Carrabelle, Fla	Aug. 19, 1904	Do.
Venice	74	1905		1900		Fogartyville, Fla	Mar. 10, 1905	Fogartyville, Fla	First inspn.	
W. H. Hales	36	1904		1904		Blountstown, Fla	Oct. 6, 1905	Apalachicola, Fla	Sept. 20, 1904	Do.
Ocean towing steamer.										
Geo. W. Childs	107	1872	1890	1896		Camden, N. J	June 29, 1905	Key West, Fla	June 11, 1904	Apalachicola, Fla.
Inland towing steamers.										
Alexander Wyllie	51	1904		1904		Scranton, Miss	Sept. 13, 1905	Inglis, Fla	Sept. 30, 1904	Mobile, Ala.
Blazer	46	1893		1901		Apalachicola, Fla	Mar. 23, 1905	Apalachicola, Fla	Mar. 9, 1904	Apalachicola, Fla.
Burton E. Coe	42	1897		1901		Tampa, Fla	Sept. 29, 1905	Crystal, Fla	Sept. 22, 1904	Do.

a Estimated.

DOMESTIC VESSELS INSPECTED, YEAR ENDED DECEMBER 31, 1905—TENTH SUPERVISING DISTRICT—APALACHICOLA, FLA.—Continued.

Names of vessels and class.	Gross tonnage.	Hull built.	Hull rebuilt.	Boilers built.	Boilers rebuilt.	Where built	Date of inspection.	Where inspected.	Date of previous inspection.	Local district where previously inspected.
Inland towing steamers—Con.										
City of Carrabelle	12	1892	1904	1891		Carrabelle, Fla.	Mar. 31, 1905	Carrabelle, Fla.	Mar. 19, 1904	Apalachicola, Fla.
Chas. W. Tilden	23	1881		1889		do	Aug. 12, 1905	Apalachicola, Fla.	Aug. 11, 1904	Do.
Catherine L. Kennedy	39	1881	1900	1900		Apalachicola, Fla.	Nov. 3, 1905	do	Oct. 8, 1904	Do.
Dewey	30	1899		1905		Portland, Fla.	June 2, 1905	St. Andrews, Fla.	May 20, 1904	Do.
Gertrude	a 2	1890		1890		Apalachicola, Fla.	July 28, 1905	Apalachicola, Fla.	July 26, 1904	Do.
Little Belle	a 2	1886	1903	1903		Boston, Mass.	Mar. 25, 1905	Wewahitchka, Fla.	Mar. 8, 1904	Do.
Overtime	a 2	1904		1895		Wewahitchka, Fla.	Feb. 27, 1905	do	Mar. 9, 1904	Do.
Orono	97	1900		1904		Carrabelle, Fla.	Mar. 14, 1905	Carrabelle, Fla.	Mar. 19, 1904	Do.
Police	a 1	1902		1905		Braidentown, Fla.	Oct. 16, 1905	Manatee, Fla.	First inspn.	
Ralph Barker	229	1900		1899		Port Inglis, Fla.	Jan. 27, 1905	Inglis, Fla.	Jan. 26, 1904	Do.
Sam Pyles	31	1885	1901	1901		Panasoffkee, Fla.	Oct. 14, 1905	Cedar Keys, Fla.	Aug. 9, 1904	Do.
T. C. Drake	a 4	1900		1895		Bainbridge, Ga.	Apr. 25, 1905	Apalachicola, Fla.	May 11, 1904	Do.
Steam pleasure yachts.										
Aroostook	78	1903		1903		Morris Heights, N. Y.	Nov. 11, 1905	Punta Gorda, Fla.	Nov. 13, 1904	Apalachicola, Fla.
Fortuna	150	1903		1903		Chicago, Ill.	Jan. 22, 1905	Tampa, Fla.	May 28, 1904	Do.
Gopher	98	1895		1895		Jacksonville, Fla.	Nov. 3, 1905	Apalachicola, Fla.	Oct. 27, 1904	Do.
Vessels propelled by gas motors.										
Florida	48	1886				West Haven, Conn.	May 7, 1905	Myers, Fla.	Apr. 25, 1904	Apalachicola, Fla.
Doctor Lykes	89	1900				Tampa, Fla.	Nov. 12, 1905	do	Apr. 26, 1900	Do.
Mermaid	20	1891				Fogartyville, Fla.	Dec. 7, 1905	Tampa, Fla.	First inspn.	
Pilot	20	1901				Tampa, Fla.	Jan. 25, 1905	Port Tampa, Fla.	Jan. 24, 1904	Do.
Traveler	43	1904				Marco, Fla.	Nov. 11, 1905	Punta Gorda, Fla.	First inspn.	
Undine	18	1900	1904			Key West, Fla.	Oct. 19, 1905	Key West, Fla.	Sept. 27, 1904	Do.
Freight sail vessel of over 700 tons.										
Francis S. Humphries	1,079	1881				Richmond, Me.	Feb. 18, 1905	Tampa, Fla.	June 17, 1903	New York, N. Y.

LOCAL DISTRICT OF GALVESTON, TEX.

Names of vessels and class.	Gross tonnage.	Hull built.	Hull rebuilt.	Boilers built.	Boilers rebuilt.	Where built	Date of inspection.	Where inspected.	Date of previous inspection.	Local district where previously inspected.
Ocean passenger steamer.										
Manteo	719	1887	1902	1887	1902	Wilmington, Del.	Apr. 20, 1905	Galveston, Tex.	Apr. 30, 1904	Galveston, Tex.

Inland passenger steamers.										
Alberta	8	1899		1896		Franklin, La	Mar. 8, 1905	Beaumont, Tex	Mar. 8, 1904	Galveston, Tex.
Albert N. Hughes	92	1887		1899		Philadelphia, Pa	Mar. 14, 1905	Galveston, Tex	Mar. 14, 1904	Do.
Chas. Clarke	211	1899		1899		Camden, N. J	Oct. 2, 1905	do	Oct. 6, 1904	Do.
Della	55	1902		1902		Scranton, Miss	May 10, 1905	Port Arthur, Tex	May 7, 1904	Do.
Eugene	70	1889		1889		Lynchburg, Tex	Sept. 1, 1905	Houston, Tex	July 11, 1904	Do.
Gertrude	34	1897		1893		Scranton, Miss	July 24, 1905	Galveston, Tex	June 23, 1904	Do.
George Sealey	9	1884	1901	1901		Clear Creek, Tex	Aug. 10, 1905	Orange, Tex	Aug. 10, 1904	Do.
Hygeia	47	1884		1897		Philadelphia, Pa	July 16, 1905	Galveston, Tex	July 11, 1904	Do.
Ima Hogg [b]	99	1872	1905	1905		do	June 5, 1905	do	Feb. 27, 1903	Do.
J. N. Gilbert	42	1902		1902		Scranton, Miss	Sept. 12, 1905	do	Sept. 12, 1904	Do.
Katharine	45	1902		1889		Orange, Tex	May 9, 1905	Orange, Tex	May 9, 1904	Do.
Little Fay	6	1903		1903		Chicago, Ill	Apr. 12, 1905	Beaumont, Tex	Apr. 25, 1904	Do.
Olive	91	1891		1892	1903	Mermentau, La	Nov. 16, 1905	Mermentau, La	Nov. 25, 1904	Do.
Romeo	61	1889	1901	1901		West Bay Mich	Mar. 9, 1905	Lake Charles, La	Mar. 9, 1904	Do.
Sadie	25	1902		1902		Scranton, Miss	Dec. 4, 1905	Galveston, Tex	Dec. 7, 1904	Do.
Texas	220	1901		1901		Philadelphia Pa	Aug. 17, 1905	do	Sept. 4, 1904	Do.
Ferry steamer.										
Hazel	78	1888		1895		Lake Charles, La	Oct. 25, 1905	Lake Charles, La	Aug. 10, 1904	Galveston, Tex.
Ocean freight steamers.										
El Valle	4,605	1901		1901		Newport News, Va	June 1, 1905	Galveston, Tex	May 31, 1904	Galveston, Tex.
El Sud	4,572	1899		1899		do	June 10, 1905	do	June 4, 1904	New York, N. Y.
El Norte	4,604	1899		1899		do	July 11, 1905	do	July 12, 1904	Galveston, Tex.
El Rio	4,604	1899		1899		do	Aug. 26, 1905	do	Sept. 5, 1904	Do.
El Siglo	4,616	1901		1901		do	Nov. 3, 1905	do	Nov. 4, 1904	New Orleans, La.
Missouri	7,914	1901		1901		Sparrow Point, Md	Dec. 29, 1905	do	Dec. 21, 1904	Do.
Inland freight steamers.										
Annie P	55	1904		1885		Compte, La	Apr. 27, 1905	Denison, Tex	Apr. 3, 1904	New Orleans, La.
Luzon	98	1895		1893		Scranton, Miss	July 26, 1905	Point Isabel, Tex	July 24, 1904	Galveston, Tex.
Nicholaus	43	1904		1904		Wallisville, Tex	Sept. 7, 1905	Galveston, Tex	First inspn	
Ocean towing steamers.										
Capt. Sam	92	1873	1896	1900		Philadelphia, Pa	Apr. 5, 1905	Port Arthur, Tex	Apr. 2, 1904	Galveston, Tex.
Higgins	119	1903		1903		Scranton, Miss	Mar. [illegible]	Galveston, Tex	Apr. 11, 1904	Do.
Seminole	78	1871	1902	1895	1902	Philadelphia, Pa	July 7, [illegible]	do	June 22, 1904	Do.
Inland towing steamers.										
Albania	13	1893	1902	1902		Chicago, Ill	Jan. 16, 1905	Orange, Tex	Jan. 13, 1904	Galveston, Tex.
Alamo	10	1890	1902	1895		Lake Charles, La	Mar. 9, 1905	Beaumont, Tex	Mar. 8, 1904	Do.
Annie	23	1892		1892		Ceder Bayou, Tex	Oct. 9, 1905	Houston, Tex	Oct. 10, 1904	Do.
Boston	11	1893		1900		Chicago, Ill	Sept. 25, 1905	Beaumont, Tex	Sept. 22, 1904	Do.

[a] Estimated.

[b] Formerly Cynthia, 1903.

DOMESTIC VESSELS INSPECTED, YEAR ENDED DECEMBER 31, 1905—TENTH SUPERVISING DISTRICT—GALVESTON, TEX.—Continued.

Names of vessels and class.	Gross tonnage.	Hull built.	Hull rebuilt.	Boilers built.	Boilers rebuilt.	Where built.	Date of inspection.	Where inspected.	Date of previous inspection.	Local district where previously inspected.
Inland towing steamers—Con.										
Bernie Holmes	24	1892		1892		Berwick, La	Nov. 16, 1905	Mermentau, La	Nov. 26, 1904	Galveston, Tex.
Charles McFarlin	a 4	1902		1902		Orange, Tex	Jan. 27, 1905	Orange, Tex	Sept. 25, 1903	Do.
Clara May	21	1882	1899	1900		Lake Charles, La	May 23, 1905	Galveston, Tex	May 20, 1904	Do.
Caprice	a 4	1887	1902	1891		Galveston, Tex	Aug. 24, 1905	Beaumont, Tex	Aug. 19, 1904	Do.
Dorothy	33	1901		1901		Scranton, Miss	Sept. 13, 1905	Galveston, Tex	Sept. 13, 1904	Do.
Dura	22	1905		1893	1901	Deweyville, Tex	Dec. 20, 1905	Deweyville, Tex	First inspn	
Eva L. Mernan	6	1899	1902	1902		Franklin, La	Oct. 26, 1905	Lake Charles, La	Oct. 13, 1904	Do.
Fannie	16	1872	1901	1899		Newark, N. J	Feb. 4, 1905	Houston, Tex	Feb. 4, 1904	Do.
Frankie	a 4	1896	1905	1894	1905	Chicago, Ill	July 17, 1905	Orange, Tex	First inspn	
Gertrude	13	1901		1902		Berwick, La	June 20, 1905	Mermentau, La	June 20, 1904	Do.
Germ	70	1882		1892		New York, N. Y	July 26, 1905	Point Isabel, Tex	July 24, 1904	Do.
Goldie	a 4	1899		1904		Lake Charles, La	Nov. 16, 1905	Mermentau, La	Nov. 25, 1904	Do.
Helen	43	1904		1904		Wallisville, Tex	Feb. 28, 1905	Houston, Tex	First inspn	
Horatia	98	1891	1902	1891	1902	Corpus Christi, Tex	Oct. 31, 1905	Galveston, Tex	Aug. 12, 1904	Do.
Ida	a 4	1903		1903		Lake Arthur, La	Feb. 24, 1905	Mermentau, La	Feb. 23, 1904	Do.
Josephine	a 4	1903		1903		Mermentau, La	do	do	do	Do.
Josephine	32	1892	1903	1892	1903	Scranton, Miss	May 15, 1905	Galveston, Tex	May 12, 1904	Do.
Jemmie	21	1902		1902		Mobile, Ala	May 22, 1905	do	May 20, 1904	Do.
J. B. Griffith	15	1898		1898		Johnsons Bayou, Tex	May 26, 1905	Orange, Tex	May, 18, 1904	Do.
John P. Smith	46	1893		1896		Brashear, La	June 26, 1905	Houston, Tex	May 13, 1904	Do.
Juno	80	1878	1897	1904		Camden, N. J	Aug. 18, 1905	do	Sept. 16, 1904	Do.
J. H. Sterrett	29	1876	1902	1894		Lynchburg, Tex	Nov. 14, 1905	do	Nov. 19, 1904	Do.
Katharine	19	1902		1893		Scranton, Miss	Oct. 25, 1905	Lake Charles, La	Aug. 10, 1904	Do.
Lillian T	7	1895		1895		Detroit, Mich	Mar. 8, 1905	Beaumont, Tex	Mar. 8, 1904	Do.
Leonore	27	1894		1894		Lake Charles, La	Mar. 9, 1905	Lake Charles, La	Mar. 9, 1904	Do.
Little Joe	a 4	1895		1902		Mermentau, La	May 19, 1905	Mermentau, La	Oct. 20, 1903	Do.
Lee	a 4	1905		1905		do	June 20, 1905	do	First inspn	
Louise	105	1880	1902	1894		Camden, N. J	July 19, 1905	Houston, Tex	June 24, 1904	Do.
Larbano	6	1889		1900		Shel Bank, La	Sept. 25, 1905	Orange, Tex	Sept. 22, 1904	Do.
Mina	56	1893		1888		Lake Charles, La	June 15, 1905	Galveston, Tex	June 16, 1904	Do.
Margaret	17	1875	1902	1902		do	Sept. 22, 1905	do	Sept. 23, 1904	Do
Molyneaux	17	1873	1893	1886	1900	Bordentown, N. J	Dec. 5, 1905	Lake Charles, La	Dec. 8, 1904	Do.
Ontario	21	1872	1902	1899		Lynchburg, Tex	Oct. 25, 1905	do	Aug. 10, 1904	Do.
Oscar G	27	1890	1901	1898		Berwick, La	Oct. 26, 1905	Mermentau, La	Oct. 19, 1904	Do.
Piasa	5	1881	1903	1892		St. Louis, Mo	Sept. 27, 1905	Orange, Tex	Sept. 22, 1904	Do.
Picayune	23	1875	1901	1901		New Orleans, La	Dec. 6, 1905	Houston, Tex	Dec. 7, 1904	Do.
S. G. Rosamond	12	1884	1900	1884		Cedar Bayou, Tex	Oct. 25, 1905	Lake Charles, La	Aug. 10, 1904	Do.
Two Brothers	12	1897		1897		Mermentau, La	Nov. 15, 1905	do	Nov. 25, 1904	Do.
Viva	30	1882	1902	1882	1902	Chicago, Ill	Mar. 8, 1905	Beaumont, Tex	Apr. 15, 1904	Do.
Willie C	16	1884	1902	1890	1901	New York, N. Y	Feb. 14, 1905	Lake Charles, La	Mar 9, 1904	Do.

Steam pleasure yachts.										
John H. Kirby	99	1902		1902		Chicago, Ill	Nov. 9, 1905	Beaumont, Tex	Oct. 26, 1904	Galveston, Tex.
Two Georges	[a]3	1905		1905		Orange, Tex	Oct. 3, 1905	Orange, Tex	First inspn	
Miscellaneous steam vessel.										
Mamie Higgins (pilot)	77	1879	1904	1904		Buffalo, N. Y	Jan. 19, 1905	Galveston, Tex	Aug. 19, 1903	Galveston, Tex.
Vessels propelled by gas motors.										
Dulcena	30	1902				Cedar Bayou, Tex	Dec. 20, 1905	Houston, Tex	Dec. 22, 1904	Galveston, Tex.
Echo	42	1906				do	Oct. 16, 1905	Galveston, Tex	First inspn	
Folly	19	1891	1905			New Orleans, La	Nov. 21, 1905	do	do	
Hard Times	28	1867	1899			Galveston, Tex	Aug. 8, 1905	do	do	
Henrietta	23	1905				Wallisville, Tex	Oct. 17, 1905	do	do	
Logger	103	1905				Orange, Tex	Apr. 24, 1905	Orange, Tex	do	
Matilda	30	1888				Clear Creek, Tex	July 21, 1905	Galveston, Tex	do	
Mary Alma	55	1904				Cove, Tex	Aug. 15, 1905	do	Aug. 12, 1904	Do.
Maud	28	1904				Cedar Bayou, Tex	Aug. 16, 1905	do	Aug. 19, 1904	Do.
M. L. Weaver	27	1877	1902			Madison, La	Oct. 30, 1905	do	Oct. 28, 1904	Do.
Naulahka	27	1903				Byonne, N. Y	Apr. 3, 1905	do	Oct. 16, 1903	Do.
Robert E. Lee	15	1901				Grand Rapids, Mich	Feb. 13, 1905	Beaumont, Tex	Feb. 4, 1904	Do.
Rosa T	20	1893				Old River, Tex	Apr. 1, 1905	Galveston, Tex	Mar. 4, 1904	Do.
Ruth [b]	17	1896				Peekskill, N. Y	Nov. 14, 1905	Houston, Tex	Nov. 19, 1904	Do.
Sun Flower	17	1905				Galveston, Tex	June 19, 1905	Galveston, Tex	First inspn	
Stella	18	1900				Stienway, R. I	June 26, 1905	Houston, Tex	Mar. 24, 1904	Do.
Sousie	20	1882				Clear Creek, Tex	July 20, 1905	Galveston, Tex	First inspn	
Yevette	34	1903				Wooster, Tex	Jan. 18, 1905	do	Jan. 12, 1904	Do.
Yilliah	18	1903				New York, N. Y	Aug. 30, 1905	do	Aug. 29, 1904	Do.
Freight sail vessel of over 700 tons.										
C. P. Dixon (schooner)	728	1881				Belfast, Me	Mar. 11, 1905	Sabine Pass, Tex	Feb. 10, 1904	New York, N. Y.

LOCAL DISTRICT OF MOBILE, ALA.

Ocean passenger steamer.										
Tarpon	449	1887	1891	1899		Wilmington, Del	Jan. 17, 1905	Mobile, Ala	Jan. 18, 1904	Mobile, Ala.
Inland passenger steamers.										
Annie D [c]	85	1893	1903	1904		Stockton, Ala	Dec. 31, 1904	Mobile, Ala	Dec. 29, 1903	Mobile, Ala.
Angelo	122	1893	1898	1898		Pensacola, Fla	Jan. 5, 1905	Pensacola, Fla	Dec. 14, 1903	Do.
Amelia	29	1903		1891		Mobile, Ala	Mar. 8, 1905	Mobile, Ala	Feb. 10, 1904	Do.

[a] Estimated. [b] Formerly Pherabe, 1904. [c] Certificated Jan. 3, 1905.

DOMESTIC VESSELS INSPECTED, YEAR ENDED DECEMBER 31, 1905—TENTH SUPERVISING DISTRICT—MOBILE, ALA.—Continued.

Names of vessels and class.	Gross tonnage.	Hull built.	Hull rebuilt.	Boilers built.	Boilers rebuilt.	Where built.	Date of inspection.	Where inspected.	Date of previous inspection.	Local district where previously inspected.
Inland passenger steamers—Continued.										
Amelia	16	1904		1904		Scranton, Miss	Nov. 14, 1905	Moss Point, Miss	Oct. 8, 1904	Mobile, Ala.
Annie D	85	1893	1903	1904		Stockton, Ala	Dec. 27, 1905	Mobile, Ala	Dec. 31, 1904	Do.
Baldwin	218	1905		1905		Mobile, Ala	July 7, 1905	do	First inspn.	
Cornelia C	26	1904		1904		Columbus, Miss	Jan. 24, 1905	Columbus, Miss	do	
City of Tampa	125	1887		1896		Mason City, W. Va	Apr. 20, 1905	Pensacola, Fla	Apr. 20, 1904	Do.
Columbia	156	1900		1900		Pensacola, Fla	Aug. 2, 1905	do	Aug. 1, 1904	Do.
City of Mobile	209	1898		1898		Mobile, Ala	Oct. 30, 1905	Mobile, Ala	Nov. 4, 1904	Do.
Capt. Fritz	57	1892	1904	1904		Moss Point, Miss	Nov. 28, 1905	Pensacola, Fla	Dec. 14, 1904	Do.
Dawn	23	1897		1896		Scranton, Miss	Mar. 22, 1905	Mobile, Ala	Jan. 12, 1904	Do.
Dixie	72	1904		1904		Rome, Ga	Oct. 17, 1905	Rome, Ga	Nov. 21, 1904	Do.
El Rio	16	1897		1897		Mobile, Ala	Feb. 25, 1905	Mobile, Ala	Feb. 27, 1904	Do.
Enterprise	40	1896		1895		Tottenville, N. Y	June 7, 1905	Pensacola, Fla	June 7, 1904	Do.
Eran Dantzler	27	1904		1903		Scranton, Miss	Nov. 13, 1905	Scranton, Miss	Sept. 10, 1904	Do.
Ethel	25	1893		1904		do	Dec. 11, 1905	Mobile, Ala	Dec. 24, 1904	Do.
F. C. Loxley	32	1900		1900		do	Jan. 28, 1905	Gulfport, Miss	Jan. 29, 1904	Do.
Florence Witherbee [a]	84	1873	1889	1894		Williamsburg, N. Y	Mar. 13, 1905	Pensacola, Fla	Mar. 11, 1904	Do.
Fairhope	93	1901	1905	1902	1905	Fairhope, Ala	Sept. 15, 1905	Mobile, Ala	Aug. 5, 1904	Do.
Florence	29	1874	1901	1901		New York, N. Y	Nov. 29, 1905	Pensacola, Fla	Dec. 13, 1904	Do.
Farnsworth	41	1902		1901		Scranton, Miss	Dec. 19, 1905	Scranton, Miss	Dec. 22, 1904	Do.
Gertrude	39	1900		1899		do	Jan. 11, 1905	Mobile, Ala	Jan. 11, 1904	Do.
Gulfport	224	1903		1903		Philadelphia, Pa	Jan. 28, 1905	Gulfport, Miss	Jan. 29, 1904	Do.
Gladys	30	1901		1901		Moss Point, Miss	Mar. 8, 1905	Mobile, Ala	Mar. 1, 1904	Do.
Hard Cash	248	1876		1892		Pittsburg, Pa	Feb. 3, 1905	do	Feb. 5, 1904	Do.
Harry Greenwood	27	1900		1900		Scranton, Miss	Apr. 17, 1905	do	Apr. 15, 1904	Do.
Helen	20	1884	1903	1901		Buffalo, N. Y	Aug. 3, 1905	Pensacola, Fla	Aug. 1, 1904	Do.
Hustler	16	1901		1901		Scranton, Miss	Oct. 11, 1905	Mobile, Ala	Oct. 20, 1904	Do.
Ida	11	1902		1902		Bon Secour, Ala	Feb. 9, 1905	do	Feb. 9, 1904	Do.
Isabel	12	1896		1896		Moss Point, Miss	Mar. 11, 1905	do	Feb. 29, 1904	Do.
Iva	27	1904		1904		Mobile, Ala	Mar. 15, 1905	do	Mar. 18, 1904	Do.
Jumbo	14	1883		1891		Bay Point, Fla	Jan. 4, 1905	do	Jan. 4, 1904	Do.
J. C. Watson [b]	58	1879	1897	1893		Camden, N. J	Mar. 2, 1905	do	Feb. 26, 1904	Do.
Jas. A. Carney	199	1894	1905	1898		Mobile, Ala	July 27, 1905	do	May 11, 1904	Do.
Kimball	23	1903	1905	1903		Scranton, Miss	July 28, 1905	do	Oct. 26, 1904	Do.
Lee Kimball, jr	58	1904		1904		do	Jan. 7, 1905	do	First inspn.	
Laura	56	1901		1901		do	May 2, 1905	Moss Point, Miss	May 3, 1904	Do.
Lapwing	34	1901		1901		Mobile, Ala	May 16, 1905	Mobile, Ala	May 21, 1904	Do.
Louis Dolive	314	1861	1889	1888		Wilmington, Del	May 26, 1905	do	Mar. 30, 1904	Do.
Liberty	218	1889		1889		Harmar, Ohio	Aug. 26, 1905	do	Oct. 18, 1902	Memphis, Tenn.
Monarch [c]	143	1882		1894		Charleston, S. C	Dec. 13, 1904	Pensacola, Fla	Dec. 13, 1903	Mobile, Ala.
Mary S. Blees	214	1899		1899		Mobile, Ala	Jan. 9, 1905	Mobile, Ala	Jan. 9, 1904	Do.
Mary	27	1897		1897		Scranton, Miss	Jan. 13, 1905	Bay St. Louis, Miss	Jan. 12, 1904	Do.

Mary Wittich	126	1882		1902		Camden, N. J	Feb. 20, 1905	Mobile, Ala	Feb. 15, 1904	Do.
Mary Louisa	87	1871		1898		Philadelphia, Pa	Mar. 6, 1905	do	Feb. 23, 1903	Apalachicola, Fla.
Mary E. Staples	201	1905		1905		Mobile, Ala	Oct. 26, 1905	do	First inspn.	
Mary	198	1899		1899		Jeffersonville, Ind	Dec. 6, 1905	do	June 15, 1904	Mobile, Ala.
Monarch [c]	143	1882		1894		Charleston, S. C	Dec. 13, 1905	Pensacola, Fla	Dec. 13, 1904	Do.
Neptune	17	1896		1896		Scranton, Miss	Jan. 27, 1905	Scranton, Miss	Jan. 19, 1904	Do
Nimrod	116	1890	1893	1903		Athens, N. Y	Feb. 17, 1905	Mobile, Ala	Feb. 17, 1904	Do.
Nellie	61	1879	1901	1901		Camden, N. J	Apr. 13, 1905	Pensacola, Fla	Jan. 14, 1904	Do.
Nelley Keyser	42	1885	1894	1897		New Orleans, La	Nov. 28, 1905	do	Dec. 14, 1904	Do.
Nettie Quill	299	1896		1886		Mobile, Ala	Dec. 7, 1905	Mobile, Ala	Dec. 15, 1904	Do.
Okoloosa	46	1886		1895		Milton, Fla	June 9, 1905	Bagdad, Fla	June 8, 1904	Do.
Ouachita	98	1899		1899		Jeffersonville, Ind	Sept. 1, 1905	Mobile, Ala	Aug. 1, 1904	Do.
Pic	4	1888		1896		Handsboro, Miss	May 1, 1905	Moss Point, Miss	May 14, 1904	Do.
Pat	16	1902		1902		Mobile, Ala	May 10, 1905	Mobile, Ala	May 10, 1904	Do.
Pascagoula	65	1904		1904		Scranton, Miss	Nov. 13, 1905	Scranton, Miss	Aug. 1, 1904	Do.
Rosalia	8	1886		1888	1902	Moss Point, Miss	May 1, 1905	Moss Point, Miss	May 14, 1904	Do.
Vienna	176	1898		1885		Columbus, Miss	Feb. 28, 1905	Columbus, Miss	Feb. 22, 1904	Do.
Wm. McGee	24	1898		1898		Buffalo, N. Y	Feb. 13, 1905	Mobile, Ala	Feb. 5, 1904	Do.
Water Witch	11	1874	1890	1886	1904	Green Bay, Wis	Mar. 24, 1905	do	Mar. 24, 1904	Do.
Wm. M. Flanders	58	1872		1891		East Boston, Mass	May 18, 1905	Pensacola, Fla	May 20, 1904	Do.
Wasp	17	1904		1903		Mobile, Ala	July 8, 1905	Gulfport, Miss	July 7, 1904	Do.
W. J. Bethea	242	1897		1897		do	Aug. 1, 1905	Mobile, Ala	Aug. 1, 1904	Do.
Zoe	42	1903		1902		do	Apr. 24, 1905	do	Apr. 23, 1904	Do.
Ziyara	9	1890	1905	1899		Rome, N. Y	July 3, 1905	do	June 16, 1904	Do.
Ocean freight steamers.										
Pensacola	1,696	1888		1888		West Hartlepool, England.	Aug. 24, 1905	Mobile, Ala	Sept. 25, 1904	Mobile, Ala.
Roanoke	546	1871		1883		Wilmington, Del	Jan. 7, 1905	do	Dec. 31, 1903	Do.
Inland freight steamers.										
Alabama	137	1904		1884		Gadsden, Ala	Oct. 17, 1905	Rome, Ga	Oct. 18, 1904	Mobile, Ala.
Aid	28	1902		1895		Apalachicola, Fla	Dec. 14, 1905	Caryville, Fla	Sept. 12, 1904	Do.
Belle	74	1903		1903		Vernon, Fla	June 22, 1905	Pensacola, Fla	June 8, 1904	Do.
City of Gadsden, Ala	14	1905		1899		Gadsden, Ala	Sept. 13, 1905	Gadsden, Ala	First inspn.	
Connasauga	39	1897		1894		Rome, Ga	Oct. 17, 1905	Rome, Ga	Nov. 21, 1904	Do.
Edna C	124	1904		1903		Pensacola, Fla	Aug. 3, 1905	Pensacola, Fla	Aug. 1, 1904	Do.
Mary C. Byrne	28	1903		1903		Stockton, Ala	May 2, 1905	Mobile, Ala	Mar. 14, 1904	Do.
Owl	32	1899		1901		Scranton, Miss	May 15, 1905	Scranton, Miss	May 14, 1904	Do.
Vernon	61	1897		1897		Geneva, Ala	Feb. 24, 1905	Pensacola, Fla	Feb. 1, 1904	Do.
Willie C. Wagnon	151	1897		1897		Gadsden, Ala	Mar. 20, 1905	Rome, Ga	Mar. 21, 1904	Do.
Ocean towing steamers.										
Bessie H. Dantzler	108	1901		1901		Scranton, Miss	Nov. 14, 1905	Scranton, Miss	Nov. 18, 1904	Mobile, Ala.
E. E. Simpson	109	1877		1904		Camden, N. J	Apr. 21, 1905	Pensacola, Fla	Apr. 20, 1904	Do.
Echo	136	1883		1891		do	Dec. 15, 1905	Mobile, Ala	Dec. 21, 1904	Do.
Mary Lee	34	1896		1903		Scranton, Miss	Dec. 13, 1905	Pensacola, Fla	Dec. 13, 1904	Do.
Sybil	76	1905		1905		do	Nov. 18, 1905	Mobile, Ala	First inspn.	

a Formerly U. S. S. Maud, 1904. b Formerly Italian, 1903. c Certificated Jan. 7, 1905.

DOMESTIC VESSELS INSPECTED, YEAR ENDED DECEMBER 31, 1905—TENTH SUPERVISING DISTRICT—MOBILE, ALA.—Continued.

Names of vessels and class.	Gross tonnage.	Hull built.	Hull rebuilt.	Boilers built.	Boilers rebuilt.	Where built.	Date of inspection.	Where inspected.	Date of previous inspection.	Local district where previously inspected.
Inland towing steamers.										
Alberta B	9	1893		1892		Scranton, Miss	Jan. 12, 1905	Mobile, Ala	Jan. 11, 1904	Mobile, Ala.
Allie R	17	1894	1899	1899		Milton, Fla	May 18, 1905	Pensacola, Fla	May 16, 1904	Do.
Alert	158	1885	1905	1885		Jeffersonville, Ind	June 16, 1905	Tuscaloosa, Ala	May 30, 1904	Do.
Clarence	3	1888	1905	1901		Mobile, Ala	July 7, 1905	Mobile, Ala	Apr. 7, 1904	Do.
Celestine	23	1883		1887		Newburgh, N. Y	July 18, 1905	Pensacola, Fla	July 18, 1904	Do.
Captain Taifor	43	1905		1905		Scranton, Miss	Dec. 11, 1905	Mobile, Ala	First inspn.	
Deo Volente	40	1873	1891	1905		New London, Conn	Nov. 21, 1905	do	July 18, 1904	Do.
Eva	27	1889		1889		Moss Point, Miss	Mar. 10, 1905	Moss Point, Miss	Mar. 1, 1904	Do.
Edna	28	1902		1902		Mobile, Ala	Oct. 6, 1905	Mobile, Ala	Oct. 3, 1904	Do.
Elma	4	1893		1903		Scranton, Miss	Nov. 14, 1905	Scranton, Miss	Oct. 8, 1904	Do.
Eleanor	28	1894		1904		do	Dec. 19, 1905	do	Dec. 21, 1904	Do.
Florida	301	1890		1903		Pensacola, Fla	Jan. 20, 1905	Pensacola, Fla	Jan. 14, 1904	Do.
Fidget	82	1894	1899	1904		do	Nov. 27, 1905	do	Sept. 13, 1904	Do.
Gus Shammel	42	1903		1903		Freeport, Fla	Apr. 20, 1905	do	Apr. 20, 1904	Do.
Hero	4	1894		1892		Mobile, Ala	Jan. 2, 1905	Mobile, Ala	Dec. 30, 1903	Do.
Julius Elbert	42	1893		1899		Biloxi, Miss	Nov. 15, 1905	Biloxi, Miss	Sept. 17, 1904	Do.
Linus	28	1890		1897		Port Washington, Fla	Jan. 21, 1905	Millview, Fla	Jan. 26, 1904	Do.
Lizzie Frank	36	1880		1889		Grand Haven, Mich	Jan. 20, 1905	Pensacola, Fla	Jan. 14, 1904	Do.
Lady Jane	21	1895		1905		Charlevoix, Mich	May 15, 1905	Gulfport, Miss	Apr. 4, 1904	Do.
Le Baron	102	1893		1902		Wilmington, Del	Aug. 9, 1905	Mobile, Ala	Aug. 1, 1904	Do.
Linnet	7	1904		1904		Mobile, Ala	Oct. 7, 1905	do	Oct. 28, 1904	Do.
Minnie R	30	1903		1904		do	Jan. 23, 1905	do	Jan. 20, 1904	Do.
Maggie	19	1893		1892	1905	Scranton, Miss	June 8, 1905	Pensacola, Fla	June 7, 1904	Do.
Nellie	14	1900		1900		Bon Secour, Ala	Jan. 12, 1905	Mobile, Ala	Jan. 12, 1904	Do.
Native	10	1891		1904		Scranton, Miss	Oct. 21, 1905	do	Oct. 20, 1904	Do.
Nemesis	11	1903		1903		Biloxi, Miss	Nov. 16, 1905	Biloxi, Miss	Aug. 23, 1904	Do.
Olivilo	37	1901		1897		Geneva, Ala	Jan. 14, 1905	Freeport, Fla	Dec. 2, 1903	Do.
Ottawa	20	1897	1904	1893		Mobile, Ala	Dec. 16, 1905	Demopolis, Ala	May 4, 1904	Do.
Portland	11	1893		1901		Chicago, Ill	Aug. 31, 1905	Bayou La Batre, Ala	Aug. 24, 1904	Do.
Rowena	31	1897		1897		Biloxi, Miss	Nov. 15, 1905	Biloxi, Miss	Dec. 11, 1904	Do.
Telephone	18	1904		1904		Scranton, Miss	Feb. 21, 1905	Moss Point, Miss	Feb. 19, 1904	Do.
Toiler	22	1875		1897		Newburgh, N. Y	Nov. 13, 1905	Scranton, Miss	Sept. 10, 1904	Do.
Vivian	25	1903		1903		Mobile, Ala	Oct. 5, 1905	Mobile, Ala	Oct. 11, 1904	Do.
Victor [a]	18	1893	1903	1893	1903	Scranton, Miss	Nov. 18, 1904	Scranton, Miss	Nov. 2, 1903	Do.
Venture	7	1889		1898		New Orleans, La	July 20, 1905	Mobile, Ala	July 18, 1904	Do.
Vera	41	1896		1897		Handsboro, Miss	Nov. 15, 1905	Biloxi, Miss	Dec. 11, 1904	Do.
Victor	18	1893	1903	1893	1905	Scranton, Miss	Nov. 20, 1905	Moss Point, Miss	Nov. 18, 1904	Do.

Steam pleasure yachts.										
Cyclone	8	1893		1893		Montgomery, Ala	July 12,1905	Demopolis, Ala	July 17,1904	Mobile, Ala.
Ernest G	4	1905			1905	Scranton, Miss	Nov. 14,1905	Scranton, Miss	First inspn.	
Folly	4	1891		1904		Pass Christian, Miss	June 28,1905	Bay St. Louis, Miss	June 13,1904	Do.
Iona	22	1904		1904		Beauvoir, Miss	do	Beauvoir, Miss	June 14,1904	Do.
Lillie	4	1900		1903		Pensacola, Fla	June 8,1905	Pensacola, Fla	June 7,1904	Do.
Mecca	5	1892		1904		Bristol, R. I	May 23,1905	Mobile, Ala	May 24,1904	Do.
Meriwana	7	1905		1905		Josephine, Ala	June 8,1905	Millview, Fla	First inspn.	
Mary C	4	1898		1899		Cahaba, Ala	Oct. 14,1905	Mobile, Ala	June 22,1904	Do.
Reva	17	1895		1904		Biloxi, Miss	May 25,1905	Biloxi, Miss	May 26,1904	Do.
Thistle	12	1901		1903		Beauvoir, Miss	do	do	do	Do.
Vixen	4	1900		1900		Manatee, Fla	Feb. 16,1905	Mobile, Ala	Dec. 7,1902	New Orleans, La.
Miscellaneous steam vessels.										
Alice (water boat)	25	1889		1889		Pensacola, Fla	Nov. 27,1905	Pensacola, Fla	Dec. 14,1904	Mobile, Ala.
E. W. Menefee (oyster dredge)	80	1889		1897		Caryville, Fla	June 28,1905	Biloxi, Miss	June 14,1904	Do.
Florida (pilot)	57	1900		1898		Scranton, Miss	May 13,1905	Pensacola, Fla	May 25,1904	Do.
Vessels propelled by gasoline motors.										
Anna Long (oyster dredge)	25	1904				Biloxi, Miss	Nov. 15,1905	Biloxi, Miss	Nov. 5,1904	Mobile, Ala.
Emma (oyster dredge)	27	1901				Scranton, Miss	Jan. 29,1905	Bay St. Louis, Miss	Jan. 18,1904	Do.
Fairchild (oyster dredge)	27	1901				do	do	do	Jan. 16,1904	New Orleans, La.
Harry Cage (oyster dredge)	25	1904				Biloxi, Miss	Nov. 15,1905	Biloxi, Miss	Nov. 5,1904	Mobile, Ala.
Little Annie (oyster dredge)	18	1888	1904			Freeport, Fla	Jan. 27,1905	do	First inspn.	
Lillie L. (oyster dredge)	25	1904				Biloxi, Miss	Nov. 15,1905	do	Nov. 5,1904	Do.
Peerless (freight)	45	1904				Handsboro, Miss	Jan. 29,1905	Bay St. Louis, Miss	Feb. 8,1904	Do.
Pilot (pilot boat)	35	1903				Scranton, Miss	Nov. 13,1905	Scranton, Miss	Aug. 17,1904	Do.
Rambler (passenger)	21	1905				Holly, Fla	June 20,1905	Pensacola, Fla	First inspn.	
Rita J. (freight)	28	1901				Scranton, Miss	July 8,1905	Scranton, Miss	May 14,1904	Do.
Sylph (freight)	34	1899				Demopolis, Ala	May 8,1905	Demopolis, Ala	May 4,1904	Do.
Sea Em (passenger)	19	1900				Shieldsboro, Miss	Aug. 28,1905	Mobile, Ala	July 1,1904	Do.
Willie N. Johnson, jr., (oyster dredge).	19	1901				Biloxi, Miss	Dec. 19,1905	Biloxi, Miss	Dec. 21,1904	Do.
Freight sail vessels of over 700 tons.										
Charles G. Rice (bark)	715	1879				Yarmouth, Me	Jan. 5,1905	Pensacola, Fla	July 1,1903	New York, N. Y.
Thomas A. Ward (schooner)	805	1891				Camden, N. J	Feb. 10,1905	Gulfport, Miss	Jan. 4,1904	Jacksonville, Fla.

[a] Certificated January 11, 1905.

SUMMARY OF CASUALTIES, VIOLATIONS OF LAW, AND INVESTIGATIONS FOR THE YEAR ENDED DECEMBER 31, 1905.

FIRST SUPERVISING DISTRICT.

LOCAL DISTRICT OF SAN FRANCISCO, CAL.

January 1.—Steamer *Lakme* struck on bar at Humboldt Bay, Cal., lost her rudder, and engines were disabled. The spar buoy, marking the end of north jetty, had drifted from position, thereby causing the master of the steamer to be misled as to the channel. Damage to steamer about $20,000. Master exonerated.

January 6.—H. C. Worth, chief mate of bark *Kaiulani*, charged with intoxication while on duty September 9 and November 14, 1904. Case investigated; charges not sustained.

January 28.—On appeal, November 15, 1904, of Peter C. Hedvall, chief mate of steam vessels, from the decision of the local inspectors rendered October 18, 1904, revoking his license in connection with casualty to steamer *Northland* on September 19, 1904. the supervising inspector, first district, on January 28, 1905, modified said revocation to a suspension of license for the period of 12 months from October 18, 1904.

January 30.—In the case of loss of a passenger overboard from steamer *W. H. Kruger* on November 24, 1904, reported in annual report, year 1904, upon investigation thereof, the master and chief mate of the steamer were exonerated.

February 14.—In the case of the collision between the steamers *Grace Dollar* and *St. Helena*, on December 15, 1904, reported in annual report, year 1904, upon investigation thereof, the masters and pilots of the respective steamers were exonerated.

February 14.—While steamer *Jacinto* was at landing, Colusa, Cal., a deck hand named E. Segnanini fell overboard and drowned before a boat which was promptly lowered could reach him.

February 14.—A. W. Howard, chief mate of schooner *Annie E. Smale*, charged with misconduct in December, 1904, and January 15, 1905. Case dismissed April 21, 1905.

February 16.—Chris Jensen, seaman on gasoline boat *Ida A.*, fell overboard in Drakes Bay, Cal., and drowned before a boat which was lowered could reach him.

February 23.—Steamers *Point Arena* and *Berkeley* collided on Bay of San Francisco. Case investigated. License of Frederick Miller, master and pilot of steamer *Point Arena*, suspended March 16 for 5 days; and that of James Blaker, master and pilot of steamer *Berkeley*, suspended for 15 days. Damage to steamer *Berkeley*, $60; to steamer *Point Arena*, $1,000.

February 27.—The steamship *Oregon*, 2,335 gross tons, became afire in her after-between decks while at sea off Crescent City, Cal. The fire was extinguished by the officers and crew. Case investigated by the supervising inspector, first district. The testimony did not establish the cause of the fire. Captain Warner and his officers were exonerated from blame and awarded great credit in battling successfully with the fire for 48 hours. Damage to steamer about $16,000; to cargo, $60,000.

March 1.—Steamers *Transit* and *Oakland* collided in a dense fog on Bay of San Francisco. Damage to the *Oakland*, about $150; to the *Transit*, $700.

March 2.—Steamers *Alert* and *San Jose* collided in a dense fog on Bay of San Francisco. Case investigated. License of O. O. W. Parker, pilot of steamer *San Jose*, suspended for 15 days, and that of M. R. Downey, of the *Alert*, suspended for 5 days, March 20. Captain Parker appealed, March 20, to the supervising inspector, first district who, on March 24, sustained the decision of the local inspectors. Damage to the *Alert*, $250; to the *San Jose*, nominal.

March 7.—Steamer *Cascade* grounded in a thick fog near Point Dunne, Cal., and was towed to San Pedro for temporary repairs, and subsequently to San Francisco for permanent repairs. Case investigated. License of Edward Jahnsen, master, suspended April 17 for 30 days. Damage to steamer, about $4,000.

April 9.—Steamer *Amelia* caught fire in her upper engine room while lying at her berth in San Francisco. Damage slight.

Casualties, Violations of Law, and Investigations, Year ended December 31, 1905—First Supervising District—San Francisco, Cal.—Continued.

April 22.—Steamer *Sea Foam* collided with schooner *Del Norte* at sea off Coquille River, Oreg. Case investigated and the master and chief mate of the steamer were exonerated May 23. The *Del Norte* became a total loss and was valued at $4,000. Damage to the steamer, about $100.

April 30.—Steamer *Roanoke*, charged with violation of the rules of navigation at sea off Point Arena, Cal., April 29. Case investigated and R. J. Dunham, master of the *Roanoke*, was censured May 12.

May 3.—While steamer *Northland* was at Redondo, Cal., one of her lifeboats with 4 men was capsized on way to moorings and 2 of the men were drowned before assistance could be rendered.

May 4.—The steamer *Meteor* collided with schooner *A. B. Johnson* in Bay of San Francisco. Case investigated and the master of the steamer was exonerated, June 17. Damage to schooner, about $8,000.

May 12.—Steamer *H. E. Wright* struck on rocks near San Pablo Point, Cal., the vessel refusing to answer her helm. Damage to steamer, about $150.

May 17.—Steamer *Tamalpais* collided with her ferry slip at Sausalito, Cal., her engines refusing to reverse. Case investigated and the licenses of Richard S. Wosser, chief engineer, and John T. Babue, assistant engineer, were each suspended, June 1, for 15 days. Damage nominal.

May 18.—Two deck hands (colored) of steamer *Mary Garratt*, while scuffling in play, went overboard in Stockton Channel and were drowned before aid could be given them.

May 28.—Steamer *Arctic* collided with the gasoline launch *Dewey* (under 15 tons) in Bay of San Francisco. The launch sunk and the engineer, R. R. Hawley, and Mr. Miller, a baggage agent, were drowned. No blame could be attached to the steamer.

June 2.—While steamer *Breakwater* was lying at Coos Bay, Oreg., a fireman, F. Patuso, was drowned. It is believed that deceased was fishing at the side of the vessel and fell overboard.

June 7.—While steamer *State of California* was lying at her berth in San Francisco, a fire broke out in cargo in forward hold and was extinguished by the ship's pumps and the aid of the city fire department. Damage to cargo estimated at $3,000; to steamer, about $1,000.

June 10.—Steamer *Relief* charged with violation of the rules of the road. Complainant was notified but did not answer.

June 12.—Harry O. Clark, second mate of steamer *George Loomis*, charged with intoxication and violation of section 4449, Revised Statutes, June 7. Case investigated. Defendant waived trial and threw himself upon the mercy of the court. Charges virtually sustained, and license of Mr. Clark was suspended, June 20, for 30 days.

June 18.—While steamer *Acme* was at Mill wharf, Eureka, Cal., receiving cargo, a fire originated at her donkey boiler. Fire extinguished.

July 1.—The barge *Argus*, in tow of steamer *A. C. Freese*, collided with schooner *Mabel and Edith*, which was aground on river bank with a line across stream in Stockton slough. The schooner sunk in 10 feet of water.

July 9.—The freight steamer *Celia* broke a blade of her propeller at sea off Port Harford, Cal. Damage about $250.

July 11.—Steamer *W. G. Hall* collided with the United States transport *Sherman* in channel leading out of Honolulu Harbor, causing one of the boats of the *W. G. Hall* to be smashed. Case investigated by the supervising inspector, first district, and the license of George H. Piltz, master of the *W. G. Hall*, suspended, August 3, for 10 days.

July 13.—Steamer *Robert Dollar* collided with a barge in tow of steamer *Tiger* on bay of San Francisco, causing the barge to capsize. Case investigated and the license of Henry M. Hughes, master and pilot of the steamer *Tiger*, suspended, September 8, for 10 days. Damage to steamer nominal; to barge, $3,500.

July 29.—Mr. Watson Berry, a passenger on steamer *Brunswick*, committed suicide at sea off Point Arena, Cal., by jumping overboard. A boat was promptly lowered and search made, without finding Mr. Berry.

August 15.—Mr. George Sargent, a passenger on ferry steamer *Ellen*, fell from the rail at ferry slip, Vallejo, Cal., and was fatally crusht between the guard rail and the slip.

August 19.—The freight sail vessel *Spartan* was wrecked on a shoal near Kahului. Case investigated and the master exonerated, November 16. The *Spartan* was valued at $15,000 and her cargo at $5,000.

CASUALTIES, VIOLATIONS OF LAW, AND INVESTIGATIONS, YEAR ENDED DECEMBER 31, 1905—FIRST SUPERVISING DISTRICT—SAN FRANCISCO, CAL.—Continued.

August 23.—A passenger, name unknown, jumped overboard from the steamer *General Frisbie* in bay of San Pablo, Cal. A boat was promptly lowered and the man rescued from the water, but he died one-half hour later.

August 29.—Harry F. McMullen, chief engineer of the steamer *Newport*, charged with intoxication and insubordination at Panama, Acupulco, and Manzanillo in August dates at those ports. Case investigated; charges not sustained. Defendant, however, admitted a neglect of duty on his part and his license was suspended, October 10, for 90 days.

September 5.—The steamers *Gipsy* and *Apache* collided on bay of San Francisco. Case investigated by the supervising inspector, first district. License of Carl Saulit, master and pilot of the *Apache*, was suspended, September 23, for 30 days, and that of Herman D. Leland, master and pilot of the *Gipsy*, for same period. Damage to the *Apache* about $800; to the *Gipsy*, about $400.

September 8.—Steamer *F. A. Kilburn* struck on the bar at Coos Bay, Oreg. Case investigated and the license of Albert Thompson, master and pilot of the steamer, was suspended, November 10, for 6 months. Damage to steamer, about $6,000. Captain Thompson, on November 14, appealed to the supervising inspector, first district, who, on November 25, modified the above suspension to one of 5 months.

September 17.—At sea, 4 days out from New York, the tubes in after port boiler of the steamship *Californian* collapsed, causing injuries to the chief engineer, 1 fireman, 1 oiler, and 2 coal passers. Mr. A. L. Blanchfowler, a water tender, fell from the upper fireroom grating and was killed. Case investigated, and license of Hugh W. Salbador, chief engineer, suspended, December 26, for 3 months. On December 26, Mr. Salbador appealed to the supervising inspector, first district, who, on January 3, 1906, reversed the decision of the local inspectors.

September 21.—Steamer *Del Norte* collided with *Car Float No. 2* in Oakland Creek, Cal. Case investigated by the supervising inspector, first district, and the license of Herman T. Payne, master and pilot of steamer *Del Norte*, suspended, October 10, for 30 days. Steamer *Del Norte* was damaged to extent of about $1,500.

September 23.—The gasoline boat *Sotoyome* sprung a leak at sea, near Greenwood, Cal.; became water-logged and was towed to San Francisco.

September 27.—The freight steamer *Gipsy* struck near China Point, Monterey Bay Cal., and became a total wreck. Case investigated and the license of Thomas Boyd, master and pilot, was suspended, October 25, for 12 months. No lives lost. The *Gipsy* was valued at $20,000; and her cargo at $5,000.

September 30.—The steamship *Alameda* stranded on rocks at Fort Point, bay of San Francisco; was gotten off and repaired at a cost of about $60,000. Case investigated. Thomas Dowdell, master, was exonerated, and the license of Charles B. Johnson, master and pilot, who was in charge as State pilot, was suspended, November 1, for 6 months.

October 1.—Steamer *Santa Barbara* struck on rocks near Gualala, Cal. Case investigated and the licenses of her following officers were suspended, October 19, viz: Frank B. Zoddart, master and pilot, for 3 months; Edward E. Johnson, chief mate, for 6 months; and Arthur Self, second mate, for 3 months. Damage to steamer estimated at $20,000; to cargo, $5,000. Edward E. Johnson, chief mate, appealed, October 25, to the supervising inspector, first district, who, on November 6, affirmed the above suspension of 6 months.

October 4.—The bark *Vidette*, in tow of steamer *National City*, collided with the bark *Himalaya*, at anchor in bay of San Francisco. Collision caused by the steamer losing control of her tow. Damage to the *Vidette* estimated at $800; to the *Himalaya*, $1,000.

October 5.—The steamship *St. Paul* stranded on rocks at Point Gorda, Cal., and became a total loss. Case investigated, and on November 8, the license of Clement Randall, master and pilot, was suspended for 18 months and that of William Holmes, as second mate (who was in charge on the bridge as third mate) was suspended likewise for 18 months. The *St. Paul* was valued at $284,000, and her cargo at $166,000.

October 5.—The steamers *Brooklyn* and *San Gabriel* collided lightly in a dense fog at sea off Point Arena, Cal. Damage nominal.

October 8.—While swinging out the working boat of steamer *Chico* near her anchorage at Noyo, Cal., a seaman named A. Nyland lost his balance and fell overboard and drowned, tho immediate efforts were made to rescue him.

October 15.—Mr. D. McGowan, passenger on steamer *Sea Foam*, was drowned at sea off Little River, Cal. Mr. McGowan was observed as soon as he was in the water and a boat in the davits was lowered and sent to the rescue, but without success in finding deceased.

CASUALTIES, VIOLATIONS OF LAW, AND INVESTIGATIONS, YEAR ENDED DECEMBER 31, 1905—FIRST SUPERVISING DISTRICT—SAN FRANCISCO, CAL.—Continued.

October 19.—The gasoline boat *W. P. Fuller* collided with a rowboat of the barkentine *Arago* in bay of San Francisco. P. Peterson, one of the two occupants of the rowboat, was drowned. The rowboat displayed no light, but the *W. P. Fuller* made active efforts to avert the collision and sounded signals.

October 27.—The steamers *Aurelia* and *Umatilla* collided while the latter was backing from her wharf at San Francisco. Case investigated and no blame attached to the master in charge of either steamer, a misunderstanding having evidently arisen in the exchange of signals between the two vessels. Damage to the *Aurelia* about $4,000; to the *Umatilla* about $1,500.

November 4.—Steamer *Potrero* collided in dense fog with the schooner *King Cyrus* at anchor in bay of San Francisco, carrying away the head gear of the schooner. No bell from the schooner was heard by the officers and lookout on the steamer.

November 4.—The schooner *Transit*, in tow of steamer *Pilot*, collided in a dense fog with the United States steamer *General Mifflin*. The *Pilot* was backing her engines, and the engines of the *General Mifflin* were apparently going astern at the time the two vessels came in view of each other.

November 6.—Steamer *Arrow* collided with schooner *Rock of Cashel* in bay of San Pablo. The steamer was on her course to clear the schooner when the latter came about in a manner to cause the collision.

November 13.—The light-house tender *Madrono* collided with the gasoline boat *Nonpareil* on bay of San Francisco. Mr. J. Boer, a deck hand of the *Nonpareil*, was knocked overboard by the force of collision and drowned. Case investigated and the masters of the respective vessels exonerated, November 27.

November 27.—The working boat of steamer *Gualala* was capsized by a heavy swell at Rockport, Cal., and one seaman, S. Seger, was drowned before a lifeboat from the steamer came to the rescue.

November 27.—Steamer *Roanoke* lost her rudder and struck on the bar at Humboldt Bay, Cal. With jury rudder twice rigged she made her way to locality of Point Arena, and was thence towed to San Francisco. Case investigated. Master exonerated, December 26. Damage to vessel estimated at $5,000.

December 8.—The steamer *Despatch* at San Francisco, Cal., caught fire from gases originated from her petroleum fuel. These gases ignited from open lamps used by employees on board. James Mitchell, a boy engaged in scaling the boiler, was killed. Case investigated and the licenses of Henry Weber, master, and James M. Spencer, chief engineer, were suspended December 29, each for 90 days. Damage to vessel estimated at about $6,000. The master and the chief engineer appealed, respectively, January 2 and 3, 1906, from the above suspensions of their licenses, to the supervising inspector, first district, who modified same, January 9, 1906, to a period of 45 days each.

December 15.—One of the boats of steamer *Greenwood*, with two seamen, engaged in letting go a breast line of the vessel at Bowen's landing, Cal., was capsized by a heavy breaker, and one seaman, Carl Peters, was drowned before assistance could be given him.

December 16.—Harry Vahlbusch, second mate of steamer *Costa Rica*, charged with intoxication while on duty, December 14, at San Francisco. Charge admitted and license of Mr. Vahlbusch suspended, January 2, 1906, for 30 days.

December 20.—Frank Connors, in attempting to board the steamer *H. E. Wright* at her wharf in Stockton, fell on the deck, striking his head and rolled into the water. He was rescued, but died 30 minutes afterwards.

December 25.—The crown sheet of port furnace in main boiler of steamer *Acme* came down while the vessel was off the north coast of California, causing the steamer to be disabled. She was hove to under sail and taken in tow by steamer *Chehalis* to San Francisco.

December 29.—Martin Oldenborg, third officer of the steamer *Costa Rica*, charged with neglect of duty, causing water to flow into her forward hold, December 14, at San Francisco. Case to be investigated.

December 29.—The steamer *City of Pueblo* on voyage from Seattle to San Francisco broke her tail shaft in a storm off the Columbia River, Oreg., and was taken in tow by steamers *Chehalis* and *Norwood* to San Francisco.

LOCAL DISTRICT OF PORTLAND, OREG.

January 10.—While en route from The Dalles, Oreg., to Portland, Oreg., steamer *Dalles City*, owing to the extreme low water, struck a submerged rock, breaking a hole in the hull forward, on port side. Steamer was immediately beached. No one injured. No damage to cargo. Estimated damage to steamer, $1,000.

CASUALTIES, VIOLATIONS OF LAW, AND INVESTIGATIONS, YEAR ENDED DECEMBER 31, 1905—FIRST SUPERVISING DISTRICT—PORTLAND, OREG.—Continued.

January 14.—Investigation as to the cause of the blocking, with an accumulation of dirt and scale, necessitating the removal of the tubes to clear same, of the steamer *Undine's* boiler, was held and the license of John H. Epler, chief engineer, suspended for 30 days. License of Herbert O. Rima, assistant engineer, suspended for 10 days for negligence.

January 21.—The steamship *Geo. W. Elder*, while in charge of pilot W. C. Snow, en route from Portland, Oreg., to San Francisco, Cal., struck a rock at Reuben, Columbia River, Oregon, and sunk. Case investigated February 2, and from the evidence submitted it was found that the tiller quadrant jammed immediately prior to the accident. Pilot W. C. Snow was exonerated from all blame. (Damage to steamer can not be reported at this time as the steamer has not been raised as yet.)

April 21.—Steamer *Star*, while tied to her dock at Portland, Oreg., for the night, was damaged by fire to the extent of $500. Cause of fire not known. No one injured.

May 1.—Near Hoffmans landing, Columbia River, Oregon, E. Fleming, fireman, accidentally fell overboard and was drowned during fire and boat drill on the steamer *Harvest Queen*. Body not recovered.

May 31.—Steamers *Dalles City* and *Chas. R. Spencer* collided on Willamette River, near Linnton, Oreg. Estimated damage to steamer *Dalles City*, $2,500; to cargo, $100. Estimated damage to steamer *Chas. R. Spencer*, $100. Miss M. Young, a passenger on the steamer *Dalles City*, was slightly injured by falling over a hog chain. Case investigated June 2, and license of E. W. Spencer, master and pilot, pilot of the steamer *Chas. R. Spencer*, suspended from June 14, to December 5, 1905. License of Sidney H. Scammon, master and pilot, master steamer *Dalles City*, suspended from June 14 to December, 1905. Case appealed to supervising inspector first district, who, in the case of E. W. Spencer, sustained the decision of the local inspectors. The license of Sidney H. Scammon was ordered returned on September 16.

June 1.—Near Pillar rock, Columbia River, steamer *Samson*, with rock barge in tow, and steamer *Toledo* collided. No damage to steamer *Samson*. Damage to steamer *Toledo*, about $500.

July 10.—En route from San Francisco, Cal., to Portland, Oreg., Johan Johanson, seaman on steamship *Despatch*, while taking in reefed foresail during heavy gale, accidentally fell overboard and was drowned. Body not recovered.

August 18.—Near Ranier, Columbia River, Oreg., en route to Portland, Oreg., steamer *Hassalo* broke her main shaft in the starboard bearing, causing the breaking of three cylinder heads, two in the high-pressure engine and one in the low-pressure engine. No one injured. No damage to cargo. Estimated damage to engine and shaft, $2,000.

September 2.—While en route from Wallula to Ainsworth siding, Snake River, Washington, steamer *Gerome*, while going through Little Homely rapids, struck a submerged rock and sunk. No one injured. Estimated damage to steamer and cargo, $4,000.

September 22.—While crossing in over Alsea River bar steamship *W. H. Harrison* struck on bar and was carried by strong wind and tide onto the South spit and is a total wreck. No one injured. Estimated damage to cargo, $2,500. Estimated value of steamer, $10,000.

October 6.—U. S. light-house tender *Manzanita* collided with dredge *Columbia* in tow of the steamer *John McCracken* on Columbia River, near Waterford post light. *Manzanita* sunk. No damage to steamer *John McCracken* or dredge *Columbia*. No one injured. Damage to U. S. light-house tender *Manzanita* not known at this time. Investigation held October 13, and license of Eugene Hayden, master and pilot, master steamer *John McCracken*, suspended for 6 months for a violation of Rule II. Master of the U. S. light-house tender *Manzanita* exonerated from all blame.

October 16.—Near Maygers, Columbia River, en route from Portland to Astoria, Oreg., crosshead on port engine of the steamer *Lurline* gave way, knocking out forward cylinder head. A piece of the cylinder head struck the Chinese cook (Chin Lung), breaking two of his ribs. Estimated damage to steamer *Lurline's* engines, $200.

LOCAL DISTRICT OF SEATTLE, WASH.

January 11.—Investigation of collision, December 15, 1904, between the steamers *Sehome* and *Geo. E. Starr*. Decision January 28, suspending the license of W. H. Mangan, master of *Sehome*, and Chas. E. Brydsen, master of *Geo. E. Starr*, each 5 days, for violation of Rule VIII of pilot rules.

January 18.—The steamer *Alexander Griggs* stranded on rocks in Entiat Rapids, Columbia River. Hull a total loss. Estimated loss, $6,000.

CASUALTIES, VIOLATIONS OF LAW, AND INVESTIGATIONS, YEAR ENDED DECEMBER 31, 1905—FIRST SUPERVISING DISTRICT—SEATTLE, WASH.—Continued.

January 20.—The crown sheet in combustion chamber of one of the furnaces of the port boiler of the steamer *Olympia* collapsed. The chief engineer and the third assistant engineer were badly burned by escaping steam. Third assistant engineer, Oliver Van Tassel, died from the effects of his injuries. Investigated January 24 and February 24. Decision, February 27, revoking the licenses of Samuel C. Snyder, chief engineer, and Frank J. Aiken, first assistant engineer, and suspending the license of Geo. G. Murphy, second assistant engineer, until its expiration, July 30, 1905, each for negligence.

February 8.—Daniel B. Jackson, master and pilot of steamer *Dix*, charged with violation of section 15 of Rule V. Case investigated February 8. His license suspended 30 days for failure to hold and log the boat and fire drills, as required by law.

February 15.—In the matter of charges against H. Ohlemutz, master, Ernest F. Miller, engineer, and Ralph A. Gaertner, engineer, investigation begun on December 20, 1904. The charges having been withdrawn, the case was dismissed.

February 28.—The steamer *Portland* struck on an uncharted rock near Ellamar, Alaska, tearing away a portion of her keel. Damage, about $600.

April 12.—While attempting to board a launch in tow of the steamer *Gazelle*, on Lake Washington, W. B. Frazier, owner of the launch, fell overboard and was drowned.

April 20.—The license of Percy Lermond, master and pilot, was suspended 30 days for violation of sections 13 and 14 of Rule IV, rules and regulations.

May 22.—While towing near Shelton, Wash., the steamer *Irene* broke a cylinder head and wrist pin. Damage, about $200.

May 26.—A fire occurred on board bark *Coloma* while at sea. The fire originated in the galley. Damage, about $300.

May 27.—While proceeding from Everett, Wash., to Seattle, Wash., the steamer *Athlon* broke her tail shaft and lost propeller. Damage, about $600.

June 2.—The steamer *Telegraph*, en route from Seattle to Edmonds, Wash., broke both cylinder heads and crosshead on starboard engine. Damage, about $400.

June 17.—The steamer *Garden City* burned at the wharf at Port Orchard, Wash. Origin of fire unknown. Estimated loss, $12,000.

June 29.—The license of James Brownfield, assistant engineer, suspended until its expiration, July 2, 1905, for intemperance.

July 6.—While fishing on the halibut banks, Queen Charlotte Sound, John Larsen, a seaman on the fishing steamer *Zapora*, was drowned thru the capsizing of one of the boats.

July 24.—The steam tug *Reef* burned at Pontiac, Wash. Origin of fire unknown. Loss, $1,500.

July 24.—The steamship *Dakota* left Seattle this date bound to Oriental ports. While yet in the Strait of Fuca the stern gland was found to be very hot; this condition continuing, the ship returned to Seattle, and, after discharging cargo, was docked at Bremerton, Wash. The neck bush was found split the entire length and froze to the shaft casing on shaft, and casing showed numerous cracks, which necessitated putting in new tail shaft and new bush. The stern frame was found to be cracked in the arch; this was repaired by strong backs.

August 9.—Edward C. Smith, master and pilot, charged with having navigated the steamer *Thistle* without having the proper equipment on board. Case investigated and his license was suspended August 31 for 60 days.

August 16.—Steamer *Edith* struck a sunken rock in Seymour Narrows, carrying away her sternpost, rudder, and rudder post. She was towed to Quartermaster, Wash., where she was docked and repaired. Damage, $3,500.

August 18.—While the steamship *Olympia* was docking at pier 8, Seattle, Wash., she collided with the fishing schooners *J. F. Conner* and *Jennie Decker*, causing some damage to both vessels by jamming them against the piles. Amount of damage not known.

August 20.—George Bartsch, master and pilot, charged with having navigated the steamer *Success* without displaying the lights required by the rules and regulations for the government of pilots. Investigated August 29 and license suspended for 60 days.

August 23.—Alexander McConnell, chief engineer, charged with having been intoxicated and incapable of performing his duties as first assistant engineer of the steamer *Leelanaw* at Treadwell, Alaska, on March 16 and 17, 1905, pleaded guilty and his license was suspended for 90 days.

CASUALTIES, VIOLATIONS OF LAW, AND INVESTIGATIONS, YEAR ENDED DECEMBER 31, 1905—FIRST SUPERVISING DISTRICT—SEATTLE, WASH.—Continued.

August 26.—It having been reported that Edward Benson, first assistant engineer, acting as assistant engineer, on the steamer *Melville Dollar*, was unable to attend to his duties on account of drunkenness, he was cited to appear for investigation. He failed to appear, and continued on a prolonged debauch. Having verified his condition by personal observation, his license was revoked.

August 29.—Philip Spidzen, a seaman on steamer *Melville Dollar*, was killed by the breaking of the mainmast during the loading on the ship of a flat car.

August 29.—A slight collision occurred between the steamer *Norwood* and the steamer *Port Orchard;* the accident was due to the breaking of the steering gear on the *Norwood.*

August 29.—Thos. Sidworth, a waiter on the steamship *Humboldt*, jumped overboard in Seymour Narrows, and was drowned.

August 30.—The steamship *Tampico* encountered a heavy gale in Bering Sea, during which she labored heavily. Upon being docked at Seattle, Wash., her stern frame was found to be broken.

September 1.—The steamer *Humboldt* collided with an iceberg near the southeastern end of Douglas Island. Alaska, crushing her stern.

September 3.—The steamers *Enterprise* and *Magic* were in collision off Jefferson Head, Puget Sound, resulting in minor damages to the *Magic* and carrying away the *Enterprise's* stem. Investigated September 18; decision September 25, 1905, suspending the license of Tennes Olsen, master and pilot of steamer *Enterprise*, 15 days for violation of articles 22 and 23, pilot rules, and that of Andrew Benson, second-class pilot, acting mate of steamer *Magic*, 15 days for violation of Rule 3, pilot rules.

September 3.—The steamer *Flyer* collided with her dock at Seattle, Wash. The accident was due to the breaking of the pin holding the handwheel controlling clamp nut attached to throttle valve lever, the engineer being unable to reverse the engine in time to avoid collision. Estimated damage to *Flyer*, $1,500.

September 15.—A fire occurred in the coal bunker of the steamer *Rainier* on voyage from San Francisco to Puget Sound. The steamer was not seriously damaged.

September 19.—While in Christie Passage, British Columbia, September 19, 1905, the steamer *Cottage City* broke her tail shaft. Estimated damage, $3,500.

September 22.—The steamship *San Mateo* grounded on West Point, Puget Sound, during a dense fog; the ship came off at high water without damage. The accident appears to have been due to the fact that the fog trumpet on West Point was not blowing at the time.

September 26.—While attempting to dock at Seattle, Wash., the steamer *Portland* collided slightly with the the steamer *Advance*, owing to a misunderstanding of the bells by the engineer. Damage to *Advance*, about $50.

October 6.—While making a landing at pier 4, Seattle, Wash., the steamship *Ohio* drifted down against the steamer *Perdita*, crushing her against the dock. The *Perdita* was not seriously damaged. Accident apparently due to the strong wind blowing at the time.

October 12.—As the steamer *City of Everett* was leaving her wharf at Seattle, Wash., she collided with the steamer *Reliance*. Damage to the *Reliance*, about $200. Investigated October 20. It appearing that there was no violation of the rules the case was dismissed.

October 16.—During a thick snowstorm the steamship *Valencia* stranded on Broad Point, St. Michael Island. The vessel was successfully floated after having jettisoned some 75 tons of cargo. The ship sustained no apparent damage.

October 17.—The license of Andrew Dixon, master of steamers, No. 29069, dated January 1, 1904, was revoked for reason of the cancellation of his naturalization papers.

October 17.—The license of Chance E. Wiman, master and pilot, was suspended 10 days for having navigated the steamer *Vashon* while her lifeboats were not ready for immediate use.

October 18.—Charges preferred against William Clark, assistant engineer, investigated this date, and his license suspended October 20, 10 days for misconduct in having left his position and vessel without giving notice of his intentions.

October 21.—The license of Jens A. Jensen, master and pilot, and that of Ebenezer Franks, chief engineer, were each suspended 5 days for violation of section 7, Rule IV, rules and regulations, while serving in their respective capacities on the steamer *Florence K.*

October 21.—The license of Robert W. Jackson, master and pilot, was suspended 5 days for violation of section 5, Rule III, and section 3, Rule IV, rules and regulations, while in charge of the steamer *Dix.*

CASUALTIES, VIOLATIONS OF LAW, AND INVESTIGATIONS, YEAR ENDED DECEMBER 31, 1905—FIRST SUPERVISING DISTRICT—SEATTLE, WASH.—Continued.

October 25.—Arthur Morrison, pilot of the steamer *Progress*, and Jesse W. Wagner, chief engineer of the steamer *Fleetwood*, charged with misconduct. Case investigated at Aberdeen, Wash., November 23 and 24. Charges not sustained and case dismissed.

October 26.—The license of Wells Green, second-class pilot, was suspended for 30 days for violation of section 5, Rule III, rules and regulations, while in charge of steamer *Dorothy*.

October 27.—The license of Samuel Y. Hall, master and pilot, was suspended 30 days for violation of section 5, Rule III, rules and regulations, while in charge of the steamer *Vashon*.

October 27.—A collision occurred between the steamer *Ilwaco* and the schooner *Sequoia* in tow of the tug *J. E. Boyden*. Damage slight. Investigated December 22 and case dismissed.

October 28.—While the crew of the steamship *Victoria* were mustered for fire and boat drill, a quartermaster named Emil Abrahamson slipped an fell overboard. Life buoys were thrown to him, the engines were reversed and a boat lowered, but he was not found. After cruising around until darkness set in, the ship proceeded on her voyage.

October 28.—The steamer *Port Orchard* broke her shaft while near Port Orchard. Damage, $670.

November 1.—Wm. E. Trevorah, master and pilot of steamer *Inland Flyer*, charged with violation of section 4482, Revised Statutes. Investigated and license suspended November 6 for 25 days.

November 2.—The license of John E. Jackman, chief engineer, was suspended 30 days for having permitted the boiler of the steamer *Dorothy* to become in bad condition.

November 3.—While passing through Icy Straits, southeastern Alaska, the steamer *Corwin* collided with a submerged cake of ice, crushing her stem. Damage about $300.

November 10.—The steamer *City of Everett* collided with the ferry steamer *City of Seattle* during a dense fog. Estimated amount of damage $200. Investigated December 8 and case dismissed.

November 13.—John Phillips, chief engineer of the steamer *Skookum*, charged with having been intoxicated while on duty. Case investigated at Aberdeen, Wash., November 23, and license suspended December 6 for 15 days.

November 16.—Philip G. Groves, acting as chief mate, charged with negligence in making the required inspections of the life-saving equipment of the steamship *Olympia*. Investigated November 11, and license suspended November 16, 1905, for 30 days.

November 18.—The license of Herbert M. Parker, master and pilot, was suspended 15 days for negligence in the care of the equipments of the steamer *Vashon*.

November 21.—The license of Ole Borrisen, chief mate, was suspended 8 days for negligence in the care of the equipments of the steamer *Santa Clara*.

November 22.—The steamers *Ramona* and *T. W. Lake* were in collision in Tacoma Harbor. No damage to *Ramona*. Damage to *T. W. Lake*, $300. Investigated December 4; case dismissed.

December 15.—The license of Philip G. Groves, master of steamer, No. 29080, dated January 27, 1904, was revoked for reason of the cancellation of his naturalization papers.

December 15.—The license of Duncan E. Morris, master of steamer, No. 23262, dated October 16, 1902, was revoked for reason of the cancellation of his naturalization papers.

December 15.—The steamship *Umatilla* collided with the schooner *Geo. E. Billings* anchored in Tacoma Harbor, during a dense fog. Damage to *Geo. E. Billings*, $1,000.

December 19.—The steamer *Fleetwood* collided with the drawbridge in the Chehalis River. Damage to steamer about $50.

December 21.—The license of George G. Swan, chief engineer, suspended 1 year for violation of section 14, Rule IX, rules and regulations, while acting as chief engineer of the steamer *Multnomah*.

December 22.—The intermediate shaft of the steamer *Athlon* broke, and the engine was badly wrecked before it could be stopt. Damage about $2,000.

December 23.—The steamer *Alice Gertrude* broke her tail shaft; the stuffing box bearing was also damaged. Damage about $400.

December 24.—The tug *Bahada* collided with the French bark *Boïldieu* while towing her from Bremerton to Seattle; the bark had two frames broken and two plates cracked. Slight damage to the tug.

December 27.—The license of Wm. McKenzie, master of steamer, was suspended 15 days for negligence while acting as chief mate of the steamship *Eureka*.

Casualties, Violations of Law, and Investigations, Year ended December 31, 1905—First Supervising District—Continued.

LOCAL DISTRICT OF JUNEAU, ALASKA.

April 5.—Anton Pederson, sailor on bark *J. D. Peters*, en route from Seattle to Alaska, fell from foreyard while furling sail during heavy gale. Very high sea running and impossible to save him.

May 7.—Collapse of furnace, steamer *Vigilant*, J. T. Martin, master, Richmond S. Dodge, chief engineer. Vessel en route from Juneau to Wrangel, Alaska; on noticing damage, vessel returned to Juneau. Boiler examined by local board May 8; case investigated May 15, 1905, and officers exonerated. Estimated amount of damage, $750.

May 16.—While steamer *Kaiulani* was discharging freight at Papaikou landing, Island of Hawaii, boat was carried on rock by heavy sea and upset. Prompt effort made to save men, but Nisamura, a Japanese seaman, was drowned.

June 8.—Man drowned from steamer *Tanana Chief*, operating on Tanana River, Alaska, without licensed officers. Victim's name unknown and cause of accident unknown. Case reported to deputy collector of customs at St. Michael, Alaska.

July 23 to August 5.—Visited steamer *Tanana Chief* at Fairbanks on August 8, 1905, and found her without licensed officers, legal boiler, fire-fighting or life-saving equipment. Sworn report received from Albert Hughes, chief engineer, of trip made on Tanana and Kantischna Rivers as a passenger vessel while in this condition. Case reported to deputy collector of customs at Eagle, Alaska, and United States district attorney at Fairbanks, Alaska. Reported vessel fined $500, which was paid.

June, July, and August.—Steamer *Independence*, John Leech, master, operating without full complement of engineers during major portion of season of 1905; running without any licensed engineers on trip from St. Michael to Chena, Alaska, leaving St. Michael July 25, 1905. Case reported to deputy collector of customs at St. Michael, Alaska.

July 11.—Steamer *Ella*, Joel P. Geer, master, operating on upper Tanana River, Alaska. Willard Converse, deck hand, was in a small boat running a cable to assist vessel over swift water and his foot caught in the cable and he was pulled overboard. Line was immediately pulled in and every effort made to resuscitate him, but without avail. Vessel running without inspection at the time and case reported to United States district attorney at Fairbanks, Alaska.

July 13.—Steamer *Governor Perkins*, Thos. A. Whistler, master, was anchored off Nome, Alaska, with no crew aboard. Storm arose suddenly and crew unable to get off to steamer. Vessel parted moorings and was washed ashore. Total wreck; value of steamer, $6,000. No investigation.

June and July.—Steamer *White Seal*, operating on Yukon and Tanana rivers, Alaska, without licensed master, mate, or engineer; with license sufficient to cover tonnage, and without inspection until August 17, 1905. Case reported to United States district attorney at Fairbanks, Alaska.

June 20 to September 6.—Milton H. Hartzell, acting as assistant engineer on steamer *Koyukuk*, of 286 gross tons, operating on Koyukuk River, Alaska, licensed as engineer in charge of steamers of 100 gross tons and under. Affidavit of loss of license stated license to be as chief of river steamers. Apparent case of perjury and referred to supervising inspector, first district, for investigation by local board of Portland, Oreg., where license was issued.

July 29 to September 16.—Steamer *Elk No. 1*, Frederick Lupp, master, inspected at St. Michael, Alaska, July 23, 1905, and certain equipment ordered, which was not on board September 16, 1905; also running without assistant engineer required from July 29 to September 16. Case reported to deputy collector of customs at St. Michael, Alaska, September 16, and vessel fined $200. Case investigated September 16 and master exonerated from blame. Visited steamer September 17 and canceled passenger license, changing character to that of a freight steamer.

August 12.—T. S. Davis, employed to look after cattle on barge being shoved ahead of steamer *Rock Island* en route from Fort Gibbon to Fairbanks, Alaska, while carrying a bale of hay from steamer onto barge, attempted to cross on starboard side, where there was an opening of about 4 feet, instead of taking regular crossing amidships, and fell overboard. Had been warned not to cross at that place. Lifeboat immediately lowered and search made for an hour, but body could not be found. Accident apparently due to the man's own carelessness. No investigation.

August 16.—Gasoline freight vessel *Tana* George W. Beers, master, left Fairbanks, Alaska, on August 16 with passengers small passenger barge in tow. Left barge at Chena, and proceeded with passengers to Kantischna River. Case reported to collector of customs at Eagle City and United States district attorney at Fairbanks, Alaska. Vessel running without licensed mate this trip.

Casualties, Violations of Law, and Investigations, Year ended December 31, 1905—First Supervising District—Juneau, Alaska—Continued.

August 28.—Steamer *Monarch*, D. W. Dobbins, master, left Tanana, Alaska, for Dawson, Yukon Territory, on August 28 without licensed second mate. Case reported to deputy collector of customs at Eagle City, Alaska, same date.

August 28.—Steamer *Robert Kerr*, A. E. LeBallister, master, left Tanana, Alaska, for Fairbanks, Alaska, on August 28, without licensed second mate. Case reported to deputy collector of customs at Eagle City, Alaska, same date.

August 9.—Visited steamer *Dusty Diamond* at Chena, Alaska, and found her without licensed officers and short of equipment. Reported as running from St. Michael to Chena, Alaska, in September, 1904, and landing boats at Russian Mission, Yukon River, and completing voyage without them. Vessel since laid up. Case reported to deputy collector of customs at Eagle City, Alaska.

Steamer *Annawanda*, uninspected vessel operating on Kuskokwim River, Alaska. No application for inspection filed this year. No licensed officers so far as known. Report received from Christian Betsch that water glass broke, and the crew became frightened, and left vessel in a small boat, which was overturned, and 6 persons drowned—3 boys named Lynn and 3 Indians, names unknown. Date of accident unknown. Case reported to United States district attorney at Nome, Alaska, on September 14, 1905.

April 9.—Steamer *Dora*, O. A. Johansen, master, while leaving Chignik Bay, Alaska, on April 9, struck uncharted rock. Damage temporarily repaired, and vessel proceeded on her voyage. Estimated amount of damage, $125. Case not investigated.

July 29.—Ship *Star of Russia*, K. Lindberg, master, struck on sand beach on northwest end of Chirikof Island, Alaska, during very thick fog. Was floated 8 days later, and towed to Alitak Bay, where she was temporarily repaired, and then proceeded to San Francisco without cargo or passengers. Estimated damage to vessel, $20,000; estimated damage to cargo, $36,000. No loss of life. Case not investigated, by reason of our inability to find master or officers on our return from the Yukon River district.

October 3.—Steamer *Monarch*, D. W. Dobbins, master. Barney McRea, working his way from Chena, Alaska, to. Dawson, Yukon Territory, as deck hand, while suffering from delirium tremens, escaped his watchman and fell overboard while steamer was lying at bank taking on wood, 15 miles south of Fort Gibbon, Tanana River. Boat lowered and immediate effort made to save him, but body could not be found. Case not investigated.

November 23.—Revoked license of George F. Dudley, second assistant engineer of ocean steamers and chief of inland steamers of 100 gross tons and under, on the grounds of intoxication and neglect of duty. Case appealed to supervising inspector, first district, December 10. Decision rendered by supervising inspector, December 30, reducing penalty from revocation of license to suspension for a period of 70 days.

October 2.—Suspended license of Thomas F. Shipsey, chief mate of ocean steamers, for a period of 90 days, on account of intoxication.

November 17.—Suspended license of J. E. Sayles, second-class pilot, for a period of 10 days for violation of Rule V, section 50, Rules and Regulations, and section 4405, Revised Statutes, in not keeping up proper fire drills and entering same in log book on steamer *Canta*, of which he was master.

December 18.—Suspended license of Frederick J. Caffyn, chief engineer of ocean steamers, until July 1, 1906, on account of misbehavior and neglect of duty while acting as chief engineer of steamer *Schwatka*, on the Yukon River, Alaska, during summer of 1905. Case investigated at Seattle, Wash., October 30 and 31.

December 18.—Suspended license of James G. Bennett, first assistant engineer of ocean steamers, until June 19, 1906, on account of misbehavior and neglect of duty while acting as assistant engineer of steamer *Schwatka*, on the Yukon River, Alaska, during summer of 1905. Case investigated at Seattle, Wash., October 31.

December 22.—While steamer *Kaiulani*, J. J. Dower, master, was discharging cargo at Honohina landing, island of Hawaii, on December 22, one of the surf boats was struck by three heavy swells, riding the first two, but was swamped by the third and became unmanageable. Two of the men in the boat jumped overboard. Another boat came to their assistance, and picked up one of them, but the other, a South Sea islander, Antone by name, was drowned. Boat searched for a half hour, but body could not be found.

CASUALTIES, VIOLATIONS OF LAW, AND INVESTIGATIONS, YEAR ENDED DECEMBER 31, 1905—Continued.

SECOND SUPERVISING DISTRICT.

LOCAL DISTRICT OF NEW YORK, N. Y.

January 3.—About 5.15 p. m., car float in tow of tug *Edmund L. Levy* collided off Hoboken, N. J., with car float in tow of tug *New York Central No. 7*, causing slight damage. No one hurt.

January 10.—About 9.15 p. m., while steamer *Larchmont* was on her way from New York to Providence, and in Long Island Sound, a slight fire occurred, caused by the electric light wire fuse burning out. Only about 50 cents damage done before fire was put out by the crew of the steamer. No one hurt.

January 12.—About 10.10 p. m., canal boat in tow of tug *Pottsville* collided off Governors Island, New York, with tugboat *J. Fred Lohman*, causing the canal boat to sink. No one injured.

January 14.—About 4.10 a. m., towboats *Baltimore* and *New York Central No. 10* collided off Harrison street, Brooklyn, N. Y., causing very slight damage. The *Baltimore* was backing out from pier and a mud digger hid the other boat from view. No one hurt.

January 17.—Ferry steamer *Middletown* inspected May 12, 1904; certificate issued with restriction as follows: "This vessel not permitted to navigate after the ice forms in the bay." Steamer has been navigating since the ice formed. We believe this is a technical violation, as the steamer has been extensively repaired while on dry dock since the certificate with the above restriction was issued. Above restriction canceled this date, January 17.

January 20.—About 12 noon, tugboat *Slatington*, with boats in tow, collided with sailing lighter *T. W. Ladd* off Fifty-fifth street, North River; damage very slight. The lighter drifted down upon the tow. No one hurt.

January 20.—About 6.05 a. m., float in tow of tug *Nonpariel* collided in the North River with towboat *New York Central No. 12*, causing slight damage. No one hurt.

January 21.—About 9.15 a. m., ferry steamers *Chicago* and *Washington* collided in the North River, causing slight damage. No one on the *Chicago* hurt. Four passengers on the *Washington* claimed to be injured. Investigated January 26; decision February 9; license of L. H. Phillips, pilot of the *Chicago*, suspended for 10 days.

January 24.—About 4.30 a. m., canal boat in tow of tug *Wm. E. Cleary* and car float in tow of tug *New York Central No. 21* collided, causing some slight damage. No one injured.

January 25.—The freight steamer *Clarence* sunk in New York Harbor, near Robbins Reef. The steamer was located by a wrecking company and was raised, but the divers did not discover any bodies of the crew. The steamer had a crew of 7, all of whom it is believed were drowned. The steamer was on her way from Bayonne, N. J., to Brooklyn, N. Y., and at the time there was a very severe storm. The owners of the steamer reported the circumstances to this office.

January 25.—While towing, steamer *Patience*, on her way from Philadelphia, bound to Fall River and Boston, with two barges loaded with coal in tow, and when off Barnegat. encountered a severe gale with snowstorm. The barges were astern on hawser and broke loose. The gale became so heavy that the tug had to leave the barges and to be put before the wind. On the 26th the tug sought the barges and discovered the topmast of the *S. D. Carlton* projecting from the water, she having meanwhile sunk, and, as believed by the master of the tug *Patience*, with her cargo and crew. The tug took the other barge in tow and brought her to New York. The *S. D. Carlton* had a crew of 4 men.

January 25.—About 10.40 a. m., ferry steamers *Susquehanna* and *John G. McCullough* collided in the North River, causing very slight damage. The accident occurred during a severe snowstorm. No one hurt.

January 25.—About 11.15 a. m., towboat *Daniel Willard* collided in the North River with ferry steamer *Princeton*, causing slight damage. The accident was due to thick fog and snowstorm. The steamers were going slowly and blowing fog whistles at the time. No one hurt.

January 28.—About 10.05 a. m., ferry steamers *Wilkesbarre* and *Middletown* collided off Whitehall street, New York, causing very slight damage. No one hurt.

January 28.—About 11.15 a. m., car float in tow of tugboats *New York Central No. 17*, *Maria Hoffman*, and *Robert Rogers*, collided in the North River with tugboat *Daniel Wheeler*, causing some damage, but of slight amount. There was a snowstorm at the time, which was the cause of the accident. No one hurt.

Casualties, Violations of Law, and Investigations, Year ended December 31, 1905—Second Supervising District—New York, N. Y.—Continued.

January 30.—About 7.15 p. m., towboats *De Witt C. Ivins* and *Rochester* collided in the North River, causing very slight damage.

February 1.—About 12.50 p. m., barge in tow of tug *Mercy B.* collided off the Battery, New York, with steamer *H. F. Dimock.* The damage was slight. Accident was due to great quantity of ice. No one hurt.

February 1.—About 8 p. m., float in tow of tug *Charles E. Matthews* collided in the North River with scow in tow of tug *Eugene F. Moran*, turning the scow over. The scow was towed back to Hoboken, N. J. No one hurt. There was a great deal of ice in the river.

February 4.—About 2.30 a. m., during a blinding snowstorm, the steamer *Lewis Luckenbach*, when near Cape Hatteras shoals, evidently struck some obstruction, as soundings taken showed plenty of water under her bottom, but was unable to find out the character of same. The ship apparently sustained no damage.

February 4.—About 7.20 p. m., float in tow of tug *New York Central No. 21* collided in the North River with ferry steamer *Newburgh*, causing very slight damage. No one hurt. The ferry steamer was coming out of her slip. Investigated February 9; decision February 15; license of John Durning, master of the tug *New York Central No. 21*, and of William Thompson, pilot of the ferry steamer *Newburgh* suspended for 10 days.

February 4.—About 2 p. m., while the steamer *City of Everett* was in latitude 32° 52½′ N., and longitude 78° 54½′ W., she struck the steamship *Lief Eriksson* during a thick fog. The *City of Everett* was at a standstill when the other ship ran in front of her, and when the sea lifted her bow she came down on the *Eriksson*, whose crew left their boat and were rescued by the *City of Everett* with the exception of 2, which were lost. 20 men were saved and 2 lost.

February 8.—About 3 p. m., the tug *Unique*, while off Liberty Island, New York Bay, collided with the steamship *Citta di Napoli*, the latter boat striking the *Unique* on the starboard quarter, doing slight damage. No damage to the steamer. No one hurt.

February 10.—About 5.40 p. m., car float in tow of tug *Gladiator* collided off pier 5, East River, with steamship *Phœnix*, causing considerable damage to the float. No one hurt.

February 13.—About 5.30 p. m., the steamer *John H. Starin* collided in the East River with the ferryboat *Jamaica*, both bound for points in the North River. The *Starin's* bow was somewhat injured. Slight damage to the ferryboat. No one hurt.

February 13.—About 8.30 p. m., fire broke out on the steam yacht *Delaware* while lying at her berth at Fifteenth street, Hoboken, N. J., causing considerable damage to the boat by fire and water. Hull but slightly damaged, but great damage to deck houses, cabins, masts, rigging, and furnishings. No one hurt. A watchman and oiler on board the yacht at the time.

February 14.—About 4.15 a. m., the ferryboat *Wyoming* collided with the tugboat *Harry G. Runkle* in the East River, resulting in damages to the tugboat to the amount of $2,500. Damage to the *Wyoming* slight. No one hurt.

February 14.—About 8.40 a. m., tugboat *Transfer No. 18*, with two floats in tow, bound down the East River, collided with tug *S. O. Co. No. 3*, with lighter No. 53 in tow bound up river. One of the floats collided with the lighter, with considerable damage to the lighter. No damage to the float. No one hurt.

February 16.—About 4.20 a. m., towboats *John S. Smith* and *Owasco* collided in the North River, causing such damage to the *Owasco* that she had to return to pier, where she sunk soon afterwards. The *Smith* sustained no damage. No one hurt. The *Owasco* was raised and put on dry dock and repaired. Both the tugs had car floats in tow.

February 17.—About 7.30 p. m., towboat *William Orr* took fire while in Newtown Creek, N. Y., and was beached. The crew of 4 escaped in the boat. No one hurt. Cause of fire unknown.

February 20.—Investigation was held in the matter of charges made against John O'Rourke, engineer of towing steamer *Henry L. Wait*, for having a bucket of scrap iron hung on lever of safety valve to increase steam pressure. Decision rendered February 21, and engineer license of O'Rourke revoked. The license of Henry Morris, engineer of this same steamer, also revoked for similar offense after investigation of facts brought out in O'Rourke's case. (See item of March 10.)

February 23.—About 9.40 p. m., while towboat *Royal* was tied up at Java street, Brooklyn, N. Y., fire broke out, causing damage estimated at $2,000. Cause of fire unknown. No one hurt.

CASUALTIES, VIOLATIONS OF LAW, AND INVESTIGATIONS, YEAR ENDED DECEMBER 31, 1905—SECOND SUPERVISING DISTRICT—NEW YORK, N. Y.—Continued.

March 5.—About 9.15 p. m., ferry steamers *Sag Harbor* and *Harry B. Hollins* collided off Thirty-fourth street, East River, causing considerable damage to the *Harry B. Hollins*, but slight damage to the *Sag Harbor;* the *Sag Harbor* had just left her slip. No one hurt.

March 8.—About 1.23 a. m., steamer *North Star* collided off Harts Island, Long Island Sound, with schooner *Clifford L. White*, causing very slight damage. The accident was due to a fog. The *North Star* proceeded on her trip to Portsmouth.

March 8.—About 12.45 a. m., scow in tow of tug *Mattie* collided off Ninety-third street, East River, with a float in tow of tug *Transfer No. 4*, causing damage to the scow of about $700. Damage to the float slight. No one hurt.

March 10.—About 4 p. m., scow in tow of tug *Mattie* collided off Sixty-second street, East River, with steamer *General Henry J. Hunt*. The scow filled with water and sunk. After the tug had landed the rest of her tow she returned and got fast to the damaged scow and towed her into slip at Sixty-first street and made her fast. No one hurt.

March 10.—Investigation was held in the matter of charges made by this office against Henry Morris, engineer of towing steamer *Henry L. Wait*, for carrying an overpressure of steam on the boiler, which fact was brought out at a previous investigation of similar charges against one John O'Rourke, engineer of this same boat, whose license was revoked. (See item of February 20.) Decision rendered March 16, and license of Henry Morris revoked.

March 22.—About 4.45 p. m., ferry steamer *Columbia* and towboat *George W. Elder* collided off Wall street, East River, causing very slight damage. The mate in charge of the tugboat had his arm broken. No passengers injured. The collision occurred just as the ferryboat had left her slip.

March 24.—About 2.15 p. m., car float in tow of tug *New York Central No. 20*, collided off pier 73, North River, with steamer *Sarah A. Jenks*, causing damage to the car float. The *Sarah A. Jenks* was on her way up the river and the tug was preparing to swing into slip. No one hurt.

March 24.—About 4.45 p. m., car float in tow of tug *Transfer No. 15* collided off Thirteenth street, East River, with ferry steamer *Greenpoint*, causing slight damage. The accident was due to a thick fog. No one injured.

March 27.—Investigation was held in the matter of charge against Hendrick L. Bennett, chief engineer, for leaving steamer *Shackamaxon* on February 28, 1905, when there was another trip to be made; decision, April 5; case dismissed.

March 31.—About 8.30 a. m., towboat *New York Central No. 18* and ferry steamer *Colorado* collided off pier 34, East River, causing very slight damage. Accident was due to schooner getting in the way. No one injured.

April 3.—Passenger steamer *John H. Starin* carried cartridges on the deck outside of the magazine on a trip from New Haven, Conn., to New York, N. Y., ending at New York on April 3, 1905. The steamer had a permit to carry cartridges in a properly constructed magazine from the local inspectors at New York, N. Y., but cartridges were carried on the deck outside of magazine; violation of section 4424, Revised Statutes. Investigated April 8; decision, April 17; license of Robert McAllister, master of the steamer, suspended for 60 days, and the collector of customs at New York, and United States district attorney at New York notified of violation of law. The owners of the steamer were fined $100, which they paid to the collector on April 25, 1905. McAllister's license restored May 24.

April 3.—About 7.30 a. m., freight steamer *Daniel Wheeler* collided off pier 16, East River, New York, with towboat *Alison Briggs*, causing considerable damage to the *Alison Briggs*. The *Briggs* was headed for the pier when it was discovered that she was damaged, and she sunk just off pier 19, East River. No one hurt. The *Alison Briggs* was raised and repaired.

April 3.—About 6.55 a. m., ferry steamer *Cincinnati* and tugboat *Idlewild* collided off pier G, Jersey City, North River, causing very slight damage. No one hurt.

April 4.—The collector of customs at New York was notified of the following: The last certificate of inspection of the barkentine *Mannie Swan* expired October 20, 1904. When the vessel was inspected on April 3, 1905, the master told the assistant inspector who made the inspection that the vessel had been running, thru some oversight of the agent who did not get the certificate last year. The fine was mitigated to $50.

April 5.—About 11.30 p. m., while the ferry steamer *Westfield* was entering her slip at St. George, Staten Island, she struck on the corner of the dock, damaging her guard and cabin. The accident was due to bad tides and strong wind. No one hurt. Steamer was afterwards placed on dry dock for repairs.

CASUALTIES, VIOLATIONS OF LAW, AND INVESTIGATIONS, YEAR ENDED DECEMBER 31, 1905—SECOND SUPERVISING DISTRICT—NEW YORK, N. Y.—Continued.

April 6.—About 8.10 a. m., while the ferry steamers *Newark* and *Princeton* were entering their slips at Jersey City, N. J., they sagged together, causing very slight damage. No one hurt. Steamers continued in service.

April 7.—Investigation was held in the matter of assault on Robert Miller, master of steamer *John Tygert*, on the engineer, Harry Hoffman, on March 27, 1905, on trip from New York to Elizabethport, N. J., on complaint of Hoffman. Decision April 19; case dismissed.

April 8.—About 10 a. m., tugboat *Greenville* sunk in the North River, off Bloomfield street, and 3 of the crew drowned (Christopher C. Tull, pilot; Nelson Crapser, engineer; and Hans Eysen, deck hand). The crew consisted of 6 men, but 3 were rescued. The tug *Eugene F. Moran* was going up the river with scows and the *Greenville* coming down the river, threw a line to one of the scows and directed the scowman to make it fast to the scow, as the tug was to take the scow in tow. The line was made fast but the *Greenville* continued down the river, and when she tightened the line up the sudden strain pulled her over and she filled with water and sunk. The tug was afterwards raised. Investigated April 15; decision July 3; officers of the *Moran* exonerated from blame in connection with this accident.

April 11.—About 2 p. m., towboats *Joanna* and *Sentinel* collided in the East River, causing very slight damage. No one hurt.

April 12.—A deck hand named John Maloney, on the steamer *S. S. Wyckoff*, in stepping from the dock to the boat at Perth Amboy, N. J., fell overboard and was drowned.

April 16.—About 3.30 p. m., towboats *R. J. Moran* and *Transfer No. 5* collided in the East River off Astoria ferry slip, causing slight damage. Both tugs had tows. No one hurt.

April 17.—About 2.15 p. m., a canal boat in tow of tug *Hudson* collided off the stake light off Elizabethport, N. J., with a canal boat in tow of tug *Orville A. Crandall*, causing slight damage. No one hurt. Investigated May 22; decision May 31; license of W. T. Cox (master of the *Hudson*) suspended for 30 days, and of M. C. Prout (master of the *Crandall*) for 10 days.

April 17.—The collector of customs at New York was notified of the following: Sailing ship *Henry Lippitt*, certificate of inspection expiring February 16, 1905, lay at Charleston, S. C., from January 24, 1905, until March 21, 1905. Arrived at New York on March 31, 1905, and inspected at New York on April 15, 1905. Vessel navigated from Charleston to New York on an expired certificate of inspection.

April 19.—About 4.30 p. m., towboats *Maria Hoffman* and *Rover* collided in Newtown Creek, N. Y., causing the *Rover* to roll over so that she filled and sunk. No one hurt. The vessel was raised.

April 19.—About 10.10 p. m., ferry steamer *Montclair* collided off Christopher street, North River, with towboat *H. B. Chamberlain*, causing slight damage. Two men passengers on the ferryboat claimed to have been slightly injured.

April 25.—Investigation held in the matter of license obtained by fraud, by George Stutt, as first assistant engineer, 500-ton condensing steamers, and in charge of steamers of 100 tons. Investigation continued August 1; decision August 4; license of George W. Stutt revoked.

April 27.—About 4.30 p. m., schooner *Eliza A. Schribner* collided off Barnegat with a barge in tow of the tug *Concord*, causing very slight damage. No one hurt. There was a dense fog at the time of the accident.

May 4.—About 2.30 p. m., while the towboat *John Fleming* was in the lower bay, New York Harbor, with dumpers in tow on her way to sea, one of the dumpers sunk, and the man in charge was drowned. His name not known.

May 4.—About 5.50 a. m., during a thick fog, the ferry steamers *Binghamton* and *New Jersey* collided in the North River, causing slight damage. No one hurt.

May 8.—About 7.30 p. m., ferry steamers *New York* and *Maryland* collided in the East River, causing slight damage. The *Maryland* was on her way from New York, New Haven and Hartford Railroad depot to Jersey City, with passenger cars on board. The damage to the *New York* was on the port side. Very slight damage to the *Maryland*. No one injured.

May 8.—About 6.15 p. m., canal boat in tow of tug *Media* collided in the East River with the ferry steamer *Winona*, causing slight damage. No one injured.

May 9.—About 5.15 p. m., ferry steamer *Easton* collided off the Battery, New York Harbor, with excursion steamer *Angler*, causing damage to the *Angler* of about $860. The accident was due to both steamers trying to keep clear of a ferryboat, as stated in the reports of the officers of both steamers. No one hurt. Investigated May 22;

CASUALTIES, VIOLATIONS OF LAW, AND INVESTIGATIONS, YEAR ENDED DECEMBER 31, 1905—SECOND SUPERVISING DISTRICT—NEW YORK, N. Y.—Continued.

decision May 31, suspending for 30 days the license of George Simms, pilot of the ferry ferry steamer *Easton*. On June 22 Ira Harris, supervising inspector second district, restored his license on appeal, 23 days having elapsed.

May 13.—About 7.31 a. m., freight steamer *Gypsum King* and excursion steamer *Taurus* collided off Fortieth street, North River, causing some damage to the *Taurus*. No damage to the freight steamer. No one hurt.

May 14.—About 12 o'clock, at midnight, while steam canal boat *H. and A. Morse* was lying in dock in the Raritan River, New Jersey, fire broke out around the fire room. The crew tried to put the fire out, but were unable to do so. The hull was burned Damage, $3,000. Cause of fire unknown. No one hurt.

May 15.—About 10.15 a. m., canal boat in tow of tug *Charles J. Davis* collided in the East River with the steam yacht *Surf*. Considerable damage to the canal boat, but trifling damage to the yacht. No one hurt.

May 16.—About 7.20 a. m., towboats *Eddie H. Garrison* and *Castor* collided off pier 27, East River, causing slight damage. No one hurt. Investigated May 23; decision June 5 suspending licenses of William H. Flannery (master of *Eddie H. Garrison*) and of William A. Newman (master of the *Castor*) for 20 days each.

May 19.—About 8.05 a. m., ferryboat *Rockaway* collided off slip 4, Long Island City, East River, with passenger steamer *Nassua*, causing slight damage. No one hurt.

May 24.—Investigation held in the matter of complaint made by Douglass G. Moore, part owner of the tug *Wilkesbarre*, against chief engineer E. J. Wilgus and assistant engineer J. E. Derrickson, of neglecting the boiler and machinery of the said tug. Decision June 5; complaint dismissed.

May 26.—At 2.30 p. m., at sea, latitude 33° 45′, longitude 76° 33′, the second mate of the steamer *Northwestern* was swept overboard by a heavy sea and drowned. His name, John P. Metzig. The master of the vessel in his report says that the accident occurred while the mate and 2 seamen were endeavoring to fasten down the after cofferdam hatch; life-preservers and planks thrown overboard and boat cleared away and swung out, and when ship backed within 100 or 200 feet of the mate he sunk and never came up, and the ship lay until 3.15 p. m., and then proceeded on her way. Fresh southeast gale; ship laboring heavily. Investigated by Nforolk local board.

June 1.—About 8.10 a. m., ferry steamer *Baltimore* collided in the North River with the tugboat *Edwin Dayton*, causing very slight damage. No one hurt.

June 2.—About 1.30 p. m., towing steamers *Admiral* and *Arthur W. Palmer* collided off North Fourth street, Brooklyn, N. Y., causing considerable damage to the *Admiral* and slight damage to the other steamer. No one hurt. Investigated June 20; decision July 5, suspending the license of Frank Cassidy (master of the *Palmer*) for 10 days. Appealed to the supervising inspector of the second district, who rendered decision July 13, remitting remainder of suspension of Frank Cassidy's license, and license was returned to him.

June 5.—About 8.39 p. m., steam dredge *Caucus* went aground in Long Island Sound, off Jones inlet. The vessel was on her trial trip from Greenport, N. Y., to New York; said vessel was constructed for the U. S. Engineers Department. Vessel was floated at 8.20 p. m., June 6, and proceeded at once for New York. Slight damage to vessel. No one hurt.

June 7.—About 8 p. m., float in tow of tug *New York Dock Co.* collided in Buttermilk channel New York Harbor, with ferryboat *South Brooklyn*, causing slight damage. No one hurt. Investigated July 25; decision August 3; case dismissed.

June 9.—About 6.20 a. m., while the steamer *Hartford* was in the East River, on her way to New York, it was reported to the master of the steamer that about 10 minutes previously the form of a woman was seen in the water, having either jumped or fallen overboard from the steamer. No one had seen her go overboard. On investigation the passenger list showed that a woman named L. Leitman was missing.

June 10.—About 7.30 a. m., fire boat *William L. Strong* collided in the East River with barge in tow of tug *Border City*, causing slight damage. No one hurt. Investigated July 13; decision July 26, suspending license of Hugo G. Weinert, pilot in charge of the *Strong*, for 30 days.

June 10.—About 3 p. m., wrecking steamer *Champion* collided off Tottenville, N. Y., with a small launch, causing the launch to sink. There was one man in the launch, but he was taken on board the *Champion* and afterwards transferred to a small boat. Name of man not known. No name on launch. No one injured.

June 13.—About 8.20 p. m., ferry steamers *Jersey City* and *Tuxedo* collided in the North River, causing very slight damage (about $5). No one hurt.

Casualties, Violations of Law, and Investigations, Year ended December 31, 1905—Second Supervising District—New York, N. Y.—Continued.

June 16.—About 11 a. m., excursion steamers *Cepheus* and *Cygnus* collided off Coney Island Point, N. Y., causing very slight damage. No one hurt. There was a thick fog at the time of the collision. The steamers were both backing when they came together.

June 16.—About 3.49 a. m., car float in tow of tug *Transfer No. 8* collided off Halletts Point, East River, with steamer *Allan Joy*, causing very slight damage. There was no one hurt.

June 18.—About 11.20 p. m., steamer *Sunshine* collided with gasoline launch in Canarsie Bay, N. Y., damaging the launch and causing her to leak. The passengers on the launch were taken on board the *Sunshine* and the launch was towed to her dock. No one hurt. Investigated June 27; decision July 5; case dismissed.

June 19.—Investigation held in the matter of complaints of light-house inspectors against Harry D. Quillen, of steamer *Emma Kate Ross*, Phillip Le Maistre, same steamer, and Florian Romard, of steamer *William H. Taylor*, for damage done buoys and Scotland light-ship by tows of steamers under their command. Decision, July 5, suspending license of Harry D. Quillen for 90 days, Phillip Le Maistre for 60 days, and of Florian Romard for 30 days. On appeal of Florian Romard the supervising inspector of the second district reversed decision on July 12 and license returned to Mr. Romard same date. On appeal of Harry D. Quillen the supervising inspector modified the decision on July 14 and reduced the suspension to 20 days.

June 20.—Investigation held in the matter of a complaint made against William Flagg, master of the tug *Rescue*, of navigating said vessel without the proper number of licensed officers on board. Decision September 5: case dismissed.

June 21.—About 3 p. m., while ferry steamer *Fannie McKane* was being towed by the tugboat *Hornet* from Canarsie to Barren Island to have repairs made, a man was seen to jump from the deck of the *Fannie McKane* into the waters of Canarsie Bay and was drowned. The pilot of the *Fannie McKane* reports that the man who "jumped overboard" was not a passenger on the *Fannie McKane* or aboard by permission of any one who had authority.

June 23.—About 1.45 p. m., float in tow of tug *Transfer No. 12* collided in the East River with barge in tow of tug *Edward J. Berwind*, causing slight damage. No one hurt.

June 23.—Anonymous complaint was made that the steamer *Daisy* was being navigated without licensed pilot. Assistant Inspector Charlton was detailed to investigate the matter, and he reports that David Murray, the master and owner of the vessel, stated that he *did* "allow a man without a license to run the boat for him while absent on Friday, June 23, 1905." Reported to the collector of customs at New York July 1. Investigated, and the license of David Murray, pilot, suspended for 10 days from July 17.

June 24.—About 8.48 p. m., steamer *Nantasket* collided with small naphtha launch off One hundred and thirty-fourth street, East River, causing the launch to sink. There were 3 men in the launch, and they were rescued by the lifeboat which had been launched from the port side of the *Nantasket* after the accident occurred. The master of the *Nantasket* reports that the launch had no lights.

June 26.—About 5.30 p. m. steam yachts *Tarantula* and *Norman* collided off Stepping Stone, Long Island Sound, causing very slight damage to the yachts. There was no one hurt.

June 26.—A scow in tow of tug *Henry S. Beard* collided with the Scotland light-ship as reported by the master of the tug, John A. Terney, said report being dated July 6: Investigated July 20; decision July 27, suspending the license of John A. Terney, master of said tug, for a period of 60 days. On August 5 the supervising inspector of second district reduced the suspension to 30 days.

July 3.—About 8.15 a. m. ferry steamers *Long Beach* and *Virginia* collided off Grand street, East River, causing slight damage. No one hurt.

July 4.—About 4.15 p. m. ferry steamer *Annex*, while leaving slip at Fulton street, Brooklyn, N. Y. (East River), collided with tugboat *Confidence*, causing slight damage. No one hurt. Investigated August 2; decision August 11; case dismissed.

July 5.—Reported to the collector of customs the following: Last certificate of inspection of the steamer *Eddie H. Garrison* expired on October 29, 1904. Vessel was again inspected on June 30, 1905. In the interim (between October 29, 1904, and June 30, 1905) vessel was navigated. Investigated July 6; decision same date; master and pilot's license of Albert Anderson suspended for 10 days. Department of Commerce and Labor mitigated the penalty to $25, which was paid by the owners on September 25, 1905.

CASUALTIES, VIOLATIONS OF LAW, AND INVESTIGATIONS, YEAR ENDED DECEMBER 31, 1905—SECOND SUPERVISING DISTRICT—NEW YORK, N. Y.—Continued.

July 6.—Mr. John Erickson, master of the tugboat *Franklin N. Brown*, reports that a scow in tow of the said tug collided with the West End bank buoy No.11, on June 20, 1905.

July 7.—About 11.30 p. m. excursion steamer *J. S. Warden*, in a dense fog, grounded at Constable Hook. The steamer laid there 24 hours, then came off without assistance. Master reports that there was no damage done and that the steamer resumed her regular trips. No one hurt.

July 8.—Mr. F. Bouchard, pilot of the tug *John Fleming*, reports that while towing scows he fouled red can buoy No. 10, at 4 a. m. on that date, off Upper Middle.

July 8.—About 3.10 p. m., ferry steamer *Atlantic* and steam yacht *Golden Rod* collided off Whitehall street, New York, causing very slight damage. One man, a passenger on the *Atlantic*, was slightly cut by flying glass, as reported by the pilot of that steamer. Investigated July 31; decision August 7, suspending the license of Onslow Ludlow, master of the *Golden Rod*, for 20 days, and the case reported to the collector of customs and the United States district attorney, the master and owners also being guilty of violation of section 4438, Revised Statutes.

July 10.—About 4.40 p. m. ferry steamer *Wilkesbarre* collided in the North River with tugboat *Queen Mab*. The crew of the *Queen Mab* were thrown into the river by the force of the collision, but they were all rescued. No one seriously injured. Investigated August 18; decision August 28; case dismissed.

July 11.—About 9 p. m. the steam yacht *Normandie* collided off Dobbs Ferry, Hudson River, with the Norwegian tramp steamer *Volund*, causing the *Normandie* to sink. Three persons on the yacht were drowned: William Storms, pilot; Stewart Gracie, engineer, and Miss Gladys Dodge, a guest. There were 3 more persons on the *Normandie*, but they were rescued. Report of the accident was furnished by the owner of the yacht. The yacht at the time of the accident was chartered from the owner by one of the persons rescued.

July 11.—About 2.25 a. m. tugboat *S. L'Hommedieu* collided in Gowanus Creek, Brooklyn, N. Y., with a launch, causing the launch to capsize. The men who were in the launch were rescued by the crew of the tugboat. The pilot of the tugboat reports: "There were no lights on board the launch except a white light in the bottom of the boat." Name of launch not known.

July 17.—About 1.05 p. m. ferry steamer *Lackawanna* collided off Twenty-third street, North River, with excursion steamer *Dreamland*, causing slight damage. No one hurt.

July 17.—About 5.05 a. m. ferry steamer *Baltimore* and tugboat *John D. Dailey* collided off Desbrosses street, North River, causing slight damage. No one hurt.

July 17.—About 9.20 a. m. excursion steamer *Monmouth* and steamer *Wm. E. Chapman* collided off pier 3, North River causing slight damage. No one hurt.

July 18.—About 5.40 p. m. ferry steamers *Rockaway* and *John Englis* collided off Thirty-fourth street, East River, causing slight damage. No one hurt. Investigated July 28; decision August 3, suspending the license of the pilots (John Thorson, *Rockaway;* C. E. Underhill, *John Englis*), each for 10 days.

July 19.—About 2.45 p. m. ferry steamer *America* and tugboat *Wyomissing* collided in the East River, causing very slight damage. No one hurt.

July 19.—About 2.13 p. m. ferry steamer *Greenpoint* collided in Hell Gate with derrick in tow of tug *Wm. E. Chapman*, causing slight damage to the derrick. No damage to the steamer. No one hurt.

July 21.—While the excursion steamer *Sirius* was passing thru the East River, she struck a rock on the southwest side of North Brother Island and broke her bottom. The master had an examination made and found the steamer leaking. There were 541 passengers on board, which were transferred to the steamers *Dreamland* and *Massasoit*. No one hurt and master reports that there was "no excitement." The *Sirius* was backed off and brought to dry dock at Erie basin for repairs.

July 24.—Reported to the collector of customs at New York, the following: Steamer *John Wise* was inspected as a passenger steamer on June 30, 1905, and found short in equipment. Owner notified by letter July 1 of "shorts;" affidavit made on July 20 that equipment had been supplied and certificate of inspection issued. Steamer was navigated from July 2 to July 20 without certificate of inspection. The steamer during this period was in command of Mr. Ambrose W. Jayne, who holds license as master and pilot of towing steamers only. Investigated July 22 and the license of Mr. Jayne suspended for a period of 10 days, commencing July 23.

July 26.—About 8 a. m. the tugboats *New York Central No. 15* and *Robert White* collided off the Battery, New York, causing the *Robert White* to sink. No lives lost. The *New York Central No. 15* was slightly damaged. Both tugs were heading for the

CASUALTIES, VIOLATIONS OF LAW, AND INVESTIGATIONS, YEAR ENDED DECEMBER 31, 1905—SECOND SUPERVISING DISTRICT, NEW YORK, N. Y.—Continued.

East River. The tug *Robert White* was raised. Investigated August 4; decision August 16, suspending the license of William Davies, master of the *New York Central No. 15*, and of Frank St. Clair, master of the *Robert White*, for a period of 30 days.

July 28.—About 11.45 a. m. freight steamer *Martha Stevens* and U. S. Government steam lighter *Williams* collided in New York Harbor near Liberty Island, causing considerable damage to the *Martha Stevens*, which began to fill with water, and her master ran her ashore on the mud flats. No one hurt.

July 29.—About 8.35 p. m. ferry steamer *Newtown* collided in the East River with tugboat *Transfer No. 7*, causing very slight damage. No one hurt.

July 31.—Reported to the collector of customs at New York the following: Certificate of inspection of water steamer *Croton* expired on July 23, 1905, and on July 24 owners' agent applied to have vessel reinspected on July 25. Inspection made by this office on July 25, upon which occasion the assistant inspector making inspection was informed by master of the vessel that she had been navigated on July 24. This was confirmed by letter from the master written July 29.

July 31.—About 11 p. m. ferryboats *Hopatcong* and *Philadelphia* collided in North River. Slight damage. No one hurt.

August 3.—Reported to the collector of customs at New York the following: The last certificate of inspection of the tug *Chas. J. Davis* expired April 25, 1905. On July 20, 1905, owners applied to have vessel reinspected on July 24, which was done. Owners state that vessel was navigated continuously since April 25, due to error on copy of certificate; skeleton stamp on same gives "July 25" as date of expiration, but correct date of expiration is "April 25," the latter date appearing on lower part of certificate.

August 6.—About 5 a. m. while freight steamer *Rancocas* was laid up at One hundred and fortieth street, Harlem River, discharging freight, fire was discovered in the fireroom. Fire was put out by the crew of the steamer. Damage about $700. No one injured. Cause of fire unknown.

August 7.—About 8 p. m. the ferryboat *Hopatcong* was laid up at the dock at Hoboken with no licensed officers aboard. The crew left her in perfect order, so stated, and in charge of the regular watchman, and nothing unusual was discovered when she was laid up. Fire was discovered about 11 p. m., down stairs. In spite of all that could be done the fire spread rapidly so that the boat was destroyed. The fire spread to the *Binghamton*, which was laid up next to the *Hopatcong*, and she was considerably damaged above the deck. No lives lost.

August 8.—About 3 p. m. tugboat *Lucerne* collided in Hell Gate with float in tow of tug *Transfer No. 17*, causing very slight damage. No one hurt.

August 8.—Reported the following to the collector of customs at New York: Last certificate of inspection of the towing steamer *H. B. Rawson* expired on August 5, 1905. On August 3 owners' representative applied to have vessel reinspected on August 7, stating that the vessel would be laid up on August 6 and could not be inspected until August 7, altho this office could have made the inspection August 4 or 5. Vessel was reinspected by this office on August 7, at which time the pilot of said vessel informed the inspector that the vessel had been run from Barren Island to New York since the expiration of the certificate.

August 9.—About 2.20 a. m. float in tow of tug *Hazelton* collided in the East River with the tug *John Fleming*, causing some damage. No one hurt. The *John Fleeming* had a scow in tow.

August 13.—About 12.15 a. m. ferryboat *Chicago* collided in the North River with towing steamer *Wm. C. Redfield*, causing very slight damage. No one hurt.

August 13.—About 2.10 p. m. passenger barge *Andrew M. Church*, in tow of the tug *Harry G. Runkle*, collided off North Beach, East River, with the ferry steamer *North Beach*, causing damage of about $50. A couple of boys who were on the rail of the barge were knocked overboard but were rescued. No one hurt.

August 14.—Investigation was held in the matter of charges made by H. L. Des Anges, superintendent of floating equipment of the Long Island Railroad Company. that cross whistles were blown from the tug *John Harlan* on July 31, 1905, to the steamer *Sagamore*. Decision August 25; case dismissed.

August 15.—While the ferry steamer *Montauk* was on her trip from Brooklyn to New York a man who was a passenger on the steamer jumped overboard and was drowned. His name not known.

August 16.—W. A. Kinyon, master of the tugboat *Col. John F. Gaynor*, reports as follows: "While passing in to the eastward of the Scotland light-ship with three light dump scows our stern scow collided with the light-ship, the side of scow about amidships striking the stern of ship, doing no damage to the scow. The wind was

CASUALTIES, VIOLATIONS OF LAW, AND INVESTIGATIONS, YEAR ENDED DECEMBER 31, 1905—SECOND SUPERVISING DISTRICT—NEW YORK, N. Y.—Continued.

northeast, blowing about 20 miles per hour. The tug past not less than one-half mile to the eastward of ship. Capt. James F. Decker, the mate in charge of the watch at the wheel at the time, thought he had ample room to clear the ship, and I thought the same, but they were making more leeway than he thought." Investigated August 30; decision September 30. Decker's license suspended for 30 days. License restored to him by the supervising inspector's letter of October 7.

August 18.—About 7 a. m., while tugboat *Stella* was about 5 miles to the southeast of the Scotland light-ship, fire was discovered in the cross bunker. Fire was subdued and tug towed to Erie basin by tugs *Reliance* and *Jacob M. Heath*. No one hurt.

August 21.—About 9 p. m. the towing steamers *Nanticoke* and *New York Central No. 9* had a very slight collision in the Passaic River. The damage was very slight. No one was hurt.

August 23.—Reported to the collector of customs at New York the following: The last certificate of inspection of the pleasure steamer *Trifle* expired on June 28, 1902. The owner states that owing to an oversight the vessel has been navigated after the certificate expired. The vessel was reinspected on August 21, 1905. The Department of Commerce and Labor mitigated the penalty to $10, which was paid on September 25.

August 23.—Investigation was held in the matter of illegal navigation of pleasure steamer *Aileen*, on the coast of Maine, by Henry S. Wicks, master of the vessel. Decision August 28; referred to the supervising inspector, second district, and reported to the collector of customs at New York.

August 26.—Investigation was held in the matter of complaint by Capt. M. R. S. Mackenzie, U. S. N., light-house inspector, against tug *H. B. Chamberlain* fouling Gedney channel gas buoy No. 3 on the 2d of May, 1905. Decision, September 25; case dismissed.

August 27.—About 9.45 a. m. a man who was on board the motor boat *Dora*, when vessel was off Midland Beach, N. Y., fell overboard and was drowned. His name was John Burley. Investigated August 30; decision September 30. The case reported to the collector of customs and the United States district attorney at New York as George Cotterell, who was acting as pilot, was navigating on waters not covered by his license, and August Grap, owner, was acting as engineer without a license authorizing him to act as an engineer.

September 1.—About 8.09 a. m. barge in tow of tug *Manhattan* collided off pier 35, East River, with steamer *Maine*, causing the barge to sink. No one hurt.

September 1.—At nighttime the steamer *City of Hudson* collided off Hastings, Hudson River, with a small naphtha launch, causing the launch to fill with water and sink. A man and boy who were in the launch were taken on board the *City of Hudson*. The pilot of the steamer reports that the launch took a sudden shear across the bow of the steamer. Steamer was going up the river and the launch down.

September 1.—Investigation was held in the matter of a charge made by Mr. Roland Allwork, inspecting engineer of the Panama Railroad Company, against Thomas Carey, who signed as first assistant engineer on the steamer *City of Savannah* and then deserted the ship just before sailing for her trip to Colon and return. Decision September 6; case dismissed.

September 5.—About 7.10 p. m., while the tugboat *H. B. Rawson* was towing 2 scows, and when a little above the outer anchorage buoy off Jersey Flats, the foreign steamer *Prince Adelbert* came in contact with the scows, scraping the first scow and striking the other scow on the port bow, causing her to sink. No one hurt.

September 6.—About 11 p. m. a man who was a passenger on the ferry steamer *Chicago* jumped overboard and was drowned. His name not known. The steamer was on her route from New York to Jersey City, N. J.

September 7.—About 11.40 p. m. scow in tow of tug *George W. Elder* collided off Thirty-third street, East River, with ferry steamer *Rockaway*, causing considerable damage. No one hurt. Investigated September 27; decision September 30, suspending the license of L. A. Johnson, pilot of the tug *George W. Elder*, for a period of 30 days, commencing October 4, 1905.

September 7.—About 2.30 p. m., while the tugboat *John K. Cowen* was in New York Harbor, deck hand S. Swensen accidently fell overboard and was drowned.

September 9.—About 7.30 a. m. deck hand Thomas Doran fell overboard from the excursion steamer *Mount Desert* and was drowned. Steamer was on her way from West Twenty-first street, North River, New York.

September 22.—About 5 p. m. barge in tow of tug *S. O. Co. 14* collided off the Battery, New York, with the excursion steamer *Taurus*, causing slight damage. No one hurt.

CASUALTIES, VIOLATIONS OF LAW, AND INVESTIGATIONS, YEAR ENDED DECEMBER 31, 1905—SECOND SUPERVISING DISTRICT—NEW YORK, N. Y.—Continued.

September 23.—About 7 p. m. towing steamers *Ira M. Hedges* and *Dennis Valentine* collided off pier 20, East River, causing slight damage. No one hurt.

September 25.—About 12.45 p. m. ferry steamer *Manhattan Beach* collided in the East River with schooner *Racer*. Slight damage. No one injured.

September 28.—The following was reported to the collector of customs at Perth Amboy, N. J., relative to the towing steamer *Woodbridge* navigating on an expired certificate of inspection. Vessel was inspected September 16, 1904, and certificate issued, expiring September 16, 1905. Copies of certificate issued from Perth Amboy custom-house on September 28, 1904, were erroneously stamped "This certificate expires September 28, 1905." Vessel was reinspected September 26, 1905; in the interim—from September 16 to September 28—she was navigated due to this error in stamping the certificate as above.

September 29.—Investigation was held in the matter of pilot of ferryboat *New Jersey* neglecting to blow one long blast of the whistle leaving the ferry slip at Jersey City on 8.27 a. m. trip, September 25; decision September 30; license of pilot A. K. Reeves suspended for 5 days. License restored to Mr. Reeves by letter of the supervising inspector, second district, dated October 3.

September 30.—About 3.45 p. m. ferry steamer *Jersey City* collided in the North River with freight steamer *Express*, causing very slight damage. No one hurt.

October 2.—About 7.20 a. m., while freight steamer *Meteor* was on her way from New Brunswick, N. J., to New York, N. Y., one of the deck hands (while under the influence of liquor, so stated by the master), fell overboard and was drowned while the steamer was in the Raritan River. Efforts were made to rescue him, but unsuccessfully.

October 2.—The collector of customs at New York was notified that the pleasure steamer *Scout* was reported to have been running with only 1 boat, while the certificate of inspection requires 2; this alleged violation, running without proper boat equipment, during the season of 1905.

October 2.—About 8.35 a. m., schooner *Lawrence Haines*, in tow of tug *Emma J. Kennedy*, collided off West Farms Creek, East River, with steamer *Nantasket*, causing the steamer to sink a few minutes after the collision. No lives lost. No one hurt.

October 3.—About 6.30 a. m. tugboat *Kate Buckley* and steam yacht *Sayonara* collided off Mannings basin, Brooklyn, N. Y., causing slight damage. No one hurt.

October 6.—Investigation was held in the matter of the complaint made by Lieut. K. W. Perry, of the U. S. revenue-cutter *Manhattan*, against the tug *Frank* for violation of the rules of the road in not displaying the proper towing lights, etc. Decision October 23; reported to the collector of customs.

October 18.—About 1.13 p. m., steamer *Massasoit* collided in the East River with a small schooner (name unknown), causing slight damage. No one hurt.

October 18.—The fire boat *The New Yorker* and tugboat *Richmond* collided in the North River, causing slight damage. No one hurt. Investigated November 20; decision November 9; case dismissed.

October 22.—While the steamer *Benjamin Franklin* was lying at her dock at Yonkers, N. Y., fire broke out in the kitchen and dining room on upper deck, burning out the same. Cause of fire unknown. No one injured.

October 24.—About 6.35 a. m., while tug *C. C. Clarke* was backing out of slip at Hoboken, N. J., with a car float, the float collided with tugboat *W. H. Flannery*, causing very slight damage. No one hurt.

October 24.—About 8 a. m., barge in tow of tug *C. J. Saxe* collided in the North River with the Holland steamship *Statendam*, crushing in the bow of the barge and causing her to fill. The barge was towed to Jersey City. No one hurt.

October 25.—The tug *James D. Leary* burned up while in Newark Bay. Cause of fire unknown. No one hurt. The tug was a total loss.

October 25.—Investigation was held in the matter of complaint that Edward T. Russell, pilot of the ferryboat *Jersey City* did not blow proper whistle on leaving his slip, etc. Decision October 30; no action taken against his license.

October 27.—Reported the following to the collector of customs at Cold Spring, N. Y., relative to gas vessel *Siva* navigating on expired certificate of inspection. Vessel was inspected by this office on October 27, 1905. The previous inspection was made September 27, 1904, certificate on that inspection expiring September 27, 1905. The collector of customs at Cold Spring, N. Y., in issuing the copies of certificate for said inspection, erroneously stamped same "Expires October 27, 1905," instead of "September 27, 1905," and the vessel was navigated after September 27.

October 28.—About 10.47 a. m., while steamship *Seneca*, from Habana, was entering the port of New York she collided with sail lighter *Alpha*. No one hurt.

CASUALTIES, VIOLATIONS OF LAW, AND INVESTIGATIONS, YEAR ENDED DECEMBER 31, 1905—SECOND SUPERVISING DISTRICT—NEW YORK, N. Y.—Continued.

October 29.—About 6.30 a. m., while tugboat *Ben* was lying at Atlantic dock, Brooklyn, N. Y., fireman Martin Wilcarba was found scalded, lying in the coal bunker. The man was brought up on deck and sent to the hospital. The engineer of the tug stated that he first heard steam blowing in the engine room and went to find where it came from, and found that it came from the injector, and then shut off the valve on the injector steam pipe. It was then that he found the injured man. The injector and its connections were examined by Local Inspector Mersereau and Assistant Coleman, and they found everything in order, as reported at the regular inspection made the previous Saturday.

November 1.—About 4.40 a. m., the tug *Catasaqua* (Lehigh Valley Railroad) with 2 car floats, collided in the North River, off Twenty-third street, with the tug *Flemington* (Central Railroad of New Jersey), with a car float, the floats coming in contact, but resulted in no damage either to the floats or the tugs. The tide was ebb, the weather thick and foggy, and both boats were bound up the river from Jersey City, the *Flemington* being on the starboard side of the other boat when the collision occurred. No one hurt.

November 2.—About 6 p. m., while the steamship *Horatio Hall* was on her way up the East River, bound to Portland, Me., and while abreast of Wards Island, she collided with coal boats in tow of the tug *Zouave*, damaging 3 out of the 11 she had in tow. No damage was done to the *Horatio Hall*, and no one was injured.

November 2.—About 12.45 p. m., while the tugboat *Geo. F. Randolph* was landing float at pier 22, North River, deck hand N. Milovech fell overboard and was drowned. Efforts were made to rescue him. Investigated November 25; decision, December 4, the master of the tug, Andrew Bohlen, exonerated from blame.

November 3.—About 12.15 p. m., while the tugboat *Frank* was proceeding up the Harlem River with 3 canal boats in tow alongside, she collided with the tug *Three Brothers*, which was traveling in the same direction with a scow in tow, causing slight damage to said scow. This occurred near the Willis Avenue Bridge, and the river was crowded at this point at the time. No one hurt.

November 6.—About 5.35 a. m., float in tow of tug *Transfer No. 12* collided when off Sunken Meadows, East River, with the towing steamer *Wm. S. Anderson*, causing slight damage. No one hurt.

November 8.—About 5.35 a. m., the tugboat *Olympia*, towing a sand scow, going up the East River to Newtown Creek, collided off Atlantic avenue, Brooklyn, with the ferryboat *Winona*, bound from New York, resulting in some damage to the tugboat. No damage to the *Winona*. No one hurt.

November 9.—About 1.30 p. m., scow in tow of tug *Joel D. Smith* collided in the East River with float in tow of tug *S. R. Callaway*, causing very slight damage. No one hurt.

November 13.—About 3 p. m., the pilot boats *New Jersey* and *New York*, when off Sandy Hook, while transferring pilots, collided. Damage slight. No one hurt.

November 15.—About 6 p. m., ferry steamers *Atlantic* and *Brooklyn* collided in the East River, causing very slight damage. No one hurt.

November 15.—About 10.15 a. m., ferry steamer *Baltimore* collided in the North River with the excursion steamer *Cetus*, causing slight damage to the *Cetus* and no damage to the ferryboat. No one hurt.

November 16.—About 5.27 p. m., steamer *Warren* left New York bound east. When off Wards Island, East River, check valve on one of the boilers blew out. Steamer anchored and made temporary repairs. Got under way at 1.48 a. m. and returned to pier at New York under her own steam. Repairs made and steamer left for Fall River at 11.14 a. m., November 17. No one injured.

November 17.—About 4.30 p. m., towing steamers *John D. Dailey* and *Jamestown* collided off the Battery, New York, and the tug *Erin* collided with the barge in tow of the tug *Jamestown*. Slight damage. No one hurt. Investigated December 7; decision, December 18, pilot license of William J. Walsh suspended for 20 days. Walsh was acting as mate of the tug *John D. Dailey* and also as pilot.

November 19.—About 6.30 p. m., while steam lighter *Shooter Island* was tied up at Atlantic dock, Brooklyn, N. Y., she caught fire in the engine room. Damage slight. Cause of fire unknown. No one hurt.

November 20.—Investigation was held in the matter of the complaint made by Lieut. Wm. C. Ward, Revenue-Cutter Service, in that the steamer *Cygnus* and *Sarah A. Jenks* proceeded thru the course of the International Motor Boat Carnival, ignoring the hail of the revenue cutter, on September 14. Decision December 4; no action taken against the licenses of the officers in charge of said steamers.

CASUALTIES, VIOLATIONS OF LAW, AND INVESTIGATIONS, YEAR ENDED DECEMBER 31, 1905—SECOND SUPERVISING DISTRICT—NEW YORK, N. Y.—Continued.

November 21.—Investigation was held on that date, and on November 25, in the matter of ferryboats *Cincinnati* and others cutting thru the line of war ships composing the North Atlantic Fleet, and the British Second Cruiser Squadron, in the North River, on November 8 and 9, 1905. Decision December 7; no action taken against licenses of the pilots of ferryboats. Complaint of the above was made by Rear-Admiral R. D. Evans, commander in chief, North Atlantic Fleet.

November 21.—Investigation was held in the matter of complaints made by the second lieutenant of U. S. revenue cutter *Mohican*, Thos. M. Molloy, against the master of the tugboat *Elsie K.*, of hindering him in his lawful duty, etc., while he was patrolling the course of the motor-boat races on the Hudson River. Decision December 11; no action taken against the master's license. Guilty of violation of rule 1, article 18, etc., and reported to the collectors of customs at Newark, N. J., and New York, N. Y.

November 25.—About 5.40 p. m. passenger steamer *William Fletcher* collided in the North River with steam lighter *Douglas Alexander*, causing considerable damage to the *William Fletcher*. No one hurt.

November 25.—About 2.50 p. m. freight steamer *Climax* collided off Grand street, East River, with the light-house tender *Cactus*, causing a good deal of damage to the *Climax*. No one hurt. Investigated December 5; decision December 18. Master of the *Cactus* reported to the collector of customs at New York.

November 25.—About 6.30 a. m. ferry steamer *Somerset* and tugboat *W. Freeland Dalzell* collided in the East River, causing considerable damage. No one hurt.

November 28.—About 1 a. m. scow in tow of tug *George W. Elder* collided off Governors Island, New York Harbor, with coal barge in tow of the tugs *Ashbourne* and *Pencoyd*, causing a scow and coal barge to turn over. No one hurt.

November 28.—About 5 a. m., while towing, steamer *Ivanhoe* was at the dumping grounds off light-ship, one of the scows turned over and sunk and man on board was drowned. Cause of sinking unknown. The master of the tug reports that the scow was heading the sea at the time, and could only have turned over because water was allowed to leak in the bilge and not properly pumped out. They searched around for an honr for the man on the scow, but could not find him.

December 2.—About 10.30 a. m. towing steamer *New York Dock Co.* collided in the North River with the German steamship *Prinzess Irene*, causing damage to the float in tow of the tugboat. The steamship was bound up the river and the tug was coming down. No one hurt.

December 2.—Investigation was held on this date, and on December 12, in the matter of a charge against Fred C. Walter that he obtained an engineer's license without having had the proper preliminary experience. Decision December 18; license revoked.

December 5.—About 8.40 a. m. ferry steamer *Garden City* collided in the East River with the schooner *Michael C. Collins*, the bowsprit of the schooner going thru the outer and inner walls and into horse gangway. No one hurt on board the ferryboat, but the captain of the schooner had his head slightly injured. The tug *Royal* pulled the schooner clear of the ferryboat.

December 5.—About 10.20 a. m. float in tow of tug *Transfer No. 19* collided off pier 50, East River, with the steam lighter *Shooter Island*, causing very slight damage. No one hurt.

December 7.—About 1 a. m., while the steamer *Rosalie* was at the foot of Fifty-sixth street, Brooklyn, N. Y., laid up, undergoing repairs, fire broke out on board. The fire was put out by the assistance of the U. S. transport *McClellan* and the New York city fire department. Within five minutes of when the fire started the *McClellan*, which was alongside the *Rosalie*, had 6 streams of water playing on the fire. Steamer filled and rested on the bottom. No one hurt. Cause of fire unknown.

December 11.—About 6.15 a. m. the ferry steamer *Kingston* collided with the pier at foot of Franklin street, North River, while making her slip, causing considerable damage to the forward men's cabin on the port side. The wind was blowing strong from the southwest and tide flood. No one injured.

December 11.—About 3.30 p. m., while towing steamer *Crescent* was off St. George, Staten Island, N. Y., she collided with a submerged wreck, causing loss of propeller and shaft. Damage about $1,000. No one hurt.

December 13.—An investigation was held in the matter of the navigation of the freight steamer *S. S. Wyckoff*, of 267 gross tons, from New York to Keyport and return to New York, on December 7 and 8, in command of Charles S. Thompson, who only holds a license as second-class pilot of 100 gross tons, and Mr. Thompson admitted that he did

Casualties, Violations of Law, and Investigations, Year ended December 31, 1905—Second Supervising District—New York, N. Y.—Continued.

so navigate the steamer. The case was reported to the collector of customs at New York by decision of December 13.

December 13.—Towing steamer *John J. Sweeney* was reported to the collector of customs at New York for navigating on the waters of the New York Harbor in command of Thomas Leahy, pilot, Mr. Leahy only holding a license of second-class pilot of 100 gross tons for the Hudson River between Troy, N. Y., and Cornwall, N. Y. Gross tonnage of the tug, 28. (Violation of sec. 4438, Revised Statutes.) Reported to the collector of customs, New York.

December 16.—About 8.55 a. m. float in tow of the tug *Transfer No. 7* collided off Blackwells Island, East River, with freight steamer *Alert*, causing the *Alert* to sink almost immediately. The crew of the *Alert* got on the float. No one injured.

December 16.—An investigation was held in the matter of charges of misconduct against David H. Hudson, of Philadelphia, in assisting to take the steamer *Asa W. Hughes* from New York to Philadelphia on or about September 20, when the route or waters given upon that vessel's certificate of inspection at that time limited her to Delaware River and Bay. Decision December 19; case dismissed.

December 20.—About 5 p. m. float in tow of tugboat *John Harlin*, collided off the Battery, New York City, with excursion steamer *Mount Desert*, causing slight damage to float and excursion steamer. One of the crew of the *Mount Desert* was slightly injured.

December 22.—An investigation was held on this date in the following matter: Upon information from the local inspectors at Philadelphia, Pa., that the towing steamer, *Asa W. Hughes*, on September 20, 1905, was navigated on the waters of the Atlantic coast between New York and Philadelphia, without being certificated for such waters. Decision December 28; reported the steamer to the collector of customs at New York for violation of the statutes. This investigation was somewhat delayed, owing to failure to obtain the presence of witnesses at an earlier date.

December 23.—About 7.45 a. m. the towboat *N. B. Starbuck* collided off Whitehall street, New York, N. Y., with the ferry steamer *Queens*, causing considerable damage to the *N. B. Starbuck*, but no damage to the *Queens*. The fireman on the *N. B. Starbuck* was knocked overboard, but he was uninjured. There was no one hurt on the ferryboat.

December 23.—About 8.30 a. m. ferry steamer *Annex* and the tugboat *Royal* collided off Fulton street, Brooklyn, N. Y., causing very little damage. No one hurt.

December 24.—About 12.45 p. m., while freight steamer *Westover* was bound from Stockton, Me., to New York, N. Y., she grounded on Execution rock, Long Island Sound. The steamer was floated by a wrecking company on January 1, 1906. She had a full cargo of potatoes. No one hurt.

December 26.—During the night schooner *Bessie Whiting* collided in the lower bay, New York Harbor, with dumper in tow of the tug *John Fleming*, causing the dumper to sink. No one hurt.

December 28.—About 9 a. m. canal boat in tow of tug *Coleraine* collided off Bayonne, N. J., with tugboat *S. O. Co. No. 3*, causing the canal boat to sink. No one hurt.

December 30.—About 5 p. m. ferry steamer *Shinnecock* and water boat *F. H. Grove* collided in the East River. No damage done either boat and no one injured.

LOCAL DISTRICT OF BOSTON, MASS.

January 3.—Steam tug *Cornelia* sunk at her wharf in the Charles River at Boston. She was raised and it was discovered that the ice had chafed a hole thru her planking. No lives lost or personal injury. Amount of loss not reported.

January 23.—A collision occurred between ferryboat *City of Boston* and tug *Hamilton A. Mathes* in Boston Harbor. Neither steamer was very seriously injured. No personal injury resulted. Amount of loss not reported.

January 25.—During a gale of wind and snow the steamship *Georgetown* was driven on shore on Great Point beach, Nantucket, and stranded. Ship was subsequently floated by the Merritt & Chapman Wrecking Company and proceeded to New York for repairs. No lives lost or personal injury. Amount of loss not reported.

February 17.—Tug *Nonpareil* was reported to the collector of customs at Boston for carrying persons in addition to her crew, her permit for doing so having expired. A fine was paid by the master for this violation of section 4427, Revised Statutes.

February 25.—While lying at her wharf in East Boston in the night, the tug *Emily* took fire and was damaged to the extent of about $500. Cause of fire unknown. No loss of life or personal injury.

Casualties, Violations of Law, and Investigations, Year ended December 31, 1905—Second Supervising District—Boston, Mass.—Continued.

May 4.—A collision occurred between steamship *Ontario* and schooner *John C. Gregory* during a thick fog, about 11¼ miles W. ¾ S. from Gay Head. Steamer was running slowly under one bell at the time.

Schooner's crew was saved and taken on board of steamer but no more was seen of the schooner.

May 7.—During a dense fog the steamship *Aransas*, while on her passage from Boston to New York and in the vicinity of Pollock Rip shoal, came into collision with barge *Glendower*, the third barge in tow of tug *Patience*, and injured to that extent that she sunk in about 15 minutes, and with her cargo became a total loss.

The life of one passenger was lost from the *Aransas*, the balance of her passengers and crew were saved by her own boats and taken on board the *Glendower*.

The case was duly investigated and the officers of both steamers were exonerated from blame.

May 19.—Steamship *City of Memphis* collided with the Clyde Line wharf in Boston, damaging the wharf to some extent, also slight damage to stem of steamship *New York*, and cracking one plate in the bow of the *Memphis*. No personal injury; caused by some mistake in signals.

May 25.—Steamship *Bay Port* from Chicago to Boston, struck bottom at entrance to Cardinal canal, Galoo rapids, St. Lawrence River, causing ship to leak, but was kept free by her own pumps until voyage was completed, when she went on dry dock for repairs. No personal injury or amount of loss stated.

July 3.—Steamer *Calvin Austin* came into collision with schooner *Chromo* during a dense fog in Boston Bay, sinking the schooner. Ship immediately lowered a boat and rescued 4 of the crew, 1 man being lost. Report states schooner was not blowing a fog horn. Amount of loss not stated.

July 4.—Steamship *Nantucket* collided with a barge in tow of tug *Blue Bell* in Vineyard Sound. Master's report states ship was jammed between the barge and the Cross Rip light-ship, and to avoid striking the light-ship attempted to pass between the tug and barge and in doing so was struck by the barge, damaging his ship about $1,500. No personal injury or loss of life.

Cause seems to have been confusion of Great Point light and red light of barge.

July 5, 10.—Steamer *Joppaite* running from Newburyport, was navigated after expiration of her certificate of inspection. Pilot's license suspended and case reported to collector of customs at Newburyport, who collected a fine.

July 6.—During foggy weather at sea, between Halifax, N. S., and Boston, Mass., steamship *Olivette* collided with an unknown brigantine, carrying away the latter's jib boom. The steamer was stopt but the vessel had disappeared in the fog. No personal injury. Damage to steamer slight.

July 8, 15.—Steamer *Maylu*, running from Vineyard Haven, was navigated after expiration of her certificate of inspection. The engineer's license was suspended, as he was the only licensed officer permanently employed on the steamer and the case reported to the collector of customs at Edgartown.

July 11.—During a dense fog steamers *Winthrop* and *Sylvan Shore* collided in the channel between Lynn, Mass., and Nahant; both steamers were backing engines at the time and the damage was not serious to either steamer. No personal injury.

July 15.—A collision occurred between a barge in tow of tug *International* and schooner *Nimrod*, off Pollock Rip light-ship. The weather was foggy.

The schooner was struck by the middle barge of three and sunk at about 2.30 a. m., and the master of tug did not know of the mishap until 7.45 a. m. Crew of schooner picked up by another tug and landed at Vineyard Haven. No lives lost.

August 4.—Charges being made against Assistant Engineer Edward Walsh, of insubordination and misbehavior toward the chief engineer on steamer *Monitor* of Boston, the case was investigated, charges sustained, and the license of Mr. Walsh was suspended for 15 days.

August 7.—The cargo in upper between decks of steamship *Kershaw* was discovered to be on fire while ship was off Winter Quarter shoal light-ship bound to Boston. Holes were cut in saloon deck and 5 streams of water turned on. The fire was extinguished after 5 hours' work.

Cause of fire supposed to be spontaneous combustion. Damage to ship about $1,500; to cargo unknown. No personal injury.

August 15.—Charges were made against Assistant Engineer, Geo. H. Doyle, jr., of being intoxicated while on duty and refusing to serve in his official capacity, thereby detaining the steamer *Massasoit* about 4 hours at the wharf in Boston.

CASUALTIES, VIOLATIONS OF LAW, AND INVESTIGATIONS, YEAR ENDED DECEMBER 31, 1905—SECOND SUPERVISING DISTRICT—BOSTON, MASS.—Continued.

The case was investigated and the charges as to detaining the ship were fully sustained and the license of Mr. Doyle suspended for 30 days.

September 9.—Steamer *Favorite* while on the passage from Boston to Nahant broke tail shaft of starboard engine; steamer made her way to Nahant, landed passengers and returned to Boston with port engine alone. No personal injury.

September 15.—An explosion, setting the gasoline motor vessel *Veda M. McKown* on fire, took place at sea off Cape Cod. The fire was kept under control until they arrived at Provincetown, where it was extinguished.

Damage to vessel about $500. No personal injury.

This case was investigated and it was found that in filling the gasoline tank before leaving Gloucester a large amount of gasoline was accidentally run into the vessel instead of the tank. The engineer being absent at the time no blame was attached to him. The vessel was aired out for two days before sailing but we concluded there was enough gasoline left, when steamer got warmed up to cause the trouble, especially as the engine subsequently was found to be in perfect order.

September 17.—During a thick fog the tug *Boswell* ran aground in Vineyard Sound and while using the engine to get the vessel afloat the crank shaft and bedplate were broken, doing considerable other damage to the machinery. No personal injury resulted.

September 20.—A collision occurred about 25 miles off Cape Cod, during foggy weather, between steamship *Juniata* and schooner *Harwood Palmer*. The steamship heard the schooner's fog horn on starboard bow and immediately put helm to starboard and slowed engine, and then on sighting schooner coming directly for him, stopt and backed engines full speed, but schooner struck steamer on starboard side doing considerable damage to steamer and breaking off bowsprit of the schooner. Several persons on steamer injured but none thought to be serious. Amount of loss not stated.

September 23.—A collision occurred between steamship *Indian* and schooner *Viola*. The latter filled with water but being lumber laden, did not sink. Master of steamer states schooner *Viola* was not seen in time to prevent the collision. It happened at 8.22 p. m.; steamer stopt and backed engine but was unable to avoid schooner. Steamer stood by until schooner was safely in Vineyard Haven. No damage to steamer or personal injury.

November 8.—A collision occurred between a mud scow in tow of tug *Minot I. Wilcox* and a sailing vessel. The scow was being towed on a long line astern and the sailing vessel (a fisherman) attempted to pass between the tug and scow. Damage to sail vessel $500. No personal injury reported.

November 14.—A report, accompanied by a complaint, was made to the collector of customs at Boston by this board that the barge *Margery*, 152 gross tons, did on September 17, 1905, carry passengers for hire, said vessel not having complied with the Revised Statutes relating to inspection.

The case is not yet settled.

November 30.—Barge *Delawanna*, in tow of tug *Scranton*, foundered 8 miles E. by S. from Minot light in Massachusetts Bay. Master of steamer unable to account for the accident, as he only knew of it after the hawser parted, when he immediately turned back and saved 1 man; the balance of the crew, 3 men, and 1 woman were drowned.

November 30.—Martin Paschal, mate and pilot on tug *Hamilton A. Mathes*, accidentally fell overboard and was drowned, while towing mud scows at Nantucket, Mass.

December 17.—The tug *Thomas J. Yorke, jr.*, sunk at her wharf at East Boston during the nighttime. Cause found to be the accidental leaving open of the valve in a 2-inch siphon; steamer was immediately raised; only damage by water.

December 29.—Steamer *Penobscot* collided with fishing schooner *Shepard King* in Boston Harbor. The steamer's stem was injured and she returned to her wharf for repairs.

Master's report states schooner changed her course when he was doing all he could to avoid him.

LOCAL DISTRICT OF PHILADELPHIA, PA.

January 6.—At or about 1 p. m. towing steamer *Harriet*, 55 gross tons, of Wilmington, Del., when turning around in river opposite Harlan & Hollingsworth wharf, river filled with heavy and packed ice, engines working ahead slow, pilot gave engineer 3 bells, directing him to stop engines and come astern slow, which order was promptly obeyed; but, owing to the miscalculated distance and momentum, vessel's bow collided with an oil barge, cutting thru her guard and damaging a plate; amount of damage not stated. No one injured; no loss of life.

CASUALTIES, VIOLATIONS OF LAW, AND INVESTIGATIONS, YEAR ENDED DECEMBER 31, 1905—SECOND SUPERVISING DISTRICT—PHILADELPHIA, PA.—Continued.

January 11.—It was reported to us that on December 9, 1904, the towing steamer *Convoy*, 78 gross tons, of Baltimore, Md., when backing out between piers 11 and 12, North wharves, thru floating ice, propeller struck floating log under same, breaking off one blade. Vessel was placed in dock and same renewed. No one injured; no loss of life.

January 18.—At 7.05 p. m. steamer *Paraguay*, 2,201 gross tons, of Philadelphia, while proceeding down river at full speed, keeping a little to westward of channel to avoid heavy ice in same, when about one-fourth of a mile off pier opposite Quarryville, struck on bottom or some submerged obstruction. 7.15 p. m. slowed engine, number 3 starboard water bottom having filled with water. Continued down channel until opposite Christiana Creek, when master decided to return. On helm being put to starboard, ship did not respond, owing to strong flood tide and heavy ice floes. While working engines full speed ahead and full speed astern ship again grounded at 7.50 p. m. on lower end of Cherry Island flats. January 19, assisted by towing steamers *John A. Hughes* and *Asa W. Hughes*, vessel floated and proceeded up river to Marcus Hook. From there was towed to Philadelphia and put in dry dock. Case investigated January 24, and decision rendered same date, suspending for a period of 15 days each the licenses of J. Nevius Kay, master, and C. A. Laimer, mate and pilot.

January 18.—At about 7 p. m. towing steamer *Eureka*, 353 gross tons, of Fall River, Mass., while towing 4 ocean-going coal barges from Philadelphia to Eastern ports, owing to floating ice in river found it necessary to dock same at ice piers off Marcus Hook. Owing to strong flood tide, while steamer was turning her stern struck the sterm of the towing steamer *Mollie*, 36 gross tons, of Philadelphia, that was made fast at ice piers. Damage reported as slight; no one injured. No loss of life.

February 1.—On the morning of February 1 steel ferryboat *Goshen* (new), while proceeding from Wilmington, Del., for New York on builders' certificate, owing to heavy ice in channel, while attempting to make fast at ice pier opposite New Castle, Del., collided with same, tearing off 6 pieces of staving and breaking iron opposite of same. No one injured; no loss of life.

February 5.—At or about 5.35 a. m. *City Ice Boat No. 3*, 635 gross tons, of Philadelphia, Pa., built in year 1872 of iron (side-wheel vessel with two single horizontal surface condensing engines, 50 inches diameter cylinder and 9 feet stroke of piston, supplied with 8 boilers 12 feet long, 120 inches diameter, allowed a steam pressure of 60 pounds per square inch), struck a submerged obstruction, supposed to be a wreck. Effort was made to beach vessel, but she immediately began to fill with water; inside of 10 minutes fires were put out by same. Boats cleared away, dividing the crew equally, and vessel abandoned in a sinking condition. Crew rescued from lifeboats by steamers *Gettysburg*, *Teaser*, and *Boxer*. No one injured; no loss of life.

February 5.—At about 11 p. m. passenger steamer *Admiral Sampson*, 2,104 gross tons, of Perth Amboy, N. J., while bound for Philadelphia, having on board State branch pilot Enoch Eldrige, acting as pilot at times, during heavy rain and sleet, channel full of very heavy floating ice, strong flood tide running; while trying to avoid heavy field of ice ship took bottom on Pea Patch shoal, and heavy ice striking vessel aft carried away steering gear and forced ship high onto shoal. February 8 at 2.40 a. m., with the assistance of the tugs *Juno*, *New Castle*, and *City Ice Boat No. 2*, was hauled off. While on shore cargo of bananas was jettisoned. No loss of life; no one injured. Vessel to be placed on dry dock.

February 8.—At 7.15 p. m. towing steamer *Sea King*, 123 gross tons, of Philadelphia, Pa., while docking barge *Logan*, collided with heavy floating ice, breaking propeller. Vessel placed in dock and examined and found in good condition otherwise. No loss of life; no one injured.

February 8.—Passenger steamer *Berkshire*, 2,014 gross tons, of Baltimore, Md., while proceeding upriver, when opposite Eagle Point took bottom. As soon as tide swelled came off without assistance. Master reports grounding was caused in attempting to avoid heavy floating ice. No damage sustained by vessel. No loss of life; no one injured.

February 11.—On the morning of February 11 towing steamer *Waltham*, 353 gross tons, of Fall River, Mass., when making up tow, opposite Greenwich coal piers, collided with heavy floating ice, breaking propeller. No one injured; loss of life.

February 14.—It was reported to us that on February 9 at 10.30 a. m. the freight steamer *Northman*, 2,210 gross tons, of Cleveland, Ohio, while bound down river, channel filled with heavy floating ice, propeller was disabled by same. Vessel continued with disabled propeller until abreast Tinicum Island ranges, when ship became unmanageable, being jammed in ice floe. On February 10 at about 3 a. m. ice began to

CASUALTIES, VIOLATIONS OF LAW, AND INVESTIGATIONS, YEAR ENDED DECEMBER 31, 1905—SECOND SUPERVISING DISTRICT—PHILADELPHIA, PA.—Continued.

move, forcing ship across the channel. Ship not being under control of engines, grounded on upper end of Tinicum Island, on soft bottom. Attempt was made to anchor vessel without success. Vessel remained aground until February 11, 5.30 p. m., when she floated, cargo having been unloaded. Vessel proceeded to Philadelphia, but no damage sustained excepting to propeller. No one injured; no loss of life.

February 14.—At about 7 p. m. towing steamer *Covington*, 401 gross tons, of New York, N. Y., struck a submerged object, carrying away rudder and rudder frame. Vessel was bound from Providence, R. I., to Newport News, Va. After having lost rudder, vessel was steered with bight of hawser over stern to destination. No loss of life; no one injured.

February 18.—Towing steamer *Waltham*, 353 gross tons, of Fall River, Mass., lost all the blades on the propeller by same striking submerged obstruction, supposed to be ice, when opposite Fort Mifflin, Delaware River. Vessel left Philadelphia at 7.30 a. m. with barges *Sharon* and *Whitman* in tow for Eastern ports; ice in river very heavy; was proceeding down river in channel made by city ice boat when accident occurred. No one injured; no loss of life.

February 18.—Towing steamer *Harry M. Wall*, 60 gross tons, of Philadelphia, Pa., while proceeding up the Schuylkill with tow, vessel was jammed in field of heavy ice, which crushed in two strakes of plating along starboard side, damaging several frames. Vessel placed on railway. Amount of damage not stated. No loss of life; no one injured.

February 21.—Towing steamer *Willie*, 15 gross tons, of Philadelphia, Pa., while proceeding from Port Richmond down the river with tow of canal barges, assisted by towing steamers *William Cramp* and *Harry M. Wall*, ran into very heavy floating ice at mouth of Schuylkill River, which carried away rudder stock and damaged planking on starboard bow. Amount of damage not stated. No loss of life; no one injured.

February 21.—Towing steamer *Taurus*, 50 gross tons, of Wilmington, Del., while navigating Christiana River, which was full of heavy floating ice, when about 1 mile above mouth of same, carried away propeller and fractured tail shaft. Amount of damage not stated. No loss of life; no one injured.

February 22.—At about 4 p. m. towing steamer *Mary McIlvaine*, 34 gross tons, of Philadelphia, Pa., while proceeding down river in heavy ice, when opposite Philadelphia propeller struck submerged ice and broke two blades of propeller. Amount of damage approximated at $300. No loss of life; no one injured.

February 23.—At 1.30 p. m. passenger steamer *Yemassee*, 1,879 gross tons, of Philadelphia, Pa., while proceeding down Delaware Bay, destination Norfolk, Va., broke after crank pin of engine. Steamer *Goldsboro* towed vessel to Delaware breakwater, where she anchored. February 24, vessel was towed by steamers *North America* and *Somers N. Smith* to destination. Amount of damage not stated. No loss of life; no one injured.

February 24.—At about 5.30 p. m. towing steamer *J. S. W. Holton*, 62 gross tons, of Philadelphia, Pa., when opposite Horse Shoe buoy, became jammed in heavy ice floe, and her tow (schooner *Madeline Cooney*) ran up on her, damaging joiner work and carrying away smokestack. No damage sustained by schooner. No loss of life; no one injured.

February 25.—At about 3.30 p. m. towing steamer *S. A. McCaulley*, 92 gross tons, of Philadelphia, Pa., while jammed in heavy floating ice at mouth of Mantua Creek, Delaware River, had plating of hull on both sides badly bent inboard, causing vessel to leak badly. Vessel at the time was assisting towing steamer *Southwark* in towing the lighter *Haverford* into Mantua Creek. *City Ice Boat No. 1* came to assistance of vessel and at about 6 p. m. succeeded in breaking channel. Steamer *S. A. McCaulley* was then beached to prevent her sinking. Amount of damage not stated. No loss of life; no one injured.

February 25.—At or about 3.30 p. m. towing steamer *Southwark*, 52 gross tons, of Philadelphia, Pa., became jammed in heavy moving ice off the mouth of Mantua Creek, Delaware River. Pressure of ice crusht in sides of vessel, causing her to leak badly, and at 5 p. m. she sunk in 20 feet of water. This vessel was towing the lighter *Haverford*, and was assisted by the towing steamer *S. A. McCaulley* when both vessels became jammed in the ice. Crew, after abandoning vessel, walked across ice to the shore, taking lifeboat with them. No loss of life; no one injured; amount of damage not stated.

February 25.—Towing steamer *Boxer*, 216 gross tons, Philadelphia, Pa., while proceeding down Delaware River with tow of barges (river full of heavy floating ice),

Casualties, Violations of Law, and Investigations, Year ended December 31, 1905—Second Supervising District—Philadelphia, Pa.—Continued.

damaged stem at and above water line. Returned to Philadelphia and went on dry dock. Amount of damage not stated; no loss of life; no one injured.

February 26.—At 9.30 a. m., Absecon light-house bearing NNW., 10 miles, passenger steamer *Powhatan*, 2,098 gross tons, of Baltimore, Md., and schooner *Jose Olaverri*, 661 gross tons, of New York, N. Y., came in collision, damaging boat hung in davits on stern of schooner and also davits. Steamer received no damage. Cause of accident: Schooner had set a signal and steamer in maneuvering around drifted on schooner. No loss of life; no one injured.

February 26.—Towing steamer *Meteor*, 95 gross tons, of Wilmington, Del., proceeding down Delaware River, towing barge *Nine*, channel filled with heavy floating ice, when opposite Thompson's Point, New Jersey, became jammed in the ice and barge ran up on stern, damaging fantail and guard irons. Amount of damage not stated; no loss of life; no one injured.

March 5.—At about 8.20 a. m. towing steamer *Active*, 60 gross tons, of Philadelphia, Pa., and ferry steamer *Coopers Point*, 389 gross tons, of Camden, N. J., were in collision. Steamer *Active* was proceeding up river and steamer *Coopers Point* was proceeding across river from Camden to Philadelphia. Steamer *Coopers Point* struck steamer *Active* on starboard side abreast of forward part of house, damaging same and breaking rail and carrying away wheel chains of steamer *Coopers Point*. Amount of damage not stated; no loss of life; no one injured. Case investigated March 8, and second-class-pilot license of John M. Taylor, pilot of the steamer *Active*, suspended for a period of 14 days, for violation of article 29, inland pilot rules.

March 17.—At about 6.45 a. m. steamer *Convoy*, 78 gross tons, of Philadelphia, Pa., while working at pier 62, south wharves, struck a submerged log, breaking off one blade of propeller and bending the studs of same. Vessel placed on dry dock for repairs. No loss of life; no one injured.

April 11.—Affidavit having been filed at this office that the pleasure steamer *Alan Gray*, of Millsboro, Del., 2 gross tons, last inspected by us June 2, 1904, was being navigated on Indian River without licensed pilot or engineer, in violation of section 4438, Revised Statutes, the case was reported to the collector of customs, Wilmington, Del., that penalty might be imposed.

April 14.—It was reported to us that on November 5, 1904, during heavy weather, slight depression was discovered in deck of steamer *Texan*, vessel at time being on voyage to Kobe, Japan. On arrival at Kobe, after cargo was discharged, bolts were found sheared off of head of stanchion abreast No. 1 hatch in lower hold; also the two stanchions in No. 1 orlop deck. On arrival at Manila jacked up deck and rebolted 6 stanchions and put toms under the other beams where bolts were sheared off. On arrival at Honolulu decks were reenforced with heavy shores, under beams, before loading cargo of sugar. Vessel arrived at Philadelphia with cargo in good condition, ship showing no signs of leaking during the voyage. No one injured; no loss of life.

April 19.—At or about 3 a. m. towing steamer *Sweepstakes*, L. B. Tilton, master, bound from Philadelphia to New England port with two barges (*Elk Garden* and *Hampshire*) and schooner *William L. Walker* in tow; when opposite Lincoln Park, schooner *William L. Walker* collided with a small motor launch. The launch received no damage, and at time of collision she was not showing any light whatever. It has since been reported that 2 of the men in launch jumped overboard before the collision occurred. No injury received by schooner. Case investigated May 18, at which it was shown that 2 of the 8 occupants of motor boat were drowned. Decision rendered same date, exonerating licensed officers from all blame.

April 28.—At 8.20 p. m. fire was discovered in the fireroom of the oil-carrying freight steamer *Catania*, 3,269 gross tons, of Galveston, Tex. Crew, under direction of chief officer, used every effort to extinguish same until the arrival of city fire boats *Samuel H. Ashbridge* and *Edwin S. Stuart*. Fire was extinguished at 11.30 p. m. Damage was confined to fireroom and engine room. Amount of damage not stated; no loss of life; no one injured.

May 4.—At 10.40 a. m. fishing steamer *Adroit*, 92 gross tons, of Tuckerton, N. J., while proceeding in to Absecon inlet grounded on bar, vessel at time being in channel. Remained on bar about ten minutes, when she proceeded under her own steam to Little Egg Harbor, N. J. Vessel leaks slightly and rudder was damaged; will be hauled out and repaired. No loss of life; no one injured.

May 10.—During daylight, steamer *Toledo*, 2,277 gross tons, of Philadelphia, Pa., while bound down river, when opposite mouth of Christiana Creek and passing towing steamer *Boxer*, 216 gross tons, of Philadelphia, Pa., which had barge *E. W. Stetson*,

CASUALTIES, VIOLATIONS OF LAW, AND INVESTIGATIONS, YEAR ENDED DECEMBER 31, 1905—SECOND SUPERVISING DISTRICT—PHILADELPHIA, PA.—Continued.

1,141 gross tons, of New York, N. Y., in tow, and bound up river, steering gear of *Toledo* became disabled, leaving helm to port, which caused her to collide with barge *E. W. Stetson*, doing some damage. Amount of damage not stated; no loss of life; no one injured.

May 17.—Steamer *Twilight*, 466 gross tons, after leaving Burlington on her down trip for Philadelphia broke her crosshead. Vessel towed back to Burlington by steamer *Bristol*, to which vessel passengers were transferred. No other damage was done.

May 30.—At or about 5.30 p. m. steamer *Pleasant Valley*, 400 gross tons, of Camden, N. J., proceeding down the river, and the steamer *Riverside*, 452 gross tons, of Philadelphia, Pa., proceeding up the river, came in collision off Washington Park, N. J., thru a misunderstanding of the whistle signals, resulting in slight damage to both vessels. No one injured; no loss of life. Pilot of steamer *Pleasant Valley* censured by this office.

June 1.—At or about 11 p. m. towing steamer *John Reese*, 57 gross tons, Philadelphia, Pa., pilot house caught fire from unknown cause. Damage slight. No loss of life; no one injured.

June 8.—At or about 7 p. m. passenger steamer *Twilight*, 636 gross tons, of Philadelphia, Pa., proceeding across the river from Philadelphia, and towing steamer *Mary J. Walker*, 61 gross tons, of Philadelphia, proceeding down the river towing car float, came in collision, the bow of the car float striking the *Twilight* on the port side at paddle-wheel box, breaking the A frame and letting shaft down. The *Twilight* was towed back to her wharf; no damage sustained by car float. No loss of life; no one injured. Case investigated June 19 and decision rendered June 20, suspending master and pilot license of James Blocksom, master steamer *Twilight*, and second-class pilot license of George F. Murray, pilot steamer *Mary J. Walker*, each for a period of 15 days, for violation of the inland pilot rules.

June 19.—At or about 4.30 a. m. towing steamer *Somers N. Smith*, 211 gross tons, of Philadelphia, when attempting to take in tow the schooner *Nathaniel T. Palmer*, 2,240 gross tons, of Portland, Me., schooner being under sail at time, wind blowing fresh, jib boom of schooner fouled mainmast of steamer, carrying same away, and damaging steamer's lifeboat. No loss of life; no one injured. Estimated damage to steamer, about $150. Damage to schooner not stated.

June 27.—The towing steamer *Laura*, 28 gross tons, of Philadelphia, Pa., when in vicinity of Callowhill street wharf, propeller struck submerged obstruction and was broken. Vessel put on dock and otherwise found in good condition. No loss of life; no one injured.

July 3.—Reported David G. Hallinger to the collector of customs at Somers Point, N. J., and to the United States attorney at Newark, N. J., for violation of section 4438, Revised Statutes, in navigating the motor passenger vessel *Arrow*, 41 gross tons, of Philadelphia, Pa., on the waters of Hereford inlet, New Jersey, without holding a license permitting him to do so.

July 3.—At or about 7 p. m. towing steamer *Eva Belle Cain*, 20 gross tons, of Philadelphia, Pa., while lying at shipyard at wharf in Camden, N. J., a fire occurred in forward cabin, which was put out immediately, having caused but slight damage. No loss of life; no one injured.

July 15.—At or about 10.30 p. m. towing steamer *Lenape*, 627 gross tons, of Philadelphia, Pa., having in tow barges *Preston* and *Brookside*, while proceeding up Delaware River, when opposite upper end of Chester Island and passing U. S. Government dredge *Hell Gate*, which was moored in midchannel, the barge *Brookside*, 841 gross tons, being the after barge of tow, came in collision with dredge *Hell Gate*, damaging dredge *Hell Gate* yawl boat, parting her lines and knocking one eye and chock out of position. Damage sustained by barge *Brookside* was confined to port bow, there being a large hole knocked in same. Amount of damage not stated; no loss of life; no one injured. Case investigated August 10 and decision rendered August 11, exonerating licensed officers of steamer *Lenape* from blame.

July 19.—At 1.48 p. m. Manuel S. Lewis of Providence, R. I., employed as seaman on wrecking steamer *Somerset*, 179 gross tons, of Fall River, Mass., while off duty, was standing directly under cargo derrick, which was supporting several lengths of spiral pipe, combined weight estimated at 3,000 pounds, safe working load of said derrick being 10 tons. As derrick was slacked away, pin worked loose from shackle in block, block falling and striking said Manuel S. Lewis back of shoulders and causing instant death.

CASUALTIES, VIOLATIONS OF LAW, AND INVESTIGATIONS, YEAR ENDED DECEMBER 31, 1905—SECOND SUPERVISING DISTRICT—PHILADELPHIA, PA.—Continued.

July 28.—Reported the passenger steamer *Nada*, 44 gross tons, of Atlantic City, N. J., to the collector of customs at Somers Point, N. J., for violation of section 4417, Revised Statutes, in navigating as a steamer on an expired certificate of inspection.

July 28.—On investigation Jesse L. Williams, master and pilot, steamer *Nada*, was found guilty of operating that vessel without equipment required by Title LII, Revised Statutes, and without certificate of inspection being posted; also indifference to duty in connection with fire and boat drills. His license was suspended for a period of 30 days from this date.

August 2.—It was reported to us that on July 26, 1905, the steamer *Esther*, 27 gross tons, of Philadelphia, Pa., was boarded by officers from the Revenue-Cutter Service and reported to the custom-house service as being navigated without a certificate of inspection being posted as required by section 4423, Revised Statutes. Collector of customs notified this board on August 2. August 5 case investigated by this board as required by section 4450, Revised Statutes. Decision rendered August 5 censuring licensed officers for neglect to conform with section 4423, Revised Statutes.

August 7.—Assistant engineer in charge, William R. Reynolds, reported to this board that he had, knowing water to be low in boiler, ordered fires to be hauled down and steam raised on steamer *Maurice*, which was done, resulting in blowing out fusible plug. Investigated August 8 and decision rendered same date, suspending license of William P. Reynolds for a period of 15 days.

August 13.—At or about 2.45 p. m. steamer *Peconic*, 1,795 gross tons, while bound up Delaware River, just below Horse Shoe buoy No. 37, and making the turn, in order to avoid collision with schooner *Minnehaha* (tonnage not stated), under 37 gross tons, directed her course to starboard, which resulted in vessel grounding on starboard side of channel (bottom soft). At 10.10 p. m., August 13, vessel floated with assistance of towing steamer *New Castle.* No damage sustained; no one injured; no loss of life.

August 15.—It was reported to us that on August 4, at about 11 p. m., passenger steamer *Mary M. Vinyard*, 220 gross tons, Milton, Del., proceeding down Delaware River, when opposite the lower end of Tinicum Island, collided with wire mooring cable of U. S. dredge *Hell Gate.* Damage confined to one masthead block on dredge; no one injured; no loss of life.

August 21.—Licensed officers of steamer *Madeira* having been reported to this office as operating said steamer without the complement of officers named in vessel's certificate of inspection, investigation was held August 21, and decision rendered suspending for a period of 1 year the licenses of Joseph T. Long, pilot, and David H. Derrickson and John H. Hazel, engineers, steamer *Madeira.*

August 22.—Reported passenger steamer *Harriet*, 55 gross tons, of Wilmington, Del., owned by the E. I. Du Pont Company, to the U. S. district attorney and collector of customs at Philadelphia, Pa., for violation of section 4472, Revised Statutes, in having landed two boxes of Atlas powder at consumer's wharf at Chester, Pa., on August 21, 1905. August 25 licensed officers investigated and decision rendered same date, exonerating them from all blame.

August 29.—On August 11 Stephen H. Beers attempted to obtain an indorsement on license No. 17333 by presenting to this board lower half of license No. 3068, which the records showed was issued to Clarence L. Tingle. Matter laid before supervising inspector of second district, who, on August 14, directed this office to issue notices of revocation of license No. 17333. On August 18 notified by telegram from supervising inspector, second district, that he had restored license to Beers and directing this office to recall notices of revocation. On August 26 supervising inspector, second district, notified this office that after investigation he found that Stephen Beers simply made a mistake in taking wrong license from frame, and therefore exonerated him from all blame in charge of attempting to obtain license by fraud.

September 1.—Licensed officers of steamer *Lizzie Crawford* having been reported to this office as operating said steamer on route not permitted by vessel's current certificate of inspection, investigation was held August 21 and September 1 and decision rendered September 1 suspending for a period of 1 year the pilot license of Albert Olsen and the engineer license of Benjamin M. Donovan.

September 1.—Reported to collector of customs at Philadelphia, Pa., towing steamer *Lizzie Crawford*, 52 gross tons, of Philadelphia, Pa., Charles L. Walker, owner, for having violated section 4400, Revised Statutes, in operating on Delaware Bay, her certificate of inspection limiting route to Delaware River and tributaries. Vessel was therefore navigated on route not permitted by certificate of inspection.

CASUALTIES, VIOLATIONS OF LAW, AND INVESTIGATIONS, YEAR ENDED DECEMBER 31, 1905—SECOND SUPERVISING DISTRICT—PHILADELPHIA, PA.—Continued.

September 3.—At or about 11 a. m. towing steamer *Juno*, 62 gross tons, of Philadelphia, Pa., while assisting in towing steamer *Aral*, Marcus Hook, Pa., the high-pressure cylinder of engine cracked, thus disabling engine so the same could not be operated. Amount of damage not stated; no loss of life; no one injured.

September 16.—Reported to collector of customs at Philadelphia, Pa., steamer *Maderia*, 51 gross tons, of Philadelphia, for operating without the complement of licensed officers named in current certificate of inspection.

September 18.—Reported to collector of customs, Philadelphia, Pa., towing steamer *Asa W. Hughes*, 106 gross tons, of Philadelphia, Pa., Justus L. Williamson, master, for having violated section 4400, Revised Statutes, in navigating on Atlantic coast between Cape Henlopen, Del., and Sandy Hook, N. J., her certificate of inspection limiting route to Delaware River and Bay. Vessel was therefore navigated on route not permitted by current certificate of inspection. Licensed officers investigated September 26 and decision rendered same date suspending for a period of 6 months master and pilot license of Justus L. Williamson and chief engineer license of Elisha D. Jarvis.

September 18.—Investigation held in matter of accident to auxiliary boiler steamer *Philadelphia*. Decision rendered on this date suspending for a period of 30 days license of James C. Hudson, first assistant engineer.

September 20.—It was reported to us that on September 5, 1905, towing steamer *Maurice*, 36 gross tons, of Camden, N. J., Clarence Chamberlain, pilot, proceeding across Delaware River from Camden, N. J., and towing steamer *Lillie M. Graham*, 49 gross tons, of Philadelphia, William McKeever, pilot, proceeding up Delaware River when oposite Otis street wharf, towing steamer *Lillie M. Graham*, collided with barge in tow of steamer *Maurice*. Damage sustained by barge estimated at $50; no loss of life; no one injured. Case investigated September 25 and decision rendered same date suspending license of William McKeever, pilot, steamer *Lillie M. Graham*, and Clarence Chamberlain, pilot, steamer *Maurice*, each for a period of 7 days.

September 21.—It was reported to us that on September 1, 9 p. m., as ferry steamer *Atlantic*, 451 gross tons, of Camden, N. J., J. R. Keene, pilot, was leaving Vine street, Philadelphia, ferry slip, an unknown man jumped over iron gates of steamer and dived into the river from the bow of the boat when boat was just outside of ends of slip. Alarm was given and pilot immediately stopt steamer, but person could not be seen or heard.

September 23.—It was reported to us that on September 4 passenger steamer *Penn*, 445 gross tons, of Philadelphia, Pa., Alex McNamee, master, while bound from Philadelphia to Baltimore, Md., as vessel was leaving wharf at Chester, Pa., engines working ahead one bell, a passenger, one Lake Collins, leaned out of the midship gangway in order to catch a bottle of beer some friend tossed him, was caught between the vessel and wharf piling and crushed to death. Master as soon as notified reversed engines and body fell overboard. Licensed officers immediately reported facts to Chester police department, who recovered the body shortly after.

September 26.—Reported Seldon N. Gibble, second class pilot, and G. A. Hitchens, chief engineer, to U. S. attorney, Philadelphia, Pa., for violation of section 4438, Revised Statutes, in operating the steamer *Asa W. Hughes* on a route for which they had no license.

September 26.—Reported James E. Hughes, owner towing steamer *Asa W. Hughes*, 106 gross tons, of Philadelphia, Pa., to collector of customs at Philadelphia, Pa., for violation of section 4438, Revised Statutes, in employing persons as mate and engineer on this vessel who are not licensed by the inspectors.

September 29.—Investigation held on September 5 and 28 into charges preferred by James W. Elwell & Co., of New York, against Axel Hedlund, a licensed chief mate, for desertion and neglect of duty, in leaving the steamer *Peconic*, without notice, on August 22, 1905. Decision rendered September 29, exonerating Axel Hedlund from the charges preferred against him, and dismissing case.

October 2.—It was reported to us that on September 26, 1905, steamer *Hainesport*, 57 gross tons, of Baltimore, Md., while proceeding down Rancocas Creek, having in tow barges *Samuel Thomas*, *Hainesport No. 8*, and *Ella*, the last named being the after barge, when just above Bridgeboro bridge barge *Ella* began to settle by the head. Pilot of steamer *Hainesport* immediately stopped, and gave orders for master of barge *Samuel Thomas* to let go *Ella's* line, she being near the shore. Richard Krauss, master of barge *Ella*, failed to direct her course toward shore, and *Ella* sunk. Krauss endeavored to save himself by holding onto a floating log, but before steamer *Hainesport* reached him he released his hold, and was drowned.

CASUALTIES, VIOLATIONS OF LAW, AND INVESTIGATIONS, YEAR ENDED DECEMBER 31, 1905—SECOND SUPERVISING DISTRICT—PHILADELPHIA, PA.—Continued.

October 2.—It was reported to us that on September 13, at or about 4.30 a. m., while towing steamer *Swatara*, 625 gross tons, of Philadelphia, Pa., and her tow of 3 barges, was proceeding up the Delaware River, and towing steamer *White Rose*, 74 gross tons, and her tow of 2 barges, one on either side, was proceeding down the river, barge in tow of steamer *White Rose* collided with steamer *Swatara*, slightly damaging both vessels. No one injured; no loss of life. Case investigated September 22 and 29 and decision rendered October 2, exonerating from all blame John Sablich, master of steamer *Swatara*, and suspending for a period of 30 days from September 29 master license of Thomas C. Hickman, master of steamer *White Rose*.

October 4.—At or about 3.30 p. m., while steamer *Frederick*, 1,872 gross tons, of Baltimore, Md., was being towed down the river by towing steamer *F. A. Churchman*, 54 gross tons, made fast on starboard quarter, and towing steamer *Bryn Mawr*, 74 gross tons, of Philadelphia, made fast on port quarter, Eli Walls, master of towing steamer *F. A. Churchman*, when opposite pier 10, north wharves (about 100 feet from same), steamer *Chester*, while backing out of said wharves, collided with steamer *Frederick*, slightly damaging her own starboard side. No damage to steamer *Frederick*; no one injured; no loss of life. Necessary whistle signals given and answered, and when collision was inevitable master of each vessel did all in their power to avert same.

October 10.—At or about 5 p. m., Capt. Stokley Warrington, master of towing steamer *Cumberland*, 377 gross tons, of Baltimore, Md., disappeared from vessel; vessel at time being at sea, off Delaware capes. Thoro search was instituted, and vessel cruised around for 1 hour and 45 minutes, but unable to locate him. W. G. Michalskie, mate of the vessel, in his report states "Am mystified how he got lost;" "don't know of any cause for self-destruction."

October 14.—At or about 11.10 a. m., Joe Lawrence, a Spaniard, one of the coal passers on the steamship *Waccamaw*, 1,359 gross tons, of Buffalo, N. Y., in attempting to go on board vessel, which was moored at pier 11, Port Richmond, fell between vessel and wharf and was drowned. Vessel at time had suitable gangway from vessel to shore; but, owing to said Lawrence being under the influence of liquor, he attempted to board vessel by climbing up side. Every effort to save him without avail.

October 22.—At or about 7 p. m., steamer *Bristol*, 48 gross tons, of Philadelphia, Pa., John Mott, pilot in charge, having in tow 5 light sand scows, proceeding up river, when opposite Beverly, N. J., a small motor power launch attempted to cross river between the *Bristol* and her tow, which resulted in motor vessel colliding with the tow, carrying away her deckhouse and drowning 6 of the 9 persons on board, 3 members of the party being saved by crew of *Bristol*. Wreck examined by this board on October 23. Case investigated October 28, and decision rendered same date, exonerating the licensed officers from all blame.

October 24.—It was reported to us that on October 1, 1905, at or about 1 p. m., towing steamer *Lenape*, 637 gross tons, of Philadelphia, towing barges *Enterprise*, 901 gross tons, *Alaska*, 853 gross tons, and *Girard*, 841 gross tons, all of Philadelphia, down the Delaware River, when opposite buoy No. 28, the after barge of tow (*Girard*) took a sudden sheer, which caused her to collide with schooner *C. P. Dixon*, 717 gross tons, of New York, N. Y., lying at anchor, carrying away that vessel's head gear and damaging a lifeboat on the *Girard*. Weather clear; strong flood tide. Amount of damage not stated; no loss of life; no one injured.

November 11.—At or about 10.45 a. m., freight steamer *Georgetown*, 1,358 gross tons, of Buffalo, N. Y., while at anchor two ship's lengths NE. of Lower Anchorage buoy, opposite Greenwich Point, Pa., was run into by the Belgian passenger steamer *Friesland*, 7,116 gross tons, of Antwerp, Belgium. Steamer *Friesland* while proceeding down the river, when opposite Greenwich Point, sheered across channel, colliding with the *Georgetown*, head on, damaging the latter vessel's rails and guards, tearing out starboard rigging, starboard side of bridge, and damaging plating of vessel under guard. Amount of damage not stated; no one injured; no loss of life. As the *Friesland* is a foreign vessel, and not required to carry U. S. licensed officers, case not investigated.

November 11.—Steamer *J. L. Luckenbach*, 4,920 gross tons, of New York, N. Y., while proceeding from Delaware River to Girard Point, just above mouth of Schuylkill River, under her own steam and assisted by towing steamer *Bristol*, 48 gross tons, of Philadelphia, John Mott, pilot on port quarter, and towing steamer *Majestic*, 55 gross tons, of Philadelphia, Theo. Dolbow, pilot on starboard quarter, when opposite entrance to Schuylkill River, took bottom. Telegraph between bridge and engine room being out of order, way was not gotten off vessel in sufficient time to avoid her grounding heavily on east side of channel. Vessel was in charge of State pilot. No one injured; no loss of life. It was necessary to lighten vessel before she was floated. Hull was uninjured.

CASUALTIES, VIOLATIONS OF LAW, AND INVESTIGATIONS, YEAR ENDED DECEMBER 31, 1905—SECOND SUPERVISING DISTRICT—PHILADELPHIA, PA.—Continued.

November 14.—It was reported to us that steamer *J. L. Luckenbach*, 4,920 gross tons, of New York, N. Y., on March 21, while on voyage from Norfolk, Va., to Port Natal, South Africa, in latitude 17° 29′ S., longitude 9° 45′ W., explosion occurred in middle furnace of port boiler, forcing open connection doors and blowing portion of the fire into after fireroom. George Peters, fireman, who was in front of furnace door at time of explosion, was so badly burned and injured that he died at 11.15 a. m., without having regained consciousness. Firemen Ramon Gonzales and Ramon Ramises, who were also on duty at the time, were slightly injured. Repairs made to boiler at Port Natal.

November 14.—It was reported to us that steamer *J. L. Luckenbach*, 4,920 gross tons, of New York, N. Y., on May 13, latitude 7° 10′ S., longitude 85° 10′ E., while on voyage from Port Natal, South Africa, to Cavite, P. I., via Singapore, explosion occurred in the furnace of the port boiler. N. Mitchell, a coal passer, who was near the furnace door at the time, was slightly burned about the feet. Repairs made to boiler at Singapore. Explosion is attributed to overheating of furnace sheet, due to deposit of salt.

November 22.—On November 20, at or about 3 a. m., towing steamer *Rebecca*, 39 gross tons, of Philadelphia, coming up Delaware River with 1 lighter in tow, ran into wharf at pier 70 South, scow in tow running up on steamer, causing the tug to careen over and sink immediately; crew escaped without injury. No loss of life; no one injured. Amount of damage not known, as tug has not yet been raised. Case investigated December 27, and decision rendered December 29, suspending for a period of 60 days the second-class pilot license of George Kerbaugh, who was the pilot in charge of steamer when accident occurred.

November 29.—It was reported to us that on November 23, at 9.30 a. m., steamer *Shawmut*, 1,624 gross tons, in charge of first-class pilot Henry C. Perring, grounded in the Horse Shoe, Delaware River, and was floated at 11.36 p. m., same day. Considerable damage done to vessel's bottom. Case to be investigated.

December 1.—On the night of November 27, the towing steamer *Majestic*, 55 gross tons, of Philadelphia, Pa., while lying tied up at Burlington, N. J., after towing the barge *B. Y. Donaldson* from Delaware City to Burlington, arriving there at 12 o'clock midnight, the tug was made fast alongside of the barge for the remainder of the night and the crew retired. At 2 a. m., November 28, crew were awakened by the boat being on fire in vicinity of boiler room. Every effort was made by crew, assisted by Burlington fire department, to extinguish fire, until vessel finally sunk. Cause of fire unknown; no loss of life; no one injured; amount of damage not stated.

December 16.—At 4 p. m. steamship *Northman*, 2,210 gross tons, of Cleveland, Ohio, while on voyage from Sabine Pass, Tex., to Philadelphia, Pa., when 15 miles S. by E. from Winter Quarter light vessel, during strong gale, accompanied by heavy sea, was compelled to jettison about 1,500 barrels of crude oil to prevent foundering. Prior to jettisoning cargo, large amount of heavy water was shipped on after deck, causing same to settle. Chief engineer was knocked down by heavy sea and seriously injured, and, upon arrival at Philadelphia, December 17, he was at once sent to the Marine Hospital. Examination of vessel showed deck badly sprung and 4 vertical between-deck stanchions bent; doors in after house smashed in by sea. Necessary repairs being made; no loss of life; amount of damage not stated.

December 20.—Between 11 and 12 p. m. pilot boat *Philadelphia*, 359 gross tons, of Philadelphia, Pa., while on her station was in collision with schooner *Viking*, 1,017 gross tons, of Bath, Me. Amount of damage sustained by schooner unknown. Steamer *Philadelphia* was swept fore and aft, losing pilot house, boats, smokestack, and masts. Vessel now in dock undergoing repairs. No loss of life; no one injured. Case to be investigated.

December 23.—At or about 6.25 a. m. passenger steamer *Riverside*, 72 gross tons, of Philadelphia, Pa., proceeding from Camden, N. J., to Philadelphia, Pa., and towing steamer *Ogontz*, 113 gross tons, of Philadelphia, Pa., proceeding from Philadelphia to Camden, N. J., when opposite Otis street wharf, Philadelphia, came in collision at right angles. Stem of steamer *Riverside* and shell plating B, C, and D badly bent to port; all damage being above water line. Steamer *Ogontz* damaged on port side amidships, about guard, waist, and rail; damage all above water line. No loss of life; no one injured. Case to be investigated.

December 28.—At or about 8 a. m., during dense fog, the ferry steamer *Columbia*, 663 gross tons, of Philadelphia, Pa., and the ferry steamer *Arctic*, 394 gross tons, of Philadelphia, Pa., came in collision, slightly damaging the joiner work on steamer *Columbia*. Vessels proceeding slow at time of collision. No loss of life; no one injured.

CASUALTIES, VIOLATIONS OF LAW, AND INVESTIGATIONS, YEAR ENDED DECEMBER 31, 1905—SECOND SUPERVISING DISTRICT—PHILADELPHIA, PA.—Continued.

December 28.—At or about 7.25 a. m., during dense fog, ferry steamer *Columbia*, 663 gross tons, of Philadelphia, Pa., proceeding from Philadelphia to Camden, and steamer *Camden*, 757 gross tons, of Camden, N. J., proceeding from Camden, N. J., to Philadelphia, came in collision, doing slight damage to cabin of steamer *Camden*. Both vessels proceeding slow at time. No less of life; no one injured.

December 28.—At or about 7.45 a. m. passenger steamer *City of Chester*, 611 gross tons, of Wilmington, Del., bound from Wilmington to Philadelphia, during dense fog, when passing thru Philadelphia, Wilmington and Baltimore Railroad bridge, Christiana River, collided with south wing, carrying away rail on port side forward and damaging port forward end of house. No loss of life; no one injured. Amount of damage not stated.

December 28.—Charges having been made by Frank J. Deebold, under oath, that Dominick McBride, pilot in charge of steamer *Riverside*, had on December 9, while in charge of said vessel, squeezed the naptha motor boat *Anna*, which is operated by said Frank J. Deebold, against the pier at Pyne Point, N. J., damaging said motor boat to the extent of about $25 investigation was held December 28, and decision rendered December 29. Charges not sustained and case dismissed.

December 30.—Charges having been preferred, under oath, by William C. Wilson, that Charles W. Fleetwood, engineer of steamer *Alert*, was intoxicated while on duty on December 26, 1905, case was investigated on December 30, and decision rendered same date. Mr. Fleetwood, having pleaded guilty, his license was suspended for a period of 15 days, the circumstances in the case being such as to permit of some leniency being shown the accused.

LOCAL DISTRICT OF NEW LONDON, CONN.

January 2.—Ferry steamer *Col. Ledyard*, en route from Groton to New London, Conn., in dense fog, collided with freight steamer *Mohegan* on morning of January 2. Estimated damage to *Col. Ledyard*, $700. Damage to *Mohegan*, not given. No lives lost or persons injured. Case investigated, and decision rendered January 13, exonerating licensed officers from all responsibility.

January 28.—Steamer *Manhanset*, while lying at New York, New Haven and Hartford Railroad wharf, New London, Conn., took fire from unknown cause at midnight on January 28. Superstructure amidships, also lower engine room and interior of hull badly burned. Vessel filled and sunk. No lives lost or persons injured. Amount of damage not given.

March 19.—Steamer *Spartan*, while proceeding thru Block Island Sound, grounded during a dense fog on the south end of Block Island, R. I. Amount of damage not stated. No lives lost or persons injured.

April 6.—Tug *Covington*, en route from Newport News, Va., to Fall River, Mass., with barge *Texas* in tow, struck on Block Island, R. I., during dense fog on morning of April 6. Tug backed off unaided and proceeded to New London in damaged condition and dry docked. *Texas* also grounded, and was total loss; estimated value, $40,000. John L. Toole, cook, and Joseph Berne, deck hand, on *Texas*, lost. Case investigated, and decision rendered April 15, exonerating William B. Perry, master of *Covington*, from all responsibility.

May 3.—Barge *Moonbeam*, in tow of tug *Gertrude*, Capt. George W. Halyburton, foundered off Point Judith, R. I., on the night of May 3. Charles Eckert, master, his daughter, aged 13, a son, aged 7, one Bowen, cook, and a seaman, name unknown, drowned. Case investigated, and decision rendered June 26, exonerating George W. Halyburton, master of *Gertrude*, from all responsibility.

May 29.—Fishing steamer *Seaconnet*, eastbound from fishing ground on back side of Long Island, near Shinnecock light, struck on the bar opposite Shinnecock light during thick fog on afternoon of May 29. No lives lost or persons injured. Vessel total loss; value not stated. Case investigated, and decision rendered December 13, suspending license of James H. Fish, master of *Seaconnet* for 30 days for careless navigation.

June 1.—Steamer *Nashua*, en route from New York, N. Y., to Providence, R. I., collided on morning of June 1st in Long Island Sound, with schooner *L. L. Hamlin*, of Northport, Long Island. No lives lost or persons injured. Damage to steamer not stated. Damage to schooner, estimated $700.

June 15.—Tug *James Hughes*, en route from Promised Land, Long Island, with barge *Essie Flannery* in tow, took fire off Plum Island, Long Island Sound, at 4.45 a. m., and was totally destroyed and sunk. No lives lost or persons injured. Origin of fire unknown. Case investigated, and decision rendered October 7, exonerating licensed officers from all responsibility.

CASUALTIES, VIOLATIONS OF LAW, AND INVESTIGATIONS, YEAR ENDED DECEMBER 31, 1905—SECOND SUPERVISING DISTRICT—NEW LONDON, CONN.—Continued.

June 16.—Steamer *Chelsea*, in backing out from her slip at Norwich, Conn., on afternoon of June 15, swamped a small boat which contained a man, whose name was afterwards ascertained to be Harry Johnson. Boat destroyed; man drowned. Case investigated, and decision rendered August 17, exonerating Martin A. Colberg, master of *Chelsea*, from all responsibility.

June 17.—Reported to collector of customs at Stonington, Conn., and U. S. district attorney at Hartford, Conn., with recommendation of leniency, violation by Edward H. Beebe of section 4426, Revised Statutes, in navigating motor vessel *Laura Reed* from May 28 to June 13, after expiration of certificate of inspection. Cause, ignorance of laws governing Steamboat-Inspection Service on part of master.

June 29.—Steamer *Restless*, while passing down New London Harbor, collided with ferry steamer *Col. Ledyard*, Frank E. Thompson, master. Estimated damage to *Restless*, $75; to *Col. Ledyard*, $500. No lives lost or persons injured. Case investigated and decision rendered September 1, suspending for 10 days license of Frank E. Thompson, master of *Col. Ledyard*, for violation of Rules II and V and unskilful navigation.

July 6.—Steamer *Providence*, en route from New York to Providence, when off Faulkners Island, Long Island Sound, on morning of July 6, broke port shaft; was towed into New London by steamers *Maine* and *City of Taunton*. No lives lost or persons injured. Amount of damage not given.

July 9.—Steamer *Surprise*, en route from New York, N. Y., to Fall River, Mass., with freight and passengers, grounded during dense fog near Orient Point, Long Island Sound, at 1.45 a. m. of July 9. At 2.45 a. m., same date, steamer floated without assistance and proceeded to destination. No lives lost or persons injured. Case investigated and decision rendered November 11, suspending for 20 days license of John P. Webber, first pilot of *Surprise*, for careless and unskilful navigation.

July 13.—Steam yacht *Senator*, laid up out of commission during previous year at Wickford, R. I., took fire, burned, and sunk at dock. Cause of fire unknown. No lives lost or persons injured. Valuation not given.

July 25.—Steamer *Osprey*, while proceeding down New London Harbor during a thick fog on morning of July 25, collided with steam yacht *Parthenia*. No lives lost or persons injured. Damage to each vessel estimated at $100. Case investigated and decision rendered October 5, suspending for 8 days license of Anderson L. Crandall, master of *Osprey*, for violation of Rule III and unskilful navigation. Also, as result of testimony taken at this investigation, reported to collector of customs at New London, Conn., and United States district attorney at Hartford, Conn., the violation by Harry E. Converse, owner and master of *Parthenia*, of section 4426, Revised Statutes, by navigating said *Parthenia* on waters of New London Harbor on July 25, 1905, without licensed authority.

August 6.—Lake steamer *Bay View*, with barges *Bavaria* and *Badger* in tow, en route from Newport News, Va., to New London, Conn., grounded during thick fog on Race Point, Fishers Island, N. Y. No lives lost or persons injured. Estimated damage to steamer not stated. Case investigated and decision rendered August 16, exonerating licensed officers from responsibility.

August 15.—Steamer *New Shoreham*, en route from Providence, R. I., to Block Island, R. I., while passing thru entrance to Great Salt pond, struck a sunken scow; damaged bottom, which caused steamer to sink 5 minutes later. No lives lost or persons injured. Case investigated and decision rendered November 7, exonerating licensed officers from all responsibility.

September 19.—Tug *Cora L. Staples*, while lying at New York, New Haven and Hartford Railroad wharf, New London, Conn., took fire in boiler room from causes unknown on afternoon of September 19. Estimated damage from $3,000 to $4,000. No lives lost or persons injured. Case investigated and decision rendered November 7, exonerating licensed officers from all responsibility.

October 18.—Steam yacht *Nautilus*, while moored at wharf at Fishers Island, N. Y., took fire and was totally destroyed. Origin of fire unknown. No lives lost or persons injured. Case investigated, and decision rendered November 7, exonerating licensed officers from all responsibility.

October 6–24.—Investigated charges preferred against E. H. McDonald, master of steamer *City of Lowell*, by Thomas M. Molloy, second lieutenant, revenue cutter service, alleging violation of the provisions of act of Congress, entitled "An act to provide for the safety of passengers on excursion steamers," on the occasion of the Yale-Harvard regatta at New London, Conn., June 29, 1905. Decision rendered October 30, acquitting said E. H. McDonald, the evidence adduced being deemed insufficient to prove the violation alleged.

CASUALTIES, VIOLATIONS OF LAW, AND INVESTIGATIONS, YEAR ENDED DECEMBER 31, 1905—SECOND SUPERVISING DISTRICT—NEW LONDON, CONN.—Continued.

October 30.—Reported to collector of customs at Sag Harbor, N. Y., and United States district attorney at Hartford, Conn., the navigation of steamer *Sarah Thorp* from October 19 to October 30 after expiration of certificate of inspection. Case investigated, and decision rendered November 7, suspending the license of Thomas Corcoran, master of *Sarah Thorp*, for 10 days for this violation.

November 23.—Reported to collector of customs at New London, Conn., and United States district attorney at Hartford, Conn., the navigation from November 11 to November 22 of steamer *J. E. Randerson* after expiration of certificate of inspection. Case investigated, and decision rendered November 29, suspending for 10 days the license of Arthur F. Taylor, master of *J. E. Randerson*, for this violation.

November 24.—On p. m. of November 24 steamer *Henry C. Rowe* collided with unknown steamship at a point in Long Island Sound about 3 miles north of Hortons Point light. Damage to *Henry C. Rowe* not stated. Case investigated, and decision rendered December 5 suspending for 10 days the license of James Howard, master of *Henry C. Rowe*, for careless navigation and violation of pilot rules.

LOCAL DISTRICT OF ALBANY, N. Y.

July 8.—The tug *Roys J. Cram*, while lying at the dock at New Baltimore, N. Y., laid up for the night, caught fire from some unknown cause, and was totally destroyed. Valued at $2,000. Insurance carried, $1,500.

September 3.—The ferry steamer *George H. Power* and passenger steamer *Young America*, bound from Athens, N. Y., to Hudson, N. Y., came in collision near the dug way at Hudson light. The steamer *Young America* was sunk and 4 passengers were drowned. An investigation was held on September 12 to ascertain the cause of collision, and the pilot license of Ernest McKnight, pilot of ferry steamer *George H. Power*, and Alexander Rainey, pilot of steamer *Young America*, was revoked for a violation of pilot rules and reckless navigation. An appeal was made to the supervising inspector and our decision in the case of Alexander Rainey was sustained. In the case of Ernest McKnight our decision was modified to suspension to 18 months.

October 11.—The steamer *John McCausland*, bound from Tivoli, N. Y., to Rondout, N. Y., when abreast of Turkey Point was discovered to be on fire. The vessel was run ashore and was totally destroyed. No lives were lost or persons injured. Amount of loss, $6,000. Insurance carried, $6,000.

LOCAL DISTRICT OF PORTLAND, ME.

January 8.—Steamer *Alice Howard*, while on route between Portsmouth, N. H., and Kittery, Me., Piscataqua River, broke propeller shaft. No other damage.

February 2.—Schooner *Eliza J. Pendleton* found running on an expired certificate of inspection. Case reported to collector of customs at Portland, Me., February 2, and the matter was settled by the Department on payment of a fine of $25.

February 12.—Towing steamer *Catawissa*, while approaching Portland Harbor with 3 loaded barges in tow, at night and thick snowstorm, struck on Cushings Island Point. Came off without serious damage.

February 27.—Small fishing steamer *Arthur B*, left at dock with banked fire, burned and sunk at dock. Hull total loss, value estimated at $400.

May 27.—Steamer *Vinal Haven*, while crossing Penobscot Bay, Me., broke crank shaft. No other damage.

June 2.—Steamer *Emita*, while proceeding down Portland Harbor in dense fog, made steamer *Georgetown* ahead, at anchor, and struck her a glancing blow, slightly damaging *Emita's* stem. No other damage.

June 30.—New steamer *Roosevelt* left Portland, Me., for New York, N. Y., without certificate or inspection. Case reported to collector of customs, Portland, Me.

July 8.—Steamer *Governor Dingley*, while approaching Portland Head in dense fog and strong breeze, collided with and sunk schooner *Sarah C. Smith*. Owing to conditions, schooner was not located in season to clear her. No one lost or injured. Very slight damage to steamer.

July 10.—Steamers *Emita* and *Scandinavia*, while navigating close to dock in Portland Harbor, came in collision through misunderstanding of signals. Slight damage to *Emita; Scandinavia* not damaged. No one lost or injured.

July 29.—Towing steamer *Falmouth*, laid up for the night at Portland, Me., banked fires, no lights left burning, discovered on fire at 3.30 a. m. Cause not known. Small damage to deck frame, deck, port bunker, and house over boiler, estimated at $150.

CASUALTIES, VIOLATIONS OF LAW, AND INVESTIGATIONS, YEAR ENDED DECEMBER 31, 1905—SECOND SUPERVISING DISTRICT—PORTLAND, ME.—Continued.

August 19.—Steamer *Ransom B. Fuller*, on passage from Boston to Gardiner, Me., stranded in Fiddlers reach, Kennebec River, remaining ashore about 5 hours, when she floated and proceeded to Bath, where bottom was examined by diver, who reported very slight damage to planking. Caused by steamer taking quick sheer in narrow channel in thick fog and strong current.

October 14.—U. S. Quartermaster's Department steamer *Henry Wilson*, while attempting to pass towing steamer *Willard* in White Head passage, Portland Harbor, sheered on account of shoal water and struck the *Willard* a glancing blow, damaged guard, covering board, and starting clamp. Damage to *Willard* estimated at $100. No one lost or injured.

November 29.—Tug *Howell* while backing out from coaling dock at Portland, Me., fouled hoisting gear, causing slight damage to guys, stack, and escape pipe, and fireman struck by stack guy. No serious injury.

LOCAL DISTRICT OF PROVIDENCE, R. I.

January 3.—At 3.50 a. m., during thick fog, passenger steamer *Pilgrim* collided with oyster schooner *Winslow Morse*, near Gull rocks, Narragansett Bay. Damage to both vessels slight.

March 14.—Upon investigation concluded this date, suspended for 10 days the license of Abel W. Underhill, as engineer in charge, for drunkenness.

May 10.—After investigation held this date, suspended for 5 days the second-class pilot's license of Joseph W. Rose for running motor vessel *Fosstena* without inspection on November 19, 1904, and March 30 to April 6, 1905. Case referred to the collector of customs at Fall River, Mass., and the U. S. district attorney at Boston, Mass.

May 13.—About 1.30 p. m., barge *General Knox*, in tow of tugs *Carrie A. Ramsey* and *Eben Hodge*, collided with tug *Tormentor*, in Providence River, causing slight damage to latter tug. Whistle signals correctly given and answered. Accident apparently due to a slight miscalculation of distance between vessels.

July 25.—John Lucas, sailor, aged 22 years, was killed on board of steam yacht *Aida*, lying at Pawtuxet, R. I., by the accidental discharge of a cannon on board the steamer.

August 26.—Suspended for 10 days the license, as master and pilot, of Edward M. Millikin for permitting, on July 9 and 16, 1905, more passengers to be carried on steamer *Mary* than allowed by her certificate of inspection. Collector of customs at Providence imposed a fine upon the vessel.

September 26.—Passenger steamer *Queen City* collided with a steam dredger at Stone Bridge, R. I., damaging house of *Queen City*. Accident due to strong tide in narrow, newly dredged channel. No one hurt. Loss, about $500.

September 28.—"Jack" Joseph, a fireman employed on passenger steamer *Warwick*, was accidentally scalded by the parting of a tube rod which he attempted to screw up, said rod being used for the purpose of plugging one of the tubes in the boiler. Accident occurred at Providence.

September 29.—A slight fire occurred on steamer *Windber* during her passage between Newport News and Providence. Broke out in a small place aft, used as a storeroom. Due, in the opinion of the captain, to spontaneous combustion. Was extinguished with little difficulty. No one injured.

October 6.—At 6.15 a. m., passenger steamer *Kennebec* collided with a naphtha launch at Fall River, Mass., causing launch, which had been lying at anchor, to sink, also damaging yacht clubhouse. Practically no damage to the steamer. Accident due to engine hooks of the *Kennebec* dropping as she was making her dock. No lives lost. No one injured. Loss of launch and clubhouse estimated at $1,500.

October 30.—At about 9.15 a. m., fire broke out on passenger steamer *Mary* while she was lying at her dock at Providence. Fire started between bulkhead in fireroom and water tank in hold. Cause not known. The steamer's own streams, with help of city fire department, put out the fire. Estimated loss, $5,000. No one hurt.

November 1.—About 6.50 p. m., in coming out of Block Island, passenger steamer *Mary* struck an obstruction in the Gap and broke her propeller. Accident due to difficulty in handling vessel at time and place of accident on account of strong northwest wind prevailing. Loss, about $1,000.

November 12.—About 1.30 a. m., passenger steamer *Powhatan* collided with barge *Ira A. Allen* in tow of steamer *H. A. Baxter*, near Pomham light, Providence River, sinking said barge and also barge *Elheurah*. Whistle signals properly exchanged. Master of *Powhatan* says collision was caused by barge *Allen* sheering into *Powhatan*,

CASUALTIES, VIOLATIONS OF LAW, AND INVESTIGATIONS, YEAR ENDED DECEMBER 31, 1905—SECOND SUPERVISING DISTRICT—PROVIDENCE, R. I.—Continued.

which had given her all the chance possible and was going astern at time of collision. Crew of barges saved in small boat belonging to barge *Allen*. Barges afterwards raised. Loss, about $3,000.

December 11.—Investigated complaint of E. B. Swett, master of schooner *Mary E. Palmer*, against Alfred F. Gray, mate of same, for misconduct in leaving schooner without notifying master. Case dismissed, with caution to Gray.

LOCAL DISTRICT OF BANGOR, ME.

January 7.—While steamer *Sappho* was attempting to make landing at Bar Harbor, Me., she was thrown against wharf by heavy sea, breaking in guard on port side and breaking flange on auxiliary steam pipe. Entire damage estimated at $125. No one lost or injured.

January 13.—A rehearing on appeal of William D. Bennett and Charles Shute, whose licenses as master and pilot were suspended by this board on December 14, 1904, for 4 months, was held at Belfast, Me., before the supervising inspector, second district, who modified the time of suspension in each case to 2 months.

June 3.—At 11.30 p. m., during thick fog, steamer *Henry F. Eaton* was in collision with wharf on Canadian side of St. Croix River, while proceeding downstream on ebb tide. Steamer grounded, but was floated next high water without damage.

July 2.—During evening, in thick rain, the fishing steamer *Escort* was approaching landing on St. Croix River below St. Stephen, New Brunswick, when bells to back steamer were not answered and steamer went aground.

Investigation showed the engineer, Alonzo C. Ray, to be missing and no trace of him could be found. His body was afterwards found on the New Brunswick shore below the landing. Coroner's verdict, "accidental drowning." Very slight damage to steamer.

July 19.—Steamer *Penobscot*, on passage from St. John, New Brunswick, to Eastport, Me., was in collision with small sailboat containing 2 men. Cries were heard apparently on port bow of steamer and wheel was immediately put hard to port and engines reversed, but it was impossible to avoid collision. Boat was at once lowered from steamer, but no trace of men could be found. No damage to steamer and no blame attached to officers.

August 23.—At 2.30 a. m. fire was discovered by crew of steam yacht *Monaloa*, lying on owner's private railway at Camden, Me.

Fire was extinguished by crew with apparatus on board, but not until steamer was badly damaged. Fire apparently originated under forward end of boiler from unknown cause. No one injured. Loss estimated at $5,000.

September 11.—While steamer *Lubec* was approaching wharf at Lubec, steamer proceeding slow in dense fog, she was in collision with sail vessel lying at end of wharf. No one injured and no damage to sail vessel. Damage to steamer slight.

December 1.—On passage from Swans Island to Rockland, Me., intermediate shaft broke on steamer *Vinal Haven*. Towed to Rockland for new shaft.

No other damage and no one injured.

LOCAL DISTRICT OF NEW HAVEN, CONN.

January 17.—While steamer *Jack Jewett* was moored at Dolphins in East Haven River, the bow of said steamer was crushed by ice. Steamer was run on flats and now lies submerged. No lives lost.

January 28.—Towing steamer *Edna Murray* took fire in the forward end of boiler room, while vessel was in the harbor of Milford, Conn., and was not discovered until it was too late for the engineer to reach the fire pump and start it working. Steamer was burned to the water's edge. No lives lost.

February 27.—As steamer *Amanda* was navigating at the mouth of New Haven Harbor, the planking of said steamer was crusht in by floating ice and steamer foundered in about 18 feet of water. Steamer was subsequently raised and towed to dock. No lives lost.

June 16.—Steamer *John H. Starin* collided with an unknown vessel off Bridgeport Harbor. Damage to unknown vessel not ascertained as vessel proceeded on its way; no damage to steamer *John H. Starin*, and no one injured. A dense fog prevailed at time of accident, and circumstances did not warrant an investigation.

July 18.—Towing steamer *Arthur* reported to the collector of customs at New Haven, Conn., for navigating on expired certificate of inspection from June 21 to July 15, and

CASUALTIES, VIOLATIONS OF LAW, AND INVESTIGATIONS, YEAR ENDED DECEMBER 31, 1905—SECOND SUPERVISING DISTRICT—NEW HAVEN, CONN.—Continued.

after receipt of statement of repairs and equipment necessary before certificate of inspection would be issued. The case was investigated and the licenses of William Kelly, pilot, and Thomas E. Hempstock, engineer, were suspended for 10 days.

October 31.—Charges of unprovoked assault were preferred by Captain H. Eugene Lockwood, pilot of the steamer *Alice R.*, against George Van Heusen, engineer of said steamer. The charges were investigated on November 28 and sustained, and his license as engineer in charge of river steamers was revoked.

November 20.—Towing steamer *Atkins Hughes*, while coming west from Point Judith, R. I., to Sachem Head, Conn., with scow in tow, grounded on the north shore of Falkner Island. Steamer was hauled off with no damage done and no personal injury. The case was investigated and the license of Fred W. Rich, pilot in charge of said steamer, was suspended for 15 days.

December 6.—Motor vessel *Commander* was in collision with schooner *H. T. Hedges* about 3 miles off Stratford Point. Slight damage done and no personal injury. Case was investigated and the license of Royal C. Decker, pilot in charge of the *Commander*, suspended for 10 days.

December 15.—At 6.35 p. m., steamer *City of Laurence*, bound east from New York to Bridgeport, was in collision with the three-masted schooner *Basutoland* (British) between Stamford and Greens Ledge lights, damaging the schooner so that she leaked badly and was abandoned by the crew. Schooner was awash when picked up by tug and towed to port. Damage to *City of Laurence*, small hole in port bow and 12 stanchions broken. Case will be investigated.

THIRD SUPERVISING DISTRICT.

LOCAL DISTRICT OF NORFOLK, VA.

December 27, 1904 (reported in January, 1905).—Steamship *Northeastern*, W. J. Lynch, master, bound to Philadelphia from Sabine Pass, during gale with high seas and frequent rain squalls, mistook Cape Hatteras light for the lightship, and, owing to incorrect sounding, ship struck the shoal and went to pieces. Crew saved.

January 22.—During thick fog, steamer *Ocracoke* ran into and sunk gasoline boat *Ray*, due to the latter's sounding 3 blasts of the fog horn, which is the signal given by a sail vessel running free. The *Ray* does not carry a licensed crew and at this time had several passengers on board, but no lives were lost.

January 25.—Steamer *Conqueror*, G. T. Powell, master, during northwest gale, while trying to rescue barges that were anchored off lee shore, steamer lost her rudder and was blown ashore. No lives lost.

January 31.—At 4.45 p. m., when off Old Point bound in, seaman Sivanus Pizostu fell overboard from the forecastle head of steamer *J. L. Luckenbach*, while hauling in the fish tackle, and was drowned before help could reach him.

February 3.—About 6 a. m., while about 10 miles from Washington, N. C., one Augustus Blount (colored), a passenger on steamer *Shiloh*, was mist, and it is presumed that he fell overboard and was drowned. His wife states he was nearsighted and subject to giddiness.

February 10.—It having come to the knowledge of this board that Owen Mallon was acting as assistant engineer on steamer *A. J. Beardsley* without proper license, the case was investigated and his license was suspended for a period of 10 days.

February 20.—Second engineer of steamer *Alice* filed report stating that chief engineer, William Marshall, fastened down safety valve on boiler in this vessel and steam rose above the amount allowed by certificate of inspection. Case investigated; charges not sustained.

December 20, 1904 (reported in March, 1905).—While entering Oracabessa, Jamaica, under guidance of pilot, steamer *Buckman*, A. Madden, master, backed into ledge; broke rudderpost and blade to propeller; proceeded next day in tow for Port Antonia. At entrance to this harbor towline parted and anchor dragged, causing vessel to drift ashore. Vessel temporarily repaired at Kingston and proceeded to Newport News, where she arrived March 8, 1905.

March 21.—Steamer *Helen*, passing up river with a tow, struck steamer *Luray* amidships; slight damage to both vessels; strong ebb tide and crowded channel. No lives lost.

April 10.—Steamer *Sophie Wood*, Robert S. Griffin, master, is reported to have sunk thru siphon pipe, and hull in bad condition from result of sinking. Examined April 18, under authority of section 4453, Revised Statutes.

CASUALTIES, VIOLATIONS OF LAW, AND INVESTIGATIONS, YEAR ENDED DECEMBER 31, 1905—THIRD SUPERVISING DISTRICT—NORFOLK, VA.—Continued.

April 13.—Fire broke out while steamer *Haven Belle*, T. W. Tillery, master, was made fast at dock for the night, consuming all woodwork of said vessel above deck. Cause of fire unknown. No lives lost.

April 13.—While rounding bend in river after giving proper signals and hearing no answer, steamer *R. L. Myers*, W. A. Powers, master, sighted a gasoline launch. In trying to clear launch struck same and ran into bank, damaging bow of steamer *R. L. Myers*. No lives lost.

April 18.—At entrance of Elizabeth River, steamer *George W. Clyde*, coming from Newport News, and steamer *Crisfield*, with *N. Y. P. and N. R. R. Barge No. 8*, in tow from Norfolk, came together, doing considerable damage to both vessels. No lives lost and no persons injured.

April 29.—At 11.30 p. m., while steamer *Dorothea* was proceeding across river, sloop *Harry & Ralph* tacked ship under *Dorothea's* bow and the two came together, doing considerable damage to sloop. No lives lost or injured. Case investigated and Master George B. Downing, of steamer *Dorothea*, exonerated from all blame.

May 11.—Steamer *Sara Louise*, while proceeding down the river, colored deck hand, who was amusing himself by riding around deck on a truck, slipt overboard and was drowned.

May 28.—Steamer *Hamilton*, A. B. Boaz, master, left Norfolk at 4.45 a. m., and at 8.50 a. m., same day, fire was discovered in fore hold. Water and steam were turned in to extinguish fire, and ship returned to Norfolk. Spontaneous combustion in cargo of cotton presumed to be cause of fire. Lower deck beams warped by heat. No lives lost; no one injured.

May 28.—At 2 a. m. steamer *Mollie L. Farmer* was burned while lying at her dock at Newbern, N. C. Cause of fire unknown; damage estimated at $300.

June 11.—Fire occurred on steamer *Pennsylvania*, caused by upsetting a pan of grease on cook stove. Fire was immediately put out by chemicals and hose. Very little damage was done. No lives lost. No one injured.

June 14.—While steamer *Mohican* was maneuvering for her berth, tide cut her down onto *N. Y. P. and N. R. R. Barge No. 12*, proceeding down the harbor in tow of tug *Philadelphia*. Stem of *Mohican* cut part way thru 2 fender guards on barge, doing very little damage. No damage to *Mohican*, and no lives lost; no one injured.

June 16.—When ferry steamer *Superior* had started to leave her slip at Berkley, J. W. Jones, deck hand, age 23 years, while in the act of pulling up the rudder pin, fell to the deck and rolled overboard, presumably taken with apoplexy. All efforts to save him failed. He was not seen to come to the surface. Body was recovered a few hours late.

June 16.—While steamer *Volunteer*, Joseph J. Jones, master, was under way, was put in charge of an unlicensed man while pilot went about deck collecting fares from the passengers. Case set for investigation.

June 30.—At 1.15 a. m., while steamer *Martha E. Dickerman* was proceeding up Pasquotank River, collided with tug *Armorica*, coming down river. No lives lost.

August 25.—Steamer *Neuse* collided with steamer *Blanche* in Neuse River, sinking steamer *Blanche*. No lives lost. Damage to steamer *Blanche* not known. Case investigated and decision rendered.

September 1.—In Blades Creek, North Carolina, while Robert Custer, deck hand on steamer *Hatteras*, was leaning over the rail, he lost his balance and went overboard and was drowned. All efforts to save him failed.

July, 1905 (reported September 8, 1905).—Ruffin Cofield was charged with acting as assistant engineer on steamer *Guide* without holding proper license. Case investigated and decision rendered.

September 4.—Steamer *Aragon* stranded on False Cape, coast of Virginia. Electric storm affected compass, causing the vessel to be off her course. Vessel floated with no damage. No lives lost; no one injured.

September 11.—Steamer *R. L. Myers*, while proceeding down Tar River from Greenville to Washington, struck a submerged log, breaking one blade of propeller and starting sternpost, causing boat to leak. No lives lost; no one injured.

September 25.—In Chesapeake Bay, while proceeding out of harbor, steamer *Bay Port*, Capt. K. A. Jensen, master, collided with schooner *Job H. Jackson*, Captain Williamson, master. Schooner turned turtle and crew were picked off her bottom and taken on board steamer, with the exception of one man, who could not be found (name not known). Steamer then anchored and early next morning a schooner bound in collided with the steamer. Case investigated and decision rendered.

CASUALTIES, VIOLATIONS OF LAW, AND INVESTIGATIONS, YEAR ENDED DECEMBER 31, 1905—THIRD SUPERVISING DISTRICT—NORFOLK, VA.—Continued.

October 15.—Steamer *Louisville*, while lying at dock, Pinners Point, about 4 a. m., sunk. No person on board. Cause of sinking unknown. Case investigated and decision rendered.

October 4 to October 27.—Steamer *Marietta* was found with expired certificate of inspection on board and boat being navigated, no application having been made for inspection. Case reported to collector of customs, Norfolk, Va.

October 31.—Barge in tow of steamer *Piedmont*, while maneuvering about dock in Norfolk Harbor, was struck by U. S. torpedo boat *Truxton*, Lieut. Clark D. Stearns, commanding. Case to be investigated.

November 3.—While ferry steamer *City of Portsmouth* was entering dock steamer *Defiance* backed into her. Damage slight.

November 16.—Steamer *Kershaw*, Capt. Wm. J. Bond, master, while proceeding up Norfolk Harbor about 6 a. m. collided with barge *Frank Pendleton*, anchored off Lamberts Point, causing barge to sink. Steamer damaged on both bows. No lives lost. Captain Bond, of steamer *Kershaw*, reports shat his steering gear refused to work causing the collision. Case investigated and decision rendered.

December 1.—While steamer *Mobjack* was backing from Bay Line dock, Norfolk Harbor, struck a gasoline launch containing 4 persons; 1 man lost. Case investigated and decision rendered.

December 4.—In Norfolk Harbor tug *Alice* (of navy-yard), while swinging from end of Old Dominion pier, came ahead and struck steamer *Accomack* on port side while the latter vessel was entering her slip. No lives lost; no one injured. Slight damage to steamer *Accomack*.

December 9.—Steamer *Aragon*, Capt. Charles Blackley, master, on Atlantic coast, near Kitty Hawk, N. C., during easterly gale, ship, with barge in tow, bound south, light, was unable to head up enough to keep offshore. *Aragon* is a lake type steamer, with no means of getting her bow down when light; consequently in a gale of wind can only run before it. No lives lost; no one injured. Steamer sustained considerable damage, but was gotten off and towed to Norfolk. Her own pumps helped to keep her free.

November 24 and previous.—Walter S. Williams, master of steamer *E. V. McCauley*, was reported as acting as master of steamer *E. V. McCauley*, of 136 gross tons, under a first-class pilot's license. Case investigated and decision rendered.

December 15.—Between Old Point and Thimbles, in Chesapeake Bay, steamer *Joseph M. Clark*, Capt. Jackson Miller, master, collided with steamer *Jack Twohy*. Damage to steamer *Joseph M. Clark* about $300. Case to be investigated.

November 22 (reported December 19, 1905).—Capt. Edmund Parkin, master of steamer *Edmund Parkin*, reports the drowning of one Willie Rogerson, after making lines fast to the hoister and float in tow of above steamer. Body recovered December 7.

December 15.—Steamer *Bay View*, Capt. Leslie J. Cummings, master, left Newport News with load of coal, and barge *Bath* in tow, also loaded. Encountered bad weather, and when off Winter Quarter light-ship barge, signaled that she was leaking. The tow was then turned around and headed back for Cape Henry. When south of Cape Charles, the steel hawser parted. The *Bay View* stood by the vicinity, but when daylight came barge was not to be seen. The steamer came into Hampton Roads, and after weather moderated went out to search. Report to-day (December 27) is that barge has been reported by incoming vessel, and *Bay View* has left port to locate her and tow her in.

December 18.—Steamer *John Scully*, Capt. H. W. Gregg, master, while proceeding from Newport News to sea, when in Hampton Roads, steamer lost rudder, rudderpost, and shoe, and returned to Newport News under jury rig. Cause of accident unknown.

LOCAL DISTRICT OF BALTIMORE, MD.

February 7.—Steam tug *Chas. J. Baker*, while assisting in towing a car float tandem, in Baltimore Harbor, port hawser parted and starboard hawser jammed, causing her to heel over and sink. Was raised. Estimated damage, $500. No lives lost.

February 8.—Tug *Ivanhoe* collided with scow in tow of tug *Greyhound* in Baltimore Harbor. Collision due to heavy ice in harbor. Estimated damage to scow, $45. No lives lost.

February 13.—Tug *Imperial* collided with ice boat *F. C. Latrobe* in Chesapeake Bay, off Magothy River. Estimated damage to *F. C. Latrobe*, $300. No lives lost.

March 2.—Tug *Hanson H. Keys* partially burned while lying at foot of Bond street, Baltimore Harbor. Origin of fire unknown. Estimated damage, $3,500. No lives lost.

CASUALTIES, VIOLATIONS OF LAW, AND INVESTIGATIONS, YEAR ENDED DECEMBER 31, 1905—THIRD SUPERVISING DISTRICT—BALTIMORE, MD.—Continued.

March 12.—Steamship *Essex* collided with schooner *Sunny South* in Chesapeake Bay near Sandy Point light, damaging the schooner to the extent of about $150. No lives lost.

March 31–April 1.—The Baltimore, Chesapeake and Atlantic Railway Company, owners of steamer *Cambridge*, reported to collector of customs, Baltimore, Md., for violation of section 4438, Revised Statutes, by having in their employ St. Elmo Todd, who acted as master and pilot of steamer *Cambridge* on March 31 and April 1, 1905, his license as master and first-class pilot having expired February 6, 1905, and same not having been renewed.

March 31–April 1.—St. Elmo Todd reported to collector of customs, Baltimore, Md., for violation of section 4438, Revised Statutes, by acting as master and pilot of steamer *Cambridge* on March 31 and April 1, 1905, his license as master and first-class pilot having expired February 6, 1905, and same not having been renewed.

April 6.—Steamer *Harry Randall* was afire on Potomac River, caused by overturning of pot of grease in kitchen. Estimated damage, $300. No lives lost.

April 20.—Steamer *Georges Creek* collided with bugeye *Ray* in Curtis Bay. Estimated damage to bugeye, $50; damage to tug, slight. Arthur Rothwell, one of crew of bugeye, either fell or jumped overboard at the time of collision and was drowned. The case was investigated May 9, and the license of John N. Kelley, master of steamer *Georges Creek*, suspended for a period of 30 days for unskilful navigation.

May 19.—Tug *Columbia* collided with steamship *Dania* in Curtis Bay. Damage to steamship, slight. No lives lost. Case was investigated May 29, and the license of Benjamin F. Evans, master of tug *Columbia*, was suspended for 30 days for being intoxicated while on board the tug in the capacity of captain.

May 27.—Tug *H. J. Hoole* overturned at Wilkerson wharf, Va., while coaling, and filled with water. No damage except by water. No lives lost.

May 31.—While steamer *Charles Macalester* was lying at her berth in Washington, D. C., Joseph Briscoe, a fireman and member of the crew, was struck by the main crank, causing his death. Not investigated.

June 14.—Schooner *Alice P. Turner*, in tow of tug *Peerless*, collided with bugeye *G. A. Zirckel*. Weather was misty at the time. Estimated damage to bugeye, $100; to schooner, none. No lives lost.

July 3.—Jack Brown (colored), deck hand on steamer *Harry Randall*, fell overboard while said steamer was making a landing at River Side, Md., and was drowned. The officers of the steamer stated that he was intoxicated and lost his balance. Case not investigated.

July 7.—Tug *Rescue* collided with steamer *Legonia* in Baltimore Harbor. Collision due to engine of tug *Rescue* catching in center. Estimated damage to *Legonia*, $100; to *Rescue*, none. No lives lost.

July 14.—William Crowley, a member of the crew of steamer *Estelle Randall*, was drowned in the harbor of Washington. Case investigated October 12, and found that no licensed officer was responsible for said drowning while acting under the authority of his license.

July 18.—Charges preferred against Herbert A. Bohannon, master of steamer *Calvert*, for having oil, paint, etc., outside of metal-lined oil locker on July 15, 1905. Case investigated August 3, and dismissed.

July 18.—Charges preferred against R. Bailey Reed, master of steamer *Pocahontas*, for having paints, oils, driers, etc., outside of metal-lined locker on July 15, 1905. Case investigated September 2, and dismissed.

July 23.—Tug *Defiance* collided with bugeye *M. Blanche Hayward* in Potomac River, near Hallowing Point. No damage to tug; estimated damage to bugeye, $300. No lives lost. Case investigated September 26, and Edward P. Snyder, master of tug *Defiance*, exonerated from responsibility of the collision.

August 21.—John Pinn, member of crew of steamer *Wm. S. Brusstar*, fell overboard from said vessel while vessel was lying at wharf at Mila, Va., and was drowned. Finn was under the influence of liquor at the time. Case not investigated.

August.—Steamer *Doc Reh* violated section 4426, Revised Statutes, by navigating without inspection being completed. Case reported to collector of customs, Washington, D. C., on November 29, 1905.

September 6.—Tug *Walter F. Mead* damaged by fire to the extent of about $200 in Potomac River. Believed fire originated from spark from galley stove. No lives lost.

September 8.—Tug *Annie* damaged by fire to the extent of about $500, at Queenstown, Md. Origin of fire unknown. No lives lost.

CASUALTIES, VIOLATIONS OF LAW, AND INVESTIGATIONS, YEAR ENDED DECEMBER 31, 1905—THIRD SUPERVISING DISTRICT—BALTIMORE, MD.—Continued.

September 16.—Simon Jones, a passenger, committed suicide by jumping overboard from main deck of steamer *Charles Macalester* while en route from Marshall Hall to Washington, D. C. Case not investigated.

September 19.—Tug *Little Nora* collided with tug *Columbia* in Baltimore Harbor. Estimated damage to *Little Nora*, $75; to *Columbia*, none. No lives lost.

October 2.—Joel H. Drummond, charged with unlawfully raising the tonnage on his license as chief engineer, was reported to district attorney. Case dismissed for want of evidence.

October 4.—Steamer *Peerless* collided with a sailing vessel (name unknown) in Chesapeake Bay below Sandy Point. Cause of collision stated to be unskilful navigation of sail vessel. Estimated damage to *Peerless*, $25; to sail vessel, not known. No lives lost. Case not investigated.

October 10.—The schooner *Pearl* collided with the steamer *Vesper* in Chesapeake Bay about 1 mile below Seven Foot knoll. Estimated damage to schooner, $250; to steamer, $20. No lives lost.

October 24.—Tug *Irene* collided with motor vessel *Sunbeam* in Baltimore Harbor. Estimated damage to motor vessel, $30, to tug. none. No lives lost.

October 31.—Steamer *Ericsson* collided with a scow in tow of tug *Southern* in Baltimore Harbor. Estimated damage to *Southern* and scow, $1,500, to *Ericsson*, none. No lives lost. Case investigated November 14, and license of John H. Brown, master of tug *Southern*, suspended for 15 days for unskilful navigation; and license of John W. Grace, master of steamer *Ericsson*, suspended for 10 days for unskilful navigation.

November 6.—Steamer *T. V. Arrowsmith* reinspected and it was found that there was a shortage in the required number of life preservers. Alfred A. Richards, master of said steamer, was charged with negligence. Case investigated November 25 and dismissed.

November 7.—Tug *Sea King* collided with steamer *Calvert* near junction of Cut-off and Craighill channels. Estimated damage to *Sea King*, $200, to *Calvert*, slight. No lives lost.

November 9.—Fire was discovered in port coal bunkers of steamer *Emma* in Great Wicomico River. Efforts to extinguish the fire by using fire buckets and axes proved fruitless, and O. A. Thompson, the master of the *Emma*, caused the vessel to be sunk, in order to save as much as possible of the boat. Estimated damage, $8,500. No lives lost. Case not investigated.

November 13.—Tug *Maryland* collided with a scow in tow of tug *Southern*, in Baltimore Harbor. Estimated damage to tug *Maryland*, $250; to tug *Southern*, none; to scow, slight. No lives lost. Case investigated November 28, and the license of William J. Johnson, pilot of tug *Maryland*, was suspended for 5 days; the license of John H. Brown, master and pilot of tug *Southern*, being also suspended for 5 days for negligence.

November 21.—Investigated charges of incompetency preferred against Young D. Griffis, pilot of fire boat *Cataract*, which charges were based upon his actions on the morning of November 2, 1905, while in charge of fire boat *Cataract*, proceeding from Commercial wharf to coal pier of the Quemahoning Coal Company, in giving wrong signals from pilot house to engine room. Mr. Griffis exonerated of the charge of being incompetent.

November 29.—Steamer *Dispatch*, McMullen & McDermott, owners, reported to collector of customs, Baltimore, Md., for navigating the Susquehanna River November 24, 1905, before inspection was completed and certificate issued, in violation of section 4426, Revised Statutes.

December 19.—Steamer *Baltimore* collided with schooner *Amelia M. Price*, in Chesapeake Bay, about 4 miles northward of Point No Point. One man drowned. Estimated damage to steamer, $500; to schooner, unknown. Case will be investigated.

December 21.—Motor vessel *Pioneer* sprung a leak while lying at anchor in Love Point Harbor and was run ashore. Estimated damage to motor vessel, $150. No lives lost.

December 26.—Tug *J. W. Thompson*, while passing thru the Western Maryland drawbridge, Spring Gardens, was struck by the drawbridge closing before the tug was clear. Estimated damage to tug, $500. No lives lost.

LOCAL DISTRICT OF CHARLESTON, S. C.

January 3.—Charles St. George, master and pilot, blew cross whistle to steamer *Navahoe* on Cape Fear River from steamer *Alexander Jones*. License supended 15 days.

CASUALTIES, VIOLATIONS OF LAW, AND INVESTIGATIONS, YEAR ENDED DECEMBER 31, 1905—THIRD SUPERVISING DISTRICT—CHARLESTON, S. C.—Continued.

January 5.—On the night of this date, off Cape Romain, fire was discovered on board the steamship *Iroquois*, in the lower hold abaft the forward hatch. The hatches were battened down and steam turned into the hold. The steamer came to port, where the fire was soon extinguished by flooding the lower hold. The damage was mostly confined to cargo, the extent of which is not known. The steamer was bound to Jacksonville via Charleston, but discontinued her trip and returned to New York, with ballast, for repairs. The passengers were all called, and boats cleared as a precaution on discovery of fire.

February 23.—On the night of this date Engineer Robert Sellers, of steamer *Mayflower*, fell overboard at Gibson's mill, Town Creek, N. C., and was drowned.

February 28.—Steamer *Alexander Jones*, towing schooner *Elizabeth T. Doyle*, was struck by schooner, carrying away the smokestack and both masts. Damages to extent of $1,000. No one hurt.

March 2.—While towing scow into Town Creek, steamer *Ava* was driven down upon the jetty and sunk. Estimated damage, $75. No one hurt.

May 8.—James Doward, assistant engineer, deserted steamer *Lulu E*, with cargo on board and steamer ready to sail, causing the loss of cargo and delay of steamer. Case investigated, and license of James Doward suspended for 30 days.

June 21.—Steamers *Wilmington* and *Sea Gate*, proceeding up Cape Fear River, collided on June 21, damaging the *Sea Gate* to the extent of $300 and the *Wilmington* $10. No one hurt. Case investigated, and, owing to disagreement in decision by inspectors, referred to supervising inspector, third district, for settlement.

July 3.—At a point on the Cape Fear River, near Blenheim landing, Richard Winn (colored), age 23, a deck hand on the steamer *Tar Heel*, fell overboard and was drowned. He was seen to fall overboard by other hands, and the steamer was immediately stopt and the yawl boat launched, but the man was never seen to rise after falling into the water. A careful search was made, but the body was not recovered.

July 14.—Charges filed against William H. Ward for drunkenness, insubordination, and exceeding the provisions of his engineer's license. Charges investigated, and his license as chief engineer suspended for 6 months; also his license as master and pilot suspended 6 months.

July 19.—While steamer *A. J. Johnson* was making landing at W. M. Corbett's mill on Cape Fear River, S. C., she struck a stump projecting from the land, tearing a rent in her side about 2 feet long, sinking the steamer. The steamer has been raised and damages, including the damage to cargo, found to approximate $300. No lives lost.

August 1.—On trip from Morehead City, N. C., to Wilmington, N. C., Daniel E. Strickland, engineer in charge of steamer *Grayling*, of Detroit, Mich., allowed boiler to become salted and burn, causing serious damage to boiler. Charges filed by master and admitted to be true by engineer. On examination of boiler by inspectors, and admission of the charges by engineer, said engineer's license was suspended 12 months, from September 8, 1905.

August 20.—August Redd, passenger on steamer *Wilmington*, en route from Carolina Beach pier to Wilmington, committed suicide by jumping overboard. When the cry "man overboard" was given the steamer was quickly stopt and boat lowered, but without avail.

September 11.—On the night of this date steamer *Thistle*, while lying at her dock at Santee, S. C., caught fire from some unknown cause, burning her pilot house and forward main deck. Fire was extinguished by the crew of the steamer with fire buckets.

November 29.—Charges filed against Samuel Robinson for drunkenness while on duty as engineer on board steamer *Charles M. Whitlock*. Case investigated, and his license as engineer suspended for 6 months.

LOCAL DISTRICT OF SAVANNAH, GA.

May 15.—Tug *Harold*, while lying at her dock at Savannah at 3 a. m., damaged by fire to extent of $300. The fire was supposed to have originated on board. No lives were lost.

June 1.—Steamship *City of Macon* collided with coal barge 20 miles southeast of Highland light. Slight injury to barge; none to ship. No lives were lost.

August 28.—Steamship *Peconic*, of New York, 1,855 tons, David N. E. Jones, owner, C. R. Jones, master, bound from Philadelphia for New Orleans with coal, foundered in a gale off the northeast coast of Florida. All of the officers and crew,

CASUALTIES, VIOLATIONS OF LAW, AND INVESTIGATIONS, YEAR ENDED DECEMBER 31, 1905—THIRD SUPERVISING DISTRICT—SAVANNAH, GA.—Continued.

except two Spanish seamen who were on watch, 20 men all told, were lost. The survivors escaped in a lifeboat and landed on Amelia beach near Fernandina, Fla. Their statement was that during the night while the ship was being put about and was in the trough of the sea a heavy wave struck her broadside, and she went down.

September 30.—Tug *Grantham I. Taggart* collided with open naphtha launch, which ran across the steamer's bow in Savannah River. The launch was sunk and 1 occupant drowned. The launch carried neither lights nor signals, the collision having occurred in the night.

December 5.—Tug *Iris*, of Brunswick, reported to collector of customs at Brunswick for navigating without the complement of officers required by the certificate of inspection. The license of Andrew J. Kopperad, master, was suspended.

December 16.—Steamer *C. H. Evans*, of Brunswick, reported to collector of customs for navigating without the required number of officers on board as called for by the steamer's certificate of inspection. The license of Benjamin A. White, jr., master, was suspended.

LOCAL DISTRICT OF JACKSONVILLE, FLA.

April 7.—While steamer *Hoo Hoo* was lying at dock at Palatka, Fla., on the night of April 7, W. B. Lucas, cook on said vessel, fell overboard and was drowned. Body was seen floating in water on Sunday and recovered. Cause unknown.

April 11.—At 7 p. m., a little white smoke was discovered coming from under boiler of steamer *Harry Lee*. Thinking there might be a fire, a stream of water was turned on under boiler and ash pan, which stopped the smoke, and no damage was sustained.

May 21.—On Sunday, Lee Finnell, occupying Room 233 on the steamer *City of Jacksonville* was mist when the steamer was near Sanford, Fla. His body was afterwards found, but it was impossible to state whether it was accidental drowning or whether he committed suicide.

May 24.—Alex McPherson, a colored man, boarded steamer *Lavinia* at Fort Gates, Fla., en route to Welaka, Fla., to receive medical attention, account of suffering with indigestion. Shortly after vessel left dock at Fort Gates he died from above cause.

May 15.—Steamship *David*, Capt. L. H. Warncke, of the Donald Steamship Company, of New York, went aground about 12 miles north of Cape Florida, Fla.; was aground 10 hours; assisted off by steam tug *Martha Helen*, of Jacksonville, Fla., and proceeded to Pensacola, Fla., to discharge cargo and haul out for repairs. Damage unknown. No one injured.

June 1.—About 5 p. m., steamship *Arapahoe*, Capt. E. Kemble, of the Clyde Steamship Company, collided with the U. S. dredge *Jacksonville* off or near the mouth of Dunns Creek, St. Johns River, Florida. No lives lost nor persons injured. Damaged plating of steamship on starboard side above water line. Estimated cost of repairs unknown. Damage to dredge slight.

June 11.—About 11 o'clock steamer *St. Johns* caught fire near bulkhead aft of boiler from cause unknown. Damage to vessel estimated at $400. No lives lost and no damage to anything else done.

July 2.—About 2.30 p. m., while steamer *Annie H.* with 2 lighters in tow, was passing thru Florida East Coast Railway drawbridge, at Jacksonville, Fla., an unknown man in rowboat came from under the bridge and lighter struck the rowboat; it being ascertained afterwards that man was drowned.

July 4.—About 7.15 p. m., Clifford Sturdevant, colored deck hand on steamer *Heck*, while in bathing near Curry & Allen's landing on Wekiva River, was accidentally drowned. Every effort was made to find body, but without success.

July 6.—The cook on boad steamer *Kathleen*, while bound for Cuba, fell overboard off Mayport, Fla., and was drowned. He was intoxicated; name unknown. Steamer proceeded on voyage after being unable to find body.

July 30.—Between 11 and 12 p. m., steam yacht *Augusta* caught on fire in engine room from cause unknown. No one injured; damage to yacht estimated at $500.

August 8.—Steamer *Hessie*, David R. Floyd, captain, was tied up to dock at Mayport, Fla., about 6 p. m. Engineer and 3 other men were aboard until about 6 p. m. Between 1 and 2 a. m. vessel sunk from causes unknown. No lives lost; approximate damage, $300.

August 9.—The steamer *City of Jacksonville*, Thomas Creaser, captain, on her downward trip from Sanford to Jacksonville, Fla., broke her starboard shaft near Welaka, Fla. Vessel was repaired; damage nominal; no one injured.

August 14.—Sandy Alvarez, colored, age 70, residing at Picolata, Fla., wa passe ger on steamer *Crescent*. About 2.15 p. m., opposite Green Cove Springs, Fla., while

CASUALTIES, VIOLATIONS OF LAW, AND INVESTIGATIONS, YEAR ENDED DECEMBER 31, 1905—THIRD SUPERVISING DISTRICT—JACKSONVILLE, FLA.—Continued.

sitting on after rail he suddenly fell into the water and was drowned. Every effort was made to recover body, but without success.

August 15.—R. L. Terrell made affidavit that Jefferson D. Robeson, licensed master and pilot of steamer *L. McNeill*, 145 gross tons, employed Bert R. Brown as assistant engineer and in charge of watch on board said steamer, who only had license for vessels of 12 gross tons. License of Jefferson D. Robeson, master, was suspended for 15 days, and that of Bert R. Brown was suspended for 30 days, violation section 4450, Revised Statutes.

October 4.—Boatswain Francisco Rodrequez while running hose on forward saloon deck of steamship *Martinique* for fire drill endeavored to straighten out a kink, when the pressure of water threw the bight out with a jerk, striking Rodrequez in the abdomen. He was given every medical attention possible on board ship, but upon arrival at Habana he walked down stairs and was taken to the hospital, where he died about noon October 7.

October 7.—About 5 a. m., steamer *S. S. Brewster* collided with steamer *Rosa* on St. Johns River opposite the city of Jacksonville, Fla. No lives lost; damage slight.

November 7.—On voyage from Key West to Miami, Fla., on steamship *Martinique*, the infant of a Mrs. Small died at 9 a. m., of some child's sickness, of which the child had been suffering for several days.

November 21.—About 5.30 p. m., steamer *City of Jacksonville* collided with Florida East Coast Railway drawbridge at Jacksonville, Fla., breaking in the side house and guards. No lives lost; damage approximately $75.

December 12.—While auxiliary motor vessel *Mount Pleasant* was lying alongside of barge anchored off Plantation Key in Bay of Florida, while filling vessel's tanks with gasoline from drums on barge, a tremendous explosion occurred in the inside of the vessel which totally wrecked the whole after-part of the vessel, inflicting painful burns on captain and engineer. No lives lost; approximate loss, $1,000.

December 15.—Steamer *Biscayne* collided with steamer *St. Lucie* while making landing at Miami, Fla., owing to misunderstanding in signals from pilot house to engine room. Damage about $20; no lives lost.

FOURTH SUPERVISING DISTRICT.

LOCAL DISTRICT OF ST. LOUIS, MO.

January 31.—While the steamer *Anderson* was laid up for the night, with watchman on board, fire was discovered at 11.45 p. m., origin unknown; steamer total loss, estimated at $6,000. Grand Tower, Ill.

February 16.—While the steamer *Wm. K. Kavanaugh* was lying at the bank at St. Louis, Mo., about 6.30 p. m., sprung a leak and sunk. Steamer has been raised and is now in service. Amount of damage unknown.

February 17.—While steamer *D'Artagnan* was lying at St. Louis, Mo., anticipating the breaking up of ice gorge, a workman was sent to thaw out the pipes and raise steam, and using a salamander in heating the boiler room, absented himself; set fire to woodwork. Damage about $200.

April 12.—Steamer *Jessie Bill*, John Otto Shertz, owner, navigating without a licensed pilot, Illinois River, Beardstown, Ill., case turned over to U. S. district attorney for prosecution and surveyor of customs, Peoria, Ill., notified.

April 12.—While local inspectors were at Beardstown, Ill., inspecting steamer *City of Pekin, No. 2*, they were approached by George C. McComas while in a drunken condition; they were also informed that while the said McComas was acting as pilot of steamer *Bimini* he was guilty of such misbehavior and intemperance. Licenses as pilot and engineer suspended 60 days of probationary period. Since returned to him and reports are in his favor.

May 5.—While lying at the bank at Beardstown, Ill., the steamer *Mary* was capsized by a high windstorm and sunk. Steamer has since been raised; damage about $500.

May 12.—While navigating near Squaw Island, Mississippi River, steamer *Belle of Calhoun* struck a log and sunk. Steamer has since been raised and in service. Damage unknown. No lives lost.

May 14.—In the taking of evidence at the investigation into the collision of the steamers *Robt. E. Carr* and *Corwin H. Spencer*, May 14, for which violation the license of Frank J. Maglio, pilot in charge of the towing steamer *Robt. E. Carr*, was suspended for a period of 30 days, it was admitted that passengers were carried in pilot house of said steamer *Robt. E. Carr* in violation of law. The case was turned over to the U. S. district attorney and surveyor of customs, St. Louis, Mo., notified.

CASUALTIES, VIOLATIONS OF LAW, AND INVESTIGATIONS, YEAR ENDED DECEMBER 31, 1905—FOURTH SUPERVISING DISTRICT—ST. LOUIS, MO.—Continued.

June 2.—John Smith, engineer in charge of steamer *Annie Russell*, charged with intemperance and drunkenness, while steamer was lying at St. Louis, Mo., with steam up and ready to pull out. Case investigated and dismissed, the officer exonerated with a reprimand.

June 5.—On or about June 5, steamer *Messenger Boy*, Thos. M. Jones, owner, navigating without licensed officers, Missouri River, 5 miles above Vermillion, S. Dak. Case turned over to U. S. district attorney, and surveyor of customs, Sioux City, Iowa, notified.

June 30.—While steamer *Dubuque* was rounding to, to land at Louisiana, Mo., during a heavy rain storm, Thomas Galagher, roustabout, stumbled on forward cavil, fell overboard, and was drowned. Lifeboats were lowered and every effort made to save him; two skiffs also put out from shore, but could not find him.

June 30.—In making landing of steamer *Florence*, just as headline was made fast and ferry prepared to back into landing, man, name unknown, attempted to get on; attempting to jump a space of about 5 feet and fell into the river. Another man, name unknown, jumped into the water and attempted to save him, but failed. Several life floats were thrown overboard and lifeboat lowered, which resulted in saving the second man, but the first man had disappeared.

June to September.—George W. Redeforth, pilot, admitted in letters to the local inspectors that he had been navigating without a license from June to September, 1905, license having expired. The case was turned over to U. S. district attorney and surveyor of customs, Peoria, Ill., notified.

July 17.—While steamer *India Givens* was lying at bank at Calhoun Landing, Ill., the fireman, George Manion, colored, in going out on fantail to cool off, having been overheated, fell overboard and was drowned. Captain and engineer rushed back to assist him; the mate, on shore, shouted for a light so that he could get him, but the body never came to the surface.

July 18.—Charges having been filed with local inspectors, St. Louis, Mo., that Pilot Rule No. VII had been violated on July 18, in the navigation of the steamers *Corwin H. Spencer* and *City of Providence*, the case was investigated on various dates, resulting in a disagreement between the local inspectors, and the case was turned over to the supervising inspector, as required by section 4452, Revised Statutes, with the following result: The licenses of Harry Brolaski and William H. Thorwegen, masters, Seldon T. Wadlington and James Donohue, pilots, were ordered suspended for 30 days; and on appeal to the Department the licenses were ordered returned October 10, which order was complied with October 12.

July 18.—It having developed at the investigations of the above (last) mentioned case, "Violation of Pilot Rule VII, steamers *Corwin H. Spencer* and *City of Providence*, July 18, 1905, and the suspension of licenses incident thereto," that William H. Thorwegen violated section 4438, Revised Statutes, in acting and serving as master of the steamer *City of Providence* while without license on July 18, 1905, license as master previously issued to him having expired some time prior thereto and not renewed, the case was turned over to the U. S. district attorney for prosecution and the surveyor of customs, St. Louis, Mo., duly notified.

August 2.—While steamer *Harry Reid* was lying at the bank at Winneberg, Ill., 3 a. m., from some cause unknown, sprung a leak and sunk. Steamer has since been raised and is in service. The steamer was in charge of watchman. No lives lost.

August 20.—While steamer *Silver Crescent* was underway, about opposite Meyer, Ill., a woman, Mrs. Pearl Kohl, jumped from roof with suicidal intent and was drowned. Boats were promptly lowered and every effort made to save her, but to no avail.

September 5.—While steamer *Corwin H. Spencer* was backing out from shore at Chautauqua, Ill., fire was discovered in the texas; steamer was immediately landed and all passengers left the steamer, and fire extinguished by the prompt action of the drilled crew; damage about $25. No disorder and no lives lost.

October 12.—Steamer *Corwin H. Spencer*, while lying at the bank, just south of city limits of St. Louis, Mo., undergoing repainting, was destroyed by fire. Steamer was in charge of mate; origin unknown; no lives lost; damage about $120,000; total loss.

October 13.—While steamer *Wm. McClellan* was lying at bank at St. Louis, Mo., in charge of watchman, was damaged by fire to the extent of about $6,000; origin unknown Vessel has since been rebuilt and is now in service. No lives lost.

October 28.—While steamer *Esther* was lying at the bank at East St. Louis, Ill., fire was discovered about 5.15 p. m., origin unknown, and totally destroyed; damage about $1,500.

Casualties, Violations of Law, and Investigations, Year ended December 31, 1905—Fourth Supervising District—St. Louis, Mo.—Continued.

November 25.—While steamer *Meeker* was lying at dock, fire was discovered about 4 a. m., and partially destroyed, at Warsaw, Ill. Steamer is now being rebuilt; damage about $1,200.

December 16.—In making landing, the steamer *Jessie Bill* in backing into shore, ice may have only pushed in some oakum, causing vessel to take water and sink, at La Grange, Ill. Steamer has been raised and is now in service. Damage unknown.

FIFTH SUPERVISING DISTRICT.

LOCAL DISTRICT OF DUBUQUE, IOWA.

March 18.—While steamer *Arctic* was lying at Muscatine, Iowa, and not yet in commission, the ice crowded her onto the bank, and she careened and filled with water and sunk. Steamer was raised and repaired at a cost of about $200.

April 9 to 12.—Motor boat *Iowa*, master, Abner Ayres, was navigated after expiration of certificate of inspection, in violation of section 4417, Revised Statutes. Violation reported to surveyor of customs, Sioux City, Iowa.

June 13.—While motor boat *Scotty Philip* was navigating the Missouri River near Grass, S. Dak., said vessel collided with a skiff containing 2 men, upsetting the skiff and throwing the men out, one of whom swam ashore, the other one, Ole Oppegaard, being drowned. Lifeboat was lowered, and every effort possible was made to save the man, but without effect.

June 16 to 24.—Motor boat *Lillian*, master, John C. Gear, was navigated after expiration of certificate of inspection, in violation of section 4417, Revised Statutes. Violation reported to surveyor of customs, Galena, Ill.

July 17.—Steamer *Clyde*, while near Minneiska, Minn., was capsized by a sudden severe wind. Damage estimated at $6,000.

August 20.—While steamer *Quincy* was lying at Eagle Point, Dubuque, Iowa, about 9 p. m., an altercation occurred between Mate J. H. Brinker and Julius Davis, a colored roustabout, during which the latter was shot in the abdomen and groin, Charles Hanthorn, a white deck hand, was shot in the neck by the negro, and Mate Brinker was shot in the forearm. Davis died from the effects of the wound on August 22

September 12.—Marcus L. Henderson, officer in charge of steamers *Davenport* and *T. J. Robinson*, was reported to the surveyor of customs at Rock Island, Ill., for violation of section 4467, Revised Statutes, and section 50, Rule V, general rules and regulations, in failing to report passengers carried and drills held on said vessels during the months of July and August, after being repeatedly requested to do so, and his license as master was suspended for 30 days. On appeal to the supervising inspector he was reinstated.

December 1.—While steamer *Verana* was laid up at the bank at Lake City, Minn., she caught fire in the early morning, in some manner unknown, the upper works being destroyed. Damage estimated at $2,000.

LOCAL DISTRICT OF DULUTH, MINN.

January 7.—Tug *Superior*, of Duluth, Minn., caught fire in some unknown manner in the compartment between the fireroom and engine room. The vessel was damaged to the extent of $500.

April 25.—Tug *Sylph*, while lying at Superior, Wis., was damaged by fire, the origin of which is unknown. Damage estimated at $150.

May 3.—Steamer *Hesper*, while bound up Lake Superior, encountered a severe windstorm and stranded on Beaver Bay reef, north shore of Lake Superior, and is a total wreck. Value of vessel, $80,000.

May 4.—Thomas Bettis, employed as watchman on steamer *J. S. Keefe*, was mist and is supposed to have been washt overboard and drowned while the vessel was approaching the port of Duluth, there being a heavy sea at the time.

June 12.—Steamer *City of Genoa*, while en route from Superior to Ashland, Wis., ran on Sand Island, due to heavy fog. The vessel was released and brought to Superior, where repairs were made. Damage estimated at $1,200.

July 10.—Alphonse Boutin, employed as a deck hand on steamer *Senator*, accidentally fell in the hold of the vessel at Two Harbors, Minn., and was killed.

August 2.—Steamer *Hiawatha*, of St. Paul, Minn., was reported to the chief officer of customs at St. Paul, Minn., with violation of section 4417, United States Revised Statutes.

CASUALTIES, VIOLATIONS OF LAW, AND INVESTIGATIONS, YEAR ENDED DECEMBER 31, 1905—FIFTH SUPERVISING DISTRICT—DULUTH, MINN.—Continued.

August 3.—Steamer *G. A. Mower*, of St. Paul, Minn., for violation of section 4463, Revised Statutes, was reported to the chief officer of customs at St. Paul, Minn.

August 3.—While steamer *Hiawatha* was being loaded with iron ore at Duluth, Minn., fire broke out in the hall way, and was damaged to the amount of about $200. Origin of fire unknown.

August 11.—While steamer *E. Rutledge* was about 4 miles above Prescott, Wis., on the St. Croix River, the breaking of a gib in the crosshead caused the piston rod and both cylinder heads of the engine to break. Damage estimated at about $1,000.

August 23.—Steamer *H. B. Hawgood* collided with the Duluth-Superior bridge, caused by a strong current. Damage to vessel estimated at $1,000.

September 2.—Steamer *Sevona*, while bound down Lake Superior, encountered a severe gale, and in seeking shelter among the Apostle Islands struck a reef in the vicinity of York Island and broke in two. All the members of the crew who were on the forward part of the vessel, 7 in number, consisting of D. S. McDonald, master; Louis Darwin, first mate; George Hamilton, second mate; Nels Salverson and O. Vallette, wheelsmen; Gus Drews, watchman, and another watchman, whose name is unknown, lost their lives. Those on the after-end of the vessel, consisting of 2 engineers, 3 firemen, 2 oilers, 4 deck hands, 2 cooks, 1 porter, and 3 women passengers, were saved by means of the lifeboats. The vessel, which is a total loss, was valued at $220,000.

September 2.—John Lindquist, who was employed as watchman on steamer *Samuel Mather*, was washt overboard by a big sea and was drowned. The accident occurred while the vessel was abreast of Knife Island, Lake Superior.

September 2.—Steamer *Hiawatha* was navigated without a certificate of inspection, in violation of section 4417, Revised Statutes. Violation reported to the chief officer of customs at St. Paul, Minn.

September 3.—Steamer *North Wind* in entering the Duluth Harbor sheered against the concrete pier, which was caused by strong wind and current. The vessel soon filled with water and sunk immediately upon reaching the harbor. Damage estimated at $5,000.

September 13.—Steamer *Tempest*, while lying at her dock in the Duluth Harbor, sunk, the cause of which is unknown. Damage to vessel estimated at $100.

October 31.—While steamer *Peter White* was en route to Duluth her crank shaft broke. The vessel was picked up by the steamer *Troy* and towed to her destination. Damage estimated at $500.

November 11.—George Kressin, employed as second assistant engineer on steamer *Peter White*, in some unknown manner, was caught between the connecting rod and crank web while the engine was in motion and received injuries from which he died.

November 24.—Tug *Spirit* struck a submerged obstruction in Duluth Harbor and sunk. The vessel was subsequently raised. Damage estimated at $100.

November 28.—Steamer *Mataafa*, while bound down Lake Superior, was forced to return to Duluth for shelter, owing to the hatches having commenced to give way, due to a severe wind and snow storm. In attempting to enter the harbor the vessel struck bottom, lost her steerageway, and then struck the pier. An effort was then made to head the vessel out into the lake, but the engine had to be stopt for reasons unknown, and the vessel drifted helplessly on the beach directly north of the canal and about 700 feet from shore. She broke in two amidships about an hour and twenty minutes later, and was settling in the sand, with the sea going over her and with a freezing temperature; 9 members of the crew who were aft perished. Their anmes are as follows: William Most, chief engineer, Cleveland, Ohio; C. A. Farenger, second engineer, Cleveland, Ohio; James Early, third engineer, Buffalo, N. Y.; Carl Carlson, oiler, Chicago, Ill.; William Gilchrist, oiler, Wiarton, Ontario; Thomas Woodgate, fireman, Toronto, Ontario; Henry Wright, (colored), steward, Cleveland, Ohio; Walter Bush (colored), second cook, Amherstburg, Ontario; Thomas McCloud, deck hand, Kentucky. All the bodies have been found except C. A. Farenger, James Early, and William Gilchrist. All the crew in the forward part of the vessel, 15 in number, were taken ashore in an almost exhausted condition, after 20 hours of exposure to the sea and freezing temperature. The vessel was valued at $300,000, but operations have begun to float her, and in that event the damage will be about $100,000.

November 28.—Steamer *William Edenborn*, while bound up Lake Superior, was driven ashore near Split Rock, Minn., during a severe wind and snow storm. James Johnson, second assistant engineer, lost his life by falling in the hold of the vessel immediately after the vessel stranded. The vessel is valued at $300,000, but will be floated and repaired, in which event the loss will be about $100,000.

CASUALTIES, VIOLATIONS OF LAW, AND INVESTIGATIONS, YEAR ENDED DECEMBER 31, 1905—FIFTH SUPERVISING DISTRICT—DULUTH, MINN.—Continued.

November 28.—Steamer *Lafayette* was driven ashore at Encampment Island, north shore of Lake Superior, in the midst of a blinding snow and wind storm, and is a total loss. Valuation of vessel, $300,000. Patrick Wade, a fireman, fell between the vessel and the rocks and was either killed or drowned while attempting to get ashore. All the rest of the crew reached the shore safely.

November 28.—Steamer *R. W. England* went ashore on Minnesota Point, midway between Duluth Canal and Superior entry, during a gale. The vessel, which was released by tugs on December 1, 1905, was damaged to the amount of $60,000.

November 28.—Steamer *George Spencer*, bound up Lake Superior during a gale of wind and snow, stranded at Thomasville, Minn., north shore of Lake Superior. Loss, $30,000.

November 28.—Steamer *Crescent City* was driven ashore in a storm about 7 miles east of Duluth. The vessel is valued at $300,000, but can be floated and repaired. Loss estimated at $100,000.

November 28.—Steamer *Isaac L. Ellwood*, in entering Duluth Harbor, struck the piers twice, owing to the high seas and current. She sunk immediately upon reaching the harbor. Damage estimated at $50,000.

November 28.—Steamer *Perry G. Walker* was damaged to the amount of about $4,000 by the seas washing over her while laboring in the sea on the western end of Lake Superior.

November 28.—Steamer *Umbria*, while en route for Duluth, encountered severe weather and had to turn around and head into the sea, and while in this condition the seas damaged her to the extent of about $2,000.

November 28.—Steamer *E. C. Pope* was damaged to the extent of about $1,500 while riding out a severe wind and snow storm. The steering gear became foul, which caused the vessel to drop in the trough of the sea, where she was tossed about while the stearing gear was being repaired.

November 28.—Steamer *Yosemite* was damaged by a raging wind and snow storm on Lake Superior. Damage estimated at $1,000.

November 28.—Steamer *Mariposa*, while laboring in a heavy sea on Lake Superior, received damages amounting to $300.

November 28.—Steamer *William E. Corey*, while en route up Lake Superior during a wind and snow storm, fetched up on Gull Island, one of the Apostle group. The vessel was released December 10, 1905, and taken to Superior, where she will undergo repairs. Damage to vessel estimated at $100,000.

December 6.—Steamer *Sir William Siemens*, while pulling on steamer *William E. Corey*, ashore on Gull Island, was driven on the rocks due to the wind shifting, and was damaged to the extent of about $5,000.

December 6.—Tug *Edna G.* while holding up the bow of steamer *Sir William Siemens*, which was pulling on steamer *William E. Corey*, ashore on Gull Island, was dragged astern onto a reef and damaged to the extent of $1,000.

SIXTH SUPERVISING DISTRICT.

LOCAL DISTRICT OF LOUISVILLE, KY.

January 24.—Decision rendered in the investigation of explosion of boilers on the towing steamer *Fred Wilson*, that occurred May 26, 1904, causing the loss of 11 lives. The evidence submitted could not with any degree of certainty place the responsibility of this disaster on any of the licensed officers. However, there could be no doubt that the vessel had been wilfully navigated at various times in violation of sections 4441 and 4437, Revised Statutes, for which violation the chief engineer license of Lewis A. Walker was revoked and the case referred to the U. S. district attorney for prosecution.

March 4.—Steamer *Egan*, Harry Regan, master, and Chas. DeGraw, acting mate, was reported to the U. S. district attorney and surveyor of customs for having navigated said vessel without a licensed mate. Violation of section 4438, Revised Statutes.

March 15.—Steamer *Louise*, S. J. Preston, master, was reported to the U. S. district attorney and surveyor of customs for navigating said vessel without a licensed engineer. Violation of section 4438, Revised Statutes.

April 17.—John George's chief engineer license suspended 90 days for intemperance. Violation of section 4441, Revised Statutes.

CASUALTIES, VIOLATIONS OF LAW, AND INVESTIGATIONS, YEAR ENDED DECEMBER 31, 1905—SIXTH SUPERVISING DISTRICT—LOUISVILLE, KY.—Continued.

April 21.—Decision rendered in the investigation of collision that occurred May 22, 1904, between steamer *Sunshine* and gasoline yacht *Dixie.* Case investigated and dismissed.

June 20.—Aris Gregory (colored), deck passenger, while under the influence of cocaine, jumped overboard off the steamer *Peters Lee* and drowned.

June 26.—W. A. Robinson, a deck hand, accidentally fell overboard off the steamer *James Moren* near this harbor and drowned.

July 3.—Steamer *Louise*, out of commission on Kentucky River, sprung a leak and sunk. Vessel subsequently raised and repaired at a cost of $100. No lives lost.

July 5.—Joseph B. Fields, cabin watchman on the steamer *Peters Lee*, fell overboard while intoxicated and drowned near Westport, Ky.

July 8.—The towing steamer *W. W. O'Neil* struck a hidden obstruction in the Louisville and Portland Canal near this harbor and sunk. Vessel subsequently raised and repaired. No lives lost. Damage, $2,975.

August 22.—The chief engineer license of John George revoked for drunkenness. This violation came under the observation of the local inspectors while the accused was engineer on the steamer *Nellie Willett.* Violation of section 4441, Revised Statutes.

August 24.—The passenger vessel *Hanover* caught fire from a lamp while gasolene was being transferred from a cask to a tank in the hold and burned to the water's edge. No lives lost. Amount of damage, $1,700. Casualty investigated and officers exonerated.

October 27.—The license of Thomas Neal, assistant engineer, was suspended 18 months for intemperance. Violation of section 4441, Revised Statutes.

October 30.—James King, deck hand on the steamer *John A. Wood*, was accidentally killed by a check line slipping from a coal boat in tow of the steamer while lying at this port.

November 14.—Louis F. Bergenroth, master and pilot license suspended 10 days for inattention to duty. Violation of sections 4439 and 4442, Revised Statutes.

December 2.—Charges of intemperance preferred against William H. Weber, chief engineer of the steam tug *Daisy.* Investigation now pending.

December 11.—Charges of intemperance preferred against George W. Shields, a licensed chief engineer, investigated and dismissed.

December 16.—Steamer *Gladys* foundered under the cribbing of the wharf at Frankfort, Ky., and sank. No lives lost. Damage estimated at $250.

LOCAL DISTRICT OF EVANSVILLE, IND.

January 25.—W. Frank Anderson, licensed master, pleaded guilty to the charge of intemperance and his license was suspended for 90 days.

February 25.—While the steamer *Conveyor* was laid up at the bank opposite the city of Evansville, Ind., in the ice she was struck by a heavy cake of ice and sunk. No lives lost. Damage estimated at $2,000. Later hull was raised, docked, and repaired.

February 27.—While the ferry steamer *Katherine* was en route from Cairo, Ill., to Birds Point, Mo., she struck heavy ice or some obstruction and sank. No lives lost. Cost of damage about $1,000. Later, was raised, docked, and put in commission.

March 27.—While the steamer *Key City* was making a landing at Belgrade, 2 miles above Metropolis, Ill., she struck a hidden obstruction and sank. No lives lost. Later, wrecked and total loss. Estimated value, $1,200.

May 1.—George Boos, assistant engineer on steamer *Ruth*, pleaded guilty of negligence and his license was suspended for 60 days.

June 1.—The steamer *Henrietta* was found to have run on an expired certificate of inspection from May 20 to June 1, 1905, and the case was reported to the surveyor of customs at the port of Cairo, Ill., and the U. S. attorney at East St. Louis. Ill., for action.

June 20.—While attempting to jump from a barge to the steamer *Wabash*, at Evansville, Ind., on June 20, 1905, Robert Browder, one of the crew, fell in the river and was drowned before assistance could reach him.

July 3.—While the steamer *Stacker Lee* was taking a coal flat in tow at Cairo, Ill., Foe Jones, a colored deck hand, fell overboard and was drowned.

July 12.—Clarence B. Baker, chief engineer, was found guilty of negligence on the steamer *Louisiana*, and his license was suspended for 90 days.

August 5.—While the steamer *Fred Herold* was lying at the wharf boat at Cairo, Ill., Nelson Larkin, a deck hand, going from the wharf boat to the steamer, stumbled and fell overboard and drowned.

CASUALTIES, VIOLATIONS OF LAW, AND INVESTIGATIONS, YEAR ENDED DECEMBER 31, 1905—SIXTH SUPERVISING DISTRICT—EVANSVILLE, IND.—Continued.

August 10.—The steamer *Joseph B. Williams*, en route up the Ohio River, struck a snag at Sisters Island, near Bay City, Ill., and sunk. The boat was raised and placed on the ways for repairs. The damage was estimated at $25,000. No lives lost.

August 15.—Louis Heyden acted as pilot on the gasoline boat *Tecumseh*, of a greater tonnage than that named on his license, and his license was suspended for a period of 90 days.

August 24.—The steamer *Jessie B.* was navigated from Fairview, Ill., to Golconda, Ill., without a licensed pilot on board. The case was reported to the U. S. district attorney of the State of Illinois and the surveyor of customs at Paducah, Ky.

August 24.—Joe M. St. John admitted that he had left his post as engineer of the steamer *Jessie B.* in charge of an unlicensed man. His license as chief engineer was suspended for 90 days.

August 24.—Joe M. St. John admitted that he had acted as pilot of the steamer *Jessie B.* without license. The case was reported to the U. S. district attorney of the State of Illinois and the surveyor of customs at Paducah, Ky.

August 24.—Sufficient evidence having reached this office that Edward Lizinsky had acted as engineer of the steamer *Jessie B.* without license the case was reported to the U. S. district attorney of the State of Illinois and the surveyor of customs at the port of Paducah, Ky.

September 2.—The license of Alvin T. Collier, master and pilot, was suspended for 30 days for intemperance.

LOCAL DISTRICT OF NASHVILLE, TENN.

January 27.—The steamer *Charley Hook* struck the dike at Canton, Ky., on the Cumberland River, and sunk in 8 feet of water. No loss of life. Damage to property estimated at $1,500.

February 10.—The steamer *Mary N.* sunk during the night at the wharf at Paducah, Ky. No loss of life. Damage estimated at $1,000.

February 12.—Bud Hunter, colored, deck hand on steamer *R. Dunbar*, fell overboard and was drowned at Bluffs Landing, Ky., on the Cumberland River. Every effort was made to save the unfortunate man, but without avail.

February 18.—Charges were preferred against Thomas B. Allison on February 13 for violation of section 4441, Revised Statutes. Accused pleaded guilty and submitted his case. His license as chief engineer was suspended for a period of 6 months for intemperance.

March 9.—Charges were preferred against James H. Christley, March 2, for violation of section 4441, Revised Statutes. Accused pleaded guilty and submitted his case. His license as assistant engineer was suspended for a period of 6 months for intemperance.

March 25.—Charges were preferred against William H. Shouse, March 22, for violation of section 4441, Revised Statutes. Accused pleaded guilty and submitted his case. His license as chief engineer was suspended for a period of 6 months for intemperance.

March 25.—Charges were preferred against Albert J. Cowlishaw, February 25, for violation of sections 4442 and 4449, Revised Statutes. Accused pleaded guilty and submitted his case. His license as first-class pilot was suspended for a period of 6 months for intemperance. No violation of section 4449, Revised Statutes.

April 1.—Reported steamer *Pavonia* to the U. S. district attorney and surveyor of customs for navigating without a licensed pilot, in violation of section 4438, Revised Statutes.

April 1.—Reported Thomas E. Buckingham to the U. S. district attorney and surveyor of customs for acting as pilot on steamer *Pavonia* without a license, in violation of section 4438, Revised Statutes.

April 6.—The steamer *Bart E. Linehan* was totally destroyed by fire while lying at the elevator at Nashville, Tenn., March 30. No loss of life. Estimated loss of property, $20,000.

April 15.—Reported W. J. Carroll to the U. S. district attorney and surveyor of customs for causing the safety valves on boiler of steamer *I. N. Hook* to be loaded, on February 25, in violation of section 4437, Revised Statutes.

April 21.—Walter Bonnet, colored, deck hand on steamer *Henry Harley*, fell overboard at Rome, Tenn., and was drowned. Every effort was made to save the unfortunate man, but without avail.

April 26.—The license of Joseph Farrell, mate, was suspended for 90 days for intemperance. This violation came under our immediate observation.

CASUALTIES, VIOLATIONS OF LAW, AND INVESTIGATIONS, YEAR ENDED DECEMBER 31, 1905—SIXTH SUPERVISING DISTRICT—NASHVILLE, TENN.—Continued.

April 26.—Edward Howell, colored, deck hand on steamer *J. T. Reeder*, fell overboard at Sheffield, Ala., and was drowned. Every effort was made to save the unfortunate man, but without avail.

May 11.—The license of Shepard Green, master and pilot, was suspended for 90 days for drunkenness. This violation came under our immediate observation.

May 22.—The steamer *H. W. Buttorff* broke her water-wheel shaft at Burksville, Ky., on the Cumberland River. No loss of life. Estimated damage to property, $600.

June 6.—Reported steamer *W. T. Scovell* to the U. S. district attorney and surveyor of customs for navigating with loose granulated cork life-preservers on board in violation of Rule III, section 20, rules and regulations.

June 16.—Reported steamer *Pavonia* to the U. S. district attorney and surveyor of customs for carrying more steam than allowed by the certificate of inspection in violation of section 4437, Revised Statutes.

June 19.—Coffe Patton, colored, deck hand on steamer *Bob Dudley*, fell overboard and was drowned near Hartsville, Tenn., on May 21. He was not missed until steamer reached Nashville, Tenn., and body was found next trip.

August 12.—John Jordan, operator of sand-digging machine on steamer *Mackie*, fell into sand screen at Nashville, Tenn., and was killed on August 3. Accident reported to have been caused through his own carelessness.

August 23.—Frank Banta, fireman on steamer *Condor*, fell overboard while steamer was lying at wharf at Joppa, Ill., on August 20, and was drowned. The man never came to the surface and there was no opportunity to render any assistance. Body was recovered a few hours later.

August 25.—Ollie Stall, passenger on steamer *H. W. Buttorff*, was drowned at Canton, Ky., on August 22. He was last seen going down forward stairway and in an intoxicated condition. Body was found at landing next day.

September 1.—Reported steamer *Kentucky*, S. K. Hale, master, John H. Reynolds, chief engineer, and Fred McCandless, assistant engineer, to the U. S. district attorney and surveyor of customs for carrying more steam than allowed by the certificate of inspection, in violation of section 4437, Revised Statutes.

September 1.—Revoked the license of John H. Reynolds, chief engineer on steamer *Kentucky*, for carrying more steam than allowed by the certificate of inspection, in violation of section 4437, Revised Statutes. This violation came under the observation of local inspector. The case was appealed to the supervising inspector of the sixth district, who sustained the action of the local board. A subsequent appeal was made to the supervising inspector-general, September 29, who modified the action of the local and supervising inspector from a revocation to that of a suspension for a period of 90 days for violation of section 4441, Revised Statutes.

September 1.—Suspended for 6 months the license of Fred McCandless, assistant engineer of the steamer *Kentucky*, for failing to report the steamer for carrying more steam than allowed by her certificate of inspection, in violation of section 4441, Revised Statutes. This case was appealed to the supervising inspector of the sixth district, who revoked the action of the local inspectors.

September 19.—Charges were preferred against Allard M. Jones, June 20, for violation of sections 4437 and 4441, Revised Statutes. The accused pleaded guilty to the charge and his license as chief engineer was revoked for carrying steam in excess of the amount allowed boilers on steamer *Pavonia*.

September 19.—Charges were preferred against Pat H. Cox for violation of sections 4437 and 4441, Revised Statutes. The accused appeared and pleaded guilty to the charge and his assistant engineer license was suspended 30 days for failing to report an excess of steam on boilers on the steamer *Pavonia*.

September 19.—Charges were preferred against Thomas E. Buckingham for violation of sections 4437 and 4439, Revised Statutes. The accused appeared and pleaded guilty to the charge and his master's license was suspended 90 days for allowing an excess of steam to be carried on boilers of the steamer *Pavonia*.

October 4.—Charges were preferred against Omar O. Huskey for violation of sections 4438 and 4441, Revised Statutes. The accused appeared and pleaded guilty and his assistant engineer license was revoked for acting in the capacity of chief engineer.

October 4.—Charges were preferred against Fred Huskey for violation of sections 4438 and 4442, Revised Statutes. The accused appeared, pleaded guilty, and his second-class pilot license was suspended 60 days for navigating steamer *Almande* without a licensed chief engineer.

October 4.—Reported steamer *Almande* to the U. S. district attorney and surveyor of customs for navigating without a licensed chief engineer, in violation of section 4438, Revised Statutes.

CASUALTIES, VIOLATIONS OF LAW, AND INVESTIGATIONS, YEAR ENDED DECEMBER 31, 1905—SIXTH SUPERVISING DISTRICT—NASHVILLE, TENN.—Continued.

October 4.—Reported Omar O. Huskey to the U. S. district attorney and surveyor of customs for acting as chief engineer on the steamer *Almande* without a license, in violation of section 4438, Revised Statutes.

October 25.—Assistant engineer license of Sargent Moss was suspended 12 months for intemperance, violation of section 4441, Revised Statutes.

November 13.—Suspended the license of William T. Rhea, assistant engineer, 90 days for intemperance. This violation came under the observation of the local inspectors.

LOCAL DISTRICT OF MEMPHIS, TENN.

February 27.—Sam Jackson, a deck hand on the steamer *Sadie Lee*, fell overboard near New Madrid, Mo., and drowned.

March 3.—Steamer *Delta* was destroyed by fire at Harwood landing, Ark. No lives lost. Damage $40,000.

March 28.—Charles Johnson (colored), deck hand on the steamer *Ferd Herold*, fell overboard near Tiptonville, Tenn., and drowned.

April 7.—George Washington, deck hand on gasoline boat *Peerless*, fell overboard near Duvalls bluff, Ark., and drowned.

May 22.—Mrs. Sexton, passenger on a small gasoline boat (not named), lost her life in collision between said vessel and steamer *Grace Smith* near the mouth of Red River.

July 16.—James Rockwell, passenger on the steamer *Gate City*, fell overboard near Dyersburg, Tenn., and drowned.

July 17.—John A. Bandy, chief engineer, license revoked for intemperance. Violation of section 4441 Revised Statutes.

July 22.—The license of George F. Carvell, master of the steamer *City of St. Joseph*, was revoked and said vessel reported to the U. S. district attorney for having been navigated in violation of section 4477 Revised Statutes.

July 25.—Deck passenger (name unknown) fell overboard off the steamer *Sadie Lee* near Hopefield, Ark., and drowned.

August 7.—The license of Wm. T. Warner, master of the steamer *Hazel Rice*, was suspended 60 days and said vessel reported to the U. S. district attorney for having been navigated without a licensed mate, violating her certificate of inspection and section 4438 Revised Statutes.

August 8.—Gasoline boat *Peerless* reported for having been navigated without a complement of officers. Case investigated, charges not sustained.

August 12.—Steamer *Meter* reported for having been navigated without a licensed engineer. Case investigated and dismissed for want of evidence to prosecute.

September 2.—The license of Bond O. Nichols, engineer of motor vessels, revoked for negligence. Violation of section 4441 Revised Statutes.

October 11.—Steamer *Gate City* struck a snag near Reelfoot landing, Tenn., causing damage to the extent of $150. No lives lost.

October 17.—H. T. Dean, deck hand, fell overboard from the steamer *Pacific* near Idaho landing, Ark., and drowned before assistance could reach him.

October 30.—Steamer *Nettie* struck a drift log at Little Rock, Ark., and sunk. No lives lost. Damage, $3,000.

November 6.—Steamer *Dewet* reported to the U. S. district attorney and surveyor of customs for having been navigated without licensed officers.

December 9.—The license of Walter Howard, pilot, and H. S. Junk, engineer, was suspended 60 and 90 days, respectively, for refusing to serve on the steamer *Mary D.* in the capacity for which they were licensed. Violation of section 4449, Revised Statutes.

December 16.—John Arms, passenger on the steamer *Sadie Lee*, fell overboard near Caruthersville, Mo., and before assistance could reach him drowned.

December 18.—The pilot license of Wm. W. Butler was suspended 90 days for negligence. Violation of section 4442, Revised Statutes.

SEVENTH SUPERVISING DISTRICT.

LOCAL DISTRICT OF CINCINNATI, OHIO.

January 10.—Steamer *Ollie Neville*, while laid up for the night, at Ripley, Ohio, with no one on board, from some unknown cause, sprung a leak and sunk.

January 10.—Steamer *Frank Miller*, descending, and steamer *Avalon*, ascending, the Ohio River, at Cincinnati, Ohio, near the Chesapeake and Ohio Railroad bridge, collided. Slight damage to steamer *Frank Miller*.

CASUALTIES, VIOLATIONS OF LAW, AND INVESTIGATIONS, YEAR ENDED DECEMBER 31, 1905—SEVENTH SUPERVISING DISTRICT—CINCINNATI, OHIO—Continued.

February 9.—Peter H. Wagner, chief engineer, accused of intemperance; pleaded guilty and license suspended for a period of 30 days.

March 9.—Steamer *Delta*, laid up for the night at foot of Lawrence street, sprung a leak and sunk. Steamer was immediately raised and is now in commission.

March 9.—Steamer *Relief* was cut down by ice at foot of Lawrence street. Total loss. Valuation, $20,000. No lives lost.

March 9.—Steamer *Geo. Matheson* was cut down by ice at foot of Congress avenue. Total loss. Valuation, $18,000. No lives lost.

July 6.—Steamer *Courier*, while ascending the Ohio River near Smiths landing, Ohio, broke her main shaft. No one injured. Cost of repairs, $1,000.

July 6.—Steamer *City of Louisville*, while ascending the Ohio River near Norths landing, Ohio, broke her main shaft. No one injured. Cost of repairs, $2,000.

July 11.—Steamer *Val P. Collins*, while ascending the Ohio River near Coal Haven, Ky., broke her main shaft. No one injured.

August 9.—George Wilson, deck hand on steamer *Exporter*, fell overboard from barge in tow and drowned.

October 9.—Charles H. Hewett, owner of steamer *Dan Patch*, pleaded guilty to violation of section 4426, Revised Statutes. He being an unlicensed man, the case was referred to the U. S. district attorney.

October 27.—Tom Coates, a deck hand on steamer *J. B. Finley*, fell from boiler deck, striking the guard of the Cincinnati wharfboat, then falling into river. Body never came to the surface.

December 8.—Steamer *Lizzie Bay*, while descending the Ohio River in fog, collided with coal fleet at Ludlow, Ky., and sunk in 7 feet of water. No one injured. Damage, $1,000.

LOCAL DISTRICT OF GALLIPOLIS, OHIO.

January 3.—Steamer *Defender* was ascending the Ohio River with a tow of coal barges and passing Huntington, W. Va., when 2 of her 6 boilers exploded and she sunk over her main deck and everything above water was burned. Nine of the crew were killed and 3 injured. On investigation January 5, it was found that the starboard boiler had stretched to a feather edge and ruptured below the fire line over the furnace, from low water, and the boiler next to it had also exploded while the 4 remained in place. The license of chief engineer, Hernando W. Allis, was revoked.

February 10.—Steamer *Chevalier*, cut down by ice, was raised, docked and repaired; cost $2,000.

April 5.—John Adams, deck hand on steamer *Charlie Jutte*, accidentally fell overboard near Parkersburg, W. Va., and drowned before yawl could rescue him.

May 18.—Steamer *Louise*, thru a mistake in bells, ran into steamer *Ironsides* while landing at Middleport, Ohio. The *Louise* had her stem crusht and ran ashore and settled where she was afterwards wrecked. *Ironsides* was not damaged. Loss, $800.

June 16.—Steamer *Florence Marmet*, ascending the Great Kanawha River at Red House shoals, with a tow of barges, about 1 a. m., ran over a log raft on which Charles Wears and E. Safereed were floating without a light and had gone to sleep. Charles Wears was rescued by the boat's yawl but E. Safereed was drowned.

June 24.—Steamer *Boaz* with tow had laid up for the night at Hockingport, Ohio, and her fleet man, Mike Smith, while walking over the barges fell between them and drowned.

July 2.—Lewis S. Clark, assistant engineer on steamer *Greyhound*, fell overboard at Portsmouth, Ohio, and drowned.

July 17.—William Vance, deck hand on steamer *Henry M. Stanley*, fell overboard near Leon, W. Va., and drowned before boat's yawl could reach him.

September 14.—Steamer *Nina Paden* was reported to the U. S. district attorney at Parkersburg, W. Va., for navigating under an expired certificate from September 7 to September 14.

September 16.—Steamer *Kanawha* was reported to the U. S. district attorney at Parkersburg, W. Va., for navigating without a valid certificate on board from September 13 to September 16.

September 27.—Steamer *Francis* backed into steamer *Neva* at Gallipolis, Ohio, breaking her guard; damage about $50. License of pilot, Joseph B. Gilpin, of the *Francis*, was suspended for 30 days.

October 20.—William E. Roe, master of steamer *Kanawha*, charged with navigating her without a valid certificate on board, in violation of sections 4423, 4439, Revised Statutes, appeared for investigation, and the local inspectors failing to agree, referred

CASUALTIES, VIOLATIONS OF LAW, AND INVESTIGATIONS, YEAR ENDED DECEMBER 31, 1905—SEVENTH SUPERVISING DISTRICT—GALLIPOLIS, OHIO—Continued.

the case to the supervising inspector under section 4452, Revised Statutes, who, after a hearing on December 6, suspended the licenses of William E. Roe, master and pilot, for 60 days, from January 1, 1906.

November 24.—John Stone, pilot, charged with navigating the steamer *Nina Paden* under an expired certificate, was, on investigation, exonerated from all blame.

December 1.—Steamer *Laynesville*, out of service, sunk in the mouth of Big Sandy River. Has been raised; loss, $300.

LOCAL DISTRICT OF WHEELING, W. VA.

February 12.—Steamer *Gazelle* was wrecked by ice at Wheeling Island, W. Va. Total loss; valuation, $10,000. No lives lost.

March 13.—Steamer *Mildred* was caught on top land wall at Lock 13, Ohio River, and sunk. Damage, $1,500. No lives lost.

March 23.—Steamer *Josh Cook* with tow struck pier of Baltimore and Ohio Railroad bridge at Bellaire, Ohio, and during the excitement Dod Lynch, a deck hand, jumped overboard and drowned.

April 16.—Frank Horton, deck hand, fell overboard from steamer *Queen City* at Bellaire, Ohio, and drowned.

June 9.—Joseph Sirlock, deck hand, fell overboard from steamer *Tom Dodsworth* above Marietta, Ohio, and drowned.

July 3.—A colored passenger (name unknown) while intoxicated fell overboard from steamer *Bessie Smith* below East Liverpool, Ohio, and drowned before they could reach him.

July 8.—John Llowshow fell overboard from the ferryboat *Charon* at Bellaire, Ohio, and drowned.

August 16.—Steamer *Ruth* while navigating the Ohio River at Powhattan, Ohio, broke her main shaft. Cost of repairs, $400.

September 25.—Thomas Nealon, deck hand on steamer *Tom Dodsworth*, fell overboard and drowned at Allegheny City.

October 30.—Frederick Bartruff, master and pilot of steamer *Progress* had his license suspended for a period of 90 days for navigating his steamer without valid certificate of inspection.

October 30.—Charles A. Leezer, master and pilot of steamer *Cascade*, had his license suspended for a period of 90 days for navigating his steamer without valid certificate of inspection.

November 5.—The ferry steamer *Grace Virginia* burned to the waters' edge and sunk at New Matamoras, Ohio. No loss of life. Damage, $6,000.

December 2.—William Carter, deck hand on steamer *Ben Hur*, fell overboard at Bellaire, Ohio, and drowned.

LOCAL DISTRICT OF PITTSBURG, PA.

February 9.—Steamer *F. K. Hulings* was cut down by ice at Greensboro, Pa., on Monongahela River. No one lost. Damage, $3,500.

February 10.—Ferry steamer *Portsmouth* cut down by ice at Lashells landing, Ohio River. No lives lost. Damage, $1,000.

March 4.—Steamer *Jim Brown*, ascending the Ohio River, near McKeesport, James Riley, a fireman, was mist from the steamer; supposed to have fallen overboard and drowned.

March 7.—Capt. W. O. Rhodes, of the steamer *John F. Klein* fell overboard and drowned.

March 23.—William Gilmore, a deck hand on steamer *Carbon*, was drowned at Lock 3, Monongahela River.

April 12.—Charges were preferred by the local inspectors against Capt. Frank Gilmore of the steamer *Iron Age*, upon information received, for making remarks reflecting upon the integrity of the Service, and demanding an excess of steam to be carried. The case was investigated, the local inspectors disagreeing, and the testimony was submitted to the supervising inspector for decision. By instructions of the supervising inspector, the license of Frank Gilmore, master and pilot, and of Ulysses K. Riggs, chief engineer, were suspended for a period of 60 days each, from December 15, 1905.

April 15.—The steamer *Cyclone* was totally destroyed by fire at Dravosburg, Pa. Loss, $1,500. No lives lost.

April 27.—Thomas Nixon, steward of steamer *Andrew Axton*, fell overboard near McKeesport, Pa., and drowned.

CASUALTIES, VIOLATIONS OF LAW, AND INVESTIGATIONS, YEAR ENDED DECEMBER 31, 1905—SEVENTH SUPERVISING DISTRICT—PITTSBURG, PA.—Continued.

May 5.—Steamer *John F. Klein* collided with the steamer *Charlie Clark* at Pittsburg wharf. Damage to steamer *Charlie Clark,* $500.

May 17.—Charlie White, watchman on steamer *Independent,* fell overboard below Sharpsburg, Pa., and drowned.

May 25.—Steamer *P. M. Pfeil* collided with steamer *J. C. Risher* above Lock 1, Monongahela River; damage to both steamers, $240.

June 18.—Steamer *Hazel L. Watson* and *Gazelle,* descending the Monongahela River, running side by side, collided below Rices landing, Pa., damaging the *Hazel L. Watson* to the extent of $250. No one injured. The case was investigated and the license of Isaiah P. Faddis, pilot, in charge of the *Gazelle,* was suspended for a period of 60 days.

June 19.———— Cousins, colored passenger, fell from barge *Beauty* in tow of steamer *John F. Klein,* near Davis Island dam and drowned.

June 20.—Steamer *Vulcan* descending the Monongahela River below Coal Center, Pa., with an empty barge in tow, capsized and sunk. Was raised and repaired at a cost of $2,000.

June 22.—Isaac Harris, preferred charges against Geo. E. Berry, engineer of the steamer *National,* for overweighting the safety valves and carrying excessive steam. The case was investigated and the license of Geo. E. Berry was suspended for a period of 6 months, and the license of Geo. R. Bollman, master and pilot of said steamer, was suspended for a period of 120 days, both for violation of section 4437, Revised Statutes, suspensions taking effect August 25, 1905. Messrs. Berry and Bollman were returned to the U. S. district attorney for prosecution, but no action was taken against them owing to the refusal of the local inspectors to furnish a copy of the evidence in the case. A lockup safety valve was placed on the boilers of the steamer. Captain Bollman appealed to the supervising inspector, who affirmed the decision of the local inspectors.

June 22.—James Dougherty, fireman on the steamer *Little Fred,* fell out of yawl at Pittsburg wharf and drowned.

June 23.—Steamer *J. E. Leonard* was totally destroyed by fire near Redstone Creek, Monongahela River. No lives lost. Loss, $13,000.

July 4.—James Snyder, a passenger, fell overboard from steamer *Island Queen* opposite Elizabeth marine ways and drowned.

July 6.—Steamers *J. C. Risher* and *Sailor* collided at Lock 3, Monongahela River. Damage, $50.

July 17.—Steamer *Harry Brown* struck a rock below Lock 2, Ohio River, and sunk. Raised and repaired at a cost of $1,000.

August 5.—John Drake, a deck hand, fell overboard from steamer *Harmony* at Pittsburg, Pa., and drowned.

August 31.—Steamer *Bessie Smith* struck an obstruction at Dam No. 2, Ohio River, and sunk. Raised and repaired at a cost of $500.

September 7.—Steamer *Pastime* sprung a leak and sunk at Sewickley, Pa. Was raised and repaired at a cost of $100.

September 9.—Henry Holden, a deck hand of steamer *W. C. Jutte,* while hitching up to barge near Dravosburg, Pa., was crushed between barge and steamer. Taken to hospital and died next day.

September 12.—The dredge steamer *Fay S.* was sunk above Manoca, Pa., on the Ohio River. No lives lost. Damage, $4,000.

October 5.—Steamer *Clyde* collided with steamer *Vesta* near McKeesport, Pa. No lives lost. Damage, $200.

October 27.—Steamer *Slackwater* and steamer *P. M. Pfeil* collided at Lock No. 2, Monongahela River. Damage to steamer *Slackwater,* $300.

November 1.—Steamers *Vulcan* and *Cascade,* descending the Monongahela River, collided at Lock No. 2. Case was investigated and the license of Chas. A. Leezer, master and pilot of steamer *Cascade,* was revoked.

November 13.—Creed May preferred charges against William Cullen, engineer of steamer *Harmony,* for carrying excess pressure of steam. At an investigation, after taking the testimony of the captain of the boat, Engineer Cullen refused to answer any questions or be sworn. The case was submitted to the supervising inspector, and at his suggestion, the license of Engineer Cullen was suspended for a period of 6 months, for refusal to answer questions, and a lockup safety valve was ordered placed on the boilers of the steamer *Harmony.* The engineer brought suit for a preliminary injunction in U. S. court, thru an attorney, but at the completion of this report, no decision has been given.

November 27.—The steamer *Rose Hite* ascending the Monongahela River, near Lock No. 6, struck a sunken flat and damaged her hull to the extent of $500.

Casualties, Violations of Law, and Investigations, Year ended December 31, 1905—Seventh Supervising District—Pittsburg, Pa.—Continued.

December 3.—Steamer *Twilight* and loaded tow was carried over the dam at Lock No. 2 and wrecked. No lives lost. Damage, $5,000.

December 14.—Steamer *John F. Klein* descending with a loaded tow, and steamer *Rose Hite* ascending, collided near Thompson's landing, Monongahela River, sinking coal flat and steamer *Rose Hite;* 2 white and 2 colored deck hands were drowned. Damage to coal flat, $1,500; loss of steamer *Rose Hite* and cargo, $1,500.

December 20.—While passenger steamer *Gazelle* was ascending the Monongahela River near Millsboro, Pa., a passenger (a foreigner), name unknown, fell overboard and drowned.

EIGHTH SUPERVISING DISTRICT.

LOCAL DISTRICT OF DETROIT, MICH.

February 17.—Completed investigation of collision between steamers *Chili* and *City of Berlin*, August 7, 1904. As there was no wilful violation of the rules and regulations, case was dismissed.

May 22.—While en route from Huron, Ohio, to Sandwich, Ontario. the crank pin on engine of steamer *Rube Richards* broke close to after crank. Estimated damage, $1,000.

May 28.—While the steamer *P. J. Ralph* was bound down Detroit River the cylinder head and piston broke. Damage estimated at $1.500.

June 5.—An unknown man, while intoxicated, going aboard the ferry steamer *Victoria* staggered and fell off gang plank and was drowned. All efforts made to save him were in vain.

June 9.—While leaving Bates street dock, steamer *Columbia* backed into the steamer *Pappoose*. Estimated damage to the *Pappoose*, $25. No damage to the *Columbia*.

July 2.—While trying to pass the steamer *George Spencer*, the stern of the steamer *Aurania* struck the *George Spencer*, abreast of the engine room, damaging the latter to the extent of $1,000. No damage to the *Aurania*.

July 2.—While crossing Lime Kiln crossing, Detroit River, the steamer *W. P. Thew* grounded on rocky bottom, breaking wheel and shoe. Damage, about $400.

July 7.—Steamer *Saturn* stranded by getting out of channel. Released after lightering 700 tons. No damage to steamer.

July 20.—While making a landing alongside the steamer *City of Toledo*, at the White Star Line dock, Detroit, George Wollencheck, a deck hand on the steamer *Owana*, after taking out the pins holding the grating guarding the after port gangway, attempted to talk to some one on board the *City of Toledo*, at the same time leaning against the grating, which fell out, letting him into the water. All efforts made to save him were unsuccessful.

August 16.—The steamers *Hancock* and *Binghampton* met in collision in Lake St. Clair, resulting in the sinking of the *Hancock*. Estimated damage to the *Hancock*, $10,000. No damage to the *Binghampton*. No lives lost. Investigation pending.

August 24.—While passing the steamer *Francis Hinton* in Detroit River, the wheel chains of the steamer *Binghampton* parted, causing the two steamers to collide. Estimated damage to the *Francis Hinton*, $500; to the *Binghampton*, $1,400.

August 28.—While leaning over the rail in the act of unhooking a fall attached to the kedge anchor, Wallace Asphba, a deck hand on the steamer *R. E. Doville*, lost his balance, fell overboard, and was drowned. All efforts made to rescue him were without success.

August 29.—While passing Mullin's coal dock, Sandwich, Ontario, the steamer *Lily* took a sheer, struck a wreck, and sunk. Estimated damage, $1,000.

August 30.—In trying to avoid a collision with the schooner *Abby L. Andrews*, in the Detroit River, the steamer *Frank L. Robbins* struck a dump scow, sustaining damage amounting to about $2,000.

September 22.—While bound down Detroit River the shaft of the steamer *Ella G. Wood* broke, doing damage estimated at $75. Steamer was towed to Toledo, Ohio.

October 1. The steamer *Fannie Tuthill* was sunk in collison with the steamer *D. C. Whitney*. Estimated damage to the *Fannie Tuthill* $2,500; to the *D. C. Whitney*, $3,000. One life lost. Investigation pending.

October 1.—While the steamers *Anna C. Minch* and *Viking* were approaching each other in the Detroit River, the steamer *Viking* took a sheer, causing the sterns of the two steamers to collide. No damage to either steamer.

October 4.—While bound up Detroit River the steamer *Saxona* collided with an unknown barge in tow of a steamer bound down, and which was rounding to. On account of a heavy smoke which was overhanging the water the barge was not seen until the *Saxona* was close upon it. No damage to the *Saxona*.

CASUALTIES, VIOLATIONS OF LAW, AND INVESTIGATIONS, YEAR ENDED DECEMBER 31, 1905—EIGHTH SUPERVISING DISTRICT—DETROIT, MICH.—Continued.

October 5.—The steering gear of the steamer *Brazil* became disabled, and could not get hand gear in in time to save steamer from stranding. Damage estimated at $4,000.

October 19.—While bound down the Detroit River the steamer *D. M. Clemson* struck an obstruction near Bois Blanc Island, beileved to have been thrown up by dredges at work at that place. Estimated damage, $12,000.

December 9.—While lying at the dock at the foot of McKinstry avenue, Detroit, the steamer *Tempest* caught fire from some unknown cause and was damaged to the extent of $3,500.

December 19.—Completed investigation of the collision between the steamers *Fannie Tuthill* and *D. C. Whitney*. License of Charles Abair, master of the *Fannie Tuthill* was suspended for 9 months for violation of rule 15 of the pilot rules for the Great Lakes, and for carrying passengers on a towing certificate. Case reported to the proper authorities.

LOCAL DISTRICT OF CHICAGO, ILL.

February 20.—Steamer *Joseph C. Suit* collided with Van Buren Street Bridge, Chicago, at 7.30 p. m., due to engine stopping on center and steamer being carried against bridge by current. Estimated damage to steamer, $30.

May 9.—Steamer *John W. Gates* ran on expired certificate of inspection on voyage from Duluth, due to delay by fog. Case reported to collector of customs.

May 11.—Steamer *Pere Marquette 18* collided with Pennsylvania Railroad bridge at South Chicago, Ill., caused by strong wind and current. No damage.

May 31.—While passing the schooner *Annie M. Peterson* in Chicago River, the steamer *Batavia* took a sheer, caused by suction of steamer *Fred Drews*, and struck schooner *Annie M. Peterson*. No damage to steamer *Batavia*.

June 7.—While the steamer *William Edenborn* was about 15 miles northeast of Grosse Point, Lake Michigan, in a fog, an unknown steamer collided slightly with said vessel. No damage to steamer *William Edenborn*.

June 20.—Suspended license of Robert Regan, engineer, for 30 days, for not making repairs ordered to boiler under his charge, as ordered at time of annual inspection.

June 24.—While steamer *Christopher Columbus* was being towed out of Chicago River by 2 tugs, tow line parted and steamer collided with schooner *Ralph Campbell*. No damage to steamer *Christopher Columbus*.

June 30.—Steamer *Commodore* entered harbor of South Chicago, Ill., arriving from Chicago, Ill., with 30, more or less, persons other than crew on board. Said steamer certificated as a freight steamer. Case reported to district attorney and collector of customs.

July 3.—While steamer *Iriquois* was en route from Chicago to South Haven, Mich., return bend in pipe boiler gave way, and escaping steam blew flame and hot ashes out of fire door and ash pan, burning Otto Adler, a coal passer, about the head and shoulders.

July 8.—On the morning of July 8, steamer *Welcome* sunk at her dock in Chicago River, caused by a need of calking. After being raised and while being towed to dry dock, steamer collided with Sixteenth Street Bridge, tearing off roof of pilot house. Total amount of damage, $300.

July 14.—While tied up to the bank of the Illinois and Michigan Canal at Channahon, the steamer *Walwarth*, at 2 a. m., caught fire from some unknown cause and was totally destroyed. Loss, $3,500.

July 21.—While landing at dock, steamer *Soo City* struck schooner *Iver Lawson*, lying at dock at foot of Franklin street, Chicago. No damage to steamer *Soo City*.

July 23.—While the steamer *Puritan* was in midlake, a passenger, evidently intoxicated, fell overboard and was drowned. Every effort was made to save him but without avail.

July 27.—Steamers *Syracuse* and *Batavia* met in Chicago River at Twelfth Street Bridge. After exchanging proper signals and in passing, steamers collided. Damage to steamer *Batavia*, $500. No damage to steamer *Syracuse*.

August 2.—On trip from Chicago on steamer *Manitou*, a Miss Burgess and sister, of Mattoon, Ill., were passengers. It appears that sometime during the night one of the ladies jumped overboard through the porthole, but was not missed until the following morning. A note was left by the deceased announcing her contemplated act, showing a clear case of suicide.

August 3.—Steamer *Yosemite* reported to have carried 30 policemen on a trip from Ninety-second street, South Chicago, into Lake Michigan and return. Steamer certificated as a "fire" steamer and not allowed to carry passengers. Case reported to proper authorities.

CASUALTIES, VIOLATIONS OF LAW, AND INVESTIGATIONS, YEAR ENDED DECEMBER 31, 1905—EIGHTH SUPERVISING DISTRICT—CHICAGO, ILL.—Continued.

August 16.—Steamer *Charles H. Hackley* left her dock at Rush Street Bridge, Chicago, to take an excursion party to view yacht races off Chicago Harbor on Lake Michigan, taking on the party at foot of Randolph street. Upon landing at Randolph street, Captain Barry, master, was called ashore upon urgent personal matters and left the ship in charge of Thomas M. Madden, master, and Joseph Oliver, also licensed as master; these two men being the only licensed men employed on board the vessel having authority to navigate the ship. Case reported to proper authorities.

August 20.—Complaint was made, alleging that while on duty, Thomas M. Madden, a licensed pilot on steamer *Charles H. Hackley*, was intoxicated. Upon investigation, it was found that Mr. Madden, while able to handle the vessel properly, had been drinking and his license was suspended for 30 days.

August 20.—Complaint was made, alleging that while on duty, Charles St. John Sherwood, a pilot on steamer *Charles H. Hackley*, was intoxicated. Upon investigation found that charges were not correct, but that Mr. Sherwood had exceeded his authority in attempting to navigate said steamer, and his license was suspended for 6 months.

August 20.—Charges made, alleging that upon August 20, steamer *Charles H. Hackley* had been navigated without proper complement of officers. Upon investigation found charges incorrect and case was dismissed.

August 20.—While winding in the Chicago River, steamer *Charles H. Hackley* collided with a dump scow. Scow was sunk. Steamer then struck Goodrich dock with her stern, doing slight damage. Steamer *Charles H. Hackley* not damaged.

August 29.—A young man, name unknown, jumped overboard from steamer *Eagle* while steamer was moving about 2 miles per hour. Every effort was made to save him, but without success.

September 8.—Suspended license of John F. Johns, master and pilot, for 30 days, for intemperance while acting as master of steamer *John Sharpies*.

September 9.—Complaint made that John Lavell, a licensed engineer, was intoxicated while on duty on September 9, 1905. Attempts to locate Mr. Lavell were unsuccessful, and the case was dropt on November 27.

September 11.—When off Grosse Point, Lake Michigan, steamer *Manitou* struck an uncharted obstruction, evidently a submerged wreck, breaking one of the buckets of her propeller. Estimated damage, $500.

September 27.—While en route from South Chicago to Chicago, steamer *Hattie* broke coupling on shaft. Estimated damage, $15.

October 7.—While steamer *Iroquois* was leaving Chicago Harbor, John McHughes, a deck hand, who had climbed overboard to clear a heel rope on a fender, slipt and fell into the river. A boat put out from the dock and attempted to rescue him, but he drowned before the boat reached him. Upon investigation of the case, Capt. F. W. Swails, master of the steamer, was found guilty of neglect in not attempting to rescue the man with the life-saving appliances required by law to be on his vessel, and his license was suspended for 6 months.

October 15.—Steamer *Ferdinand Schlessinger*, in attempting to find entrance to South Chicago Harbor, mist entrance and struck light-house pier, owing to smoky conditions. No damage to steamer. Case reported to light-house inspector, Chicago.

October 19.—While steamer *Schuylkill* was passing thru Adams Street Bridge, Chicago River, bridge was swung against steamer, damaging vessel to the extent of about $1,000.

October 20.—While steamer *Nyanza* was leaving port of South Chicago, main steam-pipe throttle casting broke. Steamer returned to South Chicago and had a new casting made at an expense of $222.

October 20.—Suspended license of Bernard J. McCabe, engineer, for 30 days, for failure to report necessary repairs to boilers of steamer *Maurice B. Grover*, under his charge, before making said repairs.

October 26.—Steamers *City of Kalamazoo* and *Rochester* collided at the mouth of Chicago River, caused by inability of wheelsman on steamer *Rochester* not being able to give the ship the wheel quick enough to avoid collision. Damage to *City of Kalamazoo*, $350; to *Rochester*, none.

November 3 and 6.—Pleasure steamer *Vernon Jr.*, 33 gross tons, was navigated on Chicago River and Lake Michigan without having the certificate of inspection exposed to view, as required by section 4423, Revised Statutes. License of Vernon C. Seaver revoked. On appeal to supervising inspector, decision of this board reversed.

November 3 and 6.—Steamer *Vernon Jr.*, Vernon C. Seaver, master, navigated on Chicago River and Lake Michigan without having certificate of inspection exposed to view, as required. Case reported to proper authorities.

CASUALTIES, VIOLATIONS OF LAW, AND INVESTIGATIONS, YEAR ENDED DECEMBER 31, 1905—EIGHTH SUPERVISING DISTRICT—CHICAGO, ILL.—Continued.

November 3 and 6.—Steamer *Vernon Jr.*, was navigated on Chicago River and Lake Michigan without having on board the proper equipment, as required by Rules III and IV, general rules and regulations. December 21, license of Vernon C. Seaver revoked, and license of William Brown, pilot, suspended for 6 months.

November 4.—Suspended license of L. L. Hill, master and pilot, for 30 days, for failure to provide equipment for steamer *City of Marquette*, as ordered at time of annual inspection.

November 6.—Steamer *Starruca* collided with Metropolitan Elevated Railway bridge, Chicago. Damage to steamer, $750.

November 6.—When about 18 miles from Chicago, something went wrong with port engine of steamer *Virginia*. Proceeded to Milwaukee with starboard engine and later discovered bracket on outboard end of port shaft broken. Damage, $300.

November 11.—John Mooney, engineer of steamer *M. G. Hauslet*, was slightly scalded by escaping steam from the boiler, caused by stay bolts in combustion chamber giving way, due to grooved and thin sheet. Estimated damage, $300.

November 23.—John Rounds, a deck hand on steamer *John B. Trevor*, in boarding the vessel, which was lying at the dock in Chicago River, fell into the river and was drowned. Every effort was made to save him, but without success.

November 23.—Steamer *Phillip Minch*, in attempting to make the harbor of South Chicago in very thick and smoky weather, collided with Rockefeller Shoal gas buoy. No damage to steamer. Case reported to light-house inspector, Chicago.

November 27.—In entering Chicago River steamer *Pasadena* grounded on La Salle street tunnel, and was damaged to the amount of $200.

December 3.—Steamer *German* stranded near Glencoe, Ill., on an uncharted reef. Damage estimated at $20,000.

December 4.—Steamer *Andrew H. Green*, in towing scows in Chicago River, collided with steamer *Fire Queen*. Damage to steamer *Fire Queen*, $50.

December 18.—Gustaf E. Anderson, master, steamer *Hendrick S. Holden*, failed to report the dry docking of his steamer, as required by section 5, Rule VI, general rules and regulations. His license was suspended for 30 days. Appeal made to the supervising inspector.

December 21.—Revoked license of Vernon C. Seaver, special pilot, for failure to have the steamer *Vernon Jr.*, equipped as required by the rules and regulations and the certificate of inspection.

LOCAL DISTRICT OF MILWAUKEE, WIS.

February 24.—When about 7 miles out from Milwaukee Harbor, the steamer *Dan Costello* broke her shaft and lost wheel. Estimated damage, $200.

May 11.—Steamer *Pere Marquette 19* collided with railroad bridge, Milwaukee River. No damage to steamer.

May 11.—Steamer *Mauch Chunk*, in tow of 2 tugs, collided with Sixth Street Bridge in Milwaukee River, twisting rudder stock and breaking 3 buckets off wheel. Estimated damage, $1,000.

May 11.—When about 32 miles northeast of Milwaukee, on Lake Michigan, steamer *Pere Marquette 17* lost port wheel and outboard shaft. Estimated damage, $3,000.

May 11.—Steamer *Kearsarge* collided with tug *W. H. Simpson* in Milwaukee River. Tug was lying at dock and steamer was coming down river when she took a sudden sheer from her course and struck tug on bow. Cause supposed to have been heavy current on account of rains. Estimated damage to tug, $1,000.

May 20.—While navigating Fox River the steamer *Le Fevre* carried more passengers than allowed by her certificate of inspection. Case reported to proper authorities.

May 23.—Steamer *Evelyn* navigated with an engineer whose license was not of sufficient tonnage to cover steamer. Case reported to proper authorities.

May 23.—Steamer *Tuscarora* collided with a bridge in Milwaukee River. No damage to steamer.

May 25.—Suspended license of John Velte, master and pilot, for 10 days for failing to render monthly report of fire and boat drills, as required by section 50, Rule V, general rules and regulations.

May 29.—While the steamer *Pere Marquette 20* was leaving Milwaukee Harbor she collided with the sand scow *Hiram R. Bond*, which was entering the harbor. A thick fog was reported outside the harbor and none in the harbor. Collision occurred just after steamer *Pere Marquette 20* had entered fog. No damage to *Pere Marquette 20*. Steamer *Hiram R. Bond* sunk. Crew of the latter left steamer in a small boat. Estimated loss, $15,000.

CASUALTIES, VIOLATIONS OF LAW, AND INVESTIGATIONS, YEAR ENDED DECEMBER 31, 1905—EIGHTH SUPERVISING DISTRICT—MILWAUKEE, WIS.—Continued.

June 5.—During a heavy fog the steamer *Harlem* stranded one-half mile north of Fox Point, Lake Michigan. Steamer released next day and proceeded to Milwaukee under her own power. Estimated damage, $2,000.

June 7.—While lying at the dock at Oshkosh, Wis., fire broke out on the steamer *Tia Juana* aft of boiler. Estimated damage, $1,500.

June 12.—While at Appleton, Wis., one of the crew of the steamer *J. H. Marston* in lowering the yawl fell overboard and was drowned. All efforts made to save him were without avail.

June 17.—During a heavy fog on Lake Michigan the schooner *Eliza Day* collided with the steamer *Mohawk*. Estimated damage to steamer, $5. Schooner was towed to Milwaukee, considerably damaged.

June 20.—Revoked license of James Egbert, first assistant engineer and engineer in charge of 100 gross tons and under, for altering his license. Case reported to district attorney.

June 23.—Steamer *H. S. Pickands* destroyed buoy No. 24, abreast of Depere docks, Fox River. Reported to U. S. Engineer Department.

June 24.—Steamer *Neosho* navigated on an expired certificate of inspection. Case reported to proper authorities.

June 25.—Steamer *Naomi* collided with steamer *Empire State* in Milwaukee River. Estimated damage to *Empire State*, $200. Accident unavoidable.

June 28.—While returning to Marinette, Wis., an elbow in the water-tube boiler of the steamer *Bonita* burst. No one hurt. Estimated damage, $50.

July 1.—When steamer *Virginia* was about 3 miles off Milwaukee she struck some unknown object and broke off bucket from port wheel. Estimated damage, $100.

July 19.—Steamer *Kearsarge* collided with a bridge in Milwaukee River. No damage to steamer.

July 26.—While on Green Bay, near Washington Island, the steamer *George Presley* caught fire from some unknown cause and was totally destroyed. Estimated value, $40,000. No lives lost.

July 27.—Steam pleasure yacht *Ensign* carried more passengers than allowed by certificate of inspection. Case reported to proper authorities.

August 7.—When steamer *Conemaugh* was about 8 miles S. by W. of Beaver Island, Lake Michigan, one of the crew was lost overboard. Reported to have jumped overboard. All efforts made to save him were without success.

September 17.—During a heavy fog steamer *City of Glasgow* stranded on North Point, 3 miles north of Milwaukee. Released next day by aid of tug. No damage to steamer.

October 3.—Steamer *Amazonas* failed to comply with letter of instructions regarding equipment and repairs, dated June 22, 1905. Case reported to proper authorities.

October 9.—On account of a misunderstanding of signals between master and engineer, the steamer *Manistee* collided with bridge in Milwaukee River. Estimated damage to steamer, $2,000.

October 25.—Steamer *Hendrick S. Holden* stranded in the middle of river at Sheboygan, Wis. Steamer ran a line ashore, and fishing tug *Elizabeth G*, coming up the river at dusk, did not see the line and ran into it, tearing off part of pilot house. No one hurt. Estimated damage to tug, $300.

November 1.—When tug *W. H. Meyer* was entering Manitowoc Harbor it was discovered that the starboard furnace of the boiler bulged down several inches over the grates in the lowest place and extended fore and aft 3 feet and around the circle of the furnace 18 inches. Estimated damage, $250.

November 2.—On account of thick smoke from the city of Milwaukee the steamer *Iowa* stranded north of North Point, Lake Michigan. Estimated damage, $6,500.

November 2.—On account of thick smoke from the city of Milwaukee the steamer *Appomattox* stranded north of North Point, Lake Michigan. Steamer a total loss. Valuation, $75,000.

November 7.—Steamer *Evelyn* demolished her wheel on Wolf River. Estimated damage, $100.

November 15.—Rudder of steamer *Tioga* touched spring piling in Milwaukee River, causing extra strain on wheel chain, pulling down starboard quarter shear bracket. Estimated damage, $45.

November 28.—Steamer *D. C. Whitney* was stranded near Port Washington, Wis., to prevent her from foundering in deep water. Wind was blowing 50 miles per hour. No lives lost. Steamer was released later and towed to Milwaukee. Estimated damage, $4,500.

CASUALTIES, VIOLATIONS OF LAW, AND INVESTIGATIONS, YEAR ENDED DECEMBER 31, 1905—EIGHTH SUPERVISING DISTRICT—Continued.

LOCAL DISTRICT OF MARQUETTE, MICH.

February 6.—Completed the investigation, begun November 4, 1904, of the causes that led to the collision between the steamers *Ira H. Owen* and *Henry W. Oliver* on October 13, 1904, and suspended the license of George Graham, master and pilot, for a period of 4 months for violation of Rules III and VIII, pilot rules for the Great Lakes. Upon appeal this suspension was modified by the supervising inspector eighth district to a period of 60 days.

April 15.—Owing to defect in machinery of bridge at Houghton, Mich., the steamer *Northern Wave* collided with draw of said bridge. Estimated damage to steamer, $500.

April 17.—The steamer *Admiral*, while making a landing at Sault Ste. Marie, Mich., struck the steamer *Superior*, which was lying alongside of the steamer *Corsica*, breaking shell plate and frame in the latter vessel. Estimated damage, $300.

April 18.—While the steamer *Frontenac* was lying in the ice in White Fish Bay, Lake Superior, the wind suddenly shifted, forcing a large field of ice against her port side, damaging steamer's frame and plates to the amount of about $2,000.

April 19.—While on Lake Superior, bound for Lake Erie ports, the steamer *Maruba* had one plate and one frame broken by collision with floating ice. Estimated damage to steamer, $200.

April 20.—While in the ice in Mud Lake, St. Marys River, the steamer *John Sharples* was struck on port quarter by steamer *D. M. Clemson*, sustaining damage estimated at $2,000.

April 28.—While on Lake Superior the steamer *Andaste* collided with a heavy field of ice, denting 1 plate on port bow and cracking 2 plates and 7 frames. Damage, $2,000.

April 28.—While in the ice off White Fish Point, Lake Superior, the steamer *Admiral* collided with the steamer *Mariposa*, damaging the latter to the estimated amount of $4,000.

May 1.—While in the Canadian Canal, Sault Ste. Marie, Ontario, the steamer *Maritana* collided with the tow barge *G. W. Roby*. No damage sustained by steamer.

May 1.—While on White Fish Bay, Lake Superior, steamer *Douglas-Houghton* was struck on the stern by her consort, *Thomas*, the steamer sustaining damage to the amount of $1,000.

May 2.—While in St. Marys Canal, Sault Ste. Marie, Mich., the steamer *Sir William Siemens* was struck by the barge *Smeaton* and damaged to the amount of $1,000.

May 6.—While on Lake Superior, in a dense fog, the steamer *William P. Rend* stranded on a rocky reef off Manitou Island, owing to alleged failure of light-keeper to sound fog whistle. Estimated damage to steamer, $15,000.

May 16.—While en route from Ashland, Wis., to Cleveland, Ohio, the steamer *Harvard*, in a heavy fog, collided with the steamer *Thomas W. Palmer*, about 30 miles past Manitou Island light, Lake Superior, sinking the latter steamer in a few moments. The entire crew of the steamer *Palmer* was taken aboard the steamer *Harvard*, no lives being lost or persons injured. The *Harvard* sustained an estimated loss of $15,000. Estimated loss on the steamer *Thomas W. Palmer*, $100,000.

May 18.—Investigated the causes that led to the collision between the steamers *Harvard* and *Thomas W. Palmer* on May 16, and on July 8 completed the investigation and suspended the master and pilot's license of Carleton D. Secord and the first-class pilot's license of Benjamin Broderick, each for a period of 60 days, for violation of Rule XV, act of Congress approved February 8, 1895.

June 1.—While en route from Chicago to Duluth, on arrival at Sault Ste. Marie, Mich., the steamer *Douglas-Houghton* was discovered to have lost her shoe. Estimated damage to steamer, $3,500.

June 5.—While en route from Milwaukee, Wis., to Marquette, Mich., the steamer *G. J. Grammer*, running under check in a heavy fog, struck on St. Martins reef, Lake Huron, puncturing her plates and breaking one bucket off wheel. Estimated damage, $5,000.

June 8.—Suspended the master and pilot's license of Joseph Taylor, jr., for misconduct, viz, being intoxicated while on duty and acting as master of the steamer *William Maxwell* at Houghton, Mich.

June 10.—Steamer *The Tramp* violated section 4417, Revised Statutes, viz, running on an expired certificate of inspection. Violation reported to the collector of customs at Marquette after investigation.

June 11.—The steamer *George B. Leonard* stranded on Point Iroquois, Lake Superior, and while trying to back off broke outboard shaft and 1 bucket off wheel. Estimated damage, $2,000.

Casualties, Violations of Law, and Investigations, Year ended December 31, 1905—Eighth Supervising District—Marquette, Mich.—Continued.

June 13.—In a dense fog on Lake Michigan the steamer *W. H. Gilbert* stranded on Helena Island, sustaining damages to the amount of $4,000.

June 13.—While off White Fish Point, Lake Superior, the steamer *Sylvania*, owing to alleged misunderstanding of passing signals, collided with the steamer *Sir Henry Bessemer*. Damage to *Sylvania*, $10,000; to *Sir Henry Bessemer*, $40,000.

June 15.—Investigated causes that led to the collision between the steamers *Sylvania* and *Sir Henry Bessemer* on June 13. Investigation pending.

June 15.—While en route from Cheboygan to Sault Ste. Marie the steamer *Harriet A. Hart* caught fire from some unknown cause and was burned to the water's edge. The passengers and crew were safely placed in lifeboats and rafts, subsequently taken aboard the steamer *Juniata* and landed at Mackinac Island. No lives lost or persons injured. Estimated loss on the steamer *Harriet A. Hart*, $50,000.

June 16.—Investigated the causes that led to the burning of the steamer *Harriet A. Hart*, and on November 2 completed the investigation, resulting in the suspension of the master and pilot's license of Joseph W. Carrigan and the master and pilot's license of Joseph T. Roulett for 30 days, and the chief engineer's license of Rufus Spaulding and the assistant engineer's license of Bertrand W. Neeland for 90 days, all being off and employed on the steamer *Harriet A. Hart* at the time of burning.

June 17.—While en route from Conneaut, Ohio, to Ashland, Wis., the steamer *John J. Albright*, in a dense fog, stranded on the east end of Espanore Island, Lake Huron, sustaining damage estimated at $10,000.

June 19.—Investigated charges preferred against Henry A. Pocock, master and pilot of the steamer *Fortune*, for alleged violation of section 4131, Revised Statutes, viz, not being a citizen of the United States. These charges were dismissed, as per report rendered July 29, 1905.

June 25.—While lying at anchor in a dense fog in St. Marys River the steamer *W. C. Richardson* was struck by the steamer *Lewis Woodruff*, sustaining damage estimated at $3,500. Damage to the *Lewis Woodruff*, $3,400.

July 8.—While en route from Milwaukee to Duluth the steamer *William Nottingham* stranded on St. Martins reef, Lake Huron, sustaining damages to the estimated amount of $3,500.

July 14.—While on Lake Superior, off Outer Island, John Seabrooks, first officer of the steamer *Sir William Fairbairn*, in some unknown manner fell overboard and was drowned. Every effort was made to save him, but without avail.

July 16.—While en route from Fairport to Two Harbors the steamer *James B. Neilson*, in a dense fog, collided with the steamer *Neshoto*, downbound, damaging the latter vessel to the amount of $10,000.

August 3.—While the tug *Hattie Jordan* was towing a scow loaded with gravel on Little Bay De Noquette, near Escanaba, Mich., Fred Diebolt, a deck hand, fell over board, was drawn under the scow before help could reach him, and was drowned.

August 10.—Steamer *Charles B. Hill* stranded on St. Martins reef, Lake Michigan, sustaining damage estimated at $1,000.

August 17.—While steamer *Ann Arbor No. 3* was swinging away from the dock at Menominee, Mich., Charles Reed, a deck hand, attempted to jump from the stern of said steamer to the dock, lost his balance, fell into the river, and was drowned.

August 18.—While en route from Escanaba to Buffalo, the steamer *Louisiana* struck off the end of Gull Island, Lake Michigan, starting a leak, and subsequently breaking the wrist pin of air pump to engine. Estimated damage, $6,000.

August 26.—Investigated charges preferred against Edwin Smith, master and pilot, for violation of Rule VIII, pilot rules for the Great Lakes. Charges not being sustained by the evidence, case was dismissed.

August 29.—Investigated causes of the collision between the steamers *Neshoto* and *James B. Neilson*, and on December 22 completed the investigation, and suspended the license of John Dunn, master and pilot of the steamer *Neshoto*, and the license of Oscar Olsen, master and pilot for the steamer *James B. Neilson*, each for a period of 5 months, for violation of Rule XV, pilot rules for the Great Lakes.

September 3.—While in the vicinity of Huron Islands, Lake Superior, steamer *Iosco* foundered, and the officers and crew, supposed to consist of 19 persons, were all drowned. Estimated loss on steamer, $65,000.

September 3.—While the steamer *R. L. Ireland* was laboring in a heavy sea on Lake Superior, Frank Smith, second mate of said steamer, was caught by a wave, carried overboard, and was drowned.

September 3.—While proceeding up St. Marys River with barge *John Roebling* in tow, the steamer *George Stephenson* ran aground, and the tow barge collided with her stern, damaging said steamer to the amount of $3,000.

CASUALTIES, VIOLATIONS OF LAW, AND INVESTIGATIONS, YEAR ENDED DECEMBER 31, 1905—EIGHTH SUPERVISING DISTRICT—MARQUETTE, MICH.—Continued.

September 5.—While en route from Sault Ste. Marie, Mich., to Duluth, Minn., the steamer *W. C. Richardson*, when about 2 miles above the ship canal on St. Marys River, collided with the foreign towing steamer *Shamrock*, sinking the said *Shamrock* and drowning the master and engineer thereof.

September 10.—Investigated the causes leading to the collision between the steamers *W. C. Richardson* and *Shamrock*, and the evidence showing no violation of law by the officers of the steamer *W. C. Richardson*, the case was dismissed without further action on November 3.

September 12.—While navigating on Lake Superior near White Fish Point, the fishing steamer *C. W. Endress* broke the crank to engine. Estimated damage, $300.

September 16.—While navigating St. Marys River in a dense fog, the steamer *Sultana* stranded on Vidal shoal. Estimated damage, $2,500.

September 18.—While en route from Lorain, Ohio, to Marquette, Mich., the steamer *Maritana* stranded on Grand Island reef. Estimated damage, $15,000.

October 7.—Steamer *J. J. Evans* violated section 4325, Revised Statutes, viz, non-surrender of steamer's expired license. Violation reported to collector of customs at Marquette, after investigation.

October 14.—Steamer *L. Q. Rawson* violated section 4424, Revised Statutes, viz, carrying passengers on a towing certificate. As a result of the investigation of this violation, the license of James T. Tilley, second-class pilot, was suspended for a period of 60 days and the violation reported to the collector of customs at Marquette.

October 19.—While en route from Sault Ste. Marie to Green Bay, during a gale of wind, accompanied by sleet and snow, the steamer *Frank Perry* stranded on a rocky reef off Boot Island, Lake Huron, sustaining damages to the amount of $10,000.

October 20.—While laboring in a heavy sea, in the vicinity of Stannard rock, Lake Superior, the engine of the steamer *Oregon* was disabled, and the steamer subsequently drifted ashore. Estimated damage, $15,000.

November 3.—While en route from Two Harbors, Minn., with tow, the steamer *Frank Rockefeller* stranded on Rainbow Cove reef, Lake Superior, sustaining damages to the amount of $9,000.

November 9.—While the steamer *Joliet* was lying at the dock at Marquette, Mich., loading iron ore, George Harden, employed as a fireman aboard, accidentally fell thru the after hatch of the steamer, sustaining injuries from which he died on November 10, at Marquette, Mich.

November 12.—While en route from Lorain, Ohio, to Marinette, Wis., loaded with coal, the steamer *R. J. Hackett* caught fire from some unknown cause, proving a total loss. The officers and crew of 13 men got into lifeboats and were picked up by the fishing steamer *Stewart Edward* and safely landed at Cedar River, Mich. Estimated loss on steamer, $16,000.

November 15.—While lying at anchor under Point Seul Croix, Lake Michigan, the steamer *Rochester* dragged ashore, sustaining damages to the amount of $20,000.

November 15.—While the steamer *Marina* was lying at the dock at Detour, Mich., the steamer *Mariposa* approached with barge in tow, the barge colliding with the steamer *Marina*, doing damage to said steamer to the estimated amount of $2,000.

November 20.—While engaged in dredging at Grand Marais, Mich., the steamer *George Rogers* broke the out-board shaft. Estimated damage, $125.

November 24.—While on Lake Superior, en route from South Chicago, the steamer *Charlemagne Tower, Jr.*, encountered a heavy wind and snowstorm, the sea breaking on her deck, doing damage to steamer to the estimated amount of $1,500.

November 27.—While en route from Duluth to Buffalo, the steamer *Harold B. Nye* encountered a heavy gale of wind on Lake Superior, the seas staving in her houses, cabin, and decks, and washing overboard and drowning William Sturtevant, the first officer. Estimated damage to steamer, $30,000.

November 28.—While en route on Lake Superior, during a terrific gale of wind, Gunder Hanson, a deck hand aboard the steamer *Victory*, was mist, and is supposed to have been washt overboard and drowned.

November 28.—During a terrific gale of wind, accompanied by snow, the steamer *Bransford* struck a reef off the west end of Isle Royale, Lake Superior, sustaining damages to the amount of $15,000.

November 28.—The steamer *Ira H. Owne* foundered on Lake Superior, and the officers and crew, consisting of 19 men, were all drowned. Estimated loss on steamer, $40,000.

November 29.—While on Lake Superior, in a terrific gale of wind, the steamer *Coralia* stranded on Point Isabelle, sustaining damages to the amount of $10,000.

CASUALTIES, VIOLATIONS OF LAW, AND INVESTIGATIONS, YEAR ENDED DECEMBER 31, 1905—EIGHTH SUPERVISING DISTRICT—MARQUETTE, MICH.—Continued.

November 29.—In a heavy gale of wind and snowstorm on Lake Superior, the steamer *Western Star* stranded near Fourteen Mile Point, sustaining damages to the amount of $20,000.

December 9.—Investigated misconduct of George E. Hursley, master of the steamer *Wisconsin*, at Marquette, Mich., viz, being intoxicated while acting under authority of his license, resulting in the suspension of his license as master and pilot for a period of 6 months.

LOCAL DISTRICT OF GRAND HAVEN, MICH.

February 17.—While breaking ice in Grand River, the steamer *H. J. Dornbos* lost her wheel. Damage estimated at $150.

February 21.—While assisting the steamer *Manistique, Marquette & Northern 1*, which was stuck in the ice at Ludington, Mich., the steamer *Geo. D. Nau* was struck by a heavy field of floating ice, causing the *Nau* to collide with the *Manistique, Marquette & Northern 1*. Estimated damage to the *Nau*, $300.

February 24.—While working in heavy ice about 8 miles off Manistique, the steamer *Manistique, Marquette & Northern 1* broke off one propeller blade from starboard wheel. Damage estimated at $450.

March 6.—While on Lake Michigan, the steamer *Nyack* struck an obstruction and stove 2 holes in her bow. Arriving at Grand Haven, the steamer sunk opposite her dock. Steamer was unloaded and temporarily repaired; then taken to Milwaukee, Wis., and placed in dry dock. Estimated damage, $5,000.

March 7.—While working in heavy ice off Ludington, the steamer *Pere Marquette 17* twisted her rudder stock. Estimated damage, $1,500.

April 1.—While en route from Ludington to Manitowoc, Edward J. Decker, jr., a passenger on the steamer *Pere Marquette 18*, was lost overboard in some unknown manner and drowned.

April 3.—While at Charlevoix, Mich., the steamer *Inna L. Wheeler* caught fire from some unknown cause and was totally destroyed. Estimated loss, $4,000.

April 4.—The steamer *Sprite* was wrecked about 3 miles north of Whitehall, Mich. Estimated loss, $1,500.

May 18.—The steamer *Superior City* struck a rock between North Manitou and Pyramid Rock. Estimated damage, $10,000.

June 5.—Steamer *Ella* navigated on an expired certificate of inspection. Case reported to the collector of customs at Grand Haven, Mich.

August 8.—While at Holland, Mich., the steamer *Post Boy* caught fire from some unknown cause and was totally destroyed. Estimated loss, $8,000.

August 16.—Steamer *Juniata* navigated on expired certificate of inspection and without licensed engineer. Case reported to the collector of customs.

September 12.—While in Ludington Harbor, a brisk wind caught the steamer *Manistique, Marquette & Northern 1* and carried her against the steamer *Lizzie Walsh*, which was lying at the Pere Marquette docks. No damage to former; steamer *Lizzie Walsh* damaged to the extent of $300.

September 13.—Steamer *Clara A. Elliott* navigated on an expired certificate of inspection. Case reported to the collector of customs at Grand Haven, Mich.

October 19.—Steamer *N. McGraft*, at Petosky Harbor, Mich., parted lines and drifted on beach. Estimated damage to steamer, $300.

October 25.—Steamer *Chequamegon* was navigated without having a metal lifeboat on board, as required by the rules and regulations. The license of C. C. Fowler, master and pilot, was suspended on November 7, for a period of 60 days, and case reported to the collector of customs. Upon appeal to the supervising inspector, decision was sustained.

November 2.—While navigating Ludington Harbor, the steamer *Pere Marquette 16* struck an obstruction and loosened propeller wheel. Estimated damage, $600.

November 7.—While en route on Lake Michigan, the steamer *William P. Rend* broke inboard shaft. Steamer was taken in tow by steamer *Black Rock* and towed to Mackinaw. Estimated damage, $2,000,

November 24.—While en route from Chicago to Holland, Mich., during a severe storm, the steamer *Argo* stranded on shore at entrance to Holland Harbor. Estimated damage to steamer, $25,000.

CASUALTIES, VIOLATIONS OF LAW, AND INVESTIGATIONS, YEAR ENDED DECEMBER 31, 1905—EIGHTH SUPERVISING DISTRICT—GRAND HAVEN, MICH.—Continued.

November 26.—Steamer *Joseph L. Hurd* dumped deck load of stone in Grand Haven Harbor. Estimated damage to steamer, $3,500.

November 27.—While en route from Escanaba to Cleveland, during a severe storm, the steamer *J. H. Outhwaite* stranded near Little Point Sable, Mich., broke in two, and burned. Estimated loss on steamer, $40,000.

November 28.—While en route from Ashland to South Chicago, Ill., during a severe storm, the steamer *Vega* stranded on South Fox Island, Lake Michigan, and broke in two. No lives lost. Estimated loss on steamer, $140,000.

November 30.—The steamer *Hum* navigated without having a metallic lifeboat on board, as required by the rules and regulations. The license of J. P. Partridge, master and pilot, was suspended for 60 days, and the case reported to the collector of customs at Grand Haven.

December 10.—While entering Manitowoc Harbor, Wis., the steamer *Pere Marquette 18* struck a log, loosening wheel. Estimated damage to wheel, $600.

December 18.—Suspended the license of John B. Mondor, master and first-class pilot, for 6 months, for misconduct in not having proper equipment on board steamer *Elva*, as directed at annual inspection.

LOCAL DISTRICT OF PORT HURON, MICH.

January 30.—Complaint having been made against Capt. D. A. Curran for violation of section 6, Rule V, general rules and regulations, and Rule I of the pilot rule for the Great Lakes, upon investigation he was found guilty of the above violations, but as he had already been fined he was considered to have been sufficiently punished.

April 22.—While steamer *Bethlehem* was bound down St. Clair River her steering gear became disabled and she collided with the steamer *Saturn*, sustaining damage estimated at $3,000. Estimated damage to steamer *Saturn*, $10,000.

May 2.—While bound up Lake Huron, the steamer *Edward P. Recor* stranded on Black River reef and was damaged to the extent of $3,100.

May 14.—While bound up Lake Huron, between Port Hope and East Tawas, Henry Kutcher, a deck hand on the steamer *City of Holland*, fell overboard and was drowned.

May 31.—While the steamer *George T. Burroughs* was bound down St. Clair River, she collided with an unknown steamer and sunk. Estimated loss, $4,000. No lives lost. Investigation pending.

June 13.—While stranded at the head of Stag Island, the steamer *Yakima* caught fire and was totally destroyed. Loss, $50,000.

June 14.—While being towed down St. Clair River, the steamer *George B. Leonard* stranded at the head of Stag Island and was damaged to the extent of $500.

June 17.—While bound up Lake Huron in a dense fog, the steamer *Minnie E. Kelton* stranded on North Point of Hammonds Bay. Estimated damage, $1,000.

June 18.—While bound down Lake Huron, a short distance above Presque Isle, the steamer *Amasa Stone* collided with the steamer *Eturia*, upbound, sinking the latter. Damage to the *Amasa Stone*, $7,000. Loss on *Eturia*, $280,000. No lives lost. Investigation pending.

June 23.—While bound up St. Clair River, the steamer *Linden* collided with the steamer *City of Rome*, resulting in the sinking of the former. Loss on the *Linden*, $35,000. Estimated damage to the *City of Rome*, $10,000. Two lives lost.

June 29.—While the steamer *Ramapo* was lying at anchor in St. Clair River the steamer *Brazil* drifted into her, causing damage to the former estimated at $800. Estimated damage to the *Brazil*, $300.

July 25.—The steamer *Shamrock* water-logged on Lake Huron, and was towed into Thunder Bay, where she sunk, being a total loss. Loss, $7,000.

July 28.—The towing steamer *A. B. Watson* violated section 4417, Revised Statutes, carrying passengers without a passenger certificate of inspection. Steamer was attending dredge, which broke down, and carried owner out to her. Case reported to the proper authorities after investigation.

August 5.—Complaint having been made against R. P. Thomson for violation of section 4446, Revised Statutes, the case was investigated and charges dismissed.

August 13.—While at Bay City, Mich., the steamer *Charles W. Liken* caught fire from some unknown cause and was damaged to the extent of $3,000.

August 15.—While springing away from the dock at Harbor Beach the steamer *City of Mackinac* pulled out a pile and stringer from the dock, damaging the steamer to the amount of $1,000.

August 16.—While bound up Lake Huron, Patrick Whelan, a fireman on board the steamer *John W. Gates*, jumped overboard and was drowned.

Casualties, Violations of Law, and Investigations, Year ended December 31, 1905—Eighth Supervising District—Port Huron, Mich.—Continued.

August 24.—While the steamer *Omar D. Conger* had an excursion party on board her after compartment filled with water. On investigation William S. Major, master, and William Waugh, chief engineer, were found guilty of violation of sections 4439 and 4441, Revised Statutes, and their licenses were suspended for 30 days.

September 2.—The steamer *William R. Linn* collided with the steamer *Ball Bros.*, near St. Clair Flats and was damaged to the extent of $4,000.

September 16.—The steamer *Sarah E. Sheldon* stranded on North Point in a dense fog. Released without damage.

September 30.—While lying at the dock at Alpena, Mich., the steamer *P. H. Birckhead* caught fire and was damaged to the extent of $1,200.

October 18.—As the steamer *Alvin A. Turner* was going thru Little Detroit passage her wheel chains parted, causing steamer to ground on rocks. She afterwards took fire and was totally destroyed. Loss, $5,000.

October 19.—The steamer *Kaliyuga* foundered on Lake Huron, and her crew of 17 was lost. Loss, $70,000.

October 19.—While bound down Lake Huron, the steamer *Joseph S. Fay* sprung a leak and was beached about half a mile from Forty-mile Point, becoming a total loss. Loss, $30,000. One life lost.

November 11.—While bound down St. Clair River, the steamer *John J. Albright* collided with an unknown barge, sustaining damage amounting to $2,000.

November 14.—While bound up Lake St. Clair, near the flats, the steamer *Point Abino* sprung a leak and had to be beached, becoming a total loss. Loss, $2,500.

November 15.—While bound up St. Clair River, the steamer *Canisteo* collided with the steamer *Wawatan* and was damaged to the extent of $1,200.

November 21.—Complaint having been made that Edward N. Stevens, chief engineer, was intoxicated while on duty, the case was investigated and his license revoked.

November 24.—While bound up St. Clair River, abreast of Port Huron, the steamer *Saginaw* caught fire and was damaged to the extent of $25,000.

November 26.—While bound up St. Clair River, the steamer *L. C. Smith* collided with the Canadian steamer *Silma*, sustaining damage estimated at $5,000.

November 28.—While bound up Lake Huron, in a heavy snowstorm and gale, the steamer *Charles M. Warner* stranded on Nine-mile Point, sustaining damage estimated at $20,000.

November 28.—The steamer *City of Holland* parted her lines while at the dock at Rogers City, Mich., and was blown ashore, sustaining damage estimated at $2,500.

November 29.—The steamer *Ferdinand Schlessinger* stranded on False Presque Isle in a snowstorm, sustaining damage estimated at $5,000.

December 5.—While bound down St. Clair River, the steamer *James B. Colgate* collided with the schooner *Duval*, sustaining damage estimated at $500.

NINTH SUPERVISING DISTRICT.

LOCAL DISTRICT OF CLEVELAND, OHIO.

May 3.—Fish tug *Rocket*, 36 gross tons, while leaving Lorain Harbor, struck a sunken crib that was being used by contractors for public work, causing the tug to sink. The tug was raised. Estimated damage, $1,000. No person injured.

May 12.—While steamer *H. B. Hawgood*, 4,655 gross tons, was on Lake Erie, 50 miles above Long Point, Capt. T. C. Ellis, of said steamer, accidentally fell overboard and was drowned. The steamer *H. B. Hawgood* traversed the course for 55 minutes, but the body could not be seen, which was picked up later by the steamer *Lizzie Madden*. The first mate took charge of the steamer and brought her to her port of destination, viz, Buffalo, N. Y.

September 7.—Steamer *Livingston*, 2,134 gross tons, while passing down the Cuyahoga River, Main street bridge having been opened to let her pass, and as the *Livingston* was passing through, the bridge was also being closed, and the end of the bridge struck the steamer aft, knocking down her stack, and damaging some of her steam pipes. One of the firemen was scalded.

October 13.—While steamer *Robert Fulton*, 4,219 gross tons, was picking up her consort on Lake Erie off Ashtabula, Ohio, in a heavy sea, her anchor chain parted; she then swung around against her consort, barge *Krupp*, breaking a hole in the steamer's side. The steamer came to Cleveland for repairs. Estimated damage to steamer *Robert Fulton*, $2,000. Estimated damage to barge *Krupp*, $1,000.

CASUALTIES, VIOLATIONS OF LAW, AND INVESTIGATIONS, YEAR ENDED DECEMBER 31, 1905—NINTH SUPERVISING DISTRICT—CLEVELAND, OHIO—Continued.

October 17.—It having come to our knowledge that Henry L. Mitchell, chief engineer of steamer *Geo. H. Russel* was carrying more steam pressure on the boilers of said steamer than allowed by her certificate of inspection, we traveled to Fairport, Ohio, and there made a complete examination and test of those boilers, and found that said Henry L. Mitchell, the chief engineer of the steamer *Geo. H. Russel* was carrying more steam pressure than allowed by the certificate of inspection. For thus violating the law we suspended the chief engineer license of Henry L. Mitchell for 5 months. Before leaving the steamer we set the safety valves for the pressure allowed by the certificate of inspection. Have also reported the matter to the U. S. district attorney.

October 20.—Steamer *Sarah E. Sheldon*, 517 gross tons, while on Lake Erie, about 6 miles east of Lorain, Ohio, a heavy sea running, sprung a leak, which gained rapidly, so that her pumps could not keep her free; she was run on the beach to keep her from sinking, being distant therefrom about 600 feet. While making for the shore a lifeboat was being lowered, into which 2 wheelsmen had got. They were wearing life preservers. The boat capsized, throwing the 2 men into the water, which rapidly washed them out beyond reach and they were drowned. The balance of the crew were taken to Lorain, Ohio, by 2 tugs that had come to their assistance. Meanwhile the wind had developed into a gale, which had pounded the steamer *Sarah E. Sheldon* so badly that she is a total loss.

October 20.—Steamer *Wisconsin*, 4,858 gross tons, while leaving Lorain Harbor, and when just outside the piers, encountered a heavy wind; was driven against the breakwater, damaging several plates and frames. She returned to Lorain, and went into dry dock for repairs. Estimated damage, $4,000.

LOCAL DISTRICT OF BUFFALO, N. Y.

April 8.—While bucking ice on Lake Erie, about 6 miles from Buffalo breakwater, steamer *Martin Mullen* struck stern of steamer *Sonora*, damaging latter vessel to the extent of $1,000.

April 10.—When steamer *Hurlbut W. Smith* was abreast of Long Point, Lake Erie, en route from Buffalo to Chicago, the weather being foggy at the time, she encountered a heavy field of ice, damaging plates and frames to the amount of $1,000. The steamer was running under check.

April 10.—When steamer *William Nottingham* was about 45 miles from Buffalo, on Lake Erie, running half speed, the weather being very foggy, the steamer ran into a field of ice, which stove in some plates and bent some frames, doing damage to the amount of $1,000.

April 10.—When steamer *B. Lyman Smith* was about 45 miles from Buffalo, on Lake Erie, running at a slow speed on account of fog, she encountered a field of very hard ice, damaging bow plates by corrugation and bending some of the light frames. Damage estimated at $1,000.

April 27.—Steamer *Appomattox*, en route from Escanaba to Buffalo, when abreast of Wind Mill Point, Lake Erie, struck a rocky ledge, and part of the cargo had to be lightered in order to release the vessel. The steamer was running slowly at the time, there being a fog and heavy ice. Damage, $4,000.

May 17.—While steamer *Niagara* was in the Niagara River opposite Buffalo, en route from Duluth to Tonawanda, she struck some obstruction, causing a leak and doing damage estimated at $3,500.

May 25.—While steamer *Alcona* was in the Niagara River at Tonawanda she struck an obstruction in the bottom of the river, breaking shoe, stern post, and wheel. The vessel managed to get to her dock, where she sunk. Damage, $3,000.

June 17.—While steamer *P. J. Ralph* was en route to Niagara Falls she struck an obstruction in the Niagara River near Navy Island, damaging hull to the amount of $1,500.

August 15.—While steamer *Idlewild* was en route from Buffalo to Crystal Beach the sleeve coupling on rudder post broke, rendering rudder useless. Other steamers attempted to get lines to the *Idlewild*, and in so doing one came in contact with her, damaging plates somewhat. A portion of the smokestack was lost, occasioned by the steamer rolling in the heavy sea while she was being towed back to Buffalo. Damage, $1,500.

August 24.—While steamer *W. J. Warwick* was coaling up at the Buffalo Fuel Company's dock, Blackwell Canal, Buffalo Harbor, too much coal was dumped on one side and the tug capsized, drowning the engineer, Wm. Bodamor.

September 12.—While steamer *J. T. Hutchinson* was lying at the Eastern Elevator, Charles Merz, a fireman, fell overboard and was drowned.

CASUALTIES, VIOLATIONS OF LAW, AND INVESTIGATIONS, YEAR ENDED DECEMBER 31, 1905—NINTH SUPERVISING DISTRICT—BUFFALO, N. Y.—Continued.

September 21.—While steamer *L. L. Barth* was making a landing at the Government breakwater, she struck her stem, opening a scarf, and necessitating going into dry dock for repairs. Damage, $250.

October 9.—While steamer *J. F. Eddy* was at the Anchor Line dock, in Buffalo Creek, Herman Davies, a wheelman, fell into the hold of the vessel and was instantly killed.

October 20.—Steamer *Western States* was caught in the severe storm that prevailed on Lake Erie, and being unable to make Buffalo Harbor with safety, was obliged to run back under Long Point for shelter. Damage caused by the heavy seas to staterooms, bulwarks, etc., $8,000.

October 20.—Steamer *Siberia* was on Lake Erie about 30 miles west of Long Point, en route to Buffalo. While the steamer was laboring in the heavy seas the machinery became disabled. Repairs were made and steamer *H. S. Wilkinson* stayed by until the *Siberia* got around Long Point. Water continued to gain in the hold and steamer *J. H. Wade* shoved the *Siberia* toward the shore, where she sunk in 22 feet of water. Before she could be refloated another gale sprung up and she went to pieces. Loss of vessel, $45,000.

October 23.—Steamer *Huron* was coming up Buffalo Creek and when passing Commercial slip the tug *Hudson* came out and attempted to pass between the *Huron* and steamer *Ramapo*, which was lying at dock. The tug was caught between the two steamers and sunk, and fireman Thomas Smith drowned. Case investigated October 24 to 28; decision, November 2, suspending license of Simon Staley, master of the tug *Hudson*, for a period of 6 months, for a violation of the pilot rules.

November 15.—Towing steamers *Robert H. Hebard* and *Puritan* collided in Buffalo Harbor. Case investigated November 20, and license of David Hazen, pilot of steamer *Puritan*, suspended for 6 months for violation of the pilot rules.

November 16.—Complaint was made against steamer *Lizzie Madden* for being navigated from Duluth to Tonawanda with a fireman acting as second engineer. Matter investigated November 27 and license of Wm. J. Lynn, master, suspended for 15 days. Case also referred to the U. S. district attorney and collector of customs for the imposition of penalties incurred.

December 10.—Fire broke out on steamer *John Mahar*, which was moored to a dock in Black Rock Harbor, Buffalo, destroying engine room and upper works. Origin of fire unknown; damage, $500.

LOCAL DISTRICT OF OSWEGO, N. Y.

June 18.—Steamer *Samuel Marshall*, bound down Lake Ontario, stranded on the Main Duck Islands during a dense fog. Was lightered and pulled off. Damage to vessel estimated at $500.

August 10.—As steamer *Lookout* was coming out of a bay between Point Lookout and Newport, on Irondequoit Bay, a skiff, with 4 occupants, crossing her bow was not seen until too late to avoid a collision. The skiff was sunk and 1 person (Fred McCormick) drowned.

August 30.—Steamer *Calumet*, when about 150 yards westward of Duck Island, river St. Lawrence, and running at reduced speed, the propeller struck on point of reef. Damage estimated at $300.

September 12.—Steamer *Nicaragua*, bound west in Soulonge Canal, and when about half a mile from the Canada Atlantic Railroad bridge, saw a green light displayed, indicating that the bridge was open. Steamer approached slowly, after blowing three whistles. When within 300 or 400 feet Captain Owens noticed that the bridge was closed. Reversed full speed, but struck bridge lightly. No damage to vessel.

September 20.—Steamer *Sophia*, of Alexandria Bay, N. Y., while lying at the dock at Rockport, Ontario, was totally destroyed by fire. Origin of fire unknown, the crew being at supper on shore at the time. Reported value of vessel, $7,000.

LOCAL DISTRICT OF TOLEDO, OHIO.

March 24.—On November 26, last, we reported to your office on form 2161 that, November 19, 1904, steamer *Philip Minch* was destroyed by fire when on Lake Erie near Marblehead Point, which, however, resulted in no loss of life. We have since concluded the investigation of this case, and as a result thereof have, on the 24th day of March, suspended the license of Bernard A. Benson, master and pilot, and Myron W. Sweet, chief engineer, for violation of that part of section 4450, Revised Statutes, relating to negligence, in that said licensed officers who were in charge of said steamer at time of fire did not stand by the steamer, and made no apparent effort to extinguish

CASUALTIES, VIOLATIONS OF LAW, AND INVESTIGATIONS, YEAR ENDED DECEMBER 31, 1905—NINTH SUPERVISING DISTRICT—TOLEDO, OHIO—Continued.

the flames. Said suspension covers a period of 6 months, commencing March 24 and ending September 24, 1905.

May 6.—Sand-dredge steamer *Commerce*, of Toledo, Ohio, 112 gross tons, while lying at anchor on Maumee River, was collided with by the sand-dredge steamer *L. G. Powell*, of Toledo, Ohio. Estimated damage to steamer *Commerce*, $300; to steamer *L. G. Powell*, $100. No lives lost. There was a strong current running at the time of collision, and, in our opinion, the master of steamer *L. G. Powell* lost control of his steamer.

May 19.—Steamer *Lily*, 104 gross tons, while lying at the Hocking Valley dock, Toledo, Ohio, caught fire from some unknown cause. Loss, $5,000. No lives lost.

June 7.—Fishing steamer *Grace M*, 12 gross tons, when about 6 miles east of Middle Island, Lake Erie, was collided with by the Canadian government steamer *Vigilant*, resulting in the sinking and total loss of the steamer *Grace M* and the drowning of 2 of her crew.

July 15.—Steamer *James P. Donaldson*, 521 gross tons, while lying at dock, Midland, Ontario, caught fire and was damaged to the extent of about $500. Origin of fire unknown. No loss of life reported.

July 18.—Towing steamer *Sheboygan*, of Buffalo, 63 gross tons, while lying at dock on Maumee River, was damaged by fire to the extent of $400. Origin of fire unknown. No lives lost.

August 15.—Steamer *State of New York*, 807 gross tons, while en route from Cleveland to Toledo, Ohio, and when 10 miles east of Middle Island, Lake Erie, the starboard shaft broke. The anchor was let go and temporary repairs made. The steamer then proceeded to Detroit, Mich., where permanent repairs are now being made. Estimated damage, $10,000.

September 16.—While the steamer *Louise*, 83 gross tons, was near Middle Island, Lake Erie, her intermediate shaft broke. The steamer was towed to Toledo, Ohio, for repairs. No person injured; estimated damage, $100.

November 3.—Steamer *Pluto*, of Toledo, Ohio, 4 gross tons, while at Edgewater, Ohio, was damaged by fire to the extent of $350. No lives lost. Origin of fire unknown.

November 23.—Steamer *City of Rome*, 1,908 gross tons, stranded on a shoal near Middle Island, Lake Erie, owing to a smoky haze which existed at the time, the distance thereby being miscalculated. The steamer was released and towed to Cleveland for repairs. No lives lost.

November 28.—Steamer *Sheldon Bros.*, of Cleveland, Ohio, 13 gross tons, was navigated in the vicinity of Vermilion Ohio, without having her certificate of inspection on board. The case was reported to the district attorney and collector of customs.

LOCAL DISTRICT OF BURLINGTON, VT.

June 30.—Steamer *Mariquita*, returning from Plattsburg, N. Y., to Burlington, with 22 passengers, grounded on hogback reef. Passengers were taken ashore in small boats without accident. Steamer was pulled off the next morning; no damage done to vessel.

July 5.—Steamer *Liberty*, while lying at her dock, St. Albans Bay, Vt., caught fire and was totally destroyed. No loss of life; damage to steamer, $3,000.

TENTH SUPERVISING DISTRICT.

LOCAL DISTRICT OF NEW ORLEANS, LA.

January 22.—About 9 a. m. there occurred a collision between the tug *R. C. Veit* and the transfer ferry *Gouldsboro* in the harbor of New Orleans, in which the *Veit* was injured to the extent of about $500. The *Gouldsboro* was uninjured. No lives lost.

February 6.—About 8 p. m., while attempting to pass the traffic bridge at Monroe, La., the stage and boom of the steamer *Frank B. Hayne* struck the bridge. S. E. Swayze was hurt by being struck with a piece of timber, and afterwards died. Pilot rang the backing bell, but the boat could not be checked in time to prevent the accident. Boat injured to the extent of about $400.

February 15.—About 7 p. m., in the Mississippi River, about 26 miles below New Orleans, steamer *William Cliff* was coming upstream when she sighted gasoline vessel *Empire* about 800 yards distant and sounded one blast of the whistle. Instead of keeping proper position, the *Empire* swung her bow towards the *William Cliff*. The

CASUALTIES, VIOLATIONS OF LAW, AND INVESTIGATIONS, YEAR ENDED DECEMBER 31, 1905—TENTH SUPERVISING DISTRICT—NEW ORLEANS, LA.—Continued.

William Cliff then blew the danger signal to warn the *Empire*, which vessel continued on her course, striking the *William Cliff* a glancing blow. The *Empire* then made for the right bank of the river. There was an inexperienced man at the wheel of the *Empire*, and when the master of the *Empire*, Michael Lorko, heard the danger signal blown by the *William Cliff* he got up from eating supper, ran on deck and was thrown overboard by the shock of the impact when the *Empire* struck the *William Cliff*, and was drowned.

March 7.—While moored at landing in Bayou Courant, La., gasoline motor vessel *Empire* was burned with exception of hull. Cause of fire unknown. No lives lost. Loss reported to be $3,500.

March 12.—While steamer *Natchez* was backing out from Grand Bay landing, about 8.30 p. m., Jacob Blinn, white deck passenger, fell overboard and was drowned. Was drunk when he came on board, and drunk when he fell overboard. Was repeatedly warned to keep in deck room, but refused. Boat was lowered, but efforts at rescue were fruitless.

April 7.—About 3.20 p. m. while taking on cargo for Habana, Cuba, steamship *Louisiana* listed to starboard (toward wharf) until ports were under water, when she filled and sunk rapidly. Cause of accident not ascertained with certainty. Matthew Solbach, a machinist helper, who was working on the vessel at the time was missing, supposed to be drowned. Estimated loss, $300,000.

April 10.—About 3 p. m. steamer *J. E. Trudeau* backed out into the river preparatory to leaving for trip up the river; when thru backing, and started up the river, she was struck by a strong wind, and blown against mast of sunken steamship *Louisiana* and considerably damaged. Amount of damage unknown. No lives lost.

June 2.—About 10.15 p. m. steamer *H. M. Carter* collided with bridge just below Alexandria, La., and sunk. No lives lost, and amount of damage unknown.

June 12.—About 3 p. m. as steamer *Roberta* was descending the river near Brunswick landing, Ed. Leslie, negro roustabout, who had been sleeping on some cotton on the guards, either became frightened in his sleep and jumped in the river or rolled in the river and was drowned. Boat was stopt and search made, but the body was not recovered.

June 22.—About 2 p. m. during a cloudburst in Lake Verret, steamer *Hustler* was overturned by the wind 2½ miles from shore in 11 feet of water. No lives lost. Loss reported to be $5,000.

June 22.—Steamer *Archon* sunk off Plum Island Point, just outside of Atchafalaya River.. Property loss estimated at $3,000 to $4,000.

July 8.—About 12.50 p. m. tug *Ella Andrews* had been towing steamship *Vera* to Stuyvesant docks; when about the middle of docks, being on the starboard side, the tug loosed her lines and it was discovered that the tug was riding one of the laps of the ship's plating, so much that she listed hard to starboard and began taking water. All the crew jumped on the ship, except Chief Engineer William Gould, who jumped overboard and was drowned. Skiff put out from the shore, but all efforts at rescue were fruitless. Altho it seemed she would capsize, she righted herself in a few minutes.

July 21.—While en route down the Mississippi River, opposite Jackson street, tug *Independent* lost her rudder and shoe, caused by wheel striking the shoe. Damage about $700.

July 22.—At 12.30 a. m., while lying at J. W. Thompson's plant with a barge on port side of steamer *John F. May*, Sidney Sanford, deck hand on said steamer, fell off the port bow of the steamer and was drowned. The body was not recovered.

August 3.—Steamer *Peruna* was going down Bayou Lafourche, about 4 miles below Lockport, when Maurice Lefort, cabin boy, while playing with deck hand, fell overboard from lower deck and was drowned. Efforts at rescue were futile. Body recovered 3 hours after the accident by the boat's crew.

August 7.—About 6 p. m., while about 44 miles above New Orleans, the shaft of the steamer *St. James* broke. Steamer was towed to New Orleans by the tug *Ella Andrews*. No lives lost. Estimated damage, $1,200.

August 9.—Steamer *Export*, which was inspected on April 15 and found short in equipment and whose certificate of inspection was withheld, was reported to the collector of customs, Vicksburg, Miss., for running under expired certificate of inspection, in violation of section 4400, Title LII, Revised Statutes.

August 22.—Motor vessel *Grace* was reported on this date to collector of customs, New Orleans, La., for navigating without licensed engineer.

August 25.—On information received at this office, the steamer *Iris* was reported to the collector of customs, New Orleans, as having had entirely new set of tubes installed

CASUALTIES, VIOLATIONS OF LAW, AND INVESTIGATIONS, YEAR ENDED DECEMBER 31, 1905—TENTH SUPERVISING DISTRICT—NEW ORLEANS, LA.—Continued.

at Key West, Fla., no notice, coupon, or affidavit having been filed with the local inspectors.

August 26.—While underway, 10 miles below Barbre's landing, Bob Swain, one of the owners of steamer *Wade*, fell overboard and was drowned. Body was found next day. No one saw him fall and it was not known until too late to save him.

August 30.—On information had by this office that the steamer *Guy Hunter*, which was inspected on August 10 and whose certificate of inspection was withheld for completion of equipment and repairs, had been navigating since that date, altho certificate had not been issued, in violation of section 4400, Revised Statutes, we reported this case to the collector of customs, New Orleans.

September 10.—While steamer *Alice* was moored to her landing at Algiers, La., a fire started in the engine room and she burned to the main deck. Loss about $7,000.

September 15.—As steamer *Albert Baldwin* was going into the Gretna wharf, John Fletcher, handy man on said steamer, deliberately jumped overboard and was drowned before assistance could be rendered.

September 15.—The license of George W. Knight, master of steamer *T. K. Green*, was this day revoked, under section 4439, Revised Statutes, for navigating a steam vessel without a certificate of inspection.

September 15.—The steamer *T. K. Green* was this day reported to the U. S. attorney for the eastern district of Louisiana, for violation of section 4453 of the Revised Statutes, navigating without a certificate of inspection.

September 15.—License of H. D. Wagnon, master of steamer *Wm. J. Kelly* was this day suspended for 15 days, for wilful violation of Title LII, Revised Statutes, navigating steamer without equipment on board required by certificate of inspection (section 4439, Revised Statutes).

September 30.—Frank Zeh, one of the deck hands of the tug *W. M. Wood*, was supposed to have drowned, as tug was towing the schooner *Nimbros* from the city to the Gulf. Search for him proved futile. He disappeared during the night.

October 13.—About 1.25 p. m. steamer *Elk* was backing from wharf at Vicksburg under slow bell to prevent shaking up the dock in which was the tug *Vanguard*. When opposite the *Vanguard*, the *Elk* struck some hidden obstruction on the west side of the canal and sunk in 4 minutes, water covering the deck until the pilot house touched the water, part of the cargo being dumped off. Succeeded in getting a line ashore and hauled the boat to the east shore. Starboard knuckle is on bank; stern in 30 feet of water. Six of crew jumped overboard, and 4 drowned. Property loss unknown.

October 14.—At 3.20 p. m. steerage passenger, Thomas Smith, fell overboard from steamship *Chalmette* and was drowned. Ship was stopt and boat lowered and cruised about for an hour, but no trace of the man was found.

October 16.—About 1.45 on the night of the 16th, while moored at landing of Capital City Oil Mill, Baton Rouge, La., without steam, boat filled and sunk, engineer and watchman, sleeping on board, barely escaping with their lives. Cause of filling and sinking unknown. No lives lost. Loss, $7,500.

October 18.—Steamer *Laura* was reported to the collector of customs, Morgan City, for running on expired certificate of inspection. Inspectors could not make inspection at proper time on account of quarantine restrictions.

October 19.—Steamer *Istrouma* was reported to the collector of customs, New Orleans, La., for running on expired certificate of inspection. Inspectors could not make inspection when due on account of quarantine restrictions.

October 19.—At 6.30 p. m., 42 miles below New Orleans, while making a landing, steamer *Louise* commenced taking water freely. On investigation it was found there was a large hole amidships; pumps were set to work, but the water gained, and the crew commenced discharging cargo at once. Distress signal was blown to attract attention of the tug *R. C. Veit*, which was at that time passing, but before the tug got alongside and got her pumps into the *Louise* she careened to port and filled and sunk, parting her mooring and sinking out of sight. No lives lost. Steamer a total loss, amounting to $20,000, with $6,500 insurance. Cargo loss, $3,422.

October 25.—Steamer *J. P. Schuh* operated between August 4 and October 25 under expired certificate of inspection, inspectors not being able to inspect at proper time on account of quarantine restrictions. Steamer reported to collector of customs, New Orleans.

October 26.—At Sixty Mile Point, 60 miles below New Orleans, La., about 11 p. m., as a result of violation of Rules I and III by steamer *Esparta*, steamers *Magnolia*, light-house tender, and *Esparta*, British steamship, collided, resulting in a damage to the *Magnolia* of about $20,000.

CASUALTIES, VIOLATIONS OF LAW, AND INVESTIGATIONS, YEAR ENDED DECEMBER 31, 1905—TENTH SUPERVISING DISTRICT—NEW ORLEANS, LA.—Continued.

October 27.—The steamer *Ed. Dilley* was this day reported to collector of customs, New Orleans, La., for the following reason: Steamer was notified to be at Logtown for inspection on October 27, but on arrival inspectors learned that, notwithstanding this notice, vessel left the day before, persisting in running on expired certificate of inspection when ordered by inspectors to remain at Logtown.

October 27.—Steamer *Edgar* reported to the collector of customs for operating under expired certificate of inspection since August 4, 1905, inspectors being unable to inspect at the proper time on account of quarantine restrictions.

November 2.—Steamer *Baton Rouge Belle* was burned to extent of $700. No one injured. Origin of fire unknown, as no one was on the steamer at the time.

November 11.—Steamers *Dorothy, Cecile, Thelma, Sunbeam, Sparrow, Robbie, H. W. Crady, Hornet*, and *Laura Sutcliff* reported to collectors of customs for operating under expired certificates of inspection, inspectors being unable to inspect at proper time on account of quarantine restrictions.

November 14.—This office reported to collector of customs New Orleans, La., a steamer, name unknown, marked on side *U. S. M. C.*, navigating Ouachita River and tributaries without license, enrollment, inspection, or measurement, in violation of the navigation laws, and in violation of Title LII, Revised Statutes, from sections 4439 to 4500, inclusive; also section 4438, operating without licensed officers.

November 15.—Charges against John Gomellon, pilot of steamer *Frank B. Hayne*, charging him with drunkenness on watch, February 5, 1905, which resulted in collision of said steamer with the traffic bridge at Monroe, La., and injuring S. E. Swayze, so that he died, were filed on August 5, by M. D. and L. H. Swayze, jr. On investigation of said charges Gomellon was found not guilty as charged.

November 20.—This office reported steamer *Millie W.* to collector of customs at Morgan City, La., for operating under expired certificate of inspection. Inspectors were prevented from making inspection at the proper time on account of quarantine restrictions.

November 23.—Investigaton of charges filed by J. L. Ross, pilot of steamer *Columbia*, against steamer *St. James*, charging violation of pilot rules, almost causing collision between the two vessels on evening of October 30, resulted in the licenses of pilots E. R. Daigre, of the *St. James*, and Ross, of the *Columbia*, being suspended for a period of 10 days each.

November 25.—As a result of the investigation held of the collision which occurred on October 26 between steamers *Magnolia* and *Esparta* at Roosevelts Point, 60 miles below New Orleans, it was found that said collision was due to violation of inland pilot Rules I and III by the pilot of steamer *Esparta*. This steamer being a British steamer, under Department decisions No. 19115, March 18, 1898, and No. 6665, November 29, 1884, the pilot of the steamer *Esparta* was not acting under the authority of his license, and the board of local inspectors has no authority to inflict any penalty.

November 25.—While steamer *America* was en route Vicksburg to New Orleans, La., just below Bruinsburg, Miss., Andy Rubmer, roustabout, shipped at Natchez, Miss., fell overboard and was drowned. The alarm was given, life float thrown overboard, boat lowered and proceeded astern, but no trace was found of the man.

November 30.—Steamer *Natalbany* was notified to be at Springfield, La., on November 24, 1905, for inspection. When inspectors proceeded to Ponchatoula, en route to Springfield, they were informed that the steamer had left Springfield for New Orleans. On arrival at New Orleans the steamer failed to notify inspectors, but returned to Springfield without being inspected, at which place she was subsequently inspected, owners paying expenses of inspection trip. Case was reported to collector of customs, and licenses of master and engineer suspended for 30 days each.

December 8.—While gasoline motor vessel *Robert Bruce* was towing cane on Bayou Lafourche 6 or 7 miles below Lockport, she took fire from gasoline stove in the kitchen and was destroyed. Machinery may possibly be saved.

LOCAL DISTRICT OF APALACHICOLA, FLA.

January 27.—While the steamer *Crescent City* was making the wharf at East Point, Fla., Mathew Grand (colored), deck hand, got his foot in the line and cavil and cut off.

July 5.—Steamer *Forest*, being navigated on Flint River without a licensed engineer from Newton to Albany, Ga., in violation of section 4438, Revised Statutes, was reported to collector of customs, Apalachicola, Fla. Fine and penalty enforced of $100.

July 10.—The steamer *Little Belle* was reported being navigated without a licensed pilot and engineer on the Chipola River and Dead Lakes, Fla., on July 1 and 2, 1905,

CASUALTIES, VIOLATIONS OF LAW, AND INVESTIGATIONS, YEAR ENDED DECEMBER 31, 1905—TENTH SUPERVISING DISTRICT—APALACHICOLA, FLA.—Continued.

in violation of section 4438, Revised Statutes. Was reported to the collector of customs and United States district attorney. Steamer was fined and penalty enforced.

August 11.—Steamer *Sego*, while lying at the wharf at Carrabelle, Fla., at 4.45 a. m., sunk from a defective pipe connection with water tanks in the hold. Steamer has been raised. Amount of damage to steamer, $500.

August 28.—At 3 p. m., while the steamer *W. C. Bradley* was descending and steamer *Queen City* ascending, met at Cold Shades bend on the Apalachicola River and collided. Steamer *Queen City* starboard bow damaged $200. No damage to steamer *W. C. Bradley.*

September 21.—At 1 a. m. steamer *Three States*, while lying at Millport landing on the Chattahoochee River, Sidney Culver (colored), deck hand, accidentally fell overboard, striking his head on guards, and was drowned. Body was recovered in about ten minutes, but failed to resuscitate him.

September 30.—While the steamer *Miama* was on trip from Habana, Cuba, to Key West, Fla., broke her port shaft. Steamer proceeded on her trip with one propeller.

November 13.—Steamer *Ocean Gem*, while lying at the wharf at Apalachicola, Fla., accidently caught fire and burned the pilot house and forward part of cabin. Damage, $400.

November 20.—While the steamer *Three States* was under way on the Chattahoochee River in Slick Bluff shoals, Milton Seale (colored), deck hand, accidentally fell overboard and was drowned.

LOCAL DISTRICT OF GALVESTON, TEX.

April 1.—Steamship *Lampasas*, bound to New York from Galveston, discovered fire in main hold and returned to Galveston April 2, discharged cargo, and by survey found 60 bales of cotton more or less burned. Estimated damage, $3,500.

June 3.—Steamship *Manteo*, while on a voyage from Brazos Santiago to Galveston, broke her tail shaft and was towed into port. Amount of damage unknown.

August 17.—The steamer *Lawrence* was reported to the collector of customs and the U. S. attorney of this district for navigating on an expired certificate of inspection.

August 17.—The steamer *Lawrence* was reported to the collector of customs of this district for receiving passengers on board and navigating without having a certified copy of certificate of inspection on board.

October 28.—The steamers *Rosamond, Hazel, Ontario, Katherine* were reported to the collector of customs at Morgan City for violation of Title LII, Revised Statutes, navigating with an expired certificate of inspection. Owing to quarantine regulations these vessels could not be inspected at the time applications were made.

November 22.—From some unknown cause the steamer *Agnes T. Parks* took fire while lying at Lowry, La., and burned to the water's edge. No lives lost. Loss about $1,200.

December 2.—The tug *Margaret* saw the signal for open drawbridge in the grade-raising canal at Galveston, Tex. The bridge being closed the tug in backing away fouled the dredge *Leviathan*, which was towing astern, thereby damaging the tug to the extent of $600. The collision was caused by the neglect of the drawbridge tender.

December 10.—The gasoline motor vessel *Zillah*, while lying at the pier at Port Boliver, was destroyed by fire at 11.40 a. m. Fire caused by the explosion of a lamp. Vessel valued at $6,000. No lives lost or persons injured.

LOCAL DISTRICT OF MOBILE, ALA.

January 16.—American schooner *Charles G. Rice*, G. C. McLaughlin, master, was reported by this office to the collector of customs, Pensacola, Fla., for a violation of section 4417, Revised Statutes. Application was made for the inspection of this boat January 4, 1905, 6 months after the date of expiration of her certificate of inspection, July 1, 1904, during which time she was regularly engaged in trade. (This $500 fine was mitigated by the Department to $100.)

January 16.—O. C. Gliddon, engineer of steamer *Eleanor*, reported that on night of January 8, 1905, while his vessel was proceeding down Mobile Bay bound for Bon Secour, Ala., with the schooner *Hilda S.* in tow, Capt. Thomas H. Benton, who was in command of his vessel, accidentally fell overboard and was drowned. The deceased was last seen on board of the tow, and the cause and time of the accident are not known.

January 16.—Steamship *Roanoke*, G. Hansen, master, was reported by this office to the collector of customs, Mobile, Ala, for a violation of section 4417, Revised Statutes.

CASUALTIES, VIOLATIONS OF LAW, AND INVESTIGATIONS, YEAR ENDED DECEMBER 31, 1905—TENTH SUPERVISING DISTRICT—MOBILE, ALA.—Continued.

This vessel exceeded her legal time by 7 days, having entered and left Tampa, Fla., after the expiration of her certificate of inspection. (This fine of $500 was remitted by the Department.)

February 13.—Steamship *Lee Kimball, Jr.*, J. W. McDowell, master, reported that on the night of February 12, 1905, while proceeding down Mobile Bay, bound for the dredge *Herndon*, Daniel Solien, a passenger, who was bound for said dredge, accidentally fell overboard and was drowned before assistance could reach him. The exact cause of the accident is not known.

February 18.—Steam packet *City of Mobile*, G. W. Quarels, master, reported that while proceeding up the Alabama River, Sebe McMillian, a deck hand, was caught robbing a case of brandy, and to avoid being arrested jumped overboard and attempted to swim ashore, but sunk before reaching there. Effort was made to reach him, but without avail.

March 11.—Gasoline steamer *J. F. Fink*, master unknown, owned by J. F. Fink, was reported by this office to the collector of customs, Mobile, Ala., for a violation of Rule VIII, pilot rules for the western rivers, and section 4413, Revised Statutes. On the day preceding our report we witnessed this vessel back out of a slip, both ends of which were occupied by steamers, making it necessary for a vessel to be well out into the stream before approaching vessels could be seen, without giving any warning whatever, thereby hazarding the lives of its passengers, who numbered about 15, mostly women. The operators of this particular class of vessel, almost without exception, completely ignore our laws, and if such practice is allowed to continue a serious loss of life will follow, hence our report.

March 24.—Steam packet *Ouachita*, W. H. Gray, master, reported that on the night of March 17, while nearing Bells Landing, Alabama River, Alfred Hamlin, an aged passenger, accidentally fell from the roof to the deck of that vessel and was killed. The deceased was seen to rise from his chair in a startled manner, no cause being apparent, and stagger to the edge of the roof and fall.

April 6 (reported April 8).—Steamship *Clarence*, M. Myers, master, was partially destroyed by fire at Stockton, Ala., on the night of April 6. Cause of same can not be accounted for. Damages, $600. No lives lost and no one injured.

April 26.—Steam packet *Dixie*, G. H. Gould, master, was deprived of its fireman, Hamp Cousby, by accidental drowning. The deceased was lying asleep on deck when he was seen to roll overboard. Every effort was made to rescue him, but without success.

April 26.—Steam packet *Dixie*, G. H. Gould, master, was deprived of its fireman, John Espy, by accidental drowning on night of April 5. The deceased was off watch at the time, and it is supposed that he was intoxicated and fell overboard.

May 23.—Mr. Arthur Kimball, owner of steamship *Zoe*, reported Captain Edward Dorgan for refusing to serve in his official capacity on April 14. The alleged cause being on account of personal dislike the accused harbored against Mr. J. M. Walsh, one of the owners of the vessel. The case was investigated by us May 26, and dismissed for lack of evidence against the accused.

May 31.—Steamship *Kimball*, C. S. Tompkins, master, was partially destroyed by fire at Stockton, Ala., on night of May 24. The steamer was laid up for the night, no one being on board at the time but the watchman, and the barge to which she was moored caught fire from some unknown cause, setting fire to the steamer, damaging it to the amount of $1,200. No lives lost and no one injured. (This vessel has since been repaired.)

July 10.—Steam packet *New Haven*, W. M. Eans, master. The certificate of inspection of this vessel was revoked for failure to supply certain equipment and make repairs ordered—violation of section 4453, Revised Statutes. Verbal and written notices were given the master of this vessel to cease navigating until these requirements had been complied with, but the vessel proceeded on her regular run, which act was duly reported to the collector of customs, Mobile, Ala. The certificate of inspection was returned to the vessel on July 18, the order for the repairs and equipment having been satisfactorily complied with.

August 25.—Steam packet *New Haven*, W. M. Eans, master. Captain Eans was reported by the ex-engineer of that vessel for a violation of section 4439, Revised Statutes—Inattention to duty—in allowing the second mate to direct the affairs of the boat. The case was investigated August 28, and dismissed for lack of evidence, as per our report of September 1.

CASUALTIES, VIOLATIONS OF LAW, AND INVESTIGATIONS, YEAR ENDED DECEMBER 31, 1905—TENTH SUPERVISING DISTRICT—MOBILE, ALA.—Continued.

August 25.—Steam packet *New Haven*, W. M. Eans, master, was reported by the ex-engineer of that vessel for carrying passengers without license. This case, together with several other charges filed against this vessel by the same complainant, were investigated on August 28, viz: Failure to have certificates of inspection exposed, section 4423, Revised Statutes; carrying passengers without license, section 4424; and failure to keep a list of passengers carried, section 4468, Revised Statutes, all of which were dismissed for lack of evidence, as per our report of September 1.

August 25.—Steam packet *Alabama*, E. G. La Follette, master. Jack Wilson, deck hand on this vessel, lost his life by accidental drowning. The accident happened on the Coosa River, August 19, and was caused by the deceased becoming frightened at the blowing out of a plug. Thinking something serious had happened, he jumped overboard. Steps were immediately taken for his rescue but he could not be located.

September 23.—Steamship *Gertrude*, Wm. C. Clark, master, collided with the U. S. quartermaster's steamer *General R. N. Bachelder*, while the latter was lying at her dock, Mobile River, September 17, at 3.45 a. m. Captain Clark's report shows that his vessel was descending the river, and when opposite the *Bachelder* several logs appeared ahead, and to avoid them the vessel was brought hard to starboard, causing the wheel ropes to become jammed. In his effort to port the vessel a wheel spoke broke, causing him to fall out of the wheel house. This prevented his giving the backing signal, except by cries, which were answered by the engineer, but not in time to prevent the collision. Damages not stated. No lives lost and no one injured. (This case was informally investigated by us, and we learned that the circumstances were the same as those stated by Captain Clark, making the collision unavoidable.)

November 18.—Steamship *Elma*, R. C. Avent, master, was reported by us to the collector of customs, Gulfport, Miss., for violating section 4427, Revised Statutes, viz, navigating on an expired certificate of inspection, from October 8 to November 14. This vessel was prevented from undergoing inspection by reason of quarantine.

November 18.—Steamship *Toiler*, J. G. Swain, master, was reported to the collector of customs, Gulfport, Miss., for navigating on expired certificate of inspection from September 10 to November 13; violation of section 4427, Revised Statutes. (Confined in the quarantined district.)

November 18.—Steamship *Pascagoula*, H. Colle, master, was reported to the collector of customs, Gulfport, Miss., for navigating on an expired certificate from August 1 to November 13; violation of section 4417, Revised Statutes. (Confined in the quarantined district.)

November 18.—Steamship *Evan Dantzler*, A. Bugge, master, was reported to the collector of customs, Gulfport, Miss., for navigating on an expired certificate from September 10 to November 13; violation of section 4417, Revised Statutes. (Confined in the quarantined district.)

November 18.—Steamship *Amelia*, H. Colle, master, was reported to the collector of customs, Gulfport, Miss., for navigating on expired certificate from October 8 to November 14; violation of section 4417, Revised Statutes. (Confined in the quarantined district.)

November 18.—Gasoline steamer *Harry Cage*, J. Lipscomb, master, was reported to the collector of customs, Gulfport, Miss., for navigating on an expired certificate from November 5 to November 15; violation of section 4427, Revised Statutes. (Confined in the quarantined district.)

November 18.—Gasoline steamer *Lilly L.*, H. A. McLeod, master, was reported to the collector of customs, Gulfport, Miss., for navigating on an expired certificate from November 5 to November 15; violation of section 4427, Revised Statutes. (Confined in the quarantined district.)

November 18.—Steamship *Julius Elbert*, P. Harvey, master, was reported to the collector of customs, Gulfport, Miss., for navigating on an expired certificate from September 17 to November 15; violation of section 4427, Revised Statutes. (Confined in the quarantined district.

November 18.—Gasoline steamer *Anna Long*, F. Enlenterius, master, was reported to the collector of customs, Gulfport, Miss., for navigating on an expired certificate from November 5 to November 15; violation of section 4427, Revised Statutes. (Confined in the quarantined district.)

November 18.—Gasoline steamer *Eureka*, Lopez & Dugate, owners, no master, was reported to the collector of customs, Gulfport, Miss., for navigating on an expired certificate from August 23 to November 16; violation of section 4427, Revised Statutes. (Confined in the quarantined district.)

CASUALTIES, VIOLATIONS OF LAW, AND INVESTIGATIONS, YEAR ENDED DECEMBER 31, 1905—TENTH SUPERVISING DISTRICT—MOBILE, ALA.—Continued.

November 20.—Steam packet *Vienna*, S. A. Cosper, master, Abe Jackson, a deck hand on this steamer, was accidentally drowned by the overturning of a working boat. The accident happened on the Bigbee River, while the deceased was running a tow line.

November 27.—Steamship *Isabel*, L. W. Hogan, master, collided with the gasoline launch *Scimitar*. Captain Hogan's report shows that his vessel was descending Mobile River, and when he had just about cleared a schooner which was anchored in the river, midstream, the launch suddenly appeared directly across his bow, having come from behind the moored schooner. The launch was lasht alongside of the steamer and carried to the wharf. No one injured. Damages to steamer about $50. No report has been made by the launch, and the extent of her damages is not known.

December 1.—Steamship *Celestine*, J. J. McKee, master, was reported to the collector of customs, Pensacola, Fla., for violating section 4427, Revised Statutes. The inspection of this vessel was commenced July 18 and completed November 27, during which time the vessel was regularly navigated without the required certificate of inspection. (The completion of this inspection was prevented by quarantine.)

December 1.—Steamship *Fidget*, W. M. Baker, master, was reported to the collector of customs, Pensacola, Fla., for violating section 4427, Revised Statutes. This vessel was navigated on an expired certificate of inspection from September 13 to November 27. (Confined in the quarantined district.)

December 8.—Steam packets *Pleasure Bay*, W. B. Curran, master, and *Jas. A. Carney*, F. A. Lumsden, master, collided at Daphne's landing, Mobile Bay. It appears that both these vessels tried to make the landing at the same time. The *Pleasure Bay* was slightly damaged, while the *Jas. A. Carney* escaped without any damages. No lives lost and no one injured. The case will be investigated as soon as practicable.

INSPECTIONS OF BOILERS OF UNITED STATES GOVERNMENT STEAMERS AND BUILDINGS.

In addition to the regular annual inspections, boilers on or for United States Government steamers and in United States Government buildings were inspected by officers of the Steamboat-Inspection Service during the year ended December 31, 1905, as follows:

Local inspection district, and name of steamer or building.	Port where inspected.	Date inspected.	Boilers inspected.
San Francisco, Cal.:			
Steamers—			
George M. Sternberg	Oakland, Cal	Jan. 21	1
Buford	San Francisco, Cal	Feb. 21	3
Buford No. 1	do	do	1
Dix	do	Mar. 13	3
Dix No. 1	do	do	1
Dix	do	Mar. 28	1
Light-ship No. 70	do	Apr. 20	3
Warren	do	May 4	3
Do	do	May 11	1
Sherman	do	July 22	4
Sherman No. 1	do	July 31	1
Sherman No. 2	do	do	1
Steam launch of steamer McArthur	Alameda, Cal	Sept. 1	1
Thomas	San Francisco, Cal	Sept. 5	4
Thomas Jr. No. 2	do	Sept. 30	1
Thomas Jr. No. 3	do	do	1
Logan	do	Nov. 4	4
Logan No. 2	do	do	1
Logan No. 3	do	do	1
Sheridan	do	Dec. 13	4
Buildings—			
Indian Industrial School	Phoenix, Ariz	Apr. 6 Apr. 7	3
Marine hospital	San Francisco, Cal	June 28	3
Total			46
Portland, Oreg.:			
Steamers—			
Geo. H. Mendell	Portland, Oreg	Jan. 26	1
Arago	do	Feb. 3	1
Manzanita	do	Feb. 25	1
Total			3

INSPECTIONS OF BOILERS OF UNITED STATES GOVERNMENT STEAMERS AND BUILDINGS—Continued.

Local inspection district, and name of steamer or building.	Port where inspected.	Date inspected.	Boilers inspected.
Seattle, Wash.:			
Steamers—			
Burnside	Tacoma, Wash	Apr. 19	2
Do	do	Apr. 26	1
Gedney	Seattle, Wash	Apr. 28	1
McArthur	do	May 2	1
Lieut. Elliott	Port Townsend, Wash	July 28	1
Lieut. Geo. M. Harris	Seattle, Wash	Sept. 8	1
Lieut. Elliott	do	Nov. 23	1
Patterson	do	Nov. 24	1
Do	do	Dec. 14	1
Total			10
New York, N. Y.:			
Steamers—			
Bache	Jersey City, N. J	Jan. 30	2
Ellis Island	Ellis Island, N. Y	May 10	2
Mistletoe	Tompkinsville, N. Y	Aug. 28	1
Canby	Brooklyn, N. Y	Sept. 12	1
Iris	Port Richmond, N. Y	Sept. 16	2
Havana	Hoboken, N. J	Dec. 21	5
Buildings—			
Appraisers' warehouse	New York, N. Y	May 15, May 17, May 19, May 25, June 13	4
Immigration station	Ellis Island, N. Y	May 23, July 6	8
Barge office	New York, N. Y	June 1	1
Subtreasury	do	do	1
Custom-house	do	June 6, June 8, June 13, June 20	4
Post-office	Brooklyn, N. Y	June 6, July 13	4
Court-house and post-office	New York, N. Y. (boilers examined at Bayonne, N. J.).	June 9, July 28, Aug. 26	2
Do	Newark, N. J	June 27, June 30	3
Military Academy	West Point, N. Y	July 10, July 12, July 14, July 17, Nov. 25	25
Marine hospital	Stapleton, N. Y	Aug. 4, Aug. 9	2
Total			67
Boston, Mass.:			
Steamers—			
Verbena	do	Jan. 23	1
Captain Reilly	do	Dec. 27	1
Buildings—		May 17	2
Post-office	Boston, Mass	May 24	2
Do	do	June 7	3
Do	do	Sept. 23	1
Marine hospital	Chelsea, Mass	Sept. 28	1
Do	do	Oct. 4	1
Do	do	do	1
Immigration station	Boston, Mass		
Total			13
Philadelphia, Pa.:			
Steamers—			
Immigrant	Wilmington, Del	Mar. 20	1
Lieutenant Ord	Camden, N. J	May 19	1
Robert H. Swartwout	do	do	1
General Timothy Pickering	Philadelphia, Pa	May 29	1
Lieutenant Lewis	Camden, N. J	June 6	1
Zizania	Philadelphia, Pa	June 16	2
Lieutenant Benchley	Camden, N. J	do	1
General R. L. Batchelder	Philadelphia, Pa	June 21	1
General Howe	Wilmington, Del	Aug. 9	1
Uncle Sam	Camden, N. J	Aug. 10	1

INSPECTIONS OF BOILERS OF UNITED STATES GOVERNMENT STEAMERS AND BUILDINGS—Continued.

Local inspection district, and name of steamer or building.	Port where inspected.	Date inspected.	Boilers inspected.
Philadelphia, Pa.—Continued.			
Buildings—			
Mint	Philadelphia, Pa	Mar. 14	4
Do	do	Aug. 16	4
Total			19
Albany, N. Y.: Building—Post-office	Albany, N. Y	June 26	3
Portland, Me.: Building—Court-house and post-office.	Rockland, Me	Aug. 29	1
Providence, R. I.:			
Steamer—Azalea	Fairhaven, Mass	Nov. 27	1
Buildings—			
Fort Wetherill	Fort Wetherill, R. I	Mar. 27	1
Post-office	Providence, R. I	July 17	2
Total			4
New Haven, Conn.:			
Buildings—			
Custom-house and post-office	New Haven, Conn	June 29	2
Do	Bridgeport, Conn	Sept. 23	2
Total			4
Norfolk, Va.:			
Steamers—			
Endeavor	Norfolk, Va	Jan. 4	1
Trent	Newbern, N. C	Mar. 29	1
General George Thom	Norfolk, Va	Mar. 30	1
Scuppernong	Harlow Creek, N. C	do	1
Roanoke	Norfolk, Va	May 16	1
Phillips	do	June 19	1
Total			6
Baltimore, Md.:			
Steamers—			
Gibbon	Washington, D. C	June 29	1
Explorer	Baltimore, Md	Dec. 15	2
Bache	do	Dec. 18	2
Endeavor	do	Dec. 19	2
Buildings—			
Marine hospital	do	{July 5 July 8}	3
Government Printing Office	Washington, D. C	Oct. 24	4
Total			14
Charleston, S. C.:			
Steamers—			
Ajax	Wilmington, N. C	Feb. 26	1
Cape Fear	do	do	1
Cynthia	do	do	1
General H. G. Wright	do	Feb. 27	1
Mercur	do	Mar. 8	1
Total			5
St. Louis, Mo.:			
Steamers—			
Lily	St. Louis, Mo	Mar. 27	2
Wright	do	May 23	4
Phoenix	Keokuk, Iowa	June 3	1
Lucia	do	do	1
David Tipton	do	July 19	1
Atalanta	Gasconade, Mo	July 31	1
Coal Bluff	Louisiana, Mo	Aug. 10	3
James B. McPherson	St. Louis, Mo	Aug. 15	1
Col. A. Mackenzie	do	Sept. 19	3
Roberts	Sioux City, Iowa	Aug. 22	1
Pile driver	do	do	1
Building—Custom-house	St. Louis, Mo. (heater)	Feb. 15	1
Total			20

INSPECTIONS OF BOILERS OF UNITED STATES GOVERNMENT STEAMERS AND BUILDINGS—Continued.

Local inspection district, and name of steamer or building.	Port where inspected.	Date inspected.	Boilers inspected.
Dubuque, Iowa:			
Steamers—			
Alert	Fountain City, Wis	June 13	1
Elsie	do	do	1
Hecla (dredge)	Sandusky, Ohio	June 18	3
Mac	Rock Island Rapids, Moline, Ill., and vicinity.	June 27	1
Ruth	do	do	2
Ajax (dredge)	do	do	1
Drill boat No. 6	do	do	1
Drill boat No. 103	do	do	1
Curlew	Dubuque, Iowa	July 10	1
Fury	Fountain City, Wis	Aug. 8	2
Ada	do	do	1
Emily	Clayton, Iowa	Sept. 1	1
Vulcan (dredge)	do	do	1
Geyser (dredge)	Guttenberg, Iowa	do	1
Louise	Dubuque, Iowa	Sept. 26	1
Total			19
Duluth, Minn:			
Steamers—			
Vidette	Duluth, Minn	Jan. 4	1
Do	do	Apr. 24	1
Do	do	Dec. 15	1
Building—Station, Bureau of Fisheries	do	Sept. 28	2
Total			5
Louisville, Ky.:			
Steamers—			
Green River (dredge)	Louisville, Ky	Apr. 24	1
Canal dredge No. 2	do	May 1	1
Derrick boat	do	do	1
Major Mackenzie	do	do	4
Canal dredge No. 1	do	do	1
Dredge Wabash	do	May 10	1
Gen. O. M. Poe	Frankfort, Ky	Aug. 14	3
Drill scow No. 1	Louisville, Ky	Aug. 30	1
Drill scow No. 2	do	do	1
Wave Rock	do	do	1
Col. G. L. Gillespie	do	do	2
Buildings—			
Canal machine shop	do	May 1	2
Marine hospital	do	May 16	2
Total			21
Nashville, Tenn.:			
Steamers—			
Wm. Preston Dixon	Bowling Green, Ky	Apr. 17	3
Emerald	do	do	1
Derrick boat No. 1	do	do	1
Derrick boat No. 2	do	do	1
Dredge boat No. 1	do	do	1
Colbert	Lock No. 6, Tennessee River	Nov. 4	2
Kingman	do	do	1
Total			10
Memphis, Tenn.: Steamer—John N. Macomb	Memphis, Tenn	Aug. 1	5
Cincinnati, Ohio:			
Steamers—			
Goldenrod	Cincinnati, Ohio	June 27	2
E. A. Woodruff	do	Dec. 11	6
Total			8
Pittsburg, Pa.:			
Steamers—			
Loma	Pittsburg, Pa	Aug. 26	1
Wenonah	do	do	1
Gen'l Theodore Schwan	do	Sept. 5	4
Buildings—			
Post-office	do	Apr. 19	3
Do	do	May 5	3
Total			12

INSPECTIONS OF BOILERS OF UNITED STATES GOVERNMENT STEAMERS AND BUILDINGS—Continued.

Local inspection district, and name of steamer or building.	Port where inspected.	Date inspected.	Boilers inspected.
Wheeling, W. Va.:			
Steamers—			
Vega	Zanesville, Ohio	Oct. 9	2
Malta (dredge)	do	do	1
Total			3
Detroit, Mich.:			
Steamers—			
Haze	Detroit, Mich	Mar. 29	2
Light-ship No. 59	do	do	1
Amaranth	do	Apr. 10	1
Do	do	Apr. 14	1
John Johnson	do	do	1
Buildings—			
Post-office	do	Oct. 2	5
Old Federal building	do	Oct. 5	1
Do	do	Oct. 10	1
Post-office	do	Dec. 18	1
Total			14
Chicago, Ill.:			
Steamer—Dearborn	Chicago, Ill	Aug. 4	1
Buildings—			
Marine hospital	do	June 3	2
Do	do	Aug. 14	1
Total			4
Grand Haven, Mich.:			
Steamers—			
Light-ship No. 55	Cheboygan, Mich	Mar. 23	1
Light-ship No. 56	do	do	1
Light-ship No. 57	do	do	1
Total			3
Cleveland, Ohio: Building—Marine hospital	Cleveland, Ohio	July 31 Sept. 15	2
Buffalo, N. Y.:			
Steamer—General John M. Wilson	Buffalo, N. Y	June 9	1
Buildings—			
Court-house and post-office	Rochester, N. Y	June 26	4
Isthmian Canal Commission	Erie, Pa	Nov. 28	3
Total			8
Burlington, Vt.: Steamer—Nettle	Burlington, Vt	Sept. 16	1
New Orleans, La.:			
Steamers—			
Picket	New Orleans, La	Oct. 27	1
General John Newton	do	Dec. 8	1
General Comstock	do	do	1
Ram	do	do	3
Total			6
Mobile, Ala.:			
Steamers—			
Ivy	Mobile, Ala	July 1	2
Rossell	do	Aug. 19	1
General R. N. Bachelder	do	Sept. 18	1
Arbutus	do	Oct. 8	2
Mangrove	do	Dec. 8	2
Total			8
Grand total			344

Hulls of United States Government Steamers Inspected.

In addition to the regular annual inspections, hulls of United States Government steamers were inspected by officers of the Steamboat-Inspection Service during the year ended December 31, 1905, as follows:

Local inspection district.	Name of steamer.	Port where inspected.	Date inspected.
Norfolk, Va	Trent	Newbern, N. C	Mar. 29
Do	General George Thom	Norfolk, Va	Mar. 30
Do	Scuppernong	Harlow Creek, N. C	Do.
Do	Roanoke	Norfolk, Va	May 16
Dubuque, Iowa	Curlew	Dubuque, Iowa	July 10
Burlington, Vt	Nettle	Burlington, Vt	Sept. 16

DETAILED LIST OF FOREIGN STEAM VESSELS INSPECTED DURING THE FISCAL YEAR ENDED JUNE 30, 1906.

BY THE LOCAL INSPECTORS AT NEW YORK, N. Y.

Name.	Gross tonnage.	Nationality.	Date of inspection.
Algeria	4,484	British	Aug. 24, 1905
Alleghany	2,494	German	Aug. 11, 1905
African Prince	4,915	British	Oct. 23, 1905
Amerika [a]	22,314	German	Oct. 25, 1905
Atrato [a]	5,346	British	Nov. 11, 1905
Amazonense	2,828	....do	Jan. 13, 1906
Antonio Lopez	5,975	Spanish	Mar. 15, 1906
Altai	2,480	German	May 5, 1906
Astoria [a]	5,049	British	June 7, 1906
Baltic [a]	23,875	....do	July 24, 1905
Batavia [a]	11,045	German	July 11, 1905
Bulgaria [a]	11,077	....do	Aug. 8, 1905
Burmudian	5,530	British	Dec. 18, 1905
Bremen [a]	11,570	German	Nov. 20, 1905
Buenos Aires	5,311	Spanish	Nov. 11, 1905
Baker	1,930	German	Mar. 6, 1906
Barbarossa [a]	10,915	....do	Feb. 21, 1906
Blucher [a]	12,334	....do	Mar. 17, 1906
Boniface [a]	3,504	British	Feb. 8, 1906
Braslie	5,269	Italian	Jan. 18, 1906
Breslau [a]	7,524	German	Feb. 28, 1906
Brighton	1,126	Norwegian	Feb. 16, 1906
Byron [a] [b]	3,909	British	Apr. 28, 1906
Campania [a] [b]	12,950	....do	July 25, 1905
Campania	12,950	....do	Sept. 19, 1905
Caribbee [d]	1,944	....do	June 30, 1905
Cretic	13,507	....do	Sept. 20, 1905
Calabria	4,375	....do	Oct. 27, 1905
Carmania [a]	19,524	....do	Dec. 14, 1905
Carpathia [a]	13,564	....do	Nov. 16, 1905
Clarense	2,704	....do	Nov. 24, 1905
Celtic [a]	20,904	....do	Oct. 25, 1905
Cornwall [a]	5,498	....do	Oct. 9, 1905
Cusityba	2,363	Cuban	Do.
Camatense [a]	2,183	British	Feb. 28, 1906
Campania [a] [b]	12,950	....do	Mar. 27, 1906
Cedric [a] [c]	21,034	....do	Mar. 22, 1906
Celtic [a] [c]	20,904	....do	Mar. 23, 1906
Citta di Napoli	4,125	Italian	Mar. 9, 1906
Columbia [a]	8,292	British	Mar. 22, 1906
C. F. Tietgen [a]	8,139	Danish	May 15, 1906
Caledonia [a]	9,222	British	Apr. 4, 1906
Caronia [a] [b]	19,593	....do	Apr. 21, 1906
Caronia [a] [c]	19,593	....do	June 15, 1906
Cedric [a] [c]	21,034	....do	May 29, 1906
Citta di Torino	3,435	Italian	May 30, 1906
Cornwall [a] [c]	5,498	British	June 25, 1906
Deutschland [a] [c]	16,502	German	July 18, 1905
Devon [a]	3,546	British	Aug. 16, 1905
Deutschland [a] [c]	16,502	German	Apr. 27, 1906
Etruria [a] [c]	8,119	British	Nov. 9, 1905
Etruria [a] [c]	8,119	....do	Apr. 3, 1906
Ethiopia [a]	4,005	....do	Jan. 9, 1906
Everton Grange [a]	7,201	....do	Feb. 26, 1906
Fontabelle	2,646	....do	Aug. 8, 1905
Francesca	4,945	Austrian	Sept. 20, 1905

[a] Act Feb. 15, 1902.
[b] Thrice examined during the year.
[c] Twice examined during the year.
[d] Certificate issued July 3, 1905.

Detailed List of Foreign Steam Vessels Inspected, Fiscal Year ended June 30, 1906—Continued.

BY THE LOCAL INSPECTORS AT NEW YORK, N. Y.—Continued.

Name.	Gross tonnage.	Nationality.	Date of inspection.
Fuerst Bismarck [a]	8,332	German	Sept. 2, 1905
Furnessia [a] [b]	5,494	British	July 19, 1905
Flandria	2,041	German	[d] May 29, 1905
Florida	5,112	Italian	Dec. 9, 1905
Fluminense [a]	2,154	British	Mar. 27, 1906
Furnessia [a] [b]	5,494	....do	Mar. 29, 1906
Friedrich der Grosse [a]	10,695	German	May 26, 1906
Gerty	4,212	Austrian	Sept. 28, 1905
Guilia	4,336	....do	Sept. 7, 1905
Gallia [a]	4,133	French	Oct. 19, 1905
Georgia	2,811	Austrian	Feb. 5, 1906
Germania [a]	4,897	British	Mar. 6, 1906
Gneisenau [a]	8,081	German	Mar. 16, 1906
Graecia	2,799	....do	Mar. 6, 1906
Graf Waldersee [a]	13,193	....do	Feb. 20, 1906
Grangense [a]	2,161	British	Jan. 31, 1906
Grosser Kurfuerst [a]	13,182	German	Mar. 28, 1906
Gunther	3,037	....do	June 18, 1906
Gutrune	3,039	....do	May 14, 1906
Hellig Olav [a]	10,085	Danish	Apr. 5, 1906
Hohenzollern [a]	6,668	German	May 3, 1906
Hubert [a]	1,922	British	May 26, 1906
Indiana	5,106	Italian	Feb. 26, 1906
Italia	5,300	....do	Apr. 6, 1906
Italia	4,806	British	May 14, 1906
Justin [a]	3,498	....do	Nov. 8, 1905
Konigin Luise [a]	10,710	German	Sept. 9, 1905
Kaiser Wilhelm II [a]	19,361	....do	Mar. 24, 1906
Kaiser Wilhelm der Grosse [a]	14,349	....do	Feb. 2, 1906
Konig Albert [a]	10,643	....do	Feb. 16, 1906
Kaiserin Auguste Victoria [a]	24,581	....do	May 22, 1906
Korona	2,874	British	Apr. 24, 1906
Kronprinz Wilhelm [a]	14,908	German	Apr. 7, 1906
La Touraine [a]	8,892	French	Aug. 1, 1905
Langton Grange [a]	5,805	British	Dec. 14, 1905
La Plata [a]	4,464	....do	Nov. 25, 1905
Lombardia	5,126	Italian	Nov. 7, 1905
La Bretagne [a]	7,112	French	Feb. 21, 1906
La Champagne [a]	7,087	....do	Mar. 22, 1906
La Lorraine [a]	8,385	....do	Mar. 13, 1906
La Savoie [a]	11,639	....do	Mar. 28, 1906
Lucania [a]	12,952	British	Jan. 17, 1906
La Gascogne [a]	7,395	French	Apr. 11, 1906
La Provence [a]	13,787	....do	May 2, 1906
Lazio	9,196	Italian	Apr. 11, 1906
Lucania [a] [b]	12,952	British	June 5, 1906
Luisiana	4,982	Italian	Apr. 27, 1906
Majestic [a] [b]	9,965	British	Sept. 9, 1905
Minnehaha [a] [b]	13,403	....do	Sept. 5, 1905
Montevideo	5,296	Spanish	Aug. 11, 1905
Montserrat	4,146	....do	Dec. 12, 1905
Magdalena [a]	5,372	British	Feb. 21, 1906
Manuel Calvo	5,139	Spanish	Feb. 12, 1906
Maracas	2,925	British	Jan. 29, 1906
Merchant Prince	3,031	....do	Jan. 27, 1906
Mesaba [a]	6,833	....do	Mar. 23, 1906
Minneapolis [a] [b]	13,401	....do	Jan. 4, 1906
Minnehaha [a] [b]	13,403	....do	Feb. 27, 1906
Minnetonka [a]	13,403	....do	Mar. 13, 1906
Madonna	5,551	....do	May 21, 1906
Majestic [a] [b]	9,965	....do	May 12, 1906
Maranhense	2,680	....do	Apr. 24, 1906
Minneapolis [a] [b]	13,401	....do	Do.
Moltke [a]	12,334	German	June 8, 1906
Nord America	4,828	Italian	Sept. 11, 1905
Norman Prince	3,464	British	Dec. 5, 1905
Napolitan Prince	2,900	....do	Mar. 13, 1906
Noordam [a]	12,530	Dutch	Feb. 2, 1906
Nieuw Amsterdam [a]	16,967	....do	Apr. 23, 1906
Oscar II [a] [b]	9,956	Danish	July 15, 1905
Oswestry Grange [a]	6,674	British	July 20, 1905
Oceanic [a] [b]	17,273	....do	Oct. 28, 1905
Olinda	2,376	Cuban	Oct. 23, 1905
Orinoco [a] [b]	4,571	British	Dec. 23, 1905
Oceana [a]	7,859	German	June 21, 1906

[a] Act Feb. 15, 1902.
[b] Twice examined during the year.
[c] Thrice examined during the year.
[d] Certificate issued Oct. 11, 1905.

DETAILED LIST OF FOREIGN STEAM VESSELS INSPECTED, FISCAL YEAR ENDED JUNE 30, 1906—Continued.

BY THE LOCAL INSPECTORS AT NEW YORK, N. Y.—Continued.

Name.	Gross tonnage.	Nationality.	Date of inspection.
Oceanic [a] [b]	17,273	British	Apr. 23, 1906
Orinoco [a] [b]	4,581	....do	May 18, 1906
Oscar II [a] [b]	9,956	Danish	May 4, 1906
Pannonia	9,851	British	July 28, 1905
Parisian [a]	5,395	....do	Aug. 29, 1905
Prins Der Nederlanden	2,100	Dutch	Sept. 25, 1905
Prinzess Irene [a]	10,881	German	Aug. 16, 1905
Prins Oskar [a]	6,026	....do	Aug. 12, 1905
Peninsular	2,744	Portuguese	Dec. 23, 1905
Perthshire [a]	5,550	British	Dec. 27, 1905
Prins Frederik Hendrik [a]	2,164	Dutch	Nov. 22, 1905
Prins Willam I [a]	1,765	....do	Dec. 20, 1905
Prins Willem IV [a]	1,713	....do	Oct. 9, 1905
Prinz Adalbert [a]	6,029	German	Dec. 18, 1905
Pennsylvania [a]	13,333	....do	Mar. 6, 1906
Perugia	4,348	British	Feb. 8, 1906
Pretoria [a]	13,189	German	Mar. 27, 1906
Prins Maurits [a]	1,777	Dutch	Jan. 2, 1906
Prins Willem II [a]	1,621	....do	Feb. 13, 1906
Prins Willem III [a]	1,663	....do	Feb. 28, 1906
Prins Willem V [a]	1,777	....do	Mar. 26, 1906
Prinz August Wilhelm [a]	4,733	German	Feb. 8, 1906
Prinzessin Victoria Luise [a]	4,419	....do	Jan. 13, 1906
Parima	2,990	British	May 21, 1906
Patricia [a]	13,424	German	May 2, 1906
Potsdam [a]	12,522	Dutch	Apr. 6, 1906
Pretoria	3,303	British	June 5, 1906
Prince Arthur [a]	2,041	....do	June 22, 1906
Prinzess Alice [a]	10,911	German	June 21, 1906
Prinz Eitel Frederich [a]	4,650	....do	May 1, 1906
Rhein [a]	10,058	....do	Oct. 24, 1905
Rotterdam [a]	8,139	Dutch	Oct. 5, 1905
Ryndam [a]	12,527	....do	Sept. 28, 1905
Rosalind	2,567	British	June 15, 1906
Rugia [a]	6,598	German	Apr. 10, 1906
Soldier Prince	3,118	British	Aug. 14, 1905
Sarnia	3,402	German	Dec. 22, 1905
Siberia	3,347	....do	Dec. 7, 1905
Sicilian Prince	2,783	British	Dec. 27, 1905
Southwark [a]	8,606	....do	Dec. 2, 1905
Statendam [a]	10,491	Dutch	Dec. 5, 1905
Sieglinde	3,037	German	Mar. 24, 1906
Siegmund	3,378	....do	Feb. 26, 1906
Sofia Hohenberg	5,491	Austrian	Jan. 11, 1906
Seydlitz [a]	7,942	German	Apr. 14, 1906
Sicilia	5,602	Italian	May 1, 1906
Silvia	1,707	British	June 5, 1906
Slavonia [a]	10,606	....do	May 18, 1906
Tagus [a] [b]	5,544	....do	Oct. 27, 1905
Trent [a] [b]	5,524	....do	Dec. 9, 1905
Tagus [a] [b]	5,544	....do	Jan. 5, 1906
Teutonic [a]	9,984	....do	Feb. 3, 1906
Trave [a]	5,271	German	Mar. 26, 1906
Trinidad	2,592	British	Mar. 28, 1906
Tennyson	3,901	....do	Apr. 3, 1906
Trent [a] [b]	5,524	....do	May 4, 1906
Ultonia	10,402	....do	July 5, 1905
Umbria [a] [b]	8,128	....do	Aug. 30, 1905
United States [a] [b]	10,095	Danish	[d] June 30, 1905
Umbria [a] [b]	8,128	British	Oct. 25, 1905
Uller	1,860	Norwegian	Mar. 6, 1906
Ultonia [a]	10,402	British	Mar. 19, 1906
Umbria [a] [d]	8,128	....do	Apr. 19, 1906
United States [a] [b]	10,095	Danish	Apr. 23, 1906
Valdivia	2,176	German	Nov. 21, 1905
Venetia [a]	2,987	....do	Nov. 15, 1905
Virginia [a]	2,543	....do	Oct. 17, 1905
Vaderland	12,017	Belgian	Mar. 9, 1906
Virginia [d]	2,543	German	Mar. 22, 1906
Weimar [a]	4,996	....do	Mar. 18, 1906
Wurzburg [a]	5,085	....do	Apr. 6, 1906
Zeeland [a]	11,904	British	Dec. 28, 1905

[a] Act Feb. 15, 1902.
[b] Twice examined during the year.
[c] Thrice examined during the year.
[d] Certificated July 3, 1905.

DETAILED LIST OF FOREIGN STEAM VESSELS INSPECTED, FISCAL YEAR ENDED JUNE 30, 1906—Continued.

BY THE LOCAL INSPECTORS AT BOSTON, MASS.

Name.	Gross tonnage.	Nationality.	Date of inspection.
Arabic	15,800	British	Aug. 22, 1905
Aranmore	1,169	....do	Dec. 8, 1905
Arabic [a]	15,801	....do	May 8, 1906
Bohemian	8,547	....do	Dec. 27, 1905
Beverly	1,516	....do	May 12, 1906
Boston	1,694	....do	June 9, 1906
Cymric [b] [c]	13,096	....do	Sept. 12, 1905
Cymric [b] [c]	13,096	....do	Nov. 8, 1905
Canopic	12,096	....do	Nov. 15, 1905
Cestrian [b] [c]	8,823	....do	Jan. 8, 1906
Corinthian	6,226	....do	Apr. 17, 1906
Cestrian [b] [c]	8,823	....do	Apr. 24, 1906
Canadian	9,301	....do	May 14, 1906
Devonian [b] [d]	10,417	....do	Jan. 15, 1906
Devonian [b] [d]	10,417	....do	Feb. 19, 1906
Devonian [b] [d]	10,417	....do	Apr. 25, 1906
Halifax	1,874	....do	Apr. 28, 1906
Ivernia [b] [d]	14,058	....do	July 1, 1905
Ivernia [b] [d]	14,058	....do	Dec. 15, 1905
Ivernia [b] [d]	14,058	....do	June 9, 1906
Mongolian [b] [c]	4,837	....do	Jan. 24, 1906
Mongolian [b] [c]	4,837	....do	Apr. 11, 1906
Numidian	4,835	....do	Mar. 31, 1906
Prince George	2,040	....do	May 14, 1906
Parisian [b]	5,395	....do	June 17, 1906
Republic	15,378	....do	Oct. 4, 1905
Romanic	11,394	....do	Oct. 25, 1905
Saxonia [b] [d]	14,280	....do	Aug. 14, 1905
Saxonia [b] [d]	14,280	....do	Dec. 4, 1905
Sardinian	4,348	....do	Jan. 11, 1906
Siberian	3,845	....do	Mar. 22, 1906
Saxonia [b] [d]	14,280	....do	May 25, 1906
Sicilian	5,615	....do	Apr. 21, 1906
Toronto	6,035	....do	July 24, 1905
Winifredian [b] [c]	10,404	....do	Jan. 1, 1906
Winifredian [b] [c]	10,404	....do	Apr. 13, 1906

BY THE LOCAL INSPECTORS AT PHILADELPHIA, PA.

Name.	Gross tonnage.	Nationality.	Date of inspection.
Carthagenian	2,856	British	Nov. 13, 1905
City of Vienna	4,672	....do	June 4, 1906
City of Bombay	4,548	....do	June 18, 1906
Freisland	7,116	....do	Aug. 31, 1905
Haverford [b] [d]	11,635	....do	Oct. 31, 1905
Haverford [b] [d]	11,635	....do	Dec. 8, 1905
Haverford [b] [d]	11,635	....do	Apr. 27, 1906
Laurentian	4,522	....do	Apr. 20, 1906
Menominee	6,918	....do	Sept. 27, 1905
Marquette	7,056	Belgian	Oct. 11, 1905
Manitou	6,849	British	Jan. 26, 1906
Merion	11,621	....do	Jan. 31, 1906
Noordland	5,129	....do	May 25, 1906
Westernland [b] [c]	5,665	....do	Aug. 1, 1905
Westernland [b] [c]	5,665	....do	May 14, 1906

BY THE LOCAL INSPECTORS AT PORTLAND, ME.

Name.	Gross tonnage.	Nationality.	Date of inspection.
Canada	9,413	British	Apr. 11, 1906
Dominion	7,008	....do	Feb. 16, 1906
Kensington	8,668	....do	Apr. 19, 1906
Norseman	9,545	....do	May 31, 1906

[a] Twice certificated during the year.
[b] Act Feb. 15, 1902.
[c] Twice examined during the year.
[d] Thrice examined during the year.

Detailed List of Foreign Steam Vessels Inspected, Fiscal Year ended June 30, 1906—Continued.

BY THE LOCAL INSPECTORS AT BANGOR, ME.

Name.	Gross tonnage.	Nationality.	Date of inspection.
Aurora [a] [b]	364	British	Aug. 2, 1905
Aurora [a] [b]	364	....do	Oct. 26, 1905
Viking	127	....do	Oct. 2, 1905

BY THE LOCAL INSPECTORS AT ALBANY, N. Y.

Name.	Gross tonnage.	Nationality.	Date of inspection.
Julia [c]	1,811	Cuban	Jan. 20, 1906

BY THE LOCAL INSPECTORS AT BALTIMORE, MD.

Name.	Gross tonnage.	Nationality.	Date of inspection.
Barnstable [b]	1,356	British	[e] June 13, 1905
Brookline [b]	1,356	....do	[f] June 20, 1905
Barnstable [b]	1,356	....do	June 5, 1906
Brandenburg	7,532	....do	June 11, 1906
Brookline [b]	1,356	....do	June 12, 1906
Cassel	7,543	German	Nov. 17, 1905
Darmstadt	5,012	....do	Feb. 12, 1906
Frankfurt	7,431	....do	July 20, 1905
Joseph Di Giorgio	1,249	Norwegian	Sept. 29, 1905
Karlsruhe	5,057	German	Apr. 18, 1906
Main	10,067	....do	June 4, 1906
Neckar	9,835	....do	Sept. 15, 1906
Oldenburg	5,005	....do	Feb. 27, 1906
Roland	3,602	....do	Mar. 5, 1906
Rhein	10,058	....do	Apr. 4, 1906
Salvatore Di Giorgio	1,249	Norwegian	Aug. 22, 1905
Wittekind	5,736	German	May 5, 1906

BY THE LOCAL INSPECTORS AT SAN FRANCISCO, CAL.

Name.	Gross tonnage.	Nationality.	Date of inspection.
Ammon	4,553	German	Aug. 9, 1905
America Maru	6,307	Japanese	Oct. 20, 1905
Coptic [a]	4,352	British	Oct. 10, 1905
Coptic	4,352	....do	Jan. 3, 1906
Doric	4,675	....do	Sept. 11, 1905
Doric [a]	4,675	....do	Dec. 1, 1905
Hong Kong Maru	6,159	Japanese	Mar. 2, 1906
Mera	4,797	German	Feb. 23, 1906
Nippon Maru	6,168	Japanese	Feb. 10, 1906
Stanley Dollar [g]	2,903	British	July 15, 1905
St. Denis	515	....do	Apr. 5, 1906
Theben	4,613	German	July 28, 1905

BY THE LOCAL INSPECTORS AT SEATTLE, WASH.

Name.	Gross tonnage.	Nationality.	Date of inspection.
Iroquois	195	British	Aug. 17, 1905
Iyo Maru	6,319	Japanese	Dec. 4, 1905
Kanagawa Maru	6,160	....do	Aug. 12, 1905
Machaon	6,737	British	Sept. 27, 1905
Maheno	5,282	....do	May 22, 1906
Princess Victoria	1,943	....do	Aug. 11, 1905
Princess Beatrice	1,289	....do	Jan. 12, 1906
Princess May	1,717	....do	June 20, 1906
Riojun Maru	4,805	Japanese	June 22, 1906
Shinano Maru	6,387	....do	Feb. 9, 1906
Tydens	7,441	British	Nov. 20, 1905
Telemachus	7,449	....do	Feb. 12, 1906
Tango Maru	7,463	Japanese	May 19, 1906
Teucer	9,019	British	June 7, 1906

[a] Act Feb. 15, 1902.
[b] Twice examined during the year.
[c] Inspected in Porto Rican waters.
[d] Certificate issued Oct. 11, 1905.
[e] Certificated July 24, 1905.
[f] Certificated July 19, 1905.
[g] Inspected in Hawaiian waters.

DETAILED LIST OF FOREIGN STEAM VESSELS INSPECTED, FISCAL YEAR ENDED JUNE 30, 1906—Continued.

BY THE LOCAL INSPECTORS AT DETROIT, MICH.

Name.	Gross tonnage.	Nationality.	Date of inspection.
City of Chatham [a]	362	British	[b]June 8, 1905
Winona [a]	231	....do	July 27, 1905

BY THE LOCAL INSPECTORS AT MARQUETTE, MICH.

Name.	Gross tonnage.	Nationality.	Date of inspection.
Algoma [a]	156	British	Aug. 4, 1905
Algoma [a] [g]	156	....do	June 16, 1906
City of Midland [a]	974	....do	June 15, 1906
King Edward [a]	570	....do	Aug. 2, 1905
Manitou [a]	470	....do	July 1, 1905
Manitou [a]	470	....do	Sept. 9, 1905
Minnie M. [a]	612	....do	July 12, 1905
Ossifrage [a]	632	....do	July 14, 1905

BY THE LOCAL INSPECTORS AT PORT HURON, MICH.

Name.	Gross tonnage.	Nationality.	Date of inspection.
Hiawatha [a]	162	British	July 29, 1905
Hiawatha [a] [d]	162	....do	June 8, 1906
Huronic [a]	3,330	....do	Apr. 13, 1906
Monarch [a]	2,017	....do	July 1, 1905
Monarch [a] [d]	2,017	....do	Apr. 13, 1906
Saronic [a]	1,960	....do	July 18, 1905

BY THE LOCAL INSPECTORS AT BUFFALO, N. Y.

Name.	Gross tonnage.	Nationality.	Date of inspection.
Alexandria [a]	863	British	May 6, 1906
City of Montreal [a]	1,554	....do	[e]June 19, 1905
Corona [a]	1,273	....do	Apr. 24, 1906
Chicora [a]	930	....do	Do.
Chippewa [a]	1,513	....do	Apr. 25, 1906
Kingston [a]	2,925	....do	May 18, 1906
Majestic [a]	1,577	....do	[f]June 20, 1905
Ongiara [a]	97	....do	Apr. 24, 1906
Toronto [a]	2,779	....do	May 18, 1906
White Star [a]	450	....do	Aug. 10, 1905
White Star [a]	629	....do	May 30, 1906

BY THE LOCAL INSPECTORS AT OSWEGO, N. Y.

Name.	Gross tonnage.	Nationality.	Date of inspection.
Antelope [a]	24	British	Aug. 9, 1905
America [a]	520	....do	May 23, 1906
Argyle [a]	700	....do	May 24, 1906
Aletha [a]	171	....do	June 13, 1906
City of Belleville [a]	101	....do	Sept. 14, 1905
Caspian [a]	957	....do	June 22, 1906
M. & W. [a]	8	....do	May 11, 1906
Niagara [a]	396	....do	July 27, 1905
North King [a]	872	....do	May 24, 1906
Pierrepont [a]	251	....do	May 17, 1906
Reliance [a]	239	....do	July 1, 1905
Resolute [a]	371	....do	Sept. 6, 1905
Reliance [a] [d]	239	....do	Apr. 19, 1906
Rideau Queen [a]	350	....do	June 13, 1906
Rideau King [a]	265	....do	Do.
Varuna [a]	134	....do	July 29, 1905
Victoria [a]	58	....do	Aug. 8, 1905
Valeria [a]	51	....do	June 4, 1906
Where Now [a]	47	....do	July 10, 1905
Where Now [a] [d]	47	....do	May 5, 1906

[a] Act Feb. 15, 1902.
[b] Certificated July 6, 1905
[c] Certificate issued Oct. 11, 1905.
[d] Twice examined during the year.
[e] Certificated July 12, 1905.
[f] Certificated July 6, 1905.
[g] Twice certificated during the year.

Detailed List of Foreign Steam Vessels Inspected, Fiscal Year ended June 30, 1906—Continued.

BY THE LOCAL INSPECTORS AT BURLINGTON, VT.

Name.	Gross tonnage.	Nationality.	Date of inspection.
Alma [a]	6	British	May 30, 1906
Lady of the Lake [a]	607	....do	July 20, 1905
Missisquoi [a]	159	....do	July 13, 1905

BY THE LOCAL INSPECTORS AT TOLEDO, OHIO.

Name.	Gross tonnage.	Nationality.	Date of inspection.
Cuba [a]	931	British	July 5, 1905
City of Dresden [a]	193	....do	Aug. 11, 1905

BY THE LOCAL INSPECTORS AT NEW ORLEANS, LA.

Name.	Gross tonnage.	Nationality.	Date of inspection.
Antillian	5,608	British	July 3, 1905
Atlantian [a]	6,175	....do	Aug. 25, 1905
Anselm	1,562	....do	Nov. 7, 1905
Asian [a]	3,680	....do	Dec. 19, 1905
Asian [a] [b]	5,613	....do	May 11, 1906
Brewster	1,620	German	Dec. 27, 1905
Bertha	1,680	Norwegian	Mar. 29, 1906
Bluefields	1,001	....do	June 25, 1906
Californian	6,222	British	July 18, 1905
City of Tampico	1,513	Norwegian	Oct. 5, 1905
City of Mexico	1,511	....do	Nov. 11, 1905
Californie [a]	7,000	French	Apr. 16, 1906
Colonian [a]	6,443	British	Apr. 20, 1906
Darien [a]	2,178	....do	Dec. 12, 1905
Darien [a]	3,299	....do	May 3, 1906
Ellis	2,011	Norwegian	July 15, 1905
Esparta	3,297	British	Jan. 5, 1906
Floridian [a]	2,098	....do	Nov. 22, 1905
Hiram	602	Norwegian	Nov. 6, 1905
Imperator	989	....do	Apr. 25, 1906
Joseph Vaccaro	1,661	British	Jan. 26, 1906
Karen	1,689	Norwegian	Mar. 22, 1906
Louisianian [a]	3,642	British	July 31, 1905
Louisiane [a]	9,300	French	Nov. 9, 1905
Limon	3,297	British	Nov. 29, 1905
Mexico [a]	3,100	French	Dec. 11, 1905
Nicaraguan [a]	2,385	British	Sept. 28, 1905
Nor	1,409	Norwegian	Nov. 15, 1905
Nicaragua	561	....do	Apr. 9, 1906
Nicaraguan [a]	3,642	British	May 28, 1906
Olympia	1,658	....do	Jan. 16, 1906
Preston	1,443	Norwegian	Sept. 22, 1905
Rosina [a]	1,094	British	Nov. 20, 1905
Vincenzo Florio	2,840	Italian	Jan. 30, 1906
William Cliff [a] [b]	3,287	British	Aug. 14, 1905
William Cliff [a] [b]	3,287	....do	Apr. 18, 1906

BY THE LOCAL INSPECTORS AT MOBILE, ALA.

Name.	Gross tonnage.	Nationality.	Date of inspection.
Alm	1,617	Norwegian	July 25, 1905
Belize	1,002	....do	Feb. 15, 1906
Corinto	998	....do	Oct. 2, 1905
Colombia	825	....do	Apr. 6, 1906
Espana	528	....do	Dec. 7, 1905
Fort Gaines	1,121	....do	[c] May 22, 1906
Fort Morgan	1,120	....do	Jan. 4, 1906
Hellas	1,380	....do	Mar. 28, 1906
Harald	851	....do	Mar. 24, 1906
Helen	1,098	....do	June 4, 1906
Katie	1,098	....do	Oct. 19, 1905
Mobila	2,167	Cuban	Apr. 16, 1906
San Jose	3,296	British	Nov. 20, 1905
Suldal	439	Norwegian	Feb. 2, 1906
Taunton	1,329	....do	Nov. 2, 1905
Vueltabajo	794	Cuban	Oct. 20, 1905

[a] Act Feb. 15, 1902.
[b] Twice examined during the year.
[c] Certificated Sept. 27, 1905.

Detailed List of Foreign Steam Vessels Inspected, Fiscal Year ended June 30, 1906—Continued.

BY THE LOCAL INSPECTORS AT GALVESTON, TEX.

Name.	Gross tonnage.	Nationality.	Date of inspection.
Cuthbert	3,563	British	June 29, 1906
Carrigan Head	4,200	.....do	Oct. 2, 1905
Galveston	1,254	Norwegian	Apr. 10, 1906
Irak	8,116	British	Nov. 2, 1905
Irada	8,119	.....do	Apr. 23, 1906
Justin	3,498	.....do	July 14, 1905
Köln	7,409	German	July 3, 1905
Louisianian	3,642	British	Apr. 17, 1906
Morlina	1,122	Norwegian	Mar. 16, 1906
Norheim	1,403	.....do	Mar. 9, 1906
Progreso	1,620	.....do	Apr. 14, 1906
Texan	3,183	British	May 28, 1906

Annual Certificates of Inspection and Certificates of Examination Issued to Foreign Steam Vessels by the Inspectors During the Fiscal Year ended June 30, 1906.

Nationality.	Number.	Gross tonnage.
British	251	1,418,673
German	69	555,795
Norwegian	32	38,698
Dutch	14	87,756
Italian	12	60,921
French	11	87,830
Japanese	8	49,777
Danish	6	58,326
Austrian	5	21,795
Spanish	5	25,867
Cuban	5	9,511
Belgian	2	19,073
Portuguese	1	2,744
Total	421	2,436,766

O

CPSIA information can be obtained at www.ICGtesting.com
Printed in the USA
LVOW110736181112
307814LV00004B/27/P